The SAGE Guide to
Educational
Leadership
and Management

SAGE was founded in 1965 by Sara Miller McCune to support the dissemination of usable knowledge by publishing innovative and high-quality research and teaching content. Today, we publish more than 750 journals, including those of more than 300 learned societies, more than 800 new books per year, and a growing range of library products including archives, data, case studies, reports, conference highlights, and video. SAGE remains majority-owned by our founder, and after Sara's lifetime will become owned by a charitable trust that secures our continued independence.

Los Angeles | London | Washington DC | New Delhi | Singapore | Boston

The SAGE Guide to
Educational
Leadership
and Management

Editor

Fenwick W. English
University of North Carolina at Chapel Hill

Associate Editors

JoAnn Danelo Barbour
Gonzaga University

Rosemary Papa
Northern Arizona University

$SAGE reference

Los Angeles | London | New Delhi
Singapore | Washington DC | Boston

Los Angeles | London | New Delhi
Singapore | Washington DC | Boston

FOR INFORMATION:

SAGE Publications, Inc.
2455 Teller Road
Thousand Oaks, California 91320
E-mail: order@sagepub.com

SAGE Publications Ltd.
1 Oliver's Yard
55 City Road
London, EC1Y 1SP
United Kingdom

SAGE Publications India Pvt. Ltd.
B 1/I 1 Mohan Cooperative Industrial Area
Mathura Road, New Delhi 110 044
India

SAGE Publications Asia-Pacific Pte. Ltd.
3 Church Street
#10-04 Samsung Hub
Singapore 049483

Acquisitions Editor: Jim Brace-Thompson
Production Editor: Jane Haenel
Reference Systems Manager: Leticia Gutierrez
Reference Systems Coordinator: Anna Villaseñor
Typesetter: Hurix Systems Pvt. Ltd.
Copyeditors: Kristin Bergstad, Neil Womack
Proofreader: Ellen Howard
Indexer: Virgil Diodato
Cover Designer: Candice Harman
Marketing Manager: Carmel Schrire

Printed in the United States of America.

A catalog record of this book is available from the Library of Congress.

978-1-4522-8192-6

15 16 17 18 19 10 9 8 7 6 5 4 3 2 1

Summary Contents

List of Figures, Tables, and Sidebars   xvii

About the Editors   xxi

Contributors   xxv

Acknowledgments   xxxiii

Introduction   xxxv

PART I. LEADERSHIP AND MANAGEMENT   1

PART II. TEACHING AND LEARNING   53

PART III. CURRICULUM AND INSTRUCTION   101

PART IV. TESTING AND ASSESSMENT   151

PART V. TECHNOLOGY, THE INTERNET, AND ONLINE LEARNING   197

PART VI. BUDGETING, FINANCE, AND FUND-RAISING   237

PART VII. SCHOOL LAW, SAFETY, AND THE LIMITS OF REGULATION   287

PART VIII. STUDENTS, PARENTS, AND SPECIAL POPULATIONS   341

PART IX. SCHOOL CLIMATE, CULTURE, AND HIGH PERFORMANCE   387

PART X. POLITICS, ELECTIONS, AND ACCOUNTABILITY   433

Appendix: Getting Started in Your Educational Leadership Career: Associations and Journals   487

Index   491

CONTENTS

List of Figures, Tables, and Sidebars   xvii

About the Editors   xxi

Contributors   xxv

Acknowledgments   xxxiii

Introduction   xxxv

PART I. LEADERSHIP AND MANAGEMENT

1. Unraveling the Leadership/Management Paradox   3
   Ira Bogotch

   Uncertainty and the Language of Scientific Management   3

   A Century of Scientific Management   5

   The Dimensions and Behaviors of School Managerial Control Explored   6

   Standards Versus Developing Standards: Murphy's Two Laws Centered?   8

   Improving Schools From Within   10

   Managerial Virtues of Necessity: Little Things and Big Things   13

   What Are the Odds That Little Comes Up Big? Big "L" Versus Little "l"   13

   The Challenge of Reclaiming Our Voices and Our Ideals   15

   Conclusion: Keeping Uncertainty and Risk in Our Sights   15

   Key Chapter Terms   16

   References   16

   Further Readings   18

2. The Emerging Wisdom of Educational Leadership   21
   Fenwick W. English and Rosemary Papa

   Parsing Out the Leadership/Management Opposites   22

   The Concept of *Accoutrements* as Artful Leadership and the Key for Imagination   25

   Machine Metaphors and Unrealistic Expectations   28

   The Lenses of Practice   29

   How to Discern *Best Practice* From Ordinary Practice, Common Sense, and Kitsch Texts   30

   Key Chapter Terms   33

   References   34

   Further Readings   35

3. **Understanding How the Bureaucratic Maze Works**   **39**
   Autumn Tooms Cyprès

   Welcome to Wonderland: A Primer on Bureaucratic Networks   39

   Back to the Beginning: How Networks Are Formed   40

   What Does Fit Have to Do With Membership in Networks?   41

   The Family Trees Where We Fit: A Look at n/networks and N/networks   42

   Navigating Networks by Understanding the Panopticon and the Johari Window   42

   Conclusion   47

   Key Chapter Terms   48

   References   49

   Further Readings   50

PART II. TEACHING AND LEARNING

4. **What Makes a Good Teacher? Models of Effective Teaching**   **55**
   Jennifer Prior

   Classroom Management   55

   Teaching Strategies   58

   Building Family Partnerships   61

   Making a Plan for Family Involvement   63

   Reflective Teaching   66

   Conclusion   67

   Key Chapter Terms   68

   References   68

   Further Readings   69

5. **Overcoming Learning Barriers for All Students**   **71**
   Jane Clark Lindle and Beth Parrott Reynolds

   Learning Barriers and Their Sources   73

   Resources for Overcoming Learning Barriers   81

   Key Chapter Terms   82

   References   85

   Further Readings   85

6. **Response to Intervention and Its Impact on Classroom Performance**   **87**
   Alicia Valero-Kerrick

   RTI and Systemic Reform   87

   Components of Response to Intervention Programs   88

   Expanded Roles in RTI   90

   RTI and English Language Learners   92

   RTI in Middle and High School   93

   RTI Impact on Classroom Performance   94

The Future of RTI   94

Conclusion   97

Key Chapter Terms   98

References   99

Further Readings   100

PART III. CURRICULUM AND INSTRUCTION

7. Multiculturalism Versus the Common Core   **103**
Fenwick W. English

An Earlier Conflict With a Common Curriculum   104

The Contemporary Common Core Movement Briefly Reviewed   105

Flash Points: Pushback, Problems, and Politics With the Common Core   109

Curriculum Alignment   114

Conclusion   115

Key Chapter Terms   116

References   116

Further Readings   117

8. The Growing Hispanic Population in U.S. Schools: Challenges and Solutions **119**
Claudia Sanchez

A Decade of Continued Growth   119

Latinos and Education   120

Solutions and Strategies for School Leaders   122

Conclusion   129

Key Chapter Terms   129

References   131

Further Readings   132

9. The Continuing Search for Best Practices in Classroom Instruction   **135**
Kimberly Kappler Hewitt

"Best Practice" Defined   135

Looking Backward: From Where Does the Concept of Best Practice Come?   136

Best Practices: A Critique   136

Best Practices for the Use of Best Practices   142

Best Practices   144

Field-Specific Best Practices   146

Approach-Specific and Technique-Specific Best Practices   146

Conclusion   147

Key Chapter Terms   147

References   148

Further Readings   149

PART IV. TESTING AND ASSESSMENT

10. What Is This Test Really Testing? Validity, Reliability, and Test Ethics   **153**
Launcelot I. Brown

Ethics and Testing   154

The Scientific Method   155

Conclusion   164

Key Chapter Terms   165

References   165

Further Readings   166

11. Achievement Gaps: Causes, False Promises, and Bogus Reforms   **169**
Connie M. Moss

Achievement: Misunderstandings and Misconceptions   169

Fifty Years of Reforms Yield a Widening Achievement Gap   171

No Child Left Behind: 21st-Century, High-Stakes, Test-Driven Accountability   174

Race to the Top: Competitive Grants for Educational Innovation   177

Test or Invest?   178

Conclusion   180

Key Chapter Terms   182

References   182

Further Readings   183

12. Cheater, Cheater, I Declare: The Prevalence, Causes, and Effects of, and Solutions to, School Cheating Scandals   **185**
Gail L. Thompson

Prevalence   185

The Worst Cheating Scandal in U.S. History   186

Causes   187

Effects   189

Solutions   191

Conclusion   192

Key Chapter Terms   192

References   193

Further Readings   194

PART V. TECHNOLOGY, THE INTERNET, AND ONLINE LEARNING

13. The Expanding Wireless World of Schooling   **199**
James E. Berry

Disruptive Innovation: Decentralization of Learning   200

The Infrastructure of Global Learning   200

The Future School   202

Flattening Education Through Technology   202

The Locus of Learning: Individualized and Personalized Learning in a Digital School   203

Individualized and Personalized Learning: Opportunity and Access 205

Learning: A Global Commodity 205

Ubiquitous Learning 206

Conclusion 207

Key Chapter Terms 208

References 209

Further Readings 210

14. The Opportunities and Challenges of Online and Blended Learning **211**
  Brad E. Bizzell

Background 211

Growth of Online and Blended Learning 212

Defining Online and Blended Learning 212

Online and Blended Learning: Benefits and Concerns 213

Productivity of Online and Blended Learning 217

Planning for Online and Blended Programs 218

Conclusion 221

Key Chapter Terms 221

References 222

Further Readings 223

15. Social Media and Texting: The Law and Considerations for School Policy **225**
  Theodore B. Creighton and M. David Alexander

Students 226

Teachers 231

Conclusion 235

Key Chapter Terms 235

References 236

Further Readings 236

PART VI. BUDGETING, FINANCE, AND FUND-RAISING

16. Understanding School Finance Laws and Practices **239**
  Eric A. Houck

The Context of School Funding 240

Trends in School Finance: Moving Toward Resource Allocation 240

Competing Values in School Finance 241

Understanding School Finance Laws 242

Using Educational Funds at the District and School Level 249

Does Money Matter? 250

Conclusion 252

Key Chapter Terms 252

References 254

Further Readings 255

17. **Expectations Exceeding Revenues: Budgeting for Increased Productivity**   **257**
William K. Poston, Jr.

    Some State Funding Structures Inhibit Equity and Disregard Inflation   257

    Funding Trend, Expectations Progression, and New Assessments   258

    The Nature of Budgeting   258

    Functions of Budgeting in Improving Productivity   260

    Expectations and Results of Performance-Based Budgeting   270

    Conclusion   270

    Key Chapter Terms   270

    References   271

    Further Readings   272

18. **A Free Public Education for All: Rediscovering the Promise**   **273**
Fred C. Lunenburg

    Misconceptions About U.S. Public Schools   273

    Equal Educational Opportunity   274

    The Achievement Gap   275

    Privatizing Education: Can the Marketplace Deliver Choice,
Efficiency, Equity, and Excellence?   280

    Conclusion   282

    Key Chapter Terms   282

    References   283

    Further Readings   285

PART VII. SCHOOL LAW, SAFETY, AND THE LIMITS OF REGULATION

19. **Today's Compelling Issues in Public School Law**   **289**
M. David Alexander, Patricia F. First, and Jennifer A. Sughrue

    Bullying/Cyberbullying and Student Free Speech Rights   290

    Seeking Justice   292

    Guidelines for Preventing and Responding to Harassment and Bullying   296

    Search and Seizure and Student Privacy Rights   296

    Conclusion   303

    Key Chapter Terms   303

    References   304

    Further Readings   305

20. **Transportation, School Safety, and Dealing With Bullies**   **307**
Jennifer A. Sughrue and M. David Alexander

    School Transportation   308

    Safety While Students Are at School   313

    Bullying   321

    School Safety Implications for School Administrators   324

    Key Chapter Terms   325

References 326

Further Readings 327

21. Charter Schools and the Privatization of Public Education: A Critical Race Theory Analysis 329
Abul Pitre and Tawannah G. Allen

Origin of Charter Schools 330

Evolution of Charter Schools 331

Arguments Advanced for Charter Schools 331

Using Critical Race Theory to Analyze the Intersection of Race and Education 334

Conclusion 337

Key Chapter Terms 338

References 338

Further Readings 340

PART VIII. STUDENTS, PARENTS, AND SPECIAL POPULATIONS

22. Student Conduct, Attendance, and Discipline: The Troika of School Safety and Stability 343
Claire E. Schonaerts and Pamela Jane Powell

Transformational Leadership 343

Why Be Concerned With Conduct, Attendance, and Discipline? 346

Supporting Positive School Conduct, Discipline, and Attendance 350

The Final Charge 354

Key Chapter Terms 355

References 356

Further Readings 357

23. Homeschooling: Parents' Rights and the Public Good 359
Jennifer A. Sughrue

The History of Homeschooling 361

The Look and Feel of Contemporary Homeschooling 362

Legal and Policy Issues Involved in Homeschooling 365

Conclusion 369

Key Chapter Terms 370

References 371

Further Readings 372

24. Emerging Trends in Student Services and Counseling 373
Kimberly A. Gordon Biddle and Shannon Dickson

Trends in General Student Services 373

Emerging Trends in Counseling 377

The Emerging Trends in Action 381

Conclusion 382

Key Chapter Terms 382

References 383

Further Readings 385

PART IX. SCHOOL CLIMATE, CULTURE, AND HIGH PERFORMANCE

25. Establishing a Climate of Performance and Success 389
Matthew T. Proto, Kathleen M. Brown, and Bradford J. Walston

Leadership in Turnaround Schools 389

Establishing a Climate of Performance and Success in North Carolina Turnaround Schools 390

Conclusion 398

Key Chapter Term 399

References 399

Further Readings 400

26. Secrets of Creating Positive Work Cultures: The Work Lives of Teachers 401
Frank Davidson

What Is Culture? 402

The Current Context 403

The Interplay of Culture and Leadership 404

A Changing Workforce and Cultural Implications 406

Five Secrets of Creating Positive Work Cultures 407

Conclusion 410

Key Chapter Terms 411

References 412

Further Readings 413

27. New South Realities: Demographics, Cultural Capital, and Diversity 417
Tawannah G. Allen and Dionne V. McLaughlin

North Carolina as a Microcosm of the Changing Complexion of the United States 419

African American and Latino Underachievement Through the Lenses
of Cultural and Social Capital 419

Descriptions of African American and Latino Underachievement 421

Effectively Educating African American and Latino Students 423

Appendix A: Interview Questions for Assistant Superintendents 428

Appendix B: Interview Questions for Principals 429

Key Chapter Terms 430

References 430

Further Readings 431

PART X. POLITICS, ELECTIONS, AND ACCOUNTABILITY

28. School Leadership and Politics 435
Catherine Marshall, Darlene C. Ryan, and Jeffrey E. Uhlenberg

Power, Conflict, and Leaders as Political Actors 435

Society's Wicked Problems Land on Principals' Shoulders 435

Power, Principals' Roles, and the Organizational Realities of Schools 436

The Actors in the Dramas of School Politics 441

Politics and the Career 445

Challenges for Women and Minorities in Administration 447

Exercising Power While Promoting Instruction, Democracy, and Community 447

Politically Astute Communications 448

Politics and Leadership for Social Justice 448

Wicked Problems Revisited 450

Key Chapter Terms 451

References 451

Further Readings 453

29. Producing "Evidence": Overcoming the Limitations of the Market, Competition, and Privatization **455**
Christopher Lubienski, Janelle Scott, and Elizabeth DeBray

Markets, Competition, and Privatization in Education 456

The Promise of Incentivism 457

Empirical Evidence on Incentivist Policies 458

A New Political Economy of Research Evidence? 459

Patterns of Strategic Efforts in Advocacy for Incentivist Policies 460

Toward a Theory of Advocacy Coalitions in Advancing Education Reforms 463

Conclusion: Caveat Emptor 465

Key Chapter Terms 466

References 466

Further Readings 470

30. The Changing Nature of Teachers' Unions and Collective Bargaining **471**
Todd A. DeMitchell

Beyond the Wisconsin Budget Repair Act: Money, Power, and Relevance 472

What Unions Do 472

The Role of Union Member and Professional Teacher 475

The Industrial Labor Model 477

Good Faith and Disputes 478

Enforcement of Rights and Responsibilities: Grievances and Unfair Labor Practices 479

The Future of Unions and Collective Bargaining 481

Key Chapter Terms 482

References 482

Further Readings 483

Appendix: Getting Started in Your Educational Leadership Career: Associations and Journals **487**

Index **491**

LIST OF FIGURES, TABLES, AND SIDEBARS

Table 1.1   Murphy's Developing Standards

Figure 2.1   Resolving the Paradoxes Between Management and Leadership

Table 2.1   A Comparison of the Papa Accoutrements of Leadership to Lessons of Leadership

Sidebar 2.1   The Nature of Leadership Accoutrements

Figure 2.2   The Context of Midlevel Managerial Decision Making

Sidebar 3.1   How to See n/networks

Figure 3.1   The Johari Window

Sidebar 3.2   Jon Thomas, the Panopticon, and the Johari Window

Sidebar 4.1   Teaching Strategies and the Common Core

Figure 4.1   Ecological Systems Theory

Figure 4.2   Sample Parent Newsletter

Sidebar 4.2   Working With Divorced Parents

Sidebar 4.3   Sample Parent/Child Activity

Sidebar 5.1   Do You Have These Barriers in Your School?

Table 7.1   Standards and Curriculum

Table 7.2   What Do Educational Leaders Need to Know?

Figure 7.1   The Requisite Curriculum Alignment for Any Plan of Accountability

Table 8.1   Number and Percentage of the Hispanic Population in the United States in 2011

Sidebar 8.1   Teaching With Dichos

Sidebar 9.1   Flipped Instruction: Possible Emerging Best Practice

Sidebar 10.1   Determining a Test's Validity

Figure 10.1   A Model of Construct Validity

Figure 11.1   An Absolute Continuum of Quality

Sidebar 11.1   Analyzing Assessments

Sidebar 12.1   How to Prevent Adult-Led Cheating on Standardized Tests

Sidebar 14.1   Online Course Standards

Figure 16.1   Current Instruction Expenditures for Public Elementary and Secondary Education, by Object and State or Jurisdiction: Fiscal Year 2009

Table 16.1   2013 Marginal Tax Rates for Citizens Filing as a Head of Household

Table 16.2   Comparison of Characteristics of Different Taxes

Sidebar 16.1   Values in Conflict

Table 16.3   Funding Weights and Corresponding Per-Pupil Amounts for the State of Georgia, Select Categories, 2009

Figure 17.1   Lawrence Schools State Aid Drop 2009 Graph

Figure 17.2   Economic Confidence

Table 17.1   Incremental Budget Modules (Music Example)

Table 17.2   Comparing Budget Levels to NCES Objectives

Figure 17.3   Budget Unit Decision Package Sample

Table 17.3   Package Ranking Example

Table 20.1   NASDPTS Stop Arm Violation Survey 2013

Figure 20.1   Broward County Public School District's New Discipline Flow Chart

Table 20.2   Percentage of Public Schools That Used Safety and Security Measures: Various School Years, 1999–2000 Through 2009–2010

Figure 20.2   Percentage of Students Ages 12 to 18 Who Reported Being Bullied at School During the Year, by Selected Bullying Problems and Sex: 2011

Figure 20.3   Percentage of Students Ages 12 to 18 Who Reported Being Cyberbullied Anywhere During the School Year, by Selected Cyberbullying Problems and Sex: 2011

Sidebar 21.1   Ten Questions on Charter Schools

Sidebar 22.1   Maintaining Good Student Conduct

Sidebar 22.2   Building School Community

Table 23.1   Percentage of Homeschooled Students, Ages 5 Through 17 With a Grade Equivalent of Kindergarten Through 12th Grade, by School Enrollment Status: 1999, 2003, and 2007

Figure 24.1   Trends in Student Services

Figure 24.2   Systems Perspective of Student Services

Sidebar 24.1   Examples of Warning Signs of a Poorly Run Student Services Program

Sidebar 24.2   Steps Administrators Can Take When Encountering Student Services Programs That Are Run Poorly

Sidebar 25.1   Challenges and Conditions at School

Sidebar 25.2   How Do Your Actions Compare?

Table 25.1   A Summary Overview of the Principals' Actions Intended to Establish a Climate of Performance and Success

Figure 26.1   Culture, as Viewed by Peterson (1999) and Schein (1992)

Figure 26.2   Sergiovanni's Hierarchy of Leadership Forces

Table 27.1   Shares of Net Population Growth, by Region, 2000–2010

Table 27.2   Growth of Latino Population in Six North Carolina Counties

Figure 27.1   North Carolina Fourth-Grade Reading Score Gaps, by Race

Sidebar 27.1   A Checklist for Working With Minority Students and Their Families

Table 28.1   Assumptive Worlds of School Administrators—The "Rules"

Sidebar 28.1   Political Realities: Who Controls Personal Days?

Sidebar 28.2   Political Realities: Parents as Lobbyists

Sidebar 28.3   Political Realities: Navigating Assumptive Worlds Rules

Sidebar 28.4   Several Strategies for Changing Beliefs and Behaviors

Sidebar 28.5   A Social Justice Advocacy Leader Is More Than Just a Good Leader

Sidebar 29.1   When Research Raises Red Flags

Sidebar 29.2   Habits of Highly Effective IOs

Sidebar 30.1   Subjects of Bargaining

Sidebar 30.2   Teacher Perceptions of Unions

Figure 30.1   Outcomes of Collective Bargaining

Sidebar 30.3   Duty to Bargain in Good Faith

ABOUT THE EDITORS

General Editor

Fenwick W. English is the R. Wendell Eaves Senior Distinguished Professor of Educational Leadership in the School of Education at the University of North Carolina at Chapel Hill, a position he has held since 2001. Dr. English has served in practitioner settings in California, Arizona, Florida, and New York as a K-12 public school teacher, middle school principal, central office coordinator, assistant superintendent, and superintendent. He has worked in the private sector as a partner in the then Big Eight accounting firm of Peat, Marwick, Mitchell & Co., in the Washington, D.C., office of the firm where he was practice director of North American Elementary and Secondary School Consulting. He was also an associate director of the American Association of School Administrators (AASA). In higher education Dr. English has been a department chair, dean, and vice-chancellor of academic affairs at the University of Cincinnati and Indiana University-Purdue University in Fort Wayne, Indiana.

Dr. English's scholarship includes more than 35 books, 25 book chapters, and over 100 articles published in both practitioner and academic/research journals. He has been recognized by his academic colleagues as a leader in his field, having been elected to the presidency of UCEA (University Council for Educational Administration) in 2006–2007 and as president of NCPEA (National Council of Professors of Educational Administration) in 2011–2012. His research and scholarship have been presented not only in North America at UCEA, AERA (American Educational Research Association), and NCPEA, but internationally at BELMAS (British Educational Leadership Management Association Society) and CCEAM (Commonwealth Council of Educational

Administration and Management). In 2013 he received the Living Legend Award for his career-long work in educational leadership from the NCPEA.

Dr. English has conducted on-site research on educational management and leadership issues in England and Australia and published in academic journals in those countries as well as on the European continent. He was editor of the 2005 *SAGE Handbook of Educational Leadership,* which was issued in a second edition in 2011; general editor of the 2006 *SAGE Encyclopedia of Educational Leadership and Management* (two volumes); and general editor of the four-volume *Educational Leadership and Administration* (part of the SAGE Library of Educational Thought and Practice series), a compilation of the most outstanding scholarship in educational leadership and administration in the past 40 years in North America, the UK, Australia, New Zealand, and Hong Kong. His recent sole authored books include *The Art of Educational Leadership: Balancing Performance and Accountability,* published by SAGE in 2008, and the best-selling *Deciding What to Teach and Test,* issued in a third edition by Corwin in 2010.

Associate Editors

JoAnn Danelo Barbour is associate professor and department chair of the Doctoral Program in Leadership Studies at Gonzaga University. Professor Barbour has a PhD (administration and policy analysis) and MA (anthropology) from Stanford University. Prior to coming to Gonzaga University, Barbour was for 22 years professor of education administration and leadership at Texas

Woman's University, where she taught courses for future school principals and superintendents, chaired to completion over 100 master's theses and professional papers, served a stint as department chair, and served one year as faculty intern in the offices of provost and chancellor. While at Texas Woman's University, Barbour was awarded the Mary Mason Lyon Award for Excellence in Scholarship, Teaching and Service, the university's highest award for a junior professor; the Ann Uhlir Endowed Fellowship for Higher Education Administration; and in 2012 the Outstanding Faculty Award for Research Mentor, College of Professional Education. In 2013 the university awarded Barbour status of Professor Emerita.

Formerly chief editor of *Academic Exchange Quarterly*, Barbour created and for several years edited the topic Teaching Leadership/Teaching Leaders for the journal. Former International Leadership Association (ILA) Leadership Education Special Interest Group Chair, Barbour coedited two ILA volumes in the *Building Leadership Bridges (BLB)* book series: *Global Leadership: Portraits of the Past, Visions for the Future* (2008) and *Leadership for Transformation* (2010), and was chief editor of *Leading in Complex Worlds* (BLB 2012). Her publications include 10 entries in *the Encyclopedia of Educational Leadership and Administration* and several journal articles and chapters in leadership texts, including recently the chapter "Critical Policy/ Practice Arenas Predicting 21st-Century Conflict" in *The SAGE Handbook of Educational Leadership* (2nd ed., 2011), and, with Claudia Sanchez, "A Critical Approach to the Teaching and Learning of Critical Social Science at the College Level" in *Critical Qualitative Research Reader* (2012). Additionally, Barbour has presented over 30 papers at professional conferences. Her research interests are qualitative in nature and include critical, philosophical, experiential, multidisciplinary, and artistic approaches to the study of leadership, organizations, and teaching. Currently Barbour is exploring the philosophical and practical underpinnings and approaches to authentic leadership. Barbour has taught in Florence, Italy, and plans to teach more courses there in the future. Courses she enjoys teaching include any in the area of leadership and leadership studies, but especially: leadership theories and

practices, organizational theories and practices, organizational culture, qualitative research courses, designing conceptual frameworks, ethics, and critical and political philosophies/theories courses. While teaching is a joy, the most sublimely gratifying part of Barbour's academic career continues to be working with doctoral and master's students on their research projects from the inception of the research questions to the completion of the thesis or dissertation.

Rosemary Papa is the Del and Jewel Lewis Endowed Chair in Learning Centered Leadership and professor of educational leadership in the College of Education at Northern Arizona University, a position she has held since 2007. In 2000 she founded the *eJournal of Education Policy*, one of the first open access, free, blind-peer-reviewed journals in the world, and serves as its executive editor. She founded the Sacramento Heart Gallery, an organization to provide adoption for older children in foster or group homes, in 2005, and in 2012 she founded Educational Leaders Without Borders, an organization focused on children not in school and on the role of economic, cultural, and political influences on schooling worldwide.

Dr. Papa's record of publications includes 14 books, more than 80 refereed journal articles, and numerous book chapters and monographs. She has been an elementary and junior high school teacher, served as a principal and chief school administrator for two districts in Nebraska, and in higher education served as California State University system level assistant vice chancellor for academic affairs, vice president for Sylvan Learning, Inc., faculty director of a university-based Center for Teaching and Learning in California, and founded two joint doctoral programs in educational leadership with University of California and the California State University.

In 1991–1992, Dr. Papa was elected as the first female president of the National Council of Professors of Educational Administration (NCPEA) and currently serves as the organization's first international ambassador. She has received the NCPEA Living Legend Award and has been invited to present their Walter D. Cocking lecture on two separate occasions.

She has worked internationally in China, Singapore, Korea, and West Africa, bringing adult learning practices and multimedia technology training to their university classrooms. She is a noted educator with expertise in leadership skills and characteristics, accoutrements, mentoring, adult learning, and multimedia technology. In recent years, she was the editor of *Technology Leadership for School Improvement* (2011), Sage Publications; associate editor of the *Handbook of Online Instruction and Programs in Education Leadership* (2012), NCPEA Publications; coauthor of *Educational Leadership at 2050: Conjectures, Challenges, and Promises* (2012), and *The Contours of Great Educational Leadership* (2013), both published by Rowman & Littlefield; and editor and chapter author, *Media Rich Instruction: Connecting Curriculum to All Learners* (2014), Springer Publishing.

CONTRIBUTORS

Tawannah G. Allen is an associate professor at Fayetteville State University (FSU). She earned her doctorate in education degree from the University of North Carolina at Chapel Hill. Prior to her role at FSU, she served as a human resources administrator with Wake County Public Schools in Cary, North Carolina, and as executive director of human resources and professional development with Bertie County Schools. Earlier she served as director of elementary education and professional development with Chapel Hill-Carrboro City Schools. Dr. Allen has facilitated trainings and presented at many conferences and lecture series pertaining to the challenges African American and Latino male students face within the public school sector. Many of these discussions focused on understanding how theoretical perspectives such as resiliency, critical race, and successful pathway theories are imperative when educating students of color. Her most recent scholarly article on the achievement of minority males was "The Resilient Ones: Voices of African American Males," in the *Journal of Urban Education: Focus on Enrichment, 1*(1), 21–31.

M. David Alexander is a professor in the Department of Educational Leadership and Policy Studies, School of Education, at Virginia Polytechnic Institute and State University. He received his EdD in educational administration from Indiana University in 1969, and joined Virginia Tech in 1972 after having taught at Western Kentucky University. Dr. Alexander was a math teacher, coach, and school board member in the public schools of Kentucky and Virginia. He is coauthor of five books, one of which, *American Public School Law,* is currently in its eighth edition and is a leading graduate textbook on education law. He is a coauthor of *The Challenges*

to School Policing, a publication of the Education Law Association. He has also written numerous research reports and articles, many of which have been presented at regional, national, and international meetings.

James E. Berry is a professor in the Department of Leadership & Counseling at Eastern Michigan University. He has served as an assistant principal, principal, assistant superintendent, department head, and associate dean. He was an American Council on Education fellow in 2001. He presently serves as the executive director of the National Council of Professors of Educational Administration. Berry has conducted research and written in the area of K-12 school reform with a focus on change leadership and the use of technology.

Kimberly A. Gordon Biddle is a university professor with over 20 years of experience. Her research interests include motivation and resilience in students who are at risk because of family income level, stressful life circumstances, ethnic minority status, learning English as a second language, and/or being a student with a special need. She is especially interested in the education and socialization of these children. She has coauthored a textbook, written more than 12 peer-reviewed articles, and presented at more than 30 peer-reviewed conferences. At Sacramento State University, she teaches students who want to advocate for, teach, and/or work with children and families in some capacity.

Brad E. Bizzell is an assistant professor and program area coordinator for the educational leadership program at Radford University. Radford's educational leadership program uses a blended learning model that includes a combination of synchronous and asynchronous online and face-to-face instruction. Bizzell completed his PhD in Educational Leadership and Policy Studies at Virginia Tech in 2011 where he also earned a Master Online Instructor Certificate. Prior to his current position, he worked for 25 years in public education as a teacher, principal, and school improvement specialist with the Virginia Department of Education. His experience includes work at all levels of education in rural, suburban, and urban school districts.

Ira Bogotch is a professor of school leadership at Florida Atlantic University. In the 1990s, he facilitated the development of leadership standards in Louisiana. In 2014, the *International Handbook of Educational Leadership and Social (In)Justice* was published by Springer, coedited by Professor Carolyn Shields and Ira. He also serves on a number of editorial boards including the SAGE journal *Urban Education,* as well as *The Scholar-Practitioner Quarterly, The Professional Educator,* and the *Journal of Research in Leadership Education.* He is the associate editor of the *Journal of Cases in Educational Leadership,* published in association with the University Council for Educational Administration, and the *International Journal of Leadership in Education.* Professor Bogotch has also held short-term visiting professorships in Malaysia, Scotland, and Australia.

Kathleen M. Brown currently serves as professor of educational leadership and policy at the University of North Carolina at Chapel Hill. Her research interests include effective, site-based servant leadership that connects theory, practice, and issues of social justice. Her most recent book, *Preparing Future Leaders for Social Justice, Equity, and Excellence*, was published as part of the Christopher-Gordon School Leadership Series. Kathleen received a bachelor of arts degree in psychology and theology with an elementary education concentration from Immaculata College, a master of arts in educational administration from Rowan University, and her EdD at Temple University.

Launcelot I. Brown, PhD, is the Barbara A. Sizemore Professor of Urban Education at Duquesne University, associate professor of educational research, and chair of the Department of Educational Foundations and Leadership. He earned his PhD in educational research, evaluation, and policy studies from Virginia

Tech. Dr. Brown is a former teacher, special educator for students with emotional and behavioral difficulties, and a former principal of a school for deaf children. He has served on many national educational boards in Trinidad and Tobago, including the National Advisory Committee on Special Education. His research interests are in the areas of school leadership, student achievement, national assessment, and teachers' use of assessment data, with a focus on the English-speaking Caribbean. In conducting his research, he utilizes both quantitative and qualitative methodologies. Dr. Brown has been an invited speaker and presented his work at several international, national, and regional conferences. He served as an associate editor for the journal *Educational Measurement: Issues and Practice* from 2006 to 2009 and is an active member of the Comparative & International Education Society, the American Educational Research Association, and the National Council on Measurement in Education.

Theodore B. Creighton was a professor of educational leadership and policy studies at Virginia Tech prior to his retirement in 2011. He has served as a teacher in the Los Angeles Unified School District and as a principal and superintendent in Fresno and Kern counties, California. Creighton is widely published in the areas of school leadership and the use of data to improve decision making in K-12 schools. He currently serves as publications director for the National Council of Professors of Educational Administration.

Autumn Tooms Cyprès is the chair of the Department of Educational Leadership in the School of Education at Virginia Commonwealth University. She is a former school principal whose research examines the politics of school leadership and school reform. Her contributions as a principal include the desegregation of a school and the implementation of a schoolwide dual language program. Autumn served as the 50th president of the University Council for Educational Administration, and her work can be found in journals for scholars and practicing school leaders such as *Educational Administration Quarterly, Kappan,* and *Educational Leadership.* She received her doctorate from Arizona State University in 1996.

Frank Davidson is the superintendent of the Casa Grande Elementary School District in Casa Grande,

Arizona, a position he has held since 1997. He has served as a teacher, principal, and assistant superintendent for curriculum and instruction. He received his doctorate in education at the University of Arizona in 2005. He coauthored *Contours of Great Leadership,* published in 2013. He received the Superintendent of the Year Award for Large School Districts from the Arizona School Administrators in 2000 and was the Arizona nominee for National Superintendent of the Year, presented by the American Association of School Administrators in 2006.

Elizabeth DeBray is a professor in the Department of Lifelong Education, Administration, and Policy in the College of Education, University of Georgia. She received her EdD in administration, planning, and social policy from the Harvard Graduate School of Education in 2001. Dr. DeBray's major interests are the implementation and effects of federal and state elementary and secondary school policies and the politics of education at the federal level. She is author of *Politics, Ideology, and Education: Federal Policy During the Clinton and Bush Administrations* (Teachers College Press, 2006), which analyzes the politics of the reauthorization of the Elementary and Secondary Education Act in the 106th and 107th Congresses. She was a 2005 recipient of the National Academy of Education/Spencer Postdoctoral Fellowship, which supported her research on education interest groups, think tanks, and Congress. With Christopher Lubienski and Janelle Scott, she is the coprincipal investigator on a William T. Grant–funded project on how intermediary organizations promote research on incentivist policies (charter schools and teacher pay for performance) in three school districts and at the national/federal level.

Todd A. DeMitchell is the John and H. Irene Peters Endowed Professor of Education at the University of New Hampshire. He was named distinguished professor of the university in 2010 and was selected as the Lamberton Professor of Justice Studies from 2010 to 2013. He earned graduate degrees from the University of La Verne (American intellectual history), University of California at Davis (philosophy of education), and the University of Southern California (education). In addition, he completed his postdoctoral study at Harvard University (school law and policy). He has published six books on school

law and labor relations in education and over 160 book chapters, law review articles, peer-reviewed journal articles, professional education articles, and case and policy commentaries. Prior to joining the faculty at the University of New Hampshire, he spent 18 years in the public schools of California, holding such positions a substitute teacher, elementary school teacher, assistant principal (K-6), principal (K-8), director of personnel amd labor relations (K-12), and superintendent (K-8). He served as the chief negotiator for two school districts and consults with school districts and teachers about collective bargaining and labor relations issues.

Shannon Dickson is a university professor and a licensed psychologist in part-time private practice in Sacramento, California, where she provides psychoeducational assessments and individual psychotherapy services to adults and youths with a special focus on children, adolescents, and families. As a member of the Sacramento Multicultural Counseling and Consulting Associates (MCCA) she provides consultation services, workshops, and trainings in K-12 schools in such areas as culturally responsive service delivery, crisis intervention, and recognizing trauma response in children. She has coauthored two book chapters and written several journal articles and has presented at two international conferences and a host of national and local conferences. Her research interests include responses of youths and families of color to traumatic experiences (e.g., child abuse and intimate partner violence) and culturally responsive mental health treatment of children and their families.

Patricia F. First is the Eugene T. Moore Distinguished Professor of Educational Leadership at Clemson University and Director of the UCEA Center for Leadership in Law and Education. Dr. First's research and teaching are focused on the legal and policy issues of the education system, particularly those issues intersecting with ethical leadership furthering justice for children, the role of school boards and the financing of education. She is the author of *Educational Policy for School Administrators,* and *School Boards: Changing Local Control.* She has written numerous legal monographs, book chapters, and articles in scholarly and practitioner journals and has presented education law topics nationally and internationally. Her current work focuses upon the legal and ethical rights of immigrant children. Dr. First received her EdD at Illinois State University and her JD at The University of Dayton School of Law.

Kimberly Kappler Hewitt serves as assistant professor of educational leadership at the University of North Carolina Greensboro. She earned her PhD in educational leadership from Miami University. Her books include *Differentiation Is an Expectation: A School Leader's Guide to Building a Culture of Differentiation* (2011) and *Postcards From the Schoolhouse: Practitioner Scholars Examine Contemporary Issues in Instructional Leadership* (2013). Her research focuses on the ethical and efficacious use of educational data. She served as a school and district administrator for 8 years in Ohio where she worked to cultivate and interrogate best practices in classroom instruction.

Eric A. Houck, is an associate professor of educational leadership and policy at the University of North Carolina at Chapel Hill. He earned his doctoral degree from Peabody College of Vanderbilt University. Dr. Houck is a specialist in school finance, having published in an array of journals on such topics as equity and efficiency in state education funding systems, and the resource allocation implications of district level policies such as student assignment.

Jane Clark Lindle, PhD, is Eugene T. Moore Professor of Educational Leadership at Clemson University. She has developed innovative leadership development programs for aspiring and practicing school leaders in rural schools. She has prepared parents and community members for their decision-making roles in school governance. Lindle has experience as a principal in two states and as a teacher in five states. She has served as a special education teacher in secondary schools. Her recent publications include work on school safety and cognitive coaching of experienced and midcareer school leaders.

Christopher Lubienski is a professor of education policy and the director of the Forum on the Future of Public Education at the University of Illinois and Sir Walter Murdoch Adjunct Professor at Murdoch University in Australia. His research focuses on education policy, reform, and the political economy of education, with a particular concern for issues of equity and access. His current work examines organizational responses to competitive conditions in local education markets, including geo-spatial analyses of charter schools and research on innovation in education markets. Lubienski was recently a Fulbright Senior Scholar for New Zealand and continues to study that country's school policies and student enrollment patterns. He is principal investigator of a multiyear project on intermediary organizations' ability to influence the use of research evidence in the policymaking process with Elizabeth DeBray and Janelle Scott. He has authored both theoretical and empirical papers, including peer-reviewed articles in the *American Journal of Education,* the *Oxford Review of Education,* the *American Educational Research Journal, Educational Policy,* and the *Congressional Quarterly Researcher.* Lubienski is the author of *The Charter School Experiment: Expectations, Evidence, and Implications* (with Peter Weitzel, Harvard Education Press, 2010) and *The Public School Advantage: Why Public Schools Outperform Private Schools* (with Sarah Theule Lubienski, University of Chicago Press, 2014).

Fred C. Lunenburg is The Jimmy N. Merchant Professor of Education at Sam Houston State University, where he teaches graduate courses in educational leadership. He has taught at the University of Louisville and Loyola University Chicago. In addition, he has served as a high school English teacher, principal, superintendent of schools, and university dean. He has authored or coauthored 25 books and more than 200 journal articles. His best known books include: *Educational Administration: Concepts and Practices* (1991, 1996, 2000, 2004, 2008, 2012), *Creating a Culture for High-Performing Schools* (2008, 2012), *Writing a Successful Thesis or Dissertation* (Corwin, 2008), *The Principalship: Vision to Action* (2006), *Shaping the Future* (2003), *The Changing World of School Administration* (2002), and *High Expectations: An Action Plan for Implementing Goals 2000* (Sage, 2000).

Catherine Marshall is the R. Wendell Eaves Distinguished Professor of Educational Leadership and Policy at the University of North Carolina, Chapel Hill. Her ten books include *Designing Qualitative Research, Reframing Educational Politics for Social Justice, Leadership for Social Justice, The Assistant Principal,* and *Activist Educators.* Marshall was president of the Politics of Education Association and vice president of politics and policy of the American Educational Research Association. Awards include the Stephen Bailey Award for Shaping the Intellectual and Research Agendas of the Field of Politics and the Campbell Lifetime Achievement Award for contributions that changed the leadership field.

Dionne V. McLaughlin, author of "Insights: How Expert Principals Make Difficult Decisions," is an assistant professor at North Carolina Central University. She is a British-born Jamaican educator and an experienced bilingual high school and elementary school principal. Dr. McLaughlin has 13 years of experience as a principal and assistant principal, five years of experience as a K-12 director, and four years of experience as a program director for a Latino community-based organization. Additionally, she has nine years of experience teaching. Her doctorate of education in educational leadership was earned from the University of North Carolina at Chapel Hill. She completed her master's in education from the Harvard Graduate School of Education. Her most recent scholarly article on effective teachers of African American and Latino high school students was "Inside Our World: How Administrators Can Improve Schools by Learning From the Experiences of African American and Latino High School Students," in the National Council of Professors of Educational Administration (NCPEA) *Education Leadership Review* Special Issue (2013),*14*(2), 28–40.

Connie M. Moss, an associate professor and director of the Center for Advancing the Study of Teaching and Learning (CASTL) at Duquesne University, earned her EdD at Duquesne. Her research, published in books, chapters, and journal articles, occurs at the nexus of classroom assessment, social justice, student learning and achievement, teacher effectiveness, and educational leadership. Her most recent book, coauthored with Susan Brookhart, is *Formative Classroom Walkthroughs: How Principals and Teachers Collaborate to Raise Student Achievement* (ASCD, 2015). The book advances a learning target theory of action to help principals and teachers use evidence from what students produce during daily lessons to develop assessment capable students, increase the effectiveness of teachers and administrators, and raise student achievement.

Abul Pitre, PhD, is professor and department head of educational leadership and counseling at Prairie View A&M University, where he teaches graduate courses. His current research interests are in the areas of multicultural education for educational leaders, critical educational theory, and the educational philosophy of Elijah Muhammad.

William K. Poston, Jr., is an emeritus professor of educational leadership and policy studies at Iowa State University in Ames, Iowa, where he served from 1990 to 2005. He taught school finance and school business management and managed the Iowa School Business Management Academy, sponsored by the Iowa Association of School Business Officials. He is the former superintendent of schools in Tucson and Phoenix, Arizona, and in Billings, Montana. He was the youngest elected international president of Phi Delta Kappa, selected as an outstanding young leader in American education in 1980. He has authored numerous professional articles and published over a dozen professional books.

Pamela Jane Powell spent over two decades as an elementary school teacher prior to coming to Northern Arizona University. Now, she is dedicated to helping teachers learn to utilize current, inclusionary, and developmentally appropriate practices in their classrooms to promote learning for all students. She serves as chair of the Department of Teaching and Learning in the College of Education at NAU. Interested in education policies that affect students in public school settings, she has studied the practice of grade retention and is interested in studying the high correlation of grade retention to subsequent high school dropout, transitions, and subsequent life trajectories.

Jennifer Prior is an associate professor of literacy and early childhood in the Department of Teaching and Learning at Northern Arizona University. She received her PhD in curriculum and instruction from Arizona State University. Her research interests include early literacy, family involvement in education, and teacher preparation. She is the author and coauthor of over 70 books and articles for teachers, including *Environmental Print in the Classroom: Meaningful Connections for Learning to Read, Family Involvement in Early Childhood Education: Research Into Practice,* and "Curriculum: The Inside Story" in *Curriculum and Teaching*

Dialogue, 14(1/2). She has 12 years of teaching experience in elementary classrooms.

Matthew T. Proto currently serves as assistant dean of admission at Stanford University. Previously, he served as director of selection for the Morehead-Cain Scholarship at the University of North Carolina at Chapel Hill, associate director of admission and college counseling at Choate Rosemary Hall, and assistant director of undergraduate admission at Yale University. Matt received a bachelor of arts in history from Yale University, a master of arts in liberal studies from Wesleyan University, and his EdD at the University of North Carolina at Chapel Hill.

Beth Parrott Reynolds, PhD, is the executive director of the National Dropout Prevention Center at Clemson University. She is a former English teacher, high school principal, and assistant superintendent with more than 30 years of experience in leading schools and districts to develop the internal capacity to drive change for student and organizational success. In addition to keynote speeches, Reynolds is often asked to lead deep work with schools and districts in areas including standards, assessment, instruction, and grading. She is a coauthor on two books about assessment.

Darlene C. Ryan is the principal of Glenwood Elementary School, Chapel Hill, North Carolina, and formerly served as the math-science coordinator. She completed her bachelor's, master's, and doctorate degrees at the University of North Carolina at Chapel Hill with a dissertation on principal mentoring. Ryan currently serves as the president of the National Science Education Leadership Association (NSELA) and has served as North Carolina Science Leadership Association (NCSLA) president. The UNC-CH School of Education honored Ryan with the Distinguished Alumni Award—Excellence in Teaching, and NCSLA honored Ryan with the Herman Gatling Distinguished Service to Science Education Award. Ryan recently completed the North Carolina Principal and Assistant Principal Association Distinguished Leadership in Practice Program.

Claudia Sanchez is associate professor of bilingual education and English as a second language at Texas Woman's University. She earned a PhD in educational psychology with an area of emphasis in bilingual education at Texas A&M University-College Station. Her publications explore culturally appropriate strategies for the instruction of English language learners in kindergarten through fifth grades and family involvement of Spanish-speaking Hispanics in public schools.

Claire E. Schonaerts taught 35 years in the PreK-12 school setting and served in the area of school administration before spending the last decade in higher education. She has brought her years of experience and passion for teaching and learning to teacher-candidates as an associate clinical professor at Northern Arizona University. Her work with pre-service teachers is fueled by her desire to support their knowledge, skills, and professional dispositions. Supporting children's early literacy development and acquisition in the United States, Asia, and Europe is an enduring interest that propels her research and outreach. Her work with teachers and administrators to support the survivors of devastating typhoons in the Philippines has provided opportunities for mutual understanding and professional development in a cross-cultural setting.

Janelle Scott is an associate professor at the University of California at Berkeley in the Graduate School of Education and African American Studies Department. A former elementary school teacher, her research explores the relationship between education, policy, and equality of opportunity through three policy strands: (a) the racial politics of public education; (b) the politics of school choice, marketization, and privatization; and (c) the role of elite and community-based advocacy in shaping public education. She was a Spencer Foundation Dissertation Year Fellow and a National Academy of Education/Spencer Foundation Postdoctoral Fellow. With Christopher Lubienski and Elizabeth DeBray, and funding from the William T. Grant Foundation, she is currently studying the role of intermediary organizations in research production, promotion, and utilization in the case of incentivist educational reforms.

Jennifer A. Sughrue is director and graduate coordinator for the Ed.D. program in educational leadership and professor at Southeastern Louisiana University. Her areas of instruction include law, policy, ethics, politics of education, history of American schooling, comparative education, social justice in education, and leadership for diverse populations. Her areas of research focus primarily on law and policy, including special education. She writes and presents extensively on the federal constitutional rights of students.

Gail L. Thompson, Fayetteville State University's Wells Fargo Endowed Professor of Education, has written six books, including the award-nominated *The Power of One: How You Can Help or Harm African American Students,* and the critically acclaimed *Through Ebony Eyes: What Teachers Need to Know But Are Afraid to Ask About African American Students. Yes, You Can! Advice for Teachers Who Want a Great Start and a Great Finish With Their Students of Color,* a book for beginning teachers that she coauthored with her husband, Rufus Thompson, was published by Corwin. Her work has also been published in newspapers and journals nationwide. She has given hundreds of presentations and workshops, and has appeared on television and radio programs. Thompson earned a doctorate from Claremont Graduate University.

Jeffrey E. Uhlenberg currently serves as an elementary school principal in Greensboro, North Carolina. He has also been a middle school principal and assistant principal, and an elementary and middle school teacher. Uhlenberg holds masters' degrees in school administration from the University of North Carolina at Chapel Hill and in elementary education from the University of North Carolina at Greensboro. Uhlenberg coauthored an article titled "Racial Gap in Teachers' Perceptions of the Achievement Gap"

published in *Education and Urban Society* (2002). He is currently enrolled as a doctoral student at the University of North Carolina at Chapel Hill.

Alicia Valero-Kerrick is a university lecturer at California State University, Sacramento, and a school psychologist. She has worked as an evaluation coordinator, a training coordinator, and a private educational consultant. Her interests include early literacy development, best practice for students with special needs, and the professionalization of educators in the field of early childhood education to promote advanced learning and development experiences for young children. She has coauthored a textbook, *Early Childhood Education: Becoming a Professional,* and presented at various conferences. She has delivered staff development and training for early childhood education teachers working with infants, toddlers, preschoolers, and kindergartners. She has knowledge of effective instruction, consultation and coordination, mental health, behavior, school organization, prevention, and program evaluation.

Bradford J. Walston is principal at Providence Grove High School in the Randolph County School System in Central North Carolina. He earned his BA in history from East Carolina University, and he holds a master of arts in school administration and an EdD from the University of North Carolina at Chapel Hill. His research interests are in exploring school turnaround as well as the adaptive leadership capabilities of school-based administrators.

ACKNOWLEDGMENTS

The general editor acknowledges the encouragement and support of three deans in the School of Education at the University of North Carolina at Chapel Hill since 2001: Madeleine Grumet, Thomas James, and Bill McDiarmid. Thank you for making it possible to serve as general editor of the first and second editions of the *SAGE Handbook of Educational Leadership* (2005, 2011); the *Encyclopedia of Educational Leadership and Administration* (two volumes) in 2006, and the four-volume *Educational Leadership and Administration,* part of the SAGE Library of Educational Thought and Practice major works series, in 2009.

Thanks also to Robert Eaves Jr. for endowing the School of Education with funds to support research and development in educational leadership in the memory of his late father Robert Wendell Eaves Senior, who served as executive secretary of the National Association of Elementary School Principals from 1950 to 1969, and who was my professor of educational administration at the University of Southern California in 1964. He was a remarkable national educational leader.

Fenwick W. English, General Editor

INTRODUCTION

The SAGE Guide to Educational Leadership and Management: A Living Reference Situated in Practice

Welcome to the third component of SAGE's unique tripartite approach to improving educational leadership and management practice in the schools. It is called a guide to differentiate it from other reference works such as SAGE's A-to-Z *Encyclopedia of Educational Leadership and Administration*, released in 2006, and *The SAGE Handbook of Educational Leadership*, published in 2005 with a second edition in 2011, all of which were edited by Fenwick W. English. The encyclopedia is very broad and includes interdisciplinary terms and concepts that have impacted school leadership over a century, while the handbook is designed to take the reader deeply into contemporary research. The concept of a guide, however, has a very different design and purpose.

The SAGE Guide to Educational Leadership and Management is designed to be a highly readable, practical, and brief treatment of foundational knowledge and information about current leadership and management issues in the schools. While research is not ignored and is included where relevant, the *Guide* is meant to distill research and good practice rather than to become involved in purely research or methodological issues. So this book is not a review of the research about leadership and management, nor about how to conduct research about leadership and management. It is about how to improve the practice of leadership and management by providing exemplars, models, perspectives, and criteria by which practice can be redefined, reshaped, and reimagined. The *Guide* is a reference work, but it is more than that. It is a living reference situated in contemporary practice, specifically aimed at the school site administrator and students at the master's degree level.

"Talking the Talk, Walking the Walk": About the Chapter Authors

A quick look at the chapter authors of *The SAGE Guide to Educational Leadership and Management* shows that some currently are practicing school administrators. A larger number are former practitioners turned professors, who currently reside at more than 20 different institutions of higher education in 13 different states. The universities represented by the chapter authors range from public research giants such as the University of Illinois at Urbana-Champaign, the University of North Carolina at Chapel Hill, and Virginia Commonwealth University in Richmond, Virginia. Others are more regionally prominent such as Sam Houston State University in Texas, Northern Arizona University in Flagstaff, Arizona, Sacramento State University in California, and Eastern Michigan University in Ypsilanti, Michigan.

There are also authors from historically Black colleges and universities such as Prairie View A&M in Texas and Fayetteville State University in North Carolina, as well as smaller private, religiously centered institutions such as Duquesne University in Pittsburgh. The institutions in which our authors work are located in densely populated California, Texas, and Florida, and in smaller, more rural states such as Iowa and New Hampshire. In short, there is great diversity represented by our chapter authors, not only in their own personal experiences and careers as educational leaders, but in their places of work. Readers can be sure that our authors "talk the talk" because most have "walked the walk." That's why they were approached to contribute to this book by the general editor, Fenwick W. English, and the two associate editors, Rosemary Papa and JoAnn Danelo Barbour.

The Layout of *The SAGE Guide to Educational Leadership and Management*

The layout for the *Guide* consists of 30 chapters clustered into 10 broad, intersecting themes within the practice of educational leadership and management in the schools. We briefly review them here and give an overview of each section and its contents. We should say at the outset that the reader can expect some overlap and blurring among the chapter contents inasmuch as the job of managing and leading schools is an interdisciplinary endeavor. The creation of conceptually pure categories to try and provide a more singular focus for presentation and discussion is therefore elusive. For example, cyberbullying is a matter of school safety, but also an emerging area of school law. Digital learning laps over several categories relating to practice. Practical problems almost always lap over more than one academic discipline or category. That is to be expected, and confronting these problems depends on how one sorts them out. If the problems in educational leadership and management are interdisciplinary, then so must be texts that purport to solve them. Each chapter ends with key terms defined and further readings recommended. Links are also provided for websites, blogs, and other types of electronic references, so that the reader can quickly learn more.

Here, we present the general flow of the book. We did not assume that a reader would sit down and chronologically read it from Chapter 1 to Chapter 30. Rather our assumption was that readers would jump into some chapters as the need for such a resource arose in their practice of school leadership, and perhaps not read other chapters because there were no problems in that area. So the context of the book is one that may be called "need" or "problem" based reflecting the old adage that, "If it ain't broke, don't fix it." Graduate programs using a case study approach to learning school administration would be especially apt to use the text, as would school practitioners.

However, the guide can also be used in a more traditional way and read sequentially. The logic of the chapter flow does reflect how the editors conceptualize the most important aspects of leadership at the school site level. The context for the chapters is distinctively American and located within the American social, cultural, and legal systems. This is not to say that educators in other nations do not have similar problems; they too might find the chapter contents interesting and useful. It simply acknowledges that the focus of the book is centered in the American experience. We now review the 10 book themes and the chapters within each theme.

The Themes and Chapters of the *Guide*

Theme 1: Leadership and Management

The initial three chapters of the *Guide* present the core notions of leadership and management that provide a conceptual framework for the remainder of the book. The initial chapter, "Unraveling the Leadership/Management Paradox," by Ira Bogotch of Florida Atlantic University, confronts the paradox of whether improving schools is an issue for management or for leadership. He observes that American school administration was, and remains, in thrall to the tenets of scientific management and specifically to the ideas of Franklin Bobbitt. Dr. Bogotch indicates how these tenets are reflected in leadership standards, but proffers the notion that leadership cannot be improved without a reengagement in school management and that is the paradox to be confronted in improving and reforming schools.

The second chapter, "The Emerging Wisdom of Educational Leadership" by the guide's Editor Fenwick W. English of the University of North Carolina at Chapel Hill and Associate Editor Rosemary Papa of Northern Arizona University, picks up the themes developed in Chapter 1, and posits that both leadership and management are required to improve schools. It is not a choice to be captured by one or the other, but rather a dynamic dyad that must be taken together. The chapter then examines six dimensions of this dyad and explores the concept of artful leadership within Dr. Papa's concept of *accoutrements* as a perspective regarding how experience and knowledge are woven together to improve actual leadership practice. Effective decision making involves balancing three factors: personal risk, uncertainty, and emotionality in context.

Chapter 3 is "Understanding How the Bureaucratic Maze Works," by Autumn Tooms Cyprès of Virginia Commonwealth University in Richmond, Virginia. Dr. Cyprès opens this chapter by dealing with the negative halo surrounding the term "bureaucracy" and moves to present the organizational complexity facing school site leaders by substituting the term "network" for it. School site leaders (principals, assistant principals, department or grade-level chairs, and instructional coaches) have to leverage their change agendas within formal and informal networks, collectively referenced as a kind of *stammbaum*, a German term for network or family tree. The notion of political "fit" is explored as a way to consider membership in a network and to successfully negotiate school system networks.

Theme 2: Teaching and Learning

Teaching and learning are the heart of the school and its raison d'être. The three chapters (Chapters 4, 5, and 6) within this theme concentrate on issues and practices central to teaching and learning. Chapter 4 is "What Makes a Good Teacher? Models of Effective Teaching," by Jennifer Prior of Northern Arizona University. The components of being an effective teacher are carefully reviewed and include classroom management, teaching strategies, building family partnerships, and reflective teaching. The need for differentiated instruction is discussed along with the concept of building family partnerships.

Chapter 5 is "Overcoming Learning Barriers for All Students," by Jane Clark Lindle and Beth Parrott Reynolds from Clemson University in South Carolina. The framing for the chapter is a bio-ecological understanding of students' worlds, which offers a lens for attending to multiple aspects of the learner's ecology (social, cultural, political, institutional, interpersonal, and individual). This broader approach requires analysis of four ecologies in the following order: (a) social, cultural, and economic, (b) policies and rules, (c) teaching strategies, and then (d) learning strategies for individual students' use. When school leaders confront barriers to learning, they have multiple resources in their school ecologies. The key is to confront the barriers with an optimistic,

rather than a deficit, approach. One of the keys is the idea of a community audit, which is described in detail.

Chapter 6 is "Response to Intervention and Its Impact on Classroom Performance," by Alicia Valero-Kerrick of California State University at Sacramento. As Dr. Valero-Kerrick explains, Response to Intervention (RTI) is an innovative service delivery model designed to help all students succeed academically. It is a tiered intervention framework where students are provided with *research-based instruction,* and *evidence-based interventions* that are student unique. RTI addresses long-standing concerns with educating students with learning challenges, including English language learners, students from impoverished backgrounds, and students with learning disabilities. Since all 50 states allow RTI as a method for learning disability identification, this chapter is timely and relevant everywhere in the United States.

Theme 3: Curriculum and Instruction

Practical concerns with matters pertaining to curriculum and instruction are the theme of Chapters 7 to 9. Chapter 7, first under this theme, is Fenwick English's "Multiculturalism Versus the Common Core." As the nation moves toward a common curriculum with a common set of tests for the first time in its history, several important issues have emerged. The first is the question, "Whose common curriculum is common?" The enormous cultural diversity of the U.S. school population means that some children would inevitably find the idea of knowledge that is common to all not to be true of their different cultural experience. The idea of multiculturalism is severely challenged with a one size fits all assumption behind the Common Core State Standards. Other issues with the Common Core revolve around the control of the curriculum, which up to this time has been reserved to the respective states. Will there end up being a common national curriculum, and will this be unconstitutional?

Chapter 8 is "The Growing Hispanic Population in U.S. Schools: Challenges and Solutions" from Claudia Sanchez, a professor of bilingual education at Texas Woman's University. The author identifies the four main challenges facing school leaders as a result of the growth in the numbers of Hispanic students, along with five potential solutions that include strategies school leaders can use to overcome them. The challenges are the importance of responding to school enrollment projections, the need to educate children of poverty, the urgency of meeting the needs of language minority children, and the need to reduce dropout rates and increase college completion rates. Among the many program options for English language learners, bilingual education is more effective than all-English approaches (submersion, structured English immersion, ESL), especially in cases where ELLs' native language is stronger than their second language. Dr. Sanchez concludes with an exploration of the critical assumptions behind effective programs for non-English language speakers.

Chapter 9 is by Kimberly Kappler Hewitt, a professor of educational leadership at the University of North Carolina at Greensboro, who explores the topic of "The Continuing Search for Best Practices in Classroom Instruction." The concept of best practices reflects the 17th- and 18th-century Enlightenment notion of betterment through change grounded in scientific knowledge. Dr. Hewitt indicates that while the concept of best practices has notable merits, there are also substantive concerns about it that fall into four broad categories: theoretical challenges, issues of social justice and equity, challenges of practice, and misuse of best practices. Among the most serious is that best practices work toward oversimplifying and ultimately deskilling teaching. Dr. Hewitt says that when considering best practices, we must ask, "Best for whom, in what context, under what conditions, for what goals/ends/purposes and best as determined by whom, using what criteria and evidence, and selected over what alternatives?" Context is key and includes historical, social, political, and cultural elements. There is no best practice that serves all students' needs at any given time in any given setting.

Theme 4: Testing and Assessment

There are few more heated issues in education today than matters concerning testing and assessment and their use in accountability and pay for performance schemes. Three chapters in this theme (Chapters 10, 11 and 12) explore these issues and more. Chapter 10 is "What Is This Test Really Testing? Validity, Reliability, and Test Ethics" by Launcelot I. Brown, a professor at Duquesne

University. Dr. Brown differentiates between tests and assessments, indicating that assessment is the process of documenting, describing, quantifying, and interpreting the data from a test to retrieve the information hidden therein about an individual's learning, attitudes, and beliefs. The overarching questions posed in this chapter are, "Is the test really capturing the data it was designed to capture?" and "Is the test being used with the appropriate population?" The answers to these questions address issues of the reliability of the data generated by the test and, as a consequence, the validity of the conclusions drawn from the test. But, foundational to each question is an ethical concern. Thus issues of reliability and validity are ethical issues and are integral to the code of ethical standards that delineate the social responsibility that guides a profession and the personal responsibility of practitioners within the profession.

Chapter 11 is "Achievement Gaps: Causes, False Promises, and Bogus Reforms," by Dr. Connie M. Moss, also from Duquesne University. In the first part of this chapter, Dr. Moss discusses the question "What is achievement?" The answer is not obvious. Achievement can have numerous definitions depending on content, grade level, and expectations for success. The chapter examines the historic achievement gap over several decades and offers a wide and penetrating review of the adequacies and inadequacies of the No Child Left Behind Act (NCLB) as well as Race to the Top (RTT). Various types of gaps are also discussed, including those attributed to race, opportunity, and competency.

In Chapter 12, "Cheater, Cheater, I Declare: The Prevalence, Causes, and Effects of, and the Solutions to, School Cheating Scandals," Dr. Gail L. Thompson of Fayetteville State University in Fayetteville, North Carolina, discusses causes of the escalating cheating scandals, which appear to be becoming more prevalent. Described are scandals in Atlanta, Georgia, Washington, D.C., and El Paso, Texas, and the draconian approaches of the chief school administrators in these school systems who had allegedly created a climate of fear and retribution to the point where educators engaged in unethical behavior rather than face being punished or humiliated for low test scores. In El Paso, Texas, a superintendent was even sent to federal prison for schemes to defraud the district and federal government that included his involvement in inflating student test scores. Dr. Thompson closes by presenting some of the solutions that can be pursued by school leaders and teachers to counteract the new pressure to improve test scores.

Theme 5: Technology, the Internet, and Online Learning

Educators are slowly becoming aware of the enormous impact the digital world has had on students and the schools. Chapters 13, 14, and 15 explore and expose some of those impacts. In Chapter 13, "The Expanding Wireless World of Schooling" James E. Berry of Eastern Michigan University characterizes technology as a "disruptive innovation" that has already led to the decentralization and global expansion of learning. Dr. Berry examines the infrastructure of global learning and how the traditional brick-and-mortar concept of schooling is being penetrated by digitally infused structures that challenge conventional bureaucratic concepts. He then sketches out the future school as an example of a disruptive innovation in which education is "flattened" through technology. This development will create a much more individualized and personalized type of learning that is still not the norm in conventional schools.

Chapter 14 is "The Opportunities and Challenges of Online and Blended Learning," by Brad E. Bizzell of Radford University in Virginia. Dr. Bizzell observes that online learning is a fifth-generation distance learning technology, following mail, radio, television, and videoconferencing. However, unlike the previous generations of distance learning, the growth of online and blended learning is occurring at a rapid pace. Online learning is defined as teacher-led education that occurs entirely or mostly online. Online learning includes static content, multimedia, and links to various resources in addition to the online delivery of instruction. Blended learning, also referred to as hybrid learning, includes a mix, or blend, of online instruction with face-to-face instruction. Blended learning is not simply the use of Web-based resources in the conduct of a traditional class; rather, it occurs when a significant portion of the instruction is delivered in the online environment. The chapter closes with a presentation of planning for online and blended programs.

Chapter 15 is "Social Media and Texting: The Law and Considerations for School Policy" by Theodore B. Creighton and M. David Alexander, both professors at Virginia Tech. The chapter focuses on the most ubiquitous social media tools, Facebook, Myspace, and Twitter. The authors of this chapter use existing case law to help teachers and principals in the schools understand and utilize legal decisions related to social media in dealing with the enormous impact social media is having in their schools. In the past 10 years, there have been numerous cases involving students and electronic media or communication. These cases have involved student blogging, Facebook, YouTube, Myspace, email, instant messaging, and texting. The courts have been faced with numerous questions, such as, "Do the student free speech cases apply to student activity off-campus?" and "Do the student free speech cases apply if the student uses his grandmother's computer to post derogative statements about a principal or fellow student?" The authors review the most recent and important court decisions in the arena of social media and indicate that new rules are being written for communication in cyberspace.

Theme 6: Budgeting, Finance and Fund-Raising

Money for support of public education at all levels has never been tighter than in the years since the Great Recession. Chapter 16 is "Understanding School Finance Laws and Practices" by Eric A. Houck of the University of North Carolina at Chapel Hill. Dr. Houck first briefly describes the context of educational funding and then introduces four values that frame discussions of school finance issues and have implications for school administrators: equity, efficiency, liberty, and adequacy. The chapter also introduces a conceptual shift from "school finance" to "resource allocation" as a profitable framework from which school administrators may work, even in the face of the limited resources of tightly controlled school budgets.

Chapter 17, "Expectations Exceeding Revenues: Budgeting for Increased Productivity," is by William K. Poston, Jr., of Iowa State University. He describes budgeting as an art—specifically the creation of a quantified financial strategy to implement organizational plans and goals for a specified future accounting period. Moreover, it requires constraining planned expenditures to no more than tangible revenues available for the allocation process. Included are the four basic steps for budgeting and an explanation of the new requisites. These requisites pertain to including cost-benefit analyses, utilizing knowledge of the results of budgeted activities, and implementing participatory decision making for organizational allocations. The author concludes with a step-by-step outline of how to implement performance-based budgeting.

Chapter 18 is "A Free Public Education for All: Rediscovering the Promise," by Fred C. Lunenburg of Sam Houston State University in Texas. Dr. Lunenburg provides a unique perspective on much of the current commentary about the alleged failures of public education by declaring that all of the pronouncements about the crisis in education are largely a myth. He concedes, however, that there are huge disparities for children who are poor and for African American, Native American, and Latino students, compared to White students and those from certain Asian groups. Dr. Lunenburg examines the achievement gap, its causes linked to social class, poverty, racial isolation, and child-rearing and health-related barriers to school learning. He argues that NCLB does not address education inequality, and instead has had negative effects on schools. He closes the chapter by reviewing current means of privatizing public education in the form of school choice programs, including tuition tax credits, vouchers, and charter schools.

Theme 7: School Law, Safety, and the Limits of Regulation

Under this theme, the first chapter is "Today's Compelling Issues in Public School Law," written by M. David Alexander of Virginia Tech, Patricia F. First of Clemson University, and Jennifer A. Sughrue of Southeastern Louisiana University. Chapter 19 highlights two important current areas: (1) bullying and cyberbullying; and (2) search and seizure. These areas are very important to the school site administrator for several reasons, but school safety is paramount. Bullying and cyberbullying have led to students being injured and, in several cases, have been cited as at least one reason for victims committing suicide. Knowledge of when search and seizure procedures are permissible in schools is important for school administrators since these procedures relate to the need to promote school safety through measures such as removal of alcohol, drugs, and weapons from school property.

Chapter 20, "Transportation, School Safety, and Dealing With Bullies," by Jennifer A. Sughrue and M. David Alexander, examines the issue of what is a safe school? Safe schools are not only about physical safety, but about emotional and psychological safety, as well. Child safety starts when a parent takes the youngster to catch the "big yellow bus" to school. More than 450,000 school buses transport approximately 25 million students per day, which represents over 55% of the K-12 enrollment. The chapter reviews what the school site leader has to know regarding transportation, including why there was a debate regarding the use of seat belts on school buses. The authors also discuss the general matter of school violence, including the major forms of school violence—verbal, social or indirect, sexual, physical, and property-related violence; cyberbullying (also discussed in the previous chapter); and corporal punishment. The need to reexamine so-called zero-tolerance policies is also part of this very practical chapter.

In Chapter 21, "Charter Schools and the Privatization of Public Education: A Critical Race Theory Analysis," Abul Pitre of Prairie View A&M in Texas and Tawannah G. Allen of Fayetteville State University in North Carolina examine the growth of the charter school movement through the lens of critical race theory (CRT). Emerging in the mid-1970s with the work of legal scholars who were distressed over the slow pace of racial reform in the United States, CRT attempts to provide a greater understanding of the intersection of race and education. On the surface, charter schools appear to offer minority students a better educational option and thus appear to be the great equalizer for historically underserved groups. As the authors illustrate, however, analysis from an interest convergence perspective reveals that the charter school movement serves the interest of the powerful and has very little to do with education for the empowerment of disenfranchised groups. The charter school movement and the privatization of public education are not new in education. As this chapter illustrates, these movements have taken different names at different times, but the outcome remains remarkably the same.

Theme 8: Students, Parents, and Special Populations

Chapter 22 is "Student Conduct, Attendance, and Discipline: The Troika of School Safety and Stability," by Claire E. Schonaerts and Pamela Jane Powell of Northern Arizona University. The troika of positive student conduct, consistent attendance, and the cultivation of self-discipline is a major challenge of school site leaders. The ability to harness these three essential student responses—conduct, attendance, and discipline—often requires behaviors that demand professional practice. At the heart of this challenge, school leaders must be motivators, communicators, and strategists; in short, transformational leaders. As this chapter illustrates, the school community that is built on collaborative practices provides a frame that is both dynamic and stable. The chapter authors illustrate the need for systems building and the intersection of multiple systems to construct a true and reliable community school.

Chapter 23 is "Homeschooling: Parents' Rights and the Public Good," by Jennifer A. Sughrue of Southeastern Louisiana University. Dr. Sughrue explores the homeschooling movement and its current place in K-12 education across the states. The chapter begins with a look at the recent growth in homeschooling and a brief history of homeschooling in the United States to provide some background for the debate on the subject. This is followed by descriptions of some of the homeschooling options available to home educators, and then by a discussion of the legal debate over the rights of the parents versus the authority and responsibility of the state in the matter of educating children. The author adds an overview of the primary concerns associated with homeschooling, such as socialization, civic and citizenship education, and the impact of homeschooling as a social movement.

Chapter 24 is "Emerging Trends in Student Services and Counseling" by Kimberly A. Gordon Biddle and Shannon Dickson of Sacramento State University. The authors review trends in student services, such as the focus on student mental health, the emphasis on gifted and talented students, and the increased emphasis on data collection and storage in both elementary and secondary schools. More data are being archived, transferred, and communicated electronically. Because such data are easily accessible and permanent, issues have arisen concerning the privacy of the individual families and children involved. The authors also review the role of the 21st-century elementary and secondary (K-12) counselor. Counselors today are involved in preparing and supporting students' academic readiness and overall school success, thus assisting in closing the ever-widening achievement gap. Additionally, they play a major role in delivering mental health services to the students in their charge. Leadership is fast becoming

a prominent responsibility for professional school counselors as they influence and effect change in ways that teachers and administrators cannot, given their other responsibilities and duties. Counselors are trained to assess, identify areas of concern, and develop strategies to address obstacles that hinder children and adolescents' academic success. Learning to use the special talents and skills of a trained school counselor is critical in accomplishing the overall mission of a school.

Theme 9: School Climate, Culture, and High Performance

The first chapter under this theme (Chapter 25) is "Establishing a Climate of Performance and Success," by Matthew T. Proto of Stanford University in California, Kathleen M. Brown of the University of North Carolina at Chapel Hill, and Bradford J. Walston, a high school principal in North Carolina. Of particular importance is the challenge for leadership of turnaround schools, that is, chronically low-performing schools that are mandated to generate higher student achievement outcomes in very restricted time frames. Turnaround schools are placed under federal, state, or district mandate to increase student achievement within one to three years. If they are unable to do so, the principal and other staff members often face strict accountability measures (sometimes including the removal of the principal). Many school turnaround efforts have significantly increased student achievement while others have failed to generate positive results. The authors identify specific practices that have been shown to significantly impact transforming a school from a low-performing site to a high-performing site.

Chapter 26 is "Secrets of Creating Positive Work Cultures: The Work Lives of Teachers" by Frank Davidson, who is the superintendent of the Casa Grande Elementary School District in Arizona. He explains that teachers' beliefs and attitudes are central to school quality. Additionally, despite the history of teaching as work that is independent and autonomous, both researchers and practitioners agree that students experience greater success in schools where teachers work together in meaningful ways, sharing the responsibility for planning, carrying out, and assessing the outcomes of instruction. Creating school workplaces where collaboration is an expected norm must, of necessity, take into account the historical and sociological reality of schools and the organizational supports needed to foster a collegial and collaborative environment. The author highlights the impact of current school accountability policies promulgated by those who want instant and simple fixes and cheap solutions. These are often barriers to establishing a true work culture based on collaboration, which take a longer period of time and solid transformational leadership to establish. The chapter closes with an explanation of the five secrets of creating positive work cultures.

Chapter 27 is "New South Realities: Demographics, Cultural Capital, and Diversity" by Tawannah G. Allen of Fayetteville State University and Dionne V. McLaughlin of North Carolina Central University. Racial and ethnic minority populations are growing in the United States. Projections generated by the U.S. Census Bureau indicate that members of minority groups represented 37% of the population in the United States in 2011 and are expected to reach 57% by 2060. If current growth rates continue, the United States will be transformed into a "majority minority" nation by 2043. This demographic projection represents a sea change for public educational systems. The authors discuss the ways in which underachievement by minority students is characterized and how school site leaders can engage in the creation of counternarratives for these students that will lead to their academic success. The necessity of using culturally relevant curriculum content and classroom practices is also discussed.

Theme 10: Politics, Elections, and Accountability

The last theme of the *Guide* deals with "big picture" issues that impact school site leadership. Chapter 28 is "School Leadership and Politics" by Catherine Marshall of the University of North Carolina at Chapel Hill and Darlene C. Ryan and Jeffrey E. Uhlenberg, who are currently elementary school principals in North Carolina. The authors posit that school politics is mostly about manipulating and bargaining over who gets what—and who controls who gets what. They argue that school principals who ignore politics, or perform as if school leadership centers on technical competencies, will leave themselves, their staffs, their parents and communities, and their students vulnerable. The most serious problems are those that are characterized as "wicked." Wicked problems have characteristics such as no

clear solution and involve conflicting values, and perceived mistakes can carry serious consequences. The problems rarely go away because they come from chronic challenges, such as poverty, violence, and the tendency for people to take care of their self-interests and ignore others. To be politically wise and strategic means actively engaging in the political environment. To do this the authors identify three roles a politically wise leader takes to manage issues and problems: the diplomat/negotiator, the political strategist, and the executive. The authors close with a discussion of the school leader pursuing social justice and the context and implications of the choices involved.

Chapter 29 is "Producing 'Evidence': Overcoming the Limitations of the Market, Competition, and Privatization," by Christopher Lubienski of the University of Illinois at Urbana-Champaign; Janelle Scott of the University of California, Berkeley, and Elizabeth DeBray of the University of Georgia. One of the current major national debates in the United States concerns the appropriate role of the government vis-à-vis the private sector in public education. This debate around schooling has become acrimonious, with participants making moral claims for their perspectives on issues like choice and competition, or accusations about the unethical position of their opponents. The authors focus on issues for which there are some emerging empirical insights. As they point out, the empirical evidence itself not only is often disputed, but frequently serves as the center of a new political economy of knowledge production for use in public policy making. At the center of the chapter is an analysis of what the authors call "incentivist" policies in education such as the use of vouchers, charter schools, merit pay for teachers, and pay for performance. This chapter will be of enormous value to school site leaders seeking to understand the nature of the debate over incentivist policies and practices, which are beginning to be mandated in state legislation and are already impacting school leaders in many states.

Chapter 30 is "The Changing Nature of Teachers' Unions and Collective Bargaining," by Todd A. DeMitchell of the University of New Hampshire. Teachers' unions are under siege. They have been attacked as self-serving at the expense of the children. As Dr. DeMitchell notes, collective bargaining is a creature of the law: created by law, changed by law, and eliminated by law. Such laws are also under attack. The struggle is really about money, power, and influence. Dr. DeMitchell provides a concise history of unionism and points out that the major conundrum for teachers is that while their union advocates and bargains for their self-interests, teachers are professionals who provide a valuable service in the best interests of their students. Teachers tend to see themselves and describe themselves as professionals. Typically, they do not define themselves as union members but become union members when threats to their work, their livelihood, and their security arise. The chapter focuses on how teachers deal with this dilemma and how it plays out in schools. Upon the resolution of this dilemma lies the future of unions and collective bargaining.

A Final Note From the Editors

It has been a challenge to put together this initial *SAGE Guide to Educational Leadership and Management*. The editors had to keep one eye on how our academic disciplines sort out issues for analysis and inquiry and the other eye on how such knowledge can be applied in practical school site settings. The tension between these two antipodes is palpable and means that the boundaries of the disciplines sometimes become blurred and the arena of practice is not always in absolute alignment so that some advice or guidance does not always seem practical. In the end in balancing these two requirements we accepted the consequence that there is no ultimate response that everyone will find 100% satisfactory. This is another reason to view the *Guide* as a "living reference" and one that will inevitably be changed in the years ahead as the nation continues to debate and resolve the continuing dilemma of finding a form of schooling that provides justice, equality, and excellence for all of its future citizens.

PART I

Leadership and Management

1

Unraveling the Leadership/ Management Paradox

Ira Bogotch

Florida Atlantic University

One doesn't have to be a baseball fan to believe that with every spring comes a rebirth. Last year's won-lost record is wiped clean. Everyone has a chance to be this year's champion. So it is with books and articles on the topic of leadership and management. There is always hope that the next book will open one's mind to new beginnings and new insights to improve public education. That continuing search is represented in this chapter. What is not needed is a recipe for success, for, even if there were such a thing, it should be resisted, in part because context matters. We should follow ideas grounded in our own experiences rather than slavishly follow and deliver someone else's pet solution. Wheels can be reinvented if done so smartly, building on the many good ideas of others who help us to see familiar things differently.

The truth is that most educational leaders work under a lot of pressure and they want to be good and make a difference; nearly all have the desire somewhere inside themselves to change the world, for if not, why would they struggle every day? Another reality is that there is a whole lot written on leadership and management and wading through it, even superficially, can be daunting. It's best not to accept anything written on education uncritically, whether Franklin Bobbitt on **scientific management**, Joseph Murphy on standards, Thomas Sergiovanni on the

moral leadership and **the managerial mystique**, Roland Barth on improving schools, even the lead editor of this guide, Fenwick English, on critique. These are movers and shakers in the field of educational theory and practice, along with many individuals cited and not cited in this chapter. But one's own experiences and instincts are the only arbiter of truth about one's professional self.

Uncertainty and the Language of Scientific Management

According to English (1994), American educational administration was captured by the language and ideas of scientific management shortly after the beginning of the 20th century. These remain firmly entrenched—if not in its theories, then in its practice. English wrote that scientific management promotes the illusion that leadership knowledge is objective and that there are specific managerial behaviors that produce results that are true and of value. The big questions this raises are: (1) true for what purpose? and (2) of value for whom? (Bogotch, Miron, & Biesta, 2007).

Schools can be judged any number of different ways. For example, they can be assessed on indices of "financial efficiency, student attendance, student enjoyment of education, future student participation in education, student aspiration, preparation for citizenship, and so on" (Gorard, 2011, pp. 745–746). And of course they can be assessed using achievement tests, which measure one dimension of within-school learning. However, the critical issue with this latter criterion is, as Elliot Eisner (2002) reminds us, "the function of schooling is not to enable students to do better in school. The function of schooling is to enable students to do better in life" (p. 369).

Sergiovanni (1992) said the reason we forget this is due to (1) trained incapacities and (2) displacement of goals (pp. 4–5). Trained incapacity is the "tendency to focus knowledge, attention, and skills so narrowly that principals and teachers become incapable of thinking and acting beyond their prescribed roles" (p. 5). And, through goal displacement, principals and teachers "lose sight of their purposes, allowing instrumental processes and procedures to become ends in themselves" (p. 5). Together, these two concepts make up "the managerial mystique"—a phrase Sergiovanni borrowed from Abraham Zaleznik (1989) of the Harvard Business School (p. 3).

To counter this managerial mystique, we would need to focus on "personal and social development, creativity, social justice, democratic awareness or lifelong learning, reminding us that different stakeholders have varying expectations of what schools are and what they should, and should not, do" (Townsend, MacBeath, & Bogotch, in press). To which it could be asked, "Do the numbers measure the quality of teaching, learning, and leadership or rather the frequency or correlated frequencies of behaviors? Do the numbers measure learning or performance on a multiple choice examination?" (Bogotch et al., 2007, pp. 102–103).

The work of statistician Nate Silver is instructive here. Silver (2012) developed a system (PECOTA, Player Empirical Comparison and Optimization Test Algorithm) to forecast baseball performance. According to Silver, a lot of numbers are just noise (i.e., random patterns) and only a few numbers signal meaningful events and actions to which we ought to pay close attention. For Silver, the signals are underlying truths behind a statistical problem. Nowhere in his book does he talk about education or school. Nevertheless, Silver's argument is that we must interpret data in context, not just as patterns found in the data, but also in what is happening outside the data. All too often, organizations seek to maintain and sustain themselves as they are. As a result, large organizations, especially, tend to define their successes based on the needs of the system's hierarchy and protocols, ignoring signals.

This, according to Sir Ken Robinson (2006), is one reason why alternative ideas in education remain on the margins as alternatives. Robinson has said many times that schools need to reframe alternative ideas that work in practice as the new norm. Silver explains why we don't; he says that our data are based on what we know, not on what is unobservable or at present unknown. We narrow our thinking and choices to within-school variables on which we have a whole lot of data, but about which we cannot make accurate predictions. While most of us can imagine better schools and better futures for students, we don't act on these imagined ideas because they represent an unknown. But Silver reminds us that they are really known unknowns.

So what does this have to do with management and leadership? Silver makes the case for analyzing existing data in order to establish probabilities of outcomes, not certain solutions. In fact, probabilities admit that we are uncertain of the results. Or, in his words,

> Our brains process information by means of approximations. . . . With experience, the simplifications and approximations will be a useful guide and will constitute our working knowledge. But they are not perfect, and we often do not realize how rough they are. (Silver, 2012, p. 449)

School administrators instead select specific programs and materials and put all their hopes for school improvement on that set of practices supported by existing within-school correlational data. To do otherwise might be mistaken for weakness, and what we tell ourselves and the public is that we need to have strong educational leaders. In other words, "the problem comes when we mistake the approximation for the reality" (Silver, 2012, p. 450) and act accordingly. The progressive educator John Dewey (1909) asked us to make tentative hypotheses and to learn from our mistakes. In many contexts, however, to do so might get an administrator relieved of his or her position. Further, it might stain the reputation of a school improvement researcher. What is central to a status quo mindset is the belief that a product will lead to certain results in neat and easy-to-follow steps (Thrupp & Willmott, 2003, p. 54). Both administrators and researchers want to be viewed as being certain and right.

To help differentiate the issues involved, Silver (2012) makes a distinction between two concepts that all leaders face: risk and uncertainty. Silver says that risk is "something that you can put a price on" (p. 29), as in a bet in a poker game. In the game or in life, you know the odds and can account for them. Uncertainty, however, is hard to measure because you have only "some vague awareness of the demons lurking out there" (p. 29). The problem arises in all human endeavors when we mistake uncertainty for risk. That is, we calculate that which is incalculable—at present. Encouraging a school leader to take a risk without calculating the odds of success is dangerous advice, but that is precisely what many authors, experts, and trainers do in the name of innovation and improvement.

This discussion of Silver's ideas on risk and uncertainty helps us see how scientific management and similar approaches substitute certainty where there is none and why; for English, these approaches create an illusion, if not also a deception. The illusion is that each successive school reform will improve public education. In fact, existing data tell us that there is a persistent pattern of sameness in public schools across generations adding up to a century that now inscribes sameness into the theories and practices (including biases) that make up the field of educational administration.

And yet, just maybe, our understanding of uncertainties—along with calculated risks—may also be the source for us to create opportunities to develop different strategic mindsets and new actions for changes—if and only if we are willing to struggle against sameness and develop new alternative patterns, starting small and with ourselves as the primary unit of analysis. Thus, the ideas and concepts presented here are meant to make the familiar, that is, the sameness of public schools, strange so that we can rethink and reposition ourselves as public educators to enhance social, political, and economic opportunities and not just work hard to raise standardized test scores (Duke & Landahl, 2011).

A Century of Scientific Management

In 1913, Franklin Bobbitt, an instructor at the University of Chicago, wrote that "the fundamental tasks of management, direction, and supervision are always about the same" (p. 7). In other words, Bobbitt promoted the idea of general principles of

management "that have universal applicability" (p. 8) regardless of organizational settings and contexts; and, therefore, educational administrators, whom he considered to be "rather backward" (p. 8), needed to learn the general principles from business lessons. His premise for both management and education was an analogy that "education is a shaping process as much as the manufacture of steel rails" (p. 12).

Bobbitt (1913) instructed educational administrators to learn to define standards in the most specific and measureable terms. For "so long as education is content merely to set the conditions of growth in a general way with reference to standards of growth, the educational supervisor . . . is in his turn relatively helpless" (p. 14). Bobbitt cited the pioneering works of university professors of educational administration and superintendents, among them, Clarence Stone, Stuart Appleton Courtis, Edward Thorndike, and Leonard Ayres, educators who had all developed data-driven scales to measure student performance subject by subject, grade by grade.

One set of scales, a *Manual of Instructions* (Courtis, 1914), presented benchmarks for each subject in each grade. Classroom teachers could, therefore, be informed of their progress and then evaluated based on how they were able to raise students' performance based on these measureable standards. "This putting of the educational product in the forefront of education means the establishment of a continuous record of progress in the case of each of the products" (Bobbitt, 1913, p. 23). Bobbitt included data charts along with instructions to readers on how teachers should enter the data and interpret the results. Thus, it is made clear to all which child is falling behind, which child is making normal progress, and which child is above expectation. The same procedures apply to measuring teachers and supervisors.

Bobbitt (1913) recognized the need to differentiate standards based on a child's "native ability" (p. 26). A child's performance determines the standards that need to be measured and met. However, such native ability was to be used in determining the child's "vocational and social destiny" (p. 26).

In other words, schools should prevent any child "from entering any field of work" (p. 27) not consistent with his or her school performance. Thus, performance standards are of value to teachers and to their supervising principals in terms of how to improve school grades. Without belaboring the obvious, Bobbitt's scientific management has provided today's rationale for accountability systems under the No Child Left Behind Act of 2001; that is,

> with scales of measurement and standards of performance . . . , it is no longer possible for a principal to hide behind the plea that he (sic) has an inferior social class in his school, and, therefore, high performance should not be expected of him or of his teachers. (Bobbitt, 1913, p. 29)

This reads like a "no excuses" approach to management although it was written in 1913.

In 1913, education already had subject area standards for every educational product, from English composition, spelling, handwriting, stenography, arithmetic, algebra, history, and science to the many top vocations of the time. "Our problem is simply the replacement of vague, indefinite estimation with more exact methods of measurement, and the substitution of definite standards of attainment for the uncertain, fluctuating ones now used" (Bobbitt, 1913, p. 44).

While the major work of the day was still to discover the exact scientific methods of management, Bobbitt (1913) envisioned a day soon when "the [cost and time] saving in teaching labor required that is affected by the one matter of continuous records will perhaps be very much greater than the increased amount of labor necessary to make the records" (p. 48). But for that to happen, Bobbitt understood and assured readers that the distance between standards and standardization would have to decrease, if not disappear.

> In other words, the need for standards on the training side [will] serve as bases for standardizing costs in the field of physical administration . . . which will result in great improvements in methods. . . . of placing educational money, in economy and in efficiency. . . . It is but one step in the . . . direction of effective procedure. (p. 48)
> We cannot standardize teaching costs until we standardize teaching product. (p. 49)

Bobbitt explicitly says that in order to accomplish this standardization, all curriculum and classroom lessons would have to be standardized grade by grade, level by level, including the delivery of instructional materials. Thus, what is essentially an economic argument used to justify cost efficiencies in the manufacturing industry should now, analogously, drive the curriculum and pedagogies of public schools, from 1913 forward to 2014.

This efficiency-effectiveness program described in detail by Bobbitt came directly from the research writings of Frederick Taylor (March 20, 1856–March 21, 1915), a mechanical engineer, whose industrial ideas of scientific management were a practical extension of Max Weber's (April 21, 1864–June 14, 1920) ideal model for bureaucracy. At the time of Bobbitt's essay, he estimated that public education was a quarter of a century behind the world of machine shops. Using a general principle of bureaucracy, that is, the division of labor, it is up to management to use science and for teachers to put that science into practice (Bobbitt, 1913, p. 53). To do so requires continued research conducted by practitioners and universities. Scientific management requires cooperative research teams for "the isolation of the two forms of organization is, in fact, disastrous to the efficiency of both. . . . It is time to get together" (p. 61). And while even today we continue to struggle in building partnerships between K-12 systems and higher education, Bobbitt followed up rhetorically not by citing any actual school-university partnership, but instead by citing words he said were taken from a declaration by an association of German brewers as his example for public education: "science is the golden guide-star of practice. Without it there is nothing but blind groping in the unbounded realm of possibilities" (p. 62).

Clearly, by reading Bobbitt's words, or what English calls the language of scientific management, we can see how today's accountability movement essentially had been devised a century ago. We continue to promote and use business and management principles for public schools, measurement standards or benchmarks with grade-level scales, data and data-driven decision making, continuous record keeping, monitoring of student progress, student and teacher products, ideas of effectiveness and efficiency, and the notion that benchmarks and standards lead necessarily to standardization.

The Dimensions and Behaviors of School Managerial Control Explored

If this author's understanding of Bobbitt is correct, then standards and accountability are both managerial process issues. Standards and accountability have been described as two of four behavioral processes comprising a managerial control model, the other two processes being information sharing and incentives (Bogotch, 1989; Bogotch, Williams, & Hale, 1995). This model described how standards and accountability worked in concert with information and incentives, but differentiated how teachers interpreted supervisory activities.

It was found that the four processes of standards, information sharing, assessment/accountability, and incentives were perceived by teachers as operating along two almost contradictory dimensions: structural sameness versus discretionary differences. In other words, for each of the four managerial processes, teachers could distinguish between "by the book" administrative rules and regulations and the distinctive qualities by which administrators related "socially" to them. For example, when it came to setting standards and enforcing accountability, teachers paid more attention to how administrators communicated the messages and treated them. In fact, information sharing and intangible incentives influenced teachers more than either structural dimensions of standards or assessment systems. The structural dimensions of standards and accountability, at least in the 1980s and 1990s, were not particularly salient to teachers. Alas, how times have changed and how we have reverted back to the 1900s and scientific management principles.

Educational policymakers have used the two behavioral processes of standards and accountability to externally drive school reforms going forward into the 21st century, although neither control mechanism had been shown to be robust nor rigorous enough to move teacher performance prior to today's era of accountability. Moreover, whenever we see the word *standards*, it is affixed to the term *leadership*, not management. The **Interstate School Leaders Licensure Consortium (ISLLC)** 1996 standards directed the "school administrator" to act across six specific domains. By 2008, the Council of Chief State School Officers (CCSSO), in concert with the National Policy Board of Educational Administration (NPBEA), revised these standards, changing "school administrator" to "educational leader" for all six leadership standards.

This was not an isolated action. A search for the words *management* and *leadership* in Google's Ngram Viewer, which allows users to search for the frequency of words in books and then see the corresponding book titles, found that the number of book titles using the word "management" outnumbered the book titles using "leadership" by 3:1 from 1900 to 2007. During the early 1940s, books on leadership almost caught up to those of management; but, from the early 1960s on, management books took off dramatically while the number of books with "leadership" in the title remained flat.

This ratio is somewhat peculiar given that the field of educational leadership has been inundated with leadership textbooks for quite some time. A search for "school management" and "school leadership" in the Ngram Viewer shows a different picture. In 1995, school leadership titles caught up to school management titles, and then in 2002, leadership books surpassed management books for the first time. By 2005, there were almost twice as many school leadership book titles as there were books about school management. What does this language shift mean?

Were schools before 1995, before national leadership standards, run by managers, while today, our schools require educational leaders? Did this switch in terms between management and leadership actually lead to changes in the way schools operated? Can we put Franklin Bobbitt and scientific management to rest or have schools become even more managerial today (Thrupp & Willmott, 2003) even as we are reading more books and articles about leadership?

How words are used matters, and sometimes by repeating words, phrases, and talking points over and over again, new realities are created. That's certainly true for advertising and politics. But is this also the case for public education? Perhaps the author's experience with the development of leadership standards in Louisiana may help to illuminate this issue.

A year or two after the ISLLC 1996 standards were circulated, the individual states were asked if they wanted to develop their own state leadership/principal standards or follow the national ISLLC standards as written; Louisiana opted to develop its own standards.

In one statewide meeting, a school district superintendent sitting in the back of a large auditorium in Baton Rouge asked whether or not the standards for school principals dealing with technology would apply specifically to his rural classrooms (see Bogotch, 2002, p. 511). He emphatically reminded his administrator colleagues (about 150 were present that day) that most of his teachers still considered blackboards, white chalk, erasers, and students with pencils as his system's current level of technology.

At the time, he was assured that the interpretations (meaning the subsequent actions to be taken by the State Department of Education) for all the leadership standards would be flexible and adaptable to the many different contexts and students. At that time, the thought among those developing the standards was that they would be open to multiple meanings and especially to local interpretations (Bogotch, 2002, p. 512). And we had solid educational change theories with empirical evidence to support this view from a range of studies conducted by top researchers such as Paul Berman and Milbrey Wallin McLaughlin, Michael Fullan, and Karen Louis. The understanding was that through negotiating, the tense change forces within schools and through mutual adaptations, educators would successfully overcome obstacles and barriers to change and school improvement. However, a different reality emerged as soon as the development stage stopped.

A follow-up study with the very same administrators told a different story. The same school administrators who at first made enthusiastic comments such as: "I'd like to think I'm already implementing these standards. I put my professional growth plans to guidelines of these standards every year," were now saying how implementation processes were not creative, joyful, growth oriented, or exciting.

A similar phenomenon occurred in a longitudinal project sponsored by the University Council for Educational Administration called Voices From the Field, with results published in a series of articles from 1999 to 2005 (Bogotch, 2012, p. 193). Nowhere in this large data set were the terms *exciting*, *creative*, *stimulating*, *enjoyable*, *meaningful*, and *trusting* as used by the Louisiana participants in developing leadership standards. Instead, the dispositions of the school administrators reflected what was referred to by them as "if-only realities," as in the clause "if only administrators had the following":

1. more latitude through government waivers;

2. more funding to meet the demands of mandated programs;

3. more workplace autonomy to tap the creativity of teachers and staff;

4. collaborative voices of teachers, parents, and community members participating in messy decision-making processes;

5. permission as well as freedom to break rules when necessary; and

6. the courage to lead. (p. 193)

Standards Versus Developing Standards: Murphy's Two Laws Centered?

One of the principal architects of the original ISLLC Standards for School Leaders, Joseph Murphy, presented an invited lecture at the 1999 American Educational Research Association conference in Montreal, Canada. He titled his talk "The Quest for a Center: Notes on the State of the Profession of Educational Leadership" (Murphy, 1999). Near the end of the written version (on pp. 72–73), Murphy listed seven developing "standards" (see **Table 1.1**).

In both purpose and language, these "developing standards" are very different from either the ISLLC standards of 1996 or the revised 2008 ISLLC leadership standards. Murphy makes as powerful an argument for school leadership to correspond to the needs of communities through educational processes as did Ralph Tyler, a curriculum theorist, 50 years ago. In correspondence, these authors both meant that whatever standards or objectives are developed in education, they ought to correspond to life in society in the present.

Whereas Bobbitt asserted that education was a good quarter of a century behind competent business practices, Murphy's quest for a center came 50 years after what became known as the Tyler Rationale. Tyler eschewed the term *standards* and preferred to use the word *objectives*. Yet the parallels in language to scientific management are striking. According to Herbert Kliebard (2004), Tyler believed that stating objectives was the "crucial first step in the development of a curriculum" (p. 184).

> Objectives, in other words, should not be stated in vague terms such as knowing, appreciating, and understanding, but in terms that described in rather precise terms how the student would behave after a period of study. Moreover, the success of the program would be determined by the extent to which the behaviors embodied in the objectives would be achieved. (p. 184)

Quest for the Center Standards
1. It [educational leadership] should acknowledge and respect the diversity of work afoot in educational administration yet exercise sufficient magnetic force . . . to pull much of that work in certain directions.
2. It should be informed by and help organize the labor and the ideas from the current era of ferment.
3. It should promote the development of a body of ideas and concepts that define school administration as an applied field.
4. It should provide hope for fusing the enduring dualisms . . . that have bedeviled the profession for so long (e.g., knowledge vs. values., academic knowledge vs. practice knowledge).
5. It should provide a crucible where civility among shop merchants in the big tent gives way to productive dialogue and exchange.
6. It should be clear about the outcomes upon which to forge a redefined profession of school administration; in other words, it should provide the vehicle for linking the profession to valued outcomes.
7. It should establish a framework that ensures that the "standard for what is taught lies not with bodies of subject matter" (Kliebard, 2004, p. 72) but with valued ends.

Table 1.1 Murphy's Developing Standards

SOURCE: Murphy, J. (1999/2000). The quest for a center: Notes on the state of the profession of educational leadership. In P. Jenlink (Ed.), *Marching into a new millennium: Challenges to educational leadership.* The Eighth Yearbook of the National Council of Professors of Educational Administration (pp. 16–81). Lanham, MD: Scarecrow Press, Inc.

Again, both the logic and language of Franklin Bobbitt are evident. According to Kliebard (2004), Tyler's vision reinforces the argument of Bobbitt:

> The idea that, in curriculum development, exact specifications ought to be drawn up in advance and that success would be measured in terms of the extent to which those blueprints were followed is derived from the root metaphor of social efficiency, production, by which educational products are manufactured by the school-factory according to the particulars demanded by a modern industrial society. (p. 185)

In contrast, Murphy's "developing standards" argued that while educational administration is an applied field, the processes by which it comes to understand "valued outcomes" are more complex than what either Bobbitt or Tyler called for. Educational leadership—as a steward of moral responsibilities—would set criteria for determining valid research outcomes and for building communities in and beyond school buildings.

That said, the pragmatics of an applied field called for specifying management and leadership functions, that is, standards that should be translated into school building and school improvement practices. They

should also be translated in the managing of school operations regarding other functions such as school budgeting, personnel, compliance, facilities, and so on. The answer to these questions, according to Murphy (1999), would have to be found in the correspondence between society, the profession, and the purpose of schooling. Unfortunately, all of today's school improvement models have emphasized a different concept, one grounded in intercorrelations of within-school variables presenting a coherent picture of school improvement. In the literature, the word *comprehensive* is substituted for "coherent" and what is ignored is correspondence with the needs of society. As a result, coherent school improvement models, while neat, internally reliable, and, therefore, appealing on the surface, have delimited the purposes of schooling to within-school issues such as raising test scores and establishing fair schoolwide disciplinary procedures. As for a model of school improvement that corresponds to the needs of society, that is considered, by many, as outside the control of a school administrator.

The 2008 ISLLC Standards no longer list specific indicators that ipso facto fixed standards to specific behaviors and objectives, such that technology use in classes would be the same across urban, suburban, and rural school districts regardless of funding. At the same time, however, many of the 50 states in their interpretations of standards have become more, not less, prescriptive. That is, precision indicators have actually increased exponentially, and implementation within school districts has become even more restricted to the language and behaviors of specific indicators.

Fast forward to the 2014 draft for public comment of the new ISLLC standards. Given the contradiction between "developing standards" and the root metaphor of standards for "social efficiency," the ISLLC Standards Refresh Project of 2014 explicitly states that it is to be used as a developing and implementation guide—the so-called North Star (p. 8)—by each of the 50 states for developing effective policies and practices. The most noticeable revisions, according to the authors, can be found in

> the leadership domains that pertain to a school's instructional program, culture, and human capital management, and in the enrichment of the core dynamic of the Standards. Collectively, this prioritization can be characterized as leadership for learning. This leadership for learning requires school leaders to primarily focus on supporting student and adult learning. (p. 6)

However, coherence and alignment still define the system for school leadership as it moves from policy to content, to performance to tools. To be sure, adapting, developing, and implementing—within specific contexts—are called for. And clearly, the 2014 version provides a more realistic district perspective of leadership development with a recognition that cultural relevance, the wider communities' diversity, democracy, advocacy, equity, and asset-based mindsets are all to be built into a more inclusive school system.

That said, the 2014 ISLLC Standards repeat the mantra of high expectations without explaining how the expanded 11 standards can be transformed from noise to signals (Silver, 2012). How exactly will leadership for learning transform climates of fear, failure, and mistrust when the systemic causes of such conditions have not been empirically tested or questioned? How will the inclusive and wider conceptualizations of Refresh be translated into "tools" by monopolistic companies such as Microsoft, Apple, and Pearson? Surely, the educators who participated in developing standards will not be offered positions within these for-profit companies. And even if some were, how will their fingers shore up the dike against global capitalistic profits and resulting policies?

Most other fields have long ago made paradigmatic shifts in thinking, attitudes, systems' analysis, and their everyday work. In organizational theory, broad classifications of organizations document the transformations from simple structures to machine bureaucracy to professional bureaucracy to divisionalized form (e.g., loosely coupled systems) to adhocracy (Carlson, 1996; Shapiro, 2013, p. 18). Public schools have not successfully been transformed beyond the stage of machine bureaucracy. Can we take the 2014 ISLLC Standards on faith? Should we?

Nevertheless, Bobbitt's predictions that the work itself would make teachers and principals more efficient and effective have not come true at all. Administrators today report more time on the job, more frustration, and feeling more stress (Krzemienski, 2013). English's 1994 text called for a *nouvelle critique* (p. 233) where educational leadership would develop theories from the study of history, literature, and biographies coupled with administrative science. Similarly, Bobbitt called on educators to live "in a family in natural human fashion; not in the isolation of the boarding- or rooming house" (Bobbitt, 1913, p. 86).

> [H]e must have the means for travel. If he is to have a cultivated appreciation of the various humanities, then he must have money for the purchase of books and music and pictures. He must be able to attend the drama, the opera, the concert, the lecture. (p. 86)

Efficiency should lead to tangible incentives of time and space for "privacy and quiet, for study and meditation" (p. 86). Social and educational reformers have always argued that separating school from society is a mistake and not giving educators the time to enjoy neighborhoods, communities, the arts, and visiting schools, kept them isolated from the affairs of the world (Bruner, 1960). The 2014 ISLLC Standards shine a Dewey-like light, pointing educators to a door to a different future. But the emphasis on coherence and alignment seems like a choral response to closed system thinking (i.e., the noise) and not a signal for a *nouvelle critique*.

Improving Schools From Within

Some may recognize the heading for this section as the title of a 1991 book by Roland Barth, the founder of Harvard's Principal Center and active in developing leadership learning through International Principal Centers. We are aware from experiences how external authorities have deskilled public school educators by delivering instructional materials as print and digitally with accompanying standardized tests. Barth has been a staunch advocate for mining the talents of teachers within each school in terms of visioning, leadership, and management.

In this sense, Barth (1991) is on the same page as Neil Shipman and Murphy (1996), that is, educators have to be "enmeshed in the work" (Shipman & Murphy, p. 8). In today's parlance, we see this as job-embedded pre-service and in-service learning. It combines the best of workshops, mentoring, clinical education, classrooms, internships, and apprenticeships. It is the on-the-job practice that brings together the multiple tasks of not only teaching and learning, but also budgeting, personnel, discipline, safety, and crisis management.

Improving schools from within begins with changes in our own leadership and management behaviors. It also requires a deeper knowledge of U.S. history, U.S. culture, democracy with a small "d" (and leadership with a small "l"). One way to consider potential changes in leadership behavior is through the metaphor of turning "right on red" and what it means to be the change we want to see in others, particularly in those we might consider our "least preferred coworkers."

Right on Red: Local Customs

Many of us travel by car to different towns and cities. At one time or another, at an intersection where we have stopped in the right lane for a red light, we hear a horn honking. At first, we ignore it. But if it continues, we quickly understand that the person honking in the car directly behind us is signaling for us to make the right turn. At first, we interpret the honking as noise. It was only upon reflection and awareness that the noise becomes a signal that we may legally proceed with a right on red.

Throughout life, there are signals indicating local conditions and customs, differing from town to town, city to city, state to state. The information comes to us through experience and practices that work, not as universal theories or generalizable rules. Of course, we all first stop at a red light, but in some locales, we can then turn right with permission from local authorities. That's the difference between rules and cultures. Educational standards should be sophisticated enough

to clarify this difference and permit educators to make adjustments based on rules and cultures, at least after the first honk.

This same metaphor can be applied to the very beginnings of the United States. Historically, James Madison, Alexander Hamilton, and John Jay convinced the people of the 13 colonies to make a right on red based on evidence that the original governance model of the Articles of Confederation did not work well locally or nationally. They wrote essay after essay persuading the populace to reconvene a new convention and draft the U.S. Constitution. And in that Constitution, public education was left to the states. Today, there are more than 13,000 school districts in the United States; but for some reason, maybe the dominance of scientific management or the emergence of an ideology that school control should be centralized, external authorities have not given superintendents permission, nor do superintendents believe that they have the power, to turn right on red or ask for forgiveness in bending rules and regulations to fit local situations. As English has noted:

> The American superintendency was an especially vulnerable public position to the legacy of scientific management. . . . [S]chool superintendents are especially prone to adapt new "fads" such as scientific management in order to prolong their tenure; in the process, they turn attention away from strictly personality-political variables working against them by indicating they are responsive to criticisms of cost and inefficiencies. (English, 1994, pp. 19–20)

Culturally, this vulnerability shouldn't have continued as it has. Many of today's educational leaders at the very top of the educational hierarchy are from the baby boomer generation, which coined phrases such as "question authority" and "you can't trust anyone over 30"; but this generation of educational leaders seems to have grown into perhaps the most authoritarian, compliance-demanding generation in U.S. educational history. If it can be said that they made a "right on red," it certainly was not in the direction of progressive and joyful educational reforms.

But this critique is not limited to those at the top of the educational hierarchy. In 1956, a prominent sociologist, C. Wright Mills, situated education in the United States as follows:

> Within American society, major national power now resides in the economic, the political, and the military

domains. Other institutions seem off to the side of modern history, and, on occasion, duly subordinated to these. . . . Religious, educational and family institutions are not autonomous centers of national power; on the contrary, these decentralized areas are increasingly shaped by the big three, in which developments of decisive and immediate consequences now occur. . . . Families and churches and schools adapt to modern life; governments and armies and corporations shape it. . . . Schools select and train men for their jobs in corporations and their specialized tasks in the armed forces. (p. 8)

Mills's thesis was confirmed by educational researchers Raymond Callahan (1962) and David Tyack (1974). These gentlemen stopped short of Mills's conclusion that the big three of the power elite operate on a level of higher immorality. Yet Mills makes a powerful argument, laying the blame of immorality on the fact that knowledge was separated from power in U.S. culture. He wrote that:

Knowledge is no longer widely felt as an ideal; it is seen as an instrument. In a society of power and wealth, knowledge is valued as an instrument of power and wealth, and also, of course, as an ornament in conversation. (1956, p. 352)

To illustrate his point, Mills (1956) noted that George Washington in 1783 relaxed with Voltaire's "letters" and John Locke's "On Human Understanding," whereas Dwight Eisenhower read cowboy tales and detective stories (p. 350). Robert Starratt (2014) attributes this separation of knowledge from power to U.S. culture and education, claiming that American educators are intellectually behind foreign-born educators in their ability to connect postmodern complexities to school practices (pp. 75–76). Given the compliance orientation of today's public school teacher-administrators, what contributes, too, to the managerial mystique is that much of the new thinking in education is done primarily by experts for consulting, hired in the service of those in power. In other words, school districts bring in experts from afar, on a fee-for-service basis, ignoring "native eyes" who have deep knowledge of local communities and culture or the thesis of Barth's text, "improving schools from within."

The issue, then, is not whether school people know much of value, but under what conditions they will reveal their rich knowledge of their craft so that it may become part of the discussion of school improvement (Mills, 1956, p. 106).

Well-funded think tanks, foundations, and international publishing companies recruit the best and brightest to work under their branded logos and to lend their well-earned reputations. Educational policies are left to government officials, educational consultants, and corporate publishing industries to provide instructional materials, tests, and even to purchase and run for-profit K-12 schools. But how smart is it really to leave education to noneducator "experts"? A *New York Times Magazine* article (Davidson, 2013), brought together two of the most influential economic policy experts in the United States: Glenn Hubbard, who worked in the administrations of both George H. W. Bush and George W. Bush, and Larry Summers, who worked in the Clinton and Obama administrations. Writing for the *Times*, Adam Davidson said Hubbard argued that "once the big fiscal problem is solved, the government can redouble its efforts on education and help the truly needy" (p. 32). Summers lumped the costs of education in with rising healthcare costs, subsuming educational needs within overall government costs. When we leave education to economists or to politicians, education remains a backburner issue in world affairs.

This illustrates a point made by Brian Beabout (2014), who described the notion of "expertism" as "the historical tendency of the powerful to design social arrangements, institutions, and programs that will benefit themselves but harm others" (p. 561). One challenge for educational leaders collectively is to reclaim education as the dominant investment for both economic prosperity and democracy. Educational leaders should continuously remind the electorate of their responsibilities to pay taxes to support world-class schools for all children regardless of whether they themselves have children within the public schools. Public education is a public responsibility that comes with public accountability for funding. The role of educational leadership is to inform neighborhoods, communities, states, and the nation as a whole that the education of children is the best financial investment anyone can make in the future of the country. Following managerial rules or promoting instructional leadership is not the central purpose of education in a democracy.

Schools are by and large meant to be conservative, but by conservative we should not think of school as regressive or retrospective. Most educators believe that schools have to address the next generation, and if we hold to that view, then we have to label our leadership and management as progressive. Labels, of course, are sticky in that adhesive puts us in contact with views, people, and policies we may not agree with—so we strive to do what we think is right as individual leaders. Yet, whenever we act solely as individuals, then the stress we put on ourselves to be heroes does not lead to sustainable or systemic changes. It is easy for us to work hard, stay focused on teachers and students, and in a very real sense perpetuate the status quo by doing what we have been told to do.

But right on red holds out another decision-making possibility. If we accept Silver's argument of uncertainty, ambiguity, and probabilities, then we understand that there are valid arguments for and against what we decide almost every day. Important skills for educational leaders include how we manage ourselves and others, stay under control, control our temper, keep our voices down, and encourage others to put forth their best ideas.

At the same time, context matters. Educational leaders might function in a different way in a high-wealth and homogenous community than they would in an impoverished one. In one setting, the leader might be highly influenced by parent groups, extracurricular events, and community priorities. But in another setting, the leader may be more concerned with the breakfast program, providing a safe and stable environment for students with chaotic home lives, and "ensuring that teachers hold all students to high expectations while, at the same time, being sensitive to diverse cultural backgrounds and expectations" (Shields, 2013). To attain high levels of academic success, the educational leader must understand the influence of socioeconomic and cultural realities in which students are embedded.

Managerial Virtues of Necessity: Little Things and Big Things

Management is making a virtue of necessity (i.e., working within existing structures and rules) alongside choices and discretion (i.e., qualitative behaviors and measures). A school principal might say, "I have very little control of the system (e.g., evaluation) that is used and I must do it by a certain procedure." But in

point of fact, principals have a great deal of latitude in working with teachers (Bogotch, 1992). Leadership is an art because managerial tasks and school situations are far too numerous for a precise calculus mode of when to do this or how to do that. "The art is to systematically arrange managerial behaviors to improve the performance of others. It is in this fundamental human endeavor that managerial activities are deemed [to be] virtuous" (Bogotch, 1992, p. 264).

What the debate over the terms *leadership* and *management* has ignored is that within the daily managerial role of a school administrator lie matters of educational functions and educational qualities. As in so many human enterprises, success depends upon attention to both, with adjustments made moment by moment. It adds up to doing many little things, not just one big thing.

Prior to the enactment of No Child Left Behind, public educators had multiple opportunities to make sense of the many little things that they do during the day, week, month, and year. School leaders might have reclaimed functional/managerial control of curricula and pedagogy from external authorities had they integrated themselves into communities and collaboratively defined the meaning of educational leadership and the role of public schools in a democracy. School leaders' professional failures throughout the 1970s, 1980s, and 1990s created opportunities for consultants, publishing houses, and State Department bureaucrats to jump on standards and accountability as leverage to control public education. Concurrently, with centralization policies, education has become an even more profitable industry/venture as states, districts, and schools become bulk consumers of educational products.

What Are the Odds That Little Comes Up Big? Big "L" Versus Little "l"

To date, traditional leadership theories (Big "L") have failed educators. From a learning and teaching perspective, it seems unlikely that practitioners apply already developed theories to their practices with both adults and children. What they actually do every day is based on theories-in-practice that reflect what they learn day by day that works. Leadership and management are in the doing; learning from experience results from our reflection and subsequent learned actions.

Written theories of leadership, as Silver helps us to see, are not predictive of outcomes. What predicts outcomes are the organizational sameness and the managerial control mechanisms of administration that allow us to predict behaviors within acceptable margins of risk. We know outcomes from school reforms based on past practices. To date, leadership theories have not disrupted the status quo. It is not leadership theory per se that has unleashed the talents of students or enabled teachers to teach imaginatively. That is what "developing standards" always have the potential to do and what fixed standards with accountability, which have led to standardization, can never do.

John Dewey is still relevant today, and his ideas on education as experiences and democracy have never been needed more in the United States and for reforming our schools. Even if Robert Starratt was correct that American educators lack the intellectual background to understand Classical and Continental philosophies, we can understand the pragmatic and practical ideas of Dewey, who throughout his career explained, again and again, that not all experiences in life are educative (1938/1965).

Trying to capture the richness of ideas of John Dewey in this chapter is impossible, but it is important for educational leaders to distinguish between what Dewey would refer to as educative and miseducative experiences in and out of schools. The bottom line, for Dewey, is that the world is always in a state of becoming; that is, life is made up of dynamic experiences—some promoting growth and others preventing it—that we as individuals and socially have to make sense of while also participating in knowledge creation. To do so, experiences have to be internalized so that everyone makes education relevant for herself or himself. As a result, knowledge that emanates from external authorities is, according to Dewey (1920/1952), "suspect and obnoxious" (p. 118).

What leads to growth is what we experience ourselves, not what we do to someone (such as teaching to the test). Development is experience with a purpose—not a fixed purpose or goal, but rather a goal that is continuously constructed and reconstructed to make ourselves and society better. It is in this sense that all education, according to Dewey, is moral. The purpose or end of school is so that youths (and people from economically depressed classes) see that they can become the masters of their own development, and in so doing practice democratic citizenship—in schools—at all times. That seems to be a lot to ask of schools, school leaders, and teachers; thus, it is not surprising that Dewey always seemed to be disappointed that his ideas were never taken to heart by American educators.

When we apply Dewey's ideas to leadership learning, a different unit of analysis comes to mind, one that accounts for complexity and uncertainty by deliberately making the familiar strange and at the same time ending strangeness among those with whom we work (Bogotch, 2011). The idea of leadership encompasses all situations for all people, even our least preferred coworkers. Our work, therefore, is in the everydayness of before, during, and after school. But practically, how might we connect the best ideas and learn from experiences within our daily activities? For Dewey, the means and ends are inseparable. So, what should we be thinking about on our commutes to and from schools and on to-do lists or checklists, and what are the connections between our school agendas and the problems of society? With such thoughts come calculable measures, that is, risk. How should leaders assess those risks?

Years ago an organizational researcher, Henry Mintzberg (1970), recommended "structured observations" to document what we actually do during the day. Today, there are research studies that use technology and handheld devices to record the doing, talking, and moving of school leaders. Collectively, these data points are what we call routines that over time become habits and comfort zones for all of us. We repeat cycles as sameness. How do we challenge ourselves to go beyond "playing it safe" and begin to reflect on daily routines?

For many of us, our days begin with commutes, parking the car, entering the building, meeting people, and beginning our work. What if we considered variations that provide us with multiple and different perspectives on the routines, the work, and the people we work with? When we choose to interact with those we agree with (our best preferred coworkers) more often than with those with whom we disagree, over time, we limit our growth and development by narrowing our networks and continuously reinforcing our biases. In routine practices, strangers remain strangers, and that includes students, teachers, and other staff members. There cannot be trust and excellence in educational climates and cultures when they are populated by strangers, regardless of what philosophers such as Kwame Anthony Appiah (2006) opine.

Our schools have subcultures that we need to know more intimately. Outside our schools are other subcultures presenting different leadership and research challenges that we need to embrace professionally. The idea of leadership as little "l" is that instead of getting more and more comfortable with experiences in our roles as school administrators, the challenge is to unlearn, discover, and relearn new experiences about people, places, and processes and to do this continuously every day. This is leadership with a small "l."

The Challenge of Reclaiming Our Voices and Our Ideals

Every generation is charged with the responsibility to discuss and debate its commitment to public education and then garner support for policies and programs. Some generations meet this challenge better than others. This author has criticized his own baby boomer generation for how it gravitated to authoritarian policies and practices, despite the generation's 1960s' legacy of free speech and protest against unjust policies. The challenge is where and how educational leaders can reclaim their voices even as they are confronted by unprecedented sanctions and public scrutiny leading to fear and distrust in too many instances. When parental or student complaints seem to have more power than administrative and teacher voices within hierarchical systems, reclaiming our voices can seem hopeless. When there are meetings where only one voice can be heard, but immediately upon leaving that meeting there is a cacophony of voices decrying the hypocrisies and blindness of leadership, then reclaiming our voices seems hopeless. So what can we learn to practice differently based on the ideas discussed in this chapter?

Ironically, it may be very healthy for educational leadership researchers-authors-trainers to reclaim the word "management" to its rightful place in directing school operations. While it is easy to say that we lead people but manage processes, we all know, having sat in the office, that our work is messy and detailed. It's all management, but not in

terms of promoting the processes that "further intensify inequalities" (Thrupp & Willmott, 2003, p. 3). As for repositioning leadership, Dewey may have said it best in 1909 when connecting leadership not just to schooling, but also to society and to children's needs and interests:

> The society of which the child is to be a member is, in the United States, a democratic and progressive society. The child must be educated for leadership as well as for obedience. He must have power of self-direction and power of directing others, administration, ability to assume positions of responsibility. This necessity of educating for leadership is as great on the industrial as it is on the political side. (p. 10)

School quality matters most in difficult circumstances. And here is where school is undoubtedly political and where the United States needs to target and invest serious resources as a priority. The words of economists can be heard whenever superintendents tell principals, teachers, students, and parents to "do more with less." That is not what any democratic society should ever hear from an educational leader!

Conclusion: Keeping Uncertainty and Risk in Our Sights

Educators, whether working in K-12 or university settings, need to reclaim education, professionally. But to do so, we must be clear on both the risks and uncertainties. We must first question whether the science-driven managerial strategies that fall under the umbrella of coherent school improvement models will give U.S. society a competitive edge. Why? We need to emphasize educational contexts within schools that allow for dynamic growth, not mechanistic lessons inside the world of uncertainties and promises. We can address managerial risks by identifying the known unknowns through research and development and gather the courage to face unknown unknowns through experimentation and innovations that may sometimes fail, but always teach us how to do better the next time, day by day, maybe even minute by minute. The message of this chapter is that one person can make a difference. It comes down to self-control while working inside a huge public institution designed to promote knowledge and freedom of thought.

While it is so important for us to think big, for right now, we must take small steps such as turning right on red and doing little "l" activities with those with whom we work. It will take time for us to relearn how to rebuild our professional capacities, displace today's standardized goals, and return to more diverse goals of democracy and citizenship, but that is the challenge of educational leadership defined in this chapter. This chapter has shown why the history of educational leadership is critical to our work and to our survival as a profession (Bogotch, 2011). By connecting to the past successes and mistakes of our predecessors we can begin to more clearly see how to negotiate and build on the leadership/management paradox. It is done in the everyday work school administrators do in schools, but that must be connected to a larger vision of what schools must do to promote social justice beyond schools. There's nothing paradoxical about that.

Key Chapter Terms

Interstate School Leaders Licensure Consortium (ISLLC): Developed a framework of six school leadership standards: Setting a widely shared vision for learning; developing a school culture and instructional program conducive to student learning and staff professional growth; ensuring effective management of the organization, operation, and resources for a safe, efficient, and effective learning environment; collaborating with faculty and community members, responding to diverse community interests and needs, and mobilizing community resources; acting with integrity, fairness, and in an ethical manner; and understanding, responding to, and influencing the political, social, legal, and cultural contexts.

The managerial mystique: Coined in 1989 by Abraham Zaleznik for the world of business, the phrase entered education by way of Tom Sergiovanni in his now classic 1992 book, *Moral Leadership: Getting to the Heart of School Improvement.* Both Zaleznik and Sergiovanni believed that the character of a person mattered and that business practices that ignore human character are flawed. Both authors opposed the dominant practices of scientific management. According to Zaleznik (1989, p. 2), "As it evolved in practice, the mystique required managers to dedicate themselves to processes, structures, roles and indirect forms of communication and to ignore ideas, people, emotion and direct talk. It deflected attention from the realities of business [and schools], while it reassured and rewarded those who believed in the mystique" (cited in Sergiovanni, 1992, p. 4; bracketed words added by Sergiovanni). In Sergiovanni's analysis, the managerial mystique contributed to "trained incapacities" of educators and "goal displacement" in schools, which "represents a conspiracy of mediocrity" (Sergiovanni, 1992, p. 5), and thus, the challenge of this chapter, is to reclaim educators' own voices.

Scientific management: A term describing the work of Frederick Taylor (1856–1915), who created a body of work centered on the idea of efficiency. Taylor's idea was based on a five-step procedure in which the work was shifted from the worker to management based on an analysis of the work to be performed. The result of Taylor's studies led to simplifying the work via standardization, and hiring less skilled workers and paying them less except for those who exceeded daily work tasks.

References

Appiah, K. A. (2006). *Cosmopolitanism: Ethics in a world of strangers.* New York, NY: Norton.

Barth R. (1991). *Improving schools from within.* San Francisco, CA: Jossey-Bass.

Beabout, B. (2014). Community leadership: Seeking social justice while re-creating public schools in post-Katrina New Orleans. In I. Bogotch & C. Shields (Eds.), *The international handbook of educational leadership and social (in)justice* (chap. 30, pp. 543–570). Dordrecht, Netherlands: Springer.

Bobbitt, F. (1913). *Some general principles of management applied to the problems of city-school systems: The twelfth yearbook of the National Society for the Study of Education, part I. The Supervision of City Schools* (pp. 7–96). Chicago, IL: University of Chicago Press.

Bogotch, I. (1989). *A model of school managerial control.* Unpublished doctoral dissertation, Florida International University.

Bogotch, I. (1992). Managerial virtues of necessity and choice. In P. F. First, *Educational policy for school administrators* (pp. 260–266). Boston, MA: Allyn & Bacon.

Bogotch, I. (2002). "Enmeshed in the work": The educative power of developing standards. *Journal of School Leadership, 12*(5), 503–525.

Bogotch, I. (2011). Democracy is little "l" leadership: For every day at any time. *The Scholar-Practitioner Quarterly, 5*(1), 93–98.

Bogotch, I. (2012). Social justice in middle passage: The voyage from frustrations to hope. In M. Acker-Hocevar, J. Ballenger, W. Place, & G. Ivory (Eds.), *Snapshots of school leadership in the 21st century: The UCEA Voices from the Field Project* (pp. 189–208). Charlotte, NC: Information Age.

Bogotch, I., Miron, L., & Biesta, G. (2007). "Effective for what; effective for whom?" Two questions SESI should not ignore. In T. Townsend (Ed.), *International handbook of school effectiveness and improvement* (Vol. 17, Sec. 1, pp. 93–110). Dordrecht, Netherlands: Springer International Handbooks of Education.

Bogotch, I., Williams, P., & Hale, J. (1995). School managerial control: Validating a social concept. *Journal of Educational Administration, 33*(1), 44–62.

Bruner, J. (1960). *The process of education.* New York, NY: Vintage Books.

Callahan, R. (1962). *Education and the cult of efficiency.* Chicago, IL: University of Chicago Press.

Carlson, R. (1996). *Reframing and reform: Perspectives on organization, leadership, and change.* White Plains, NY: Longman Publishing.

Council of Chief State School Officers. (2008). *Educational Leadership Policy Standards, 2008.* Washington, DC: National Policy Board for Educational Administration. Retrieved from http://www.ccsso.org/documents/2008/educational_leadership_policy_standards_2008.pdf

Courtis, S. A. (1914). *Manual of instructions for giving and scoring the Courtis standards tests in the three R's.* Detroit, MI: Department of Cooperative Research.

Davidson, A. (2013, May 5). Boom, bust or what? Larry Summers and Glenn Hubbard square off on our economic future. *New York Times Magazine.* Retrieved from http://www.nytimes.com/2013/05/05/magazine/larry-summers-and-glenn-hubbard-square-off-on-our-economic-future.html?pagewanted=all&_r=0

Dewey, J. (1909). *Moral principles in education.* Boston, MA: Houghton Mifflin.

Dewey, J. (1952). *Reconstruction in philosophy.* New York, NY: Mentor Books. (Original work published 1920)

Dewey, J. (1965). *Experience and education.* New York, NY: Macmillan. (Original work published 1938)

Duke, D., & Landahl, M. (2011). "Raising tests scores was the easy part": A case study of the third year of school turnaround. *International Studies in Educational Administration, 39*(3), 91–114.

Eisner, E. (2002). *The arts and the creation of mind.* New Haven, CT: Yale University Press.

English, F. (1994). *Theory in educational administration.* New York, NY: HarperCollins College.

Gorard, S. (2011). Serious doubts about school effectiveness. *British Educational Research Journal, 36*(5), 745–766.

Kliebard, H. (2004). *The struggle for the American curriculum: 1893–1958 (3rd ed).* New York, NY: Routledge Falmer.

Krzemienski, J. (2013). *The impact of stress on elementary school principals and their effective coping mechanisms.* Unpublished doctoral dissertation, Florida Atlantic University.

Mills, C. W. (1956). *The power elite.* New York, NY: Oxford University Press.

Mintzberg, H. (1970). Structured observation as a method to study managerial work. *Journal of Management Studies, 7*(1), pp. 87–104.

Mintzberg, H. (1992). *Structure in fives: Designing effective organizations.* Upper Saddle River, NJ: Prentice Hall.

Murphy, J. (1999, April 19–23). *The quest for a center: Notes on the state of the profession of educational leadership.* Paper presented at the Annual Meeting of the American Educational Research Association, Montreal, Quebec, Canada. Retrieved from http://files.eric.ed.gov/fulltext/ED433620.pdf

No Child Left Behind Act, 20 U.S.C. §§ 6301 *et seq.* (Jan 8, 2002). Retrieved from U.S. Education Department information page on Elementary and Secondary Education Act http://www.ed.gov/esea

Robinson, K. (2006). *How schools kill creativity* [Video]. Retrieved from http://www.ted.com/talks/ken_robinson_says_schools_kill_creativity.html

Sergiovanni, T. (1992). *Moral leadership: Getting to the heart of school improvement.* San Francisco, CA: Jossey-Bass.

Shapiro, P. (2013). *Emergent behavior of the US government workforce: An agent-based model of worker departure.* Unpublished doctoral dissertation, George Washington University. Retrieved May 7, 2013, from http://search.proquest.com.ezproxy.fau.edu/pqdtft/docview/1346219213/fulltextPDF/13E4D4F935D54C532C7/2?accountid=10902

Shields, C. (2013). Leadership for social justice education: A critical transformative approach. In I. Bogotch & C. Shields (Eds.), *The international handbook of educational leadership and social (in)justice* (chap. 19, pp. 323–340). Dordrecht, Netherlands: Springer.

Shipman, N., & Murphy, J. (1996, November 2). Preface. Interstate School Leadership Licensure Consortium standards for school leaders, (pp. 5–8). Washington, DC: Chief State School Officers.

Silver, N. (2012). *The signal and the noise: Why so many predictions fail—but some don't.* New York, NY: Penguin.

Starratt, R. (2014). Ethics and social justice: Strangers passing in the night? In I. Bogotch & C. Shields (Eds.), *The international handbook of educational leadership and social (in)justice* (pp. 67–80). Dordrecht, Netherlands: Springer.

Taylor, F. (1911). *The principles of scientific management.* New York, NY: Harper & Brothers.

Thrupp, M., & Willmott, R. (2003): *Education management in managerialist times: Beyond the textual apologists.* Maidenhead, England: Open University Press.

Townsend, T., MacBeath, J., & Bogotch, I. (2015). Critical and alternative perspectives on educational effectiveness research (EER). In C. Chapman, D., Muijs, D. Reynolds, P. Sammons, & C. Teddlie (Eds.), *Routledge international handbook of educational effectiveness* (chap. 18). New York, NY: Routledge.

Tyack, D. (1974). *The one best system.* Cambridge, MA: Harvard University Press.

Zaleznik, A. (1989*). The managerial mystique: Restoring leadership in business.* New York, NY: HarperCollins.

Further Readings

Barth, R. (1991). *Improving schools from within: Teachers, parents, and principals can make the difference.* San Francisco, CA: Jossey-Bass.

Barth's focus is not on children, but rather on the adults who help children to learn. Unlike the lessons of Taylorism and standardization, the work of a school administrator is filled with uncertainties. In fact, "uncertainties are many and resolutions few" (p. 5). This book conceptualizes the meanings of a good school and what a principal can do collectively with teachers, parents, and staff to build it. Success for Barth depends on the quality of these interactions. This now classic text anticipates the very best ideas the field of educational leadership has to offer our society.

Blount, J. (2008). History as a way of understanding and motivating. In I. Bogotch, F. Beachum, J. Blount, J. Brooks, & F. English (Eds.), *Radicalizing educational leadership: Dimensions of social justice* (pp. 17–38). Taipei, Taiwan: Sense Publishers

Jackie Blount's objective is to bring historical awareness to the field of educational leadership and administration, and she does so by bringing history to life, not as insular chronological dates, but rather by elucidating the social contexts and social relations of the people who make history, such as Ella Flagg Young. For Blount, history inspires actions, the first of which is to increase our abilities to ask provocative questions.

Through history, Blount motivates us to work together for "true social, political, and economic fairness for all persons" (p. 37).

Bogotch, I. (2011). A history of public school leadership: The first century, 1837–1942. In F. English (Ed.), *The SAGE handbook of educational leadership* (pp. 3–26). Thousand Oaks, CA: Sage.

This chapter traces the first century of school leadership in the United States. It reviews the major issues and personalities who were the trailblazers, such as Horace Mann, Cyrus Pierce (Mann's first principal), and Ella Flagg Young. The careers and controversies of William Maxwell, superintendent of schools in New York City; Angelo Patri, an exemplary school principal in New York City; and T. H. Harris, former state superintendent of schools in Louisiana, are analyzed. These portraits of our predecessors give us glimpses of the challenges, then and now, that continue to confront school leaders.

Callahan, R. (1962). *Education and the cult of efficiency.* Chicago, IL: University of Chicago Press.

This is an excellent source for understanding why educators have been viewed as vulnerable to government and business practices. Raymond Callahan provides the details of the historical transition from school management practice prior to the impact of Taylorism and tracks in detail how the basic ideas of scientific management were introduced into educational management practice, especially via the newly founded departments of educational administration at the leading U.S. universities.

With this newfound awareness of our vulnerability, however, we need to see in practical terms how educators can and have reclaimed their voices.

Dewey, J. (1897). *My pedagogic creed.* New York, NY: E. L. Kellogg & Co.

Even though the citations in this chapter came from three other Dewey sources, his 1909 Ethics, *his* Reconstruction in Philosophy *written originally in 1920, and his 1938 essay "Experience and Education,"* My Pedagogic Creed, *which predates the others, anticipates many of the ideas developed at book length throughout his illustrious career. What is remarkable about* My Pedagogic Creed *is not just the range of ideas: theory as experiences, theory of art, play and aesthetics, the connections between local problems to societal problems, the relevance of all the subject areas in a traditional school curriculum, and the unity morality and education; but also that it is written in the* format and tone of a manifesto, a call to educators to rethink, reflect, and act. My Pedagogic Creed *demonstrates Dewey's faith in the power of education and educators.*

Taylor, F. (1911). *The principles of science management.* New York: Harper.

This is clearly the work that has dominated management thinking in the United States and in education since Bobbitt's 1913 essay. And while many scholars believe Taylor's ghost haunts us, the pop cultural image of zombies seems more apt a description of the hold scientific management has had on our political leaders and public education. Other books that explain Taylor's influence are D. Nelson (1980) Frederick W. Taylor and the rise of scientific management, *Madison: University of Wisconsin Press; and R. Kanigel (1997)* The one best way: Frederick Winslow Taylor and the enigma of efficiency, *New York: Viking Penguin.*

2

THE EMERGING WISDOM OF EDUCATIONAL LEADERSHIP

FENWICK W. ENGLISH

University of North Carolina at Chapel Hill

ROSEMARY PAPA

Northern Arizona University

School leadership is a bounded activity that occurs within physical and conceptual spaces. It is bounded usually by a physical and material presence, that is, a school plant with classrooms and other types of architectural features (although there are continuing attempts to create virtual schools that do not have such properties), and within that space are ideas and schemes regarding what should go on within them.

The activities that are supposed to be transacted within classrooms contain a **pedagogy**, and by that is meant more than simply the kinds of methods used in teaching. The use of the term *pedagogy* is used to connote the broad sweep of political, cultural, and curricular decisions that impact what schools do, both overtly and covertly. The term *critical pedagogy* refers to a type of discourse described by Henry Giroux (1988) that "can be understood as historical constructions related to economic, social, and political events in a particular space and time" (p. 132). Giroux indicates that this concept is "absolutely essential in order to be able to think about how specific instances of schooling and curriculum theory may represent one form among the many possible"

(p. 132). In short, change or reform is not truly possible until one understands how the status quo has been constructed and situated within a discourse and that it contains particular histories.

The management and/or leadership of the collection of classrooms contain a second set of assumptions or an **ideology**. An ideology is a set of beliefs or tenets, as they are sometimes called, that forms a platform from which various political or pedagogical actions are proposed or enacted. Ideologies are not scientific statements or theories because they rarely are open to contrary evidence upon which they may be refuted. Most often, they are advanced as a kind of self-evident common sense.

Despite many attempts to make leadership into a science over the last 100 years, that goal remains elusive today because, as William Foster (1986) noted over 25 years ago, "The scientific study of leadership has essentially faltered, partly because the wrong phenomenon has been studied and partly because the functionalist paradigm that houses the studies has gone bankrupt" (p. 3). It is because of this criticism that this chapter intends to more clearly define the boundaries of effective leadership and management.

Parsing Out the Leadership/ Management Opposites

It has long been observed that there is a connection between systems of **authority** and the allocation and management of space and the nature of what teachers do in classrooms. This chapter argues that the structure of schools and classrooms is compatible with some ideas of school leadership and management and not so compatible with others. This understanding is central to appreciating why Robert Dreeben (1973) commented that "schools appear to be among the most conservative and unbending of institutions, maintaining traditional ways of doing things in the face of intense pressures to change" (p. 455).

First, this chapter deconstructs the idea that the terms *leadership* and *management* are antipodes, contending that both are required to effectively turn around underperforming schools (Papa & English, 2011), because one cannot lead an organization if it is not first managed well. In an institutionalized setting, leadership must work thorough the structures, rules, expectations, and discourses that already exist in order to improve them. Ric Brown, Paul Noble, and Rosemary Papa (2009) call this the false dichotomy. While management is essential to operationalize leadership, leadership is essential to changing forms

of management. So there is a dialogic connection between the two that is shown in **Figure 2.1**.

On the left of Figure 2.1 are the benchmarks of functioning within a hierarchical, bureaucratic organization that is a school or a school system. School administrators are state functionaries. They are licensed and in some states examined by tests to determine if they have the state-approved skills, knowledge, and attitudes to be responsible for operating a state-approved school. The state compels students to attend school, and so the state has the responsibility of creating institutions that carry out the schooling mission.

All of the legal and coercive **power** of the state is embodied in its structure and operations. School administrative authority is contained in legal documents, rules, and regulations. The state imposes on systems of schools, in the United States called school districts, stipulations within which the jurisdictional authority of school boards (elected or appointed by the people or representatives of the people such as mayors in some large cities) carry out policy and/or oversight duties.

The authority of the local site administrator is defined and confined to that unit. The position of the school site administrator is thus organizationally centered and dependent upon the very unit that person is

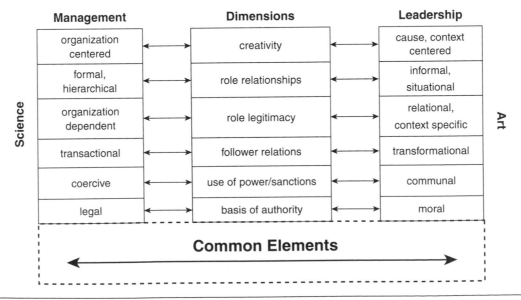

Figure 2.1   Resolving the Paradoxes Between Management and Leadership

SOURCE: English, F. W. (2008). *The art of educational leadership: Balancing performance and accountability*. Thousand Oaks, CA: Sage, p. 13.

responsible to lead or direct. School site administrators are considered midlevel functionaries since teachers are typically arranged in a subordinate organizational layer beneath them and there are normally layers of administrative officers above them. The basis of the power of the site administrator is legal, which is also the basis of bureaucratic authority. It is within this theoretical, political, and practical matrix that the science of administration or management is believed to exist.

In contrast to the mantle of management is that of leadership, which may not be confined to bureaucratic entities. The fact that leadership involves management but is not confined or defined by an organization is why former U.S. Army General Colin Powell (2013) once remarked that "leadership is the art of accomplishing more than the science of management says is possible" (p. 17). Here is a brief commentary regarding the dimensions of the management/leadership dyad.

Creativity

Creativity is stressed as a vital dimension to improve schools (Senge et al., 1999, p. 153). The fact is, however, that creativity within a management lens is confined to the unit that is managed, in this case a school. The manager would look for ways to improve or change schools within the structure of the school and within its organizational boundaries. A leadership perspective would call any such structures or boundaries into question. Managers would accept the legitimacy of schools as a given. Leaders would have no such presumptions and not necessarily accept school structure of boundaries as ipso facto legitimate. Managers would confine creativity to inside the schooling box. Leaders would not only not accept the current definitions of schooling but also not accept its history or current boundaries or functions.

This distinction regarding creativity, however, involves both perspectives. A historical examination of school changes shows that both management and leadership were involved. For example, the creation of the graded school in Quincy, Massachusetts, in 1848 was an effort to create a more orderly and efficient classification of children. It led to the "egg crate" school that has dominated the American landscape for over 150 years and with it graded curriculum, standard courses of study, and later standardized

tests. This "cellular structure of the school" as it has been called (Lortie, 1975, p. 23) is the principal basis for imposing factory models of schooling as the major metaphor for a "good school" becoming dominant. It is also the foundation upon which the role of school principal was created as the "principal-teacher" who had supervisory duties akin to duties of factory supervisors. Later, the role of school superintendent emerged as the apex of bureaucratic power, all resting on the structure of the graded school.

One could argue that John Philbrick, the educator who convinced the Boston School Committee to initially construct the first graded school, was a leader. He broke the mold. He had to think outside of the existing structure of the Lancastrian model of schooling and envision a different way to engage the ordering of students and teaching within them. According to the management/leadership distinction, administrators who came after Philbrick accepted all of the tenets of the graded schools and therefore they were merely managers. This addition to the two-level structure (elementary, or K-8, and secondary, or Grades 9–12) was designed to provide students with one year of the old high school curriculum before entering high school, in order to introduce students to high school content and cut the dropout rate between the elementary and secondary levels. And how would one classify the creators of the junior high school? Based on the connection between leadership and management shown earlier, they can be seen as both. It can also be argued that without boundaries it is difficult even to judge what is creative at all. A measure of creativity is how one overcomes boundaries or barriers.

Role Relationships

Schools as formal, bureaucratized organizations have developed, over time, a series of hierarchically situated roles. These roles are arranged so that they are enmeshed in superior/subordinate dyads, each accompanied by differences in legal, formal authority, and compensation differences based on how important, complex, and/or overarching the duties of one compared to another may happen to be.

In the past, all teachers were located on the same salary schedule irrespective of their competence or ability. The only differences between them that counted for salary purposes were seniority and formal training beyond the bachelor's degree. The salary schedule has long been a criticism of those who see it as a major obstacle to installing forms of merit pay that take into account superior teaching or the ability to obtain better results, usually defined as higher test scores. Many states have moved to require student test scores to be part of formal teacher evaluation schemes. These proposals have been stoutly resisted by teachers' unions and by other professional groups who see them as a method for obtaining increased managerial control over teacher autonomy.

In contrast to managerial approaches, leaders may employ more informal and situational means to deal with role relationships; this may be especially true if leaders are recognized outside of bureaucratic organizations where role authority is based on charisma or where they are what is termed *grassroots leaders* working in volunteer organizations. Grassroots or volunteer leaders have four common features. First they don't occupy any formal role within their respective community or organization. Second, they are concerned with certain kinds of change, or what are viewed as improvements that are promoted by either conflict-based approaches or by consensual models of engagement. Third, they have no institutionalized power. Fourth, they focus on a particular issue or change, and for this reason their leadership activity tends to be temporary and task focused (Ehrich & English, 2012, pp. 87–88).

Role Legitimacy

Role legitimacy refers to the perception by those associated with a role to accept the role and its attendant duties and responsibilities as sanctioned and not to be seriously questioned. This does not mean that competency to perform the role may not be questioned. But the role itself is not to be questioned. Role legitimacy from a management perspective in schools is rooted in the law, beginning with the power of an elected or appointed board of education to exercise citizen or lay oversight over educational systems and/or schools.

Contemporary approaches to role legitimacy that employ so-called distributive leadership are simply a means to rearrange duties among existing roles within the existing organization. Philip Woods (2005) has contrasted this perspective with true democratic leadership, which is much more relational and context specific. Democratic leadership is not so much concerned with organizational boundaries as with matters of equality and creating open boundaries and an "equal distribution of externalized authority, voice, esteem, and internal authority" (Woods, 2005, p. 34). Woods contrasts two types of needs. The first is met with management and is focused on getting "people to commit themselves to working in ways consistent with organizational requirements and powerful interests in the wider socioeconomic system" compared to the second need which is "the human need . . . for a re-enchantment of labour, imbuing work with a sense of meaning, worth and validity rooted in enduring truths and values concerning human living" (p. 37).

Follower Relations

Franklin Roosevelt once remarked, "It's a terrible thing to look over your shoulder when you are trying to lead and find no one there" (Peters, 2005, p. 17). By definition one cannot lead if no one is following. Leaders and followers are a dynamic dyad. Howard Gardner (1995) indicates that leaders compete for followers by the telling of stories or narratives. The most essential stories are those dealing with identity in answer to the question, "who are we" followed by "what are we about?" Leaders weave patterns of potential meaning for human actions. Prospective followers find connections with the stories leaders tell and decide to go with them or not. Gardner indicates that the most effective narratives are simple stories that have wide appeal and are understood. Thus, we find that stories from Aesop's fables, Grimms' Fairy Tales, the Bible, and Greek mythology are frequently employed in leadership narratives. These anecdotes require little explanation and if the fit to the overall story line is good, add much emotional and cognitive satisfaction to potential followers.

Leaders are storytellers. They are also teachers. They work to make complex problems appear to be resolvable. Because we all know that human attention spans are limited, especially in the contemporary world of instant Internet messages and Twitter, brevity is the rule of the day. It is almost impossible to believe that over 150 years ago, Abraham Lincoln gave a 7,000-word speech that made him U.S. president at New York City's Cooper Union in 1860. But

Lincoln's speech was a masterful example of teaching, and it ended with his immortal line that "right makes might" (Holzer, 2004, p. xxii).

Transactional leadership is an approach to leading that is based on formalized bureaucratic concerns. The emphasis is on the system. Transformational leadership is based on the self-interests of the employees and how the leader is able to connect with them and link those interests to the overall goals of the organization. Managers emphasize rule conformance, while leaders look for ways to connect with followers so that what they find intrinsically rewarding also is beneficial to the system. The stories leaders tell and the fables and metaphors they employ greatly support revealing to which drummers the leader is marching. Transformational leaders understand that followers are an integral part of leadership and they must be persuaded and motivated. Transactional leaders want them to be merely obedient.

Use of Power and Sanctions

The difference between management and leadership is also expressed in how one uses power to obtain influence. Management tends to be centered on forms of coercive power centered on punishment. Thus, the emerging approach of tying teacher salary and tenure to student standardized test scores is highly coercive. The ability of a teacher to exert any control or to resist this pressure by being lodged in a group norm is negated. A group norm might have heretofore existed within the confines of a union contract that placed some restrictions on the actions of administration. In states where the ability of a union to compel the administration to accept some limitations on its coercive power has been vitiated, the manipulation of salary is a powerful kind of reward power for management to employ. Leadership is more apt to use what John French and Bertram Raven (1959) have called "expert power" and that is influence based on knowledge. Research-based practice is an expression of this type of approach. Management approaches legitimacy by stressing its legal authority. Leadership rests its legitimacy on knowledge, and it works to influence individuals by stressing common attributes of highly effective groups, groups that are held together by a common purpose and vision and not merely institutional structures.

The Basis of Authority

Management's authority and its power to govern and compel conformance is centered in organization, largely bureaucracies. Bureaucracies are ideally suited for managers to compel compliance because of their hierarchical structure and the linkage of salary and other forms of compensation to specific roles within a hierarchy. Bureaucracies also stress forms of accomplishment that are tied to entry and advancement within a set of linked superior and subordinate roles.

Conversely, leadership stresses moral authority, and its norms are rooted in the cultural norms of what is good for the entire community. Conformity is acquired by stressing how behavior will or will not advance or retard the group or community as a whole.

The reality is that persons occupying roles of managers in bureaucracies can be managers without being leaders. What that means is that if it were not for the legal authority embedded in a managerial role in a school or school system, few persons would pay much attention to the office holder and what he or she thought or wanted. Managers can be office holders without being leaders of any real influence. On the other hand, if leaders are going to lead within a bureaucracy they have to also be good managers or employ people who are to assist them to be so. Leaders can lead outside bureaucracies, that is, be grassroots leaders who occupy roles that are very much more fluid than those inside of school organizations. We now turn to a discussion of leadership.

The Concept of *Accoutrements* as Artful Leadership and the Key for Imagination

Leadership has been written about from many perspectives found in the dyad of management and leadership. The so-called scientific methods of researching leadership lend a focus solely on the techniques and skills that can be linked in measurable ways to our preparation programs and perhaps serve as a fulcrum for determining some forms of job performance. However, the traditional research focus on what principals do has been heavily lopsided on skills and behaviors to the detriment of issues of interiority within a leader.

As Papa and Fenwick English discuss in their 2011 book on principals in underperforming schools, a comparison of research in different international schools depicts seven commonalities of leaders. Leaders are self-constructed and not born; they are the sum total of their life experiences. Effective leadership is centered in a moral values base, and that also is an anchor for the leader's vision. Leadership is about working with and through others, drawing the best out of the people with whom one works. While leaders work with a sense of purpose based on a commitment to their ideals, they remain open-minded intellectually and curious about how things work and what moves people and can change their minds when the facts do not match the situation. Because leadership is a projection of self, the first lesson of leadership is to understand oneself; a leader cannot lead without understanding what motivates himself or herself. Leadership is about a journey taken with others and lived with and through others; it is not a destination but a quest. Finally, leadership involves the total human being—not just the rational side but the emotional and feeling side as well (pp. 76, 78).

The essence of leadership begins with the formation of identity. A purely behavioral or structural view of leadership fails to deal with this quintessential human question of how identity is formed. Unless the human dimension is considered as an integral aspect of developing effective leadership, the skill lists (which up to now have been the way leadership has been characterized for testing and licensing purposes) amount to preparing and evaluating robots instead of the flesh and blood human beings who are necessary to make schools human and humane places.

The authors of this chapter have written about the artfulness that the leader needs to develop (English, 2008; Papa, 2011; Papa & English, 2011). This chapter contends the focus of neoliberal education policies on linking leadership effectiveness with test scores is a far too narrow perspective and is leading to a broad culture of corruption that is already beginning to emerge in education. Unfortunately, preparation programs for educational leadership have begun to emphasize performance on testable measures.

Papa has researched these artful qualities that the school leader needs and refers to them as **accoutrements** (Papa, 2011; Papa & Fortune, 2002). Accoutrements represent a combination of reflective and reflexive experiences acquired within specific contexts and culture. Most important, the concept of accoutrements rests on the fundamental claim that leadership is a socially constructed agenda of purposeful action exercised within specific contexts. These accoutrements were developed over 12 years of empirical data gathering, including field-based observations, surveys, interviews, and document collection, through site-based visits by teams of professors, superintendents, and principals. Classroom observation and interviews with all school staff members and parents, along with the results of other researchers' work on school leadership, served as the basis for the accoutrements. High-performing schools in California and Arizona that were high poverty and high minority formed the research database. Similar results can be found in international studies, such as the research done by Neil Cranston and Lisa Ehrich (2007) in Australia. These findings are noted in **Table 2.1**.

Accoutrements develop through the years of professional reflection and reflexivity. These attributes are predicated on the concept that leaders are made; that is, leadership does not come from birth, is not a trait gene that some have and others do not. It does mean that understanding and growing the accoutrements requires one to change, continuously, while continuing reflexivity is practiced. These accoutrements are (a) understanding adult learners; (b) developing human agency (social justice through fairness, care, compassion); (c) acknowledging intended but ignored dimensions, such as listening, as critical to develop; (d) expanding your intellectual curiosity and those of others you teach and lead; (e) cultivating a tolerance for ambiguity that will support challenging the status quo by visioning a different future; and (f) expansion of the imagination so that thinking outside the box becomes a path that can lead to new and creative solutions to the daily and long-term issues faced by educational leaders. (See **Sidebar 2.1**.)

The criticality of imagination was underscored by N. Scott Momaday (2009) who remarked, "We are what we imagine. Our very existence consists in our imagination of ourselves. The greatest tragedy

Papa Accoutrements	*Papa Characteristics*	*Cranston & Ehrich Leadership of Lessons*	*Commentary*
Leading adult learners	Leadership preparation is grounded in theory and practice and occurs on a "need to know" basis.	Formal and informal learning is critical to leadership development.	Learning to be a leader should be multidimensional and involve more than formal course work in a university or agency setting.
Human agency	Focus on the totality of human existence, rejection of a "one size fits all" mental model.	Leadership is values driven; it ought to be about seeking equity and tolerance.	Leadership is concerned with human existence and social justice and working toward a better world. It is a moral endeavor.
Ignored but intended skills	Leadership skills are not all reducible to discrete behaviors, a rejection of reductionism.	Life forces, experiences and opportunities explored are fundamental to leadership development.	Leadership is more than the technical acquisition of discrete skill sets, it is a value-defined and -driven enterprise enacted with and through followers.
Intellectual curiosity	Leaders should be curious about all aspects of leading and learning.	Leadership is a journey of discovery, seeking answers to intriguing questions.	Closed minds do not see leadership as open-ended and therefore are not interested in the unanswered questions. Leadership is quest.
Futurity	Leadership involves multiple frames of knowing and understanding in order to grasp a future that is different from the status quo.	A quest to effect change for a better future is the critical challenge for leaders.	Being able to more fully understand the challenges of the future requires the ability to reframe the field.
Imaginativeness	This facet of leadership is also connected to creativity, originality, and inspiration.	Leadership draws on creativity, risk taking, and a capacity to lead and develop others in collaborative work.	Leaders are required to have a vision, but visions are anchored to imagination and creativity.

Table 2.1 A Comparison of the Papa Accoutrements of Leadership to Lessons of Leadership

SOURCE: Papa, R., & English, F. (2011), p. 77.

that can befall us is to go unimagined" (p. 100). While performing day-to-day tasks is encouraged or discouraged by the limits we might place on our thinking about the actions we might wish to take, it has been customary to see the expression of imagination as "thinking outside the box." In a twist on this notion, Drew Boyd and Jacob Goldenberg (2013) take the position that some of the most innovative solutions and radical breakthroughs have

occurred when leaders think inside the box, but in different ways than before. They review several strategies that include the idea of *subtraction,* the removal of what were viewed as essential elements that led to the creation of the Sony Walkman. Another strategy is *task unification* in which apparently unrelated tasks or functions are united. This approach led Samsonite to produce backpacks with straps that it claimed also provided a massage

Sidebar 2.1   The Nature of Leadership Accoutrements

These are the attributes combined with your experiences that lead to **artful leadership** practice. Think about how you are aware of them in your perspective on leadership and where you might need to acquire more knowledge and practice.

- Consider your capacity for human agency, social justice, and compassion to those around you and decisions understanding who may be harmed, who benefits and who doesn't.
- Consider how well you listen to those who come to you; active listening takes practice.
- Consider your curious intellect by thinking about how reflective you are when you think of options and possibilities.
- Consider how forward thinking you are in the face of current wisdom and practices; anticipation and risk are considerations.
- Consider what you can imagine and hope for as in what we are becoming, who we are—visioning a better and more hopeful future and taking the steps to move forward.

Now, what do you need to do to put together your own career in educational leadership that will lead to you becoming an "artful practitioner"?

sensation, because the straps were located at shiatsu points in the back.

This notion of reimagining and recombining elements within the box requires a shift in imagination. Boyd and Goldenberg (2013) suggest, "Most people think innovation starts with establishing a well-defined problem and then thinking of solutions. Our method is just the opposite: We take an abstract, conceptual solution and find a problem that it can solve."

Machine Metaphors and Unrealistic Expectations

Another important leadership issue is the type of metaphors the leader employs. There has been a tendency to use the **machine metaphor** in the pursuit of what Stephen Pattison (1997) has called *managerial perfectionism*. This tendency not only destroys the concept of leadership and reduces it to mechanical and dehumanizing theorizing, it also results in a pervasive cynicism about how effective leaders really do their work.

Managerial perfectionism is the misguided and irrational belief that the actions of management can somehow always be right if we are wise enough, have

enough data, have enough courage, plan carefully enough, and are bold enough; then, everything will work out right. The idea that somehow human foibles and imperfections always can be overcome or that management can become omniscient borders on an improbable and irrational myth that involves large doses of mysticism, perhaps akin to reading Tarot cards.

> Although management is strewn about with tough, practical-sounding talk and scientific-seeming techniques and technologies, it is full of metaphysical beliefs and assumptions. These are often unsupported by any kind of evidence; sometimes they exist in flat contradiction to such evidence as is available. (Pattison, 1997, p. 26)

One way that contextual complexities can be overcome is to adopt an approach that ignores them or erases them with magical solutions. Medical doctors are sometimes prone to this, as seen when they make a diagnosis based on erroneous thinking and then stick to it despite evidence to the contrary (Groopman, 2007, p. 261). This phenomenon has occurred in education with the passage of the No Child Left Behind Act in 2001, which declared that all children would be proficient at grade-level math and reading by 2014. The inability to meet this expectation has led most states to seek waivers from some of the law's provisions, including the 2014 proficiency deadline.

Managerial perfectionism is rampant in education. Yet perfectionism is rarely possible; rather, leaders should be expected to consistently work toward good results without becoming robots and/or machine parts or replacements.

Often leadership skill acquisition is given in a metaphor of the toolbox. School leaders learn a new skill and declare, "just something I can put in my toolbox" for future use. This is a decidedly mechanistic and artificial view of leadership and a deterministic metaphor for management. Tools are for machines. The metaphor that one acquires specific skills or techniques and puts them in his or her toolbox is simplistic, mechanistic, and reductionist.

Lumby and English (2010) have compared the nature of a machine to a human. A machine always performs exactly the same; that is, there is little variance in performance, and it will produce identical results. The machine functions the same as long as its energy source lasts. It produces faster than humans with greater consistency; it never gets tired or sick, does not have to be motivated, and does not have to believe in a better future to keep working hard (Lumby & English, 2010, p. 13).

The assumption that educational leaders can become machines and attain heretofore "perfect" responses is embedded in political statements and job descriptions that employ machine metaphors to describe the expectations for school leadership. For example, in 2006, the North Carolina State Board of Education (NSCBE) adopted the *North Carolina Standards for School Executives*. A close examination of the standards finds these examples of machine metaphors and assumptions included in the commentary below the standard:

"The goal of school leadership is to transform schools so that large-scale, sustainable, continuous improvement becomes built in to their mode of operation" (NCSBE, 2006, p. 1).

[*Commentary:* Something that never rests and runs *continuously* without stopping is the embodiment of a machine, and when it is "built in to their mode of operation" it is a decidedly mechanical notion.]

"Leadership is not a position or a person. It is a practice that must be embedded in all job roles at all levels of the school district" (NCSBE, 2006, p. 1).

[*Commentary:* This idea completely strips leadership away from human interaction and replaces it with the idea that leadership is simply a part within a machine.]

"Influences the evolution of the culture to support the continuous improvement of the school as outlined in the school improvement plan" (NCSBE, 2006, p. 4).

[*Commentary:* The idea is that from the specifications within a plan, the leader embeds the required and desired "culture" that will lead to continuous improvement without cessation in the school.]

"Designs protocols and processes that ensure compliance with state and district mandates" (NCSBE, 2006, p. 6).

[*Commentary:* The idea is to ensure conformance by duplicating procedures (the working parts of a machine) with state and district mandates (the overall machine design)].

The continued use of machine metaphors to describe desired leadership behaviors and actions sets up a leader to fail because humans are not machines and will have bad days where emotionless machines do not. Think about our greatest athletes. No matter how talented or great, they do drop balls, miss goals, strike out, fumble the ball, and flat out fail. To insist that educators "do it right the first time and every time" is to compare us to machines where we will never outperform them and we will always come up short. This is pure folly.

School leaders should avoid being compared to machines and avoid using machine metaphors to establish school goals and processes. In education, as with most professions, the perfect is the enemy of the good. Good performance is for humans. Perfect performance is for machines. Beginning with realistic expectations goes a long way in defining success. We can never succeed if we are bound to fail from the beginning. The wisdom of practice means that practice will rarely, if ever, attain perfection. It is important to have high standards. But there is a difference between high standards and impossible standards.

The Lenses of Practice

Leadership practice does not occur in a vacuum. Leadership and its actions are deeply embedded in culture and context. Leadership practice also swims in a sea of larger narratives or stories: stories about what is valuable or not; what is worth doing; what is beautiful; what is the purpose of getting an education and learning and the meaning and nature of work.

The lens through which educational leadership has been historically defined since it was established as a specific field near the turn of the last century has been founded on claims that management was or ought to be a science and that school administrators should be "scientifically trained" so as to gain maximum efficiency (the reduction of cost) in operating schools.

So-called scientific management was the creation of Frederick Taylor, one of the country's first management consultants, who brought time and motion studies to the study of work to discern the most efficient way to do anything on a job. His path-breaking book published in 1911, *The Principles of Scientific Management,* laid the foundation for establishing departments of educational administration in the newly emerging schools of education.

Taylorism had a profound impact on ideas of administrative practice in schools and, for that matter, in business. Taylor (1911/1947) believed that with enough study there was one "right way" to do most everything. So the "one right way" became a kind of powerful assumption behind thinking about administrative practice. It survives today in the form of the concept of **best practice**, which is not always the same as research-based practice. More often than not, best practice refers to a sort of "rule of thumb" or heuristic passed on from one administrator to the next, sometimes in the form of popular off-the-shelf **kitsch** management **books**, which are glossy treatises with happy endings always promised with implementation of the remedies described between the covers. Airport book nooks are awash with them (Papa, Kain, & Brown, 2013).

How to Discern *Best Practice* From Ordinary Practice, Common Sense, and Kitsch Texts

When someone declares that something is best practice the reader needs to beware. All too often best practice is simply the author's or advocate's personal opinion about how best to handle a situation, and all too often the advocate fails to divulge his or her own biases when revealing best practice. Perhaps one of the most blatant examples is the bestselling book by Stephen Covey, *The 7 Habits of Highly Effective People,* first published in 1989. Covey has sold about 10 million copies of his book, which has been translated into 28 languages.

While Covey claimed that his book was based on a thorough study of the relevant thought regarding American "success" literature since 1776, a close read of his actual research study showed something else. While Covey advanced the claim of comprehensiveness, his "success" literature consisted of 108 references of which nearly 25 percent were other doctoral dissertations completed in the time period 1963 to 1974. Twenty-two percent of Covey's citations were from journal articles in the time period 1945 to 1975. Of the secular books cited in Covey's research, none bore copyrights earlier than 1938 or older than 1975. Secular books comprised 38 percent of his literature base, 46 percent of these were citations from the sixties with 34 percent in the period 1970 to 1975. The remainder of Covey's research base were sacred writings, including the *King James Version of the Bible* and major sources of Mormon literature, including *The Book of Mormon,* originally released in 1830.

Covey (1991) claimed to have been brought into contact with "hundreds of books . . . the majority of it appears to have originally come out of the study of the Bible by many individuals" (p. 153). Additionally, Covey's empirical research consisted of 222 business students at Brigham Young University (BYU) who were divided into two groups. One group was taught using "traditional" methods and content. The second group was instructed with religious principles of the Mormon Church and they were called "stewardship classes." These classes were heavily loaded with Church doctrine. After instruction had ended, Covey administered a 30-item questionnaire on three aspects of personal development. They were the *social dimension,* the *emotional dimension*, and the *moral dimension.* After performing a rudimentary statistical analysis, Covey's findings showed *no significant difference* between the groups.

What is important about this revelation is that Covey never tells readers of *7 Habits* any of this. And he never explains that his research was not conducted in the school of education nor the school of business, but within the Department of Church History and Doctrine at BYU and that his doctorate was in religious education. Our discussion of these facts is not a condemnation of the Mormon faith nor its teachings. Rather it is to illustrate that this widely popular book, which advanced seven principles, was not in fact based on any substantive research that supported its claims. Covey's (1991) claim of "effectiveness" was not empirically based, but rather centered on the teachings of the Mormon Church, which begs the question of the truth of his claims. He simply asserts, "They are . . . unarguable because they are self-evident" (p. 35). *7 Habits* is larded with social science jargon to give it the veneer of respectability, but

> Covey's social science is no science at all. He fails to adequately define his terms, fully disclose his sources, forthrightly identify his biases and assumptions, carefully pursue a logical approach to clearly identified problems, and offer empirical evidence to support his claims. (English, 2003, p. 170)

7 Habits is not the only example of nonempirical work being advanced as a base for "best practice." Other examples, which are compilations of slogans, metaphors, and anecdotes, have been identified by Papa et al. (2013), such as Spencer Johnson's (1998) *Who Moved My Cheese?;* Kenneth Blanchard and Johnson's (1983) *The One Minute Manager;* Stephen C. Lundin, Harry Paul, and John Christensen's (2000) *Fish! A Remarkable Way to Boost Morale and Improve Results.*

These books are examples of kitsch management texts; they are highly sentimental, cheap, superficial treatments of complex situations. Kitsch management texts require no in-depth knowledge, need no hard reading, reinforce our existing prejudices, "avoid unpleasant conflicts, and promise a happy ending" (Samier, 2005, p. 38). They are a kind of managerial pulp fiction. Some are outright frauds. Thomas Peters, one of the authors of the best-selling business management book *In Search of Excellence* (Peters & Waterman, 1982), stated in a 2001 article that he and coauthor Robert Waterman "faked the data" cited in the book (Lieberman, 2001) .

Some Questions to Ask About *Best Managerial Practice*

When a practice is identified as a "best practice" and reduced to the form of maxims, proverbs, or

commandants, certain questions should be asked about how they were derived. This chapter poses these questions within the context of a study of organizational decision making. The study reveals not only the complexity of decision making, but also the kinds of benchmarks a study of practice should meet to be considered "best practice," especially with regard to administrative "best practice."

What Is the Context and the Theoretical Perspective in Defining a Practice?

One of the key issues in determining a "best" managerial practice is the definition and a solid presentation of the background and context of the practice. Few practices in administration are good for all times and all places. There are too many "what ifs" and "it all depends" scenarios that create contingencies and exceptions to a practice for it to be applicable for every kind of situation facing an administrator.

Some prior empirical studies of school superintendents showed that "the reputationally successful [superintendents]—those who can be considered as expert performers—have larger amounts of if-then scenarios to draw on in navigating the superintendency, allowing them a seemingly intuitive orientation to the tasks at hand" (Nestor-Baker & Hoy, 2001, p. 123).

Any study in which "best practices" are the result must be fully forthcoming about not only the context in which the study was conducted but also how the study was theoretically framed. A study that does not reveal its theoretical underpinnings should not be trusted because too often the researcher obtains what he or she assumed was already there. Such a study amounts to the exercise of a tautology; that is, it was true by definition and really didn't even need a study to be considered "true."

To explicate our point, English and Cheryl Bolton (2008) conducted a study of decision-making practices in England and the United States to determine whether educational decision makers at the mid-management level engaged in "heuristics" or "rules of thumb" to aid them. The study was grounded in preliminary evidence compiled from education and medicine that showed not all decisions in both fields were always rational, that professionals face situations in which there is a large amount of uncertainty, and that time is limited for accurate and prolonged diagnosis. The acquisition of rules of thumb enabled decision makers to "chunk" complex situations into smaller pieces. By rules of thumb was meant that information, "is organized mentally via predetermined metarules that are category based and whole pattern in structure" (Davis, 2004, p. 631).

In the English and Bolton (2008) study, the context was identified (midlevel managers in largely higher education situations in the United States and the United Kingdom) along with the initial theoretical lens. The explication of the theoretical lens is significant because the use of a lens is the way a study of practice is framed. The framing of a study means that some facets of a situation or context are included while others are excluded. For example, the framing of this study involved **rational choice theory** or RCT. RCT was employed because administrator preparation has been almost exclusively grounded in rational choice theory (Bolton & English, 2010). RCT requires a separation of logic and emotion and it is centered on game theory, which is linked to a hard analysis of risk and value.

The Logic of a Practice and Understanding Contextual Complexities

Decision making within an organization is a complex interplay between the decision maker and the context in which he or she is working. Persons working at the midmanagement level such as school principals or persons occupying positions at central offices or larger educational institutions do not make decisions in isolation. The context of decision making is therefore connected to other roles.

The English and Bolton (2008) study asked questions of midlevel managers to determine if they used heuristics and, if so, under what circumstances. What emerged from the interviews of 13 middle-line managers over a five-month period was that instead of a separation of logic and emotion required by the tenets of rational choice theory, emotion was present in nearly every decision that midlevel managers made. The supposed binary of separating logic from emotion in the day-to-day business of running an educational institution turned out to be a myth.

While it was discovered midlevel managers did make decisions, the interview data also showed a more complex reality facing them. What the researchers discerned were not heuristics per se but rather a sorting out of the issues within a matrix of other roles. The researchers found that a midlevel manager differs from a medical doctor or a school superintendent who make decisions alone on some matters.

The interview data revealed that decisions by midlevel managers were made on the cognitive/intellectual side that would be supported by the tenets of rational choice theory, but they also made decisions based on their own sense of what was proper and right. These were primarily nonrational (emotional). They came to be called "core values" and were composed of personal moral decisions, connections to larger values outside the organization that existed in the connecting tissue to society, culture, or a linguistic heritage, or connections to a set of values of other institutions such as a church or synagogue or mosque.

The data showed that this personal, emotional side was always present in decision making by midlevel managers. In a sort of personal heuristic, the respondents sometimes refused to make a decision when they felt a heavy emotional burden because one of their core values was broached. These disjunctions in decision making were called *circuit breakers*. In scenarios where midlevel managers perceived a transgression of their core values, or they perceived that a particular kind of decision posed too much job risk, they found ways to avoid making a decision at all. In these cases midlevel managers would kick the decision upstairs, that is, pass it on to their bosses or refer it back to those who sent it by asking for more information before rendering any decision. A key component was the extent to which there was a climate of trust in the organization, meaning the extent to which a midlevel manager could expect not to be fired if a decision went badly. A key factor here was the extent to which uncertainty was present; that is, if the personal risks were high with strong levels of uncertainty, an individual decision maker refused to render a decision. This was a circuit breaker.

The English and Bolton (2008) study concluded that midlevel administrators make decisions, or choose not to make them, on two levels. The first is their organizational, positional level and where they "fit in" to the overall structure. The second is at a highly personal level that might be called a sort of moral plane. The data illustrated that midlevel administrators might not always render a decision that was good for the organization or that was required to be made at their level, but they almost always made a decision that was good for themselves (Bolton & English, 2010). In retrospect, this makes perfect sense, and it is a kind of heuristic, but not exactly how the researchers initially conceptualized the nature of a heuristic.

Toward an Improved Grasp of Administrative Practice

The actual decision-making context of midlevel administrators in practice is shown in **Figure 2.2.**

The decision-making context for midlevel managers indicates that within the dynamic interplay of the individual and the organization the administrator renders or defers a decision by constant balancing of three factors: personal risk, uncertainty, and emotionality based on personally held values. These three factors are in constant tension and are codependent. By *risk* is meant the possible negative consequences of a decision that will arise to the decision maker if a decision goes badly. By *uncertainty* is meant the unknown elements that will impact a decision, some of which could be known with more time and others not. By *emotionality* is meant the organization's climate and, with an individual, the extent "to which any leader must deal with his or her feelings, including intuition, hunches, and even suspicions" (English & Bolton, 2008, p. 108).

When viewing what might be best managerial practice, one has to know the theoretical lens through which such practice is defined and implemented. Rational choice models will define best practice as one in which profit is maximized and cost is minimized. Other lenses will stress other factors. The context in which administrative decisions are rendered really defines the efficacy of a decision.

Before anyone should accept certain managerial axioms or decisions as best, one must know something about the factors discussed in this section. It should also be obvious why the kitsch management books are so ambiguous. Their proverbs and advice must remain general and contextually bland or the nuances of real organizational life quickly invalidate their utility.

Any real consideration of best practices in educational management and leadership is contextually dependent on many variables. It has been the purpose of this chapter to highlight some of them.

Key Chapter Terms

Accoutrements: Those artful skills, insights, and characteristics that the school leader needs to develop to become an effective educational leader. The concept is both artful and one based on social science approaches and also takes into account context and culture.

Artful leadership: An approach to leadership based on the idea that leading is an act of performing because it involves actions, movement, rituals, and the use of symbols, chief of which is language.

Authority: The source of power within organizations. In schools, the basis of authority is legal, which is one of the classic earmarks of a bureaucracy.

Best practice: The idea that some managerial practices optimize results over all other practices that may be possible. The forerunner of "best practice" is Frederick Taylor's "one best method" outcome with scientific management. In management, the idea of best practice rests on the assumption that there are no significant differences in context that will reduce the effectiveness of a practice.

Ideology: A closed system of beliefs or values in which the original assumptions of those beliefs or values are rarely, if ever, questioned, but instead

Figure 2.2   The Context of Midlevel Managerial Decision Making

SOURCE: English, F.W., & Bolton, C.L. (2008).

accepted as givens. Those most difficult to discern are cultural ideologies.

Kitsch and kitsch management books: Kitsch is a slang term that means "rubbish" or "trash" and is usually applied to inexpensive "knock offs" of art or artistic products. It can also mean in "bad taste." Kitsch management books are highly simplified descriptions and other bromides that can be taken as organizational "pep pills" without regard to any subtle nuances in context. Such management books are simplistic prescriptions for happiness at the end of the organizational rainbow.

Machine metaphors: Descriptors of management or leadership in which such words as *continuous improvement* appear, implying rest is not necessary and that human foibles are erased when management is put together properly and running well. In such models of leadership, the major descriptors are "smooth running," as in a well-oiled machine.

Managerial perfectionism: An approach toward describing the goals of management as 100% of all possible outcomes or results. It is the idea that

perfection is not only possible but attainable, even when dealing with organizations in which such an outcome is impossible if for no other reason than management does not control the variables used to judge its performance.

Pedagogy: Narrowly defined pedagogy refers to the science of teaching children. However, in the more modern sense it refers to the discourse in which education and educational matters are defined, refined, and applied. It also refers to the historical deconstruction of ideas, patterns, and themes undergirding educational issues.

Power: The legitimization and authorization within law and social institutions to define the shape of education (schooling) and to compel its use and impose its form on the remainder of those inhabiting any given social system.

Rational choice theory: A narrative in which human choice is portrayed as a process of maximizing outputs within the constraints imposed by specific situations and those employing the choices of others, as in game theory.

References

Blanchard, K., & Johnson, S. (1983). *The one minute manager.* New York, NY: Berkeley Books.

Bolton, C. L., & English, F. W. (2010). Exploring the dynamics of work-place trust, personal agency, and administrative heuristics. In E. Samier & M. Schmidt (Eds.), *Trust and betrayal in educational administration and leadership* (pp. 29–42). New York, NY: Routledge.

Boyd, D., & Goldenberg, J. (2013, June 15–16). Thinking inside the box. *Wall Street Journal,* C1.

Brown, R., Noble, P., & Papa, R. (2009). *So you want to be a higher education administrator? Avoid crossing to the dark side or what they don't teach in summer leadership institutes.* Lancaster, PA: Proactive.

Covey, S. (1991). *The 7 habits of highly effective people.* New York, NY: Simon & Schuster.

Cranston, N., & Ehrich, L. (2007). *What is this thing called leadership?* Brisbane, Australia: Australian Academic Press.

Davis, S. H. (2004). The myth of the rational decision maker: A framework for applying and enhancing

heuristic and intuitive decision making by school leaders. *Journal of School Leadership, 14*(6), 621–652.

Dreeben, R. (1973). The school as a workplace. In R. M. W. Travers (Ed.), *Second handbook of research on teaching* (pp. 450–473). Chicago, IL: Rand McNally.

Ehrich, L. C., & English, F. W. (2012). What can grassroots leadership teach us about school leadership? *Halduskultuur-Administrative Culture, 13*(2), 85–108.

English, F. W. (2003). The denouement of a contemporary management guru. In F. English (Ed.), *The postmodern challenge to the theory and practice of educational administration* (pp. 145–174). Springfield, IL: Charles C Thomas.

English, F. W. (2008). *The art of educational leadership: Balancing performance and accountability.* Thousand Oaks, CA: Sage.

English, F. W., & Bolton, C. L. (2008). An exploration of administrative heuristics in the United States and the United Kingdom. *Journal of School Leadership, 18*(2), 96–119.

Foster, W. (1986). *The reconstruction of leadership.* Victoria, New South Wales, Australia: Deakin University Press.

French, J., & Raven, B. (1959). The bases of social power. In D. Cartwright (Ed.), *Studies in social power* (pp. 150–167). Ann Arbor: University of Michigan.

Gardner, H. (1995). *Leading minds: An anatomy of leadership.* New York, NY: HarperCollins.

Giroux, H. (1988). *Teachers as intellectuals: Toward a critical pedagogy of learning.* New York, NY: Bergin & Garvey.

Groopman, J. (2007). *How doctors think.* Boston, MA: Houghton Mifflin.

Holzer, H. (2004). *Lincoln at Cooper Union.* New York, NY: Simon & Schuster.

Johnson, S. (1998). *Who moved my cheese?* New York, NY: G. P. Putnam.

Lieberman, D. (2001, November 19). Author: Data on successful firms "faked" but still valid. *USA Today,* p. A1.

Lortie, D. C. (1975). *School-teacher.* Chicago, IL: University of Chicago Press.

Lumby, J., & English, F. W. (2010). *Leadership as lunacy: And other metaphors for educational leadership.* Thousand Oaks, CA: Corwin.

Lundin, S. C., Paul, H., & Christensen, J. (2000). *Fish! A remarkable way to boost morale and improve results.* New York, NY: Hyperion.

Momaday, N. S. (2009). Wisdom. In T. Nguyen (Ed.), *Language is a place of struggle: Great quotes by people of color.* Boston, MA: Beacon Press.

Nestor-Baker, N. S., & Hoy, W. K. (2001). Tacit knowledge of school superintendents: Its nature, meaning, and content. *Educational Administration Quarterly, 37*(1), 86–129.

North Carolina State Board of Education. (2006). *North Carolina standards for school executives.* Raleigh, NC: Author.

Papa, R. (2011). Standards for educational leadership: Promises, paradoxes and pitfalls. In F. English (Ed.), *Handbook of educational leadership* (2nd ed., pp. 195–209). Thousand Oaks, CA: Sage.

Papa, R., & English, F. W. (2011). *Turnaround principals for underperforming schools.* Lanham, MD: Rowman & Littlefield.

Papa, R., English, F., Davidson, F., Culver, M., & Brown, R. (2013). *Contours of great leadership: The science, art and wisdom of outstanding practice.* Lanham, MD: Rowman & Littlefield.

Papa, R., & Fortune, R. (2002). *Leadership on purpose: Promising practices for African American and Hispanic students.* Thousand Oaks, CA: Corwin.

Papa, R., Kain, D., & Brown, R. (2013). Who moved my theory? A kitsch exploration of kitsch leadership texts. In B. Irby, G. Brown, R. Lara-Alecio, & S. Jackson (Eds.), *The handbook of educational theories* (pp. 969–973). Charlotte, NC: Information Age.

Pattison, S. (1997). *The faith of the managers: When management becomes religion.* London, England: Cassell.

Peters, G. (2005). *Five days in Philadelphia.* New York, NY: Public Affairs.

Peters, T., & Waterman, R. (1982). *In search of excellence: Lessons from America's best-run companies.* New York, NY: Harper & Row.

Powell, C. (2013, April 5). Wit and wisdom. *The Week, 13*(611), 17.

Samier, E. (2005). Toward public administration as a humanities discipline: A humanistic manifesto. *Halduskultuur: Administrative Culture, 6,* 6–59.

Senge, P., Kleiner, A., Roberts, C., Ross, R., Roght, G., & Smith, B. (1999). *The dance of change: The challenges to sustaining momentum in learning organizations.* New York, NY: Doubleday.

Taylor, F. W. (1947). *The principles of scientific management.* New York, NY: W.W. Norton. (Original work published 1911)

Woods, P. A. (2005). *Democratic leadership in education.* London, England: Paul Chapman.

Further Readings

Ackerman, R. H., & Maslin-Ostrowski, P. (2002). *The wounded leader: How real leadership emerges in times of crisis.* San Francisco, CA: Jossey-Bass.

For a school leader who wants to understand the nature of the battles in educational leadership and how to survive them when "wounded" from them, this book based on interviews of educators who have endured them is helpful and hopeful. As the authors note, it's not "if" you are wounded, rather it is "when" you are wounded.

Bell, T. H. (1988). *The thirteenth man: A Reagan cabinet memoir.* New York, NY: Free Press.

Terrel H. Bell was brought in to abolish the U.S. Department of Education by the Reagan administration but ended up finding that a federal department was necessary in the Washington, D.C., bureaucratic wars. His battles with Reagan ideologues are described in some detail, as is his decision to form and fund a national group that released the groundbreaking federal report A Nation at Risk. For school administrators who really want to understand the nature of educational conflict at the national level, this is as up close and personal as it gets.

Berliner, D. C., & Biddle, B. J. (1995). *The manufactured crisis: Myths, fraud, and the attack on America's public schools.* Reading, MA: Addison-Wesley.

One of the first comprehensive rebuttals of the neoconservative attacks on public education. It exposes the myths about achievement and aptitude, criticizes poor ideas for reform, and explains the real problems of American education. The authors also explain how to examine the fundamentals of school improvement through research and compassion.

Bohman, J. (1992). The limits of rational choice explanation. In J. Coleman & T. Fararo (Eds.), *Rational choice theory: Advocacy and critique* (pp. 207–228). Newbury Park, CA: Sage.

In this chapter in a book devoted to rational choice theory, James Bohman succinctly critiques the basic structure of rational choice explanations and the assumptions that lie behind it. He then summarizes and describes the limits of those assumptions. Bohman does not contend that rational choice theory is wrong but rather that it cannot be a comprehensive social theory or even serve as the basis of one. This is a very brief but comprehensive account of rational choice theory.

Drucker, P. (1974). *Management: Tasks, responsibilities, practices.* New York, NY: Harper & Row.

This is the classic book on management by the acknowledged "dean" of managerial thinkers. Peter Drucker describes the emergence of management and the tasks which comprise the dimensions of management. He separates performance into business performance and performance in service institutions. He goes into detail in describing the manager's work tasks and jobs, effective skills, and the building blocks of organization. The final part of the book deals with the tasks, organization, and strategies of top management. It concludes with a discussion of the legitimacy of management.

English, F. W. (2014). *Educational leadership in the age of greed: A requiem for res publica.* Ypsilanti, MI: National Council of Professors of Educational Administration.

This book is a detailed analysis of the forces of neoliberalism and what groups, agencies, and foundations are funding the neoliberal attack on public education. The book includes an expose of the Broad Foundation and its graduates, many of whom were not educators but were placed in positions of educational leadership in school systems around the United States. The coming culture of corruption caused by linking teacher and administrative pay to standardized student test scores is included as well.

Kanigel, R. (1997). *The one best way: Frederick Winslow Taylor and the enigma of efficiency.* New York, NY: Viking.

This is must book for any reader who wants to really understand the continuing influence of Frederick Taylor and the scientific management movement that today has morphed into accountability and is embodied in the No Child Left Behind Act and the Race to the Top federal grant program. The book is a comprehensive biography and offers a rare glimpse into the life and mind of one of the earliest management consultants in the United States, whose influence is still profound.

Lumby, J., & English, F. W. (2010). *Leadership as lunacy: And other metaphors for educational leadership.* Thousand Oaks, CA: Sage.

Included are seven basic metaphors in which leadership is described: machine, accounting, war, sport, theater, religion, and lunacy. Each of these various metaphors is illustrated in some detail with a discussion of the strengths and weaknesses of each.

Mintzberg, H. (1983). *Structure in fives: Designing effective organizations.* Englewood Cliffs, NJ: Prentice Hall.

This is the classic book on organization design. It establishes a model of how to understand the key parts of any organization composed of the operating core, the middle line, and strategic apex with relationships to the technostructure and the support staff. Henry Mintzberg shows how organizational design is related to the nature of the tasks embedded in an organization. Of key importance is his discussion of the machine bureaucracy compared to the adhocracy. The reader will be provided with a very practical way of thinking about why organizations contain what they do and are shaped the way they are.

Papa, R., & English, F. W. (2011). *Turnaround principals for underperforming schools.* Lanham, MD: Rowman & Littlefield Education.

Based on Rosemary Papa's early research in California of outstanding schools serving minority students, the book expands the research into understanding activist leadership to improve schooling and life chances and how to create socially just schools. Chapters close with a description of heuristics for activist leaders. Book appendices include explicit leader beliefs and actions and a troubleshooting guide that contains advice for school leaders who want to implement the ideas in the book.

Papa, R., English, F. W., Davidson, F., Culver, M. K., & Brown, R. (2013). *Contours of great leadership: The science, art, and wisdom of outstanding practice.* Lanham, MD: Rowman & Littlefield.

Based on Rosemary Papa's decade-long pursuit of the keys to effective school leadership, the book presents a prism for understanding the nature of educational leadership, the nature of accoutrements, habits of reflection, and a focus on instruction, the acquisition and refinement of skills and insights anchored to leadership identity, practice, and wisdom. Chapters include learning extensions and a method for testing one's beliefs about great leaders.

Pattison, S. (1997). *The faith of the managers: When management becomes religion.* London, England: Cassell.

Stephen Pattison is a trained theologian who analyzed contemporary managerial propositions as forms of religion replete with visions and missions. Pattison says, "Although management has no official deity of a traditional, metaphysical kind, it is laden with the kinds of faith presuppositions, irrationalities, paradoxes and symbols that are often directly associated with religion" (p. 2). This book will open one's eyes to the mysticism that lies behind much of the contemporary management movement in education and elsewhere.

Ravitch, D. (2010). *The death and life of the great American school system: How testing and choice are undermining education.* New York, NY: Basic Books.

Once a member of the neoconservative camp in advocating national testing, Diane Ravitch had a change of heart when she saw the direction neoconservative policies were taking public education. She takes on the business model and its shortcomings in San Diego and New York City and critiques No Child Left Behind. In addition, she critiques the neoliberal philanthrocapitalists such as Bill Gates, Eli Broad, and others and discusses why their notions of reform work against public education.

Starratt, R. J. (1996). *Transforming educational administration: Meaning, community, and excellence.* New York, NY: McGraw-Hill.

This book begins with an explication of the unique calling of a school administrator and presents a picture of pathology and health in school administration. There is an excellent discussion of the way meaning is administered in schools, including the pursuit of meaning in a learning community. There are also chapters on empowerment and organic management as well as how to administer excellence with a moral community.

3

Understanding How the Bureaucratic Maze Works

Autumn Tooms Cyprès

Virginia Commonwealth University

Unfortunately, no one can be told what the Matrix is. You have to see it for yourself. . . . You take the blue pill, the story ends, you wake up in your bed and believe whatever you want to believe. You take the red pill, you stay in Wonderland and I show you how deep the rabbit hole goes.

—Morpheus introducing his purpose to Neo in *The Matrix* (Silver, Cracchiolo, Wachowski, & Wachowski, 1999).

This chapter discusses bureaucracies, their value to school leaders, and how to navigate them. First, bureaucratic networks are defined and explored. Then a look at the politics associated with how such networks are built is offered. Finally, suggestions and examples of expert navigation are examined as way to inspire and support both new and seasoned school leaders.

Welcome to Wonderland: A Primer on Bureaucratic Networks

Historically, *bureaucracy* was a term with many positive connotations as it referred to government/ public administration managed by units of non-elected officials. This definition implied that the most noble and pure forms of government systems are those that serve their people and are free from politics (Weber, 1922/1978). Current understandings and implications of the term are significantly different and typically negative. They connote red tape,

the labyrinth of administrivia, and a large amorphous monster that sometimes is policy and sometimes is politics. Because arguments about the "goodness" or "badness" of the concept of bureaucracy will muddle the points in this chapter, the term *network* is used in this discussion. *Network* provides a more concrete set of understandings, which can be visualized by recalling the scene in the 1999 film *The Matrix* (Silver et. al., 1999) in which Neo decides to swallow the red pill and learns about a whole new world (or matrix) of power relationships between people. A *matrix* refers to an array of numbers, symbols, or expressions arranged in rows or columns. In this chapter, the concept is extended to illustrate that bureaucracies, and the power wielded within them, are simply tapestries woven from networks of people.

At their core, networks are intricately arranged daisy chains of people. Experiences, politics, and job titles weave the chains together to form the fabric (or matrix) of education systems at the local, state, and national level. If one person exists metaphorically as a carefully placed stitch within such a fabric, it is hard for him or her to look beyond the immediate environment to see the entire matrix of stitches, warp, and weft threads that constrains or empowers his or her daily work. However, taking stock of one's environment is vital to understanding (and therefore navigating) a network.

The first step to successful leveraging of an agenda is to understand that in the United States, all education systems are built on formal and informal networks because education is a political endeavor (Spring, 1993). Thus, a leader must first understand who has the ability to help or hinder his or her vision and agenda. This leadership skill set is something deeper than the usual Administration 101 class in strategic planning that outlines a recipe for creating a time line and holding meetings to allow for all stakeholders to give input. All stakeholders involved in change do not need to understand the networks that undergird the bureaucratic system of education. The person leveraging the agenda, however, does, for these reasons.

- People are not always forthright in a public meeting with their opinions (Goffman, 1959).
- The meeting held after the meeting (usually in the parking lot, over the telephone, or via social media such as Facebook) is where clusters of people express their honest reactions to ideas and events along with a willingness to hinder or help a leader's vision and agenda (Harvey, 1988).
- Relationships between people are not always obvious, and they can influence group opinion.

These factors are key to understanding networks and leverage points, an essential understanding for leaders so they can inspire people to support and follow their ideas. These truths are applicable to the spectrum of group dynamics found everywhere, from PTA meetings to the U.S. Congress.

Back to the Beginning: How Networks Are Formed

A film that illustrates how large-scale professional and political networks are formed is *The Good Shepherd* (De Niro, 2006). It examines the birth of the Central Intelligence Agency as viewed through the life of one man. Although a fictional movie, it illustrates how relationships formed through college fraternities, social clubs, marriage, and the military

all contributed to the selection and placement of intelligence officers and administrators for the Central Intelligence Agency and to the advancement of politicians' careers. This same formula could be easily applied to the formation of school district leadership teams, local school boards, state legislative bodies, and national policy-making groups. In other words, the formula explains how networks are constructed. A more pragmatic way to visualize the arrangement of formal and informal relationships is to consider a German term, *Stammbaum,* which literally means "family tree." When considering the Stammbaum of networks in education, it is useful to visualize a forest of family trees (Tooms, 2012).

In this chapter, two species of family tree are considered. In order to best define them, a general understanding of what a family tree is must be established: In this context, a family tree is best understood as a historical chart depicting generations of marriages and the offspring produced within (and out of) those relationships. The first species of family tree central to the ideas in this chapter is a historical chart that chronicles generations of relationships centered on the geography of a person's education and training. This type of tree is particularly important because school leadership is a relatively small discipline grounded in politics (Spring, 1993). For example, school district superintendents tend to reach back to classmates and professors to ask for the names of good candidates for leadership positions for the teams they form in school districts. Thus, school district administrations can (although they do not always) consist of administrators who are similar to one another because administrators turn to people they knew in college or during stints as teachers to ask for recommended candidates. Those the administrators turn to for recommendations are often similar to them, and they in turn recommend candidates who are similar. Membership in some of these family trees is obvious through the display of college alumni and fraternity or sorority paraphernalia or professional organization service awards.

About Fit

The second species of family tree forming the Stammbaum of educational leadership chronicles generations of mentors, protégés, and groups of people who work together. The identification of these relationships is a more nuanced process that has to do with a political construct called **fit**. Fit is best understood as a game specific to the politics and relationships between school administrators and the community they serve (Tooms, Lugg, & Bogotch, 2010). In this game, the community, which ultimately governs a school, sets the rules for how an administrator is to behave and not behave. The administrator seeks to understand, obey, and perpetuate these rules because this is the necessary currency to obtain support and therefore job security (Anderson, 1990; Iannocone & Lutz, 1970; Stout, 1986).

When one is selected from a pool of equally qualified candidates as a new principal, superintendent, or state secretary of education, the values of a community (be that a community of district office administrators or a legislative district) directly impact the selection and retention of a leader. For example, it is probably a rare occurrence that an openly gay school principal would be hired in a small conservative Christian town in Mississippi; however, in a more socially progressive area of the United States, such as Madison, Wisconsin, or Los Angeles, California, openly gay school principals might be more prevalent. *Fit* can also be explained as the nexus point between three frames of understanding relative to politics and society. They are identity theory, social construction, and **hegemony**. Below is a brief description of each.

Identity

The definition of identity used in this chapter refers to parts of a self that are composed of meanings attached to the roles people play in society. Identity is a social construct related to interaction of people in the varying contexts of one's life. In the case of a male professor who identifies as a Democrat, for instance, his children would primarily identify him as their father, rather than as "Democrat" or "professor." A visual metaphor of this phenomenon is to consider each context as an empty picture frame that we wear around our necks. In the context of parenting, our frame says "mother" or "father" on its identifying placard. In a different context, such as at the voting booth, the picture frame might say "Democrat" or "Republican." While we "wear" these frames of identity all at the same time, context typically pushes one of these frames to the forefront. That is why third graders are shocked to see their teacher in the grocery store. The identity frame of

"teacher" typically is entrenched with the environmental context of the classroom. It does not occur to young children that teachers are also parents or consumers who buy groceries.

Social Construction

Social construction refers to how parts of the social world, such as a role, practice, or type of behavior, are products of a particular society rather than natural or inevitable. This can be the case with identity because, ultimately, how we see ourselves relates to constructions of reality that we create with others (Gergen, 1999). This means that, in terms of social construction, how we present and understand ourselves depends on our audience and circumstances (Jung & Hect, 2004). Rather than having a single identity, we possess a framework of multiple identities and behaviors; which identities and behaviors are at play depends on the context.

Hegemony

Sociopolitical philosophers such as Michel Foucault (1975) and Jacques Derrida (1982) argued that identity cannot be considered without the influence of hegemony. Hegemony explains how groups or individuals can maintain their dominance over other groups of individuals in a society via coercion rather than violence (Gramsci, 1971). This phenomenon is achieved through persuading those in the subordinate group to accept, adopt, and internalize the dominant group's definition of what is normal. Mechanisms such as the media and school teach, reinforce, and maintain this viewpoint, achieving a kind of veiled oppression. Therefore, the power of a dominant group of people in a society is also maintained (Apple, 1993). Those who are subjected to hegemony are rarely aware of it because messages of what is normal permeate every pore of society through symbols, language, and other cultural structures influenced by the dominant group.

What Does Fit Have to Do With Membership in Networks?

Think about the water cooler talk about an administrator in his or her first year. Often, we say things like, "Oh she fits right in." Or we say, "Oh man,

I don't know if he fits yet." We are not even aware that in truth we are affirming that this person replicates the norms and values of a dominant group in our community. Or consider a statement that countless human resource officers have uttered during a school administrator's application process, "This one is a rock star. I can't put my finger on why. I just know my gut tells me he is a good fit for the job." In truth, the recognition of fit doesn't come from a mysterious gut feeling. It is a barometer of how a community defines school leadership.

This definition comes by way of the convergence of how we understand and construct the rules of society and identity (i.e., what a "good leader" looks and acts like). An example of how this dynamic works would be the consideration of women in school leadership positions. In the mid-20th century, classes for girls in high school included home economics, which focused on the study of maintaining a home in the role of wife. Classes, television, and pop culture did not include explorations of leadership (or any other work-related roles) outside of the home for women. A woman did not "fit" a community's idea of what a superintendent was. Schools and universities are mechanisms in which students, teachers, and administrators are taught the margins of tolerance as prescribed by the communities they serve. This happens directly via constructed definitions and derivations of the words *good, normal,* and *legitimate.* To really drive this point home, consider that until 1959, a *good* school administrator in Alabama was one who kept schools segregated. Or until the last decade, a good school administrator could easily ignore the bullying of a gay student because the student did not fit (Lugg, 2003).

The Family Trees Where We Fit: A Look at n/networks and N/networks

James Paul Gee (1996) described discourse as "big D discourse" (which is represented in writing as *D/discourse*) and "little d discourse" (which is represented in writing as *d/discourse*). D/discourse refers to the large messages that we get in society such as what a good student is or what a good leader does. Small everyday conversations that are embedded in our everyday lives are referred to as d/discourse. Both of these kinds of discourse influence each other. Change happens when one of these is leveraged. For example, when Ryan White's family went public in the 1980s about how he was shunned at school because he had

AIDS, the D/discourse in society changed concerning how children with AIDS should be regarded in schools. This in turn affected (to some degree) the everyday actions of educators in terms of setting and reinforcing the culture of school and how AIDS victims of all ages are regarded. This section borrows from the construct of d/D and uses the idea of **n/networks and N/networks**. Networks centered around a school community and school districts are known as n/networks. N/networks exist on a larger scale and are specific to statewide and national daisy chains of those who serve education. Understanding and identifying n/networks and N/networks is an extremely useful skill set for school leaders for these reasons.

It helps professionals in the field seek and seize opportunities in terms of school leadership.

It helps professionals in the field seek and seize opportunities in terms of career trajectory.

It helps professionals assess and navigate their leadership goals in relationship to national and statewide reform efforts such as the Common Core State Standards.

Navigating Networks by Understanding the Panopticon and the Johari Window

Thus far, arguments have been offered that explain how networks are formed, and why it is useful to understand and use them in school leadership. This section is dedicated to exploring two ideas that come from the worlds of philosophy and sociology and play a large part in how leaders understand and navigate networks in schools, education systems, and society. By understanding the panopticon and using the **Johari Window**, school leaders can more effectively navigate networks. This section begins with an explanation of the panopticon. This is followed by a discussion of the Johari Window. Last, a case study outlines how one of the most successful school superintendents in Tennessee uses these tools to navigate the n/networks and N/networks in his state.

The Panopticon

Foucault (1975) argued that social and political institutions such as schools, prisons, and hospitals produce and reproduce power structures in society by defining what is normal, good, and tolerable. As stated previously, these societal ideals can change

Sidebar 3.1 How to See n/networks

To understand how n/networks work, this sidebar presents a fictional scenario featuring a teacher with leadership ambitions. Beth Hinton was always a go-getter as a teacher. This was evidenced by her willingness to do the most mundane jobs, like extra bus duty or detention supervision, without complaint. Ms. Hinton asked for and received professional critique with grace and made a point to happily volunteer for staff development activities, such as curriculum committees. Ms. Hinton was also an excellent teacher who had few classroom discipline issues and worked well with parents. All of these facets of Ms. Hinton's professional contributions got the attention of her supervisor, the principal of her school.

In October of Ms. Hinton's third year as a teacher, the principal asked her to give a presentation about her class at a February meeting of the school district's governing board. As usual Ms. Hinton went about this assignment with intensity, humility, and a keen attention to detail. During the months of November, December, and January, Ms. Hinton attended all the meetings of the governing board. She took notes of what the board members, administrators, teachers, and audience members wore at the meetings. She sat in the back and watched to see who would approach the superintendent during breaks or immediately after the conclusion of the board meeting. She noted who the superintendent approached during breaks and at the conclusion of the meetings. Ms. Hinton noticed a man in the audience at every meeting, a lawyer named Jack Gray. She found out from the superintendent's secretary that Mr. Gray was a community fund-raiser and "plugged in." In January, Ms. Hinton was at a meeting of a statewide school coalition. She noticed in the back corner of the large audience was that same lawyer sitting next to her superintendent.

Two weeks before she was scheduled to make her presentation, Ms. Hinton made an appointment to see Mr. Gray. She introduced herself, explained that she was preparing to make a presentation at an upcoming school board meeting, and said that she thought someday she might want to serve her district in a leadership role. She said she noticed he attended the meetings frequently and asked if he had any advice on how she could best represent her school and the superintendent at the meeting.

Three days later, Ms. Hinton had a similar meeting with her supervising principal. A day after that, she had the same kind of meeting with the assistant superintendent of instruction. Ms. Hinton asked in each meeting what she should wear, what the relationships were between the lawyer, the community, and the superintendent; how long her presentation should be; and what it was that made a memorable presentation. Ms. Hinton gave her presentation to the school board. Her superintendent was impressed, her principal was very proud, and members of the school board complimented her effort. The day after the meeting, Ms. Hinton was careful to write a note to Mr. Gray (the lawyer), her principal, and the assistant superintendent to thank them for their mentoring. After she mailed her last thank you letter, Ms. Hinton wrote this on the inside of a card in her wallet:

RECIPE FOR SUCCESS

a. Look for patterns of who interacts informally with whom.

b. Verify understandings of this information with a member or two of the network.

c. Solicit feedback and mentoring from a circle of people who are part of the network.

d. Sincerely thank people for their time and insights.

e. Engage in a level of professionalism and preparation far above colleagues.

f. Check in with network members regularly to help you consider your career trajectory.

Ms. Hinton used this strategy often during her third and fourth years as a teacher. Her recipe for success can be summarized as an activity called **GASing**, which stands for "Getting the Attention of a Superior." The term was coined by Dan Griffiths (1963) in his groundbreaking study of how teachers move up the organizational ladder in New York City school districts. Aspiring administrators are not the only leaders who find GASing a useful tool. School leaders who are interested in sorting out the merits of a community agenda, vetting the perceptions of an idea or candidate for a position, or gathering supportive momentum for a reform agenda can engage in a similar activity to GASing. The only difference is the target. This author offers the acronym of **GAMEing**, or "Getting the Attention of Movers Early," as a way to build networks and therefore leadership capacity in schools. The recipe for successful GAMEing is the same as for GASing; the only difference is that the targets are relative to moving an agenda forward. GAMEing can be used to collect a reference list of people who may be helpful in sorting out the truth of an agenda, vetting the street perceptions of a candidate for a job, and gathering momentum for a public discussion of a strategic plan.

over time. Two kinds of power fuel the mechanism within a school that reproduces the power structures that form margins of tolerance and deem who fits and who does not. The first is sovereign power, and it refers to those who are in formal positions of power, such as elected and hired officials in school and community systems. Sovereign power is typically enacted through the formal chain of command and authority in an organization with teachers answering to principals, principals answering to superintendents, and superintendents answering to governing boards of education.

Disciplinary power is a less discussed dynamic in society and is enacted by way of **panoptic mechanisms**. Foucault coined this phrase in reference to the panopticon, a prison building designed by English philosopher Jeremy Bentham in the late 18th century. The panopticon allowed a guard to observe all the prisoners without the prisoners knowing whether or not they were being watched. An organizational environment of this kind resulted in a "sentiment of invisible omniscience" (Foucault, 1975, p. 195). This dynamic creates a culture of self-monitoring and regulates prisoner behavior because the threat of being seen is always imminent.

School communities define what a school administrator *is* and make hiring and firing decisions based on that construction. Thus, the community is a panoptic mechanism because it is composed of complex seen and unseen networks that are ever present in a school administrator's life. An administrator never knows who is watching and judging his or her actions and who is taking those impressions back to those who have the power to terminate. Thus, these leaders both act and are acted upon (Hamilton, 1989). To understand a panoptic mechanism in action in everyday terms of school leadership, consider these questions.

What would happened to a school principal who was caught engaging in a sexual activity with a member of the same gender in a car parked in his or her school district?

What would happen to a school superintendent if a picture appeared on Facebook of him drinking heavily and the superintendent works in a conservative community that bans the sale of alcohol?

What would happen if a grocery store cashier overheard a school principal using racial epithets while speaking on the phone?

Any seasoned administrator should be shuddering at the thought of these events because the ramifications of such activity depend on the invisible and visible network of people involved in the incident. For example, unbeknownst to the racist principal in line at the grocery store, the cashier may be married to the sister of the president of the school board. And the president of the school board may be grossly offended by such comments. The cashier could call his brother-in-law and share what he witnessed, and the principal would never know who witnessed his inappropriate remarks. The same could be said for the other two scenarios. The bartender could be a former student who was amused to see her superintendent drunk. Or the jogger who caught the principal in a tryst might be homophobic and still resentful that this principal refused to let her daughter go to the prom. Administrators learn early on that they are always being watched and that one can never be sure who will learn about their actions outside of their daily lives at work. Savvy administrators self-regulate their choices. Sadly, some of these choices result in the loss of personal freedoms in order to fit (and therefore lead) within the networks to which they are beholden.

The Johari Window

The Johari Window (Luft & Ingham, 1955) is a tool for understanding group dynamics and how people behave. It is used often in the field of counseling. The name, Johari, refers to the originators, Joe Luft and Harry Ingham. Essentially, the window illustrates that people behave in ways that can be conceptualized in four quadrants to varying degrees. The Johari Window also recognizes that people don't always understand how they might behave or the ramifications of behaviors they exhibit. The window looks like the image shown in **Figure 3.1**. The first quadrant centers on the public self, or what Goffman (1959) refers to as "front stage behavior." Front stage behavior refers to kinds of behaviors that are purposeful and are in the forefront of conscious actions. Examples of front stage behavior can be found in the observance of school administrators conducting a press conference or participating in a television interview. The quadrant of the public self is where people put their best face forward.

The second quadrant is known as the blind to self area. The blind to self area is where we engage in

I. Front Stage Behavior	II. Blind to Self Area
III. Back Stage Behavior	IV. Quadrant of the Unknown

Figure 3.1 The Johari Window

SOURCE: Adapted by Autumn Tooms Cyprès from Luft, J., & Ingham, H. (1955).

behavior whose effects on other people cannot be seen by us. Similar to having bad breath and not knowing it, blind to self behavior is a phenomenon where a person's words or actions affect others' perceptions of that person. An example of this occurred in October 2012 during the U.S. presidential race between President Barack Obama and Republican presidential nominee Mitt Romney. A town hall debate was held between the two of them as part of the presidential campaign. During that debate, a question was raised about how each candidate would address salary equity issues for women. Romney responded to this question by telling a story from when he was governor of Massachusetts. He said he was considering positions for his cabinet and noticed that almost all of them were men. And then he said,

> And—and so we—we took a concerted effort to go out and find women who had backgrounds that could be qualified to become members of our cabinet. I went to a number of women's groups and said, "Can you help us find folks?" and they brought us whole binders full of women. (Washington Post, 2012)

Romney's odd turn of phrase, "binders full of women" inspired immediate commentary from the Internet. Many stated his words objectified women, turning them into things crammed into notebooks. Some suggested images of little black books of girlfriends. True, his comments could be categorized as a slip of the tongue. But to some, they also illustrated his lack of understanding, knowledge, and comfort level on women's equality (Cardona, 2012). His blind to self behavior in the form of "binders full of women" underscored his inability to connect with many voters. Skepticism of his leadership abilities was evidenced by the immediate deluge of comments in the news media and social media platforms such as Twitter, Tumblr, and Facebook.

Blind to self behavior plays a large role in *fit,* and therefore access to networks. A school superintendent who speaks fondly of his love for martinis might not earn the kind of political carte blanche he had hoped for if the prominent members of his community are teetotalers. What is maddening about blind to self behavior and fit is that one may have no idea why one is refused support from a network.

The third quadrant of the Johari Window centers on what Goffman (1959) referred to as "back stage behavior." This quadrant encompasses all of the actions that are a part of our private selves. Behavior of this kind is the sociological equivalent of running around the house in one's underwear. Back stage behavior is the stuff of casual moments between people who trust each other. One might scratch an itch without a second thought if the only other person in the room was one's spouse. However, if that same person realized there was an itch to be scratched during a school board meeting, they might refrain from doing so in public. Savvy administrators looking to understand networks understand the incredible opportunities and dangers that exist in social events shared with colleagues or potential political allies.

For example, many school faculties celebrate the end of a semester with a happy hour gathering. This provides a quandary for the school administrator. He or she runs the risk of being understood as aloof by not attending. If he or she does attend, there is a risk of confusing happy hour shared with subordinates (in which front stage behavior must be maintained) with happy hour in the presence of friends (in which back stage behavior is acceptable). This dynamic plays both ways: A savvy principal at a happy hour is keen to refrain from losing focus and so consumes minimal alcohol, or none at all, while still appearing engaged in back stage behavior. This fosters camaraderie and esprit de corps. As the evening progresses and people loosen up, the principal has a chance to look for blind to self and back stage behaviors in his or her subordinates. This is an opportune time to listen to the stories colleagues are sharing in order to understand relationships (family trees) within networks and the political baggage that may be attached.

The fourth quadrant, the quadrant of the unknown, is a category that addresses how people behave in situations unknown to them. For example, a principal may announce at a faculty meeting that if a student were to arrive on campus with a loaded shotgun, he or she would ensure the campus is safe for everyone. What does that really mean? Will the principal calmly confront the student and try to remove the weapon? Or will that principal, in the heat of the moment, actually run quickly to the nearest office and call the police? Or will the principal nervously ask for help from the first adult he or she sees? No one (including the principal) knows what this leader will do. The quadrant of the unknown is the category that looks at how people behave in novel and unpredictable situations. An illustration of this phenomenon is the scenario where a teacher witnesses the principal berating and yelling at the assistant principal. Does the teacher intervene? Does the teacher call someone at the district office and inform them of this event? Does the teacher say nothing?

The rules of the Johari Window note that people rarely exhibit behaviors in just one quadrant, and they often shift from one quadrant to another during the day. Sometimes we spend more time in one quadrant than in others. The amount of time and effort in each quadrant changes depending on the dynamics of those involved in a particular moment or event. For example, if a teacher was a friend of a principal who was yelling, he or she might find the principal later and ask what happened to cause such a dramatic moment. Or if the teacher was in his or her first year, he or she might say nothing at all in the hopes of staying out of a firestorm. Blind to self behavior is where our actions most affect politics, in terms of our own reputations and how we understand others.

Sidebar 3.2 Jon Thomas, the Panopticon, and the Johari Window

To understand how a school leader might conduct his career while keeping in mind the principles outlined in this chapter of the panopticon and the Johari Window, let's return to the fictional school district of teacher Beth Hinton in Sidebar 3.1 and examine the career of the district's superintendent, whom we'll call Jon Thomas. Tall with a boyish face, he grew up in Boston and was selected from a national search to serve as superintendent of one of the largest school systems in the Appalachian region of the United States. After five years as superintendent there, Dr. Thomas has established himself in his adopted hometown and has already become known around the country as a leader in school reform. One reason for his success is his education at prestigious schools (as this chapter argues, connections are important). But a pedigree does not necessarily affect the day-to-day interactions of the superintendency. Perhaps it was luck that the mayor, who was undoubtedly involved in the superintendent's hire, won his state's gubernatorial race two years into Dr. Thomas's tenure as superintendent. But it takes more than knowing the mayor of a midsize town in the South to reform schools and build such a strong reputation in education. Dr. Thomas certainly could not have predicted that the mayor would win; however, Dr. Thomas might have spent some energy trying to learn what the odds were of the mayor winning the governor's seat. And he might have spent some time learning who the mayor trusted while they were still working together in the same town.

Dr. Thomas watched the mayor (who would become governor) with an eye for detail. He made a point to sit at the back of the audience at council meetings and notice patterns of who spoke with whom and when. With some regularity, the mayor engaged in sidebars with a local attorney, Jack Gray, who was known for his fund-raising efforts. Counselor Gray had graduated from one of the most prestigious law schools in the United States, and his father was a politician. Dr. Thomas sought Mr. Gray out for advice on building relationships with the community. By the end of Dr. Thomas's first year, the two had formed a solid and trusting camaraderie.

Dr. Thomas was doing a good job by all accounts. He built relationships with the local university, he kept his word, and he acted with integrity. The teacher's union, the school board, and the community liked him. So when it became time for the newly elected governor to name a secretary of education for his state, many in the community assumed it would be Dr. Thomas.

Why did he seem like a natural choice?

- He had an academic pedigree from a prestigious university.
- It was hard for anyone to say anything negative about him.

- He had been superintendent for three years and had made positive changes in his district without alienating the school board or the community.
- People knew him around the state because he had been active in several coalitions, particularly ones led by the mayor and Jack Gray.

A couple of things about Dr. Thomas come to mind immediately when you watch him at a school board meeting. First and foremost, the man loves kids. He lights up whenever there is a student present. Second he is always a very polished professional in his appearance, his actions, and his delivery of speech. He conforms to many expectations of people in the area in that he attends church with his family and his children attend a public school in his school district. He is on constant front stage behavior, as evidenced by the lack of negative gossip around anything related to his persona, his leadership style, and his background. These attributes did not just happen. They are the result of an understanding that one is always the center of attention in educational administration.

Dr. Thomas made a point to learn the culture of his adopted hometown. As an example, he was quick to open his speech at a community breakfast by asking that someone save him the local morning indulgence, a chicken biscuit. And he made sure to eat that chicken biscuit while he was at the meeting. He rarely discussed with anyone stories of his family, his life in Boston, or how other districts he served went about the daily work of education.

Because of this, there is no personal controversy surrounding his individual likes, dislikes, or behavior. That he is a Yankee from a well-off family up north who vacations on Martha's Vineyard is a fact blurred into the background because Dr. Thomas proudly sports the colors of the local university football team, eats once a week at the local barbeque shack, and visits schools to cheer on teachers whenever he can. His office is not filled with flashy furniture, and he is happy to admit that he gets his suits on sale at the Men's Warehouse. In sum, Dr. Thomas is a lethal combination politically because he is brilliant, disciplined, savvy, and above all, humble. Working in a panopticon does not scare Dr. Thomas, but he is always aware that there may be someone witnessing his actions with the ability and connections to scuttle his career.

Dr. Thomas not only subscribes to disciplined front stage behavior, he is keenly observant of the other quadrants of the Johari Window relative to others. This information helps him to understand how the people in his community interact and are related. This information also allows him to pace those behaviors in order to fit (i.e., asking for and eating a chicken biscuit for breakfast). All of these attributes can be distilled down to one very important leadership trait: Dr. Thomas sees himself as a reflection of his school community and profession rather than a beacon. And if there are moments when his ego gets the best of him, few know it because he is so committed to his front stage behavior.

Conclusion

The most important two sentences in this chapter appeared early. They explained that a school administrator never knows who is watching and judging his or her actions and who is taking those impressions back to those who have the power to terminate. Thus, school leaders both act and are acted upon (Hamilton, 1989).

School leaders who are able to build successful careers understand they simultaneously *act* and are *acted upon*. The ominous implications here center on the idea that leadership encompasses every action a leader makes in his or her daily life. Thus, the personal and the professional meld into one combustible environment waiting for a series of small events to spark a political firestorm. This is why public leadership is so stressful and challenging. When they enter the profession, many school administrators accept that they must negotiate fit while still stretching the boundaries of what is thinkable.

Which brings this discussion back to the film *The Matrix* (Silver et al., 1999) and Neo's choice between the contented ignorance of illusion and the embrace of a tough reality. Neo and his colleague Cypher choose the difficult path of working within the truth of society held in the red pill. Later on, Cypher regrets his choice to live in such a harsh world and wished he had stayed ignorant of the challenges and problems brought on by the Matrix.

Morpheus cautions Neo that not many people are ready to act in a world of easy-to-digest explanations; thus taking a pill to stay in a world ignorant of power relationships may be a more comfortable choice. Many are accustomed to a world that is oblivious to the matrix of power relationships, to the point that the disruption of entrenched structures is unthinkable. The same argument can be made for those who are in the profession of school leadership because many get caught up in the entrenched structures to the point that they are not able to look beyond day-to-day leadership tasks to see the larger matrix of political structures that affect their profession.

Consider the principal who is deluged with complaints about a teacher and knows that the teacher should be fired but who chooses not to do so because it involves the stress of confrontation and the hard work of documentation. Or think about the school superintendent who enjoys travel and lobbying all over her home state, but really doesn't want to get her hands dirty with the difficult work of implementing a new teacher evaluation model. While these professionals have the credentials of leadership on paper, they have made a conscious choice to take the blue pill. Turning a blind eye to the difficult challenges of leadership within the political world of education begs observers to wonder if this is a form of mindless complicity, Machiavellian self-preservation, or both.

Hegemony, fit, and the social construction of what a school leader is all play a part in how school administrators go about the business of leading. As stated before, truths about what a leader is and does are often not understood. Even worse, they are sometimes dismissed. Such is the stuff of the blue pill of blissful ignorance. This chapter discussed how bureaucracies are successfully navigated based on real stories from the field and the examination of sociopolitical theory and school leadership research. The bridge between theory and practice is not an easy one to construct, but it is a very necessary component to effective school leadership. When theory and authentic research are contextualized by experience, school leadership is understood in a way that empowers leaders to authentically lead with confidence as opposed to hollow swagger. This discussion does not seek to calibrate a moral compass for the reader. Rather, the focus is on the recognition that

leaders who engage in authentic, quality leadership depend on the support of the networks they serve and that surround them. Earning such support requires an understanding of how one's behaviors are interpreted and acknowledging the price one is willing to pay. How much of one's personal time and identity is appropriate to sacrifice in order to fit? How much energy is one willing to devote to ensure professional vitality?

The terms used in this discussion are ideas meant to be included in a school leader's repertoire of skills. They do not take the place of stellar attention to detail, fidelity to a moral compass, and consistent focus on manifesting a vision. A rigorous work ethic is only the entrée to a world of opportunities waiting to be found and seized in the name of school leadership and reform.

Key Chapter Terms

Fit: A game of being specific to the politics and relationships between school administrators and the community they serve (Tooms et al., 2010). In this game, the community, which ultimately governs a school, assigns administrative personnel both a role and identity, which are embedded with rules for how to behave and not behave. Researchers in educational administration have noted that administrators seek daily to understand, obey, and perpetuate these rules within the margins of their own leadership agenda because this is the necessary currency to obtain support for leadership decisions and therefore job security.

GAMEing: This term is coined by the author and is an extension of GASing. It refers literally to Getting the Attention of Movers Early in a network. This is done via producing work above and beyond standard expectations.

GASing: A term coined by Dan Griffiths (1963) in reference to a study of how teachers moved upward into positions of administration in New York City schools. GASing translates to Getting the Attention of a Superior. It refers to behaviors beyond the teaching workday, such as supervision of nighttime activities, coaching, sponsoring clubs, and leading curriculum committees.

Hegemony: A sociopolitical construct that explains how groups or individuals can maintain their dominance over other groups of individuals in a society via coercion rather than violence. This phenomenon is achieved through persuading those in the subordinate group to accept, adopt, and internalize the dominant group's definition of what is normal.

Johari Window: A tool used to understand group dynamics and how people behave. The name, Johari, refers to the originators, Joseph Luft and Harry Ingham. This chapter uses the author's interpretation of the Johari Window (Luft & Ingham, 1955). In this interpretation, the window illustrates that people behave in ways that, to varying degrees, can be categorized into four quadrants. While we are aware of some of these behaviors, we are unaware of others.

n/network and N/networks: These terms are based on James Paul Gee's construct of d/Discourse. n/networks are those centered around a school community and school districts. N/networks exist on a larger scale and are specific to statewide and national daisy chains of those who serve education. Both kinds influence each other.

Panoptic mechanism: Coined by philosopher Michel Foucault, this phrase references the panopticon, a prison building designed by English philosopher Jeremy Bentham in the late 18th century. The panopticon allows a guard to observe all the prisoners without the prisoners knowing whether or not they were being watched. An organizational environment of this kind results in a "sentiment of invisible omniscience" (Foucault, 1975, p. 195). This dynamic creates a culture of self-monitoring and regulates prisoner behavior because the threat of being seen is always imminent. For example, a school administrator never knows who is watching and judging his or her actions and who is taking those impressions back to people who have the power to terminate. Therefore, they lead and are constrained by a panoptic mechanism.

References

Anderson, G. (1990). Toward a critical constructivist approach to school administration: Invisibility, legitimation, and the study of non-events. *Educational Administration Quarterly, 26*(1), 38–59.

Apple, M. (1993). *Official knowledge: Democratic education in a conservative age.* London, England: Routledge.

Cardona, M. (2012, October 18). Romney's empty "binder full of women." *CNN.* Retrieved 5/26/2013 from http://www.cnn.com/2012/10/17/opinion/cardona-binders-women

De Niro, R. (Producer & Director). (2006). *The Good Shepherd* [Motion picture]. United States: Universal Pictures.

Derrida, J. (1982). *Of grammatology.* Baltimore, MD: Johns Hopkins University Press.

Foucault, M. (1975). *Discipline and punish: The birth of a prison.* New York, NY: Vintage Books.

Gee, J. P. (1996). *Social linguistics and literacies.* New York, NY: Routledge.

Gergen, K. (1999). *An invitation to social construction.* Thousand Oaks, CA: Sage.

Goffman, E. (1959). *The presentation of self in everyday life.* Garden City, NY: Anchor/Doubleday.

Gramsci, A. (1971) *Selections from the Prison Notebooks.* London, England: Lawrence and Wishart.

Griffiths, D. (1963). Teacher mobility in New York City. *Educational Administration Quarterly, 6*(1), 15–31.

Hamilton, D. (1989). *Towards a theory of schooling.* Philadelphia, PA: Falmer.

Harvey, J. (1988). *The Abilene Paradox and other meditations on management.* New York, NY: Jossey-Bass.

Iannocone, L., & Lutz, R. (1970). *Politics, power, and policy: The governing of local school districts.* Columbus, OH: Charles E. Merrill.

Jung, E., & Hecht, M. (2004). Elaborating the communication theory of identity: Identity gaps and communication outcomes. *Communication Quarterly, 52*(3), 265–283.

Luft, J., & Ingham, H. (1955). *The Johari Window, a graphic model of interpersonal awareness.* Proceedings of the Western Training Laboratory in Group Development. Los Angeles, CA: UCLA.

Lugg, C. A. (2003). Sissies, faggots, lezzies and dykes: Gender, sexual orientation and the new politics of education. *Educational Administration Quarterly, 39*(1), 95–134.

Silver, J., & Cracchiolo, D. (Producers), Wachowski, A. & Wachowski, L. (Directors). (1999). *The Matrix.* United States: Warner Brothers Pictures.

Spring, J. (1993). *Conflict of interest: The politics of American education.* New York, NY: Longman.

Stout, R. (1986). Executive action and values. *Issues in Education, 4*(3), 198–214.

Tooms, A. K. (2012). The importance of leadership legacies. *The UCEA Review, 53*(1), 1–6.

Tooms, A. K., Lugg, C., & Bogotch, I. (2010). School leadership and the politics of fit. *Educational Administration Quarterly, 46*(1), 96–131.

Washington Post Wonkblog. (2012, October 16). Full transcript of the second presidential debate. Retrieved from http://www.washingtonpost.com/blogs/wonkblog/wp/2012/10/16/full-transcript-of-the-second-presidential-debate/

Weber, M. (1978). *Economy and society* (G. Roth, trans.). Los Angeles, CA: University of California Press. (Original work published 1922)

Further Readings

Anderson, G. (1990). Toward a critical constructivist approach to school administration: Invisibility, legitimation, and the study of non-events. *Educational Administration Quarterly, 26*(1), 38–59.

This article examines the everydayness of a school leader's life and explains how seemingly nonevents contribute to larger messages and actions of school leadership.

Black, H., & English, F. (1997). *What they don't tell you in schools of education about school administration.* Baltimore, MD: Scarecrow.

This is a practical volume that outlines the unspoken rules of change management for school leaders.

Blau, P. (1964). *Exchange and power in social life.* New York, NY: Wiley.

This classic work explores power relationships in society.

Butler, J. (1997). *Excitable speech: A politics of the performative.* New York, NY: Routledge.

This book explains and quantifies specific kinds of words and explains how they shape meaning in conversations.

Counts, G. (1932). *Dare the school build a new social order?* Carbondale: Southern Illinois University Press.

This classic book is one of the touchstones in the profession of education and explores schools' role in a society.

Debray, E. (2006). *Politics, ideology, and education.* New York, NY: Teachers College Press.

This book looks at the intersections of idealism and education and how they play out in social politics.

Derrida, J. (1982). *Of grammatology.* Baltimore, MD: Johns Hopkins University Press.

This book is a seminal work by one of the most prolific philosophers in the postmodern movement of the 20th century. It explores how language and words are used to change understanding of reality and reinforce, create, or interrupt power structures.

Foucault, M. (1975). *Discipline and punish: The birth of a prison.* New York, NY: Vintage Books.

This book is a seminal work by one of the most influential philosophers in the last quarter of the 20th century. It explored how school, prisons, and hospitals contour societal norms.

Goffman, E. (1959). *The presentation of self in everyday life.* Garden City, NY: Anchor/Doubleday.

This classic sociologic work is the first to examine the rituals of interaction between people on an everyday basis.

Gramsci, A. (1971). *Selections from the Prison Notebooks.* London, England: Lawrence and Wishart.

This important work outlines the notion of hegemony and explains how society is manipulated by groups of people and politics.

Harvey, J. (1988). *The Abilene Paradox and other meditations on management.* Lexington, MA: Lexington Books.

A critical text that uses easy to read narrative to explain how groups of people subvert charges of leadership behind the scenes and contribute to dysfunction in an organization.

Iannocone, L., & Lutz, R. (1970). *Politics, power, and policy: The governing of local school districts.* Columbus, OH: Charles E. Merrill.

A classic book that was the first to coin the term micro politics *and is a foundational text on how school districts are governed.*

Lyman, L., Ashby, D., & Tripses, J. (2005). *Leaders who dare: Pushing the boundaries.* Landham, MD: Rowman & Littlefield.

This book examines women in school leadership positions in Chicago and explains how they used networks in their leadership contributions.

Sacks, H. (1985). On doing being ordinary. In J. Maxwell Atkinson & John Heritage (Eds), *Structures of social action: Studies in conversation analysis.* New York, NY: Cambridge University Press.

This lecture is a seminal discussion of how people trivialize events in their day-to-day lives that in truth are not trivial and have great effect on social systems.

Spring, J. (1993). *Conflict of interest: The politics of American education.* New York, NY: Longman.

This book concisely explains how large global policies and economics affect schools and school systems in the United States.

Tooms, A. K., Lugg, C., & Bogotch, I. (2010). School leadership and the politics of fit. *Educational Administration Quarterly, 46*(1), 96–131.

This article demonstrates in specific detail the politics related to fit in education.

PART II

TEACHING AND LEARNING

4

WHAT MAKES A GOOD TEACHER?

Models of Effective Teaching

JENNIFER PRIOR

Northern Arizona University

There are great teachers, good teachers, and certainly some duds in the field of education, but what makes them so? Most teachers enter the field because they care about children, and they are excited to inspire the minds of their future students. Some, maybe, enter the field because they think it will be an easy job with summers off. Most have good intentions to educate and impact the lives of children. This chapter includes several scenarios showing the challenges teachers face. All of the scenarios describe actual events, but all names have been changed to pseudonyms. In the first scenario, Miss O'Neal conveys a story from her student teaching:

> When I did my student teaching, I was enthusiastic and wanted to be the most effective teacher in the *world!* I remember planning a unit about space for my second graders. I went to a nearby geological survey office to get the most recent photos of planets taken by a NASA space probe. I created a beautiful bulletin board and engaged my students in hands-on projects, including making solar system models out of salt dough. I was doing amazing things, or so I thought. A little girl named Lynette was in that class, and Lynette was an apathetic learner. Nothing much seemed to capture her interest. So, when I found Lynette looking intently at the planet photos on the bulletin board I thought, "Aha! I have finally gotten through to her." I walked over and stood beside her. Lynette asked, "Miss O'Neal, is that

> what Jupiter really looks like?" "Yes," I said. "All those colors and everything?" "That's what it looks like," I said as I secretly patted myself on the back for being such a good teacher. Then, Lynette looked up at me and said, "Miss O'Neal, is Jupiter a city or a state?" So much for being a great teacher.

Most teachers enter the field of education thinking that teaching is about teaching, and while that is true to some degree, there is certainly much more to it than that. This chapter examines the components of being an effective teacher, including classroom management, teaching strategies, building family partnerships, and **reflective teaching**. Educational leaders can use this information as a guide to support teachers as they grow as professionals.

Classroom Management

Managing the classroom environment is one of the most important things a teacher can do. After all, an unruly classroom is not going to be conducive to learning. Kristin L. Sayeski and Monica R. Brown (2011) point out that "poor classroom management results in lost instructional time, feelings of inadequacy, and stress" (p. 8). So in order to maximize student learning and minimize teacher stress, classroom management is imperative. Teachers often think of this as discipline, but there are many things that can be done to structure the environment so behavior problems are reduced. Management is key. Harry K. Wong and Rosemary T. Wong (2009) state,

> Classroom management consists of the practices and procedures that a teacher uses to maintain an environment in which instruction and learning can occur. For this to happen, the teacher must create a well-ordered environment. Discipline has very little to do with classroom management. You don't discipline a store; you manage it. The same is true of a classroom. (pp. 11–12)

It can be difficult for effective teachers to identify the specific strategies they use that make them successful classroom managers. Most realized that they were not successful at the beginning. In fact, many teachers remember their first group of students as the worst behaved classes they have had. In reality, it is the lack of strategies that lead to ineffectiveness. For this reason, an underlying foundation or philosophy of classroom management is important. This section details four specific areas that lead to successful classroom management—relationship, fun, support, and consistency.

Develop Relationships

Children need to feel valued in the classroom, which is why this section starts with addressing relationships. In their article, "The Key to Classroom Management," Robert J. Marzano and Jana S. Marzano (2003) emphasize the importance of quality relationships between teachers and students. They cite these relationships as "the keystone for all other aspects of classroom management" (p. 6). Think about it. If there are people in your life who you don't particularly care for, you're probably not terribly motivated to please them. On the other hand, we tend not to want to disappoint those people we love. When caring relationships are established between the teacher and students, there is a level of respect that develops and that leads to an overall cohesiveness in the classroom. Alfie Kohn reported in a 2005 interview, "Children need to feel loved and valued even when they aren't succeeding or behaving. When kids don't feel trusted and accepted, behavior problems become worse" (Bryner, 2005, p. 20). Furthermore, Nel Noddings (2012) states, "A climate in which caring relations can flourish should be a

goal for all teachers and educational policymakers. In such a climate, we can best meet individual needs, impart knowledge, and encourage the development of moral people" (p. 777). She goes on to say, "A climate of care and trust is one in which most people will want to do the right thing, will want to be good" (p. 777). For these reasons, quality relationships between teachers and students are a strong piece of the foundation for effective classroom management.

Create Fun Experiences

A fun and stimulating classroom environment is another element that builds a strong foundation for classroom management. This doesn't mean that every teacher needs to be wacky or put on a show in order to be effective, but rather that the teacher can have a little fun and still maximize learning. Students spend several hours a day in school and these hours should be pleasurable as well as productive. Former high school teacher, Jonathan C. Erwin (2005), claims in his article, "Put the Fun in Classrooms," "That old adage, 'All work and no play makes Johnny a dull boy' needs amending: It also creates the conditions for him to be absent, shut down, give up, or disrupt" (p. 16). Keep in mind that children need to understand the limits of having fun in the classroom. Spontaneous activities can bring about disorder, so the teacher must establish boundaries even in the midst of novel experiences so as not to distract students from learning. That said, adding fun, humor, and interest to the classroom is a great way to minimize behavior problems and capture students' attention.

Offer Support

The next foundational element for effective classroom management is support. This means supporting students' behavior by showing them and practicing with them what they should do instead of punishing them for what they shouldn't do. Adults tell children what to do all the time, and children learn to ignore them. It's important that adults stop talking at children and start talking and working with them. Many researchers agree that teachers need to make clear their expectations for student behavior and that if they do this, students are more likely to meet those expectations. Teachers should establish a delicate balance between structure and cooperation, combined with an understanding of individual student needs. This results in a positive and effective classroom environment. It's about teaching children what they should do and then reinforcing these behaviors over and over again.

In their book, *The First Days of School*, Harry K. Wong and Rosemary T. Wong (2009) emphasize the need for teaching procedures for the classroom that will become well-practiced routines. For example, a teacher might become upset when students enter the classroom in a noisy and out-of-control way. He or she might scold or yell at them to try to get them to quiet down. While the students may quiet down (or not), typically they will do the same thing day after day, causing great frustration for the teacher. The better thing to do is to teach the students a procedure for entering the classroom. For example, the teacher might tell the students that they are to come in the room quietly, put away their backpacks, and begin working on an assignment that is written on the board. The teacher would then have the students practice this procedure several times. If the students do not follow it on a particular day, the teacher does not need to scold them, but rather remind them of the procedure and practice it again. With enough practice and reinforcement, the procedure becomes a routine.

One of the most common things observed among pre-service teachers is that they try to continue teaching even when children are not paying attention or when they are misbehaving. They seem to think that stopping a lesson to address behavior makes for a failed lesson. The truth is quite the opposite. Effective teachers address student behavior all the time. Before beginning a lesson, an effective teacher might speak to the children about how they should sit during a lesson—what they should do with their hands and feet and what they should do if they want to speak. The teacher might ask students to demonstrate these behaviors. During the lesson, a teacher will likely notice a student or two not meeting those expectations, in which case, he or she would pause the lesson to address them, "Remember what we said we would do with our hands during the lesson? I'm noticing a few people who are not doing that right now. Let's practice keeping our hands to ourselves as we continue." By addressing procedures and not being afraid to stop a lesson to discuss expectations, potential problems can be reduced.

It is often thought that students should just know what to do, when in reality, they often don't know. They might know what they should not do, but they don't know what to do instead. The effective teacher does not constantly harp on the children, telling them over and over what they are doing wrong. Instead, he or she supports them—teaches them—what they should do and how they should behave.

Focus on Consistency

Consistency is the last element to address for classroom management. The effective teacher is consistent with expectations. Expectations are reinforced all the time, not just when it's convenient or only with children who get in trouble a lot. Children notice when a teacher's expectations are not consistent for all students, which can be frustrating for those who may struggle with controlling their behavior. Pre-service teachers will often state an expectation to students, wait until most of them are doing it, and then move on. So, the new teacher might say, "I need everyone to look up here at me." She waits until all but two children in the back are looking and then begins the lesson. This communicates to the children that she does not mean what she says, and the two children in the back continue to misbehave and will likely have increased behavior issues or lack of attention as the lesson progresses. The effective teacher waits until every single student follows the stated expectation before she proceeds.

New or ineffective teachers often make idle threats to try to make students behave. These are often born out of frustration. Mr. Thompson recalls such an experience during his first year of teaching.

> I remember during my first year of teaching, I threatened to cancel the Valentine party if the students didn't do what I had asked. Well, they didn't do what I asked. So what was I to do? I knew I was never going to cancel the party. Parents would have been furious with me. So, I had to figure out a way to have them earn it back. What was the most important lesson I learned from this? Don't make threats, and don't say something you can't follow through on.

The students of effective teachers know that expectations are for all of the students, and that their teacher will be consistent in upholding those expectations. This is not always easy, and not something teachers learn in the first few years and never have to think about again. Teachers often find that consistency is something they struggle with throughout their careers, as illustrated by a story Mrs. Kay tells of a second-grade class during her 12th year of teaching.

> Every day at 10:00 we would go to recess. The students would get their snacks (which they ate outside before playing) and stood in line by the door. Each day, I would say, "As soon as you're quiet, we'll go out to recess." At one point in the year, I found myself saying that an awful lot. The kids would get their snacks and line up and then stand there and talk. "As soon as you're quiet, we'll go out to recess. Okay, I'm waiting. As soon as you're quiet, we'll go out to recess." One day, as I continued to harp on them about being quiet, I said to myself, "I wonder how long they'll stand there and just keep talking?" I waited. I waited some more. Then I went over to my computer and began to work on some things. The kids continued to talk. I continued to work. Finally, I looked at my watch. It was 10:15 and recess was over. So, I said the students, "Okay, recess is over. Put your snacks away and go back to your seats." The room became absolutely silent. A few of the children smiled and chuckled, "She's just being silly, right?" I repeated, "It's 10:15 and recess is over. Put your snacks away and go sit down. And tomorrow, if you would like to stand in line for fifteen minutes, holding your snacks, we can do it again. It's your choice." Do you know I never had a problem with that again? I had reinforced to my students over time that I didn't mean what I said. They knew that I would take them outside to recess whether they were quiet or not. It was not until I was consistent with my expectation that their behavior changed.

Relationship, fun, support, consistency—those four elements create a solid philosophy for classroom management. Teachers usually have behavior systems in their classrooms—programs with rewards and consequences. Those are fine, but without relationship and support, without consistency and a little bit of fun, those systems usually don't work very well. Some children just don't care about earning a sticker, but they do care about being valued. The philosophy a teacher holds and the way it is implemented in the classroom makes all the difference.

Teaching Strategies

Once a classroom environment is established for optimal learning, it is important to focus on the kinds of teaching strategies that best facilitate student learning. The strategies teachers use when actually teaching lessons are extremely important and part of what separate effective teachers from average teachers. While there are numerous strategies that can be employed in a classroom, too many to address in detail in a single chapter, there are things to keep in mind when planning for instruction.

Interactive Learning

Children benefit from interactive learning experiences. "Effective teachers develop student learning through interactive instruction. Effective teachers increase students' accomplishments by facilitating active learning" (Dibapile, 2012, p. 81). Lev Vygotsky's **sociocultural theory** (1981), in particular, focuses on the acquisition of mental functions through social interaction. He emphasized the social and cultural factors involved in development and learning. While Vygotsky is categorized as a **constructivist**, his ideas did not just address the child's need to construct meaning, but rather he added that social interaction is of great importance in that process. He claimed that in order for children to internalize new knowledge, they need involvement in social activities. Much research highlights the effectiveness of interaction between peers. Children bring different perspectives to learning experiences, which brings about increased cognitive development. When looking at children's success in school, it is important to look at the factors that lead to this success. Vygotsky (1981), John Dewey (1916/1966), and Jean Piaget and Barbel Inhelder (1969), suggest that social interactions and intellectual development cannot be separated and that children end up with higher levels of understanding and cognitive development when social interaction is part of the learning process.

Piaget's (1985) theory of cognitive development emphasizes the continual drive children have to match their views of the world to the realities they encounter in the world. They assimilate and accommodate, meaning they rework and revise their understandings as they encounter problems. Peers and adults, along with the social setting, are important influences in the environment and bring about cognitive development. "The more actively involved children are with people and things in their world, the more quickly they will assimilate new learning and accommodate their own incorrect views of the world"

(Prior & Gerard, 2006, p. 3). Dewey also stressed the importance of learning through experience, emphasizing learning that interests, stimulates, and engages the student. Along with Piaget and Vygotsky, Dewey recognized that educational experiences are interwoven with social experiences. Learning experiences become interesting and personally captivating when they involve others. The effective teacher considers ways to combine instruction with social interaction to maximize learning.

Integrated Instruction

Children benefit from integrated instruction. The Interstate Teacher Assessment Support Consortium (InTASC, 2013) provides standards for ongoing development in teaching. InTASC Standard 8 emphasizes instructional strategies stating, "The teacher understands and uses a variety of instructional strategies to encourage learners to develop deep understanding of content areas and their connections, and to build skills to apply knowledge in meaningful ways." One way to create meaningful connections in the classroom is through subject integration. Dewey addresses the importance of tapping into student interest. Effective teachers focus on areas of interest and weave in different subject areas. For example, a second-grade teacher using Judi Barrett's *Cloudy With a Chance of Meatballs* for teaching reading skills

---

Sidebar 4.1 Teaching Strategies and the Common Core

The Common Core State Standards address the knowledge and skills children should attain through their K-12 education. As teachers implement the standards, they should keep in mind the effective teaching strategies of interactive learning, integrated instruction, adult input, and differentiated instruction. The following are key points to consider related to the English language arts and mathematics standards addressed in the Common Core.

Reading

- The reading standards emphasize increasing complexity of text levels and students' levels of comprehension.
- Students are encouraged to read and interact with both literature and informational texts.

Writing

- Students need to develop the ability to write narrative, persuasive, and informational works.
- Students learn to conduct research as part of the writing process.

Listening/Speaking

- Students are required to develop speaking and listening skills and participate in small- and large-group academic discussions.
- Students also learn to present ideas through various forms of media.

Language

- The importance of vocabulary development is emphasized and encouraged through reading and conversation as well as through direct instruction.
- Vocabulary and conventions should be taught through reading, writing, listening, and speaking, rather than in isolation.

Mathematics

- Emphasis should be placed on procedures, but also on conceptual understanding.
- Students develop foundational concepts, which are built upon throughout K-12 with the intention of preparing them for college and future careers.

SOURCES: Common Core Standards Initiative (2012a, 2012b).

could extend the idea of the book's genre into learning about and writing tall tales. Then, after reading about the rather strange weather conditions described in the literature selection, the students could learn about real weather patterns as part of a science lesson. By participating in this unit, students are able to make connections to the theme across subject areas throughout the day, and the transition from one subject to the next is seamless as the theme weaves all curricular areas together. In their book *Meeting Standards Through Integrated Curriculum,* Susan M. Drake and Rebecca C. Burns (2004) state that integrated curriculum serves as a bridge to meaningful and relevant learning experiences, resulting in increased student achievement. Integration can connect numerous subject areas or just a few. By learning from an integrated curriculum, students see the connection between subjects and focus on one integrated theme throughout the day.

Adult Input

Children benefit from adult input in learning. While interactive learning and experiences are important, this does not discount the role of direct instruction. Effective teachers understand that direct instruction is necessary in some instances and can lead to opportunities for further intellectual development. From this point of view, instruction cannot be identified as development, but properly organized instruction "will result in the child's intellectual development, will bring into being an entire series of such developmental processes, which were not at all possible without instruction" (Vygotsky, 1978, p. 121).

Vygotsky (1978) describes the zone of proximal development as "the distance between the actual developmental level as determined by independent problem solving and the level of potential development as determined through problem solving under adult guidance or in collaboration with more capable peers" (p. 86). This interaction and scaffolding between student and adult help the child to grow more than he or she might if working alone. A teacher can do this easily by circulating the room as students work in groups. A group might get to a point of frustration and feel stuck. The teacher then simply drops a breadcrumb, "I wonder what would

happen if you tried. . . ." The lightbulb flashes on, and the students are back to their exploration with new inspiration and excitement.

Differentiated Instruction

Differentiated instruction is another area to consider when planning for instructional experiences. Often people tend to think of differentiated instruction as ability grouping or tracking students. While adapting instruction to meet the needs of all students, this is not just another term for ability grouping, which can serve to be a damaging practice, causing children to lose confidence and forever lag behind their peers. Differentiated instruction encourages the teacher to recognize the varying levels of the students—who needs specific attention and who needs more of a challenge.

In thinking about ways to provide instruction that caters to students' needs, it is cautioned not to fall into the ability-grouping trap. For example, three first graders with advanced reading skills would quite naturally fall into the "high" group (in a classroom using ability grouping). Anna and Keith read on a fifth-grade level. While both read books on a similar level, Anna's understanding of concepts and curiosity about the nuances of the story far exceed Keith's. Keith is a typical first grader with interests that most 6-year-olds have. So even though he is an advanced reader, he needs topics that are interesting to a boy of his age. The third student is Dana, who according to her parents taught herself to read and reads at a third- or fourth-grade level. The interesting thing about Dana is that, even though she can read quite well, she lacks phonic knowledge in many areas and often finds herself stuck on a word with no word-attack skills to decode it. In a classroom with ability grouping, these three would have be in a group together—the high group—because they are all reading above grade level. But really these three children are not equally matched for a group. No two children learn in the same way. So putting Anna, Keith, and Dana in a group together for reading instruction would be making the assumption that they all have similar needs, which they clearly do not. They are not all "high" in the same way, just as other students in the class are not all "low" or "medium" in the same way. Mixing up ability levels in instructional groups forces the teacher to see each child as an individual and provide additional guidance and challenges to the students as it is necessary. All too often what happens in a "low" reading group is that so much attention is focused on the basics that the teacher dumbs down the thinking level of instruction as well. Just because a child reads slowly, has difficulty decoding, or is learning a second language, does not mean he or she is unable to think at a higher level. For example, a third-grade boy who has trouble with reading and has a documented learning disability might be fascinated with airplanes and aerodynamics. He can discuss high-level concepts and has a strong desire to learn. It is important to meet his reading skill needs, while not squelching his curiosity. Simply because he has difficulty reading a word like *aerodynamics* is not a reason not to talk and learn about it. Mixed-ability grouping encourages the teacher to maintain a high level of critical thinking while offering differentiated instruction as needed.

There are numerous strategies for effective teaching. Interactive learning, integrated instruction, direct instruction, and differentiated instruction are only a few. Effective teachers will want to consider other strategies and theories about how to teach effectively. The important thing is to consider the needs and interests of all students, and design instruction and instructional means that address these needs.

Building Family Partnerships

When thinking about effective teachers, family involvement may not be the first topic that comes to mind, but a focus on families and their role in children's education has been shown to bring about great benefits for children. Family involvement is more than just asking parents to help out in the classroom. It's about building partnerships with families so both the home environment and the school experience are working together to support children's academic and social development. While many teacher preparation programs place little emphasis on family involvement, this is not a new idea. In fact, in the past 50 years or more, researchers have emphasized its importance. The sociocultural theory, for example, emphasizes the interrelatedness and interdependence of individual and social processes in development and learning. This relates back to the home because

it underscores a fundamental principle for sociocultural pedagogical perspectives—the recognition of children's learning processes before children come to school and of the ongoing learning outside school. Vygtosky claimed that any learning a child encounters in school has a previous history. (Mahn, 1999, p. 347)

Urie Bronfenbrenner's (1995) **ecological systems theory** addresses the spheres of influence that impact a child's development—the microsystem, the mesosystem, the exosystem, and the macrosystem. These spheres are shown in **Figure 4.1.** Children are most closely impacted by their interactions with family members. They are then influenced by the neighborhoods and schools. More distantly, children are influenced by media, a parent's work environment, and friends of the family. Bronfenbrenner notes the reciprocal relationship between the child and these spheres of influence. For example, the child impacts the family and the family impacts the child. The child influences the school and the school influences the child. When thinking about the importance of building partnerships with families, it is necessary to think about all the things that impact children outside of school.

The microsystem is the layer that most closely affects and includes the child. The child is impacted by his or her family and friends. The child likely encounters areas of the neighborhood, health services, church, and at a certain age, school. These are all in the child's immediate surroundings. The microsystem is where the child experiences face-to-face interaction with people and institutions. There exists a reciprocal relationship where the child is not only influenced but also has influence on these people and places. For example, the child's family affects the growth and development of the child, and in return, the child has influence on his or her family. Institutions within the microsystem are also affected by one another. Family members are influenced by interactions with the school and events that take place at the school, and the school is influenced by families and the neighborhood community. All of these people and settings interact with one another.

The exosystem is comprised of people, places, and institutions that more indirectly impact the child's life. These include members of the extended family, friends of the family, people in the surrounding neighborhood, the parent's workplace, media, and institutions in the community offering social services. While

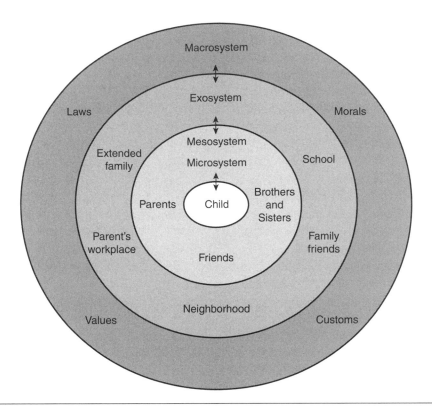

Figure 4.1 Ecological Systems Theory

SOURCE: Jennifer Prior, based on Urie Bronfenbrenner's (1995) ecological systems theory.

these do not directly touch the child on a daily basis, they have an impact on the child's life. A parent's workplace, for example, has an indirect influence on the child. A parent whose work environment is positive and whose earnings adequately support the family is likely to come home with a positive attitude. On the other hand, a work environment that is stressful might cause a parent to bring negative attitudes into the home, which is likely to influence the overall environment in a negative way.

The mesosystem connects the microsystem and exosystem. This system is not made up of people and institutions, but rather consists of the connections between two or more settings in which the child actively participates. For example, the child's relationships with family members in the home, friends and teachers at school, and peers and families in the neighborhood make up the mesosystem. In order for a child's development to be enhanced, positive connections between these layers must exist.

The macrosystem is the final layer of ecological systems. This layer includes attitudes and ideologies of the culture. Laws, morals, values, customs, and worldviews all make up the macrosystem. These may not impact the child's immediate world, but they have great impact on the family and community in which he or she lives. Values of a particular society certainly affect parenting styles or work habits, for example, which have a direct effect on the child's upbringing.

This broad perspective of the ecological systems theory of child development relates to family involvement and building partnerships with parents in education. The school experience involves an interrelated system that includes not just the teacher and the child but also the family and the surrounding community. In more recent years, research has revealed the benefits of family involvement on children's academic success. Suzanne Carter (2002) investigated 70 studies of parent involvement programs and found several common themes:

Parents who are involved in their children's education tend to have children who are more successful in school.

Regardless of ethnicity, cultural background, or socioeconomic status, the achievement gap is minimized for children whose families are involved in their education.

For young children, family involvement in education makes the school experience less frightening.

Math and literacy skills tend to improve when families are involved in the academic process.

Overall student achievement and school improvement happens when parents work together with schools.

Anne T. Henderson and Nancy Berla (1994) identified four areas of change that happen as a result of parent involvement—increased student achievement, improved student attitudes, improved attendance, and a decrease in discipline problems. Family involvement brings about long-term effects that benefit children throughout the span of their school experience. It is also noted that there is increased communication and a greater understanding of their responsibility in children's success in school.

Family involvement also brings about benefits for parents as well as for teachers. Joyce L. Epstein (2000) found that teachers who formed partnerships with families had a greater understanding of the family culture and gained appreciation for the value of parents in the academic process. Epstein also reports a higher level of confidence with parenting among those who involve themselves with their children's education.

Ms. Ansel reports her feelings about interacting with parents as a new teacher:

When I first began teaching, it didn't occur to me that I would have a lot of involvement with families. In fact, I was scared to death of them. I avoided them whenever I could. I was 21, so maybe I was a little naïve, but what I found was that the more I avoided, the more they wanted to talk to me. Most parents just want to know what their children are learning in school and how they are doing academically. My avoidance of interaction merely caused parents to be more concerned. Within the first few years, I began to warm up to parents, making efforts to chat with them informally after school. This simple effort at communication made a world of difference and helped to build trusting relationships. I later began sending home a weekly newsletter, letting parents know what we would be learning that week. This small and regular form of communication had an incredible impact on the trust level parents had with me. They didn't worry about what was happening at school because they were informed.

Making a Plan for Family Involvement

Effective teachers plan for family involvement in a variety of ways. They make personal connections, communicate regularly, provide ideas for involvement in the home environment, create a welcoming environment, and prepare for parent conferences. Let's take a closer look at some of these.

Personal Connections

Communication is the foundation of successful family involvement programs. For this reason, it is important to communicate to families who you are as a person. A letter sent home at the beginning of the year might communicate to parents that the teacher has two dogs, loves skiing, and likes to paint in his or her free time. By telling parents a few things about his or her life, the teacher may find things in common with them, which will lead to future conversations, opening the doors of partnership and trust.

Regular Communication

Most schools have some form of a back-to-school night at the beginning of the school year. This is a great time for the teacher to tell parents about his or her philosophy of education, classroom expectations, and particular things children will learn during the year. The teacher should let parents know how and how often to expect communication and provide information for how they can best reciprocate this communication.

The weekly newsletter, as shown in **Figure 4.2,** is an outstanding way to connect with parents regularly. Some teachers send a newsletter at the end of the week, while some send it at the beginning. The teacher can use weekly newsletters as a means of sending reminders of upcoming events, notifying parents of weekly homework assignments, and letting them know what their children will be learning in the days to come. Teachers can provide questions parents can ask their children about specific learning experiences in order to facilitate conversation at home. When parents know that communication will be sent home consistently, they look for it, read it, and ask their children about specific things they're learning. The key is to be consistent.

Parent phone calls are another effective means of communication. It is helpful to call every parent within the first week or two of the school year. If there is a particularly difficult child in class, make the call before issues arise. The first phone call should be positive and communicate how well the child is doing in class. Leaving time for parent questions is helpful as well. Mrs. Gomez was the parent of a first grader. She had been a teacher for many years and was nervous about her son's first-grade experience. She overwhelmed her son's teacher with questions at a meet-the-teacher night, wanting to know her philosophy of education, her beliefs about teaching reading, and how she planned to challenge him. These were questions the teacher could not answer with the limited time and numerous distractions in the classroom. So a few days later, the first-grade teacher gave her a call. "Mrs. Gomez," she said, "I know you're not going to rest easy until your questions are answered. So fire away." The two talked for a while about their teaching philosophies, the boy's learning needs, the teacher's beliefs about teaching reading. They spent the next hour just talking about life. Mrs. Gomez became one of the greatest advocates for her son's first-grade teacher and a wonderful support to the classroom community for the rest of the year. Remember that most parents anticipate that a phone call from the teacher is going to be negative, so a positive first call lays the foundation for a positive partnership.

Weekly News

Announcements	Math
Picture day is on Thursday! Don't forget to send in your child's permission slip for next week's field trip.	In math we will continue learning to subtract two-digit numbers with regrouping.
Reading/Writing	**Homework**
This week we will read Judi Barrett's book, *Cloudy With a Chance of Meatballs*. We will learn about contractions and learn to write tall tale stories.	1. Read to your child each day. 2. Have a family discussion about the uses of math in your home.
Science	**Donations**
We will begin a unit about weather. The children will learn to use thermometers and make predictions about the weather. Ask your child about the visit from a local weatherman on Wednesday.	Next week we will make a project with salt dough. If you have any salt or flour you could donate, please send it in!

Figure 4.2 Sample Parent Newsletter

Encouraging Involvement at Home

Teachers often provide opportunities for parents to volunteer in the classroom, and while this can be helpful, research shows that the greatest benefits of parent involvement happen as a result of what parents do with their children in the home. David B. Yaden, Deborah W. Rowe, and Laurie MacGillivray (2000) cite an increase in literacy skills among children whose families participate in literacy activities with

Sidebar 4.2 Working With Divorced Parents

Parent-teacher partnerships are often complicated when a child's parents are divorced. This can create an uncomfortable situation for the teacher, the parents, and the child. If the noncustodial parent has permission to be involved in the child's life, the teacher can use the following tips for helping with his or her involvement:

1. Reserve judgment about the family situation.
2. Offer to mail newsletters and other school communication on a weekly basis.
3. Offer to schedule separate parent/teacher conferences.
4. Engage both parents equally in conversations about the child's progress.
5. Avoid negative conversations about the parent who is not present.
6. Keep your focus on supporting the child.

SOURCE: Adapted from Prior and Gerard (2006).

them in the home. Jones (2001) states, "While school officials are enthusiastic about recruiting parents as volunteers, they should be aware that the cookie-baking, word-processing, candy-selling, paper-shuffling, showing-up activities traditionally associated with parent involvement are not likely to have much impact on student achievement" (p. 37). Jones emphasizes, rather, that it is the interaction between parent and child in the home that makes the most difference. So, effective teachers communicate to parents about the value of their involvement and the kinds of things they can do at home. A teacher might send home a backpack activity that parents and children complete together. For older students, the teacher might encourage family participation in conducting a simple science experiment or discuss a news program they watch on television. A teacher might include a family involvement suggestion in the newsletter each week or send home a monthly list of suggested activities. In her article *Mathematics Backpacks: Making the Home-School Connection,* Sheryl Orman (1993) reports the use of school-to-home math backpacks as a way to connect with parents. Each backpack she created contained markers, pencils, paper, and other necessary mathematics supplies, an inventory of supplies, an informational letter to parents, and a journal. Children took turns taking the backpacks home and were permitted to keep them for a few days. The purpose was for parents and children to work together to complete a math-related activity and then report their experiences in the journal. Orman explains that the use of these backpack activities helps connect parents with school activities and provides them with engaging and interactive experiences with their children. For students who are older, the teacher can send home a set of instructions for a game, experiment, or interactive discussion between parent and child. Letters to parents suggesting general ideas for involvement in the home can be used as well.

Create a Welcoming Environment

The way a classroom is set up creates an environment that welcomes students and their families. The room should be decorated in a way that is comfortable, uncluttered, and allows for easy movement throughout the space. It is important to communicate

---

Sidebar 4.3   Sample Parent/Child Activity

Show a parent a letter with the following text:

Dear Parent,

A fun way to follow-up the reading of a story is to interact with your child in different ways. Talk about two of the characters in the story. Discuss their personalities and the things that happened to them in the story. Then draw your child's attention to the setting of the story. Was the setting realistic? Was it make-believe? Re-create the setting one of the following ways:

—Draw a picture of the setting.
—Use clay or dough (see recipe below) to create different objects in the story's setting.
—Pour a layer of salt or sugar in the bottom of a cake pan. Use your finger to draw objects from the story.

Salt Dough Recipe

Ingredients:
1 cup of flour
½ cup of salt
1 cup of water

Mix ingredients together to make pliable dough. Add more flour or water, if necessary, to create desired consistency.

through the environment that you are happy to have children and parents in the classroom. Be careful not to have too much on the walls as this gives the classroom a cluttered feel that is not conducive to learning. Also, leave space to display students' projects. They should feel that this is their classroom and that they have valuable things to contribute to the overall appearance of the classroom. Manipulatives and materials should be stored in cabinets or on shelves in a neat and organized way. If materials from previous teachers have been left behind, neatly store the things you think you will use and give the rest away to other teachers in the school. You might even consider giving students some of the unneeded materials if they do not belong to the school. Label seating areas with students' names so parents and students can immediately sense that you are ready to include them as part of the classroom community.

Parent/Family Conferences

It is important to communicate to parents that your goal is to develop partnerships with them for the benefit of their children's overall success in school. When parents come to meet with you, schedule enough time to engage in a quality discussion. Be prepared to speak about the child's progress in your class and how he or she is doing and offer anecdotes of the child's interactions with peers and successes in particular subject areas. In addition, encourage a two-way conversation, allowing the parent to ask questions and address concerns. Create a seating arrangement that is comfortable and engaging. Consider placing some adult-sized chairs around a table rather than sitting behind a desk, which will create a physical barrier that is not conducive to relationship building. Be prepared to show student work samples from various points of the school year to give an indication of the child's progress over time. Indicate expected milestones of academic progress and how the child has moved from one milestone to the next, rather than merely making comparisons between the child and his or her peers. Invite the parent to share the progress seen at home, both academically and socially, and encourage the parent to express goals he or she has for the child. Be sure to allow time for the parent to address questions and concerns, and make note of these in the parent's presence to show that you value the parent's input.

Then communicate with the parent in the coming weeks to show you have given thought to the discussion and how you have addressed some of the concerns or goals. This expresses to the parent that you care about the child and that his or her input in the **parent/teacher partnership** is valuable.

The benefits of family involvement are far-reaching, but it is the teacher's responsibility to work closely with families and work to build effective partnerships. Teachers can also encourage natural and meaningful engagement between parents and children in the home. There is nothing a teacher can do to force families to actively participate in their children's educational development, but he or she can try to make family involvement opportunities appealing and fun (Prior, 2011).

Reflective Teaching

Being a reflective practitioner involves stepping back from what we do to examine why we do it. So often the job of a teacher is about accomplishing tasks and allows little time for reflection, yet reflecting on practice is becoming more of a focus for effective teachers. The InTASC standards, in particular, place a strong emphasis on teacher reflection, encouraging teachers to keep journals reflecting on personal biases, children's responses to instruction, the decisions made about teaching, and how to improve practice. In his book, *The Reflective Practitioner* (1983), Donald Schon emphasizes the importance of reflection and states that in the reflective process

> the practitioner allows himself to experience surprise, puzzlement, or confusion in a situation which he finds uncertain or unique. He reflects on the phenomena before him, and on the prior understandings which have been implicit in his behavior. He carries out an experiment which serves to generate both a new understanding of the phenomena and a change in the situation. (p. 68)

Schon (1983) comments on the shift in our thinking as practitioners when engaging in reflection and how a teacher "must expand the scope of her interest in students. What they know how to do in the world outside the school becomes deeply interesting to her, for it suggests the intuitive competences on which she can build" (p. 333). The understanding of students' prior knowledge can be better understood when engaging in reflection about what students know and what they are ready to learn.

Tools for Reflection

In their book, *Teachers as Curriculum Planners: Narratives of Experience,* F. Michael Connelly and D. Jean Clandinin (1988) describe tools teachers can use for engaging in reflection. The first involves keeping a journal. It is important to note that a journal of this kind should not be an evaluative tool for judging the teaching of lessons. Rather, a reflective journal is used to record what the teacher does, why particular decisions are made, and what is noticed about students and for wrestling with experiences that are confusing or surprising. Connelly and Clandinin also describe the idea of writing a personal autobiography about one's journey to and practice in teaching, allowing the teacher to understand himself or herself as a teacher. They also suggest ideas for reflecting with others through written dialogue with colleagues or more formal interviews between teachers. While there are many ways to participate in reflection, the point is to take a step back and think about teaching and students in a different way—a more thoughtful way.

The *Standards Continuum Guide for Reflective Teaching Practice* (Arizona K12 Center, 2011) is a publication created by the Arizona K12 Center and is based on the InTASC Standards. The guide encourages reflection about the performances, essential knowledge, and critical dispositions related to teaching. While teachers may choose to reflect on their practice in many different ways, some of the reflective prompts from the guide are listed here:

Standard 1: Learner Development—Why do I vary my teaching methods?

Standards 2: Learning Differences—Why do I create opportunities for all learners to communicate and work with one another?

Standard 3: Learning Environments—Why do I create opportunities for students to navigate their own learning?

Standard 3: Learning Environments—Why do I value student opinions?

Standard 4: Content Knowledge—Why do I value learners' knowledge and experience when planning instruction?

Standard 4: Content Knowledge—Why do I create a learning environment that scaffolds instruction?

Standard 6: Assessment—Why do I challenge learners to become more aware of connecting their learning across the curriculum areas?

Standard 6: Assessment—Why do I teach learners to build their skills in self-reflection?

Standard 7: Planning for Instruction—Why do I reflect on instructional successes and challenges?

Standard 7: Planning for Instruction—Why do I analyze instructional data and learners' strengths and needs?

Standard 8: Instructional Strategies—Why do I build upon learners' strengths, interests, and needs when establishing expectations and setting learning outcomes?

Standard 9: Professional Learning and Ethical Practice—Why do I accept personal responsibility for student learning?

Standard 9: Professional Learning and Ethical Practice—Why do I commit to reflecting on instruction and student learning daily?

Standard 9: Professional Learning and Ethical Practice—Why do I create an environment that enhances students' life experiences, prior knowledge, and interests?

Standard 10: Leadership and Collaboration—Why do I value family backgrounds and their role in student learning?

The effective teacher thoughtfully considers his or her students and all aspects and decisions involved in the teaching process and classroom environment. These reflections assist the teacher in adapting curriculum, teaching strategies, and the physical environment in order to bring about the best possible educational experience for children.

Conclusion

What separates great teachers from good teachers is actually quite a lot. Because great teachers don't just stand in front of a group of students and deliver dynamic content. Great teachers make purposeful decisions about the classroom environment. They consider the instructional strategies that will best meet the needs of their students. Great teachers recognize the importance of their students' families and strive to involve them in the educational experience, and they make the time to thoughtfully reflect on what they do and why they do it. Great teachers focus on the whole classroom and the whole child. A good number of teachers choose to focus only on teaching, but great teachers recognize quality education as a combination of a variety of things that enhance each child's learning. Of course, each person will decide what kind of teacher he or she will be, but a strong, supportive leader can guide him or her in the right direction.

Key Chapter Terms

Constructivist: A proponent of constructivism, a theory emphasizing that children construct knowledge from active experiences.

Ecological systems theory: Urie Bronfenbrenner's (1995) theory, emphasizing the multiple influences on a child's development.

Parent/teacher partnership: A working relationship between parents and the teacher that focuses on the progress of the child. Emphasis is placed on the joint contribution of input by both teacher and family.

Reflective teaching: The process of exploring one's own teaching and decisions and practices related to teaching and children.

Sociocultural theory: Lev Vygotsky's theory that emphasizes social interaction in the development of children's thought.

References

Arizona K12 Center. (2011). *Standards continuum guide for reflective teaching practice.* Flagstaff: Northern Arizona University.

Barrett, J., & Barrett, R. (1988). *Cloudy with a chance of meatballs.* New York, NY: Atheneum.

Bronfenbrenner, U. (1995). The bioecological perspective from a life course perspective: Reflections of a participant observer. In P. Moen, G. H. Edler, & K. Luscher (Eds.), *Examining lives in context* (pp. 599–618). Washington, DC: American Psychological Association.

Bryner, J. (2005). Rewards not working? *Instructor, 155*(4), 19–20.

Carter, S. (2002). *The impact of parent/family involvement on student outcomes: An annotated bibliography of research from the past decade.* Eugene, OR: Consortium for Appropriate Dispute Resolution in Special Education.

Common Core Standards Initiative. (2012a) *English language arts standards.* Retrieved from http://www.corestandards.org/assets/KeyPointsELA.pdf

Common Core Standards Initiative. (2012b) *English mathematics standards.* Retrieved from http://www.corestandards.org/assets/KeyPointsMath.pdf

Connelly, F. M., & Clandinin, D. J. (1988). *Teachers as curriculum planners: Narratives of experience.* New York, NY: Teachers College Press.

Dewey, J. (1966). *Democracy and education.* New York, NY: Free Press. (Original work published 1916)

Dibapile, W. T. S. (2012). A review of literature on teacher efficacy and classroom management. *Journal of College Teaching and Learning, 9*(2), 81.

Drake, S. M., & Burns, R. C. (2004). *Meeting standards through integrated curriculum.* Alexandria, VA: Association for Supervision & Curriculum Development.

Epstein, J. L. (2000). *School and family partnerships: Preparing educators and improving schools.* Boulder, CO: Westview.

Erwin, J. (2005). Put back the fun in classrooms. *Education Digest: Essential Readings Condensed for Quick Review, 70*(5), 14–19.

Henderson, A. T., & Berla, N. (1994). *A new generation of evidence: The family is critical to student achievement.* St. Louis, MO: Danforth Foundation and Flint, MI: Mott (C. S.) Foundation.

Interstate Teacher Assessment Support Consortium. (2013). *InTASC model core teaching standards and learning progressions for teachers 1.0.* Washington, DC: Council of Chief State School Officers.

Jones, R. (2001). Involving parents is a whole new game: Be sure you win! *The Education Digest, 67*(3), 36–43.

Mahn, H. (1999). Vygotsky's methodological contribution to sociocultural theory. *Remedial and Special Education, 20*(6), 341–350.

Marzano, R. J., & Marzano, J. S. (2003). The key to classroom management. *Educational Leadership, 61*(1), 6–13.

Noddings, N. (2012). The caring relation in teaching. *Oxford Review of Education, 38*(6), 771–781.

Orman, S. A. (1993). Mathematics backpacks: Making the home-school connection. *Arithmetic Teacher, 40*(6), 306–309.

Piaget, J. (1985). *The equilibration of cognitive structures: The central problem of intellectual development.* Chicago, IL: University of Chicago Press.

Piaget, J., & Inhelder, B. (1969). *The psychology of the child.* New York, NY: Basic Books.

Prior, J. (2011). *An educator's guide to family involvement in early literacy.* Huntington Beach, CA: Shell Education.

Prior, J., & Gerard, M. R. (2006). *Family involvement in early childhood education: Research into practice.* Belmont, CA: Wadsworth.

Sayeski, K .L., & Brown, M. R. (2011). Developing a classroom management plan using a tiered approach. *Teaching Exceptional Children, 44*(1), 8–17.

Schon, D. A. (1983). *The reflective practitioner.* New York, NY: Basic Books.

Vygotsky, L. S. (1978). *Mind in society: The development of higher psychological processes* (M. Cole, V. John-Steiner, S. Scribner, & E. Souberman, Eds.). Cambridge, MA: Harvard University Press.

Vygotsky, L. S. (1981). The genesis of higher mental functions. In J. J. Wertsch (Ed.), *The concept of activity in Soviet psychology* (pp. 144–188). White Plains, NY: M. E. Sharpe.

Wong, H. K., & Wong, R. T. (2009). *The first days of school: How to be an effective teacher.* Mountain View, CA: Harry K. Wong.

Yaden, D. B., Rowe, D. W., & MacGillivray, L. (2000). Emergent literacy: A matter (polyphony) of perspectives. In M. L. Kamil, P. B. Mosental, P. D. Pearson, & R. Barr (Eds.), *Handbook of reading research* (pp. 425–454). Mahwah, NJ: Erlbaum.

Further Readings

Connelly, F. M., & Clandinin, D. J. (1988). *Teachers as curriculum planners: Narratives of experience.* New York, NY: Teachers College Press.

This book provides hands-on exercises teachers can use to assist with the development of their beliefs and philosophies as they plan curriculum in their classrooms.

Prior, J. (2011). *An educator's guide to family involvement in early literacy.* Huntington Beach, CA: Shell Education.

This book provides a wealth of strategies teachers can use to help families involve themselves in strengthening early literacy in the home.

Wong, H. K., & Wong, R. T. (2009). *The first days of school: How to be an effective teacher.* Mountain View, CA: Harry K. Wong.

This book assists teachers with strategies for structuring their classrooms for effective classroom management and optimal student learning.

5

Overcoming Learning Barriers for All Students

Jane Clark Lindle

Clemson University

Beth Parrott Reynolds

Clemson University

Students are as individual as their fingerprints. Their individuality is expressed in their appearance, their rates of growth and learning, their backgrounds, and their personalities. The complexity of collecting a group of individuals into a single space, such as school, is compounded by the individuality of adults (professionals, staff, parents, and community members) and their backgrounds, rates of development and learning, and personalities. Furthermore, all these individuals belong to groups, cultures, and communities, and those group dynamics and cultural norms create even more complexity. This complex mixture does not even require a stir for it to bubble and stew, even spew. In short, at any given moment, the combination of adults and students and all their individual talents and needs will create moments that impede learning.

Larger sociocultural events with media interpretations shape school circumstances and provide more dynamics that affect schools' learning environments and ultimately raise barriers to learning. These barriers range from individuals' **cognitive developmental differences** to **social-emotional development** to historic cultural influences on schools, such as **racism** and **gendered roles** along with social media's expansion of bullying into **cyberbullying** and **social/ moral panic** about media reports of school violence. For school leaders, the issue of reducing learning barriers may also be a question of how to address the complexity of cultural, social, and school dynamics in order to focus on any given student's or groups of students' needs.

For the purposes of this chapter, a bio-social-ecological understanding of students' worlds, as first described by Urie Bronfenbrenner (1979), offers a lens for attending to multiple aspects of the learner's ecology (social, cultural, political, institutional, interpersonal, and individual). This ecological focus will be explained through a lens of an individual's development. Then that lens will be enhanced with emerging knowledge of expanding social-cultural influences, such as social media and **funds of knowledge** in diverse cultures (González, Moll, & Armanti, 2005; Moll, 1992).

Bronfenbrenner (1979) suggested that any person's development corresponded to a set of ever-expanding social and institutional ecologies. For example, a baby's ecology includes the family and medical personnel and, from baby to baby, the dominance of family or the medical personnel varies

Sidebar 5.1 Do You Have These Barriers in Your School?

A *yes* answer to any one of these questions can be a signal that a barrier exists that may be a critical aspect in affecting any student's or groups of students' success.

1. Does your school's surrounding neighborhood, community, or municipality set up, even inadvertently, barriers to students' and families' health, safety, or other aspects of their well-being?

2. Is your school distant from the homes and neighborhoods of the students and their families?

3. Is your school's student body experiencing any economic changes (booms or busts) that affect students and their families' access to transportation, health, housing, or other services?

4. Has your student body experienced any forms of cyberbullying, on-campus violence, neighborhood violence, natural disasters, or other crises?

5. Does your school staff lack sufficient preparation or ability to work with students and families with different cultural backgrounds or language heritages?

6. Does your school and school staff lack sufficient knowledge about access to school system and community services that any student may need?

7. Does your school staff lack awareness or preparation for working with family and community volunteers in the school?

8. Does your school staff lack ability or preparation for shared decision making about students' well-being with parents, guardians, and other service professionals or organizations?

9. Are your school's or school systems' policies too restrictive to accommodate individual differences among students and their families?

10. Does your school or system have any zero-tolerance policies?

11. Does your school staff lack preparation and skills in developing appropriate teaching/learning relationships with students and their families?

12. Does your school staff fail to monitor discipline or absentee data to address escalating issues?

13. Do the school's teachers lack the ability to differentiate instruction?

14. Does the school's academic assessment system fail to differentiate for developmental differences?

15. Does the school fail to support students' development of self-awareness of learning and healthy and productive learning strategies?

based on culture, financial resources, and availability of medical services. The young child's world expands to playmates, preschool, and religious institutions, depending on socioeconomic status and cultural mores. School-age children's ecologies expand to teachers and classmates as well as before- and after-school activities surrounding the school or in other areas of the neighborhood and larger community. Older students also become more involved in institutional, commercial, and governmental services as they learn to drive on public roads, expand their work and purchasing power, earn the right to vote, and grow into other aspects of adult life. For school leaders, the images of these increasingly expanding ecologies can be useful for analyzing both

barriers to learning and the possible assets among those ecologies that might mitigate learning barriers.

The ecologies for all students range from family to community members to community and governmental agencies and institutions. For more than 30 years, an extensive research base on family and community involvement attests to its power in lowering barriers to learning and creating student success. Joyce Epstein and her associates have developed a model for increasing parent, family, and community involvement (Epstein, Galindo, & Sheldon, 2011). According to this model, school leaders can have an effect on how well students learn by engaging all aspects of the community and empowering parents in meaningful ways that suit their varying interests and talents.

Some family members are more suited to caring for their children at home, ensuring that the student goes to school well fed, clean, clothed, and rested, which is termed **parenting** in Epstein's model (Epstein et al., 2011). Other families parent well plus **support learning at home**. In these cases, such families not only help with homework but also provide educational experiences such as trips to museums and libraries, summer camps, or other enriching activities. Still other families have individual members, historically mothers or grandparents, who engage with school by **volunteering**. More and more men and businesses seek to mentor young people through schools and expand the concepts of volunteering in this manner.

Epstein's model (Epstein et al., 2011) also includes **two-way communication**, where both school and home make efforts for clarifying expectations about learning. Realistically, school professionals may need to make the first move to truly engage some families and to elicit a two-way exchange about student progress and welfare. Another form of engagement in Epstein's model includes families and community members in **decision-making** processes. Much of U.S. law on student education already mandates the inclusion of parents and guardians in decisions about each student, but Epstein's work, as well as other research, has shown the value of parent and community input and participation in other decisions about schooling. The final portion of Epstein's model is **community engagement**. The diversity of student needs across years of growth as well as throughout his or her expanding ecologies indicates ways in which schools need to collaborate with other community and government agencies.

As noted, Epstein's model holds some general notions about the diversity of ways that families and communities must be involved in schools, but as each neighborhood and community is different, school personnel may require more specific understanding of those differences. The concept of *funds of knowledge* (Moll, 1992) is useful for understanding distinctive communities. Funds of knowledge focus on the idea that households are part of a social network that can ensure a community's and its members' continued success. Moll and colleagues noted that historically, school policies and curriculum have emphasized an assimilative approach that has a side effect of relegating student differences to a **deficit**

model. That is, students who do not conform to the majority are seen not only as different but as problems to be solved. Sometimes, the approach is so narrowly concentrated on a single student that the important social networks that support him or her are broken. When these relationships are broken, students' opportunities to thrive diminish.

Using a combination of Bronfenbrenner's (1979) bioecological model and Epstein and her associates' (Epstein et al., 2011) extensive research on the positive effects of parenting and community collaboration, enhanced by an understanding of funds of knowledge, school leaders have many tools to analyze and address each and every student's needs. When a student seems to fail at learning, the school leader can explore the student's current ecology from classroom to home and throughout the community to find both the cause and the remedy. Learning barriers can be as diverse as the students who face them, but each student's family and community also have assets that can be employed to lower those barriers. With Epstein's six types of involvement and an understanding of funds of knowledge in the community, the school leader can both diagnose and explore how to leverage the assets within the family and community to help the student succeed and learn.

Learning Barriers and Their Sources

In most schools, the typical response to identification of learning barriers is to focus on the child and try to fix him or her. Most of the time, this approach is frustrating because of the dynamics in the students' ecology; that is, sometimes more than the child needs to be fixed. Even the notion of fixing a student is a barrier to helping and supporting a student since a fixing approach is a deficit approach. Among the lists of deficits, a lot of well-meaning professional literature lists poverty, race, nationality or ethnicity, language, and sexual identity as deviations from normal. Many of the notions of abnormality slip into stereotypes and profiling of deficits in students, families, and cultures. Especially for students with disabilities, the concept of normal can be a barrier and that deficit approach is known as **ableism** (Hehir, 2002). Because a high percentage of students identified for special education include racial minorities, ableism lapses into racism (Beratan, 2006). The danger of labeling differences in students' backgrounds and personal characteristics is that none of these labels provide guidance on supporting or helping the students. Labels are not useful because they promote biases and stereotypes.

Another social development affecting students' learning is technology and social media. While these developments can be used to enhance learning environments, the unfortunate side of these developments includes the expansion of bullying from physical and verbal confrontations on school grounds to cyberbullying. Both bullying and cyberbullying offer another form of exploiting students' diversity as a deficit. Many of the publicized examples of cyberbullying have focused on gender socialization and sexual identity. Bullying identifies victims based on their differences, and the normalizing environment of schools, including the habit of labeling differences, may inadvertently foster bullies' prejudiced assaults.

In these publicized cases, global exposure leads to a public reaction known as moral panic. Moral panic can exacerbate students' and their parents' fear of schools. This kind of panic also illustrates the connection of communities to schools, as well as how a social network works both for and against students' opportunities for schooling.

Moral panic is associated frequently with publicity about school shootings. School violence is not a new phenomenon with examples, although rare, of mass shootings, bombings, fires, and other forms of school disasters dating at least to the early decades of the 20th century. Nevertheless, pervasive social expectations of an ideal normality promote an overreaction to these rare events. Moral panic often fuels intolerance for diversity, and generates a view of natural differences among students with more sinister interpretations—a deficit view.

A deficit focus thwarts any opportunities to perceive or use the assets and talents that pupils, families, and communities can contribute. As a more positive approach, Bronfenbrenner's (1979) bioecological model can illuminate strategies for learning supports from the largest ecology to the smallest, instead of the traditional deficit-oriented origins that start from the smallest sphere, individual student characteristics or background. This broader approach requires analysis of four ecologies in the following order: (a) social, cultural, and economic; (b) policies

and rules; (c) teaching strategies; and (d) learning strategies for individual students' use.

Social, Cultural, and Economic Ecologies

Sometimes schools are ensconced in the same local culture and socioeconomic conditions that students and families share. Other times, schools are located in different neighborhoods away from the students' homes and cultural wealth; in other words, they are removed from their funds of knowledge. Some schools have a great mix of different communities, cultures, languages, and a variety of different socioeconomic strata among the students and teachers. In all cases, schools' environments are different from students' home environments, and those differences may affect students' comfort, confidence, and readiness to learn. School leaders need to pay attention to differences that need to be bridged rather than deficits to overcome. Deficit thinking may prevent principals, assistant principals, and teacher leaders from finding the wealth of assets that can bridge differences, facilitating diversity to support learning.

Most students need support to navigate between home and school. When school leaders understand that home and school may be more than miles apart, then they bridge those differences and support student learning.

For example, language differences are difficult to address without translators. Hiring translators and training school personnel might be possible, but can strain school funds. One simple contribution from the community can be the availability of local translators, such as friends, neighbors, or other students who can bridge the language gap. Based on the kinship and area relationships, these local translators also can make a student and his or her family more comfortable in school.

Although an initiative about bridging language differences seems clear in schools where U.S. English is the dominant language and immigrants speak a different language, U.S. Standard English is not the dialect or cultural form of English spoken in many homes. In some schools, the differences in home-forms of English and school-forms are a matter of pronunciation and accents. Even though these differences seem minimal, emphasis on so-called proper pronunciation can convey a deficit approach rather than a supportive one. In such situations, what might seem to a teacher to be restrained instruction to a pupil about how an educated person speaks instead entails a **micro-aggression** (Pierce, 1970) to a child. "Micro-aggression is the continuous, insidious, display of racially motivated hostility acted out in benign insensitivity" (Dyson, 1990, p. 21). Hidden in the notion of proper is that the school form is implicitly better than the home form of language. Students (and all educated people) need to understand differences as normal rather than as choices between one as favorable and any others as unfavorable. School leaders may need to help other school personnel recognize and avoid micro-aggression in their own professional practices and especially in their communication with students, families, and communities.

All communities possess assets in different amounts and in ways perhaps different from the usual stereotypes. For example, urban communities may have a large number of social groups, organizations, businesses, and community agencies dedicated to helping families and schools. Yet many urban communities also can have isolating features such as large apartment complexes where families may not know their neighbors on either side of their unit, much less anyone on the floors above or below them. Rural communities frequently have fewer formal groups, industry, or agencies dedicated to social services, but neighbors may be very tightly aware and involved in each other's lives even though the physical distances between their homes might be acres or miles. School leaders must be able to understand their communities and how the social networks fit together to support students.

A community services audit is a long-standing recommendation for understanding how a school's surrounding community can help with student learning. Such an audit ranges from generating a convenient contact list for various kinds of needs from health to food to homework and tutoring volunteers to a list of parents, family, and community members' special talents and skills that can be shared during classroom lessons or school events, such as science or art fairs. A community services audit can be completed by school staff; by community or parent volunteers; or as a social studies project in upper elementary, middle, or high school levels.

In generating the community audit, school leaders can use at least three of Epstein's types of involvement

to apply community support for student learning. Two, *volunteering* and *decision making* may fall under the umbrella of the third, *community engagement.*

The volunteering form of community engagement may range from individual volunteers to groups. Individual community members may volunteer as tutors and mentors during or outside of school hours. These community members may have important life lessons to help individually struggling students with what John Dewey (1938) termed, **habits of mind.** According to Dewey, these qualities include a number of habits that help with learning, such as awareness of one's own learning strategies, persistence, dependability, responsibility, and resilience. When individual community members work as mentors, they typically work one-to-one with individual students either during or after school hours.

Some community members also have subject matter expertise since they use math, reading, and other so-called academic skills on their jobs. They can mentor by helping individual students with specific homework and class assignments and share habits of mind that increase literacies from reading to technologies. On the other hand, they may work with groups of students. Such community members can co-teach certain lessons with teachers or offer special presentations to groups of students. These community members can help students understand the relevance of school work to work after school and in their future lives.

In the case where communities exhibit cultural diversity, school leaders can activate volunteers to help students and families celebrate and accept differences among different groups. School leaders may need to begin these steps with exposing school personnel to the variety of community groups and leaders. When schools, rural or urban, are isolated by distances from students' homes and neighborhoods, teachers and other school personnel may also be unfamiliar with the community. School leaders may enlist community leaders' help in escorting school personnel as they visit unfamiliar neighborhoods and community centers to meet the people of the students' social networks. For example, owners of grocery stores, gas stations, restaurants, and other small businesses might host parent-teacher conferences or meet-the-teacher receptions to kick off a new school year. Many schools have used school buses for teachers to tour the routes their students ride and even make stops so teachers can walk the neighborhoods and meet neighborhood members. In some neighborhoods, community leaders such as church ministers or neighborhood association members greet the teachers and arrange home visits. Other groups of teachers have used summer time to visit their incoming students' homes, offering books, pencils, and contact information to parents and other family members before the school year starts with all its hectic moments. These kinds of personal experiences often alleviate teachers' and students' or families' misperceptions and erroneous stereotypes. Enlisting community leaders in these efforts activates students' social networks in a positive direction.

Other community members would prefer to work in groups to support students. Sometimes civic organizations and church groups would like to provide services for students and families, such as funding for and/or transportation to and from special school events or field trips. Other contributions can include a series of backpack programs ranging from a once or twice a year program of backpacks stuffed with school supplies to a weekly program where ready-to-eat meals are placed in backpacks to go home on weekends and other nonschool days.

Finally, any community audit that shows gaps in services should be addressed by school leaders, who are the first responders in addressing student needs. That is, school personnel may be the first to recognize the absence of community services because students are too young and their families too embarrassed or unaware to ask for the help they need. Thus, school leaders need to call other community leaders together to discuss the issues and develop solutions. This approach leads into the kind of involvement that Epstein termed, *decision making*.

Schools customarily hold a cultural and institutional responsibility to educate students, but the nature of learning barriers may include responsibilities that other parts of the community traditionally address. Many students face custodial conflicts due to divorce or other legal interventions in their family relationships. Some schools have found that inviting court services into or near their campuses help keep such students' absences for legal procedures to a minimum. Even when school personnel cannot be included in these proceedings due to matters of confidentiality, the court's decision structure is literally closer to the school, which may decrease delays in

managing custodial matters. The proximity of educational services may enable the court to use a more productive approach to juvenile adjudication, thus providing less disruption in the students' education.

Further examples of community inclusion in decision making can encompass decisions about the school calendar, the school's daily hours, and how the community, including law enforcement, can handle students' out-of-school time. When key groups such as the public library and law enforcement work with schools to manage time out of school, they can minimize the number of students who must be home alone as well as reduce petty crimes that have resulted from extended unsupervised out-of-school hours.

By working from the outermost ring of Bronfenbrenner's (1979) ecologies and applying half of the six types in Epstein's model to community involvement, schools can manage their own ecologies for student learning more effectively. When school leaders act to recognize and develop stronger links in students' social networks, then the divisions between school and home can be bridged. School leaders have a professional obligation to scan the learning environment vigilantly for microaggressions and the constraints of normalizing curriculum or instruction and the arrogance of ableism. These are the sociocultural impediments of student learning, and none of these conditions originates with the students. Instead, these issues require adults to refocus their efforts, connections, and attention to improving the social network for students. In many situations, learning barriers are not obstacles for individual students, but for all of them, and those learning barriers are created by the school or its personnel. In such situations, the divide between school and community destroys opportunities for learning. A positive and complementary relationship between schools and their communities can reduce barriers to learning.

Policies and Rules Ecologies

School leadership positions historically include responsibilities for enforcement of rules and policies that were intended to enhance the learning environment. Nevertheless, on any given occasion, a rule may enhance the learning environment for some students and yet impede learning for others. For example, some students prefer total silence for their schoolwork, but others feel more engaged with background music or by humming to themselves. Some learners need to sit still to concentrate, but others need to walk around to think. A rule to sit still and be quiet will help some learners and hinder others. School leaders' enforcement of rules and policies need to be informed by professional judgment about learning and in particular judgments about balancing individual rights while maximizing the common good for all students. Such a requirement is a balancing act, and given the ebb and flow between individual rights and the common good, informed professional judgment is necessary.

Jacqueline A. Stefkovich (2006) argued that policies in the best interests of students offer school leaders options in enforcement and implementation. These rules allow the application of professional judgment in determining next steps or meting out penalties. She referred to the differences between zero-tolerance or restrictive rules and those that permit professional discretion. School leaders cannot exercise professional judgments under policies or rules that require or prohibit specific actions. Among restrictive or prohibitive rules are the most restrictive versions known as zero-tolerance policies, which offer any school leader an extremely limited list of specific responses. This list is so restrictive that a school leader is required to execute those responses, no matter whether specific circumstances might suggest a more reasonable response. The school leader is much closer to the circumstances of any rule infraction, and the policymakers are far removed. Sometimes these policymakers are reacting to the public's moral panic about school violence or other sensationalized events near schools. Reams of paperwork, legal cases, research results, and lots of media airtime have documented the unwise and unintended consequences of zero-tolerance policies. Most of these results have severely hampered learning, not merely for any students directly involved in the case but also for many of the students who were not initially involved. The narrow lists of responses required of school leaders in zero-tolerance policies are an example of removing professional discretion about learning from the professionals. Stefkovich argued for policies that support the ethical and professional discretionary judgments of school leaders who understand how a learning environment can be preserved for all the students, even when a student breaks a rule.

School leaders need to evaluate school rules and policies for their discretionary opportunities for the leaders to exercise professional judgment about enhanced learning for all students and for each student. In the case of most school rules and policies, a rule that made sense years in the past might not be appropriate currently. Again, the decision making involvement portion of Epstein's model may provide a guide to garnering student, teacher, parent, and community input on how to revise outdated rules to address current issues in the school's learning environment.

School leaders can look at their discipline records and determine which rules generate the most infractions. The volume of infractions needs further investigation. Are these infractions due to serious disruptions of the learning environment? Does everyone, or just a handful of students, commit these infractions repeatedly? If everyone is caught by the rule, then is the rule outdated? Is it a time-wasting rule since so many students are caught and some school leader has to mete out punishments, which often results in students missing learning time? Is it a rule that only some students repeatedly bump into because the rule has some trap that lures in students who have particular learning or other special needs?

Depending on the volume of infractions for a particular rule, when the next student is caught by that rule, that student's case may require deeper investigation than usual. For example, sometimes students want to avoid a particular class and quickly discover they can miss instruction by breaking a particular rule that the class's teacher has shown to be a trigger for sending students to the office. This kind of class avoidance is a vicious cycle since the teacher is aiding the student in missing instruction. The school leader may need to spend time with the teacher to develop a different response than sending students out of the room.

Many schoolwide discipline programs wane in effectiveness, not because students are not responsive, but due to teachers' inconsistency in implementation. Typically, teachers begin to drop their implementation strategies about the time of the fall and winter holidays. Workload issues with the special events of November and December may provide an excuse for teachers' lack of consistency. For school leaders, the reliability of school year routines can help them with reinforcing teachers' commitment to schoolwide discipline policies during the seasons teachers might be distracted or forgetful.

Another aspect of helping teachers with classroom management rests on individual teachers' struggles with both power and deficit approaches to student behavior. Teachers face a class size fact: There is only one teacher and as many as 30 other human beings in the same classroom. Teachers' jobs require supervision of an outsized group of people. Most other occupations cap supervisory requirements at 15 people. The size of classes in most U.S. school systems is a feature of funding restrictions and not necessarily the optimum capacity for building healthy teaching-learning relationships. Without a doubt, a sense of being outnumbered can make a teacher interpret his or her role as one of control and power over students rather than building healthy relationships for a supportive learning environment.

The power and control dynamic often makes the teaching and learning relationship unhealthy. Students may view teacher dominance as a challenge to their own rights. While some children will challenge the teacher directly, others may react in fear. Both reactions are those of distrust. Since learning requires trust, a distrustful environment is a barrier to learning.

Teachers who feel challenged by their students may react defensively and thus escalate misunderstandings and power struggles. The escalation can be micro-aggressions or overt verbal abuse. Regardless of the form, these escalations represent a form of deficit thinking. A school leader needs to help teachers move past these reactions, and if a teacher resists this help, the best interests of students must supersede the teacher's interests. A defensive, reactive, and power-oriented teacher cannot teach, and consequently, should not remain employed as a teacher.

Teachers' individual classroom policies and rules can raise barriers to learning. If teachers are unfamiliar with their students' cultural and social backgrounds, homes, or neighborhoods, the teachers' rules might be inadvertently offensive. School leaders might uncover this problem before much of the school year passes by reviewing teachers' classroom policies for ways of enhancing home and school communication as well as accessing students' funds of knowledge. If this preventative approach is not taken,

then a review of which teachers' students seem to have the most infractions might reveal this problem.

Teachers' classroom rules and schoolwide discipline policies should be supportive of a strong curriculum that supports positive learning environments. Students need an understanding of how to work in groups, how to move in crowded places, and how to enjoy sporting and musical events. School activities can teach these kinds of skills. Businesses and other future employers as well as municipalities want safe environments with people who can work together and also enjoy social gatherings at sports and entertainment venues. When teachers and schools approach rules as educative rather than as control mechanisms, then students can learn more about group work and public safety.

If a classroom or school rule is generating a good deal of infractions across all students or perhaps trapping only certain students repeatedly, then the rule may need to be changed. Students can provide insights into how the rule affects them. Teachers and parents will have other perspectives on how the rule and its enforcement affects student learning and the environment for learning. The involvement of these stakeholders can enhance decisions about what rules can be helpful and effective in maintaining an environment for learning. In addition, these groups can provide suggestions about strategies for helping students follow any rule. When rules are useful teaching tools and ensure a positive learning environment, barriers to learning are lowered.

Teaching Strategies

When a student fails, the first line of investigation should be instructional rather than diagnostic. In other words, the initial analysis of why a pupil failed should involve consideration of how well instruction had been diversified for differences in student learning strengths and weaknesses (Tomlinson & Imbeau, 2010). Teachers and school leaders can serve as partners in this line of instructional investigation. They can observe students and teacher interactions. They can monitor teacher language and the degree of trust the teacher has generated with students. They also can support a teacher's reteaching strategies when students misunderstand or misconstrue concepts.

If students have few opportunities for work during class time, the instruction may be too teacher focused.

That is, the teacher may be doing more work than the students by lecturing rather than taking the time to listen and observe student understanding. Students' work during class can illustrate their understanding and misunderstanding. Observations of teaching should emphasize a variety of teaching strategies and not only the model of teacher as lecturer.

Another line of instructional investigation should include the quality of the measure signaling the student's failure. Was that measure a test that was well designed for learning or merely a measure of effort rather than learning? For example, some teachers focus on the act of turning in homework rather than assessing the quality of the work (Stiggins, 2002). If there is no opportunity for student work during class time, then the measure of learning, either tests or homework, is not directly connected to class instruction. The consequential issues of making judgments about student learning based on tests are huge. The limits of the tests must be considered before exercising any decision that affects any student's continued progress.

Other limits of instruction concerning literacy must be considered before any decision about a student's progress is made. Often, the problems with testing and instruction may lie in issues of literacy rather than concepts or knowledge. For example, the teaching strategies, textbooks, and other learning activities may use different vocabulary than the test. Literacy issues for any subject area tend to be tied to vocabulary and students' depth and extent of vocabulary (Marzano, 2004). Thus, the primary instructional remedy for most learning barriers is vocabulary development. In the analysis of instructional barriers to learning, the teacher's development of student comprehension of appropriate vocabulary for all subject areas must be considered.

Regardless of age, students are active participants in learning. However, their awareness of learning and their engagement in the process may vary. **Metacognition** and habits of mind require student-based awareness of their own style and preferences for how they learn. **Cognitive demand** requires that students develop persistence in the face of learning new or difficult material. Persistence in the face of difficulty or even after making an error is an important habit of mind for student development. Mentors and tutors may help students with developing persistence. Teachers also need to let students know that

errors and error analysis are an important form of learning, rather than an inescapable fatal sign of failure. Gloria Ladson-Billings (1995) noted that teachers of any race may adopt a culturally sensitive approach, and she borrowed Judith Kleinfeld's (1975) term, **warm demander**, to describe teachers who encourage learning while keeping the cognitive demand rigorous.

Unfortunately, many lessons are developed and delivered without attention to how students engage in learning. That is, lessons may focus solely on a topic and never offer students explicit tips for understanding the topic. Lessons with a mere focus on topical information also fail to support students' own awareness of how to find out more or practice application of that knowledge. Over years in school, some students are left with the impression that lessons and knowledge are completely teachers' responsibilities, and these pupils have no skills to use in enhancing their own learning.

Yet technology now offers students an alternative online means of learning. Students using technology outside the classroom may be disconnected from classroom learning. They, and some of their teachers, may perceive digital learning as a variety of colorful, fast action entertainment. Thus, even though students may like technology-based learning, they remain just as unaware of how to learn and how their learning strategies can be different in the class, whether reading a book or even staring at digital information. Teachers need to build in learning time for helping students to become more aware of how they learn with print, with a teacher, and with other media. Lessons can be developed to optimize technology's applications for learning diversely with diverse learners (Rose, Meyer, Strangman, & Rappolt, 2002).

Because each subject requires different kinds of thinking, students need to be taught how to learn math and how to learn science or social studies. They need to learn how to think like a writer, mathematician, or scientist. Teachers need to help students develop these strategies.

Teachers can help each other in analyzing the strength of lesson strategies for diverse learners, sharing common assessments that are both reliable and valid in measuring learning, as well as observing each other's instruction during classes. Peer feedback can help teachers investigate whether instruction is sufficient for all learners. School leaders also should provide monitoring of lessons, assessment strategies, and classroom observations to build collegial support for improving teaching that enhances learning. Students' strategies for learning are not intuitive, and teachers need to build lessons to raise students' awareness of their own learning. Once these instructional supports for learning are in place, then the final investigation about student failure can turn to students and their abilities and strategies for learning.

Learning Strategies

Students' learning approaches vary with their experiences and background (Marzano, 2004). Once the support system across all ecologies has been enhanced for student learning, then persistent student failure requires a focus on individual needs. Students' needs can include academic, emotional, or behavioral requirements. All of these needs require a team approach, which involves both family and school, and in many cases, needs to tap into the students' communities and its funds of knowledge.

Most schools now include teams of teachers, social workers, and school psychologists dedicated to diagnosis and intervention for students' persisting academic and social issues. Such teams consult with teachers of students who fail to thrive in the classroom. The purpose of these teams is to help teachers design student-specific interventions and then monitor how well the particular student responds to the interventions.

One of the key considerations about any intervention is to allow enough time to elapse to see the strength of the student's response. Any change may produce a worsening of the problem before a student can adjust to the new situation. That is, when changing any habit, enough time must elapse to allow a person to change his or her typical, habitual reaction. That time involves the person's developing an awareness of the reaction and then time for learning how to prevent it as well as learning an alternate habit or reaction. Depending on how long the habit has existed, the change time might take as much as three to seven times longer to break that cycle of trigger and reaction.

Interventions that take place in a very short term, less than a month, will not be successful because they do not provide enough time for a new habit to develop. Systematic monitoring of the student

response is necessary for the team to determine if the desired change is occurring or not. Several models exist that help monitor the chain of trigger and reaction and then intervention and response. Perhaps the most common monitoring process is a behavioral approach to monitoring. This model is referred to the A-B-A-B approach. The behavioral model includes a baseline (A) of how often the habit occurs without intervention. Sometimes the baseline involves the teacher or another observer, such as another school professional or a family member. To develop a student's awareness of his or her own learning strategies, sometimes the student also keeps a baseline and self-monitors. Then the intervention (B) is tried, and the monitoring with the intervention continues. Finally, another period of monitoring without the intervention (A) is completed. This process can be repeated as often as necessary to assess progress and success of the intervention.

Sometimes the issue involves a group of students, and intervention teams should include group assessments and observations. Unfortunately, most school teams fail to investigate the degree to which peer influence plays a role in an individual student's failure to thrive in the classroom. Peer feedback has an influence on a student's sense of confidence, both academically and socially. The degree to which peers influence an individual student's motivation and engagement in school increases with age and varies across individuals. That is, middle and high school students are more likely to be influenced by their peers' opinions than elementary students are. Students in upper elementary grades are more influenced by peers than are students in primary grades. The degree of influence of peers on any given student varies. Interventions in the degree of peer influence must be designed around the particular student's development and reactions to peers.

The team approach also must include the family and the student. Students who need to develop a deeper awareness of their own behavior and learning need support from at least two of their ecologies, the home and the school, although the community ecology can be an important component as well. Two-way communication between home and school may provide more information for the team's systematic monitoring process. Some parents can help students self-monitor and help them become more independent and self-aware about their own habits and how those habits help or hinder learning. Some parents may be able to help the team understand how certain student habits developed, and that history may give the team clues about how to change nonproductive habits. If families are unwilling or unable to help the team, then community members may be willing and able to help students with learning through mentoring and tutoring programs. The school's community audit can provide the team a list of resources that may enhance any interventions for any individual student.

A focus on individual students is the last step in an ecological approach to addressing barriers to learning and teaching. Once the community's capacity for supporting homes and families and their abilities to thrive has been established, then the ecologies of school and classroom must be investigated for appropriate supports for teaching and learning. School and classroom environments require policies that enhance teachers' and students' interactions. Teaching strategies also must be monitored for supporting development of students' awareness of their learning strategies and for maintaining rigor in students' productivity. After these ecologies have been investigated for capacity and strategies to support learning, then any given student's persisting academic or social delays can be best addressed through a team approach.

Resources for Overcoming Learning Barriers

When school leaders confront barriers to learning, they have multiple resources in their school ecologies. The key is to confront the barriers with an optimistic and ecologically sensitive, rather than a deficit, approach. An ecologically sensitive approach respects diversity by honoring differences in race, language, ethnicity, religion, and gender or sexual identity. Schools also are ecologically sensitive when they prevent and intervene in normalizing acts such as bullying or micro-aggressions. Effective school leaders focus on fixing negative elements in school and students' environments first. The most effective strategy is to prevent any barrier to learning at any level of the students' ecologies. The resources for student learning reside in all of the ecologies surrounding students and schools. As with the analysis of barriers to learning, the analysis of strategies starts with the

largest part of a student's ecology, the community, and then moves to the smallest part, the student.

Community Connections and Supports for Students and Schools

With a community audit, school leaders create a toolbox of resources that can offer positive learning experiences. All communities represent a social network that includes funds of knowledge through which each part of the community provides families a means of thriving. Different sectors of the community can include businesses, government, health, religion, and other social services. Among these sectors are funds of knowledge for the communities' households. These funds of knowledge may be as different as each community is from another.

For any given community, the community audit likely will have gaps. Urban communities may have fewer sector gaps than rural communities may, but even with gaps, rural communities may be more tightly focused on the school as a social or sporting event center in their communities. Schools need to know where help resides for their students in any kind of community because schools cannot provide all the services and support that every child may need. On the other hand, as schools are often a location for community events, schools also can be a location where other agencies can deliver services directly to students and their families. In some regions, the school is a community center. In other places, a school may need to develop a reputation as a safe place and earn its standing as an authentic center of the community.

Schools need to reach out into their students' communities to become a part of the social network of support. Teachers and other school personnel need to develop relationships with families and neighbors. They do so when they become visible in locations outside of school such as grocery stores, gas stations, and other places where students and their families frequent. School personnel also become more visible if partnering with churches and other social groups as a place to host parent-teacher meetings or student performances or other school events. When schools become a part of the community, they can draw on community leaders, groups, businesses, agencies, and organizations for supporting students. Community members can work as individual or group volunteers focused on providing the necessary support for learning from food, shelter, health, and recreation to individual mentoring or tutoring. Communities, whether urban or rural, have different assets that students need, and a school's community audit can help school leaders identify and use assets for any learning need.

Learning-Friendly Policies and Rules

Schools must be learner-, family-, and community-friendly. Many schools have rigid policies and rules that may detract from a positive learning environment. Some of these rules conflict with the students' home rules or cultures.

School leaders need to take a preventative stance by vetting the rules for how they might be racist, sexist, or even narrowly normative. Some teachers' approaches to classroom rules can set up and escalate conflicts with students instead of building trust and enhancing the learning environment. School leaders can regularly review classroom rules to help teachers establish optimum learning time and avoid power struggles with students.

School leaders can use school discipline records to monitor the effects of school rules on students. School leaders should investigate which students are referred most often for breaking such rules and which teachers make the referrals. In many schools, males are referred most often for breaking rules, and Black males have a particularly high rate of discipline referrals. Emerging research on working with male students shows ways that students can engage in learning and avoid discipline referrals where the classroom is structured for their needs. In any adjustment for student differences, individual needs offer better clues about changing the rules or environment than does a one-size-fits-all approach. That is, just because some male students need more physical activity doesn't mean that all males will share that preference or need. Instead, teachers need a variety of strategies that encourage individual and group work. Teachers are more likely to be effective with culturally sensitive and culturally responsive pedagogy. When students are engaged in a learning environment that suits their learning, they have fewer referrals for disciplinary infractions.

School leaders need to study how school and classroom rules affect learning and to what extent they can be changed to be more educational. School leaders need to see that rules do not disintegrate into a time-out-of-the-classroom routine. To address the value of rules for promoting student learning, school leaders need the insights of teachers, students, and community members.

Tools and Strategies for Increasing the Quality of Instruction

The nature of good instruction has been long investigated and well studied. Measures of learning must be well constructed, reliable, and valid indicators of learning and student progress. Measures of effective teaching also must be varied and must be used reliably in conjunction with professional learning. Teachers and school leaders must work as colleagues in monitoring the quality of instruction to ensure that all students have opportunities to learn. Students also need to be taught how to be aware of and monitor their own learning and how to develop strategies appropriate to each subject area.

Enabling and Empowering Student Learning

When individual students persistently struggle, then students need individual support. Intervention teams, which provide collaboration in monitoring change in instruction with a goal for change in learning, should include professionals as well as the student and his or her family. Community members also may provide support for ongoing strategies to help students overcome learning barriers.

Key Chapter Terms

Ableism: A deficit approach to diversity. Ableism promotes the belief that normal is a narrow range of acceptable behaviors or development.

Cognitive demand: Indicates the level of difficulty of learning a concept or performing a skill. The higher the cognitive demand is, the more difficult the standard or requirements.

Cognitive developmental differences: Refers to individuals' different rates of brain development. Some of the differences in rates are temporary and idiosyncratic to each person's awareness. Other differences may have physical, medical, or environmental causes.

For the majority of students, differences in background, pre- and out-of-school experiences affect their rates of learning. Teachers must be able to address the diversity of learning and cognitive development among the students in their classrooms. School leaders must support teachers in addressing these developmental differences.

Community engagement: From Joyce Epstein's (Epstein et al., 2011) model, the term refers to a variety of partnerships that schools may have with different sectors of the community. For example, public health agencies may have health fairs on school grounds as well as provide the state-required inoculations for students. Alternatively, a business may provide equipment for labs and perhaps guest speakers on curriculum topics. Volunteering may overlap with this form of involvement as well.

Cyberbullying: Includes a form of verbal and even visual/auditory abuse that takes place through a variety of digital platforms and social media. The participants include the same players as in schoolyard bullying, but the actions are often not during school hours and expand the school campus to cell phones and the World Wide Web. Given the very open nature of the web, additional bullies who have nothing to do with the school, and often are not even school-age, can join in the abuse. The legal role of school personnel in preventing and addressing this kind of abuse of their students is still evolving.

Decision making: Among the six types of involvement, refers to the process of determining school rules and practices. Officially, nearly every school system is run by a board, which appoints the superintendent. Most of these boards are elected or appointed and represent the larger public that funds the schools. In terms of school-level involvement, some schools have required parent advisory or decision-making groups; others set up their own because when parents participate in the decisions, their children are more likely to succeed.

Deficit model: Sometimes deficit thinking, refers to a perception that if something is different, then it is not normal, and if it is not normal, then it is a problem. The framing of a student's behavior or cognitive development as a problem often leads to removal from classrooms and thus limited access to learning.

When students are identified as a problem, then some of their funds of knowledge might be ignored as a group of professionals may intimidate or ignore the students' parents, families, and communities.

Funds of knowledge: A term that recognizes the shared heritage and wisdom of a group's culture and history. Each cultural group shares ideas through stories, songs, and other means of transmission about how a family can thrive. The definition of the family structure comes from the culture's funds of knowledge. For some cultures, the family depends on generations of women who help each other. The women may pass on their advice and help with short sayings or quiet actions, depending on the traditions of their culture. In other cultures, a male patriarch makes major decisions for generations of children, grandchildren, even great-grandchildren. School personnel who understand and respect these funds of knowledge can use them to help with students' learning.

Gendered roles: Those roles that are socially determined to be male or female. School statistics still show that teaching young children appears to be a female role. Gendered roles create a set of norms that imply that one sex may have more power than the other. In addition, in schools, that power differential is often demonstrated by the fact that men are principals and women are teachers. These social norms, however inadvertently, may teach students to expect a narrow range of options for themselves. Further, especially in middle and high schools, students who are becoming more aware of their sexual identity may feel a stigma based on the strong messages of what is normal for males and females. School personnel need to be aware that gender and sexual identity may cause students to suffer bullying and fear based on the normalized environment of schools.

Habits of mind: A phrase from the work of progressive educator John Dewey. Among the habits necessary for success in and beyond school are the following five: (a) awareness of one's own learning strategies; (b) persistence; (c) dependability; (d) responsibility; and (e) resilience.

Metacognition: Refers to awareness of one's own approach to learning. Students who are aware of how they learn generally achieve more. Conversely, students who believe that they cannot learn often are not aware of how they do learn. If they are not aware of their learning, students who believe they cannot learn often fail.

Micro-aggression: Generally, refers to a comment that on the surface may seem normal, but can be interpreted as disrespectful. So-called normal remarks are normal from one perspective, but not necessarily appropriate for the diversity found in public spaces, such as schools in the United States or globally.

Parenting: One of Joyce Epstein's six forms of school and community involvement. Parenting refers to primary care for the student, including meals, clothing, hygiene, and shelter. Many well-meaning parents may not have the resources for one or all of these caregiving responsibilities, and school personnel may be the first responders in identifying these needs.

Racism: Refers to social stigma and segregation of people based on the color of their skin or their ethnic or national origins. For some communities, racism comes from the cultural heritage of the region. In schools, racism can be very subtle but may underlie such phenomena as the disproportionately high rates of school discipline among African American males; disproportionate representation of African American males in special education, particularly for emotional and behavioral disorders; and the underrepresentation of African American and Hispanic students in honors and Advanced Placement classes. Racism can appear among school staff, where more minorities provide support services such as teacher aides, school meal workers, or facilities service workers than appear among the professional teaching staff. Racism can also manifest itself in social patterns within the school, such as voluntary segregation when students and staff members of different races do not socialize with one another during meals or breaks. If school staff members are segregated, simply integrating the students will not eliminate racism. School personnel have a responsibility to identify and address racism and its effects on students.

Social/moral panic: Refers to a crowd phenomenon where information about a crime or disaster causes widespread concern that violence and tragedy is very close to home. In school shootings, the widespread identification with victims and their families can cause immediate action and precautions in locales far from the event and well after the event has been resolved.

Social-emotional development: A term that references how people learn to make friends, work in groups, and cope with their feelings in socially appropriate ways. Businesses refer to these kinds of good citizenship behaviors as soft skills. Most municipalities and employers want students to graduate from school with these skills. School personnel try to develop these behaviors among students through classroom management and schoolwide discipline programs.

Support for learning at home: In Joyce Epstein's model, extends the parenting role to support for students' cognitive development. These activities can range from providing space and time for a student to concentrate on homework and helping check that the work is done to arranging trips or other learning experiences outside of school time. These outside school activities can include visits to museums, local events, sightseeing, and the opportunity to learn funds of knowledge from the culture and community. These parents may provide opportunities for their children to visit and learn about other cultures as well.

Two-way communication: Refers to Joyce Epstein's and associates' expansion of schools' information dissemination and advertising of school events to a stronger relationship where parents and families keep schools informed of their needs and events. Most families require schools to reach out to them, and school personnel will need to develop strategies to encourage family communication. Some families may be reluctant to approach school officials, even teachers, and that means school personnel need to make sure that they are welcoming and approachable. Two-way communication is fundamental to student success.

Volunteering: The participation in school activities by adults in the community who are not school personnel. Traditionally, students' mothers provided support, from cookies to art supplies, for classroom activities. That traditional support also included school fund-raising by parent-teacher groups and club supporters. Today, volunteering with schools has spread to tutoring and mentoring programs for the students. Additionally, out-of-school time includes volunteers to help with homework or to provide meals when school is not in session.

Warm demander: A teacher who remains encouraging while still setting a high standard for learning and achievement. The teacher has the students' trust and expresses a belief that the students will be successful even though the work requires a higher level of cognitive engagement.

References

Beratan, G. D. (2006). Institutionalizing inequity: Ableism, racism and IDEA 2004. *Disability Studies Quarterly, 26*(2), 3.

Bronfenbrenner, U. (1979). *The ecology of human development: Experiments by nature and design.* Cambridge, MA: Harvard University Press.

Dewey, J. (1938). *Experience and education.* New York, NY: Collier.

Dyson, J. L. (1990). The effect of family violence on children's academic performance and behavior. *Journal of the National Medical Association, 82*(1), 17–22.

Epstein, J. L., Galindo, C. L., & Sheldon, S. B. (2011). Levels of leadership effects of district and school leaders on the quality of school programs of family and community involvement. *Educational Administration Quarterly, 47*(3), 462–495.

González, N., Moll, L. C., & Amanti, C. (Eds.). (2005). *Funds of knowledge: Theorizing practices in households, communities and classrooms.* Mahwah, NJ: Erlbaum.

Hehir, T. (2002). Eliminating ableism in education. *Harvard Educational Review, 72*(1), 1–33.

Kleinfeld, J. (1975). Effective teachers of Eskimo and Indian students. *School Review, 83,* 301–344.

Ladson-Billings, G. (1995). Toward a theory of culturally relevant pedagogy. *American Educational Research Journal, 32*(3), 465–491.

Marzano, R. J. (2004). *Building background knowledge for academic achievement: Research on what works in schools.* Alexandria, VA: ASCD.

Moll, L. C. (1992). Bilingual classroom studies and community analysis: Some recent trends. *Educational Researcher, 21*(2), 20–24. doi:10.3102/0013189X021002020

Pierce, C. M. (1970). Offensive mechanisms: The vehicle for micro-aggression. In F. B. Barbour (Ed.), *The Black 70s* (pp. 265–282). Boston, MA: Porter Sargent.

Rose, D. H., Meyer, A., Strangman, N., & Rappolt, G. (2002). *Teaching every student in the digital age: Universal Design for Learning.* Alexandria, VA: ASCD.

Stefkovich, J. A. (2006). *Best interests of the student: Applying ethical constructs to legal cases in education.* Mahwah, NJ: Erlbaum.

Stiggins, R. J. (2002.) Assessment crisis: The absence of assessment *FOR* learning. *Phi Delta Kappan, 83*(10), 758–765.

Tomlinson, C. A., & Imbeau, M. B. (2010). *Leading and managing a differentiated classroom.* Alexandria, VA: ASCD.

Further Readings

Brookhart, S. M. (2013). *How to create and use rubrics for formative assessment and grading.* Alexandria, VA: ASCD.

This book is a teacher-friendly volume that explains how to set up grading strategies that accommodate developmental differences.

Dana, N. F., Thomas, C. M., & Boynton, S. S. (2011). *Inquiry: A districtwide approach to staff and student learning.* Thousand Oaks, CA: Corwin.

The purpose of this book is to provide action-oriented, evidence-based strategies for schools to use in increasing the cognitive development of both students and their teachers.

Davies, A., Herbst, S., & Reynolds, B. P. (2012). *Transforming schools and systems using assessment: A practical guide.* Courtenay, Canada: Connections.

This guide offers a systemic strategy for using and interpreting test data to make instructional decisions to support diverse learners.

Dean, C. B., Hubbell, E. R., Pitler, H., & Stone, B. J. (2012). *Classroom instruction that works: Research-based strategies for increasing student achievement* (2nd ed.). Alexandria, VA: ASCD.

The second edition of the popular research-based instructional strategies guide provides specific information to teachers about how to apply diverse strategies to support learners.

Iddings, A. C. D., Combs, M. C., & Moll, L. (2012). In the arid zone: Drying out educational resources for English language learners through policy and practice. *Urban Education, 47*(2), 495–514.

This journal article explains a variety of important concepts useful in differentiating the classroom environment to support students whose first language is not English.

Rose, D. H., Meyer, A., Strangman, N., & Rappolt, G. (2002). *Teaching every student in the digital age: Universal design for learning.* Alexandria, VA: ASCD.

The authors of this book explain how to design lessons that accommodate every learner's needs.

Tomlinson, C. A., & Imbeau, M. B. (2010). *Leading and managing a differentiated classroom.* Alexandria, VA: ASCD.

The first author of this popular book for teachers has a solid reputation built on creating classroom environments, lessons, and assessments that support the needs of each and every student.

6

RESPONSE TO INTERVENTION AND ITS IMPACT ON CLASSROOM PERFORMANCE

ALICIA VALERO-KERRICK

California State University, Sacramento

Response to intervention (RTI) is an innovative service delivery model designed to help all students succeed academically. RTI is a tiered intervention framework where students are provided with *research-based instruction* and **evidence-based interventions** that vary in duration and intensity based on individual student needs. RTI is used for prevention, intervention, and determination of a learning disability (LD). Currently, all 50 states allow RTI as a method for learning disability identification. RTI addresses long-standing concerns with educating students with learning challenges, including English language learners (ELLs), students from impoverished backgrounds, and students with learning disabilities. Since its inception in 2003, RTI has changed the way that schools respond to student instruction, assessment, and data collection.

Studies show that there is no universal RTI implementation framework as each school has flexibility in how it specifies its RTI system and then provides professional development to its staff (Barnes & Harlacher, 2008; Fuchs, Fuchs, & Compton, 2012). RTI has expanded the role of school administrators, generalists (i.e., general education teachers) and specialists (e.g., special education teachers, reading specialists, speech and language pathologists, and school psychologists). Recent studies suggest that RTI is a promising practice, but more research is needed to determine its impact on classroom performance (Al Otaiba & Torgesen, 2007; Hughes & Dexter, 2011; Vaughn & Fletcher, 2012). Researchers have proposed solutions to address some of the challenges of utilizing the RTI model to improve instruction and intervention (Denton, 2012; Fuchs et al., 2012; Vaughn & Fletcher, 2012). RTI has brought about systemic reform within the educational system, and its future greatly depends on effective leadership, collaboration, and commitment among school personnel.

RTI and Systemic Reform

Lynn Fuchs and Sharon Vaughn (2012) state that "RTI has become a major force in education reform" (p. 195). RTI holds implications for curriculum, assessment, instruction, and professional development. The reform of education continues as a major focus of federal legislation. Schools, districts, and states are making systemic changes to comply with the provisions and requirements of the No Child Left Behind (NCLB) Act of 2001 and the **Individuals with Disabilities Education Improvement Act (IDEA) of 2004.** NCLB requires states to develop curriculum standards for K-12 that translate into high-quality instruction in general education classrooms.

States must administer annual, state-standards assessments to 95% of students in reading and math for Grades 3 to 8 and once during high school. With the alignment of NCLB and IDEA, students with special needs are expected to achieve the same learning outcomes as their typically developing peers but with adaptations and accommodations to the curriculum.

RTI emerged as a response to the dissatisfaction with traditional approaches to identify and serve students with learning disabilities—the largest population of students served in special education. Traditionally, schools have relied upon an IQ and academic achievement **discrepancy formula** to determine special education eligibility under a specific learning disability. The Response to Intervention Action Network cites concerns over the need to prevent the overidentification of students with learning disabilities, overrepresentation of minorities in special education, reliability issues surrounding **norm-referenced tests**, and variability of identification rates across both states and districts. IDEA 2004 states that a student cannot be diagnosed with a learning disability as a result of poor reading instruction. Moreover, a student cannot be learning disabled if the determining factor in reading delay is a variation in language, culture, or race.

Under IDEA, schools can use 15% of their special education money to implement general education interventions. Schools now use RTI to provide intervention services earlier to students who are struggling instead of continuing the **wait-to-fail model** (Fuchs & Fuchs, 2006, p. 96). According to the National Research Center on Learning Disabilities (NRCLD) (2003), the discrepancy formula relegated schools to wait until the third grade or later before students could receive intensive intervention. RTI expands the identification procedure to include RTI as part of the determination process for special education placement. This authorization is noted in the following provision of IDEA 2004:

> Local education agencies (LEAs) may use a student's response to scientifically based instruction as part of the evaluation process; and (b) when identifying a disability. LEAs shall not be required to take into consideration whether a child has a severe discrepancy between achievement and intellectual ability. [P.L. 108–446, 614(b)(6)(A)]

NCLB and IDEA emphasize the use of evidence-based instruction and intervention for all students. The rise in poverty and poor test scores in some school districts have fueled reform measures. When a school district's composite test score is low, it is often the impetus that drives the district's strategic plan to raise student performance levels in English and math. Education reform efforts need to move beyond simply looking at evidence-based interventions to examining the entire system to promote change and sustainability (Ervin, Schaughency, Goodman, McGlinchey, & Matthews, 2006). Ruth A. Ervin and colleagues view each school as an evolving system with diverse needs and varying levels of readiness for schoolwide innovations. Ervin and colleagues (2006) contend that many school reform efforts fail, but there are three factors that sustain evidence-based interventions: staff commitment, administrator support, and facilitators who promote practice mastery. These factors are critical within the RTI framework. The next section presents the principles and essential components of RTI.

Components of Response to Intervention Programs

Aaron Barnes and Jason Harlacher (2008) contend that practitioners need to understand both the principles behind why RTI is needed as well as the components of what RTI looks like. They found that while there is variation in how the components are implemented across schools, the principles of RTI do not change. Following are the principles that they found were consistent across research studies:

- A proactive and preventative approach to address the needs of all students;
- An instructional match between student skills, curriculum, and instruction;
- A problem-solving orientation and data-based decision making;
- Use of effective practices that are evidence based; and
- A systems-level approach emphasizing the entire school as opposed to a single student or classroom. (p. 419)

The essential components of RTI programs include multitiered approach, research-based instruction, **universal screening**, evidence-based intervention, and progress monitoring. These components can vary in execution at school and district levels.

A Multitiered Model

One of the components of the RTI prevention system is a multitiered intervention approach. Some schools use from two tiers to four or more tiers. The three-tiered model is most commonly used and will be described here. Tier 1 (i.e., primary prevention) is research-based core reading instruction where universal screening of all students is used to determine proficiency levels and identify students at risk for reading problems. RTI implementation across schools in the United States has focused on reading intervention in the primary grades. However, more schools are beginning to address math and behavior problems as part of primary prevention. Tier 2 (i.e., secondary intervention or secondary prevention) incorporates supplemental empirically validated instruction for students who are not making adequate academic progress in Tier 1. Students receive evidence-based intervention in small groups to address specific skill development while they continue Tier 1 core instruction. Tier 3 (i.e., tertiary intervention or tertiary prevention) provides students who have not responded to Tier 1 interventions with more intensive and sustained intervention (Fletcher & Vaughn, 2009). Some RTI prevention systems move to a formal evaluation for learning disability classification for students at Tier 3.

Research-Based Reading Instruction

Under NCLB, the Reading First initiative was implemented to ensure that schools use **research-based reading instruction** to get all students to read by the end of third grade. The Reading First initiative emerged as a response to the National Reading Panel report (National Institute of Child Health and Human Development, 2000) that highlighted five essential components of effective reading instruction: phonemic awareness, phonics, fluency, vocabulary, and comprehension. All students must receive a high-quality core instructional program based on these five components of reading. The reading programs are packaged commercially to schools and require systematic and explicit instruction of skills and concepts in a hierarchical order. This provides the foundation

for effective instruction at Tier 1 and is based on the principle that a proactive and preventative approach is necessary to address the needs of all students. Typically, the goal is that 80% of students will require only the core reading program to meet grade-level expectations (Vaughn & Fletcher, 2012).

Universal Screening

Universal screening is administered to assess the effectiveness of the curriculum and instruction, as well as to address academic problems in a timely manner. RTI emphasizes that schools administer universal screenings to all children to identify those who are at risk for poor reading performance. There is variation in the number of screenings administered, ranging from one screening to three screenings throughout the school year. Some school administrators have also moved to screen children in the areas of math and behavior that were not originally part of RTI. Benchmarks are set at the school, district, or state level to ensure that student outcomes or goals for a particular domain are achieved during the course of the year. **Curriculum-based measurement** (CBM) (Fuchs & Fuchs, 2006; Stecker, Fuchs, & Fuchs, 2005) screenings are used as they are closely aligned with classroom instruction because they are designed to measure progress in basic skill areas of reading, math, and written language.

Examples of research-based standardized measures that schools use to screen students include the Dynamic Indicators of Basic Early Literacy Skills and the Developmental Reading Assessment. The DIBELS are short fluency measures used to monitor development of early literacy and early reading skills. The measures assess phonological awareness, the alphabetic principle, fluency with connected text, vocabulary, and comprehension. The DRA is a **formative assessment** that allows teachers to observe, record, and evaluate student reading performance over time. The DRA includes an individual instructional plan to increase reading proficiency. These benchmark-based screening assessments should provide teachers with information so that they can differentiate instruction to improve student achievement. The International Reading Association and the National Council of Teachers of English (IRA-NCTE, 2009) indicate that assessment should serve the purpose of improving teaching and learning.

Evidence-Based Intervention

Evidence-based intervention refers to the use of scientific, empirically based intervention directed at students who are at risk for learning problems based on universal screening. Small-group instruction offered within Tier 2 emerges from experimental studies validating its efficacy. An instructional match between student skills, curriculum, and instruction is critical. At the secondary prevention level, schools may use the standard protocol model to address reading difficulties. Douglas Fuchs and Lynn S. Fuchs (2007) indicate that standardized treatment protocols rely on small-group tutoring to ensure mastery for most students. These tutoring protocols are scripted and "do not rely on local professionals, who may have uneven training and background in instructional design" (Fuchs, Fuchs, & Zumeta, 2008, p. 122).

Sharon Vaughn and Greg Roberts (2007) provide some guidelines for determining the level of intervention intensity for students at Tier 2 and Tier 3. At Tier 2, instructional intervention is designed as a supplement to core instruction. Students can participate in instructional blocks at each grade level. Students receive instruction in small groups of four or five students based on ability level, three to five times weekly for 20 to 30 minutes per day. Ongoing assessment is recommended twice a month on the target skill identified for intervention. The interventionists can include the classroom teacher, reading specialist, or other trained personnel. Tier 3 intervention is determined when students have not responded well to Tier 1 and Tier 2 instruction. Instruction at the tertiary level is delivered by a reading specialist or special education teacher, either individually or in small groups of two to three students. The emphasis is on explicit and systematic instruction that is sustained and intensive. Tier 3 students are viewed as the most likely candidates for special education.

Progress Monitoring

Progress monitoring is a scientifically based practice used to generate data about children's short-term academic progress and to evaluate the effectiveness of instruction. Typically, schools screen an entire class three times a year to monitor student performance. Progress monitoring increases once a student has been identified by screening measures as at risk for achievement delay. One question that a school

must answer is how frequently progress monitoring should take place for an individual student. Fuchs and Fuchs (2006) recommend that students designated at risk be monitored weekly within a time frame of 8 to 10 weeks during Tier 1 core instruction using curriculum-based measurement. The National Center on Student Progress Monitoring (MPACT, 2013) indicates that when progress monitoring is implemented well it has potential benefits:

- Accelerated learning because students are receiving more appropriate instruction
- More informed instructional decisions
- Documentation of student progress for accountability purposes
- More efficient communication with families and other professionals about students' progress
- Higher expectations for students by teachers
- Fewer special education referrals

RTI incorporates a problem-solving orientation and data-based decision making. Data-based decision making is central at all levels of RTI implementation and instruction. School personnel participate in grade-level teams or multidisciplinary teams to work collaboratively to analyze student data and make decisions about the intervention process. The data collected during screening and progress monitoring is used to make decisions about student learning and instruction. School personnel use data to decide when students will move from one tier to another or when a student will be evaluated for special education.

Expanded Roles in RTI

As schools and school districts implement RTI programs, new and changing roles are emerging for school administrators, general education teachers, and specialists, such as special educators, school psychologists, and speech and language pathologists. RTI presents more opportunities for collaborative teaming among school personnel to help improve students' academic skills and behavior. Successful implementation of RTI programs requires strong leadership at all levels of school administration. The RTI approach also requires that general education teachers and specialists collaborate to engage in assessment and intervention activities to address individual student needs. This section describes how the roles of school personnel have changed and expanded within the RTI framework.

The Role of School Administrators

School administrators at every level provide leadership in the planning, implementation, and evaluation of the RTI service delivery model. The strong focus on effective classroom teaching has become central to the role of school administrators. Principals, for example, are spending more time as instructional leaders engaging staff in early literacy development and instruction. School administrators have the role of implementing educational reform efforts that require the need to structure professional development to maximize resources. School districts have moved from separate professional development based on categorical programs to an integrative system of training that underscores both the principles and components of RTI to ensure fidelity in program implementation. Vaughn and Roberts (2007) indicate that leaders should support prevention-oriented practices and ongoing professional development to assure personnel is knowledgeable about effective interventions.

Part of the evaluation process of the RTI model requires that principals determine the effectiveness of the RTI delivery model in reducing the number of students referred for special education. When the RTI program simply delays the referral of students for formalized testing, the effectiveness of the model needs to be addressed. This requires an emphasis on effective communication and collaboration among school administrators, generalists, and specialists.

The Role of General Education Teachers

The RTI model places high expectations for general education teachers who have seen an expansion of their role within the classroom. Teachers are expected to be trained in various reading and behavior interventions. RTI has increased the role of teachers as interventionists in that now they need to focus more time on making accommodations and differentiating instruction for diverse learners. Because the majority of students identified for special education have learning disabilities, teachers require foundational knowledge and understanding of atypical development and learning. Teachers also have to demonstrate competency in the use of screening and assessment tools, data collection, and decision making. For example, general education teachers use data collection to make informed decisions that guide instruction for students designated at risk for reading, math, or behavior problems. Teachers have a significant role in providing supplemental instruction and monitoring progress to ensure that students are reading by the third grade. One of the positive consequences of RTI is the availability of supports to allow teachers to carry out their role. General education teachers work collaboratively with specialists to improve educational and behavioral outcomes of students.

The Role of Specialists

Special Education Teachers

The RTI approach has afforded many opportunities for special education teachers to take leadership roles and work collaboratively with generalists and with students in various settings. Prior to RTI, special education teachers worked specifically with students identified with a disability. Today, special educators are increasingly called on to provide intervention to students without special needs. Special education teachers have expertise in teaching strategies that can enhance learning of all students. According to William Bender (2009), special educators have developed the skills required for RTI that include individual, curriculum-based measurement for progress monitoring and individualized tutoring. These interventions, along with high-quality, effective instruction in the classroom, can reduce the number of students identified as learning disabled.

Speech and Language Pathologists

Speech and language pathologists have had the traditional role of intervention within the special education program but will need to expand that role to include prevention and identification of at-risk students in general education. This requires consultation and collaboration with general education teachers, decreasing the time spent on a traditional **pullout program** where students are removed from the general education classroom to receive intervention.

Ehren, Montgomery, Rudebusch, and Whitmore (n.d.) identify the contributions that speech and language pathologists can make within the RTI model:

- Explain the role that language plays in curriculum, assessment, and instruction, as a basis for appropriate program design.
- Explain the interconnection between spoken and written language.
- Identify and analyze existing literature on scientifically based literacy assessment and intervention approaches.
- Assist in the selection of screening measures.
- Help identify systemic patterns of student need with respect to language skills.
- Assist in the selection of scientifically based literacy intervention.
- Plan for and conduct professional development on the language basis of literacy and learning.
- Interpret a school's progress in meeting the intervention needs of its students.

Speech and language pathologists have expertise in the development of speech and language skills that can be used to support students in general education and those who move on to special education.

School Psychologists

Similar to speech and language pathologists, school psychologists are closely connected to special education programs. School psychologists have traditionally spent the majority of their time conducting psychological and educational evaluations to determine special education eligibility. The RTI framework can reallocate more time for school psychologists to address academic and mental health concerns early in primary prevention to reduce time spent on special education evaluations. Direct contact with students has traditionally involved short-term counseling and behavioral interventions. According to the National Association of School Psychologists (NASP, 2010), RTI has created new opportunities for school psychologists to work directly with generalists and students:

- Consulting with teachers and parents regarding early intervention activities in the classroom and at home
- Observing students in the instructional environment in order to help identify appropriate intervention strategies, to identify barriers to intervention, and to collect response to intervention data

- Evaluating the student's cognitive functioning
- Determining the most useful procedures to address referral concerns and the needs of the individual student
- Evaluating the student's relevant academic, behavioral, and mental health functioning
- Working with team members and service providers to set realistic goals, design appropriate instructional strategies and progress-monitoring procedures, and periodically evaluate student progress for those receiving special education services, using RTI and other data

School psychologists have knowledge in data collection strategies, instruction, behavior support, and behavioral assessment that can be used at all levels of RTI. This knowledge base can also support programs for preschool children. Robin Hojnoski and Kristen Missall (2006) advocate for a contemporary model of school psychology that expands the role of the school psychologist to include a collaborative effort with early education to emphasize a prevention-oriented approach that prepares all children for school readiness.

RTI and English Language Learners

IDEA 2004 made specific recommendations for the assessment and instruction of students with limited English proficiency. These recommendations speak to the need to take into account the experiences and cultural background of students, as well as their English language proficiency. NCLB requires that all students be taught by highly qualified teachers. However, as Shernaz B. Garcia and Alba A. Ortiz (2006) report, many students from culturally and linguistically diverse backgrounds are "being educated in low-income and urban schools staffed with teachers who are relatively inexperienced with culturally and linguistically diverse learners, teaching out-of-field, and/or on emergency certification plans" (p. 65). Debra Kamps and colleagues (2007) found that in urban schools there are limited resources available to address both language and literacy instruction for ELLs. Kenji Hakuta (2011) argues that ELLs have the challenge of learning a new language while mastering academic content.

Robert Rueda and Michelle P. Windmueller (2006) contend that it is important to look at multiple-level approaches to address educational intervention and remediation. The focus on intervention with students in special education with learning disabilities has primarily centered on the cognitive framework. It is critical to examine the diverse sociocultural context of schools that serve children. Daniel J. Losen and Gary Orfield (2002) affirm that children with special needs from racial minorities and children with special needs who are ELLs often receive inadequate special education services, have limited access to a high-quality curriculum and high-quality instruction, and are often isolated from their peers who are non-disabled. These studies provide a context in which to examine an RTI intervention service delivery model for culturally and linguistically diverse students.

RTI emphasizes the need to support struggling learners early to reduce inappropriate special education referrals. One of the concerns is that educators lack the pedagogical knowledge and skills to determine if an English language learner may be struggling to read due to a learning disability or second-language issues. It is often difficult to make eligibility decisions about ELLs. Oftentimes, schools make the determination to wait until a child has acquired English proficiency before beginning the process of early intervention. The decision to wait places many ELLs at a disadvantage since they would benefit from research-based interventions (Klingner, Artiles, & Mendez Barletta, 2006).

Claudia Rinaldi and Jennifer Samson (2008) have proposed a three-tiered RTI model to address the needs of ELLs. At Tier 1, universal screening of all students entails curriculum-based measurement where information on oral language proficiency and **academic language proficiency** is collected by examining a student's level of interpersonal English language proficiency and native language proficiency. Academic language includes comprehension and vocabulary development that can be assessed in the native language and compared to English. It is important to address any recommendations made by bilingual education personnel. Progress monitoring of at-risk ELLs should include informal measures. At Tier 2, students receive small-group tutoring and continued progress monitoring. Once instruction is delivered, the ELL's rate of progress and level of English language proficiency are measured. Additionally, informal measures are used to collect data and track academic language proficiency.

Students who have not responded to secondary-tiered intervention are referred for a special education evaluation to determine the need for more intensive tertiary-tiered intervention.

Garcia and Ortiz (2006) suggest that an important element of preventing school achievement and failure for ELLs is for educators to have the expectation that all students can learn. This is one of the underlying principles of RTI discussed earlier. Klinger and colleagues (2006) state that experts in second-language acquisition should form part of collaborative teams to support students' learning needs and help implement research-based interventions.

RTI in Middle and High School

The principles and the essential components of RTI are not as well understood by school personnel within secondary (middle and high school) levels. Few research studies have examined the implementation of RTI at the secondary level. Bender (2009) states that wide variation between elementary and secondary schools makes it more challenging to implement RTI at the secondary level. Secondary schools deliver a departmentalized curriculum in which students have various classes and teachers focus on a single subject area. Secondary teachers instruct a significantly higher number of students than elementary teachers, giving them less knowledge of individual students. Teachers express concerns that, when time is spent on teaching students to read, it takes time away from delivering content material. An additional concern is that secondary teachers may not have the training to provide intensive remediation.

Sharon Vaughn and Jack Fletcher (2012) conducted a multiyear study with secondary (i.e., middle school) students, Grades 6 to 8, with reading difficulties. They found that the multitiered approach to instruction and intervention was different as compared to its implementation in elementary schools. Secondary students do not need to progress through tiers but can progress to less or more intensive interventions based on their current performance and instructional needs rather than responsiveness to intervention. Furthermore, documentation of less intensive interventions are not required with secondary students with the lowest scores since "the best predictor of low RTI in Year 3 of treatment is very low reading achievement at the beginning of Year 1" (p. 252). These students can move directly into intensive remediation.

RTI Impact on Classroom Performance

Reviews and meta-analyses provide documentation of the role of RTI in improving classroom performance (Al Otaiba & Torgesen, 2007; Denton, 2012; Hughes & Dexter, 2011; Vaughn & Fletcher, 2012). This research suggests that RTI has led to decreases in special education referrals and increases in reading performance. However, experimental and quasi-experimental research is still needed to increase validation of RTI.

Reduction in Special Education Referrals

The Data Accountability Center (U.S. Department of Education, 2011) states that since 2004 there has been a 3.9% drop in the number of students aged 6 to 21 who receive special education services and a 12.4% drop in the number of students identified as having a specific learning disability. Stephanie Al Otaiba and Joseph K. Torgesen (2007) indicate that some RTI programs have reduced the number of students with significant difficulty learning to read to 1% to 2% of the population. This data shows that RTI may be increasing the options within general education to support underachieving students while at the same time it is decreasing the number of students moving into special education.

Reading Outcomes

Carolyn Denton (2012) reviewed the research on RTI programs and reading difficulties in primary grades and found that supplemental interventions at Tiers 2 and 3 are most effective when provided in the early grades (i.e., kindergarten to first grade). This underscores the importance of early intervention in preventing serious reading problems. For example, a student with a decoding problem has decreased opportunities to read text and this may evolve into a learning disability "characterized by low fluency, poor vocabulary, and limited world knowledge, all contributing to impaired reading comprehension" (p. 233).

While positive effects are seen with students in second through fifth grades, reading difficulties are more challenging to remediate. In a review of the research, Vaughn and Fletcher (2012) found that only moderate reading gains and limited effects are noted for secondary level students with very low reading achievement. They contend that a better understanding is needed of "the instructional demands of secondary students with persistent reading disabilities" (p. 253).

In a review of field studies of RTI programs, Charles Hughes and Douglas D. Dexter (2011) report on findings on the impact on classroom performance. The first finding is that all of the studies reported improvement in academic achievement of at-risk students as a result of RTI programs. The second finding indicates that improvements in academic skills are relegated to early reading skills for students in elementary school. The third finding shows that referral and placement rates for special education have remained constant, with some studies showing decreases.

Kamps and colleagues (2007) reported that ELLs who participated in a three-tiered RTI process showed significantly more academic growth in early literacy skills than students receiving only English as a second-language (ESL) instruction. Students who participated in the RTI process received evidence-based secondary-tier interventions that included small-group tutoring.

Overall, studies of multitiered interventions reveal that students who participate in treatment groups where a standard protocol reading intervention is administered, individually or in small groups, perform better on measures of reading. These studies also report a reduction in the percentages of students who remain at risk for reading difficulties.

The Future of RTI

Several obstacles still challenge RTI implementation. RTI can be costly and schools have limited resources; there is confusion regarding IDEA regulations and RTI implementation; and the responsibilities for generalists and specialists have expanded. However, RTI implementation has led to several positive accomplishments that include universal screenings and progress monitoring; early evidence-based intervention for struggling students; a move away from a **child deficit model**; and an alternative to discrepancy formula for LD identification. Researchers have reflected on the last 10 years of RTI implementation and have proposed recommendations to improve RTI intervention and prevention delivery systems.

Challenges of Response to Intervention

Costly Interventions and Limited Resources

RTI is costly both in time and resources. Schools have to use their resources in the most efficient way while maximizing the opportunities for student academic and behavioral success. Prior to RTI, schools did not engage in universal screening. One of the concerns with universal screening is that it can produce a large number of false positives, or students who are considered at risk and placed in Tier 2 intervention unnecessarily. False positives can lead to costly interventions such as small-group tutoring. Progress monitoring also requires frequent costly testing. Schools are expending resources to ensure that effective interventions are provided to students not responding to instruction. School administrators have to spend time selecting a variety of measurement tools that are reasonable in cost and easy to administer.

Confusion Over IDEA Regulations

The use of RTI for LD identification has led to confusion and myths about the special education referral process. The National Dissemination Center for Children with Disabilities (2013) cautions that RTI cannot be used by schools to delay or refuse an evaluation for special education. The 2004 reauthorization of IDEA included a mandate known as **child find** that requires public school districts to locate students, birth through age 21 years, with suspected disabilities and who are in need of special education services, and refer them for evaluation within a reasonable time. RTI has evolved within the context of legal requirements for special education referrals and evaluations, posing challenges for educators. While one goal of RTI is to identify students at risk for reading problems, the trend is toward providing Tier 2 high-quality research-based interventions before

special education testing is started. However, when the parent or an agency makes a formal request for an evaluation, the school district must comply and begin the formal evaluation process. Schools cannot deny the parent an evaluation if the child has not participated in the RTI process as this would violate the child find mandate. IDEA allows schools to document whether a student has responded to RTI interventions for special education eligibility, but it is not a federal requirement. Edward J. Kame'enui (2007) states that "RTI will require careful federal guidance and direction which is still forthcoming, particularly in the due process procedures invoked in identifying or failing to identify students who may have a learning disability."

Cecil R. Reynolds and Sally E. Shaywitz (2009) caution against the use of the RTI model to determine a specific learning disability, such as dyslexia. Dyslexia is defined as having a reading problem despite normal cognitive ability, therefore "a full evaluation including consideration of their history, oral language acquisition, literacy skills (including fluency), and cognitive ability is necessary" (p. 142). The authors go on to say that a comprehensive evaluation is needed to identify areas of strength and weakness.

Expansion of Roles

A successful RTI model requires that school personnel expand their roles to support new demands for intervention and assessment. This may be a challenge as traditional roles already place time constraints on generalists and specialists. General education teachers may not have the classroom management skills to provide intervention services for struggling students while the rest of the students engage in independent work. General education teachers also require a high level of expertise in various areas such as literacy development and instruction, second-language acquisition, and assessment. This requires a commitment from school administrators and districts to provide professional development and opportunities for collaborative consultation.

Specialists, such as school psychologists, have high caseloads and may not have the time to engage in the development and implementation of an RTI model. Despite federal legislation that no longer requires a significant discrepancy between aptitude and academic achievement or the use of intelligence tests, school psychologists continue to spend the majority of their time conducting psychoeducational assessments to determine eligibility for special education placement. Allocating more time to primary prevention will require that specialists, generalists, and school administrators have an open mind to how students are identified for intervention and the willingness to adapt a more systemic approach to serving schools.

Lack of Universal RTI Framework

The 2004 IDEA legislation introduced response to intervention terminology and encouraged schools to use 15% of their special education money to provide intervention within regular education. IDEA required that schools use evidence-based instruction and administer regular assessments to measure student progress. What IDEA did not do was specify how an RTI model should be designed, implemented, or evaluated. Furthermore, it did not require a structure with tiers or levels. IDEA also did not specify how often student progress should be assessed. This high degree of flexibility has led researchers and practitioners to use various approaches to developing models of RTI.

Accomplishments of RTI

Universal Screening and Progress Monitoring

One of RTI's greatest accomplishments to date is the use of informal screening for the purpose of early identification with students who require some additional help. While achievement monitoring has always been a hallmark of special education, RTI requires progress monitoring in general education as well. During instruction, schools must administer formal achievement assessments at reasonable intervals and provide this information to the child's parents. Progress monitoring can inform intervention design, implementation, and modification. Teachers make decisions about data collection to determine if students are benefiting from the instructional program.

Evidence-Based Interventions

RTI began as a model for K-3 and reading intervention. This is due to the extensive research base on the prevention of reading difficulties through early intervention, along with the knowledge that most students in special education have a specific learning disability in reading. Early in the RTI process, students are provided with evidence-based intervention to prevent severe reading problems that may lead to learning disabilities. More schools are now using evidence-based intervention to support students with math and behavior problems.

Move Away From Child Deficit Model

School personnel have had to conceptualize student learning and behavior problems from an ecological and cultural perspective. Response to intervention takes the focus away from a *child deficit model* where a learning disability is thought to exist in the child and places it on the student's learning environment and his or her access to research-based instruction.

Alternative to LD Discrepancy Formula Identification

In 2003, Sharon Vaughn and Lynn S. Fuchs conceived of RTI as a viable alternative to LD discrepancy formula. They noted that RTI would lead to earlier identification of struggling students, prevention of academic problems, and progress assessment with clear implication for academic programming. According to Dawn Flanagan and Vincent Alfonso (2011), using an RTI service delivery system to identify specific learning disabilities has an advantage in that the "instructional response components are embedded in the identification process, streamlining eligibility decisions and directly linking special education services with those provided in general education" (p. 127). RTI has also led to the use of multiple sources of data to address student academic delays, minimizing the impact of biases and limitations of standardized norm-referenced IQ measures.

Improving RTI Service Delivery Models

Smart RTI

Douglas Fuchs and colleagues (2012) offer recommendations for how to improve RTI. They advocate for a Smart RTI model that emphasizes three levels of prevention. Primary prevention refers to the first level of instruction that students receive within the regular education classroom. Secondary prevention refers to the intervention services students receive that typically involve small-group instruction based on an empirically validated tutoring program. Tertiary prevention refers to the more intensive services provided by special education personnel. Fuchs et al. (2012) clarify the assumptions behind Smart RTI.

One assumption behind Smart RTI is that the model should not be used to prevent special education placement. The overall goal of Smart RTI is for educators to address the more global consequences of school failure such as school dropout, unemployment, and incarceration. The second assumption assumes that a comprehensive framework will reduce but does not eliminate the need for tertiary prevention. Some students will need temporary services from special education while other students with severe learning problems will require more intensive remediation from a special educator. The third assumption is that specialized expertise is necessary within every level of Smart RTI. The authors argue that the regular education teacher cannot be held responsible for all of the instructional interventions needed at the multiple levels of Smart RTI. At the tertiary level, specialized expertise is needed in the areas of instructional approaches, curricula, data collection, and data-based instruction for students with serious learning disabilities. Special educators have unique knowledge and skills needed not only at the tertiary level when working alone but also when working in collaboration with generalists within the primary and secondary prevention levels.

The assumptions behind Smart RTI align with the recommendations for a more effective RTI implementation process. Under a Smart RTI model, a two-stage screening process is recommended to reduce false positives and identify students who are more likely to experience academic difficulty during primary prevention. Students identified as at risk are administered a thorough second screening following 6 weeks of core instruction. This minimizes the need to provide costly secondary intervention services to students who do not require Tier 2 intervention.

Smart RTI also advocates for multistage assessment within the primary prevention level to avoid an RTI wait-to-fail model that relegates students to spend time within the secondary intervention level before receiving more intensive special education services within the tertiary prevention level. Studies show that a more in-depth assessment can accurately identify students who are reliably predicted not to respond to small-group tutoring. A multistage assessment should include data collection from universal screening; 6 weeks of progress monitoring within primary prevention; teacher ratings of student attention and behavior; and a battery of norm-referenced tests.

Sustainability

Hughes and Dexter (2011) report on critical factors that relate to the sustainability of RTI programs,

- Extensive, ongoing professional development
- Administrative support at the system and building level
- Teacher buy-in and willingness to adjust their traditional instructional roles
- Involvement of all school personnel
- Adequate meeting time for coordination (p. 10)

Parent Involvement

Parent involvement is critical at all levels of the RTI prevention and intervention process. Parents need to receive information about how the school is implementing RTI to be enabled to support learning both at home and school. Information about a family's ecological and cultural environment can support the school's ability to support families. The school has the responsibility to inform a parent about assessment results, interventions being used, and the grade-level expectations for the child. When a child is having academic or behavioral difficulties, the parent plays an important role in working with school personnel to make decisions about how long to wait for an intervention to work. In this way, parents can help make the determination about when a special education evaluation is warranted.

Conclusion

RTI is both an instructional and prevention framework, characterized by successively more intensive tiers of intervention to correspond to students' instructional needs. RTI has brought about systemic reform at all levels of the educational process. Most states have developed or are developing RTI models to address academic delays and behavior challenges. One of the assumptions of RTI is that all students can learn. The essential components of RTI include universal screening, research-based instruction, evidence-based intervention, progress monitoring and a multitiered approach to intervention. The 2004 reauthorization of IDEA allows RTI as a strategy to use in the identification of learning disabilities. Part of the goal of RTI is to identify students who are struggling academically and to provide support for those students who may or may not qualify for special education services. The focus is redirected to eliminate poor instruction as the cause of disability. RTI implementation has primarily addressed primary grade reading. While RTI programs may have already made some positive changes in both general and special education overall, more research studies are needed to address the impact of RTI on classroom performance and behavior. In addition, more studies would inform how RTI can be conceptualized at the secondary level.

Key Chapter Terms

Academic language proficiency: Language needed to access content from the academic curriculum. Academic language includes comprehension and vocabulary.

Child deficit model: Based on the medical model that assumes a disability exists within a child while excluding environmental influences.

Child find: A federal mandate of Individuals with Disabilities Act (IDEA) that requires states to identify, locate, evaluate, and track students with special needs from birth through age 21.

Curriculum-based measurement (CBM): Assessments used for measuring student competency and progress in the areas of reading fluency, spelling, mathematics, and written language.

Discrepancy formula: A formula used by schools to determine if a student meets state eligibility criteria for special education. A student must have a significant discrepancy between intellectual ability and

academic achievement in one or more areas—oral expression, listening comprehension, written expression, basic reading skills, reading comprehension, mathematics calculation, and mathematics reasoning.

Evidence-based intervention: Intervention that has empirical evidence of effectiveness related to improved outcomes for students.

Formative assessment: Assessment designed to evaluate progress on specific learning objectives during instruction.

Individuals with Disabilities Education Improvement Act (IDEA) 2004: Legislation that ensures all children with special needs receive comprehensive and individualized services through special education or related services.

Norm-referenced tests: Standardized measurements designed to compare an individual student's performance to an appropriate peer group.

Pullout program: Instruction is delivered outside of the general education classroom.

Research-based reading instruction: Under the No Child Left Behind Act of 2001, instructional programs primarily used in kindergarten through third grade should be based on rigorous scientific research.

Response to Intervention (RTI): An approach to intervention for and assessment of students struggling academically or socially. RTI is used to determine eligibility for special education services.

Universal screening: Schools administer universal screenings to all children that include low-cost, quick testing from one to three times during the academic year in order to assess the effectiveness of the curriculum and instruction as well as to address academic problems in a timely manner.

Wait-to-fail model: Students with academic problems need to wait for intensive interventions within entitlement programs until they demonstrate a significant discrepancy between intellectual ability and academic achievement in one or more areas.

References

Al Otaiba, S., & Torgesen, J. (2007). Effects from intensive standardized kindergarten and first-grade interventions for the prevention of reading difficulties. In S. R. Jumerson, M. K. Burns, & A. M. VanDerHeyden (Eds.), *Handbook of response to intervention: The science and practice of assessment and intervention* (pp. 212–222). New York, NY: Springer.

Barnes, A. C., & Harlacher, J. E. (2008). Clearing the confusion: Response-to-intervention as a set of principles. *Education and Treatment of Children, 31*(3), 417–431.

Bender, W. N. (2009). *Beyond the RTI pyramid: Solutions for the first years of implementation.* Bloomington, IN: Solution Tree Press.

Denton, C. (2012). Response to intervention for reading difficulties in the primary grades: Some answers and lingering questions. *Journal of Learning Disabilities, 45*(3), 232–243.

Ehren, B., Montgomery, J., Rudebusch, J., & Whitmore, K., (n.d.). *Responsiveness to intervention: New roles for speech-language pathologists.* Retrieved from http://www.asha.org/SLP/schools/prof-consult/NewRolesSLP/

Ervin, R. A., Schaughency, A., Goodman, S. D., McGlinchey, M. T., & Matthews, A. (2006). Merging research and practice to address reading and behavior school-wide. *School Psychology Review, 35*(2), 198–223.

Flanagan, D. P., & Alfonso, V. C. (2011). *Essentials of specific learning disability identification.* Hoboken, NJ: Wiley.

Fletcher, J. M., & Vaughn, S. (2009). Response to intervention: Preventing and remediating academic difficulties. *Child Development Perspectives, 3*(1), 30–37.

Fuchs, D., & Fuchs, L. S. (2006). Introduction to response to intervention: What, why, and how valid is it? *Reading Research Quarterly, 41*(1), 93–99.

Fuchs, D., Fuchs, L. S., & Compton, D. L. (2012). Smart RTI: A next-generation approach to multilevel prevention. *Exceptional Children, 78*(3), 263–279.

Fuchs, L. S., & Fuchs, D. (2007). A model for implementing responsiveness to intervention. *Teaching Exceptional Children, 39*(5), 14–20.

Fuchs, L. S., Fuchs, D., & Zumeta, R. O. (2008). Response to intervention: A strategy for the prevention and identification of learning disabilities. In E. L. Grigorenko (Ed.), *Educating individuals with disabilities* (pp. 115–136). New York, NY: Springer.

Fuchs, L. S., & Vaughn, S. (2012). Responsiveness-to-intervention: A decade later. *Journal of Learning Disabilities, 45*(3), 195–203.

Garcia, S. B., & Ortiz, A. A. (2006). Preventing disproportionate representation: Culturally and linguistically responsive prereferral interventions. *Teaching Exceptional Children, 38*(4), 64–68.

Hakuta, K. (2011). Educating language minority students and affirming their equal rights: Research and practical perspectives. *Educational Researcher, 40*(4), 163–174.

Hojnoski, R. L., & Missall, K. N. (2006). Addressing school readiness: Expanding school psychology in early education. *School Psychology Review, 35*(4), 602–614.

Hughes, C. A., & Dexter, D. D. (2011). Response to intervention: A research-based summary, *Theory Into Practice, 50*(1), 4–11.

Individuals with Disabilities Education Act, 20 U.S.C. §§108-446 (2004).

International Reading Association and National Council of Teachers of English. (2009). *Standards for the assessment of reading and writing.* Retrieved from http://www.ncte.org/standards/assessmentstandards

Kame'enui, E. J. (2007). A new paradigm: Responsiveness to intervention. *Teaching Exceptional Children, 39*(5), 6–7.

Kamps, D., Abbott, M., Greenwood, C., Arreaga-Mayer, C., Wills, H., Longstaff, J., . . . Walton, C. (2007). Use of evidence-based, small-group reading instruction for English Language Learners in elementary grades: Secondary-tier intervention. *Learning Disability Quarterly, 30*(3), 153–168.

Klingner, J. K., Artiles, A. J., & Mendez Barletta, L. (2006). English language learners who struggle with reading: Language acquisition or LD? *Journal of Learning Disabilities, 39*(2), 108–128.

Losen, D. J., & Orfield, G. (Eds.). (2002). *Racial inequality in special education.* Cambridge, MA: Harvard Education Publishing Group.

MPACT. (2013.) *RTI resources.* Retrieved from http://ptimpact.org/eSource/RTI.aspx

National Association of School Psychologists. (2010). *Model of comprehensive and integrative school psychological services.* Retrieved from http://www.nasponline.org/standards/practice-model/index.aspx

National Dissemination Center for Children With Disabilities. (2013, May). *Response to intervention.* Retrieved from http://www.parentcenterhub.org/repository/rti

National Institute of Child Health and Human Development. (2000). *Report of the national reading panel: Teaching children to read: An evidence-based assessment of the scientific research literature on reading and its implications for reading instruction.* Washington, DC: Government Printing Office.

National Research Center on Learning Disabilities. (2003). *Executive summary of the NRCLD symposium on response to intervention.* Retrieved from http://www.marylandpublicschools.org/NR/rdonlyres/2A7BF936-8572-44A7-9FFD-B2D44E1990F9/6684/EXSUMNRC.pdf

No Child Left Behind Act of 2001, Pub. L. No. 107–110, § 115 Stat. 1425 (2002).

Reynolds, C. P., & Shaywitz, S. E. (2009). Response to intervention: Ready or not? Or, from wait-to-fail to watch-them-fail. *School Psychology Quarterly, 24*(2), 130–145.

Rinaldi, C., & Samson, J. (2008). English language learners and response to intervention: Referral considerations. *Teaching Exceptional Children, 40*(5), 6–14.

Rueda, R., & Windmueller, M. P. (2006). English language learners, LD, and overrepresentation: A multiple-level analysis. *Journal of Learning Disabilities, 39*(2), 99–107.

Stecker, P. M., Fuchs, L. S., & Fuchs, D. (2005). Using curriculum-based measurement to improve student achievement: Review of research. *Psychology in the Schools, 42*(8), 795–819.

U.S. Department of Education, Data Accountability Center. (2011). [IDEA 618 data tables]. Retrieved from www.ideadata.org

Vaughn, S., & Fletcher, J. M. (2012). Response to intervention with secondary school students with reading difficulties. *Journal of Learning Disabilities, 45*(3), 244–256.

Vaughn, S., & Fuchs, L. (2003). Redefining learning disabilities as inadequate response to instruction: The promise and potential problems. *Learning Disabilities Research & Practice, 18*(3), 137–146.

Vaughn, S., & Roberts, G. (2007). Secondary interventions in reading: Providing additional instruction for students at risk. *Teaching Exceptional Children, 39*(5), 40–46.

Further Readings

Buysse, V., & Peisner-Fienberg, E. S. (2013). *Handbook of response to intervention in early childhood.* Baltimore, MD: Paul H. Brooks.

This book is a foundational resource for early childhood educators and administrators working to improve academic and social success of young learners. The authors present current research on best practices in applying the RTI model in early childhood settings to address early intervention.

Compton, D. L., Fuchs, D., Fuchs, L. S., Bouton, B., Gilbert, J. Barquero, L. A., Cho, E., & Crouch, R. C. (2010). Selecting at-risk first graders for early intervention: Eliminating false positives and exploring the promise of a two-stage gated screening process. *Journal of Educational Psychology, 102*(2), 327–341.

One of the concerns with the RTI model is the persistent high number of false positives that emerge from universal screening. The authors offer solutions to the problem by illustrating a two-stage screening process that a school can incorporate within its RTI service delivery model to reduce unnecessary interventions.

Knoff, H. M. (2009). *Implementing response-to-intervention at the school, district, and state levels: Functional assessment, data-based problem solving, and evidence-based academic and behavioral interventions.* Bethesda, MD: National Association of School Psychologists.

Written from a practitioner's perspective, this resource e-book provides much-needed direction in the incorporation of a data-based, functional assessment problem-solving approach to Response to Intervention implementation.

PART III

CURRICULUM AND INSTRUCTION

7

Multiculturalism Versus the Common Core

Fenwick W. English

University of North Carolina at Chapel Hill

The idea of a common state **curriculum** that might become a national model of curriculum is not new. In 1779 Thomas Jefferson drafted a plan for education for the state of Virginia that provided 3 years of public elementary education for all children of free men at public expense. The most advanced boys could then attend a grammar school with public support. Jefferson included in his model curriculum "reading, writing, arithmetic, and history substituted for religious instruction" (Tanner & Tanner, 1990, p. 34).

The difference today is that the respective states, via a number of national associations and other groups with financial backing from the Gates Foundation, have crafted a set of standards that through incentives for adoption would become a de facto national (though, it is argued, not a federal) curriculum. Called the Common Core, these standards currently allow state and local school officials to "retrofit" some curriculum content to implement them. The assumption is that the standards will require new rigor and richness in the curriculum (Hansel, 2013, p. 32).

The wisdom of a common national curriculum has been debated for many decades, complicated by the fact that the individual states each set their own curriculum content, testing protocols, and standards, and

no individual state has the authority to impose its own standards on the other 49. Only the federal government has the authority and policy reach to create and impose such a national curriculum, but it was barred by the United States Constitution from doing so. In creating a truly national curriculum, this has been the proverbial "rock and the hard place" in U.S. education; that is, how to have a national but not federal curriculum when only the federal government has the power to impose standards, rules, laws, and policies on all the states.

The move toward a common national curriculum by starting with a common set of standards has been prompted by perceptions that: (1) the curriculum in U.S. schools, particularly the academic curriculum, is not demanding enough of American students as reflected in international test score comparisons that show the United States is at the average or below average standing in selected academic areas such as math, science, and reading compared to other developed countries (Rotberg, 2011); (2) the difficulty the respective states have in setting their own curriculum content and standards and the quandary state legislators and taxpayers have in understanding how good their respective state's curriculum really is when there is no common yardstick upon which to compare themselves to the others; and (3) continuing calls for improved accountability and cost controls because of political resistance to imposing any increase in taxes to support public education.

This latter objective is one aimed at improving the efficiency of public schooling by creating common benchmarks for rating schooling effectiveness. A common curriculum is required to create a companion common test. Such a test becomes the anvil upon which to engage in collective disciplinary and fiscal decisions regarding the potential laggards. As more states use the test scores to evaluate teachers, the more these tests are considered punitive as opposed to helpful in improving teaching and instruction. Early results of state tests based on the Common Core State Standards show that in New York state, for example, only 31% of students in third through eighth grade met or exceeded the proficiency standard in math and reading on state exams in 2013. This was down from 65% in math and 55% in English on different tests given a year earlier (Fleisher & Banchero, 2013). When test scores are also used to hold students back from promotion, parents also become alarmed (Toppo, 2013). Another more cynical view of the motivation behind the Common Core State Standards is that it will allow commercial companies to make huge profits in selling more tests and new books and supplementary materials as well as new technologies by which it will be implemented (English, 2014). Education is "a $650 billion industry, making it America's second-largest economic sector" (Anderson & Pini, 2011, p. 185). As Gene Glass, a respected and long-time educational researcher observed, "The corporations just woke up a few years ago to the billions and billions of dollars that exist in public education, and they just decided to go for it. The incredible thing is how easy it is" (Davis, 2013, p. 52).

But perhaps the most troublesome issue with the move toward a common curriculum is who decides what is "common"? The idea that there is or should be a singular curriculum that is good for everyone, at all times and in all places, is deeply presumptuous and ignorant of the fact that the selection of curriculum content is an act of choice of many potential facts, figures, and cultures, especially for a country that is growing ever more diverse and where the White population is expected to be the minority population within the next three decades or sooner. It is estimated that new immigrants and their children

and grandchildren born in the United States will account for 82% of the population increase in the United States from 2005 through 2050 (Nasser, 2008). A single curriculum for everyone flies in the face of the growing diversity that will be coming to school in the years ahead.

Pierre Bourdieu and Jean-Claude Passeron (2000) called the idea that one curriculum was good for everyone the **cultural arbitrary,** and by that they meant that human culture is a construct; it is neither good nor bad or true nor false. It just is. To elevate one culture above others is essentially a political act taken by those who are in dominant sociopolitical positions to ensure that the school's curriculum advances their own social position within the larger social structure (Brantlinger, 2003). This means that neither the school nor its curriculum is a neutral agent in the process of education, neither in the United States nor anywhere else in the world. It is also a key to understanding some of the causes of the achievement gap.

An Earlier Conflict With a Common Curriculum

One of the earliest conflicts in American curriculum that involved the idea of a "common core" was a scheme put forward by Franklin Bobbitt (1918/1971) in 1912. Bobbitt argued for a scientific approach to creating curriculum. He wanted businessmen to have more influence on education, especially in shaping curriculum outcomes. Instead of the curriculum simply being the traditional subjects in schools, Bobbitt argued for a different model. He advocated that curriculum developers should go into the real world, analyze the jobs that exist in the world, and design curriculum so that once students graduated from school, they could step right into the real world and be productive citizens.

Bobbitt (1918/1971) began with a survey of

the science-needs of each social class; and to each they would teach only the facts needed; only those that are to be put to work. In an age of efficiency and economy they would seek definitely to eliminate the useless and the wasteful. (p. 4)

Bobbitt summarized this approach when he said to a group of elementary school teachers, "Work up the raw material into that finished product for which it is best adapted" (Tanner & Tanner, 1990, p. 180).

As was done during the creation of the Common Core State Standards, Bobbitt analyzed jobs of the day to determine "the abilities, attitudes, habits, appreciations, and forms of knowledge that men need. These will be the objectives of the curriculum" (p. 42). The same posture of designing a curriculum so that students will be "career ready" or "ready for college" was a part of Bobbitt's "scientific" method of curriculum. He denied that the model he employed was narrow, saying that it would be as "wide as life itself" (p. 43).

Bobbitt's proposed procedure for developing a common curriculum was opposed by Ohio State University education professor Boyd Bode (1930), who pointed out that Bobbitt's approach was deeply antidemocratic because by using existing skill sets he also froze the social status quo. Bode wrote:

> The genius of democracy expresses itself precisely in this continuous remaking of the social fabric. With regard to curriculum construction it requires, first of all, a type of education that enables the individual, not only to adapt himself to the existing social order, but to take part in its remaking in the interests of a greater freedom. (pp. 19–20)

Creating a common curriculum based on existing jobs and roles in the "real world" also mirrored the division of labor in that world that was skewed along racial and gender lines. Training people for the existing world of work reproduces that world. School systems and other educational agencies that used Bobbitt's approach soon had to abandon it because the jobs the curriculum was designed to prepare students to do were changed or vanished.

The Contemporary Common Core Movement Briefly Reviewed

Robert Rothman (2011) has indicated that the movement to create the Common Core State Standards began in 2006 when former North Carolina governor James B. Hunt convened a small band of educators and policy developers in a meeting in Raleigh to consider creating national curriculum standards. Following this meeting scholarly papers were commissioned to examine the impact of having national curriculum standards. After this the Hunt Institute

began to develop an approach to creating national standards in 2008.

The move was accelerated when the National Governors Association (NGA) and the Council of Chief State School Officers (CCSSO) joined together and forged a joint agenda. In 2009 a coalition of the NGA, CCSO, the National Association of State Boards of Education, the Alliance for Excellent Education, the Hunt Institute, and the Business Roundtable forged ahead with the Common Core State Standards. Only the governors of Alaska and Texas refused to participate in the initial development of the Common Core.

From this impetus it can be seen that the creation of the Common Core State Standards (CCSS) represented a collaborative response to the assumption that all children should be career and college ready when they exit high school (a similar assumption was employed earlier by Franklin Bobbitt). Even as this assumption has been questioned (Emery & Ohanian, 2004) as emerging from a value-laden perspective, the framers of the CCSS document began to define the important outcomes such a goal would entail.

At least 50% of writing a curriculum begins with specifying the outcomes to be obtained. Such outcomes can be called goals, objectives, benchmarks or standards. Imagine a standard being a plan to travel to a specific destination, say from New York City to Madrid, Spain. The standard might include not only the destination but the need to reach it in a specific time period, say 2 days. About the only way to accomplish this standard would be to fly. The way this standard is stipulated limits the means to achieve it. So, while in theory there are optional decisions in the use of standards, the options are circumscribed.

Curricular outcomes are always deeply entrenched in sets of values and assumptions about what knowledge is best suited to accomplish them. In this respect the classic book *The Saber-Tooth Curriculum* written by J. Abner Peddiwell (aka Harold Benjamin) in 1939 remains the enduring example and still a worthwhile read for any contemporary educational leader to understand how curriculum, or the delineation of the classroom content to be taught, is a product of what the framers believe schools or education should be about. It is a far cry from a culturally neutral position about what knowledge and values are most worthy to be included in the school's curriculum.

The developers of the CCSS began by drafting a target set of outcomes: the College and Career Readiness (CCR) Standards for all students. Beginning with the end in mind allowed for the development of step-by-step understandings throughout K-12 schooling. They used the CCR Standards to anchor their thinking as they determined grade-level expectations beginning with high school and moving backward to kindergarten. This created a trajectory from kindergarten to Grade 12 and formed a progression of skills that builds by grade level to the CCR Standards.

The CCR workgroups used existing state standards, international benchmarks from top-performing countries, and research from college entrance exams and reports to inform their thinking. Using these documents allowed the workgroups to meet several important goals. Though relying on the best of the state standards available, they sought to create a succinct set of standards that were clear and rigorous. Using international benchmarks allowed the framers to focus on developing standards that would prepare students for competition in a global economy and society. Depending on research and evidence from college entrance exams and reports helped them align the standards to college and career readiness expectations.

In addition to taking existing standards, benchmarks, and research into consideration, the framers gathered advice and feedback from several stakeholders. Important to the process was the development of a Validation Committee (VC) made up of school personnel and experts on academic standards. VC members were selected by governors and CCSSO members to review the process for developing the standards and determine whether the evidence used to create the standards was sufficient. The VC met for one day and provided feedback.

The framers also worked with an advisory group with members from Achieve, Inc.; the College Board; the National Association of State Boards of Education; and the State Higher Education Executive Officers. Additional feedback was gathered from teachers, parents, school administrators, business leaders, and content experts. The NGA and CCSSO received nearly 10,000 comments during the two time periods when written comments from the public were accepted. The intent was, and continues to be, for the feedback process to be an avenue for review

and revision of the document as new research is conducted and the standards are implemented.

Basic Premise: Purpose for the CCSS

The perceived need for a common set of standards that prepare students for college and careers was the primary rationale for the CCSS document. Drawing on the intended purpose, the standards outline specific expectations for student learning on this path. They are intended to be rigorous and set high expectations for applying knowledge in real-world situations. In addition, the writers of the standards worked with a goal to provide clear and precise language so the standards would be easily understood and applicable to all stakeholders. While taking pains to point out that the CCSS were not initiated by the federal government, the developers of CCSS promote the benefits of common standards for all students across the nation.

The proposed benefits of common educational standards include a high-quality education for all students regardless of where they live. The hope is that as families move from state to state and from school to school, their educational experience will be based on the same standards and therefore be consistent. It is hoped that the standards will provide opportunities for sharing resources as schools, districts, and states implement common standards. The common standards are also expected to create a more informed, globally competitive citizenry and society.

What Educational Leaders Need to Know

Standards and Curriculum

It is important to make a distinction between standards and curriculum. Standards are a set of guidelines that describe what students need to know and be able to do. Standards are not curriculum, but are aligned with curricular materials and practices. This means standards do not include instructions for teaching, lesson plans for delivering content, or directions for assessing students' understanding. They are the what (to teach), but not the how (to teach or assess it). **Table 7.1** further explains the distinction between standards and curriculum.

Since the release of the CCSS, some supplementary materials (outside of the standards and document review process) have been released to inform stakeholders regarding curricular materials and practices.

Standards—The What	Curriculum—The How
Describes what students need to know and be able to do	Describes how students will learn the standards
Adopted by the State Board of Education as state level policy (mandated) and usually referred to as the Standard Course of Study	Adopted by local education agencies as local policy (often mandated) and usually referred to as curriculum maps, pacing guides, curriculum frameworks, and so forth
The Standard Course of Study in most states includes the Common Core State Standards for English language arts and math and standards for additional disciplines	Includes all goals, objectives, and plans as well as lessons, activities, and tasks
	Encompasses students' strategies for learning and teachers' methods for instructing
	Includes demonstration of progress toward outcomes (various assessments—formative, summative)
	Includes materials used to teach the standards (all texts, digital devices, organizers, etc.)

Table 7.1   Standards and Curriculum

SOURCE: Cynthia Dewey

These materials included several sets of publishers' criteria, which were written by the developers of the CCSS to guide educational publishers in aligning their English and math materials to the standards. Educational researchers and practitioners labeled some of these materials, including the initial drafts of the publishers' criteria, as inconsistent with the body of research and practice in the field. These materials were also incongruent with the intent of the standards document, which is clear throughout in differentiating standards and curriculum, and states that the CCSS do not tell teachers *how* to teach, but *what* to teach.

Recommendations considered inconsistent with research findings were: avoiding or limiting pre-teaching practices when introducing texts; teaching students at their frustration level, or using texts that require some assistance from the instructor to understand; and drastically reducing teaching narrative writing and literature in the English language arts classroom. Researchers and practitioners are calling for evidence-based practice recommendations to support teaching of the CCSS and have criticized the supplementary curricular documents and videos that recommend practice outside of current research and evidence-based understandings.

Educational administrators, as instructional leaders acting within the guidelines and policies of their local education agencies, make curricular decisions regarding teaching practices, materials, and assessments that align with state adopted standards. They support and guide educators as they plan and implement lessons and tasks that provide the educational experiences students need in order to reach the outcomes defined by the standards. They ensure educators have the necessary curricular materials to accomplish this work. They assist educators in establishing and reaching goals for student achievement based upon collaboratively monitoring and analyzing student data toward meeting outcomes.

In order to serve as informed instructional leaders, educational administrators need to have a working knowledge of the CCSS and recognition of curricular alignment to the standards (**Table 7.2**). More precisely, instructional leaders need to be able to observe a lesson and document whether or not the teaching observed is preparing students for the desired outcome defined by the CCSS and whether or not the assessment administered is measuring student achievement of the desired standard.

Standards: What is being taught	Look for a small set of standards for a task or lesson and analyze them closely. The CCSS are intended to be fewer, clearer, and more demanding than previous standards. This should decrease the number of standards taught in each task or lesson and provide more focused instruction. Be sure to analyze the standards closely to gain an understanding of what the standards are expecting students to know and be able to do.
Curriculum: How the standards are addressed	Look for clear alignment to the standards. Are the standards listed in the task or lesson completely addressed within the lesson? Are students demonstrating the skills and abilities to meet the outcomes described within the standards listed?
Assessments: How the standards are assessed	Look for clear alignment to the standards. Are students demonstrating the outcomes described in the standards listed? Are data gathered regarding students' progress toward meeting these outcomes?

Table 7.2 What Do Educational Leaders Need to Know?

SOURCE: Cynthia Dewey

For example, suppose an educator has planned a task that focuses on Reading Standard for Informational Text for Grade 5, Standard #6 (RI.5.6): "Analyze multiple accounts of the same event or topic, noting important similarities and differences in the point of view they represent" (NGA & CCSO, 2010, p. 14). The educational administrator needs to be able to recognize the intent of the standard and look for ways the educator is teaching and assessing this standard within the task. It is important that the administrator can tease out what the standard is specifying.

This standard requires a particular understanding of *point of view* with informational text. With literature, point of view is most likely taught as identification of first-person, second-person, and third-person point of view. The standard requires students to analyze the content of multiple texts by comparing and contrasting them focused on viewpoints presented about a topic or event. It is this type of analysis of the standards that is necessary to determine alignment of standards to teaching and assessment. It is not enough to align teaching and assessment to a concept within the standard without addressing the intended outcome of the standard.

Building Capacity

The CCSS are a new set of educational standards. They are intended to be different than previous standards in order to better prepare students for college and career, largely based upon ACT studies from 2006 and 2009 that revealed students were underprepared to meet these challenges. This necessitates changes in teaching to meet the outcomes described in the standards. In order to prepare for these changes, educational leaders will need to plan for capacity building. Educators will need professional knowledge and materials in order to meet the tasks ahead. The role of the educational leader will be to provide opportunities for educators to build the professional knowledge and skills necessary and will need to provide access to different curricular materials.

Educators will need to read and analyze the standards with the intended purpose and guiding framework of the standards in mind. Since the standards were designed to prepare students for college and career readiness, educators will need to study the progression of standards to understand how teaching their grade-level standards contributes to the progression of skills necessary in reaching the intended readiness outcomes.

For example, understanding how *point of view* is described in Reading Standard 6 for both literature and informational texts across grade levels will impact how teachers instruct students at their particular grade level. It will provide insight into how the skills build from one year to the next so that students are able to meet the intended outcomes by the time they graduate from high school. More specifically, fifth-grade teachers will need to know that students compare and contrast first and third person point of view when reading literature and first-hand and second-hand accounts of the same events or topics and describe differences in focus when reading informational texts in Grade 4. They will also need to know how the author develops point of view in literature and how to determine an author's point of view in informational text in Grade 6. This is just the first small step, however. Reading across all of the grade-level standards will help build an understanding of the intent of the standards as educators go about the work of designing tasks and lessons.

Professional development can build capacity by focusing on reading across the standards to gain these connected understandings through defining key concepts and the desired outcomes. The appendices of the CCSS documents are also important and can inform this work. For English language arts, for example, educators can work together to define what is intended for each grade level for important key concepts, such as: point of view, textual evidence, theme, central idea, objective summary, text structure, diverse formats, media, argument, claims, sufficiency of evidence, and complex texts, to name a few. This collaborative work will provide a common understanding and support the trajectory of the standards progression.

After a thorough examination of the intent of the standards to build college and career readiness through a progression of skills, educators can analyze their grade-level standards to determine ways to design tasks and lessons that align with the desired outcomes. In doing so, they will have in mind what their students will need to know and be able to do for the grade they instruct and also the skills and abilities that come before and after. This will support their ability to develop differentiated lessons for students. They will also gain an understanding of ways to match curricular materials to the tasks and lessons they design. If this step is also collaborative, it will allow for sharing of materials and realignment to best match their newly designed tasks and lessons. It is probable that different and new materials will be required to meet their goals and educators will need support in gaining access to the materials they need.

One of the proposed benefits of the CCSS is the abundance of implementation materials concurrently under development. Each state that has adopted the CCSS is creating a storehouse of resources for implementation that includes lesson plans and materials. Searching state education websites will provide insight into the implementation process and access to exemplar lessons and resources for teaching that can serve as either benchmarks or models for lesson design.

Flash Points: Pushback, Problems, and Politics With the Common Core

The Common Core, and with it the distinct possibility of an emerging common national curriculum, revolves around several critical flash points. They are:

- Lack of political agreement over the "proper" curriculum content to be included, sometimes referred to as the "culture wars"
- Disputes regarding the jurisdictional political boundaries between federal, state, and local educational authorities
- Questions regarding the so-called rigor of the U.S. curriculum, if it can be considered as a collective entity of the 50 states, and the extent to which curriculum should be an instrument of maintaining national economic dominance
- Issues concerning testing and assessment and the continuing existence of the achievement gap
- Issues concerning where to set test-score cutoffs to be fair to all students

These issues are now reviewed in greater detail.

Curriculum Flash Point 1: Right Knowledge and Curriculum Content Selection

The creation of a curriculum involves the identification of a specific form, type, and set of cultural values advanced by the creators. There is no value-free curriculum. Curriculum construction per se may be considered a form of engineering, but the inclusion of the content within it involves a consideration of what is worth knowing. And the question about which knowledge is of most worth was forcefully asked in 1860 by Herbert Spencer in a prescient essay. His answer was that certain "life activities" ranked in the following order should form the basis of selecting the "right" knowledge:

1. Knowledge that relates to self-preservation

2. Knowledge regarding obtaining life's necessities

3. Knowledge in the rearing and disciplining of offspring (children)

4. Knowledge in maintaining one's social and political relations

5. Knowledge regarding the spending of leisure time in pursuit of one's tastes and feelings (p. 32)

It should be obvious rather immediately that the answers to Spencer's questions would be deeply embedded in a person's culture. For example, to respond to the question regarding self-preservation would involve the matter of food. Bourdieu (2009) has pointed out that what one culture considers delicious food another culture may consider barbaric or even quite repulsive. Take sushi. The idea of eating raw fish is decidedly a matter of cultural conditioning.

And what one culture considers a necessity another considers a luxury. Owning two cars may be a matter of economic survival in the United States when both a mother and father work. In other cultures automobile ownership itself is reserved only for the extremely wealthy. There is no way around the matter of culture, class structure, or wealth in designing an appropriate curriculum. Values such as those related to class structure, religion, and race/ethnicity, as well as those identified as liberal or conservative, or right or left, permeate U.S. public life. Cultural values inevitably shape curriculum, and as Ira Shor (1986) has argued, the imposition of a curriculum by a dominant group can be seen as a form of culture war in which those in power seek to maintain the status quo.

The issue of whose interests are being pursued in the designation of curriculum content was highlighted when the Texas State Board of Education declined to require third graders to know about Dolores Huerta, who was a key figure in the fight for farm workers' rights but also was "a prominent advocate of unrestricted abortion and socialism, the honorary chair of the Democratic Socialists of America, and therefore, arguably, not a role model for third graders" (Upham, 2010, p. A17). And why would Huerta not be appropriate as a role model? Because the cultural values of the groups who control the curriculum find her a threat to their own social position. Disputes in some states over whether evolution should be taught in schools, and whether creationism should be taught as a plausible alternative to evolution, also illustrate the conflict over values in curriculum design. The culture wars will continue to break out in the future over points of conflict with school curriculum.

Curriculum Flash Point 2: Conflict Over Political Boundaries and the Role of Government

How the Common Core was developed is fairly clear. What isn't clear, at least to many conservatives, is how the Obama administration, which encouraged the adoption of the Common Core through the Race to the Top grant competition and waivers to the requirements of the No Child Left Behind Act, could be involved without being in charge of it (see Ujifusa, 2013). The Common Core has been opposed by the Republican National Committee, tea party activists, and some free-market think tanks (Stern & Klein, 2013). The governor of South Carolina, Nikki Hawley, said that the state should not "relinquish control of education to the federal government, neither should we cede it to the consensus of other states" (Banchero, 2012). Despite the fact that the National Governors Association and the Council of Chief State School Officers pushed hard for the Common Core State Standards, some conservative think tank pundits, such as Michael McShane of the American Enterprise Institute, believe that "the Obama administration's vocal support for the initiative [Common Core] is 'actually unbelievably harmful to the common-core effort moving forward'" (Ujifusa, 2013). Some states have halted implementation of the Common Core and, as of June 2014, Indiana, Oklahoma, and South Carolina had dropped the standards altogether.

Curriculum Flash Point 3: What Constitutes Curricular Rigor and Why It Is Important

Another potent flash point with the Common Core has been the debate over how rigorous the **Common Core standards** actually are. Here the contestation centers on opinions regarding what constitutes "rigor," which in arguments over the Common Core has been defined in at least two different ways. The first is to compare books or texts used in states that have adopted the Common Core against what those states used before, and to note which set of books or texts is more advanced or intellectually difficult. The second is to fall back on international test score comparisons and use them as the basis to support the need for the Common Core.

For example, proponents of the Common Core argue that it is rigorous because

> one of the Common Core's reading standards for grades 9–10 calls for students to analyze and understand the arguments in "seminal U.S. texts, including the application of constitutional principles and use of legal reasoning." How many American public schools do that today? (Stern & Klein, 2013, p. A13)

A study completed by the neoconservative Thomas B. Fordham Institute indicated that the "Common Core standards 'are clearly superior to those currently in use in 39 states in math and 37 states in English. For 33 states, the Common Core is superior in both math and reading'" (Banchero, 2012, p. A6).

Others have argued against the idea that the Common Core is rigorous, and noted that in some cases students will read less fiction than they had previously. Massachusetts has scored "best in the nation" on all grades and assessments of the National Assessment of Educational Progress for several years in a row. But in the Bay State, as Jamie Gass and Charles Chieppo (2013) point out, "Common Core's English standards reduce by 60% the amount of classic literature, poetry and drama that students will read. For example, the Common Core ignores the

novels of Charles Dickens, Edith Wharton and Mark Twain's *Huckleberry Finn*."

For some Common Core advocates, curricular rigor is also determined by international test score comparisons. For example, Edward Frenkel and Hung-Hsi Wu (2013) warn that "Mathematical education in the U.S. is in deep crisis." They noted that the World Economic Forum ranked the United States 48th in the quality of math and science education. Frenkel and Wu also noted a report from the National Academies "warned that America's ability to compete effectively with other nations is fading."

Yet it is important to remember that every time international test scores are released that show the United States is not ranked very high, a broad spectrum of critics and "reformers" create doomsday scenarios. This began with the 1983 classic work *A Nation at Risk*, issued by the National Commission on Excellence in Education headed by Terrel (Ted) Bell, and has continued to the present day, with neoconservative education critic Chester Finn (2010) calling Shanghai outperforming the United States on the Programme for International Student Assessment (PISA) a "Sputnik moment for U.S. education."

The persistent emphasis on only a few subjects in the curriculum also has led to concern regarding how much time is spent on certain subjects to the detriment or exclusion of other subjects. This tension involves the issue of whether schooling should prepare students for an enduring and lifelong quest for understanding, and/or whether schooling should be primarily interested in the economic values to be obtained by graduating skilled workers to be expert in the trades and vocations of the moment. The place of the arts in the curriculum is also a matter of value preferences. While the ancient Greeks always considered art, music, and physical education part of the basic curriculum, the Puritans disavowed art, music, and drama as sinful and therefore excluded them from being taught in schools. To this day, art, music, and other culturally specific topics or subjects are often neglected because they cannot be easily compared with nation-to-nation test results. The bottom line appears to be "if it isn't tested, it doesn't count."

Whether it is called the Common Core and irrespective of the rationale for creating it, that is, the expressed need to enable the nation to continue to be economically dominant in the international marketplaces of the world, the issues involved with creating a curriculum are profound and are politically sensitive.

Curriculum Flash Point 4: Assessment Issues and the Achievement Gap

The persistence of the achievement gap as revealed in test scores displayed by race and social class continues to be used by proponents as a justification for the Common Core. Many critics of U.S. education give the impression that we are the only nation on earth to have such a problem. Nothing could be further from the truth, as Richard Rothstein (2004) notes:

> The inability of schools to overcome the disadvantage of less literate home backgrounds is not a peculiar American failure but a universal reality. The number of books in students' homes, for example, consistently predicts their test scores in almost every country. Turkish immigrant students suffer from an achievement gap in Germany; as do Algerians in France, as do Caribbean, African, Pakistani, and Bangladeshi pupils in Great Britain, and as do Okinawans and low-caste Buraku in Japan. (p. 20)

What are the common elements of these groups from different nations' gaps with their more mainstream student counterparts? In nearly all cases the groups that are not performing as well as the more mainstream students exhibit these characteristics:

- They are of lower socioeconomic position in the existing social hierarchy.
- They are of a different language and/or cultural system.
- They often exhibit attitudes that are, if not hostile, resistant to "fitting in" to the norms of the school and are disciplined at higher rates than their proportionate numbers in the schools, often receiving harsher penalties than their more privileged counterparts.
- They have higher dropout rates from school and lower graduation rates.
- Parents often have attitudes of helplessness, indifference, or antagonism to school and school authorities.

These commonalities should suggest that the achievement gap is more than a school issue. It is a larger socioeconomic cultural issue (English, 2010).

What we have is a cultural difference. It should suggest that the schools are not neutral cultural grounds. It should also suggest that those groups that find themselves more at odds with the culture and language embedded in schools, their routines and assumptions, will find their achievement more difficult. Many will also find their place problematic and perceive their difficulties as a matter of personal rejection of who they are as human beings. That their skin color, their language, their religion, clothing, and food customs are also not valued or are frowned upon become the breeding grounds of apathy toward school. The perception that these differences cannot be overcome even if they try hard results in a group-based anomie in which members of the group become permanent outcasts. Such a state was captured very well in Jay MacLeod's 1987 book *Ain't No Makin' It: Leveled Aspirations in a Low-Income Neighborhood.*

Bourdieu (2009) has called the differences between groups a matter of **cultural capital**. By that he meant the way any particular social group and the individuals in it relate to life, move their bodies, dress, engage in certain social customs regarding courtship, marriage, entertainment, music, and more.

It should be recalled that human culture is a construct, that is, an artificial creation of beliefs, attitudes, customs, and actions. Cultures are not better or worse than each other; they are *different*, however. Much of human culture is learned unconsciously and so it is invisible to those who possess it; that is, they don't think about it and they are not consciously aware of how their culture shapes their views, or advances or inhibits their thinking or attitudes.

Most people think they confront the world as "it is," not realizing that their cultural lens is shaping what they see and don't see. Their cultural lens also tells them that what they do see is "natural" and the way things are. When others don't see things the way they do, it is not uncommon for them to come to believe such people are "wrong" or "misguided" or in earlier times that such people were *inferior, barbaric, savage, uncivilized, animals, lazy, stupid, infidels,* and other such historic descriptors of cultural and human inferiority.

Any discussion about cultural capital has to avoid a deficit mindset. It has not been an easy thing to do in the past, and many educators have succumbed to the belief that culturally different children are simply *inferior* in one or more ways. The important thing to understand when it comes to schools is that the school and its curriculum privileges

> the cultural capital (which includes world views, linguistic codes, certain types of knowledge, and material objects—such as books) of a particular social class, the dominant social class. The school does not act primarily, however to teach children anything they don't already know, but to certify the knowledge of the children of the dominant class by giving them high marks, certificates, and diplomas. (Reed-Danahay, 2005, p. 47)

For this reason, Bourdieu and Passeron (1979) discerned in their study of which groups of children succeeded best in schools that it was the children of the wealthier or more privileged groups who did well in schools, so much so that they "inherited" the school as if it were a birthright. This phenomenon is repeated all over the world where there is an achievement gap. And it means that the achievement gap is also a gap between social group distinctions and is unlikely to be erased anytime soon because of it.

Another realization should be that the achievement gap is about a lot more than stuff on tests and test scores. Tested information is connected to the expectations of the dominant social class via the curriculum that it is supposed to assess. Members of the dominant social class would not permit the school to teach or test anything they did not find important to their own sense of what is important and worth knowing. They will fight very hard to make sure the school maintains their perspectives and interests (Brantlinger, 2003).

Deborah Reed-Danahay (2005) comments about the often misrecognized purpose of schooling when she observes, "the function of education is to produce a social hierarchy and that this conflicts with the value of a 'truly democratic' system that would enable all students to have access to skills leading to school success" (p. 47). Despite the rhetoric about "all children learning in school," the school is set up so that all children do not learn equally well in school. Unmasking this rather ugly truth means that given the conditions that exist in schools today, all children will never be successful in them. The schools will continue to privilege what they do with the interests of the dominant social class.

The perspective of Bourdieu and others regarding cultural capital is beyond the idea that the tests in use are biased because they consistently show that some social groups usually underperform on them when compared to others. Tests are skewed to assess what is privileged as curriculum, and in turn, the entire school, its expectations, routines, view of difference and exceptionality are similarly biased. The problem with the Common Core is that it is "common" only to a certain select group of parents and students. It is simply imposed on everyone else, something Bourdieu and Passeron have called the cultural arbitrary. While the cultural capital embedded in the Common Core State Standards and ultimately the curriculum content is "natural" for some students, for others it is an alien and arbitrary choice to which they are subjected and some are never successful with it and leave school as early as possible.

The Common Core privileges one form of cultural capital over many others. School ought to be a place where various forms of cultural capital are respected and the children represented from that distinction are not de-privileged or made to feel inferior or less human because of who and what they are. Once an important understanding is reached that the sources of the achievement gap encompass more factors than the school, but also that the school itself produces some factors leading to the gap, then a deeper understanding of the gap and how it can be confronted can be reached. Unless this occurs, no amount of money or effort aimed at "reforming" schools will fully erase the achievement gap, because they will not deal with its true sources.

Curriculum Flash Point 5: The Issue of Where to Set Test Cutoff Scores

While there seems to be a general consensus about educational standards, the issue of where to set test cutoff scores for a state's students is less an educational problem than a political one. For example, in Texas, when the state adopted a new more demanding set of expectations, the legislature responded by lowering test and curriculum requirements (Gewertz, 2013).

The very tricky issue of raising the bar is fraught with a state's officials determining how many students may fail or be graded as "not proficient" or "minimal." If such terms result in politically unacceptable large groups of students being ranked in the lower categories, such numbers can led to widespread pessimism about the value of the test and the curriculum it is supposed to assess. One alternative is to set the bar higher in stages so that school systems have a chance to ramp up their systems of teaching to avoid the public perception that their schools were not very good after all. This approach appears to have been taken in Louisiana where the state superintendent put forth a plan that "the full impact of new common-core-aligned tests wouldn't be felt on school grades until 2025" (Ujifusa, 2013).

Curriculum Alignment

A partial solution to the problem of the use of selective classes of students and their form of cultural capital is that of **curriculum alignment.** Curriculum alignment was earlier called either *curriculum overlap* or *instructional alignment (*English & Steffy, 2001, p. 90). It emerged from a variety of attempts to improve pupil test performance in the 1980s. It was discovered that, if the curriculum "overlapped" with the test, pupil scores were better. The first statewide use of alignment was in Missouri in 1991.

Curriculum alignment is a concept that the curriculum, the test, and teaching should be matched or congruent. This would be especially true if the test were the kind of high-stakes instrument that was connected to measures of schooling effectiveness and remuneration for teachers and school leaders.

Think of a three-legged stool as shown in **Figure 7.1**. One is teaching, the other is curriculum, and the third is testing. They are all connected in a common structure. A teacher is supposed to teach the approved curriculum, perhaps one based on the Common Core. In turn, curriculum and teaching are assessed by the test. Put another way, one teaches to the curriculum and since the curriculum is already matched to the test, when one is teaching to that curriculum one is also teaching to the test.

Curriculum alignment helps students who do not belong to the cultural majority perform better because it ensures that the tested curriculum will be taught. As a practice, then, alignment ensures that the disadvantages of some home environments that accrue because some are less apt to be matched to school expectations, routines, and content than others, will decrease. Alignment creates a more level testing playing field as a result (Moss-Mitchell, 1998).

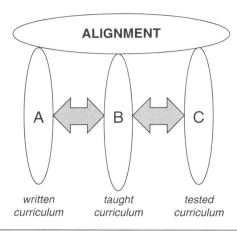

Figure 7.1   The Requisite Curriculum Alignment for Any Plan of Accountability

Since majority children already come to school with a huge advantage—according to Barry (2005), the achievement gap is estimated to start at 22 months—students who lack the legitimated cultural capital embodied in the school have increased access to that which is assessed. Preliminary results show that under these circumstances, minority achievement improves (Moss-Mitchell, 1998).

Today curriculum alignment is an accepted concept, especially with various accountability approaches that can either reward or punish teachers, school leaders, or school systems for test score gains or losses. For accountability to be fair, the content of tests must be connected to a curriculum to which all students have access. Teachers and school leaders must be provided with curriculum, textbooks, and other materials that are aligned with the assessment instruments so that they will know what will be assessed. In addition, sample test items should be available so that teachers understand *how* students will be assessed, sometimes referred to as the *performance conditions* under which students will be tested. The idea is that testing should be assessing what is business as usual in a school and not some atypical set of conditions. Within this idea is that students should not be surprised by the test. It should be a fair and reliable measure of the learning they have acquired in a typical school year.

There are two ways a school leader working with teachers can approach curriculum alignment. Referring again to Figure 7.1, one can attain alignment by adopting the approach A-B-C, which means that first a written curriculum is developed, then it is taught, and lastly it is tested. That approach is called **frontloading** (English & Larson, 1996). Frontloading is the typical sequence that connects the written to the tested curricula. This approach was followed in the development of the Common Core standards. It ensures that the testing tail never wags the curriculum dog.

However, it ought to be obvious that the sequence can be reversed. So, for example, the sequence C-A-B or C-B-A can be employed by beginning with the test and working back to the written and/or taught. That is the idea of **backloading** (English & Larson, 1996). As a practice, backloading will work when the state of the curriculum is of very poor quality and/or specificity. This occurred in many states when they initially created a state-level curriculum, often with very poor levels of specific content and with wide ambiguity in what was actually desired to be learned. The actual alignment to state level assessments turned out to be very low (Rothman, 2004; Webb, 2002). In such cases, the largest factors of predicting student performance are socioeconomic ones, an indicator of cultural capital acquisition.

As a practice, backloading involves a thorough analysis of test items *as a type* of assessment with an eye toward discerning whether the content being assessed matches the existing curriculum and whether the *performance conditions* in the item have been taught in the classroom. In other words, if the test involves the use of multiple-choice items, students should have practice with multiple-choice items as a way of learning how to respond appropriately. Similarly, students should practice writing essays to prepare for a test where an essay response is desired. Testing formats should be familiar to students.

In addition, backloading should involve an analysis of the cognitive levels involved in the assessment. Using *Bloom's Taxonomy* (1956) for example, if the test item is at level 5, synthesis, but classroom instruction has been at much lower levels, say level 1 factual recall, there is a mismatch between how students were taught and how they are going to be assessed. Under these circumstances teachers will often say, "I taught that," but the teaching was not at the same or higher level of cognition as the assessment. Students are then surprised when faced with a test item for which they have no prior experience.

The testing situation should be a fair measure of pupil learning when they have been adequately prepared.

The simple truth is that for students to be fairly and reliably assessed, the school, its curriculum, and its teaching should be aligned to the assessment. There should be few surprises for students when taking a test. Whatever differences are revealed in test performance should be those connected to student learning and ability, and not to being unprepared for the test because the school, its curriculum, and its teaching staff failed to adequately provide an aligned curriculum in which A-B-C were connected.

In summary, the teaching staff teaches what is tested and it teaches the curriculum the way it is going to be tested. Both the tested curriculum and its *performance conditions* should be part of sound test preparation practices in use in the school. If the first time a student encounters curriculum content or a specific test item format is on the day the test is given, then the school has failed that student. A low test score is not due to inadequate learning, but to inadequate preparation for learning to be correctly and fairly assessed.

Finally, even with curriculum alignment in place, curriculum content that fails to recognize differences in cultural capital and the influence of the home environment on the development of that capital will not erase the achievement gap. In that respect, neither will the Common Core, since it is an example of Bourdieu and Passeron's cultural arbitrary. The gap is the product of that arbitrary being imposed on all children irrespective of their cultural backgrounds.

The Common Core, regardless of whether in political terms it was created from the ground up, is still only one possible cultural lens among many other possibilities. The antidote is a multicultural lens, within one beam of light broken into a rainbow.

Conclusion

Even in states that have not formally backed away from the Common Core standards because of the political backlash, states and schools face challenges in implementing them. It is also highly doubtful any new set of single standards will erase the achievement gap anytime soon, and it will be some time before the Common Core standards can be determined to have improved international test score comparisons upon which so much political capital has been expended. The simple fact is that one cannot test excellence into a curriculum or the schools. One can only test what is in the curriculum and in the schools in the first place.

Key Chapter Terms

Backloading: The practice of reaching alignment by starting with the test of form of assessment in use and creating a written curriculum from the test-designated content and also influencing teachers to use it as a focus for teaching.

Common Core standards: The expectations or expected outcomes of learning desired when there is a common curriculum in place. The Common Core standards have been internationally benchmarked and represent desired academic competencies.

Cultural arbitrary: Since human culture is an artifact, that is, a social construction, there is no "natural" culture. The selection and imposition of one form of

culture upon others is an arbitrary act, usually with political dominance, to engage in its application to all other cultures.

Cultural capital: A form of noneconomic capital that represents modes of living and thinking, deportment, dress, linguistic patterns and accents, as well as manners. It is the cultural capital of the political elites that dominate the selection of the formal curriculum in schools of the state.

Curriculum: The actual designation of the content (or plan of studies) to be taught and that is expected to represent the means by which the expectations (standards) are realized.

Curriculum alignment: The match or congruence between the written curriculum, the taught curriculum, and the tested curriculum. Alignment includes not only the content of the curriculum and the test, but the match between cognitive levels as well.

Frontloading: The attainment of alignment to assessment/tests and/or teaching by starting with the designation of the curriculum content prior to teaching or testing.

References

Anderson, G., & Pini, M. (2011). Educational leadership and the new economy: Keeping the "public" in the public schools. In F. W. English (Ed.), *The Sage handbook of educational Leadership* (2nd ed., pp. 176–222). Thousand Oaks, CA: Sage.

Banchero, S. (2012, May 9). School-standards pushback. *The Wall Street Journal,* A6.

Barry, B. (2005). *Why social justice matters.* Cambridge, England: Polity Press.

Benjamin, H. (1939). *The saber-tooth curriculum.* New York, NY: McGraw-Hill.

Bloom, B. S. (1956). *Taxonomy of educational objectives: Cognitive domain.* New York, NY: Longman.

Bobbitt, F. (1971). *The curriculum.* Arno Press & The New York Times. (Original work published 1918)

Bode, B. H. (1930). *Modern educational theories.* New York, NY: Macmillan.

Bourdieu, P. (2009). *Distinction: A social critique of the judgment of taste* (R. Nice, Trans.). New York, NY: Routledge.

Bourdieu, P., & Passeron, J.-C. (1979). *The inheritors: French students and their relation to culture*

(R. Nice, Trans.). Chicago. IL: University of Chicago Press.

Bourdieu, P., & Passeron, J.-C. (2000). *Reproduction in education, society, and culture* (2nd ed.). Thousand Oaks, CA: Sage.

Brantlinger, E. (2003). *Dividing classes: How the middle class negotiates and rationalizes school advantage.* New York, NY: RoutledgeFalmer.

Davis, M. R. (2013, April 24). Education industry players exert public-policy influence. *Education Week, 32*(29), 52–53.

Emery, K., & Ohanian, S. (2004). *Why is corporate America bashing our public schools?* Portsmouth, NH: Heinemann.

English, F. W. (2010). *Deciding what to teach and test: Developing, aligning, and leading the curriculum* (3rd ed.). Thousand Oaks, CA: Corwin.

English, F. W. (2014). *Educational leadership in the age of greed: A requiem for res publica.* Ypsilanti, MI: National Council of Professors of Educational Administration.

English, F. W., & Larson, R. L. (1996). *Curriculum management for educational and social service organizations.* Springfield, IL: Charles C Thomas.

English, F. W., & Steffy, B. E. (2001). *Deep curriculum alignment: Creating a level playing field for all children on high-stakes tests of educational accountability.* Lanham, MD: Scarecrow Press.

Finn, C. E. (2010, December 8). A sputnik moment for U.S. education. *The Wall Street Journal,* A21.

Fleisher, L., & Banchero, S. (2013, August 7). New York test scores bode ill for rest of U.S. *The Wall Street Journal,* A5. Retrieved from http://online.wsj.com/news/articles/SB10001424127887323420604578652450468865758

Frenkel, E., & Wu, H-H. (2013, May 7). Republicans should love "common core." *The Wall Street Journal,* A15.

Gass, J., & Chieppo, C. (2013, May 28). Common core education is uncommonly inadequate. *The Wall Street Journal,* A15.

Gewertz, C. (2013, December 11). States grapple with setting common test-score cutoffs. *Education Week, 33*(14), 6.

Hansel, L. (2013, May 22). The common core needs a common curriculum. *Education Week, 33*(32), 32.

MacLeod, J. (1987). *Ain't no makin' it: Leveled aspirations in a low-income neighborhood.* Boulder, CO: Westview.

Moss-Mitchell, F. (1998, May). *The effects of curriculum alignment on the mathematics achievement of third-grade students as measured by the Iowa Test of Basic Skills: Implications for educational administrators.* Unpublished doctoral dissertation, Clark University.

Nasser, H. E. (2008, February 12). U.S. Hispanic population to triple by 2050. *USA Today.* Retrieved March 12, 2011, from http://www.Usatoday.com/news/nation/2008-02-11—population study_N.htm

National Commission on Excellence in Education. (1983). *A nation at risk: The imperative of educational reform.* Washington, DC: U.S. Department of Education.

National Governors Association Center for Best Practices & Council of Chief State School Officers. (2010). *Common Core State Standards for English*

language arts and literacy in history/social studies, science, and technical subjects. Washington, DC: Authors.

Peddiwell, J. A. (1939). *The saber-tooth curriculum.* New York, NY: McGraw-Hill.

Reed-Danahay, D. (2005). *Locating Bourdieu.* Bloomington: Indiana University Press.

Rotberg, I. C. (2011, September 14). International test scores, irrelevant policies. *Education Week, 31*(3), 32.

Rothman, R. (2004). Benchmarking and alignment of state standards and assessments. In S. Fuhrman & R. Elmore (Eds.), *Redesigning accountability systems for education,* (pp. 96–114). New York, NY: Teachers College Press.

Rothman, R. (2011). *Something in common: The common core standards and the next chapter in American education.* Cambridge, MA: Harvard University Press.

Rothstein, R. (2004). *Class and schools: Using social, economic, and educational reform to close the Black-White achievement gap.* New York, NY: Teachers College Press.

Shor, I. (1986). *Culture wars: School and society in the conservative restoration 1969–1984.* Boston, MA: Routledge & Kegan Paul.

Spencer, H. (1860). What knowledge is of most worth? In *Education* (chap. 1). New York, NY: Appleton.

Stern, S., & Klein, J. (2013, May 4). Conservatives and the common core. *The Wall Street Journal,* A13.

Tanner, D., & Tanner, L. (1990). *History of the school curriculum.* New York, NY: Macmillan.

Toppo, G. (2013, August 8). Tougher exams pressure public schools. *USA Today,* 3A.

Ujifusa, A. (2013, June 12). State opposition jeopardizes common-core future. *Education Week, 32*(35), 36.

Upham, D. (2010, April 27). Is Texas messing with history? *The Wall Street Journal,* A17.

Webb, N. (2002, April). *An analysis of the alignment between mathematics standards and assessment for three states.* Paper presented at the American Education Research Association, New Orleans, LA.

Further Readings

ACT, Inc. (2006). *Reading between the lines: What the ACT reveals about college readiness in reading.* Iowa City, IA: Author.

This research report was used to validate the need for the standards and was used to inform the College and Career Readiness Standards.

ACT, Inc. (2009). *The condition of college readiness 2009.* Iowa City, IA: Author.

This research report was used to validate the need for the standards and was used to inform the College and Career Readiness Standards.

Bode, B. (1930). *Modern educational theories.* New York, NY: Macmillan.

Bode, a professor at Ohio State, criticized the work of Franklin Bobbit in a classic analysis that is still modern when thinking about the Common Core debates of our times. However, for a good understanding, the reader may want to become familiar with Bobbit's proposals to develop a "relevant" curriculum by using "real world" data.

English, F. W. (2010). *Deciding what to teach and test* (3rd ed.). Thousand Oaks, CA: Corwin.

This book focuses on issues of curriculum design and validation and brings issues of cultural capital and the cultural arbitrary into focus on matters of creating a "one size fits all" curriculum as in the case of the Common Core.

English, F. W. & Steffy, B. E. (2001). *Deep curriculum alignment.* Lanham, MD: Scarecrow Education.

This book provides the rationale for, and a step-by-step guide to, curriculum alignment, frontloading, and back-loading, as well as test item deconstruction.

NGA & CCSSO. (2009). *Common core state standards initiative standards-setting criteria [online].* Retrieved from http://www.corestandards.org/assets/Criteria.pdf

This document outlines the criteria used by the workgroups as they developed the College and Career Readiness Standards.

NGA & CCSSO. (2010, March). *Common core state standards initiative frequently asked questions [online].* Retrieved from http://www.corestandards.org/assets/CoreFAQ.pdf

This document defines educational standards and discusses the CCSS Initiative, who developed the CCSS, and the adoption and implementation process.

NGA & CCSSO. (2010, June). *Reaching higher: The common core state standards validation committee [online].* Retrieved from http://www.corestandards.org/assets/CommonCoreReport_6.10.pdf

This document describes the role of the Validation Committee, how members were chosen, and who members were, and reports summary feedback.

NGA & CCSSO. (2010, June). *Reactions to the March 2010 draft common core state standards: Highlights and themes from the public feedback [online].*

Retrieved from http://www.corestandards.org/assets/k-12-feedback-summary.pdf

This document describes the feedback process and reports themes in feedback gathered.

NGA & CCSSO. (2010, June). *Summary of public feedback on the draft college- and career-readiness standards for English-language arts and mathematics [online].* Retrieved from http://www.corestandards.org/assets/CorePublicFeedback.pdf

This document describes the feedback process and reports themes in feedback gathered.

Peddiwell, J. A. (1939). *The saber-tooth curriculum.* New York, NY: McGraw-Hill.

The reader of this chapter might wonder how a book published almost half a century ago could possibly be relevant today. This little paperback book will surprise, amuse, and provide keen insights into the nature of knowledge and how it is selected and the rationale for that selection.

Perna, D. M., & Davis, J. R. (2007). *Aligning standards & curriculum for classroom success* (2nd ed.). Thousand Oaks, CA: Corwin.

This is a very practical book that shows in detail how to move from a standards-based curriculum into classroom practice. It provides examples of how to work curriculum standards into lesson planning and provides sample charts and graphs.

Rothman, R. (2011). *Something in common: The common core standards and the next chapter in American education.* Cambridge, MA: Harvard Education Press.

For an educational leader who wants to get the "big picture" of how the Common Core came into being and the contemporary challenges it faces with implementation, this small and readable book is just a superb source.

Tanner, D., & Tanner, L. (1990). *History of the school curriculum.* New York, NY: Macmillan.

For the serious practitioner who wants to delve deeply into past curricular controversies, movements, names, and places, this resource would be hard to top. It is complete and concise, and it will illustrate the continuing flash points in curriculum development in the United States.

8

THE GROWING HISPANIC POPULATION IN U.S. SCHOOLS

Challenges and Solutions

CLAUDIA SANCHEZ

Texas Woman's University

The chapter examines the demographic context of the Hispanic population and the educational implications of its steady growth in the United States. It also depicts four main challenges facing school leaders from this development along with five potential solutions that include strategies school leaders can use to overcome the stated challenges. Although the term *Hispanic* appears more often than *Latino* in this chapter, for the purposes of this chapter, the terms are used interchangeably.

A Decade of Continued Growth

According to the Pew Hispanic Center (now called the Pew Research Center's Hispanic Trends Project), which used the U.S. Census Bureau's 2011 American Community Survey to analyze the Hispanic population, the Hispanic population increased from 35.2 million in 2000 to 51.9 million in 2011 (Motel & Patten, 2013). This signifies an increase of 48% in a little over a decade. Today, Hispanics make up 17% of the U.S. population, up 4 percentage points from the 13% they represented in 2000. Compare this

growth to the 6 percentage point decrease in the White population, which went from 69% in 2000 to 63% in 2011.

Among Hispanics, two thirds of the population is of Mexican origin and one third is of Puerto Rican, Salvadoran, Cuban, Dominican, and other origins. Two thirds of the Hispanic population in the United States is concentrated in five states: California, Texas, Florida, New York, and Illinois. **Table 8.1** shows the number of the Hispanic population in these states in 2011 and the percentage these figures represented based on the overall number of the Hispanic population in the United States. As Table 8.1 shows, as of 2011, about half of the Hispanic population in the United States (47%) lived in the two states of California and Texas. Data from the analysis conducted by the Pew Hispanic Center also revealed that since 2000, five other states (South Carolina, Kentucky, Arkansas, Minnesota, and North Carolina) have experienced the fastest growth of the Hispanic population in the United States to date. The rates of growth in these states between 2000 and 2011 ranged from 120% to 154%.

The Hispanic population is the nation's youngest major racial or ethnic group, with a median age

State	Number of Hispanics (millions)	% of the Total U.S. Hispanic Population*
California	14.4	28%
Texas	9.8	19%
Florida	4.4	8%
New York	3.5	7%
Illinois	2.1	4%

Table 8.1 Number and Percentage of the Hispanic Population in the United States in 2011

SOURCE: Claudia Sanchez, using statistics from Pew Hispanic Center's analysis of the U.S. Census Bureau's 2011 American Community Survey, http://www.pewhispanic.org/2013/02/15/hispanic-population-trends/ph_13-01-23_ss_hispanics6/

*The total Hispanic population in the United States in 2011 was estimated at 51.9 million.

of 27, while the median ages of Blacks, Asians, and Whites, are 33, 36, and 42, respectively. The Hispanic population in the United States predominantly speaks Spanish and English at home, with about 25% of the Hispanic population ages 5 and older reporting they speak only the English language at home.

Educational Attainment

Among Hispanics ages 25 and older, the rate of high school diploma attainment grew from 52% in 2000 to 63% in 2011 (Motel & Patten, 2013). Further, rates of college attainment and enrollment among Hispanics also rose in the last decade. The percentage of Hispanic adults ages 25 and older who attained a bachelor's degree or more grew from 10% in 2000 to 13% in 2011. As well, the percentage of Hispanics ages 18 to 24 who were enrolled as an undergraduate or graduate student went from 20% in 2000 to 33% in 2011.

Household Income

Median household income is lower among Hispanics ($39,000) than the United States overall ($50,000) (Motel & Patten, 2013). Depending on how the poverty rate is calculated, Hispanics had

either the largest poverty rate of any racial group in the United States, or the second largest, in 2011 (Lopez & Cohn, 2011). Consequently, Hispanic households are more likely to receive food stamps than all U.S. households, and fewer than half of Hispanic households own their homes. Also, a staggering 30% of the Hispanic population lacks health insurance, compared to 15% of the U.S. population.

Latinos and Education

As discussed in the previous section, the past decade has been one of continued growth for the Hispanic population in the United States. The issues that face Hispanic children are not unique to them, but are severely exacerbated in this group. School leaders face challenges to educate children of poverty, meet the needs of language minority children, reduce **dropout** rates, and prepare students for college. In many schools, Hispanic children make up most of the children in poverty and language minority children. Hispanic children also face particular issues with regard to finishing school and going on to graduate from college. The remainder of this chapter discusses these challenges and, later, presents culturally appropriate strategies that can aid school leaders in addressing these issues.

Challenge No. 1: Preparing to Respond to School Enrollment Projections

School leaders must be ready to respond to the needs of a steadily growing Hispanic population in public schools. According to *The Condition of Education 2014* report (Kena et al., 2014) issued by the National Center for Education Statistics (NCES), the total public school enrollment for prekindergarten through 12th grade grew from 47.7 million in 2001 to 49.5 million in 2011. By 2023, the total public school enrollment is estimated to increase by 7% to 52.1 million (Kena et al., 2014).

From fall 2001 through fall 2011, the share of enrollment of White students in grades PreK-12 decreased from 60% to 52%. Conversely, the share of enrollment of Hispanics, the fastest growing group of students in U.S. schools, increased from 17% to 24%. By 2023, the share of Hispanic enrollment is projected to increase by 6 percentage points, to 30%, while the share of White enrollment is projected to continue its downward trend by 7 percentage points, to 45%. The share of Black student enrollment is expected to decrease slightly from 16% to 15%. According to the projections, beginning in 2014 and continuing through 2023, the percentage of public school students who are White will be less than 50% while the enrollment of Hispanics and Asians/Pacific Islanders will continue its upward trend (Kena et al., 2014).

Challenge No. 2: Educating Children of Poverty

A second challenge facing school leaders today is the education of children of poverty. According to *The Condition of Education 2014,* in school year 2011–2012, 19% of public school students attended a high-poverty school while only 12% did during school year 1999–2000 (Kena et al., 2014). In fact, the percentage of school-age children living in poverty across the nation increased from 16% in the year 2000 to 21% in 2011. In 2012, all regions of the United States (Northeast, South, Midwest, and West) reported an increase in poverty rates for school-age children. The South had the highest rate of poverty for school-age children (23%), followed by the West (21%), Midwest (19%), and Northeast (17%).

In 2011, the South also included two of the three states with the largest percentage of Hispanics in the nation (Texas and Florida) as well as states with the largest rate of increase in the Hispanic population (South Carolina, Kentucky, Arkansas, and North Carolina) (Motel & Patten, 2013). The *Condition of Education 2014* reports that in 2012 the poverty rate for Hispanic children under the age of 18 (33%) was lower than the rate for Black children (39%) and American Indian/Alaska Native children (36%) (Kena et al., 2014). However, because of their higher numbers in the population, as of 2010 more Hispanic children under 18 were living in poverty—6.1 million that year—than children of any other racial or ethnic group. An analysis of U.S. Census Bureau data by the Pew Hispanic Center showed that in 2010, 37.3% of poor children were Latino, 30.5% were White, and 26.6% were Black (Lopez & Velasco, 2011).

These figures are similar to data released in a report by the NCES (Ross et al., 2012) that indicated that while 6% of White students were enrolled in high-poverty schools for the school year 2010–2011, the rate of Hispanic enrollment in high-poverty public elementary and secondary schools for that same year was 38%, second only to that of Blacks (41%).

Challenge No. 3: Addressing the Needs of Language Minority Children

A third challenge for school leaders is the education of children whose native language is other than English. According to the 2012 NCES report *Higher Education: Gaps in Access and Persistence Study* (Ross et al., 2012), 22% of the student population ages 5 to 17 spoke a language other than English at home in 2010. Among the student population that speaks a language other than English at home, a smaller group is designated as **English language learners (ELL)**. The term ELL applies to students being served in PreK-12 public school programs of language assistance such as bilingual education or **English as a second language (ESL)**. The percentage of U.S. public school students who were English language learners was 9.1% in 2011–2012, up from 8.7% in 2002–2003 (Kena et al., 2014).

One of the issues public education has yet to conquer is the successful academic preparation of students whose native language is other than English. Results from state-mandated tests continue to reveal a disparity in the achievement of native English speakers or non-English language learners and that of non-native English speakers or English language learners. In 2011, for instance, the National Assessment of Educational Progress (NAEP) reading scale scores for non-ELL students in Grades 4 and 8 were higher than their ELL peers' scores. The fourth grade score difference between non-ELL and ELL students was 36 points and the eighth grade score difference was 44 points. The disparity between average scores of two student groups is known as the **achievement gap** in NAEP reading scores (Aud et al., 2013). These results confirmed the long-standing disparity in reading scores between non-ELLs and ELLs that NAEP has identified since 2002.

Challenge No. 4: Reducing Dropout Rates and Increasing College Completion Rates

A fourth challenge in public education is the need to decrease dropout rates and increase college completion rates.

Status and Event Dropout Rates

Status dropout rates represent the percentage of individuals ages 16 through 24 who are not enrolled in school and have not received a high school credential (either a diploma or an **equivalency certificate** such as a **GED certificate**). In 2012, the status dropout rate for Hispanics was 13%, compared to 8% for Blacks and 4% for Whites (Kena et al., 2014).

Event dropout rates, on the other hand, represent the proportion of students who leave school each year without completing a high school program (Aud et al., 2013). While event dropout rates provide a picture of the proportion of students who at one point participated in a high school program, status dropout rates provide cumulative data on dropouts among all young adults within a specified age range (whether or not they participated in a high school program at some point). Status rates are therefore higher than event rates because they include all dropouts ages 16 through 24, regardless of when they last attended school (Aud et al., 2013).

A report from the NCES (Chapman, Laird, Ifill, & KewalRamani, 2011) indicated that during 2009, a higher percentage of Hispanic students dropped out of high school than any other **racial/ethnic group**. The event dropout rate was 5.8% for Hispanics and 4.8% for Blacks, compared to 2.4% for Whites. While Whites and Blacks experienced a downward trend in event dropout rates for nearly two decades (1972 through 1990), Hispanics' dropout rates remained unchanged during that period. Hispanic event dropout rates did begin to decline in 1995, for the first time since 1972, and continued to decline through 2009.

Ross et al.'s (2012) study reported on postsecondary attainment in the United States. Only 52% of Hispanics who became full-time students attending a 4-year institution of higher education in 2003–2004 attained bachelor's degrees by 2009, while 73% of Whites achieved this goal.

A 2009 survey conducted by the Pew Hispanic Center found that Latinos in general recognize the importance of a college education (Lopez, 2009). The survey found that the main reasons behind the low educational attainment of Latinos were financial struggles and pressure to support their families. Other reasons for the lag in educational attainment among Latinos included poor English skills, a dislike of school, and a perception that additional education was not required for the career paths they preferred.

Solutions and Strategies for School Leaders

The previous section discussed four main challenges school leaders must consider, namely, the importance to respond to school enrollment projections, the need to educate children of poverty, the urgency to meet the needs of language minority children, and the need to reduce dropout rates and increase college completion rates. This section suggests strategies to help school leaders address the aforementioned challenges.

Solution No. 1: Fully Acknowledge Your Responsibility to Step Up to the Challenge

School leaders must be ready to respond to school enrollment projections. The question is not if, but when, a school leader will need to address the issue of cultural and linguistic diversity in the school setting. All projections suggest cultural and linguistic diversity in public schools is on the rise and the Latino population continues to be an important part of this growth. In urban, suburban, and rural school settings, the influx of Latino children into U.S. schools will continue, and as a result, school leaders who can respond to the demands of our schools' new reality become a must. So how is a school leader to prepare for an increasing Latino school population? The first step is for school leaders to fully acknowledge their responsibility to equip themselves with the tools that will enable them to build schools that can prepare academically successful students. The second step is to actively do what is necessary to acquire such tools. The remainder of this section suggests concrete steps that can help school leaders prepare to meet the challenges discussed earlier.

Solution No. 2: Implement Solid Education Programs for Language Minority Children

To respond to the challenge of addressing the needs of language minority children, school leaders must support the implementation of strong education programs. In the broad menu of program options for English language learners (ELLs), bilingual education is more effective than all-English approaches (**submersion**, **structured English immersion**, ESL), especially in cases where ELLs' native language is stronger than their second language (De Jong, 2013; Thomas & Collier, 2002). James Crawford and Stephen Krashen (2007) define bilingual education as

> the use of students' native language to accelerate English-language development. Children receive content-area instruction in both languages, although the proportions may vary (with English phased in rapidly or gradually). Goals include developing "academic English," promoting academic achievement in English, and in some models, cultivating proficiency in both languages. (p. 15)

The philosophy behind bilingual programs stresses the need to build on the linguistic foundation students already have in their native language to develop students' cognitive and linguistic skills in two languages. Bilingual education programs distinguish between conversational and academic language proficiency and bilingual program types include the following, listed from more effective to less effective according to findings from a 2002 national study of effective programs for the long-term academic achievement of language minority students (Thomas & Collier, 2002):

- Two-way bilingual or dual language education consists of classrooms with native English speakers and limited English speakers who acquire a second language while they learn academic content.
- "Late exit" bilingual education consists of classrooms where the goals are (a) to prepare students who are bilingual and biliterate in English and students' native language and (b) to succeed academically. Late exit programs typically run from kindergarten through fifth grade.

- "Early exit" bilingual education programs temporarily support limited English speakers in their native language. The main goal of early exit programs is to mainstream limited English speakers as soon as possible.

In contrast to bilingual programs, all-English programs either make no use of students' native language, or may use students' first language incidentally to clarify a concept. The delivery of content, however, is done only in the second language since the use of the students' native language is deemed a distraction from the acquisition of the English language.

School leaders who aim for successful student outcomes must build on the linguistic foundation ELLs bring with them. Developing ELLs' first language not only develops ELLs' ability in the language they acquired first, but also could improve their cognitive skills (Bialystok, 2011; Engel de Abreu, Cruz-Santos, Tourinho, Martin, & Bialystok, 2012). These developed cognitive skills, in turn, have the potential to accelerate the acquisition of the English language both socially and academically.

Solution No. 3: Promote High-Quality Instruction for Children of Poverty and Language Minority Children

As the school's instructional leader and lead administrator, a principal's duty is to promote a school culture that encourages instruction of high quality for all children, where teachers do not blame students and their families for existing academic shortcomings but instead recognize

> the role of economic change (including a decrease in factory and skilled labor jobs to which one could aspire and with which one could support a family) and structural inequalities related to access to education; housing; healthcare; and basic nutrition (Trumbull & Pacheco, 2005b, p. 109).

Hold and Communicate High Expectations

High-quality instruction is not possible without having high academic expectations for students and communicating such expectations to students and their families. High expectations alone do not suffice; they must be combined with adequate support systems for student learning. In fact, the more teachers attribute failure to students' backgrounds and the more students' backgrounds are viewed as barriers to academic achievement, the less teachers tend to take responsibility for students' success (Trumbull & Pacheco, 2005b).

Promote a Collective Responsibility for Students' Learning

Instructional leaders promote a collective responsibility for students' learning, so that everyone finds ways to adjust instruction to students' needs and everyone also finds ways to effectively engage students by using strategies that connect to students and their interests. Instructional leaders support teachers to renew themselves within collaborative learning communities that examine student and adult work in addition to serving as a forum for the sharing of teachers' ideas on maintaining high expectations in addition to strategies for high-quality instruction. To this end, school leaders encourage professional development opportunities that are carefully designed for educators and school staff.

To better serve an increasingly diverse student population, six main assumptions can guide the design of strong professional development opportunities for educators. First, competent leadership should buffer teachers from outside stressors and foster their professional life, including ongoing professional development focused on student success (Trumbull & Pacheco, 2005b). The second assumption is that the school community has norms in which teachers are responsible for student success (Trumbull & Pacheco, 2005b). Third, the school culture should foster and develop a common understanding among educators and all other instructional personnel of the ways in which particular instructional practices help learners achieve high academic goals (Vialpando & Yedlin, 2005). The fourth assumption is that all professional development efforts should represent

- Meaningful opportunities for educators and other school staff. Participants must identify the importance and relevance of the professional development activities (Vialpando & Yedlin, 2005).
- Opportunities to learn useful strategies educators can use to increase their knowledge of students and their cultures (Vialpando & Yedlin, 2005).

- Opportunities to practice strategies that encourage interaction among students from different backgrounds where group formation is not always assigned by the teacher, but also determined by the students (Trumbull & Pacheco, 2005b).

The fifth assumption of professional development for educators is that schools should actively promote specialized training (Vialpando & Yedlin, 2005) in the following areas:

- All aspects of school-based assessment, from test administration to interpretation of results;
- English as a second language (ESL) and bilingual education;
- Principles of language and literacy acquisition for first and second languages;
- Culturally responsive pedagogy; and
- Multicultural training for school administrators and staff members.

The sixth assumption is that all professional development efforts should encourage repeating cycles of collaboration and reflection among educators. The purpose of this type of collaboration is to

- Find out what has worked for students from different backgrounds with different skills (Trumbull & Pacheco, 2005b).
- Design culturally responsive curriculum, instruction, and assessment, taking into account the students educators are teaching (Trumbull & Pacheco, 2005b).
- Provide educators with opportunities to do microteaching, or short practice teaching sessions with colleagues, in order to practice the new strategies they learn (Vialpando & Yedlin, 2005).
- Provide educators guidance on how to adapt and modify instruction to meet the needs of learners (Vialpando & Yedlin, 2005).
- Provide educators opportunities to describe, reflect upon, and support the curriculum (Vialpando & Yedlin, 2005).
- Observe how different students participate in classroom activities to determine what strategies reach which students, and involve students in choice about their work (Trumbull & Pacheco, 2005b).

Solution No. 4: Advocate for Children and Families of Poverty

A school leader is not only an instructional leader and lead administrator but a leader advocate for the students, their families, and the community at large. Strategies to assist school leaders in advocating for children and families of poverty include forming and participating in multicultural school committees for family advocacy, having a system in place to identify and advise families in need, informing families about the way the school system works, and encouraging professional development activities focused on student and family advocacy.

Form and Participate in Multicultural School Committees for Family and Advocacy

The vital role of teachers' advocacy for students and families is well documented in the literature, and is also part of teacher education standards and competencies (Trumbull & Pacheco, 2005a). School leaders are well aware of teachers' role as advocates and consequently support the development of teacher advocates by promoting the creation of committees whose purpose is to advocate for students and their families. The committees can consist of teachers, aides, administrators, and parent representatives. To get started, members can define their general goal for advocacy as well as specific objectives with corresponding tasks and benchmarks. Advocacy committees can assist in bridging the gap between the school culture and families' cultures by promoting deeper understanding.

Establish a System to Identify and Advise Families in Need

From parent support and education to health care and financial assistance, today's school leaders, teachers, and personnel must be knowledgeable of community resources that can assist families in need. Further, schools must find ways to make families aware of such resources and to advise families on how to access help. School leaders are well aware that all assistance to families must be communicated in the language families speak well.

Inform Students and Families About the Way the School System Works

Family involvement in children's schooling is successful if it results in teachers' increased understanding of their students' families and communities, as well as families' increased understanding of how

schools operate (Trumbull, Rothstein-Fisch, & Hernandez, 2003). Rather than assuming families know their way through the school system, school leaders investigate how much they really do know. To this end, school leaders conduct informal group talks and share any vital information parents may wish to know.

Parents familiar with the way the school system works understand the meaning of schooling concepts such as homework, desirable reading habits, report cards, standardized tests, and the PTA. Families unfamiliar with the system may not be aware of the meaning or implications of these concepts, so may need plenty of information and guidance to successfully internalize new meanings of schooling.

Encourage Professional Development Activities Focused on Advocacy

School leaders committed to student and family advocacy actively promote professional development activities where teachers and other school personnel can constantly explore and reshape their perceptions of advocacy. These professional development activities allow educators to examine ways in which they can promote justice and equity. For example, as Trumbull and Pacheco (2005b) suggest, they can

- Advocate for equitable allocation of resources within the school and the district.
- Collaborate with other teachers to evaluate the adequacy and cultural representativeness of the school library.
- Oppose tracking systems that group high achievers and low achievers separately.
- Support district's efforts to gather data in ways that will allow disaggregating by race and ethnicity (as well as other aspects of identity such as gender and socioeconomic status) for examination of patterns of privilege and differential access to programs and courses.

Professional development activities focused on student and family advocacy encourage educators to take a stand. When role play is incorporated into professional development exercises, for example, educators can gain practice speaking out when they see that low expectations of certain groups are accepted (Trumbull & Pacheco, 2005b). Professional development exercises can provide opportunities for teachers and school staff to create, monitor, and enforce a school policy that supports correcting racial or ethnic slurs and using them as an opportunity to educate students about their impact and the fact that they will not be tolerated in the school (Trumbull & Pacheco, 2005b).

As is the case in all strong professional development activities, efforts directed toward promoting family advocacy among educators should promote teamwork where educators could

- engage in conversations about race with colleagues and community members;
- listen to what others have to say, and work hard to recognize other perspectives;
- collaborate with other teachers, administrators, and parents to establish a conflict resolution plan that is culturally appropriate;
- cultivate opportunities to learn from people unlike one's self; and
- examine one's own values, and evaluate whether one's behaviors are in line with these values (Trumbull & Pacheco, 2005b).

Solution No. 5: Develop and Support Strong Family Involvement Programs

To respond to a couple of challenges mentioned earlier, namely, the urgency to meet the needs of language minority children and the need to reduce dropout rates and increase college completion rates, school leaders can develop and support solid family involvement programs that echo the importance of academic success in grades PreK through 12 and beyond. The involvement of parents in their children's education is a strong predictor of students' success in school (Delgado-Gaitán, 2004; Hamilton, Roach, & Riley, 2003). Unless there is evidence of a successful home–school two-way communication that is sustained throughout the school year every school year, no school could claim that it is successful in involving families in their children's education or that it knows the languages and cultures of its students and families well.

Parental or family involvement is often a difficult goal to achieve. Differences between minority families' and school's cultures frequently become barriers that hinder effective communication and prevent schools and families from developing successful partnerships (Delgado-Gaitán, 2004; Hamilton et al., 2003). Barriers to family involvement often include

family's contextual factors, school and home language barriers, families' and schools' cultural beliefs with respect to the roles of parents and schools, families' lack of familiarity with U.S. schools' practices and policies, families' lack of knowledge about the subject matter of homework, and families' exclusion and discrimination by school staff or school organizations (Boethel, 2003; Trumbull & Pacheco, 2005b). Although research shows that most parental involvement efforts launched by schools are directed to minority parents and families, these efforts often have a low rate of success due to the ways in which schools attempt parental and family involvement approaches (Boethel, 2003; Trumbull & Pacheco, 2005b).

To help close the education gap facing Hispanic students, a stronger alliance becomes a must between schools and Hispanic families. Such alliance is perhaps even more crucial in the case of Spanish-speaking families with limited English proficiency, since they may be more vulnerable to becoming alienated from school due to language differences (De Gaetano, 2007). To develop into effective allies, schools must work with families to promote children's acquisition of language and content while making parents aware of the ways in which their involvement is a major factor influencing students' academic success (Delgado-Gaitán, 2004).

Effective family involvement strategies for the Hispanic Spanish-speaking population have included personalized phone calls (Delgado-Gaitán, 2004); warm and positive face-to-face conversations with parents (Espinosa, 1995); as well as monthly parent meetings and newsletters. Also, informal interactions with teachers, along with personal relationships with them have been identified as Hispanic parents' preferred ways of communicating (Trumbull & Pacheco, 2005b).

Trumbull and Pacheco's (2005b) guidelines for maximizing family involvement include four suggestions. First, have informal and personal interactions with families that make families feel more comfortable asking questions or sharing information than they would be in a formal meeting. Second, be flexible about scheduling conferences, meetings, and volunteer opportunities to allow for more parental responsiveness. Third, the authors recommend close work with paraprofessional and school volunteers from students' communities, as well as staff from community-based organizations, to facilitate communication and a real two-way understanding. The fourth suggestion is that schools reach out to families both formally and informally.

Perhaps the first step toward creating solid family involvement programs is for school leaders to relate to students' and families' cultures. School leaders can relate to Hispanic students' cultures by immersing themselves in Hispanic families' cultures, recognizing that families' and school's understanding of parental involvement may differ from one another, identifying the ways in which families prefer to communicate with the school, and validating families' home language.

Immerse Yourself in Families' Cultures

To engage families in linguistically and culturally sensitive ways (De Gaetano 2007), school leaders need to know the cultures of the children's families. Learning about culture is an inside-out process that starts by examining and re-examining one's own values and beliefs in light of the similarities and differences between one's culture and that of the other. Immersing one's self in another culture requires engaging in experiences that will teach one about families' values, customs, beliefs, and communication patterns. Some examples of how this can be done are

- visiting students' neighborhoods and their homes;
- learning from families when conducting home visits and talking to students' family members (grandparents, extended family members);
- going to places where the community gathers socially, such as churches and temples;
- shopping at grocery stores of families' communities;
- watching television or listening to the radio with students and families; and
- listening to the music grandparents, parents, and children like and asking what the lyrics say.

Once engaged in these experiences, one can reflect on the ways in which one is culturally similar to and different from students' families. This reflection has the potential to promote intercultural understanding.

Recognize That Families' Understanding of Parental Involvement May Differ From the School's

Different cultural groups understand the role of parents in children's education in different ways. Culturally diverse families' beliefs and practices often differ from schools' expectations (Barton, Drake, Perez, St. Louis, & George, 2004).

Many Hispanic families, especially recent immigrants from rural areas, may understand that their role is not interfering with the school's or teacher's work. For instance, this may mean refraining from visiting the school or classroom and not expressing their opinions or asking questions of the teacher or school staff. To many Hispanic families, these behaviors are often synonymous with respect for and trust in the teacher's work. Many educators, however, will often mistake these behaviors for disengagement and indifference.

As a school leader, find out how families perceive involvement, and do not assume families will share the school's beliefs. Ask families how they wish to participate in their children's education; let them know what the school recommends they do to become involved, and assure them that it is appropriate—and expected—to visit, ask questions, and share their opinions about their children's schooling. Also, once you have understood whether the school's and family's expectations may differ, be flexible in terms of what you expect from families and take cues from parents and families as to what they feel is appropriate for them in terms of their involvement in children's education (Trumbull & Pacheco, 2005b).

Identify the Ways in Which Families Prefer to Interact With Schools

Families have different preferences about communicating with schools, and teachers and schools need to know what they are (Orozco, 2008). In general, Hispanic families favor warm, inviting classroom and school environments. As stated earlier, families feel more comfortable communicating with the teacher or school staff in small groups, at informal, face-to-face talks, rather than in one-on-one, formal meetings. When rapport has been established, families may prefer home visits.

Before the school year begins, lead school efforts to survey families about how they prefer to communicate. Give families options such as formal or informal meetings, individual or small-group talks, phone calls, written notes, flyers, email, and an interactive website.

Validate Families' Home Language

Validating families' native language is a way to involve parents by acknowledging and celebrating their cultural and linguistic identity (De Gaetano,

2007). To relate to families' culture, it is important to communicate in their native language. Below are some strategies that can help school leaders validate and relate to families' language.

Take a Survival Spanish Course. Learning another language takes a long time, but one does not have to learn the new language perfectly to start communicating in it. Survival Spanish courses allow learning basic communication skills. As a school leader, you can make sure the school offers a survival Spanish course for teachers and school staff. If a course of this nature is not an option at your school, you can lead a one-on-one language tutoring course. All you need is a well-defined goal, such as a list of words and phrases you want to learn and a willing native speaker eager to trade tutoring hours with you. That speaker may be a bilingual teacher aide, a volunteer, a parent, a colleague, or a member of the community. This person could teach you what you want to learn in Spanish, and you could teach the person something he or she wants to learn in English.

Having one-on-one tutoring sessions with a native speaker of the language you want to learn will give you a good language model in addition to a great opportunity for interacting and further exploring the new culture.

Use Live Translators or Interpreters. Identify people in your school and community who speak Spanish and English, and who are willing to serve as translators during face-to-face parent-teacher conferences and other situations such as phone conferences and online communication. Translators are usually members of the community, such as parents and older members of the students' extended families.

Use Electronic Translators and Apps. Two online translators are Google Translate, which is also available as an iPhone and Android smartphone app, and Bing Translator. When using these online tools and apps, it is a good idea to ask a native speaker for input on the accuracy and appropriateness of your translation before sharing the translated message with your audience.

Share Traditional and Technology-Enhanced Bilingual Newsletters. Communication with families needs to be in the language families speak and understand best. In many cases, this means communicating in Spanish. To encourage family involvement, consider sending home short and informative bilingual (English and Spanish) newsletters, which can be in paper, electronic, or video formats. In designing the newsletter, always consider the literacy levels of families and the technology available in families' homes. Contrary to common belief, Spanish-speaking parents with low incomes and low levels of education often have access to multiple technological methods (Walsh, Buckley, Rose, Sanchez, & Gillum, 2008).

Ensure Access to Bilingual Books in School and Classroom Libraries. Bilingual books are critical literacy tools in bilingual classrooms, and they also validate the students' and families' cultural backgrounds and language. By incorporating bilingual books in your classroom library, many Spanish-speaking parents will be able to relate to the language and will be likely to share the book with their child.

Use Spanish Proverbs or Dichos. To be successful, parental involvement programs must relate to the many sociocultural contexts present in families (Souto-Manning, 2006), and consider these contexts when promoting awareness of the benefits associated with parental participation in children's education. One possible way to counter two of the obstacles cited in the published literature (namely, schools' and homes' language barriers and families' lack of familiarity with U.S. schools' practices and policies) in a culturally and linguistically appropriate way may be the use of *dichos* or folk sayings in the Spanish language (Sanchez, 2009). A key component of the Hispanic oral culture and Spanish language discourse, *dichos* have been identified as culturally and linguistically appropriate tools for family involvement. *Dichos,* or popular sayings, may prove effective in enhancing communication between the school and Spanish-speaking families. Rooted in oral tradition (Zúñiga, 1992), *dichos* are commonly used by Spanish-speaking people to express their values, attitudes, and perceptions (Espinoza-Herold, 2007). The concept of *dichos* is explained in greater detail in **Sidebar 8.1.**

Sidebar 8.1   Teaching With *Dichos*

As short traditional guides of conduct, *dichos* endorse moral and ethical values (Delgado-Gaitán, 2004). They transmit cultural values and beliefs to younger generations by teaching lessons about life, offering advice, summarizing ideas, and expressing a specific perspective on a given situation (Chahin, Villarruel, & Viramontez, 1999). These metaphorical images of cultural values and beliefs are spontaneous, brief, and often developed with rhyme (Zúñiga, 1992). They are funds of knowledge of a people and part of the historically accumulated body of knowledge essential for household functioning and well-being among native speakers of Spanish (González, Andrade, Civil, & Moll, 2001). Given their cultural and linguistic relevance among Hispanics, and their potential to impact individuals' belief systems, *dichos* may also influence the ways parents bring up a child, their style of communication, and their thoughts about formal education (Espinosa, 1995).

Dichos can be used as slogans or mottos to encourage behaviors conducive to family involvement (Sanchez, Plata, Grosso, & Leird, 2010). Teachers, administrators, and other school staff can incorporate the slogans or mottos in settings where Spanish is spoken to communicate with families. For example, assume that teachers wish to invite parents to talk about the importance of working together in children's education. One *dicho* to help persuade parents to become involved is *"Dos cabezas piensan mejor que una,"* which means "Two minds are better than one." Another helpful *dicho* is *"En la unión está la fuerza,"* which means "In unity, there is strength." Both *dichos* can be interpreted as conveying the need to have the teacher working alongside families to encourage children to learn.

In settings where Spanish is not commonly used, teachers and school staff could integrate *dichos* into their communication efforts with families, provided that *dichos* are applied within appropriate contexts. Bilingual resource books can assist non-Spanish-speaking teachers and school staff in understanding and interpreting most commonly used *dichos*. Popular resource books for *dichos* include the *Dictionary of Proverbs: Spanish/English and English/Spanish* (Carbonell-Basset, 1996), *101 Spanish Proverbs* (Aparicio, 1998), and *My First Book of Proverbs/Mi Primer Libro de Dichos* (González, Ruiz, & Cisneros, 2002).

Conclusion

The Hispanic population in the United States continues to grow at unprecedented rates. This shift in the demographic landscape of this country requires that public education respond to four urgent challenges. The first challenge is the need to prepare for the demands of current school enrollment and projected enrollment rates indicating a substantial and growing presence of Hispanic children in U.S. classrooms. Second, public schools must successfully prepare an increasing number of children of poverty from Hispanic origin. Third, schools must meet the needs of an increasing number of language minority children, an important subgroup among Hispanic students. Finally, reducing dropout rates and increasing college completion rates among the Hispanic population is an ongoing challenge.

This chapter proposes five solutions for school leaders to step up to the aforementioned challenges. School leaders' acknowledgment of their responsibility and their commitment to actively engage in doing what is necessary to better serve an increasing Hispanic student population is the first step toward overcoming these challenges. Next, it is a must to implement strong education programs for language minority children and high-quality instruction for economically disadvantaged children. It is also important to advocate for children and families of poverty and to develop and support strong family involvement programs that are both linguistically and culturally appropriate. By implementing these solutions and the strategies suggested in this chapter, school leaders will be better prepared to face the demands of an increasingly diverse student population.

Key Chapter Terms

Achievement gap: Occurs when one group of students outperforms another group, and the difference in average scores for the two groups is statistically significant.

Dropout: Term used to describe both the event of leaving school before completing high school and the status of an individual who is not in school and who is not a high school completer. High school completers include both graduates of high school programs as well as those who complete equivalency programs, such as those that prepare students for the General Educational Development (GED) test. Transferring from a public school to a private school, for example, is not regarded as a dropout event. A person who drops out of school may later return and graduate but is called a "dropout" at the time he or she leaves school. Measures to describe these behaviors include the event dropout rate (or the closely related school persistence rate), the status dropout rate, and the high school completion rate.

English as a second language (ESL): Designates the programs and instructional strategies used to teach the English language to non-English speakers. The programs and strategies do not use the student's native language for instructional purposes.

English language learner (ELL): An individual who, due to any of the reasons listed below, has sufficient difficulty speaking, reading, writing, or understanding the English language to be denied the opportunity to learn successfully in classrooms where the language of instruction is English or to participate fully in the larger U.S. society. Such an individual (1) was not born in the United States or has a native language other than English; (2) comes from environments where a language other than English is dominant; or (3) is an American Indian or Alaska Native and comes from environments where a language other than English has had a significant impact on the individual's level of English language proficiency.

Equivalency certificate: A formal document certifying that an individual has met the state requirements for high school graduation equivalency by obtaining satisfactory scores on an approved examination and meeting other performance requirements (if any) set by a state education agency or other appropriate body. One particular version of this certificate is earned by passing the General Educational Development (GED) test. The GED test is a comprehensive test used primarily to appraise the educational development of students who have not completed their formal high school education and who may earn a high school equivalency certificate by achieving satisfactory scores. GED certificates are awarded by the states or other agencies, and the test is developed and distributed by the GED Testing Service of the American Council on Education and education publisher Pearson.

Event dropout rate: Estimates the percentage of high school students who left high school between the beginning of one school year and the beginning of the next without earning a high school diploma or an alternative credential (e.g., a General Educational Development [GED] certificate).

GED certificate: This award is received following successful completion of the General Educational Development (GED) test. The GED program, sponsored by the American Council on Education, enables individuals to demonstrate that they have acquired a level of learning comparable to that of high school graduates.

Racial/ethnic group: Classification indicating general racial or ethnic heritage. Race/ethnicity data are based on the *Hispanic* ethnic category and the race categories listed below (five single-race categories, plus the *two or more races* category). Race categories exclude persons of Hispanic ethnicity unless otherwise noted. *White:* A person having origins in any of the original peoples of Europe, the Middle East, or North Africa; *Black or African American:* A person having origins in any of the black racial groups of Africa. Used interchangeably with the shortened term *Black; Hispanic or Latino:* A person of Cuban, Mexican, Puerto Rican, South or Central American, or other Spanish culture or origin, regardless of race. Used interchangeably with the shortened term *Hispanic; Asian:* A person having origins in any of the original peoples of the Far East, Southeast Asia, or the Indian subcontinent, including, for example, Cambodia, China, India, Japan, Korea, Malaysia, Pakistan, the Philippine Islands, Thailand, and Vietnam. Prior to 2010–2011, the Common Core of Data (CCD) combined Asian and Pacific Islander categories; *Native Hawaiian or Other Pacific Islander:* A person having origins in any of the original peoples of Hawaii, Guam, Samoa, or other

Pacific Islands. Prior to 2010–2011, the Common Core of Data (CCD) combined Asian and Pacific Islander categories; *American Indian or Alaska Native:* A person having origins in any of the original peoples of North and South America (including Central America), and who maintains tribal affiliation or community attachment.

Status dropout rate: Reports the percentage of individuals in a given age range who are not in school (public or private) and have not earned a high school diploma or an alternative credential.

Structured English Immersion: Designates programs and instructional techniques whose goal is ELLs' rapid acquisition of the English language at the expense of the students' native language. SEI programs use structured and sequential lessons that are largely based on the mainstream curricula and taught exclusively in the English language.

Submersion: Also known as "sink or swim." In these classrooms, English language learners do not receive support in the form of ESL instruction or native language instruction.

References

Aparicio, E. (1998). *101 Spanish proverbs.* Lincolnwood, IL: Passport Books, NTC/Contemporary Publishing Group.

Aud, S., Wilkinson-Flicker, S., Kristapovich, P., Rathbun, A., Wang, X., & Zhang, J. (2013). *The condition of education 2013* (NCES 2013-037). U.S. Department of Education, National Center for Education Statistics, Washington, DC. Retrieved May 3, 2013, from http://nces.ed.gov/pubsearch/pubsinfo.asp?pubid=2013037

Barton, A. C., Drake, C., Perez, J. G., St. Louis, K., & George, M. (2004). Ecologies of parental engagement in urban education. *Educational Researcher, 33*(4), 3–12.

Bialystok, E. (2011). Reshaping the mind: The benefits of bilingualism. *Canadian Journal of Experimental Psychology, 65*(4), 229–235.

Boethel, M. (2003). *Diversity: School, family and community connections.* Southwest Educational Development Laboratory. Retrieved from http://www.sedl.org/connections/resources/diversity-synthesis.pdf

Carbonell-Basset, D. (1996). *Dictionary of proverbs: Spanish/English and English/Spanish.* Hauppauge, NY: Barron's Educational Series.

Chahin, J., Villarruel, F. A., & Viramontez, R. A. (1999). Dichos y refranes: An alternative approach to understanding the values and beliefs of Mexican families. In H. P. McAdoo (Ed.), *Family ethnicity: Strength in diversity* (pp. 153–167). Thousand Oaks, CA: Sage.

Chapman, C., Laird, J., Ifill, N., & KewalRamani, A. (2011). *Trends in high school dropout and completion rates in the United States: 1972–2009*

(NCES 2012-006). U.S. Department of Education. Washington, DC: National Center for Education Statistics. Available from http://nces.ed.gov/pubsearch

Crawford, J., & Krashen, S. (2007). *English learners in American classrooms: 101 questions, 101 answers.* New York, NY: Scholastic.

De Gaetano, Y. (2007). The role of culture in engaging Latino parents' involvement in school. *Urban Education, 42*(2), 145–162.

De Jong, E. J. (2013). Effective bilingual education: From theory to academic achievement in a two-way bilingual program. *Bilingual Research Journal, 26*(1), 65–84.

Delgado-Gaitán, C. (2004). *Involving Latino families in schools: Raising student achievement through home-school partnerships.* Thousand Oaks, CA: Corwin.

Engel de Abreu, P. M. J., Cruz-Santos, A., Tourinho, C. J., Martin, R., & Bialystok, E. (2012). Bilingualism enriches the poor: Enhanced cognitive control in low-income minority children. *Psychological Science, 23*(11), 1364–1371.

Espinosa, L. M. (1995). *Hispanic parent involvement in early childhood programs* (ERIC Digest, EDO-PS-95-3). Urbana, IL: ERIC Clearinghouse on Elementary and Early Childhood Education.

Espinoza-Herold, M. (2007). Stepping beyond *sí se puede: Dichos* as a cultural resource in mother-daughter interaction in a Latino family. *Anthropology & Education Quarterly, 38*(3), 260–277.

González, N., Andrade, R., Civil, M., & Moll, L. (2001). Bridging funds of distributed knowledge: Creating zones of practices in mathematics. *Journal of Education for Students Placed at Risk, 6*(1–2), 115–132.

Gonzalez, R., Ruiz, A., & Cisneros, S. (2002). *My first book of proverbs/Mi Primer Libro de Dichos.* San Francisco, CA: Children's Book Press.

Hamilton, M. E., Roach, M. A., & Riley, D. A. (2003). Moving toward family-centered early care and education: The past, the present, and a glimpse of the future. *Early Childhood Education Journal, 30*(4), 225–232.

Kena, G., Aud, S., Johnson, F., Wang, X., Zhang, J., Rathbun, A., . . . Kristapovich, P. (2014). *The condition of education 2014* (NCES 2014-083). Washington, DC: U.S. Department of Education, National Center for Education Statistics. Retrieved from http://nces.ed.gov/pubs2014/2014083.pdf

Lopez, M. H. (2009). *Latinos and education: Explaining the attainment gap* (Report by the Pew Hispanic Center). Retrieved May 3, 2013, from http://www.pewhispanic.org/2009/10/07/latinos-and-education-explaining-the-attainment-gap/

Lopez, M. H., & Cohn, D. (2011). *Hispanic poverty rate highest in new supplemental census measure.* Retrieved on July 17, 2014, from http://www.pewhispanic.org/2011/11/08/hispanic-poverty-rate-highest-in-new-supplemental-census-measure/

Lopez, M. H., & Velasco, G. (2011). *Childhood poverty among Hispanics sets record, leads nation: The toll of the Great Recession* (Report by the Pew Hispanic Center). Retrieved from http://www.pewhispanic.org/2011/09/28/childhood-poverty-among-hispanics-sets-record-leads-nation/

Motel, S., & Patten, E. (2013). *Statistical portrait of Hispanics in the United States, 2011.* Pew Hispanic Center. Retrieved on July 17, 2014 from http://www.pewhispanic.org/2013/02/15/statistical-portrait-of-hispanics-in-the-united-states-2011/

Orozco, G. L. (2008). Understanding the culture of low-income immigrant Latino parents: The key to involvement. *The School Community Journal, 18*(1), 21–37.

Ross, T., Kena, G., Rathbun, A., KewalRamani, A., Zhang, J., Kristapovich, P., & Manning, E. (2012). *Higher education: Gaps in Access and Persistence Study* (NCES 2012-046). U.S. Department of Education, National Center for Education Statistics. Washington, DC: Government Printing Office. Retrieved from http://nces.ed.gov/pubs2012/2012046.pdf

Sanchez, C. (2009). Learning about students' culture and language through family stories elicited by "dichos." *Early Childhood Education Journal, 37*(2), 161–169.

Sanchez, C., Plata, V., Grosso, L., & Leird, B. (2010). Encouraging Spanish-speaking families' involvement through dichos. *Journal of Latinos and Education, 9*(3), 239–248.

Souto-Manning, M. (2006). Families learn together: Reconceptualizing linguistic diversity as a resource. *Early Childhood Education Journal, 33*(6), 443–446.

Thomas, W. P., & Collier, V. P. (2002). *A national study of school effectiveness for language minority students' long-term academic achievement.* Santa Cruz, CA: Center for Research on Education, Diversity and Excellence, University of California-Santa Cruz.

Trumbull, E., & Pacheco, M. (2005a). *Leading with diversity: Cultural competencies for teacher preparation and professional development.* Providence, RI: Brown University and Pacific Resources for Education and Learning.

Trumbull, E., & Pacheco, M. (2005b). *The teacher's guide to diversity: Building a knowledge base.* Providence, RI: The Education Alliance at Brown University.

Trumbull, E., Rothstein-Fisch, C., & Hernandez, E. (2003). Parent involvement in schooling: According to whose values? *The School Community Journal, 13*(2), 45–72.

Vialpando, J. & Yedlin, J. (2005). *Educating English language learners: Implementing instructional practices.* Washington, DC: National Council of La Raza.

Walsh, B. A., Buckley, R. R., Rose, K. K., Sanchez, C., & Gillum, N. L. (2008). Innovative school-family communication: Parent's perceptions of the use of monthly classroom DVD newsletters. In P. G. Grotewell & Y. R. Burton (Eds.), *Early childhood education: Issues and developments* (pp. 211–221). Hauppauge, NY: Nova Science.

Zúñiga, M. E. (1992). Using metaphors in therapy: *Dichos* and Latino clients. *Social Work, 37*(1); 55–60.

Further Readings

Cloud, N., Genesee, F., & Hamayan, E. (2000). *Dual language instruction: A handbook for enriched education.* Boston, MA: Heinle & Heinle.

This book details ways to develop and sustain high-quality instruction in the context of dual-immersion education.

Crawford, J. (2004). *Educating English learners: Language diversity in the classroom* (5th ed.) Los Angeles, CA: Bilingual Education Services.

This book gives a comprehensive overview of history, politics, theory, and practice regarding the education of English language learners.

Freeman, R. D. (2004). *Building on community bilingualism: Promoting bilingualism through schooling.* Philadelphia, PA: Caslon.

This book demonstrates how schools can promote English language development, high academic achievement, and multilingual expertise within bilingual communities.

Genesee, F., Lindholm-Leary, K., Saunders, W. M., & Christian, D. (2006). *Educating English language learners: A synthesis of research evidence.* New York, NY: Cambridge University Press.

This report by the Center for Research on Education, Diversity, and Excellence (CREDE) presents research findings on English learners' language, literacy, and general academic development.

Lindholm-Leary, K. J. (2001). *Dual language education.* Clevedon, England: Multilingual Matters.

This book was one of the first in the field of bilingual education to present a thorough overview of a variety of dual language programs from the United States.

Ross, R. (2013). School climate and equity. In T. Dary & T. Pickeral (Eds.), *School climate: Practices for implementation and sustainability* (School Climate Practice Brief, No. 1). New York, NY: National School Climate Center.

This report suggests the following strategies for creating equitable communities in schools: encouraging reflective practice of students and adults, increasing multicultural understanding, keeping diverse schools physically and emotionally safe, promoting cultural responsiveness regarding high expectations, ensuring diverse participation, and attending to students' emotional needs.

Zarate, M. E. (2007). *Understanding Latino parental involvement in education.* Los Angeles. CA: The Tomas Rivera Policy Institute. Retrieved on May 30 from http://files.eric.ed.gov/fulltext/ED502065.pdf

This study explored the different definitions and perceptions of parental involvement in education from the perspective of a variety of stakeholders. School administrators will find this report helpful as they seek to promote parental involvement in schools.

9

The Continuing Search for Best Practices in Classroom Instruction

Kimberly Kappler Hewitt

University of North Carolina Greensboro

Consider a principal newly assigned to a struggling, "majority minority" middle school. She pores over the school's achievement and demographic data, along with data from surveys, and learns all she can from school faculty and other stakeholders, including students and parents. She recognizes that students are struggling to master grade-level math content, especially in the areas of complex problem-solving and algebraic concepts. Additionally, she learns that many of the school's African American students derisively equate math success with "acting White." Alongside the school improvement team and with input from a subgroup of students and parents, she works to identify root causes of these challenges and to draft a thoughtful, intentional plan, drawing upon available research and the wisdom of the faculty, including their expertise about the local context. This principal embodies a commitment to **best practices**.

This chapter defines best practices, provides a critique of the concept, and identifies general, field-specific, and approach-specific defensible teaching practices. Additionally, it offers concrete strategies that educational leaders can use to leverage best practices to serve students effectively, ethically, and equitably.

"Best Practice" Defined

In their seminal work, *Best Practice: New Standards for Teaching and Learning in America's Schools* (2012), now in its 4th edition, Steven Zemelman, Harvey Daniels, and Arthur Hyde note that the terms "good practice" and "best practice" are "everyday phrases used to describe solid, reputable, state-of-the-art work in a field" (p. 1). Their use of the term underscores several concepts: (a) best practices are state of the art, reflecting current research and underscoring the notion that what constitutes best practice will change over time as more is learned and understood about teaching and learning; (b) the word *reputable* reflects the notion that best practices represent consensus (or as close to it as we get in education) of professionals in the field; (c) best practices are based on research, and; (d) best practices represent mindful practice.

Often, the terms "good practice," "best practice," "promising practice," "evidence-based practice," "research-based practice," "scientifically based practice," and "excellent practice" are conflated and used interchangeably. Grover J. Whitehurst, who served as assistant secretary for educational research and improvement at the U.S. Department of Education during the George W. Bush administration, in 2002 defined evidence-based practice as the "integration of professional wisdom with the best available empirical evidence in making decisions about how to deliver instruction" (p. 3). He recognizes the role of professional expertise and judgment that considers context alongside research in shaping instruction. Essentially, best practices are intentional, considered approaches that reflect educator judgment and research. Additionally, best practices are *defensible practices* (Skelton, 2009). Nothing we do as educators is value-free. As such, educators must be mindful of the values underscored in their judgments and must ensure that practices are ethically defensible.

Looking Backward: From Where Does the Concept of Best Practice Come?

The **discourse** of best practices reflects the 17th- and 18th-century Enlightenment notion of betterment through change grounded in scientific knowledge. Enlightenment—or modernist—values include certainty, objectivity, and the belief that science provides a linear arc of progress toward ever better ways of doing and being. Further, modernist thinking eschews ideology and privileges a belief in value-free, objective reasoning (and by extension research) and the application of "correct" (identified by research) practices.

In the early 20th century, F. W. Taylor (1911) ushered in the era of scientific management or Taylorism, the aims of which were focused on efficiency of management and production. The attending results were devaluation of worker creativity and agency. In the 1960s and 1970s, process/product researchers worked to map specific teacher behaviors to student achievement, resulting, for example, in attention to teacher behaviors that promoted time on task. Discourses of best practice can be found today in manufacturing, business, finance, medicine, law, architecture, and the social services, including the treatment of mental illness and substance abuse. Vestiges of Taylorism are reflected in a contemporary tendency to apply science in a myopic way to improve efficiency and achieve ends.

This assumption that what is best is knowable and can be applied universally to bring about predicted outcomes underscores a commitment to evidence-based practices, where evidence comes from scientifically based research, which privileges quantitative, experimental design as the "gold standard" for research and marginalizes qualitative and mixed methods research. This is manifest in the federal government's What Works Clearinghouse, which acts as a powerful arbiter of what do and do not constitute best practices in education. Taken further, this approach manifests itself in the mantra that "what counts is what works," where value is indicated by the ability to effect certain ends, and concerns about ethical and moral dimensions and the value-ladenness of knowledge and assumptions are elided.

Best Practices: A Critique

While the concept of best practices has notable merits, there are also substantive concerns about it that fall into four broad categories: theoretical challenges, issues of **social justice** and equity, challenges of practice, and misuse of best practices.

Theoretical Challenges

Best Practices as a Neoliberal Mechanism for Control and Accountability

Neoliberalism involves the privileging of economic values over social values and the privileging of market forces, including competition and privatization of social institutions, including education. This discourse is inextricable from the discourse of accountability, which emphasizes measurable outcomes as a mechanism of surveillance, usually in the form of standardized achievement test scores. Here best practices are those that increase test scores, and best practices are advanced within the framework of accountability.

Neoliberalism tends to elide issues of power, ethics, equity, and social justice. It promotes external reward and punishment and marginalizes discourses that speak to democratic roles of education, including the development of an educated citizenry and freedom from oppression, and to humanistic roles of education, including attending to the needs of the whole child—intellectually/academically, socially, emotionally, and physically. To the extent that the language of best practices is used to reify neoliberal discourse, it does a disservice to the multifaceted role of education in society and to students.

What Constitutes Evidence: "Scientific" Evidence for Best Practices

An aspect of modernism is the notion that reality is external, objective, and both knowable and verifiable through the application of (quantitative) empirical research. Such scientific evidence serves to identify best practices. Within the modernist and neoliberal discourses, there is a clear hierarchy of scientific evidence promulgated by the U.S. Department of Education that places quantitative experimental research at the pinnacle and—in descending order of worth—comparison groups (quasi-experimental design), pre-post treatment comparison, correlational studies, case studies, and anecdotes (Whitehurst, 2002). Qualitative research is severely marginalized. This is misguided at best and dangerous at worst. While random trials may help to establish causal links between certain practices and outcomes, they cannot attend to issues of how and why something "works," nor can they address issues of appropriateness or value. This hierarchy of evidence excludes whole worlds of research and severely limits our access to actionable data.

Best Practices as Simplifying and Deskilling Teaching

As Louise Anderson Allen argues in her entry on best practices in the *Encyclopedia of Curriculum Studies* (2010), best practices are leveraged in an attempt to "teacher proof" curriculum and instruction and, in doing so, oversimplify teaching and disenfranchise educators:

> Clearly, the concept of best practices was conceived of and touted to be the simplification of the complex task of teaching. As a nonlinear task, however, teaching does not easily lend itself to being reduced to a formula or to a recipe. . . . Best practice also deskills teachers. . . . Teachers are now encouraged in fact, required to be compliant deliverers. (p. 81)

To the extent that disembodied best practices are valued over the expertise and experience of educators, they are coercive and serve as technologies of control over educators. Only by cultivating critically reflective educators can the diverse needs of diverse students in diverse context be ethically and effectively met.

Resistant to Change and Antithetical to Innovation: Fixed Versus Dynamic Best Practices

The phrase *best practice* connotes status. Once identified and adopted, best practices are codified such that they are resistant to change. Consider the five-paragraph essay, math problem sets, and book reports. There are innumerable practices to which educators remain committed, even as more innovative approaches are developed. We must think of best practices as fluid and dynamic as opposed to fixed. What might have served as a best practice at one point in time may no longer be best practice. For example, in the second edition of the aforementioned *Best Practice: New Standards for Teaching and Learning in America's Schools* (1998), Zemelman and colleagues illustrate an "exemplary" whole language program. In the fourth edition (2012) the authors articulate instead a balanced approach to literacy. What is once a best practice will not always be a best practice, as new methods and research may support different practices. Additionally, nascent fields, like that of neuroscience, provide new direction for best practices, although some researchers think that unwarranted conclusions are often drawn from brain research and that the findings don't support all the specific practices that are advocated as "brain-based." Still, what we know about the brain can positively influence classroom practice. For example, in the second edition of Patricia Wolfe's *Brain Matters: Translating Research Into Classroom Practice* (2010), she emphasizes the role of exercise and nutrition in healthy brain functioning; advocates the use of problems, projects, and simulations; and identifies specific "brain-compatible" strategies, such as mnemonic strategies to aid memory and "active rehearsal" strategies, such as peer teaching, to promote long-term retention of learning.

Another risk is that teachers will be averse to experimenting and trying emerging methods and technologies because they have not been vetted as best practice. Overemphasis on best practices can stifle innovation. See **Sidebar 9.1** about flipped instruction as an emerging method for leveraging technology to radically rethink the use of class time.

Sidebar 9.1 Flipped Instruction: Possible Emerging Best Practice

Flipped or reverse instruction basically "flips" traditional school and home learning roles. Traditionally, a teacher might provide direct instruction in class while students take notes. Then the teacher leads the class in guided practice, and afterwards students complete independent practice as homework. In a flipped model, instruction that can be delivered outside of the classroom using technology is pushed to the home, where it is learned in advance of class, freeing up class time for discussion, collaboration, student-teacher conferencing, application, problem solving and student questions. Often in flipped instruction, the teacher will create or identify videos, applets (interactive, web-based software applications), podcasts, websites, or online simulations that serve to provide instruction that would typically take place in the classroom.

Within the emerging best practice of flipped instruction, there are "best practices" for flipping. For example, flipped videos are typically short—often no more than 10 or so minutes—and feature a picture-within-picture of the teacher explaining what the student is seeing in the larger frame. Additionally, best practices in flipped instruction include identifying a purpose for learning; using engaging and well-considered audio and video; tying content accessed outside the classroom to classroom work; embedding flipped content into an effective pedagogical model, such as inquiry learning; promoting student reflection and metacognition of flipped content; and attending to issues of equity due to the digital divide (Bergmann & Sams, 2012).

Educators must be mindful of the digital divide that privileges some students and marginalizes others, based on access to an Internet-enabled device (e.g., desktop or laptop computer, tablet, or smartphone) with quality video and audio capabilities and high speed Internet access. Flipped instruction pioneers Jonathan Bergmann and Aaron Sams, authors of *Flip Your Classroom: Reach Every Student in Every Class Every Day* (2012), identify strategies that promote access, including "burning" flipped content to DVDs or CD-ROMs or making technology available to students before and after school.

There is, however, little systematic research on flipped instruction to date, and evidence of the benefits of flipped instruction are largely anecdotal. As such, educators must be critical practitioners when considering moving to flipped instruction. That said, flipped instruction is the type of innovation that can be squelched if we maintain a fixed notion of best practices, as opposed to a more fluid or dynamic approach that recognizes the need for experimentation in teaching and learning. Flipped instruction is a fruitful area for action research at the classroom or school level.

Best Suggests Just One Way

The very phrase "best practice" implies that there is a single best way to do something and that as educators we must seek out this pinnacle of performance and replicate it. In this respect, the *best* is very much the enemy of *good*. Additionally, the notion that there is one best way to teach is countered by a good deal of research. There is, in fact, a multiplicity of good, defensible ways to approach instruction. A landmark study by Guy L. Bond and Robert Dykstra (1967) of first-grade reading methods and materials found that "no one approach is so distinctly better in all situations and respects than the others that it should be considered the one best method and the one to be used exclusively" (p. 123). Additionally, in a number of large-scale, federally funded studies of exemplary teaching, researchers have found that there is no single "one right way" to teach; instead, what constitutes exemplary teaching can vary across schools and classrooms (Gabriel & Allington, 2012).

Issues of Power, Equity, and Social Justice

The Ecological Fallacy and Attention to the Mean Versus Outlier

Ecological fallacy refers to the act of making inferences or assumptions about individuals based on collective data on groups to which the individual belongs. When we too greatly emphasize the central tendency of data (i.e., what the average student's achievement or profile looks like for a certain group) and underemphasize outliers or individuals, we risk committing ecological fallacy. Ecological fallacies come in many varieties, from assuming that a specific girl will prefer fiction to nonfiction to inferring that all students who were not proficient on a standardized achievement test require the same interventions. While central tendencies, like averages, can give us part of the picture, we must recognize that any group is comprised of diverse, unique individuals who may have different strengths and needs and as such require different approaches and strategies. Being equitable means doing different things to meet different students' needs.

Attention to Context

When considering best practices, we must ask, "Best for whom, in what context, under what conditions, for what goals/ends/purposes and best as determined by whom, using what criteria and evidence, and selected over what alternatives?" Context is key and includes historical, social, political, and cultural elements. There is no best practice that serves all students' needs at any given time in any given setting. It is imperative that teachers, as critically reflective experts, consider the particulars of context in making instructional decisions—drawing upon their knowledge of their field of practice and their knowledge of the particular case. An approach or strategy that was successful in one setting may be ineffective or even counterproductive in another. Alternatively, a different setting might require dissimilar or additional supports—reinvention and adaptation, instead of adoption. For example, many schools are implementing professional learning communities (PLCs). PLC initiatives are not uniformly successful. In some cases, this is because cultural work needs to be done in a school to ready educators for the kind of collegial relationships that PLCs both require and enhance. In other cases, it is because there is an emphasis on strict compliance to a particular PLC model instead of more flexible adaption of the model to suit the particular needs of a group of educators.

The converse concern here is that educators dismiss a promising practice because *it can't work here.* While context is key, it should not be used to dismiss ideas and strategies before they are afforded thoughtful consideration. Sometimes dismissal of ideas as irrelevant or inappropriate for a given context reflects ungrounded assumptions or a failure of imagination that keeps educators from seeing and embracing potentially powerful strategies.

For example, in response to the idea that kindergarteners can begin to write their own books, some educators might respond, "That might work in some rich White neighborhood but certainly not here." Educational leaders must take care to allow context to inform instructional decisions but not limit them.

Best Practices Located Primarily at the Practitioner Level

Most works on best practices in education focus on classroom-level practice. This is reasonable given that substantial research shows that the teacher—not materials or facilities or programs or principals—has the greatest impact on student learning of any school-related factor. As such, it stands to reason that much of the discourse of best practices focuses on teacher-level strategies.

The danger here is twofold. First, the myopic focus on teacher-level best practices ignores the fact that larger, systemic issues can greatly magnify, constrain, or corrupt the influence of teachers. As such, by focusing solely on the teacher level, the discourse of best practices elides the responsibility of educational leaders to ensure systems are aligned with best practices. Additionally, educational leaders must leverage best practices at the program level for whole school improvement.

Second, teachers enacting individually selected practices fail to capitalize on the power of teacher collaboration and shared goals. When all educators in a school have a shared vision for student success and work collaboratively together to enact that vision, teachers' efforts are synergistically magnified. As such, attention must be given to teaching as a collaborative endeavor, including cultivating a shared vision; collaborative planning, assessing, and reflection; and the role of teacher leadership within a framework of distributed leadership.

Lack of Focus on Systemic Issues of Equity, Bias, and Marginalization

Linda Darling-Hammond, in her influential book *The Flat World and Education: How America's Commitment to Equity Will Determine Our Future* (2010) argues that as a society, our attention should be focused not on the achievement gap but on the opportunity gap, the "accumulated differences in access to key educational resources—expert teachers, personalized attention, high-quality curriculum opportunities, good educational materials, and plentiful information resources" (p. 28), which is compounded over generations. Best practices, when focused on compartmentalized instructional strategies, omit attention to larger and more compelling issues of institutional and systemic bias and marginalization. For example, best practices such as accessing and building upon prior knowledge, writing across the curriculum, or hands-on learning will never resolve or ameliorate systemic problems of low expectations for poor students, stratifying or segregating students by "ability," limiting access to high-level, rigorous coursework, inequitable distribution of quality teachers, and the absence of culturally relevant pedagogy (Murphy, 2010). In the context of these powerful forces, best practices seem insignificant or even moot.

Perverse Effects: Costs of Best Practices

When looking at "what works" or at best practices for achieving a certain end, we need to examine intended and unintended consequences. For example, in working to raise Advanced Placement (AP) exam scores, a school might restrict access to the courses to only those students who are likely to score well. This might indeed result in higher AP scores, but it unjustly restricts other students from access to rigorous, deep content. This is a social justice issue, as all students should have access to and should be encouraged to challenge themselves with rigorous content. Educators must be ever vigilant about the use of best practices at the expense of other desirables.

Best Practices Encourage Abdication of Critique

Because best practices are ostensibly the best—as determined by some external and assumed trustworthy entity—they are taken as given and therefore uncontested. This encourages abdication of critique. In other words, because best practices have some figurative stamp of approval, educators may be reluctant to challenge, critically examine, or question these practices. This is dangerous. As previously discussed, sometimes "best" practices result in perverse, unintended consequences or may not be appropriate for a certain context. Judgment regarding instructional practices must always reside in critically

mindful, reflective practitioners. Best practices should be used at the service of such teachers, never as their masters.

Challenges of Practice

When Best Practices Aren't: Poor Implementation

Even the best ideas can be bastardized upon implementation. While a practice must be reinvented and adapted as opposed to mindlessly adopted, we must take care to implement a practice fully and with fidelity; otherwise, the expected benefits or outcomes may be undermined. The challenge comes in balancing the need to fit the practice or program to a specific context and not the other way around, while also recognizing that there are elements or components of an initiative that must be implemented with fidelity in order to see results. For example, perhaps school faculty decide to implement a universal program on prevention of substance abuse that research has shown to be effective, but they recognize that a component of the program—nine weekly 90-minute evening parent sessions—is not a good fit for their community where a substantial number of parents work second shift at a local steel mill. If the faculty cut out the part of the program that engages parents, then the program may not be as effective. Instead, if the faculty offer sessions every other Saturday for 3 hours, they may be adapting the program in a way that is sensitive to the local context but still maintains fidelity to a critical component of the program. Reinvention and adaptation of practices must be a function of context and not a function of educator convenience.

Additionally, if practices—for example a writing workshop—are implemented haphazardly or inconsistently, then the effects are likely to be disappointing. At the school level, deep implementation of a program or reform—by 90% or more of faculty—is needed to effect real change. As practices are implemented, attention should be paid not only to the impact of the practices but the degree, adaptation, and consistency of implementation.

Best Practices as Too Particularistic

In *What Successful Teachers Do: 91 Research-Based Classroom Strategies for New and Veteran Teachers,* authors Neal A. Glasgow and Cathy D. Hicks (2003) introduce each of 91 strategies, identify classroom applications of and research on each, and call attention to precautions and pitfalls. Many of the strategies included in the book are laudable, such as those related to student collaboration, using assessment and feedback, and integrating technology. At the same time, there is a real concern that focusing on isolated, particular strategies, such as the "jigsaw technique" (strategy no. 2), may elide or overshadow larger principles of service, as Joe Osburn, Guy Caruso, and Wolf Wolfensberger argue in "The Concept of 'Best Practice': A Brief Overview of its Meanings, Scope, Uses, and Shortcomings" (2011):

> There is a danger in particularizing as this obscures high-order principles such as a positive relationship of the server to the served, holding and conveying positive high expectations of the party served, and countering negative stereotypes to which the party may be vulnerable. (p. 218)

In the example featured at the beginning of the chapter, analysis of assessment data indicated weak math performance by African American students. Without attention to the root causes of this underperformance, educators might invoke certain best practices in math—such as having students illustrate or act out word problems—when the real issues may lie in students' cultural construct of strong math performance as "acting White" and the prevalence among educators of a deficit model that perseverates on and pathologizes students' weaknesses instead of leveraging their strengths. Sometimes focusing on micro best practices obscures the need to focus on macro issues like systemic bias and cultural misalignment.

The Misuse of Best Practices

Best Practice of Terrible Practices

There are arguably better and worse ways to do just about anything, including practices that are themselves far from best. Even those things that are less desirable in education—a management approach to leadership or a direct instruction approach to pedagogy—have best practices. Indeed, there are entire books written on how best to do these things that are themselves suspect. Educational leaders must ensure not just that things are being *done right* but that *right things* are being done.

Best Practices: Appropriate Versus Effective

What is effective in producing an outcome—such as increases in test scores—can be inappropriate or even perverse. Certainly, a teacher who extracts from students higher test scores by threatening, bullying, and punishing would be roundly condemned. That which is "best" at obtaining certain ends may not be appropriate or ethical. Consider these findings from research on effective teaching for at-risk students:

> Teachers who ask the most high-level and the fewest low-level questions, teachers whose pupils ask more questions and get more feedback from their teachers, teachers who tend to amplify or discuss pupil-initiated comments most are the ones who are *least* effective. (Medley, 1979, p. 24, emphasis added)

If a teacher were to act on this research and focus solely on lower-level questions, she would be guilty of what George W. Bush (2000) referred to as the "soft bigotry of low expectations." She would be teaching students that their questions and comments do not matter, that their work does not warrant her thoughtful feedback. Such "teaching" would be unethical and would mis-serve her students. There are two issues here: The first is that our practices must always be ethical and defensible. To borrow from the medical profession, *primum non nocere—*first, do no harm. Appropriate instruction is that which is fitting (context-relevant) and ethical. Second, we must be mindful about what "ends" or "outcomes" we aim for in education. When considering best practices, we must ask, "Best at what?" In other words, we need to have a sense of what we want to accomplish in order to critically consider practices to bring about the intended result. For example, if the end goal of instruction is to cultivate students who are creative, collaborative problem solvers, instruction will look quite different than if the end goal is success on state standardized achievement tests. Unfortunately, in this era of accountability, what is "best" is generally considered in terms of raising test scores.

Best Practices as Those That Lift Test Scores

Often, best practices are defined in terms of demonstrated impact on raising achievement test scores. This is often the "evidence" used for "evidence-based practice" or "scientifically based practice." This is a narrow view of the role of teaching and learning. It inappropriately elevates certain practices, such as test preparation, narrowing of the curriculum, and short chunking of instruction (instruction in short, limited, skill-based activities, as opposed to multilesson learning on larger concepts), over practices such as interdisciplinary, collaborative, inquiry-based projects as well as a more comprehensive focus on the whole child. If we want students to be nimble, collaborative, creative problem-solvers, as the goals of 21st-century teaching and learning (e.g., Partnership for 21st Century Learning, n.d.) suggest, then using test scores as both the goal of and evidence of best practices is imprudent. Educational leaders must be mindful of the larger picture for teaching and learning. Once that vision has been articulated, then best practices for achieving that vision can be considered.

Supervision Concern: Best Practices as Checklist

Best practices can help school and district leaders make decisions on how to invest resources (e.g., on group sets of leveled books, or books based on students' individual reading levels, instead of basal readers for primary literacy classrooms), on professional development (e.g., on providing rich, job-embedded, ongoing professional development on enduring pedagogical approaches versus one-shot sessions on education fads), and on what to look for in classrooms. Leaders should know what good instruction looks like, how to identify it, and how to cultivate it. Best practices can help to do these things. That said, there is a risk that educational leaders will reduce best practices to a checklist of observables and mindlessly evaluate educators against the checklist. This would be inappropriate for a number of reasons. First, as discussed above, context is key. Educators need the "discretionary space" (Hlebowitsh, 2012, p. 3) to make instructional decisions based on the particular needs of their particular students at a particular point in time. Second, teaching is a complex practice—both art and science—and any reduction of that complexity to a checklist is misguided and both oversimplifies and deprofessionalizes teaching. Thus while educational leaders should be well versed in practitioner dialogue and research about best practices, they must also recognize that doing what is best for students is never

a technical exercise in applying a list of best practices. How, then, should educational leaders approach the use of best practices? The section that follows focuses on this question.

Best Practices for the Use of Best Practices

Given the extensive critique of best practices in this chapter, the reader may well wonder whether the concept of best practices is ruined or at least emasculated. The preceding critique notwithstanding, the discourse of best practices can be generative and productive—and can even promote equity and social justice—when approached critically and reflectively. The following section provides strategies for utilizing best practices in an ethically defensible manner.

Leverage Best Practices to Promote Equity and Social Justice

Certain best practices, such as holding high expectations, heterogeneous and flexible grouping, and differentiation, when provided to *all students,* can actually promote equity and social justice. Additionally, best practice in data use involves analysis of data to uncover and address hidden inequities, such as the common overrepresentation of African American students in discipline referrals and underrepresentation of female students in advanced science courses.

Additionally, the discourse of best practices itself should be reoriented toward—and best practices should be defined as—those practices that abolish marginalization, reduce the opportunity gap, and promote social justice, as opposed to those practices that increase test scores. Further, best practices for social justice require educators to serve as transformative intellectuals who ask hard questions, point out issues of injustice, and challenge orthodoxy.

Promote Educators' "Critical Intelligence" and "Creative Intelligence"

In "Evaluation as Practical Hermeneutics," Thomas A. Schwandt (1997) defines critical intelligence as the ability to question whether the [end] is worth getting to. It requires not simply knowledge of effects, strategies, procedures and the like but the willingness and capacity to debate the value of various ends of a practice. . . . This is fundamentally an exercise in practical-moral reasoning. (p. 79)

Educators must cultivate this critical intelligence in order to judge various best practices and to avoid being positioned as passive drones who mindlessly employ this or that "best practice" as defined by an external entity. Actualizing critical intelligence frames educators as agentic in considering values and evaluating ends. This is difficult to do in highly directive school districts that require compliance with "best practices" as defined or adopted by the school district and thus may require strategic resistance by educators.

Aligned with the need for critical intelligence is what John Dewey referred to as creative intelligence in a book by that name (1917/1970). Creative intelligence is

an intelligence which is not the faculty of intellect honored in text-books and neglected elsewhere, but which is the sum-total of impulses, habits, emotions, records, and discoveries which forecast what is desirable and undesirable in future possibilities, and which contribute ingeniously in behalf of imagined good. (p. 67–68)

Here Dewey liberates intelligence from inert knowledge and exhorts its use for envisioning a better world and transforming the current world toward that vision of the future. Further, he frames creative intelligence as an amalgam of external (records, discoveries) and internal (impulses, habits, emotions) sources of knowing. Again, here the educator is positioned as an empowered, capable, agentic being responsible for imagining and bringing about future good. This discursive positioning of the educator is a major shift from educator as automaton implementing a teacher-proof curriculum using externally identified, prescribed best practices.

Promote Teacher Inquiry

Praxis is the integration of theory into reflective practice, and one vehicle for advancing praxis is teacher inquiry. The cycle of inquiry includes questioning, planning, acting, assessing, reflecting, and adjusting—cycling through the inquiry process continually. Inquiry involves teachers raising questions and identifying challenges, looking to both external evidence as well as their own experience and expertise, making thoughtful decisions, acting upon those decisions, then reflecting on the data (formal and informal) that speak to the intended and unintended consequences of those decisions and then responding appropriately. Joe L. Kincheloe, in his book *Teachers as Researchers: Qualitative Inquiry as a Path to Empowerment* (1991) argues that educators must "push their knowledge to new levels via new questions involving topics which transcend mere teaching technique" (p. 4). Action research is systematic inquiry by educators for educators, the goals of which, according to action research expert Geoffrey E. Mills in *Action Research: A Guide for the Teacher Researcher* (4th edition, 2011), include "gaining insight, developing reflective practice, effecting positive changes in the school environment (and on educational practices in general), and improving student outcomes and the lives of those involved" (p. 5). Action researchers are reflective practitioners.

Promote Collegial Dialogue on Best Practices

Educators are most powerful and effective at advancing student learning when they work collaboratively. Crucial to this collaboration is an ongoing, critical dialogue about best practices, including their potential, limitations, and discursive situatedness, as discussed previously. Indeed, educator collaboration is itself a best practice and can be cultivated within professional learning communities, which are collaborative learning groups orientated toward sharing and applying learning to advance student growth. PLC expert Shirley M. Hord, in her book *Learning Together, Leading Together: Changing Schools Through Professional Learning Communities* (2004), identifies five principles of mature PLCs: shared and supportive leadership, shared values and vision, collective learning and application of learning, supportive conditions, and shared personal practice. Within PLCs, best practices are a focus for dialogue as opposed to a checklist of observable teaching behaviors.

Best Practices

What follows in these sections is an introduction to three dimensions of best practices: general (across multiple grades and content areas), field specific (discipline-specific), and approach or technique specific. A comprehensive treatment of best practices at each of these levels is beyond the scope of this chapter; however, the Further Readings section at the end of the chapter provides additional resources.

General Best Practices

General best practices refer to those that span multiple grades and content areas. In the 4th edition of *Best Practice: Bringing Standards to Life in America's Classrooms* (2012), Zemelman and colleagues identify what they call progressive and constructivist principles of best practice: Learning is student-centered, authentic, holistic, experiential, and challenging; higher-order cognition is emphasized through developmental and constructivist teaching that encourages students to express and reflect on learning; and learning is interactive, reflecting a social, collaborative, and democratic classroom community (pp. 8–9). Additionally, they identify seven structures of best practice teaching, including:

1. *gradual release of responsibility,* the intentional, staged transfer of responsibility from teacher to students through modeling, shared practice, guided practice, and independent practice;

2. *classroom reading-writing workshop,* in which students select their own focus for reading and writing, collaborate with classmates, keep their own records, and self-assess, and where teachers model, conference with students, and conduct mini-lessons based on students' needs;

3. *strategic reading,* which includes metacognition and pre-reading, during-reading, and after-reading comprehension and meaning-making strategies;

4. *collaboration,* in which classroom instruction is decentralized and the role of the teacher shifts from front-of-class commander to supporter of flexible groupings of students, including ad hoc groups and teams of students who work together in long-term teams for projects, novel studies, writing groups, and inquiry-based learning;

5. *integrative (trans-disciplinary) units,* which may be theme-based and which focus on big ideas that cross content areas;

6. *representing to learn,* which requires students to talk, write, draw, act out, and in other ways represent their learning; and

7. *the use of formative-reflective assessment,* which involves assessment *for* learning and assessment *as* learning, where observational records, student portfolios, learning exhibitions, and other assessments not only reflect student learning but foster it as well.

In their book *How Learning Works: Seven Research-Based Principles for Smart Teaching* (2010), Susan A. Ambrose, Michael W. Bridges, Michele DiPietro, Marsha C. Lovett, and Marie K. Norman identify strategies for teaching and learning that stretch across grade levels and content areas, each of which is introduced here.

Prior Knowledge

The activation of students' prior knowledge serves to anchor and filter new learning. Teachers can identify student prior knowledge by dialoging with colleagues, administering diagnostic assessments, having students self-assess their prior knowledge, and by examining student work for patterns of error. The authors offer a number of strategies for activating student prior knowledge, including brainstorming, concept mapping, explicitly linking new content to previously learned content, using analogies and examples, and having students reason through new material based on their prior knowledge. Additionally, teachers must address insufficient, inappropriate, and inaccurate student prior knowledge before and during instruction of new content.

Organization of Knowledge

The second general strategy involves recognizing that "how students organize knowledge influences how they learn and apply what they know" (p. 44) and that experts and novices organize knowledge differently, where experts have rich, meaningful knowledge structures that support learning and performance and novices tend to build sparse, superficial knowledge structures (p. 45). To enhance the way students organize knowledge, teachers can utilize concept maps; provide students with a "big picture" sense of key learning in their course; analyze tasks to determine the type of knowledge organization that will best facilitate learning (linear approach, use of tables, etc.); use contrasting cases (two examples that share features but also differ in important ways) and boundary cases (anomalies); have students categorize using multiple schemas; and make connections among concepts explicit.

Motivation

The third strategy focuses on leveraging principles of motivation to promote learning. This involves recognizing that goals "serve as the basic organizing feature of motivated behavior" (pp. 70–71) and hold subjective value, including attainment value (satisfaction gained from mastery), intrinsic value (satisfaction from the process of doing), and instrumental value (accomplishment of other goals, usually involving extrinsic rewards). In order for students to be motivated to accomplish goals, they must not only value them but also have positive outcome expectations, which are beliefs that "specific actions will bring about a desired outcome" (p. 76). Motivation is promoted when students perceive their environment as supportive of their pursuit and achievement of valued goals. Teachers can stimulate motivation by connecting content to student interests; providing authentic, real-world tasks; articulating relevance of content to students' current academic lives and future professional lives; demonstrating passion and enthusiasm for content; ensuring that objectives, instructional activities, and assessments are well aligned; providing early opportunities for students to be successful; articulating expectations and providing rubrics to establish clear performance targets; and allowing student choice of learning activities, reading materials, resources, and more.

Promoting Mastery

The fourth strategy involves fostering mastery by helping students acquire component skills and integrate and apply skills appropriately. Teachers can do this by deconstructing complex skills into their component parts; diagnosing and addressing missing or weak component skills; providing practice to increase fluency and automaticity of skill integration; and providing diverse contexts in which students can apply skills.

Targeted Feedback

The fifth strategy focuses on the use of feedback to aid learning. Targeted, specific, and timely feedback on deliberate practice can guide successive practice. Teachers provide instructional scaffolding within the zone of proximal development, which refers to a level of challenge such that students cannot yet perform successfully on their own but can with support; this is also known as students' instructional (as opposed to independent) level. Students need sufficient goal-focused practice at an appropriate challenge level coupled with feedback that communicates progress and directs subsequent efforts. Feedback is generally more effective when it comes soon after performance and when it is frequent. Teachers can use rubrics to articulate performance expectations; provide models and nonexamples of performance aligned to rubrics; and provide feedback in relation to the rubric performance criteria. Teachers should prioritize their feedback, perhaps providing feedback on one dimension at a time in order to avoid overwhelming students. Additionally, teachers should balance positive feedback with constructive feedback, provide opportunities for peer feedback, and require students to articulate how they used feedback to inform subsequent efforts.

Classroom Climate

The sixth strategy is based on the importance of the intellectual, social, and emotional climate of the learning environment. Learning climates can be centralizing (inclusive and welcoming) or marginalizing (exclusive and discouraging) to groups and individuals. Particularly toxic are classroom environments in which stereotypes operate or in which stereotype threat—the "tension that arises in members of a stereotyped group when they fear being judged according to stereotypes" (Ambrose et al., 2010, p. 174) is activated. Additionally, students' perceptions about how approachable the teacher is and whether their teacher is interested in and cares about them influence their views of climate. To promote a healthy classroom climate, teachers can communicate that ambiguity is acceptable; encourage multiple approaches; be mindful of unintentional messages being sent to students (e.g., about their ability); avoid expecting an individual to represent his or her minority group; reduce anonymity; model inclusive attitudes, language, and behavior; establish and reinforce norms for interaction; avoid marginalizing students; seek feedback on climate; address tensions directly, and use discord as a teachable moment; and model active listening.

Self-Directed Learners

The last strategy involves helping students become self-directed learners, capable of assessing what a task requires, planning their approach, monitoring progress, and making adjustments as needed. This requires metacognition. In order to promote metacognition for self-directed learning, teachers may model metacognition and have students do guided self-assessments and reflect on and annotate their work.

Field-Specific Best Practices

Each discipline or field has best practices specific and unique to it. Here the field of natural sciences is used as an example. Best practice in science involves inquiry, which ostensibly reflects the way in which "real" scientists "do science." Inquiry labs fall along a continuum (Brickman, Gormally, Armstrong, & Hallar, 2009). At one end of the continuum is closed inquiry in which students are provided the research question, protocol, and materials and are given directions regarding what data to collect and how to analyze it. Closed inquiry is sometimes referred to as cookbook or recipe inquiry. Further along the continuum is guided inquiry, in which the teacher may pose the problem or question and then provide support and guidance to students as they select variables, establish the experimental design, plan procedures, collect and make meaning of data, and report findings. On the other end of the continuum is authentic or open inquiry, in which students choose their own research question, identify variables, design experimentation, collect and analyze data, and then report the data vis-à-vis other studies or theories. Best practice science instruction moves toward more authentic inquiry and away from closed inquiry.

Additionally, educators must cultivate science literacy, which requires the recognition that experts in different fields read differently, attending to varying text features and utilizing differing strategies to make meaning of complex texts. For example, in the subfield of chemistry, students are expected to attend to a text's narrative and to "read" alternative representations (e.g., graphics, figures, diagrams, etc.) in a recursive, repeated back-and-forth way (Shanahan & Shanahan, 2008). Also, as students progress through school and move into higher levels of science, skills and routines are less general across the sciences and more particular to subfields, such as chemistry, due to specific organization of subfield knowledge, increased abstraction, and progressively more sophisticated and technical vocabulary. Additionally, fields and subfields have differing rhetorical structures and implicit understandings about ways of doing and speaking the discipline. To the extent possible, these need to be explicitly spelled out for students, and field-specific expectations must be articulated, modeled, and practiced.

The National Research Council, in 2011, released its *Framework for K-12 Science Education: Practices, Crosscutting Concepts, and Core Idea*s, which served as the conceptual framework for the *Next Generation Science Standards* (Achieve, 2013), released in spring of 2013. The framework includes eight instructional practices for science and engineering, including asking questions (science) and defining problems (engineering); developing and using models; planning and carrying out investigations; analyzing and interpreting data; using math, information technology, and computational thinking; constructing explanations (science) and designing solutions (engineering); engaging in argument; and obtaining, evaluating, and communicating information.

Zemelman and colleagues (2012) offer additional best practices for the natural sciences, which include building on students' innate curiosity about the natural world; providing students with opportunities to "construct, defend, and critique arguments with empirical evidence" (p. 202); integrating science and engineering; and providing opportunities for scientific discussion and debate.

Approach-Specific and Technique-Specific Best Practices

Best practice pedagogical approaches, such as problem-based learning (PBL), themselves have best practices. John R. Savery (2006), in the inaugural issue of the *Interdisciplinary Journal of Problem-based Learning,* defines PBL as an "instructional (and curricular) learner-centered approach that empowers learners to conduct research, integrate theory and practice, and apply knowledge and skills to develop a viable solution to a defined problem" (p. 12). He further identifies 10 best practices, what he frames as PBL essentials, that are paraphrased here:

1. Students must take ownership of their learning.

2. Problem simulations must be messy and permit free inquiry.

3. Learning must be trans-disciplinary.

4. Student collaboration is critical.

5. Student self-directed learning must be applied to the resolution of the problem.

6. The PBL must close with a reflective debriefing exercise designed to consolidate learning.

7. Self- and peer-assessment is an integral part of PBL.

8. PBL activities must be transferable to and valued in the real world.

9. Student evaluation must incorporate knowledge-based and process-based dimensions.

10. PBL must serve as the pedagogical foundation of curriculum and not be a component of a didactic curriculum. (pp. 12–14)

This is merely one example of approach-specific best practices. Technique-specific practices for everything from collaborative learning groups to jigsawing to development of formative assessments abound.

Conclusion

Educators can leverage best practices, those practices that reflect professional wisdom and existing research and evidence, to maximize student learning. With roots in Enlightenment thinking and modernist commitments, best practices are associated with an approach that privileges efficiency and attaining ends. There are a number of critiques leveled against best practice discourse, and these fall into the four broad categories of theoretical challenges; issues of power, equity, and social justice; challenges of practice; and misuse of best practices. The aforementioned concerns notwithstanding, the discourse of best practices can be generative and productive when used in an ethically defensible manner, which involves leveraging best practices to promote equity and social justice, educators' "critical intelligence" and "creative intelligence," teacher inquiry, and collegial dialogue on best practices.

Best practices can be found along three dimensions of practice: (1) general best practices that span multiple grades and content areas and include practices such as strategic reading, integrative units, and the use of timely, frequent, and specific feedback; (2) field-specific best practices, such as those particular to the natural sciences, which include inquiry, science literacy, and additional strategies such as developing and using models, integrating science and engineering, and building on students' innate curiosity regarding the natural world; and (3) approach-specific and technique-specific best practices, such as those for problem-based learning, which include, for example, students' responsibility for their own learning, messy problem simulations that permit free inquiry, and the incorporation of student collaboration.

Key Chapter Terms

Best practices: Sometimes used interchangeably with good practice, excellent practice, promising practice, evidence-based practice, research-based practice, and scientifically based practice, the term refers to the assimilation of professional wisdom with available research.

Discourse: A way of thinking and viewing the world that is embedded in language; we function within and through multiple discourses, which tend to be so taken for granted that we are not aware of them. An example of a dominant discourse in contemporary American education is the discourse of accountability.

Social justice: Concept that includes the notions of liberty for all people and freedom from oppression. It refers to efforts to thwart and remedy inequities, especially those that are institutionally sanctioned, as well as violations of civil and human rights, especially of traditionally marginalized groups.

References

Achieve, Inc. (2013). *The next generation science standards.* Retrieved from http://www .nextgenscience.org/next-generation-science-standards

Allen, L. A. (2010). Best practices. In E. Kridel (Ed.), *Encyclopedia of curriculum studies* (pp. 80–81). Thousand Oaks, CA: Sage.

Ambrose, S. A., Bridges, M. W., DiPietro, M., Lovett, M. S., & Normal, M. K. (2010). *How learning works: Seven research-based principles for smart teaching.* San Francisco, CA: Jossey-Bass.

Bergman, J., & Sams, A. (2012*). Flip your classroom: Reach every student in every class every single day.* Washington, DC: ISTE and ASCD.

Bond, G. L., & Dykstra, R. (1967). The Cooperative Research Program in first-grade reading instruction. *Reading Research Quarterly, 2*(4), 5–142.

Brickman, P., Gormally, C., Armstrong, N., & Hallar, B. (2009). Effects of inquiry-based learning on students' science literacy skills and confidence. *International Journal for the Scholarship of Teaching and Learning, 3*(2), 1–22.

Bush, G. W. (2000). Speech before the 91st annual convention of the NAACP. *Washington Post.* Retrieved from http://www.washingtonpost.com/ wp-srv/onpolitics/elections/bushtext071000.htm

Darling-Hammond, L. (2010). *The flat world and education: How America's commitment to equity will determine our future.* New York, NY: Teachers College Press.

Dewey, J. (1970). The need for a recovery of philosophy. In J. Dewey, A. W. Moore, H. C. Brown, G. H. Mead, B. H. Bode, H. W. Stuart, . . . H. M. Kallen (Eds.), *Creative intelligence: Essays in the pragmatic attitude* (pp. 3–69). New York, NY: Octagon Books. (Original work published 1917)

Gabriel, R., & Allington, R. (2012). The MET project: The wrong $45 million question. *Educational Leadership, 70*(3), 44–49.

Glasgow, N. A., & Hicks, C. D. (2003). *What successful teachers do: 91 research-based classroom strategies for new and veteran teachers.* Thousand Oaks, CA: Corwin.

Hlebowitsh, P. (2012). When best practices aren't: A Schwabian perspective on teaching. *Journal of Curriculum Studies, 44*(1), 1–12.

Hord, S. M. (Ed.). (2004). *Learning together, leading together: Changing schools though professional learning communities.* New York, NY: Teachers College Press.

Kincheloe, J. L. (1991). *Teachers as researchers: Qualitative inquiry as a path to empowerment.* London, England: Falmer.

Medley, D. M. (1979). The effectiveness of teachers. In P. L. Paterson & H. J. Walberg (Eds.), *Research on teaching: Concepts, findings, and implications* (pp. 11–27). Berkeley, CA: McCutchan.

Mills, G. E. (2011). *Action research: A guide for the teacher researcher* (4th ed.). Boston, MA: Pearson.

Murphy, J. (2010). *The educator's handbook for understanding and closing achievement gaps.* Thousand Oaks, CA: Corwin.

National Research Council. (2011). *Framework for K-12 science education: Practices, crosscutting concepts, and core ideas.* Washington, DC: Author.

Osburn, J., Caruso, G., & Wolfensberger, W. (2011). The concept of "best practice": A brief overview of its meanings, scope, uses, and shortcomings. *International Journal of Disability, Development and Education, 58*(2), 213–222.

Partnership for 21st century learning. (n.d.). *Framework for 21st century learning.* Retrieved from http:// www.p21.org/about-us/p21-framework

Savery, J. R. (2006). Overview of problem-based learning: Definitions and distinctions. *Interdisciplinary Journal of Problem-based Learning, 1*(1), 9–20.

Schwandt, T. A. (1997). Evaluation as practical hermeneutics. *Evaluation, 3*(1), 69–83.

Shanahan, T., & Shanahan, C. (2008). Teaching disciplinary literacy to adolescents. *Harvard Educational Review, 78*(1), 40–59.

Skelton, A. M. (2009). A "teaching excellence" for the times we live in? *Teaching in Higher Education, 14*(1), 107–112.

Taylor, F. W. (1911). *The principles of scientific management.* New York, NY: Harper & Brothers.

Whitehurst, G. J. (2002, October). *Evidence-based education.* Presentation at the Student Achievement and School Accountability Conference, Washington, D.C.

Wolfe, P. (2010). *Brain matters: Translating research into classroom practice* (2nd ed.). Alexandria, VA: ASCD.

Zemelman, S., Daniels, H. S., & Hyde, A. (1998). *Best practice: New standards for teaching and learning in American's schools* (2nd ed.). Portsmouth, NH: Heinemann.

Zemelman, S., Daniels, H. S., & Hyde, A. (2012). *Best practice: Bringing standards to life in America's classrooms* (4th ed.). Portsmouth, NH: Heinemann.

Further Readings

Ambrose, S. A., Bridges, M. W., DiPietro, M., Lovett, M. S., & Normal, M. K. (2010). *How learning works: Seven research-based principles for smart teaching.* San Francisco, CA: Jossey-Bass.

This book outlines seven research-based best practices and offers for each introductory anecdotes that illustrate the principle, articulation of what the principle is and what research says about it, a graphical representation of how the principle operates, and practical strategies suggested by the research.

Bergman, J., & Sams, A. (2012). *Flip your classroom: Reach every student in every class every single day.* Washington, DC: ISTE and ASCD.

Flipping pioneers Bergman and Sam tell the story of how they developed flipped instruction, provide cogent arguments for flipping, describe how to implement flipping, and introduce their "flipped mastery model."

Hord, S. M. (Ed.). (2004). *Learning together, leading together: Changing schools through professional learning communities.* New York, NY: Teachers College Press.

In this edited book, Hord and her chapter authors introduce the reader to research on professional learning communities (PLCs) and offer practical ideas from 22 schools using PLCs.

Kincheloe, J. L. (1991). *Teachers as researchers: Qualitative inquiry as a path to empowerment.* London, England: Falmer.

Kincheloe argues that inquiry is a component of educators' "good work" and that critical inquiry is an act of empowerment. He explores assumptions behind educational research, considers the nature of knowledge and purposes for research, and argues for the use of qualitative inquiry.

Mills, G. E. (2011). *Action research: A guide for the teacher researcher* (4th ed.). Boston, MA: Pearson.

Where Kincheloe's aforementioned book is more theoretical in nature, Mills's book is a practical guide for educators seeking to conduct action research.

Savery, J. R. (2006). Overview of problem-based learning: Definitions and distinctions. *Interdisciplinary Journal of Problem-based Learning, 1*(1), 9–20.

In this article, Savery defines problem-based learning (PBL), provides a brief history of the approach, identifies essential elements of PBL, distinguishes between PBL and case-, project-based, and inquiry-based pedagogical approaches, and ends the article with ruminations about the future of PBL.

Wolfe, P. (2010). *Brain matters: Translating research into classroom practice* (2nd ed.). Alexandria, VA: ASCD.

Wolfe introduces readers to the brain's anatomy and development and then describes the brain's information storage processes of sensory memory, working memory, and long-term memory. She identifies teaching practices that leverage what is known about learning from cognitive science.

Zemelman, S., Daniels, H. S., & Hyde, A. (2012). *Best practice: Bringing standards to life in America's classrooms* (4th ed.). Portsmouth, NH: Heinemann.

This seminal work, now in its fourth edition, identifies progressive, constructivist best practices that are "enduring" and yet "evolving." The book provides indicators of best practice instruction; identifies, describes, and illustrates seven structures of best practice teaching that transcend grade-level and content boundaries; and identifies content-specific best practices in the areas of reading, writing, math, science, and social studies.

Websites

Center for Data-Driven Reform in Education. (n.d.). *Best evidence encyclopedia.* Retrieved from http://www.bestevidence.org

Through its Best Evidence Encyclopedia, *the Center for Data-Driven Reform in Education disseminates findings from analyses of programs in the areas of math, reading, elementary science, early childhood education, and comprehensive school reform.*

Institute of Education Sciences. (n.d.). *What Works Clearinghouse.* Retrieved from http://ies.ed.gov/ncee/wwc/

This massive repository contains findings from the U.S. Department of Education's Institute of Education Sciences analyses of individual research studies as well as practices and programs on a number of educational

topics, including math, school choice, and student behavior.

U. S. Department of Education. (n.d.). *Doing what works.* Retrieved from http://www2.ed.gov/nclb/methods/whatworks/edpicks.jhtml

This site contains a number of resources to help educators understand what evidence-based education is and to identify and implement evidence-based practices. The site contains graphics, video, and short explanations to make content accessible.

PART IV

Testing and Assessment

10

WHAT IS THIS TEST REALLY TESTING?

Validity, Reliability, and Test Ethics

LAUNCELOT I. BROWN

Duquesne University

Here is a conversation between a grandmother and her 8-year-old grandson that illustrates some of the concerns about K-12 testing (names are pseudonyms):

Grandmother:	Tell me about school. What do you do in school?
Derrin:	We take tests.
Grandmother:	And what are these tests for?
Derrin:	I don't know. Maybe she wants to see if we know the work.
Grandmother:	You don't like to take tests, do you?
Derrin:	No. But Marcia does because she always gets everything right. She can write fast and Miss Davis likes her.

Derrin's last statement is instructive but not unique. From his statement we can deduce what the test means to him. To what extent do you think his writing speed and his perception of teacher bias factors into his test performance?

This conversation, although based on one that took place sometime in 1978 and in a culture foreign to the United States, could happen today. The fact is, some form of testing is common to all societies. These tests can range from a test of skill that qualifies as a rite of passage for acceptance into a community, to the more sophisticated cognition demanding tests that provide opportunities to pursue further education or the right to append certain credentials to your name. A common factor in all our lives is we have all taken tests.

Nevertheless, it may be necessary to differentiate between a **test** and **assessment**. In today's discourse, these words are often used interchangeably but they are not the same and do not convey the same meaning. A test is a tool or instrument used for capturing data. An assessment is the judgment, or process of making a judgment, based on the data. A camera—a tool used for capturing images—is analogous to a test in certain ways. The image can be blurred or detailed depending on, among other things, the quality of the camera, the number of megapixels per image, and the photographer's skill and knowledge of the limitations of the particular camera.

Additionally, there are environmental factors that can impinge on the quality of the image requiring that the photographer make adjustments either to the camera or the context to mitigate the effects of the existing conditions. These are all critical elements that impact the quality and, therefore, the utility of the image (data) collected and could have consequential effects on the final outcome. It is from the examination of the image that we make an assessment, that is, pass judgment. The clearer and more detailed the image, the more we can learn from it and, consequently, the more accurate our interpretation of what we see.

This analogy to a large extent captures the main characteristics of a test and differentiates between a test and an assessment. In an educational setting, the test is an instrument or systematic procedure that consists of a set of questions or activities designed specifically to measure an individual's ability, skill level, or knowledge to determine what she or he knows—that is, the extent of the knowledge—or has learned. The results of the tests usually are represented by some score and these scores comprise the data.

But data have to be interpreted in order to provide information that then can be turned into actionable knowledge (Halverson, 2010) and this happens through assessment. Therefore assessment is the process of documenting, describing, quantifying, and interpreting the data from a test to retrieve the information hidden therein about an individual's learning, attitudes, and beliefs. As with the camera, the quality of the test, the skill of the testing professional, and the existing conditions—both internal and external to the test-taker—impact the accuracy of the assessment and the usefulness of the actionable knowledge that can be inferred from the data.

The overarching question then becomes: Is the test really capturing the data it was designed to capture? If not, then we have to interrogate further and deeper. For example: Is it because we are not using the test for its intended purpose or the way it was intended to be used? Is it because the test is poorly constructed in terms of its length, the difficulty level of the language, or the clarity of instructions? Is the test being used with the appropriate population?

The answers to these questions address issues of the **reliability** of the data generated by the test and, as a consequence, the **validity** of the conclusions drawn from the test. But, undergirding each question is an ethical concern. Thus issues of reliability and validity are ethical issues and are integral to the code of ethical standards that delineates the social responsibility that guides a profession and the personal responsibility of practitioners within the profession (Iliescu, Ispas, & Harris, 2009; Leach & Oakland, 2007).

Ethics and Testing

Ethical codes establish the minimum acceptable behaviors expected of members of a particular profession to which the members are honor bound to abide. As stated in a paper on the social implications and ethics of testing issued by the International Test Commission (Iliescu et al., 2009), "ethics describe criteria for assessing the appropriateness of behaviors, be they actions, decisions, or intellectual stances" (para. 1). But, there is a moral element to being ethical that goes beyond what is required by law or the code of **ethics.** This moral element has to do with individuals' moral principles and sense of right and wrong.

Thus, even in the absence of a code or enforceable laws, there is a moral imperative to do what one believes to be right; to do no harm; to minimize any unforeseen effects that could be harmful. Therefore being ethical transcends compliance with a code or laws. It is an individual choice (Iliescu et al., 2009) that grounds the testing professional, especially in situations in which there are no simple answers and no prescriptive "to-do list." It is in such situations of ethical dilemma that an individual's ethical principles define her or his behaviors.

Relative to the previous statements, the concern about ethics, while central to the debate about testing, has nothing to do with the test itself but the use to which the test is put. So for example, using a camera to take a picture is fine; but if the photographer in taking the picture invades someone's privacy then the issue of ethics becomes a concern. Iliescu et al. (2009) captures this distinction in asserting that "being 'ethical' is a characteristic of a behavior and not a product of a behavior" (para. 19). Clearly then, tests are neither ethical nor unethical. It is the person conducting the test who has to be ethical in her or his use of the test by making sure all ethical standards are met.

While definitions of ethics seem fairly straightforward, and we all have assumptions of what constitutes ethical and even more so, unethical behavior, the fact is, it is not always a simple exercise in determining whether a behavior or procedure is ethical or not. Different organizations have different codes of ethics and so too do different governments. Therefore, a behavior that might be in breach of the ethical code of one organization or country might be within the accepted practices in another. This should be expected because ethical codes are grounded on value statements of morality, rightness, and wrongness, which to a large extent are reflective of the particular society and culture. Certainly, then, it is imperative that to ensure ethical behavior, test-users at a minimum should adhere to the code of ethics that governs them. Such adherence does not preclude anyone going above and beyond the behaviors dictated by the code or laws; what it does is make sure that the testing professional is operating within the established boundaries delineated by the code or laws.

Specifically with regard to the **ethics of testing** there are two overriding principles that govern testing procedures and to which all testing professionals must adhere. The first is that testing professionals must adhere to the general principles of the *scientific model,* the focus of which is the evaluation of evidence to confirm or support the test's psychometric properties (Iliescu et al., 2009; Messick, 1980). The second is that the interaction process between the testing professional and the other stakeholders involved in the testing process must be respectful, fair, procedurally just, transparent, and equitable (Iliescu et al., 2009; International Testing Commission (ITC), 2000; Messick. 1980).

The Scientific Method

The scientific method assumes objectivity of procedure and the instrument. The warrants supporting this assumption are that adherence to the scientific method of testing allows for generating data that are objective, reliable, and valid. These are essential characteristics of data to be used for decision making, which is the overall purpose of testing. Thus the scientific method addresses issues of objectivity, reliability, and validity by presenting the evidence that the test is accurately measuring what it purports to measure in a manner that is equitable and fair.

Objectivity

Is the test objective? If not, how do we control for subjectivity and bias? **Objectivity** is both a procedure and characteristic (McMillan & Schumacher, 2010, p. 8). It implies that the testing procedure and testing conditions are fair and unbiased, or controls for subjectivity. Using more technical and precise language, Westhoff and Kluck (2008) define objectivity as "inter-user consistency in the execution, scoring and interpretation of standardized assessment procedures" (p. 68).

It is accepted by the scientific community that objectivity is a key principle of the scientific method; however, it is also an accepted fact that no test is 100% objective. Populations and conditions change across time. Knowledge and facts that may have been accepted as true, correct, or objective at one time may no longer fit those descriptors. (For example, as of 2006, based on the decision of the International Astronomical Union, Pluto is no longer a planet as we understand planets to be.) Therefore, one has to think of objectivity as confined to the current context as evidenced by the testing procedures, the population being tested, and the conditions under which the test is executed. The evidence has to demonstrate that for all stakeholders—test-users and test-takers—the procedures for administration, scoring, and interpretation are standardized and constant across time, populations, conditions, and time of testing (Iliescu et al., 2009; Kline, 1993). All test-takers must have an equal chance to perform that is not influenced by characteristics independent of the testing instrument or procedure.

Concerns about **test bias** relate to the technical aspects of test development and construction. However, the issue of objectivity also has to do with professional judgment in the interpretation of the test scores. The fact is, even for the best constructed test, the results have to be interpreted and interpretation is always influenced by some level of subjectivity. Therefore, even when using the camera as an analogy, there is the awareness that the photograph is simultaneously objective and subjective; for while the reproduced image is objective, different people looking at the image observe different aspects, or place greater emphasis on certain elements within the image. This inevitably results in varying judgments with regard to the quality and usefulness of the image, which are then extrapolated to the competence of the photographer. Thus, the testing professionals have to be cognizant of the fact that interpreting the results of a test is really making a judgment call and therefore must be willing to reflect on and acknowledge their "self-knowledge regarding how their own values, attitudes, experiences, and social contexts influence their actions, interpretations, choices, and recommendations" (The Universal Declaration of Ethical Principles for Psychologists [UDEPP], 2008, Principle II, f).

The focus on objectivity is also about minimizing error in the testing process. While in the behavioral sciences there will always be error in measurement, the test should not maximally add to the error. This is analogous to using a faulty camera but expecting to get a perfect picture. Thus, it is incumbent on whoever is selecting or interpreting a test to be current with scientific developments in the field and apply that knowledge to the selection of the testing instrument, or the critique of the construction, administration, scoring, and interpretation of the test. As alluded to in UDEPP (2008), testing professionals have an *ethical responsibility* to use instruments that meet current standards and to ensure that procedures are well documented and the psychometric properties of the test are clearly stated.

However, meeting the criteria of consistency in the scoring and execution of the test is not a guarantee of objectivity. As Iliescu et al. (2009) contend, "Objectivity is not simply a characteristic of the test but also of the situation" (Section 4, para. 9). This is an important point and one that is not always given due consideration as part of the process in the interpretation of test scores. The fact is, a test may function differently in different situations or for different groups within the same population. Adherence to ethical standards demands that those with the power to make judgments be aware that items on a test may function differently for males and females, or minority groups, or for students of different educational levels. Therefore, it is important that theoretical support and empirical evidence be provided showing that the use of the test is appropriate for the target population.

But theoretical support and the related empirical evidence presuppose that there is a clear understanding of the underpinning theory that validates the use of the test. As such, a reliance on empirical evidence, while critically important, is not a sufficient indicator of test objectivity. There should be equal interest in generating theoretical definitions, the process of which allows for the examination of the theories that support the construct or concept being measured.

Theoretical and Empirical Definitions

Lee Cronbach and Paul Meehl (1955), capture the importance of generating **theoretical** and empirical (operational) **definitions.** As they explain, a construct derives its meaning from its connections with other constructs in a **nomological network,** that is, a network of hypothesized relationships to other constructs in a theoretical context (Shepard, 1993). Thus, interrogating the literature allows for the examination of competing theories and further allows for a refining of the variables of interest and the consequent formulation of the **operational definition**. The impact of not having a theoretical definition includes that the findings of the test cannot be defended in any meaningful way and unexpected results could be due to inappropriate operational definitions. Also, the observed measures might not be measuring the desired trait and might not be appropriate or relevant for the tested population or the purpose of the test. Overall, inadequate examination of the theory suggests a lack of preparation and increases the possibility that even expected results may be unreliable.

Emphasizing the importance of theoretical definitions in no way diminishes the essentiality of generating empirical or operational definitions. For a construct to be measured, it first has to be operationalized, that is, the theoretical definition has to be translated into observable characteristics that can be measured. Many of us have come across the phrase "as measured by" performance on some test or a score on some instrument. As explained by Lorraine R. Gay and Peter W. Airasian (2003), operational definitions ask questions such as, "what observable characteristics define" (p. 64) for example, student math achievement? Most likely, student math achievement would be operationally defined in terms of a score or scores on an achievement test. Most persons can relate to and attach some meaning to a score. Therefore, what the operational definition does is simplify and clarify the variables of interest so that there is common understanding across stakeholders of the construct being measured.

Reliability and Validity

Does the test provide reliable data? If not, on what are we basing our decisions? Critical to the ethics of testing is evidence of the reliability of the test. To most persons, reliability connotes *trustworthiness, dependability, and consistency.* Even in testing, evidence of reliability says to the test-user that the results are consistent and most likely trustworthy. Returning to the camera analogy, a camera that consistently captures the images the photographer intended to capture can be considered reliable.

Gay and Airasian define reliability as the "degree to which a test consistently measures whatever it is measuring" (2003, p. 141). This definition in simple terms makes it clear that reliability is about consistency, the consistency of obtaining the *same or similar* scores across *multiple measures* of the *same population* under *similar conditions* using the *same test* or to be more formal, "the consistency of measurements when the testing procedure is repeated on a population of individuals or groups" (AERA, APA, & NCME, 1999). While all these variations of the same concept are accurate, they do not include a fundamental aspect of reliability: It is a measure of the extent to which test scores are free from random errors of measurement (Pedhazur & Pedhazur-Schmelkin, 1991). This means that the score reflects the trait or construct being measured and not random error. Making this clear is important because a test with high random error would have low reliability and therefore would provide inconsistent information from one testing occasion to another.

Measurement Error

It is impossible to construct a test that is error-free because there are always unaccounted-for factors that influence test scores by introducing error into the process. An example of this can be seen in the following story about a hypothetical student named Cindy. On Monday she scored 85 on her math achievement test, on the same test on Wednesday she scored 83, and on Friday her score was 87. There is variability among the scores, but that is expected because all test scores have some degree of measurement error. Reasons for such variability could be she might have been a little tired on Wednesday or, the mere fact that she had taken the test on two previous occasions had resulted in some learning and as a result helped her improve her score on Friday. Based on these scores, we can say that Cindy's math achievement score is probably in the low to mid eighties.

There are two types of measurement error. There is **random error,** which can be defined as sources of extraneous variance that occur with no discernible pattern. This results in inconsistency among scores affecting the reliability of the test. There is **systematic or constant error,** which is a "characteristic of a test or testing situation that will affect all measurement

equally" (de Klerk, 2008, p. 2), and consequently the validity of the conclusions drawn from the test. A camera may take clear pictures but anything blue has a greenish hue and red appears orange. The background sky has a tinge of yellow, which makes it seem that the air is polluted.

No test is error-free. Accordingly, the pertinent question becomes, to what extent should we rely on the results of the test? This question is crucial for it addresses a serious ethical concern with regard to the use of the test in decision making. As Iliescu et al. (2009) contend, "the degree of reliance on the test result describes the limits of its ethical usage" (Section 5, para. 3). Therefore, using the results from a test with low reliability is unethical because the score may not be reflective of the construct being measured.

Extending the previous question, there is also need to answer the question: What is an acceptable level of reliability? The answer to this question depends on whether the test is being used for high-stake or low-stake decisions. Reliability is expressed numerically as a reliability coefficient with values ranging between 0—no relationship between the observed scores and the trait being measured and 1—observed scores perfectly reflect the trait being measured. The higher the reliability coefficient, the more confident one can be in the results of the test.

Underlying estimation of reliability is classical test theory, also called the **true score** model. The logic underlying the true score model is an *observed score* consisting of two components—a true component and an error component. Therefore an individual's test score can be represented in Equation 10.1 as:

$$X = T + E \qquad \text{(Eq. 10.1)}$$

where X is the observed score, T is the true score, and E is the random error associated with the person's score.

Leo Harvill (1991) defines *true score* as "that part of an examinee's *observed score* uninfluenced by random events" (p. 33). Conceptually, the true score can be conceived of as the score that would be obtained over an infinite number of trials (assuming that the individual remains unchanged between each trial), or under ideal or perfect conditions of measurement that in reality never exist. Because conducting infinite numbers of trials is untenable and perfect conditions do not exist, observed scores always contain error resulting from myriad factors, unrelated to the trait being measured, that influence the individual's test performance. For example: Let us say Cindy's true score is 85 but her test score is 87. In that case, the random error in her score can be determined by Equation 10.2:

$$87 - 85 = 2 \ (X - T = E) \qquad \text{(Eq.10.2)}$$

Ross Traub and Glenn Rowley (1991) explain that "the average of a set of repeated measurements provides a more precise estimate of what is being measured than a single measurement" (p. 37). But as already stated such a proposition is untenable. Therefore the alternative is instead of measuring one individual repeatedly, many individuals are measured and the observed scores are used in the estimation of the *reliability coefficient.* Should we take Cindy's class as a group, we know that all scores comprise composites of true scores and error scores. Therefore, we can say that observed differences among a group of test-takers reflect true differences in their abilities and attitudes plus random factors affecting their test performance.

But the purpose for estimating the reliability of a measure is to determine the extent to which random error is associated with the measure. A highly reliable measure indicates that observed variance is primarily due to true score variance and little error variance. Equation 10.3 shows the conceptual model of reliability:

$$r_{xx} = \frac{\sigma_T^2}{\sigma_X^2} \qquad \text{(Eq.10.3)}$$

where r_{xx} = reliability of the measure, σ_T^2 = true score variance, and σ_X^2 = observed score variance.

In terms of the true score model, reliability therefore can be defined as the ratio of true score variance to observed score variance. As such, the reliability coefficient can be interpreted as the proportion of systematic variance in an observed score. For example, if the reliability of a measure of math achievement is .85, (r_{xx} = .85), that means that 85% of the variance of the observed score is due to true score variance and 15% (1 − .85) is the proportion of variance due to random error. However, it is accepted by the field that neither the true score nor the error score

can ever be known; we can only estimate reliability based on observed behavior.

Methods of Estimating Reliability

Robert Gable and Marian Wolf (1993) have reminded us that "reliability like validity is a generic term that refers to different research questions and types of evidence" (p. 205). They further explain that classical test theory allows for considering only one definition and source of error at a time. For example, Cronbach's (1946) alpha coefficient provides information regarding item sampling. However, this reliability does not give information on the stability of the scores across time and occasions. As such, classical theory does not allow for the simultaneous examination of the relative importance of various sources of error. It is important for researchers to recognize that they have an ethical responsibility to specify the type of reliability they report because "estimates of reliability would differ, to a greater or lesser extent, depending on the specific sources of error being addressed" (Pedhazur & Pedhazur-Schmelkin, 1991, p. 88).

Basically there a two approaches to estimating reliability. One approach estimates the correspondence between the results of tests taken at different times or equivalent forms of the same test either taken at the same time or on different occasions. The second approach addresses the internal consistency of the instrument and estimates the relationship among items on the test. The assumption is that items measuring the same construct should correspond to each other.

Test-retest reliability is a statistical technique used to determine how stable or consistent scores are across time. Of interest is the reliability of the consistency, stability, or repeatability of measurement. Using this approach, the same group of people is measured twice on the same instrument. The two sets of scores are correlated to give the *coefficient of stability,* which is taken as an estimate of the reliability of the measure. The underlying assumption is that true scores remain constant between testing occasions. As such, test-retest reliability is relevant to cognitive and trait scales that are stable and therefore not expected to change significantly over time. It is not appropriate for scales in the affective domain—for example: attitude, mood, anxiety—or for estimating consistency of a measure of knowledge following an intervention where change is expected (DeVon et al., 2007).

A challenge with this type of reliability is that the reliability coefficient depends on the length of time between testing occasions. If there is too little time intervening there is risk of practice or memory effects. With too much time intervening there is chance that persons have changed with respect to the trait being measured. Therefore in order to aid in the interpretation, it is necessary when reporting the coefficient of stability to provide the time interval between the two testing occasions.

Equivalent or alternate forms reliability is used to determine if two versions of the same test are comparable. The two versions must measure the same construct and have the same level of difficulty; the same number of items, and the same directions for administration, scoring, and interpretation. The challenge is in developing two versions of the same test that are truly parallel. Traub and Rowley (1991) advise that items could be written in matched pairs so each item in a pair will more likely be similar both in the skill or knowledge being tested and in the level of difficulty.

The reliability coefficient is obtained by administering the two versions of the test to the same group, on the same occasion, with a brief interval between the two tests. The two sets of scores are correlated. The resulting coefficient, called the *coefficient of equivalence* or *alternate-form reliability,* is taken as an estimate of the reliability of the measure but also as a measure of the extent to which the two forms measure the same trait. However, if the two forms are not parallel, the reliability would be underestimated. The advantage of using alternative forms is there are no practice or memory effects since the items differ.

Equivalence and stability reliability combines the test-retest and equivalent forms of reliability. The procedures are basically the same. One form is administered to the group, and after a period of time, the other form is administered. The scores are then correlated. The resulting estimate is called the *coefficient of stability and equivalence.* Gay and Airasian (2003) caution that with this form of reliability, more sources of measurement error are possible than with either method alone.

Internal consistency reliability is concerned with the extent to which items within a test or subsection of the test measure the same construct, trait, or attribute. The internal consistency approach requires one administration of the test and so eliminates random error due to alternative testing conditions, testing on different occasions, and alternative forms. There are three methods for estimating internal consistency reliability: split-half, KR-20, and Cronbach's alpha. Reliability methods for estimating internal consistency reliability should not be used with speeded tests. The focus of speeded tests is the number of responses within a specified time.

Split-half reliability is determined using two steps. The first step involves splitting the test into halves and correlating responses from the two halves to estimate the reliability. This form of reliability can be useful when a test is very long or when administering a test on two occasions or two different forms to the same group is not possible. Split-half reliability can be viewed as a variation of the alternate-forms reliability where each half is treated as an alternate form. Because longer tests tend to be more reliable, the correlation of the two halves will underestimate the reliability since the correlation coefficient is based on only half the original number of items. To correct for this reduction in test length, we apply the *Spearman-Brown prophecy formula.* For instance, for a 40-item test we could correlate the odd 20 items with the even 20 items. Therefore an estimated reliability of .90 is based on 20 items.

Equations 4a and 4b show the Spearman-Brown prophecy formula (often referred to as Spearman-Brown formula) used to estimate the reliability for a 40-item test.

$$r_{xx} = \frac{2r_{old}}{1+r_{old}} \qquad (\text{Eq.10.4a})$$

$$r_{xx} = \frac{2(.90)}{1+.90} = \frac{1.80}{1.90} = .95 \qquad (\text{Eq.10.4b})$$

There is also the General Spearman-Brown prophesy formula, which may be used to estimate the change in reliability resulting from an increase or decrease in the test length. In this formula, 2 (2 times the length) is replaced by k, where k is the factor by which the test length is increased or decreased. An example is shown in Equations 5a and 5b.

General Spearman-Brown Prophesy Formula

For example: A teacher has a 75-item test with a reliability of .86. She wants to know how reliable a 25-item reduced version of the test would be. The reduction in length results in a reliability coefficient of .67.

$$r_{xx} = \frac{kr_{old}}{1+(k-1)r_{old}} \qquad \text{(Eq.10.5a)}$$

$$r_{xx} = \frac{\frac{1}{3}(.86)}{1+(\frac{1}{3}-1)(.86)} = .67 \qquad \text{(Eq.10.5b)}$$

Kuder-Richardson 20 (KR-20) is a method for estimating reliability when items (e.g., multiple-choice items) are dichotomously scored. This method of estimating reliability assumes that items are parallel. To the extent that items are not parallel, KR-20 will underestimate the reliability.

Cronbach's alpha (aka coefficient alpha) is the most frequently used method for estimating reliability by researchers in the behavioral sciences. In general, Cronbach's alpha and KR-20 will yield the highest reliability estimates of all the methods. Because it is a measure of the internal consistency for the test responses from the specific group or sample, alpha coefficients should be computed each time the test is administered. For both KR-20 and Cronbach's alpha it is more convenient to use statistical software.

Scorer/rater reliability is not often classified with the other types of reliability because the focus is on the scoring of the test. Of interest is the *subjectivity* when different scorers on a test do not agree. This is more likely to happen with short answer or essay-type tests, performance and product tests, and observations. The concern is with interscorer, interrater, or interobserver reliability, especially when used for making far-reaching decisions. It is critically important that there be consensus among raters/scorers. As stated by Gay and Airasian (2003), "subjective scoring reduces reliability and in turn, diminishes the

validity of the interpretations one wished to make from the scores" (p. 145).

Factors That Can Affect Reliability

There are a number of factors that can and do introduce error into the process to which the researcher must pay particular attention:

Characteristics of the sample or group: The reliability coefficient resulting from a given test is specific to the sample that did the test.

Characteristics of the testing environment: Conditions under which the test is administered. These may include physical conditions such as temperature and lighting, the attitude of the testing professional, the instructions given, and whether time limits are set. Speeded tests require the ability to work quickly and therefore might not be measuring the construct of interest.

Characteristics of the test: There is a relationship between reliability and *test length*. Longer tests tend to yield higher reliability estimates. Too small a sample of items will most likely lower reliability (de Klerk, 2008). *Item type* also affects reliability. Tests on which items are scored objectively are more reliable than tests on which the scoring is subjective. Also, *item quality* has to be considered with regard to its effect on reliability. Items that are too hard, too easy, or ambiguous, will lower reliability.

Reliability is *not* a characteristic of the test itself; a test is neither reliable nor unreliable. Reliability is a characteristic of the scores for a specific sample on a specific test under specific testing conditions (de Klerk, 2008; Green, Chen, Helms, & Henze, 2011; Iliescu et al., 2009; Traub & Rowley, 1991). This is because reliability is based on correlations, and correlations are sample specific.

What is a "good" reliability? That depends on the purpose and use of the test. For high-stakes tests used for making decisions about individuals, the level of reliability should be at least .90 and up (Nunnally & Bernstein, 1994). For group-administered measures used for research, it should be .80 and up. For all other decisions, reliability should be at least .70.

Decisions based on reliability under .70 should be made with extreme caution.

Standard Error of Measurement

The **standard error of measurement** (SEM) is an estimate of the average amount by which we would overestimate or underestimate true scores on a given test. In statistical terms, it can be defined as the "standard deviation of errors of measurement associated with test scores for a specified group of test-takers" (Harvill, 1991, p. 34). It allows for the estimation of the difference between an individual's obtained score and true score. This difference is a function of the reliability of the test. The more reliable the test is, the smaller the SEM. The SEM is used to construct confidence intervals around test scores. What this does is provide a range within which the true score is located with a certain probability. Equation 6 shows the formula for the standard error of measurement.

$$SEM = SD\sqrt{1 - r_{xx}} \qquad \text{(Eq.10.6)}$$

The standard error of measurement can be used for constructing confidence intervals around test scores. In the behavioral sciences we usually calculate the 95% (Z = 1.96) or 99% (Z = 2.58) confidence intervals. The confidence interval simply indicates one's level of certainty that the range of values include the true mean.

$$CI_{95\%} = X \pm 1.96 \, (SEM) \qquad \text{(Eq.10.7a)}$$

$$CI_{99\%} = X \pm 2.58 \, (SEM) \qquad \text{(Eq.10.7b)}$$

The following shows how to construct a confidence interval for Cindy, the hypothetical student introduced earlier. Cindy scored 83 on the 40-item math achievement test. The standard deviation (SD) for the test is 8 and the reliability coefficient is .91. Equations 8a and 8b would be used to construct a 95% confidence interval around Cindy's score.

$$SEM = 8\sqrt{1 - .91} \qquad \text{(Eq.10.8a)}$$

$$SEM = 8\sqrt{.09} = 8(.3) = 2.4 \qquad \text{(Eq.10.8b)}$$

The SEM = 2.4. Therefore with 95% confidence Cindy's score is between 78.3 and 87.7, as shown in Equation 9.

$$83 \pm 1.96(2.4) = 83 \pm 4.7 = 78.3 \text{ and } 87.7 \quad \text{(Eq.10.9)}$$

Logically, someone with Cindy's ability could score as high as 87.7 or as low as 78.3 on the math achievement test. This has implications with regard to decision making. If, for instance, only students who scored 85 and higher were being selected for an Advanced Placement class, the question one has to ask is whether that will be fair to Cindy. Iliescu et al. (2009) are correct when they insist that "*good practice* (emphasis added) will take the SEM into account when communicating test scores or when reaching decisions" (Section 5, para. 9).

Validity

Validity refers to the appropriateness, meaningfulness, and usefulness of judgment or inferences one makes from scores obtained from tests and measures. The core element of validity is encapsulated in Samuel Messick's (1989) question: "To what degree, if at all, on the basis of evidence and rationales, should the test scores be interpreted and used in the manner proposed?" (p. 5). The implication that derives from this question is that the valid use of a particular test must be evidenced based and must give due consideration to the context, how the scores are interpreted for a particular group of people under a specific set of circumstances and for a given purpose. Essentially, a test is neither valid nor invalid. It is the *use* and/or *interpretation* of the *scores* that is valid or not. This is shown in **Sidebar 10.1**.

Validity relates to the use and interpretation of a test, and inferences drawn from the interpretation, and is not a characteristic of any given test. As a result, no test is valid for all situations and purposes, or for all populations (AERA, APA, & NCME, 1999). Therefore, any statement about a test's validity must be qualified by evidence of the test's appropriateness for a particular population and purpose and the particular situation or context (Iliescu et al., 2009). Consequently, no one should ever make a statement about a test being valid or "prior research has *proven* the validity of test B." Validity is inferred and not measured; it is something that is judged as

Sidebar 10.1 Determining a Test's Validity

A middle school uses a "well-established" standardized test of math achievement for placing students into an Advanced Placement (AP) class. The test includes word problems and assumes a seventh-grade reading level. Two students who have recently moved to the United States from non-English-speaking countries perform poorly on the test. Based on their performance, the teacher concludes that they do not possess the aptitude necessary for AP placement, and so they were not selected for the class.

- On the basis of the information provided, what has the teacher inferred from the test scores?
- If you were to make a statement about the validity of this test, how would you qualify the statement?
- Would you describe her decision as reflecting ethical behavior?

That the test is described as "well-established" suggests that the scores would be highly reliable, and indeed they may have been. However, reliability is a necessary but not sufficient condition for validity. Therefore, whereas a test must be reliable in order to be valid, reliability does not guarantee validity. Reliability is related to the stability or consistency of test scores, whereas validity attaches meaning to the scores.

---

adequate, or marginal, or unsatisfactory (Messick, 1989). We look for a test with evidence—both *theoretical and empirical*—supporting its use for our population and purpose (AERA, APA, & NCME, 1999; Messick, 1989). Additionally, contexts change and people change; therefore, no test is permanently certified as valid (Gable & Wolf, 1993). Validation is an ongoing process based on results of numerous validation studies.

Messick (1980) stresses that "different kinds of inferences from test scores require different kinds of evidence, not different kinds of validity" (p. 1014) and therefore the categories should not be construed as *validity types*. Indeed, all types of validity evidence contribute to the construct validity of the test. However, Holli A. DeVon and colleagues differentiate content and face validity, which they refer to as translational validity, from concurrent, predictive, convergent, and discriminant, which they refer to as criterion validity (DeVon et al., 2007, p. 156). **Figure 10.1** presents a model of construct validity.

Construct-Related Validity Evidence

Construct-related validity evidence refers to the degree to which an instrument measures the construct it is intended to measure (Cronbach & Meehl, 1955). It asks the question: What is this test really measuring? Construct-related validity is the core of the validation process because all other types of validity-related evidence are in support of the construct validity of the test. The construct validity is supported if the test items are "related to its operationally defined theory and concepts" (DeVon et al., 2007, p. 156). There are two broad types of construct-related validity evidence: *internal methods*, which examine the structure of the measure to be validated; and *external methods*, which examine relationships between the measure of interest and other traits.

Internal analysis for supporting construct validity provides the evidential basis of the extent to which items of a scale relate to each other in such a way that they may be added up to form a total, or a subscale score. It provides evidence that the items of a scale or subscale are measuring one trait. Additionally, it confirms whether the underlying structure of the scale is in congruence with the theoretical definition of the trait as suggested in the literature.

But even if internal analyses indicate that the measure reflects the structure hypothesized by a theoretical definition, this is not sufficient for construct validation. It is also necessary to conduct external analyses to examine relationships between the measure and other variables in a *nomological network*. If the test is truly measuring what it's supposed to be measuring, it should be related to other variables in predictable ways.

There are two types of external validity: convergent validity and discriminant validity, which fall under the umbrella of *criterion validity*, which is discussed later. Convergent validity compares a measure with other measures of the same construct. As stated by Elazar J.

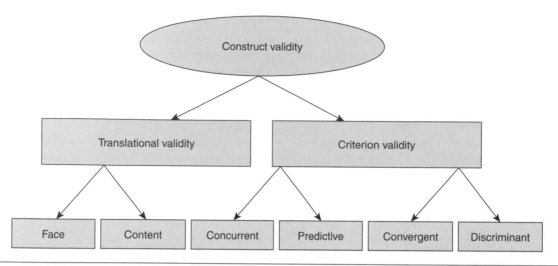

Figure 10.1 A Model of Construct Validity

SOURCE: DeVon, H. A., et al. (2007). A Psychometric Toolbox for Testing Validity and Reliability. *Journal of Nursing Scholarship, 39*(2), 155–164. Reproduced with permission from John Wiley and Sons Publishers. Based on Trochim, W. (2001). *The Research Methods Knowledge Base*, 2nd ed. Cincinnati, OH: Atomic Dog Publishing.

Pedhazur and Liora Pedhazur-Schmelkin (1991, p. 74), "convergent validity refers to the confirmation of a construct by the use of multiple methods" of the same trait based on distinctive methods. Discriminant validity demonstrates that the trait measured by your test is distinctive from other related traits. Discriminant validity studies involve examination of correlations between measures of several different traits. The correlation is then examined to determine if it conforms to theoretical expectations.

Translational validity, as proffered by DeVon and colleagues, simply explains the construct, thus making it understandable. This is done through the appropriateness of the test items—content-related evidence—and whether the items on their face value, give a sense of what is being measured—face validity.

Content-related validity evidence refers to whether test items cover what was taught or the attribute to be measured. As the name suggests, content-related validity provides evidence of appropriate breadth and depth of content. It refers to the "relevance and representativeness of the task content used in test construction" (Messick, 1980, p. 1015). In other words, test items must be relevant to, and must sample the complete range of the attribute under study (DeVon et al., 2007). For achievement tests, this refers to a match between test content and instructional objectives. For affective measures this means that items are included that address all relevant aspects or dimensions of the

trait. For aptitude or selection tests, content evidence reflects coverage of all relevant aspects of the skills or competencies being evaluated.

Content-related validity also includes evidence of appropriate language and cognitive level. Items should be free of culturally biased language. The reading level of the test should match the reading ability of the examinees. Establishing content validity is a logical rather than empirical process. Typically it involves defining the construct of interest and its dimensions by searching the literature, or asking a "panel of experts" to review the items (Netemeyer, Bearden, & Sharma, 2003). Content-related validity evidence is particularly important for achievement tests. As Gay and Airasian (2003) assert, "a test score cannot accurately reflect a student's achievement if it does not measure what the student was taught and is supposed to learn" (p. 136).

Face validity is the degree to which a test appears to measure what it purports to measure. It is subjective, not psychometrically sound. It simply makes the claim that the items on the test are linked to the construct being measured (de Klerk, 2008).

Criterion-related validity evidence pertains to evidence of the extent to which a measure is related to some other measure that serves as the criterion (DeVon et al., 2007; Messick, 1989). It comprises convergent and discriminant validity evidence (already discussed) and predictive and concurrent validity evidence. The two types of related validity differ in terms of whether the test and criterion data were collected at the same time or at different times.

Predictive validity seeks to determine the extent to which test scores predict some future behavior. Predictive validity evidence is established by examining the Pearson correlation between the test one is attempting to validate and the criterion of interest. High correlations between the original measure and criterion variables suggest that the tool is a valid predictor of the specified criterion (de Klerk, 2008; DeVon et al., 2007). Predictive validity is what would be measured if a principal wants to know whether a newly developed English learning inventory is a valid predictor of students' performance on the English component on the statewide assessment (the criterion).

Concurrent validity assesses the extent to which test scores are related to some criterion (usually another test) measured at the same time. Validity is supported by the correlation between a measure and the criterion of interest. For both predictive and concurrent validity, the Pearson correlation is called the *validity coefficient.*

For criterion-related validity, the criterion needs to be reliable and meaningful. As Messick (1980) states, "the simple demonstration of an empirical relationship between a measure and a criterion is a dubious basis for justifying relevance and use" (p. 1017). The utility of criterion-related validity evidence depends not only on how one operationally defines the variable of interest, but also on how one operationally defines the criterion.

However, there are limitations to content and criterion-related validity evidence:

- Neither attaches any meaning to the score, that is, they don't tell us what we're measuring.
- Good match between instructional objectives and test content doesn't guarantee that the objectives were appropriate in the first place.
- High correlation between the measure and a criterion does not tell us what the correlation represents; for example, high correlation between the SAT and grade point average might have more to do with the schools attended than academic ability.

*Factors Affecting Score Reliability
(and, in Turn, Validity)*

There are many factors that can affect the reliability coefficient. Among these are: low reliability between the test and the criterion, student test anxiety, test and item bias that could be gender or culturally focused, response set (a biased set of responses on self-report measures), and student guessing. Therefore, to answer the question, "What is the test really testing?" requires knowing whether (a) the test is appropriate for the construct being measured, (b) the test is appropriate for the population of interest, (c) the items work the same for all subgroups, and (d) the conditions of testing are the same for all groups. In other words, it requires knowing that the test scores are reliable and valid and indicators of ethical behavior are transparent.

Consequential Validity

Having addressed the technical aspects of the test to ensure that interpretations are evidenced based, we now look at the consequences of the decision (Messick, 1989), both intended and unintended (Haertel, 2013). In a special issue of *Measurement: Interdisciplinary Research and Perspectives*, Edward Haertel in the article "How Is Testing Supposed to Improve Schooling?" provides an expanded concept of validation, making a distinction between what he calls *direct mechanisms* and *indirect mechanisms.* Of particular interest are the indirect mechanisms. As Mary Garner (2013) in her commentary in the same issue explains, indirect mechanisms are the "intended, anticipated effects of testing that have no direct dependence on the information particular scores provide about underlying constructs" (p. 36). Nevertheless, these indirect mechanisms are often the rationale for the testing.

This argument is not much different from that of Mary Lee Smith and Patricia Fey (2000), who remind us that "validity is the standard of quality that professionals place on tests" (p. 334). Meanwhile, accountability decisions premised on test scores are political. This is an issue of continuing debate because of the unintended consequences, especially those emanating from political decisions, that often leave school administrators caught in the middle.

Conclusion

So what are school administrators supposed to do? School administrators may have very little, if any, control over the choice of the test used and the intentional use of the test by policymakers for decisions unrelated to the intended use of the test. What they do have control over is the ethical use of tests in their institutions. They have a responsibility to understand the limits or defined parameters of test use and the properties of the test that lend support to the decisions derived from interpretation of the test scores.

Therefore, it is incumbent that principals understand at least the basic properties of tests used in their schools and be cognizant of the strengths and limitations of these tests. They must be able to articulate these strengths and limitations to parents and the various audiences with whom they interface and also be able to defend their use of tests in the decision-making process. There is no magic to learning how to do this; it simply requires experience, dialoguing with colleagues, and reading some of the more accessible literature.

Key Chapter Terms

Assessment: The process of documenting, describing, quantifying, and interpreting the data from a test to determine an individual's or group's learning, attitudes, and beliefs.

Ethics: Standards for assessing the rightness and wrongness of behaviors based on values relating to human conduct.

Ethics of testing: Refers to testing behaviors and the use of testing instruments that are fair, procedurally just, transparent, and equitable.

Nomological network: A network of hypothesized relationships that link observable measurements to constructs within a theoretical framework.

Objectivity: Refers to consistency with which the testing procedure and testing conditions are fair, unbiased, or control for subjectivity.

Operational definition: Identifying and defining the variables of interest in terms of observable behaviors or actions that can be measured.

Random error: Unexplained errors in measurement that affect the testing process in unpredictable ways.

Reliability: The consistency of obtaining the same or similar scores across multiple measures of the same population under similar conditions using the same test.

Standard error of measurement: The standard deviation of scores from a test of examinees on a single test.

Systematic or constant error: Constant or consistent error due most likely to an inaccuracy in the testing instrument, conditions, or procedure.

Test: An instrument or systematic procedure that consists of a set of questions or activities designed to capture data.

Test bias: Systematic differences in the functioning of test items based on group membership, for example, gender differences or cultural differences

Theoretical definition: Defines the terms or variables, showing their relationship to the theory, or within the context of a theoretical framework.

True score: The part of an observed score that is not influenced by random error.

Validity: The appropriateness, meaningfulness, and usefulness of inferences one makes from scores obtained from tests and measures.

References

AERA, APA, & NCME, (1999). *Standards for educational and psychological testing.* Washington, DC: AERA.

Cronbach, L. J. (1946). Response sets and test validity. *Educational and Psychological Measurement, 6,* 475–494. Retrieved February 21, 2013, from http://epm.sagepub.com/content/6/4/475

Cronbach, L. J., & Meehl, P. E. (1955). Construct validity in psychological tests. *Psychological Bulletin, 52,* 281–302.

de Klerk, G. (2008). Classical test theory (CTT). In M. Born, C. D. Foxcroft, & R. Butter (Eds.), *Online readings in testing and assessment.* International Test Commission. Retrieved from http://www.intestcom.org/Publications/ORTA.php

DeVon, H. A., Block, M. E., Moyle-Wright, P., Ernst, D. M., Hayden, S. J., Lazzara, D. J., . . . Kostas-Polston, E. (2007). A psychometric toolbox for testing validity and reliability. *Journal of Nursing Scholarship, 39*(2), 155–164.

Gable, R. K., & Wolf, M. B. (1993). *Instrument development in the affective domain: Measuring attitudes and values in corporate and school settings* (2nd ed.). Boston, MA: Kluwer Academic Publishers.

Garner, M. (2013). Lies, damn lies and tests. *Measurement: Interdisciplinary Research and Perspectives, 11,* 36–39.

Gay, L. R., & Airasian, P. (2003). *Educational research: Competencies for analysis and applications* (7th ed.). Saddle River, NJ: Merrill-Prentice Hall.

Green, C. E., Chen, C. E., Helms, J. E., & Henze, K. T. (2011). Recent reliability reporting practices in psychological assessment: Recognizing the people behind the data. *Psychological Assessment, 23*(3), 656–669.

Haertel, E. (2013). How is testing supposed to improve schooling? *Measurement: Interdisciplinary Research and Perspectives, 11,* 1–18.

Halverson, R. (2010). Mapping the terrain of interim assessments: School formative feedback systems. *Peabody Journal of Education, 85,* 130–146.

Harvill, L. M. (1991). Standard error of measurement. An NCME Instructional Module. *Instructional Topics in Educational Measurement (ITEMS), 10*(2), 33–41.

Iliescu, D., Ispas, D., & Harris, M. (2009). Social implications and ethics of testing. *International Test Commission.* Retrieved from http://www.intestcom.org/publications/orta/social%20implications%20and%20ethics%20of%20testing.php

International Testing Commission (ITC). (2000). International guidelines for test use. Retrieved from http://www.intestcom.org/Publications/ORTA/Social

Kline, P. (1993). *The handbook of psychological testing.* London, England: Routledge.

Leach, M. M., & Oakland, T. (2007). Ethics standards impacting test development and use: A review of 31 ethics codes impacting practices in 35 countries. *International Journal of Testing, 7*(1), 77–88.

McMillan, J. H., & Schumacher, S. (2010). *Research in education: Evidence-based inquiry* (7th ed.). Boston, MA: Pearson Education.

Messick, S. (1980). Test validity and the ethics of testing. *American Psychologist, 35*(11), 1012–1027.

Messick, S. (1989). Meaning and values in test validation: The science and ethics of assessment. *Educational Researcher, 18*(2), 5–11.

Netemeyer, R. G., Bearden, W. O., & Sharma, S. (2003). *Scaling procedures: Issues and applications.* Thousand Oaks, CA: Sage.

Nunnally, J. C., & Bernstein, I. H. (1994). *Psychometric theory* (3rd ed.). New York, NY: McGraw-Hill.

Pedhazur, E. J., & Pedhazur-Schmelkin, L. (1991). *Measurement design and analysis: An integrated approach.* Hillsdale, NJ: Erlbaum.

Shepard, L. (1993). Evaluating test validity. *Review of Research in Education, 19,* 405–450. Retrieved from http://www.jstor.org/stable/1167347

Smith, M., & Fey, P. (2000). Validity and accountability in high-stakes testing. *Journal of Teacher Education, 51*(5), 334–344.

Traub, R. E., & Rowley, G. L. (1991). Understanding reliability. An NCME Instructional Module, Instructional Topics in Educational Measurement (ITEMS). Retrieved from: http://ncme.org/linkservid/65F3B451-1320-5CAE-6E5A1C4257CFDA23/showMeta/0/

The Universal Declaration of Ethical Principles for Psychologists. (2008). Retrieved from http://www.iupsys.net/about/governance/universal-declaration-of-ethical-principles-for-psychologists.html

Westhoff, K., & Kluck, M. L. (2008). *Psychological reports* (5th ed.). Heidelberg, Germany: Springer.

Further Readings

Borsboom, D., Mellenbergh, G. J., & van Heerden, J. (2004). The concept of validity. *Psychological Review, 111*(4), 1061–1071.

This article challenges the current conception of validity by proposing a simpler conception of validity that is premised on the attribute the test is measuring and not on its consistency with a nomological or theoretical network.

Kane, M. (2010). Validity and fairness. *Language Testing, 27*(2), 177–182.

The article makes explicit the relationship between fairness and validity in that they both attempt to answer the question: Are the proposed interpretations and uses of the test scores appropriate for a population over some range of context? Fairness is the interpretive component focusing on absence of bias and equitable treatment of all examinees, whereas validity relies on empirical evidence to draw conclusions with regard to confidence in the test scores.

*Measurement: Interdisciplinary Research and
Perspectives.* (2013). Vol. 11 (1/2), 1–70.

This issue is a must read. It comprises 12 comprehensive commentaries on Haertel's article "How Is Testing Supposed to Improve Schooling?" in which he expands the concept of validation, making a distinction between what he calls direct mechanisms and indirect mechanisms. The commentaries are from top experts in the field. They include Daniel Koretz, Andrew Ho, Kadriye Ercikan, Suzanne Lane, Lyle Bachman, Robert Mislevy, Lorrie Shepard, Dylan Wiliam, Derek Briggs, George Engelhard, Jr., and Stefanie Wind.

Moss, P. A. (1992). Shifting conceptions of validity in educational measurement: Implications for performance assessment. *Review of Educational Research, 62*(3), 229–258.

This article is both historical in that it traces the changes in the conception of validity, and current in that the arguments are relevant to today's challenges with regard to alternative forms of assessment and the validity of high-stakes tests. Moss argues that new technologies and developments in education require alternative assessment procedures to measure skills such as critical thinking and creativity as a result of shifting attitudes toward performance assessment that are designed to help both the student and the educator. The article expands the concept of validity beyond that of the social consequences of assessment-based interpretations and actions to questioning why particular methods of inquiry are privileged and what the effects are of that privileging on the community.

Smith, M., & Fey, P. (2000). Validity and accountability in high-stakes testing. *Journal of Teacher Education, 51*(5), 334–344.

The authors differentiate between validity and accountability. They argue that validity is about the psychometric properties of the test, whereas accountability exists in a political community with a different set of priorities and values. The article then addresses lack of validity and the weak foundation for the decisions made from the results of standardized tests and the effects of these decisions on the most disadvantaged students.

11

Achievement Gaps

Causes, False Promises, and Bogus Reforms

Connie M. Moss

Duquesne University

In his speeches about helping people and regions to prosper, President John F. Kennedy liked to use the hopeful metaphor, "A rising tide lifts all boats." It merged ideas of equity and growth into a singular assurance that strategic thinking could promote upward mobility for all. For Americans, even those born into poverty or marginalized groups, a quality education was the great equalizer. Their free, public education not only put them on a boat and but also equipped them to navigate the rising tides of opportunity. From 1950 to 1980, most boats rose and intergenerational mobility increased. But that upward trend stalled in the 1990s giving way to a sharp decline. Currently, the tides of the 21st century are lifting fewer boats and allowing many to run aground. And, the achievement **gap** shows little change despite a half-century of reform efforts designed to shrink it.

This chapter examines those reforms through a particular lens of inquiry: *How did each reform define and measure* **achievement**? The question helps educational leaders critically examine each reform effort to discern what worked, what didn't, and why, in order to distinguish lofty intentions from meaningful impacts.

Achievement: Misunderstandings and Misconceptions

Initiatives to improve student achievement at the system-, school-, and classroom-level launch regularly with each changing of the guard at the White House and with leadership changes in statehouses and school district offices across the country. The design of each reform effort is guided by the question—*What can be done to close the achievement gap?*—met with varying levels of success. Perhaps the guiding question puts the cart before the horse by assuming that educators, policymakers, politicians, and parents shared the same understanding of "achievement." This chapter suggests that a more powerful line of inquiry results from a pair of guiding questions: *Achievement of what?* and *What will count as evidence that students achieved it?* It further suggests that how you frame an argument is just as important, and many times, more important that the argument you make.

What Is Meant by "Achievement"?

According to Thomas Guskey (2007), a leading expert in assessment, achievement simply means that we are looking for evidence of "something." In educational settings that "something" is commonly defined as learning goals or objectives that can describe outcomes across grade levels (PreK-12), domains (e.g., cognitive, psychometric, affective), subjects (e.g., English, math, science), courses (e.g., Earth Science, U.S. History, spelling), and units (e.g., telling time, balancing chemical equations, writing a friendly letter). Some goals span content and contexts (e.g., problem-solving, analytical thinking), while others describe skills and proficiencies (e.g., using the scientific method, speaking a foreign language). Achievement, then, can have numerous definitions depending on content, grade level, and expectations for success. Achievement in high school algebra means something very different, for example, than achievement in a first grade reading class.

Standards and Criteria—"Achievement of What?"

To assess understanding and skill two things are required: a standard and criteria. A standard describes what students must know and/or be able to do. For example, the Pennsylvania Department of Education (PDE) lists the following standard for all ninth grade world history students: They must be able to "demonstrate an understanding of how the PA Constitution and the US Constitution co-exist." By 12th grade all students must be able to "analyze and assess the rights of people as written in the PA Constitution and the US Constitution" (PDE, 2009).

The standard is the bull's-eye for which students aim, and criteria define their degree of mastery or accuracy—how close they came to the bull's-eye. Descriptions of where a student ranks in relation to a particular standard fall somewhere along a continuum of competence, as shown in **Figure 11.1**, ranging from absence of the skill or understanding to absolute understanding or perfect performance.

Standards and grade-level standards provide the goals against which to benchmark what students are supposed to learn. But without criteria, it is impossible to conclude where a student is in relation to a particular standard or whether the student made sufficient progress.

Grasp or Growth? The Difference Makes All the Difference

There is a significant difference between expecting students to grasp certain content or skills, and expecting them to show growth with the content or skill over time. Understanding the distinction between grasp and growth is pivotal for those who seek to improve and measure student success.

Consider this example: A student enters the ninth grade already able to explain in detail how the Pennsylvania State Constitution and the United States Constitution coexist. In other words, on the first day of school, this student has already attained or grasped the standard. Describing achievement as simply grasping or attaining something, answers the question *"Has the student mastered it or not?"*

In contrast, achievement can be described as the growth or progress a student demonstrates as a result of school effectiveness—the influence of the learning experiences the school provides on the quality/degree of the student's learning. Douglas Ready (2013), an educational researcher examining the history of educational reforms, suggests that meaningful measures of student success require the use of learning progressions/trajectories and "value-added" models that provide measurements of progress and growth with the content or skill for the same student or group of students over time.

While the examination of grasp versus growth yields fundamentally different measures of achievement, combining the two helps educational leaders develop a sophisticated picture. For example,

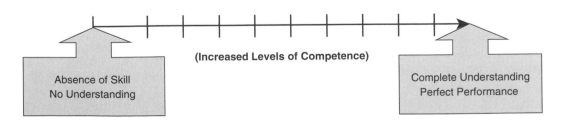

Figure 11.1   An Absolute Continuum of Quality

Sidebar 11.1   Analyzing Assessments

When reviewing the results of any measure of student achievement, school leaders should ask themselves the following:

- Does this measure conceptualize student achievement as attainment? Does it provide information about what students know or do not know compared to criteria?
- Does this measure conceptualize achievement as improvement? Does it compare what the student knew before the educational experience to what the student knows as a result of the learning experience to determine the degree of impact of schooling?

---

it is possible for gifted students to demonstrate the same grasp of something on both pre- and post-measures of their learning, thereby demonstrating no progress. On the other hand, students with learning challenges can demonstrate significant learning progress over a period of instruction but never meet the criteria for mastery of the standard—a phenomenon explained by the **Matthew Effect**.

The Matthew Effect and Achievement Gaps

Matters of achievement and reforms designed to close achievement gaps are better understood using what researchers call the *Matthew Effect*. Originally, Robert Merton (1968) coined the term to highlight the phenomenon that already eminent scientists routinely garnered disproportionate credit over their collaborators or colleagues by virtue of their status, allowing them to enjoy a cumulative advantage over time. In educational research, the term refers to the cumulative advantage enjoyed by high-achieving students: the rich get richer and the poor get poorer. That is to say, students who begin cognitively rich becoming increasingly richer, while slow starters experience a progressive decline that yields an ever-widening gap between them and the students who make good initial progress.

Through their research, Paul Morgan, George Farkas, and Jacob Hibel (2008) found that low-achieving students continued to fall further behind even while differences between their high-achieving and average ability peers remained constant. Stated another way, students who come to learning experiences with fuller understandings of the concepts being taught enjoy an important cumulative advantage allowing them to learn more quickly and learn more than students with no knowledge of, or early misconceptions about, the

content. As a result, the gap between higher achieving and struggling students can remain constant even when struggling students make progress.

Considering the Matthew Effect challenges leaders to critically examine reform efforts that attempt to raise achievement through a focus on educational standards and accountability but that ignore other salient factors.

Fifty Years of Reforms Yield a Widening Achievement Gap

Douglas Harris and Carolyn Herrington (2006) examined a half-century of research to investigate the interrelationships among accountability, standards, and improved student achievement. To explain their finding that the achievement gap shrank significantly between 1950 and 1980, only for progress on closing the gap to stall, followed by the gap widening in the 1990s, they point to a core economic casual factor. As they explained, "income and status . . . become increasingly determined by educational success . . . and the gap in achievement . . . shifted steadily from being an indicator of educational inequality to being a direct cause of socioeconomic inequality" (p. 210). In other words, they found educational equity and student achievement to be positively correlated.

What follows is a description of the major economic and cultural forces that drove reforms and influenced changes in the achievement gap between 1950 and 2000.

1950 Through 1979: The Achievement Gap Decreases

Beginning in 1950 there was a significant decrease in the achievement gap. Policy reforms increased the time students spent in school mastering challenging content. Social and political forces, combined with reform efforts, ushered in a period of increased equity. During the decades following World War II, minority students prospered from resources and academic content historically previously available only to White students.

The G.I. Bill

Following World War II, minority servicemen took advantage of the Servicemen's Readjustment Act of 1944 (Public Law 78-346, 58 Stat. 284m), commonly known as the G.I. Bill. Among other provisions, veterans who had seen active duty for at least 90 days received direct funds for tuition and living expenses to attend high school, college, or vocational schools. Additionally, servicemen were given a year of unemployment compensation to provide them both the time and the resources needed to further their education. Many G.I Bill recipients were the first in their families to graduate. Their increased educational status caused a rise in their expectations for their own educational futures and careers and those of their children.

Brown v. Board of Education *(1954)*

In 1954 *Brown v. Board of Education* ended legal segregation in public schools to become one of the most important decisions ever rendered by the U.S. Supreme Court. The law was a catalyst for significant change in national and social policies. School desegregation meant that some African American students could attend the same schools as their White peers, gaining access to better teachers and resources. The law outlawed **de jure segregation**—legal mandates that were commonly thought of as "separate but equal" segregation laws sanctioned by the states, but many African American children were (and many still are) subjected to **de facto segregation**—inequalities that existed in practice but were not officially established or ordained by law.

The Economic Punches of 1965

In 1965 two separate government initiatives to combat poverty delivered a one-two punch that helped shrink the achievement gap for all students. Though the funds were meant to alleviate conditions of poverty, many children living in poverty were also African American.

The first punch was the Elementary and Secondary Education Act (ESEA; 20 §§ U.S.C. 6301 *et seq.*). Part of President Lyndon B. Johnson's War on Poverty, the ESEA was designed to help poor and disadvantaged students reach their full potential. ESEA's Title I (Public Law 89-10, Section 201), originally called Title I: Better Schooling for Educationally Deprived Children, provided resources to schools and districts with high percentages of students from low-income families. The second punch was the Head Start program, also part of the War on Poverty. At its inception, Head Start delivered a 6-week summer program that helped prepare low-income children for kindergarten by bolstering their physical and emotional well-being, and helping them develop stronger cognitive skills.

Both economic initiatives significantly increased resources to elementary schools with large low-income populations, and put a greater focus on these schools. Minority children, who made up a significant percentage of the poor and disadvantaged, saw their educational options increase quantitatively and qualitatively. The concentration on underfunded schools and children from low-income families helped to ease conditions that often diluted what was happening in the classroom, thus improving the academic achievement of the poor and marginalized.

The 1980s

Toward the beginning of the 1980s, average scores on what was then called the Scholastic Aptitude Test (now known simply as the SAT) began to decline. Many pointed the finger at twin culprits: the socially permissive culture of the 1970s and the increased efforts to address economic and racial inequities. They hypothesized that in order to raise standards for minorities and the disadvantaged, schools had deviated from a core of rigorous content to, in effect, decrease academic standards for all students. High inflation rates (18% by 1980) and unemployment (11% by 1982) added to widespread, general dissatisfaction and further fueled calls for a return to "high standards" through sweeping educational reform.

A Nation at Risk

In response to a chorus of growing concerns, the National Commission on Excellence in Education

(NCEE) released *A Nation at Risk* in 1983. The report, commissioned by Secretary of Education Terrel Bell under President Ronald Reagan, spanned 36 pages and used heated rhetoric to describe the dangerous direction taken by American schools and the resulting dire consequences. "If an unfriendly foreign power had attempted to impose on America the mediocre educational performance that exists today, we might well have viewed it as an act of war," the report stated. "As it stands, we have allowed this to happen to ourselves." Schools, the report said, were force-feeding an "incoherent, outdated patchwork quilt" of classroom learning experiences to America's children through a "cafeteria style curriculum" of choices that diluted content and permitted students to move through schooling with minimal effort.

A Nation at Risk took education from the sidelines to the forefront of the national agenda to galvanize perspectives that still influence today's high-stakes accountability landscape. Harris and Herrington (2006) draw particular attention to its warning about the consequences of permissiveness: "our once unchallenged preeminence in commerce, industry, science, and technological innovation . . . [will be] overtaken by our competitors in the world" (NCEE, 1983). The quote underscores the report's primary objective: increasing achievement for the "average" student (NCEE, 1983). And though the report mentioned equal treatment for diverse student populations (NCEE, 1983, p. 13), it did so as a preemptive strike against those who might oppose the report. The commission had little interest in promoting educational equity and excellence through political action, yet the recommendations the report put into place caused a positive shift in those conditions and increased academic opportunity (Harris & Herrington, 2006).

In their detailed study of *A Nation at Risk* and its recommendations, James Guthrie and Matthew Springer (2004) concluded that despite a misdiagnosis of the problem, student achievement was not lower in 1983 than any time in history, nor was the U.S. economy being sabotaged by the nation's schools. Even though it ignored inequities faced by the disadvantaged, the commission got some solutions right.

A Nation at Risk focused on three main themes: more rigorous academic content, greater resources, and increased time spent learning. Consequently, the

National Center for Education Statistics (NCES, 2001) found significantly more students taking core academic classes in the years following the report, resulting in increased instructional time—a condition that is positively correlated with raising achievement of disadvantaged students. As African American and Hispanic students took an increased number of core academic classes during the 1980s, they experienced the largest gains in instructional time to date and had increased exposure to more academically challenging content, helping to raise their achievement. In fact, the positive relationship between high-quality, challenging content and student achievement level is even stronger than the positive relationship between a student's grade point average and achievement. Earning good grades by sailing through easy content does not shrink the achievement gap. Rather, achievement rises when we give all students the respect of high expectations along with the differentiated support they need to reach those challenges.

Particularly in the high schools, *A Nation at Risk*'s curriculum improvements, measured by changes in **Carnegie units**, or time-based references that each represent one year of work in a high school subject, brought more stringent demands for all students. NCES (2001) reported gains for African American and Hispanic students as especially significant. High schools required a base combination of four units of English, three units of social studies, two units of science, and two units of math. Other rigorous requirements added additional units in math, computers, and foreign languages.

Finally, *A Nation at Risk* changed the criteria for judging quality schools. Prior to the report, quality was used to describe schools that were rich in resources; because of the report school quality became tightly lashed to student achievement. The report's agenda, improving the country's productivity through high-quality graduates who would secure the nation's global economic preeminence and increase its scientific and military dominance, birthed a cultural trend of examining achievement scores. As a result, there were increased demands that scores for those at the bottom of the achievement distribution improve as well—a view that certainly has merit. Yet even good ideas, when taken too far, can have detrimental effects.

A Nation at Risk initiated several trends that still influence today's schools. Guthrie and Springer

(2004) point to its influence on the history of American education through its acceleration of a "federalization of education policy" (p. 9), a trend the authors said affects public schools by limiting their options, creativity, and decision making. Before this federalization, local schools enjoyed the freedom to tailor their curriculum to the needs and talents of their student population. For better or worse, *A Nation at Risk* caused control to shift from the states to the federal government, which assumed a greater leadership and accountability role for educational policy.

A second trend, a belief that scores on standardized tests are the gold standard for certifying student achievement, has been especially harmful. Reducing achievement to this sole measure meant that other reform policies and initiatives focused on racial, economic, and social inequalities that were equally or perhaps more important to achievement than raising test scores were increasingly ignored and often abandoned.

Finally, *A Nation at Risk* reinforced a growing cultural trend that while failures and inequalities in other social institutions such as government, finance, and business could be tolerated, failures and inequalities in schools required decisive action. The rhetoric in the report convinced the general public the schools were at the root cause of the country's problems and solving those problems meant "fixing" schools. Raising achievement became the alpha and omega of popular initiatives to raise the quality of life in the United States, allowing other social reform policies to recede into the background.

The 1990s: Achievement Stalls and Then Falls

The United States entered the 1990s with achievement trending upward. Recommendations from *a Nation at Risk* led to increased percentages of students taking core academic courses, and the nation enjoyed a decade of growth. But the 1990s also brought increased "carrot and stick" policies of a federal government that measured achievement according to standardized tests and used those test scores to mete out specific rewards and punishments. The political and financial pressures, intended to make schools accountable to the public, promoted educational decisions based largely on standardized test results rather than on careful consideration of the

many factors that contribute to or deter meaningful student learning.

The Scarlet Letter of Accountability

Beginning in the 1990s, reformers sought to pressure low-achieving schools to raise the achievement of struggling students by publishing the school's achievement scores. Their purpose was to create a "scarlet letter" effect that would force educators to do everything and anything to avoid the stigma of being labeled failures. Harris and Herrington (2006), who conducted extensive research on government-based accountability measures during the 1990s, disagreed with that perspective. They argued that schools with necessary financial and human capital were able to use their resources to adequately respond to government pressures but poorer schools could not. In fact, students who gained the most from increased government accountability pressures already attended schools with records of high performance, contributing to a widened achievement gap and a Matthew Effect. Achievement for average students increased, while achievement for low-performing students in schools with few resources saw less impact. And, while the trend toward government accountability measures cannot bear the blame as the sole cause of a widening achievement gap, it is clear that when the nation shifted its focus from helping schools build capacity by providing all students with more challenging content, student achievement stalled and the achievement gap grew.

No Child Left Behind: 21st-Century, High-Stakes, Test-Driven Accountability

On January 8, 2002, President George W. Bush signed the No Child Left Behind Act of 2001 (NCLB; Public Law 107-110), promising to raise student proficiency in reading and mathematics and close the achievement gap between identifiable groups of children. Promising scientifically based measures for identifying and stimulating low-performing schools, NCLB's impact over more than a decade has been the subject of tough questions: Has NCLB lived up to its promise? Is adequate yearly progress (AYP) a valid and reliable indicator of improvement in low-performing schools? Did NCLB promote academic excellence and equity across the United States? Countless studies examined NCLB's measures, incentives, and mandates against the sobering reality that in 2014 American children of color, along with those who are poor or disadvantaged, still find themselves well behind those who are White and wealthy.

What NCLB Mandated

NCLB relied heavily on high-stakes testing to hold all schools accountable for making adequate yearly progress (AYP) toward the goal of 100% student proficiency in math and reading by the year 2014. Borrowing a theory of action from *A Nation at Risk*, it used incentives and punishments to transform educational conditions and motivate schools, teachers, and students to do better. Researchers Jaekyung Lee and Todd Reeves (2012) explain that NCLB was supposed to build on the alleged success of government accountability movements in states such as Texas and North Carolina, although the researchers noted that evidence of gains in student achievement in those states was mixed and contradictory.

NCLB emphasized a four-pronged approach: "research-based" educational policy, pedagogy and curriculum that were "measurable," increased funding for poor schools, and assurances that all students would be educated by highly qualified teachers. New regulations stipulated that any school receiving federal funds would be accountable for raising the achievement of all students by "disaggregating" achievement data. The intent of forcing schools to break data apart to report specific impacts was to expose inequality and eliminate the common shell game many schools used to hide their failure to help the very students the federal funds were supposed to reach: students of color, those living in conditions of poverty, and students with disabilities.

In addition, NCLB required federal approval of each state's plan for raising student achievement. This granted the federal government the power to mandate the specific "standards" for key areas of education and select the measures used to certify attainment of those standards. NCLB also described the specific and standard penalties to be levied on districts that underperformed.

Finally, NCLB demanded 100% accountability from schools without assuming 100% of the bill for the measures required by the law, thereby placing heavy financial and bureaucratic reporting burdens on states, districts, and schools, without providing financial assistance. Although the federal government provided $412 million a year for additional testing required by the law, many states had to divert funds from other programs to pay for testing and other NCLB provisions.

Hobbled From the Start

NCLB was enacted through a bipartisan bargain that promised a large increase in federal aid to high-poverty schools in order to fund the reforms, and strict requirements for accountability measures intended to reveal and eliminate achievement disparity by race, ethnicity, language, and special education status. The first leg of the plan, demanding strict accountability through high-stakes testing, remained untouched, but the increased funds for high-poverty schools promised by the law vanished after the first year.

LaRuth Hackney Gray (2005), a director with the Metropolitan Center for Urban Education at New York University, saw NCLB's approach as an attempt to use a deficit model to raise achievement. She noted that NCLB's core demand that all students reach the same "finish line" fails to consider that different children come to their learning from dramatically different starting points. In light of this disparity, NCLB requires minority and disadvantaged communities to play "catch up"—to expend tremendous effort to run faster in order to simply stay in place. To fully understand the uneven playing field highlighted by Hackney Gray, it is critical to examine what NCLB demanded, how it defined "achievement," and the way NCLB set about to measure it.

What NCLB Demands

Under NCLB, all schools must substantiate that their students made adequately yearly progress (AYP) using three prescribed indicators: attendance or graduation rate, academic performance, and test participation. NCLB measures AYP in complicated and confusing ways that include multiple variables in reporting, status levels, and conditions. Schools that fail to make AYP for 5 consecutive years must be "restructured" and can be taken over by the states or made into charter schools. Nationally, more than 3,500 schools were in restructuring for the 2007–2008 school year—an increase of more than 50% from the previous year (Center on Education Policy, 2009). That number increased to 7,643 schools for the 2011–2012 school year (U.S. Department of Education. 2013). While a full discussion is impractical here, the following summary provides an overview of NCLB's three major indicators and their variables.

Attendance or Graduation Rate

Attendance rate applies to schools without high school graduating classes. Based on the entire school, the rate is 90% or a target of any improvement from the previous year.

Graduation rate applies to all measurable subgroups in schools with high school graduating classes. The goal rate is 85%, or a 10% reduction of the difference between the previous year's graduation rate and 85%. Graduation rate for any year is the number of graduates divided by that year's cohort multiplied by 100. Graduates are defined as students graduating in 4 years with a regular diploma. The cohort is made up of first-time ninth graders entering the school 4 years earlier, plus students in that grade cohort transferring into the school during the 4-year period and minus those in the cohort transferring out.

Achieving Proficiency (Academic Performance)

Each state sets AYP goals for schools—the percentage of students who must meet or exceed proficiency in mathematics and reading. Under the law, these percentages had to increase gradually until 2014, when 100% of students were supposed to score proficient or higher.

Schools may meet AYP using a "safe harbor" provision where performance rate is based on only those students enrolled for the full academic year (as of October 1) who completed the test and are not in their first year of an English language learner program. Schools meet AYP under this provision if the percentage of students who scored proficient decreases by 10% from the previous year.

Taking the Test (Test Participation)

At least 95% of a school's students overall and within each subgroup must take the test. That rate covers students enrolled as of the last day when the test can be given in that school year, regardless of whether the students were enrolled for a full academic year.

How NCLB Defines and Measures Achievement

> Each State shall establish a timeline for adequate yearly progress. The timeline shall ensure that not later than 12 years after the end of the 2001–2002 school year, all students . . . will meet or exceed the State's proficient level of academic achievements on the State assessments (No Child Left Behind Act of 2001).

The language used in NCLB could lead people to believe that by "proficient," NCLB requires all students to achieve grade-level success by 2014, an assumption that is far from valid.

How NCLB Defines "Proficient"

Standardized tests define "proficient" using specific **cut scores**—the number of points students must score to certify degrees of achievement (e.g., 60 for unsatisfactory, 70 for basic, 80 for proficient, 90 for advanced). NCLB allows states to use their own federally approved assessments to both implement and evaluate their efforts to raise student achievement and to determine their own cut scores. Consider what happens in two states that administer similarly difficult standardized tests. State A sets its proficient cut score at 55 points, while State B selects 75 points to certify proficiency. As a consequence, State B, by selecting a higher cut score has less chance of making AYP than State A, which selected the lower cut scores.

NCLB's Overall Impacts

In an article based on a 4-year study by the Center on Education Policy, Jack Jennings and Diane Stark Rentner (2006) summarized NCLB's overall influences on public schools. They noted that although students were scoring higher on state tests, they were also taking more tests. In addition, the gains students demonstrated in math and reading came at the expense of their performance in other subjects. NCLB also had an impact on schools, and the researchers found that schools were using the test score data to align their curriculum and instruction to improve student test scores. This increased focus on data from the tests heightened awareness of the gaps that existed between groups of students in the same school. Not surprisingly, the impact was greater on low-performing schools. These schools made significant changes in an effort to avoid restructuring. Teachers were also impacted, with more teachers meeting the criteria for being highly qualified. Finally, the study concluded that while NCLB had resulted in an increased role of the federal government in education, there was no increase in federal funds to provide state governments and school districts with adequate financial support to perform the expanded duties required by NCLB.

Benchmarking NCLB's Assessment Results

Given that 50 different states can theoretically use 50 unique testing systems and cut scores, it comes as no surprise that states show greater gains in student achievement on their own high-stakes tests than on external, independent, low-stakes measures like the National Assessment of Educational Progress (NAEP). Hoping to minimize this condition, NCLB mandated that beginning in 2003 states must administer NAEP every other year for reading and mathematics in Grades 4 and 8 as a benchmark against which to compare their assessment results. NAEP standards for proficiency are quite rigorous by design. When the National Center for Education Statistics (McLaughlin et al., 2008) compared the measures, it found no consistent pattern of agreement between NAEP and states' NCLB assessment reports, even though those reports were used as evidence they had produced gains in achievement.

Once again, educational leaders who seek to gauge the merits of any reform focused on raising student achievement should begin by uncovering how that initiative defines the "something" it is measuring and what will count as evidence that "something" is achieved.

Acknowledging the Need for Waivers

In 2011, at the direction of President Barack Obama, the Department of Education established a

formal plan to "provide flexibility to states" seeking relief from NCLB provisions to meet AYP by 2014. That process was extended in August of 2013 so that states that had approved waivers in place that would expire in the 2013–2014 school year, could request a renewal of those waivers. Policies and procedures for requesting flexibility and securing waivers continue to develop. As of July 2014, the U.S. Department of Education posted extended guidelines to offer targeted flexibility to states that required extra support in meeting the mandates of NCLB.

Race to the Top: Competitive Grants for Educational Innovation

On February 17, 2009, President Obama signed the American Recovery and Reinvestment Act of 2009 (ARRA) to stimulate the economy, support job creation, and invest in critical sectors including education. The law provided an initial $4.35 billion for the Race to the Top (RTT) Fund, a competitive grant program to encourage states to build on years of weak reforms and spark change by creating their own reform agendas based on specific criteria. The criteria focused states on the four key priority areas:

1. Designing and implementing rigorous standards and high-quality assessments by encouraging states to work together toward a system of common academic standards benchmarked to international standards.

2. Attracting and keeping great teachers and leaders by expanding support to educators; improving teacher preparation; revising evaluation and compensation policies to encourage effectiveness; and helping to ensure that the most talented educators are placed in the schools and subjects where they are needed the most.

3. Supporting data systems that inform decisions and improve instruction by fully implementing a statewide longitudinal data system and making data more accessible to key stakeholders.

4. Using innovation and effective approaches to turn around low-performing schools.

Forty states applied during the first three phases of competition and 22 were awarded grants. Their applications embodied the priority criteria, demonstrated momentum around collaboration and reform, and promised work in key innovation areas that included expanded support for high-performing charter schools and reinvigorated math and science education.

Some states are in the early stages of their work and top research firms are in the midst of a contracted 5-year $18 million study of RTT's impact that is scheduled to last until September 2015. Yet, some indicators have emerged from the states that entered during Phases 1 and 2.

RTT's Performance Thus Far

Ulrich Boser (2012), a senior fellow at the Center for American Progress, evaluated states on their efforts by benchmarking their success against key indicators that included implementation of new teacher evaluation systems, implementation of the Common Core State Standards, establishing data systems, and garnering support of major stakeholders. Boser noted that since the RTT competition coincided with the Great Recession, states were unusually desperate for federal funds and tried to outdo each other by promising improvements prior to the competition to increase their chances of winning. As a result some states over-promised and under-delivered.

Based on an extensive state-by-state analysis, Boser reported that RTT has sparked significant reform and policy changes, particularly in implementing the Common Core and designing and employing new teacher evaluation systems. Many states were on track to meet their RTT commitments, but some states were behind due to political missteps and poor communication. Some states faltered early, due to lack of buy-in from key stakeholders like teachers unions. Finally, Boser noted the positive influence of the U.S. Department of Education in monitoring and supporting state performance.

Shortcomings of Race to the Top

While it is too early to analyze the long-range impact of Race to the Top, several concerns are arising as states implement various components. For example, even in states with promising new teacher evaluation systems, problems arise when schools try to parse out the effect of one teacher on student growth. What's more, the new evaluation systems, tied to the outcomes from standardized tests, put greater pressure on the teachers of "tested subjects" in "tested grades" than they do on the entire teaching force. States have been characterized as over-promising and under-delivering complex teacher evaluation systems due to insufficient time to develop rubrics, provide professional development to administrators, and pilot their new systems.

Secondly, the very shortfalls in education budgets that encouraged many districts to apply for Race to the Top funds, have made plans and promises impossible to keep and implement as school budgets continue to dwindle and prevent schools from acquiring the resources and expertise they need. Again, the push to do too much, too quickly, and with disappearing resources has led superintendents, principals, and teachers to express frustration and stress (Weiss, 2013).

Test or Invest?

Over the last 50 years, those who wanted to reform education experienced significant tension between a need to invest in conditions that contribute to learning versus the need to hold schools accountable for student learning through high-stakes testing. Yet, regardless of their focus, their impacts fell dramatically short of their promises. In the United States of America, one of the wealthiest nations on Earth, the dawn of the 21st century finds too many U.S. children are still poor, undereducated, and forgotten. It is abundantly clear in hindsight, and a source of significant insight, that many forces impacting student learning and achievement come from beyond the schoolhouse door and cannot be solved by nearsighted efforts that focus on schools and schooling alone.

What follows is an overview of other "gaps." Educational leaders should consider them separately and in relation to one another to construct a more comprehensive view of the complex and too rarely discussed underlying factors that we ignore at our own peril.

The Black-White Achievement Gap

Previous sections of this chapter acknowledged that from 1940 through 1990 the gap between Black students' and White students' achievement, both in terms of high school and college graduation, decreased significantly. For African American children born after 1965, on the heels of the Civil Rights Act of 1964, years of gains came to a halt. Paul Barton and Richard Coley (2010) used NAEP data, the Early Childhood Longitudinal Survey of Kindergartners (ECLS-K), Census data, and nearly 100 years of other research to examine what history and social science make of this disturbing chain of events. What made the progress stop?

Unable to uncover a smoking gun, the researchers exposed several factors to pull together a causal explanation for what happened. The ECLS-K storehouse of longitudinal data was especially meaningful since it followed the progress of children by looking at factors such as birth weight, health, participation in Head Start, and noncognitive characteristics that determine a child's approach to learning. The data revealed what common sense can conclude—the opportunity to acquire skills that help children to learn is hugely reduced in areas of concentrated poverty. This discovery caused Barton and Coley to urge policymakers, educators, and researchers to look at the health of the "smallest school"—the family.

Children who grow up in poverty experience the cumulative and corrosive impact of one disadvantaged generation raising the next. Efforts to improve the schools historically ignored the neighborhoods where the schools existed, and for Black children their neighborhoods tend to be urban areas of concentrated poverty that became isolated from the mainstream. The inner-city "blight" caused in part by urban renewal and low-income public housing allowed poverty to become further concentrated in increasingly smaller areas.

Underscoring this condition, Pedro Noguera and Jean Yonemura Wing (2006) view U.S. schools as both epicenters of unfinished business and "pockets of hope." Informed by their extensive work to close the racial achievement gap through the Berkeley High School Diversity Project, they learned lessons from the inside out to develop renewed faith in the power of public education to create equality and justice for all. As a result, they describe the "struggle to create just and equitable schools that succeed in educating all children as the most important civil rights issue of the twenty-first century" (p. viii).

The Opportunity Gap

As the children of the rich do better in school, and those who do better in school increase their prospects of becoming rich, the opportunity gap continues to produce an unequal and economically polarized society. Sean Reardon's research (2011) convinced him that family income is now a better predictor of student success in school than race, and that the **income achievement gap** is twice as large as the Black-White achievement gap. For a child born today, a given difference in family income, like the difference between those above and below the median income level, translates to a 30% to 60% larger difference in school success than it did for children born in the 1970s. This relationship between parental income and student achievement has grown sharply over the last 50 years to become a better predictor of success than level of parental education and children's achievement, which has remained stable.

The Education Debt

For years, Gloria Ladson-Billings (2013) has drawn attention to the "education debt," the results of the historical, economic, political, and moral decisions that a society makes over time. By labeling the disparities that exist between rich and poor, or White and Black, or privileged and disenfranchised as a "gap," Ladson-Billings argues that we are suggesting that there is something inherent in a person that makes that person responsible for the difference.

Ladson-Billings (2013) goes on to explain that the education debt accrues each year due to the nation's long-term failure to rectify the disparate conditions that contribute to failing schools, resulting in mounting deficits in learning and achievement. These inequities among the schools they attend mean that children in lower-funded districts, through no fault of their own, have less access to quality buildings, technology, teachers, and supports than their peers in affluent districts.

U.S. school-funding policies are inadequate, and esteem for educators is low, Ladson-Billings finds. Countries that routinely outscore the United States on measures of student achievement have schools that are equitably funded by their national budgets, and are not dependent on local property taxes.

Finland's teachers, frequently cited as the gold standard of effectiveness, are selected from the top 10% of their university classes and belong to fully unionized systems.

Assessment Competency Gap

In her review of over 50 years of research on classroom summative assessment, Connie Moss (2013) found a dangerous and enduring gap between educator confidence and competence related to testing and summarizing student achievement. Accurate descriptions of student achievement are critical to the planning and delivery of quality instruction, the framing of useful feedback, and designing effective assessments to collect evidence of student learning. While this chapter highlighted the biases and weaknesses present in high-stakes testing, Moss's review underscores the critical need to examine the impacts of daily classroom assessments as well. Educators spend one third of their professional lives engaged in summarizing student achievement—although they have only minimal university or professional development instruction in effectively designing and interpreting summative assessments. That fact becomes even more troubling since 99% of the tests students take are designed and interpreted by their teachers. And, as classrooms are increasingly impacted by the high-stakes accountability climate, teachers are making and students are taking more of those tests than ever before.

Classroom teachers routinely use a variety of assessment practices despite being inadequately trained in how to design and use them effectively. What is troubling, according to Moss (2013), is that when teachers frame and test achievement as the collection of disparate facts, they produce a "pedagogy of poverty" that perpetuates low-level thinking, rather than the development of conceptual understanding and critical thinking skills.

Conclusion

Weighing a cow does not make it fatter

—African Proverb

How we define achievement determines the methods we use to measure it, the evidence we rely on to certify it has occurred, and the interventions we pursue should achievement wane or stall. Comparisons among the reforms reviewed in this chapter reveal strong connections among the social, economic, educational, political, and measurement conditions at work. Achievement does not occur in a vacuum, nor can it be increased through testing alone. Understanding what reformers mean when they promise to raise achievement, and looking critically at how they go about auditing the impacts of their recommendations, reveals root causes of achievement gaps, as well as false promises and bogus attempts to help our nation's children achieve. Despite each wave of reform, there are still inequalities and injustices in U.S. schools. In light of the issues examined in this chapter, it may be helpful for educational leaders to consider the following suggestions.

Weed Your Own Backyard

Children do not live their learning or raise their achievement from one standardized test to the next. Rather, students live their learning one lesson and teacher at a time in their neighborhood school. Educators enter schools with the intention to do no harm, yet well-intentioned people can turn a blind eye to unequal conditions or view them as impossible to change. In a very real sense it is often easier and far less uncomfortable to identify inequities in other cities, states, and nations, than to recognize injustices flourishing in our own backyard. Educational leaders must become vigilant and skillful observers who systematically search for unfair conditions in their own school and courageously pull them out by the root.

To close gaps in achievement and opportunity across the multiple dimensions of education, educational leaders must adopt frameworks for "systemic equity." Researchers Linda Skrla, James Joseph Scheurich, and Juanita Garcia, from the University of Texas at Austin, and Glenn Nolly, director of the Austin Independent School District (2004), identified equity audits as practical tools that help leaders systematically look for and address inequitable conditions. They suggested framing the equity audit, a systematic data collection that crosses all areas of a school or district, by starting with a manageable set of key indicators from three categories—teacher quality equity, programmatic equity, and achievement equity—to create an initial audit of the school or district (p. 155). An equity audit can bring into sharp focus achievement gaps by race, gender, ethnicity, home language, socioeconomic status, and ability. A first line audit can uncover inequitable distributions of quality teachers, or inequitable patterns of students placed in special education or Advanced Placement courses.

Become an Informed Skeptic

Beliefs then are the best predictor of leadership actions and leaders, like all human beings, do not set about to do what is right. Rather, each day they do what they *believe* to be right. In a very real sense leadership actions and decisions are shaped by the beliefs leaders hold, and the beliefs that hold them. Beliefs can be very difficult to change, and human beings tend to hold fast to their beliefs, even in the face of contradictory evidence (Moss, 2005).

Almost every injustice that we now deplore in our personal, professional, and social lives was somewhere, and at some time, acceptable. Many of those whom we now consider as the world's greatest leaders embodied customs and cultures that by today's standards were discriminatory, prejudicial, and socially unjust. Our beliefs—right or wrong—drive our decisions. And, while disparity between just intentions and unjust actions can exist for any human being, it is especially common for those who lead. Leaders enjoy levels of privilege that allow them to respond only to what they intended to do, say, or promote, regardless of the impact their actions may have on people, policies, or other outcomes. These levels of privilege can lull leaders into becoming hardened to their own perspectives, satisfied with the status quo, and powerless to see flaws in their own reasoning and action. Undoubtedly, beliefs matter in matters of leading for equity and social justice. Uncovering one's own beliefs, questioning them, holding them up to scrutiny, and discarding those beliefs that prevent leaders from recognizing and eliminating unjust educational practice is a life-long pursuit. A great way to start is for leaders to ask themselves this powerful question during any decision-making process—*What do I strongly believe about this and why?*

Powerful questions help educational leaders position themselves as informed skeptics and life-long learners who intentionally pursue professional learning agendas to critically examine educational initiatives and those who promote them. The starting point for that journey is a deliberate and systematic excavation of a leader's own beliefs regarding what is meant by student achievement, how to measure it in meaningful and ethical ways, and claims and truths regarding achievement gaps.

Crack the Lid Open and Dig Deeper

Powerful questions provoke deeper understanding. Fran Peavey (1994) compared a strategically powerful question to a "lever you use to pry open the stuck lid on a paint can." A short lever will let you crack the lid open, but a powerful question—a longer lever—allows you to open the can much wider and dig much deeper to provoke thinking, stir things up, and promote informed decision making. Listed below are a few "stuck lid" issues framed as powerful questions that will clarify your thinking, help you surface underlying assumptions, and promote personal learning agendas related to understanding achievement gaps.

- Considering that the next occupant of the White House or statehouse will most certainly launch an initiative to improve schools, what assumptions do we need to test or challenge about legislating achievement? Is it possible for the government to mandate and test our way to better learning for our children?
- Since every country has issues with learning and achievement, what do we need to consider regarding the universal issues that contribute to gaps in learning for our children?
- What are the dilemmas and opportunities related to how we currently fund schools in the United States—at the federal, state, and local levels—and how can the funding process be either an engine that fuels student achievement or a shortfall that derails it? What impact would sufficient school funding, fairly distributed to districts to address and alleviate concentrated poverty, have on the ability to deliver high-quality education in all 50 states?
- As diversity in the United States increases, what role would culturally competent educational leaders and teachers—those with the skills, knowledge, and attitudes to value the diversity among students—play in creating educational systems designed to serve all students well and shrink the achievement gap? In the same vein, how might a culturally competent educational leader create conditions of learning at the building and district level to shrink the achievement gap?

- The evidence is clear that some teachers produce much larger achievement gains than others do and that differences in teacher effectiveness tend to persist from year to year. What questions should educational leaders ask as they are walking through classrooms and observing instruction that could close the achievement gaps present in each building due to differences in teacher effectiveness?
- Has a racial, gender, or socioeconomic achievement gap existed in your school for more than 3 years, and why has this gap persisted?
- Some believe the United States lags behind other countries in student achievement due to its propensity to teach and test content acquisition in its schools as if it were still the beginning of the 20th century. How might educational leaders advocate for accountability systems that promote the instruction and testing of 21st-century skills like critical thinking, communication, and collaboration?
- What role does the educational leader play in balancing the male/female ratio among elementary and middle school teachers? How does this gender imbalance contribute to the gender achievement gap that exists between boys and girls in elementary and middle schools? The U.S. Department of Education's 1999–2000 Schools and Staffing Survey reports that 91% of the nation's sixth grade reading teachers and 83% of eighth grade reading teachers are female. Most middle school teachers of math, science, and history are also female. While this may raise girls' achievement by reducing the gender gap in science and math, it may be exacerbating the gender gap in reading by handicapping boys. How should educational leaders approach hiring and staffing practices in light of these factors?

Key Chapter Terms

Achievement: The act of successfully accomplishing "something" specific. In order to gauge "achievement" it is necessary to describe exactly what that "something" is that will be assessed.

Carnegie Unit: A measure of the amount of time a student has studied a subject as developed by the Carnegie Foundation in 1906. One Carnegie Unit equals 120 hours in one subject, meeting four or five times per week for 40 to 60 minutes, 36 to 40 weeks per year. A minimum of 14 Carnegie units is required to certify 4 years of academic or high school preparation.

Cut Score: A selected point on the score scale of a test used to determine whether a particular score is sufficient for some purpose. Cut scores are used to classify student performance into categories such as basic, proficient, or advanced. The setting of cut scores requires the involvement of policymakers, educators, measurement professionals, and other stakeholders during a multistage, judgmental process. Meaningful cut scores must be based on accurate methodology and judgments of qualified people.

De Facto Segregation: Situations and practices where segregation and inequality exist in practice but are neither officially established nor ordained by law.

De Jure Segregation: Segregation mandated by law in all public institutions and facilities, creating "separate but equal" status for African Americans and other non-White racial groups.

Gap: A problematic situation resulting from a conspicuous imbalance or disparity.

Income Achievement Gap: The difference in income between a family in the 90th percentile and a family in the 10th percentile.

Matthew Effect: The positive relationship between initial academic success and later learning. Named for the gospel passage (Matthew 13:12) "To all those who have, more will be given, and they will have abundance; but from those who have nothing even what they have will be taken away."

References

Barton, P. E., & Coley, R. J. (2010). *The Black–White achievement gap: When progress stopped.* Princeton, NJ: Educational Testing Service. Available at http://www.ets.org/Media/Research/pdf/PICBWGAP.pdf

Boser, U. (2012). *Race to the Top: What have we learned from the states so far? A state-by-state evaluation of Race to the Top performance.* Washington, DC: Center for American Progress.

Center on Education Policy. (2009). *Compendium of key studies of the No Child Left Behind Act.* Washington, DC: Center on Education Policy. Retrieved from http://eric.ed.gov/?id=ED505036

Guskey, T. R. (2007). Multiple sources of evidence: An analysis of stakeholder's perceptions of various indicators of student learning. *Educational Measurement: Issues and Practice, 26*(1), 19–27.

Guthrie, J., & Springer, M. (2004). Did "wrong" reasoning result in "right" results? At what cost? *Peabody Journal of Education, 79*(1), 7–35.

Hackney Gray, L. H. (2005). The 2004 Charles H. Thompson Lecture-Colloquium Presentation: No Child Left Behind: Opportunities and threats. *The Journal of Negro Education, 74*(2), 95–111.

Harris, D. N., & Herrington, C. D. (2006). Accountability, standards, and the growing achievement gap: Lessons from the past half-century. *American Journal of Education, 112,* 209–237.

Jennings, J., & Rentner, D. S. (2006). Ten big effects of the No Child Left Behind Act on public schools. *Phi Delta Kappan, 88*(2), 110–113. Retrieved from http://www.cep-dc.org/displayDocument.cfm?DocumentID=263

Ladson-Billings, G. (2013). Lack of achievement or loss of opportunity? In P. L. Carter & K. G. Welner (Eds.), *Closing the opportunity gap: What America must do to give every child an even chance* (pp. 11–22). New York, NY: Oxford University Press.

Lee, J., & Reeves, T. (2012). Revisiting the impact of NCLB high-stakes school accountability, capacity, and resources: State NAEP 1999–2009 reading and math achievement gaps and trends. *Educational Evaluation and Policy Analysis, 4*(2), 209–231.

McLaughlin, D. H., Bandeira de Mello, V., Blankenship, C., Chaney, K., Esra, P., Hikawa, H., . . . Wolman, M. (2008). *Comparison between NAEP and state reading assessment results: 2003* (NCES 2008-474). National Center for Education Statistics, Institute of Education Sciences, U.S. Department of Education. Washington, DC.

Merton, R. (1968) The Matthew effect in science. *Science, 5*(1), 56–63.

Morgan, P. L., Farkas, G., & Hibel, J. (2008). Matthew effects for whom? *Learning Disability Quarterly, 31,* 187–198.

Moss, C. M. (2005). *A proposed foundation for a theory of leadership disposition development* (Technical Report Series No. 1-05). Pittsburgh, PA: Duquesne University, Center for Advancing the Study of Teaching and Learning. Available at http://www.duq.edu/academics/schools/education/outreach-and-research/castl/research/research-technical-reports

Moss, C. M. (2013). Research on classroom summative assessment. In J. H. McMillan (Ed.), *SAGE handbook of research on classroom assessment* (pp. 235–256). Thousand Oaks, CA: Sage.

National Center for Education Statistics (NCES). (2001). *The 1998 High School Transcript Study tabulation: Comparative data on credits earned and demographics for 1998, 1994, 1990, 1987, and 1982 high school graduates* (Report 2001-498). Office of Educational Research and Improvement, U.S. Department of Education, Washington, DC.

National Commission on Excellence in Education (NCEE). (1983). *A nation at risk: The imperative for school reform.* Retrieved from http://datacenter.spps.org/uploads/sotw_a_nation_at_risk_1983.pdf

Noguera, P. A., & Yonemura Wing, J. (Eds.). (2006). *Unfinished business: Closing the racial achievement gap in our schools.* San Francisco, CA: Jossey-Bass.

Peavey, F. (1994). *By life's grace: Musings on the essence of social change.* Gabriola Island, BC, Canada: New Society Publishers.

Pennsylvania Department of Education (PDE). (2009). *Academic standards for civics and government.* Retrieved from http://www.pdesas.org/standard/standardsdownloads

Ready, D. D. (2013). Associations between student achievement and student learning: Implications for value-added accountability models. *Educational Policy, 27*(1), 92–120.

Reardon, S. F. (2011). The widening academic achievement gap between the rich and the poor: New evidence and possible explanations. In G. J. Duncan & R. J. Murnane (Eds.), *Whither opportunity? Rising inequality, schools, and children's life chances* (pp. 91–115). New York, NY: Russell Sage Foundation.

Skrla, L., Scheurich, J. J., Garcia, J., & Nolly, G. (2004). Equity audits: A practical leadership tool for developing equitable and excellent schools. *Educational Administration Quarterly, 40(*1), 133–161.

U.S. Department of Education. (2013). Total number of schools in restructuring: 2011–12. Retrieved from http://eddataexpress.ed.gov/data-element-explorer.cfm/tab/map/deid/521/

Weiss, E. (2013). *Mismatches in Race to the Top limit educational improvement.* Economic Policy Institute. Washington, DC. Retrieved from http://www.epi.org/publication/race-to-the-top-goals/

Further Readings

Berliner, D. C., & Biddle, B. J. (1995). *The manufactured crisis: Myths, fraud, and the attack on America's public schools*. White Plains, NY: Longman.

Outraged by the scapegoating of America's public schools, David C. Berliner, Regents Professor in the College of Education at Arizona State University, and Bruce J. Biddle, professor of psychology and sociology at the University of Missouri, reinterpreted the various statistics

used to label schools as failing to cut through the rhetoric and debunk myths and false accusations. The book's arguments hold relevance for educational leaders who must traverse today's high-stakes educational terrain.

Boykin, A. W., & Noguera, P. (2011). *Creating the opportunity to learn: Moving from research to practice to close the achievement gap.* Alexandria, VA: ASCD.

A. Wade Boykin is a professor and director of the graduate program in the Department of Psychology at Howard University, and Pedro Noguera is the Peter L. Agnew Professor at New York University and internationally known for his leadership on equity and diversity in the public schools. The book critically analyzes evidence-based methods and their impact on the academic achievement gap. The authors explain how to create schools where a child's race or class no longer determines how well that child learns.

Carter, P. L, & Welner, K. G. (Eds.). (2013). *Closing the opportunity gap: What America must do to give every child an even chance.* New York, NY: Oxford University Press.

Prudence L. Carter, an associate professor of education at Stanford University, and Kevin G. Weiner, a professor of education at the University of Colorado, Boulder, coedited this book, which casts opportunity and achievement as extremely different goals. U.S. children lack important resources and opportunities both inside the classroom and outside of schools. The book contains essays from experts to highlight discrepancies in schools, policy, and life that create opportunity gaps on which achievement gaps rest. Contributors explain practical policies that can restore and enhance conditions that allow all children to reach their full potential.

Darling-Hammond, L. (2010). *The flat world and education: How America's commitment to equity will determine our future.* New York, NY: Teachers College Press.

Linda Darling-Hammond is the Charles E. Duncan Professor of Education at Stanford University. The book discusses trends affecting the United States and suggests how to build schools that are equitable and foster high achievement for all children.

Duncan, G. J., & Murnane, R. J. (Eds.) (2011). *Whither opportunity? Rising inequality, schools, and children's life chances.* New York, NY: Russell Sage Foundation.

Greg J. Duncan is distinguished professor in the Department of Education at the University of California, Irvine. Richard J. Murnane is Thompson Professor of Education at the Harvard Graduate School of Education. Their coedited volume represents the most comprehensive effort to date to examine the toll that rising economic equality is taking on education in America. The work was funded by two prestigious foundations: The Spencer Foundation, a leader in research on American education, and the Russell Sage Foundation, historically dedicated to research on the nature of poverty in America.

Freire, P. (2005). *Pedagogy of the oppressed.* New York, NY: Continuum International Publishing Group. (Original work published 1970).

Paulo Reglus Neves Freire was a Brazilian educator whose revolutionary theory of critical pedagogy still influences educational and social movements throughout the world across academic disciplines that include theology, sociology, anthropology, applied linguistics, pedagogy, and cultural studies. Freire urges both students and teachers to unlearn their race, class, and gender privileges and to engage in a dialogue with those whose experiences are very different from their own.

Hattie, J. (2009). *Visible learning: A synthesis of over 800 meta-analyses relating to achievement.* New York, NY: Routledge.

John Hattie is a professor of education and Director of the Visible Learning Labs, University of Auckland, New Zealand. This ground-breaking book resulted from 15 years of research involving millions of students and synthesizes more than 800 meta-analyses related to student achievement. In opposition to those who equate achievement with test scores, the book explains what actually works to increase learning. Areas covered include influences of the student, home, school, curricula, teacher, and teaching strategies.

Kozol, J. (1991). *Savage inequalities: Children in America's schools.* New York, NY: Crown.

In this book, Jonathan Kozol, internationally known author and advocate for equity and social justice, examined the extremes of wealth and poverty and questioned the reality of equal opportunity in our nation's schools.

Popham, W. J. (2001). *The truth about testing: An educator's call to action.* Alexandria, VA: ASCD.

W. James Popham is a renowned expert on testing and assessment. In this book he examines educational testing in the United States to argue that, in most settings, high-stakes testing, as well as poorly constructed classroom tests, are doing serious educational harm to children.

Stobart, G. (2008). *Testing times: The uses and abuses of assessment.* New York, NY: Routledge.

Gordon Stobart is a professor of education at the University of London Institute of Education. This book will help the reader understand assessment as a value-laden social activity that does not objectively measure what is already there but rather creates and determines what is measured. In doing so, assessments produce both constructive and destructive consequences that can undermine or encourage learning.

12

CHEATER, CHEATER, I DECLARE

The Prevalence, Causes, and Effects of, and Solutions to, School Cheating Scandals

GAIL L. THOMPSON

Fayetteville State University

In 2009, a federal judge sentenced financial investment manager Bernie Madoff to 150 years in prison for defrauding investors of billions of dollars. At the beginning of 2013, Lance Armstrong, the bicyclist who gained international fame for winning numerous racing competitions, shocked his supporters when he admitted that he had used performance-enhancing drugs. During the same month, Ray Nagin, the former mayor of New Orleans, Louisiana, was indicted on 21 charges, including conspiracy, filing false tax returns, bribery, fraud, and money laundering. In 2014, a jury found Nagin guilty of 20 of the 21 charges. Long before these events became public, numerous other athletes, politicians, and celebrities had "fallen from grace" as a result of some type of "cheating." In fact, a careful look at history reveals that various types of cheating have surfaced periodically throughout history. In recent years, however, one type of cheating that has received widespread publicity is the "school cheating scandals." Because these scandals have far-reaching consequences, they contain important lessons for policymakers and school leaders: the individuals who are most likely to be blamed when cheating is alleged.

School leaders face many challenges, including raising test scores, maintaining a safe school environment, and keeping parents satisfied. A 2013 MetLife report, *Challenges for School Leadership: A Survey of Teachers and Principals*, indicated that today, the job of the school principal has become more challenging, and many principals say that their jobs are very stressful as a result of budget cuts, finding ways to meet the needs of struggling students, teacher attrition, implementing the new Common Core standards, and determining how to increase parent and community involvement. The report also revealed that both teachers and school principals believe that principals are responsible for what happens at the local school site.

Consequently, since school leaders are deemed responsible for actions occurring at school, a logical conclusion is that when cheating is suspected at a school, they will be blamed. With all of the stressors that school leaders already face, the last thing that they need is for a school cheating scandal to erupt. Therefore, an examination of the prevalence of school cheating scandals, as well as their causes, effects, and ways to prevent them, can be useful to policymakers and school leaders.

Prevalence

In the last decade, so many reports of educator-involved cheating in schools have surfaced that news accounts and opinion pieces have referred to this problem as an "epidemic" (Donaldson James, 2008, p.1), and a "plague" (Bloomberg Editors, 2011). Two of the main types of cheating include teachers changing answers on students' standardized tests, and teachers providing students with answers to test questions directly or indirectly. Although the mainstream media have exposed numerous school cheating scandals in the past few years, cheating in schools—by students, teachers, or school leaders—has a long history. In fact, in previous eras, several adult-involved scandals received extensive media attention and public exposure.

In a 2013 article for the investigative journalism organization ProPublica, Lois Beckett provided a historical overview of some of the most notorious cases of cheating or suspected cheating involving principals and teachers. During the late 1980s, for example, a medical doctor from West Virginia started an investigation into the number of suspiciously high test scores in his home state, and ultimately learned that cheating on standardized tests that involved teachers and principals had occurred in numerous states. In 2000, investigators reported cheating in 32 New York City schools. Another investigation revealed that teacher cheating had occurred in many Chicago schools over a 7-year period from 1993 to 2000. In 2001, high schools in Birmingham, Alabama, allegedly encouraged a substantial number of students to drop out of school to prevent them from taking standardized tests on which they were expected to perform poorly (Beckett, 2013). In 2012, the Los Angeles Board of Education closed six charter schools after the director was accused of forcing school principals to cheat on tests (Blume, 2012). In fact, in the past few years, cheating has been confirmed in schools in 37 states and the District of Columbia (Schaeffer, 2013). One reporter concluded that cheating is not only "widespread," but it's a "nationwide problem" (Pell, 2012). The most scandalous recent case of adult-involved cheating in schools occurred in Atlanta, Georgia.

The Worst Cheating Scandal in U.S. History

While numerous school cheating scandals have surfaced throughout the years, the one that took place in Atlanta, Georgia, from 2001 to 2010 has received extensive exposure because of its magnitude. In Georgia, officials use a multiple-choice test to determine whether or not schools are meeting their adequate yearly progress (AYP) goals, as required by the **No Child Left Behind Act**. The test is administered to elementary and middle school students.

Starting in 2001, standardized test scores in the Atlanta Public Schools system (APS) began to improve dramatically (Bowers, Wilson, & Hyde, 2011), and this news was widely publicized. One result of the spotlight being shone on APS was that Beverly Hall, who had been the district's school superintendent for several years, received national attention. Because she was credited with doing what many school leaders dream of doing: narrowing the achievement gap as measured by higher standardized test scores, in 2009, Hall was named U.S. superintendent of the year by the American Association of School Administrators (AASA; Jonsson, 2011). This occurred in spite of the fact that reporters had become suspicious of APS's test scores as early as 2001. Nevertheless, throughout the years, Hall and her administrative team denied that cheating had occurred, even though at least one educator told school officials that cheating was taking place. This educator "was punished" for breaking the "code of silence" in APS (Bowers et al., 2011, p. 4).

In 2010, after rumors had circulated for years about cheating in APS, the governor intervened and appointed a special investigative team to determine whether or not the allegations of widespread cheating in APS were true. The governor ordered the investigators to look specifically at whether or not cheating had occurred on the standardized test that was administered in 2009. After examining nearly 1 million documents, and interviewing over 2,000 APS employees and individuals who were not employed by APS, the investigators delivered a three-volume report to the governor. In the report, they stated:

> Widespread cheating in the Atlanta Public School System (APS) harmed thousands of school children. In 30 schools, educators confessed to cheating. We found cheating on the 2009 Criterion-Referenced Competency Test (CRCT) in 44 of the 56 schools (78.6%) we examined, and uncovered organized and systemic misconduct within the district as far back as 2001. Superintendent Beverly Hall and her senior staff knew, or should have known, that cheating and other offenses were occurring. Many of the accolades, and much of the praise, received by APS over the last decade were ill-gotten.

We identified 178 educators as being involved in cheating. Of these, 82 confessed. Thirty-eight of the 178 were principals, from two-thirds of the schools we examined. The 2009 erasure analysis suggests that there were far more educators involved in cheating, and other improper conduct, than we were able to establish sufficiently to identify by name in this report.

Hall failed in her leadership of, and ultimate responsibility for, testing activities and for ensuring the ethical administration of the CRCT in 2009, as well as in previous years. . . . Finally, we conclude that Dr. Hall either knew or should have known cheating and other misconduct was occurring in the APS system. (Bowers et al., 2011, pp. 2, 410)

The Atlanta school cheating scandal and others that have been exposed reveal that adult-involved cheating is a huge problem in schools, and it has a long history. Just as it has occurred in many schools and in numerous states, multiple explanations have been given for its causes. Three of these explanations are described in the next section.

Causes

There are at least three causes of educator-led or educator-involved cheating at school: personal gain, fear, and high-stakes testing. An examination of the careers of two prominent school leaders illustrates the link between personal gain and school cheating. In every organization, including corporations, political groups, banks, school districts, and local schools, leaders set the tone for acceptable and unacceptable behavior (Thompson, 2007). In schools, one of the reasons the number of cases of adult-involved cheating has soared is that various leaders realized that they could personally benefit from being at the helm of a school district or school that had high standardized test scores. As previously noted, Beverly Hall of the APS received awards and widespread attention from the media and various organizations as a result of the impressive test scores in APS. However, at least two other high-profile school leaders also appeared to have benefitted from test score gains in their school districts: Michelle Rhee and Lorenzo Garcia.

In 2007, Rhee, who began her career as a Baltimore, Maryland, teacher, became the chancellor of the District of Columbia Public Schools (DCPS). At the time, most of the high school students in the district, which had an enrollment of nearly 50,000

students, were performing below grade level in reading and math (Rhee, 2010, pp. 127–128). Rhee's leadership style was guided by her beliefs that all students are capable of academic excellence and the belief that students will do well academically when educators provide them with a quality education. Before long, positive results began to take place in her district. Test scores improved and the district started attracting favorable publicity.

Within a few short years, Rhee's district became a model for other districts, and her popularity—outside of her school district—increased. A *New York Times* columnist referred to her as "the national symbol of the data-driven, take-no-prisoners education reform movement" (Winerip, 2011). Soon, Rhee became a highly sought after expert. She was featured in a documentary, interviewed by numerous reporters and talk-show hosts, widely quoted, and her photo was placed on a magazine cover. However, beneath the surface, allegations of cheating in DCPS simmered.

During Rhee's first year as chancellor, reports and news articles surfaced suggesting there was cheating on standardized tests in the form of teachers providing students with answers, as well as either teachers or principals erasing wrong answers and replacing them with correct ones. Furthermore, the rumors persisted for two more years before she finally hired investigators to conduct limited investigations to ascertain whether or not cheating had occurred in 2009 and 2010 (Merrow, 2013). Investigators concluded that in 2009, no cheating took place, but in 2010 cheating had indeed occurred at three schools (Office of the State Superintendent of Education, 2011). In 2010, Rhee resigned as chancellor. Since then, investigators have found that cheating has occurred in even more DCPS schools in 2011 and 2012 (Office of the State Superintendent of Education, 2012, 2013).

Although no *widespread* cheating was proven to have taken place under Rhee's leadership, a cloud of suspicion hovers over her reputation. Reporter John Merrow, who interviewed Rhee for PBS and who published several articles about her, said that she participated in a cover-up that is similar to the Watergate political scandal that destroyed the career of former U.S. President Richard Nixon, that she knew as early as her first year as chancellor that cheating was occurring, and that early on, at least two individuals informed Rhee about the cheating. Moreover, Merrow stated that both Rhee and her employees benefited from the cheating that occurred in terms of the personal rewards that they received. In addition to earning celebrity status, Rhee gave various school employees bonuses for ensuring that their students had higher test scores. In terms of Rhee's benefiting from the inflated scores personally, Merrow explained:

> It's easy to see how not trying to find out who had done the erasing—burying the problem—was better for Michelle Rhee personally, at least in the short-term. She had just handed out over $1.5 million in bonuses in a well-publicized celebration of the test increases. She had been praised by presidential candidates Obama and McCain . . . and she must have known that she was soon to be on the cover of Time Magazine. The public spectacle of an investigation of nearly half of the schools would have tarnished her glowing reputation, especially if the investigators proved that adults cheated—which seems likely given that their jobs depended on raising test scores. (Merrow, 2013)

In 2006, the El Paso Independent School District (EPISD) board hired Lorenzo Garcia as the district's new superintendent. Garcia quickly began to implement an ambitious program to improve low-performing schools. During this time, his popularity soared, and he became "powerful" and "highly regarded" in El Paso (Kappes, 2012). His plan appeared to work. Test scores improved and as a result of his efforts, Garcia earned nearly $60,000 in bonuses (Kappes, 2012).

By 2010, rumors had begun to circulate about cheating and other unsavory practices in the EPISD. When the full details of the EPISD cheating scandal were revealed, they involved sex, money, and an abuse of power. Not only did Garcia allegedly have a mistress who profited financially from her affair with him, but Garcia also was suspected of forcing students to leave the school district, refusing to admit various students to the district, retaining certain students in ninth grade to prevent them from taking the standardized test, and other activities that were designed to inflate test scores (Kappes, 2012; Pitman, 2012).

In 2012, 56-year-old Garcia "pleaded guilty to federal charges in connection with schemes to defraud EPISD and the federal government" (Pitman, 2012). The first charge was related to the money that his mistress received through the lucrative consulting contracts she received from the EPISD as a result of her personal relationship with Garcia. The second fraud charge involved cheating on the standardized test. Garcia pleaded guilty to ordering "staffers to manipulate state and federal mandated annual reporting statistics in order to keep EPISD compliant with requirements of the No Children [*sic*] Left Behind Act. . . . By pleading guilty, Garcia admitted that in order to achieve his contractual bonuses, he caused material, fraudulent misrepresentations regarding EPISD's AYP to be submitted . . . in order to make it appear as though the District was meeting and exceeding AYP" (Pitman, 2012).

The Role of Fear

A second cause of educator-related cheating in schools is fear. In many of the cases that have been exposed, educators claimed that fear either caused them to actually engage in various types of cheating, or prevented them from reporting that cheating was occurring.

After allegations of cheating in the EPISD refused to disappear, employees accused former superintendent Garcia of using fear as a weapon to silence dissenters or would-be whistle-blowers. A high-ranking EPISD official admitted that Garcia had the power to ruin employees' careers. "If you said no to him, you were gone" (Sanchez, 2013). A former EPISD principal revealed that "administrators retaliated against him" for opposing efforts to implement Garcia's school improvement "model," which was based on fraudulent practices (Kappes, 2012).

Likewise, Rhee was notorious for creating a climate of fear in the DCPS. One district-level administrator said that during meetings with school principals, Rhee

> would ask each of the principals, "When it comes to your test scores, what can you guarantee me?" And she would write it down. And you could cut through the air with a knife, there was so much tension. . . . Principals were scared to death that, if their test scores did not go up, they were going to be fired. And they knew that she could do it. (Merrow, 2013)

In the report that investigators submitted to the governor regarding the Atlanta Public Schools cheating scandal, fear also repeatedly surfaced as an explanation. The investigators said that not only did a "culture of fear" permeate the entire school district, but also that the climate of fear was created by Hall. In one instance, the investigators stated, a "principal forced a teacher with low [test scores] to crawl under a table at a faculty meeting" (Bowers et al., 2011, p. 18). In a detailed explanation of the effects of this fear, the investigators explained:

> Dr. Hall and her top staff created a culture of fear, intimidation and retaliation, which was usually enforced on principals and teachers by some of the . . . executive directors. Many witnesses said that after reporting cheating, or some other misconduct, they became the subject of an investigation and were disciplined. . . .
>
> This culture of fear, intimidation, and retaliation has infested the district, allowing cheating—at all levels—to go unchecked for years. Those who dared to report misconduct in the district were held in contempt and punished. (Bowers et al., 2011, pp. 356, 357)

High-Stakes Testing

A third reason why educator-involved cheating has become rampant in K-12 schools is that school leaders and teachers have felt pressured to produce outstanding test scores. This pressure intensified after *A Nation at Risk* (National Commission on Excellence in Education, 1983) was published. The report's indictment of the U.S. public school system prompted policymakers to scramble for solutions that would make K-12 students more competitive with their school-age counterparts in other nations. Since then, a series of school reforms have been implemented.

The No Child Left Behind Act of 2001 ratcheted up the pressure on schools to improve test results. When Congress passed this bill, it intended, among other goals, to improve the U.S. K-12 public school system by closing **achievement gaps**, increasing parent involvement, and ensuring that teachers received adequate professional development training. In order to demonstrate that their schools were improving, school leaders were required to show that their schools had made adequate yearly progress (AYP), as measured mainly by standardized test scores. They were also required to publicize their scores.

Schools that failed to make AYP for two consecutive years could be sanctioned under NCLB, while those that did make AYP often were rewarded. Rewards included public recognition and monetary bonuses for educators, and the possibility of a school being labeled as a "distinguished school." This label meant that the school could become a model for struggling schools, and its employees were in a position to offer advice and assistance to schools that failed to meet their AYP goals. A sanctioned school ran the risk of a state-government initiated takeover, and educators at such a school risked being replaced with new personnel.

Despite the laudable goals behind its enactment, by many accounts NCLB has failed to produce improvement in U.S. schools. Many students who have historically been underserved by the public school system, such as African Americans, continue to underperform on standardized tests in comparison to White and some Asian American groups (National Center for Education Statistics, 2011), and remain more likely to have negative schooling experiences than White and some Asian American students as measured by school dropout rates, graduation rates (Schott Foundation for Public Education 2010), and suspension and expulsion rates (National Center for Education Statistics, 2012). Furthermore, because of the consequences attached to high-stakes tests, "many schools have been turned into test-prep factories, with narrowed, distorted, and weakened curricula often dominated by mindless drilling, rote memorization exercises, and 'teaching to the test'" (Advancement Project 2010, p. 4). Moreover, many teachers are dissatisfied with the curriculum that they are required to teach (MetLife, 2012). However, one of the best indicators of the failure of NCLB is that by October 2013, 45 states and the District of Columbia had submitted requests for waivers from some of NCLB's provisions.

Additionally, the undue pressure to produce higher test scores has prompted many educators to resort to cheating. In their report to the governor, for example, the investigators of the APS school cheating allegations, wrote:

> The unreasonable pressure to meet annual "targets" was the primary motivation for teachers and administrators to cheat . . . in 2009 and previous years. Virtually every teacher who confessed to cheating spoke of the inordinate stress the district placed on meeting targets and the dire consequences for failure. (Bowers et al., 2011, p. 350)

Effects

Just as there are several causes of cheating by adults at school, there are also many effects. These effects include embarrassment for educators associated with schools and districts where cheating is suspected, negative stigmas being attached to these schools and districts, and public ridicule. Three additional effects, scapegoating, ruined careers, and harm to students are worth examining in detail.

Scapegoating

When allegations of cheating by adults surface in schools and school districts, one of the first consequences is denial. Often, the denial occurs for several years, but when media exposure makes it impossible for the denial to continue, finger-pointing begins, and in most cases, school leaders and teachers begin to scapegoat one another. Sometimes, when only one school is involved, the principal and teachers may be blamed. However, if multiple schools are involved, the scapegoating usually reaches the top echelons of school districts, and in the end everyone—district-level leaders, principals, and teachers—may be blamed.

In Atlanta, allegations of adult-involved cheating in the APS occurred for at least a decade before the scandal received national exposure. At the outset, school officials denied that cheating was occurring, but over time, when the governor launched an investigation, they created a full-fledged cover-up before the scapegoating began. When investigators submitted their report to the governor, they concluded that although 44 schools and nearly 200 teachers and principals were involved, in the end the blame rested with Hall and her administrative team. Hall, they stated, was responsible for pressuring educators to produce high test scores or risk punishment even after it became clear that her goals were unrealistic. Moreover, the majority of the educators whom the investigators interviewed, even the ones who confessed, also blamed Hall (Bowers et al., 2011, p. 3).

Hall disagreed. In a televised interview that she gave to NBC's Brian Williams, she acknowledged "responsibility for not anticipating that we needed more security and protocols" (Williams, 2011). However, Hall repeatedly denied that she had created a culture of "fear and intimidation," and insisted that she was not responsible for the widespread cheating that occurred in APS. The blame, she maintained, should be placed on the shoulders of the true culprits: the teachers and principals. According to Hall, "I can't make you cheat. . . . We did not emphasize testing at

the expense of integrity. What made people cheat, I believe, is who they are and not anything that I as an administrator can do."

In the DCPS cheating scandal, when allegations of cheating surfaced early in her tenure as chancellor, Rhee was reported to have "bur[ied] the problem" and permitted "severely limited investigations" to occur (Merrow, 2013). However, in 2011, when *USA Today* reporters tried to interview her for their exposé on rampant rumors about cheating in DCPS, Rhee declined their offer. Shortly thereafter, she allowed PBS talk show host Tavis Smiley to interview her.

During the interview, Rhee criticized the *USA Today* reporters for publishing their exposé. Furthermore, she insisted that she and her staff had "put in place . . . very strict testing security protocols." Although she agreed that teachers and school administrators were under pressure, she disagreed that the pressure was "intense enough to cause cheating." In fact, Rhee maintained, she had actually warned teachers against cheating (Rhee, 2011). Despite the fact that Rhee gave over a million dollars in bonuses to personnel at schools that had huge increases in test scores, including the majority of the schools where cheating was suspected, and the fact that she fired principals and at least 600 teachers at low-performing schools (Gillum & Bello, 2011), Rhee refused to accept responsibility for the cheating that occurred (Rhee, 2011). She did state, however, that NCLB needed to be revised.

In the EPISD cheating scandal, scapegoating occurred at multiple levels. When a state senator called for an investigation of numerous types of improprieties occurring in the district in order to give the appearance of high test scores, Garcia, other district employees, and some of Garcia's supporters questioned the senator's motives. Garcia accused him of actually harming students, and both he and various school principals denied that cheating had occurred (Reiser, 2010).

Nevertheless, after initial investigations, both Garcia and the school board were eventually blamed. According to an NPR reporter, "The scandal in El Paso . . . is not just about cheating. It's about state and local school officials running for cover and blaming each other for letting it happen" (Sanchez, 2013). At the time of Garcia's conviction, federal officials said they planned to investigate other school district employees.

Ruined Careers and Reputations

Another effect of adult-involved cheating is that the careers of those involved can be adversely affected. At the very least, teachers and principals can be reprimanded and have negative letters placed in their personnel file (Office of the State Superintendent of Education, 2012). In other cases, truth-tellers and whistle-blowers have been punished or forced to resign (Bowers et al., 2011). Even more serious consequences such as job termination can occur. When cheating was confirmed at three DCPS schools in 2010, a first-year teacher lost his job after confessing (Merrow, 2013). Numerous principals and teachers involved in scandals have also been suspended, fired, or forced to resign.

A more serious effect is criminal prosecution that could result in jail or prison time. In the EPISD, the entire school board was fired for permitting Garcia and his staff to engage in many illegal activities, and in 2012, Garcia "became the nation's first superintendent convicted of fraud and reporting bogus test scores for financial gain" (Sanchez, 2013). Furthermore, he was sentenced to 42 months in prison, and ordered to pay the EPISD nearly $200,000 (Martinez, 2012). Like Garcia, many of the nearly 200 educators who were directly involved in the APS cheating scandal also risk jail time.

Harm to Students

One of the most damaging effects of the school cheating scandals is that countless K-12 public school students have been harmed. At the very least, it is embarrassing to students to attend schools where cheating has been alleged. In El Paso, Texas, after Garcia, the former school superintendent, was arrested, an EPISD high school student told a reporter, "it does feel bad because everybody looks down on us" (Sanchez, 2013). Moreover, a logical conclusion is that when adult-involved cheating is suspected or confirmed, it is confusing to students, who have been repeatedly told by adults that cheating is bad. When their teachers and school leaders who are supposed to be positive role models are suspected of cheating, this suggests hypocrisy, and may make students lose respect for educators.

One of the most harmful effects on students is that the adult-involved cheating has actually shortchanged students academically. For example, as a result of the falsely elevated scores, students in the DCPS who needed remedial education services failed to receive them (Merrow, 2013). In fact, Merrow claimed that although DCPS received positive national exposure under Rhee's chancellorship, by the time that she resigned, students were worse off, or no better off, than they were before her arrival. According to Merrow (2013):

> The most disturbing effect of Rhee's reform effort is the widened gap in academic performance between low-income and upper-income students. . . . The gaps are so extreme that it seems clear that low-income students, most of them African-American, did not fare well during Rhee's time in Washington.

Solutions

Just as there are several causes and effects of adult-involved school cheating, there are also several solutions. Policymakers have a responsibility to discuss education reform options that are realistic and will truly improve student achievement rather than encourage cheating. At the same time, school leaders, and teachers, the classroom leaders, can act to prevent adult-involved cheating.

What School Leaders Can Do

The school cheating scandals contain important lessons for school leaders. One of those lessons is that school leaders must not lose sight of the main purpose of education: to educate students (Advancement Project, 2010). When school leaders become blinded by the potential to receive rewards as a result of students' standardized test performance, they will also become susceptible to corruption.

A second lesson that school leaders can learn from the cheating scandals is that when cheating is suspected at one or more of the school sites under their authority, they must quickly launch a thorough and independent investigation, and present the findings to school district employees, the local community, the media, and state and federal authorities. Moreover, instead of blaming others, school leaders must accept responsibility for any lapses of test security that occurred under their leadership, and for any undue pressure that they placed on educators and students.

Sidebar 12.1   How to Prevent Adult-Led Cheating on Standardized Tests

- Make sure that the school and district remain student-centered, instead of administrator-centered.
- Remember that test scores are one indicator of student learning, and that multiple assessments should be used.
- Do not pressure teachers to raise test scores at all costs.
- Keep the lines of communication open, so that teachers, parents, staff, and students can express concerns to school leaders.
- Investigate suspiciously high test scores immediately.
- Investigate sudden and dramatic surges in test scores.
- Investigate all allegations of testing irregularities and misconduct.
- Make sure that testing-related investigations are conducted by independent organizations.
- Beware of a school leader or teacher who is hungry for media attention, rewards, and accolades.
- Listen to educators and students who express concerns about testing procedures, practices, and so on.
- Don't punish truth-tellers.
- Remember that the existence of a climate of fear in a school or district is correlated with cheating on standardized tests.
- Practice and emphasize the importance of all school and district stakeholders behaving with integrity.

A third lesson for school leaders is that instead of accepting every reform—especially those that are clearly destined to fail—they must share their concerns with policymakers. Research has repeatedly shown that no test can accurately measure the full extent of student learning. Therefore, multiple types of assessments are necessary (Thompson, 2007). This is a message that school leaders should have shared with policymakers long before NCLB became law.

What Teachers Can Do

As the instructional leaders in classrooms, teachers must set a positive example for students. When they feel pressured by school-site and district-level leaders to produce high test scores at all costs, even to the detriment of students, teachers must voice their concerns to school board members and to state and federal lawmakers, in writing and anonymously if necessary. They must also refuse to compromise their own integrity by capitulating to the urge to cheat. Teachers who fear retaliation or job loss for not engaging in cheating can seek legal counsel, and even join with other teachers in launching a class action lawsuit against school leaders. Sidebar 12.1 contains a checklist that can be used as a template to help school leaders protect their schools from adult-led cheating on tests.

Conclusion

The prevalence, causes, and effects of adult-involved cheating in schools underscore the message that all school leaders are responsible for stopping the spate of cheating. They must use their voices to speak up. They must behave with integrity. They must remember the true purpose of education. They must remember that all reform movements that are based on one type of assessment are destined to fail, and they must be willing to work collaboratively with teachers and students in order to create a realistic and effective education reform plan that will improve the quality of education that K-12 students receive, improve the morale of educators, and allow school leaders to create healthy and productive work environments for adults and students. Policymakers must be willing to listen to educators and students and realize that any reform that is based on high-stakes testing will lead to widespread cheating.

Key Chapter Terms

Achievement gaps: The distance or gap between the standardized test scores of one group of students and another. Historically, there have been numerous achievement gaps, most notably the Black-White achievement gap, indicating that there are statistically significant differences between the mathematics and reading standardized test scores of Black and White K-12 students.

No Child Left Behind Act: Approved by Congress in 2001, the law was designed to improve the K-12 education system by closing achievement gaps, increasing parent involvement, and providing teachers with effective professional development. A school's efficacy under NCLB is measured by its ability to make adequate yearly progress as evidenced by students' standardized test scores.

References

Advancement Project. (March, 2010). *Test, punish, and push out: How "zero tolerance" and high-stakes testing funnel youth into the school-to-prison pipeline*. Washington, DC: Advancement Project. Retrieved from http://www.advancementproject.org/resources/entry/test-punish-and-push-out-how-zero-tolerance-and-high-stakes-testing-funnel

Beckett, L. (2013, April). America's most outrageous teacher cheating scandals. *ProPublica online*. Retrieved from http://www.propublica.org/article/americas-most-outrageous-teacher-cheating-scandals

Bloomberg Editors. (2011, August). No erasure left behind is key to stopping test mischief: A view. *Bloomberg.com*. Retrieved from http://www.bloomberg.com/news/2011-08-30/no-erasure-left-behind-is-key-to-stopping-standardized-test-mischief-view.html

Blume, H. (2012, August 17). Charter school group's chief blamed for 2010 cheating scandal. *Los Angeles Times*. Retrieved from http://articles.latimes.com/2012/aug/17/local/la-me-crescendo-20120818

Bowers, M. J., Wilson, R. E., & Hyde, R. L. (2011, June). Office of the Governor special investigators report (Volumes 1 & 3). Retrieved from http://www.courthousenews.com/2011/07/27/38493.htm

Donaldson James, S. (2008, February). Cheating scandals rock three top-tier high schools. *ABC News online*. Retrieved from http://abcnews.go.com/US/story?id=4362510&page=1#.UZaCyoVJW9g

Gillum, J., & Bello, M. (2011, March). When standardized test scores soared in D.C., were the gains real? *USA Today*. Retrieved from http://usatoday30.usatoday.com/news/education/2011-03-28-1Aschooltesting28_CV_N.htm#

Jonsson, P. (2011, July). America's biggest teacher and principal cheating scandal unfolds in Atlanta. *The Christian Science Monitor online*. Retrieved from http://www.csmonitor.com/USA/Education/2011/0705/America-s-biggest-teacher-and-principal-cheating-scandal-unfolds-in-Atlanta

Kappes, H. (2012, October). Former EPISD Superintendent Lorenzo Garcia gets 42 months, offers no apologies for scandal. *El Paso Times*. Retrieved from http://www.elpasotimes.com/ci_21707413/former-episd-superintendent-lorenzo-garcia-sentenced-3-1

Martinez, J. (2012, October). Former EPISD superintendent sentenced to 3½ years in jail, must pay $180,000 in restitution. *Kfoxtv.com*. Retrieved from http://www.kfoxtv.com/news/news/former-episd-superintendence-sentenced-3-years-jai/nSWCS/

Merrow, J. (2013, April). *Michelle Rhee's reign of error*. Retrieved from http://takingnote.learningmatters.tv/?p=6232

MetLife. (2012). *The MetLife Survey of the American Teacher: Teachers, parents, and the economy*. New York, NY: Metropolitan Life Insurance Company.

MetLife. (2013). *The MetLife Survey of the American Teacher: Challenges for school leadership: A survey of teachers and principals*. New York, NY: Metropolitan Life Insurance Company. Retrieved from https://www.metlife.com/metlife-foundation/what-we-do/student-achievement/survey-american-teacher.html?WT.mc_id=vu1101

National Center for Education Statistics. (2011). *The nation's report card. Grade eight national results*. Retrieved from http://nationsreportcard.gov/reading_2011/nat_g8.asp?subtab_id=Tab_3&tab_id=tab1#chart

National Center for Education Statistics. (2012). *Youth indicators 2011. America's youth: Transitions to adulthood. Table 14. Percentage of public school students in 9th through 12th grade who had ever been suspended or expelled, by sex and race/ethnicity: 1999, 2003, and 2007*. Retrieved from http://nces.ed.gov/pubs2012/2012026/tables/table_14.asp

National Commission on Excellence in Education. (1983, April). *A nation at risk: The imperative for educational reform: A report to the nation and the Secretary of Education.* Washington, DC: U.S. Department of Education. Retrieved from http://www2.ed.gov/pubs/NatAtRisk/title.html

No Child Left Behind Act, 20 U.S.C. §§ 6301 *et seq.*

Office of the State Superintendent of Education. (2011, May). *OSSE releases DC CAS security update.* Retrieved from http://osse.dc.gov/release/osse-releases-dc-cas-security-update

Office of the State Superintendent of Education. (2012, June). *OSSE releases 2011 DC CAS test integrity investigation results.* Retrieved from http://osse.dc.gov/release/osse-releases-2011-dc-cas-test-integrity-investigation-results

Office of the State Superintendent of Education. (2013, April). *OSSE releases 2012 DC CAS test integrity investigation results.* Retrieved from http://osse.dc.gov/release/osse-releases-2012-dc-cas-test-integrity-investigation-results

Pell, M. B. (2012, September). More cheating scandals inevitable, as states can't ensure test integrity. *AJC.com.* Retrieved from http://www.ajc.com/news/news/more-cheating-scandals-inevitable-as-states-cant-e/nSPqj/

Pitman, R. (2012, June). *Former E.P.I.S.D. superintendent pleads guilty to federal charges.* U.S. Department of Justice. Retrieved from https://www2.ed.gov/about/offices/list/oig/invtreports/tx062012.html

Reiser, L. (2010, June). EPISD leaders defend practices amidst allegations. *KTSM News.* Retrieved May 27, 2013, from http://www.ktsm.com/news/episd-leaders-defend-practices-amidst-allegations

Rhee, M. (2010). Putting kids first. In K. Weber (Ed.), *Waiting for Superman: How we can save America's failing public schools* (pp. 127–141). New York, NY: Public Affairs.

Rhee, M. (2011, March). Former DC schools chancellor Michelle Rhee: Interview with Tavis Smiley. *PBS Television.* Retrieved May 27, 2013, from http://www.pbs.org/wnet/tavissmiley/interviews/former-dc-schools-chancellor-michelle-rhee/

Sanchez, C. (2013, April). *El Paso schools cheating scandal: Who's accountable?* Retrieved May 20, 2013, from http://www.npr.org/2013/04/10/176784631/el-paso-schools-cheating-scandal-probes-officials-accountability

Schaeffer, B. (2013, March). Standardized exam cheating confirmed in 37 states and D.C.; new report shows widespread test score corruption. *The National Center for Fair and Open Testing.* Retrieved May 27, 2013, from http://www.fairtest.org/2013-Cheating-Report-PressRelease

Schott Foundation for Public Education. (2010). *Yes we can: The Schott 50 state report on public education and Black males.* Cambridge, MA: Author.

Thompson, G. L. (2007). *Up where we belong: Helping African American and Latino students rise in school and in life.* San Francisco, CA: Jossey-Bass.

Williams, B. (2011, November). School cheating investigation puts Atlanta teachers, principals at center of scandal. *NBC's Rock Center with Brian Williams.* Retrieved from http://www.nbcnews.com/video/rock-center/45421829#51996072

Winerip, M. (2011, August). Eager for spotlight, but not if it is on a testing scandal. *New York Times.* Retrieved from http://www.nytimes.com/2011/08/22/education/22winerip.html?pagewanted=all&_r=0

Further Readings

Comer, J. (2004). *Leave no child behind: Preparing today's youth for tomorrow's world.* New Haven, CT: Yale University Press.

As a highly esteemed child psychiatrist and creator of the School Development Plan that has been used by countless educators for decades, Comer offers a wealth of practical and research-based information that can help educators work more effectively with students who have historically been underserved by the K-12 public school system.

English, F. (2010). *Deciding what to teach & test: Developing, aligning, and leading the curriculum.* Thousand Oaks, CA: Corwin.

English uses a reader-friendly approach to define curriculum and explain how educators can use it to truly empower students. He offers practical advice on how to design, deliver, and align the curriculum.

Kozol, J. (2005). *The shame of the nation: The restoration of apartheid schooling in America.* New York, NY: Crown Publishers.

As a result of his visits to numerous schools throughout the nation, Kozol reached some startling conclusions regarding the ways in which current education reforms have perpetuated inequality of educational opportunity for African American and Latino students.

McEwan, E. (2002). *Teach them all to read: Catching the kids who fall through the cracks.* Thousand Oaks, CA: Corwin.

As a school leader who successfully improved reading scores at her school and a literacy expert, McEwan offers research-based strategies to improve reading achievement.

Sandberg, S. (2013). *Lean in: Women, work, and the will to lead.* New York, NY: Knopf.

Sandberg describes the challenges that women leaders continue to face, and shares autobiographical vignettes from her personal and professional experiences.

Thompson, G. (2004). *Through ebony eyes: What teachers need to know but are afraid to ask about African American students.* San Francisco, CA: Jossey-Bass.

This critically acclaimed book contains seminal research, practical strategies for teachers, and answers to common questions that teachers have about African American students, such as "How can I work more effectively with African American students from challenging backgrounds?"

Thompson, G. L. (2007). *Up where we belong: Helping African American and Latino students rise in school and in life.* San Francisco, CA: Jossey-Bass.

Teachers, school leaders, parents, and policymakers will benefit from the research, stories, and recommendations that are designed to close the achievement gaps between African American and Latino students and their school-age peers.

Thompson, G. L. (2010). *The power of one: How you can help or harm African American students.* Thousand Oaks, CA: Corwin.

Thompson describes the ground-breaking "Mindset Study," that revealed what many educators, including school leaders, believe about African American K-12 students and their parents. She offers stories, and strategies to improve students' test scores, and includes

personal and professional growth exercises that can help educators increase their efficacy with African American K-12 students.

Thompson, G. L., & Allen, T. G. (2012). Four effects of the high-stakes testing movement on African American K-12 students. *Journal of Negro Education, 81*(3), 218–227.

The authors explain specific ways that the No Child Left Behind Act has had a negative effect on African American students, and contributes to low teacher morale.

Thompson, G. L., & Shamberger, C. T. (2012). What really matters: Six characteristics of outstanding teachers in challenging schools. *ASCD Express, 8*(2). Retrieved from http://www.ascd.org/ascd-express/vol8/802-thompson.aspx

The authors describe the qualities of several teachers and school leaders who have been successful with African American, low-income, and urban K-12 students.

Thompson, G. L., & Thompson, R. (2014). *Yes, you can! Advice for teachers who want a great start and a great finish with their students of color.* Thousand Oaks, CA: Corwin.

The authors present seminal research, "The Teacher Confidence Study," and offer research, stories, strategies, and professional growth activities that are designed to help beginning teachers improve the schooling experiences of students of color.

Walters, D. (2001). *The art of leadership: A practical guide for people in positions of responsibility.* New York, NY: MJF Books.

In this simple yet powerful guide, Walters describes the qualities of outstanding leaders, emphasizes the importance of integrity, and explains how good leaders bring out the best qualities in others.

PART V

Technology, the Internet, and Online Learning

13

THE EXPANDING WIRELESS WORLD OF SCHOOLING

JAMES E. BERRY

Eastern Michigan University

Technological change is outpacing pedagogical practice in K-12 classrooms. Technology innovation by the software and hardware industries races against market competition to find the next iPhone and iPad, which are among the best-selling products of all time. The latest and most dynamic versions of computer-based games such as *Tomb Raider* (by Square Enix in 2013) or *Call of Duty* (by Activision in 2007) challenge the movie industry for sales supremacy, especially for the millennial demographic. Microsoft's Office productivity suite, which includes Word, PowerPoint, and Excel, has become a dominant global force. Technology may not be *the* answer for improving education, but the adoption and use of software for engaging students to learn in a media-rich environment is changing how educators think about teaching and learning.

Whether as a productivity tool, for entertainment, communicating with students, or for building a digital school, the software emerging for use by the educational system is being adapted to improve learning across the globe. A digital school is an extension of the brick-and-mortar school and exists as a software and Internet entity. The digital school will encompass wireless and wired connectivity; face-to-face, hybrid, and virtual teaching; and anytime and anywhere learning (**ubiquitous learning**). The challenge for this kind of school will be to overcome the perceived,

and real, problems of transactional distance, or the physical and psychological distance that separates the teacher from the student. That is, the pedagogical challenges posed by virtual teaching and learning can be viewed favorably when compared to face-to-face teaching and learning.

The trend line is convincing: School systems are adopting smartphones and tablets in growing numbers for student use. Among the general public, in 2013, sales of smartphones accounted for more than half of mobile phone sales (Gartner, 2014). The smartphone will soon become the smart *classroom,* the smart *teacher,* smart *textbook,* and *smart* library.

Software applications can motivate students and enhance teaching. But how useful software turns out to be in education will be determined by the extent to which educators embrace it as a teaching and learning tool. The use of software in mobile devices, in particular, has a potential to disrupt education at a fundamental level. Until the use of digital devices and software becomes integrated into the act of learning, however, these forms of technology will be resisted by teachers who see them only as tools, and as a poor substitute for face-to-face teaching in a physical classroom. The synergy of technology adoption in education will create an environment for learning, and learning culture, that has not been experienced by educators. The transition of an entire system of learning—from teachers to students—to a digital-rich environment is the real challenge for the future.

Disruptive Innovation: Decentralization of Learning

One can point to any number of legislative acts and judicial decisions that shaped American education. The Morrill act signed by Abraham Lincoln in 1862 created the parameters for states to establish land grant universities. The Individuals with Disabilities Education Act (IDEA, Public Law 94-142) established rights for handicapped students in the United States. The *Brown v. Board of Education* decision in 1954 was a landmark decision that ended segregation of the American educational system. The Elementary and Secondary Education Act of 1965 authorized federal funds to improve the schooling of children from low-income households and led to programs such as Head Start.

However, the most significant legislative act to hasten the development of education worldwide was enacted by the Massachusetts legislature in 1647. The Old Deluder Satan Act of 1647 was the first governmentally legislated act to hold a community responsible for managing education at the local level. This legislative act by Massachusetts became the basis for the *decentralized, locally controlled educational system* that has so defined the American system of schooling. This decentralized governance model of learning has been sustained by the underlying belief that educational access and opportunity are fundamental rights of people. An Internet-based educational system is an extension of the opportunity and access that was granted to the citizens of Massachusetts and then spread across America state by state in the westward expansion after the 1803 Louisiana Purchase by Thomas Jefferson.

The Old Deluder Satan Act of 1647 required that every town of 50 houses tax its citizens and spend money for the education of a community's children. This resulted in a decentralized educational governance system that formalized the one-room school to ensure local citizens provided an education to every child at every crossroad, hamlet, and rural village. The decentralized system of education is an extension

of opportunity, access, and *self-education*. Ultimately, every state would have a provision in its constitution establishing public schools. Determining one's destiny by getting an education is the story of Horatio Alger and "pull yourself up by the bootstraps" success that is an archetype for American education and a belief in oneself. The provision of free, public education for all children, governed by locally elected officials, was to become the law of the land and gateway to success.

The advent of the digital school expands the reach, access, opportunity, and right of the individual to take advantage of education. The digital school—and the opportunity to access knowledge and learn at one's own rate and level—in the 21st century is a clear affirmation of the individual and reflects John Locke's belief in natural law.

> To understand political power right, and derive it from its original, we must consider, what state all men are naturally in, and that is, a state of perfect freedom to order their actions, and dispose of their possessions and persons, as they think fit, within the bounds of the law of nature, without asking leave, or depending upon the will of any other man. (Locke, 1764/1980, p. 8)

The digital school will reach beyond borders to make education a global enterprise with a more distinctive form of personalized learning. The Internet-based school is as significant an education reform as the milestones mentioned earlier in this chapter, and will perhaps turn out to be more significant. The Internet-based school is the software school that will operate as a networked system of mobile devices linked by personalized teaching and learning.

The Infrastructure of Global Learning

The digital school will be as real as the brick-and-mortar school but exist as an entity based upon virtual organizational structures. Virtual teaching will be supported by an infrastructure built upon servers. The virtual educational organization is an emerging software system of education networked for learning. It is a virtual structure built upon the brick-and-mortar structures of 20th-century educational organizations. According to diffusion theory, technology and software innovation will be adopted by the way educators communicate through the "members of the social system" (Rogers, 2003, p. 70). Rogers (2003) refers to diffusion through a social system—in this case the global educational system—as "social change, defined as the process by which alteration occurs in the structure and function of a social system" (p. 73).

The forces of educational change together with changes to accommodate the digital learner will mean that today's educational system will go through a fundamental decentralization that is little understood at the present time. However, *some* of the organizational features of virtual education can already be observed:

1. Learning is embedded in software through personal mobile devices. Ubiquitous learning, which refers to the use of mobile devices to allow for learning anytime and anyplace, will become an accepted teaching and learning structural and pedagogical approach.

2. The Internet is accessed through browsers (Safari, Internet Explorer, Chrome, etc.) to exchange information, capture knowledge, and connect with the student.

3. Student engagement will shift from a teacher-driven lecture/discussion format to a software-enhanced, facilitative approach to teaching and learning.

4. Learning will be based on performance rather than content and time.

5. The educational organization will become a more virtual organization with its own systems to support learning. A library, for example, will be more of a virtual rather than a physical resource.

6. The act of teaching will be reshaped by software that will change the structure of teaching. The Technological Pedagogical Content Knowledge (TPACK) model developed by Punya Mishra and Matthew J. Koehler in 2006 defines teaching as an act that will require technological skill as well as face-to-face pedagogical ability that will be combined with content knowledge mastery.

The structures of education are the enduring patterns in which software will shape the emerging virtual educational organization. The software itself will be designed and utilized to support a virtual educational organization in order to facilitate teaching and learning. The very nature of schooling was embedded in time- and place-bound learning that defined bureaucratic education for the entire 20th century. The teacher lecturing in a room big enough to hold six rows of desks and 30 students was the model of education that framed the current paradigm for learning. Emerging software for education will shape the virtual classroom:

- Brick-and-mortar classrooms of 30 children sitting in neat rows facing a teacher who lectures from the front of the classroom will give way to virtual schools and virtual cubicles linked to individuals by the Internet.
- Time-bound learning based upon 55-minute lessons within an eight-period day will shift to performance and mastery of skills in an asynchronous and synchronous learning environment.
- Grade-level age-based learning will shift to individualized and personalized growth.
- Individualized growth will be measured by software that monitors and adjusts learning for each child, which is facilitated by the teacher.

The structure of the virtual educational system will also have to merge the cultural, professional, and organizationally embedded ideas and beliefs that are stitched into the present-day educational system. The historical and cultural beliefs about learning have been so deeply ingrained in the American psyche that it will take a generation to shift from these closely held beliefs about where and how one must learn. Education is still organized around the bureaucratic structures that were "designed to minimize or at least regulate the influence of individual variations on the organization" (Hall, 1991, p. 85).

The path education takes in the next 10 years will change schooling as we know it. Over the next decade, technology will be integrated into the structure of schooling. But, the changes shaping the structures of education are like the slow drip of water on rock over time. The penetration of digitally infused structures will be blunted by traditional beliefs about bureaucratic organizations and deeply held notions concerning the conditions of schooling that are slow to change. Teaching pedagogy, for example, will be infused with software to enhance the traditional classroom lecture as a school structure. It is this adoption of software as an extension of teaching pedagogy that will redefine teaching in the next decade.

The Future School

Technology—or more correctly software—will be a disruptive innovation that reshapes the organizational architecture of today's school (Christensen, Horn, & Johnson, 2011). A disruptive innovation in education such as **massive open online courses (MOOCs)** redefines what a classroom is and how many students can take a class at one time. A teacher can teach synchronously or asynchronously and reach across great distances. Restructuring the traditional educational system into a virtual educational organization means developing an architecture through which subject matter is learned. It is the very development of this new architecture that threatens the existence of the brick-and-mortar K-12 school system.

Using Everett Rogers's (2003) diffusion framework as a guide for determining technology adoption in education, one is able to track the likely rate of its penetration. Thus, using the characteristics of innovation one must determine

- the potency and impact of the innovation;
- the way in which it is communicated and discussed throughout the entire system of education;
- the time, or lack thereof, given to the use and acceptance of an innovation; and
- the social system of education and the expectations, motivation, values, and beliefs of the key constituents involved in the adoption of the innovation.

However, as Rogers also pointed out, the best ideas or clearly superior innovations may not make it through the filtering and winnowing process that leads to adoption. If the social system doesn't embrace the innovation, it may falter and fall under the competing structures within the system itself. There are no sure things when it comes to predicting change. The challenge in bringing about substantive change within education has always rested with the forces pulling and pushing schools, classrooms, teachers, and children to improve achievement. Whether the forces of politics, economics, society and education align to bring about a more digital system will play out in the national and international culture of learning that is now emerging.

Compared to the other prominent reforms and changes that shaped education over the past 200 years, how does technological change compare as a force for educational improvement? Is the implementation of technology a paradigm shift, in the sense that Thomas Kuhn wrote about in *The Structure of Scientific Revolutions* (1962), and a significant innovation reshaping education as we know it? Can technology make significant improvements in learning and achievement?

Flattening Education Through Technology

Thomas Friedman wrote *The World Is Flat* (2005) as a handbook for understanding global innovation and change in the 21st century. The 10 forces that "flattened" the world were the key elements, according to Friedman, that had collectively "leveled the playing field" for any country (or company) that understood and took advantage of the 10 flatteners in a new global marketplace (p. 7). Quoting Nandan Nilekani, the CEO of Infosys Technologies in Bangalore, India, Friedman captured the fundamental shift that occurred. These ten flatteners, according to Nilekani, "created a platform where intellectual work, intellectual capital, could be delivered from anywhere. It could be disaggregated, delivered, distributed, produced, and put back together again—and this gave a whole new degree of freedom to the way we do work, especially work of an intellectual nature" (p. 7). The flatteners, as Friedman described them, were global game changers. He outlined them as:

1. 11/9/89—The fall of the Berlin wall, which led to the collapse of communism, and was soon followed by the rise of the Windows-enabled personal computer

2. 8/9/95—When Netscape, the first widely popular commercial browser, went public, leading to the use of the Internet by a wider swath of the public;

3. Workflow software—The emergence of software that adds value to work or individual productivity anywhere in the world

4. Uploading—Software code is made available across the Internet that can be accessed by anyone and used for free

5. Outsourcing—Exporting jobs through e-commerce to countries around the world for higher skills and lower wages displaces workers in the home country

6. Offshoring—Taking the infrastructure of commerce and producing "the very same product in the very same way, only with cheaper labor, lower taxes, subsidized energy, and lower health-care costs" (p. 137)

7. Supply chaining—The distribution of manufactured goods through suppliers, transportation carriers, and customs brokers, and the tracking and monitoring of the supply chain itself

8. Insourcing—FedEx and UPS don't just ship packages around the world. These companies handle the logistics for coordinating the movement of goods and services for other companies. The key to insourcing is that smaller companies, without the resources of a Walmart, are able maintain the same high-quality product or service in order to compete with larger companies.

9. In-Forming—Google is an example of in-forming. Search engines such as Google can gather information on topics that, to find information on, one once had to navigate library aisles and the Dewey decimal system. Type in a topic and Google gathers the source information. Watching broadcast TV over the Internet, playing videos on YouTube, or downloading music onto an iPhone are all ways in which people have a more direct way of informing their personal and professional lives.

10. The Steroids—The tenth flattener describes the synergy of digital, mobile, personal, and virtual devices that will take advantage of the increasing power and utility of hand-held devices to communicate and do work from remote locations.

The 10 forces, as Friedman indicated, allowed intellectual capital to be delivered to and from anywhere in the world. In extrapolating these *flatteners*, one can outline and translate the impact they have on an expanding global educational system. The effect of the global forces outlined in Friedman's book 9 years after its publication are a blueprint for thinking about the future American educational system. Some of the trends that may pick up steam and disrupt the educational system are the following:

1. Free market education: There is a growing competition for students globally, not just locally.

2. Online K-12 schools: Schooling is emerging as an online browser bureaucracy. Virtual online K-12 schools are becoming an accepted option to brick-and-mortar schooling for any student connected to the Internet. Thus, any student may enter the virtual

school through Internet connectivity by way of a software browser such as Google Chrome, Firefox, or Safari.

3. Software pedagogy: Teaching in the virtual environment using tools such as presentation software and multimedia extend the teacher's pedagogy beyond directed teaching and the physical classroom.

4. Knowledge access: General knowledge is free and accessible through open educational resources.

5. Changes in the job of the teacher: With the advent of the Internet, teaching is changed from a profession dependent upon the real-time physical presence of children being taught in a classroom to a pedagogy that is informed by software to shape lessons and instruction.

6. Teachers from other states and countries: The professional skill set to become a teacher can be acquired through preparation programs anywhere in the world. School districts will be able to hire highly qualified teachers who meet local requirements.

7. Knowledge linking: Books will be changed to digital modules and academic material will become embedded in webpages that link networked content to learning. The Internet browser opens access to a robust and dynamic multimedia presentation of content that the traditional book cannot compete with as a process for learning.

8. Insourcing: Small school systems will be able to access the best knowledge available. A few students living in a rural location will be able to take physics or other low enrollment classes because the virtual course will meet class size requirements for purposes of efficiency.

9. Using the Web for knowledge gathering: Google, Facebook, Twitter, and other social media networks and search engines will aggregate sources for information and data gathering.

10. The Steroids: Projecting the Steroids to education means that individualized personal learning isn't time or place sensitive. Ubiquitous learning via wireless networks will be 24/7 on hand-held devices.

The Locus of Learning: Individualized and Personalized Learning in a Digital School

Two fundamental issues are driving digital learning. One is that a global educational system will expand access and opportunity for an education—formal and informal. An online/digital/virtual learning environment will draw students to an educational marketplace that will be regulated, but not controlled, by the state. The global Internet learning environment will be based upon a free exchange of ideas. The other issue is that the individual will become the focus (the unit of analysis) by which teaching and learning are measured. Customization of teaching and learning made possible by software advances will displace (not replace) the direct instruction model of face-to-face teaching, which will result in a more engaged student who delivers upon an emerging global standard for learning and achievement.

Leah Hamilton and Anne Mackinnon (2013) wrote in the Carnegie Foundation's report *Opportunity by Design* of the need to redesign American high schools to teach all students at the level required by the Common Core State Standards. The challenge is straightforward:

> High schools will be charged with educating all students to achieve much higher levels of skill and knowledge, a monumental challenge. At the same time, high schools will continue to be responsible for meeting the learning needs of large numbers of students who enter ninth grade performing significantly below grade level. (pp. 1–2)

The report further outlines the difficulty the current system of education will have in meeting the high expectations required for success—defined as acquiring the skills necessary for holding a job—in the global marketplace. The model of learning and the model of schooling that will deliver that learning will be designed to elevate the more pedantic approach taken in the "sit and get" of the traditional classroom. It is a clear and concise premise based upon a convergence of educational flatteners that, taken together, restructure educational delivery. For some educators, face-to-face lecture and discussion in a physical classroom will be the singular definition of teaching and learning. However, as education tracks toward the future, computer software will open up teaching and learning to multimedia books, game-based learning, simulations that replicate real-world skills like flying a plane, and networking with students from around the world. Hamilton and Mackinnon discuss the potential of blended learning, which incorporates face-to-face teaching and online classes, to engage students and teach high-order content and complex skills.

Some critics of online learning make the case that the Socratic method of questioning by a teacher—and the give-and take-responses by the learner—cannot be replicated in an online environment. Online learning, as this argument goes, cannot fully take into account the gestures, voice inflections, and body cues that one communicates in language between a teacher and student. A person sees and internalizes much more than the words through the gestures and facial expressions within the face-to-face acts of teaching and learning, so goes the argument. This view dismisses and discounts the possibility that the same Socratic questioning can be replicated in an online environment to equal the quality of learning that takes place in the physical presence of the teacher with the student.

Although few rigorous studies have been done on online learning among K-12 students, evidence of high-quality learning in online classes is undeniable. In a meta-analysis funded by the U.S. Department of Education (Means, 2010), students taking online courses showed evidence of learning that was substantive and compelling. The meta-analysis of 50 study effects, 43 of which were drawn from research with older learners (students in higher education and career training programs), found that

> students in online conditions performed modestly better, on average, than those learning the same material through traditional face-to-face instruction. Learning outcomes for students who engaged in online learning exceeded those of students receiving face-to-face instruction, with an average effect size of +0.20 favoring online conditions.
>
> The mean difference between online and face-to-face conditions across the 50 contrasts is statistically significant at the p < .001 level. (p. xiv)

The report went on to caution that factors other than the instructional delivery method, such as the amount of time students spent on task, could be responsible for the advantages found for online learning.

Software-based learning is becoming an integral component of education. It is a pedagogy that does work, with attendant growing pains. Software-enhanced pedagogy is being developed by teachers and sought out by students seeking novel forms of learning. It is evident that students do extract knowledge from this virtual teaching. The engagement of students by software that challenges and enhances the learning experience through game-based graphics, music, video, physical dexterity, and emotional connection is, for many students, a much better learning opportunity—and more fun—than a face-to-face classroom lesson.

Individualized and Personalized Learning: Opportunity and Access

Technological change will continue to expand and refine learning in an age of computer-mediated instruction. However, it is not the technology driving educational change. Technology is the catalyst for the means to an education. Technology can fulfill the individual's desire to learn meaningful knowledge to apply to his or her job or life. More fundamentally, it is the primacy of the individual within the global social context that is emerging as the driver behind expanded digital learning. Locke, in *The Second Treatise of Government* (1764/1980), articulated the natural right of a person "to do whatsoever he thinks fit for the preservation of himself" (p. 67). One may, on the face of it, see technology leading change when, in fact, what leads change is access to technology by people who use knowledge as a way up, out, over, or through personal and societal conditions that constrain their growth. Anya Kamenetz (2010) makes the claim, "In the future, with the increasing availability of online courses and other resources, individuals will increasingly forge a personal learning path, combining classroom and online learning, work and other experiences."

It is opportunity and access that will drive educational change in a way that fundamentally alters the definition of learning as a time- and place-bound activity for 30 children in a brick-and-mortar classroom doing the same thing at the same time. Significantly, it also has the potential to erase the physical and emotional borders and boundaries that have shaped the educational system. The unit of analysis for learning has, in the United States, been historically focused upon the school building (Edmonds, 1979). More recently the unit of analysis for implementing educational change has centered on the school district (Supovitz, 2006) and each of the individual states (Smith, O'Day, & Cohen, 1990). The No Child Left Behind Act of 2001 made the state accountable for improving minimum levels of student achievement.

In the digital age, which is presently in a formative stage, the unit of analysis for learning will fundamentally shift to the individual. Modules and badges will testify to a student's mastery of skill and ability. Schools will continue to offer students a social, place-bound experience. However, as the child ages the pedagogy will be become more software based, teacher facilitated, and student centered. Students will still hear lectures and take part in discussions, but this type of pedagogy and a technology-infused curriculum will prepare them for lifelong learning. Karl Popper (1999) stated that two values seemed "the most important for the evolution of knowledge." The two most important values, he claimed, were having (1) a self-critical attitude, and (2) truth (p. 73).

The advent of the wireless school is an opportunity to advance learning across the globe for those who can take advantage of the emerging digital structures and the digital conditions transforming education. A critical analysis of learning in a virtual educational system will be made by digitally literate global citizens as they weigh the costs of acquiring new knowledge in order to secure a better job, a better life, and/or a higher standard of living. Students will be attracted to the wireless world as an educational delivery system only if the software tools result in higher levels of learning. From a student's perspective the pedagogy is relevant only as long as the learning experience is positive and leads to the attainment of the student's goals.

Learning: A Global Commodity

Virtual and hybrid learning, which blends face-to-face and virtual learning, are pedagogical approaches to instructional delivery. The computer and digital tools are an extension of the chalkboard that hung at the front of the 20th-century classroom. The virtual teacher will facilitate the growth of the individual through a pedagogy that takes advantage of the learning tools made available for 21st-century knowledge work.

Massive open online courses (MOOCs) are a manifestation of a global learning approach that has gained credibility and acceptance from some segments of the education community. Yet, there are many in K-12 and higher education who question the MOOC as a viable substitute for the traditional face-to-face, brick-and-mortar classroom. MOOCs are available to anyone with an Internet connection, and are usually free. Although questions abound about this new educational model, the ability to offer classes to students around the world has drawn the interest of school districts and universities. Several companies, including Coursera and Udacity, have been formed to offer MOOCs in collaboration with universities. By fall 2013, Coursera, founded at Stanford University, had 532 courses enrolling 5.2 million students in 190 countries.

The monetization of MOOCs is an evolutionary next step into the future of the digital school. Daphne Koller, one of the founders of Coursera, has discussed several possible ways for its courses to bring in revenues: an optional fee for completed courses, licensing fees paid by smaller colleges for courses developed by larger universities, and employer subsidies for workers who take courses to build skills (Smale, 2013). Both Coursera and Udacity have started offering students the chance to earn a verified certificate for certain courses for a fee. Yet the most compelling aspect about MOOCs isn't that most of them are free, but that they have attracted so many students from around the world who have taken advantage of the opportunity to access first-rate knowledge from highly respected institutions.

Global education is in its infancy. Yet there is a rush to fill the void for an obvious market for learning. Public education in America has traditionally been viewed as a public good. It is in transition as a global commodity with many evolutionary steps following the first truly global learning platform in the form of MOOCs.

Ubiquitous Learning

The global communication network is the infrastructure for a nascent educational delivery system. Kuhn (1962) described a paradigm shift as a shift in thinking about how one views an idea, concept, cultural norm, or accepted way of knowing because of an emerging idea, concept, or cultural norm that challenges the previously accepted norm, or ultimately renders it obsolete.

The landline phone was the means by which people conducted long-distance communication during the 20th century. Thus the paradigm for communication with wireless devices has, in the span of 30 years—with accelerating speed in the last 10—begun to render an entire physical infrastructure obsolete. Today, one not only looks at the cell phone—and the more robust laptop computer and tablet computer—as a voice communication device but also a multidimensional communication and media device used for listening to music, watching movies, purchasing products with a credit card, and transacting business between continents. Students can also use their phones to take courses from a university or K-12 school district, with the help of software that offers educational content.

Present-day mobile devices—wireless phones, tablet computers, and laptop computers—are part of an emerging virtual educational infrastructure that supports a more individualized and personalized form of communication for learning. More significantly, the infrastructure that was built as a system of support for wireless cell phones, is now being expanded to support *anytime and anyplace learning* in an expanding array of wireless devices. Around us a global educational infrastructure is extending its reach to students through an ever-expanding and more robust wireless network. The virtual educational system is slowly following technology and software that converts mobile devices into learning devices. They are mobile instructional tutors and teaching devices in the pockets of learners wherever they are and whenever they want to use the device as a learning tool. As online and asynchronous learning become more widespread, face-to-face learning will continue to take place, but new digital learning environments will allow for a more individualized teacher-facilitated learning experience.

It is evident the physical classroom environment will migrate to a virtual environment. **Transactional theory** describes "the interplay among the environment, the individuals and the patterns of behaviors in a situation" (Boyd & Apps, 1980, p. 5). In a virtual environment the physical distance between the teacher and learner is the transactional distance and is defined as the "gap of understanding and communication between the teachers and learners caused by geographic distance that must be bridged through distinctive procedures in instructional design and the facilitation of interaction" (Moore & Kearsley, 2005, p. 223).

The emerging virtual environment challenges educators to rethink pedagogy. Research on computer-mediated instruction is in its infancy. Criticism of the format often is benchmarked against face-to-face learning (which is idealized as the standard upon which all teacher and student learning should occur).

> Today, most studies tend to view transactional distance as the psychological separation between the learner and instructor, in a particular educational environment, where this separation or distance is mitigated by dialogue, and where it is also a measure of responsiveness to the learner's needs and the amount of autonomy allowed or present. (Shearer, 2009, p. 21)

Regardless of distance—psychological or physical—the goal of the teaching and learning experience is to narrow the separation between what is being taught and what is being learned. Psychological distance is often described as the ultimate barrier to online learning. Face-to-face learning is the standard by which all learning tends to be measured. Educators are in the throes of understanding what it means to learn, and how to learn, in something other than a traditional classroom using face-to-face instruction. Ubiquitous anytime and anywhere learning is a pedagogical approach that eliminates the physical learning environment as a barrier to education. Real-time and place-bound learning restricts student participation to a real-time and place-bound presence. By changing the realm of learning to anytime and anywhere, the physical barriers of learning are removed. In fact, the learning environment is something "that disappears" (Weiser, 1991, p. 94). Once the physical barrier is removed as a barrier, the learning environment is no longer a relevant factor. In ubiquitous learning, the technology is integral but absorbed into the background of daily life (Park, 2011). Ubiquitous learning, in fact, may be viewed as removing some of the barriers of learning associated with traditional schooling.

The transaction costs associated with transporting children to school every day, passing out papers, sitting in study hall, and handling discipline are just a few of the barriers that might be addressed by eliminating the learning distance between the teacher and the student based upon the real-time, brick-and-mortar form of schooling that has prevailed up to the present era of schooling.

Conclusion

Significant reforms, and technological reforms in particular, have been cited as critical, and necessary, for transforming the traditional bureaucratically arranged school system into an effective and efficient system of learning. As Jal Mehta described it:

> How schools are organized, and what happens in classrooms, hasn't changed much in the century since the Progressive Era. On the whole, we still have the same teachers, in the same roles, with the same level of knowledge, in the same schools, with the same materials, and much the same level of parental involvement. (Mehta, 2013)

Wired schooling, or the introduction of computers and slow ascent of the use of technology for learning starting in the 1970s, changed educational pedagogy on the margins for children in the second decade of the 21st century. Wireless schooling will change educational pedagogy as digital schools adopt software and mobile devices that facilitate individual learning. Wireless learning combined with the dynamic use of software and ubiquitous learning will accelerate educational reform over the next few decades. The use of electronic software for teaching is an emergent pedagogy supporting change in the educational system as it adapts to anywhere and anytime learning in the nascent educational digital age.

As the educational system adapts to the use of technology as a fundamental organizational structure for virtual learning, it is increasingly evident that technology is not a supplement to education but an integral component of education. One cannot separate the technology from the organization because it is becoming the organization. Similarly, one cannot separate technology from pedagogy. Educators committed to the traditional classroom as time and place bound will miss an opportunity to utilize technology as a tool for learning. However, using software as a tool for learning ignores the dynamic and robust applications of that software. Using software isn't the same as using chalk on the blackboard. Software in today's school is becoming the blackboard that accesses academic content through a web portal that is managed by a teacher from another country. This same software blackboard is able to individualize and personalize learning while the teacher monitors and facilitates this same student's progress through the curriculum. The technology is becoming the pedagogy.

The unique nature of technology in education is that it has evolved from an external resource for education to an organizational component—a structure—of education. What was once viewed as a resource or tool has become the institution itself. Technology is becoming so broadly used and adapted that it is recasting the system of education across the globe within a different paradigm that is fundamentally challenging what society thought it knew about schools, schooling, teaching, and learning.

The emerging global educational marketplace will sort out technology's merits as a delivery system and pedagogy. A teaching pedagogy based on software will extend and redefine teaching and learning. K-12 schools, universities, and educational enterprises will vie to meet the needs of these educationally savvy global citizens who will weigh the value of a technology-infused learning system. A *self-critical analysis* made by many individuals will collectively decide whether or not virtual organizations will expand digital teaching and learning.

The *truth* about the wired world of schooling is, at the present time, only partially clear. What is known is that:

- Wired and wireless learning have a place in education.
- Digital instruction has achieved recognition as a teaching pedagogy.
- Virtual learning has become an accepted way to receive instruction and is a viable way to learn.
- K-12 school systems and universities have built infrastructure to support digital courses, entire digital programs, and the digital ancillary services to support teaching and learning (e.g., library services, advising and counseling services, technical software support).
- The Internet-based school opens up opportunity and access for students across the globe.

Virtual schooling may not exist into the future as we now know it, but opportunity and access to education are a manifestation of the person using a digital device to get a meaningful personalized education. The rise of the learned individual of many nations is the tide that raises global social, economic, political, and personal conditions for daily living. When one looks at the reform agenda in education over the past 100 years, the surest way to track change—and its effect—is to follow how the individual was served by the educational system. The measure of the digital world of schooling isn't in how it impacts the learning of the few, but of the many. There may be many aspects of technology use in education that compromise quality or come up short of its potential. However, across an expanding educational platform delivered around the globe, it is clear that opportunity and access to knowledge are increasing as a result of technology. The expanding wireless world of schooling is the manifestation of the convenience, ease, value, and quality of an educational system that is responsive to, and fulfills the needs of individuals across the globe to access education. What is true at the present time is that the wireless world of schooling is expanding and is here to stay. The level and use of technology-infused learning delivered through an evolving virtual educational system is in a formative stage in a global marketplace. The viability of virtual teaching is being debated, criticized, and sorted out—even as it is implemented—in a global system of education that is still seeking credibility as a viable approach to learning.

Key Chapter Terms

Massive open online courses (MOOCs): As defined by Educause, a model for delivering learning content online to any person who wants to take a course, with no limit on enrollment numbers. In their present form, MOOCs are usually free to the student.

Transactional theory: Describes the distance between the student and instruction in a distance-learning environment. This distance, whether physical, virtual, or psychological, requires an adaptation of the pedagogy to overcome the barriers that arise because of this distance.

Ubiquitous learning: Refers to anytime and anywhere learning that is made possible through mobile connectivity and robust capabilities of phones, tablets, and laptop computers. Teaching and learning are incorporating synchronous and asynchronous learning anywhere there is wireless connectivity through sophisticated browsers such as Google Chrome, Safari, Firefox, and Microsoft's Internet Explorer.

References

Boyd, R. D., & Apps, J. W. (1980). *Redefining the discipline of adult education*. San Francisco, CA: Jossey-Bass.

Christensen, C. M., Horn, M., & Johnson, C. M. (2011). *Disrupting class: How disruptive innovation will change how the world learns*. New York, NY: McGraw-Hill.

Edmonds, R. (1979). Effective schools for the urban poor. *Educational Leadership, 37*(1), 15–24.

Friedman, T. L. (2005). *The world is flat 3.0: A brief history of the twenty-first century*. New York, NY: Picador.

Gartner (2014, February). *Market share analysis: Mobile phones worldwide, 4Q13 and 2013*. Retrieved from http://www.gartner.com/newsroom/id/2573415

Hall, R. H. (1991). *Organizations: Structures, processes, and outcomes* (5th ed.). Englewood Cliffs, NJ: Prentice Hall.

Hamilton, L., & Mackinnon, A. (2013). *Opportunity by design*. New York NY: Carnegie Corporation.

Kamenetz, A. (2010). *Diy u: Edupunks, edupreneurs, and the coming transformation of higher education*. White River Junction, VT: Chelsea Green.

Kuhn. T. (1962). *The structure of scientific revolutions*. Chicago, IL: University of Chicago Press.

Locke, J. (1980). *Second treatise of government* (C. B. Macpherson, Ed.). Indianapolis, IN: Hackett Publishing. (Original work published 1764)

Means, B., SRI International, et al. (2010). *Evaluation of evidence-based practices in online learning: A meta-analysis and review of online learning studies*. Washington, DC: U.S. Department of Education, Office of Planning, Evaluation and Policy Development, Policy and Programs Study Service.

Mehta, J. (2013, April 13). Teachers: Will we ever learn? *The New York Times*. Retrieved from http://www.nytimes.com/2013/04/13/opinion/teachers-will-we-ever-learn.html

Mishra, P., & Koehler, M. J. (2006). Technological pedagogical content knowledge: A framework for teacher knowledge. *Teachers College Record, 108*(6), 1017–1054.

Moore, M. G. & Kearsley, G. (2005). *Distance education* (2nd ed.). Belmont, CA: Thomson Wadsworth.

No Child Left Behind (NCLB) Act of 2001, Pub. L. No. 107-110, § 115, Stat. 1425 (2002).

Park, Y. (2011, February). A pedagogical framework for mobile learning: Categorizing educational applications of mobile technologies into four types. *The International Review of Research in Open and Distance Learning, 12*(2). Retrieved from http://http://www.irrodl.org/index.php/irrodl/article/view/791/1699

Popper, K. (1999). *All life is problem solving*. London, England: Routledge.

Rogers, E. M. (2003). *Diffusion of innovations* (5th ed.). New York, NY: Free Press.

Shearer, R. L. (2009). *Transactional distance and dialogue: An exploratory study to refine the theoretical construct of dialogue in online learning* (Doctoral dissertation, Pennsylvania State University, University Park). Available at http://www.ed.psu.edu/lps/adult-education/dissertations-directed-by-adult-education-faculty-1/dissertations-from-2009-directed-by-adult-education-faculty

Smale, A. (2013, January 28). Davos forum considers learning's next wave. *The New York Times, p. B2*.

Smith, M. S., O'Day, J., & Cohen, D. K. (1990). National curriculum American style: What might it look like? *American Educator, 14*(4), pp. 10–17.

Supovitz, J. A. (2006). *The case for district-based reform*. Cambridge, MA: Harvard Education Press.

Weiser, M. (1991). The computer for the 21st century. *Scientific American, 265*(3), 94–104.

Further Readings

Florida, R. (2002). *The rise of the creative class: And how it's transforming work, leisure, community, and everyday life*. New York, NY: Basic Books.

This book explores the emergence of the creative class as the 21st-century equivalent—in terms of income—to the 20th-century factory worker who forged the middle class in America.

Friedman, T. L. (2005). *The world is flat 3.0: A brief history of the twenty-first century.* New York, NY: Picador.

Friedman's book outlines the way in which the world has become a global marketplace through the confluence of 10 "flatterners" that reshaped global commerce.

Kamenetz, A. (2010). *Diy u: Edupunks, edupreneurs, and the coming transformation of higher education.* White River Junction, VT: Chelsea Green.

Kamenetz challenges the value of the traditional route through higher education. She outlines how one can gain an education through alternative routes. Free, open-source, vocational, experiential, and self-directed learning are potential options for gaining the knowledge one needs to succeed in the future.

Moore, M. G., & Kearsley, G. (2005). *Distance education* (2nd ed.). Belmont, CA: Thomson Wadsworth.

This book reviews how distance education has grown from correspondence courses in the 1800s to the modern online course offered through the Internet. The book explores the evolution, growth, and future of education offered somewhere other than in the physical presence of the teacher.

Park, Y. (2011, February). A pedagogical framework for mobile learning: Categorizing educational applications of mobile technologies into four types. *The International Review of Research in Open and Distance Learning, 12*(2), Retrieved from http:// http://www.irrodl.org/index.php/irrodl/article/view/791/1699

Park explains ubiquitous learning as the nexus between technology and the opportunity and access provided by global Internet connectivity. The challenges for learning in a virtual environment have to be overcome in order to make virtual learning of high quality.

Pink, D. H. (2005). *A whole new mind.* New York, NY: Riverhead Books.

Pink makes the case that 20th-century success as a student and job seeker favored the left-brained concrete sequential learner. The 21st-century learner will succeed by developing the more creative centers of the brain.

Thomas, D., & Brown, J. S. (2011). *A new culture of learning: Cultivating the imagination for a world of constant change.* Lexinton, KY: CreateSpace.

The future of education looks very different with technology as a catalyst for developing an educational system that truly enhances individual skills.

14

The Opportunities and Challenges of Online and Blended Learning

Brad E. Bizzell

Radford University

"Draw Me" beckoned the magazine advertisement used for many years by Art Instruction Schools. Founded in 1914, Art Instruction Schools still provide art instruction in the correspondence school fashion of assignments and feedback delivered by the U.S. Postal Service (Art Instruction Schools, 2013). Until recently, Art Instruction Schools was one of many that provided instruction through the mail in correspondence courses. Today, it is estimated that several million K-12 students take part in **online learning**, the modern correspondence course.

Online and blended learning may become the disruptive innovation that radically alters K-12 schooling or may simply continue as an alternative education option for a relatively small number of students, having little influence on the basic structure of schools and schooling. In this chapter, we will explore the evolution of online and blended learning, how the model may benefit students, and the issues that must be addressed when the model is implemented in K-12 school districts.

Background

Distance learning, originally in the form of the correspondence course, has been an educational option since the early 1800s. A student would enroll in university courses, complete course work on his or her own schedule, and mail completed assignments to the professor. The professor would then grade the assignments and return them via mail. While use of mail correspondence resulted in significant time lags when compared with on-campus classes, these courses provided educational opportunities to those who were geographically separated from universities, holding full-time jobs, or could not attend classes for other reasons.

In the 20th century, educators took advantage of radio and then television to provide educational programming (Reiser, 2001). Educational television (ETV) programs were provided to students both at school and in homes through public television stations. Many will recall programs such as *Sesame Street,* which has aired continuously since 1969 (Sesame Workshop, 2013). *Sesame Street,* with its high production values and aim to entertain as well as instruct, is not typical of most ETV programs of the 1960s and 1970s. Televised programs were produced for all academic areas and were shown in classrooms across the country. Most were of poor instructional quality, relying heavily on lecture, and accordingly ceased to air soon after their introduction. In the 1980s, videoconferencing, which allowed interaction between instructors and students, was viewed as an improvement over ETV but was unable to demonstrate positive effects on student learning. Online learning joined the other distance learning options in the mid-1990s.

Growth of Online and Blended Learning

Online learning is referred to as a fifth-generation distance learning technology following mail, radio, television, and videoconferencing (Means, Toyama, Murphy, & Bakia, 2013). Unlike the previous generations of distance learning, the growth of online and blended learning is occurring at a rapid pace. The Florida Virtual School has grown from 10,050 course enrollments in the 2001–2002 school year to over 300,000 by 2012 (iNACOL, 2013). The Florida Virtual School is by far the largest state online program, but double-digit annual growth rates are common for other state, multidistrict, and single-district online programs. Because of inconsistencies in defining terms and reporting of data, the numbers of K-12 students served through online and blended learning programs are only estimates, but significant growth is clearly occurring. In *Disrupting Class: How Disruptive Innovation Will Change the Way the World Learns* (2011), Clayton Christensen and colleagues predict significant growth in online learning over the next few years: "When viewed from the logarithmic perspective, the data suggest that by 2019, about 50 percent of high school courses will be delivered online" (Christensen, Horn, & Johnson, p. 98).

The Evergreen Education Group publishes an annual report on K-12 online learning, *Keeping Pace With K-12 Online and Blended Learning: An Annual Review of Policy and Practice* (Watson, Murin, Vashaw, Gemin, & Rapp, 2012), that includes growth statistics. The 2012 report estimates more than 5% of K-12 students in the United States took at least one online or blended learning course, with some of these students enrolling in courses outside of the school and some enrolled in fully online programs. The National Center for Education Statistics (NCES) reported that in the 2009–2010 school year, there were an estimated 1.8 million enrollments in distance education courses in the 55% of public school districts that offered these courses (Queen & Lewis, 2011). The majority of these districts planned to increase enrollments in the 3 years following the NCES survey. Although the NCES data are reported as distance education rather than specifically online courses, fully 90% of the distance education in public schools is now provided online.

Overall, the data on online programs reveal significant growth, but not all individual programs are experiencing success. State virtual schools in Kentucky, Nebraska, and Tennessee closed in 2012 (Watson et al., 2012). The local school board operating Virginia's statewide virtual school voted in 2013 to discontinue its contract with K^{12}, Incorporated, the school district's partner in operating the school (Chandler, 2013). However, at the same time, Virginia has become one of several states to require students to participate in an online course before high school graduation. Online and blended learning is evolving in a dynamic environment.

Defining Online and Blended Learning

There are many ways the Internet is currently accessed to support teaching and learning. School districts are purchasing online professional learning opportunities for teachers and tools supporting online collaborative work among teachers. Teachers are using web-based resources to plan and support traditional face-to-face classroom instruction, including resources that both enrich and expand learning as well as remediate. Public school districts, private schools, and homeschoolers are accessing individual courses, both credit and noncredit bearing, and entire educational programs online. With the diversity of online educational opportunities and the pace of technological changes, it is important to clarify the terms used in this field.

For the purposes of this chapter, *online learning* is defined as teacher-led education that occurs entirely or mostly online. Online learning includes static content, multimedia, and links to various resources in addition to the online delivery of instruction. Static content can include text documents and graphical material maintained within a **learning management system (LMS)**. Multimedia include audio, video, animation, and gaming content. An infinite number of links to other websites can be archived within the LMS as resources for an online course. The online delivery of instruction can occur in multiple ways with multiple tools.

Instruction in online learning can be delivered *synchronously, asynchronously,* or through a combination of the two. In **synchronous instruction**, the teacher and students meet together in an online space in real time. Software allows teacher-to-student and student-to-student interaction in the online classroom through audio, video, and chat, and the sharing of documents, presentations, and interactive white boards. Students can listen to minilectures delivered by the teacher with presentation slides, watch demonstrations, engage in question-and-answer sessions, contribute to whole class discussions, and participate in breakout sessions for small-group discussions. Teachers can give students control through the software to share their own documents and deliver presentations just as they might do in a face-to-face classroom. Both students and teachers can be located anywhere there is access to the Internet; a classroom in the neighborhood school, a public library in another part of the country, or their home half way around the world.

Using **asynchronous instruction**, the teacher creates opportunities for student learning and interaction that do not require everyone to be online at the same time. Discussion boards, email, wikis (which allow people to collaborate on web content), blogs, and video logs, or vlogs, are among the tools that allow teachers and students to share information, engage in discussions, ask and answer questions, and work collaboratively without the necessity of being together, either physically or virtually, at the same time. Asynchronous, online learning is the most widely used approach in public school districts.

Blended learning, also referred to as hybrid, includes a mix, or blend, of online instruction with face-to-face instruction. Blended learning is not simply use of web-based resources in the conduct of a traditional class, but rather, occurs when a significant portion of the instruction is delivered in the online environment. Again, the online portion of instruction can be provided either synchronously or asynchronously in the blended learning course. The face-to-face component can also take different forms. For example, in one state that offers online courses through a state-operated virtual school, students take an online class in a computer lab in their neighborhood school and are visited by a certified teacher weekly or biweekly during the class time for additional instruction or one-on-one support. In other

settings teachers are assigned to blended classes where students receive instruction and access content online at a time and place of their choosing and spend daily face-to-face time interacting with the teacher and classmates to apply knowledge or receive supplementary instruction. The **flipped classroom**, a recent instructional model that utilizes online video lectures and other online resources for homework and in-class application of content or small-group instruction, is an example of this type of blended learning that is growing in popularity. In blended learning, teachers, when face-to-face with students, spend their time assisting individual learners or creating opportunities for student collaborative work rather than delivering lessons to large groups designed for the average learner.

Online learning can also be classified according to other practices such as who provides the instruction. The providers of online courses vary considerably. The NCES distance education report indicated that half of the public school districts were receiving courses provided by postsecondary institutions (Queen & Lewis, 2011). This is frequently a local community college offering dual-credit courses to high school students. Commercial vendors and state virtual schools also provide online courses to districts. A large majority of districts offering online courses do not develop and deliver any using in-district resources; however, single- and multidistrict programs are among the fastest growing. Regardless of the provider, online and blended learning offers both opportunities and challenges.

Online and Blended Learning: Benefits and Concerns

Initially, like earlier forms of distance learning, online and blended learning was seen as a way to offer educational opportunities or expand offerings to students for whom the traditional classroom was not available. A student who had been injured or was ill and unable to attend school for a lengthy period could receive instruction in his or her home. A student who was traveling on a long-term basis could continue with his or her education. Incarcerated youth could have access to learning opportunities with the potential to improve their outcomes upon release. Relatively few students were covered by these categories. As online and blended learning become available to a much broader population of students, it is bringing about new opportunities as well as raising concerns.

The ubiquitous nature of the Internet makes it a natural medium for reaching a broad population of students. The Federal Communications Commission in 2012 reported that in 2011, 64% of all U.S. households had broadband Internet service, and the percentage was growing. This figure included only fixed wire broadband and accordingly did not count those households with satellite Internet or wireless phone data plans. Additionally, virtually all public schools, libraries, and community centers in the United States provide computer and Internet access that is available to students. Now nearly all schools have the opportunity to offer online and blended learning.

However, that opportunity comes along with a challenge: Low-income households disproportionately represent those households without broadband service. These same households are less likely to have computers. Students from these households, as a group, are also more likely to experience academic difficulties. While students can access online courses through school computer labs or other public terminals, the equity and logistical issues for students unable to access online courses at home must still be addressed.

There are also households without access to broadband services regardless of cost. These households are disproportionately rural. Satellite Internet providers are attempting to market to those in rural areas, but currently do not offer service at the same level of performance offered through fixed wire services. Addressing both the infrastructure and equity issues is no small matter and will require both economic and policy solutions.

Student Achievement

The first consideration in selecting any instructional approach should be the effectiveness of the approach in meeting instructional objectives. As with much research in the field of education, results for online learning are mixed. Anecdotally, educators report that self-motivated students are at least as successful online as they are in traditional settings while less motivated students tend to perform poorly online with teacher-led interventions more difficult to implement when the teacher doesn't see the student

daily. Individual research studies may produce varied results. A research technique known as meta-analysis synthesizes results from a number of studies revealing broader, more generalizable results. A recent study applied this technique to the study of online and blended learning (Means et al., 2013).

In *The Effectiveness of Online and Blended Learning: A Meta-Analysis of the Empirical Literature,* Means et al. (2013) found that distance learning approaches used prior to online learning, in terms of student achievement, were, at best, no better than traditional classroom instruction and in some cases, such as videoconferencing, worse. Their meta-analysis utilized 45 studies conducted between 1996 and 2008 following the implementation of online learning. The researchers found online approaches overall to be as effective as traditional face-to-face classes, and blended approaches slightly better. They cautioned that the blended approaches examined in the studies typically included additional resources above what was offered in either the purely online or face-to-face classes, making it difficult to discern what actually caused the increase in student achievement. One wonders what future research will show as online pedagogy is addressed in teacher education and in-service professional learning, and new teachers who were themselves online learners join the profession.

Small Schools

Small, neighborhood schools are often close-knit communities where students and teachers know each other both within and outside school. The relationships that develop can improve learning outcomes and lead to long-term mentoring and friendship. The small school, especially at the high school level, can also be limited in the courses that can be offered to students. Beyond the basic core academic courses, there must be enough student demand to warrant offering certain courses. Additionally, there must be enough courses in a particular area to warrant the hiring of a teacher. These two conditions can leave students in small schools with limited opportunities for advanced courses in mathematics and science, Advanced Placement courses, foreign languages, and career and technical courses.

Larger urban or suburban districts can justify hiring itinerant teachers who travel to multiple small schools to teach. Still, the district incurs additional costs as the teacher must be provided time to travel between schools and be reimbursed for travel costs. For small schools in rural districts, itinerant teachers may not be an option. The distances between schools can be large, making travel time-consuming and costly. Rural schools may also find it difficult to attract teachers licensed in hard-to-staff subjects such as advanced mathematics and science. Online courses present an opportunity for students in these schools.

When providing courses online, school districts can pool student demand for courses from multiple schools, increasing opportunities for students without necessarily increasing costs. District personnel can develop and deliver these online courses in-house where expertise exists or purchase commercially developed and delivered courses. In either case, courses not otherwise available to students are now an option. For students who wish to continue with a traditional schooling experience while having access to additional courses, the classes can be scheduled in students' neighborhood schools as part of the regular school day using existing computer labs. In this arrangement, students retain the benefits of a small learning community while gaining opportunities previously unavailable.

Personalized Instruction

In schools and districts where the student population does not create limits on traditional course offerings, online and blended courses can still increase learning options for students. The nonprofit Khan Academy (n.d.) offers more than 4,000 free online video lessons on a variety of academic topics geared toward K-12 students. Some of the world's most prestigious universities have begun to offer free college-level courses as MOOCs, or massive open online courses. Personalized learning, viewed as a major benefit of the online model, encompasses more than expanded content choice. Online and blended learning can offer opportunities for personalized learning by giving students choice and control over certain aspects of their learning and responding to individual student learning needs.

Students in traditional school settings have little control over their learning. Students are assigned to teachers and courses for specific periods of time in specific classrooms. The school calendar is created for all students in the district, indicating the beginning and ending dates of the school year and vacation

days within. Teachers follow pacing guides that describe what must be done on a daily or weekly basis to complete the required curriculum within a prescribed number of days. Rigid calendars and strict adherence to pacing guides can result in students being passive objects of education rather than active participants. Online learning creates the opportunity for students to exercise some choice and control over the time, place, and pace of instruction.

Traditional daily starting and ending times, controlled in part by tradition, bus routes, school locations, and high school athletics, do not apply in the online environment. High schools that start early in the morning in order to accommodate afternoon sports schedules are not being responsive to the sleep patterns of many adolescents. Schools at all levels generally establish rigid daily class schedules with 50, 70, or 90 minutes per class and 90 or 180 classes per year. Teachers in a traditional classroom setting strive to differentiate instruction to meet the needs of learners, some who learn slower and some who learn faster, but are often frustrated by the diversity of their students' readiness levels and learning profiles. Students in online courses can choose to work on multiple content areas daily or spend extended time with one subject. They may work early in the morning or late at night. A student can vary his or her schedule on a daily basis to address need or interest. Wireless connectivity and mobile devices allow learning to occur virtually anywhere and at anytime.

Asynchronous tools such as discussion boards allow students time to think deeply and reflectively, composing and editing before responding to prompts from the instructor or posts from other students. Students can review recorded minilectures and other online resources as often as necessary. Such an abundance of "think time" is seldom available in the traditional classroom. Questions posed during face-to-face classes are often answered by the quickest thinker in the room before others have had adequate time to even process the question or mentally prepare a response.

The freedom students have in planning when they will engage in course activities and how much time they will spend on individual tasks also presents challenges. Teachers must work with students to ensure progress in a given course. Just as teachers must learn new skills to teach in the online environment, so too must students be taught and learn new skills such as planning and scheduling their work.

Learning management systems have tools that allow instructors to monitor and encourage students' progress. Use of these tools and frequent communication with students and parents will help keep students progressing.

Online learning does not require a student to be physically present in a particular school building or classroom. Computer labs in traditional brick-and-mortar schools are frequently used to access online and blended courses but students may engage in learning activities from other locations such as homes, public libraries, or community centers. In fact, some schools are now using distance technologies along with traditional face-to-face courses to replace snow days with "e-learning days." Students with home Internet access are able to continue learning when getting to school is not safe or possible.

As previously noted, not all students have ready access to online learning in their homes. Students from families with low incomes may have no Internet access or computers in their homes. Students living in some rural areas have limited access to broadband. Schools attempt to address these issues with computer lab hours that extend beyond the typical school day and by providing laptops that can be borrowed. Some schools have a one-to-one laptop or tablet program, providing computers for all students. The one-to-one programs are generally instituted to replace textbooks and enhance in-school instruction, but can also benefit those students enrolled in online courses. In order for students to truly exercise control over the "place" of their learning, these access issues must be addressed.

Data collection systems within some online systems allow for real-time adjustment of instruction based on students' performance. Assessments are the basis for quickly moving students past content they have already mastered and into new content or to identify when additional instruction is needed. In the online or blended classroom, the data systems provide teachers with the information needed to plan individual or small-group instruction that focuses upon students' particular needs. This is theoretically possible in the traditional classroom, but seldom occurs as teachers are designing instruction for large groups of students and following pacing guides dictating daily content objectives. The availability of data in online systems, while of instructional value, also raises concerns about student privacy that must be addressed by school districts.

The challenge to personalizing the pace of instruction lies within our traditional structures and policies. Course credit, in most states, is not only a function of a student's achievement in a particular content but also a function of meeting a required minimum number of seat hours in a course. State testing systems also complicate a student's ability to move at his or her own pace. High-stakes, end-of-course tests are set at particular times of the year, and in traditional school settings instruction is planned in order to finish the curriculum just before the test is administered. If students in online courses are subject to these same, unaltered policies, they lose some of the control over the pace of instruction that online learning is able to offer.

Credit Recovery

Online learning is being used extensively for credit recovery in high schools. Credit recovery includes both courses that were taken but not successfully completed by students and courses missed by students when originally offered. Driven by state and federal accountability measures related to graduation rates, schools are increasingly focused on credit recovery courses. Credit recovery courses are the single largest category of online K-12 course enrollment. The International Association for K-12 Online Learning (iNACOL, 2013) reported that in the 2009–2010 school year, credit recovery courses were provided online by 62% of school districts using online learning. Most often, students attending traditional brick-and-mortar schools are the students taking online credit recovery courses. Here again, the opportunity to assess and personalize the program for the student so that instruction matches his or her need is an important feature.

Typically, students taking credit recovery courses have been unsuccessful in earlier attempts at a course or are behind in credits due to prior failures in other courses. Before online options were available, students repeating courses would either take a time-condensed version of the course in summer school or repeat the entire course in a subsequent school year, often taught by the same teacher in the same way. Without online options, the number of credits that a student can accumulate in a school year is limited by the number of class periods. Students who find themselves behind in credits after ninth grade may have little hope to graduate with their peers.

Online credit recovery has the potential to offer personalized instruction that focuses on areas within the content where the student has yet to demonstrate competence. In the state-sponsored Michigan Virtual School (MVS), students take pretests that can allow them to skip content already mastered (Davis, 2011). Additionally, MVS's courses are designed to present academic content in real-world contexts, such as music and driving, which are appealing to students. Reducing the amount of time a student must engage in the course by focusing solely on content not yet mastered and creating interest in the content enhances a student's chance of successfully completing and earning credit for the course.

A potential challenge to success with online credit recovery courses relates to the student typically enrolled in credit recovery courses. The student characteristics generally associated with success in the online environment, such as being self-motivated, are often not attributed to students taking credit recovery courses. In fact, lack of student motivation is often linked to course failures. Because of this, structures to ensure frequent communication between the teacher and student and monitoring of student progress are essential. The blended model where students enrolled in the credit recovery course take the course in a school computer lab and have access to teachers on a daily basis could be a successful structure. Research is currently lacking comparing the effectiveness of online credit recovery courses with traditional summer or repeat courses, but school leaders report that increasing options for students in these circumstances is a good thing.

Productivity of Online and Blended Learning

Online learning is considered to have cost-saving potential. In order to measure and reach appropriate conclusions, one must not consider costs in isolation but rather in relation to course or program effectiveness. This ratio of educational productivity, cost to effectiveness, can inform policy and practice decisions in online and blended learning. Productivity can be increased by decreasing costs while maintaining outcomes, keeping costs constant while improving outcomes, or both decreasing costs and improving outcomes. Current research examining both costs and effectiveness is limited but does show potential

for significant productivity increases with online courses through both cost savings and improvement of student outcomes (Bakia, Shear, Toyama, & Lasseter, 2012).

Several of the mechanisms through which productivity may be increased (lowered costs or increased effectiveness) have already been identified in this chapter. Being able to combine students from remote locations or small schools through an online offering of courses that cannot be offered in traditional schools due to limited numbers is one such mechanism. Combining these students to reach numbers that will support the hiring of a teacher or the adding of a course costs no more than hiring a teacher to meet the course demand in a physical building yet adds learning that would not otherwise be available to students. Another mechanism to potentially increase productivity is the ability to personalize learning by differentiating instruction based on student readiness and building on students' interests. Doing so can increase student motivation and lead to improved learning at faster rates.

As in other industries, technology can be utilized in education to make better use of teacher time. In an online model, once a course has been developed, a teacher can spend time interacting with individual students to provide feedback on assignments, extend learning, and additional learning opportunities as determined by formative assessments. Data collection, including assessment data, activity completion, time interacting with course materials, and even next steps in instruction, can be automated and thus completed in a more efficient manner. A challenge, or caution, exists here as well. Some believe that in online or blended courses teachers can work with much larger numbers of students than in the traditional face-to-face class due to the efficiencies in online learning models and the lack of classroom management issues. Increasing the student-teacher ratio could very well negate the educational benefit of the enhanced student-teacher interaction described earlier.

Online learning also has the potential for increased productivity through economies of scale. The large-scale production of online course material or entire courses is possible. Many of the commercial vendors of online learning hire instructional designers to develop courses and then hire teachers to teach those courses to students across the country. In larger school districts, a similar model can be used where many teach online courses developed by a few. Instructional designers and teachers each develop expertise that increases their efficiency.

The Common Core State Standards in mathematics and English Language Arts, adopted by 45 states and the District of Columbia, creates even greater potential for economies of scale to be realized (National Governors Association Center & Council of Chief State School Officers, 2013). A challenge is ensuring that courses are developed and delivered in such a way that the unique needs of the district, school, and student are addressed. The flexibility to customize must be thoughtfully considered during course development or purchase.

A final area of potential productivity improvement is related to school facility costs. Shifting education to homes or to public spaces such as libraries or community centers lessens wear and tear on current school facilities and, long term, may reduce the need for new facilities. The other side of this argument is that schools must invest more in technology infrastructure and software to support online learning. These are complex and dynamic circumstances that make decision making difficult but critical. Blended learning does not offer the same potential savings in facilities that fully online courses or programs do, but, according to current research, it offers greater potential for improved student outcomes.

Another caution is warranted in this discussion of the productivity of online learning. With the perceived, though yet undocumented, cost-savings of online instruction, some states are adjusting funding formulas to reduce reimbursements to localities for students enrolled in online courses or programs. Some states provide funding for full-time online students at the same rate as in brick-and-mortar schools, some at a reduced rate, and some fund only for successful completion of online courses. Both reductions in funding and uncertainty in funding can serve as disincentives to explore and develop innovative approaches to teaching and learning such as an online or blended model. Clearly, districts must be aware of state policies regarding funding.

Planning for Online and Blended Programs

Planning for online and blended learning must include learning about best practices for course and program design, instruction, administrative functions, and policy development. Several organizations

have been involved in the development of standards for online programs. iNACOL (2011a, 2011b) published the second iteration of their *National Standards for Quality Online Courses* (see **Sidebar 14.1**) and *National Standards for Online Teaching* in 2011 following the first sets in 2007 and 2008 respectively. iNACOL (NACOL at the time) partnered with the National Education Association (NEA, n.d.) to develop the *Guide to Teaching Online Courses,* in which the NEA makes recommendations on the development of online courses, teaching skills needed, and administrative and policy issues that must be addressed. The *Quality Matters Grades 6–12 Rubric Standards* integrates the standards from iNACOL, the Southern Regional Education Board, and The Partnership for 21st Century Skills (Quality Matters, 2010). Accrediting agency AdvancEd (2013) has also adapted its *Standards for Quality* for, as they describe, digital learning institutions. Each of these sets of standards includes information easily recognizable as good instructional design and delivery for the traditional face-to-face course and addresses the unique environment and circumstances of online courses. Recognized standards should be used to guide the development and evaluation of online programs.

Design and Delivery of Online and Blended Programs

Planning for the design and delivery of online and blended models should begin with conversations about students and desired educational outcomes. Online learning has the potential to increase choice and opportunities for students, but the process is not as simple as moving the components of a traditional face-to-face class to an online space. Thorough discussions are needed about students and how their learning needs can be met or enhanced through the use of online or blended learning.

In planning online or blended courses or programs, a multitude of questions must be answered at both the practice and policy levels. While by no means is this an exhaustive list, the following questions should be considered as districts decide whether and how to implement online programs.

Related to Practice

- How will online offerings improve learning opportunities for students?
- What courses or programs will be offered and in what online format?

> ## Sidebar 14.1   Online Course Standards
>
> The five standards below are drawn from iNACOL's *The National Standards for Quality Online Courses.* According to iNACOL, a quality online course:
>
> 1. Provides online learners with multiple ways of engaging with learning experiences that promote their mastery of content;
> 2. Uses learning activities that engage students in active learning;
> 3. Uses multiple strategies and activities to assess student readiness for and progress in course content;
> 4. Takes full advantage of a variety of technology tools, has a user-friendly interface, and meets accessibility standards for interoperability and access to learners with special needs; and
> 5. Is evaluated regularly for effectiveness and the findings are used as a basis for improvement (iNACOL, 2011a).

- What is our time line for developing an online program?
- Who will develop and teach the online courses?
- How will we ensure quality of instruction and delivery of special education services?
- What are the professional learning needs of our staff?
- How will we administer state tests?
- What will we do for students who do not have broadband access to the Internet or computer hardware?
- How will we evaluate teachers of online courses?
- How will we evaluate the costs and effectiveness of online courses or programs as compared with traditional face-to-face courses or programs?

Related to Policy

- Will online courses be noted as such on student transcripts?
- Will we accept enrollment of students from outside our district, and if so, will state funding follow the student or will we charge tuition?
- How many online courses for credit can a student take in any academic term?
- Will students be allowed to earn credit for online courses taken outside the district and, if so, what restrictions may be imposed?
- What personnel, finance, instruction, or other policies may need adjustment?

Related to Areas Outside Control of the District

- Will the offering of online courses impact our state funding?
- Do online courses require minimum seat-time hours or can they be competency-based?
- If purchasing courses developed and delivered by national vendors, will teachers licensed in another state be eligible to teach in our state?

- Will the offering of online courses impact accreditation from the state or outside accrediting agencies?
- What are the college entrance implications for students taking online courses or programs?
- What are the NCAA eligibility implications for students taking online courses or programs?

These questions are just a starting point when considering online and blended programs. Two areas, special education and teacher evaluation, warrant additional discussion.

Special Education

Any plans for online learning must consider best practices and legal requirements for students with disabilities. Just as in a brick-and-mortar school, districts must comply with the Individuals with Disabilities Education Act, the Americans with Disabilities Act, and Section 504 of the Rehabilitation Act in providing educational services to and protecting the civil rights of students with disabilities. Section 508 of the Rehabilitation Act additionally provides a mandate for federal agencies, and best practice for others, related to physical and sensory accessibility issues. Offering courses or requiring use of a technology not accessible to students with disabilities is a violation of the law and exposes school districts to liability.

In theory, the personalization made possible through online learning could be ideal for students with learning, cognitive, emotional, sensory, or physical disabilities. In reality, many districts complying fully with the law and engaging in best practices in traditional face-to-face instruction have not yet developed the capacity to do so in the online environment. One of the reasons cited by the local school district in Virginia for discontinuing operation of the state virtual school was the additional administrative work and complications from attempting to provide special education services to students from multiple school districts from all areas of the state.

Over the four decades since the Individuals with Disabilities Education Act was first enacted, teachers have developed and passed on skills in retrofitting traditional educational materials, such as textbooks, to accommodate learning differences of students with disabilities. Retrofitting is often not possible with technology-based materials that include multimedia and interactive capabilities. Developing digital materials that meet accessibility standards can also be complicated. Some, but not all, commercially developed digital educational materials are compliant with the National Instructional Materials Accessibility Standard and can be of benefit to all students, with or without disabilities. Accessible instructional materials, or AIM, centers are available to provide some digital content for students with disabilities at the state level, but these materials are not available for use with students without disabilities. Program development time lines must consider the time to ensure educational materials and activities for online courses are accessible to students with disabilities.

Universal design for learning, or UDL, is a concept that suggests instruction should be designed from the outset to meet the needs of diverse learners rather than retrofitting instruction intended for the masses (CAST, 2011). UDL's framework for guiding educational practices has its origins in the field of neuroscience. When utilizing the principles of UDL, a teacher or instructional designer plans for engaging students by stimulating student interest and motivation, presents and represents content in different ways, and differentiates how students may demonstrate their learning. The National Center on Universal Design for Learning, part of CAST (originally the Center for Applied Special Technology), offers guidelines, examples, and resources supporting the use of UDL. UDL's framework would be a useful tool in planning online programs that are responsive to students with disabilities.

Most students with disabilities in traditional schools receive their special education services, instruction, and accommodations within the general education

setting. A model used extensively is co-teaching, where a general teacher and special educator are paired in a classroom with a group of students including both those with and without disabilities. The teachers plan, instruct, and assess together. In a blended learning model, this arrangement could easily continue as skilled, traditional co-teachers are already utilizing small-group and individual instruction to a great extent in the face-to-face co-taught classroom. In the fully online model, both general and special educators will have to learn new collaborative skills to meet the needs of students with disabilities.

Teacher Evaluation

Teacher evaluation has garnered much recent attention with many states changing evaluation processes to include a greater emphasis on student growth as a measure of teacher effectiveness. In addition to student growth, evaluation models generally include other areas to be evaluated such as content knowledge, instructional planning and delivery, classroom environment, and professionalism. Typical evaluation processes or tools rely heavily on observation of teaching and include review of student achievement data, examination of instructional plans, recognition of contributions made outside the classroom, and may also include portfolios of teacher-selected artifacts, teacher self-assessments, and student surveys.

Principals are now, and have always been, responsible for evaluating the performance of teachers. Regardless of a principal's teaching background, she or he is expected to evaluate teachers of all content areas and grade levels under her or his supervision. Some might argue a principal with no specific training related to online instruction evaluating a teacher of an online course is no different than a former English teacher evaluating a Spanish teacher. Others would suggest that online teaching is a radical departure from the traditional face-to-face class and must be evaluated by someone with a deep understanding of this model of education. Online instruction does require skills of teachers to be effective in that particular context. It would therefore stand to reason that principals would need to understand this model deeply in order to properly evaluate a teacher's effectiveness in that context. Preparing teachers to deliver instruction in the online setting is not enough; administrators must be prepared to evaluate that instruction.

The observation of large-group instruction as the primary means of evaluating teacher effectiveness in face-to-face classes is not appropriate for evaluation of the online teacher. While it is possible to design synchronous instruction with a typical class-size group that is similar to the traditional model, use of these strategies in the online class fails to take advantage of the benefits offered through the online model and should certainly not be done just for evaluative purposes. The online course and teaching standards noted above are a good starting place for school districts to begin considering appropriate models of teacher evaluation.

Evaluators must spend time within the online space occupied by the teacher. They should examine the layout and accessibility of the course content, the means through which the teacher communicates with students individually and in groups, how the teacher facilitates student-to-student interaction and student engagement with content, the timeliness and quality of feedback to students, the monitoring of student progress, and the use of a variety of appropriate online tools and resources. Each of these areas is appropriately evaluated for traditional teachers as well, but the nature of each changes substantially in the online setting where students are exerting more control over their learning, and teachers do not have daily contact with students.

learning and increase learning opportunities for students in our K-12 schools, but those opportunities come with challenges.

The report, *Understanding the Implications of Online Learning for Educational Productivity*, produced for the U.S. Department of Education, Office of Educational Technology (Bakia et al., 2012), discusses some of the changes that need to occur for online learning to realize its potential:

> The realization of productivity improvements in education will most likely require a transformation of conventional processes to leverage new capabilities supported by information and communications technologies. Basic assumptions about the need for seat time and age-based cohorts may need to be reevaluated to sharpen focus on the needs and interests of all students as individuals. And as a rigorous evidence accumulates around effective practices that may require institutional change, systemic incentives may be needed to spur the adoption of efficient, effective paths to learning. (p. viii)

Online and blended learning may turn out not just to change processes, but also to be a disruptive innovation that will drive an even greater transformation in education as a whole. Education could today be at the intersection of harsh economic reality and technological innovation that, in the near future, results in major changes in education not accomplished by decades of reform efforts. Envisioning and planning for such a shift is the challenge of today's educational leader.

Conclusion

Technology, and specifically technology associated with the Internet, is impacting every aspect of our society from economic activity to political activism, from entertainment to relationships, and, of course, education. We are shopping, banking, and paying our monthly bills online. We argue our political beliefs and support causes while reconnecting with high school friends on Facebook and with 140-character tweets. At the same time, many of us worry about the vulnerability of government systems and the power grid to hackers, and about our own privacy online. Time spent online for entertainment and shopping can cut into productivity, and the benefits of technology are not distributed equitably. Likewise, online and blended learning has the potential to enhance

Key Chapter Terms

Asynchronous instruction: Occurs when the teacher and students are not in the online environment together at the same time for either instruction or interaction. Recorded minilectures, discussion boards, email, wikis, blogs, and v-logs are among the tools that allow teachers and students to share information, discuss topics, ask and answer questions, and work collaboratively without the necessity of being together at the same time. Asynchronous, online learning is the most widely used approach in public school districts.

Blended learning: Also referred to as hybrid learning, includes a mix, or blend, of online instruction with face-to-face instruction. Blended learning is not simply use of web-based resources in the conduct of a traditional class, but rather, occurs when a significant portion of the instruction is delivered in the online environment either synchronously or asynchronously. The face-to-face component can take different forms, including daily interaction with a teacher or only intermittent (e.g., weekly, monthly) interaction. In blended learning, teachers, when face-to-face with students, should spend their time assisting individual learners or creating opportunities for small-group instruction.

Flipped classroom: A recent instructional model that introduces students to content through online video lectures and other online resources as homework and uses face-to-face time to engage students with application of content or to provide individual or small-group instruction. The flipped classroom is an example of blended learning.

Learning management system (LMS): A software application used to organize the various elements of an online course. A typical LMS includes space for static content that includes text documents and graphical material, and multimedia including audio, video, animation, and gaming content. Organizational tools within the LMS provide the ability to receive, assess, and offer feedback on assignments, administer assessments, assign grades, facilitate interaction and collaboration, manage student groups, build student portfolios, link to other websites, and communicate.

Online learning: Teacher-led education that occurs entirely or mostly online. Online learning includes static content, and multimedia, and links to various resources in addition to the online delivery of instruction using a variety of tools within a learning management system.

Synchronous instruction: Instruction in which the teacher and students meet together in an online space in real time. Software allows interaction through audio, video, and chat, and the sharing of documents, presentations, and interactive white boards. Students can listen to minilectures, watch demonstrations, engage in question-and-answer sessions, contribute to class discussions, and participate in breakout groups for small-group discussion. Teachers can give students control through the software to share their own documents and deliver presentations to the class just as they might do in a face-to-face classroom.

References

AdvancEd. (2013). *AdvancEd standards for quality: Digital learning institutions.* Atlanta, GA: Author. Retrieved from http://advanc-ed.org/webfm_send/412

Americans with Disabilities Act, 42 U.S.C. § 12201 (2008).

Art Instruction Schools. (2013). *Our history.* Minneapolis, MN: Author. Retrieved from http://www.artists-ais.com/curriculum/

Bakia, M., Shear, L., Toyama, Y., & Lasseter, A. (2012). *Understanding the implications of online learning for educational productivity.* Washington, DC: U.S. Department of Education, Office of Educational Technology.

CAST. (2011). *Universal design for learning guidelines version 2.0.* Wakefield, MA: Author. Retrieved from http://www.udlcenter.org/aboutudl/udlguidelines

Chandler, M. A. (2013, May 1). Virginia's first statewide virtual school likely to close. *The Washington Post.* Retrieved from http://articles.washingtonpost.com/2013-05-01/local/38950588_1_virtual-schools-carroll-county-school-board-northern-virginia

Christensen, C. M., Horn, M. B., & Johnson, C. W. (2011). *Disrupting class: How disruptive innovation will change the way the world learns.* New York, NY: McGraw-Hill.

Davis, M. (2011, January 12). Credit recovery classes take a personal approach. Education Week Special Report: Crafting e-curriculum that inspires. *Education Week, 30*(15).

Federal Communications Commission. (2012). *Eighth broadband progress report.* Retrieved from http://hraunfoss.fcc.gov/edocs_public/attachmatch/FCC-12-90A1.pdf

iNACOL. (2011a). *National standards for quality online courses: Version 2.* Vienna, VA: Author. Retrieved from http://www.inacol.org/resources/publications/national-quality-standards/

iNACOL. (2011b). *National standards for quality online teaching: Version 2.* Vienna, VA: Author. Retrieved from http://www.inacol.org/resources/publications/national-quality-standards/

iNACOL. (2013). *Fast facts about online learning.* Vienna, VA: Author. Retrieved from http://www.inacol.org/cms/wp-content/uploads/2013/04/iNACOL_FastFacts_Feb2013.pdf

Individuals with Disabilities Education Improvement Act, 20 U.S.C. § 1400 (2004).

Khan Academy. (n.d.). *A free world-class education for anyone anywhere.* Mountain View, CA: Author. Retrieved from https://www.khanacademy.org/about

Means, B., Toyama, Y., Murphy, R., & Bakia, M. (2013). The effectiveness of online and blended learning: A meta-analysis of the empirical literature. *Teachers College Record, 115,* 1–47.

National Education Association. (n.d.). *NEA guide to teaching online courses.* Washington, DC: Author. Retrieved from http://www.nea.org/assets/docs/onlineteachguide.pdf

National Governors Association Center and Council of Chief State School Officers. (2013). *Common core state standards initiative: In the states.* Author. Retrieved from http://www.corestandards.org/in-the-states

Quality Matters. (2010). *The QM grades 6–12 rubric standards: 2010 edition.* Annapolis, MD: Author. Retrieved from https://www.qualitymatters.org/g6-12-rubric-standards-0

Queen, B., & Lewis, L. (2011). *Distance education courses for public elementary and secondary school students: 2009–10* (NCES 2012–009). Washington, DC: U.S. Department of Education, National Center for Education Statistics. Retrieved from http://nces.ed.gov/pubsearch/pubsinfo.asp?pubid=2012009

The Rehabilitation Act, 29 U.S.C. § 701 (1973).

Reiser, R. A. (2001). A history of instructional design and technology: Part 1. A history of instructional media. *Educational Technology Research and Development, 49*(1), 53–64.

Sesame Workshop. (2013). *40 years and counting.* New York, NY: Author. Retrieved from http://www.sesameworkshop.org/about-us/40-years-and-counting/

Watson, J., Murin, A., Vashaw, L., Gemin, B., & Rapp, C. (2012). *Keeping pace with K-12 online and blended learning: An annual review of policy and practice.* Durango, CO.: Evergreen Education Group. Retrieved from http://kpk12.com/cms/wp-content/uploads/KeepingPace2012.pdf

Further Readings

Archambault, L., & Crippen, K. (2009). K-12 distance educators at work: Who's teaching online across the United States. *Journal of Research on Technology in Education, 41*(4), 363–391.

This research article reports on a study of teachers teaching online courses. They report demographic data as well as perceived advantages and challenges of teaching online.

Ash, K., (2011, August 24). At-risk students' virtual challenges. Education Week Special Report: E-learning for special populations. *Education Week.*

The article describes how online educational environments can be of use to at-risk students living in the United States. Emphasis is placed on how virtual learning environments can help struggling students by offering them a new beginning and providing flexibility to account for work or family obligations. Credit-recovery programs that help students who have fallen behind get the credits needed to graduate are also discussed.

Barnes, S. B. (2012). *Socializing the classroom: Social networks and online learning.* Plymouth, England: Lexington Books.

This book provides readers with an understanding of how students use social media and online learning environments to communicate and interact. Itsuggests ways social media may be best utilized for educational purposes.

The Center on Online Learning and Students with Disabilities. (2012). *The foundation of online learning for students with disabilities.* Lawrence, KA: Author. Retrieved from http://centerononlinelearning.org/wp-content/uploads/Foundation_7_2012.pdf

This white paper includes information on providing accommodations, complying with federal law including statutory mandates for accessibility, and provides an accessibility template. A section with links to many resources on the topic of accessibility is provided.

Engvig M. (2006). *Online learning: All you need to know to facilitate and administer online courses.* Cresskill, NJ: Hampton Press.

This book offers a "how-to" guide coupled with theory on educational innovation, pedagogy, and instructional design. A large section provides information from the students' perspective.

Hall, T. E., Meyer, A., & Rose, D. H. (Eds.). (2012). *Universal design for learning in the classroom: Practical applications.* New York, NY: Guilford Press.

This book describes practical ways to apply the principles of UDL across subject areas and grade levels. Innovative uses of technology are highlighted.

Thormann, J., & Zimmerman, I. K. (2012). *The complete step-by-step guide to designing and teaching online courses.* New York, NY: Teachers College Press.

As the title says, this book is a guide to designing and teaching online. Included is information on course design, instructional strategies, community building, assessment and evaluation, and teaching diverse students. Templates and examples are offered.

Wright, V. H., Sunal, C. S., & Wilson, E. K. (Eds.). (2006). *Research on enhancing the interactivity of online learning.* Greenwich, CT: Information Age.

This edited book provides 11 chapters of studies ranging from assessment of student work to problem solving in the online environment, and creating collaborative learning environments.

15

SOCIAL MEDIA AND TEXTING

The Law and Considerations for School Policy

THEODORE B. CREIGHTON

Virginia Tech

M. DAVID ALEXANDER

Virginia Tech

Social media include a multitude of tools used for communicating via the Internet. Facebook, LinkedIn, Myspace, Twitter, YouTube and similar websites allow people to create profiles and connect with friends and those who share common interests. The services have exploded in popularity over the past decade; as of 2014, Facebook had more than 1 billion monthly users and Twitter had more than 270 million monthly users. People of all ages use social media, and teachers, students, and principals are no exception. A 2009 study of pre-service teachers found 98% of them were acquainted with various social networking sites and 88% had at least one social media account (Fulmer, 2011).

While students get most of the attention in discussions of schools and social media, some teachers have run into problems because of what they have posted online. As noted in an article in the *Duke Law and Technology Review*, "Public school teachers have little opportunity for redress if they are dismissed for their activities on social networking websites" (Fulmer, 2011, p. 1). The article concluded by arguing for legal protection for teachers to allow them to express themselves on social networking websites without fear of professional discipline. However,

holding teachers and other public school employees to a higher moral standard is nothing new. Teacher and administrator licensure include committing to moral codes prohibiting any conduct that might discredit the teaching profession.

Schools and school districts have begun to offer guidance for staff in using social media. On the Chicago Public Schools website, a page devoted to appropriate use of social media notes that only a school's principal can authorize an official school social media account and that principals are ultimately responsible for what the school posts on social media (Chicago Public Schools, n.d.). On the same webpage, the Chicago Public Schools has posted YouTube videos with suggestions on teaching social media etiquette and managing a school Twitter account.

This chapter uses existing **case law** on social media to help teachers and principals understand and utilize court decisions as they deal with the enormous impact social media are having in their schools. Legal precedents play a critical role in education and these court cases can help school leaders develop new policy or refine existing policy in regard to social media. Understanding precedents allows school leaders to analyze laws, policies, and practices and determine whether they are vulnerable to legal challenges (Sughrue & Driscoll, 2012).

However, the law has lagged behind technology, as it has throughout history. The printing press caused concerns that led to copyright laws. Telephones ushered in the concerns of privacy, especially over the early party lines that were shared by multiple phone service subscribers. Lyria Bennett Moses noted that "As technology changes and creates new possibilities, lawyers and legal scholars struggle to deal with the implications" (Moses, 2007, p. 239).

One of the first Supreme Court cases to deal with electronic communications and privacy was *City of Ontario v. Quon* (2010), in which the Court ruled the city had the authority to audit texts sent and received on a city pager. After finding a city police officer, Jeff Quon, sent an excessive amount of texts on a city-issued pager, it conducted an audit and found personal messages, some of them sexual in nature, on Quon's pager.

Several city employees, including Quon, filed suit claiming a violation of fundamental rights of privacy. The Court found that Quon's privacy rights were not violated but expressed concern that this decision should be narrowly drawn. Writing for the majority, Justice Anthony Kennedy stated, "The judiciary risks error by elaborating too fully on the Fourth Amendment implications of emerging technology before its role in society has become clear" (*Quon*, at pp. 2629–2630).

He continued:

Rapid changes in the dynamics of communication and information transmission are evident not just in the technology itself but in what society accepts as proper behavior. As one *amici* brief notes, many employers expect or at least tolerate personal use of such equipment by employees because it often increases worker efficiency. . . . At present, it is uncertain how workplace norms, and the law's treatment of them, will evolve. (*Quon,* at pp. 2629–2630)

Students

Legal Precedents Involving Students' Free Speech Rights

This explosion of technology has impacted decisions regarding student disciplinary matters. Therefore, school leaders have been making discipline decisions

about a new phenomenon without legal certainty. The Supreme Court has ruled that students have constitutional rights to free speech, in the landmark 1969 case *Tinker v. Des Moines Independent School District.* The students in this case wore black armbands to school to protest the Vietnam War. They were sent home and suspended until they would come back to school without their armbands. The Court ruled in favor of the students, stating that schools could regulate student speech only when it would interfere "materially and substantially" with the operation of the school and not simply to avoid "discomfort and unpleasantness." The Court also stated that the students' First Amendment rights did not extend if school officials could show "facts which might reasonably have led [them] to forecast substantial disruption of or material interference with school activities" (*Tinker* at p. 738).

Then, in 1986, the U.S. Supreme Court ruled in *Bethel School District v. Fraser* that lewd and indecent speech was not covered under the First Amendment. Mathew Fraser made a speech at a high school assembly that was filled with sexual innuendo, and the principal suspended him. The Court ruled for the school, determined that schools could discipline students for lewd and obscene language used while at school. The Court said that older students and teachers are role models and distinguished this case from *Tinker,* saying that *Tinker* involved political speech.

In 1988, the Supreme Court ruled in *Hazelwood School District v. Kuhlmeier* that the school could regulate the student newspaper and any other speech that related to the curriculum.

There is no magic number of students or classrooms that must be impacted in order to determine whether the disruption or potential disruption from students' speech meets what has become known as the *Tinker* test. In *J.S. ex rel v. Bethlehem Area School District* (2002) the Supreme Court of Pennsylvania noted disruption had to be more than "a mild distraction or curiosity created by the speech" but did not need to be "complete chaos."

The courts have considered several factors when determining whether the material and substantial disruption test has been met. The mere fact that students are discussing a particular subject in school is not sufficient to meet the substantial disruption standard. In *J.S.,* a student's website included violent and threatening comments and images, such as a drawing showing the teacher's head cut off with the caption, "why she should die." The court ruled the website caused disorder and impaired the delivery of instruction.

In 2007, the Supreme Court ruled in favor of the school in *Morse v. Frederick.* Joseph Frederick sued, claiming violation of his First Amendment rights, after he was disciplined for unfurling a banner that stated "Bong Hits for Jesus" while students were watching the Olympic torch pass through Juneau, Alaska. In the majority opinion, Chief Justice John Roberts wrote:

> School principals have a difficult job, and a vitally important one. When Frederick suddenly and unexpectedly unfurled his banner, Morse had to decide to act—or not act—on the spot. It was reasonable for her to conclude that the banner promoted illegal drug use—in violation of established school policy—and that failing to act would send a powerful message to the students in her charge, including Frederick, about how serious the school was about the danger of illegal drug use. The First Amendment does not require schools to tolerate at school events student expression that contributes to those dangers. (*Morse* at p. 2629)

Based on the *Tinker, Bethel, Hazelwood,* and *Morse* decisions, the limits on freedom of expression for students while in school can be described as follows: First, vulgar or plainly offensive speech may be prohibited without showing disruption or substantial interference with the operation of the school. Second, school-sponsored speech may be restricted when the limitation is reasonably related to legitimate educational concerns. Third, speech that is neither vulgar nor school-sponsored may be prohibited only if it causes a substantial and material disruption of the school's operation or a reasonable forecast of disruption. Fourth, school officials can limit speech that undermines efforts to discourage illegal drug use.

In the past 10 years, numerous court cases have involved students and social media or other forms of electronic communication. These cases have involved student blogging, Facebook, YouTube, Myspace, email, instant messaging, and text messaging. The courts have uniformly ruled that the *Bethel* standard applies only to lewd and obscene language if used on school property, not to vulgar electronic communication that originated off-campus. The Supreme Court in *Bethel v. Fraser* recognized that it did not extend "outside the school context." *Hazelwood* applies only to curriculum matters or items that pertain to "legitimate pedagogical concerns" and does not address

off-campus student activity. Likewise, *Morse* did not apply to off-campus activity. The only case that would apply to students who post online or send text messages while off campus would be *Tinker v. Des Moines.* School officials may take an action against the student if it "materially or substantially disrupts" the school or it can be factually shown that it is reasonable to cause disruption.

Cases Decided in Favor of the School

The following cases involved situations in which, courts ruled, the school could show disruption or forecast disruption. Therefore, the courts upheld the disciplinary actions taken by the schools.

S.J.W. v. Lee's Summit *(2012)*

The Lee's Summit R-7 School District in Missouri suspended twin brothers, Steven and Sean Wilson, for 180 days because of disruption caused by a website they created. The brothers created a blog called NorthPress that contained "offensive and racist comments as well as sexually explicit and degrading comments about particular female classmates, whom they identified by name" (*S.J.W.,* at p. 773). The brothers stated they only wanted a few friends to access the website but it quickly spread through the school, with the website being accessed from school computers.

The Wilsons filed suit against the district, alleging it violated their rights to free speech. They argued that "all off-campus speech is protected and cannot be the subject of school discipline, even if the speech is directed at the school or specified student" (at p. 776). The U.S. Court of Appeals for the Eighth Circuit ruled for the school district, noting the brothers' speech targeted the high school and could reasonably be expected to reach the school or impact the environment. Its ruling quoted *Tinker:*

> Conduct by the student, in class or out of it, which for any reason—whether it stems from time, place, or type of behavior—materially disrupts class work or involves substantial disorder or invasion of the rights of others is not immunized by the constitutional guarantee of freedom of speech. (393 U.S. 513, at 777–778).

Bell v. Itawamba County School Board *(2012)*

Taylor Bell, a senior at Itawamba Agricultural School in Mississippi, composed and published a rap song and posted it on Facebook, where his 1,300 "friends" could listen to it, and to YouTube, where anyone could listen. The rap song contained vulgar language and criticized two coaches, alleging improper conduct with female students.

The student was suspended for 7 days and transferred to an alternative school because the board found his action "threatened, harassed, and intimidated school employees." One coach heard about the rap song when his wife texted him. He testified that his teaching style had been adversely affected; the other coach testified he had lost student respect. Taylor Bell and his mother sued, arguing that school officials violated Taylor's First Amendment rights and his mother's 14th Amendment due-process rights.

U.S. District Court Judge Neal Biggers ruled in favor of the school district, saying that Bell intended for the song to reach the school as evidenced by his posting it for his Facebook friends, many of whom were students at the school. The court ruled that *Tinker* applied to this case and stated that the material and substantial disruption test can apply when the disruption is "reasonably foreseeable."

Kowalski v. Berkeley County Schools *(2011)*

Kara Kowalski, a high school senior in West Virginia, was suspended for creating and posting to a Myspace webpage on her home computer, "Students Against Sluts Herpes," which targeted a particular student for ridicule. After investigating, the school administration concluded Kowalski had created a "hate website." She was suspended for 10 days, and not allowed to attend school events. She also was prevented from crowning the next "Queen of Charm" as the student who was elected to the position the year before. Kowalski sued, contending the district violated her free speech and due process rights under the First and 14th Amendments.

The U.S. Court of Appeals for the Fourth Circuit ruled Kowalski's actions disrupted the school environment and her constitutional rights were not violated. When addressing her argument that this happened after school and at home the court stated,

> This argument, however, raises the metaphysical question of where her speech occurred when she used the Internet as the medium. Kowalski indeed pushed her computer's keys in her home, but she knew that the electronic response would be, as it in fact was, published beyond her home and could reasonably be expected to reach the school or impact the school environment.

Doninger v. Niehoff *(2011)*

A Connecticut school scheduled an event called "Jamfest," which featured a battle-of-the-bands concert. Avery Doninger and other students were involved in planning this event. After the date was selected, the administration found out that the individual who was responsible for lighting and sound in the auditorium could not attend. The administration gave the students the option of holding it in the cafeteria or finding a new date. This upset Doninger and fellow students who wanted the event in the auditorium on the scheduled date.

Doninger and several of the students decided to act; they gained access to an email account on a school computer, which was restricted by policy for school purposes only, and sent a mass email to parents and students, stating, "The Central Office [had] decided that the Student Council could not hold its annual Jamfest/Battle of the Bands in the auditorium." Please "contact [the] Central Office and ask that we be let [sic] to use the auditorium." The email listed phone numbers and urged people to call the central office.

The principal met with Doninger and told her the email had incorrect information and that sending the email from a school computer rather than working with the principal was "unbecoming" to a class officer. That night at home Doninger posted an item on her blog criticizing administrators. The principal called Doninger to the office and informed her that she was being removed as a candidate for senior class officer. Doninger sued, claiming a violation of her free speech.

The U.S. Court of Appeals for the Second Circuit ruled that the *Tinker* case applied and the facts supported disruption, citing a "deluge" of phone calls and emails, upset students gathered outside of administration offices, and students called out of class to discuss the emails. The facts also supported

> that Doninger's blog post directly pertained to an event at [the high school], that it invited other students to read and respond to it by contacting school officials, that students did in fact post comments on the post, and that school administrators demonstrated that it was reasonably foreseeable that Doninger's post would reach school property and have disruptive consequences here. (p. 348)

Wynar v. Douglas County School District *(2011)*

Landon Wynar, a high school student in Nevada, threatened several female students on his "hit list" during an instant message exchange with his friend,

J., another student. Concerned about the messages, J. forwarded them to another student, who contacted the high school administration. Wynar was subsequently arrested and removed from school pending an investigation.

Wynar argued that his First Amendment rights were violated because he was disciplined for off-campus speech. In his ruling, U.S. District Court Judge Larry R. Hicks upheld Wynar's expulsion and said: "A school may discipline or suppress speech if there are sufficient facts for school authorities to reasonably forecast the substantial disruption of, or material interference with, school activities."

The court found a reasonable basis for forecasting disruption of school activities. The ruling also noted that Wynar spoke of the Virginia Tech massacre, said he had access to guns and ammunition, and mentioned he was going to get the "record." He also mentioned a specific date. In 2013, the U.S. Court of Appeals for the Ninth Circuit upheld the lower court ruling.

Wisniewski v. Board of Education *(2007)*

From his parent's computer, Aaron Wisniewski, an eighth-grade student in upstate New York, used AOL Instant Messaging software to exchange messages with his buddies. Aaron's "buddy icon," or avatar, showed a bullet being fired at a person's head with corresponding blood splatter. The words that appeared underneath the drawing were "Kill Mr. VandeMolen," who was Aaron's English teacher. Students at Aaron's school had been instructed that threats were not allowed by school rules. A student who received the IM told Mr. VandeMolen, who was upset when he viewed the icon. The police investigated and concluded it was a joke; a psychologist found Aaron posed no threat. A hearing officer acknowledged the police and psychologist reports, and recommended Aaron be suspended and placed in an alternative school for one semester. The superintendent and school board confirmed the discipline.

The U.S. Court of Appeals, Second Circuit, ruled that even if the transmission of the icon were protected speech under *Tinker,* it had

> cross[ed] the boundary of protected speech and constitutes student conduct that poses a reasonable foreseeable risk that the icon would come to the attention of school authorities and that it would materially and substantially disrupt the work and discipline of the school. (*Wisniewski* at p. 38)

Cases Decided in Favor of the Student

R.S. v. Minnewaska Area School District *(2012)*

R.S., a 12 year old, sixth-grade student in Minnesota, posted disparaging comments about an adult hall monitor on her Facebook page while at home. The message was discovered by the principal, who called R.S. to his office and told her this was bullying. R.S. received detention and was made to apologize, and was later disciplined again for another post on Facebook complaining about whoever revealed the earlier post on the hall monitor. R.S. then was given a one-day suspension for "dangerously harmful and nuisance substances and articles."

Later, a boy's guardian told school administrators R.S. and the boy were communicating about sexual topics. A counselor, a deputy sheriff, and another school employee met with R.S. and demanded she provide them with her email and Facebook passwords; school officials logged on to her accounts and spent approximately 15 minutes searching through her communications. U.S. District Judge Michael J. Davis ruled there was no disruption, as per *Tinker,* and that school officials had violated R.S.'s First Amendment rights.

J.S. v. Blue Mountain School District *(2011)*

Eighth-grade student J.S. in Pennsylvania violated the school dress code twice, then created a fake profile of the principal on Myspace. The profile did not identify the school but did have a picture of the principal cut and pasted from the school website. The profile was presented as a self-portrayal of a bisexual Alabama middle school principal: "The profile contained crude content and vulgar language, ranging from nonsense and juvenile humor to profanity and shameful personal attacks aimed at the principal and his family" (*J. S.,* at p. 920).

J.S. was suspended for 10 days and prohibited from attending school dances. After a meeting where J.S.'s parent apologized, J.S. wrote an apology letter to the principal and his wife, but the parents filed suit claiming a violation of J.S.'s rights. The suspension was upheld by the superintendent. U.S. District Judge James M. Munley found for the student, saying that the student's speech "did not cause a substantial disruption in the school." The court also ruled that *Bethel* and *Morse* did not apply to student activity that occurs off campus.

The Third Circuit Court of Appeals heard the case and voted 8–6 to uphold. The majority noted that no one took the content of the fake profile seriously and stated, "The authority of public school officials is not boundless. . . . The First Amendment unquestionably protects the free speech rights of students in public schools." Several concurring judges went so far as to say that *Tinker* did not apply to off-campus student activities. "I would hold that [*Tinker*] does not [apply], and that the First Amendment protects students engaging in off-campus speech to the same extent it protects speech by citizens in the community-at-large."

The dissenting judges stated, "Today's holding severely undermines schools' authority to regulate students who materially and substantially disrupt the work and discipline of the school."

> The majority holds that [t]he facts in this case do not support the conclusion that a forecast of substantial disruption was reasonable. . . . But the majority makes light of the harmful effects of J.S.'s speech and the serious nature of allegations of sexual misconduct. Broadcasting a personal attack against a school official and his family online to the school community not only causes psychological harm to the targeted individuals but also undermines the authority of the school. It was permissible for the School District to discipline J.S. because substantial disruption was reasonably foreseeable. (*J. S.*, at p. 941)

The above dissenting judges stated that there was a lack of uniformity among the courts in measuring what is the standard for "material and substantial disruption."

Layshock v. Hermitage School District *(2011)*

The same day that the Third Circuit Court of Appeals handed down the decision in *J.S. v. Blue Mountain School District,* the same court also decided the *Layshock* case. Whereas in *J.S.* the decision was an 8–6 vote for the student, *Layshock* was a 14–0 vote for the student.

Justin Layshock, a senior at Hickory High School in Pennsylvania, sat at his grandmother's computer during nonschool hours and created a "parody profile" of his principal on Myspace. The profile gave bogus answers to a survey with questions about favorite shoes, pizza, and the like. The Q&A included: "Birthday: too drunk to remember," and "Are you a health freak: big steroid freak." Justin also took the principal's picture off the school website and posted it on Myspace.

The principal consulted the police, but no charges were filed. Justin was suspended for 10 days, placed in an alternative education program, banned from all extracurricular activities, and not allowed to participate in graduation.

The Layshocks filed suit, claiming violations of free speech and due process. The school argued that the Supreme Court's *Fraser* decision applied because the Myspace site was lewd and vulgar. The court rejected this argument and stated:

> It would be an unseemly and dangerous precedent to allow the state, in the guise of school authorities, to reach into a child's home and control his/her actions there to the same extent that it can control that child when he/she participates in school sponsored activities. Allowing the District to punish Justin for conduct he engaged in while at his grandmother's house using his grandmother's computer would create just such a precedent, and we therefore conclude that the district court correctly ruled that the District's response to Justin's expressive conduct violated the First Amendment guarantee of free expression. (*Layshock*, at p. 216)

T.V. v. Smith-Green Community School Corporation *(2011)*

During summer vacation two high school girls in Indiana had a slumber party and posted racy photos on Facebook, Myspace, and Photobucket. A parent brought the online pictures to the superintendent. The girls were suspended from cocurricular and extracurricular activities such as volleyball and show choir. The girls sued, arguing that school officials violated the First Amendment by punishing them for off-campus behavior. U.S. District Chief Judge Philip P. Simon ruled for the students, saying the activity was juvenile, silly, and provocative but nonetheless was protected by the First Amendment. In his ruling, Simon wrote: "The fact that adult school officials may not appreciate the approach to sexual themes the girls displayed actually supports the determination that the conduct was inherently expressive." Simon also stated the case did not meet the *Tinker* standard and that while there may have been disagreements among the volleyball players, that did not establish disruption.

Evans v. Bayer *(2010)*

Katherine Evans, a high school senior in Florida, posted on her Facebook page: "Ms. Sarah Phelps is the worst teacher I've ever met! To those select students who have had the displeasure of having Ms. Sarah Phelps, or simply knowing her and her insane antics: Here is the place to express your feelings of hatred." The page included Phelps's photo; some students posted comments supporting Phelps; some students agreed with the posting.

The principal suspended Evans for 3 days and removed her from her Advanced Placement classes. The principal cited the previously decided *Doninger* case where the court stated:

> If courts and legal scholars cannot discern the contours of First Amendment protections for student internet speech, then it is certainly unreasonable to expect school administrators, such as Defendants, to predict where the line between on- and off-campus speech will be drawn in this new digital era. (Doninger v. Niehoff, 594 F. Supp. 2d 211, 224 (D. Conn. 2009))

Evans claimed she was engaged in an off-campus activity that was protected by free speech. The court ruled that Evans's speech was protected and that it had been abridged by the principal. There was no finding of disruption as per *Tinker,* and U.S. Magistrate Judge Barry L. Garber stated in his ruling: "A mere desire to avoid discomfort or unpleasantness will not suffice. . . . [T]he government may not prohibit student speech based solely upon the emotive impact that its offensive content may have on the listener."

J.C. v. Beverly Hills Unified School District *(2010)*

J.C., a high school student in California, and several students gathered in a local restaurant after school, and J.C. recorded a 4-minute and 30-second video of her friends talking. A friend used profanity during the recording. J. C. encouraged the others to continue.

That evening, J.C. posted the video on YouTube from her home computer. J.C. contacted her friends and told them to look at the video. School officials investigated the video and J.C. was suspended. J.C. sued, claiming a violation of her First Amendment rights by punishing her for the YouTube posting. The U.S. District Court for the Central District of California found the school's discipline violated the student's First Amendment rights, stating:

> Based on the undisputed facts, and viewing all reasonable inferences in favor of the [school], the Court finds no reasonable jury could conclude that J. C.'s YouTube

video caused a substantial disruption of school activities, or that there was a reasonably foreseeable risk of substantial disruption as a result of the YouTube video.

Teachers

The news media have reported on many instances of teachers who have been disciplined or dismissed for posting on social media or other forms of electronic communication. Some teachers have claimed it was a violation of their free speech rights when they were dismissed over online postings or communications with students. If a student claims a free speech right, the court generally accepts it as free speech whether it is a Facebook or Myspace posting or passing out literature at school. But as relates to their employment, teachers' speech is protected only when they are speaking as citizens and it is a matter of public concern. Students' speech rights are more closely akin to those the general public, whereas teachers' speech is constrained by the fact that they are public employees. The Supreme Court has rendered decisions on the free speech rights of students; likewise it has decided on free speech issues involving teachers. The Supreme Court in *Garcetti v. Ceballos* (2006) emphasized this point when they said:

> Many citizens do much of their talking inside their respective workplaces, and it would not serve the goal of treating public employees like "any member of the general public," . . . to hold that all speech within the office is automatically exposed to restriction.

One of the first cases involving public employees' speech rights went before the Supreme Court in 1968 (*Pickering v. Board of Education,* 1968). Marvin Pickering, a high school teacher in Illinois, was dissatisfied with the way the school board allocated funding and wrote to the local newspaper criticizing the board. The school board dismissed Pickering for writing the letter because it "impugned the motives, honesty, integrity, truthfulness, responsibility and competence" of the school board and superintendent.

The Court determined that a teacher had the right to speak out without being dismissed from his or her position, but only as a citizen on matters of public concern. Writing for the majority, Justice Thurgood Marshall said: "This Court [Supreme] has also indicated that statements by public officials on matters of public concern must be accorded First Amendment protection despite the fact that the statements are directed at their nominal superiors." It was also important that the *Pickering* criticism was not aimed directly at someone with whom the teacher worked closely.

> The statements are in no way directed towards any person with whom [the Teacher] would normally be in contact in the course of his daily work as a teacher. Thus no question of maintaining either discipline by immediate superiors or harmony among coworkers is presented here. [The Teacher's] employment relationships with the Board and, to a somewhat lesser extent, with the superintendent are not the kind of close working relationships for which it can persuasively be claimed that personal loyalty and confidence are necessary to their proper functioning. (*Pickering*, at p. 1735)

Therefore, a school has a right to have an orderly organization even if the teacher is speaking on a matter of public concern. In the majority opinion, Marshall wrote:

> The problem in any case is to arrive at a balance between the interests of the teacher, as a citizen, in commenting upon matters of public concern and the interest of the State, as an employer, in promoting the efficiency of the public services it performs through its employees.

The teacher who claims that being disciplined over a Facebook posting was a violation of his or her free speech rights must show that he or she was speaking a as citizen on a matter of public concern, and that it did not disrupt the educational environment.

In 1977, the Supreme Court again addressed the free speech rights of public employees in *Mt. Healthy City School District v. Doyle* (1977). This case was different from *Pickering* in that it raised the issue of a free speech constitutional right being present at the same time that a nonconstitutional right was involved. This case illustrates the Court's development of the *mixed motive test,* in which there are constitutional rights and nonconstitutional rights involved in the same incident. In these instances, the school board needs to set aside the constitutional rights and ask the question: "Is there enough evidence based on the nonconstitutional rights to terminate the employee?" In other words, if constitutional rights are involved, and the teacher is speaking out as a citizen on a matter of public concern, then the board must show disruption to negate these rights or have other nonconstitutional issues to dismiss.

Fred Doyle, an untenured teacher, was elected president of the teacher's association and then served on its executive committee. There was a history of tension between Doyle and the school board. Several incidents occurred before his contract was nonrenewed; he was involved in an argument with another teacher and the teacher slapped Doyle, and both were suspended for one day; he then argued with school cafeteria workers over the amount of spaghetti he was served; he called some students "sons of bitches"; and he made obscene gestures toward two female students when they did not obey him in the cafeteria. And, when the principal sent out a memo relating to teacher dress and appearance, Doyle conveyed the substance of the memo to a local radio station and called the station to discuss the teacher dress policy.

Subsequently, the superintendent recommended not rehiring Doyle. The letter read:

> You have shown a notable lack of tact in handling professional matters which leaves much doubt as to your sincerity in establishing good school relationships. A. You assumed the responsibility to notify W.S.A.I. Radio Station in regards to the suggestion of the Board of Education that teachers establish an appropriate dress code for professional people. This raised much concern not only within this community, but also in neighboring communities. B. You used obscene gestures to correct students in a situation in the cafeteria causing considerable concern among those students present. (*Mt. Healthy*, at p. 574)

Since a free speech issue was involved, the legal question was Doyle's speaking out at the radio station criticizing the dress policy. If this issue were not considered, would the school board have fired Doyle for the other incidents, such as obscene gestures, fighting with cafeteria workers, and so on? If a free speech issue is involved, then it must not be considered separately unless the action disrupts the school environment; therefore, the mixed motive test.

The Supreme Court again took up free speech rights for public employees in *Connick v. Myers* (1983). Sheila Myers, an assistant district attorney in New Orleans, received notification of her transfer to another division within the district attorney's office. After expressing reluctance to accept the transfer, she arrived at the office with a questionnaire for fellow assistant district attorneys with questions about morale, level of confidence in supervisors, and other questions about how the office was run.

The Court found that these were not matters of public concern. In a 5–4 vote, the Court held Myers's dismissal to be constitutional. The Court, citing *Pickering v. Board of Education,* said, "a public employee does not relinquish First Amendment rights to comment on matters of public interest by virtue of government employment" (*Connick,* at p. 1686). But, the state also has an interest in regulating the speech of public employees and this state need "differs significantly from those it possesses in connection with regulation of the speech of the citizenry in general" (*Connick,* at p. 1686).

The majority of the Court found that the manner, time, and place of passing out the questionnaire had great potential for disruption of the office. In this case, the employer did not need to tolerate office disruption undermining authority or destroying work relationships. The majority opinion, in discussing matters of public concern, stated: "Whether an employee's speech addresses a matter of public concern must be determined by the content, form, and context of a given statement, as revealed by the whole record." If, after reviewing the content, form, and context, the matter an employee discussed is determined to be a matter of public concern, then the *Pickering* balance test is introduced. The balance is between having an orderly organization with no disruption and the employee's free speech. Free speech ends where disruption begins.

In 2006, the Supreme Court decided *Garcetti v. Ceballos,* which established a new element regarding whether an issue is of public concern. "When public employees make statements pursuant to their official duties, they are not speaking as citizens for First Amendment purposes, and the Constitution does not insulate their communications from employer discipline." Therefore, speech "pursuant to official duties" entered into public employee free speech litigation.

Richard Ceballos was a deputy district attorney with supervisory responsibilities. He was asked by a defense attorney to review apparent inaccuracies in an affidavit to obtain a search warrant. After examining the affidavit Ceballos determined there were serious misrepresentations that led him to conclude the warrant was not valid.

After presenting this information to District Attorney Gil Garcetti and to the sheriff and his staff, a heated discussion took place as to the validity of the affidavit; Garcetti agreed with the sheriff instead of Ceballos. The district attorney's office

proceeded with prosecuting the case that involved the search warrant and Ceballos was called as a defense witness to discuss the warrant's affidavit. Ceballos was then reassigned from his position to a trial position in another location at another courthouse. Ceballos filed suit, saying his free speech rights had been abridged and this had been a retaliatory action.

In a 5–4 decision, the Court rejected Ceballos's argument and in its majority opinion stated Ceballos was not speaking as a citizen but rather as part of his duties. The Court in *Garcetti v. Ceballos* addressed a public employee's free speech rights when it stated:

> *Pickering* and the cases decided in its wake identify two inquiries to guide interpretation of the constitutional protections accorded to public employee speech. The *first* requires determining whether the employee spoke as a citizen on a matter of public concern. . . . If the answer is *no* [emphasis], the employee has no First Amendment cause of action based on his or her employer's reaction to the speech. . . . If the answer is *yes* then the possibility of a First Amendment claim arises. The question becomes whether the relevant government entity had an adequate justification for treating the employee differently from any other member of the general public.
>
> This consideration reflects the importance of the relationship between the speaker's expressions and employment. A government entity has broader discretion to restrict speech when it acts in its role as employer, but the restrictions it imposes must be directed at speech that has some potential to affect the entity's operations.

The majority opinion went on to note that those who enter government service must accept certain limitations on their freedom.

> Government offices could **not** function if every employment decision became a constitutional matter. Public employees, moreover, often occupy trusted positions in society. When they speak out, they can express views that contravene governmental policies or impair the proper performance of governmental functions. (*Garcetti,* at p. 1958)

Cases Decided in Favor of the School

In re O'Brien *(2013)*

Jennifer O'Brien, a teacher in New Jersey, posted two statements on Facebook: "I'm not a teacher— I'm a warden for future criminals," and "They had a scared straight program in school—why couldn't [I] bring [first] graders." O'Brien was recommended for dismissal based on "conduct unbecoming a teacher." At a hearing, O'Brien stated she posted on Facebook out of frustration. She had recently been hit by a student, had students hitting each other, and had items stolen from her classroom; she said six or seven students contributed to the majority of the behavior problems. She also apologized for the postings.

O'Brien appealed the decision of the state commissioner of education upholding her dismissal, and claimed her Facebook postings were protected by the First Amendment. The Superior Court of New Jersey Appellate Division ruled that O'Brien was not speaking as a citizen on a matter of public concern, which is constitutionally protected; but, even if her speech were a matter of public concern and therefore protected, she still would have been dismissed because of the disruption caused by the postings.

San Diego Unified School District v. Commission on Professional Competence *(2011)*

Frank Lampedusa, a San Diego Unified School District tenured teacher, was terminated for immoral conduct. The teacher had posted on Craigslist an ad soliciting sex in the "Men seeking Men" category; also included were graphic photos showing his genitalia and anus. The teacher testified he did not believe his actions were immoral, and he acknowledged he would continue to place ads soliciting sex. The Fourth District Court of Appeal ruled the teacher's actions were immoral and upheld his firing.

Spanierman v. Hughes *(2008)*

Jeffrey Spanierman, a nontenured teacher in Connecticut, created a Myspace page called "Mr. Spiderman" that he used to communicate with students about homework and conduct casual discussions. After receiving student complaints, another teacher and the school counselor looked at the account and were disturbed by, among other things, pictures of naked men. The teacher was asked to communicate with students using the school email account instead of MySpace. The teacher removed

the page, but then put up another page as "Apollo 68" with the same material.

The school decided not to renew the teacher's contract. The school presented several pieces of evidence, which included communications between the teacher and his students that included joking about sex.

U.S. District Court Judge Dominic J. Squatrito ruled that it was not unreasonable for the defendants to find that the plaintiff's conduct on Myspace was disruptive to school activities. In his ruling, Squatrito wrote:

> The online exchanges the Plaintiff had with students show a potentially unprofessional rapport with students, and the court can see how a school's administration would disapprove of, and find disruptive, a teacher's discussion with a student about "getting any" (presumably sex), or a threat made to a student (albeit a facetious one) about detention. (*Spanierman*, p. 312)

Cases Decided in Favor of the Teacher

Land v. L'Anse Creuse Public School Board of Education *(2010)*

A school board in Michigan terminated Anna Land, a tenured middle school teacher, after students gained access to photographs of the teacher at a summer party. The photos showed the teacher engaged in a simulated act of fellatio with a male mannequin at a bachelor/bachelorette party. The party took place at an annual public gathering of boats on an island approximately 10 minutes from the school district. The photos were taken approximately 2 years before they surfaced, were taken without the teacher's knowledge, and were posted without her consent. The photos were subsequently removed, but the superintendent recommended she be dismissed and was backed by an administrative law judge. Land appealed to the state Tenure Commission, which ruled in her favor, and the school board then appealed its ruling.

The Michigan Court of Appeals found for the teacher, noting the photo was taken 2 years prior at a public event, was not an illegal act, did not involve students or any school personnel, and was not part of the teacher's duties. It was noted she was an excellent teacher who went above and beyond to assist students and parents.

Rubino v. City of New York *(2013)*

A New York City student drowned on a school-sponsored field trip. Christine Rubino, a tenured teacher at another New York City school, posted on Facebook, "After today, I am thinking the beach sounds like a wonderful idea for my 5th graders! I HATE THEIR GUTS! They are devils [*sic*] spawn." A friend replied, "oh you would let little Kwame float away." The teacher responded, "Yes, I wld [*sic*] not throw a life jacket in for a million!!"

Rubino was recommended for termination. She sued claiming, among other things, that her dismissal violated her First Amendment right to free speech. New York state Supreme Court Justice Barbara Jaffe ruled in 2012 that Rubino should not have been terminated. Addressing the free speech argument, the ruling stated: "[The] Facebook postings do not constitute protected speech insofar as [it]. . . . was decided that [the teacher] posted the comments as a teacher and that the comments did not pertain to a matter of public concern" (*Rubino*, at p. 1).

However, even though no First Amendment right was involved, the court ruled that the teacher's dismissal was "shocking to one's sense of fairness" given the teacher's lack of prior disciplinary history. While stating that the comments were inappropriate, the court noted that she was discussing an incident involving a different school, none of her students or their parents were part of her friends network on Facebook, and she had since deleted the comments. In 2013, the New York Appellate Division, First Department, upheld the lower court's ruling.

Cases Involving Criminal Charges Against Teachers

There have been several cases where teachers are charged with criminal offenses resulting from their communication with students using social media or text messages. Teachers are not only at risk of losing their teaching licenses but also of serving prison sentences. In one case, *Hammons v. State* (2010), Sherman Lee Hammons, a Texas high school teacher who sent sexually explicit text messages to a student, was convicted of an improper relationship with a student and sentenced to 10 years in prison. The teacher claimed he had a First Amendment right of free speech to text a student if he and the student were

not in school, but the Court of Appeals for the Sixth Appellate District in Texas upheld his conviction.

Conclusion

Teachers and principals in U.S. schools are charged with and expected to do many things. Some would posit that each of the two roles and responsibilities have mushroomed in scope over the last decade to a daunting level. The authors of this chapter have spent their professional lives preparing teachers and principals for the many tasks and responsibilities they face daily in schools, and have observed that the elements and components of effective teacher and principal preparation change dramatically from year to year. In recent years, preparing teachers and principals for the ramifications of social media on schools has been added to the list.

This chapter reviews the challenges faced by teachers and principals in the area of social media and provides information about case law to help administrators dealing with these ramifications in their schools. Schools also can educate students about social media so that they fully understand the risks involved. Many may not understand that, for example, sharing an item on Facebook with "friends of friends" could expose the post to tens of thousands of other Facebook users. By helping students better understand social media, schools can not only head off potential disruption at school but help students prevent their posts from causing problems in their own lives.

Key Chapter Terms

Case law: Legal decision serving as an authoritative rule or pattern in future similar or analogous cases. Case law provides guidance to those who enact and execute statutory law; case law produces precedents, which provide guidance to lower courts that will adjudicate the legal issue in the future.

Social media: Include a multitude of tools used for communicating via the Internet. Social media sites allow users to create profiles and connect with friends, those with shared interests, or both.

References

Alexander, K., & Alexander, M. D. (2012). *American public school law.* Belmont, CA: Wadsworth Cengage Learning.

Chicago Public Schools (n.d.). *Guidance on school social media.* Retrieved from http://www.cps.edu/pages/socialmediatoolkit.aspx

Fulmer, E. (2011). Privacy expectations and protections for teachers in the Internet age. *Duke Law and Technology Review, 9*(1), 1–31. Available at http://scholarship.law.duke.edu/dltr/vol9/iss1/13/

Moses, L. B. (2007). Recurring dilemmas: The law's race to keep up with technological change. *University of Illinois Journal of Law, Technology and Policy,* 239–285. Retrieved from http://www.jltp.uiuc.edu/archives/moses.pdf.

Sughrue, J., & Driscoll, L. (2012). Legal research in the context of educational leadership and policy studies. *Education Leadership Review, 13*(2). Retrieved from http://www.ncpeapublications.org/vol-13-no-2-october-2012/511-legal-research-in-the-context-of-educational-leadership-and-policy-studies.html

Court Decisions

Bell v. Itawamba County School Board, 859 F.Supp.2d 834 (M.D. Miss. 2012)

Bethel School District v. Fraser, 478 U.S. 675 (1986)

Chaney v. Fayette County Public School District, ___F. Supp.2d ___, 2013 WL 5486829 (N.D. Ga. 2013)

City of Ontario, California v. Quon, 130 S.Ct. 2619 (2010)

City of San Diego v. Roe, 125 S.Ct. 521 (2004)

Connick v. Myers, 461 U.S. 138 (1983)

Doe v. Fournier, 851 F.Supp2d 207 (D.Mass. 2102)

Doninger v. Niehoff, 594 F.Supp.2d 211, 224 (D. Conn.2009)

Evans v. Bayer, 684 F.Supp.2d 1365 (S.D. Fla.2010)

Garcetti v. Ceballos, 547 U.S.410, 126 S.Ct. 1951 (2006)

Hammons v. State, ___S.W. 3d__, 2010 WL 241577 (Tex.App.—Texarkana 2010)

Hazelwood School District v. Kuhlmeier, 484 U.S.260, 108 S.Ct. 562 (1988)

J.C. v. Beverly Hills Unified School District, __ F.Supp. 2d__, 2010 WL1914215 (C.D.Cal 2010)

J.S. ex rel v. Bethlehem Area Sch. Dist., 807 A. 2d 847 (S.Ct. Pa 2002)

J.S. v. Blue Mountain School District, 650 F.3d 915 (3rd Cir. 2011)

Kowalski v. Berkeley County Schools, 652 F.3d 565 (4th Cir. 2011)

Land v. L'Anse Creuse Public School Board of Education, __N.W. 2d__, 2010 WL 2135356 (Mich.App. 2010)

Layshock v. Hermitage School District, 650 F.3d 205 (3rd Cir. 2011)

Morse v. Frederick, 551 U.S.393, 127 S.Ct. 2618 (2007)

Mt. Healthy City School District Board of Education v. Doyle, 429 US 274, 97 S.Ct. 568, (1977)

In re O'Brien, __A 3d__, 2013 WL 132508 (S.Ct. N.J. App. Div 2013)

Pickering v. Board of Education of Township High School District 205, 361 U.S. 563, 88 S.Ct. 1731 (1968)

R.S. v. Minnewaska Area School District No. 2149, 894 F.Supp. 2d 1129, 2012 WL 3870868 (D. Minn. 2012)

Rubino v. City of New York, N.Y.S.2d, 2013 WL 1876235 (N.Y.A.D. 1 Dept. 2013).

San Diego Unified School District v. Commission of Professional Competence, 194 Cal.Rptr. 4th 1454 (Cal.Ct.App. 4th Dist, Div. 1, 2011)

S.J.W. v. Lee's Summit R-7 School District, 696 F3d 771 (8th Cir. 2012)

Spanierman v. Hughes, 576 F.Supp. 2d 292 (D.Conn. 2008)

Tinker v. Des Moines Independent School District, 393 U.S. 503, 89 S.Ct. 733 (1969)

T.V. v. Smith-Green Community School Corporation, 807 F.Supp2d 767, (N.D. Ind. 2011).

Wisniewski v. Board of Education of the Weedsport Central School District, 494 F.3d 34 (2nd Cir. 2007)

Wynar v. Douglas County School District, __F. Supp.2d__, 2011 WL 3512534(D.Nev. 2011)

Further Readings

Alexander, K., & Alexander, M. D. (2012). *American public school law.* Belmont, CA: Wadsworth Cengage Learning.

This seminal text on school law reviews key laws and court decisions and their implications for educational leaders.

Sughrue, J., & Driscoll, L. (2012). Legal research in the context of educational leadership and policy studies. *Education Leadership Review, 13*(2). Retrieved from http://www.ncpeapublications.org/vol-13-no-2-october-2012/511-legal-research-in-the-context-of-educational-leadership-and-policy-studies.html

The article asserts the critical role legal research plays in education policy and practice and unmasks the supposed mystery that averts many graduate students from conducting legal research.

PART VI

BUDGETING, FINANCE, AND FUND-RAISING

16

UNDERSTANDING SCHOOL FINANCE LAWS AND PRACTICES

ERIC A. HOUCK

University of North Carolina at Chapel Hill

The dynamics of school finance encompass broader political agendas and activities as well as a broad array of funding streams and expenditure categories; each, it seems, with its own subset of regulations and traditions. School-level administrators experiencing the funding formula from a practitioner's perspective may feel as if they are attempting to drink water from a fire hose. How can they be expected to spend undefined sums of cash in their last month of school operations with an admonition to "use it or lose it"? How can it be that funds in one category cannot be used to replace vital school supplies at a vital time in the school year? Similarly, central office administrators must feel as if they are confronted with a Byzantine set of rules and regulations such as: Who decides how many teacher and staff positions are to exist at a given school? Why is **Title I** funding allocated per pupil but distributed as the district decides? And, will funding lost to charter enrollments be offset by fewer children attending traditional public schools?

The purpose of this chapter is to illuminate—to the extent possible—the manner in which educational funds are collected and distributed. The chapter first briefly describes the context of educational funding and then introduces four values that bound discussions of school finance issues and have implications for school administrators: **equity**, **efficiency**, **liberty**, and **adequacy**. The chapter also introduces a conceptual shift from school finance to **resource allocation** as a profitable framework from which school administrators may work, even in the face of limited resources and tightly controlled school budgets. Despite the wide array of policies across all 50 U.S. states, considering finance policies via these lenses provides administrators with a useful tool for considering how they can allocate fiscal and human resources in educational environments.

One of the subtexts of this chapter is that schools may be understood via nonrational or "garbage can" theories of organizations as well as from public choice theories in economics (Cohen, March, & Olsen, 1972; Ostrom, 1998). In each of these theoretical approaches, policy actors such as school administrators often—individually or collectively—respond to a complicated set of conflicting external stimuli. This basket of stimuli may broadly be considered a market, albeit not an economic one, in the sense that administrators attempt to find an equilibrium point between conflicting pressures.

Therefore, while external observers may disagree with—or be confused by—the actions of an administrator, more often than not those actions are internally logically consistent. This chapter seeks to make explicit for administrators the forces at work on their decision making from a school finance perspective and to provide a set of touchstones by which administrators can make their decisions transparent—to both themselves and their constituencies.

The Context of School Funding

Before describing the manifold laws and policies that bound school administrators' experience of school finance in public education, it is important to take a moment to understand the policy context within which administrators now find themselves. Administrators will acknowledge that we live in an era of "big data" more generally, and of **standards-based reform** in education specifically. By understanding this context, administrators may be able to understand the impact of school finance policies on their daily work. The sections that follow outline the development of the particular set of circumstances that contributed to the development and spread of this school reform paradigm.

Many scholars identify a shift in public and academic thinking about public education occurring around 1983, the year in which the National Commission on Excellence in Education published *A Nation at Risk,* a report that lamented the state of public education in America on the basis of international comparisons and curricular and public opinion surveys (National Commission on Excellence in Education, 1983). While some feel as if the purpose of the report was more to manipulate public opinion than to inform it (see, for example, Berliner & Biddle, 1996), most agree that it effectively placed public education reform squarely in the public's mind.

Not surprisingly, this shift affected the field of school finance as well. Until the early 1980s, the field of school finance was mostly concerned with the way in which money was raised and distributed across states and districts. Critical topics of inquiry involved the disparity of funding across states, the disparity of funding within states, and the development of appropriate models to allocate funds while acknowledging the fact that some classes of students entered school with significant social disadvantages. While researchers still examine these topics today, the focus of school finance studies has shifted to examinations of the manner in which money is used in schools, and the results of that overall spending in terms of student academic achievement. This has been termed the shift from equity to adequacy in school finance (Clune, 1994). This shift has implications for the funding of nontraditional educational alternatives such as charter schools, virtual schools, and voucher programs.

The critiques of school systems in *A Nation at Risk* also reflect a shift in values for school finance scholars. After *A Nation at Risk,* the focus of educational reformers shifted toward values of efficiency, adequacy, and liberty, and away from the value of equity.

Trends in School Finance: Moving Toward Resource Allocation

Understanding school finance is founded upon one core contradiction—that although school finance lies, as Ellwood Cubberley noted in 1905, "aback" of almost every other initiative in education policy and reform, the ability of administrators to make change by leveraging large amounts of available funds is almost nonexistent (Cubberley, 1905). Put another way: The allocation of actual dollars to educational initiatives usually occurs only at the highest levels of the policy process, far away from the **street-level bureaucrats** of district and school administrators (Lipsky, 2010). School- and district-level administrators are far more likely to have authority to work with the human and physical resources purchased by these dollars through school funding formulas than to have control over actual dollars. Therefore, a significant part of the work of school finance researchers is engaged with the notion of resource allocation—finding ways that administrators can manipulate the **purchased inputs** that result from school funding decisions. In many cases, this means teachers and personnel. The implication is that finance policy, when practiced by administrators, is human resource policy—the allocation of humans across educational systems to best benefit children and their learning. As **Figure 16.1** illustrates, personnel salaries and benefits consistently account for approximately 85 cents of every instructional dollar spent on public education in the United States.

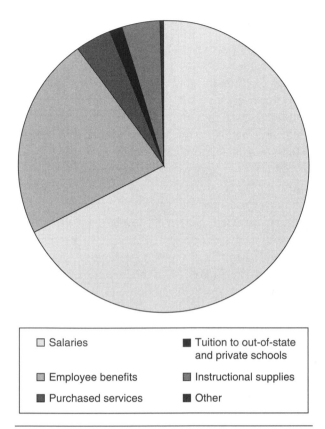

Salaries

Employee benefits

Purchased services

Tuition to out-of-state and private schools

Instructional supplies

Other

Figure 16.1 Current Instruction Expenditures for Public Elementary and Secondary Education, by Object and State or Jurisdiction: Fiscal Year 2009

SOURCE: U.S. Department of Education, National Center for Education Statistics, Common Core of Data (CCD), "National Public Education Financial Survey (NPEFS)," fiscal year 2009, Version 1a.

Whether measured in actual dollars or school personnel, the work of school finance research is bounded by four key values—often in tension with each other—that define the compromises and tradeoffs administrators must make.

Competing Values in School Finance

Many leadership preparation programs for educational administrators place the primary value orientation of their programs on the value of equity. However, scholars of school finance see most policy decisions as points located in tension (or equilibrium) between four values. This chapter endeavors to develop a broad notion of resource allocation and of the ideas encompassed by the four values represent a

resource allocation heuristic that may be helpful to administrators across many different systems. The sections that follow provide an overview of the four values that bound the field of school finance: equity, efficiency, adequacy, and liberty.

Equity: The value of equity refers to the degree of fairness of the allocation of resources across schools and districts. In school finance, scholars distinguish between different types of equity. **Horizontal equity** is often conceived of as simple fairness. It can be considered the "kindergarten rule"—you need to have a cookie for everyone. Horizontal equity is considered a baseline of fairness in the allocation of resources. A stricter definition of equity, however, demands more of educational systems. The concept of **vertical equity** is used to define the idea that differently situated students need to be treated differently; specifically, higher needs students ought to receive additional resources. Federal Title I legislation, which provides federal funding for impoverished students, is one example of a vertically equitable funding policy. Some states also include vertically equitable funding provisions in their state funding policies.

Efficiency: **Technical efficiency** refers to the amount of output or level of performance one gains from a specific investment of resources. In this conception of efficiency, an additional dollar invested in school systems should result in some marginal uptick in overall system performance. Although this conception works well in private and corporate environments, determining the efficiency of public systems such as public schools is significantly more complicated. Therefore, school finance researchers also focus on a notion of **allocative efficiency**, which examines the range of outputs produced for a specific investment level. These additional outputs would include not only test scores, but other measures such as overall climate, health, safety, and more.

Adequacy: The concept of adequacy in school finance is relatively new and is contested. Some experts consider adequacy to be an output-oriented notion of equity, and refer to it as **"equity II"** (Guthrie, Springer, Rolle, & Houck, 2006). Others consider adequacy to be a notion of sufficiency, in the manner of an amount of funding sufficient for a student to learn one year's worth of material in the span of one academic year, with adjustments made for different student types and backgrounds (Reschovsky & Imazeki, 2003). Great strides in school finance around notions of adequacy have resulted from an increasing reliance upon standardized performance measures that have developed since *A Nation at Risk*.

Liberty: Most educators today equate the notion of liberty with that of "school choice" and current controversies around charter schools, private school vouchers, and other choice-based programs and policies. Such policies reflect transfers of public funds away from the traditional public education finance system and are therefore not discussed here. There is another conception of liberty, incorporated into the **federalist** system whereby educational authority is devolved to the states and from the states to local districts: the notion of **subsidiarity**—that each layer of educational governance will want maximum freedom to act from the layer of governance above it. Here we see that school principals want maximum discretion from districts, districts from states, and states from the federal government. This notion of liberty is part of the political underpinning of the policies discussed in this chapter.

The Values in Tension

School finance researchers assert that formal and informal policies exist in tension among these four values. Take the issue of class size, for an example. The ratio of pupils to teachers in schools and districts is often used as a proxy resource allocation. Research suggests that smaller class sizes benefit student learning, especially among high-needs students (Fredriksson, Öckert, & Oosterbeek, 2013). Therefore, it would seem that reducing class sizes and pupil-teacher ratios is an unmitigated good. Yet some research suggests that reducing class sizes to 18 students is sufficient to boost student learning, and that additional class-size reduction results in the hiring of higher proportions of ineffective teachers (Jepsen & Rivkin, 2009).

Is it equitable, then, to reduce class sizes to 20 students per teacher, or is that effort simply an inefficient use of funds? Should class size be mandated from state or district central offices? Or are decisions on pupil-teacher ratios best made by principals given the flexibility to make the best educational

decisions possible? There are of course, no right answers to these questions. Administrators who prefer one value over others will locate their preferred policies at different points. It is important to recognize, however, that identifying and articulating the manner in which concepts of equity, efficiency, adequacy, and liberty inform educational policy debates at state, district, and school levels is a helpful framework for educators to have at their disposal.

Understanding School Finance Laws

Revenue for public school operations is generated via **taxes**. The modern federal **income tax** system, combined with the state income tax, **sales tax**, and local **property tax**, can sometimes seem hopelessly complex and labyrinthine. Sadly, for this reason, many school and district administrators show little concern for the manner in which revenue is generated, understandably concerning themselves more with the critical issue of whether the revenue generated is of a sufficient amount to support a high-quality instructional program. However, different kinds of taxes have different characteristics that, when examined, come to have important implications for school administrators. This section discusses the types of taxes that generally are used to raise funds for school operations, and then discusses the different methods of generating revenue for school construction and maintenance.

Revenue Generation

Schools are funded from multiple sources for multiple reasons. The first point to understand is that federal funding for public education is restrained by the **10th Amendment to the U.S. Constitution**, which states that "The powers not delegated to the United States by the Constitution, nor prohibited by it to the States, are reserved to the States respectively, or to the people." While a federal role in funding public education has developed over time—mostly through Title I of the Elementary and Secondary Education Act (ESEA) of 1965—the net result of the 10th Amendment has been that public education finance is an experiment in federalism, with each of the 50 states maintaining a system of state and local provision for public education. The degree to which states provide funding for education, the manner in which that support is provided, and the parameters by which local districts raise their own revenues is the principal focus of the rest of this section. Understanding revenue generation for schools can help administrators serve as an outward face to the community, a buffer against threats to the core technology of the organization, and an advocate for those policies and practices that result in a healthy public school environment for children. An administrator who stood idly by while his or her local district shifted the burden of revenue generation away from homeowners and onto consumers through a greater reliance on the sales tax, for example, would not be fulfilling these roles.

While the federalist nature of education funding ensures wide variation across states, data from the Education Finance Statistics Center of the National Center for Education Statistics indicates that in the 2010–2011 academic year, of all funds generated for education, approximately 43% came from local sources (the minimum from local sources was 2.6%—Hawaii, and the maximum local contribution was the District of Columbia's 88.2%); the revenue contribution from state sources was 44.1% (minimum of 29.1%—South Dakota—and a maximum of 83.4%—Hawaii); and educational revenue from federal sources averaged 12.5% (with a minimum of 5.3%—New Jersey—and a maximum of 20.3%—South Dakota) (NCES, 2013a, 2013b).

A vast majority of this revenue is generated via taxes. Much like school finance laws, however, not all taxes are created equal. Each type of tax used to generate educational revenue has particular characteristics that make that tax more or less desirable under certain conditions. The goal of any revenue generation system for public goods and services is to create a balanced "portfolio" of taxation whereby the positive qualities of taxes are emphasized while their pitfalls are minimized.

Revenue for public education is generated via three main forms of taxation: the income tax, the property tax, and the sales tax. Generally speaking, income taxes are used to generate funds at the state level, property taxes are used to generate funds at the local level, and sales taxes are used to generate funds at the state level.

Income taxes are based on wages earned. State and federal governments set up brackets of wealth with different percentages of taxation attached to each. Income taxes provide a high **yield** but are sensitive to economic downturns. An example of income tax rates is found in **Table 16.1**. Note that each bracket is a tax rate only for a specific band of income and not overall income.

Politicians have utilized income tax policy to advocate for specific values through a series of deductions (mortgage interest, marriage, child deductions, etc.). The cost of administering the income tax, therefore, is high.

If Taxable Income Is Over—	But Not Over—	The Tax Is:	of the Amount Over—
$0	$12,750	10%	$0
$12,750	$48,600	$1,275.00 + 15%	$12,750
$48,600	$125,450	$6,625.50 + 25%	$48,600
$125,450	$203,150	$25,838.00 + 28%	$125,450
$203,150	$398,350	$47,594.00 + 33%	$203,150
$398,350	$425,000	$112,010.00 + 35%	$398,350
$425,000		$121,337.50 + 39.6%	$425,000

Table 16.1 2013 Marginal Tax Rates for Citizens Filing as a Head of Household

SOURCE: Eric A. Houck, adapted from Table: 2013 Tax Rates and Brackets by Nick Kasprak, January 3, 2013. Tax Foundation. http://taxfoundation.org/blog/2013-tax-brackets

Property taxes are based on the wealth of property owners. Typically, this rate is expressed as a fraction of assessed value of the property. Property taxes generate significant yield and are less vulnerable to immediate economic downturns. Although property taxes are aimed at those wealthy enough to own land, property owners of apartments or other leases find ways to pass property tax burdens on to their tenants.

A sales tax is a **consumption tax**. It has a broad base and considerable yield. Like income taxes, sales tax revenues can dive steeply in tough economic times, as citizens scale back consumption. The sales tax disproportionally impacts the poor, although some states make efforts to address this concern. Sales taxes are easy and cheap to administer. Many states are beginning to pass legislation allowing local districts to also take advantage of the more desirable aspects of sales taxes for building renovation and construction plans.

Each tax presented has positive and negative aspects in terms of ease of understanding, amount of money brought in, and responsiveness (or lack thereof) to economic downturns. The next section outlines how the characteristics of taxes map onto the values of education finance.

Adequacy: The notion of adequacy in education finance maps onto one of the most basic elements of taxation—sufficiency. Any revenue stream must provide sufficient funds, which economists term *yield*. Each of three taxes used to generate educational revenue provides revenue sufficient for the policymakers who design them. Sufficiency for the actual work of educating students is a different topic and is discussed later in the chapter.

Liberty: The notion of liberty relates to the political responsiveness of taxes to voter input. At the theoretical level, policymakers are beholden to their constituents for a variety of policies they implement, taxation policy being one of these. Currently, advocates for tax reform advocate for broadening consumption taxes while reducing income taxes. Politicians' willingness to undertake this type of tax reform has implications for maximizing taxpayer freedom, but also has implications for equity.

Equity: The notion of equity in school finance is linked to the notion of progressivity of taxes.

A **progressive tax** is one that generates more revenue from the wealthier segments of a population; a **regressive tax** is one that either directly asks more of poorer population segments or, under the guise of treating all segments of the population equally, places a greater fiscal burden on the poor. Perhaps the purest example of a progressive tax in the United States is the income tax. As all wage-earning taxpayers know, the graduated income tax demands higher percentages of tax as one moves up the income distribution. Higher earners pay a larger share of their marginal earnings; this is an example of the progressivity of the income tax.

Traditionally, sales taxes are used as the regressive counterpoint to income taxes. Since sales taxes are based on consumption, and since poorer families spend a higher proportion of their overall incomes on basics and have a generally low savings rates, a sales tax of a uniform rate will garner a higher proportion of poorer families' incomes. Many states that rely on sales taxes attempt to ameliorate this regressivity by exempting certain categories of items or taxing some categories of goods at lower rates than others. This tends to reduce the taxes' regressivity. States with tourist attractions (i.e., Florida, Tennessee) tend to rely on sales taxes as a method for shifting the cost of state operations away from residents and onto visitors and tourists. Property taxes have elements of progressivity and regressivity. The very nature of a property tax assumes one is wealthy enough to own property and therefore targets higher-income elements of the population. However, the property tax is usually universal, although as with sales taxes, some localities have experimented successfully with exemptions for the elderly or other classes of citizens.

Efficiency: The notion of efficiency relates to the responsiveness or **elasticity** of a tax. Usually, this notion is used to explain how changes in the overall economy will affect revenues. For example, sales of cigarettes seem to be unresponsive to taxes; demand for cigarettes remains level despite increases in taxes (probably because smokers are addicted to nicotine and unconcerned about small increases in cigarette prices). However, we can also discuss this notion from a policy perspective by considering how a particular tax responds to changes in the overall economy.

Table 16.2 presents a summary of the properties of different taxes: yield, administration cost, and sensitivity to economic downturn. The goal of taxation from a public policy perspective is to require taxes from a mix of sources so that a government will reap benefits during good economic times and will be cushioned from tax revenues "bottoming out" in economic downturns. A government that goes broke when its citizens do is ineffective in that it is unable to continue to provide goods and services in times of economic difficulty.

The type of tax policy used to generate revenue for schools matters. Policies that shift increasing amounts of funding to use taxes or sales taxes are more likely to be less stable in relation to short-term economic downturns. Responsible administrators will advocate for balanced approaches to funding that provide revenues during good times and bad. Administrators may also wish to examine the progressivity and regressivity of tax structures, as these qualities may impact the families providing funding for public schools.

Funding Capital Construction

One example of a shift in the tax burden in education has to do with raising funds for school construction and maintenance. These funds are acquired separately from, and used separately from, funds for operational expenses. These are called **capital expenses**. Traditionally, funds for school construction were raised via bonding, a process whereby voters approved tax money for school construction that would be paid back by selling **bonds** on the bond market, which reduced costs. Bond referenda were always fraught with tension

because voters often viewed them as referenda on the school system as a whole instead of just as a building program. Increasingly, therefore, municipalities have begun to fund school construction via a **local option sales tax** (LOST). This initiative adds a small amount to the preexisting sales tax rate over a long period of time to provide funds for school construction needs. However, this shift in policy is also a shift in tax burden: from the more progressive property tax used to front bond money to the more regressive sales tax used in LOST programs.

Tax issues aside, administrators can sometimes benefit their school or districts by the manner in which they fund specific initiatives. Technology is one example where there is a great deal of confusion as to whether specific items fall under current operational expenditure frameworks or capital expenditure frameworks. This confusion might provide opportunities for administrators to move some items into the capital budget, thereby freeing up funds for other operational necessities. While this might work for some forms of technology such as wiring or machines, administrators who contemplate including technology as a capital expense must consider that technology often comes with additional recurring operating expenses, such as funds for repair or software upgrades.

How Is the Money Distributed?

If the multiple, interlocking layers of revenue generation for schools seem hopelessly complicated and intractably political, the methods states have derived for distributing those funds to school districts are perhaps even more complicated. The sections that

Tax Type	Yield	Responsiveness	Progressivity	Cost of Administration
Income		High	Progressive	High
Sales	High	High	Regressive	Moderate
Property	High	Low	Progressive	Low

Table 16.2 Comparison of Characteristics of Different Taxes

SOURCE: Eric A. Houck, adapted from Guthrie, J. W., Springer, M. G., Rolle, R. A., & Houck, E. A. (2006). *Modern Education Finance and Policy*. Boston, MA: Allyn & Bacon.

follow provide a general overview of the mechanics of school funding distribution formulas. Again, the role of school administrators in these machinations is limited; the importance of presenting this information is so that administrators may be informed of the manner in which their funding is allocated and begin to consider options for optimizing their resources. The sections that follow address the idea of per-pupil funding amounts, how states ensure equalized funding for wealthy and poor school districts, how student needs are addressed in funding formulas, and the distribution of funds from districts to schools. This will set up a discussion of the idea of resource allocation as a framework for administrators. The first task in such an enterprise is to outline the manner in which funding is distributed by different levels of government.

The Federal Role

State funding formulas define the manner in which state and local policies intermix to provide funds for public schools. Strict language in Title I of the ESEA commanded that federal funds be used to **supplement** school funding instead of **supplanting** it, a discussion of state funding formulas is often made without reference to federal funding streams. One issue of federal distribution that administrators will have to address is the issue of **comparability.** In order to ensure that districts did not supplant local funding with federal funding at high-needs schools, federal officials demanded that Title I funded schools proved their comparability to non-Title I schools. Federal regulations demanded schools have equally qualified teachers by asking that licensure rates and percentages of teachers teaching outside of their fields were comparable across the different types of schools. However, the cost of teachers at Title I and non-Title I schools within the same districts can vary widely.

Administrators can have a hand in determining the way that teachers are assigned into schools and can blunt the potentially deleterious consequences left open by the comparability loophole. (See **Sidebar 16.1** for a discussion of this loophole and the competing values involved in weighing teachers' preferences against the needs of schools.)

Sidebar 16.1   Values in Conflict

Equity Versus Liberty

- *Property taxes:* The most equitable finance resource distribution system is one in which the state controls the distribution of all educational resources. Since districts vary greatly in their ability to raise revenues from property tax wealth, it is this very ability that drives huge inequalities across districts. However, local support for education via property tax rates is one of the most direct connections the population of a district can have to its schools. How can an administrator balance the concept of equity with the political liberty of districts to provide funds for their own schools?
- *Student assignment to schools:* Research indicates that parents feel empowered by being able to choose their students' schools. In addition, parents seem to indicate preferences for schooling close to home. However, research also indicates the benefits of integrated environments, particularly when that integration occurs via student socioeconomic status. How can administrators work to create schools with balanced needs while respecting parental desires for choice and proximity?
- *Title I comparability:* Title I schools can have a majority of new teachers and still pass the federal government's comparability provisions. However, teachers view access to transfer policies as a perquisite of their employment. Allowing teachers to transfer from schools seems to perpetuate patterns of employment in which the most ineffective teachers work in the highest needs schools. How can administrators create policies and procedures to respect teacher preferences while still ensuring that the best teachers have a high chance of working with a district's neediest schools?

Equity Versus Efficiency

- *Ability grouping:* Grouping students by ability is very efficient for teachers and administrators: Students are paced relatively equally through the curriculum, and administrators can match teacher strengths to student needs. However, research indicates great benefits accrue to lower performing students in mixed ability environments, with no harm done to higher performing students. How can an administrator balance the equity of mixed ability grouping with the efficiency of instruction provided by tracking classrooms by student academic ability?
- *Student assignment to classrooms:* Parents often call principals to request a favorite teacher for a host of reasons. It is usually in a principal's best interest to respect these requests. However, usually, the requests come from those parents with the time and comfort level to interact with authority figures, thereby silencing significant parts of school populations. Additionally, assignment by parent negates professional knowledge of teacher strengths. How can school-level administrators respect the wishes of parents and still provide the best teachers in all of their classrooms?

Mechanisms for Funding

Flat grant: The original method for states to distribute money to school districts was to provide the same amount of funding to each district. This was a primitive approach to funding. Later iterations of this **flat grant** approach were designed to provide a specific level of funding per pupil enrolled in schools, which created more equity across districts. All states have some notion of a flat grant built into their school funding formula. This allocation of a per-pupil flat grant still does not address the diversity of students—or student needs—that come into classrooms. Students are different and have different needs based on, among other reasons, their race, socioeconomic status, level of schooling, language abilities, and disabilities.

Student weights: To address these issues and to provide more vertical equity, many states provide a set of **student weights** in their funding model. To do this, a state sets a typical child as a per-pupil weight of "1"—and ranks different types of pupils as "more than 1." **Table 16.3** shows a list of pupil weights and the corresponding per-pupil amounts for select pupil categories for the state of Georgia in 2009.

Some states, such as North Carolina, use a student-teacher ratio method that is conceptually linked to a per-pupil weight. Important points to note about pupil weights are that (1) these numbers represent attempts to achieve a type of vertical equity, not

adequacy—there is little in the academic literature to suggest that these weights are related to the actual cost of teaching a student; (2) the proportions are not based in any social scientific inquiry; that is, there is no proof that a kindergarten student costs 0.6587 more to teach than a high school student; and (3) that these weights are politically negotiated—all the way out too the fourth decimal! The irony here is that, although the pupil weights are based on thin and emerging research, politicians sure spend a lot of time debating them!

Foundation Plans. If flat grants and student weights set the amount a state commits to fund districts on a per-pupil basis, the **foundation** components of school funding plans outline the relationship between states and districts in providing that funding. Foundation plans work by requiring a fixed amount of local district effort before the state component of a funding formula can be activated. In many states, this requirement is defined in terms of effort instead of amount for reasons of fairness. By doing this, a state engages districts in partnering to provide a combination of state and local revenues for supporting public education.

The issues of local taxation to raise money for public education can be more problematic in some states than in others. In some states, districts are **fiscally independent**—that is; they have the authority to levy taxes and set tax rates. In other states, school districts are **fiscally dependent**; they set only policy and rely

Program	Per-Pupil Weight	Per-Pupil Funding Amount
Kindergarten	1.6587	$4,476.00
Primary Grades 1–3	1.2855	$3,468.92
Upper Elementary Grades 4–5	1.0323	$2,785.66
Middle Grades 6–8	1.0162	$2,742.22
Base Program—High School 9–12	1.0000	$2,698.50
Vocational Lab 9–12	1.1847	$3,196.91
Special Education I	2.3940	$6,460.21
Special Education II	2.8156	$7,597.90
Special Education III	3.5868	$9,678.98
Special Education IV	5.8176	$15,698.79
Special Education V	2.4583	$6,633.72
Gifted	1.6673	$4,499.21
Remedial Education	1.3128	$3,542.59
Alternative Education	1.6025	$4,324.35
ESOL	2.5306	$6,828.82

Table 16.3   Funding Weights and Corresponding Per-Pupil Amounts for the State of Georgia, Select Categories, 2009

SOURCE: Eric A. Houck, with data from Georgia Department of Education.

NOTE: In 2009, the base per-pupil allocation was $2,698.50.

upon other governmental bodies to provide revenues. The negotiations necessary for fiscally dependent districts to obtain increases in property tax rates add an additional level of political complexity to efforts to provide local funding for schools.

Equalizing Plans. Recognizing that foundation demands can be difficult for property-poor districts, some states build in a tax base equalization provision. This provision is an attempt to equalize the fiscal burden of foundation requirements on local districts. This simple impulse leads to the creation of a fairly controversial policy. In these plans, the state selects a specific district with average or median tax revenue per pupil and seeks to ensure that all districts are funded as though they had the same property tax base; this is known as guaranteed wealth. Districts below the median level of tax revenues are provided money to the state-sponsored amount, and districts with wealth above this amount are left alone. States do not usually provide this amount for every unit of taxation; they usually do so at least for the required foundation amount and for some specified number of tax units thereafter. In this way, states provide vertically equitable support for poorer districts via manipulation of guaranteed wealth.

The foundation amount, required contribution, and equalization components form the core of the funding mechanism in many states. Additional funding comes from specific programs known as **categorical programs**.

Categorical Funding. An additional element of many state funding formulas is added after foundation amounts and equalization levels have been calculated. This element consists of categorical funding—where funds are distributed based on particular characteristics or subformulas and added onto the per-pupil revenue amounts allocated to districts. Some states reserve categorical funding to address nuts and bolts issues such as transportation, dramatic changes in district student populations, and special education. Other states use categorical funds to address issues of equity such as funding for rural or sparsely populated districts, additional support for low-wealth districts, and so forth. Some of these categories are simple per-pupil amounts while other categories have their own formulas attached to them.

Local Funding. In addition to meeting the requirement of local funding effort, states allow districts to raise additional funds. These funds can be used to hire additional classroom teachers or provide salary "top offs" for existing teachers. The provision of local funding is a controversial aspect of school funding formulas in the United States. On the one hand, local control brought about by property taxes can enhance liberty by placing some funding discretion in the hands of local officials, which may enhance a community's connection to schools (see, for example, Fischel, 1996). On the other hand, property wealth variance across districts within states is one of the primary drivers of general inequality, and reliance upon local funding all but ensures broad disparities in funding by district across states. This violates the proposition espoused by John Coons, William Clune, and Stephen Sugarman as school finance proposition number 1: "public education expenditures should not be a function of wealth, other than the wealth of the state as a whole" (quoted in Guthrie et al., 2006, pp. 174). (See **Sidebar 16.1** for a discussion of the liberty versus equity tradeoff in local property taxes for schools.)

Off-Formula Funding—Charters and Vouchers

New school paradigms—specifically, the creation of charter schools and, to a much more limited extent, voucher programs—have challenged the school funding mechanisms just described.

Charter schools—public schools that usually are run independently of school districts and are free from many state regulations—often receive a per-pupil allocation that is tied to their state or district funding levels and arrives relatively untouched by budgeting requirements, thereby providing greater spending flexibility for charter school leaders. As charter schools gain in popularity, charter school advocates seek to obtain more funding to conform to the categories of funds received by traditional public schools; construction and transportation are common areas of request.

Voucher plans are essentially a transfer of public funds to a family to support its purchase of private educational services. Voucher monies are not always directly drawn from education revenue funds; however, as was discussed earlier, state budgets represent a zero-sum game.

The foundation, equalization, categorical, and local provision components of the generic school funding structure described in this section provide a framework for understanding almost every state's funding mechanism.

Using Educational Funds at the District and School Level

Having discussed the manner in which educational funds are collected and the complex mechanisms by which they are distributed, it is time to turn our attention to a topic of more immediate interest to school administrators at the district and school level—the manner in which educational funds are utilized. This discussion brings into play a whole host of other policies that are not usually considered under the umbrella of school finance and represents a conscious turn toward a resource allocation perspective. To understand the basis for the sections that follow, it is time to discuss the broader topic of resource allocation in schools.

The truth of the matter—as shown in Figure 16.1—is that education in the United States is an intensely personal enterprise that takes places at an incredibly large scale. School districts across the country employ approximately 3 million educators—almost 1% of the entire U.S. population.

Most industries or organizations in the private or nonprofit spheres seek to control costs and increase profit through an application of economics 101: substituting capital for labor. The more an organization or industry can rely on machines, the less it has to worry about the vagaries of personnel: retirement, sick days, training and replacement costs, and the like. To date, there has been no adequate substitute found for replacing a classroom teacher. Therefore, a great majority of money spent in education—over 85% of every educational dollar—is spent on the salaries and benefits of educators. This means that any decisions made about personnel can be considered expenditures and have resource implications. For many administrators, it also means that very few choices about funding are left to their discretion. The sections that follow establish the relationship more clearly and outline examples of ways in which personnel and assignment decisions impact resource allocation patterns in schools.

Does Money Matter?

The "Equality of Equal Opportunity" report released in 1966 (more commonly known as the **Coleman Report** after its lead researcher, James S. Coleman) addressed the impact that schooling—and school expenditures—had on student achievement. It found that environmental factors trumped school factors and that marginal increases in educational spending did not seem to have a corresponding effect on student achievement (Coleman, 1968). In the 1980s, researchers began using econometric models to examine this question in greater detail; finding across a number of studies that increases in per-pupil spending did not seem associated with increases in student performance (Hanushek, 1989).

This controversial finding spawned a host of additional studies and challenged educators to think more deeply about the relationship between dollars and student performance (Burtless, 1996; Greenwald, Hedges, & Laine, 1996). One of the key insights from this line of analysis is that, while the addition of raw dollars might not correspond to increased learning, additional investment in items purchased with those dollars can. One clear example of this can be seen in the literature on class size. Reducing class sizes below an established threshold has been shown to improve the academic performance of all students, but particularly high-needs students. However, if

funds are spent to provide teachers but do not result in reducing the class size threshold, those funds may not been seen as being effectively used.

One of the reasons researchers may not see a tight corresponding relationship between dollars and performance is that administrators rarely experience any of the money invested in their schools as discretionary funds. This is due to the tightly controlled mechanism of education budgeting and the extremely high proportion of education finding invested in salaries and benefits. The allocation of resources into schools consists mainly of "purchased inputs"—programs and personnel—that are hard to monetize and that often go disproportionately to schools with higher needs, thereby possibly blunting their effect in school improvement.

Purpose and Object Codes

One of the reasons district and school administrators may feel limited in their ability to creatively and purposefully utilize educational funds is that they see so little of them. This is not a comment on low levels of education funding; rather, it is an observation that in most states, the use of purpose and object codes at the state level presents administrators with a series of "buckets" of funding that are narrowly conceived and bureaucratically enforced. Each state has a manual that outlines the purposes and objects of educational spending. While this method of accounting is very useful in gaining a clear understanding of how funds are used, it also makes it difficult for administrators to innovate or spend in unanticipated matters. Few consider the use of purpose and object codes as a school finance policy, but the very structure presents administrators with few options for fiscal innovation.

Only Fifteen Percent

As noted earlier, another constraint on administrators when it comes to creative use of funds is that many of the largest expenditure items in education walk through the doors of classrooms every day. Since over 85 cents out of every educational dollar is going to salaries and benefits, administrators are left with little else monetarily to innovate with.

The strict controls of the purpose and object code accounting system, combined with the heavy reliance on personnel to deliver educational services, contribute to a notion in the wider field of educational administration that school finance and budgeting are "managerial" tasks as opposed to "strategic" tasks and, subsequently, are why these issues receive little attention in administrator preparation programs. Applying a resource allocation frame, however, allows administrators to begin to see the fiscal and educational consequences of the decisions they make—and to begin to apply the insights gained from an appreciation of the contentious relationships between the educational finance values of equity, efficiency, liberty, and adequacy.

Teachers Matter

Some of the strongest recent research in education productivity has focused on the critical role of teachers to student learning (Sanders & Horn, 1994; Sanders, Wright, & Horn, 1997). Researchers have consistently found that teachers are the single greatest in-school determinant in student achievement. Research indicates that a series of consecutive good teachers in elementary grades can set a student on a pathway to school success, and that a sequence of consecutive bad teachers can stifle a student's budding academic career. One takeaway from a review of this research is that educators should invest more in teacher salaries to attract and retain excellent classroom teachers. However, teachers in most school districts are currently compensated on a **single salary schedule** that rewards teachers for characteristics that research does not support. It is not always the case that a more highly paid teacher is a better teacher.

For example, many state salary schedules provide an increased salary for teachers with a graduate degree. Research indicates the relationship between possessing an advanced degree and being a better teacher is shaky (see, for example, Goldhaber & Brewer, 1996). Teachers with advanced degrees in their subject area tend to be more effective at raising student achievement than teachers with administrative or omnibus "education" master's degrees (Clotfelter, Ladd, & Vigdor, 2007).

Similarly, salary schedules provide increasingly higher salaries to teachers based on their years of experience. Again, research indicates that this relationship is not as strong as one might expect. Teachers seem to get much better around year 5 and sustain

their effectiveness until it plateaus around year 12 or so (Rice, 2003). In addition, the rate of teachers departing the profession in the first few years of their career is very high (Ingersoll, 2001). A salary schedule that responded to the benefits of teacher experience would invest greater salary gains in the early years of a teacher's career, with salary increases leveling off over time, instead of increasing incrementally year after year. In many ways this is a moot point from an administrative perspective; since administrators do not have money with which to hire teachers, anyway. Often, administrators hire for "positions" without regard to actual salary amounts, which are paid for by the state. It is an important takeaway for administrators, however, that teacher quality is based on factors not fully acknowledged in current salary structures. Nevertheless, the manner in which teachers are placed within systems can be one of the most powerful fiscal decisions an administrator makes.

Assignment

For administrators, the clearest manner in which they can move dollars around in schools and districts is to move those things that money purchases. This is why school finance researchers often use the term *resource allocation* to address the strategic ways in which administrators can use money in schools. Oftentimes, the way to move resources around is through assignment. Two of the most important allocation decisions an administrator can make are assigning teachers to schools and assigning students to teachers. Far too often, these decisions are seen through a political lens and not a resource allocation lens. (See **Sidebar 16.1** for a discussion of the values that can come into conflict in these decisions.) In order to create more equitable learning environments for students, administrators can move any of the following resources around: money, students, or teachers (Houck, 2010).

Teachers to schools: Many school district human resource policies work against getting the best teachers to the neediest students. Researchers have identified a cycle whereby new teachers are often hired at high-needs schools where their earliest years are spent facing numerous challenges (Houck, 2010; Jackson, 2009; Lankford, Loeb, & Wyckoff, 2002; Scafidi, Sjoquist, & Stinebrickner, 2007). Once they attain tenure, district policies allow these teachers to transfer schools, and teachers select into schools that they consider safer or easier to teach in, thus creating more teacher vacancies at high-needs schools, which then hire more novice teachers. This dynamic and the human resource policies that undergird it have the cumulative effect of placing less effective teachers in higher needs schools. While this makes sense from a human resources perspective, it makes limited sense from a resource allocation perspective, where the value of equity might demand pairing a district's best resources with its highest needs. Getting teachers into schools where they can be optimally effective can occur via many different routes. Directly assigning teachers into schools can be politically complicated. Administrators in union states will find that labor contracts severely restrict administrators' control over teacher transfers.

Students to teachers: Teachers are not the only resource in education systems assigned to schools. As was noted earlier, states acknowledge the differences presented by student backgrounds and exceptionalities via the use of student weights. Administrators at the district level, then, have the opportunity to assign these students into schools based on their needs and backgrounds in ways that allow for the creation of equitable educational environments. In fact, managing the student composition of a school may create the conditions that allow for the equitable distribution of teacher qualities across schools. That is, if all schools in a system have relatively heterogeneous student populations in terms of the challenges students face, teachers will not attempt to secure jobs in schools on the basis of the student makeup and good teachers should be more evenly divided across schools in a system.

Assigning students to schools can cause political problems for school administrators. Parents may feel entitled to a greater say in their choices and selections for a classroom experience. First, many parents in suburban areas have expressed a desire for "neighborhood schools" despite the fact that few schools actually are accessible by walking from students' neighborhoods. Nevertheless, the specter of "forced busing" seems anathema to many parents. Second, the U.S. Supreme Court has ruled in the 2007 case *Parents Involved in Community Schools v. Seattle School District No. 1* that race cannot be a primary factor in student assignment, and the U.S. Department of Agriculture has issued guidance indicating that school lunch eligibility is not be used as a proxy for a student's social class in making student assignment decisions.

Conclusion

The workings of policies that regulate the generation and distribution of educational funds can seem complex and far removed from administrators' day-to-day experiences in running schools. Unfortunately, too often this remoteness and complexity leads to a lack of curiosity among administrators about how their resources are derived. By understanding these policies from within a resource allocation framework, administrators should feel better prepared to understand the critical connections between daily decision making and the implications for the four values that define the field of school finance studies.

The following is a checklist of sorts for administrators who wish to be informed about state- and district-level policies while at the same time making wise decisions about the human and instructional factors they have control over.

1. Educate yourself on your state's funding formula.

2. Advocate for broad-based taxes to provide steady revenue for education.

3. Develop a position on the liberty versus equity tradeoffs brought about by local property taxation (unless you live in Hawaii).

4. Develop a strategic vision and spend to implement it.

5. Resist buying technology with one-time funds.

6. Thoughtfully allocate teachers into schools and students to teachers; this is the most important resource allocation you do!

Utilizing such frameworks should help administrators become more effective in their work to promote academic equity by understanding the forces that work against such notions.

Key Chapter Terms

A Nation at Risk: Published in 1983, this federal report catalyzed frustration with public education and launched what would become the standards based reform movement.

Adequacy: Value in school finance focused on discovering sufficient levels of resources necessary for students to make appropriate academic progress based upon a standards-based framework

Allocative efficiency: Notion of efficiency that focuses on overall effectiveness across a range of outcomes

Bonds: Method of raising capital revenue by selling debt in the market.

Capital expenses: Funds used for school building construction and maintenance; raised and expended separately from operating expenses.

Categorical programs: Funding in a state's school finance formula that is targeted for a specific purpose.

Coleman Report: An influential 1966 report that raised important questions about family effects of student performance and the issue of school district efficiency.

Comparability: in Title I funding, the regulation requiring that Title I and non-Title I schools be resourced at similar levels.

Consumption tax: Tax on use; that is, a sales tax.

Efficiency: Value in school finance focused on the relationship between resource allocation and overall performance.

Elasticity: Responsiveness; used here to connote the responsiveness of a tax to changing economic conditions.

Equity: Value in school finance focused on the equality or fairness of the distribution of resources.

Equity II: Term used in place of adequacy to connote an affinity with the value of equity around performance and outcomes.

Federalist: System of governance whereby power is shared by a central government and constituent political entities (in the U.S. case, a federal government and state governments).

Fiscally dependent: Describes a school district that cannot raise its own revenue and is dependent upon another government entity to set tax rates and provide funds.

Fiscally independent: Describes a school district that can set tax rates and bring in its own revenue.

Flat grant: Horizontally equitable level of funding per pupil that serves as the basis of many state-level school finance mechanisms.

Foundation: Component of a school funding mechanism that demands local contributions in exchange for state support; designed to provide horizontally equitable levels of district effort.

Horizontal equity: Notion of fairness whereby all are treated equally.

Income tax: Tax on earned income; assessed per pay period

Liberty: Politically, the notion of subsidiarity between levels of governance. More commonly invoked in discussions of family choice in school selection, but also pertains to the selection of teachers, curricula, and so forth.

Local option sales tax: Method of raising capital revenue by adding a marginal increment to local sales tax rates.

Progressive tax: Tax that differentiates based on wealth; specifically one that increases yield based on wealth.

Property tax: Tax on assessed owned property; assessed annually.

Purchased inputs: Human resources such as teachers, technology, and curriculum that are examined within a resource allocation framework.

Regressive tax: Tax that does not differentiate based on wealth, with the effect of demanding higher proportions of said tax from lower income populations.

Resource allocation: School finance paradigm that focuses on the totality of human resources provided to students and not just the dollars used.

Sales tax: Tax on consumption of products assessed at point of sale.

Single salary schedule: System of salary levels tied to teacher experience and credentialing that is standardized across a district or state.

Standards-based reform: Set of educational policies that focus on student academic achievement—usually proxied by standardized test scores—relative to articulated policymaker expectations and tied to various accountability consequences.

Street-level bureaucrats: The idea that teachers exercise considerable authority in the policy implementation process by their commitment to implementing various ideas.

Student weights: Set of multipliers used to provide vertical equity in school funding mechanisms.

Subsidiarity: An organizational principle that seeks to place greater control with smaller or more local units within an organization.

Supplement, not supplant: Shorthand for the basic philosophy guiding Title I fund implementation designed to assist impoverished students and not free up state and local funding for other purposes.

Taxes: Monies paid to government to fund basic services.

Technical efficiency: Notion of efficiency that focuses on the responsiveness of system productivity to marginal increases in funding.

10th Amendment to the U.S. Constitution: The last amendment of the Bill of Rights holds that all powers not enumerated in the federal Constitution are reserved to the states; this includes the function of education.

Title I: Part of the Elementary and Secondary Education Act of 1965 that provides federal funds to impoverished students.

Vertical equity: Notion of fairness whereby differently situated units are treated differently to compensate for disadvantage.

Yield: Amount of revenue brought in by any given tax.

References

Berliner, D. C., & Biddle, B. J. (1996). *The manufactured crisis: Myths, fraud, and the attack on America's public schools.* Reading, MA: Addison-Wesley.

Burtless, G. T. (1996). *Does money matter?: The effect of school resources on student achievement and adult success.* Washington, DC: Brookings Institution Press.

Clotfelter, C. T., Ladd, H. F., & Vigdor, J. L. (2007). *How and why do teacher credentials matter for student achievement?* (Working Paper No. 12828). National Bureau of Economic Research. Retrieved from http://www.nber.org/papers/w12828

Clune, W. H. (1994). The shift from equity to adequacy in school finance. *Educational Policy, 8*(4), 376–394.

Cohen, M. D., March, J. G., & Olsen, J. P. (1972). A garbage can model of organizational choice. *Administrative Science Quarterly, 17*(1), 1.

Coleman, J. S. (1968). Equality of educational opportunity. *Equity & Excellence in Education, 6*(5), 19–28.

Cubberley, E. P. (1905). *School funds and their apportionment: A consideration of the subject with reference to a more general equalization of both the burdens and the advantages of education.* New York, NY: Columbia University.

Fischel, W. A. (1996). How *Serrano* caused Proposition 13. *Journal of Law & Politics, 12,* 607.

Fredriksson, P., Öckert, B., & Oosterbeek, H. (2013). Long-term effects of class size. *The Quarterly Journal of Economics, 128*(1), 249–285.

Goldhaber, D. D., & Brewer, D. J. (1996). *Evaluating the effect of teacher degree level on educational performance.* Retrieved from http://www.eric.ed.gov/ERICWebPortal/detail?accno=ED406400

Greenwald, R., Hedges, L. V., & Laine, R. D. (1996). The effect of school resources on student achievement. *Review of Educational Research, 66*(3), 361–396.

Guthrie, J. W., Springer, M. G., Rolle, R. A., & Houck, E. A. (2006). *Modern education finance and policy* . Boston, MA: Allyn & Bacon.

Hanushek, E. A. (1989). Expenditures, efficiency, and equity in education: The federal government's role. *The American Economic Review, 79*(2), 46–51.

Houck, E. A. (2010). Teacher quality and school resegregation: A resource allocation case study. *Leadership and Policy in Schools, 9*(1), 49–77.

Ingersoll, R. M. (2001). Teacher turnover and teacher shortages: An organizational analysis. *American Educational Research Journal, 38*(3), 499–534.

Jackson, C. K. (2009). Student demographics, teacher sorting, and teacher quality: Evidence from the end of school desegregation. *Journal of Labor Economics, 27*(2), 213–256.

Jepsen, C., & Rivkin, S. (2009). Class size reduction and student achievement: The potential tradeoff between teacher quality and class size. *Journal of Human Resources, 44*(1), 223–250.

Lankford, H., Loeb, S., & Wyckoff, J. (2002). Teacher sorting and the plight of urban schools: A descriptive analysis. *Educational Evaluation and Policy Analysis, 24*(1), 37–62.

Lipsky, M. (2010). *Street-level bureaucracy* (30th anniversary ed.). New York, NY: Russell Sage Foundation.

National Center for Education Statistics. (2013a). Table 235.10. *Revenues for public elementary and secondary schools, by source of funds: Selected years, 1919–20 through 2010–11.* Retrieved from http://nces.ed.gov/programs/digest/d13/tables/dt13_235.10.asp

National Center for Education Statistics. (2013b). Table 235.20. *Revenues for public elementary and secondary schools, by source of funds and state or jurisdiction: 2010–11.* Retrieved from http://nces.ed.gov/programs/digest/d13/tables/dt13_235.20.asp

National Commission on Excellence in Education. (1983). *A nation at risk.* Retrieved from http://eric.ed.gov/?id=ED226006

Ostrom, E. (1998). A behavioral approach to the rational choice theory of collective action: Presidential Address, American Political Science Association, 1997. *The American Political Science Review, 92*(1), 1.

Parents Involved in Community Schools v. Seattle School District No. 1, 551 U.S. 701 (2007).

Reschovsky, A., & Imazeki, J. (2003). Let no child be left behind: Determining the cost of improving student performance. *Public Finance Review, 31*(3), 263–290.

Rice, J. K. (2003). *Teacher quality: Understanding the effectiveness of teacher attributes.* Washington, DC: Economic Policy Institute.

Sanders, W. L., & Horn, S. P. (1994). The Tennessee value-added assessment system (TVAAS): Mixed-model methodology in educational assessment. *Journal of Personnel Evaluation in Education, 8*(3), 299–311.

Sanders, W. L., Wright, S. P., & Horn, S. P. (1997). Teacher and classroom context effects on student achievement: Implications for teacher evaluation. *Journal of Personnel Evaluation in Education, 11*(1), 57–67.

Scafidi, B., Sjoquist, D. L., & Stinebrickner, T. R. (2007). Race, poverty, and teacher mobility. *Economics of Education Review, 26*(2), 145–159.

Further Readings

Brewer, D. J., & McEwan, P. J. (Eds.) (2010). *Economics of education.* Oxford, England: Elsevier.

This textbook outlines current issues and methods in the field of economics of education.

Grubb, W. N. (2009). *The money myth: School resources, outcomes, and equity.* New York, NY: Russell Sage Foundation.

This provocative work outlines the implications of applying a resource allocation framework to school finance issues.

Guthrie, J. W. (2007). *Modern education finance and policy.* Boston, MA: Pearson/Allyn and Bacon.

This textbook outlines many of the key issues in school finance and serves as an important basic text in the field.

Ladd, H. F., Chalk, R. A., Hansen, J. S., & National Research Council. (1999). *Equity and adequacy in education finance: Issues and perspectives.* Washington, DC: National Academy Press.

This compilation focuses on issues of fairness and sufficiency in the provision of educational funding to districts and schools.

Ladd, H. F., & Fiske, E. B. (2008). *Handbook of research in education finance and policy.* New York, NY: Routledge.

This comprehensive handbook addresses current issues, methodological approaches, and important historical context for understanding the role of school finance in education reform as well as educational policy making.

Ladd, H. F., Hansen, J. S., National Research Council, & Committee on Education Finance. (1999). *Making money matter: Financing America's schools.* Washington, DC: National Academy Press.

This compilation addresses best practice policies for attaining maximum leverage of educational funding.

Rice, J. K. (2003). *Teacher quality: Understanding the effectiveness of teacher attributes.* Washington, DC: Economic Policy Institute.

This monograph identifies the ways in which teachers as educational resources impact student performance.

Rodriguez, G. M., & Rolle, R. A. (2007). *To what ends and by what means?: The social justice implications of contemporary school finance theory and policy.* New York, NY: Routledge.

This compilation addresses critical issues of equity and social justice from within a school finance/resource allocation framework.

Thompson, D. C., Crampton, & Wood, R. C. (2012). *Money and schools.* Larchmont, NY: Eye on Education.

This book provides an important and critical overview of school finance in the United States.

17

EXPECTATIONS EXCEEDING REVENUES

Budgeting for Increased Productivity

WILLIAM K. POSTON, JR.
Iowa State University

How do school leaders, who are regularly confronted with more to do but with fewer resources with which to do it, meet escalating expectations with diminishing resources? During tough financial times over the last few decades, it hasn't been unusual for states or school boards either (1) to issue broad **mandates** that the school system must cut its **budgets** by a specific percentage or (2) to construct fiscal budgets equal to or less than current allocation levels. Generally, such mandates offer precious little guidance about exactly how school operations should achieve those cost savings and cutbacks or how to protect the quality of the system's operations and functions. Moreover, it is also common that increasing **revenues** with taxation and/or reductions in certain programs or services are not permitted. Given such impossibilities, educational leaders are left to their own devices in coping with the financial shortfall, despite increasing demands for improved or expanded service to meet challenging needs of clientele or groups.

After years of strong economic growth, the effects of a national recession beginning in 2008 accompanied by state tax cuts caused state revenues to decline. At the same time, the cost of education and other government services continued to increase. In one state, Kansas, the combination of rising costs and declining revenues dropped the state's year-end fiscal

balance from over $1 billion in 2007 to nearly zero in 2009. Only by delaying state aid payments to public schools was Kansas able to avoid a deficit at the end of the fiscal year.

Some State Funding Structures Inhibit Equity and Disregard Inflation

Many states fund their public schools with complex school finance formulas resulting in some level of uniform funding, most generally on a per-pupil basis. Frequently, state laws have placed limits on the ability of local school boards to increase local tax revenues. Under state restrictions, the fiscal balancing act becomes even more difficult to manage. When state revenues decline, local funding for public education is often reduced or allocations from states for increased costs and special needs may be deferred or disregarded. This presents a commonly found conundrum for school leaders—how to provide for escalating educational needs with diminishing financial resources.

Dramatic drops in school funding in Kansas in 2009 caused the Lawrence public school system's budget planning serious and troubling complications during the school year as a result of frequent reductions in estimates for state aid over a 6-month period, dropping from $4,433 in January to $4,012 in November—nearly a 10% reduction (Lawrence Public Schools, 2010).

Figure 17.1 shows the precipitous drop in state aid. School boards and superintendents had to cope with this eroding financial situation almost daily, creating enormous problems.

Unfortunately, the devastating financial problems haven't been unique to Kansas, nor have the problems abated over time in school systems. Employees in one Pennsylvania school district had a bizarre experience when the district was faced with the need to reduce the amount of the budget. Two school board members, without board authorization, showed up in the human resources department, demanded a list of all employees, their positions, and their salaries. With that information, they developed their own "cut list," which included a proposal to eliminate all assistant principals—even in schools with over 2,000 students!

In recent years and months, many states have reported similar situations in school funding. While the scope of this chapter doesn't extend to the thorny economic conditions underlying the financial situation facing schools, it is clear that the national economy is part of the problem with adequately funding public institutions, but much of the responsibility for shortfalls centers on inequitable tax structures (Emerson, 2009).

Funding Trend, Expectations Progression, and New Assessments

In 2011, a national study estimated that states were on track to spend $2.5 billion less on K-12 education during the 2012 fiscal year than they did in 2011 (National Governors Association, 2011). There's little doubt that budget pressures will continue to be vexatious for school administrators, since the issues of rising expectations and diminishing resources don't appear to be vanishing anytime soon (Cavanagh, 2011).

Expectations have continued to rise since the No Child Left Behind Act emerged on the national scene in 2001. For example, most states have decided to stiffen standards in English language arts and mathematics, communities and public leaders are demanding improved quality in schooling, and there have been attempts to shift public funds to private, parochial, and charter schools with voucher programs, grants, and other means. Of course, the culture of republican democracy demands greater literacy and numeracy as the society becomes more complex and technological.

More recently, the move to stiffen standards is generating even greater financial pressures for school systems. Most states have adopted a common, voluntary set of curriculum standards known as the Common Core, which has resulted in increased costs for new instructional materials, professional development for educators, new tests aligned to the standards, and technological upgrades needed to administer the tests.

Expectations are that the quantity and quality of testing will increase with corresponding increases in states' costs for testing. One state pulled out of one of the testing developmental partnerships when its costs were predicted to be $2.5 million more than current costs. Other states have reportedly withdrawn from the testing consortia, or decided not to use the tests for reasons of costs and/or other reasons (Strauss, 2013).

Aside from the Common Core, there is more generally a disconnect between what school systems are now expected to provide and the resources available to fulfill the new demands and expectations. Now the question is, what can school leaders do to carry out budgeting responsibilities effectively without undue difficulty? The following section helps to answer that question.

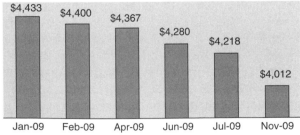

Figure 17.1   Lawrence Schools State Aid Drop 2009 Graph

SOURCE: William K. Poston, Jr., based on Lawrence Public Schools (2010, February). *Rising expectations, falling revenues.* Retrieved from http://www.usd497.org/BudgetPlanning/documents/

The Nature of Budgeting

Budgeting is an art—it is the act of creating a quantified financial strategy to implement organizational plans and goals for a specified future accounting period (Sullivan & Sheffrin, 2003). Moreover, it requires constraining planned expenditures to no more than tangible revenues available for the allocation process. Many elements control the amount of money available to a school system to use for its operations, but whatever that amount of money may be, it is normally within the allowable maximum for use within the system's governance system. Revenue and/or expenditure limitations result from state and local government (including schools) limits on tax rates, restricted or dedicated expenditures (i.e., mandates), and prohibitions of deficit spending (except in very limited circumstances, such as incurring debt over time authorized by voters for building a school).

Basically, there are four simple steps to budgeting:

1. Determining the resources the system needs or may require and for what purposes it might use them (spending requirements)

2. Identifying where and how the system may obtain revenues and funding (income availability)

3. Deciding what choices need to be made for using those revenues on programs, services, or **materiel** (what people, data, or things are needed to reach goals?)

4. Selecting and implementing a decision-making process for allocating resources available (how allocations will be decided)

The first two steps result in a simple equation that produces a balance between revenues and expenditures and, once that is mastered, the mystery of school finance is minimized (Kersten, 2012).

Of course, a major consideration in school budgeting is the need for the local community to have confidence in the financial needs and uses of funding their schools. Three factors impact **economic confidence** as depicted in **Figure 17.2** (Poston, 2011).

Figure 17.2 Economic Confidence

SOURCE: William K. Poston, Jr., adapted from W. Poston. (2011). *School Budgeting for Hard Times: Confronting Cutbacks and Critics.* Thousand Oaks, CA: Corwin, p. 24.

The first factor that the school system must satisfy requires *aligning* its expenditures within its available revenues and in effect, "living within its means." Secondly, efficiency and integrity are required to demonstrate *prudence* in the use of public funds. Any misuse of public funds will tag the system with a label of fiscal irresponsibility, which for public institutions is injurious to their integrity. Lastly, the system has to demonstrate successful results in *performance,* which means achieving adequate and appropriate progress in accomplishing the high-priority organizational goals.

It is important to remember that public school systems and private school systems are accountable to their supporting constituencies. Public schools are accountable to taxpayers, and private schools are accountable to their funding sources and supportive community members. Naturally, if a system falls down on any of these economic confidence factors, confidence in the system may be eroded and its support base may be jeopardized.

Deciding when to change budgeting processes is determined by a number of circumstances. For example, most school administrators are aware of contemporary pressures for schools to get better at what they do with the same or even less financial support. This anomaly persistently challenges educational leaders to meet often conflicting expectations.

Of course, school transformation and improvement activities have significant budget and management implications. In improving the effectiveness and quality of instruction, it is often necessary to make changes in operations without any corresponding increase in resources.

The challenge is to improve the **productivity** of schools within existing, or even diminishing, resources. Educators have had to make do with inadequate support in the way of resources for generations, but have continued to function despite the circumstances.

Budget Preparation

There's an old adage that states, "if you keep doing what you have been doing, you will get the same result." This is true in budgeting—some things have to change if different results are to be achieved. Some of the "new" requisites for budgeting focus on contemporary issues, as indicated with the following precepts.

Include Cost-Benefit Analyses in Budgeting. Most school budgets are "line-item" documents, organized by budget units, such as schools, departments, or other subdivisions of the organization. Most often, line-item budgets are difficult to use in determining whether the system is getting the most value and impact from its spending. That's because the typical budget doesn't detail the activities, objectives, or results that are funded. Sound budgeting practice requires going beyond the sector receiving funds and focusing on the nature of the outcomes that are anticipated to be realized by the program or service (activity) being funded. The simplest form of **cost-benefit analysis** requires a clear definition of the objectives of a specific endeavor, a comprehensive compilation of every resource needed in the endeavor, a thorough compilation of the activity's cost, and identification of what the activity is expected to return and at what cost. In effect, this results in a determined value of an endeavor for use in decision making.

Utilize Knowledge of Results for Budgeted Activities. W. Edwards Deming (1993), widely considered the "father of quality control," often said that the first thing an organizational leader needs to do is to figure out "what the organization is trying to accomplish." Then, he said, the second thing to determine is how well the organization is doing. Educational leaders need a clear vision of the organization's intended purposes, and feedback on how well the organizational purposes are being achieved (Murphy, 2001). By using feedback to modify organizational activities to reach the organization's purposes, the educational leader is better able to (1) measure progress, (2) modify organizational activities, and (3) formulate appropriate changes to the system with valid and dependable information. Effectively measuring or assessing how the organization is doing against its goals and objectives enables the school leader to maintain constancy of purpose in direction—an important aspect of effective organizations—and to make decisions about allocations for organizational activities on a practical foundation.

Implement Participatory Decision Making for Organizational Allocations. Budget decisions in many instances over the years have been closely held and often characterized by competition between organizational sectors. To unleash the power of the organization, collaboration has been encouraged to replace competition or arbitrary domination by management. Competition in budget decision making creates more losers than winners, but cooperative decisions provide several advantages:

- Transparency of information used in the process is widely shared.
- Decisions made accrue greater acceptance across the system.
- Quality of information is better and more extensive.
- Equitability of participation ensures all the needs of all programs and services are heard. Accountability for results is more widely shared across the organization.
- Participatory groups actually make better decisions due to collective intelligence that surpasses that of any member of the group.

Participatory management means that staff, not only the designated managers, have input and influence over the budget decisions that affect the organization. For decades in educational organizations, decisions have been demonstrated to be more successful when teachers, principals, administrators, parents, and community members work closely and harmoniously together (Pollock & Colwill, 1987). In participatory management, the designated managers (or manager) may still have final responsibility for making decisions and answering for them, but members of the staff who are affected by those decisions participate in the process by making recommendations to the chief administrator and/or governing board in the decision-making process.

The most favorable process of budget decision making incorporates the use of cost-benefit analysis, measuring and monitoring results of activities, and employing participatory decision-making processes with all important organizational stakeholders.

Functions of Budgeting in Improving Productivity

To be of value, school system budgets have to comply with two occasionally conflicting organizational purposes—efficiency and effectiveness. Efficiency is characterized by prudent use of resources to achieve the organizational mission at reasonable cost. It does not mean necessarily the cheapest use if it must achieve the school system's mission. Effectiveness is characterized by a structure and culture that supports **achievement** of the organization's mission and goals. In effect, the organization is effective if it accomplishes its defined purposes within the resources available.

The budget's functions include the following:

- Fostering achievement of long-range goals effectively
- Providing guidance to leaders in decision making and carrying out organizational activities
- Enabling choices on possibilities, use, and value of resources
- Monitoring cost-benefit connections for efficiency
- Maximizing productivity by attaining achievement of purposes within available resources
- Specifying management responsibilities for financial efficacy
- Helping control costs and ethical management of resources
- Optimizing organizational coordination and task accomplishment

Considering the widespread functions of budgeting, it's easy to see that the type of budget organization required has to include quality improvement approaches and strategies. Quality improvement is facilitated by clear connectivity between the organization's aims and purposes, organizational activities, and organizational results (Poston, 2011). That quality improvement connectivity ensures that allocations are grounded in organizational aims and purposes, are supportive of functions and activities of the organization, and ensure that budgeting decisions are justified by feedback data on results.

Maximizing productivity, or improving organizational results within available resources, requires some additional considerations. Getting more output out of the organizational inputs usually happens in one of four ways, or through a combination of them—revenue enhancement, expenditure reduction, operational efficiencies including restructuring, and **abandonment** and prioritization.

Revenue enhancement has taken many forms, including building a cash reserve for interest income, establishing a private (or public) foundation for gifts and trusts, renting facilities to other organizations, operating programs for outside organizations, implementing fees for optional programs and services, obtaining grants or contracts from other organizations, and recruiting students from other school districts who pay tuition.

Expenditure reductions generally are high on any list of budget priorities, but some approaches have serious disadvantages. For example, uniform across-the-board cutbacks in funding for all organizational units have the advantage of being relatively easy to do, but the disadvantage of using this "one size fits all" approach is that it ignores subdivisions' variability in character and needs and also ignores evaluation of the status quo. Targeted reductions, such as outsourcing some functions, consolidating facilities and services, sharing professional staff, and energy cost containment, may be more positive. Any attempt to reduce expenditures without considering staff reductions often has an excruciating effect on system effectiveness because of the large proportion of the typical school system budget that is consumed by staffing costs. Some systems expend as much as 90% of their budgets on staffing.

Operational efficiencies are similar to expenditure reductions in that both share the same goal of curbing costs, but operational efficiencies face greater hurdles in terms of broader reconfiguration. For example, operational efficiencies may accrue from privatization of some operations, joining with other systems in cooperative ventures for services such as insurance coverage, and reducing employee costs through furloughs or benefit reductions. Operational efficiency measures often require changes in organizational culture, negotiated agreement modifications, and careful scrutiny of the short- and long-range impact of any undertaking.

Despite the best efforts of budget officials, resources seem to always fall short of the organization's needs, requests, or demands. Still, the educational leader has to satisfy educational demands in the face of inadequate resources. Given continuing inadequacy of funding, school leaders have begun to turn to the principle of abandonment and restructuring. Abandonment is the process of choosing not to fund part or all of an activity, usually one of low priority. Not all program activities are successful, and termination of an activity may conceivably improve organizational performance and reduce cost. Schools are asked to do a great many things, but without adequate funding to support the spectrum of services and activities, some activities may have to be terminated.

Restructuring is modification or adaptation of an activity in order to deliver the activity in a different, perhaps better, manner at less cost. Examples might include reducing custodial services to 4 days per week instead of 5, using policy to increase the walking distance to schools to reduce transportation costs, and replacing some professional positions with trained support staff.

Whatever approach a school leader chooses in forming a budget, it's important that the process be characterized by the following attributes for productivity:

- Constancy in financial parameters to disconnect spending from resource availability and dependence upon revenue growth.
- Policy requirements for solid evidence of needs and potential results for any intervention or innovation before adoption, and objective evaluation of results for continued operation.
- Demonstrated documentation of congruity between system objectives and budget allocations.
- Adequate and relevant assessment feedback for use in budget decision making.
- Persistent demands for objective and independent data, without political influences, to drive allocation decisions.

The path to effectiveness, efficiency, and productivity diverges with each roadblock encountered along the way in the process. Leaders must exercise careful consideration of alternatives in budget development for greater assurance of success.

To carefully consider budget alternatives, educational leaders need to keep their "eye on the ball," which calls for making three important evaluative judgments in determining what activities get funded. The judgments require answering the following questions:

1. How does the budget request correspond with the organizational mission, strategic plan, or goals?

2. How do the structure, activities, and nature of the budget request facilitate achievement of the key objectives of the organization?

3. How will the budget request's results be demonstrated and validated with authentic and clear-cut evidence of usefulness and value before and after funding?

The point to be made here is that no educational leader, given the contemporary public demands for transparency, efficiency, and cost consciousness, can afford to ignore the need to focus precious resources on budget requests that enhance the efficacy of the organization.

The Pathway to Performance-Based Budgeting

Budgeting processes come in many forms, but generally may be organized into one (or more) of four levels or types of budgets that build upon each other as the process develops to higher levels. These levels are explained in this section.

Line-Item (Level 1) Budgeting

Earlier in this chapter, reference was made to line-item budgeting, which is the simplest form of budgeting in educational organizations, and without question also the most popular. Budget allocations in this level of budgeting are organized by what the funds will purchase, such as salaries, support services, benefits, materials, transportation, and so forth.

The approach, known as "level one" budgeting, is easy to organize, and the amounts allocated are frequently based on a formula using pupil enrollment as the determining factor. In level one budgeting, weighted formulas are seldom used in allocating funds for individual differences among student needs, and this level of budgeting often may use some percentage factor applied to current or previous funding levels. Of course, this practice does not take into account changing conditions and differential needs across students, buildings, and departments. Moreover, it is very difficult to conduct cost-benefit analysis at this level since the funding is not organized or tracked by end use, goal, or activity objectives.

In level one budgeting, allocations are categorized by units, department, and schools, but not by activity or what the money produces in end results or effect upon specific and measurable organizational needs. This type of budget simply describes a district's revenue and spending plan for an upcoming year as related to anticipated revenues and expenditures (Ellerson, 2013).

Key steps of a school budget process include establishing the system's objectives and priorities (Hartman, 1999). Level one budgeting seldom includes translating the organizational mission, objectives, or activities into an embodiment of how resource allocations deliver the system's goals, or provides information on how requests are evaluated before or after funding for efficacy or results. It is difficult to set priorities in line-item budgeting because of the lack of information on goals, measurable ends or outcomes, and relationships between results and costs.

Program or Activity (Level 2) Budgeting

A better way to identify relationships among costs, outcomes, and organizational aims is to identify a specific program or activity and organize all of its line items into a comprehensive view of its total costs and results, which then may be evaluated in terms of priority. Such is the advantage of program budgeting—at times called **activity budgeting** in the private sector (Cooper, 1994), and that is frequently referred to as level two (2) budgeting. Basically, a program or an activity is all or part of an endeavor carried out by an organization or a subdivision of the organization.

At this level of budgeting, most informed budget managers acknowledge that activity-based costing improves disaggregation of operational and overhead costs and helps improve efficiency, service, and results at the same or even less cost. Program budgeting, or level two budgeting, clarifies the process of setting up an activity-based, cost-benefit system process. The major advantage is that funding and allocations are no longer identified as things and items purchased, but rather as activities accomplished (or intended to be accomplished). School organizations that have moved from line-item budgets to program budgeting often for the first time became aware of the total cost of a given program or activity. It is a more descriptive approach that allows alignment of activities with objectives, making the activity more efficient, and measurement and evaluation of results. A cost-benefit analysis is much less difficult at this level of budgeting

Noticeable differences with program budgeting are that school organizations are better able to use goals and objectives derived from assessments of organizational needs and to track costs against accomplishments. Program budgeting is uncomplicated and easy to understand. It involves the following steps:

Deciding What Programs and Services Are to Be Provided. Usually, 20 to 25 program units are identified, and examples include such programs as kindergarten, athletics, and activities, elementary instruction (1–5), middle school instruction (6–8), high school instruction (9–12), custodial services, transportation, special education, maintenance, gifted and talented education, principal's office, central administration, and utilities.

Aggregating and Totaling All Costs of the Program. For example, for athletics these costs would include everything needed to conduct the program—coaching salaries, facilities maintenance, utilities for athletic venues, event security and crowd control, referees and officials, transportation, and so on. It is important to include virtually all expenditures required to conduct the program as currently configured.

Defining the Aims, Purposes, and Results Measurement for the Program. Goals, objectives, strategies, and performance measures to be used in assessing goal achievement and progress for the program are defined a priori. A major advantage of program budgeting is that it defines clearly what the organization's intentions are and it emphasizes assessment and evaluation of accomplishment of organizational intentions. Simply, the process states what and how the program is to be done, what it will cost to do it (specifically with all function-object code structures), and how results will be measured, which aids cost-benefit analysis. Moreover, program units have the advantage of providing clarity about what the funding buys and what it produces, which helps with public understanding of the budget's tangible connections.

Incremental (Level 3) Budgeting

Once the program units are defined and current costs tabulated, moving to an incremental configuration of alternative plans and costs is possible. Originally an approach used in the U.S. Department of Defense, this level of budgeting, referred to as level three (3) budgeting, takes individual program units and configures alternative versions of the program based upon analyses of the program's needs and costs. Budgets are built around defined needs of a given program, avoid blanket systemwide adjustments to costs, and produce alternative choices of program design and structure in accordance with funds available.

For example, many school systems have been faced with cutbacks in funding, requiring reductions in expenditures. In such cases, contingency alternatives are developed in accordance with different levels of funding. Frequently, at least three alternatives are planned and developed—one alternative that costs less, another alternative that matches current costs, and another alternative that provides for growth or enhancement of a program. If the needs and options of a program have changed, funding may be adjusted in accordance with the change. If a program's cost may be reduced without jeopardizing the program's goals, the funds not used are recovered by the system and may be reallocated where needed. Incremental program budgeting facilitates periodic evaluation of previous funding allocations to compare intended goals and actual results. This permits decisions about the feasibility to consider reallocations, potential elimination of outdated endeavors, and desirable changes in the scope of organizational commitments. A simple example of **incremental budgeting** is shown in **Table 17.1** (Poston, 2011).

In Table 17.1, there are three options for the music program. Each option provides a different cost level, and a different level of service. It is plain to see that the quality of the educational program changes with changes in the allocated funding, which are

important in communicating to stakeholders that money does make a difference. If the system adopted the recovery module shown in Table 17.1, a savings of $29,290 would accrue to the system, ostensibly for reallocation or to offset some unspecified portion of a revenue cutback. The tangible connection between cost and level of service is obvious. Budget discussions in incremental budgeting processes generally coalesce more often around the purpose, quality, and benefits of a module rather than around the amount of money.

When funding needs and the connection to program quality are evident, the information may be used to foster support for budget increases, program improvements, and revenue referenda as well as providing a sensible option for reduction of costs with abandonment or restructuring of program components. The conceptual grasp of incremental program budgets is heightened in level three budgets since they give a view of coherent services rather than an immersion in a blizzard of line items found in level one budgets. An unexpected advantage of this approach is that it fosters reconsideration of programs' status quo, enables creative development of workable and practical alternatives, and unleashes the potential of synergistic collaborative efforts for improvement of services despite diminished funding—an authentic ingredient of greater productivity.

Performance-Based (Level 4) Budgeting

The fourth (4th) level of budgeting incorporates the quintessence of the other three budgeting levels in its configuration (line-item, program or activity, and incremental components). It adds an important element that addresses a key issue—organizational accountability for results—a frequent reproach from critics of public institutions. According to the Gallup Poll organization, since the year 2000, more people have been dissatisfied with public schools than satisfied every year but one (Gallup Poll, 2013).

Organizational accountability is encompassed within **performance-based budgeting**, and is characterized by clear definitions of program goals and objectives grounded in measured organizational needs and valid requirements for student success in learning, planned strategies, costs, and feedback on assessments of results and outcomes. Adding the evaluation

Budget Module	Program Provisions	Module Cost
Recovery (90%)	Instrumental music begins in Grade 6	$263,610.00
Current (100%)	Instrumental music begins in Grade 4	$29,290.00
Enhancement (117%)	Add strings instruction in Grade 7 (new)	$54,370.00

Table 17.1 Incremental Budget Modules (Music Example)

SOURCE: William K. Poston, Jr., adapted from Exhibit 5.3 in W. Poston. (2011). *School Budgeting for Hard Times: Confronting Cutbacks and Critics.* Thousand Oaks, CA: Corwin, p. 65.

component by design, before and after program implementation, is a vital part of performance-based budgeting and the improvement of productivity, but valid evaluation is infrequently found in traditional budgeting practices. In configuring performance-based budgeting, the features of incremental program budgeting and its antecedents are incorporated, but an uncommon key question emerges when a program component is under consideration. That question is "so what?" If funded, what difference will result from the component, and how will its value be ascertained?

Of course, performance-based budgeting has its own set of attributes and requirements for implementation, but it has the advantage of allowing for decision making with cogent information about the efficacy of program components and services (Poston, 2011).

Comparing Budget Types

The National Center for Education Statistics published a list of objectives for budgeting, and comparing the four levels of budgeting to the objectives is illustrative of the differences as indicated in **Table 17.2**. (National Center for Education Statistics [NCES], 2004). In Table 17.2, the structure of each budget level is illustrated in clear terms as to

differences among them. Performance-driven budgeting includes and meets all the NCES objectives, and exclusively meets the budget objective for program results evaluation.

Implementing Performance-Based Budgeting

When revenues are tight, and tough decisions need to be made in allocating funds, it is helpful to use performance-based budgeting approaches. The process is extremely helpful if school organizations wish to protect or to improve the quality of teaching and learning when revenues are diminishing, unpredictable, or inadequate to meet rising expenses. Moreover, it works even when revenues are unknown because it sets priorities among program components, allowing for the determination of how much should be spent on each component to be contingent upon how much revenue becomes available. It is even more helpful when the system needs to establish a rational and effective process for determining fund allocation priorities across competing interests and endeavors.

There are many advantages to performance-based budgeting. Systems using performance-based budgeting have experienced the ever-elusive but desirable goal of cost-benefit decision making, greater credibility in financial stewardship both inside and

NCES Budget Objectives	Budget Level & Type			
	Level 1: Line-Item	Level 2: Program	Level 3: Incremental	Level 4: Performance
Compliance with federal, state, and local laws and requirements	X	X	X	X
Identification of sufficient revenues for expenditures	X	X	X	X
Verification of use of resources within legally adopted budget	X	X	X	X
Facilitation of measurement of total program costs		X	X	X
Provision of choices among multiple levels of program quality			X	X
Implementation of evaluation of program results				X

Table 17.2 Comparing Budget Levels to NCES Objectives

SOURCE: William K. Poston, Jr., based on information in National Center for Education Statistics. (2004). *Financial Accounting for Local and State School Systems: Handbook 2* (2nd Rev. ed.). Retrieved from http://nces.ed.gov/pubs2004/h2r2/ch_3.asp#2

outside the organization, better-informed decision-making processes with performance data feedback, increased organizational unity with collaborative agreement and **participatory decision making,** greater public trust and confidence given transparency in the processes of allocations and assessment, improved efficiency with use of priorities in funding decisions, and extended creativity in finding new and better ways of "doing more—with less"(Poston, 2011, p. 19). In school districts that have implemented a major change of approach to the performance-based budgeting process, system participants and observers have stated that the change was an improvement over the previous budgeting procedures (Poston, 2011, p. 171).

Creating the Performance-Based Budgeting Framework

The budgeting process ultimately results in allocations of funds to activities within the school system for a given period, usually a fiscal year. To begin a performance-based budgeting process requires answering three questions:

1. Who will make the fund allocation decisions?

2. What programs, services, or activities are in need of funding?

3. If revenue is predicted to be insufficient for all needs, how much flexibility is required in funding allocations?

The first question about budgeting participants is one for the governing body and/or the chief executive officer to answer. Budgeting may be closely held and managed by few people, or it may be a collaborative process involving a larger group of people. The case for collaboration has already been presented in this chapter. Generally, performance-based budgeting utilizes a broad representative group, including program managers (those responsible for management of the programs and services provided by the system), senior executive officers, a group of representative principals, teachers, and parents, and occasionally representatives of the Chamber of Commerce, employee unions, and student body officers. The chief executive officer (CEO) and members of the governing body (board) are not recommended for participation in this level of decision making, since the recommendations for budgeting will be made by

the budget development group to them. In school districts, the budget development group may include 12 to 15 program managers, four teachers (one each representing elementary, middle, and high schools, and special education), three or four principals, four to six parents, the chief academic officer (CAO), and the chief financial officer (CFO). The CAO usually chairs the meetings, and the CFO provides financial information and monitors the funding allocations.

The second question as to what activities are to be funded is also a decision for the CEO. It is common to begin with 20 to 25 program units. Examples of program units include: elementary, middle, and high school instruction; fine arts and music; guidance and health services; athletics and extracurricular activities; custodial and maintenance services; the school board and superintendent's office; community relations; kindergarten; utilities; media and technology; human resources; English language learners; transportation; financial services; principals' offices; preschool; and special education. The list of program or activity units may be constructed in any configuration to fit the circumstances of the school system, but each unit must be a separate, stand-alone, and distinctive entity with identifiable costs, and means for evaluating its results.

Finally, the financial circumstances confronting the school system need to determine the degree of flexibility needed to deal with the various possibilities for revenues. The system's financial projections may be dependent upon enrollment growth or decline, pending legislation, taxing limitations, or other external factors. If revenue projections are meager, program units will need to prepare funding scenarios that provide services at less cost. Program managers may be required to prepare a program or activity budget with reduced funding, but practicable and protective of program quality to the extent possible.

On the other hand, if enrollment is projected to increase along with increased revenue, packages may be prepared for *enhancement* or increments for growth—even without knowing how much growth in revenues is available at the time. For example, one district in Phoenix was growing at a rate of 2,000 to 2,500 students per year in the 1980s, and predicting the exact amount of growth was infeasible. So the district's program unit manager's prepared budget proposals at "growth" levels, which provided increased levels of program services if greater levels of state aid became available due to increased enrollment.

*Preparing Incremental Program Unit
"Packages" for Budgeting*

Once the framework has been determined, program managers are directed to prepare budget "packages" for their program activities. These are incremental packages at recovery, existing, or increased funding levels. Recovery modules or packages cost less than the program did in previous years. The number of packages may vary—some districts have had as many as five recovery packages.

Each program incremental package must be designed and configured to fit into the level of funding designated, and each must be developed and described with information sufficient to inform the budget-planning team as to the unit's nature, activities, relevance, costs, and measurable intentions. One unit package must be developed for each incremental level of funding. Each distinctive unit package must provide key information, including:

1. title of the budget unit package and package's total cost;

2. description of program activities and services to be provided by the unit package;

3. comparison of proposed activities and services with previous year(s)' operations;

4. relationship of the unit's activities with system goals and planning;

5. description of evaluation approach for ends or outcomes of the program unit package; and

6. explanation of the consequences of *not funding* the program unit package (so what?). (Poston, 2011)

Each program manager obtains and prepares the information about each program unit package, commonly using a required form for presentation to the system budget decision-making team. No additional information is necessary, but occasionally school system planning teams may wish to ask for information from the program managers for evaluation purposes. For example, the system may need to know how each package relates to or impacts organizational issues, such as legal compliance (e.g., whether funding for English language learner programs meets state and federal requirements), collective bargaining, other mandated or optional programs, health and/or safety, accreditation standards, political bodies, equity, staffing, the system's strategic planning, or facilities and maintenance. Such information is often requested and is delineated on the reverse side of the budget package form for consideration in the decision-making process.

The budget-planning form would include information needed for budget-planning team members' consideration, and the form often looks like the example in **Figure 17.3**.

In addition to the information required for the decision-making team, program managers need to prepare a list of their packages with titles, full time equivalent positions included, and the costs for each package as well as a total for all the packages. It should be understood that program unit packages are designed to be cumulative—that is, the base (or lowest funding level) package would be the starting point for cost, and each package added thereafter would show only the increment, or additional cost. For example, if the base package was a 90% cost level of the previous year's spending, and the next add on was at the 95% level of previous year's spending, the additional package cost would only be 5% to be added to the base unit package cost.

There are many considerations that need attention in program unit package planning and development. Things to consider include accountability for the validity and integrity of the proposed costs (sans overstatement or misrepresentation); equity in program design to meet differential needs of students, schools, or departments; and asymmetrical employee compensation.

Salary schedules that pay teachers based on how long a teacher has taught and how much graduate education he or she has completed mean that school and department funding levels for teacher compensation cannot be determined based strictly on head count. This is referred to as salary **compensation asymmetry**. The **teacher experience index** (longevity and training) means that some teachers make more than others for the same type of work, which makes it impossible to have equal pay from teacher to teacher and in aggregate from school to school. This problem can be ameliorated by use of the system's mean salary for various positions. That is, by budgeting positions (full-time equivalents or FTE), and using a mean salary for each type of position, the allocation of positions can be made independent of the actual cost until the final allocations are made, at which time the actual salaries can be inserted for each department or school. This "levels the playing field" in allocating positions based on need or other means of justification without undue influence of

Performance-Based Budget
Budget Unit Decision Package Description

Package Name/Title: _____

Unit Manager: _____ Package ID: _____

This is #_____of _____Packages   Package Cost: _____ FTE: _____

1. Description of program, activities, services provided by this package:

2. Description of how program activities will differ from previous year's operation:

3. Description of how this package, if funded, relates to system goals, objectives, and plans:

4. Description of the consequences of not funding this package:

5. Description of how this package will be evaluated for effectiveness and success:

Figure 17.3 Budget Unit Decision Package Sample

salaries on staffing levels or incongruous changes in staffing patterns (Cavanagh, 2011).

Given attention to these and other factors, the credibility and reliability of the data provide a solid foundation for effective budgeting development and implementation.

Setting Budget Priorities and Funding Levels

Once all package units are prepared, documented, and organized, the budget-planning group proceeds with review of proposals, appraisal of the value of each program unit package, and judging the priorities and rank order of all components for recommendation to the CEO and board.

Some ground rules are necessary for the budget-planning group, including how budget unit packages will be presented to the group by program managers for fair and equal consideration and time limits, how priority order will be established, what types of questions may be asked by group members for unbiased and objective purposes, what the role of observers would be, and the mode of nominal group procedures for the ultimate budget configuration.

Most often, the group meets at a convenient, uninterrupted time in a public venue to hear and view presentations by each program manager, with equal time and technology allotted to each manager. One district group held its meetings on Saturday mornings, in casual clothing, with refreshments and a "brown bag" lunch provided. These meetings are normally highly collegial and effectively productive. After hearing and reviewing all the program unit presentations and data, each individual member of the group proceeds to privately and confidentially rank order all program unit packages in order of perceived importance and value to the system. Procedures normally used are variations of nominal group techniques for consensus decision making, and the most popular is the **Q Sort** methodology.

Individual members' rankings are submitted to an independent person for tabulation and compilation of the overall group's consensus list of priorities among program unit packages. The group meets again to review the priority rankings, and by parliamentary procedure may accept the group consensus, or vote to repeat the process. Until a majority of the group votes to accept the priority rankings, the process continues.

Once a consensus on budget priorities is established and accepted, the resulting product is assembled and the chair of the budget group transmits the recommended priority order to the CEO for his or her consideration and transmittal to the board. The product resembles **Table 17.3,** based on the package ranking order for a Minnesota school district in 2001.

Priority Order	Program Package Description	Package Cost	Cumulative Cost
1	Media/technology: Base (Catch Up)	$1,366,244	$1,366,244
2	Guidance/Health: Base (Safety)	$2,676,843	$4,043,087
3	Elementary instruction: Base (Moderate class size)	$32,035,670	$36,078,757
4	Senior high instruction: Base (Large class size)	$14,770,359	$50,849,116
5	Custodial/Maintenance: Base (Safety)	$7,003,545	$57,852,661
6	Middle school instruction: Base (Moderate class size)	$13,903,230	$71,755,891
7	Music & fine arts: Base (6th Gr. Instrumental start)	$3,115,830	$74,871,721
8	Elementary instruction: Base + 1% (Reduce class size)	$326,916	$75,198,637

Table 17.3 Package Ranking Example

SOURCE: William K. Poston, Jr., adapted from Exhibit 8.2 in W. Poston. (2011). *School Budgeting for Hard Times: Confronting Cutbacks and Critics*. Thousand Oaks, CA: Corwin, p. 117.

NOTE: This table shows only 8 unit packages out of a total of 110 packages

The process provides a detailed list of all program unit packages and the proposed rank ordering dependent upon the amount of funding that becomes or is available. For example, if the school system in Table 17.3 had only $58 million to allocate, the budget would be cut off at priority number 5. If more funding became available, the line of budget inclusion would move down accordingly. Conversely, if additional funds were not available, programs below priority 5 would be abandoned. (Of course, the table shows an extreme example; a school district would not eliminate middle school instruction completely.) Performance-based budgeting shows clearly what programs or services are funded and those that are not. This provides a very clear picture of where the money goes, and what the consequences are on system activities when the funding available is spent before all sought-after programs and services are funded.

Certainly, this cursory overview of the process is incomplete, but it is intended to give the reader a sense of how the program works and the advantage of providing a clear depiction of what the system's funds produce—not just what the system spends.

Expectations and Results of Performance-Based Budgeting

Performance-based budgeting is a manifestation of models for **quality improvement** in organizational functions and operations. There are many features of the process that highlight its advantages and utility in public school organizations, which include the following:

- Transparency of budgeting is achieved with clear indications of how funds are used, what they produce, and what results are accrued accordingly. This information satisfies a prudent public seeking assurance that public monies are well used, and results are used to increase efficiency and productivity.
- Improvement opportunities emerge from the evaluation process employed with performance-based budgeting. Outcomes of activities are monitored, and results weighed together with costs and value to the organization. Better information about obtained results helps to improve program design and implementation over time.
- Participatory and collaborative decision making acquires greater effectiveness in allocation choices,

minimizing enmity in public organizational decisions, enhancing support for system budget processes, and creating a sense of solidarity and working toward the common goal of organizational excellence.

Conclusion

Although this chapter does not discuss every aspect of performance-based budgeting, it should give readers an idea of how it can help a school organization survive when expectations exceed available revenues. By opening up the budget process, performance-based budgeting can lead to greater credibility for the school district and more efficient uses of funds, and ultimately to value-added dimensions of productivity.

Productivity is not unintentional—it demands planning and tangible connections between costs and results, organization with flexibility to meet a shifting kaleidoscope of expectations and resources, transparency in efforts and processes leading to organizational efficacy in meeting the diverse needs of the system's clientele, and broad support from community members and system personnel. Performance-based budgeting is one option among a plethora of organizational moves that provides a well-proven approach to grasp the challenge for better schooling within limited fiscal means.

Key Chapter Terms

Abandonment: Cancelling or forsaking a work activity or project if funding is insufficient to ensure success in the undertaking.

Achievement: In education, achievement is measured learner performance against objectives, usually with some form of a test.

Activity budgeting: A methodology that identifies activities in an organization and assigns costs to each activity with resources according to the actual use by each, including indirect costs and proportionate overhead.

Budget: A plan for allocating resources that specifies how resources, chiefly money, will be allocated or spent during a particular period.

Cost-benefit analysis: A process in which comparisons are made of an activity's potential benefits with its anticipated costs.

Economic confidence: A sense of trust in public institutions by citizens and patrons of the community public entity, characterized by prudence in financial management, alignment of expenditures with revenues, and documented proficient and effective performance to stakeholders.

Incremental budgeting: Consists of establishing objectives for programs and services, and considering various options or components of cost and quality to make decisions about priority in funding.

Mandates: The requirements directed by an external governing body to school systems for operations, programs, and services, that may or may not be funded by the governing body.

Materiel: The collection of things needed or used by a school system, consisting of supplies, equipment, hardware, vehicles, and more.

Participatory decision making: A creative process in which ownership of decisions is delegated to an entire work group, each with equal authority.

Performance-based budgeting: Consists of establishing objectives for programs and services, comparing various options of quality and cost, and implementing feedback and assessment to determine funding levels and priorities by organizational groups.

Productivity: The amount of output per unit of input (labor, equipment, and capital) in an organization. In education, it is measured by learner success and costs.

Q Sort: A nominal group technique for consensus decision making by using a ranking process of budget items involving collective qualitative determinations of rank or priority effectively and quickly by a budget-planning team.

Quality improvement: A formal process of analyzing performance and initiation of systematic efforts to improve it, involving goals and feedback on results or outcomes.

Revenues: Consist of various income proceeds for schools or school systems, including tax income from local, state, and federal sources, interest on investments, sales of property, income from sales, fees, and gate receipts, and other sources.

Salary compensation asymmetry: Occurs within a group of school teachers or other employees in similar or equal positions, with variations and differences in individual compensation costs.

Teacher Experience Index: A quantification of the compensation for an individual teacher or group of teachers based upon longevity, experience, and training.

References

Cavanagh, S., (2011). Budget pressures churn workforce. *Education Week, 31*(2) 1–11.

Cooper, R. (1994). Activity-based costing for improved product costing. In B. Brinker & J. G. Kammlade (Eds.), *Handbook of cost management* (pp. B1.1–B1.51). Boston, MA: Warren Gorham & Lamont.

Deming, E. W. (1993). *The new economics: For industry, government, education.* Cambridge, MA: MIT Press.

Ellerson, N. (2013). *AASA White Paper: School budgets 101.* Retrieved from http://www.aasa.org/uploadedFiles/Policy_and_Advocacy/files/SchoolBudgetBriefFINAL.pdf

Emerson, J. (2009, June 4). *A moral framework for increasing public education funding based on a critical review of the literature.* Retrieved from OpenStax website: http://cnx.org/content/m24500/1.1/

Gallup Poll. (2013). *Gallup historical trends: Education.* Retrieved from http://www.gallup.com/poll/1612/Education.aspx

Hartman, W. (1999). *School district budgeting.* Lanham, MD: Rowman & Littlefield Education.

Kersten, T. (2012 March). *Understanding the basic school finance principle.* Retrieved from OpenStax website: http://cnx.org/content/m18331/1.9/

Lawrence Public Schools. (2010, February). *Rising expectations, falling revenues.* Retrieved from http://www.usd497.org/BudgetPlanning/documents/

Murphy, J. (2001). The changing face of leadership preparation. *School Administrator, 58*(10), 14–17.

National Center for Education Statistics. (2004). *Financial accounting for local and state school systems: Handbook 2* (2nd Rev. ed.). Retrieved from http://nces.ed.gov/pubs2004/h2r2/ch_3.asp#2

National Governors Association & National Association of State Budget Officers. (2011, Fall). The fiscal survey of states. Retrieved from http://www.nga/files/live/sites/NGA/files/pdf/FSS1111.pdf

Pollock, M., & Colwill, N. (1987). Participatory decision making in review. *Leadership & Organization Development Journal, 8*(2), 7–10.

Poston, W. (2011). *School budgeting for hard times: Confronting cutbacks and critics.* Thousand Oaks, CA: Corwin.

Strauss, V. (2013). Seven facts you should know about new Common Core tests. *The Washington Post.* Retrieved from http://www.washingtonpost.com/blogs/answer-sheet/wp/2013/09/04/seven-facts-you-should-know-about-new-common-core-tests/

Sullivan, A., & Sheffrin, S. (2003). *Economics: Principles in action.* Upper Saddle River, NJ: Pearson-Prentice Hall.

Further Readings

Ellerson, N. (2013). *AASA White Paper: School Budgets 101.* [Online]. Retrieved from http://www.aasa.org/uploadedFiles/Policy_and_Advocacy/files/SchoolBudgetBriefFINAL.pdf

This paper provides extensive but succinct descriptions of typical budgeting processes and issues, and is an excellent overview of school budgeting for the novice school administrator, current school board member, and interested member of the public.

Gallup Poll. (2013). *Gallup historical trends: Education.* Retrieved from http://www.gallup.com/poll/1612/Education.aspx

The Phi Delta Kappa (an education honor society) Gallup Poll of the Public's Attitudes Toward the Public Schools is a well-known research instrument. Conducted annually, it allows PDK members and other educators and policymakers to track public opinion about one of this nation's most important institutions, its public schools. Results from the PDK/Gallup Poll are published each year in the September issue of Kappan magazine. The most recent results of the PDK/Gallup poll and more resources are available at www.pdkpoll.org

Poston, W. (2011). *School budgeting for hard times: Confronting cutbacks and critics.* Thousand Oaks, CA: Corwin.

This book is a thorough explanation of advanced levels of school budgeting, including the application of cost-benefit analyses, organizing and implementing activity-based budgeting processes, and ways and means to monitor the results from allocations to programs and services offered by the school system. Focused on improved operations and results, it is a valuable tool in helping school personnel and the public understand what the budget delivers, what it is accountable for, and how it is supposed to work—especially when monies are hard to come by.

18

A FREE PUBLIC EDUCATION FOR ALL

Rediscovering the Promise

FRED C. LUNENBURG

Sam Houston State University

Since the middle of the 20th century, public schools have been under attack. The attackers come from all fronts: from corporate America to the religious right, to individuals who have their own political agendas. The public schools are in a crisis, we are told. American public education does not deserve the criticisms most often leveled at it (Brown, 2012). This chapter deals with misconceptions about U.S. public schools, the reasons for the **achievement gap** between high- and low-performing groups of students in public schools, the views behind the **school choice** movement, and why that movement raises concerns.

Misconceptions About U.S. Public Schools

Two myths undermine many efforts to reform U.S. public schools (Brown, 2012; Schwebel, 2003). The first myth is that the United States is faced with an educational crisis. Such a crisis does not exist and never did. What does exist is unequal educational opportunity for what has been a growing segment of the population: ethnic minorities and children living in poverty.

Data in the U.S. Department of Education's report *The Condition of Education 2013* (Aud et al., 2013) show that U.S. schools are far better than media reports would indicate. Findings include: (a) scores on SAT tests for comparable students have remained the same or increased for more than 40 years, but many more students of color and students living in poverty now take the test, causing the average score to dip slightly; (b) non-White ethnic and racial groups have maintained or improved their SAT test scores since the late 1970s; (c) scores on National Assessment of Educational Progress tests have improved; (d) scores on the Graduate Record Exam have increased significantly; (e) high school completion rates are at an all-time high. For adults ages 25 to 29, the percentage of high school graduates was roughly 50% in 1950; in 2012, about 90% had a high school diploma or its equivalent. The United States has achieved these results despite the fact that, compared to many other nations, the U.S. allocates fewer resources to education and requires students to attend school for fewer days per year.

A closer look at high school completion rates, various achievement test scores, and school expenditures indicates that, far from being in crisis, American schools continue to provide a high-quality—in many ways vastly more sophisticated—education to the type of student they have traditionally served, while greatly expanding their

273

services to larger numbers of students previously excluded from the system.

Some would argue that higher high school completion rates do not prove much if the United States is simply handing diplomas to functional illiterates who we have passed through social promotion. But scores on achievement tests, on the National Assessment of Educational Progress (NAEP), and on the SAT do not support this view. After decreasing in the late 1960s and early 1970s, scores on standardized achievement tests, including the NAEP and the SAT, began to rise. By 1986, some had attained 30-year highs, and scores have continued to rise since then. These improvements cannot be explained by charges that schools are aligning their curricula with tests or cheating. On the NAEP tests, except for the scores of 17-year-olds on the science assessments, scores have remained stable since NAEP's inception in 1969. Science scores for the older students declined from 1969 to 1982 and have recovered about half their decline since then.

As for reading and mathematics, across all three age levels tested (9, 13, and 17), overall reading performance in 2011 was as good if not slightly better than it was nearly four decades earlier. In 2011, mathematics performance had changed very little from the levels achieved in 1973 (Aud et al., 2013). This picture of stable test scores becomes noteworthy when considering the far broader range of students who now take these tests compared to earlier decades. An expanded pool of test-takers produces a distorted picture and has a tendency of reducing average test scores and how well public schools are performing.

The second myth is that the nation's public school system is not producing graduates who can meet our economic needs. This was the claim of *A Nation at Risk* (National Commission on Excellence in Education, 1983) and subsequent reform documents. Those needs are being met. When the educational system is evaluated on the basis of what leaders expect of its performance in maintaining a well-functioning economy, the nation's public school system is highly effective. School changes recommended today to reflect the economic system are misguided (Berliner & Biddle, 1995).

To believe that the American economy is suffering, because of its public education system, is to believe in a myth. Consider the following international comparisons (Bracey, 2005; Brown, 2012;

National Center for Education Statistics, 2013; Schwebel, 2003):

- The **gross domestic product (GDP)** is the market value of all officially recognized goods and services produced within a country in a given year. In 2013, the Unites States was the world leader with a per capita GDP/PPP (purchasing power parity) of $4,746, outstripping, in order, Japan at $3,276, followed by Germany, France, and the United Kingdom (U.S. Department of Commerce, 2013).
- The consumption of electricity is an indicator of economic growth and includes factors such as natural resources, climate, and standard of living. The U.S. per capita consumption in rounded kilowatt hours in 2011 was 3,886,400,000, which is 21% of the world's electricity consumption (World Development Indicators, 2013a).
- The number of persons per vehicle is a reflection of both need and affluence. For the United States, the number in 2010 was 797 (per 1,000 people) per vehicle. Italy was next at 679, while the figure for Japan was 591 (World Development Indicators, 2013b).

The United States has about 9,000 free public libraries. Its museums, theaters, opera houses, and concert halls are highly regarded worldwide and are the envy of all nations. American cinema and its television productions are consumed globally. The countless regional and local expressions of the arts and humanities indicate the widespread interest and sophistication of the population. Some 200,000 books are published in the United States annually, satisfying the needs of voracious readers. The nation is no less accomplished in the culinary arts, fashion design, and sports. And, the United States is the unquestioned leader in military power.

The United States could not be the thriving, accomplished society that it is, if it had been suffering for the last six decades from the many alleged educational crises in its history, including the present one. The United States is suffering from an inability to service effectively a growing segment of the population: children of color and children living in poverty.

Equal Educational Opportunity

The United States has a long history of providing a free public education to all children. Providing a system of compulsory, free public education for all does not necessarily render equal educational opportunity for all. There are wide differences in the physical and financial resources provided to public schools. In school facilities and expenditures per pupil, there are "savage inequalities" (Kozol, 1991). Many low-income and minority children come to school unprepared to learn (Darling-Hammond, 2010; Howard, 2010; Paige, 2010); de facto school segregation still exists (Kozol, 2011); and **tracking** still is a dominant educational practice today (Oakes, 2005).

Insightful and careful studies (Oakes 2005) document the widespread inequality that exists within public schools. Popular accounts such as those by Jonathan Kozol support the findings of empirical studies. In *The Shame of the Nation: The Restoration of Apartheid Schooling in America* (2005), Kozol describes the resegregation of many urban schools; disparities in per-pupil spending between city school districts and well-to-do suburban districts; and gross discrepancies in teacher salaries between the city and its affluent White suburbs, all of which impact the achievement gap. Schools that were deeply segregated 35 or 40 years ago are no less segregated today, while thousands of other schools around the country that had been integrated either voluntarily or by mandate have since been rapidly resegregating.

According to *The Condition of Education 2013* (Aud et al., 2013) the United States spent 7.3% of its GDP in 2009 for education at all levels combined, and 4.3% of its GDP on elementary and secondary education. The percentage of GDP spent on elementary and secondary education in the United States was higher than the 4% average for Organisation for Economic Co-operation and Development (OECD) countries reporting data for 2009 (United Nations Secretariat, 2010). But, in the United States, there are large differences in what is spent by individual school districts. According to the U.S. Census Bureau (2011), the per-pupil spending in New York City was $13,572, which may be compared with a per-pupil spending level in excess of $26,000 in the well-to-do suburban district of Manhasset, Long Island. In 2011, the median salary for teachers in New York City was $61,000, while it was $95,000 in Manhasset and exceeded $100,000 in Scarsdale.

Inequities in opportunity begin for children even before the age of 5 or 6, when they begin their years of formal education in the public schools. They start during their infant and toddler years, when hundreds of thousands of children of the very poor in much of the United States are locked out of the opportunity for preschool education, while children of the privileged are able to attend strong early childhood education programs that can cost as much as $25,000 annually for a full day program.

Many low-income children who do not have the opportunity to attend preschool enter kindergarten without the minimal social skills that children need in order to participate in class activities, such as knowing how to hold a crayon or a pencil, identify shapes and colors, or recognize that printed pages go from left to right. Three years later, in third grade, these children are introduced to what are known as high-stakes tests, which in many urban systems now determine whether students can be promoted to the next grade level. Children who have been in preschool since the age of 2 have, by now, received the benefits of 6 or 7 years of education, nearly twice as many as the children who have been denied these opportunities; yet all are required to take, and will be measured by, the same examinations.

In her studies of tracking—a system that involves assigning students to courses based on their presumed knowledge, ability, and skill level—Jeannie Oakes (2005) describes how schools in the United States perpetuate and reinforce inequality. Research by Oakes (2005) and Beth Rubin (2006) indicates that there is a high correlation between tracking, race, and class. Middle-class White and Asian students dominate the higher tracks and low-income minorities—such as African Americans and Hispanics—are disproportionately assigned to lower tracks. Track assignments are based on factors such as scores on mental ability tests, achievement tests, and teacher recommendations. Each of these indices correlates highly with social class and race.

The Achievement Gap

The term *achievement gap* usually refers to the disparity in academic outcomes between African American, Native American, and Latino students, and their White and certain Asian American peers. The gap between groups of different socioeconomic statuses seems to be related to factors such as parental education, home resources, the quality of schools, teacher experience, and preschool readiness. Children from more affluent socioeconomic backgrounds are more likely to have educated parents, resources at home, high-quality schools, and experienced teachers than children from less affluent backgrounds. Racial disparities are more puzzling. Research has shown that even when social class is held constant, sizable gaps are still present between different racial groups (Howard, 2010; Jencks & Phillips, 1998). That is, African Americans and Latino students in affluent school settings still lag behind their White and Asian counterparts. Furthermore, some research has suggested that Black and Latino students from affluent homes perform worse than poor White students on some academic measures (College Board, 1999). This suggests that race still matters (Howard, 2010).

Reducing Black-White test-score disparities inspired Christopher Jencks and Meredith Phillips to publish the landmark volume, the *Black-White Test Score Gap* in 1998. In the introduction, Jencks wrote:

> Reducing the test-score gap is probably both necessary and sufficient for substantially reducing racial inequality in educational attainment and earnings. Changes in education and earnings would in turn help reduce racial differences in crime, health, and family structure, although we do not know how large these effects would be. (p. 4)

Education has been hailed as the great "equalizer." It is seen as a way to reduce the gap between the haves and the have-nots. "If racial equality is America's goal, reducing the black-white test-score gap would probably do more to promote this goal than any other strategy that commands broad public support" (Jencks & Phillips, 1998, p. 3).

Causes of the Achievement Gap

Some researchers have indicated that the achievement gap prevalent in U.S. preK-12 public schools is merely a byproduct of gaps that exist in society at large and are only magnified in schools (Rothstein, 2004), and that any attempt to place schools at the center of closing the achievement gap is misguided, given that schools did not create the gap in the first place. Anyon (2005) reiterates this contention by claiming:

> We have been attempting educational reform in U.S. cities for over three decades. . . . As a nation we have been counting on education to solve the problems of

unemployment, joblessness, and poverty for many years. But education did not cause these problems, and education cannot solve them. (p. 3)

This was a conclusion of the Equality of Educational Opportunity study, more commonly known as the Coleman Report, more than four decades ago. James S. Coleman and colleagues (1966) argued that schools had only a negligible effect on student performance and that most of the variation in student learning was a product of differences in family background. Scholarly efforts have consistently confirmed Coleman's core finding; no analyst has been able to attribute less than two thirds of the variation in achievement among schools to the family characteristics of their students (Rothstein, 2004). In a reassessment of the Coleman Report, Jencks (1972) writes in his book *Inequality: A Reassessment of the Effect of Family and Schooling in America*:

> We have argued, in other words, that schools serve primarily as selection and certification agencies, whose job is to measure and label people, and only secondarily as socialization agencies, whose job is to change people. This implies that schools serve primarily to legitimize inequality, not to create it. (p. 135)

More recently, Richard Rothstein (2004) endeavors to show in his book, *Class and Schools: Using Social, Economic, and Educational Reform to Close the Black-White Achievement Gap*,

> why socioeconomic differences must produce an achievement gap between students from different social classes, why these differences have always produced such a gap . . . and why this unpleasant reality actually makes the most compelling common sense. Children from lower social classes and from many racial and ethnic minorities, even in the best schools, will achieve less, on average, than middle-class children. (p. 14)

It has been a finding reiterated in the research literature for more than four decades.

Social Class and the Achievement Gap

Coleman argued that schools had little effect in explaining student achievement, but instead most of the variation in student learning was a result of differences in family background (Coleman et al., 1966). Coleman's finding that family background characteristics had a greater influence on student achievement than school quality may be misinterpreted to mean that schools do not make a difference. Of course, all students learn in school, but schools have shown limited ability to affect differences in the rate at which children from different social classes progress. Children from higher social classes come to school with more skills and are more prepared to learn than children from lower social classes (Rothstein, 2004). All children learn in school, but those from lower classes, on average, do not learn so much faster that they can catch up and close the achievement gap.

Another problem in interpreting differences in achievement between student groups is that prior to the enactment of the No Child Left Behind Act of 2001 (NCLB), gaps in achievement were analyzed in norm-reference terms. Analysis of this type leads to the conclusion that average Black achievement is from one half to a full standard deviation below average White achievement. That is, if average White students are at about the 50th percentile of a national test score distribution, then average Black students would be at about the 23rd percentile in that distribution (Rothstein, 2004).

In contrast, policymakers since NCLB report achievement in criterion-referenced terms. The question now is not how do students rank in comparison to national averages (or norms), but whether they passed a specific point on a scoring scale, or the "cut point." This point is "proficiency." Policymakers ask what percentage of Blacks passed the cut point, and how this compares to the percentage of Whites who passed the designated cut point.

This shift in measurement causes problems, because the gap now depends on how difficult the cut point is. States that use more ambitious tests and have set higher cut points will experience greater failures than those with low cut points. States that set a cut score low enough can eliminate the gap without in any way changing average achievement of students from different social classes and social groups.

In the decades following the Coleman report, many researchers have studied family background factors (see, e.g., Anyon, 2005; Barton, 2003; Comer, 2004; Ferguson, 2007; Gordon, 1999; Leichter, 1975; Minow, Schweder, & Markus, 2008; Noguera, 2008; Portes, 2005; Rebell & Wolff, 2008; Rothstein, 2004; Sachs, 2007) with the goal of reducing the educational disadvantages of low-income children. Each argues that, although quality schooling is essential for closing achievement gaps,

without the amelioration of family background factors, children from poor families and ethnic/racial minorities will not be able to achieve their potential in school.

There are a number of family background factors that influence children's academic achievement (Allgood, 2006; Rebell & Wolff, 2008; Rothstein, 2004). These can be divided into the following categories: poverty and racial isolation, childrearing barriers to learning, and health-related barriers to learning.

Poverty and Racial Isolation

Although the United States is one of the wealthiest nations in the world, many Americans live in poverty. In November 2012, the U.S. Census Bureau (2012) indicated that more than 16% of the population lived in poverty, including 20% of American children (approximately 43.6 million). This is the highest level since 1993. The poverty rate is more than twice as high for Blacks and Latinos, amounting to 37.9% and 33.8%, respectively (U.S. Census Bureau, 2012).

The child poverty rate is the highest among countries with the most heterogeneous populations, like the United States (Mishel, Bernstein, & Allegrettto, 2005). UNICEF reported in 2012 that the relative childhood poverty rate in the United States was 23%, compared with 5% in Iceland and Finland, the countries with the lowest rates (Bradshaw et al., 2012). Race also enters into the child poverty rate. For example, in 2005, 14% of White children were living in poverty as compared with 34% of Black children and 28% of Latino children (Child Trends Data, 2006).

The United States also leads all other developed nations in the percentage of people who are "permanently" poor. This statistic is particularly significant because the longer a child lives in poverty, the more extreme its effects, especially if a child is poor during the early childhood years (Rebell & Wolff, 2008)). And long-term child poverty is increasing. The percentage of young children who spent 6 or more years during the past decade in poverty rose from 7% in 1977 to 13% in 2005. Black children are more likely to experience long-term poverty. One third of Black children were poor for at least 6 years of the previous decade in 2007, though less than 5% of other children experienced this extreme. In 2005, only 31% of Black children experienced no poverty at all during the past decade, compared with 75% of other children (Child Trends Data, 2006). Furthermore, there is a growing gap between the "haves" and "have-nots" in America. The top 20% of the population earn eight times as much as the bottom 20% (Mishel et al., 2005).

A related trend is that the haves and have-nots are moving farther apart physically as well as economically (Anyon, 2005; Rebell & Wolff, 2008).

> Increasingly, poor and non-poor families live in separate neighborhoods and go to separate schools. . . . As neighborhoods become dominated by joblessness, racial segregation, and single parentage, they become isolated from middle class society and the private economy. . . . A distinct society emerges with expectations and patterns of behavior that contrast heavily with middle class norms. (Orfield, 2002, p. 18)

Despite a U.S. Supreme Court decision, *Brown v. Board of Education* (1954), calling for schools to be racially integrated, public schools across the United States remain largely segregated with respect to the race and class makeup of their student populations (Noguera, 2008; Orfield & Eaton 1996). Public schools are not only segregated, but in most American cities, poor children attend these schools. Concentrated poverty is most pronounced in urban and "urbanized" suburban areas populated almost entirely by Black and Latino families (Anyon, 2005). The impact of poverty on children's learning is profound and multidimensional (Rebell & Wolff, 2008).

Poverty is also a major contributor to racial achievement gaps. Black and Latino children are much more likely than White children to live in poverty or attend segregated schools in poor neighborhoods, where concentrated poverty compounds the barriers to learning experienced by students (Orfield & Lee, 2005; Rebell & Wolff, 2008; Rumberger, 2007).

Childrearing Barriers to Learning

Children differ in how ready they are to begin school. These differences are strongly influenced by their social class backgrounds (Rothstein, 2004). The childrearing activities that are likely to affect the achievement gap between children from a higher socioeconomic status and those from a lower socioeconomic status include the following: reading to children, parental occupation, parent-child conversations, homework supervision, and grandparents' social class backgrounds.

Reading to Children. More-educated parents read to their young children daily before the children begin kindergarten. White children are more likely than Black children to be read to in pre-kindergarten years. A child who enters school recognizing some words will be easier to teach than one who has rarely held a book. At the beginning of kindergarten, large achievement gaps can already be found between Black and Hispanic children and White children, and between low socioeconomic status (SES) children and middle and high SES children. Moreover, in both fourth and eighth grades, children who are eligible for free or reduced-price lunch scored significantly lower than children who are not eligible, in reading and in mathematics (Weiner, 2006).

In 2011, only 17% of poor children demonstrated proficiency on the NAEP reading test in fourth grade, while 44% of nonpoor children performed at or above the proficient level (National Center for Education Statistics, 2011a). On the eighth grade mathematics test, only 15% of students who were eligible for free or reduced-price lunch scored at or above the proficient level in 2011, but 42% of students who were not eligible demonstrated proficiency (National Center for Education Statistics, 2011b). Moreover, the greater the percentage of low-income children in a school, the farther the average performance drops (National Center for Education Statistics, 2011c).

Parents' Occupation. Low-income households and those of certain ethnic/racial minorities have fewer books in the home and are less likely to have a computer, both of which are related to parental occupation. An international study found a strong relationship between parental occupation and student literacy. The gap between literacy of children of the highest-status workers (like doctors, professors, lawyers) and the lowest-status workers (such as waiters and waitresses, taxi drivers, mechanics) was statistically significant (Organisation for Economic Co-operation and Development, 2001).

Parent-Child Conversations. How parents read to children is important. When working-class parents read a story to their children and then ask about it, their questions are more likely to be factual. Parents who are more literate are more likely to ask questions that are creative, interpretive, or connective. Social class differences arise not only in how parents read but in how they converse. Through conversations, children develop vocabularies and become familiar with contexts for reading in school. Educated parents are more likely to engage in such talk and to begin it with infants and toddlers.

Adult conversations vary by social class and become part of infants' and toddlers' background environments. When educated parents speak to each other in children's presence, even if the children are not being addressed directly, these parents use larger vocabularies and more complex sentences than less-educated parents. These social class differences may help to explain why schools have more success in narrowing the achievement gap at lower grades, only to see it widen later in higher grades. Tests in primary years have more factual, low-order questions, identification, or simple recall, questions like those that children of lower-class families are accustomed to answering when stories are read to them. But tests in the later grades contain more questions requiring abstract reasoning or conceptualization, the kinds of questions about stories that lower-class children are not accustomed to answering but with which middle-class children have more experience.

Homework Supervision. Parents from different social classes supervise homework differently. Middle-class parents are more likely to assist children by posing questions that help children come up with the correct answers on their own. Lower-class parents are more likely to guide their children with direct instructions.

Grandparents' Social Class Backgrounds. Black grandparents are more likely than their White counterparts to be raising their grandchildren or to take care of them at least some of the time. Black grandparents also tend to have significantly less education than White grandparents or Black parents. As a result, Black children's verbal fluency, vocabulary, and later academic achievement will partly reflect the lower education level of their grandparents.

In short, there may be some overlap between social class differences in childrearing between lower-class and middle-class parents. But, on average, good schools and teachers will have more academic success with middle-class children. Childrearing deficits cannot be made up by schools alone, no matter how high the teachers' expectations. For all children to achieve the same goals, those from the lower class would have to enter school with verbal

fluency similar to that of middle-class children (Rebell & Wolff, 2008; Rothstein, 2004).

Health-Related Barriers to Learning

Lack of Adequate Health Care. Poor children are more likely than other children to lack adequate health care and, as a result, to suffer from health-related barriers to learning. Poor and minority children miss more school as a result of illness than other children (Rothstein, 2004). They are more likely to have undetected vision impairments, hearing problems, and asthma, which can affect their performance in school (Rothstein, 2004).

Hunger and Malnutrition. Poor families are more likely than other families to experience hunger or have inadequate access to a nutritionally sound diet. Hunger and malnutrition affect children's school performance. Children who are hungry are less able to concentrate in school. Malnutrition in young children can impede brain development; in older children it can lead to illness and missed school (Allgood, 2006; Rebell & Wolff, 2008). Each of these disparities is more pronounced in low-income African American and Latino families than in other families (Allgood, 2006; Lee & Burkam, 2002).

Use of Alcohol and Smoking. Alcohol use and smoking by mothers during pregnancy can result in cognitive problems for their children; both are more prevalent among low-income people.

Birth Weights and Domestic Pesticides. Low-income children are more likely to be born prematurely or with low birth weights. Studies of low-income, mostly Puerto Rican and Black women in East Harlem found that exposure to commonly used domestic pesticides was associated with children being born with smaller head circumference and much lower weight (as much as 6 ounces smaller birth weight from exposure). Head circumference, along with low birth weight, is associated with children's lower I.Q. and more behavioral problems (Rothstein, 2004).

Like poverty and racial isolation and social class differences in childrearing practices, each of the aforementioned health related differences—in vision, hearing, use of alcohol, smoking, low birth weight, and malnutrition—when considered separately may have a very small influence on the achievement gap. However, together they add up to a cumulative disadvantage for lower-class children that is likely to depress average performance of this group of students. And NCLB has not helped to alleviate educational inequalities or to close the achievement gap.

NCLB was presented as a way to ensure a high-quality education for all students, especially those in lower-performing schools. The idea was that requiring students to show proficiency on standardized tests would result in schools making improvements that would allow all students to learn at high levels. However, the law has not addressed the inequalities in the U.S. educational system. Instead, schools that have failed to meet performance goals under the law have been forced to divert funds needed for improvement of failing schools to pay for students to transfer to other schools, which may offer no higher quality education.

Privatizing Education: Can the Marketplace Deliver Choice, Efficiency, Equity, and Excellence?

Many still believe in the concept of public education as the great equalizer. The common school, initiated in the 19th century, was intended to provide a basic education for all children. The state, not the family, would assume responsibility for educating the nation's children, promising equal educational opportunity regardless of family background. The school would be the institution of the state where children would learn essential skills for productive citizenship in a democratic society (Levin, 2001).

The ideology of the common school persists despite the alleged failure of U.S. schools to fulfill the promise of equal educational opportunities for certain populations, particularly for children of color and children living in poverty. School attendance boundaries traditionally have been determined by geographic residence. Thus, wealthy families have had the benefits of choosing communities that provide good schools for their children's education. Poor families did not have such choices and their children were required to attend neighborhood schools, many of which have allegedly failed to adequately educate some student groups, in particular low-income and minority students. Through its choice provisions,

NCLB included the concept that all families—not just the wealthy—should be given the opportunity to choose the school their children will attend. Although the choice provisions of NCLB include only public schools, school choice encompasses options that involve using public money to allow families to send their children to private schools. The idea behind these choice plans is that market mechanisms will improve public schools through competition. The remainder of this section discusses a variety of choice options and why they raise concerns.

Tuition Tax Credits

Some states allow taxpayers to receive tax credits to offset the cost of sending their children to a private school or for contributions to organizations that sponsor private school scholarships. Tuition tax credit plans at the federal level also have been introduced in Congress. Advocates argue that these plans promote educational opportunity, by making it easier for low-income families to send their children to high-quality private schools. Opponents argue that **tuition tax credits** violate the constitutional separation of church and state and can increase racial and social class stratification.

Vouchers

Vouchers provide public funds to allow students to attend private schools. Economist Milton Friedman proposed the idea of vouchers (1962), and later expanded on the idea in his 1980 best-seller, *Free to Choose*. In 1990 Milwaukee became the first city to initiate a voucher program. Other voucher plans were launched in Cleveland (in 1996) and Florida (in 1999). Research indicates that vouchers do not raise academic achievement. An evaluation of the Milwaukee program for the years 1990 to 1995 "found no differences in reading and math achievement" (American Federation of Teachers, 2005, p. 3). Another annual evaluation of the Milwaukee voucher plan from 1991 to 1995 found no gains in achievement for students who used vouchers to attend private schools as compared with Milwaukee public school students as a whole (Olson, 1996).

A counter evaluation by Paul Peterson (2006), who advocates vouchers, reported students gained in achievement in their third and fourth years in the voucher plan; however Peterson's study is of a very small sample of students in only three private schools who were not compared with Milwaukee Public School students as a whole but with students who failed to get into private schools with vouchers (Olson, 1996; Peterson, 2006). As a result, the Milwaukee voucher program was terminated. Howard Fuller (2011), an architect of Milwaukee's school voucher program, admitted that the program did not produce the results he anticipated.

The Cleveland voucher program was evaluated for the years 1998 to 2003, and the researchers found "no significant difference in overall achievement between voucher students and two public school comparison groups" (American Federation of Teachers, 2005, p. 4). In Florida, a 2001 study found "no significant difference in the improvement of low-achieving (or other) schools pre- and post-vouchers" (American Federation of Teachers, 2005, p. 6). In Washington, D.C., which had the only voucher plan funded by the federal government, studies indicated that Black students had some gains but not as much as Black students in small classes in the public schools (American Federation of Teachers, 2005).

A national study conducted by Henry Braun, Frank Jenkins, and Wendy Grigg (2006) for the U.S. Department of Education found no significant differences in student achievement between public and private schools. The study made comparisons between particular types of religious private schools (Catholic, Lutheran, and conservative Christian) and public schools and found no significant differences in the achievement of students except that students in conservative Christian schools scored significantly lower in mathematics than public school students.

Diane Ravitch, an early advocate for school choice, provided a passionate defense of public schools in her 2010 book, *The Death and Life of the Great American School System*. According to Ravitch, a school with a first-rate curriculum and effective pedagogy will produce superior educational results whether it is a choice school or not. She argues that reform efforts should be rooted in high standards, strong educational values, a rigorous curriculum, and the revival of strong neighborhood public schools.

The two national teachers unions (American Federation of Teachers and National Education Association) are leading critics of vouchers and **charter schools** (Kahlenberg, 2008). Instead of vouchers, the American Federation of Teachers claims public schools can be improved with smaller class sizes, high academic and disciplinary standards, and proven, research-based academic programs. Similarly the National Education Association (NEA) argues on its website that efforts for school improvement should attempt to "reduce class size, enhance teacher quality, and provide every student with books, computers, and safe and orderly schools." The NEA offers some of the following objections to public-private choice plans that use vouchers:

A pure voucher system would only encourage economic, racial, ethnic, and religious stratification in our society. America's success has been built on our ability to unify our diverse population. . . .

About 85 percent of private schools are religious. Vouchers tend to be a means of circumventing the Constitutional prohibitions against subsidizing religious practice and instruction. (NEA, n.d.)

Charter Schools

Charter schools, which began in the early 1990s, were initially intended to spur efficiency and innovation in public schools through competition. Many proponents of charter schools see charters as vehicles to improve the academic achievement of poor minority students. The number of charter schools grew quickly and by 2011–2012, 2.1 million students in 42 states and the District of Columbia were being educated in charter schools (NCES, 2014).

Results from research studies have shown that charter schools do not show higher performance than their public school counterparts. The U.S. Department of Education conducted a national study of charter school and traditional public school students (Nelson, Rosenberg, & Van Meter, 2004). Findings of the study indicated no difference in reading and mathematics National Assessment of Educational Progress (NAEP) scores between the fourth-grade students who attended charter schools and those who attended traditional public schools. Also, poor children enrolled in public schools performed better than their charter school counterparts.

A 2002 report on the charter school movement by the American Federation of Teachers indicated that the movement is a distraction from the real business of improving public schools. The report indicates that charter schools are selective in recruiting students, fail to meet high academic standards, and erode the rights of teachers as employees. The report also indicates that charter schools contribute to racial and ethnic isolation of students by failing to educate high-cost students at the same rate as regular public schools. Consequently, these high-cost students remain in regular schools rather than transferring to charter schools. The report defines high-cost students as low-income students, **English language learners**, and special education students.

Further, two researchers, Gary Orfield and Chungmei Lee (2005), found that "charter schools are largely more segregated than [traditional] public schools" (p. 16). The authors concluded that "many charter schools across the nation are places of racial isolation, particularly for minority students" (p. 16). The national study sample consisted of schools in 11 states where 95% of the nation's charter schools are located.

An American Federation of Teachers report (Nelson et al., 2004), *Charter School Achievement on the 2003 National Assessment of Education,* indicated that compared to students in regular public schools, charter schools had lower achievement both in fourth grade (6 scale points lower in math, 7 scale points lower in reading) and eighth grade (5 points lower in math, 2 points lower in reading). These differences were all statistically significant, except for eighth-grade reading, and translate into about a half year of schooling.

A 2005 report, *America's Charter Schools: Results from the NAEP 2003 Pilot Study,* concludes that there were no significant differences between the achievement of public school and charter school students. The report stated that for students from the same racial and ethnic backgrounds, reading and mathematics performance in charter schools did not differ from that in other public schools. However, this study found lower overall mathematics performance in charter schools than in other public schools. In addition, the study indicated that in reading there was no measurable difference between the overall performance of charter school fourth-grade students as a whole and their counterparts in other public schools.

A study of urban charter schools by Ron Zimmer and Richard Buddin (2005) for RAND also concluded that achievement scores in charters are keeping pace, but not exceeding those in traditional public schools. Further, a 2006 U.S. Department of Education study, authored by Henry Braun, Frank Jenkins, and Wendy Grigg (2006), found that the achievement in reading and math of students in charter schools was lower than that of students in regular public schools. The size of these differences was smaller in reading than in mathematics.

Conclusion

Although the United States has long provided a free public education to all children, there remain inequities in the physical and financial resources made available to public schools. As Linda Darling-Hammond wrote in 2004: "Unlike most countries that fund schools centrally and equally, the wealthiest U.S. public schools spend at least ten times more than the poorest schools—ranging from over $30,000 per pupil at the wealthy schools to $3,000 at the poorest schools." The idea of school choice has been proposed as a way of improving public schools. However, the quality of schooling available to students through these options varies widely, and these options have not led to overall improvements in school performance. School choice, in itself, is not a solution to the problems of public schools.

Key Chapter Terms

Achievement gap: Refers to the disparity in academic outcomes between African American, Native American, and Latino students, and their White and certain Asian American peers. Research has shown that even when social class is held constant, sizable gaps are still present between different racial groups.

Charter schools: Elementary or secondary schools that receive public money but have been freed from some of the rules, regulations, and statutes that apply to other public schools.

English language learners (ELLs): Students who are unable to communicate fluently or learn in English, who often come from non-English-speaking homes and backgrounds, and who typically require specialized or modified instruction in both the English language and in their academic courses.

Gross domestic product (GDP): The market value of all officially recognized goods and services produced within a country in a given year.

School choice: Refers to programs that allow parents to choose the school their children will attend. The current school choice movement is based on ideas that market control in education will improve public schools.

Tracking: Involves assigning students to courses based on their presumed knowledge, ability, and skills. Research indicates that there is a high correlation between tracking, race, and class.

Tuition tax credits: Allow a credit on taxes for educational expenses, including private school tuition, incurred by parents or guardians.

Vouchers: Financial credits, sometimes called scholarships, awarded to students to pay for tuition at any school. Several cities and states have publicly funded voucher programs.

References

Allgood, W. C. (2006, August). *The need for adequate resources for at-risk children* (EPI Working Paper No. 277). Washington, DC: Economic Policy Institute.

American Federation of Teachers. (2002). *An examination of charter school performance.* Washington, DC: Author.

American Federation of Teachers. (2005). *School vouchers: The research track record.* Washington, DC: Author.

Anyon, J. (2005). *Radical possibilities: Public policy, urban education, and a new social movement.* New York, NY: Routledge.

Aud, S., Wilkinson-Flicker, S., Kristapovich, P., Rathbun, A., Wang, X., & Zhang, J. (2013). *The condition of education 2013* (NCES 2013-037). Washington, DC: U.S. Department of Education, National Center for Education Statistics. Retrieved from http://nces.ed.gov/pubsearch

Barton, P.E. (2003). *Parsing the achievement gap.* Princeton, NJ: Educational Testing Service.

Berliner, D. C., & Biddle, B. J. (1995). *The manufactured crisis: Myths, fraud, and the attack on America's public schools.* New York, NY: Perseus Books.

Bracey, G. W. (2005). *Setting the record straight: Responses to misconceptions about public education in the U.S.* Boston, MA: Heinemann.

Bradshaw, J., Chzhen, Y., de Neubourg, C., Main, G., Martorano, B., & Menchini, L. (2012). *Relative income poverty among children in rich countries* (Innocenti Working Paper 2012-01). UNICEF Innocenti Research Centre, Florence, Italy. Retrieved from http://www.unicef-irc.org/publications/pdf/iwp_2012_01.pdf

Braun, H., Jenkins, F., & Grigg, W. (2006). *A closer look at charter schools using hierarchical linear modeling.* Washington, DC: U.S. Department of Education.

Brown, D. F. (2012). *Why America's public schools are the best place for kids: Reality vs. negative perceptions.* Lanham, MD: Rowman & Littlefield.

Child Trends Data. (2006). *Race and poverty.* Bethesda, MD: Author.

Coleman, J. S., et al. (1966). *Equality of educational opportunity.* Washington, DC: Government Printing Office.

College Board. (1999). *Reaching the top: A report of the National Task Force on Minority High Achievement.* New York, NY: College Board.

Comer, P. O. (2004). *Leave no child behind: Preparing today's youth for tomorrow's world.* New Haven, CT: Yale University Press.

Darling-Hammond, L. (2004). From "separate but equal" to "no child left behind": The collision of new standards and old inequalities. In D. Meier & G. Wood (Eds.), *Many children left behind: How the No Child Left Behind Act is damaging our children and our schools* (pp. 3–32). Boston, MA: Beacon.

Darling-Hammond, L. (2010). *The flat world and education: How America's commitment to equity will determine our future.* New York, NY: Teachers College Press.

Ferguson, R. F. (2007). *Toward excellence with equity: An emerging vision for closing the achievement gap.* Cambridge, MA: Harvard Education Press.

Friedman, M. (1962). *Capitalism and freedom.* Chicago, IL: University of Chicago Press.

Friedman, M. (1980). *Free to choose.* San Diego, CA: Harcourt, Brace, Jovanovich.

Fuller, H. (2011, April 23). Keep intact the mission of choice program. *Milwaukee-Wisconsin Journal Sentinel.* Retrieved from http://wwwjsonline.com/news/opinion/120515559.html

Gordon, E.W. (1999). *Education and justice: A view of the back of the bus.* New York, NY: Teachers College Press.

Howard, T. C. (2010). *Why race and culture matter in schools: Closing the achievement gap in America's classrooms.* New York, NY: Teachers College Press.

Jencks, C. (1972). *Inequality: A reassessment of the effect of family and schooling in America.* New York, NY: Basic Books.

Jencks, C., & Phillips, M. (1998). The Black-White test score gap: An introduction. In C. Jencks & M. Phillips (Eds.), *The Black-White test score gap.* Washington, DC: Brookings Institution.

Kahlenberg, R. D. (2008). Albert Shanker and the future of teacher unions. *Phi Delta Kappan, 89*(10), 712–720.

Kozol, J. (1991). *Savage inequalities.* New York, NY: Crown.

Kozol, J. (2005). *The shame of the nation: The restoration of apartheid schooling in America.* New York, NY: Crown.

Kozol, J. (2011). Still separate, still unequal: America's educational apartheid. In E. B. Hilty (Ed.), *Thinking about schools* (pp. 445–464). Boulder, CO: Westview Press.

Lee, V., & Burkam, D. T. (2002). *Inequality at the starting gate.* Washington, DC: Economic Policy Institute.

Leichter, H. (1975). *Families as educators.* New York, NY: Teachers College Press.

Levin, H. M. (Ed.). (2001). *Privatizing education: Can the marketplace deliver choice, efficiency, equity, and social cohesion.* Boulder, CO: Westview Press.

Minow, M., Schweder, R. A., & Markus, H. (Eds.). (2008). *Just schools: Pursuing equality in societies of difference.* New York, NY: Russell Sage Foundation.

Mishel, L., Bernstein, D. C., & Allegretto, S. (2005). *The state of working America 2004/2005.* Washington, DC: Economic Policy Institute; Ithaca, NY: Cornell University Press.

National Center for Education Statistics. (2011a). National Assessment of Educational Progress (NAEP). *The nation's report card: Reading 2011.* Washington, DC: Government Printing Office.

National Center for Education Statistics. (2011b). National Assessment of Educational Progress (NAEP). *The nation's report card: Mathematics 2011.* Washington, DC: Government Printing Office.

National Center for Education Statistics. (2011c). National Assessment of Educational Progress (NAEP). *The nation's report card: 2011.* Washington, DC: Government Printing Office.

National Center for Education Statistics. (2013). *The condition of education 2013* (NCES 2013-037). Washington, DC: Government Printing Office.

National Center for Education Statistics. (2014). *Charter school enrollment.* Retrieved from http://nces.ed.gov/programs/coe/indicator_cgb.asp

National Commission on Excellence in Education. (1983). *A nation at risk: The imperative for educational reform.* Washington, DC: Government Printing Office.

National Education Association. (n.d.). *The case against vouchers.* Retrieved from http://www.nea.org/home/19133.htm

Nelson, H. (2013). *Testing more, teaching less; What America's obsession with testing costs in money and instructional time lost.* Washington, DC: American Federation of Teachers.

Nelson, H., Rosenberg, B., & Van Meter, N. (2004). *Charter school achievement on the 2003 national assessment of educational progress.* Washington, DC: American Federation of Teachers.

Noguera, P.A. (2008). *The trouble with Black boys, and other reflections on race, equity, and the public schools.* New York, NY: Wiley.

Oakes, J. (2005). *Keeping track: How schools structure inequality* (2nd ed.). New Haven, CT: Yale University Press.

Olson, L (1996, September). New studies on private choice contradict each other. *Education Week.* Retrieved from http://www.edweek.org/ew/1996/01choice.h16

Orfield, M. (2002). *American metropolitics: The new suburban reality.* Washington, DC: Brookings Institution.

Orfield, G., & Eaton, S. (1996). *Dismantling desegregation.* New York, NY: New Press.

Orfield, G, & Lee, C. (2005, January). *Why segregation matters: Poverty and educational inequality.* Cambridge, MA: Harvard Civil Rights Project.

Organisation for Economic Co-operation and Development (OECD). (2001). *Knowledge and skills for life: First results from the OECD Programme for International Student Assessment PISA 2000.* Paris, France. OECD.

Paige, R. (2010). *The Black-White achievement gap: Why closing it is the greatest civil rights issue of our time.* New York, NY: Amacom.

Peterson, P. E. (Ed.). (2006). *Generational change: Closing the test score gap.* Lanham, MD: Rowman & Littlefield.

Portes, P. R. (2005). *Dismantling educational inequality: A cultural-historical approach to closing the achievement gap.* New York, NY: Peter Lang.

Ravitch, D. (2010). *The death and life of the great American school system: How testing and choice are undermining education.* New York, NY: Basic Books.

Rebell, M. A., & Wolff, J. R. (2008). *Moving every child ahead: From NCLB hype to meaningful educational opportunity.* New York, NY: Teachers College Press.

Rothstein, R. (2004). *Class and schools: Using social, economic, and educational reform to close the Black-White achievement gap.* New York, NY: Teachers College Press.

Rubin, B. C. (2006). Detracking and heterogeneous grouping. *Theory Into Practice, 45*(1), 1–102.

Rumberger, R. W. (2007). Parsing the data on student achievement in high poverty schools. *North Carolina Law Review, 8*(5), 1293.

Sacks, P. (2007). *Tearing down the gates: Confronting the class divide in American education.* Berkeley: University of California Press.

Schwebel, M. (2003). *Remaking America's three school systems: Now separate and unequal.* Lanham, MD: Scarecrow Press.

United Nations Secretariat and United Nations Human Settlements Habitat. (2010). *OECD better life index.* Retrieved from http://www.oecdbetterlifeindex.org/countries/united-states/

U.S. Census Bureau. (2011*). Per-student spending in New York.* Washington, DC: Government Printing Office.

U.S. Census Bureau. (2012). *Poverty in the United States.* Washington, DC: Government Printing Office.

U.S. Department of Commerce. (2013). *Gross domestic product: International comparisons.* Washington, DC: Bureau of Economic Analysis.

Weiner, R. (2006, October). *Confounding evidence on achievement gaps: Understanding opportunity gaps that undermine the school success of students from poverty.* Prepared for the University of North Carolina Symposium on High Poverty Schooling in America.

World Development Indicators. (2013a). *Electricity consumption: National comparison data.* Washington, DC: World Bank Data.

World Development Indicators. (2013b). *Motor vehicle use: National comparison data.* Washington, DC: World Bank Data.

Zimmer, R., & Buddin, R. (2005). *Charter school performance in urban districts: Are they closing the achievement gap?* Santa Monica, CA: Rand Corporation. Available at http://www.rand.org/education

Further Readings

Brown, D. F. (2012). *Why America's public schools are the best place for kids.* Lanham, MD: Rowman & Littlefield.

Dave Brown's book, Why America's Public Schools Are the Best Place for Kids, *provides powerful arguments for just why American public education deserves almost none of the criticisms most often leveled at it. Public schools work as well as or better than private schools, charter schools, and voucher-based reforms.*

Darling-Hammond, L. (2010). *The flat world and education: How America's commitment to equity will determine our future.* New York, NY: Teachers College Press.

Linda Darling-Hammond has done it again. She combines vision with hands-on policy and school understanding as virtually no one else does. This is a must read.

Dyson, M. R., & Weddle, D. B. (2009). *Our promise: Achieving educational equality for America's children.* Durham, NC: Carolina Academic Press.

This book traces the numerous inequities in our educational system that continue to hinder disadvantaged groups from participating on a level playing field as they navigate the route toward academic advancement. Further, these populations continue to find themselves limited in their prospects for improvement due to ongoing discrimination and societal stratification.

Ferguson, R. F. (2007). *Toward excellence with equity: An emerging vision for closing the achievement gap.* Cambridge, MA: Harvard Education Press.

Striving to remove group identities as predicators of achievement—in other words, to close achievement gaps between groups—will help make the fruits of America's vitality more equally available. These are the goals toward which Ferguson's book is directed and that reflect the meaning of the title, Toward Excellence With Equity.

Hirsch, E. D., Jr. (2009). *The making of Americans: Democracy in our schools.* New Haven, CT: Yale University Press.

This book concerns itself with overcoming low literacy rates and narrowing the achievement gaps between demographic groups. Hirsch's goal in this book is to develop and explain neglected but fundamental principles that must guide our schools in our current historical situation if we are ever to achieve those inspiring ideals.

Howard, T. C. (2010). *Why race and culture matter in schools: Closing the achievement gap in America's classrooms.* New York, NY: Teachers College Press.

This book presents empirical data from schools that have improved achievement outcomes for racially and culturally diverse students and focuses on ways in which educators can partner with parents and communities. It is important reading for anyone who is genuinely committed to promoting educational equity and excellence for all children.

Levin, H. M. (2001). *Privatizing education: Can the marketplace deliver choice, efficiency, equity, and social cohesion?* Boulder, CO: Westview Press.

This book had its origins in the paucity of nonpartisan sources of information on a major policy issue: privatization of public education. Productive discourse in a democracy depends upon the presentation of contending views on controversial subjects, and educational privatization is one of the most contentious topics of our times.

Noguera, P. A., & Wing, J. Y. (2006). *Unfinished business: Closing the racial achievement gap in our schools.* San Francisco, CA: Jossey-Bass.

This book is about unfinished business—the nation's as yet unfulfilled commitment to equality and justice for all. The authors' focus is on the possibilities for achieving these lofty goals through public education, arguably our nation's most equitable and democratic institution.

Rebell, M. A., & Wolff, J. R. (2008). *Moving every child ahead: From NCLB hype to meaningful educational opportunity.* New York, NY: Teachers College Press.

In Moving Every Child Ahead, *Michael Rebell and Jessica Wolff begin their analysis by asking what policies and programs are needed to overcome historic inequities and current achievement gaps. They systematically analyze the major aspects of the law and provide telling recommendations for revising it in order to meet the actual needs of all students, and especially those from disadvantaged backgrounds.*

Reese, W. J. (2011). *America's public schools: From the common school to "No Child Left Behind."* Baltimore, MD: John Hopkins University Press.

William J. Reese's engrossing narrative succinctly and shrewdly analyzes nearly two centuries of American public schools, taking us from the pioneering efforts in the early 19th century through the political and cultural conflicts of today.

Rothstein, R. (2004). *Class and schools: Using social, economic, and educational reform to close the Black-White achievement gap.* Washington, D.C.: Economic Policy Institute.

In this book, Richard Rothstein asks us to view the Black-White and low- to middle-income achievement gaps with a wider lens. His revealing and persuasive analysis of how social class shapes learning outcomes forces us to look at the differences in learning styles and readiness across students as they enter school for the first time.

Sacks, P. (2007). *Tearing down the gates: Confronting the class divide in American education.* Berkeley: University of California Press.

While we often hear about the widening economic divide between the rich and the poor in modern America, this book attempts to locate the fountainhead of this growing economic disparity in one of our most cherished democratic institutions: our education system.

PART VII

SCHOOL LAW, SAFETY,
AND THE LIMITS OF REGULATION

19

Today's Compelling Issues in Public School Law

M. David Alexander

Virginia Tech

Patricia F. First

Clemson University

Jennifer A. Sughrue

Southeastern Louisiana University

The responsibilities of today's public school education leaders and administrators have never been more compelling or more complex. School leaders are focused on student achievement, but this cannot be accomplished without providing a safe learning environment. In his majority opinion for *Morse v. Frederick,* a case involving schools and the First Amendment, even Supreme Court Chief Justice John Roberts acknowledged the compounding burdens placed on educational leaders:

> School administrators have a difficult job, and we are well-aware that the job is not getting any easier. . . . Besides the teaching function, school administrators must deal with students distracted by cell phones in class and poverty at home, parental under- and over-involvement, bullying and sexting, preparing students for standardized testing, and ever-diminishing funding. When they are not focused on those issues, school administrators must inculcate students with the shared values of a civilized social order. We do not envy those

challenges, which require school administrators to make numerous difficult decisions. (*Morse v. Frederick,* 2007, p. 409)

Providing a safe learning environment requires balancing school safety policy and practice against the constitutional rights of children. As noted by the Supreme Court, public school students do not leave their constitutional rights "at the schoolhouse gate" (*Tinker v. Des Moines,* 1969). Respecting the constitutional rights of children is a moral and ethical obligation of educators, but so is maintaining an environment in which children are safe.

School safety involves a multitude of legal issues, but there are two that emerge frequently in the press and in the courts: bullying, including cyberbullying, and search and seizure. Bullying and cyberbullying impact students physically and emotionally, and often lead to poor academic performance. In several instances, bullying behavior has been cited as a reason that victims of bullying committed suicide. There is even a term for bullying-related suicides, *bullycide.* Search and seizure is not a new legal issue, yet litigation persists. Students allege violations of their Fourth Amendment rights when school administrators and school resource officers (SROs) act contrary to constitutional limits placed on them as they work to remove alcohol, drugs, and weapons from school property.

The chapter's first section, bullying and cyberbullying, defines the problem and explains the legal arguments for and against school district and administrator liability. Victims of bullying and their parents press claims against schools, usually arguing that administrators and school boards were negligent by not taking adequate measures to stop the bullying. Recent case law illustrates how the court views educator and district responsibility for stemming bullying behavior and under what circumstances one or both will be judged as liable for negligence.

The second section of this chapter addresses search and seizure. It covers the legal foundation on which school administrators can make prudent decisions to protect the students from threats of weapons and drugs in the school as well as their obligation to respect the constitutional rights of those same students and to limit their exposure, and the district's exposure, to liability suits.

Bullying/Cyberbullying and Student Free Speech Rights

The federal government defines bullying as "unwanted, aggressive behavior among school aged children that involves a real or perceived power imbalance. The behavior is repeated, or has the potential to be repeated, over time" (Stopbullying.gov, n.d., "Bullying Definition"). While the bully has been a fixture in the American school for as long as schools have existed, bullying behavior was not seen as a national concern until after the 1999 shooting at Columbine High School that killed 15 students and wounded two dozen others (Limber, 2002). Many news accounts reported that the two boys went on the killing spree in response to the harassment they received from students in the school, although other accounts later questioned whether this was the motivation behind the killings.

A newer form of bullying, cyberbullying, has emerged in the era of readily available electronic communication and social media. The federal government describes cyberbullying as "bullying that takes place using electronic technology. Examples of cyberbullying include mean text messages or emails, rumors sent by email or posted on social networking sites, and embarrassing pictures, videos, websites, or fake profiles" (Stopbullying.gov, n.d., "What Is Cyberbullying"). Cyberbullying has the same intention as face-to-face bullying, but it creates physical and social distance between the bully and the victim. It is a form of passive aggression and has the added detrimental effect of broadcasting the victimization to a broader audience.

The Seriousness of Bullying

School leaders must take bullying seriously. It is detrimental to the bully, the victim, and the bystander. Those who engage in bullying behavior are more likely to exhibit unhealthy behaviors in adulthood, such as alcohol and drug abuse; continued physical aggression, such as getting into fights or damaging or destroying property; and abusive behavior toward spouses or children (Stopbullying.gov, n.d.). Victims of bullying may experience stomachaches, headaches, depression, and moodiness. They may withdraw socially, may want to stop going to school, and may experience a decline in their academic achievement. As adults, they may manifest stress-related behaviors, such as sleep disruption, frequent absences from work, apathy, anxiousness, depression, frustration, anger, and may engage in substance abuse (Warren, 2011). Bystanders often exhibit reactions similar to those of victims. They may become depressed and exhibit physical symptoms that are consistent with stress. Witnessing bullying also may trigger repression of empathy or desensitization to abusive or other negative behaviors, as well as a sense of helplessness or ineffectiveness (Janson & Hazler, 2004).

These same behavioral outcomes occur in victims of cyberbullying. However, cyberbullying creates a different set of circumstances that make it more difficult to address in the school because most of it occurs off campus through private electronic devices and social media.

Bullying in Cyberspace

The Internet has created a virtual world in which real dangers, such as cyberbullying, can occur. It is virtual violence that results in real harm for the victim, and seeps into the school, other social venues, and the home. Cyberbullying has had a devastating impact on vulnerable teenage victims and may have driven, at least in part, a number of youths to suicide. School teachers and administrators also are targets of cyberbullying and suffer physically, emotionally, and professionally.

Cyberbullying is easily executed through multiple forms of technology, such as cell phones and computers, and communication tools, such as text messages, email, and Twitter. Those who cyberbully exploit Internet social media sites, such as Facebook and YouTube, to torment and harass their victims. Cyberbullying can occur 24 hours per day, 7 days per week, and can reach a victim at home or at a non-school related activity. Messages can be posted anonymously, sent to a very wide audience instantly, and are difficult to track. Even if the perpetrator has second thoughts and attempts to delete the offending material, it is highly problematic to purge electronic messages once they have been placed in cyberspace.

Because cyberbullying is a form of private speech, although it may be posted on a highly visible social network, it is difficult to legally quash it. Private speech enjoys federal constitutional protection and therefore is not subject to government regulation except under a very small number of exceptions (*Reno v. ACLU,* 1997).

Legislative Responses to Bullying and Cyberbullying

Almost all states have addressed bullying and cyberbullying through statute, policy, or both (Neiman, Robers, & Robers, 2012; Tefertiller, 2011). Some have adopted statutes into the criminal code and others into the education code. However, most of these laws have not yet been tested in court and legal scholars are uncertain whether all of them will pass constitutional muster. The challenges in drafting effective antibullying legislation are:

- Bullying must be defined. There is not universal agreement over what constitutes bullying behavior (Tefertiller, 2011).
- Free speech rights of students must be respected. Although the *Tinker* (1969) decision concluded that student speech rights could be circumscribed, they nonetheless exist, especially if the speech does not

cause a substantial and material disruption at school. It is a fine line to regulate "the most offensive, inappropriate, and potentially dangerous behavior" when there is "no physical contact or threats and [the speech] occurs off-campus" (p. 170).

- The range of inappropriate behavior seems infinite. Confusion exists as to the nature and scope of misbehavior and when it should be subject to school disciplinary action or to criminal prosecution.
- Many but not all states or state departments of education include some nonpunitive measures in their legislation or policies (Neiman et al., 2012; Stuart-Cassel, Bell, & Springer, 2011). In these cases, school districts are required to develop and implement proactive antibullying strategies and to integrate bullying education and prevention into the curriculum through character education programs, including Positive Behavioral Intervention (PBI) programs, or through health and wellness courses.

While 49 state legislatures have now adopted antibullying legislation, only 19 specifically identified cyberbullying in antibullying laws (Hinduja & Patchin, 2014). All but 2 states, however, have laws that prohibit electronic harassment. Among the states that require school district anticyberbullying policies, 12 also prohibit students from cyberbullying that occurs off campus. However, controlling off-campus speech has limitations.

For example, Florida allows schools to discipline students for off-campus harassment. However, the harassment must be something that "substantially interferes with or limits the victim's ability to participate in or benefit from the services, activities, or opportunities offered by a school or substantially disrupts the education process of orderly operation of a school" (Florida Department of Education, n.d., p.1). The statement "substantially disrupts" is a reference to *Tinker v. Des Moines* (1969), in which the U.S. Supreme Court ruled that students have a federal constitutional right to free speech, but that it may be restricted when the speech "materially or substantially disrupt" the educational process. Therefore, if disruption of the educational environment occurs as a result of off-campus activities, then school authorities may discipline the student for the cyberbullying (*Kowalski v. Berkeley County Schools,* 2011).

Cyberbullying and other forms of bullying are equally hurtful to victims. Student victims of all forms of bullying can suffer physical, emotional, academic, and social effects. Perhaps the one difference is that cyberbullying victims cannot escape the bullying by staying away from school or by avoiding bullies.

Today's students are technologically savvy and have had access to digital devices since a very early age. Their technological skills and the innovation and proliferation in apps have outpaced the federal and state governments' ability to access their impact on children and school personnel and to legislate against abuses (Moses, 2007). This complicates state and school district officials' efforts to limit the incidence of cyberbullying on and off campus.

Seeking Justice

When individuals seek justice for the effects of bullying or cyberbullying, they may sue in federal or state courts. Cases going to federal court are usually litigated under (a) the **liberty or property provisions of the due process clause** or the **equal protection clause of the 14th Amendment** of the U.S. Constitution, (b) Title VI of the Civil Rights Act of 1964, (c) Title IX of the Education Amendments Act of 1972, (d) the Individuals with Disabilities Education Act (IDEA) of 2004, (e) Section 504 of the Rehabilitation Act of 1973, (f) the Americans with Disabilities Act (ADA), or (g) a combination of these. When plaintiffs litigate in state court, relief is sought under the state's tort laws.

Fourteenth Amendment and Due Process

To successfully claim in federal court that a student's due process rights were violated under the 14th Amendment is very challenging. The Supreme Court set a very high standard in a noneducation case in which a child was severely injured at the hands of his abusive father (*DeShaney v. Winnebago County Department of Social Services*, 1998). In its ruling, the Court opined that "[a]s a general matter . . . we conclude that a state's failure to protect an individual against private violence simply does not constitute a violation of the Due Process Clause." The due process clause forbids government from depriving an individual of life, liberty, or property without due process, but it cannot "be extended to impose

affirmative obligation on the state to ensure that those interests do not come to harm through [third party actions]" (*DeShaney*, 1998).

For this reason, it is highly unlikely that a school board or school official would be held in violation of a student's due process rights under the federal constitution. The issue appears to be that bullying, no matter how severe, is not a federal constitutional issue under the due process clause, except under a very few exceptional circumstances. In the eyes of the Supreme Court, it is a matter to be litigated in state court under tort law.

There are a couple of narrow exceptions to the blanket rejection of a 14th Amendment claim of a due process violation (*DeShaney*, 1998). They are the "special relationship" and the "state-created danger" doctrines. The special relationship doctrine imposes an affirmative duty of care and protection under certain circumstances. Examples of a special relationship are: (a) adequate medical care for incarcerated prisoners, since the prisoners themselves have been denied the liberty to seek care, and (b) care and protection for the mentally ill who have been involuntarily committed.

Inasmuch as the Supreme Court has not ruled on a school case involving the special relationship doctrine, it has fallen to the U.S. Circuit Courts of Appeal. These courts have uniformly agreed that no special relationship exists between the public school and its students for purposes of a 14th Amendment due process claim. In numerous cases, plaintiffs have argued that requiring a student to go to school under compulsory attendance statutes creates a special relationship. This argument has been rejected by every federal circuit court in which such a claim has been made. They have asserted that compulsory attendance does not create a special relationship.

The second liability exception exists when the state creates a danger. A state-created danger is usually determined by four factors: (a) the harm was foreseeable, (b) a state actor, for example, a school official, was to blame for an act that "**shocks the conscience**," (c) a relationship existed between the state and plaintiff whereby it could have foreseen that the plaintiff was a victim, and (d) the state actor used his authority in such a way that it created a danger to the plaintiff or made the plaintiff vulnerable to danger.

The "shocks the conscience" standard has arisen several times in school cases, even though the bar to meet that standard is a high one. One example in which a plaintiff successfully sued under the 14th Amendment involved a coach who seriously injured a student in an effort to discipline him for hurting another student in a fight (*Neal ex rel. Neal v. Fulton County Board of Education,* 2000). The coach's action was considered a form of corporal punishment and was deemed as so excessive as to "shock the conscience" in violation of the 14th Amendment substantive due process protection. However, this standard is difficult to meet when the offending actions are perpetrated by a nongovernmental actor, such as a student. The failure of school officials to protect a student from bullying is not considered sufficiently egregious, brutal, or offensive to human dignity as to shock the conscience (*Smith v. Guildford Board of Education,* 2007; *Smith v. Half Hollow Hills Central School District,* 2002).

Neither of the other two exceptions, the special relations nor the state-created danger doctrine, has been applied successfully to bullying cases. In *Morrow v. Balaski* (2013), the student was excessively bullied, yet the court ruled that the school's actions neither created a special relationship nor imposed a state-created danger and, therefore, there was no substantive due process claim under the 14th Amendment. "The severity of harm caused by bullying is irrelevant to . . . constitutional judgment . . . substantive due process is not triggered" (p. 183). The court indicated that nearly every state has anti-bullying statutes, so aggrieved victims and parents should seek redress in state court.

Fourteenth Amendment and Equal Protection

School officials may be held accountable if the bullying is discriminatory. In other words, the school leader must act decisively to stem bullying that is based on characteristics such as gender, race, or religion. Not to take action is to act with **"deliberate indifference,"** which will incur liability under the equal protection clause.

The deliberate indifference standard was established by the U.S. Supreme Court in a Title IX peer-to-peer sexual harassment case, *Davis v. Monroe County Board of Education* (1999). In it, a female student became so despondent over the continual sexual harassment by a boy in her class that her grades plummeted and she no longer wanted to go to school. The Court ruled that she was denied educational benefit as the result of the harassment and the school officials' deliberate indifference to the harassment she suffered.

The key to an equal protection claim based on discrimination is that the plaintiff must show that he or she was treated differently based on his or her status as a member of a protected class. To succeed in an equal protection claim of deliberate indifference to student-on-student bullying or harassment the student must show: (a) he or she was harassed based on a protected classification, such as religion, race, or gender; (b) that school officials had knowledge of the bullying and/or harassment; and (c) that the school officials' response was unreasonable in light of the circumstances so as to imply a reasonable inference that the school official himself intended the bullying or harassment to occur. Such was the case of Jamie Nabozny, an openly gay middle school student (*Nabozny v. Podlesny,* 1996).

Nabozny was a good student and enjoyed school during his elementary years. In the seventh grade, realizing he was gay, he decided not to "closet" his sexuality. At this point other students started to bully and harass him, calling him faggot, striking him, and spitting on him. He spoke with the school counselor. The counselor managed to stop the students from bullying for a short period, but then the school hired a new counselor. When Nabozny informed the principal of a particularly egregious episode of bullying, the principal replied "boys will be boys" and "if [he is] going to be openly gay," then he should expect such treatment (p. 451). After each incident, Nabozny's parents spoke with the principal and each time nothing was done.

Nabozny sued, claiming a violation of the equal protection clause of the 14th Amendment. To successfully press an equal protection claim, Nabozny had to prove that he was treated differently from other students based on his sexual orientation and that school officials intentionally took no action to stop the discriminatory bullying. The U.S. Court of Appeals for the Seventh Circuit found that school officials violated Nabozny's equal protection rights through deliberate indifference and could not claim **qualified immunity**. Qualified immunity may be denied defendants if they do not act when they know or should have known they were required to under the law.

In another instance, a 16-year-old student became the target of bullying and harassment because he was Jewish *(G.D.S. v. Northport-East Northport Union Free School District,* 2012). Overtly anti-Semitic comments and so-called jokes were directed at the student. The students who were harassing him also posted anti-Semitic slurs on Facebook. The student and his parents met with school officials who said they would take steps to encourage religious tolerance, but never followed through. Additionally, teachers witnessed the bullying and did nothing. The bullying continued at school and on Facebook.

When the student sued, the U.S. District Court for the Eastern District of New York ruled that the school officials violated his right to equal protection. They failed in the affirmative duty to act to protect the student from bullying that was premised on his religion. The student successfully argued that the school officials were deliberately indifferent to the harassment he suffered.

The Civil Rights Act and Other Federal Statutes

Litigation regarding bullying has not only been based on violations of constitutional rights but also on violations of Title VI of the Civil Rights Act of 1964, of Title IX of the Education Amendments Act of 1972, and of the Individual with Disabilities Education Act (IDEA). The common element in these types of litigation has been whether or not the school officials acted with deliberate indifference to the discriminatory bullying or harassment.

Bullying Based on Race or Ethnicity

Title VI under the Civil Rights Act of 1964 provides "No person in the United States shall, on the grounds of race, color or national origin be excluded from participation in, be denied benefits of, or be subjected to discrimination under any program or activity receiving Federal financial assistance." Anthony Zeno, a dark-skinned White and Latino 16-year-old and his younger sister moved from Long Island to a Pine Plains, New York, school in which less than 5% of students were minority students *(Zeno v. Pine Plains Central School District,* 2012). Anthony was a freshman and was immediately confronted with verbal and physical bullying based on

race. Anthony's mother wrote to the superintendent and met with the principal about the racial attacks against Anthony, but no action was taken to address the bullying. The harassment increased in severity throughout Anthony's years at the high school.

Anthony had been previously identified as a student eligible for services under IDEA. In Anthony's senior year, an individualized education program (IEP) was developed that indicated that "Anthony has been struggling with acceptance in the school environment. There have been numerous incidents between Anthony and others with prejudicial or racial overtones" (p. 661). The special education director, although aware of the situation, never investigated the bullying and harassment even though she was also the Title IX compliance officer and was responsible for investigating Title VI and Title IX complaints. Rather than stay in school any longer than he had to, Anthony chose to leave school with a special education diploma. He would have needed to remain one more semester to earn a standard high school diploma.

Establishing liability under Title VI is based on four factors: "(1) substantial control; (2) severe and discriminatory harassment; (3) actual knowledge; and (4) deliberate indifference" *(Zeno,* p. 655). In evaluating Anthony's allegations, the court pointed to the lack of sufficient effort on the part of the school district to address the bullying, even in light of its increasing severity. More importantly, Anthony was denied full educational benefit and diminished future prospects by accepting something less than a standard high school diploma. The U.S. Court of Appeals for the Second Circuit awarded Anthony $1 million for the school's deliberate indifference to the racial harassment Anthony suffered, a violation of Title VI of the 1964 Civil Rights Act.

Bullying Based on Gender

Sexual bullying and harassment cases are commonly litigated under Title IX of the Education Amendments Act of 1972. This can be the case even when the harassment is based only on perceptions of sexual differences. H.W., the minor child of P.W., experienced peer-on-peer bullying at two different schools based solely on perceived feminine traits *(P.W. et al. v. Fairport Central School District,* 2013). Teachers and administrators failed to act in an appropriate manner at either school.

H.W. complained to the counselor almost daily about teasing, name calling, comments written on his locker, being shoved and stabbed with pencils. He was bullied and abused on numerous occasions. On one occasion a student grabbed and squeezed his nipples. There was a video recording of the incident. The assistant principal, after watching the tape, responded, "It definitely appeared as if something happened," but there was no evidence presented at trial that disciplinary action was taken. H.W. continued to be subjected to vulgar taunts and physical harassment.

The parents sued, arguing their son's substantive due process rights had been violated. Citing *DeShaney,* the U.S. District Court for the Western District of New York dismissed this argument because neither a special relationship nor a state-created danger existed. However, the suit also alleged a violation of Title IX because of the peer-to-peer sexual harassment. The court declared that it usually does not like to second-guess a school's disciplinary decisions, but in this instance it appeared the school officials' actions were clearly unreasonable and that they were deliberately indifferent to the discriminatory harassment that H.W. suffered.

Bullying Based on Disabilities

Students with disabilities are common targets for bullying and harassment in public schools. In these situations, schools may face liability for not providing a free appropriate public education (FAPE) under IDEA if they act with deliberate indifference and thereby deny victims access to educational benefit because they no longer want to go to school.

Such was the case of a 12-year-old girl, L.K., who was diagnosed as autistic and then later reclassified as learning disabled and who was subjected to bullying because of her disability (*T.K. v. New York City Department of Education,* 2011). Teacher aides testified that L.K. was ostracized, bullied, tripped, and received prank phone calls. There were also school reports of L.K. being the aggressor, with one report accusing L.K. of hitting a teacher. In a meeting with the principal, the parents sought to discuss the bullying of their daughter, but the principal said it was inappropriate and refused to discuss the matter.

Court records later revealed that no school documentation was maintained regarding the reports that

L.K. had been bullied. In ruling for the plaintiffs, the U.S. District Court for the Eastern District of New York determined that bullying based on disability can be a denial of FAPE under the IDEA. As L.K.'s father described it, "this constant bullying made her emotionally unavailable to learn" (p. 295) and, therefore, she was unable to receive any meaningful educational benefit.

In many instances, plaintiffs also allege violations of Section 504 of the Rehabilitation Act of 1973 and the American with Disabilities Act (ADA). Courts may apply the *Davis* deliberate indifference standard to peer-to-peer harassment claims under these two federal statutes.

Schools' Responsibility to Protect

Allegations of federal constitutional and statutory violations that stem from bullying have resulted in mixed outcomes. Due process claims under the 14th Amendment are the least likely to succeed. Equal protection claims may be successful if the plaintiffs are able to demonstrate that the bullying was predicated on discriminatory factors such as race, religion, or gender and that school officials acted with deliberate indifference in addressing the problem.

Cases involving federal statutory violations under Title VI and Title IX may be successful for the same reasons that equal protection claims succeed. In successful cases, the plaintiff suffered severe discriminatory harassment and school authorities failed to take reasonable measures to stem the abuse. Claims under IDEA, ADA, and Section 504 may also succeed if the student is subject to ongoing, pervasive bullying based on a disability, and the result of the harassment is denial of educational benefit.

Regardless of whether or not school officials have an affirmative duty under the law to protect students from bullying, they are not absolved of their moral and ethical responsibilities for the physical and emotional well-being of all the children in their schools. If their own personal biases and prejudices color their judgment, then it is necessary for these individuals to reflect on their fitness to lead schools. Likewise, while there may not be a special relationship, as defined by Supreme Court, between the schools and the children who attend them, there is a moral and ethical relationship that is promulgated by the professional organizations and literature that are associated with school leadership and that is rooted in the democratic and equity principles on which public education is based.

Guidelines for Preventing and Responding to Harassment and Bullying

There is substantial literature on educational programs and services to addressing bullying behavior and victimization. For the purposes of this chapter, however, it is important to highlight policy recommendations that aid school district authorities in establishing school climates that clearly communicate that bullying behavior is not tolerated.

There are legal resources that provide guidance on how to establish a climate that prevents bullying. Payne (2010) suggests that the following four types of actions—preventative, protective, punitive, and public—are helpful in protecting children from harassment and bullying and protecting school officials from possible liability (Payne, 2010, pp. 14–15):

1. Preventative Actions
   a. Adopt policies that prohibit bullying and harassment;
   b. Implement programs that promote tolerance and acceptance of all students;
   c. Provide training to both staff and students focused on educating them to recognize harassment and bullying and what is appropriate behavior;
   d. Evaluate and assess the school environment to detect harassment and/or bullying; and
   e. Have faculty and staff report regularly on aspects regarding the culture and social atmosphere of the school, such as students who are alone.

2. Protective Actions
   a. Have procedures for investigating and reporting inappropriate actions by anyone;
   b. Take immediate action to protect students who may be harassed or bullied; and
   c. Implement procedures to protect those who are bullied or harassed and those who might report harassment.

3. Punitive Action Against Wrongdoers
   a. Investigate, collect facts and immediately discipline individuals committing acts of harassment or bullying; and
   b. Punish not only the primary bully but those who have been involved, such as co-conspirators or

individuals who participated in bullying or harassment.

4. Public Action
   a. Release statement by the school officials and School Board to the public that those types of behaviors will not be tolerated, and
   b. Have press releases and transparency on your action against those individuals.

Other strategies are: (a) having staff model appropriate behavior; (b) publicizing rules prohibiting harassment and bullying and consequences to students; (c) being consistent in applying all rules; (d) reporting to proper authorities, such as law enforcement, student actions that are beyond the realm of student discipline; and (e) recognizing cultural diversity and its role in social issues (Payne, 2010).

The school leader can support all of these interventions by deciding, and acting upon the decision, that such behaviors are unacceptable in the school that he or she is leading. The administrator of the school must make clear that he or she supports the law, and is also the leader of the school who makes value-based decisions that inform his or her moral and ethical responsibilities to the child.

Search and Seizure and Student Privacy Rights

School safety measures include search and seizure policies and practices. Searches may be for drugs, weapons, or other contraband prohibited by state law or school policy, but are sometimes challenged by students who allege school officials or school resource officers (SROs) violated their right to privacy. All legal searches exit at the nexus between a student's right to privacy and school officials' need to maintain a safe and secure learning environment. The balance between these competing interests has been adjudicated under the Fourth Amendment, which provides:

The right of the people to be secure in their persons, houses, papers, and effects against unreasonable searches and seizures, shall not be violated, and no warrants shall issue but upon probable cause, supported by oath or affirmation, and particularly describing the place to be searched, and the persons or things to be seized.

Although there is no mention of the word privacy in the Fourth Amendment, the Supreme Court has determined that it implies a right to privacy and that privacy is fundamental to individual freedom (*Griswold v. Connecticut,* 1965). Just as with freedom of speech, privacy rights exist in tension with the **compelling state interest** of school districts to maintain a safe and secure learning environment in the schools. This section will use case law to explain to what extent students enjoy a right of privacy and under what conditions that right may be abridged by school officials.

School Searches and Reasonable Suspicion

The U. S. Supreme Court established guidelines for school searches in the landmark case, *New Jersey v. T.L.O.* (1985). A New Jersey high school teacher discovered two girls in the bathroom smoking, a violation of the high school's no-smoking policy. The teacher escorted the girls to the assistant principal's office where one of the girls admitted to smoking. However, T.L.O. denied smoking. The assistant principal demanded to see T.L.O.'s purse where he found cigarettes, cigarette rolling papers, a small amount of marijuana, a pipe, a number of plastic bags, a substantial amount of money in one-dollar bills, and an index card with a list of names of students who owed T.L.O. money.

T.L.O.'s mother and the police were notified. All of the items confiscated from T.L.O.'s purse were given to law enforcement. At the police station T.L.O. confessed to selling marijuana at school, a crime for which she was charged with delinquency. T.L.O. alleged that the search was illegal under the Fourth Amendment and therefore the evidence obtained by the search should be excluded.

The New Jersey Supreme Court ruled that the Fourth Amendment applied to school officials and that the evidence should be excluded under what is known as the *exclusionary rule.* The Supreme Court accepted the school district's appeal, indicating it was primarily interested in the question of "whether the exclusionary rule should operate to bar consideration in juvenile delinquency proceedings of evidence unlawfully seized by a school official without the involvement of law enforcement officers" (p. 737).

Ultimately, the Court ordered rearguments on "the broader question of what limits, if any, the Fourth Amendment places on the activities of school authorities" (p. 738). The Court justified this by observing the difficulty lower courts were having in weighing the constitutionality of searches by school officials in light of the privacy rights of students and the school authorities' obligation to provide a "safe environment conducive to education in the public schools" (p. 735).

The Supreme Court concluded that the Fourth Amendment did apply to school officials. But in the majority opinion, Justice Byron White wrote:

> But striking the balance between school children's legitimate expectation of privacy and the schools' equally legitimate need to maintain an environment in which learning can take place requires some easing of the restrictions to which search by public authorities are ordinarily subject. Thus, school officials need not obtain a warrant before searching a student who is under their authority. (p. 735)

The Justices determined that probable cause could not apply to school officials because the necessity to act when a potential danger arises in school ran counter the logistics of obtaining a search warrant. The Court replaced the probable cause and search warrant requirements with the lower standard of reasonable suspicion for school officials. Reasonableness was to be predicated on "whether the search was *justified at its inception* and whether . . . it was *reasonably related in scope to the circumstances* that justified the interference in the first place" (emphasis added) (p. 735). The court further stipulated that "a search will be permissible in its scope when the measures adopted are reasonably related to the objectives of the search and *not excessively intrusive in light of the student's age and sex and the nature of the infraction*" (emphasis added) (p. 735).

The result of the Court's crafting legal guidelines to govern searches and seizures by school officials led the Justices to conclude that the search of T.L.O.'s purse by the assistant principal was not illegal. The school administrator had a reasonable suspicion that T.L.O. had violated a school rule and that searching her purse would lead to evidence that supported that suspicion. The search itself was reasonable in nature and scope in light of the suspected violation, and it was not overly intrusive relative to the suspected violation and in light of the student's age and sex.

The lower standard of reasonable suspicion makes it easier for school authorities to find and seize evidence that may be used to discipline students as well as to criminally prosecute the offender. School administrators avoid a violation of the Fourth Amendment when:

- They have established reasonable suspicion that a violation has occurred, is occurring, or will occur.
- The suspicion is individualized; that is, suspicion is focused on a particular student. An administrator may not engage in a fishing expedition by searching a group of students in hope of finding a guilty one. However, there may be "special needs" that allow school officials to conduct nonintrusive random searches, such as metal detector or locker searches.
- The search is justified at its inception. That means that the reasonable suspicion existed prior to the search and did not emerge as a result of a search.
- The nature and scope of the search is reasonably related to the circumstances. In other words, the intrusiveness of the search must not extend beyond what is required in relationship to the suspected violation. For instance, a school administrator would violate the criteria of a reasonable search if he or she conducted a strip search to look for missing money. A strip search might be warranted if the school administrator has a strong suspicion that the student is concealing a weapon.

In the words of the Court's majority opinion in *T.L.O.,* "the reasonableness standard should ensure that the interests of students will be invaded no more than is necessary to achieve the legitimate end of preserving order in the schools" (p. 743).

Establishing Reasonable Suspicion

Reasonable suspicion should be based on facts or circumstances that would lead a reasonable person to believe a school violation has occurred or is about to occur. In *T.L.O.,* the assistant principal had the word of a teacher who caught the students in the bathroom smoking. Sometimes, school administrators get tips from students or informants.

The reliability of student information is crucial in establishing reasonable suspicion (Cox, Sughrue, Cornelius, & Alexander, 2012; Mawdsley & Cummings, 2008). Questions that the administrator should consider are: Is the information credible, reliable, and trustworthy? Is there a disciplinary record that indicates the student has been in trouble? Has the student informed on other students before? What are their grades and attendance records? Most importantly, the school administrator should attempt to corroborate the student informant's information, if there is no imminent danger (Mawdsley & Cummings, 2008). The Supreme Court has instructed lower courts to evaluate informants' tips based on the "'totality of the circumstances' while allowing for the 'lesser showing required' to meet the reasonable suspicion standard" (*Phaneuf v. Fraikin,* 2006, p. 597).

There are instances in which students provide false information solely for the purpose of getting another student in trouble (Cox et al., 2012). In one such case, a group of boys reported to the assistant principal that another in their class, Joseph Fewless, had claimed to have a dime roll of marijuana and had pulled it out of his pants pocket to show them (*Fewless v. Board of Education of Wayland Union Schools,* 2002). The assistant principal, with the assistance of the SRO, questioned Fewless and asked him to hand over anything that he should not have. He complied, pulling out a lighter and a dime roll, but the dime roll did not have any marijuana in it. He was sent back to class.

A couple of the boys returned later in the day to the assistant principal and told him that Fewless had bragged that he got away with possessing drugs because he had hidden them between his buttocks. With that information, the assistant principal and SRO returned Fewless to the office and conducted a strip search. Nothing was found. Later it was revealed that the boys had made up the story to get Fewless in trouble in retaliation for trouble they had gotten into when they purposely damaged something that he had been working on in class. The class teacher had told the assistant principal that the boys had told him the same story, but he had not witnessed anything that would lead him to believe they were telling the truth. The U.S. District Court for the Western District of Michigan held that the assistant principal and SRO had violated Fewless's civil rights by conducting an intrusive search based on unsubstantiated reports by a group of boys who reported what they suspected "en masse," and not individually. The assistant principal had failed to adequately investigate their allegations and had not checked disciplinary records, where he would have discovered that some of the boys had been in trouble previously for harassing Fewless.

Caution Regarding Strip Searches

Strip searches are extremely invasive and therefore warrant particular scrutiny by the courts. As illustrated in *Fewless,* school officials may find themselves liable for violating a student's civil rights if they have not established the threshold of reasonable suspicion based on reliable information and if the strip search is not reasonable in light of the suspected violation and the age and sex of the student. In 2009, the Supreme Court provided some guidance on strip searches in *Safford Unified School District v. Redding.* It is another example in which the principal neither vetted an informant nor properly investigated the allegations prior to conducting a strip search. Importantly, the circumstances did not indicate a need for urgency.

Safford Unified School District had a policy that prohibited "[a]ny prescription or over-the-counter drugs except those of which permission to use in school is granted" (p. 2640). The assistant principal in one of the district schools had received information from two students that Savana Redding, a 13-year-old student, had been the source of providing something akin to Advil to students. He brought Savana to his office where he had a day planner in his possession. Several days prior, he had taken the planner from another girl, Marissa Glines, at which time he opened the planner and found knives, lighters, a permanent marker, and a cigarette. Marissa insisted that the contraband was not hers because the planner was not hers. She had borrowed it from Savana.

He asked Savana if the day planner was indeed hers. She answered that it was, but that she had loaned it to Marissa several days before. He then showed her four white prescription pills and one over-the-counter pill. Denying any knowledge of the pills, Savana gave the assistant principal permission to search her backpack, but he did not find contraband. The assistant principal instructed a female administrative assistant to take Savana to the school nurse's office where she and the nurse strip searched her. Savana was asked to remove her jacket, shoes, socks, her pants, and T-shirt. She was then asked to pull out and shake her bra and to pull the elastic on her underpants, the result of which exposed her breasts and pelvic area. No pills were found.

A week prior to Savana's strip search, a male student gave the assistant principal a white pill he said Marissa had given him. Marissa was taken to the office and asked to turn her pockets out and open her wallet where a blue pill, several white pills, and a razor blade were found. She said the pills were given to her by Savana. The administrative assistant and nurse were instructed to strip search Marissa, but nothing more was found. It was based on Marissa's claim alone and a week later that the assistant principal spoke to and searched Savana and her belongings.

Savana sued, claiming her civil rights had been violated by being subjected to an unconstitutional strip search. In evaluating her claim, the Supreme Court relied on *T.L.O.,* re-emphasizing that a school search must pass the reasonableness test. The Court ruled that the assistant principal had sufficient reasonable suspicion to search Savana's backpack and outer clothing. That search was not intrusive relative to the suspected offense. However, the Court determined that there was neither adequate reasonable suspicion nor sufficiently strong circumstances to justify extending the search to Savana's person.

In the majority opinion, Justice David Souter wrote that a strip search of an adolescent is "embarrassing, frightening, and humiliating" (p. 2641) and should only occur when there is an immediate danger to the well-being of the student or others in the school. Strip searching Savana, a week after Marissa told the administrator that Savana had given her the equivalent of an over-the-counter pain reliever and in the absence of any reports of students becoming ill, was not reasonable in view of the circumstances and in light of the age and sex of the student. As stated in the majority opinion:

> [W]hat was missing from the suspected facts that pointed to Savana was any indication of danger to the students from the power of the drugs or their quantity, and any reason to suppose that Savana was carrying pills in her underwear. We think that the combination of these deficiencies was fatal to finding the search reasonable. (p. 2642)

The indignity of a strip search does not disqualify schools from ever performing them. But, strip searches require a degree of suspicion that correlates with the degree of intrusion created by the search.

[T]o limit a school search to reasonable scope requires the support of reasonable suspicion of danger or of resort to underwear for hiding evidence of wrongdoing before a search can reasonably make the quantum leap from outer clothes and backpacks to exposure of intimate parts. The meaning of such a search, and the degradation its subject may reasonably feel, *place a search that intrusive in a category of its own demanding its own specific suspicions* [emphasis added]. (p. 2643)

California, Michigan, Missouri, New Jersey, Wisconsin, South Carolina, Iowa, and Washington have prohibited or strictly limited strip searches in schools. Even in the absence of a statutory prohibition, many states authorize school districts to develop and implement policy that bans strip searches. New York City Schools was one of the first districts to place an absolute ban on strip searches. In contextualizing students dressing and undressing in school, Souter observed in the majority opinion in *Safford* that:

Changing for gym is getting ready for play; exposing for a search is responding to an accusation reserved for suspected wrongdoers and fairly understood as so degrading that a number of communities have decided that strip searches in schools are never reasonable and have banned them no matter what the facts may be. (p. 2642)

Unreasonable Searches

Regardless of the fact that the *T.L.O.* guidelines on constitutional searches have been in place for three decades, case law still is being adjudicated on the legality of school searches. This illustrates that many school leaders still do not know under what circumstances they can conduct a search of a student or of his or her things. A good example of this is *T.S. v. State of Florida* (2012).

A student, T.S., and her mother arrived at school early to meet with the school's guidance counselor. The student had a book bag, which was prohibited by school rules. After the meeting the counselor reminded the student of the rule and allowed her to leave the book bag in the counselor's office so as not to violate school rules.

On four different occasions during the day the student came to the counselor's office asking to have access to the book bag; the counselor denied the student access. The counselor testified, "I was

thinking about how many times she came to retrieve her book bag, [and] I started wondering why is it so important to her" (p. 1290), whereupon, the counselor searched the book bag and found marijuana and related paraphernalia.

The U.S. Court of Appeals for the Second Circuit ruled that the search was unreasonable and was conducted on nothing more than an "unsupported hunch that something wasn't right" (p. 1292). School officials attempted to assert that the student's disciplinary history in the school substantiated the counselor's feeling that the student might be in violation of a school rule. However, this argument was not made at trial, so it was inadmissible upon appeal. The appellate court said that such a record might support a search, but the "alleged disciplinary history cannot support the search of her book bag when no evidence of that history was presented at the trial court" (p. 1293).

Evidence secured by means of an illegal search may be excluded in court, but that does not mean that it cannot be used by the school to discipline the student. In fact, the primary concern of school leaders should be ensuring a safe and secure learning environment, not preserving evidence to prosecute a student. However, school officials may not relinquish their obligation to respect students' rights to privacy in order to search whenever and whatever they like.

An example of school authorities authorizing unreasonable searches involved two Santa Fe high schools that employed a private security service to perform pat-down searches of all students attending school proms, homecoming, and other school events (*Herrera v. Santa Fe Public Schools*, 2013). In describing the nature of the searches to which the students were subjected, one of the plaintiffs stated that

[The security guard] had me spread my arms and legs out, and she patted along my arms, touched along the waist. And then she grabbed the outer part of my bra and moved it here. And then she grabbed the inner part of my bra and moved it here. And then she cupped my breasts and shook them . . . [T]hen afterwards she moved down to my waist and then she went all the way down my leg. And then she felt over my dress and then she pulled the dress up to about mid-thigh and she felt up the bare leg, as well. (p. 1194)

Three other girls gave similar depositions. They also stated that school employees stood a few feet away while the students were patted down. School representatives argued that the pat-down search was reasonable in light of their efforts to dissuade attendees from bringing drugs, alcohol, weapons, tobacco, or other contraband to the events. Four students brought suit against the school district and the principal. The district court disagreed with the school district's position, concluding that "patting down students, without any individualized reasonable suspicion, [was] unreasonably intrusive" (p. 1249) and unconstitutional. The court noted that touching students' bodies, particularly in the absence of any suspicion that a serious offense had been committed, was an intrusive search and therefore unreasonable.

Special Needs Doctrine

The **special needs doctrine** creates exceptions to individualized suspicion, thereby allowing for random searches under certain circumstances. It was first articulated in *T.L.O.* (1985) when the Court relieved school officials of the obligation to establish probable cause and to obtain a warrant prior to conducting a search of a student in a school. The Court opined that it was burdensome to school officials to adhere to the normal requirements of the Fourth Amendment because of the unique setting and circumstances that comprise public schools. In other words, it would jeopardize the compelling state interest in maintaining order and safety in school and, therefore, there was a *special need* to dispense with the probable cause and warrant constraints on government searches and seizures under the Fourth Amendment.

The special needs doctrine has since become the legal basis with which the Supreme Court has found random drug testing of students involved with extracurricular activities to be constitutional. Random drug testing is conducted through the collection of urine samples that are then forwarded to a laboratory for testing. (It should be noted that collecting urine samples is a form of seizure; that is why random drug testing is both a search and a seizure.) Two Supreme Court search and seizure cases, *Vernonia School District 47J v. Acton* (1995) and *Board of Education of Independent School District No. 92 of Pottawatomie v. Earls* (2002), addressed school district policies that required random drug testing of students involved in extracurricular activities. *Vernonia* dictated drug testing of student athletes and *Pottawatomie* extended

testing to all students involved in sports and other competitive extracurricular activities. In both cases, the Court relied on the special needs precedent it had established in *T.L.O.*

The Court found both districts' drug testing policies to be reasonable and exempt from Fourth Amendment search requisites because (a) of the districts' special needs in ensuring the safety and well-being of students involved in competitive extracurricular activities, (b) they were not designed to detect personal and private medical conditions or information, and (c) a positive test result was not used to suspend or expel a student from school. Even prior to these decisions, lower courts upheld random drug testing of students involved in any extracurricular activity or in exercising a school privilege, such as driving a car to school. All these decisions relied on the *T.L.O.* special needs doctrine to exempt school officials from the individualized suspicion standard.

New Privacy Questions: Cell Phones in Schools

The courts have addressed several legal questions pertaining to cell phones. Specifically, they have determined that school officials may regulate or even ban cell phone use in schools. Courts have also upheld the suspension of a student whose cell phone rang during class where the school policy stated that cell phones must be kept in lockers.

One controversy regarding cell phones is if and when a school administrator may search the contents of a student's phone, including accessing its memory and contact list. In 2014 in a case involving an arrest, the Supreme Court unanimously held that searching and seizing the digital contents of a cell phone without a warrant during an arrest is unconstitutional (*Riley v. California*, 2014). The Court found profound differences between the contents of an old-fashioned cell phone and today's smartphones that can hold all of the private information associated with a person's life. The Court ruled that this abundance of personal information is protected under the Fourth Amendment from warrantless search by the police.

It is important to emphasize that *Riley* was not a case involving an educational institution. It was an incident during a police arrest of a criminal suspect. The implications of *Riley* for the schools will not be fully understood until future school cases are brought to the courts. One of the questions to be answered is whether or not there will be circumstances that allow the special needs doctrine from *T.L.O.* (1985) to overcome school administrators' restrictions on warrantless cell phone searches that may arise in school cases following *Riley* (2014).

In the meantime, school administrators, pursuing their goal of maintaining order and safety in the schools, can still obtain guidance from the three school cases regarding the legality of searching a student's cell phone for evidence of a possible school violation: (a) *Klump v. Nazareth Area School District,* 2006; (b) *J.W. v. Desoto County School District,* 2010; and (c) *G.C. v. Owensboro Public Schools,* 2013.

In *Klump,* the school had a policy that cell phones could not be used or displayed during school hours. A student's phone was confiscated by a teacher who then gave it to the assistant principal. Together they accessed the student's text messages, contact list, and voice mail. They called individuals on the list and even held a conversation with the student's brother using instant messaging by pretending to be the student. The U.S. District Court for the Eastern District of Pennsylvania ruled the school officials were justified in seizing the phone because it violated school policy prohibiting use or displaying cell phones at school. However, school officials were not justified in accessing the student's phone messages and in calling other students as "they had no reason to suspect at the outset that such a search would reveal that [the student] himself was violating another policy" (p. 640). Although the school officials ultimately found evidence of drug activity by accessing the student's messages, the court concluded that "the school officials did not see the allegedly drug-related text messages until after they initiated the search of [the] cell phone" (p. 640). The teacher and administrator were found to have violated Klump's Fourth Amendment rights through an illegal search for which the defendants had not established reasonable suspicion of illegal drug activity at the inception of the search.

The school policy in *DeSoto* (2010) prohibited students from possessing or using cell phones at school. A student, R.W. (son of J.W.), was observed using his phone and was asked to close the phone and give it to a teacher. School officials then opened the phone to look at the student's pictures. The pictures showed the student at home in the bathroom and another student pictured holding a BB gun. A second school official and a police officer examined the photos again. Based on their interpretation of the photos, R.W. was accused of having "gang pictures," which violated a school policy of "wearing or displaying in any manner on school property . . . clothing, apparel, accessories, or drawings or messages associated with any gang [that was] associated with criminal activity, as defined by law enforcement agencies" (p. 4). The police officer testified he recognized gang symbols in the photographs, which presented a threat to school safety. For this reason the student was expelled.

The U.S. District Court for the Northern District of Mississippi ruled that the school officials' and police officer's actions were justified. In evaluating the reasonableness of the defendants' actions, the court determined that a "crucial factor" was that R.W. was caught using his cell phone at school, a clear violation of school rules. The court determined that it was proper for the school official to determine why the student was using the phone when it was clearly against school policy to even have one in the school.

The court noted that the *Klump* case was distinguishable from *DeSoto* because the school in *Klump* allowed cell phones in the school, just not their use, whereas the school in *DeSoto* banned cell phones altogether. For that reason, school officials had reasonable suspicion that R.W. was violating another school rule while talking on his cell phone.

In the third case, *G.C. v. Owensboro Public Schools* (2013), the U.S. Court of Appeals for the Sixth Circuit analyzed both the *Klump* and *DeSoto* cases in reaching its decision. It determined that "the fact-based approach taken in *Klump* more accurately reflects [the] court's standard than the blanket rule set forth in *DeSoto*" (p. 633).

G.C. had had problems in school, such as being suspended for yelling, hitting a locker, fighting, and excessive tardy violations. He admitted previously that he had used drugs and that he thought of suicide. In this instance, G.C. violated the school cell phone policy by texting in class and became upset when his cell phone was confiscated by his teacher. The teacher then gave the phone to the assistant principal who read four text messages. The assistant principal said she was looking for something "to see if there was an issue with which I could help him so that he would not do something harmful to himself or someone else" (p. 627).

The court, in agreeing with *Klump,* ruled that there was no reasonable suspicion at the inception of the search, even in light of the assistant principal's justification. It determined that the circumstances that led to the teacher confiscating G.C.'s phone did not establish reasonable suspicion that there was something more going on that would require a search of his phone.

In the aftermath of *Riley v. California* (2014), other cases involving the search of students' cell phones will likely to go to federal court, and the decisions in these cases will provide further guidance to school administrators. Until then, school officials would be wise to clearly establish reasonable suspicion of the violation, or imminent violation, of a school rule in order to justify a search of photos, text messages, call logs, and other data stored in cell phones.

Conclusion

The two topics discussed in this chapter, bullying and search and seizure, continue to create legal problems for school personnel as they attempt to confront circumstances they perceive jeopardize the learning environment and well-being of students and of school personnel. In crafting and implementing school safety policies, school administrators should remain cognizant of students' rights and how the courts have weighed them against the state's compelling interest in creating and maintaining a safe teaching and learning environment. Reactive measures to confront bullying, particularly cyberbullying, may result in violations of student free speech under the First Amendment while unreasonable searches and seizures may infringe on students' privacy rights under the Fourth Amendment.

The intent here, primarily through explanations of statutory and case law, was (a) to instruct school officials on the judicial reasoning that governs how a court weighs a compelling state interest that promotes a safe and orderly learning environment against protecting the constitutional rights of students, (b) to educate school leaders about the difficulties in legislating against bullying and

cyberbullying, and (c) to explicate the standards that determine if a school search or seizure is reasonable under the Fourth Amendment.

More importantly, the purpose was to remind educators of the larger context—their moral and ethical responsibility to the child. While law and policy may not require a standard of care that anticipates all possible threats, especially those that exist outside the school or that are the acts of private individuals, school leaders should always act and make decisions that consider child welfare. Child welfare requires a safe school but also recognition for the role of government and its actors to respect constitutional rights. Society, as represented by our courts, recognizes and honors this responsibility and the herculean task of living up to it.

Key Chapter Terms

Compelling state interest: This term refers to a judicial method of determining the constitutionality of a law. Under this test, the government's interest is balanced against the individual's constitutional right that may be infringed by the law (strict scrutiny test) or the individual's right to be free of that law (rational relationship test). A law that infringes on a constitutional right will be upheld only if the government's interest is strong enough. (USLegal.com. *Compelling-state-interest-test law & legal definition.* Retrieved from http://definitions.uslegal.com/c/compelling-state-interest-test/)

Deliberate indifference: The conscious or reckless disregard of an administrator's duty to enforce policy and law at the expense of the safety and well-being of someone under his or her supervision or care. School officials who fail to respond to known acts of bullying, harassment, or discriminatory behavior are liable under the deliberate indifference standard. (*Davis v. Monroe Cnty. Bd. of Educ.,* 1999).

Equal protection clause of the 14th Amendment: The equal protection clause is a federal constitutional assurance that state government must operate within the law and must not offend the federal constitutional rights of individuals, including students. In other words, school authorities cannot abridge the equal protection rights of students by treating them differently than other students based on their status, such as their race, religion, sex, or other protected status. (Legal Information Institute, n.d. Retrieved from http://www.law.cornell.edu/wex/due_process)

Liberty and property interests under the due process clause of the 14th Amendment: Life, liberty, and property are substantive (nontrivial) rights protected under the due process clause of the 14th Amendment. School authorities may not deprive students of their liberty and property rights without first following fair procedures that apply to all students. These procedures comprise the process due the students so they are treated fairly and justly, and minimize the possibility that the government has erred and may be wrongfully depriving students of their rights (Legal Information Institute, n.d. Retrieved from http://www.law.cornell.edu/wex/due_process).

Qualified immunity: Qualified immunity shields school officials (and other state actors) from civil liability so long as they did not violate an individual's clearly established statutory or constitutional rights. The immunity turns on the concept of "clearly established" law. First, the court must determine if the government actor did indeed violate a clearly established law or right and then it must decide if a reasonable person would have known that his or her actions were in violation of that law or right (*Safford Unif. Sch. Dist. v. Redding,* 2009).

Shocks the conscience: The substantive component of the due process clause is violated by school authorities when their actions can be "characterized as arbitrary, or conscience shocking, in a constitutional sense. . . . The concept of conscience-shocking . . . points clearly away from liability, or clearly toward it." Conduct intended to deprive a student of a substantive constitutional right "in some way unjustifiable by any government interest is the sort of official action most likely to rise to the conscience-shocking level" (*Neal ex rel. Neal v. Fulton County Board of Education,* 2000, p. 1074).

Special needs doctrine: Provides school officials (and law enforcement personnel) an exemption from the normal requirements of probable cause and court-issued search warrants under the Fourth Amendment when there are exceptional circumstances that require administrators to act to protect a compelling state interest. Keeping weapons and drugs out of schools and protecting the safety and well-being of students and school personnel are considered compelling state interests that would be difficult to enforce if probable cause and search warrants were required prior to conducting any search. The doctrine was later extended to cover suspicionless and random drug searches (*New Jersey v. T.L.O.,* 1985; *Vernonia Sch. Dist. 47J v. Acton,* 1995; *Bd. of Educ. of Indep. Sch. Dist. No. 92 of Pottawatomie Cnty. v. Earls,* 2002).

References

Cox, B., Sughrue, J. A., Cornelius, L. M., & Alexander, M. D. (2012). *The challenges to school policing.* Dayton, OH: Education Law Association.

Florida Department of Education. (n.d.). *Criteria for district bullying, including cyberbullying, and harassment policies.* Retrieved from https://www.fldoe.org/safeschools/doc/CriteriaPolicies.doc

Hinduja, S., & Patchin, J. W. (2014, February). *State cyberbullying laws: A brief review of state cyberbullying laws and policies.* Retrieved from http://www.cyberbullying.us/Bullying_and_Cyberbullying_Laws.pdf

Janson, G. R., & Hazler, R. J. (2004, April). Trauma reactions of bystanders and victims to repetitive abuse experiences. *Violence and Victims, 19*(2), 239–255.

Limber, S. P. (2002). Addressing youth bullying behaviors. *Proceedings from the American Medical Association Educational Forum on Adolescent Health: Youth Bullying.* Chicago, IL: American Medical Association. Retrieved from http://www.ncdsv.org/images/AMA_EdForumAdolescentHealthYouthBullying_5-3-2002.pdf

Mawdsley, R. D., & Cummings, J. (2008). Reliability of student informants and strip searches. *West Education Law Rev. 23,* 1.

Moses, D. (2007). Westlaw, UILJL 239, 3193.

Neiman, S., Robers, B., & Robers, S. (2012). Bullying: A state of affairs. *Journal of Law & Education, 41,* 603–648.

Payne, A. M. (2010). Particular public school district liability issues arising from student or staff use of computers, Internet, or other electronic media to harass or bully students. 115 *Am. Jur. Trials, 355,* pp. 14–15.

Stopbullying.gov. (n.d.). Retrieved from http://www .stopbullying.gov/what-is-bullying/

Stuart-Cassel, V., Bell, A., & Springer, J. F. (2011). *Analysis of state bullying laws and policies.* Prepared for the U.S. Department of Education, Office of Planning, Evaluation and Policy Development. Retrieved from https://www2.ed.gov/ rschstat/eval/bullying/state-bullying-laws/state- bullying-laws.pdf

Tefertiller, T. (2011). Out of the principal's office and into the courtroom: How should California approach criminal remedies for school bullying? *Berkeley Journal of Criminal Law, 16,* 168–220.

Warren, B. J. (2011, October). Two sides of the coin: The bully and the bullied. *Journal of Psychosocial Nursing and Mental Health Services, 49*(10), 22–29.

Statutes and Court Decisions

Board of Education of Independent School District No. 92 of Pottawatomie County v. Earls, 536 U.S. 822, 122 S.Ct. 2559 (2002).

Civil Rights Act of 1964, 20 U.S.C §2000d.

Davis v. Monroe County Board of Education, 526 U.S. 629, 119 S.Ct. 1661 (1999).

DeShaney v. Winnebago County Dept. of Social Services, 489 U.S. 189 (1998).

Doe v. Covington Cnty. Sch. Dist., 675 F.3d 849 (5th Cir. 2012).

Fewless v. Board of Education of Wayland Union Schools, 204 F. Supp. 2d 806 (W.D. Mich. 2002).

G.C. v. Owensboro Public Schools, 711 F.3d 623 (6th Cir. 2013).

G.D.S. v. Northport-East Northport Union Free School District, 915 F.Supp.2d 268 (E.D. N.Y. 2012).

Griswold v. Connecticut, 381 U.S. 479 (1965).

Herrera v. Santa Fe Public Schools, 956 F.Supp 2d 1191 (D. N.M. 2013).

J.W. v. DeSoto County School District, 2010 U.S. Dist. LEXIS 116328 (N.D. Miss. 2010).

Kowalski v. Berkeley County Schools, 652 F.2d 565 (4th Cir. 2011).

Klump v. Nazareth Area School District, 425 F.Supp. 2d 622 (E.D. Pa. 2006).

Morrow v. Balaski, 719 F.3d 160 (3d Cir. 2013).

Morse v. Frederick, 551 U.S. 393, 127 S.Ct. 2618 (2007).

Nabozny v. Podlesny, 92 F.3d 446 (7th Cir. 1996).

Neal ex rel. Neal v. Fulton County Board of Education, 229 F.3d 1069 (11th Cir. 2000).

New Jersey v. T.L.O., 469 U.S.325, 105 S.Ct 733 (1985).

Phaneuf v. Fraikin, 448 F.3d 591 (2nd Cir. 2006).

P.W. et al. v. Fairport Central School District, ___F. Supp.2d___(W.D.N.Y. 2013).

Reno v. ACLU, 521 U.S. 844, 117 S. Ct. 2329 (1997).

Riley v. California, 573 U.S. ____ (2014).

Safford Unified School District v. Redding, 557 U.S. 364, 129 S.Ct. 2633 (2009).

Smith v. Guildford Bd. of Educ., 226 Fed. App'x 58 (2nd Cir. 2007).

Smith v. Half Hollow Hills Central School District, 298 F.3d 168 (2nd Cir. 2002).

Tinker v. Des Moines, 393 U.S. 503, 89 S.Ct. 733 (1969).

Title VI of the 1964 Civil Rights Act, 42 U.S.C §2000d.

Title IX, the Education Amendment Act of 1972, 20 .U.S.C. §§ 1681–1688.

T.K. v. New York City Department of Education, 779 F.Supp.2d 289 (E.D.N.Y. 2011).

T.S. v. State of Florida, 100 So.3d 1289 (Fla. Dist. Ct. App. 2012).

Veronia School Dist. 47J v. Acton, 515 U.S. 646, 115 S.Ct. 2386 (1995).

Zeno v. Pine Plains Central School District, 702 F.3d 655 (2nd Cir. 2012).

Further Readings

Cox, B., Sughrue, J. A., Cornelius, L. M., & Alexander, M. D. (2012). *The challenges to school policing.* Dayton, OH: Education Law Association.

This monograph provides comprehensive guidance on Fourth and Fifth Amendment applications in school

settings. T.L.O.'s guidelines on constitutional searches are explained, as well as judicial doctrines such as the special needs provision and the exclusionary rule. It provides considerable guidance on the case law that governs student seizures. It also describes the role of SROs in schools, including a discussion of when it is appropriate for SROs to conduct searches and interrogations of students, the latter of which is covered by the Fifth Amendment.

Hinduja, S., & Patchin, J. W. (2014, February). *State cyberbullying laws: A brief review of state cyberbullying laws and policies.* Retrieved from http://www.cyberbullying.us/Bullying_and_Cyberbullying_Laws.pdf

This website provided up-to-date information about state cyberbullying laws and policies.

King, A. V. (2010). Constitutionality of cyberbullying laws: Keeping the online playground safe for both teens and free speech. *Vanderbilt Law Review, 63*(3), 845–884.

King's article examines the phenomenon called cyberbullying and legislative attempts to provide protection for children from those who would bully them through digital technologies and social media.

Neiman, S., Robers, B., & Robers, S. (2012). Bullying: A state of affairs. *Journal of Law & Education, 41,* 603–648.

The primary focus of the authors is an exploration of definitions, prevalence, and effects of bullying, as well as a description of prevention and intervention programs and services. They also compare and contrast state laws and regulations that cover bullying and analyze them for common provisions.

Tefertiller, T. (2011). Out of the principal's office and into the courtroom: How should California approach criminal remedies for school bullying? *Berkeley Journal of Criminal Law, 16,* 168–220.

After describing the inherent difficulties of legislating against bullying and cyberbullying, Tefertiller forwards the premise that sufficient laws are already in force that can hold students criminally and civilly responsible for bullying behavior.

20

TRANSPORTATION, SCHOOL SAFETY, AND DEALING WITH BULLIES

JENNIFER A. SUGHRUE

Southeastern Louisiana University

M. DAVID ALEXANDER

Virginia Tech

The title of this chapter suggests an odd mix of topics, but they have in common the concern of parents and educators to keep children safe (a) as they travel to and from school or on field trips, (b) on the school's campus, and (c) from peers who are abusive. Hence, the organization of this chapter follows students through the day to discuss the challenges of keeping them out of harm's way. The first section of the chapter discusses school safety generally. The second section addresses student safety when the child leaves home and is transported to school on the bus. The third section discusses safety concerns and measures within the school, and a fourth section covers **bullying**, including **cyberbullying**. The last section of the chapter speaks to school safety strategies and implications for school administrators.

To plan for safety, one must first decide what a **safe school** is (Bucher & Manning, 2005). Is it defined by its school crime statistics, or by the neighborhood in which it is located? Is it safe because there are campus police patrolling the grounds? Is it safe because students pass through metal detectors and are monitored in the hallways and in the cafeteria by cameras? Or, is a safe school one in which there are relatively few serious disciplinary problems, even in the face of racial, ethnic, socioeconomic, religious, and linguistic divisions among the students that create tension in school? These questions are posed to illustrate what educators and their school communities must consider when they discuss how to identify and remedy safety concerns. Safe schools are concerned not only about physical safety, but about emotional and psychological safety, as well.

> A safe school is one in which the total school climate allows students, teachers, administrators, staff, and visitors to interact in a positive, non-threatening manner that reflect the educational mission of the school while fostering positive relationship and personal growth. (Bucher & Manning, 2005, p. 56)

A positive and caring **school climate** promotes safe schools, and safe schools contribute to a positive learning environment (Center for Social and Emotional Education, 2010; Thapa, Cohen, Higgins-D'Alessandro, & Guffey, 2012). Students engage in their education when they feel safe and supported in schools. In a multicountry study, it was concluded that "the important predictors of students' satisfaction with schools are students' feeling that they are treated fairly, that they feel safe, and that they experience that teachers are supportive" (Samdal, Nutbeam, & Wold, 1998, p. 395).

Of course, school safety is not only about school climate. There are practical considerations, such as the maintenance of the school plant and the need for safety precautions when transporting students. What follows is a discussion of student safety issues involving school transportation.

School Transportation

The U.S. Constitution does not recognize education as a fundamental right, and therefore it does not require states to provide school bus service to students (*Kadmas v. Dickinson Public Schools,* 1988). Likewise, school districts do not have a legal duty to provide school transportation unless it is required by the state legislature (*Eric M. v. Calon Valley Union School District,* 2009). Even when school districts provide transportation, it may be suspended if students are disruptive or vandalize school buses. Therefore, riding a school bus is considered a privilege and not a right (*Rose v. Nashua Board of Education,* 1982). However, if the school district does provide transportation, it must take reasonable measures to ensure the safety of students.

Child safety starts when a parent takes the youngster to catch the "big yellow bus" to school. More than 450,000 school buses transport approximately 25 million students per day, which represents over 55% of the K-12 enrollment. Public school buses travel 4.3 billion miles per year with students getting on and off the bus 20 billion times (National Association of State Directors of Pupil Transportation Services [NASDPTS], 2002).

By providing school bus transportation, school districts are keeping 17.3 million cars off the road each day, which improves student transportation safety. Many more students are injured in car accidents than in school bus accidents. A report released by the National Highway Traffic Safety Administration (NHTSA) indicated that only 1% of student fatalities during normal school travel hours are the result of traveling by school bus whereas 23% of the fatalities occur in cars driven by adults and 58% happen in cars driven by teenagers (NHTSA, 2009). Others are killed by drivers who fail to stop for the school bus or who hit children as they are going to or leaving a bus stop.

The NASDPTS conducts annual surveys to determine the size of the problem of drivers who ignore the "stop arm" and pass buses. In 2013, 29 states provided data. Bus drivers were asked to keep note of the number of drivers who passed the bus illegally while it was stopped to pick up or drop off students at their designated bus stop over the period of one day. Amazingly, bus drivers recorded over 85,000 violations in a single day. Most violations occurred during the afternoon drop offs; most of the cars passed from the front of the bus (were traveling in the opposite direction from the bus); and most violations were on the left side of the bus (see **Table 20.1**).

State	Number of Participating Buses	Illegal Passes Observed			Passed From Front	Passed From Rear	Left Side of Bus	Right Side of Bus
		AM	Midday	PM				
AL	5,180	653		804	1,134	323	1,393	64
AR	2,326	220	2	367	45	144	578	11
CA	9,147	13,974	2,241	14,419	13,351	17,283	30,634	-
CO	1,354	303	31	350	473	211	333	18
DE	1,274	314	16	342	361	311	655	17
FL	11,620	5,602	183	5,899	6,818	4,613	41,906	459
GA	12,136	6,125	65	3,617	4,633	2,170	6713	90

| State | Number of Participating Buses | Illegal Passes Observed | | | Passed From Front | Passed From Rear | Left Side of Bus | Right Side of Bus |
		AM	Midday	PM				
IA	1,596	96	7	77	120	60	179	1
ID	493	87	12	98	144	53	190	7
IL	310	42	4	46	49	66	81	3
IN	7,302	1,102	64	1,533	2,131	568	2,627	72
KS	1,858	249	50	276	413	164	559	16
MD	4,927	1,737	147	1,508	2,346	1,046	3,289	103
MI	1,395	464	24	677	813	679	1,146	13
MN	3,048	246	13	274	451	82	523	10
MO	3,747	332	20	697	476	210	667	24
MT	422	32	-	42	52	21	73	3
NC	13,361	1,449	92	1,775	2,368	948	3,213	103
NV	974	1,071	231	1,295	1,521	1,076	2,591	6
OH	3,602	557	55	664	786	393	1,139	31
OK	577	206	12	257	299	176	467	8
OR	2,834	505	134	838	1,294	239	1,451	35
SC	83	2	-	1	3	-	3	-
TN	237	24	-	44	56	12	64	1
TX	9,422	4,455	288	5,082	5,982	3,843	9,250	575
VA	1,869	911	36	927	927	870	1,737	62
WA	3,588	693	81	749	839	684	1,481	62
WV	2,600	155	10	254	364	56	401	16
WY	1,154	92	28	123	-	-	-	-
29	**108,436**	38,698	3,846	42,735	48,464	35,935	82,673	1,780
		85,279			**84,581**		**84,453**	
		45.4%	4.5%	50.1%	57.5%	42.5%	97.9%	2.1%

Table 20.1 NASDPTS Stop Arm Violation Survey 2013

SOURCE: Adapted from the National Association of State Directors of Pupil Transportation Services survey results table. Bus drivers were asked to tally the number of cars that passed their bus illegally in a single day. Twenty-nine states participated. Retrieved from http://www.nasdpts.org/stoparm/2013/documents/2013%20NASDPTS%20Stop%20Arm%20DataFINAL.pdf

How to use these data to do something more that fuel a public awareness campaign is on the minds of state and local legislators and law enforcement personnel. An emerging and popular response is to mount a camera on the stop arm that captures evidence with which to cite offending drivers. Some states are charging a hefty fine of those who are caught by police or who are captured on video illegally passing a school bus that is stopped, with the arm out and the lights flashing. For instance, a Minnesota statute levies a minimum $300 fine for those who are found guilty of a misdemeanor for (a) failing to stop a vehicle at least 20 feet from the bus, (b) failing to keep the vehicle at a complete stop until the bus stop arm has been retracted and the flashing lights stop blinking, or (c) attempting to pass the bus on the right-hand, passenger-door side when the pre-warning amber signals are flashing ("Safety of School Children; Duties of Other Drivers," 2013). Drivers are guilty of a gross misdemeanor and are prosecuted when they violate two or more of the restrictions, including trying to pass when a child is on the outside the bus and on the street, highway, or adjacent sidewalk.

History of School Bus Transportation

School bus transportation started in the late 1800s and by 1910, 30 states had school transportation systems (NASDPTS, 2000). The first school "buses" were farm wagons, later replaced by farm trucks. The school bus system did not start to expand until the 1920s and 1930s when road systems started to develop.

In 1939, the state representatives concerned with school transportation met to develop standards for buses for the purpose of implementing safer transportation systems for children. Federal standards were adopted with the passage of the National Traffic and Motor Vehicle Safety Act of 1966 and the School Bus Safety Amendments of 1974. The National Highway Traffic Safety Administration, a part of the U.S. Department of Transportation (USDOT), has issued 36 federal motor vehicle safety standards (FMVSS) that apply to school buses. These safety requirements include such items as brakes, steering, lights, secure fuel system, mirrors, heater/defroster, and many others. Several of the FMVSS are unique to school buses, such as:

- Rearview mirrors: requires inside and outside mirrors that provide the seated driver with a view in front of and along both sides of the bus
- Lamps, reflective devices, and associated equipment: requires amber and red warning lights when the bus is stopped, or about to stop, to load or unload passengers
- Bus emergency exits and window retention and release: specifies the number and operation of emergency exits
- Fuel system integrity: defines specific crash performance requirements for the entire fuel system
- School bus rollover protection: specifies the minimum structural strength of buses in rollover-type accidents
- School bus body joint strength: specifies the minimum strength of the joints between panels that comprise the bus body and the body structure
- School bus passenger seating and crash protection: establishes requirements for school bus seating systems for all sizes of school buses, provides minimum performance requirements for wheelchair securement/occupant restraint devices, and establishes a requirement that wheelchair locations be forward facing
- School bus pedestrian safety devices: requires school buses be equipped with an automatic stop signal arm on the left side of the bus to help alert motorists that they should stop their vehicles because children are boarding or leaving a stopped school bus (USDOT, 1998)

At least in part because of these safety features, school bus occupant fatality rates of 0.2 fatalities per 100 million vehicle miles traveled are significantly lower than 1.5 fatalities per 100 million miles traveled for motor vehicles overall.

Litigation

Regardless of the safety features and other precautions, such as driver training and random drug testing of drivers, and the low incidence of fatalities, accidents do happen and children are injured or killed. Parents or guardians often respond with lawsuits focusing on issues such as whether the bus stop is at a safe location or whether the bus driver was negligent.

For instances, juries will weigh factors about the appropriateness of the location of a bus stop in light of the age of the child. They take into consideration whether the bus stop location is suitable for very young children and whether the traffic conditions that surround the bus stop are too dangerous.

Driver negligence is a common allegation. For instance, a bus driver was found negligent for leaving a 6-year-old at a new bus stop without making sure the child crossed the road safely (*Slade v. New Hanover County Board of Education,* 1971). In other litigation, a bus driver was charged with negligence for failing to deploy warning signs and lights, when a state statute required drivers to operate the arm that held the stop sign and to use flashing lights to warn approaching cars (*Creshan v. Hart County Board of Education,* 1977). Bus drivers are considered negligent when they do not fulfill their responsibilities in reasonably securing the safe passage of children, even after the children have disembarked and are crossing the street (*Mikes v. Baumgartner,* 1967).

Regulation of Bus Drivers

Because of the great responsibilities placed on bus drivers, states and the federal government require local school districts to provide extensive training. This training is important not only for child safety but also to document that school districts acted with due diligence when a case is litigated. The Federal Motor Vehicle Safety Standards mandate that school bus drivers receive specialized training.

Another element in the safety of school bus transportation is the Omnibus Transportation Testing Act of 1991, which requires commercial driver license holders to be tested for alcohol, marijuana, cocaine, amphetamines, opiates (including heroin), and phencyclidine (PCP). State laws also require random drug and alcohol testing and often allow for suspicionless testing as a pre-employment requirement and as a requirement prior to taking the required safety sensitive test. Not only are bus drivers subject to random drug or alcohol testing, but supervisors can require a driver be tested if there is reasonable suspicion that he or she has shown up to work or is operating a bus under the influence of drugs or alcohol.

Seat Belts

One major safety precaution debated for years was the value of installing lap/shoulder seat belts on school buses. The National Education Association (n.d.) cited an online poll it conducted in which 53%

of respondents supported having seat belts while 47% opposed the idea. More importantly, school bus drivers strongly opposed seat belts on buses. They argued that

- Students can and do use the heavy belt buckles as weapons, injuring other riders.
- It is next to impossible to make sure that all students keep their belts properly fastened, so that they are not injured by the belts in an accident.
- If a bus has to be evacuated in an emergency, such as a fire, panicked or disoriented students might be trapped by their belts (NEA, n.d., "Bus Driver Concerns").

Bus drivers further asserted that school buses had a strong safety record because of their design and because of the way they were operated; therefore seat belts were not needed and would be an expensive modification.

Cost Issues

Another argument against the installation of seat belts in school buses has been the resulting diminished seating capacity of buses, which would have increased school transportation costs and led to children using less safe means to get to and from school. However, new "flexible seating technology" has made it possible for school buses equipped with lap/shoulder belts to maintain full seating capacity (NASDPTS, 2014), so this argument no longer applies. The NASDPTS asserts that no child should lose a place on a bus because the cost associated with installing belts reduced the overall capacity of the district to provide transportation.

Changing Perspectives on the Safety Benefits of Seat Belts

In a 2002 policy brief, NASDPTS quoted from an NHTSA report earlier that year in which the federal agency said lap/shoulder seat belts on school buses could have "unintended consequences" that may have a negative effect on student safety (NASDPTS, 2002). According to NASDPTS, the NHTSA report showed that:

Lap belts are not a good form of crash protection for children in school buses. The laboratory tests for lap-belted test dummies resulted in "Neck Injury measurements in excess of twice the maximum desirable threshold."

Additionally, the NHTSA report noted that, "it is clear that the potential for abdominal injury exists especially when lap belts are used." (NASDPTS, 2002, p. 3)

Since then, new technology, regulations, and an increased body of knowledge on lap/shoulder seat belts have shifted the debate on installing seat belts in school buses. The NHTSA now requires that school buses with a Gross Vehicle Weight Rating (GVWR) of 10,000 pounds or under to install lap/shoulder belts (NASDPTS, 2014). It further recommends that it be left to the discretion of state and local education authorities to determine whether to require lap/shoulder belts in larger buses. States and localities are in a better position to assess their needs and resources. NASDPTS (2014) also itemized several points in favor of seat belts, some of which rebut the concerns of bus drivers. Among its assertions, NASDPTS states that

(a) lap/shoulder belts provide added safety in the event of a side-impact collision or a rollover;
(b) with the new seating technology, seating capacity can be maintained;
(c) safe evacuation of students is aided because students are less likely to be injured and therefore incapacitated;
(d) lap/shoulder designs and the materials used to construct them diminish the possibility of a belt being used as a weapon;
(e) students will use them because they have been accustomed to using them from an early age;
(f) seat belts reduce school district and driver exposure to liability suits; and
(g) there may be an increase in ridership once parents believe their children are safer in buses because seat belts are required.

Discipline on School Buses

In the NEA survey cited earlier, bus drivers identified student discipline rather than a lack of seat belts as a key issue in school bus safety (NEA, n.d.). They argued that student misbehavior and violence, along with the lack of adult supervision other than the driver, contribute to unsafe conditions. Buses can carry between 50 and 70 students, many more students than a classroom teacher supervises. Yet, bus drivers are expected to operate the bus and maintain discipline at the same time. Bus drivers also complained in the same survey that they are not supported by school administrators when they report student disruptions. They believe that bus aides and disciplinary action taken by school administrators would do more to create safe school buses than seat belts.

NASDPTS (2014) disagrees, however. In its arguments in support of lap/shoulder belts, it encourages school districts to develop usage policies that will result in improved student behavior on buses, which in turn decreases the distractions for the driver. It noted that school districts with "defined and enforced lap/shoulder belt usage policies report notable improvements in student behavior and reduction in behavioral incident write-ups" (p. 5).

School districts have installed video cameras in buses to assist with discipline and order. Security cameras are ubiquitous in modern society, appearing in parking lots, stores, banks, and the hallways of schools. It is not surprising, then, that cameras have been used not only to control student behavior on school buses, but also to monitor bus drivers.

For instance, a school bus camera recording was used as evidence with which to dismiss an Ohio school bus driver for negligent duty (*Napier v. Centerville City Schools,* 2004). All bus cameras in Ohio are activated when the ignition key is turned on and continue until 4 minutes after the motor is stopped. In this instance, the video showed the bus driver leaving the bus without checking to see if all her kindergarteners had exited. The videotape showed a temperature reading on the bus of 105 degrees Fahrenheit during the ride and 122 degrees when the bus was parked. The video showed the driver leaving the bus, and then showed a 4-year-old child who had been left on the bus and was screaming for her mommy. Some time after the camera shut down, another bus driver found and removed the child. The bus supervisor confronted the negligent driver, who initially claimed that she had visually inspected the bus, as required by the Ohio Department of Education and the local school district. When confronted with the videotape, however, she admitted she had not inspected the bus, and she was subsequently terminated.

Abiding by all federal, state, and local laws governing school bus maintenance, equipment, and operation enhances student safety as well as diminishes school district and driver liability exposure. School bus drivers should be properly trained and licensed to operate a school bus and should be subject to random drug and alcohol testing to decrease the possibility that a driver may try to operate a bus while under the influence.

School personnel in charge of routing buses and of identifying bus stops must weigh factors that will determine whether bus stop locations are sufficiently safe for the children who will use them. Among the factors to be considered are the ages of the students and the traffic patterns that flow past the stops.

Having clear and enforceable policies that govern student behavior on the buses is an important step in decreasing student disruptions and bus driver distractions. This should include lap/shoulder belt usage policies, as well. Video cameras are often used to monitor student behavior, as well as that of the bus driver.

School buses continue to be the safest method of transporting students to and from school. Incident data reveal that student fatalities during transportation en route to and from school are significantly more likely to occur in a passenger car. Fatalities related to school bus transportation account for only 1% of the total number of student fatalities during normal school travel hours. Improved bus designs and technology, as well as strong regulations can continue to foster safe school transportation for children.

Safety While Students Are at School

Once children arrive safely at school, it becomes the responsibility of school personnel to make reasonable efforts to keep them safe while they are there. It is important, also, that school officials convince parents that their children are safe while they are under their care. To demonstrate their commitment to safety, school district officials have implemented a number of security features and measures in their schools. However, regardless of these efforts, it is a disservice to children, parents, and teachers to lead them to believe these policies and practices will guarantee them safety. They must be viewed as precautions indicating readiness, so that crisis planning and practice will be taken seriously by everyone.

The perceptions of parents about school violence are often founded on media coverage of horrific school tragedies. The immediacy of media coverage makes it appear that school violence appears to be on the rise, even in light of statistics that rebut that

perception (Centers for Disease Control and Prevention [CDC], 2013b; National Center for Education Statistics [NCES]. 2012). In fact, the deadliest act of school violence took place in place in Bath, Michigan, in 1927 (National Public Radio, 2009). A disgruntled farmer upset by property taxes blew up a school with dynamite, killing 38 children and six adults.

In reality, there has been a substantial decline in school-associated violent deaths, homicides, and suicides in the past two decades, with student fatalities at school comprising less than 2% of the total number of youth homicides (NCES, 2012). In fact, most of the violence that results in student deaths occurs off campus, immediately before or after school and during lunch (CDC, 2014a). Nonetheless, as parents hear and watch reports of school shootings across the country, fear for the safety of their own children at school takes root in their minds.

School violence that results in fatalities is not a phenomenon exclusive to the United States. School violence has been reported worldwide (Benbenishty & Astor, 2008). In 1996, 16 children and one teacher were killed and 10 others were wounded in a school in Scotland (Infoplease, n.d.). In 1997, six children and two adults were killed by a single gunman in two schools in Yemen. More recently, in 2012, a gunman shot and killed a rabbi, two of his children, and another child at a Jewish school in France. Shootings at schools have also occurred over the past three decades in Australia, Azerbaijan, Brazil, Canada, China, Colombia, Ethiopia, Finland, Germany, Greece, India, Israel, Japan, Jordan, Malaysia, Netherlands, Norway, Philippines, Russia, South Africa, Sweden, and Thailand.

Forms of Violence in Schools

School violence comes in many forms; it does not always result in physical harm but may cause emotional or psychological injury, and it may be perpetrated by adults as well as youth. It is also important to recognize that students may threaten or harm teachers or other adults, contributing to a negative school environment.

The major categories of school violence are verbal, social or indirect, sexual, physical, and property-related violence, cyberbullying, and corporal punishment (Plan, 2008; see also Benbenishty & Astor, 2008).

Corporal punishment is considered by many educators, psychologists, school counselors, and health professionals to be a form of violence inflicted on students by school personnel. It is outlawed in many countries around the world. Verbal violence and cyberbullying are forms of passive aggression whereas the others are forms of physical aggression.

Verbal violence includes name-calling, profanities, and derogatory comments based on race, ethnicity, religion, or other personal characteristics (Benbenishty & Astor, 2008; Plan, 2008). Adults may be as culpable of verbal violence as a student's peers. Verbal abuse that is focused on factors such as race, religion, disability, gender, and sexual orientation may expose school personnel and the district to liability under federal antidiscrimination statutes if it is not adequately addressed by school officials when it is reported. Such abuse may be found to violate legislation such as Title VI of the Civil Rights Act of 1964, Title IX of the Education Amendments of 1972, Section 504 of the Rehabilitation Act of 1973, and Title II of the Americans with Disabilities Act of 1990 (Office for Civil Rights [OCR], 2010).

Social or indirect violence and cyberbullying occur when students isolate or shun another student or a group of students. This can be exacerbated by the use of social media and text messaging, which then can cross over into cyberbullying. The fact that the victim is isolated by being socially excluded or ostracized through electronic media rather than by face-to-face verbal or physical bullying categorizes it as a form of indirect violence (Benbenishty & Astor, 2008; Stopbullying.gov, n.d.-b).

Sexual violence can be physical or verbal abuse (Benbenishty & Astor, 2008; CDC, 2014b; Plan, 2008) and includes the threat of sexual violence. In all instances, it happens against the victim's will. Sexual violence may be perpetrated by a peer or by an adult in the school. Sexual violence, whether physical or verbal, is also a form of discrimination that is covered by Title IX of the Education Amendments of 1972.

Physical violence and bullying: Fighting is a common example of physical violence, but a more insidious form is bullying. Definitions vary, but the common element is that bullying is repetitive, threatening behavior that results in physical and psychological harm. It is a form of hurtful and hostile behavior by one who is perceived as more powerful (e.g., size, age, strength, stature) against the one who is victimized (American Medical Association, 2002; Plan, 2008; Stopbullying.gov, n.d.-a).

Property-related violence includes vandalism, theft, arson, and damage to the property of students or staff. Tagging is a form of vandalism of school property (Benbenishty & Astor, 2008; Center for Problem-Oriented Policing, 2005).

Corporal punishment is the use of physical force by a person "in a position of authority against someone in his or her care with the intention of causing some degree of pain or discomfort" (Plan, 2008, p. 12). Striking a child with a paddle or hand, shaking or throwing children down or against something, pinching them or pulling their hair, forcing them to stay in uncomfortable positions, or locking or tying them up are all examples of corporal punishment. Some forms, such as paddling, are sanctioned by state law and school policy, yet many forms occur in schools illegally and may happen without repercussion for the educator who inflicts the punishment.

The physical pain may be accompanied by psychological pain and long-term negative effects (Straus, 1991). Evidence suggests that there is a relationship between corporal punishment of a child and an increase later in life of psychiatric disorders such as depression and anxiety and negative behaviors such as spousal and child abuse and participation in crimes including robberies, assaults, and murder.

In disputing myths about the corrective nature of corporal punishment, the Center for Effective Discipline (n.d.) cited studies and statistics to illustrate there is no correlation between corporal punishment and (a) reducing school violence, (b) reducing violence against teachers, or (c) reducing incarceration rates. In fact, there are significantly more fatal school shootings in states that allow corporal punishment, a decrease in violence against teachers is correlated with a decrease of paddling, and 8 of the 10 states with the highest incidences of paddling also have the highest incarceration rates nationally.

Responding to School Violence and Other Safety Concerns

Students who are subjected to violence suffer long-term health and behavioral effects. The violence can be a single traumatic experience or unrelenting passive or physical abuse; both can produce strong negative effects (CDC, 2013a; National Child Traumatic Stress Network [NCTSN]). It can result in sustained fear, anxiety, depression, alcohol and drug abuse, suicidal tendencies, and acting out, perhaps violently. In other words, children can suffer from posttraumatic stress disorder, more commonly known as PTSD. The physical results of violence are sometimes overlooked. Students can suffer cuts, bruises, and broken bones, or may have injuries, including head trauma, that result in permanent physical disabilities.

Several health, psychology, and counseling organizations urge school districts to have policies and programs in place to help students who have been the victims of school violence (CDC, 2013a; NCTSN; Stopbullying.gov, n.d.-a). Immediate and ongoing support at school can assist in alleviating some of the aftermath that victims of violence suffer.

Of course, school safety requires that schools not only stem school violence, but also prevent or punish other kinds of egregious behaviors that contribute to a negative school climate and a feeling of not being safe. One measure that was very popular in the 1990s and early 2000s was a policy of **zero tolerance**. This was originally implemented to keep weapons out of schools, but it quickly grew to encompass a number of other disciplinary offenses, such as drugs, fighting, and even truancy (Sughrue, 2003).

Zero Tolerance

In 1994, Congress passed the Gun-Free Schools Act (GFSA) to address concerns that weapons were being carried into school by students and used to harm others. As a condition of receiving federal funds, states had to enact legislation requiring that schools expel students for 365 days who brought weapons into schools (Sughrue, 2003). To tie the law to federal funding, the GFSA was enacted as an amendment to the Elementary and Secondary Education Act (ESEA), the law now known as No Child Left Behind (NCLB). This allowed the federal government to withhold Title I funds from states and school districts that did not comply.

When Congress passed NCLB in 2001, it expanded the GFSA to include disciplining students with long expulsions if they brought controlled substances into the school or if they sexually harassed or injured another student (Daniel, 2011). These actions were intended to show that schools were tough on school crime.

One incident that drew national attention to zero-tolerance policies happened in 1999, when Jesse Jackson protested the expulsion of seven African American students in Illinois for 2 years for fighting at a football game (McRoberts, 1999). Jackson complained that harsher disciplinary action was meted out to students of color under the guise of the board's zero-tolerance philosophy.

Over the decades that have followed, numerous news stories and case law have illustrated how zero-tolerance policies have been applied unreasonably by school officials who do not want to make an administrative decision to look at each case individually and weigh the circumstances in each. An example involved a 10-year-old student at Twin Peaks Charter Academy in Colorado. Her mother had put a small knife in her daughter's lunch box so that she could cut an apple. The student, recognizing it was a violation of the school zero-tolerance policy, gave the knife to a teacher. Despite her action, the student was expelled. After the case drew national attention, the student was allowed to return to school.

Case law has some examples that illustrate the mindless application of zero-tolerance policies. One of the most well-known cases is *Ratner v. Loudoun County Public Schools* (2001). In this instance, a middle school boy took a paring knife from a female friend who had brought it to school and threatened to hurt herself. He took the threat seriously because she had attempted suicide previously. He placed the knife in his locker with the intention of talking about the threat after school with her parents and his. Word got around about the knife, so the assistant principal called him into her office. He explained what happened and what his intentions were. She sent him *unaccompanied* to his locker to retrieve the knife. After he returned with the knife and handed it to the assistant principal, he was recommended for expulsion, which the school board approved. In the words of the decision by the U.S. Court of Appeals for the

Fourth Circuit, the school acted within the law and did not deny Ratner his due process rights.

> However harsh the result in the case, the federal courts are not properly called upon to judge the wisdom of a zero-tolerance policy of the sort alleged to be in place at Blue Ridge Middle School. . . . Instead, our inquiry here is limited to whether Ratner's complaint alleges sufficient facts which if proved would show that the implementation of the school's policy in this case failed to comport with the United States Constitution. We conclude that the facts alleged in this case do not so demonstrate. (p. 4)

The Fourth Circuit observed, however, that just because a school district can lawfully expel a student under its zero-tolerance policy does not mean it should. Senior Circuit Judge Clyde H. Hamilton wrote a concurring opinion, expressing his view of such policies.

> I write separately to express my compassion for Ratner, his family, and common sense. Each is the victim of good intentions run amuck. Ratner's complaint alleges that school suspensions for possession of a weapon . . . are imposed automatically, pursuant to a zero-tolerance policy that precludes consideration of the facts and circumstances of a particular student's conduct in determining a violation of stated policy and the resulting student punishment. There is no doubt that this zero-tolerance/automatic suspension policy, and others like it adopted by school officials throughout our nation were adopted in large response to the tragic school shootings that have plagued our nation's school children and those adults charged with the profound responsibility of educating them. However, as the oft repeated old English maxim recognizes, "the road to hell is paved with good intentions." The panic over school violence and the intent to stop it has caused school officials to jettison the common sense idea that a person's punishment should fit his crime in favor of a single harsh punishment, namely, mandatory school suspension. Such a policy has stripped away judgment and discretion on the part of those administering it; refuting the well-established precept that judgment is [the] better part of wisdom. (pp. 5–6)

The local newspapers wrote scathing editorials, noting that the school district was sending a message to children that no good intention goes unpunished (Sughrue, 2003). In response, the state superintendent issued a memorandum to all school district superintendents to remind them that the application of zero-tolerance policies should be restricted to violations in which students knowingly and intentionally brought a weapon to school.

Supporters of zero tolerance believe that zero-tolerance policies support a safe school environment. They believe the students will be discouraged from breaking the rules if they understand that the consequences are severe. Loose and lax discipline creates an unsafe environment.

Critics refer to these policies as *zero-intelligence* policies. They believe that taking flexibility away from school administrators promotes inequitable discipline decisions. The Rutherford Institute (n.d.), a well-established nonprofit civil liberties organization, continues to monitor and fight zero-tolerance policies and publish research on the subject. Its position is that in refusing to evaluate each situation individually, including the student's personal history and intentions that led to her or his actions, a student's "unique worth and dignity" is denied. The concept of fairness and justice is lost to those children who have been disciplined unnecessarily harshly (Sughrue, 2003).

Considerable research has also documented the increased incarceration of youths, particularly students of color, as a result of zero-tolerance policies and the presence of school resource officers (SROs) on campuses. Harsh disciplinary action prescribed, without regard to circumstances, and the involvement of police in school disciplinary matters have generated a phenomenon called the *school-to-prison pipeline.* This refers to "the policies and practices that push . . . schoolchildren, especially . . . at-risk children, out of classrooms and into the juvenile and criminal justice systems" (American Civil Liberties Union [ACLU], n.d.). In response, some school districts, particularly those in large urban centers, are beginning to take notice and revise their zero-tolerance policies.

Florida's Broward County Public Schools is one of the systems that has re-evaluated its zero-tolerance policies and how they are applied. It has formed a coalition with law enforcement, local and state courts, and the NAACP to change zero-tolerance disciplinary procedures. The outcome of the working coalition is an initiative called the PROMISE Program (Preventing Recidivism through Opportunities, Mentoring, Interventions, Supports and Education) (StateImpact, 2014). The primary objective is to redirect children who have committed minor and nonviolent violations of school rules to counseling and support services instead of suspending or expelling them under the previous zero-tolerance policies. The school district has designed a detailed discipline flow chart that is illustrated in **Figure 20.1**.

Florida's legislature is responding, too. In House Bill 7029, labeled in the media as the "Pop-Tart" bill, children will not face zero-tolerance punishments for playing with simulated weapons in schools. The fanciful nickname for the bill stems from an incident in which a 7-year-old student in Maryland was suspended from school when he nibbled his Pop-Tart into the shape of a gun.

This incident happened 11 months after the Sandy Hook Elementary School shooting in Newtown, Connecticut, in 2012. As with the aftermath of the Columbine High School shooting in Colorado in 1999, school officials were oversensitive about threats, even imaginary ones.

School Resource Officers

A popular school security measure has been to contract with local law enforcement to place police officers or sheriffs in schools. They are most commonly referred to as school resource officers (SROs), although different states have various designations for them (Cox, Sughrue, Cornelius, & Alexander, 2012). It is generally accepted that the concept of a police presence in schools originated in Flint, Michigan, in the 1950s, but it was not until the 1960s that the Miami police coined the term *school resource officer*. Many school districts, cognizant of safety, have established their own police forces (Cox et al., 2012). The first formal school police agency was created in the Los Angeles Unified School District in 1948. Several states have authorized local school boards to establish their own police forces, including Florida, Texas, California, Indiana, New Mexico, New York, Massachusetts, Maryland, Michigan, Oklahoma, Pennsylvania, and Tennessee.

New York City Public Schools has its own police force, composed of school security officers and police officers in the schools; there are 5,200 school security officers who may stop, search, and arrest children both on and off of school grounds, and 191 police officers who are trained in the same manner as police who patrol the streets of New York.

Approximately 26 states have statutes authorizing schools to have either SROs or school security, or both, and all 50 states have SROs or security in the schools. Some states distinguish between SROs (law enforcement personnel) and security officers (usually not law enforcement). For example, the Virginia Code defines each: "School resource officer means a certified law-enforcement officer hired by the local law-enforcement agency to provide law-enforcement and security services to Virginia public elementary and secondary schools" (Definitions, 2013, §9.1–101). A school security officer is defined as

> an individual who is employed by the local school board for the singular purpose of maintaining order and discipline, preventing crime, investigating violations of school board policies, and detaining students violating the law or school board policies on school property or at school-sponsored events and who is responsible solely for ensuring the safety, security, and welfare of all students, faculty, staff, and visitors in the assigned school. (Definitions, 2013, §9.1–101).

As was indicated in an earlier section of this chapter, no security measure, including armed law enforcement officers, can guarantee a completely safe school. What is less known is that there were two armed officers involved in the Columbine tragedy, both of whom were outgunned by Eric Harris, one of the teenagers responsible for the killings. One of the officers was an armed SRO at Columbine High School. A 15-year veteran of the Jefferson County, Colorado, sheriff's office, the SRO was having lunch in his car in the school parking lot when the shooting started. He came toward the building, exchanging fire with Harris, but he had to seek cover from Harris's barrage of bullets. Another officer, who was on regular patrol duty, heard the call and came to the school; he was also unable to stop Harris.

Federal funding assisted school districts to employ SROs, but as funding has dried up, so has the number of officers assigned to schools. Large districts tend to maintain their SRO numbers, but smaller districts have more difficulty (James & McCallion, 2013). However, even in tight financial times, school administrators are loath to remove officers from their schools because many students and most parents perceive that the officers make their schools safer, whether or not there is evidence to support those perceptions.

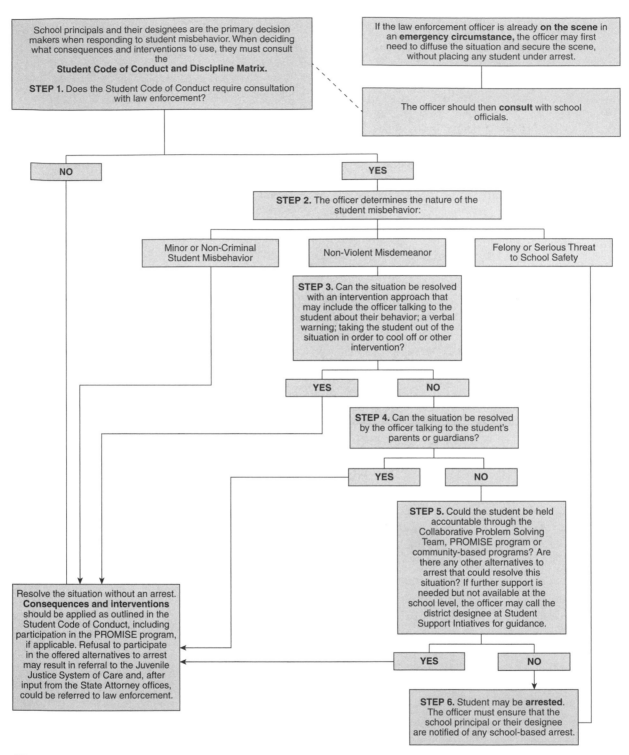

All contraband must be placed in the care and custody of the law enforcement personnel of the Department that initiates the arrest or the Broward District Schools Police Department, if no arrest is made. Nothing in this agreement is intended to limit the discretion of law enforcement. Officers responding to an incident or consulting with school officials are encouraged to use their discretion in determining the best course of action, especially when using alternatives to arrest. In addition, a student who has accumulated three incidents in a school year that fall under section 1.02 shall be referred to the Behavior Intervention Committee. Upon the fourth incident in a school year that falls under section 1.02, the student shall be referred for consultation with law enforcement, unless such referral is sooner required by the Discipline Matrix.

Figure 20.1 Broward County Public School District's New Discipline Flow Chart

SOURCE: Reprinted with permission from the Broward County Public Schools Diversity, Prevention & Intervention Department.

Critics have complaints about SROs similar to those concerning zero-tolerance policies. There is evidence to demonstrate that having law enforcement officers in schools increases the likelihood that children's misbehavior can become criminalized. What used to be disciplinary problems handled by school administrators now become matters for the court. Sassy talk now is cited by SROs as disruptive behavior. Students are given citations that require them to go to juvenile court. This is a contributing factor in the school-to-prison pipeline described previously.

If there are very clear policies, procedures, and job descriptions, SROs have a place in some schools, especially in those that have high rates of school criminality. Crimes should be investigated by the SRO, while common disciplinary problems should be handled by school personnel. The National Association of School Resource Officers (NASRO) has a series of training programs for SROs, as well as guidance on memorandums of understanding between law enforcement agencies and school districts, as well as information about supervision and evaluation of SROs (NASRO, n.d.).

Other Security Measures

Schools have implemented a variety of safety and security measures and policies in an attempt to thwart potential threats to student well-being, whether those threats come from inside or outside the school. Some of the highlights of the NCES's 2012 *Indicators of School Crime and Safety* statistics illustrate the changes that have occurred in public schools in the decade between the 1999–2000 and 2009–2010 school years (see **Table 20.2**).

For instance, there has been a substantial increase in the percentage of schools that require school personnel to wear badges or photo IDs, rising from about 25% to almost 63% in that 10-year span. Also, almost 92% of schools had locked or monitored doors to control access during school hours as of 2009–2010, up from 74.6% 10 years before. Seventy-four percent of schools had telephones in most classrooms as of 2009–2010, and

School Safety and Security Measure	1999–2000	2003–2004	2005–2006	2007–2008	2009–2010
Controlled access during school hours					
Buildings (e.g., locked or monitored doors)	74.6	83.0	84.9	89.5	91.7
Grounds (e.g., locked or monitored gates)	33.7	36.2	41.1	42.6	46.0
Closed the campus for most students during lunch	64.6	66.0	66.1	65.0	66.9
Drug testing and tobacco use					
Any students	4.1	5.3	—	—	—
Athletes	—	4.2	5.0	6.4	6.0
Students in extracurricular activities other than athletics		2.6	3.4	4.5	4.6
Any other students	—	—	3.0	3.0	3.0
Prohibited all tobacco use on school grounds	90.1	88.8	90.3	91.4	—
Required to wear badges or picture IDs					
Students	3.9	6.4	6.1	7.6	6.9
Faculty and staff	25.4	48.0	47.8	58.3	62.9

(Continued)

(Continued)

School Safety and Security Measure	1999–2000	2003–2004	2005–2006	2007–2008	2009–2010
Metal detector checks on students					
Random checks[1]	7.2	5.6	4.9	5.3	5.2
Required to pass through daily	0.9	1.1	1.1	1.3	1.4
Sweeps and technology					
Random dog sniffs to check for drugs[1]	20.6	21.3	23.0	21.5	22.9
Random sweeps for contraband[1,2]	11.8	12.8	13.1	11.4	12.1
Provided telephones in most classrooms	44.6	60.8	66.8	71.6	74.0
Electronic notification system for school-wide emergency	—	—	—	43.2	63.1
Structured, anonymous threat reporting system	—	—	—	31.2	35.9
Used security cameras to monitor the school[1]	19.4	36.0	42.8	55.0	61.1
Provided two-way radios	—	71.2	70.8	73.1	73.3
Limited access to social networking websites from school computers	—	—	—	—	93.4
Prohibited use of cell phones and text messaging devices	—	—	—	—	90.9
Visitor requirements					
Sign in or check in	96.6	98.3	97.6	98.7	99.3
Pass through metal detectors	0.9	0.9	1.0	—	—
Dress code					
Required students to wear uniforms	11.8	13.8	13.8	17.5	18.9
Enforced a strict dress code	47.4	55.1	55.3	54.8	56.9
School supplies and equipment					
Required clear book bags or banned book bags on school grounds	5.9	6.2	6.4	6.0	5.5
Provided school lockers to students	46.5	49.5	50.6	48.9	52.1

Table 20.2   Percentage of Public Schools That Used Safety and Security Measures: Various School Years, 1999–2000 Through 2009–2010

SOURCE: Table 20.1, p. 168, in Robers, S., Kemp, J., & Truman, J. (2013). *Indicators of School Crime and Safety: 2012* (NCES 2013–036/NCJ 241446). National Center for Education Statistics, U.S. Department of Education, and Bureau of Justice Statistics, Office of Justice Programs, U.S. Department of Justice. Washington, DC. http://nces.ed.gov/pubs2013/2013036.pdf

NOTE: Responses were provided by the principal or the person most knowledgeable about crime and safety issues at the school. Respondents were instructed to respond only for those times that were during normal school hours or when school activities or events were in session, unless the survey specified otherwise.

— Not available
[1] One or more checks, sweeps, or cameras
[2] For example, drugs or weapons. Does not include dog sniffs.

63% had an electronic notification system for school-wide emergencies by that year. In 1999–2000, only 19.4% of schools used security cameras to monitor activity in the school; by 2009–2010 over 61% had them. As of 2009–2010, more than 90% of schools limited access to social networking websites and restricted the use of cell phones and texting during the school day.

Interestingly, there has been a diminished reliance on metal detectors; the percentage of schools using them decreased from 7.2% in 1999–2000 to 5.2% in 2009–2010, according to NCES. Also noteworthy is that very few public schools (mostly high schools, but also some middle schools) drug test athletes and students who participate in other extracurricular activities. In 2009–2010, 6% of schools reported drug testing their athletes, up just 1.8% since 2003–2004. Only 4.6% of schools required drug tests of students in other extracurricular activates in 2009–2010.

School officials also have procedures in place to increase the probability that adults who are employed at the school will not harm the children under their supervision or those with whom they come in contact. Criminal background checks for all adults who will be in the school during the instructional day are required (U.S. Government Accountability Office [GAO], 2014). Depending on the state, this includes student teachers, parent volunteers, and outside contractors, such as construction personnel and vendors. Professional codes of conduct and state codes of ethics are designed to protect students from abuse by educators. Providing guidance to educators about boundary-setting with students is highly recommended (GAO, 2014). State laws require clear policies and procedures for investigating and reporting suspected abuse.

Bullying

Bullying is a problem that has existed for years in the United States, England, and other European countries. Although it virtually has always been a presence in schools, it was not an issue of major public concern. However, Columbine changed all that because of the belief that the motivating force behind the teen killers was the abuse they suffered from bullying, although that idea was later challenged.

After the Columbine shooting, the Secret Service investigated 37 school shootings. The findings of the study were that two thirds of the shooters were

bullied or felt threatened at school. In an address to the American Medical Association (AMA) Forum on Adolescent Health: Youth Bullying (AMA, 2002) Joseph Wright, the medical director of Advocacy and Community Affairs at Children's National Medical Center in Washington, D.C., declared that:

> If bullying were a medical issue, for example an infectious disease in my pediatrics practice, we would have the Epidemic Intelligence Service (EIS) people from the Centers for Control and Prevention investigate it. The prevalence and epidemiology of bullying is [*sic*] striking. (p. 23)

Educators realize that the problem is serious and widespread and that bullying has a serious impact not only on the victims but also on the students who engage in bullying behavior. Bullying has three forms: (1) physical (e.g., hitting); (2) verbal (e.g., taunting); and (3) psychological (e.g., engaging in social exclusion). These forms overlap with the identified forms of school violence defined earlier in the chapter. The first one has been around for years—the school yard bully pushing, shoving, and hitting other students. The second and third can be both face-to-face in school but also include the new technological bullying—cyberbullying.

The new form of bullying made possible by cell phones, computers, and other types of technology is cyberbullying, which is defined as

> bullying that takes place using electronic technology. Electronic technology includes devices and equipment such as cell phones, computers, and tablets as well as communication tools including social media sites, text messages, chat, and websites. Examples of cyberbullying include mean text messages or emails, rumors sent by email or posted on social networking sites, and embarrassing pictures, videos, websites, or fake profiles. (Stopbullying.gov, n.d.-b)

Bullying behavior, particularly physical bullying, which is direct aggression, is most often associated with male students, whereas cyberbullying, a form of passive aggression, is more often instigated by female students.

Findings from a survey reported in NCES's *Indicators of School Crime and Safety: 2012* (Robers, Kemp, & Truman, 2013) revealed that among students between the ages of 12 and 18, 24.5% of males reported being bullied at school, while a little more than 31% of females indicated they had been bullied at school (NCES, 2013). However, of the outcomes associated with bullying (i.e., being excluded from activities; being the subject of rumors; being made fun of/called names; being threatened with harm; being a target of coercion; having property destroyed; and being pushed, shoved, tripped, or spit on), the more physical acts (pushing, shoving, having property destroyed) were perpetrated more often against males. The more indirect or passive bullying was more often against females (see **Figure 20.2**). It is not known from this survey when the perpetrators were males or females

or if the bullying was male on male, female on female, or mixed.

The second part of the survey concerned cyberbullying. Cyberbullying was distinct from bullying and was defined as:

> Include[ing] students who responded that another student had posted hurtful information about them on the Internet; purposefully shared private information about them on the Internet; harassed them via instant messaging; harassed them via Short Message Service

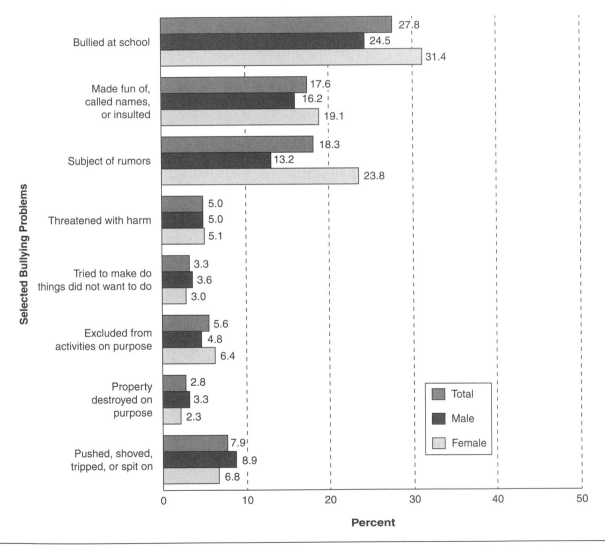

Figure 20.2 Percentage of Students Ages 12 to 18 Who Reported Being Bullied at School During the Year, by Selected Bullying Problems and Sex: 2011

SOURCE: Figure 11.1, NCES, *Indicators of School Crime and Safety: 2012*. Retrieved from http://nces.ed.gov/programs/crimeindicators/crimeindicators2012/figures/figure_11_1.asp

NOTE: "At school" includes the school building, on school property, on a school bus, or going to and from school. Bullying types do not sum to total "bullied at school" category because students could have experienced more than one type of bullying.

(SMS) text messaging; harassed them via e-mail; harassed them while gaming; or excluded them online. (Robers et al., 2013, p. 44)

Cyberbullying differs from other forms of bullying in that it can occur 24 hours per day, 7 days per week. Messages can be posted anonymously and sent to a very wide audience instantly, and they are difficult to track. Even when those who post messages online later delete them, someone else may have saved the message and it may resurface.

Cyberbullying has had a devastating impact on fragile teenagers across the United States and has led to numerous reports of teenage suicides after continuous cyberbullying. One example that has been cited is that of Rebecca Sedwick, a Florida teenager who authorities said jumped to her death in 2013 after months of bullying by two classmates. The two girls, ages 12 and 14, initially were charged with felony aggravated stalking. Some 2 weeks later the state attorney dropped the charges, as per an agreement that, since the girls were juveniles, they would go into counseling. In August 2014, Sedwick's mother filed a civil action against one of the girls and the Polk County school board.

The American Bar Association (2013) provides some guidance on the question of legal action against students who may be guilty of cyberbullying. It reminds the reader that laws and school policies surrounding cyberbullying are state-specific. It suggests there may be both criminal and civil actions, depending on the state statutes. Civil action will usually fall under traditional tort law.

It also advises that most states have some form of student cyberbullying law, under which schools must develop policies and procedures to protect students from ongoing harassment. However, it is difficult for schools to control cyberbullying because it usually happens in social media, often on private computers off campus. It is unclear under what circumstances schools can regulate off-campus speech.

Florida added cyberbullying to a bill allowing schools to discipline students for their off-campus harassment. However, because of the constitutional protection of free speech that students enjoy outside of school, the Florida statute has a provision stipulating that the school must demonstrate that the cyberbullying "substantially interferes with or limits the victim's ability to participate in or benefit from the services, activities, or opportunities offered by a school or substantially disrupts the education process or orderly operation of a school." This provision is in deference to the landmark case, *Tinker v. Des Moines Independent School District* (1969). The Supreme Court justices held that the school could regulate student speech only when it would interfere "materially and substantially" with the operation of the school. In fact, all Supreme Court cases to date that involve student speech have some nexus with the school. Off-campus speech that is unrelated to school sponsorship or that does not have an impact on the school learning environment is difficult for a school to discipline. In other words, the student who is cyberbullying from his or her grandmother's computer can claim that the school has no authority to discipline him or her for off-campus activities.

According to NCES, among students ages 12 to 18, 9% indicated they had been subjected to cyberbullying during the school year (see **Figure 20.3**). Nearly 4% reported that harmful information about them was posted on the Internet; 3% were the subject of harassing instant messages; 4% were the subject of harassing text messages; and 2% were the subject of harassing emails. The findings also showed female students were victims of cyberbullying at a higher rate than male students. Eleven percent of White students, 8% of Hispanic students, and 7% of Black students reported being victims of cyberbullying.

Because of the rise in school bullying, state legislatures have passed laws addressing this issue. Forty-nine states have enacted antibullying laws, policies, or both regarding antibullying. (As of August 2014, Montana did not have a statute specifically dealing with bullying.) At least 19 states have enacted laws or policies dealing specifically with cyberbullying.

Today's students are technologically savvy, and have had access to electronic devices since they were very young. Many young people prefer Twitter, Facebook, or some other form of social media, to email, which they find too slow. Statutes and court decisions provide some guidance to school leaders, but they are lagging behind the rapid development of technology. This explosion of technology has impacted decisions regarding student disciplinary matters, but

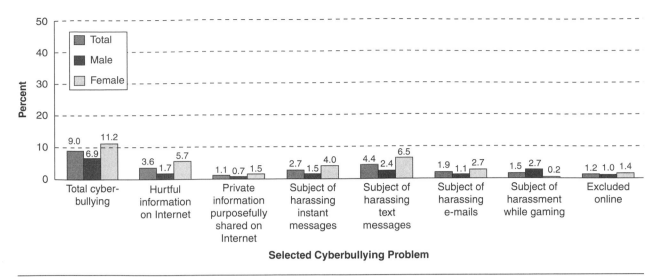

Figure 20.3   Percentage of Students Ages 12 to 18 Who Reported Being Cyberbullied Anywhere During the School Year, by Selected Cyberbullying Problems and Sex: 2011

SOURCE: Figure 11.3, NCES, *Indicators of School Crime and Safety: 2012.* Retrieved from http://nces.ed.gov/programs/crimeindicators/crimeindicators2012/figures/figure_11_3.asp

leaves school leaders making discipline decisions about a new phenomenon without legal certainty.

School Safety Implications for School Administrators

As has been amply addressed in this chapter, a wide range of serious safety and security concerns whirl around the school, its students, and its community. The first order for administrators is to always be cognizant of federal, state, and local law and policies, such as those that govern pupil transportation safety, crisis planning and management, and school threats. Administrators are well advised to work collaboratively with federal, state, and local authorities and agencies that have expertise in school safety and can offer professional development to school personnel.

Education researchers and health professionals, including school psychologists and organizational psychologists, assert that school climate is a key indicator of school safety. The more positive, respectful, and supportive the school climate, the less likely that major safety and security issues will come from within. A positive school climate is widely regarded

as the most effective preventive intervention available to school leaders. Among the sources listed at the end of this chapter is the National School Climate Center, which offers helpful advice about how to measure school climate and how to improve it.

School safety is more than physical safety. It is also about intellectual, emotional, and psychological safety.

A safe school is a place where the business of education can be conducted in a welcoming environment free of intimidation, violence, and fear. Such a setting provides an education climate that fosters a spirit of acceptance and care for every child. It is a place free of bullying where behavior expectations are clearly communicated, consistently enforced, and fairly applied. (Stephens, as cited in Bucher & Manning, 2005, p. 57)

Specific indicators of a safe school that have emerged from the research literature include:

- High academic standards
- Positive and respectful relationships
- Strong teacher support
- Systematic conflict resolution strategies (such as peer mediation and anger management training), including communication skills and cooperative problem solving

- A clean campus (including restrooms and recreational facilities) that makes a statement about "school pride, cleanliness and order, and respect for property" (Mabie, 2003, as cited in Bucher & Manning, p. 57)
- School personnel who listen to the constituents (students, parents, community, and local agencies) that they serve
- Teachers who care about students and have positive interactions with and mutual respect for students
- Commitment to civility and a positive classroom culture
- Efforts to curb bullying
- Quality environment design
- Administrators who are committed to safe schools
- A team-developed safe school plan and implementation strategy (quoted from Bucher & Manning, 2005, p. 57)

Safe schools are a function of careful planning and continuous monitoring. It is recommended that school leaders consider how to move away from a harsh and "negative product-based approach" (e.g., surveillance cameras, metal detectors) to safety, toward a process approach that emphasizes a positive school climate and supportive programs and services for students and school personnel (Bucher & Manning, 2005, p. 58). Students and staff should feel welcomed in the school and know they are valued.

Successful school safety plans and programs have both prevention and intervention characteristics. There should be programs that identify and intervene with troubled youth and provide them with the support and counseling they need to overcome their negative behaviors. In the event of a crisis, plans and strategies must be in place to respond effectively and efficiently and are the result of collaboration with first responders in the planning for emergencies. The plans must also have provisions for working with the school community to recover from trauma.

School leaders must address school disciplinary problems early and consistently and create opportunities to address these behaviors in ways that will help aggressors learn to control their behaviors or to seek help when they need it. The most effective strategy is to be proactive rather than reactive. In other words, there must be a strong school culture in which students know that certain behaviors will not be tolerated. When students know what behaviors are expected and see them modeled by the school

staff, they will contribute to the positive school climate that is necessary for safe schools.

Key Chapter Terms

Bullying: Ongoing physical and/or emotional harassment by someone in order to dominate another. Examples of bullying include threats, spreading rumors, isolation, and revealing private information.

Cyberbullying: Bullying that takes place using cell phones, computers, and social media. It is insidious in that it is easily communicated across large groups and extends beyond the school day and into the home.

Safe school: At times, *safe school* is used synonymously with *school safety,* which is really something different. The term *safe school* is more holistic and refers to the physical, emotional, and social well-being of students and staff. School safety more often refers to school violence, school criminality, crisis management, emergency drills, and other physical features of school safety. Safe schools are most often talked about in terms of a positive school climate in which students, school personnel, and the school community feel safe, communicate respectfully, and develop positive relationships that promote a healthy learning environment.

School climate: A term for which there is a variety of definitions, although they do not diverge as dramatically as do the definitions for the term *safe school.* Generally, school climate is the blend of physical, social, and academic components that determines the school environment. A positive school climate is one in which students, families, school personnel, and other members of the school community feel welcome and work together to promote the educational mission of the school

Zero tolerance: In educational settings, it commonly means that certain infractions, such as possessing weapons or drugs in schools, will not be tolerated and that, for these infractions, automatic disciplinary sanctions are imposed. For instance, a student who brings a weapon to school would be expelled for no fewer than 365 days under a zero-tolerance policy.

References

American Bar Association. (2013, July/August). Potential legal approaches to a cyberbullying case. *The Young Lawyer, 17*(9).

American Civil Liberties Union. (n.d.) *What is the school-to-prison pipeline?* Retrieved from https://www.aclu.org/racial-justice/what-school-prison-pipeline

American Medical Association. (2002). *Proceedings: Education forum on adolescent health: Youth bullying.* Retrieved from https://www.ncjrs.gov/App/Publications/abstract.aspx?ID=199699

Benbenishty, R., & Aston, R. A. (2008). School violence in an international context: A call for global collaboration in research and prevention. *International Journal on Violence and School, 7,* 59–80. Retrieved from http://www.ijvs.org/files/Revue-07/04.-Benbenishty-Ijvs-7.pdf

Bucher, K. T., & Manning, M. L. (2005, September/October). Creating safe schools. *The Clearing House, 79*(1) 55–60.

The Center for Effective Discipline. (n.d.). *Discipline at school.* Retrieved from http://www.stophitting.com/index.php?page=factsvsopinions

Center for Problem-Oriented Policing. (2005). *School vandalism and break-ins.* Retrieved from http://www.popcenter.org/problems/vandalism/print/

Centers for Disease Control and Prevention. (2013a). *About school violence.* Retrieved from http://www.cdc.gov/violenceprevention/youthviolence/schoolviolence/index.html

Centers for Disease Control and Prevention. (2013b). *Youth violence national and state statistics at a glance.* Retrieved from http://www.cdc.gov/violenceprevention/youthviolence/stats_at-a_glance/index.html

Centers for Disease Control and Prevention. (2014a). *School-associated violent deaths.* Retrieved from http://www.cdc.gov/violenceprevention/youthviolence/schoolviolence/savd.html

Centers for Disease Control and Prevention. (2014b). *Sexual violence: Definitions.* Retrieved from http://www.cdc.gov/violenceprevention/sexualviolence/definitions.html

Center for Social and Emotional Education. (2010, January). School climate research summary—January 2010. *School Climate Brief, 1.* Retrieved from http://www.schoolclimate.org/climate/documents/policy/sc-brief-v1.pdf

Cox, B., Sughrue, J. A., Cornelius, L. M., & Alexander, M. D. (2012). *The challenges to school policing* [Monograph]. Dayton, OH: Education Law Association.

Daniel, P. T. K. (2011). Bullying and cyberbullying in schools: An analysis of student free expression, zero tolerance policies, and state anti-harassment legislation. *West Education Law Reporter, 268,* 619.

Infoplease. (n.d.). Timeline of worldwide school and mass shootings. *Information Please Database, Pearson Educ., Inc.* Retrieved from http://www.infoplease.com/ipa/A0777958.html

James, N., & McCallion, G. (2013). School resource officers: Law enforcement officers in schools. *Congressional Research Service.* Retrieved from http://fas.org/sgp/crs/misc/R43126.pdf

McRoberts, F. (1999, November 8). Jackson fights expulsion of Black Decatur youths. *Chicago Tribune.* Retrieved from http://articles.chicagotribune.com/1999-11-08/news/9911080250_1_zero-tolerance-policies-eisenhower-high-school-decatur-school-board

National Association of School Resource Officers. (n.d.). Retrieved from http://www.nasro.org/

National Association of State Directors of Pupil Transportation Services. (2000). *History of school bus safety—Why are school buses built as they are?* Retrieved from http://www.nasdpts.org/Documents/Paper-SchoolBusHistory.pdf

National Association of State Directors of Pupil Transportation Services. (2002). *Enhancing school bus safety and pupil transportation safety.* Retrieved from http://www.nasdpts.org/Documents/EnhancingSBPupilTransSafety.pdf

National Association of State Directors of Pupil Transportation Services. (2014). *The equipping and use of passenger lap/shoulder belts in school buses.* Retrieved from http://www.nasdpts.org/Documents/NASDPTS%20POSITION%20PAPER%20PASSENGER%20LAP%20SHOULDER%20BELTS%20FINAL%20FEB%202014.pdf

National Center for Education Statistics. (2012). *Indicators of school crime and safety: 2011.* Retrieved from http://nces.ed.gov/programs/crimeindicators/crimeindicators2011/index.asp

National Center for Education Statistics. (2013). *Indicators of school crime and safety: 2012.* Retrieved from http://nces.ed.gov/pubs2013/2013036.pdf

National Education Association. (n.d.) *Seat belts, school buses and safety.* Retrieved from http://www.nea.org/home/19085.htm

National Highway Traffic Safety Administration. (2009). *School buses are the safest mode of transportation for getting children back and forth to school.* Retrieved from http://www.trafficsafetymarketing.gov/staticfiles/tsm/PDF/schoolbus_safety2.pdf

National Public Radio. (2009). *Survivors recall 1927 school massacre.* Retrieved from http://www.npr.org/templates/story/story.php?storyId=103186662

Office for Civil Rights. (2010, October 26). *Dear colleague letter.* Retrieved from http://www2.ed.gov/about/offices/list/ocr/letters/colleague-201010.html

Plan. (2008). *The global campaign to end violence in schools.* Retrieved from https://plan-international.org/learnwithoutfear/files/learn-without-fear-global-campaign-report-english

Robers, S., Kemp, J., & Truman, J. (2013). *Indicators of school crime and safety: 2012* (NCES 2013-036/NCJ 241446). National Center for Education Statistics, U.S. Department of Education, and Bureau of Justice Statistics, Office of Justice Programs, U.S. Department of Justice. Washington, DC. http://nces.ed.gov/pubs2013/2013036.pdf

The Rutherford Institute. (n.d.). *Zero tolerance.* Retrieved from https://www.rutherford.org/issues/zero_tolerance/

Samdal, O., Nutbeam, D., & Wold, B. (1998). Achieving health and educational goals through school—A study of the importance of the school climate and students' satisfaction with school. *Health Education Research, 13*(3), 383–397. doi:10.1093/her/13.3.383

StateImpact. (2014). *Interview: Rethinking zero tolerance discipline policies in Florida public schools.* Retrieved from https://stateimpact.npr.org/florida/2014/01/26/interview-rethinking-zero-tolerance-discipline-policies-in-florida-public-schools/

Stopbullying.gov. (n.d.-a) *Support the kids involved.* Retrieved from http://www.stopbullying.gov/respond/support-kids-involved/

Stopbullying.gov. (n.d.-b). *What is cyberbullying.* Retrieved from http://www.stopbullying.gov/cyberbullying/what-is-it/index.html

Straus, M. (1991). Discipline and deviance: Physical punishment of children and violence and other crime in adulthood. *Social Problems, 38*(2), 133–154.

Sughrue, J. A. (2003). Zero tolerance: Two wrongs do not make a right. *Educational Administration Quarterly, 39*(2), 238–258.

Thapa, A., Cohen, J., Higgins-D'Alessandro, A., & Guffey, S. (2012). School climate research summary: August 2012. *School Climate Brief, 3,* 1–23.

U.S. Department of Transportation, National Highway Safety Compliance. (1998). *Federal motor vehicle safety standards and regulations.* Retrieved from http://www.nhtsa.gov/cars/rules/import/FMVSS/

U.S. Government Accountability Office. (2014, January). *Child welfare: Federal agencies can better support state efforts to prevent and respond to sexual abuse by school personnel* (GAO-14-42). Retrieved from http://www.gao.gov/products/GAO-14-42

Statutes and Court Decisions

Creshan v. Hart County Board of Education, 549 S.W.2d 306 (Ky. App. Ct. Ky, 1977).

Definitions. Va. Code Ann. §9.1–101 (2013).

Eric M. v. Calon Valley Union School Dist., 174 Cal. App. 4th 285, 95 Cal. Rptr. 3d 428, 245 Ed. Law Rep. 941 (4th Dist. 2009).

Gun-Free Schools Act. 20 U.S.C. § 8921 (1994).

Kadmas v. Dickinson. 487 U.S. 450, 108 S. Ct. 2481, 47 Ed. Law Rep. 383 (1988).

Mikes v. Baumgartner, 152 N.W.2d 732 (Minn. 1967).

Napier v. Centerville City Schools 812 N.E.2d 311 (Ohio App. 2004).

Ratner v. Loudoun County Public Schools, 2001 WL 855606 (4th Cir. 2001). Retrieved from http://www.ca4.uscourts.gov/opinions/Unpublished/002157.U.pdf

Rose v. Nashua Bd. of Ed., 679 F.2d 279 (1st Cir. 1982).

Safety of school children; duties of other drivers. Minn. Stat. § 169.444 subd. 1–3 (2013).

Slade v. New Hanover County Board of Education, 175 S.E.2d 453 (N.C. App. 1971).

Tinker v. Des Moines Independent School District, 393 U.S. 503, 89 S.Ct. 733 (1969).

Further Readings

Brunner, J. M., & Lewis, D. K. (2009). *Safe & secure schools: 27 strategies for prevention and intervention.* Thousand Oaks, CA: Corwin.

One author is a high school principal and one is director of public safety for an urban/suburban school district; both consult with other school districts across the country about school safety. The book covers crisis planning and strategies for responding to a crisis and helping schools and students recover from a crisis. It also covers the kinds of professional development that school personnel need in order to be adequately prepared in the event of a crisis.

National Association of School Psychologists. (2002). *Threat assessment: Predicting and preventing school violence.* Retrieved from http://www.nasponline.org/resources/factsheets/threatassess_fs.aspx

This site provides useful and comprehensive information on threat assessment and the set of strategies that can be employed to evaluate the credibility or seriousness of a threat and whether the threat is likely to be carried out. It also summarizes facts about school violence and potential offenders, about establishing clear district-wide policies and procedures, and implementing interventions for potential offenders.

National Association of State Directors of Pupil Transportation Services: http://www.nasdpts.org/Security/index.html

This is an excellent resource for more information about school transportation safety and security. It had a series of position papers and association reports on topics such as (a) pupil transportation system security resources and approaches, (b) security program action items related to school bus operations, (c) bus driver training, (d) state laws on school transportation, (e) safety equipment, and much more. It also has several links to other organizations and government agencies that are associated with pupil transportation.

National Center for Education Statistics. https://nces.ed.gov/

NCES generates a plethora of reports that provide data on a variety of measures relating to school violence. The most popular of the reports is the Indicators of School Crime and Safety, which the agency publishes annually. The data are collected through surveys of school principals and youths in elementary and secondary schools. One weakness of the report has been the trend data on the number of incidents of school violence and crime. The reports have tables in which the number of incidents is reported over several decades, but it is not possible to determine if 34 student fatalities in 1994 is proportionally the same as 34 fatalities in 2010. In other words, no total student population data for each year for the schools that participated in the survey has been reported so that a ratio or percentage could be calculated, i.e. 2 fatalities per 100,000 students versus 0.5 fatalities per 100,000 students. Therefore, it has not been possible to conclude whether the percentage of students killed in school-related violence is increasing or decreasing over time.

National Child Traumatic Stress Network. *Resources for school personnel:* http://www.nctsnet.org/resources/audiences/school-personnel

This site provides resources to address the needs of children who have been traumatized by events such as a natural disaster, community violence, neglect, medical trauma, physical or sexual abuse, and school violence. The particular page identified in the URL is for school personnel who work with children who suffer from trauma, but especially from school violence. It also has links to other network sources that may be of assistance.

National School Climate Center: http://www.schoolclimate.org/guidelines/safety.php

The focus of this organization is to stress the role of school climate in improving student growth and achievement, which is inextricably linked to safety in the school. It speaks to the importance of "norms, values, and expectations that support people feeling socially, emotionally and physically safe." It summarizes the research in the field of school climate, explicates school climate improvement processes, and provides guidance on how to measure school climate.

National School Safety Center. (n.d.). http://www.schoolsafety.us/

This is a national resource that provides training in school safety leadership, safety audits, and technical assistance. It also provides strategies and suggestions for practices and programs that support safe schools.

Stopbullying.gov. http://www.stopbullying.gov/

This site is maintained by the U.S. Department of Health and Human Services and is a rich source of data on state laws on bullying and cyberbullying; what schools, communities, parents, and students can do to recognize, intervene, and stop bullying; and interventions for students who exhibit bullying behavior, as well as programs for those who are victims of bullying. It has quite a bit on the subject of students with disabilities who are victims or perpetrators of bulling behavior.

21

CHARTER SCHOOLS AND THE PRIVATIZATION OF PUBLIC EDUCATION

A Critical Race Theory Analysis

ABUL PITRE

Prairie View A&M University

TAWANNAH G. ALLEN

Fayetteville State University

The mention of the term *charter school* can elicit a variety of responses, ranging from great support to utter disgust, disdain, or blank stares (Tryjankowski, 2012). Needless to say, the charter school movement has launched educational discourse on both sides of the political aisle. President Obama indicated the prominence of **charter schools** in his 2013 State of the Union address when he called for creating more of them. U.S. Secretary of Education Arne Duncan has characterized charter schools as "one of the most profound changes in education" (Protheroe, 2011). Student enrollment in charter schools more than quadrupled during the first decade of the 21st century. As of 2011–2012, 2.1 million students in at least 40 states and the District of Columbia were being educated in charter schools (NCES, 2014).

The United States Department of Education has awarded charter school grants to states, charter school management organizations (CMOs), and groups such as the Arizona Charter Schools Association and the National Association of Charter School Authorizers (Protheroe, 2011). Indeed, the rapid ascension of charter schools has garnered federal support, while also becoming a major enterprise throughout the United States.

Charter schools receive public funding but in most cases are not run directly by school districts. They are tuition free and cannot discriminate against any student who applies. These schools are authorized by the state to operate independently under the monitoring of a state-approved agency responsible for authorizing charter schools (Tryjankowski, 2012).

Intended as incubators of educational reform, charter schools were born of commitments to social justice. Their founders were attempting to provide marginalized youths with what more privileged youths were getting in private schools—small schools, small classes, community ownership, dedicated faculty, and a multicultural and social justice curriculum (Fabricant & Fine, 2012, p. 19). Improved "customer service" would be achieved by being more responsive to the needs of students, parents, and the community, and by permitting parents to select schools that deliver the type of education they feel best meets their needs. Jack Buckley and Mark Schneider (2007) identify the following as the goals of charter schools:

- Increase opportunities for learning and access to quality education for all students
- Create choice for parents and students within the public school system
- Provide a system of accountability for results in public education
- Encourage innovative teaching practices
- Create new professional opportunities for teachers
- Encourage community and parent involvement in public education
- Leverage improved public education broadly (p. 2)

Touted as a reform strategy, charter schools are established on the basis of a contract or charter held by members of a private board. As part of the contract, charter schools are released from many of the state and district regulations by which **traditional public schools** are governed (Protheroe, 2011). Accompanying the flexibility afforded by the charter's establishment is the accountability for high-quality student outcomes. Failure to meet these expectations could warrant schools being closed by their authorizer.

Proponents maintained that charter schools would collaboratively free schools from bureaucratic red tape, while releasing new forms of practice, resulting in improved academic performance (Fabricant & Fine, 2012). The freedom from certain laws and regulations affecting regular public schools has been seen as necessary to achieve sustainable improvement within the educational setting, while also improving the culture of learning and student achievement.

The charter school conversation, including proponents and opponents, is a topic of interest among politicians across states. This topic has been a lightning rod for school reform and has been accompanied by a wave of debate filled with highly emotional rhetoric. One example is the 2010 documentary film *Waiting for Superman,* directed by Davis Guggenheim, that portrays charter schools as a possible solution to the "failing schools" that serve the historically underserved populations in the United States. This film is often used as an example of how charter schools can become beacons of hope for transforming public education. The majority of public schools in New Orleans became charter schools after Hurricane Katrina in 2005; whether that represents an improvement for the city's low-income and minority students has been hotly debated. The debate around charter schools and the privatization of public education is extremely important because the subject directly impacts the future course of the nation. This chapter uses **critical race theory** analysis to explore charter schools and the privatization of public education.

Origin of Charter Schools

The concept of public school choice came out of previous reform efforts, such as magnet schools and various small school projects (Tryjankowski, 2012). In an effort to achieve racial desegregation, magnet schools offered unique curricular programs designed to be attractive to diverse students and their families; the Small Schools Project promoted the development of small learning communities, in conjunction with focusing on student learning through relevant learning experiences and strong teacher-student relationships (Tryjankowski, 2012). To this end, the idea of charter schools, introduced by Ray Budde, has been the result of the culmination of several reform efforts.

Budde, a teacher, school administrator, and university professor, believed changing the internal organization of the school district would involve making substantial changes in the roles of teachers, principals, the superintendent, the school board, parents, and others in the community (Budde, 1988). Budde's framework of goals for charter schools was also supported by the late Albert Shanker, president of the American Federation of Teachers from 1974 to 1987, and it ultimately served as the guidepost for the implementation of charter schools. This guidepost centered on the following main tenets: local control; student responsibility; budgets for program implementation; principals as instructional leaders; research-based strategies and innovations; technology integration; and active community participation. These tenets were met with much debate between charter school proponents and detractors.

Evolution of Charter Schools

Minnesota's state legislature passed the first charter school law in 1991, and the nation's first charter school was established in Minnesota in 1992. By the late 1990s, there were more than 1,400 charter schools in 32 states and the District of Columbia. Early research on these schools focused primarily on the rate at which charter laws were adopted, differences in content across laws, and whether or not charter schools were sustainable or a passing fad that would be replaced by the next great school reform initiative (Wohlstetter, Smith, & Farrell, 2013).

The 1990s saw significant growth of charter schools, attributed to teachers, parents, and community organizations. During the 1990s, nonprofit school networks known as charter management organizations (CMOs) also emerged. At this point, questions surrounding accountability began to swirl. Some recurring questions included: Had charter schools exchanged autonomy for accountability? Against whose performance should charter school outcomes be compared? In what ways were charter school students different from the "average" district or state students? The primary questions at this point were whether charter schools "skimmed" the brightest students from noncharter public schools and whether charter schools screened out special education students (Wohlstetter et al., 2013; see **Sidebar 21.1**).

Arguments Advanced for Charter Schools

Proponents of charter schools claim that charter schools provide much-needed alternatives to traditional public schools that have failed to prepare America's youth for the challenges of the 21st century. Echoing the rhetoric of the Reagan-era report *A Nation at Risk* (National Commission on Excellence in Education, 1983), they contend that charter schools give children who attend poorly performing schools opportunities to receive a better education.

During the 1950s, economist Milton Friedman argued for limited government intervention and a voucher system in public schools, contending that competition between schools to attract and retain students would result in the best public education (Wohlstetter et al., 2013). Friedman called for disrupting what he viewed as monopolies in public services and argued that giving parents their choice of schools would allow schools in high demand to thrive, while forcing schools that are not in demand to either recreate themselves or ultimately close. Charter school advocates posited this form of healthy competition would lead to a stronger educational system that offered parents more choices for seeking the best education for their children.

Critics of charter schools contend that when the schools pull large numbers of students from traditional public schools, it can have a devastating financial

Sidebar 21.1   Ten Questions on Charter Schools

With the growing number of traditional public schools being identified as failing, it is realistic to expect the prevalence of charter schools to continue to increase. When considering the start-up or conversion of a charter school, some integral questions parents and district and building-level administrators and community leaders should pose include the following:

- On what basis was the need for a charter school decided?
- Is the establishment of a charter school the best alternative to address the current educational needs of the students?
- What geographical location will best serve the needs of students and the community?
- What will be the focus of the charter school?
- How will the governance model be structured?
- What leadership model/style will be employed with this charter school?
- How will the regulations of the Individuals with Disabilities Education Act be implemented?
- What accountability model will be utilized to measure student growth and achievement?
- What professional development opportunities will be available to teachers?
- What, if any, additional funding sources will support the charter school?

impact on the schools those students left (Buddin, 2012). Schools receive funding based on enrollment, so fewer students mean less funding (Batdorff, Maloney, & May, 2010). Batdorff et al. argue that traditional public schools spend more for special education, student support services, transportation, and food services.

Charter school opponents argue that students with special educational needs do not receive the same level of education as students enrolled in traditional public schools. Gary Orfield suggests charter schools are less likely than traditional public schools to enroll English language learners and students with learning disabilities (Orfield, 2010). Some charter school proponents have conceded the difficulties in providing services to these students. Due to the school's inability to address the needs of some students with disabilities they are encouraged to return to their district or community school to receive these services. Charter school opponents argue that charter schools show higher levels of student achievement than would be the case if they had as many students with special needs as public schools; thus, their reports of student growth—that is, student improvement on academic performance measures—and student achievement are unfair and often inaccurate (Tryjankowski, 2012).

Charter schools are generally believed to offer an array of opportunities because they are subject to fewer state regulations than traditional public schools and therefore can use more creative approaches to providing educational services. One example of such creativity is the flexibility some charter schools offer in terms of when the school day begins. Unlike traditional public schools that generally start between 7 am and 9 am, a charter school can begin the day at noon. Charter schools can also offer unique philosophical orientations or particular areas of focus such as science, technology, engineering, and math (STEM) or leadership studies. Charter schools also have the option of admitting only one type of student, for example, boys who are members of historically underserved populations.

Some supporters of charter schools, including several contributors to *Charter Schools: Answering the Call; Saving Our Children* (Esmail & Duhon-McCallum, 2012), believe they could be the answer to the educational ills that impact poor and minority student populations." Critics of the charter school movement, however, say that charter schools are a skillful way of maneuvering public schools into the private sector. In their edited volume *Defending Public Schools: Education Under the Security State* (2007), David Gabbard and E. Wayne Ross and various contributors highlight how public schools are being taken over by private corporations—a situation that will not provide students with a curriculum that makes them conscious of the social reality in which they live and thus will not produce conscious citizens who can build a more enlightened society.

These scholars contend the corporate takeover of schools will result in educational **hegemony**, a dangerous form of mis-education that will prepare students to accept oppressive societal structures rather than to challenge and repair them. In *Critical Pedagogy Primer* (2008), Joe Kincheloe referred to Antonio Gramsci's 1995 work on hegemony:

> Hegemony, Gramsci wrote from prison, involves the process used by the dominant power wielders to maintain power. The key dimension of this process is the manipulation of public opinion to gain consensus. When hegemony works best the public begins to look at dominant ways of seeing the world as simply common sense. (p. 65)

Both the Bush-era rhetoric of "leaving no child behind" and the necessity of ensuring educational equality for all U.S. children seem to support the commonsense viewpoint—that such policies were beneficial—but in reality they were a form of hegemonic control used to manipulate the public into accepting the values of an oppressive dominant class, as described by Gramsci.

Charter school advocates continue to depict the supposed failure of public schools in the United States, and what David Berliner and Bruce Biddle describe as a "manufactured crisis" has been unleashed, to be resolved by accountability measures that instead of improving public schools, maneuver them into the precarious position of being taken over by outside entities. To effectively hold schools accountable and determine if educators are meeting government-approved standards, **high-stakes testing** has become the measure of choice. In this environment, curriculum is designed by select individuals who decide which bodies of knowledge will be included and how they will be taught. High-stakes testing and accountability have thus become both normative and, in the eyes of the American public, necessary in order to correct "failing" schools. As a result, such schools may adopt increasingly punitive educational approaches as they struggle to meet mandated levels of yearly progress.

Once a school is labeled "failing" due to its below-average test scores, local newspapers report this status to the general public, which in turn demands improvement. Charter schools begin to look as if they are solutions, or at least viable alternatives to traditional public schools. Deeper questions about how to define academic achievement, however, are not thoroughly examined by the general public. Questions about *whose* knowledge is being infused into the present curriculum are also absent from the general discourse around the nation's "failing public schools."

Michael Apple (2004) has raised questions about "selective tradition" and the determination of curriculum by those in power. His analysis of the role of political and socioeconomic power in perpetuating educational inequality raises issues that are very important in understanding the charter school movement and the privatization of public schools. In terms of curriculum, relevant issues include whose knowledge is being taught, who selected this particular knowledge, and how it will be taught to a particular group of students. In critiquing the charter school movement and the privatization of public education, questions around race as well as those around political and socioeconomic status are significant.

A review of so-called failing schools indicates that the vast majority of schools labeled as such are comprised of predominantly African American or Latino students. The labels on these schools create a perception that to effectively ensure that all U.S. children have equal opportunities, more accountability measures are needed. Thus teachers and administrators must be monitored closely. In the current system, educators are so closely monitored that Michel Foucault (1977) described the situation as similar to the surveillance of prisoners advocated by Jeremy Bentham in his proposed Panopticon. Thus, accountability measures such as the **No Child Left Behind Act** and Race to the Top can be seen as creating a form of imprisonment.

The slogan **"**no child left behind**"** may have initially appealed to the public, but appears to have been designed to create a crisis that would undermine public schools, particularly those that serve African

American and Latino students (Pitre, Ray, Pitre, & Hilton-Pitre, 2009). According to Berliner and Biddle (1996), the accountability movement that culminated in No Child Left Behind was based on manufactured data and the use of this data created what Noam Chomsky (2004) calls a "necessary illusion"; this illusion became a hot topic for political conversation. In describing the political climate and the ideological forces that dominate the educational scene, Joel Spring (2010) writes that a human capitalist ideology is guiding educational policy writing:

> Today the dominant educational ideology is human capital economics, which defines the primary goal of education as economic growth, in contrast to other ideologies that might emphasize the passing on of culture or the education of students for social justice. Human capital economics contains a vision of school as a business preparing workers for business. (p. 6)

Spring's analysis reflects a political discourse where politicians make a case for improving education because it will attract more jobs. It is not unusual to hear political leaders support a human capitalist ideology, often stating that education should be about helping students find jobs. These same politicians threaten the future of public education institutions by claiming that educational institutions not focused on preparing students for jobs will find it difficult to survive.

The human capitalist ideology driving education can be explored within the context of social reproduction theory. Samuel Bowles and Herbert Gintis (1976) explored how schools reflected the larger social milieu in that they prepared students for their roles in society. Sonia Nieto and Patty Bode (2012) contend that social reproduction is a type of cyclical educational process that results in the most disenfranchised students receiving a marginal education, which in turn results in little to no social mobility. Jean Anyon's (2011) work explored social reproduction by examining four types of schools. She labeled the schools as *working-class schools, middle-class schools, executive elite schools,* and *affluent schools.* She found that each type had a hidden curriculum that prepared students for their future roles in the society. While the majority of the students she observed in these schools were White, her conclusions are alarming in that her study found that schools play a role in perpetuating the social class inequities that exist in the larger society. A highlight of her study was how working-class schools prepared students for roles as menial workers, whereas affluent schools prepared students for leadership. Regarding curriculum, the charter school movement while having some flexibility in its approach to curriculum is still bound to the state-approved curriculum. Even though charter schools have more flexibility than public schools in establishing curriculum, they too can contribute to an absence of social and economic mobility. Indeed, critics of charter schools have noted that they may be more segregated than the public schools from which charter students come and tend to reinforce existing disparities between schools in affluent and low-income neighborhoods.

Henry Giroux in his 2012 book, *Education and the Crisis of Public Values,* tackles the issue of charter schools in a chapter titled "Chartering Disaster." In this chapter, Giroux analyzes the powers behind the charter school movement and the privatization of public education. Noting that U.S. Secretary of Education Arne Duncan is an advocate of charter schools, Giroux contends that Duncan and the Obama administration advocate a market-driven model of pedagogy in which the drive for profits is the primary force behind the expansion of charter schools and privatization of public education. Giroux (2012) writes, "Also crucial to the neoliberal agenda is the channeling of public money into the hands of wealthy individuals and corporations" (p. 51).

It becomes clear that the sort of hegemony described by Gramsci may be the final nail in the coffin, taking public education completely out of the hands of the public and placing it under the total control of corporations. Giroux goes on to argue that some of the wealthy philanthropists who allegedly want to see better schools have a sinister motive: "There is a lot of money to be made in supporting charter schools, as seems evident in the number of hedge fund managers, wealthy Americans and Wall Street executives now lining up to support them" (Giroux, 2012, p. 58). He highlights the support of charter schools by the Bill and Melinda Gates Foundation, the Walton Family Foundation, and the Broad Foundation, along with their support of test scores to evaluate teachers. The emergence of charter schools and the move to privatize public education are not accidental but are products of a well-thought-out plan. The next section uses critical race theory to analyze charter schools and the privatization of public education.

Using Critical Race Theory to Analyze the Intersection of Race and Education

Many theoretical perspectives can be used to explore how race intersects the educational experiences of many youths, primarily minorities. The most commonly used perspectives include: **cultural arbitrary**, **cultural capital**, and **resiliency**.

The Cultural Arbitrary

Pierre Bourdieu and Jean-Claude Passeron (2000) coined the term *cultural arbitrary* to refer to the language, concepts, dispositions, and worldviews of the political elites who control the process of schooling and impose their values on the remainder of the socioeconomic system. The social constructions of the dominant culture are presumed to be the best for all students and are therefore imposed arbitrarily and without question (English, 2010). From this perspective, those in the dominant culture determine what concepts, terms, and historical perspectives are deemed worthy to be taught to all publicly educated students, and the voices or viewpoints of minorities are seldom heard or captured during discussions of curriculum revision or textbook adoption. Therefore, the values of minority students are rarely reflected in the adopted curriculum. Although clearly a factor to be considered when measuring race and the education of minority students, the cultural arbitrary is not the most useful concept for investigating the intersection of education and race in the context of charter schools.

Cultural Capital

Fenwick English (2010) proposes cultural capital—a form of noneconomic capital that represents the knowledge, dispositions, manners, ways of dress, values, and deportment of self of the political elites—as an explanation of why minority students may not experience academic success. Several minority students attending charter schools are products of low-wealth communities, can be characterized as underserved, and may share many of the same beliefs or cultural background. Unfortunately, the culture embodied in state exams and state-imposed curricula is not representative of the minority students who must pass high-stakes tests. Cultural capital, though a viable framework, does not offer a clear vantage point from which to support the arguments focused on the intersection of race and education in charter schools.

Critical Race Theory

Critical race theory (CRT) has emerged as the optimal theoretical perspective from which to understand the intersection of race and education. Gloria Ladson-Billings (2003) notes the origin of CRT: "Critical race theory sprang up in the mid-1970s with the early work of [legal scholars] Derrick Bell and Alan Freeman, both whom were distressed over the slow pace of racial reform in the United States" (p. 8). CRT considers racism to be so ingrained or institutionalized that it is often viewed as a normal part of American life. More importantly, critical race theorists seek to expose racism and its impact on American life. Donna M. Gollnick and Philip C. Chinn (2009) point out that CRT "focuses on racism in challenging racial oppression, racial inequities, and White privilege" (p. 11).

David Stovall (2005) identifies two major aspects of CRT as educational protest and scholarship. More importantly, Stovall links CRT to identification of White supremacy in education and of methods used to eradicate its dominance in education. Ladson-Billings and William Tate (1995) produced the first article that explored critical race theory in education. This article paved the way for the contemporary theorizing of critical race theory in education. This section applies a critical race theory perspective to the charter school movement and the privatization of public schools. It explores two major themes in critical race theory: **interest convergence** and **revisionist interpretation**. Richard Delgado and Jean Stefancic (2012) define interest convergence as a "thesis pioneered by Derrick Bell that the majority group tolerates advances for racial justice only when it suits its interest to do so" (p. 165). They define revisionist interpretation as a "view of history or an event that challenges the accepted one" (p. 172).

Interest Convergence

Interest convergence is a central theme explored by critical race theorists. They assert that those in the dominant group will make concessions to disenfranchised groups only when it serves their interest. Derrick Bell challenged the motivation for the Supreme Court's 1954 ruling on school desegregation in *Brown v. Board of Education,* arguing that it was not necessarily in the best interest of African Americans but instead served the interests of those in the dominant group by diverting attention from ongoing structural inequality. According to Bell, the decision could be seen as a defense of the image of the United States as the protector of democracy against critics who questioned it in light of the racial inequalities in American society. Those in power supported a more inclusive ideology only because projecting an image of liberty and freedom to the world was in the best interest of the dominant group in the United States. The charter school movement can be seen as a similar example of interest convergence. On the surface, charter schools may appear to be the great equalizer for historically underserved groups. For example, a charter school could have an Afrocentric philosophy undergirding everything at the school and could thus be seen as supportive of African American students. Male-only charter schools could give the appearance of ensuring equity and equality of education by providing a better educational environment than traditional public coeducational schools, but they do not necessarily lead to the type of consciousness that would make them transformative leaders. However, analysis from an interest convergence perspective suggests a different view: that the charter school movement is in the interest of the powerful and has very little to do with education for the empowerment of disenfranchised groups. They only serve as an illusion to make the general public believe that charter schools are actually improving the educational outcomes of historically underserved students. To the contrary, Diane Ravitch (2010) points out that African American and Latino students in charter schools do not outperform their peers in traditional public schools.

A RAND study of charter schools in eight states found that charter schools have difficulties raising student achievement in their first year of operation (Zimmer et al., 2009). Performance generally improves, but in many cases performance in subsequent years is still no better than that of traditional public schools (p. 85).

An unintended consequence of charter schools is the racial segregation brought about by subtle forms of student selection. This concern is documented by

Erica Frankenberg, Genevieve Siegel-Hawley, and Jia Wang (2010), who write that charter schools attract a higher percentage of Black students than traditional public schools, in part because many are in urban areas:

> At the national level, seventy percent of black charter school students attend intensely segregated minority charter schools (which enroll 90–100% of students from under-represented minority backgrounds), or *twice* as many as the share of intensely segregated black students in traditional public schools. (p. 4)

These researchers also found that half of Latino charter school students attended racially isolated minority schools, or those where 90% to 100% of students were members of minorities. Segregation patterns typically depend on the region of the country in which charter schools are located, with charter schools in the West, South, and Midwest enrolling a higher percentage of White students than charter schools in the Northeast. Concerns of racial segregation are heightened, particularly with students of color, English language learners, poor students, and special education students (Protheroe, 2011).

CRT highlights the way in which the interests of the powerful subordinate those of the masses. Charter schools are turned into sources of profit and placed on the market for sale to the highest bidder, while the students populating these charter schools become a form of property—treated as "real estate" by those seeking a workforce to support their businesses and increased revenue. Thus, the privatization of education can be seen as similar to slavery, with African Americans viewed as merely a potential labor supply. From this perspective, the education of African Americans and other historically underserved groups is not really about education for empowerment and liberation but simply meets the dominant class's need for a labor force to supply its industries. As Mwalimu Shujaa (1994) points out in his book *Too Much Schooling, Too Little Education: A Paradox of Black Life in White Societies,* historically underserved students are then equipped with training that prepares them to work for the powerful.

Critical Black educators, such as Carter G. Woodson (1933) and Elijah Muhammad (1965), questioned the rhetoric of those in powerful positions who claimed to support Black education. Historically, the education of African Americans has always been a major concern for those in positions of power. Judging from the historical record that highlights the role of wealthy philanthropists who spent considerable amounts of money in shaping the education of African Americans after the Civil War, one can draw parallels between philanthropists of yesteryear and those of the 21st century (Watkins, 2001).

Revisionist Interpretation

The education of historically underserved groups has not been left to chance. Prior to and even after the Civil War, it was a crime for African Americans to be educated. As a part of the institution of slavery, African peoples and other oppressed groups were deculturalized in order to make them see the world through the eyes of the dominant group (Spring, 2010). In the dominant narrative, education has been described as the great equalizer that would help all Americans achieve the American dream. However, the historical record of the education of oppressed groups points to careful planning on the part of those who owned the country. Even after the Civil War, the historical record indicates that the primary goal for educating African Americans was to make them more subservient to Whites. Spivey (2007) equated this to a new form of slavery that constituted a more sophisticated form of control. Countering the traditional narrative that highlights White philanthropists' support of Black education, a review of writings by critical Black educational scholars demonstrates that there was a cadre of Black leaders who argued that control of their own education was essential to Black freedom.

Woodson (1933) offered a revised interpretation of the dominant narrative regarding the role of education in keeping African Americans in the subservient position. He argued in Chapter 3 of *The Mis-Education of the Negro* that the education of African Americans was completely in the hands of those who oppressed them, saying: "Negroes have no control of their education." Woodson critiqued the educational systems of his day and argued that African Americans were being mis-educated. His arguments have been rearticulated by several critical educational scholars who, like Woodson, explored the relation between those who have power and the knowledge infused in public schools (Asante, 1991; Freire, 1970; McLaren, 2015).

Perhaps the most powerful critical Black educator was Elijah Muhammad, who, like Woodson, articulated the need for African Americans to control their own education. In his book *Message to the Blackman of America* (1965), he critiqued the educational system that he argued was a root cause of social inequities in the American society. What makes Muhammad's work in education so significant is that he created an entire educational system for African Americans, developing schools in cities throughout America. Prior to Apple's writing about the selective tradition, Muhammad discussed questions around whose knowledge is being used in the curriculum and how knowledge is taught, arguing that the knowledge made available to African Americans did not provide them with self-knowledge. Muhammad saw the knowledge of self as a prescription for eradicating the mental bondage that was a result of hundreds of years of chattel slavery. Regarding the use and application of education for empowering Black communities, he argued that African Americans were using their education primarily in the interest of their oppressors.

Conclusion

The authors have argued that the privatization of public education is a continuance of historical tradition in which those in power construct the education system to ensure that they themselves benefit from the labor of African Americans and other historically underserved groups. Jeannie Oakes and Martin Lipton (2007) pointed out a few years ago that during much of the preceding 30 years, the fastest population growth in the United States was in the South, where 38% of the nation's students are educated. Given that nearly half of U.S. public school students are non-White, in public schools one has to question if those in the dominant group who hold leadership roles would be concerned with properly educating the children of "former slaves." Molefi Kete Asante (1991) points out the historical challenge that will require a reinterpretation to the dominant historical narrative:

> Institutions such as schools are conditioned by the character of the nation in which they are developed. Just as crime and politics are different in different nations, so, too, is education. In the United States a "Whites-only"

orientation has predominated in education. This has had a profound impact on the quality of education for children of all races and ethnic groups. The African American child has suffered disproportionately, but White children are also the victims of monoculturally diseased curricula. (p. 174)

It could be argued that eventually charter schools will at some point undergo scrutiny similar to that of traditional public schools. At that point, with all of the data documenting the failure of public schools, it will become necessary to sell them to private corporations, who then will be tasked with training their future workforce. In the context of critical race theory, questions around ensuring that all U.S. students get a good education need more in-depth analysis. This should include questions such as the following:

- Who are the chief architects behind the push for charter schools and the privatization of public education?
- Will the architects of education develop a system of education that will lift those who have been historically underserved to positions of power in the society?
- Are slogans such as "No Child Left Behind" and "Race to the Top" used to support the hegemonic rule of the few over the masses?
- Have the powerful created a master narrative around achievement that does not really equate to achievement for historically underserved communities?

Questions such as these highlight critical race theorists' arguments around interest convergence and the need for a reinterpretation of the traditional historical narrative. In light of the move to privatize public education, it becomes important to assess what forces are at work to undermine public education. In the case of African Americans, the challenge continues to be the issue of control. Woodson clearly points out that education is problematic not only under White control but even when African Americans who have been shaped by a Eurocentric education system are in control:

> With mis-educated Negroes in control themselves, however it is doubtful that the system would be very much different from what is or that it would rapidly undergo change. The Negroes thus placed in charge would be the products of the same system and would

show no more conception of the task at hand than do the whites who have educated them and shaped their minds as they would have them function. . . . Taught from the book of the same bias, trained by Caucasians of the same prejudices or by Negroes of enslaved minds, one generation of Negro teachers after another have served for no higher purpose than to do what they are told to do. In other words, a Negro teacher instructing Negro children is in many respects a white teacher thus engaged, for the program in each case is about the same. (cited in Pitre, 2013, p. 47)

The charter school movement and the privatization of public education are not new in education. These movements have taken different names at different times, but the outcome remains the same—control by persons and institutions that do not have furthering the well-being of students as their goal.

Key Chapter Terms

A Nation at Risk: A report issued in 1983 by the National Commission on Excellence in Education that found poor performance at every academic level. It was the impetus for national efforts at school reform.

Charter schools: Public schools that are usually run independently from the school districts where they are located and are free from many state and local regulations.

Critical race theory: Emerging in the mid-1970s from the earlier critical legal studies movement, CRT identifies the systematic ways in which racism operates in the ideology and operation of the American legal system. The theory identifies the centrality of White privilege and White supremacy in dominant power structures that perpetuate the marginalization of people of color. Within the context of education, CRT critiques the racism underlying policies and practices that are used to control the educational system for the benefit of the dominant class.

Cultural arbitrary: The arbitrary imposition of the language, concepts, dispositions, and world views of the political and socioeconomic elites on the rest of society.

Cultural capital: Cultural practices, knowledge, and attitudes that follow and perpetuate the dominant society's cultural ideals. Schools socialize students in ways that transfer cultural capital to children of the elite by ensuring that they are positioned to assume the most favorable positions in social and occupational contexts.

Hegemony: Political and cultural dominance or authority over others.

High-stakes testing: Testing with important consequences for the test-taker. It also includes testing that has important consequences for the school and teachers.

Interest convergence: Thesis pioneered by Derrick Bell that the majority group tolerates advances in racial justice only when it is in its own interest to do so.

No Child Left Behind Act (NCLB): The 2001 reauthorization of the Elementary and Secondary Education Act, which included Title I, the government's flagship aid program for disadvantaged students. NCLB required standardized testing of students and put in place consequences for schools that fell short of proficiency goals.

Resiliency: The ability to rebound from adversity and successfully adapt in facing it. Resilient individuals survive and even thrive in the face of severe stress, developing social and academic competence.

Revisionist interpretation: View of history or event that challenges the accepted one.

Traditional public school: An elementary or secondary school in the United States supported by public funds with the purpose of providing free education for children of a community or district.

References

Anyon, J. (2011). *Marx and education.* New York, NY: Routledge.

Apple, M. (2004). *Ideology and curriculum* (3rd ed.). New York, NY: Routledge.

Asante, M. K. (1991). The Afrocentric idea in education. *Journal of Negro Education, 60*(2), 170–180.

Batdorff, M., Maloney, L., & May, J. (2010). *Charter school funding: Inequity persists.* Muncie, IN: Ball State University.

Berliner, D., & Biddle, B. (1996). *The manufactured crisis: Myths, fraud, and the attack on America's public schools.* New York, NY: Basic Books.

Bourdieu, P., & Passeron, J.-C. (2000). *Reproduction in education, society and culture* (2nd ed.). London, England: Sage.

Bowles, S., & Gintis, H. (1976). *Schooling in capitalist America: Educational reform and the contradictions of economic life.* New York, NY: Basic Books.

Buddin, R. (2012). *The impact of charter schools on public and private school enrollments.* Retrieved from http://object.cato.org/sites/cato.org/files/pubs/pdf/PA707.pdf

Budde, R. (1988). *Education by charter: Restructuring school districts. Keys to long-term continuing improvement in American education.* Andover, MA: Regional Laboratory for Educational Improvement of the Northeast & Islands.

Buckley, J., & Schneider, M. (2007). *Charter schools: Hope or hype.* Princeton, NJ: Princeton University Press.

Chomsky, N. (2004). *Chomsky on mis-education.* Lanham, MD: Rowman and Littlefield.

Delgado, R., & Stefancic, J. (2012). *Critical race theory: An introduction* (2nd ed.). New York: New York University Press.

English, F. (2010). *Deciding what to teach & test: Developing, aligning, and leading the curriculum.* Thousand Oaks, CA: Corwin.

Esmail, A., & Duhon-McCallum, A. (Eds.). (2012). *Charter schools: Answering the call; Saving our children.* Lanham, MD: University Press of America.

Fabricant, M., & Fine, M. (2012). *Charter schools and the corporate makeover of public education: What's at stake?* New York, NY: Teachers College Press.

Foucault, M. (1977). *Discipline and punish: The birth of the prison.* New York, NY: Pantheon Books.

Frankenberg, E., Siegel-Hawley, G., & Wang, J. (2010). *Choice without equity: Charter school segregation and the need for civil rights standards.* Los Angeles, CA: The Civil Rights Project/Proyecto Derechos Civiles at UCLA. Retrieved from http://www.civilrightsproject.ucla.edu/news/pressreleases/CRP-Choices-Without-Equity-report.pdf

Freire, P. (1970). *Pedagogy of the oppressed.* New York, NY: Continuum.

Gabbard, D., & Ross, E. W. (Eds.). (2007). *Defending public schools: Education under the security state.* New York, NY: Teachers College Press.

Giroux, H. (2012). *Education and the crisis of public values: Challenging the assault on teachers, students & public education.* New York, NY: Peter Lang.

Gollnick, D., & Chinn, P. (2009). *Multicultural education in a pluralistic society and exploring diversity* (8th ed.). Upper Saddle River, NJ: Prentice Hall.

Gramsci, A. (1995). *Further selections from the prison notebooks.* London, England: Lawrence & Wishart.

Guggenheim, D. (Director), & Chilcott, L. (Producer). (2010). *Waiting for Superman* [Motion picture]. US: Walden Media; Participant Media.

Kincheloe, J. (2008). *Critical pedagogy primer* (2nd ed.). New York, NY: Peter Lang.

Ladson-Billings, G. (Ed.). (2003). *Critical race theory perspectives on social studies: The profession, policies, and curriculum.* Greenwich, CT. Information Age.

Ladson-Billings, G., & Tate, W. (1995). Toward a critical race theory of education. *Teachers College Record, 97*(1), 47–68.

McLaren, P. (2015). *Life in schools: An introduction to critical pedagogy in the foundations of education* (6th ed.). Boulder, CO: Paradigm.

Muhammad, E. (1965). *Message to the Blackman in America.* Chicago, IL: Final Call.

National Center for Education Statistics. (2014). *Charter school enrollment.* Retrieved from http://nces.ed.gov/programs/coe/indicator_cgb.asp

National Commission on Excellence in Education. (1983). *A nation at risk: The imperative for educational reform.* Washington, DC: U.S. Government Printing Office. Retrieved from http://datacenter.spps.org/uploads/sotw_a_nation_at_risk_1983.pdf

Nieto, S., & Bode, P. (2012). *Affirming diversity: The sociopolitical context of multicultural education* (6th ed.). New York, NY: Longman.

Oakes, J., & Lipton, M. (2007). *Teaching to change the world* (3rd ed.). New York, NY: McGraw-Hill.

Orfield, G. (2010, March 3). *Choice without equity: Charter school segregation and the need for civil rights standards.* Los Angeles, CA: The Civil Rights Project/Proyecto Derechos Civiles at UCLA.

Pitre, A. (2013). *Educational leaders in a multicultural society: A critical perspective.* San Diego, CA: Cognella Academic Publishers.

Pitre, A., Ray, R., Pitre, E., & Hilton-Pitre, T. (2009). *Educating African American students: Foundations, curriculum, and experiences.* Lanham, MD: Rowman and Littlefield Education.

Protheroe, N. (2011). *Concerns in education: What do we know about charter schools?* Alexandria, VA: Educational Research Service.

Ravitch, D. (2010). The sound of bubbles bursting: Student gains on state test vanished into thin air. *Daily News.* Retrieved from http://articles.nydailynews.com/2010-08-01/news/29438770_1_charter-students-student-gains-national-tests

Shujaa, M. (1994). *Too much schooling, too little education: A paradox of Black life in White societies.* Trenton, NJ: Africa World Press.

Spivey, D. (2007). *Schooling for the new slavery: Black industrial education 1868–1915.* Trenton, NJ: Africa World Press.

Spring, J. (2010). *Deculturalization and the struggle for equality: A brief history of the education of dominated cultures in the United States* (6th ed.). New York, NY: McGraw-Hill.

Spring, J. (2011). *The politics of American education.* New York, NY: Routledge.

Stovall, D. (2005). Critical race theory as educational protest. In W. Watkins (Ed.), *Black protest thought and education* (pp. 197–213). New York, NY: Peter Lang.

Tryjankowski, A. M. (2012). *Charter school primer.* New York, NY: Peter Lang.

Watkins, W. (2001). *The White architects of Black education: Ideology and power in America 1865–1954.* New York, NY: Teachers College Press.

Wohlstetter, P., Smith, J., & Farrell, C. (2013). *Choices & challenges: Charter school performance in perspective.* Cambridge, MA: Harvard University Press.

Woodson, C. (1933). *The mis-education of the Negro.* Trenton, NJ: First Africa World Press.

Zimmer, R., Gill, B., Booker, K., Lavertu, S., Sass, T. T., & Witte, J. (2009). *Charter schools in eight states: Effects on achievement, attainment, integration, and competition.* Santa Monica, CA: RAND Education. Retrieved from http://www.rand.org/content /dam/rand/pubs/monographs/2009/RAND_MG869 .pdf

Further Readings

Anyon, J. (1981). Social class and school knowledge. *Curriculum Inquiry, 11*(1), 3–42.

This article contrasts the social class settings in two school districts in New Jersey and discusses how, while there were similarities in curriculum topics and materials, there were also both subtle and dramatic differences in the curriculum and the curriculum-in-use among the schools.

Bettinger, E. (2005). The effect of charter schools on charter students and public schools. *Economics of Education Review, 24*(2), 133–147.

This article estimates the effect of charter schools on both students attending them and students at neighboring public schools. The researcher purports that test scores of charter school students do not improve, and may actually decline, relative to those of public school students. Results of the study suggest that charter schools have had no significant effect on test scores in neighboring public schools.

Guggenheim, D. (2010). *Waiting for superman.* New York, NY: Public Affairs.

This powerful book offers solutions to inequities in schooling. The book disregards poverty as a factor in school performance while raising issues that demand attention, including achievement gaps, high dropout rates in some schools and districts, and the need for committed, well-prepared teachers.

Ravitch, D. (2010). The myth of charter schools. Retrieved from http://www.nybooks .com/articles/archives/2010/nov/11/myth-charter- schools/?pagination=false&printpage=true

This article offers a critique of the film Waiting for Superman *while also discussing the films* The Lottery *and* The Cartel, *all of which argue that charter schools are a solution to problems in American education.*

Woodson, C. G. (2008). *The mis-education of the Negro* (11th ed.). Trenton, NJ: First Africa World Press. (Original work published 1933)

This book points out the shortcomings of a Eurocentric teaching structure that leaves out consideration for Black culture and heritage. This has resulted in Blacks being truly mis-educated and has caused many to live in complete contradiction to their own best interests.

PART VIII

STUDENTS, PARENTS, AND SPECIAL POPULATIONS

22

STUDENT CONDUCT, ATTENDANCE, AND DISCIPLINE

The Troika of School Safety and Stability

CLAIRE E. SCHONAERTS
Northern Arizona University

PAMELA JANE POWELL
Northern Arizona University

In light of the challenges educational leaders face in the 21st century, three essential components for building school safety and stability emerge. Educational leaders must be concerned with student **conduct**, attendance, and discipline. The **troika** of positive student conduct, consistent attendance, and the cultivation of self-discipline ushers the carriage of educational management and offers multiple opportunities. For many school leaders, the ability to harness these three essential student responses—conduct, attendance, and discipline—often requires behaviors that demand professional practice. At the heart of the challenge, school leaders must be motivators, communicators, and strategists; in short, transformational leaders. The goal of educational leaders is to create a culture of excellence where administration, faculty, staff, students, and community stakeholders rely on mutual support in building and promoting schoolwide stability and quality and dynamic school **systems** rooted in positive action.

Violent student behavior disrupts learning opportunities for students involved in these incidents and has deteriorated the well-being of entire school environments (Way, 2011). Educational leaders are ultimately held accountable for the safety and stability of their schools. In an effort to support safer and more stable environments, educational leaders have implemented more restrictive and punitive disciplinary guidelines. Although stricter discipline and "zero-tolerance" measures have been used to control student conduct and discipline, "the academic community has been critical of the shift to more punitive and restrictive disciplinary approaches" (Way, 2011, p. 346). With student conduct closely aligned to discipline issues and academic stability, leaders in education debate how to create learning environments that support students academically, socially, and emotionally.

Transformational Leadership

The work of educational leaders connects student conduct, school attendance, and discipline to build school safety and stability. The management style of each leader offers a unique opportunity to incorporate an individual approach for this process. Leaders who seek to build or sustain safe and stable schools employ transformational management skills. These teacher-leaders are noted for their positive or inspirational attitudes, their ability to intellectually stimulate school community members, and their concern for overall outcomes as well as the individual success of each participant (Bass & Stogdill, 1990). Integrity, clarity of vision, and clear goals are characteristics of transformational leaders (deMarrais & LeCompte, 1999).

Transformational leaders demonstrate strong skills in communicating with all **school stakeholders** and can readily identify and provide recognition for each member's contribution (Marzano, Waters, & McNulty, 2005). As John Kotter (2012) noted, "Management makes a system work. It helps you do what you know how to do. Leadership builds systems or transforms old ones" (p. vii).

The school community that is built on **collaborative practices** provides a frame that is both dynamic and stable. "The frame also is the platform by which conversations about practice are held" (Papa, English, Davidson, Culver, & Brown, 2013, p. 5). These conversations must move the leadership team to embrace the changing academic, social, and emotional demands of the 21st century. In a school where safety and stability are honored expectations, the demonstrated strategies, skills, and techniques reveal the commitment of a shared identity that supports a shared future.

Student Conduct

The behavior habits students acquire are reflected in their personal conduct. Student conduct is the general term used to indicate how students are likely to behave given everyday circumstances. Student decorum becomes an expectation of the school culture in which students, faculty, staff, and administrators operate. To this end, educational leaders set the tone for optimal behavior. Student conduct is the layer of behavior that is often the indicator of mutual respect between the adults and the students and the students with one another. A broader sense of student conduct is based on the students' perception of discipline measures used in the school and their commitment to the school's authority (see **Sidebar 22.1**).

School Attendance

School attendance requirements are set by the state and school districts; these requirements include how many days students must attend school in a school year, how many hours per day students are required to attend, and what determines whether students are considered "tardy" or "absent." Individual schools implement these requirements. Educational leaders must be well acquainted with these policies and comply with regulations.

Since state funding is tied to attendance (deMarrais & LeCompte, 1999; EdSource, 2013), educational leaders have a unique motivation to support student attendance. Given that classrooms must be supervised by certified adults, educational leaders must also be concerned with the consistent attendance of their faculty. When teachers are absent, substitutes must be hired. Students suffer as a result of their teacher's absence. Substitute teachers cannot replace regular teachers' knowledge of their students' academic objectives and their social and emotional needs. Therefore, a record of good attendance is seen as valuable not only for students, but also for the adults in a school setting. Building a culture that encourages whole school

Sidebar 22.1   Maintaining Good Student Conduct

To maintain good student conduct, administrators should:

- Support a schoolwide discipline plan developed by all stakeholders
- Communicate behavior expectations to students, parents, and faculty
- Demonstrate desirable behaviors to clearly indicate expectations and learning goals
- Consistently uphold the behavior standards adopted by the school community
- Expect acceptable behavior in all venues of the school, including classrooms, playground, cafeteria, and elsewhere

attendance is an essential component for creating a stable environment.

Schools often implement incentives for attendance. Attendance practices require a daily accounting. Parents are informed about missed days and attendance records are reported on student evaluation communiqués such as the quarterly report card. Attendance and participation may be indicators of the regard students, faculty, staff, and leadership have for the culture of the school. Attendance reward programs have limitations. Focusing on people and practices, rather than attendance incentives, can have a positive impact on learning (Reeves, 2010). School leaders who grasp the importance of attendance find ways to support students, faculty, and staff who struggle with attendance issues.

Attendance, though, is also influenced by other factors. The health and well-being of the child are factors in attendance. Family transience, chronic illness, and older siblings staying home to care for younger siblings are factors in some students' abilities to attend school in K-12 systems. Likewise, in postsecondary school, work, health, and family concerns as well as adjustment to college life may be factors in attendance. School attendance is one variable that can be statistically calculated and hypothesized to be a factor in student success.

School Discipline

The word *discipline* emerges from the Latin verb *discere:* "to learn." The term, *discipline,* is not so much about rules and regulations as it is the process of teaching and learning the consequences of behavior and making choices that promote positive growth. Usually the educational leader establishes, defines, and refines the consequences of behavior. It is limiting to suggest that the educational leader considers discipline the punitive delivery of consequences for what is deemed inappropriate behavior. This task is often seen as the end result of poor student conduct. The expectation is that teachers and principals must *administer* discipline. John Dewey (1938/1998) succinctly addressed it this way:

> The educator has to discover as best he or she can the causes for the recalcitrant attitudes. He or she cannot, if the educational process is to go on, make it a question of pitting one will against another in order to see which is strongest, nor yet allow the unruly and

non-participating pupils to stand permanently in the way of the educative activities of others. (pp. 62–63)

If the thinking becomes one of *teaching* discipline rather than dealing with discipline, the ongoing components of discipline become daily formative habits of responsibility rather than a response to poor decision making. Engaging school communities in creating growth-producing discipline measures strengths safety and stability.

School Safety

Educational leaders face challenges in the 21st century that are unique to this era. The diversity of students and the blending of multicultural contributions provide an entire tapestry of elements that have the potential to support school safety. Schools that provide ways for students to communicate their shared differences bring a sense of cohesiveness to the school culture. When students feel there is a real connection between administration and individual students or student groups, the entire school community is supported. Differences become points of communication and celebration rather than points of isolation and conflict. School safety can emerge as communication is established.

Defining school safety is as concrete as creating a checklist of intruder deterrents or evaluating primary playground equipment. School safety is also as ethereal as the tone one feels upon entering each classroom or office space. The educational leader must embrace the expectation that both the tangible and intangible elements of school safety are present, cultivated, and routinely addressed.

The intangible environment for students, faculty, and staff is compromised by attitudes and behaviors that are counterproductive to safety. Regardless of differences in race, ethnicity, religious beliefs, or sexual orientation, the school atmosphere must provide a safe environment. Today's educational leaders are liable for allowing **bullying** and other forms of harassment to manifest on school sites. More important than any legal ramifications, bigotry and bullying erode the individual's need to feel safe and therefore deteriorate school safety and stability. Strategies for supporting the **schoolwide practice** of ensuring safety based on both procedural suggestions to cultivating an environment of mutual respect and open-mindedness are implemented by effective school leaders.

School Stability

As a school culture engenders a sense of consistent expectations for behavior, stability becomes the platform for building and deepening the honored culture of the school community. Stability of the school continues beyond the current leaders as an expectation that "great things happen here." Educational leaders at the school may move to other sites, yet the school maintains a sense of permanence, an endurance that dynamically embraces change in ways that sustain stability.

Why Be Concerned With Conduct, Attendance, and Discipline?

Educational leaders have a full plate of concerns to address as the curriculum and instructional facets of teaching and learning unfold, change, and escalate. Why be concerned with such elements as student conduct, discipline, or attendance? How will these school characteristics affect the leader who must make data-driven decisions, create meaningful professional development, contribute to the overall success of the district, and in short, fit a 24-hour workload into a reasonable 8-hour day?

Educational leaders who have established the expectation that students will conduct themselves with dignity and treat others with the same respect will attest that building these principles is time well spent. Teachers can instruct in a way that sets high expectations and facilitates students expressing their ideas, which in turn permeates the atmosphere of the school. Leaders set in motion this troika of conditions so that there is time and energy for building academic achievement and promoting socio emotional competency. Leaders build safety within their schools. Their actions demonstrate that school safety is an expectation that all children are safe and actions must be taken to support a safe environment for all students.

Neglect or violence must never be tolerated. Effective school leaders harness community efforts to investigate allegations that may diminish or compromise the safety of children. This attitude permeates the school grounds. School safety is a school goal. It can be as obvious as the posted declaration that no weapons are allowed on school property; or

as unseen as the intolerance for bullying that may occur in cyberspace. Leaders who have a clear vision of what school safety means to the child are better prepared to respond to issues *before* a crisis occurs.

Establishing guidelines for adults and children requires foresight. Bringing the school community together allows for a variety of voices to be heard. School nurses, teachers, custodial personnel, and parents, along with leaders from the community who represent law enforcement and social workers, for example, can provide avenues for discussion (Patton, 2011). Prevention is critical. When leaders are faced with difficult situations, the time to design a plan has passed. Rather, acting using the guidelines that have *already* been established, will better ensure that student safety is maintained (Way, 2011).

School stability is celebrated in these moments of decisiveness. Community response to schools where strong leadership declares a commitment to student safety can traverse moments of challenges whether these are academic or social concerns. As witnessed in the aftermath of the mass shooting at Sandy Hook School in Connecticut in 2012, the community response for the children and adults that were killed spurred a conversation regarding school safety that reached the national level. Ongoing conversations supporting school stability are echoed across our national schools. Key to this stability is the understanding that all participants have a contribution to make (York-Barr, Sommers, Ghere, & Montie, 2001).

As transformational leaders, school officials engage in conversations that demonstrate individualized consideration while bringing out the best in others. Transformational leaders "foster a collaborative, professional culture, facilitate teacher development, and help teachers solve problems" (Gordon, 2004, p. 6). School stability is everyone's goal. Garnering the ideas of community and school personnel not only fosters collaboration—the process may reveal ways for continuous improvement (Marzano et al., 2005).

School Safety and Stability: Actions of Educational Leaders

Ask a dozen teachers and staff members concerned with school safety and stability which characteristics describe an effective school leader and you will get 13 responses (or more). However, there are several key characteristics that repeatedly get mentioned. An effective education leader:

- Has a vision for the school community that can be stated, shared, and implemented by all stakeholders
- Understands the culture of the school and is committed to inclusion when building the school's impact on students and their families
- Is well organized, yet flexible when a situation requires new thinking or action
- Works collaboratively with others to promote a positive system of communication and mutual support
- Has high expectations for students, families, faculty, and staff and visibly supports the school community in reaching goals while affirming the efforts of others
- Demonstrates honesty and respect toward all school members while promoting positive teacher-student relations
- Is affable without showing favoritism; is fair and friendly, yet professional; and builds positive relationships with all school stakeholders
- Is knowledgeable in the area of safety policies at the national, state, district, and school levels and shares this information with others in a timely manner
- Is knowledgeable in the area of technological security and development, academic expectations, current research, and how these factors impact student learning
- Invests in students, teachers, and staff for the "long haul" while able to celebrate the small victories along the way
- Has a conscientious and relentless commitment to the work

The teacher-leader embraces these same qualities, particularly in the area of high expectations for students and faculty. Robert Marzano, Timothy Waters, and Brian McNulty (2005), quoting from a report of the U.S. Senate Select Committee on Equal Educational Opportunity that was first printed in 1970, have

identified the principal as the single most influential person in a school. . . . It is the principal's leadership that sets the tone of the school, the climate for teaching, the level of professionalism and morale of teachers and staff and the degree of concern for what students may or may not become. (p. 56)

An effective principal accepts these responsibilities and becomes the main link between the school and the community. Building this link is a key factor for transformational educational leaders. Principals who use strategies such as "turning a concern into a question" (Lambert, 1998, p. 27) create a culture of peer support and initiate leadership capacity building in schools.

Educational Leaders Build Communities

Community building is essential to the overall functioning of a school and its wider kinship to the locale in which it resides. Led by an effective and transformational leader, the school community is prompted by this leader who, in turn, creates multiple leaders within a school. Realizing that the time with each child at each grade level creates a sense of urgency, and making every day count can become a mantra in an environment of collegiality and shared goals. As Kotter noted (2012):

A higher rate of urgency does not imply ever-present panic, anxiety, or fear. It means a state in which complacency is virtually absent, in which people are always looking for both problems and opportunities, and in which the norm is "do it now." (p. 170)

This is particularly crucial for schools. Building a sense of community begins before the school community arrives on that first day of school. The preparations required for a smooth start to the school year begin with the entire school in mind while nearly the entire school is absent. Leading by preparedness, rather than urgency, the educational leader grabs the opportunity to "do it now."

Kimberly Strike (2011) made the point that, "as the first day of school goes, so goes the school year" (p. 51). For the educational leader, preparing for a successful first day requires the painstaking review of the mundane. Preparing school grounds, creating cleaning schedules, adding technology updates, making minor and major repairs to the facilities, all fall under a long list of deadlines. So, too, is the planning for schoolwide opportunities for building the school mission. "The principal must involve everyone in the school in recognizing, enforcing, and implementing the mission statement. The statement must become a daily concrete objective" (Papalewis & Fortune, 2002, p. 12). Implementation does not happen by accident. Focused discussions during professional development opportunities are purposefully set well in advance of that first school day.

Scheduling faculty and staff professional development opportunities to build mutual trust and support, sustainable energy, and commitment is recognizably best done before the harried onset of the first day of school. Before the arrival of students on Day One, the educational leader will have reviewed the school's schedule, the facilities, and the requests of faculty, staff, and other stakeholders. These reviews will require a prioritized examination. The school leader provides a clear, conscientious lens while inviting other stakeholders to participate. "The effective leader not only helps establish the criteria around which goals are established, but also participates in the goals' design and implementation" (Marzano et al., 2005, p. 16).

Constructing school safety and stability requires the school leader to create a school support system by capitalizing on the community at large. Reuben Jacobson, Rita A. Hodges, and Martin J. Blank (2011) tout a community school strategy where

> the community school has a set of partnerships in place that connect the school, the students' families, and the community. Community schools are more than just another model or program; they bring together community partners, parents, teachers, and administrators to assess students' needs and identify the resources that are available to meet them. Community schools have an integrated focus on academics, youth development, family support, health and social services, and community development. They address those areas by creating the structure and culture needed to ensure that the conditions for learning are fulfilled. (p. 18)

This strategy speaks to the need for **systems building** and the intersection of multiple systems. Blank, Atelia Melaville, and Jacobson (2012) also explained:

> A community school strategy recognizes that many public and private community institutions share responsibility for helping: Children develop socially, emotionally, physically, and academically; Students become motivated and engaged in learning; Families and schools work effectively together; Communities become safer and more economically vibrant. (p. 4)

Similarly, the Center for Mental Health in Schools at UCLA (2011) discussed system building in collaborations in this way:

> While every school is in a neighborhood, only a few designate themselves as Community Schools. And, those using the term vary considerably in what they do

and don't do. For some the term is adopted mainly to indicate a school's commitment to finding better ways to involve families and link with other community stakeholders. Others adopt it to reflect the implementation on campus of family centers, volunteer and mentor programs, school-based health centers, a variety of co-located health and human services, and efforts to extend the school day for learning and recreation. A few are involved in comprehensive collaborations focused on weaving together a wide range of school and community resources (including the human and social capital in a neighborhood) to enhance results for children, families, schools, and neighborhoods. (p. 1)

When teachers are given opportunities to collaborate, they see themselves as an active part of building the community school system. This builds leadership that "creates a climate of enthusiasm and flexibility, one where people feel invited to be at their most innovative, where they give their best" (Goleman, Boyatzis, & McKee, 2002, p. 248). Schools are more likely to find solutions to specific problems in school safety and stability when teachers are encouraged to share their input. Principals who readily share their power with the teaching staff create a collaborative climate (Papalewis & Fortune, 2002). "Respecting professional judgment on the part of teachers, paraprofessionals, and parent volunteers, and providing ways for everyone to do their job are critical leadership characteristics of the school administration" (Papalewis & Fortune, 2002, p. 27).

The importance of harnessing the power teachers bring to the school cannot be minimized. Teachers often see what an administrator might miss from his or her vantage point. Teachers help clarify the needs of students, parents, and other teachers. Acknowledging the contribution teachers make to the issues of safety, security, and stability provides a platform from which community building is generated and systems are cocreated.

There are several skills that school leaders might consider employing when working with teachers to positively impact student conduct, attendance, and discipline. For example, in instructional leadership, Carl Glickman (2002) suggested several elements that support collaborative community building. The initial step is listening. To build a collaborative spirit, the technique educational leaders should use is active listening. The principal "nods his or her head to show understanding" (Glickman, 2002, p. 39). The technique of actively being engaged in the listening process invites discussion. Carl Glickman also suggested the following remarks, "I understand you mean . . . I hear you saying . . ." (p. 41). These types of statements help to indicate that the principal is actively listening and inviting clarification and problem solving.

As Daniel Goleman, Richard Boyatzis, and Annie McKee (2002) note: "The best communicators are superb listeners" (p. 69). Leaders should encourage and acknowledge the contributions teachers make in the dialogue process and provide reflecting and summarizing comments. Teachers who are invited to voice their concerns and those of students support the very heart of school systems: success for every student.

Consider Urie Bronfenbrenner's ecological model (1979), which places the child in the center of concentric circles that represent all the systems the child interacts with and affects. Think, then, about all persons in this model. All are individuals who are part of systems that operate within other systems. All are part of the community whether they are engaged in the community or not. That is, we all bump against one another in ways visible and invisible.

The child within himself, within his family, within his institutions (church, school, etc.), within his community, within the world—this model is taught in early education programs but applies from the preschool years through the college experience. Bronfenbrenner's model (1979), then, can be a foundation for schools to build a sense of community and also collaborate with the greater community. Children, as contributors to the greater context, may develop a greater sense of inner locus of control through ownership of behavior in relation to self and others though service—thus impacting the communities within communities. It is often the needs of the children that bring a community together. How we support our students becomes the measure of the school's stability within the ever-expanding circle of community.

Mary Gordon (2004) speaks to the "roots of empathy" and how "children who develop social and emotional competence are happier, have more rewarding relationships with their peers, are more reliant in the face of stress, and even perform better academically" (p. xiv). Children's temperament, attachment, emotional literacy, authentic communication, and social inclusion all contribute to their development of empathy. Classrooms influence these factors and can nurture positive communication and relationships, helping to create a sense of community in the school.

These classroom communities are systems themselves working within systems that work within systems. The role of a teacher-leader as facilitator of systems includes being able to recognize the intersections and places of connection between these systems and to be intentional about connecting them for and with children. Providing multiple growth opportunities for children within these many contexts permits children to practice **self-regulation** and remain engaged in ever-changing, novel ways that stem boredom and bolster attention, which is another self-regulatory skill supporting the dynamics of school safety and security (see **Sidebar 22.2**).

Educational Leaders Support Students

In many communities, there are **partnerships** among parents, schools, and other organizations that go beyond athletics and activities such as Scouting. These communities invest heavily in children and

Sidebar 22.2   Building School Community

To help build a healthy school community, teachers should:

- Help develop a schoolwide discipline plan that involves all stakeholders
- Communicate behavior expectations to students using positive words and behavior
- Provide opportunities for students to dramatically illustrate examples of acceptable behavior
- Consistently uphold the behavior standards adopted by the school community
- Expect and inspect acceptable behavior in all venues of the school, including classrooms, playground, cafeteria, and elsewhere
- Use self-reflection as one way to examine their responses to students, peers, and the school community

have a commitment to school stability. One example is Reggio Emilia, Italy, where preschools developed an approach to early learning that has inspired similar schools around the world. By leading children in student-centered learning, Reggio-inspired classrooms engage children by listening to their questions, providing an inviting environment, and facilitating opportunities that build on children's ideas. Employing teachers, children, and families in learning, all become partners toward the goals of children. Teaching and learning in these environments are far from the rote, lockstep procedures required in some scripted endeavors in order to achieve results through fidelity to a scientifically based program. The Reggio influence serves to engage children in deep learning, promoting attendance, good conduct, and discipline through this profound engagement.

In the past, the America's Promise Alliance has named 100 cities in America as "best communities for young people" using the measurement of multiple key and collaborative factors supporting the goal of improving high school graduation rates. Also, numerous states have launched initiatives that depend on system-building intersectionality. Additionally, there is an emphasis regarding the collaboration within school systems and government organizations. This effort to work together is designed to support students in multiple contexts. Such collaboration is often required to receive grants and other types of funding due to limited resources and the desire to eliminate redundancy, share funding streams, and use money effectively.

Educational Leaders Build a Community of Learners

Building an environment where students are eager to learn can occur at any age. Beginning early, when children are first developing theory of mind, this community of learners can support the students' emotional commitment to one another. "Getting along" is not something that comes naturally and socioemotional growth needs the gentle guidance of caring adults and more-capable peers.

Daily community meetings in the early years can establish routines, encourage positive interplay, and also assist students with behavioral mores. Having students generate solutions to both simple and complex issues bolsters community building while

providing means for students to choose from several peer-generated suggestions. This builds trust and respect and provides bonding time on a daily basis, typically at the end of the day. School safety is bolstered and refined in these moments when students and teachers work collaboratively in support of community.

Supporting Positive School Conduct, Discipline, and Attendance

Supporting Student Conduct

Student conduct is the "proof of the pudding," so to speak. Students are generally happy to come to a safe place where they are reasonably challenged and encouraged to grow intellectually, socially, and emotionally. Teachers, staff, and volunteers who feel their presence adds to the positive nature of the environment generally make every effort to conduct themselves in ways that are supportive for students.

Supporting student conduct is based on meeting children's needs. In a school setting, there is a wide range of student ages, different perceptions, and a variety of experiences. The needs of each student require a thoughtful examination of what is *appropriate conduct*. Alfie Kohn (1996) suggested a focus on the questions, "Appropriate to whom? And why?" (p. 68). Without ongoing conversations with students, their teachers, and parents, the word "appropriate" may be misused as a standard for "acceptable" behavior, thus limiting students' potential to grow into responsible adults. Kohn (1996) stated that the educational leader

> models and explains and shows [students] he cares. He works with them so they will become better problem solvers and helps them see how their actions affect others. When children seem obnoxious, he is more inclined (depending on circumstances and the limits of his patience) to think in terms of providing guidance rather than enforcing rules. (p. 10)

The school environment should reflect this understanding using age-appropriate vocabulary comprehensible to the student. An important skill in developing positive student conduct is deciding as a whole school community what it means to become responsible and respectful. Other characteristics may evolve as the conversation ensues. Students of nearly every grade level can verbalize what it means to be caring and what actions reveal the inner self. These moments of clarity and conviction have a greater likelihood of happening when students, teachers, and administers work collaboratively to describe and adopt positive school conduct.

Techniques for creating a schoolwide conduct plan honor the **developmentally appropriate practice** for children respective of their needs. Schoolwide values are shared and demonstrated. The educational leader "develops a shared vision based on school community values by involving staff and community in a process that allows them to reflect upon their own cherished values" (Lambert, 1998, p. 26).

During this process, teachers, staff, volunteers, and especially the principal, need to give students explicit feedback (Denton, 2007). "Good job!" does not guide future practice. Whereas, "You helped your friend when she fell" tells a student that his or her act demonstrated conduct that revealed valued actions. When needed, describing the conduct the students *should consider* performing provides additional guidance. An example for how to correct a student found littering the school premises could be, "Next time you have trash, throw it in the correct basket the *first* time." Students who hear specific feedback along with specific guidance are left with little doubt as to the conduct that creates a positive school culture. Choosing to say words that specifically provide clarification for the child allows the reinforcement of behavior.

Verbally redirecting children so that their behavior fits within the given norms supports the reinforcement of acceptable behavior. Redirecting children is done by specifying what the child *should* be doing rather than what the child is choosing to do. An example might be during clean-up time when a child continues to play with blocks rather than follow the clean-up signal. A redirecting statement might be, "It is time to put the blocks away." This statement redirects the child and provides guidance. A firm, friendly tone is used and a note of appreciation generally follows. Example, "You put the blocks away in the right place. Thank you." A setting where children's needs are paramount noticeably impacts the environment and supports positive school conduct.

Supporting Student Discipline

Although these methods are increasingly rare, some teachers still rely on methods such as paddling or writing the names of "naughty" students on the blackboard as a means of discipline. These outward modes of disciplining students seem antithetical to those that aim to grow an inner locus of control in students starting from an early age.

Eirini Flouri (2006) reported on a British longitudinal study that indicated that inner locus of control is a predictor of later educational attainment. This finding supports the need for self-regulation enhancement and support in developmentally appropriate ways.

Promoting an inner locus of control in children, and in adults who live or work with children, may be more desirable than focusing on discipline or self-discipline. "Discipline" may be viewed as an outward attempt to manage or control the behavior of children, while "self-discipline" may connote a constant inner dampening or a regimented, breath-holding dirge. Realizing that maintaining this inner locus of control and self-regulation are part of a lifelong journey, the idea of learning and "practicing" together can become an individual and collective endeavor in schools, homes, and communities.

The transactional leader sees discipline as an opportunity to teach. Although, in the words of Kenneth T. Henson (2010), "good behavior results from good lessons that meaningfully involve students, but no lesson, however well-planned and executed, can guarantee perfect behavior" (p. 310). Understanding that every person polishes his or her skill of inner locus of control provides the underlying frame for discipline.

One technique for supporting students who have challenges in this area is to provide communication opportunities. Some of these opportunities will directly impact the educational leader's daily routine. Taking careful notes of students' exact words will help to inform future decisions. When students require more extensive discipline (teaching/learning) opportunities regarding their personal behavior, it is best if their exact words are used in the resulting dialogue. Keeping careful records of student discipline meetings also provides school leaders with a time line for progress or regress. This process can guide future decisions. What we know informs our practice and in turn our practice guides our students toward positive decision-making skills (Marzano et al., 2005).

Involving students in the discipline process is an important strategy. "Teachers should ask students to identify common behavior problems in school. The simple act of involving them in shaping the discipline/management program shows a positive concern for students, and that concern will be reciprocated" (Henson, 2010, p. 315). In other words, discipline is not something that is done "to" students, but rather a communal shaping of a desired environment. Furthermore, Henson (2010) stated:

> Today, successful discipline/management programs use positive approaches that require teachers to examine their historical, philosophical, social, and psychological beliefs. Positive discipline/management programs emphasize instruction and learning, and in doing so they de-emphasize discipline and problems. Good lessons minimize disruptive behavior. In the past, force has been used to impose discipline on students, but this approach is known to be ineffective. (pp. 330–331)

The use of positive discipline emphasizes what the student *can do* rather than enumerating penalties. Kohn (1996) stated, "Punishment actually impedes the process of ethical development" (p. 28). One element that clearly supports student discipline is the foundational assurance that students can learn and implement an ethical conviction.

Supporting School Attendance

Not until 1918 was compulsory school attendance enacted across the United States. Each state dictated the starting and ending dates of its academic year. States still hold the power to regulate compulsory school attendance laws requiring a certain number of days of school and how many hours of attendance is considered "a day" of attendance. School attendance has grown to nearly 180 days in nearly all U.S. states. This far exceeds the required "three months" of the 1800s (EdSource, 2013).

In public education, the average daily attendance (ADA) is calculated by the population of students attending the school. Attendance rates are also used to help determine whether schools meet the federal measure of adequate yearly progress (AYP) under the No Child Left Behind Act. Since federal funding and federal guidelines are related to student attendance, the educational leader must be cognizant of the factors that help motivate healthy student attendance. "Perfect attendance awards" are still highly prized by students, parents, and teachers.

Individual states have compulsory attendance laws that dictate the age students must begin school and also when students can cease to attend. Generally, attendance is mandatory for those between the ages of 7 and 17. States differ in attendance requirements. However, the terms used to describe lack of attendance are generally similar (EdSource, 2013).

Students may seek an excused absence. Excused absences may involve student illness, religious observances, extreme medical emergencies, or medical appointments that cannot be scheduled either before or after school hours. Parents/guardians are considered the primary support system for student attendance. To this point, educational leaders must build a culture within the school community emphasizing that parents hold an important key to the child's educational progress. Missing school means missing learning opportunities. Getting students to school is imperative; thus, parental support is highly valued.

Students who are sent to school by their parents and then choose to *not attend* are subject to truancy laws. Truancy is defined as the child's willful absence without having a lawful excuse for such absence. Since students also play an important part in their own attendance, the educational leader must build a system of support that involves the innermost concentric factor: student success. Motivational measures that support ongoing success require a review of attendance, student conduct, and discipline measures. In general, students attend school when they see value in learning opportunities (Patton, 2011). If schools are going to be places where students thrive and attendance is supported, teachers must be willing to review their own practice and "teach students to become active, critical, and engaged learners in an environment made stimulating" (deMarrais & LeCompte, 1999, p. 32).

The Importance of Attendance, Engagement, and Self-Regulation

It seems logical that school attendance is tied to achievement. Research indicates a correlation between chronic absence in kindergarten and performance in first grade regardless of gender, socioeconomic standing, or ethnicity (Chang & Romero, 2008). However, requiring students to attend school until age 18 does not appear to improve their persistence in school; a comparison found states with compulsory school attendance until age 18 had lower graduation rates than those that require attendance until age 16 or 17 (Whitehurst & Whitfield, 2012). It is *engagement* in school that seems to be more important than simply being there.

Students, no matter what age, need to be engaged in school. Their classrooms and the learning that is facilitated by knowledgeable, caring teacher-leaders are the means to keep students in school. The transactions that take place in carefully planned and safe environments hook the students and help them to be engaged and curious. Rather than the banking of knowledge (Freire, 1970) where the teacher deposits content into the waiting minds of receptive students, engaged learning involves students from the beginning in determining what can be, should be, and will be learned. This does not distract from the required standards, but allows students to go beyond them.

The responsibility of engaged learning, however, does not rest solely on the teacher. Students, even very young children, and adults are continuously learning and demonstrating self-regulation that affects their learning. Rather than thinking of a child's sense of self-regulation as purely controlling his or her behavior or displaying appropriate conduct, self-regulation is much broader. It can be taught and supported while embodying essential skills that assist a person over a lifetime of decisions. It is more than being in command of one's behavior; it is about being in charge of one's learning, and being in charge of one's learning can be facilitated by a teacher who creates ways for students to become involved in decisive, critical thinking at any age. After all, "a crucial step in teaching critical thinking is to develop good problems for students to think about" (Bean, 2001, p. 5).

Ellen Galinsky (2010) names seven essential life skills whose development can be assisted through parents, caregivers, teachers, and peers. These include: focus and self-control, perspective taking, communicating, making connections, critical thinking, taking on challenges, and self-directed, engaged, learning. Galinsky (2010) sees focus and self-control as "having four components: focus, flexibility, working memory, and inhibitory control" (p. 15). These elements resonate with the ideals of self-regulation. This is only part of the self-regulation story, however. Galinsky (2010) reminds us that self-regulation and focus "begin in the early childhood years, but don't become fully established until the later teen and adult years because the prefrontal cortex is among the last parts of the brain to mature" (p. 39).

This brings to mind the concept of effective developmentally appropriate practice (DAP) (NAEYC, Copple & Bredkamp, 2009). **Best practice** is based on knowledge—not assumptions—of how students learn and develop. The research base yields major principles in human development and learning. Usually relegated to early childhood classrooms (birth through Grade 3), DAP proposes the following essential points that address the needs and expectations regarding self-regulation to be appropriate to the stage of the student:

- Developmentally appropriate practice (DAP) requires meeting students where they are. Teachers must get to know their students as unique individuals, enabling them to reach goals that are both challenging and achievable.
- All teaching practices should be appropriate and responsive to the social and cultural contexts in which students live.
- Developmentally appropriate practice does not mean making things easier for students. It means ensuring that goals and experiences are suited to their learning development *and* challenging enough to promote their progress and interest.

These points can be applied to learning across a life span, especially in relation to student engagement. If students are engaged in continuous learning, and are encouraged to question and seek answers in school, will this not lead to grounded individuals in charge of their learning who are eager to participate and improve their attendance while displaying consistent self-regulation (conduct), and self-discipline? Positive student engagement supports the goals of school safety and stability.

The Importance of Attention and Learning

"Attention can be described as a cognitive process of selective concentration on one aspect of the environment while ignoring other aspects" (Kyndt, Cascaller, & Dochy, 2012, p. 287). This is an imperative condition in classrooms and school settings where multiple things may be happening and students need to focus on one thing. Galinsky (2010), in fact, uses the word *focus* instead of attention:

For young children, researchers talk about being alert and about orienting. For older children, and adults, focus includes those two aspects, plus being able to concentrate—that is to remain alert and oriented for a period of time, bringing our other skills to bear on a project or task despite internal and external distractions. (p. 16)

Attention, then, is associated with the ability to focus substantively, a trait needed for learning, collaborating, and thinking critically.

The Final Charge

Education provides each student the opportunity to meet his or her own personal goals. Student conduct, discipline, and attendance support the student's academic endeavors. This troika of essential factors is more than just *relevant* to student success; rather each element is *essential* for students, the learning institution, and the ongoing relationship with school stakeholders that builds the foundation for personal achievement. In the words of Dewey (1938/1998):

What we want and need is education pure and simple, and we shall make surer and faster progress when we devote ourselves to finding out just what education is and what conditions have to be satisfied in order that *educator* [emphasis added] may be a reality and not a name or a slogan. (p. 116)

The charge for educational leaders is to make sure their schools have the components that support school stability and safety. By supporting the entire school community (teachers, staff, parents, and most importantly, the students), the educational leader works toward this common goal. A strong, dynamic structure and well-organized system provide the conditions for this endeavor.

Systems of Capacity

Systems building from early childhood through postsecondary education is vital. Bob Wehling (2007) said, "I believe that every system is perfectly designed to get the results it gets" (p. 6). That being said, a system of education that recognizes its points of intersection, aligns its goals, employs multiple stakeholders, and keeps students engaged, may keep students in stable and safe schools. Karen Hawley Miles and Karen Baroody (2001) stated, "Only by repurposing resources currently bound by outmoded structures can we make the transformation required to

educate all students to the higher levels required for a vibrant democracy and economy in the information age" (p. 3).

This systems building can, and should, invite and employ the community in the education of all its children. "Family and community engagement helps legitimize school reform efforts in the eyes of the broader community" (Brinson & Steiner, 2012, p. 3). Additionally, this puts everyone on the same team. David Hargreaves (2011) mentioned, in regard to business, and applied here to the business of supporting students, that partnerships create solid bonds.

Inter-firm partnership competence has three core features: (1) Co-ordination—building consensus on partnership goals, ways of working, roles and responsibilities; (2) Communication—being open and honest, sharing information fully and with accuracy and in a timely way; (3) Bonding—creating trust and ensuring that people get pleasure from working together. (p. 695)

The preceding features can be positive influences in classrooms, schools, districts, and communities. As the educational leader considers actions that support a positive school environment, the charge remains to create partnerships where collaboration is prized and communication is open and welcomed.

Connecting back to Bronfenbrenner's (1979) ecological model, we are all part of systems within systems, whether we choose to acknowledge this or not. As Dewey (1938/1998) expressed, "The general conclusion I would draw is that control of individual actions is effected by the whole situation in which individuals are involved, in which they share and of which they are co-operative or interacting parts" (p. 57). Creating more intentional connections and intersections based on shared goals of purposeful conduct, self-regulation/self-discipline, and attendance is possible in a communal sense. Creating communities within communities (classrooms within schools, schools within the larger community) in more than superficial ways are means of investment. Creating community goals around students invests in multiple futures.

Relating to School Safety and Stability

School safety and stability rely more than on the expectations of suitable conduct, consistent attendance, and discipline in its multiple forms. The responsibility is not placed solely on the students, but must be shared by communities of supportive adults and communities of clear, shared goals. Parents are partners with the school community. Inter-relationships form between and among community leaders, organizations, and institutions. This is more than the shallow "program" or the latest push. It is the intentional planning together of far-reaching goals for children of a community within a community. It involves voices at tables that may not have been invited or may not have sidled up before. It involves analyzing student needs and community data to determine courses of action. It is an opportunity to build bridges, and as Neal Halfon, Kimberly Uyeda, Moira Inkelas, and Thomas Rice (2004) stated in regard to early childhood (but certainly amenable across age spans):

> A bridge is a structure created to connect what is disjointed or disconnected, to speed and enhance movement or interchange, and to encourage interactions. Bridges can facilitate and maintain relationships and connections that under ordinary circumstances might not be possible. Bridges also evoke a notion of *providing safe passage over difficult terrain and predictable hazards.* (pp. 8–9)

Furthermore, "Bridges also require common community resources to be built and remain secure" (Halfon et al., 2004, p. 9). This assertion is most appealing when discussing the notion of conduct, discipline, and attendance as the troika of school safety and stability. The onus does not rest on the shoulders of a toddler or a college senior, but rather on the collective care of the community in which all reside and all are afforded opportunities to grow to full potential. "Building a bridge opens up to everyone in the community the opportunity to achieve safe passage" (p. 9).

School safety and stability are not acquired by accident or simple longevity. The critical elements that support a vivid, productive learning environment are established by committed leadership. The teacher-leader has long recognized that schools function more effectively when every member of the community is included in the vision of excellence. Student conduct may be a measure of the support students feel regarding leadership in and out of the classroom. Engaging students with

invigorating academic stimuli and empowering each learner to find personal success supports the attendance of both students and teachers. The safe, inviting environment calls to the child. It is here where high expectations are clear and fair; where adults welcome and guide; where children are nurtured and thrive; where systems within systems provide a stable, resilient environment; in short, *where great things happen.*

Key Chapter Terms

Best practice: Practice that is based on researched principles of how children learn and develop and that produce optimum results.

Bullying: Aggressive, unwanted behavior targeting an individual or group that involves real or perceived threats or taunting, including physical, verbal, and emotional violence.

Collaborative practice: Practice in which individuals or groups work toward an identified goal with a sense of cooperation and mutual support.

Conduct: Behavior that is regulated, or measured; usually described as acceptable or unacceptable, appropriate or inappropriate.

Developmentally appropriate practice (DAP): Teaching practice that is grounded in research and addresses the most effective way to support ages and stages for students' optimal learning and potential.

Partnership: Agreed-upon arrangement between individuals or groups of individuals that will advance a mutual interest or enterprise.

School stakeholders: Individuals or groups of individuals who have a vested interest and influence in the success of the school while being connected academically, financially, or socially, such as community members, district-level personnel, and local, state, and federal government officials.

Schoolwide practice: Practice that is adopted or designed with an expectation of compliance and support from the entire school community at every organizational level, such as a schoolwide conduct code.

Self-regulation: Involves multiple skills related to multiple functions such as, but not limited to, focus, attention, and self-control. These skills develop over time, and growth can be facilitated by skillful caregivers. This developmental aspect is particularly important when one considers academic escalation, which may expect more than a child can deliver both emotionally and cognitively. For example, sitting for long periods of time with

the expectation of focusing may not be a realistic expectation for many 3-year-olds.

System: Parts that work together for a related goal.

Systems building: Intentional connecting of parts to maximize functioning of an existing system or to build a new system.

Troika: A joining of three balancing concepts or practices that results in a more effective system of support.

References

America's Promise Alliance (n.d.). *100 best communities for young people.* Retrieved from http://www .americaspromise.org/100-best-communities-young-people

Bass, B. M., & Stogdill, R. M. (1990). *Bass & Stogdill's handbook of leadership: Theory, research & managerial applications* (3rd ed.). New York, NY: Free Press.

Bean, J. (2001). *Engaging ideas: The professor's guide to integrating writing, critical thinking, and active learning in the classroom.* San Francisco, CA: Jossey-Bass.

Blank, M., Melaville, A., & Jacobson, R. (2012). *Achieving results through community school partnerships: How district and community leaders are building effective, sustainable relationships.* Washington, DC: Center for American Progress. Retrieved from http://www.americanprogress.org/ issues/education/report/2012/01/18/10987/achieving-results-through-community-school-partnerships/

Brinson, D., & Steiner, L. (2012). *Building family and community demand for dramatic change in schools.* Chapel Hill, NC: Public Impact. Retrieved from http://www.publicimpact.com/building_demand_for_ dramatic_change_in_schools-public_impact.pdf

Bronfenbrenner, U. (1979). *The ecology of human development: Experiments by nature and design.* Cambridge, MA: Harvard University Press.

Center for Mental Health in Schools at UCLA. (2011). *Community collaboration.* Retrieved from http:// smhp.psych.ucla.edu/pdfdocs/communitycollab.pdf

Chang, H., & Romero, M. (2008). *Present, engaged, and accounted for: The Critical importance of addressing chronic absence in the early grades.* New York, NY: National Center for Children in Poverty, Columbia University.

deMarrais, K. B. & LeCompte, M. D. (1999). *The way schools work: A sociological analysis of education* (3rd ed.). New York, NY: Longman.

Denton, P. (2007). *The power of our words: Teacher language that helps children learn.* Turner Falls, MA: Northeast Foundation for Children, Inc.

Dewey, J. (1998). *Experience and education.* West Lafayette, IN: Kappa Delta Pi. (Original work published 1938)

EdSource. (2013). *Highlighting strategies for student sources.* Retrieved May 15, 2013, from http://www .edsource.org

Flouri, E. (2006). Parental interest in children's education, children's self-esteem and locus of control, and later educational attainment: Twenty-six year follow-up of the 1970 British Birth Cohort. *British Journal of Educational Psychology, 76,* 41–55.

Freire, P. (1970). *Pedagogy of the oppressed.* New York: NY: Herder and Herder.

Galinsky, E. (2010). *Mind in the making: The seven essential life skills every child needs.* New York, NY: HarperCollins.

Glickman, C. D. (2002). *Leading for learning: How to help teachers succeed.* Alexandria, VA: Association for Supervision and Curriculum Development.

Goleman, D., Boyatzis, R., & McKee, A. (2002). *Primal leadership: Learning to lead with emotional intelligence.* Boston, MA: Harvard Business School Press.

Gordon, M. (2009). *Roots of empathy: Changing the world child by child.* New York, NY: The Experiment Publishing Company.

Gordon, S. P. (2004). *Professional development for school improvement: Empowering learning communities.* Boston, MA: Pearson Education.

Halfon, N., Uyeda, K., Inkelas, M., & Rice, T. (2004). *Building bridges: A comprehensive system for healthy development and school readiness* (Building

State Early Childhood Comprehensive Systems Series No. 1). Los Angeles, CA: National Center for Infant and Early Childhood Health Policy, University of California at Los Angeles.

Hargreaves, D. (2011). System redesign for system capacity building. *Journal of Educational Administration, 49*(6), 685–700.

Henson, K. T. (2010). *Supervision: A collaborative approach to instructional improvement.* Long Grove, IL: Waveland Press.

Jacobson, R., Hodges, R., & Blank, M. (2011). Mutual support: The community schools strategy. *Principal Leadership, 12*(2), 18–22. Retrieved from http:// www.communityschools.org/assets/1/AssetManager/ NASSP%20Community%20Schools.pdf

Kohn, A. (1996). *Beyond discipline: From compliance to community.* Alexandria, VA: Association for Supervision and Curriculum Development.

Kotter, J. P. (2012). *Leading change.* Boston, MA: Harvard Business School Press.

Kyndt, E., Cascaller, E., & Dochy, F. (2012). Individual differences in working memory capacity and attention, and their relationship with students' approaches to learning. *Higher Education, 64*(3), 285–297.

Lambert, L. (1998). *Building leadership capacity in schools.* Alexandria, VA: Association for Supervision and Curriculum Development.

Marzano, R. J., Waters, T., & McNulty, B. A. (2005). *School leadership that works: From research to results.* Alexandria, VA: Association for Supervision and Curriculum.

Miles, K., & Baroody, K. (2011). Act now to transform school systems. *Policy Innovators in Education.* Retrieved from http://www.erstrategies.org/cms/ files/962-milespienetworkessay.pdf

NAEYC, Copple, D., & Bredekamp, S. (2009). *Developmentally appropriate practice in early childhood programs serving children from birth through age 8.* Washington, DC: National Association for the Education of Young Children.

Papa, R., English, F., Davidson, F., Culver, M. K., & Brown, R. (2013). *Contours of great leadership: The science, art and wisdom of outstanding practice.* New York, NY: Rowman & Littlefield Education.

Papalewis, R., & Fortune, R. (2002). *Leadership on purpose: Promising practices for African American and Hispanic students.* Thousand Oaks, CA: Corwin.

Patton, J. D. (2011). Community organizations' involvement in school safety planning: Does it make a difference in school violence? *School Social Journal, 35*(2), 15–33.

Reeves, D. B. (2010). *Transforming professional development into student results.* Alexandria, VA: Association for Supervision and Curriculum Development.

Strike, K. T. (2011). *Mentoring the educational leader: A practical framework for success.* Blue Ridge Summit, PA: Rowman & Littlefield Education.

Way, S. M. (2011). School discipline and disruptive classroom behavior: The moderating effects of student perceptions. *Sociological Quarterly, 52*(3), 346–375.

Wehling, B. (2007). *Building a 21st century U.S. education system.* Washington, DC: National Commission on Teaching and America's Future.

Whitehurst, G., & Whitfield, S. (2012). *Compulsory school attendance: What research says and what it means for state policy.* Washington, DC: Brown Center on Education Policy, The Brookings Institution.

York-Barr, J., Sommers, W. A., Ghere, G. S., & Montie, J. (2001). *Reflective practice to improve schools: An action guide for educators.* Thousand Oaks, CA: Corwin.

Further Readings

Charney, R. S. (2002). *Teaching children to care: Classroom management for ethical and academic growth, K-8.* Greenfield, MA: Northeast Foundation for Children, Inc.

By setting reachable expectations, built on established schoolwide and classroom procedures, the author offers a positive approach linked to logical consequences. Teachers are guided on how to teach children to care for themselves, others, and the environment through practical wisdom.

Educational Leadership, (1997), *55*(2) [complete issue]. Schools as Safe Havens, published by ASCD. (www. ascd.org)

Schools encapsulate the community at large. Administrators across the country seek ways to make their schools a safe place for students. Building communities where everyone is greeted by name, everyone is held accountable, and everyone has a stake in the success of students is addressed in this article.

Reeves, D. B. (2006). *The learning leader: How to focus school improvement for better results.* Alexandria, VA: ASCD.

Going beyond academic leadership, the author urges teachers and administrators to go beyond the measurement of scholastic results and provide a more proactive reconceptualization of their leadership role. Great leaders are asked to consider how they motivate their colleagues and lead their schools using sound educational principles that support students and the community.

Wynne, E. A., & Ryan, K. (1997). *Reclaiming our schools: Teaching character, academics, and discipline.* Upper Saddle River, NJ: Pearson.

This publication offers dozens of suggestions on how to create a schoolwide approach to teaching character-building techniques while teaching the fundamental elements of academics through student engagement. This hands-on guide offers suggestions on classroom exercises as well as a whole-school approach to positive behavior.

23

HOMESCHOOLING

Parents' Rights and the Public Good

JENNIFER A. SUGHRUE

Southeastern Louisiana University

Although it has received considerable media attention in the past few decades, **homeschooling** is not a modern phenomenon in the United States. It was a primary method of delivering education to children during the early colonial period. This was especially evident in colonies founded by settlers seeking religious freedom. Parents had a responsibility to ensure their children learned to read for the purpose of scriptural literacy, that is, to learn to read the Bible. It was also out of necessity during the early history of the United States that parents took responsibility to provide a basic education to their children. Families in rural settings could be great distances from a town or neighbors, making it unfeasible to congregate children in a school.

The concept of parental responsibility for the nature and direction of the education of their children has endured though the centuries, although it has taken on many new forms. Traditionally, homeschooling has meant that parents assume direct responsibility for the education of children in the family, either by instructing the children themselves or by hiring a qualified person to teach in the home. The scope of parent-directed education has expanded somewhat in recent decades with the introduction of virtual schools and charter schools, which provide venues through which families who share a common purpose in homeschooling their children can unite.

The educational practice of homeschooling summons considerable passion for both its advocates and its detractors. Each faction cites some legal and moral foundation for its assertions, and each describes those who disagree as opponents of fundamental American values, such as individual liberty and self-determination. On one hand, advocates argue that parents have a substantive legal right to oversee the upbringing of their children, which they believe includes directing the children's education. Others contend that parents should be able to exercise their religious freedom by extricating their children from a government system that they believe promotes **secular humanism** or that is hostile to religion generally. On the other hand, opponents of homeschooling remind us that the concept of a system of public schools was advanced to provide an environment in which to inculcate youth to democratic ideals that are necessary to the survival of our governmental structure and to expose children to diversity, both in terms of demographics and ideas. It was also seen as a path for broadening the potential for an individual's career and economic opportunities.

What is not contested is that the percentage of students being homeschooled has steadily increased in recent years. In a 2008 issue brief, the National Center for Education Statistics (NCES) reported on the growth of homeschooling in the United States between 1999 and 2007. It was estimated in 1999 that 850,000 school-aged children (ages 5 through 17) were being homeschooled. In 2003, the number jumped to 1.1 million and in 2008, it increased to slightly more than 1.5 million. Those numbers represent 1.7%, 2.2%, and 2.9%, respectively, of all school-aged children. Those percentages indicate an increase of over 70% in the number of children being homeschooled between 1999 and 2007. Interestingly, the percentage of students who were homeschooled full time, in comparison to those who attended public schools between 9 and 25 hours per week, increased 2% for 2007 (see **Table 23.1**).

The 2003 and 2007 surveys also asked parents to cite the reasons for homeschooling their children. They were allowed to indicate multiple reasons. The two primary motives were (a) concerns about the school environment and (b) a desire to provide religious or moral instruction. Notably, the first reason, concerns about the school environment, was cited by over 84% of the parents for both survey years. The second explanation, religious or moral instruction, was cited by about 72% of parents in 2003, but that jumped to about 83% in 2007. Other reasons given were discontent with teaching at the schools and a desire to provide a nontraditional approach to education. A small percentage of parents indicated they homeschooled their children because the children had a physical or mental health–related problem or other special needs.

Whatever the reasons given by parents, there remains concern among educators and scholars that many of these children may not be receiving the education they need to direct their own futures and to participate fully as engaged citizens in a democratic republic. Many educators hold stereotypes of homeschooling parents, believing they are religious zealots, political fanatics, social outliers, or negligent parents who want to remain in control of their children's lives. They fear a great disservice is being done to these children, especially in those states that require or provide little or no oversight.

The purpose of this chapter is to explore more deeply the homeschooling movement and its current place in K-12 education across the states. It includes a brief history of homeschooling in the United States to provide some understanding for the context of the debate on the subject. This is followed by descriptions of some of the homeschooling options available to **home educators**, and then by a discussion of the legal debate over the rights of the parents versus the authority and responsibility of the state in the matter of educating children. Following that, there is an overview of the primary concerns associated with

School Enrollment Status	1999 (%)	2003 (%)	2007(%)
Total	100	100	100
Homeschooled only	82	82	84
Enrolled in school part time	18	18	16
Enrolled in school for fewer than 9 hours a week	13	12	11
Enrolled in school for 9 to 25 hours a week	5	6	5

Table 23.1 Percentage of Homeschooled Students, Ages 5 Through 17 With a Grade Equivalent of Kindergarten Through 12th Grade, by School Enrollment Status: 1999, 2003, and 2007

SOURCE: Jennifer A. Sughrue, adapted from Table 1 in Bielick, S. (2008). *1.5 Million Homeschooled Students in the United States in 2007* (NCES 2009-030). National Center for Education Statistics, Institute of Education Sciences, U.S. Department of Education, Washington, DC.

homeschooling, such as socialization, civic and citizenship education, and the impact of homeschooling as a social movement.

The History of Homeschooling

As noted previously, homeschooling is not a new idea, but it is one that has enjoyed a massive resurgence since the early 1970s. Estimates put the number of homeschoolers in the 1970s at 10,000 to 15,000, a number that is dwarfed by NCES's estimate that 1.8 million students were homeschooled in 2011–2012 (Noel, Stark, & Redford, 2013). Homeschooling is believed to be the fastest-growing form of schooling; its growth may have been encouraged by the charter school and school choice movements, as these movements have helped the idea of parent choice in education gain acceptance, and some charter schools have been created expressly for homeschoolers.

Although homeschooling is not a new form of education delivery, the reasons it exists today appear to be far different from its historical application. While teaching children at home was both a necessity and a responsibility in the early history of the United States, today it resembles more a reaction to government intrusion into familial rights and to dissatisfaction with the public school system.

Murphy (2013) categorizes the history of homeschooling into three "stages": (1) the pre-compulsory education period, (2) the institutionalized compulsory education period, and (3) the modern or contemporary homeschooling period. In the first stage, homeschooling was the principal delivery system of basic education. The family was the primary economic, religious, educational, and social mechanism in early America (Apple, 2000). Distance, religion, and the daily demands of survival in the New World required parents to provide for the education of their children. In the mid- to late-1700s, in the mid-Atlantic colonies, plantation owners and wealthy businessmen hired tutors or sent their children to Europe to be educated (Kaestle, 1983). These educational accommodations, with the addition of some rural and community schools, remained the norm until industrialization took root and converted a largely agrarian society into one that was becoming largely dependent on manufacturing and its

associated businesses. Industry and business interests required their workers to have a different set of skills and knowledge, something more than what village schools or parents could provide.

The second stage emerged during the industrial era, around the mid-1800s (Murphy, 2013). It was the period in which compulsory education through state-supported public schools took root and gained prominence. Horace Mann and others like him believed the future of a stable, more egalitarian United States resided in getting children out of factories, off the streets, and into classrooms with their more privileged peers. A surge in immigration, the industrialization of urban centers, and a fear of exaggerated economic and religious polarizations were motivating factors in requiring all children to share in an educational experience—the free universal common school (Tyack, 1974). The common school movement overshadowed homeschooling to such an extent as to nearly annihilate it (Murphy, 2013). The push for common schooling and the "professionalization" of educators cast a dark pall on families who wanted to retain the right to homeschool their children. Homeschooling was stigmatized and operated as a fringe element until recently.

The contemporary or modern homeschooling movement has roots in the era of civil protest, in the 1960s and 1970s, when anything government-operated was viewed with deep skepticism. The Vietnam War, the civil rights movement, and a cadre of progressive educational thinkers who highlighted public education's shortcomings, particularly educational inequities for children of color and females, culminated in general dissatisfaction with public schooling. In its rebirth, homeschooling was embraced by both the liberal left and by the conservative Christian right (Murphy, 2013). Both sides shared a common belief that parents had a legitimate right to direct their children's education. Both viewed homeschooling as a way to promulgate their particular cultural, political, and religious orientations that they believed were at odds with those advocated through public education.

The contemporary period deserves further attention because it is the underpinning of what today some scholars believe is a modern social movement (Apple, 2000, 2007; Murphy, 2013; Yuracko, 2008). Its supporters have successfully navigated it from the fringes of society into the mainstream through well-organized political, legal, and social strategies. As recently as the 1980s, homeschooling was illegal in most states. Now it is legal in every state.

While left-leaning liberals and right-leaning Christians were responsible for the reemergence of homeschooling, the Christian faction has come to dominate the movement in recent years, both in numbers and in visibility. Several researchers over the past decade have found that conservative Christians make up a majority of homeschoolers (Murphy, 2012). Certainly, the news media, both mainstream and Christian networks, have helped legitimize homeschooling. Coverage that advocates for homeschooling usually does so by scrutinizing how public education has failed children of color or children in poverty and then by juxtaposing those failings to happy, healthy families with smart homeschooled children. For instance, recall the news headlines of homeschooled children who outperformed their public school counterparts in national spelling bee competitions. Findings from recent studies also point to the above average academic performance of homeschooled students on standardized tests (Martin-Chang, Gould, & Meuse, 2011; Ray, 2010). The positive attributes of homeschooling have been deliberately and persuasively argued in the media and in the courts. Impassioned believers use their political, legal, and media savvy to convince the general population of the merits of homeschooling, thereby successfully moving the concept of homeschooling into the mainstream.

Two organizations are especially successful in promoting homeschooling: the Home School Legal Defense Association (HSLDA) and the National Home Education Research Institute (NHERI). Structured as nonprofit organizations, they promote information about homeschooling and provide advice to those who want to homeschool their children. It is difficult to search for information on homeschooling on the Internet and in research literature without coming upon these two associations and the research, legal victories, and other information they generate. It is important to remember when visiting their websites and reading their research and other information that they are very much homeschooling advocates and, as such, that their agenda is embedded in all their work.

Although a substantial percentage of families cite religion as one of the motivating factors for homeschooling, not all home educators are cut from the same cloth. There are those who choose to homeschool their children because they believe education should be child-centered, even child-driven (Murphy, 2013). They reject a government-operated educational system that is based on a standardized curriculum and that requires all students to pass standardized tests as the only measure of academic achievement (Apple, 2007). As one homeschooling mother observed, "Education is the lifelong search for truth, wisdom and virtue" and that "[homeschooled children] are learning what they chose to learn, when they chose to learn it, and under the guidance of the people who love them" (Cuthbert, 2002, n.p.). She and others like her view public education as indoctrination, and that tax-supported schools are a form of "educational welfarism." They see homeschooling as one way in which to "[bar] the corrupting influence of government from [their] family's life" (Cuthbert, 2002, n.p.).

> Homeschooling's greatest value is not found in academic achievement. It is found in liberty. If my son never locates Lop Nur on a map, if my daughter never correctly spells succedaneum, what does that matter? In our over-politicized, propaganda-dominated world, they have escaped the dead hand of government. Their minds are free. (Cuthbert, 2002, n.p.)

These two strands of the homeschooling population, the fundamental Christians and those who oppose government-sponsored mass education, are perhaps the least tolerant of public schools. Other homeschooling families have more moderate views on public schools and have taken advantage of more welcoming attitudes from school administrators and school choice alternatives to find a balance between their desire to direct the education of their children, yet not deprive them of advanced courses or participation in extracurricular activities. Cooperation and technological innovation have opened the door to hybrid models of homeschooling that often have some facet of public schooling attached to them.

The Look and Feel of Contemporary Homeschooling

With the advent of school choice, charter schools, and advances in technology, the homeschooling image can no longer be portrayed as a parent sitting at the kitchen table in front of the child who has her or his books open and pencil poised to write an essay or to compute figures. Today, the scene could be children and parents in front of a computer screen or in groups with other homeschooling families who congregate periodically for social and educational activities. It could capture the part-time homeschooler who goes to the public school a couple of periods a day to receive instruction in higher level or Advanced Placement math, English, and science courses or to participate in extracurricular activities and clubs.

This evolution in homeschooling is, in part, the result of a more amiable relationship between homeschoolers and public education officials. Home educators have learned to take advantage of publicly funded charter schools and **virtual schools** or **cyber schools** that cater to homeschoolers by allowing them to attend classes part time or take classes online. Public school officials have welcomed homeschoolers, even have recruited them after they realized the financial and political benefits of being more cooperative (Apple, 2007; Murphy, 2013). Most state legislatures have removed funding barriers that did not allow school districts to collect any state funds for part-time students, even on a pro-rated basis. School districts also can collect some portion of the state per-pupil funding for administrative costs that goes to charter schools in their districts, even those that are organized around homeschooling.

An examination of California law on educational alternatives brings some understanding to the multiple options that can be available to homeschooling families if the state legislature so chooses. Although there is no California statute that explicitly authorizes parents to homeschool their children, there are four sections of the California education code that detail a variety of possibilities for them. The possibilities may be organized into four options: (a) establishing a home-based private school, (b) enrolling in a private school's independent study program, (c) enrolling in a public school independent study program or in a charter school that has been established for homeschoolers, and (d) employing a credentialed tutor or becoming a credentialed tutor for the purpose of homeschooling one's children (California Homeschool Network [CHN], 2012/2013).

Under California law, the first option requires the individual home educator to file a private school affidavit (PSA) with the state superintendent of public instruction in early October each year (Affidavit by Agency Conducting Private School Instruction at Elementary or High School Level, 2013). The home school that is registered as a private school must adhere to all private school laws and must maintain certain records, such as which courses are offered, the educational qualifications of the teacher(s), and attendance records, which are to be verified by the school district's attendance supervisor (Attendance in Private School, 2013).

The second option, a private school satellite program (PSP), provides an independent study program through a private school. Of course, the school has to adhere to California law governing private schools, but it handles all the administrative tasks required by law. There are tuition costs to homeschoolers. However, families enrolled in these kinds of programs do not have to provide any personal information to the state, as they would have to if they were applying for the PSA (CHN, 2012/2013).

The third option provides free access to public school curriculum and materials through public school independent study programs (ISP) or charter schools (Educational Opportunities Offered; Limitations . . . , 2013). Children who exercise this option are considered public school students although they study at home. As such, they must abide by all state and local education laws and policies.

The final option allows a family to hire a private tutor or to have a parent be a tutor (Instruction by Tutor, 2013). The two primary obstacles for homeschooling parents under this option are the cost of a private tutor and the requirement that the tutor has to have a valid California teaching credential. If a parent wanted to be the tutor for the children, she or he would have to be a licensed teacher in the state of California.

In the view of the HSLDA, California is a low regulation state, but Texas and Oklahoma are examples of states that are considered even less bureaucratic (Home School Legal Defense Association, n.d.). These two states do not require that parents initiate contact with any educational authority if they intend to homeschool their children and neither state requires that parents be certified teachers (which is actually the case in most states now). There is virtually no oversight by either state; however, home educators are advised to offer a comparable public school education by providing instruction in the basic subjects.

With the exception of Oklahoma, which has constitutional language that has been interpreted to allow homeschooling (Compulsory School Attendance, 2013), states are not required to permit parents to homeschool. They may and do offer alternatives to public schooling, and it is through these alternatives that families legally homeschool their children. If states provide for homeschooling and there is a challenge to some aspect of it, courts will weigh in by interpreting the state's constitutional, statutory, and administrative law. Depending on the question of law under scrutiny, they will consider the definition and context of homeschooling, the extent of supervision and reporting requirements, and whether a home school qualifies as a private school or whether a parent has to be a certified teacher.

Some states allow for children to be exempted from compulsory attendance laws and to be homeschooled if the parents profess sincerely held religious beliefs. It usually resides with the individual school district to determine if the homeschooling parents in their district meet the definition of "sincerely held beliefs." This continues to be a primary source of conflict between Christian homeschoolers and the state.

Given the flexibility many states have proffered parents who want their children to learn at home, a sizeable number of private and public schools, universities, and nonprofit educational organizations have created online learning options for them or **boxed curricula** that mimic tradition school offerings but allow students to learn at home. Virtually all online or **correspondence programs** advertise flexible pacing within a structured educational program, a strong curriculum, and access to educational support. Most offer programs for elementary, middle, and high school students. Many cyber or virtual schools employ certified teachers to guide the instruction and to provide feedback online. Others enlist parents as "teachers' aides," allowing them to deliver the instruction under the supervision of a certified teacher. Others are organized around home educators who are volunteers and who provide online instruction to many homeschoolers. Cyber schools sponsored by public school districts offer online education without tuition costs. In some instances, a computer is loaned and subsidized Internet access is provided to students.

Some of the many online educational vendors tap into family fears about traditional schools in order to attract business. One such example is K^{12} International Academy, which boasts that it is "a fully accredited, private online K-12 school that liberates students from rigid schedules, classes that move too fast or too slow, bullying, and other factors that stand in the way of success" (K^{12} International Academy, n.d.). K^{12} International Academy has contracted with **K^{12},** a for-profit company that provides a curriculum, certified "learning coaches," an individualized learning plan, and links to other organizations that support online learning (K^{12}, n.d.). K^{12} offers direct programming, as well, so parents do not have to seek out a school or academy that offers K^{12} programs.

Another emerging option to homeschoolers is the **cover school**, also referred to as an **umbrella school**. It functions as a private school, but allows parents to educate their children at home. This is the only legal option for homeschoolers in Alabama. They enroll in a cover school, most often a religiously affiliated academy, yet are home educated by their parents. Most cover schools charge a nominal fee, and only require attendance verification, although it is unclear what that entails, and quarterly submission of grades and lesson plans. Some provide support services, even field trips.

As described in this section, contemporary homeschooling has little resemblance to its historical predecessor in colonial America. Parents can be as involved or as removed as they want to be in the delivery of instruction while not forsaking their commitment to direct the education of their children. They can avail themselves of the publicly supported educational materials and venues or reject them outright, opting for something free of government influence. They can differentiate the education of their children based on the children's interests and capacities. They can find a comfortable mix of homeschooling and public school experiences for their children. They can create a very insular learning environment or choose to be part of a larger organization of homeschooling families. In any case, homeschooling has taken root in the mainstream and is no longer considered the domain of society's fringe elements. However, contention still looms between those who believe they have a right to homeschool unfettered by government regulation and those who fear that states have abdicated their responsibility to provide for the well-being and future opportunities of all youths within their jurisdiction.

Legal and Policy Issues Involved in Homeschooling

It is easy to point to the fact that homeschooling has been around longer than public education as a justification that parents have an established right to direct or control the education of their children. Homeschooling was a part of the colonial fabric and existed long before the formation of the nation.

Others cite biblical passages that direct parents to educate their children, saying these passages mean they should be able to exercise their religious duty without government interference. They argue that all children belong to God but that God entrusted them to their parents "to bring them up in the discipline and instruction of the Lord" (Ephesians 6:4). Many believe that what their children learn about academic subjects should incorporate religious doctrine (Klicka, 1999). Homeschooling provides Christian families the freedom to choose a curriculum that they can infuse with a biblical worldview. To reject a public school education for their children is to reject a secular vision of their children's purpose and place in the world.

The opposing view to these justifications recalls that the leaders of Massachusetts Bay Colony issued two laws regarding education in response to the failure of parents to properly educate their children. The first law, passed in 1642, directed parents to see to the education of their children. Dissatisfied because parents were not meeting their responsibilities in this regard, the legislature passed the 1647 Old Deluder Satan Act, which required towns with 50 or more families to hire teachers and to require students to attend. These towns also were given the authority to tax families with children to fund their education. The purpose was to teach children how to read so they could be instructed by the Bible and would not fall prey to Satan. Many educational historians and legal scholars believe that this was the first evidence of government intrusion into the realm of parental rights over their children (Alexander & Alexander, 2012; Kaestle, 1983).

After the formation of the nation and as it grew, state governments took on a central role in the provision of education (Alexander & Alexander, 2012; Tyack, 1974). Through federal mandates such as the Land Ordinance of 1785 and the Northwest Ordinance of 1787 and by reasoned arguments put forth by enlightened government leaders and philosophers, any territories seeking statehood had to include education provisions in their constitutions directing the legislature to establish a system of public schools. The language of the constitutional provisions and the responsibilities for education they prescribed varied across states, but all state governments had to create and fund some form of public education. This was followed in the mid-1800s with compulsory education laws that required children within a specified age range to attend school for a prescribed number of days per year and to follow a curriculum determined to be necessary to prepare them for work and citizenship in their communities.

The legal doctrine on which state governments have been able to defend compulsory education laws is ***parens patriae,*** Latin for "parent of the country." It sanctions government to protect children's rights (and the rights of others who are not capable of taking care of themselves), even over the objections of parents. State and federal governments can pass laws that protect children from parental neglect or abuse, or from others who would do them harm. Ensuring that children receive a meaningful education safeguards their future liberty and opportunity. It is on this point that friction is created between home educators and those who believe in the role of public education and in the duty of the state to protect the interests of all children.

This section focuses on two issues: (a) the legal arguments that weigh parental rights to oversee the upbringing of their children against the state's authority to regulate education and to compel children to attend school and (b) recent concerns about the extent of deregulation of homeschooling across the United States and the potential harm to children that may result.

Parental Rights Versus State Authority

The friction between homeschooling families and state government has manifested itself in considerable litigation, but for the purpose of analyzing the legal rights of parents to direct the education of their children, three U.S. Supreme Court cases are discussed: (a) *Meyer v. Nebraska* (1923), *Pierce v. Society of the Sisters* (1925), and *Wisconsin v. Yoder* (1972). The first two established a constitutional right for parents to oversee the upbringing of their children, but this right is not without restrictions. In the third case, the Court recognized the free exercise of religion claims of the Amish to withdraw their children from school after completing the eighth grade, which indicated that the state does not have the authority to overcome legitimate religious claims with regard to schooling.

In *Meyer* (1923) and *Pierce* (1925), the Court recognized the parents' liberty interest under the 14th Amendment "to direct the upbringing and education of children under their control" (*Pierce,* 1925, p. 534). In *Meyer,* a German language teacher in a Lutheran school had been prosecuted under a new law that forbade the teaching of foreign languages to children who had not yet passed the eighth grade. While addressing the liberty interest of the teacher to pursue a career in a field for which he had been prepared, the Court's majority opinion also commented on the rights of parents to increase the educational opportunities for their children. "It is the natural duty of the parent to give his children education suitable to their station in life" (p. 400). As the facts of the case illustrated, the parents were neither trying to deprive their child of an education nor violate compulsory education laws. The Court ruled that Nebraska's foreign language law was arbitrary and that the state was unable to provide any evidence that learning a foreign language prior to passing the eighth grade was in any way harmful to the child or to the security of the state.

In *Pierce,* Oregon voters, out of fear of communism and other factors hostile to American ideals, passed an initiative that amended the **compulsory attendance law** to require all school-age children to attend public schools. This meant that private schools, including parochial schools, could no longer operate. The Society of Sisters (a corporation under Oregon law) sued, arguing that the law arbitrarily interfered with its property right to own and operate a business and illegally restricted the rights of its teachers to earn a living in their chosen field. The Society of Sisters also argued that the law hindered the rights of parents to choose schools that would provide

religious training as well as instruction in secular subjects. In ruling for the Society of Sisters, the Court restated an opinion similar to one it has expressed in *Meyer* about the rights of parents with regard to the education of their children:

> The fundamental theory of liberty upon which all governments in this Union repose excludes any general power of the State to standardize its children by forcing them to accept instruction from public teachers only. The child is not the mere creature of the State; those who nurture him and direct his destiny have the right, coupled with the high duty, to recognize and prepare him for additional obligations. (*Pierce,* p. 535)

In neither case, however, did the Court indicate that state government had no authority to compel school attendance, to determine an appropriate curriculum, and to regulate all schools to ensure children had access to an adequate education. Nor was there any suggestion that parental rights to oversee the education of their children included removing them from schools altogether for the purpose of homeschooling them.

To date the Supreme Court has not considered the question of homeschooling, per se. However, in *Wisconsin v. Yoder* (1972), a question of parents withdrawing their children from school and asking them to be exempted from compulsory attendance law for religious reasons was addressed.

Under Wisconsin compulsory attendance laws, children were expected to attend public or private school until they were 16 years old. However, the Amish community disputed this requirement, arguing that their religious order and traditions required children to withdraw from school prior to entering high school in order to protect them from experiences that promoted "contemporary secular values," which were contrary to Amish values and beliefs. They believed that "higher learning tends to develop values . . . that alienate men from God" (p. 212).

As it did in *Meyer* and *Pierce,* the Court recognized the responsibility and authority of the state to provide for education and to compel attendance, as well as other reasonable regulations. However, Chief Justice Warren Burger's majority opinion also stated that the state's authority is not without constraint: "However strong the State's interest in universal compulsory education, it is by no means absolute to the exclusion or subordination of all other interests"

(p. 215). The Court evaluated the 300 years of Amish religious dogma and traditions as evidence of something more than a personal preference; rather, it was illustrative of strongly held religious conviction.

In rejecting Wisconsin's allegations that taking children out of school after the eighth grade condemned them to ignorance, the Court commented on the Amish community's stability and on its members as highly productive and law-abiding. In ruling for the Amish families, the Court suggested there was reason to believe the State and Amish community could agree on some educational standards within the context of agricultural and vocational education the children would receive within their community that would satisfy the State's concerns for the children's futures.

It is important to note that the "Amish exception" is just that, an exception. It was based on an entire community that was organized on centuries-old religious traditions. Individual families have attempted to be exempted from compulsory attendance laws based on sincerely held religious beliefs, but they have not been successful in court for the most part. Most cannot point to religious doctrine that requires parents to withdraw from or keep their children out of public and private schools.

All three cases address some aspect of the legal arguments about parents' rights to direct the education of their children. However, in each case, the U.S. Supreme Court reiterated the "high duty" that state government has to provide for the education of all children. It asserted that nothing in its decisions was to be construed as diminishing the authority of the state to maintain compulsory education laws and to promulgate reasonable regulations applicable to all schools. Even in *Yoder,* the Court recognized the state's interest in ensuring that the vocational education the children received after leaving public school was acceptable, as long as it did not interfere with the community's free exercise of religion. In none of the cases, however, did the Court specifically address homeschooling as it is currently practiced—that is, parents who are individual home educators and who, as individuals, assume sole and direct responsibility for the education of their children without state authorization.

A state's authority and responsibility to ensure all children are receiving an adequate education in order for them to realize their potential, to direct their future, and to be engaged citizens is only one example of *parens patriae.* Another aspect of the government's duty to the children in its jurisdiction is to protect them from harm. This is a concern that is being voiced more frequently because of concern that abuse and neglect of children are more likely to go undetected if they are not attending school.

Protecting the Welfare of Children

It is usually falls to the school district to execute any regulations that govern homeschoolers in their attendance or catchment zones. There is little evidence that state education agencies or school districts are exercising much oversight (Waddell, 2010; Yuracko, 2008). Enforcement of regulations and policies relating to homeschoolers may be intermittent or absent altogether. This recent "hands off" attitude from state and school officials is worrisome to many educators, legal scholars, social scientists, and social welfare advocates.

The most pressing concern, one that strikes at the heart of *parens patriae,* is the lack of state supervision of homeschooled children to ensure their health and safety, as well as their educational progress (Barnett, 2013). Reports are beginning to emerge that reveal the dark side of homeschooling families who are allowed to operate without any public scrutiny. The *Akron Beacon* investigated reports of child fatalities in U.S. families identified as homeschooling (Barnett, 2013). In reviewing over 5,000 articles nationwide, it discovered 116 deaths of parents and children identified as homeschooling over a nearly 6-year period from 1999 to 2004. Of these, 41 were children ages 5 to 16 years old who were murdered (Willard & Oplinger, 2004). Since states do not have any mechanism to collect data on child abuse linked to homeschooling, there is no definable number of children who have suffered at the hands of their parents because they are out of sight of public scrutiny.

Bad things happen to children in public spaces such as schools, too, but perpetrators are more likely to be caught more quickly than those who operate in isolation, far from the view of education and social welfare authorities (Barnett, 2013). However, homeschooling organizations such as HSLDA bristle at any mention of increased regulation, even if its intended purpose is to protect children from abuse. They claim that increased regulation will not prevent child abuse and that the problem is much more prevalent outside the homeschooling community. Those who support some form of supervision to guard against egregious abuse dismiss these claims, noting that no law eliminates crime, but can help diminish it. They also argue that the true number of abuse cases within the homeschooling community is probably much larger than anyone knows because of lax state regulation of homeschooling and because no state agency collects data on child abuse among homeschoolers.

One group working to bring awareness to the public about the potential harm to children who are homeschooled is Homeschooling's Invisible Children (HIC). HIC has taken on the task of archiving the most egregious instances of school-aged homeschooled children who have been abused. The website, run by volunteers who are former homeschoolers, has documented cases of starvation, physical and sexual abuse, torture, extreme neglect, and home imprisonment. It has taken a position that homeschooling should be an option for parents, but "sensible safeguards" are needed to protect children's well-being as well as the credibility of homeschooling (HIC, n.d.).

It is the state that carries the duty to protect children who cannot protect themselves. In public and private schools, teachers, counselors, administrators, and anyone else who has contact with children are required by law to report suspected abuse or neglect. Sometimes abuse of children who attend school goes undetected, and suspected abuse is not always dealt with adequately. But isolating conditions created by some parents and guardians who homeschool their children makes abuse more difficult to detect. Children who have no contact with anyone but those who abuse them suffer interminably, and some die.

The tension between homeschooling advocates and detractors will not be resolved in the courts or by regulation, however. Many argue that a major court ruling against homeschooling would only drive the practice underground. Nonetheless, the state must not abdicate its responsibility to ensure that all children receive an adequate education, whether in the home or in a private or public school. Most importantly, the state has an obligation to the health and safety of all children in its jurisdiction.

Other Concerns With Homeschooling

The suitability of homeschooling in preparing students for their future and its potential impact on the role of government in education are areas of concern, as well. Specifically, the degree to which home-educated students are being properly socialized, sufficiently prepared academically, and adequately readied for engagement in civil society are long-standing concerns, with considerable research supporting opposing views on the subject. The long-term impact that homeschooling, as a social movement, may have on American society generally is a newer issue. Some warn about the potential change the homeschooling movement could have on how individuals view the role of government in creating opportunity for economic and social equality.

Early concerns about socialization were based on survey research in which school administrators opined that students were harmed by being exposed only to their parents' perspectives and did not have the opportunity to form their own opinions. In fact, some superintendents complained that home educated students would not accept any other point of view than that of their parents (Medlin, 2000). They averred that homeschooling parents taught their children that society is malevolent and government is not to be trusted.

These observations were countered by homeschooling parents who characterized public education as promoters of conformity over individuality and that as institutions, schools were rigid and authoritarian (Medlin, 2000). They further asserted that peer interactions in public schools were too often hostile and demeaning and that adults were insufficiently caring and accepting of children.

Much of this debate has dissipated, however, over time. Children, whether educated in schools or at home, have easy access to social media and the Internet. Many homeschool communities and networks create opportunities for homeschooled children to interact, and as previously discussed, many take advantage of part-time public schooling and extracurricular activities. There is no recent research that supports any claim that homeschooled children are inadequately or inappropriately socialized.

A second concern has to do with academic preparation. A problem with addressing this issue has been criticisms about poor research designs and about accessibility to a sufficiently large sample of homeschooled children to generate meaningful research findings. In one study, however, researchers attempted to compare academic achievement between similar groups of homeschoolers and those educated in public schools (Martin-Chang et al., 2011). They considered factors such as maternal education and family income, and eliminated potential participants who had experienced both forms of schooling. They created two subgroups within the homeschooling sample, those who followed a structured curriculum put together by an outside entity and those who did not. All participating children took the same standardized test, which was administered by the researchers. Findings indicated that homeschooled children who followed a structured curriculum performed better than the public school children, but that the homeschooled children who did not have a structured curriculum did poorly relative to the other two groups. Furthermore, the difference between the "structured" homeschooled students and the public school students could not be explained by maternal education level or by family income.

Other studies have focused on homeschoolers' adjustment to and performance in college. While most of these studies are conducted by advocates of homeschooling, there is a small group that comes from outside of that community (Drenovsky & Cohen, 2012; Duggan, 2010). Most of the findings are based on self-assessment on surveys, which has its own set of problems. Generally results on adjustment to college indicated that while students educated in public schools reported higher self-esteem than home-educated students, the difference was not significant (Drenovsky & Cohen, 2012). Homeschoolers, however, did have significantly lower depression scores than traditionally educated students. They also rated their achievement higher and their college experiences more positively than their traditionally educated counterparts. Other research has indicated that college students who were home educated were significantly more likely to describe themselves as good writers and speakers, as critical thinkers, and as having strong study and time-management skills (Duggan, 2010).

One enduring concern has to do with whether home educators adequately or correctly teach citizenship. Most states, even those with few regulations, require citizenship as a part of any homeschool curriculum. However, if state education agencies and school districts are not enforcing this regulation, then there is no guarantee that children are receiving this instruction.

Educating all youths in citizenship has been inextricably linked to public education's responsibility in reproducing the social contract for democracy and individual liberty. The concept that education is the primary conduit for perpetuating representative democracy preceded the common school movement. The founding fathers, in particular Thomas Jefferson, understood the importance of producing an educated citizenry as indispensable to safeguarding citizens' rights and liberties against the potential for tyranny in a self-governing republic. Contemporary educational philosophers, legal scholars, and political and social scientists value public education as the venue in which all children are exposed to diverse ideas and people, develop a sense of civic duty, and embrace core democratic values like liberty, justice, and the common good (Apple, 2000; Hamilton, 2010; Reich, 2002). As one legal scholar observed, "citizens are born, but they are also made" (Hamilton, 2010, p. 1058).

No one really understands the drawbacks, if any, that the increasing numbers of homeschoolers will have on civil society. Some fear customizing education through homeschooling may have an adverse effect on citizen participation in a democratic society and may erode the sense of public responsibility that functions to diminish inequities and injustices (Apple, 2000; Reich, 2002). Social science researchers and other scholars are concerned about the power of the homeschooling movement as a social movement that could possibly have a restructuring effect on society, one that does not benefit the general welfare of all citizens (Apple, 2000). Likewise, they are alarmed at the increasingly consumer-driven educational practices that denigrate democracy into "possessive individualism" (Apple, 2000, p. 258). However, these are fears for the future and are not yet based on any empirical evidence.

Conclusion

Homeschooling continues to be a viable form of educating children, although the degree of government supervision and regulation over homeschooling is hotly debated. Advocates and detractors argue where the boundary lies between parental rights to oversee the upbringing of their children and the state's responsibility and authority in ensuring all children receive an adequate education that prepares them for their future as productive and engaged members of society.

Research is imperative in order to measure the impact a growing and increasingly unregulated homeschooling community has on individual and collective liberty. Defending a child's liberty interest in directing her or his own future and engendering political liberty through educating all children on democratic ideals are compelling government interests, and as such, provide sufficient justification to promote research.

Gathering data will be no easy task inasmuch as most states do not require substantive data reporting on homeschoolers, and, as a group, homeschooling families resist efforts to document who they are and what they are doing unless they perceive the researchers to be friendly to homeschooling. The current hands-off approach by government may have to be reconsidered in light of the important questions that homeschooling raises.

Key Chapter Terms

Boxed curricula: Ready-made programs available for purchase that provide homeschool families with a comprehensive curriculum scope and sequence, textbooks, assessments, projects, and time lines that are grade leveled. They provide structure and guidance to parents and their children and most resemble traditional curricula found in public schools.

Compulsory attendance laws: Requires children within a specific age range (e.g., ages 6 through 16) to attend a private or public school. The laws, which are present in each state, usually specify the number of hours in a day and the number of days in a year that a child must be present in school.

Correspondence programs: Most often directed at high school level students, correspondence programs provide a full curriculum and related materials through shipping. This serves homeschoolers who may not have consistent access to a computer or to the Internet.

Cover school/umbrella school: Enrolls homeschooling children or families and offers services supportive of home education. Also known as an "umbrella school."

Cyber schools/virtual schools: Online schools that may be operated by private or public schools, universities, or other educational entities. Most contract certified teachers to oversee the delivery of the curriculum or to coach parents and help them deliver instruction. Some observers, including some homeschoolers, do not consider cyber schools to be homeschooling because the parents are not necessarily responsible for their children's education. Schools generally need an additional accreditation to be specifically allowed to provide online credits and degrees.

Home educators: Parents who educate their children at home. They take responsibility to direct the education of their children.

Homeschooling: Schooling in which parents take primary responsibility for the education of their children. They may choose to instruct their children themselves or to hire someone to teach their children. While parents may avail themselves of virtual schools or charter schools in which there may or may not be some government involvement or form of structured curriculum, they remain in control of their children's education. Homeschooling has a different legal status in each of the 50 states.

K^{12}: Well-known purveyor of online learning. It has its own online private school, but it is better known for partnering with and providing high-quality and engaging curriculum to private and public schools that offer online education.

Parens patriae: Legal doctrine that authorizes government to act as guardian to all persons who are too young or too incapacitated to care for themselves or to make decisions for themselves. Literally meaning "the parent of the country," this principle permits government to act on behalf of children and others to protect them from those who would neglect them or do them harm. It is on this basis that compulsory education laws have been upheld by courts when challenged by parents.

Secular humanism: A philosophy that advances the belief that humans can be moral and ethical in the absence of a god or deity. It relies on the human capacity to rationally discover and explain the world around them, to take responsibility for their decisions and actions, and to critically examine "truths" through scientific method and philosophical inquiry.

References

Alexander, K., & Alexander, M. D. (2012). *American public school law* (8th ed.). Belmont, CA: Wadsworth.

Apple, M. W. (2000). The cultural politics of home schooling. *Peabody Journal of Education, 75*(1/2), 256–271.

Apple, M. W. (2007, Spring). Who needs teacher education? Gender, technology and the work of home schooling. *Teacher Education Quarterly, 34*(2), 111–130.

Barnett, T. (2013). Pulling back the curtains: Undetected child abuse and the need for increased regulation of home schooling in Missouri. *Brigham Young University Education and Law Journal, 2013,* 341–356.

Bielick, S. (2008). *1.5 million homeschooled students in the United States in 2007* (NCES 2009-030). National Center for Education Statistics, Institute of Education Sciences, U.S. Department of Education. Washington, DC. Retrieved from http://nces.ed.gov/pubs2009/2009030.pdf

California Homeschool Network. (2012/2013). *Just the facts: A step by step guide to starting your homeschool* (2012–2013 ed.). Retrieved from http://californiahomeschool.net/howTo/pdf/CHNJTF2012_13.pdf

Cuthbert C. (2002, June 10). *Of spelling bees and homeschool demagoguery.* Retrieved from http://www.lewrockwell.com/2002/06/cathy-cuthbert/spelling-bees-and-homeschool-demagoguery/

Drenovsky, C. D., & Cohen, I. (2012). The impact of homeschooling on the adjustment of college students. *International Social Science Review, 87*(1/2), 19–34.

Duggan, M. (2010, January/February). Is all college preparation equal? Pre-community college experiences of home-schooled, private-school, and public-schooled students. *Community College Journal of Research and Practice, 34*(1/2), 25–38. doi:10.1080/10668920903388131

Hamilton, V. E. (2010). Immature citizens and the state. *Brigham Young University Law Review, 2010*(4), 1055–1147.

Home Schooling Legal Defense Association. (n.d.). *State laws.* Retrieved from http://www.hslda.org/laws/

Homeschooling's Invisible Children. (n.d.). *Our position.* Retrieved from http://hsinvisiblechildren.org/

K[12]. (n.d.). *What is K[12]?* Retrieved from http://www.k12.com/what-is-k12

K[12] International Academy. (n.d.) *Is your child happy in school?* Retrieved from http://landing.icademy.com/k12_icademy2/?theme=Homeschool&leadsource=sem&product_type=pay&product_interest=icad&target_audience=gen&target_grade=gen&utm_campaign=Home_-_Desktop&utm_medium=cpcgoogle-sem&utm_source=google&utm_term=virtual_homeschool&adgroup=Homeschool_Virtual&keyword_match=broad&message_class=direct_response&vendor=ef&provider=google&geo_distro=natl&ef_id=UpQuhAAABWriGwwB:20131201224235:s

Kaestle, C. (1983). *Pillars of the republic: Common schools and American society 1780–1860.* New York, NY: Hill and Wang.

Klicka, C. (1999). *Biblical reasons to home school.* Home School Legal Defense Association. Retrieved from http://www.hslda.org/docs/nche/000000/00000069.asp

Martin-Chang, S., Gould, O. N., & Meuse, R. E. (2011). The impact of schooling on academic achievement: Evidence from homeschooled and traditionally schooled students. *Canadian Journal of Behavioural Science, 43*(3), 195–202. doi:10.1037/a0022697

Medlin, R. G. (2000). Home schooling and the question of socialization. *Peabody Journal of Education, 75*(1/2), 107–123.

Murphy, J. (2012). *Homeschooling in America: Capturing and assessing the movement.* Thousand Oaks, CA: Corwin.

Murphy, J. (2013). Riding history: The organizational development of homeschooling in the U.S. *American Education History Journal, 40*(2), 335–354.

National Center for Education Statistics. (2008, December). *1.5 million homeschooled students in the United States in 2007.* Retrieved from http://nces.ed.gov/pubs2009/2009030.pdf

Noel, A., Stark, P., & Redford, J. (2013). *Parent and family involvement in education. From the National Household Education Surveys Program of 2012* (NCES 2013-028). Washington, DC: National Center for Education Statistics, Institute of Education Sciences, U.S. Department of Education.

Ray, B. (2010, Winter). Academic achievement and demographic traits of homeschool children: A nationwide study. *Academic Leadership Journal, 8*(1). Retrieved from http://contentcat.fhsu.edu/cdm/compoundobject/collection/p15732coll4/id/456

Reich, R. (2002). The civic perils of homeschooling. *Educational Leadership, 59*(7), 56–59.

Tyack, D. B. (1974). *The one best system: A history of American urban education.* Cambridge, MA: Harvard University Press.

Waddell, T. B. (2010). Bringing it all back home: Establishing a coherent constitutional framework for the re-regulation of homeschooling. *Vanderbilt Law Review, 63*(2), 541–597.

Willard, D.J. & Oplinger, D. (2004, November 17). Home schoolers may be no safer in their homes than other children. *Akron Beacon Journal.* Retrieved from http://epsl.asu.edu/epru/articles/EPRU-0503-104-OWI.pdf

Yuracko, K. A. (2008). Education off the grid: Constitutional constraints on homeschooling. *California Law Review, 96,* 123–184.

Statutes and Court Decisions

Affidavit by Agency Conducting Private School Instruction at Elementary or High School Level; List of schools. Cal. Educ. Code § 33190 (2013).

Attendance in Private School. Ca. Educ. Code § 48222 (2013).

Compulsory School Attendance. Okla. Const. art. XIII § 4 (2013).

Educational Opportunities Offered; Limitations. Ca. Educ. Code § 51745 (2013).

Instruction by Tutor. Ca. Educ. Code § 48224 (2013).

Meyer v. Nebraska, 262 U.S. 390, 43 S.Ct. 625 (1923).

Pierce v. Society of the Sisters of the Holy Names of Jesus and Mary, 268 U.S. 510, 45 S.Ct. 571 (1925).

Wisconsin v. Yoder, 406 U.S. 205, 92 S.Ct. 1526 (1972).

Further Readings

Drenovsky, C. D., & Cohen, I. (2012). The impact of homeschooling on the adjustment of college students. *International Social Science Review, 87*(1/2), 19–34.

For those interested in the relationship between homeschooling and college adjustment, this article provides findings from a study on that very subject. It reveals that homeschooled students are in some ways better prepared for college in that they have levels of self-esteem comparable to public school students and have lower levels of depression. It also documents homeschooling students' perceptions that they are stronger academically and have more positive attitudes about their college experiences.

McDowell, S., & Ray, B. (Eds.). (2000). The home education movement in context, practice, and theory [Special issue]. *Peabody Journal of Education, 75*(1/2).

This is a special issue of the journal completely focused on homeschooling. While some of the pieces on regulations and laws governing homeschooling may be dated, there is considerable literature on the history of homeschooling as well as on topics such as homeschooling and special education, socialization of homeschoolers, multiculturalism and homeschooling, and the future of public schooling in relationship to homeschooling.

Murphy, J. (2013). Riding history: The organizational development of homeschooling in the U.S. *American Education History Journal, 40*(2), 335–354.

This article traces the development of homeschooling in America from its colonial roots and through various evolutions to today's education marketplace of options. The author details how homeschooling was marginalized when compulsory education laws were introduced and how its resurgence in recent decades has been a reaction to what some perceive as too much government control over the intellectual and social growth of children. The article also follows what has been an emerging hybrid of homeschooling and public education, in which some homeschooling families use boxed curriculum or virtual schools that are provided by public schools and public schools enjoy some financial benefit.

Ray, B. (2010, Winter). Academic achievement and demographic traits of homeschool children: A nationwide study. *Academic Leadership Journal, 8*(1). Retrieved from http://contentcat.fhsu.edu/cdm/compoundobject/collection/p15732coll4/id/835/rec/1

This article provides an overview of the research literature on the academic achievement of homeschoolers as well as the attributes that are associated with this category of students as a whole. It provides a critical analysis of what the research reveals and what the gaps are in the literature.

24

EMERGING TRENDS IN STUDENT SERVICES AND COUNSELING

KIMBERLY A. GORDON BIDDLE

Sacramento State University

SHANNON DICKSON

Sacramento State University

Elementary and secondary students in the United States need support services to help them attain optimal academic achievement and overall school success. Administrative leaders and managers need to be aware of the latest trends in student services and counseling in order to facilitate the performance of their faculty, staff, and students and to be effective as leaders. These student services include learning and testing modifications, peer tutoring, peer-mediated learning, supplemental instruction in reading and math, special education, counseling, and well-trained teachers who are familiar with classroom management and behavior management strategies in addition to being trained in effective research-based pedagogical techniques. Other general student services include support and management of behavior, social work support and referrals, and home support that may include home visits. The delivery of general student services usually varies by the school level; that is, whether it is elementary, middle, or secondary school. Some of the trends in general student services are discussed in the first section of the chapter, with trends in counseling services following in the second section.

Trends in General Student Services

The delivery of general student services usually varies by school level. Elementary school trends in student services include social skills training. General student service trends in secondary school include **small learning communities**. More information about general student services can be found in the National Longitudinal Transition Study-2 (NLTS2) (2002) and the Special Education Elementary Longitudinal Study (SEELS) (2001). Special education is a general student service trend that cuts across both elementary and secondary school. Special education student services must comply with the 2004 Individuals with Disabilities Education Improvement Act and serve children with exceptionalities. Technology and electronic data are trends that also influence both elementary and secondary school student education. Other trends mentioned in the first part of this chapter focus mostly on one level of education or the other (see **Figure 24.1**).

Special Education

Within special education, there are two prominent current trends. These are a focus on the mental health

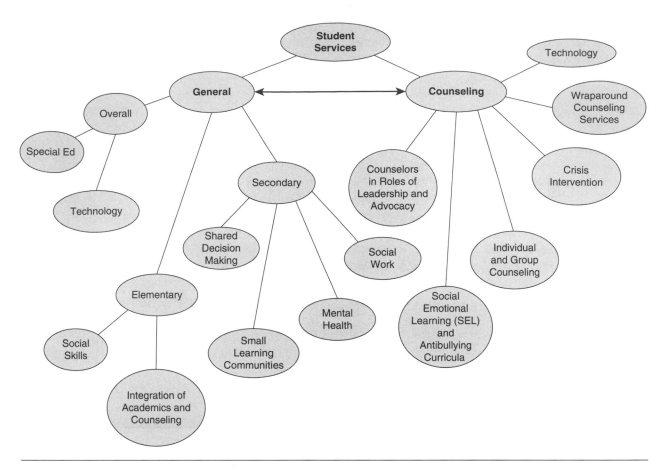

Figure 24.1 Trends in Student Services

of students (Wagner, Newman, Cameto, Levine, & Garza, 2006) and a focus on gifted and talented students (Fisher-Doiron & Irvine, 2009; Van Tassel-Baska, 2007). In terms of the mental health of students with emotional disturbances, many students with emotional disturbances spend time in general education classes. Elementary students with emotional disturbances participate in these classes less often, however, than other students with different disabilities. Most students with emotional disturbances have services that include access to a school psychologist, guidance counselors, instructional aides, social workers, and a reading specialist. In the study by Mary Wagner and colleagues (2006), high school students with emotional disturbances were less likely than their elementary counterparts to have a reading specialist, though. A majority of these students have academic resources such as tutoring, supplemental language arts, and supplemental mathematics. In elementary, they are less likely to have mathematics

supplements, and in secondary they are less likely to have reading supplements. A few of the students, especially in secondary school, have access to conflict-resolution and anger-management services. Secondary students were also more likely to have access to enrichment programs such as visual and performing arts and sports, but participation was low.

As for gifted education, teachers are being encouraged to improve instruction of all children (Fisher-Doiron & Irvine, 2009; Van Tassel-Baska, 2007), especially children who are living in an impoverished family yet show intellectual promise. Teachers are being asked to acknowledge these students' strengths, provide them with mentors, work with their families, and customize their curriculum and services. In addition, teachers are being encouraged to use evidence-based pedagogical techniques on all children, even those in poverty, that include encouraging higher levels of thinking on **Bloom's Taxonomy** (Schultz, 2005), connecting academic learning to real-life experiences, and teaching metacognition. Teachers are also being asked to differentiate instruction for learners and to form small groups of similar-ability students in which to deliver the differentiated instruction. Incorporating the visual and performing arts into education of the gifted is not new, but ensuring these disciplines are integrated into the education of all children is a current trend in reaction to the No Child Left Behind Act of 2001 (NCLB). This is because NCLB focuses on basic skills only.

Electronic Data and Privacy

There is one trend that is pervasive in general student services, whether at the elementary or secondary school level. More data are being archived, transferred, and communicated electronically. Since these data are easily accessible and quite permanent, issues have arisen concerning privacy of the individual families and children involved. This concern about general student services is in addition to the ever-present concern about the archiving, transferring, and communicating of academic achievement, attendance, and truancy data. It is imperative that leaders and managers of K-12 schools and districts keep student and family data safe, secure, and private. The National Center for Education Statistics (NCES) recommends that schools and districts keep organized files, and NCES has mandatory reporting procedures and databases that demand consistency and uniformity in how data are organized and compiled. NCES stresses safety and security at all school levels to ensure privacy of individual students and the students' families. The NCES promotes safety, security, and privacy for school leaders and managers in the K-12 system with regularly scheduled forums. These forums allow school leaders and managers to stay abreast of trends.

Elementary School Trends

General student services in elementary schools in the United States are currently focusing on social skills and the integration of academic and counseling programs with groups of children. With increasing recognition of the importance of social skills for academic success (Lane, Givner, & Pierson, 2004), students who lack social skills that teachers expect may be referred to special education services. In light of this trend, students must meet the expectations of

general educators and special educators. This is especially true because special education children are more likely to be included in the general classroom. **Self-control** seems to be the most important social skill that elementary school teachers favor, whether they are general educators or special educators. Both types of educators also favor assertion. However, general educators put more emphasis on cooperation than do special educators in elementary schools. The most critical self-control skills seem to be controlling one's temper with peers and adults, displaying appropriate responses to being hit by a peer, and getting along with others. In terms of cooperation skills, teachers want elementary students to attend to instructions, follow directions, and use free time well and productively. As students progress to higher levels of elementary school, social skills seem to be even more important in the eyes of teachers for student academic success.

Since social skills and behavior are so important for academic success, interventions that integrate the two are a trend in elementary school student services (Steen & Kaffenberger, 2007). The interventions create small groups based on the **American School Counselor Association** (ASCA; 2004, 2007) national model. In these small groups, school counselors enrich learning behaviors and social development. The learning behaviors include actions such as staying on task and completing assignments. Social skills topics include anger management, friendship, and social skills. Utilizing small groups based on the ASCA model helps counselors to reach more students effectively and efficiently in terms of student actions and academic achievement. Students in these groups usually show gains in learning behaviors and better social development. Some students even show gains in academic achievement as demonstrated by higher grades in certain subjects. Although these small groups are run by counselors, the counselors regularly communicate and cooperate with parents and teachers. The success of these types of programs demonstrates the need for school counselors in elementary schools.

Secondary School Trends

There are a number of evidence-based student service trends in secondary schools in the United States. These trends include **shared decision making** between principals and teachers, small learning communities, enhanced mental health services, and enriched social work services (Duchnowski & Kutash, 2011; Leech & Fulton, 2008; Newsome, Anderson-Butcher, Fink, Hall, & Huffer, 2008; Oxley, 2005). These trends have emerged because secondary schools and districts are generally larger than those at the elementary level. Additionally, there are usually more students per classroom, and the students are older and at a higher level of cognitive, emotional, and social development.

In order to empower teachers and students in secondary schools, especially in large urban school districts, decision making must be shared by principals and teachers (Leech & Fulton, 2008). This type of participatory leadership has the potential to transform educational culture in secondary schools. In this type of secondary school, the principal is still important as a manager and leader; indeed, the principal is held accountable for decisions, actions, behaviors, and rules associated with his or her school, teachers, students, and families. However, allowing teachers to participate in decision making empowers the teachers, students, and families who will still look to the principal for leadership and vision. In order for teachers and principals to share decision making, teachers need to be trained to increase this skill, they need to be given credible information for making their decision, and they need recognition and support from the principal and others in their environment. The actions, behaviors, and attitudes of the principal are keys to shared decision making, because he or she must challenge traditional processes and create relationships between and among teachers. In order for shared decision making to work, the principal and the teachers need training before (pre-service) and after graduating. Continual professional development for the people in both roles is the key.

Shared collaboration and learning are not just for principals and teachers. Teachers and students in secondary school settings are now collaborating and learning from each other in small learning communities (SLCs) (Oxley, 2005). It is noted that this trend is occurring in elementary schools as well. The emphasis in any SLC is collaboration among all members of the learning community with curriculum and pedagogy that focus on students. Although this idea is not entirely new, the current trend takes this idea further by introducing the concept of an interdisciplinary team in each SLC that can act with some autonomy and flexibility regarding the students in their charge. In other words, general classroom teachers, special education teachers, counselors, and social workers interact and act as a team concerning a group of students. In order for these teams and their students to flourish, they need support from the principal and district superintendent. They must keep high standards and have curriculum and pedagogy that relate to the lives of their students. All students, whether they are from low-income families or are **English language learners** or are children with special needs, must be included in these groups. Most importantly, each SLC must evaluate itself and continue to learn, grow, and improve.

Another trend in secondary schools is increased mental health services and inclusion in general classrooms for those with emotional disturbances (ED) (Duchnowski & Kutash, 2011). As a result, these students improve their test scores in academic subjects such as mathematics. In addition to services in the school, the ED students with higher achievement also receive services from mental health professionals from organizations in their neighborhood. Again, interdisciplinary teams, shared decisions, and focus on student needs characterize this trend, which Albert Duchnowski and Krista Kutash (2011) state applies to elementary and secondary schools. They also advocate that in the case of students with ED, the students themselves should perhaps participate in the decision making and planning. They also argue that this student involvement leads to significant skill development and significant increases in student learning and achievement for both elementary and secondary students.

Social workers are important team members, too, in secondary schools (Newsome et al., 2008). Social workers play a role in elementary schools, but their impact is also felt strongly in secondary schools. Social workers work with those students who are at risk for demonstrating—or who have already demonstrated—troubling behaviors, excessive absences, or truancy. School social workers usually intervene by meeting with various people related to these students. The social workers meet with the students, their parents/family members, other school staff, and other support organizations in the community. The efforts of social workers include advocating and intervening and meeting multiple times with multiple people and demonstrate effectiveness. Even in this era of accountability, social workers are needed. This is acutely true in high-risk urban secondary schools.

Although counselors play a collaborative role in general student services, there exist some student service trends that are uniquely considered counseling trends. These trends are occurring in both elementary and secondary schools. These trends are at various levels of the education process. For instance, some of the trends impact the culture of education, some impact schools, and some impact only one individual child. As the counseling strategy gets narrower in focus, it is generally more intense.

Emerging Trends in Counseling

The role of the 21st-century elementary and secondary (K-12) counselor has expanded to include more than assigned administrative duties (e.g., master scheduling, testing, class registration), discipline, and general guidance counseling (**Figure 24.2**). Counselors today are involved in preparing and supporting students' **academic readiness** and overall school success, thus, assisting in closing the ever-widening achievement gap. Additionally, they play a major role in delivering mental health services to the students in their charge (Paternite, 2005). Data from a national survey indicate that at least 60% of U.S. children and youths under the age of 17 have been exposed to violence, abuse, and crime (e.g., sexual victimization, witnessing a violent crime, child abuse, intimate partner violence; Finkelhor, Hamby, Kracke, Ormrod, & Turner, 2009). Additionally, children as young as 18 months can have socioemotional, cognitive, and behavioral problems when exposed to traumatic events (Mongillo, Briggs-Gowan, Ford, & Carter, 2009).

An increasing number of children and adolescents are facing a plethora of barriers (e.g., psychological, social, economic) that impede their ability to learn and be successful in school. Recent attempts at standards-based educational reform and school improvement initiatives such as the No Child Left Behind Act (NCLB; U.S. Department of Education, n.d.) have focused primarily on improving the academic educational standards for children and youth. NCLB legislation has also prompted professional school counselors to demonstrate how their prevention and intervention efforts support students' overall academic achievement and school success. The American School Counselor Association (ASCA) and the **Education Trust**'s **Transforming School Counseling Initiative (TSCI)** (Education Trust, 2001) have both established standards and initiatives for counseling programs to address the growing and competing developmental needs of students with the overarching goal of closing the achievement gap (ASCA, 2004; Education Trust, 2001). Both ASCA and the Education Trust recognize counselors as having a significant influence on the academic success of students. Counselors are charged with the task and responsibility of crafting and implementing holistic and developmental comprehensive counseling programs in school settings that support students in the areas of academic, career, and personal/social growth. Furthermore, in its comprehensiveness, counseling programming must demonstrate a clear relationship to the educational initiatives and mission of schools and districts (ASCA, 2004; Education Trust, 2001). Elementary and secondary counselors are best positioned by virtue of their educational background, training, and professional experience to serve as leaders, collaborators, and cultural brokers with special attention to the promotion of social justice advocacy in addressing the emotional, social, and economic needs of children (Terrion, 2006; West-Olatunji, Frazier, & Kelley, 2011).

A number of counseling trends have developed with the goal of addressing students' academic learning and psychological, social, and career development. The current trends include counselors assuming an increasingly more active role of leadership and advocacy, facilitating and delivering **social emotional learning (SEL)** and antibullying prevention curricula, individual and group counseling, **crisis intervention**, **wraparound counseling** services, and the supportive use of technology (e.g., blogs, websites, Twitter).

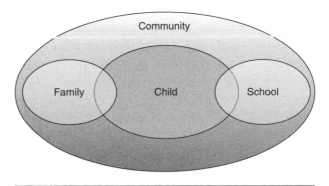

Figure 24.2 Systems Perspective of Student Services

Counselors in Roles of Leadership and Advocacy

The **National Standards for School Counseling Programs** (ASCA, 2004) and the Transforming School Counseling Initiative (Education Trust, 2001) have helped to more clearly define the roles of counselors working in K-12 settings. Leadership is fast becoming a prominent role for professional school counselors in today's schools as counselors influence and effect change in ways that teachers and administrators cannot given their other responsibilities and duties. Counselors are trained to assess, identify areas of concern, and develop strategies to address obstacles that hinder children and adolescents' academic success. In a position of leadership, counselors are afforded the opportunity to work in collaboration with administrators and teachers to accomplish the overall mission of schools and districts, which is to foster high academic achievement and success for all students (Dollarhide, 2003).

Counselors are also functioning in the role of advocate for students through challenging the status quo to ensure equal access of available resources (e.g., technology; academic enrichment activities) for all students so that students have the opportunity to be academically successful. As advocates, counselors understand how systemic conditions (e.g., poverty, inadequate resources, and inexperienced teachers) can impact students' academic success (Dollarhide, 2003; West-Olatunji et al., 2011).

Social Emotional Learning (SEL) and Antibullying Curricula

Social competence is an area in which K-12 counselors have played an important and influential role; however, given the ongoing challenges of student behavior problems (e.g., **bullying**, truancy, substance abuse, sexual acting out) that teachers, administrators, and students encounter, safety continues to be a concern (Terrion, 2006). School safety has taken the forefront of concerns given recent and past tragedies of violence occurring on school campuses across the nation (Dinkes, Kemp, Baum, & Snyder, 2009). Counselors' involvement in addressing bullying behavior has increased over the years with a shift toward counselors rather than teachers delivering antibullying curriculum to students. Traditionally, teachers were responsible for the delivery of SEL and antibullying curricula; however, since NCLB legislation their focus has shifted primarily to academic achievement. Counselors are now charged with social competence curriculum, which is congruent with national counseling standards and the school counselor initiative (ASCA, 2004; Education Trust, 2001).

SEL and antibullying, evidence-based programs developed in response to previously fragmented and uncoordinated programming and have proliferated over the last two decades with prevention and intervention aimed at decreasing and/or eliminating school violence (Greenberg et al., 2003). The general focus of SEL programs includes self-awareness (e.g., accurate self-assessment of emotions, interests, and values), self-management (e.g., emotional self-regulation), social awareness (e.g., perspective taking and empathy for others), relationship skills (e.g., cooperation and conflict resolution), and responsible decision making (e.g., making good decisions, understanding consequences of one's actions; Collaboration for Academic, Social and Emotional Learning [CASEL], 2013). Although some programs have produced successful short-term outcomes, when evaluated over time, these same results yielded unsuccessful outcomes (Durlak, Dymnicki, Weissberg, & Schellinger, 2011; Greenberg et al., 2003). The challenge associated with unsuccessful SEL programming is that many programs select and focus on one aspect of the child such as mental health, academic performance and learning, substance use, behavior problems, or truancy rather than approaching the child's challenges from a systemic perspective in which the child's environment (e.g., home, school) is viewed as interactive with the child's individual behavioral characteristics (Greenberg et al., 2003). Research suggests that social-emotional development influences and improves academic performance and learning, engenders positive school climate, and increases children's and youth's sense of belonging and safety (Durlak et al., 2011; Greenberg et al., 2003). Furthermore, data suggest that the most effective programs not only include a single aspect such as enhancing a child's social competence or decreasing internalizing/externalizing behaviors, but also include systemic and organizational change within the school, home, and community (West-Olatunji et al., 2011).

Children and youth victimization in the form of bullying is a common school problem (Farrington & Ttofi, 2011; Swearer, Espelage, Vaillancourt, & Hymel, 2010). Thirty-four percent of youth aged 12 to 17 reported being victims of moderate to severe bullying (Dinkes et al., 2009). Research findings on bullying suggest that youth who bully and youth who are bullied are at risk for mental disorders, are more likely to drop out of school, and have difficulty adjusting socially (National Association of School Psychologists [NASP], 2003). Research further revealed that 25% of teachers perceived bullying behavior as a common part of the negotiation of social relationships among youth and only 4% of teachers reported responding to bullying behavior, as reported by the National Association of School Psychologists (NASP, 2003). A factor in counselors' delivery of antibullying curriculum is their view of bullying as the interplay of the child's individual characteristics, his family, school environment, and community. This view, known as the *social ecological perspective,* purports that bullying behavior is positively reinforced and shaped by students' home, school, community, and social environment. Counselors are trained to assess, identify problem(s), and develop the appropriate treatment for addressing the problems using a systemic perspective. These skills are vital in undertaking bullying prevention given the insidious nature of bullying (e.g., cyberbullying) behavior that is often difficult to detect by teachers who are focused on academic activities and by administrators who are responsible for the overall safety of the school environment. The focus of systemic bullying programs (e.g., Olweus Bullying Prevention Program [OBPP] and Steps to Respect [STR]), in addition to teaching youth pro-social skills (e.g., social character development, problem-solving and conflict resolution skills), is to address school climate (e.g., school connectedness, bonding); collaboration between school personnel, parents, and the community agencies as well as parent involvement; teacher training; and instituting consistent school disciplinary policies.

A primary focus of counselors' efforts in the delivery of antibullying curricula is addressing factors identified as major contributors to students' bullying behaviors (e.g., poor school climate, high student-to-teacher ratios, and lack of parent involvement; Swearer et al., 2010). Building school climate

through increasing children's and adolescents' sense of bonding or connectedness to school decreases the likelihood of youth engaging in bullying and other high-risk behaviors (e.g., drug abuse, violence, sexual acting out; Beets et al., 2008). Furthermore, children and youth who believe that their teachers and other school personnel care about what happens to them as well as positively support their academic endeavors demonstrate improvement in their academic abilities (Beets et al., 2008).

Individual and Group Counseling

Brief, solution-focused group counseling is becoming increasingly popular in K-12 settings. Although the solution-focused approach is utilized in individual counseling as well, given the limited resources available and schools' focus on students' academic skills, individual counseling is losing its appeal in K-12 school settings (Campbell & Brigman, 2005). Furthermore, children and adolescents needing individual counseling are being referred to wraparound community counseling services (to be discussed later in this chapter). This brief, solution-focused approach is strength-based, short-term (four to six 50- to 90-minute sessions), and affords students the opportunity to develop solutions to their problems (Cook & Kaffenberger, 2003). In addition, the approach assists youth in learning necessary problem-solving skills that can facilitate a sense of empowerment in that they discover they have the ability to resolve their own problems as well as offer support to peers' problem-solving efforts. This brief counseling approach is attractive to administrators, teachers, and professional school counselor for several reasons: (a) given counselors' limited time and the limitation of school resources, counselors can work with 6 to 10 students at one time rather than see each child individually for a 50-minute session; (b) counselors can observe youths' interactions with one another to assess and identify problems of concern that warrant a community mental health referral; (c) one counselor can conduct several groups per day within a week's time, a cost-saving service; (d) students learn social competence skills as they interact in a safe environment with adult supervision, allowing them to work through their difficulties with one another, and (e) the approach supports the mission of the schools and districts in that teaching students social competence skills affords teachers the time to support students' academic skills to be successful students. It is important to note that some current research on group counseling with children focuses on the use of this approach to improve students' academic emotional self-regulation and social skills (Campbell & Brigham, 2005).

Crisis Intervention

Our schools are no longer the safe haven they once were; at any moment, violence can disrupt the entire school day as well as cause harm to the intended victim(s), innocent bystanders, the school itself, and the larger community. The aftermath of violence can have long-lasting psychological, emotional, and social effects on students and their families, teachers, and administrators. Schools have responded to the growing violence instituting "zero"-tolerance policies as well as developing crisis intervention plans (Studer & Salter, 2010).

The American School Counselor Association (ASCA) states that "the professional school counselor's primary role is to facilitate planning, coordinate response to and advocate for the emotional needs of all persons affected by the crisis/critical incident by providing direct counseling service during and after the incident" (2007, para. 5). According to Studer and Salter (2010), the perception of school administrators, teachers, and other school personnel is that school counselors should take the lead role in managing school crises before, during, and after a crisis ensues. As a result, professional school counselors have risen to the occasion and perform many duties related to crisis prevention, intervention, and post crisis. For example, counselors keeping abreast of up-to-date research regarding common crisis situations can assist in the development, planning, and implementation of a comprehensive crisis intervention plan. Because a crisis event can result in the loss of fellow students, friends, and teachers, counselors in crisis intervention planning have been instrumental in critical incident debriefings and in developing bereavement groups,

Wraparound Counseling

Wraparound counseling is preventive and collaborative systemic programming linking out-of-school programs such as after-school and summer school programs, on-site medical services, and social work services (West-Olatunji et al., 2011). The services are comprehensive, concentrated, and individualized, with a goal of addressing children and youth with serious psychological, emotional, and behavioral problems. Counselors work closely in collaboration with families to ensure that they have access to necessary resources, serving as the link to community-based organization that can offer a variety of supportive resources such as individual and family counseling, medical services, and academic enrichment programs (e.g., tutoring, mentoring; West-Olatunji et al., 2011). Wraparound services are available for as long as it is determined necessary to the child, thus, counselors are required to conduct ongoing assessment.

Technology

Technology (e.g., Twitter, videoconferencing, blogs, websites) is fast becoming an important force in K-12 counseling. Web-based Internet, computers, and other technological devices afford counselors numerous opportunities to reach students. For instance, counselors can use email to address student and/or parental concerns, set up chat rooms to facilitate discussions with and among students, and videoconferencing can be used to conduct meetings and share strategies with colleagues from other school districts and states. Counselors are also using technology in delivering guidance curriculum, self-assessment, and career assessments. For example, students can explore their interests, abilities, and values using web-based assessment. The results can be made available to students immediately and discussed with their guidance counselor.

According to ASCA (2004), professional school counselors must make students aware of the benefits and drawbacks of technology, advocate for all students' equal access to technology, protect students' confidentiality, and use responsible means to protect students from harmful Internet information. Counselors who have the technical skill set use web-based technology as both a professional tool to communicate with fellow colleagues regarding helpful strategies and lessons learned as well as a method to facilitate communication with students and their families, such as emailing students and their families information about a number of parenting, career, and college resources. Carey and Dimmitt (2005) found that a wide divide exists in level of proficiency in counselors' use of web-based technology. To date, there are few studies examining K-12

Sidebar 24.1   Examples of Warning Signs of a Poorly Run Student Services Program

- Unestablished or unclear goals and objectives; goals/objectives that are not in alignment with the school's mission
- Limited funding resources and/or focusing resources on programming that does not support student development and academic achievement
- No established method of program assessment and evaluation, formative and/or summative
- Lack of person(s) in charge to coordinate and manage delivery of student services
- High staff turnover or insufficient staffing
- Inadequate staff training
- Low staff morale; unwillingness of staff to work together as a team
- Poor communication among and between staff and management
- No effort to communicate with or obtain buy-in from stakeholders (i.e., teaching faculty, students, parents, community members)

counselors' use of technology; however, given the growing usage of technology in schools, counselors are being encouraged to develop and/or enhance their skills to better serve students and schools (Carey & Dimmitt, 2005).

The Emerging Trends in Action

How does the leader of a school take this information and use it? Knowing the trends in student services and counseling is not enough. How does one create an excellent student services program at an elementary or secondary school? How does one know that the student services program is not sufficient and needs improvement? (See **Sidebar 24.1**.)

After determining that the services are inadequate, what does a leader do? What if you are totally new to a school as their leader; how do you start improving student services at the school? Let's look at the following case study for some ideas.

Case Vignette

Mrs. Johnson, the new principal at High Hopes Middle School, schedules a meeting with Mr. Smith, the student services coordinator, to discuss the current status of the student services programs. She requests the following information:

- Names of people involved in the planning, managing, delivery, and evaluation of student services programming
- Demonstration of how programs support student developmental needs
- Report on alignment of vision/mission of student services with mission of High Hopes Middle School
- Statement of current goals and objectives of each student program
- Names of categories and type of direct/indirect student services provided
- Report on current program funding sources and amounts
- Numbers of students served; numbers of faculty, staff, parents, community entities involved
- Numbers of the programs offered that are or can become self-sustaining programs
- Methods of program assessment and evaluation, both formative and summative
- Frequency of program assessment and evaluation, both formative and summative
- Methods used to make modifications, improvements, and adjustments to program services
- Methods used to disseminate information to stakeholders
- Frequency of advisory council meetings in which goals, objectives, and program outcomes are discussed

Mr. Smith calls a meeting with the student services staff to prepare for his meeting with Mrs. Johnson. He discusses the information the principal is requesting and proceeds to delegate staff responsibility in collecting the information.

(Continued)

(Continued)

Some of the staff express concern that much of the information requested will be difficult to obtain since there has not been a data management procedure in place. Mr. Smith acknowledges staff concerns, asks the staff to proceed with the data collection, and prepares for his meeting with Mrs. Johnson the next week.

In his meeting with Mrs. Johnson, Mr. Smith discusses the strengths and areas of challenge. Mrs. Johnson expresses appreciation to Mr. Smith for his candor in discussing the programming challenges. In her role as principal, she also invites him to conduct a program needs assessment, draft a proposal, and schedule a future meeting in which they would discuss options that could improve and support student services programming.

Sidebar 24.2 Steps Administrators Can Take When Encountering Student Services Programs That Are Run Poorly

- Schedule a meeting early in the academic year with the student services coordinator to determine the state of student services programming
- Schedule regularly occurring meetings in the future with student services staff
- Have a general understanding about student services programs to ensure an understanding of trends, the adequacy of programming, and what resources might be needed
- Have a willingness to obtain and provide resources (i.e., funding, training, consultation) to student services staff if needed
- Provide opportunities for follow-up, informal, meetings with student services staff as needed
- Actively participate in activities supporting student services programs, including advisory council meetings
- Clearly articulate obtainable goals and objectives and vision for student services
- Cultivate relationships with community stakeholders
- Provide a direct focus for student services on student development and achievement

Conclusion

Over the last decade a number of trends have emerged in the field of student services, including counseling. Certain trends impact mostly elementary students, others affect mostly secondary students, and some impact both groups of students. These trends include, among others, focusing on mental health within special education, utilizing technology to communicate and store student service data, collaborating in interdisciplinary teams, and allowing teachers and students more say in decision making and planning. In addition, counselors are increasingly playing a larger role in implementing antibullying prevention programs and crisis intervention, as well as other counseling student services.

Key Chapter Terms

Academic readiness: A child's abilities, behaviors, and individual characteristics relative to classroom/teacher expectations and requirements.

American School Counselor Association (ASCA): The professional organization for school counselors that supports school counselors' efforts to provide students with support in the areas of academic, career, and personal/social development.

Bloom's Taxonomy: A schematic categorization of terms referring to levels of thinking depth and complexity.

Bullying: An imbalance of power resulting in psychological, verbal, and physical attack or intimidation with the intention of causing harm and/or creating fear and distress in another person. The incidents tend to be repeated over time and can occur individually (one child bullying another) or can occur in a group (two or more children bullying another child).

Crisis intervention: A short-term method used to assist individuals, groups, and communities that have experienced an event or events resulting in psychological, emotional, physical, or behavioral harm. There are three levels of crisis intervention: (1) primary, such as assessing individuals' coping skills and availability of resources, creating a safe environment, providing crisis counseling services; (2) secondary, such as conducting a critical incident stress debriefing; and (3) tertiary, such as follow-up regarding concerns of safety and available community resources.

Education Trust: Founded in 1990, this organization's mission is the promotion of high academic achievement PreK-college through creating opportunities of learning and closing the achievement gap for all youth, with specific focus on children from marginalized communities.

English language learners: Students in the educational system who speak a primary language other than English and consequently must learn English as a second language.

National Standards for School Counseling Programs: Developed in 2003, the standards for developing a comprehensive, research and data-driven school counseling program with the goal of academic, personal/social, and career development of all students to ensure their academic success.

Self-control: The ability to control and manage one's emotions and behaviors in socially accepted ways.

Shared decision making: The process by which those in authority include those without authority in deliberations that lead to policy and other decisions. In effect, shared decision making empowers those who usually have no authority.

Small learning community: A small, interdisciplinary group of teachers and other school personnel who support the education of a defined group of students.

Social emotional learning (SEL): The ability to recognize and self-regulate one's emotions; the capacity to solve one's problems, make good decisions, demonstrate empathy for another's suffering, and establish both positive and healthy relationship with others.

Transforming School Counseling Initiative (TSCI): Designed to better train and prepare school counselors to serve as advocates and leaders in developing school counseling programs that enhance students' academic, personal/social and career development.

*Wraparound counseling***:** Preventive and collaborative systemic programming linking out-of-school programs such as after-school and summer school programs, on-site medical services, and social work services. The services are comprehensive, concentrated, and individualized, with the goal of addressing children and youth with serious psychological, emotional, and behavioral problems.

References

American School Counselor Association. (2004). *ASCA national standards for students.* Alexandria, VA: Author.

American School Counselor Association. (2007). *Position statement: Crisis/critical incident response in the schools.* Alexandria, VA: Author.

Beets, M. W., Flay, B. R., Vuchinich, S., Acock, A. C., Li, K., & Allred, C. (2008). School climate and teachers' beliefs and attitudes associated with implementation of the positive action program: A diffusion of innovations model. *Society for Prevention Research, 9,* 264–275.

Campbell, C. A., & Brigman, B. (2005). Closing the achievement gap: A structured approach to group counseling. *The Journal for Specialists in Group Work, 30*(1), 67–82.

Carey, J., & Dimmitt, C. (2005). The Web and school counseling. *Computers in the Schools, 21*(3–4), 69–79.

Collaboration for Academic, Social and Emotional Learning (CASEL). (2013). What is social and emotional learning? Retrieved from http://www.casel.org/social-and-emotional-learning/

Cook, J. B., & Kaffenberger, C. J. (2003). Solution shop: A solution-focused counseling and study skills program for middle school. *Professional School Counseling, 7*(2), 116–123.

Dinkes, R., Kemp, J., Baum, K., & Snyder, T. (2009). *Indicators of school crime and safety: 2009* (NCES 2010-2012). National Center for Education Statistics,

Institute of Education Sciences, U.S. Department of Education. Washington, DC.

Dollarhide, C. T. (2003). School counselors as program leaders: Applying leadership contexts to school counseling. *Professional School Counseling, 6,* 304–309.

Duchnowski, A. J., & Kutash, K. (2011). School reform and mental health services for students with emotional disturbances educated in urban schools. *Education and Treatment of Children, 34*(3), 323–346.

Durlak, J. A., Dymnicki, A. B., Weissberg, R. P., & Schellinger, K. B. (2011). The impact of enhancing students' social and emotional learning: A meta-analysis of school-based universal interventions. *Child Development, 82*(1), 405–432.

Education Trust. (2001). *Achievement in America: 2001.* Washington, DC: Author.

Farrington, D. P., & Ttofi, M. M. (2011). Effectiveness of school-based programs to reduce bullying: A systematic and meta-analytic review. *Journal of Experimental Criminology, 7*(1), 27–56.

Finkelhor, D., Hamby, S. L., Kracke, K., Ormrod, R. K., & Turner, H. A. (2009). Children's exposure to violence: A comprehensive national study. *Juvenile Justice Bulletin,* 1–12. Washington, DC: U.S. Department of Justice. Office of Juvenile Justice and Delinquency Prevention.

Fisher-Doiron, N., & Irvine, S. (2009). Going beyond the basics to reach all children. *Principal, 88*(5), 26.

Greenberg, M. T., Weissberg, R. P., O'Brien, M. U., Zins, J. E., Fredericks, L., Resnik, H., & Elias, M. J. (2003). Enhancing school-based prevention and youth development through coordinated social, emotional, and academic learning. *American Psychologist, 58*(6/7), 466–474.

Lane, K. L., Givner, C. C., & Pierson, M. R. (2004). Teacher expectations of student behavior: Social skills necessary for success in elementary school classrooms. *The Journal of Special Education, 38*(2), 104–110.

Leech, D., & Fulton, C. R. (2008). Faculty perceptions of shared decision making and the principal's leadership behaviors in secondary schools in a large urban district. *Education, 128*(4), 630–644.

Mongillo, E. A., Briggs-Gowan, M., Ford, J. D., & Carter, A. S. (2009). Impact of traumatic life events in a community sample of toddlers. *Journal of Abnormal Child Psychology, 37,* 455–468.

National Association of School Psychologists. (2003). *Bullying: Facts for schools and parents.* Retrieved from http://www.nasponline.org/resources/factsheets/bullying_fs.aspx

Newsome, W. S., Anderson-Butcher, D., Fink, J., Hall, L., & Huffer, J. (2008). The impact of school social work services on student absenteeism and risk factors related to school truancy. *School Social Work Journal, 32*(2), 21–38.

No Child Left Behind Act, 20 U.S.C. §§ 6301 *et seq.*

Oxley, D. (2005). Small learning communities: Extending and improving practice. *Principal Leadership, 6*(3), 44–48.

Paternite, C. E. (2005). School-based mental health programs and services: Overview and introduction to the special issue. *Journal of Abnormal Child Psychology, 33*(6), 657–663.

Schultz, L. (2005). *Bloom's taxonomy.* Norfolk, VA: Old Dominion University.

Steen, S., & Kaffenberger, C. J. (2007). Integrating academic interventions into small group counseling in elementary school. *Professional School Counseling, 10*(5), 516–519.

Studer, J. R., & Salter, S. E. (2010). *The role of the school counselor in crisis planning and intervention.* Retrieved from http://counselingoutfitters.com/vistas/vistas10/Article_92.pdf

Swearer, S. W., Espelage, D. L., Vaillancourt, T., & Hymel, S. (2010). What can be done about school bullying? Linking research to educational practice. *Educational Researcher, 39*(1), 38–47.

Terrion, J. L. (2006). Building social capital in vulnerable families success markers of a school-based intervention program. *Youth and Society, 38*(2), 155–176.

U.S. Department of Education. (n.d.). Information page on No Child Left Behind. Retrieved from http://www.ed.gov/nclb/landing.jhtml

Van Tassel-Baska, J. (2007). Leadership for the future in gifted education: Presidential address, NAGC 2006. *Gifted Child Quarterly, 51*(5), 5–10.

Wagner, M., Friend, M., Bursuck, W. D., Kutash, K., Duchnowski, A. J., Sumi, W. C., & Epstein, M. H. (2006). Educating students with emotional disturbances: A national perspective on school programs and services. *Journal of Emotional and Behavioral Disorders, 14*(1), 12–30.

Wagner, M., Newman, L., Cameto, R., Levine, P., & Garza, N. (2006). *An overview of findings form wave 2 of the national longitudinal transition study-2.* Menlo Park, CA: SRI International.

West-Olatunji, C., Frazier, K. N., & Kelley, E. (2011). Wraparound counseling: An ecosystemic approach to working with economically disadvantaged students in urban school settings. *Journal of Humanistic Counseling, 50,* 222–237.

Further Readings

Catalano, R. F., Haggerty, K. P., Oesterle, S., Fleming, C. B., & Hawkins, J. D. (2004). The importance of bonding to school for healthy development: Findings from the social development research group. *Journal of School Health, 74*(7), 252–261.

The article discusses a longitudinal study, conducted in two school settings, examining school connectedness. It is posited that when youth feel a sense of belongingness in school they are more academically and socially successful. Additionally, they are less likely to engage in violent/aggressive behavior, substance use, and early aged sexual activity.

Duchnowski, A. J., & Kutash, (2011). School reform and mental health services for students with emotional disturbances educated in urban schools. *Education and Treatment of Children, 34*(3), 323–346.

This article outlines some reform efforts in urban schools that have been successful with children who have emotional disturbances. The reforms presented helped the students to achieve higher scores in subjects such as mathematics.

Farrington, D. P., & Ttofi, M. M. (2011). Effectiveness of school-based programs to reduce bullying: A systematic and meta-analytic review. *Journal of Experimental Criminology, 7*(1), 27–56.

The article presents a systematic review and meta-analysis of the effectiveness of national and international programs designed to decrease victimization and bullying. The authors discuss the limitations of previous reviews and describe how their systematic review narrows the gaps in the current bullying prevention literature.

Lane, K. L., Givner, C. C., & Pierson, M. R. (2004). Teacher expectations of student behavior: Social skills necessary for success in elementary school classrooms. *Journal of Special Education, 38*(2), 104–110.

This study demonstrates how teachers find social skills to be important in primary and intermediate classrooms. The two skills emphasized by teachers as needed for success are self-control and cooperation, with assertion skills seen as not as essential.

PART IX

SCHOOL CLIMATE, CULTURE, AND HIGH PERFORMANCE

25

Establishing a Climate of Performance and Success

Matthew T. Proto

Stanford University

Kathleen M. Brown

University of North Carolina at Chapel Hill

Bradford J. Walston

Providence Grove High School, Randolph County Schools

*A*ccountability *measures and **relational trust;** data-driven decision making and increased staff morale; a climate of high expectations* and *an orderly environment:* These phrases often seem juxtaposed, but the validity of each phrase regarding its positive impact on **student achievement** is grounded in educational research literature. This research literature also asserts that the coordinated integration of each aspect of the phrases is crucial for increased student achievement. For example, a principal who establishes a culture of accountability, but does not simultaneously increase staff morale, most likely will not be as effective in raising student achievement as a principal who manages to simultaneously integrate both concepts into his or her leadership style. This chapter provides further evidence and potential leadership strategies for coordinating and integrating these concepts to

serve as the foundation for establishing a climate of performance and success.

Leadership in Turnaround Schools

While the coordination and integration of the three concepts noted earlier emerge across many school settings, their illustration is particularly prevalent in **turnaround schools**—chronically low-performing schools that are mandated to generate higher student achievement outcomes in very restricted time frames. Turnaround schools are placed under federal, state, or district mandate to increase student achievement within 1 to 3 years. Many **school turnaround** efforts have significantly increased student achievement while others have not generated positive results. This phenomenon has been the topic of several articles and research studies, many of which focus on effective strategies to significantly increase student achievement. For example, Calkins, Guenther, Belfiore, and Lash (2007) conducted an analysis of broader school **turnaround** issues and noted that transforming the culture and climate of turnaround schools in a way that ensured the consistency of high expectations for all students was essential. In a study of chronically low-performing schools in Chicago, Bryk, Sebring, Allensworth, Luppescu, and Easton (2010) found that schools that remained focused on the "core business" of instruction by using student achievement data to drive instruction saw increased student achievement results.

Regardless of the strategies employed in turnaround schools, school leadership remains one of the single most important aspects of all school turnaround efforts. For example, in a study focused on school-related influences on student achievement conducted over a 6-year time period that included more than 180 schools across nine states and 43 school districts, Louis et al. (2010) found that school leadership was second only to classroom instruction in terms of influence on student achievement. In a separate study, Herman et al. (2008) examined turnaround initiatives across six high schools, eight middle schools, and 21 elementary schools indicating that successful school turnarounds do not occur without a strong and effective school leader managing and leading the effort. Additionally, in a study conducted for the Cleveland Public School system, the consulting firm Education First (2011) found the principal to be one of the most important factors for the success or failure of school turnaround efforts. Given this research and the purpose of this guide, the focus on school leadership in turnaround school settings and the principal's ability to simultaneously enact seemingly juxtaposed concepts establishes the foundation for this chapter.

Establishing a Climate of Performance and Success in North Carolina Turnaround Schools

Rather than generating an endless list of research studies, the authors of this chapter chose to highlight some of the information gleaned from their study of 30 turnaround schools across the state of North Carolina. It is their belief that highlighting the individual school cases and the actions taken by principals within each school setting will generate broader discussion about the intricacies involved with establishing a climate of performance and success. To gain a better understanding of the context of the individual school cases, the next section discusses North Carolina's school turnaround initiative.

The North Carolina Turnaround School Initiative

During the 2005–2006 school year, the state of North Carolina began its school turnaround initiative with a restructuring of the state's consistently low-performing high schools. At that time, 66 high schools were labeled as turnaround schools based on 2 consecutive years with fewer than 60% of students meeting the performance requirement on end-of-grade or end-of-year tests, and/or 2 consecutive years with 4-year graduation rates below 60%. During the 2006–2007 school year, 37 middle schools were added to the statewide turnaround initiative, with 25 elementary schools being added in the 2007–2008 school year. The elementary schools were soon excluded from this specific turnaround initiative because of policy shifts and funding constraints; however, the state's identification of their turnaround status allows for their classification as turnaround schools for the purposes of this study.

Five years after the inception of the statewide turnaround initiative, of the original 128 identified, 19 schools improved to a performance composite score, or combined score on end-of-grade and/or end-of-course tests, between 60% and 69%; 19 schools improved to a composite between 70% and 79%; 11 schools improved to a composite between 80% and 89%, and 3 schools improved to a 90% or higher composite (North Carolina State Board of Education, September, 2011). Although there was significant improvement in student achievement in these turnaround schools across the state, the same level of improvement did not occur for all students. For example, in March 2011, 66 elementary schools reported a performance composite below 52%, 23 middle schools reported a performance composite below 53%, 22 high schools reported a performance composite below 58%, and 9 additional high schools reported a 4-year graduation rate below 60% (North Carolina Department of Public Instruction, 2011).

Context of the Authors' Research

At the time of the authors' study (Walston, Proto, & Brown, 2013), there were approximately 120 schools, including 20 elementary schools, in six school districts that were labeled as turnaround schools in North Carolina. As the authors noted,

> Many of these schools were labeled as such because they remained under sanctions for failing to meet Adequate Yearly Progress (AYP) for three consecutive years. The remaining schools were labeled as being "in need of turnaround" because they did not meet state accountability and assessment measures as defined by North Carolina's ABC model, a statewide student achievement accountability system that measures change in student performance from one year to another. (p. 24)

In light of these results, the North Carolina Department of Public Instruction (NCDPI) allocated more resources to turning around the schools (SERVE Center, Friday Institute, and Carolina Institute for Public Policy, 2010). Similar to many other statewide school systems, the results were mixed: Some schools improved their end-of-grade test scores significantly while others did not. The North Carolina Board of Education sought to understand how the state's reform efforts would impact the school and commissioned a research team to study the school turnaround program. As Walston et al. report,

> Thompson, Brown, Townsend, Henry, and Fortner (2011) evaluated the effectiveness of the state funded District School Transformation Unit (DST): a unit established in 2007 by NCDPI to assist with the implementation of a more comprehensive and rigorous turnaround process at the school level. They found that many of the state's initiatives generated positive results, but not all of the turnaround schools experienced the same level of success. In fact, about a third of the schools studied significantly increased student achievement, a third experienced moderate growth, and another third of the schools experienced little to no growth (with a few schools showing a decline in end-of-grade assessments). (p. 24)

One of the constant themes that emerged from studying the schools that significantly increased student achievement was the importance of establishing a climate of performance and success.

Establishing a Climate of Performance and Success Across 30 Turnaround Schools

The findings of the Thompson, Brown, Townsend, Henry, and Fortner (2011) study indicated that successful school leaders simultaneously asserted strong accountability pressures as they cultivated relationships of trust. This combination of accountability pressures and strengthened professional ties brought teachers and staff behind the leadership's goals, vision, standards, and policies, and the engagement of teachers in planning and problem solving generated commitment to new goals and standards for student behavior and learning. Also, as Thompson et al. reported: "Similarly, strong and consistently enforced discipline policies together with energetic efforts to cultivate caring relationships with students combined to help schools create safer and more orderly environments" (p. viii). Assertive accountability, strengthened relationships, and shared decision making generated a schoolwide commitment to new goals and standards. This new commitment established the foundation for a more orderly environment and steps toward improved teaching and learning.

The patterns for establishing a climate of performance and success in the larger Thompson et al. (2011) study were also evident in the elementary schools. Principals in the improved schools found creative ways to simultaneously establish a climate of high expectations for all students while ensuring a more orderly and caring environment; to implement accountability measures while generating relational trust; and to adhere to data-driven decision making while increasing staff morale.

High Expectations and a More Orderly and Caring Environment

Discipline problems were just as severe at the elementary schools as in the high schools and middle schools. Constant administrator turnover contributed to a chaotic climate while the inconsistent treatment of students led to serious discipline issues. To address these issues, successful new principals worked together with teachers and staff to generate a school culture that prided itself on the orderly environment and high expectations for student behavior.

Accountability Measures and Relational Trust

As Thompson et al. noted, "Successful new principals were also credited with reversing the culture of failure that had prevailed in their schools, a culture that they found unacceptable and that they quickly challenged" (p. 69). In the schools that made progress, teachers welcomed the higher standards and worked hard to implement them in the classroom, and as a result, morale was enhanced. Internal and external staffing changes were made to build teacher teams that could and would implement a more rigorous curriculum and raise student expectations. These changes led to increased staff morale as principals continuously provided support for teachers who altered their instructional practices and showed increases in student achievement. With increased staff morale and a true sense of team, the principal and teachers worked to establish meaningful relationships with parents. In many cases, if the parents could not go to the school, the administrators and teachers would go to them.

*Data-Driven Decision Making and
Increased Staff Morale*

In several of the most improved elementary schools, as Thompson et al. (2011) noted, each grade level's academic team met and reviewed data about each classroom and each student, then teachers tailored instruction based on identified areas of weakness (**Sidebar 25.1**). They began using formative assessments, and students began receiving consistent support. Vertical and horizontal planning teams became part of teachers' routines and weekly schedules. Staff meetings were more focused on data and instructional strategies. Some schools began offering rewards to students for achievement growth (e.g., awarding field trips based on quarterly benchmark scores). Other schools made structural changes to the schedule, such as extending the reading block to 90 minutes, or extending the school day. Schools began focusing interventions on student weaknesses as shown by the data, which teachers and principals referred to as "ICUs," in reference to hospital intensive care units. Schools implemented a model known as professional learning communities (PLCs), which built collaborative relationships among grade-level teams and supported new curriculum initiatives (e.g., a new math program that includes continual review of previously covered content embedded into assignments and lessons—daily). All related personnel focused on data-driven instruction and were committed to collaborative planning.

Sidebar 25.1   Challenges and Conditions at School

Take a moment to reflect on the challenges and conditions of your school. Which of the identified factors are contributing to low performance exist at your school?

Yes	No	
		Do challenging economic and demographic conditions, whether newly developed or chronic, exist at your school?
		Are there serious and widespread discipline problems?
		Do you perceive there to be low academic demands and expectations among teachers and previous administrators?
		Is there high principal and teacher turnover?
		Is there a perception of a negative school identity in the minds of teachers, students, and the surrounding community?
		Is there a lack of parent involvement and community support?
		Do all teachers use student achievement data collection and analysis to drive differentiated instructional practices?

If you answered "yes" to any of the above questions, we encourage you to identify how the principals in the chapter's case studies either did or did not address the issues. Furthermore, if you answered "yes" to more than one question, please be aware that your school is showing signs of low performance that should be addressed.

One High-Growth School Versus One Low-Growth School

Nearly all of the schools included in both the Thompson et al. (2011) and the Walston et al. (2013) studies faced

> similar internal and external challenges. These challenges were similar to those identified by Barbour, Clifford, Corrigan-Halpern, Garcia, Maday-Karageorge, Meyer, Townsend, and Stewart (2010) who found that principals in turnaround schools face challenges associated with students performing below grade level, weak partnerships with families, parents and the community, low faculty morale, and poor instructional focus. (Walston et al., 2013, p. 25)

The challenges also were aligned with those identified in a study of 19 turnaround elementary and middle schools in the state of Virginia conducted by Duke, Tucker, Salmonowicz, and Levy (2007). With only a few exceptions related to unique circumstances, the factors contributing to low performance identified by the individuals interviewed in this study included the following (Walston et al., 2013, p. 26):

- Challenging economic and demographic conditions, whether newly developed or chronic
- Serious and widespread discipline problems
- Low academic demands and expectations among teachers and previous administrators
- High principal and teacher turnover
- A negative school identity in the minds of teachers, students, and the surrounding community
- Lack of parent involvement and community support
- Lack of student achievement data collection and analysis to drive differentiated instructional practices

Because these challenges were similar across schools, the authors now provide more detailed information on two elementary schools: one that increased its student achievement and one that did not. In facing similar circumstances, the principal of Franklin Elementary School managed to establish a climate of success and performance by coordinating and integrating accountability measures and relational trust, data-driven decision making and a culture of relational trust, and a climate of high expectations with a more orderly and caring environment. Conversely, the principal of Smith Elementary School was unsuccessful in her attempt to establish the same type of

culture. The following comparison of the two schools—whose names in this chapter have been changed to pseudonyms—can serve both as a case study and as insight into establishing a climate of success and performance.

*Franklin Elementary School:
A High-Growth School*

Franklin Elementary School is located in an urban school district in the state of North Carolina. During the 2009–2010 academic year, it served a total of 260 students, 95% of whom qualified for free and reduced lunch and 98% of whom were African American and Hispanic (Thompson et al., 2011).

Ten years prior to the studies, Franklin Elementary School was one of the top 25 performing elementary schools in North Carolina. After the departure of the principal the school's student achievement dropped significantly, such that Franklin became one of the lowest-performing schools in the state. During the time period between the high rate of success of the former principal and the high growth led by the current principal, there were high teacher and leadership turnover rates. Additionally, the student demographics changed such that a higher Hispanic and lower White student grouping emerged (e.g., 85% African American, 14% Hispanic, and 1% White). Franklin Elementary School achieved significant growth. In 3 years it doubled its performance composite score, rising from approximately 26% proficiency to 52% proficiency. In fact, Franklin Elementary is labeled as an "opt-out option" school by the school district, meaning that students from other schools within the district may "opt out" of their school and request assignment at Franklin Elementary School.

The principal at Franklin Elementary School took the following steps to create a climate of performance and success. He did so in a way that was strategic and coordinated through the integration of each piece into the culture and climate of the school.

High Expectations and a More Orderly, Caring Environment: The principal believed that if he did not have high expectations and model those expectations for his staff, that they would not require high levels of performance from their students.

He modeled for his teachers his expectations. He meets with his curriculum team and with every teacher weekly, and holds PLC meetings with every grade level. The principal used rewards to celebrate the accomplishments of students when they met expectations. After every benchmark test, students who met their goals went on field trips. According to the principal,

> A lot of these kids really don't leave the area. And so I want to give them some fun activities to keep them motivated to continue to do well. Our kids would not do as well without the activities. So not only do we do things for our kids that are overachievers, but we also do things for our kids that are making growth because not only do I talk about proficiency growth; I also talk about just growth within the skill scores. And so we celebrate all of those things.

One of the rewards systems the principal implemented at the school was Positive Behavioral Interventions and Supports (PBIS). This allowed teachers to build positive and trusting relationships with students while accentuating their positive behaviors, rather than forcefully reprimanding negative behaviors. In an effort to address discipline issues, the principal created a consistent approach for students and teachers. He mandated the implementation of a positive approach to discipline and began by serving as the primary contact for all disciplinary cases. A teacher at Franklin said,

> The principal takes the time to try to figure out why the student is acting in the way that they're acting and he builds relationships with parents. What he tries to do is come up with some sort of way in which, especially kids with major discipline problems, we can coexist and you still do what you need to do to be successful academically, socially, and in every other way. Whereas you might be at another school and as soon as you do something, you're gone. He builds those types of relationships.

Once teachers began to buy into the new program and structure, he transferred leadership of the program to them, indicating that he trusted their professional judgment.

Prior to the principal's arrival, the teachers were not using student achievement data to inform their instructional practices. So, the principal at Franklin Elementary School developed an integrated and coordinated data-based instructional structure, including the implementation of PLCs, a student achievement data board, internal professional development, and an intervention program centering instructional practice

on the collection and analysis of student achievement data. According to the principal,

> When I got here, things were kind of very scattered all over the place. A didn't connect to B. B didn't connect to C. And so what we had to do is go back and really understand how all of these pieces connect together so that we could create the kind of school we needed to create. So, we began this process of looking at all our processes in the building. One of the major things that this school wasn't really introduced to is how to look at your data and make decisions about it.

To respond to this need, the principal created an instructional structure centered on the collection and analysis of student achievement data. According to an instructional coach,

> The teachers now meet in PLCs, take the data and break it down to exactly what concepts the students fall short on. They identify the students' needs and teach to those needs. Then, (if students need more assistance) group them and then indicate it to their peers (grade-level teachers and interventionists) the specific skills the kids need to work on.

The principal also inculcated data into the structure of the school by creating a student achievement data board in the teacher's lounge, located next to the main office, that identifies every student based on his or her most recent assessment data. According to the principal,

> The data board is visual. It changes with every test. And what we actually do is we go through a process of the teachers, parents, and students coming in to this office to see where they are. They understand if they're far below proficient. They understand where their skill scores are and where they need help.

The principal understood that simply publicizing student achievement data was not enough to drive change and incorporate data into daily instructional practices. So, he developed an intervention program at each grade level to help remediate students who needed additional instructional support. According to the principal,

> A few years back the district decided that we needed to raise the classroom size. So when I raised my classroom size, I found out that as I met the ratios, I had extra teachers that really didn't have a class. So, instead of us putting these teachers back in the classroom and lowering the class size by maybe three or four students, I made the decision to let these teachers be a resource to each grade level to service those kids that were not quite getting it in class. So what was happening is the class size would be reduced by virtue of the students being pulled

out. Students were then getting that individual attention that the classroom teacher just couldn't provide. . . . And those groups were constantly rotating through in the areas of literacy, in the areas of math, and particularly in fifth grade, for science. So what we do, we do follow the district's literacy framework and doing all those things, but what we do is include intervention and remediation based on student achievement data into our schedule.

Accountability Measures and Relational Trust: The principal maintained that, to establish high expectations at the school, he had to let his staff know that he trusted them and saw them as professionals and instructional leaders in their classrooms. According to the principal,

> But every day how you talk to your kids, how you walk your kids into the cafeteria, how you conduct your parent conferences, and those things that you do outside of me, I need to trust you. And I had to start out saying, I trust you, as opposed to saying, you're going to have to prove this to me. So there's a different connotation of how you do it. You say, I trust that you're going to do this, as opposed to not believing them initially.

At the same time, the principal also identified a few teachers as low performers who were not willing to alter their instructional practices to align with his vision for the school. So, he worked with the school district to transfer those teachers and based his teacher hiring and allocation strategies on the needs of the students. According to the principal,

> There were some teachers here who, in my opinion, shouldn't have been here. And through the course of my third year as principal, we've just made some strategic changes in how we do things in terms of how we hire folks and even where folks are actually placed in their teaching capacities within the building.

In addition to transferring a few teachers, he recognized that many of his students began school without an inherent trust in their teachers. He found that many of the students were coming from difficult situations at home and, in his opinion, needed to feel safe and welcome as soon as they enrolled at the school. So, the principal placed the most nurturing teachers in the K-2 grade levels and the stricter teachers in grade levels 3 to 5. Furthermore, the principal identified individual content and instructional strengths and aligned each teacher's strengths with his intervention program. For example, according to the principal,

> For fifth grade, we have one teacher that specializes in literacy, one teacher that specializes in science, and one teacher that specializes in math. So, they each work with the kids grouped according to the content and according to what the data's showing during the intervention segment of the afternoon schedule.

This reallocation strategy appeared to indicate to teachers that the principal was trying to place teachers in a position to succeed. Because the school experienced success with the strategy, it seemed that this contributed to establishing a professional relationship based on relational trust.

Smith Elementary School: A Low-Growth School

Smith Elementary School is located in an urban school district in the state of North Carolina. In the 2009–2010 academic year, the school served a total of 441 students, a decrease of approximately 30 students from the 2007–2008 academic year. Although the number of students enrolled at the school declined during this time period, the percentage of African American and Hispanic increased from 70% to 76%. Additionally, the number of students who qualified for free and reduced lunch remained constant at 96%.

Twenty years ago, Smith Elementary was recognized as one of the top-performing schools in North Carolina. The school served a majority White and upper-middle class student population and had a consistent teaching staff. As the demographics of the community shifted to a predominantly minority and low-income population, teacher and administrator turnover significantly increased. This shift in demographics, high teacher and administrator turnover rates, and other changes appear to have contributed to a significant decline in the school's performance, such that it is currently one of the lowest-performing schools in North Carolina. Over the 3 years prior to the studies, the school's performance composite decreased from approximately 55% proficiency in both reading and math to nearly 54% proficiency in both subjects.

The principal at Smith Elementary School attempted to implement many of the same changes as the principal at Franklin Elementary School; however, she was not as successful. It seemed that her attempts did not integrate the concepts together and that they generated little to no change in the culture and climate of the school.

High Expectations and a More Orderly and Caring Environment: Unlike the principal at Franklin Elementary School, the principal at Smith Elementary indicated that the teachers had been conditioned to fail. She stated that many of her teachers exhibited deficit thinking with regard to individual student achievement. For example, the principal commented,

> They've been stressed with some behavior issues or some parent issues that continue to arise day in and day out or behaviors that they're not able to teach because they're dealing with student issues or our students do not read well enough to be in this classroom. . . . So, they're overwhelmed. I think that it's difficult for teachers to differentiate when you have a student that is in the 90th percentile and a student that's in the 5th percentile in the same classroom on a regular basis.

In addition to this feeling of being positioned to fail, teachers spoke about discipline issues that continued to be evident across all grade levels at Smith Elementary School. The school district mandated the implementation of PBIS at Smith Elementary School and allocated a behavior coach to be present at the school. According to the principal, "I think PBIS has helped our behavior and it's more of a team approach instead of just me handling every discipline problem that happens in the school." While the principal indicated a switch to a team approach, discipline continued to remain an impediment to increased student achievement across multiple grade levels. Essentially, only a few grade levels decided to implement the PBIS model with fidelity, which has led to inconsistency regarding discipline within the school. Some positive change was made, but the coordination and integration of high expectations with an orderly environment is not apparent at Smith Elementary School.

Data-Driven Decision Making and Increased Staff Morale: Similar to the principal at Franklin Elementary School, the principal at Smith Elementary required the implementation of PLCs, developed an intervention and enrichment system based on student achievement data, modified the schedule to enable more efficient planning and instructional periods, and increased the number of assessments given to students. According to the principal, the changes in scheduling also allowed students to get individual assistance during times when they would not miss class. While it appears that similar changes were put in place, unlike the teachers at Franklin Elementary who fully bought into the change, several teachers at Smith Elementary changed their

instructional strategies while others have not. For example, one teacher commented,

> It's not just a test at the end of the quarter or even the end of year or whatever. Basically, every couple of weeks you're assessing a particular objective and seeing who's got it. If they've got it, then great, you move on with those kids but if they haven't, I keep those on a little list and during IE time, intervention enrichment time, we go back to those children, work on those things.

However, another teacher stated,

> I think when they are given a textbook, some of our staff uses that textbook and only that textbook and doesn't make use of other available resources that might supplement, that might challenge, that might move those students to being able to think in higher order pathways. Sometimes I feel like maybe some of the staff doesn't know the curriculum as well as they should and know exactly what they should be teaching to focus on that year's growth for those students.

An additional teacher commented,

> I think there's a very strong core of teachers here that are very, very good teachers. And then I think on, at least, almost every grade level you have some teachers that are always going to be negative that will only teach one way and won't hear anything different. And will always be a hindrance to the school making the amount of change I think we need to be able to undergo.

It is evident that several teachers' unwillingness to change their instructional practices has limited the potential for heightened student achievement at Smith Elementary School. This unwillingness to change may have been connected to staff morale issues at the school. The feeling of helplessness coupled with negligible student achievement gains seemed to have decreased, rather than increase staff morale.

Accountability Measures and Relational Trust: It was challenging for the principal to encourage the removal of teachers at Smith Elementary School because the school district implemented a no teacher transfer policy. According to the principal, "you could talk to some of my teachers that want out but really they can't get out without losing their job because they have to have a place to go." Regardless of the no teacher transfer policy, the principal at Smith Elementary School still reallocated individual teachers across grade levels. According to the principal,

"I have moved people to different grade levels throughout the building. Sometimes they've gone kicking and screaming but then (eventually) they love it." Although the teachers at Smith Elementary School appeared to have adapted to the principal's reallocation strategy, it is evident that issues remain regarding relational trust as it relates to increased student achievement. For example, the principal did not appear to be focusing on aligning curriculum and instruction to generate higher performance composite results. According to the principal,

I'm not one that feels the need to teach the test. I feel like that is not going to get anybody where they're going. I think the kids need to be very mindful of what's coming. I don't want them to be blown away with the length or blown away with the difficulty level. So I want them to feel at ease. That's what I explain to the teachers that if you've given them the thinking strategies and the strategies that we've talked about for reading and math, let them do the best they can do. They will do fine. But if it's just skill and drill, skill and drill, I don't know that that's going to gain them what they need.

Furthermore, the principal has created a lesson plan structure that appears to have overwhelmed teachers and taken time from their instructional and planning time. According to the principal,

I check teachers' lesson plans on a weekly basis. They turn the plans in and I give them feedback and write notes to them. . . . Although, teachers did say "I'm spending 30 or 40 hours on these plans." All I could say was if you're going to have a lesson, planning is instrumental and you're going to plan a 30minute lesson, it's going to take you two hours to plan that 30 minute lesson. They didn't like that. So, they've been overwhelmed with turning in lesson plans and having them evaluated.

Although this lesson plan structure may appear to provide additional support for teachers, it is clear that many teachers believe the principal does not trust them to make professional decisions. By checking each lesson plan, the principal has not only taken away from instructional time, but also contributed to the decreased staff morale at the school. The teachers at Smith Elementary appeared to perceive this decision as a form of micromanagement rather than support. (See **Sidebar 25.2**.)

Sidebar 25.2   How Do Your Actions Compare?

How Do Your Actions Compare?

Where do your actions fall on the spectrum? Are your actions more aligned to the actions of the principal at the high-growth school or are they more aligned to the actions of the principal at the low-growth school? In the following chart, reflect on your leadership practices and provide examples as evidence of your implementing the leadership actions identified in the high-growth schools.

Leadership Actions	Your Current Practices and Examples
Setting high expectations for student achievement and discipline through consistent actions that emerge in the curriculum and discipline.	
Establishing consistent and well-enforced discipline policies.	
Establishing a "we can do this" attitude across all teachers and staff by indicating that you believe in their work and professionalism.	
Strategically assigning students to curriculum pathways matching their developing skills and the strongest teachers to end-of-course curricula.	
Building individual relationships that celebrate achievement and generate open feedback cycles.	
Actively holding teachers accountable for improving student achievement.	

Conclusion

The comparison of the principals' actions at Franklin Elementary School and Smith Elementary School serves as an illustration of successful and unsuccessful attempts of two principals trying to establish a climate of performance and success. **Table 25.1** provides a summary overview of the differences between the two principals' strategies.

Table 25.1 serves as a roadmap for principals attempting to establish a climate of performance and success at their school. While the findings indicate some of the intricacies involved in establishing a climate of performance and success, the results are not meant to be prescriptive or all-encompassing.

Table 25.1 should not be viewed as a formula for success, but instead as a tool to identify future successes and potential pitfalls.

Key Points to Consider

The integration of three themes appears to help principals establish a climate of performance and success at their school. The three themes are:

1. Coordinating and integrating accountability measures and relational trust

2. Implementing data-driven decision making and a culture of relational trust

3. Establishing a climate of high expectations with a more orderly and caring environment

Characteristics of a Climate of Performance and Success	Franklin Elementary School (High-Growth School)	Smith Elementary School (Low-Growth School)
High expectations and a more orderly and caring environment	Setting a high bar for student achievement and discipline through consistent actions that emerge in the curriculum and discipline. This, along with a tough, well-enforced discipline policy and strengthened adult-student relationships, produced an orderly environment for learning.	Indicating that individuals are not able to achieve and act in the same manner in relation to achievement and discipline. Without an assertive principal and teacher buy-in, teachers lack incentives and confidence to enforce discipline.
Data-driven decision making and increased staff morale	Establishing a "we can do this" attitude across all teachers and staff by indicating that the principal believes in their work and professionalism. Leveraging this attitude to implement the strategic assignment of students to match their areas of need with the strongest teachers in that curricular area.	Sending implicit and direct messages to students and teachers indicating that they remain in a culture of failure. This contributes to student and teacher assignments that are less strategic.
Accountability Measures and Relational Trust	Building individual relationships that celebrate achievement and generate open feedback cycles. This is coupled with a principal who actively holds teachers accountable for improving student achievement and builds positive relationships with teachers.	Making decisions that often lead to unintended consequences due to a lack of inclusion. This is illustrated through ineffective leadership, ranging from unilateral demands for improved achievement without relationship building, to nurturing relationships without accountability.

Table 25.1 A Summary Overview of the Principals' Actions Intended to Establish a Climate of Performance and Success

These three themes are fairly consistent across various types of schools. However, every principal faces a unique set of challenges relative to his or her school context. Strictly adhering to the research presented in this chapter without understanding the context and needs of the individual school may not bring about the intended result. Thus, every principal must rely on the confluence of best practices and professional judgment to implement a climate of performance and success. They must understand their school context, including the needs of their student populations, before attempting to enact these themes.

Key Chapter Terms

Relational trust: The concept that principals and teachers maintain professional relationships based on trust and open feedback cycles rather than fear.

School turnaround: A dramatic and comprehensive intervention in a low-performing school that: (a) produces significant gains in achievement within 2 years; and (b) readies the school for the longer process of transformation into a high-performance organization.

Student achievement: Represented by an individual numeric student performance indicator, measured by end-of-grade or end-of-course standardized test scores, intended to measure varying levels of comprehension within a subject area.

Turnaround: The process by which an organization experiencing decline in performance or low performance increases its performance.

Turnaround school: A school that has received state-mandated assistance and has been designated by the State Board as low performing for at least 2 of 3 consecutive years.

References

Barbour, C., Clifford, M., Corrigan-Halpern, P., Garcia, P., Maday-Karageorge, T., Meyer, C., . . . Stewart, J. (2010). *What experience from the field tells us about principalship and turnaround.* American Institutes for Research. Retrieved from http://www.learningpt.org/pdfs/leadership_turnaround_schools.pdf

Bryk, A. S., Sebring, P. B., Allensworth, E., Luppescu, S., & Easton, J. Q. (2010) *Organizing schools for improvement: Lessons from Chicago.* Chicago, IL: The University of Chicago Press.

Calkins, A., Guenther, W., Belfiore, G., & Lash, D. (2007). *The turnaround challenge: Why America's best opportunity to improve student achievement lies in our worst-performing schools.* Boston, MA: Mass Insight. Retrieved from http://www.massinsight.org/DownloadHandler.ashx?fn=~/resourcefiles/TheTurnaroundChallenge_MainReport.pdf

Duke, D. L., Tucker, P. D., Salmonowicz, M. J., & Levy, M. K. (2007). How comparable are the perceived challenges facing principals of low-performing schools? *International Studies in Educational Administration, 35*(1), 3–21.

Education First. (2011). *Developing a school turnaround strategy to help all students achieve.* Retrieved from http://www.educationfirstconsulting.com/files/Final%20Turnaround%20Strategy%20Report%20March%202011%20-%20Web%20Version.pdf

Herman, R., Dawson, P., Dee, T., Greene, J., Maynard, R., & Redding, S. (2008). *Turning around chronically low performing schools.* Washington, DC: U.S. Department of Education Institute for Education Sciences.

Louis, K. S., Leithwood, K., Wahlstrom, K. L., Anderson, S. E., Michlin, M., Mascall, B., . . . Moore, S. (2010). *Learning from leadership: Investigating the links to improved student learning.* New York, NY: The Wallace Foundation.

North Carolina Department of Public Instruction. (2011). *Many Voices, One Goal conference.* March, 2011. Retrieved from http://www.ncpublicschools.org/schooltransformation

North Carolina State Board of Education. (2011). *Where have we been and where should we go?* September, 2011. Retrieved from http://www.dpi.state.nc.us/docs/stateboard/ . . . /201109-turnaround-final.ppt

SERVE Center, Friday Institute, and Carolina Institute for Public Policy. (2010). *Race to the Top proposal* (Proposal submitted to the U.S. Department of Education). University of North Carolina at Greensboro, SERVE Center.

Thompson, C. L., Brown, K. M., Townsend, L. W., Henry, G. T., & Fortner, C. K. (2011). *Turning around North Carolina's lowest achieving schools (2006–2010).* Chapel Hill, NC: Consortium for Educational Research and Evaluation—North Carolina.

Walston, B., Proto, B., & Brown, K. (2013). Turning around North Carolina elementary schools: Lessons learned from the process of improvement. *Journal of Education Policy, Planning and Administration, 2*(2), 19–37. Retrieved from http://www.jeppa.org

Further Readings

Duke, D. L. (2010). *Differentiated principalship: Facing the challenges of practice.* Thousand Oaks, CA: Sage.

Duke argues for a type of leadership whereby a principal identifies the needs of a specific school setting and bases his or her actions and strategies on those needs. In essence, Duke advocates for school leaders to identify the larger context of the situation in which he or she is placed before determining the proper course of action.

Institute of Education Sciences—IES. (2008). *IES practice guide: Turning around chronically low performing schools* (What Works Clearinghouse, NCEE 2008-4020). Retrieved from http://ies.ed.gov/ncee/wwc/practiceguide.aspx?sid=7

This guide indicates strategies and practices to help improve student achievement in low-performing schools.

Murphy, J., & Meyers, C. V. (2008). *Turning around failing schools.* Thousand Oaks, CA: Sage.

Murphy and Meyers applied much of the general organizational literature to turning around chronically low performing schools.

Papa, R., & English, F. (2011). *Turnaround principals for underperforming schools.* Plymouth, England: Rowman & Littlefield.

Papa and English review the data collected for the What Works Clearinghouse Turning Around Chronically Low-Performing Schools Practice Guide (Institute of Education Sciences, 2008) and identify specific leadership behaviors that appear to make a significant positive impact on student achievement in turnaround school settings.

Public Impact. (2007). *School turnarounds: A review of the cross-sector evidence on dramatic organizational improvement.* Lincoln, IL: Center on Innovation and Improvement. Retrieved on from http://www.centerii.org/survey/downloads/Turnarounds-Color.pdf

Public Impact conducted a review of cross-sectional literature regarding organizational decline and turnaround initiatives and applied the relevant data to chronically low-performing schools.

Waters, J. T., Marzano, R. J., & McNulty, B. A. (2003). *Balanced leadership: What 30 years of research tells us about the effect of leadership on student achievement.* Aurora, CO: Mid-continent Research for Education and Learning.

Waters, Marzano, and McNulty reviewed over 30 years of research on the effect leadership has on student achievement and found that school leadership is one of the major determinants in student achievement.

26

SECRETS OF CREATING POSITIVE WORK CULTURES

The Work Lives of Teachers

FRANK DAVIDSON

Casa Grande Elementary School District, Arizona

The words that teachers use to describe their schools reveal a great deal about the cultures in which they work. Thankfully, some describe their workplaces as supportive, friendly, rewarding, and caring places, where both the school's principal and colleagues set a tone that is mutually supportive and that supports excellence, creativity, and innovation. Unfortunately, some teachers describe their work settings as unpleasant, hostile, oppressive, and uncaring, where neither leader nor colleagues are able to reorient the school's **culture** in a more positive direction. Problems and challenges in the latter setting have the feel of intractability, as if the everyday problems of schools are insurmountable. In contrast, in healthier settings the collective outlook and sense of collective efficacy are more robust and dynamic, and the everyday problems of schools are viewed with a "can-do" spirit of invention and **entrepreneurship**. Not only is the first of these settings a more pleasant place in which to work, but it undoubtedly is a setting more conducive to the healthy growth and development of young people. Barbara Benham Tye (2000) notes that "happy teachers who look forward to going to work each day are likely to have happy students

who enjoy being with those teachers and learning from them" (p. 125).

There are no simple recipes or quick fixes that can bring about an overnight transformation of an ailing school into a school that is an optimally healthy place for students and teachers. A wide variety of factors come together to shape the school as workplace. Despite decades of research on the culture of schools, the fact remains that schools are peopled by, after all, people, and the development of people is what schools are all about. Consequently, each school has a temperament, character, and culture that is unique and idiosyncratic. Practitioners and researchers agree that the leader's influence is critical in establishing a work culture that benefits both teacher and student. While acknowledging the uniqueness of schools and the absence of an easy path to creating a highly effective workplace, there are some high-yield practices that can be employed by leaders that have a greater likelihood of contributing to a **positive work culture**.

Teacher beliefs and attitudes are central to school quality. It is widely accepted that such attitudes and beliefs are shaped by both the workplace and by school leaders. Despite increasing interest during the first decade of the 2000s in creating the conditions for expanded collaboration on the part of teachers in planning focused on curriculum and instruction, norms for teacher interaction in schools have traditionally emphasized autonomy. Judith Warren Little (1990) notes that "school-teaching has endured largely as an assemblage of entrepreneurial individuals whose autonomy is grounded in norms of privacy and noninterference and is sustained by the very organization of teaching work" (p. 537).

Despite the history of teaching as work that is independent and autonomous, both researchers and practitioners would agree that students experience greater success in schools where teachers work together in meaningful ways, sharing the responsibility for planning, carrying out, and assessing the outcomes of instruction. One would presume that the same conclusion would be true in any field or endeavor, as it stands to reason that coworkers who share ideas, burdens, and responsibility would be more effective and more efficient, whether their end product is a car, a building, an idea, or a cure. Creating school workplaces where collaboration is an expected norm must, of necessity, take into account the historical and sociological reality of schools and the organizational supports needed to foster a collegial and collaborative environment.

As noted earlier, the work culture found in school settings varies significantly from school to school. A school's professional culture may reflect norms of persistence in the face of challenges, hard work to achieve desired ends, and honest performance appraisals. At the other extreme, the culture may reflect norms of stagnation, inconsistent work output, and unspoken yet acknowledged prohibitions against unwanted incursions into the autonomous world of the classroom. Attributes including the knowledge, values, and skills of the school leader can serve as model, catalyst, and touchstone for others in the organization and can shape and influence the culture as experienced by both students and staff.

What Is Culture?

Kent D. Peterson (1999) offers the view that culture is "the underground stream of norms, values, beliefs, traditions, and rituals that builds up over time as people work together, solve problems, and confront challenges. This set of informal expectations and values shapes how people think, feel, and act in schools" (p. 17). Although retirement and other forms of attrition will change the mixture of personnel in a given workplace, the norms, beliefs, traditions, and assumptions, both constructive and unconstructive, may endure over time. The influence of **formal** and **informal leaders** on the development of norms, beliefs, traditions, and assumptions can be quite substantial. The stories that veteran workers tell of leaders' actions contain evidence of such influence. These stories have a power and magic that appears to be most influential in schools with long histories and less so in schools that have been in existence for a short time. Yet even newer schools begin developing their stories early on, and the impact of these stories can be found in the norms, assumptions, and attitudes of school staff. Edgar H. Schein (1992) describes the role of the leader in shaping organizational culture, contending that even after some time, the assumptions and mental models of those within organizations can trace such assumptions to the beliefs and values of founders and early leaders (see **Figure 26.1**). He defines organizational culture as

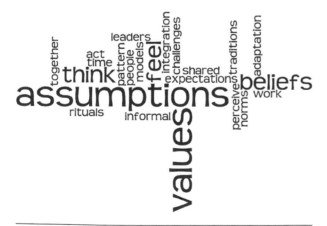

Figure 26.1   Culture, as Viewed by Peterson (1999) and Schein (1992)

SOURCES: Frank Davidson, using terms from Peterson, K. (1999). Time use flows from school culture: River of values and traditions can nurture or poison staff development hours. *Journal of Staff Development, 20*(2), 16–19; and Schein, E. H. (1992). *Organizational culture and leadership* (2nd ed.). San Francisco, CA: Jossey-Bass.

> a pattern of shared basic assumptions that the group learned as it solved its problems of external adaptation and internal integration, that has worked well enough to be considered valid and, therefore, to be taught to new members as the correct way to perceive, think, and feel in relation to those problems. (p. 12)

The Current Context

The current cultural context and the political landscape in the United States are powerful elements to consider with respect to the work culture of schools. A deeply divided nation is reflected in polarized legislative bodies across the country. On both state and national levels, lawmakers from both major political parties appear to have lost patience and faith in the abilities of educators to improve schools on their own, and evolving, untested, and sometimes risky forms of accountability measures have surfaced at a pace that practitioners find difficult to assimilate. As the **standards and accountability reform movement** continues to assume new forms and breed new policy offspring, it is increasingly apparent that the types of skills and knowledge that were embodied in successful leaders of decades past may be insufficient to meet the challenges and demands that are now faced by the nation's public schools. The ability to manage a budget, to contend with difficult personalities, to create and monitor schedules, and to directly supervise dozens of employees, while critical, scarcely scratch the surface of the skills needed to bring schools to survive or thrive in the face of today's sometimes withering and often uninformed scrutiny from state accountability systems, from parents, and from elected officials. Today's school leader must possess not only the skills to be the employer-manager of a large organization, but also the visionary-instructional leader who can instill a deep sense of purpose in teachers and support staff; who can understand and apply knowledge of curricula, assessment, and instructional practices; who can guide staff to produce constant measurable improvement in student performance; and who can do so in an environment in which the social contract that once bound a tax-paying public to the success of its schools may no longer exist.

What Kinds of Schools Does America Want?

There is an apparent mismatch between what parents want and what policymakers want. For the most part, based on the 2012 Phi Delta Kappa/Gallup Poll of the Public's Attitudes Toward the Public Schools, the public calls on today's leaders to create schools that are warm and caring places, where children learn to be problem-solving innovators and where they look out for each other and the world (Bushaw &

Lopez, 2012). A large percentage of Americans describe the teacher who was most influential in their lives using words like *caring, compassionate,* and *inspiring,* yet one would find few signs in federal or state accountability policy that *compassion* or *inspiration* are important qualities in schools. A much smaller percentage of the public describes an influential teacher as *knowledgeable, persistent, hard-working,* and *demanding.*

Teachers and principals have a palpable sense of the tension between the measurable outcomes required by accountability policies and the desire of most parents that teachers provide caring and responsive classrooms. Parents (and many medical professionals) ask for more recess and unstructured play time for children to improve physical fitness, gain social skills, and just be children. Educators defend the decision to limit recess by pointing to legislation, now in place in 32 states (Rose, 2012), requiring that students read at grade level by the end of third grade or face retention. Parents cry out for an expansion of elective classes to give students the opportunity to explore the arts, world languages, literature, and culture. School leaders point to shrinking budgets and accountability policies that distill the sum total of a school's value down to a two-digit number or a single letter grade intended to capture the performance by a diverse array of hundreds or thousands of students on a few hours of reading and mathematics tests administered each spring.

The Impact of Accountability Policies

Within the current high-stakes context, leaders at both the school and district levels are called upon to align their practices with the measurable outcomes on which they and schools will be judged. They must understand, interpret, and translate for staff a wide range of reporting and performance requirements associated with state and federal standards and accountability policy, and they must also acquire fluency in existing and emerging knowledge of topics as varied as learning styles, brain research, instructional practices, child and adolescent development, behavioral and physiological disorders, and the differentiation of instruction for students with varying capabilities. The stakes are high, and school and district leaders are challenged to provide the guidance and support needed in order for the schools under their leadership to thrive. Standardized testing, notes Richard F. Elmore (2003), "is relatively cheap and easy to implement. **Capacity building** is expensive and complex. Policymakers generally like solutions that are simple and cheap rather than those that are complex and expensive" (p. 6).

In order to create positive work cultures, one challenge that can be undertaken by leaders is to alter the formula that has influenced education policy for decades and seek to control the accountability dialogue rather than submit entirely to its control. This, understandably, is a tall order, but may become more of a trend in the coming years if distrust of simplistic, **reductionist**, and externally imposed approaches to accountability increases over time. Elmore (2003) argues for an accountability approach that is inside-out, rather than outside-in.

> Internal accountability precedes external accountability. Educators are subject to draconian and dysfunctional external accountability policies largely because they have failed to develop strong and binding professional norms about what constitutes high-quality teaching practice and a supportive organizational environment. In our society, educators are usually people to whom things happen, not people who make things happen. (p. 9)

Inside-out accountability implies a significant focus on the professional culture of schools, close attention to instructional practices, and a structured and thoughtful approach to support the development of effective instruction. The remainder of this chapter will focus on the elements of leadership that embrace the notion of personal accountability for organizational success, as well as the elements of leadership that foster both strong relationships among staff and favorable outcomes for students.

The Interplay of Culture and Leadership

Despite the challenges of leading schools in the face of daunting conditions, there is growing evidence regarding the elements of leadership that foster a culture of commitment and success, and there is a growing body of the descriptions of such leadership in practice, whereby skilled, knowledgeable, and dedicated leaders are being produced and nurtured not in isolation but in entire systems in diverse settings. Within a complex and demanding environment, many school districts manage to demonstrate a

record of continuous improvement in measurable student achievement. In such settings, leadership development efforts are underpinned with a deep appreciation of the importance of systems and culture. To develop positive work cultures, leaders must tap into what is known of those leadership skills evident in research and in practice that produce cultures capable of producing and sustaining comparably high levels of student performance.

As noted previously, the influence of formal and informal leaders can have a significant effect on the professional culture of the school. There can be little doubt that the role of the principal is critical in creating a culture of high expectations with an effective support structure for staff and students. This has been established through decades of research on the principalship. A wide variety of adjectives has been applied to principal leadership by researchers who have sought to unearth and analyze those elements of leadership that lead to favorable outcomes for students. School leaders have been called upon to provide shared leadership, distributive leadership, facilitative leadership, **instructional leadership**, and **transformational leadership**, to cite just a few such adjectives.

Research Perspectives on Leadership

Although the instructional leadership model has been influential in American schooling, it has not been free of criticism. Skeptics have questioned whether most school administrators possess the high levels of drive, knowledge, and ability needed to increase school effectiveness and student achievement through instructional leadership. Models of transformational leadership emerged in response to dissatisfaction and disillusionment with the instructional leadership model, which was seen by many as an approach that was excessively "top-down" in nature and pointed too exclusively to a single strong and assertive leader. Such models have pointed to a type of leadership centered on the engagement of staff in more distributed and collaborative leadership. Transformational leadership bears both leadership and management dimensions, emphasizes the development of individual and organizational capacity, and emphasizes school cultures marked by shared vision and collaboration, as well as administrative and organizational support.

Philip Hallinger (2003) notes that, as the control-and-coordination efforts to reform schools in the 1980s gave way to school restructuring in the 1990s, transformational leadership "overtook instructional leadership as the model of choice" (p. 342). In his view, although transformational leadership gained favor through the 1990s, increased attention in recent years on the improvement of student achievement has brought greater focus to instructional leadership. Hallinger proposes a view of leadership that integrates both the instructional and transformational models:

> When the principal elicits high levels of commitment and professionalism from teachers and works interactively with teachers in a shared instructional leadership capacity, schools have the benefit of integrated leadership; they are organizations that learn and perform at high levels. (p. 345)

Linda LaRocque and Peter Coleman (1991) analyzed the school superintendent's role in promoting a collaborative school district culture. In their work, they assert that the leadership necessary to transform organizations must be, in essence, shared leadership in which "strong executive leadership is a necessary but not sufficient element" (p. 101). They have described the leader's role as one which serves to negotiate an unwritten contract between the members of the organization which frames the organization's culture, ethos, and self-image; this contract they term the "master contract" (p. 97). Within effective school districts, they found that the typically autonomous levels within the organization find their freedom bounded by a productive professional ethos which embodies the norms and practices of the district. In their view, the creation and sustenance of a productive ethos at the district level is the most significant outcome and responsibility of the superintendent. This productive ethos at the district level "both constrains and facilitates" (p. 120), suggesting a degree of organizational coupling that reflects not so much greater bureaucratization as a greater degree of vision-focused collaboration, consensus, support, and enforcement.

In order to demonstrate not just competence but excellence in organizational effectiveness, leadership must include symbolic and cultural leadership so that what the leader and the organization stand for are clearly evident and have meaning. Sergiovanni (1984) places symbolic and cultural forces at the apex of a hierarchy of five necessary leadership forces, with the technical, human, and educational forces at the base (see **Figure 26.2**). Shaping culture, connecting staff with the larger purpose of schools, and fostering a spirit of collaboration within the school involve the types of leadership at the top of Sergiovanni's hierarchy. The skills, knowledge, and values involved in symbolic and cultural leadership would be markedly different from the skills, knowledge, and values evident in discussions about specific instructional practices or curricular materials. Again, the latter would imply skills that are necessary but not sufficient to produce culture change.

The fact is that changes in the professional culture of schools require higher levels of symbolic and cultural leadership that is capable of building capacity in organizations through developing shared vision, creating productive work cultures, and fostering distributive and collaborative leadership.

James MacGregor Burns (1978) articulates the need for leadership that would result in schools that continue to " exert moral leadership and foster needed social change long after the creative leaders are gone" (p. 454) and where leaders "induce followers to act for certain goals that represent the values and the motivations" (p. 19) of both leaders and followers. Burns's work also points to considerations of political and organizational culture that are essential to higher levels of organizational effectiveness, suggesting the development of a shared culture that sustains desired

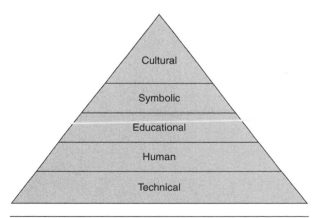

Figure 26.2 Sergiovanni's Hierarchy of Leadership Forces

SOURCE: Sergiovanni, T. J. (1984). Leadership and excellence in schooling. *Educational Leadership, 41*(5), 4–13, Figure 1, page 9.

norms. The notion of developing a shared common purpose for the organization is seen as essential to the type of leadership needed to transform institutions. Leadership that is capable of transforming organizations must first be concerned with higher order psychological needs for esteem, autonomy, and self-actualization, as well as with moral issues of goodness, righteousness, duty, and obligation.

Attributes of Positive Work Culture

Although researchers may not agree on a single definition of organizational culture or work culture, authors generally agree that the organization's culture is embodied in the shared norms of interaction, the shared values and beliefs expressed by those within the organization, and shared assumptions regarding the nature of the organization's mission and purpose. As noted previously, scholars have long assumed that strong organizational culture is a critical factor in producing higher levels of organizational performance. The assumption has also been made by scholars that, when an organization's culture is strong, this leads not only to greater work output on the part of its members but also to a stronger sense of fulfillment and commitment. While not easily measured nor highly prized in current accountability policies, the value of a sense of fulfillment and commitment on the part of staff to the professional culture of the school cannot be overstated. Individuals who find a daily reward in what they do, who feel valued and supported, and who see a relationship between what they do on a daily basis and the overarching purposes of schools are bound to be not just more effective but also more engaged, empowered, supportive, and dedicated.

What is the relationship between organizational culture and leadership style? Does the leader's style influence the culture, does the culture shape the leader, or do both culture and leadership interact upon one another? In a 1993 study, Yin Cheong Cheng found that the sharing of beliefs and values among members is an essential part of organizational culture. Irrespective of the causality of the relationship between organizational culture and organizational characteristics including strong leadership, a participative organizational structure, and positive peer interaction, there is a strong positive relationship between culture and these characteristics, and higher levels of teacher satisfaction and student

achievement are a predictable outcome. Consequently, while Cheng notes that "it is very difficult, if not impossible to confirm the causal relationship of organizational culture to leadership style, organizational structure, and social interactions" (p. 87), it is reasonable to assume that strengthening a leader's knowledge and skills is likely to lead to a more productive organizational culture, which, in turn, will likely lead to a more effective leader. Cheng found that schools with stronger organizational culture were more likely to be perceived as more effective in terms of "productivity, adaptation and flexibility" (p. 92).

Michael Fullan (2008) writes of six elements of leadership, one of which is "Connecting Peers to Purpose." He suggests a style of leadership that is more than simply fostering a spirit of collaboration, and he asserts that the role of the leader is critical. Leaders must take responsibility for providing direction, creating the conditions in which meaningful and productive peer interaction can occur, and supporting staff in a responsive and engaging manner when problems arise. An investment in individuals increases individual commitment, and an investment in conditions that enable staff to collaborate in more substantive and meaningful ways increases the collective commitment of the entire staff. Strong relationships are important, but relationships alone cannot be ends in themselves. Elsewhere, Fullan (2001) writes that "weak collaboration is always ineffective, but strong communities can make matters worse if, in their collaboration, teachers (however unwittingly) reinforce each other's bad or ineffective practice." He adds, "Collaborative cultures, which by definition have close relationships, are indeed powerful, but unless they are focusing on the right things they may end up being powerfully wrong" (p. 67).

A Changing Workforce and Cultural Implications

The fact that a significant portion of the teaching workforce began to retire over the last decade was an expected attribute of the baby boomer generation (Feistritzer, 2011). This is an important consideration for leaders. From 2005 to 2011, the proportion of teachers under 30 years of age rose dramatically, while the proportion of teachers 50 and older dropped. By 2011, there were two times as many teachers under thirty as there were just six years earlier. Older teachers are retiring, and they are being replaced by teachers in their twenties and thirties. As the nation's teaching workforce continues to change, there will be increasing importance placed on retention and support for new teachers. Historically, a substantial percentage of new teachers leave the profession for good within a few years. Despite exposure to the practicalities of classroom life through student teaching, observation, and other first-hand exposure to the classroom, it is safe to say that the vast majority of teachers experience some degree of frustration during their initial years of teaching, as a pragmatic survivalist mentality replaces pre-service idealism. The culture that new teachers experience as they begin their careers is not uniform but varies considerably school by school. A work culture that is welcoming and supportive of new teachers, with the appropriate blend of support and direction, can start teachers on a career path marked by success and fulfillment; or as is the case with far too many teachers, the work culture that they experience is neither supportive nor welcoming, yielding frustration, discouragement, and an early exit from the field.

Providing deep insights into the culture experienced by new teachers, Susan Kardos, Susan Moore Johnson, Heather G. Peske, David Kauffman, and Edward Liu (2001) conducted interviews of 50 novice teachers to better understand their experiences of the work culture in schools and the principal's role in influencing the professional culture. This research led to three different conceptualizations of professional cultures:

- *Veteran-oriented professional cultures,* in which interactions were determined principally by experienced teachers
- *Novice-oriented professional cultures,* where interactions were "generally uninformed by the expertise and wisdom of veteran teachers and
- *Integrated professional cultures,* characterized by consistent, ongoing, and mutually respectful interaction between colleagues with varying levels of experience (see pp. 260–262)

While each of the first two of these school cultures possess certain strengths, including institutional and craft knowledge in the veteran-oriented settings, and energy and enthusiasm in the novice-oriented settings, neither were characterized by the researchers as performing as well as the settings with integrated professional cultures in fostering

communication, cooperation, compassion, and collective responsibility. In such settings, "The experienced teachers made concerted efforts to orient and assist the novice teachers while remaining open to new ways of doing their work" (Kardos et al., 2001, p. 274). Notably, principals in these settings were actively engaged in attending closely to those cultures, with especially close attention paid to the needs of new teachers. Elmore (2003) emphasizes the importance of learning across roles, stating that

> schools that are improving seldom, if ever, engage exclusively in role-based professional development— that is, professional learning in which people in different roles are segregated from one another. Instead, learning takes place across roles. Improving schools pay attention to who knows what and how that knowledge can strengthen the organization. (p. 10)

This implies a work culture in which respect for varied types and levels of expertise is the norm and where professional jealousies in the extreme are held at bay. Principals play an essential role in creating a work culture that promotes such conditions. The conclusions reached by Kardos and colleagues (2001) concerning the actions of principals that successfully integrated new teachers into the workplace compare favorably with the work of other researchers, including research led by Rosemary Papa in 2011 and 2012. She and her colleagues (Papa, English, Davidson, Culver, & Brown, 2013) conducted in-depth interviews with leaders from school districts identified as highly effective, inviting leaders to describe the skills and expertise that foster exceptional performance.

Five Secrets of Creating Positive Work Cultures

Based on what we know about organizations, the factors that shape school culture, and the skills, knowledge, and values of effective leaders, what are the secrets to creating a positive work culture? Some common points emerge regarding the skills and habits of successful leaders.

Secret 1: Prioritize Teaching and Learning

Effective principals hone their knowledge of curricula, assessment practices, and instructional delivery in order not only to distinguish ineffective from effective instruction but also to help both the novice and the veteran to grow. For many teachers in many schools, the school principal is the only other professional who will actually ever have the ability to observe and comment on the teacher's developing skills. Effective principals strive to model lifelong learning, both for them individually and for the entire organization.

In schools that are effective at sustaining improvement over time, it is quite likely that this is the result of a structured system of support for instruction that has been created and refined over time. That system would include an effective feedback loop to inform instruction and a clear, agreed-upon picture of what constitutes effective instructional practice. Elmore (2003) notes,

> Schools and school systems that do well under external accountability systems are those that have consensus on norms of instructional practice, strong internal assessments of student learning, and sturdy processes for monitoring instructional practice and for providing feedback to students, teachers, and administrators about the quality of their work. Internal coherence around instructional practice is a prerequisite for strong performance, whatever the requirements of the external accountability system. (p. 9)

A leader's decisions about the use of time can have a significant impact on the organization's capacity to prioritize teaching and learning. A healthy respect for time and how precious it is to teachers can go a long way toward ensuring that their energy and their time can be dedicated to issues critical to teaching and learning.

Ask any educator. What is one of their biggest frustrations? Many will tell you it is a lack of time. There is not enough time for individual planning, for collaboration within their grade level or their department, for vertical articulation with colleagues at other grade levels, for learning how to use new curricular materials, for learning how to integrate new technologies, for professional reading, for attending professional development classes, to serve on building or district committees, for taking an active role in supporting pro-education candidates or ballot issues, for meaningful reflection on one's practice, for planning parent-teacher conferences, for entering grades, for responding to parents' emails. Yet all are deemed essential and important. There is not even enough time to eat or attend to personal needs. Notes Tye

(2000), "So powerful is the press of time on school people that even if no other deep structure forces were involved, *the lack of time alone* [italics in original] is enough to bring down a promising new program" (p. 137).

Some leaders at the school and district levels have attempted to create more time through the use of strategies such as creating more flexibility in teachers' daily schedules, by extending the school day, by making use of early-dismissal days, or by adding days to the school calendar for professional development activities. Some changes, such as early-dismissal days or no-school professional development days during the school year, help to address the need for more time, but can be very unpopular with parents who must make other arrangements for child care. There are no simple answers for solving the time problem, but a leader's decisions should be influenced by a desire to prioritize teaching and learning and to respect the many demands on a teacher's time.

Secret 2: Build Strong Connections Through Being Present and Responsive

To create a positive work culture, a leader must first have a profound understanding of the values and beliefs of teachers and support staff and of the **cultural norms** that define adult-to-adult, adult-to-student, and student-to-student interaction. Effective leaders make strong connections with others, and they constantly work to refine their interpersonal communication skills. These connections with others must be grounded in the deep purpose of the organization. One must know and purposefully learn from the informal networks that permeate and surround the school, the stories that are told, and the symbolic activities and artifacts of the school.

Building strong connections also involves creating a strong sense of purpose in the people within the organization. Fullan notes (2008), "When peers interact with purpose, they provide their own built-in accountability" (p. 32). Great leaders foster commitment to the shared vision and help people to feel that the work being done matters. Such connections foster feelings of significance and a sense of purpose.

Effective leaders pay attention to the qualities that build trust, respect, and commitment in those around them. They facilitate the development of a shared vision. They consciously and actively mentor others. They collaborate with colleagues inside and outside the organization. Openness to sharing ownership of not just the challenges that schools face but the solutions to address them is an important factor in building connections.

School leaders must also create an expectation that communication among the faculty will be open and honest, and that dissenting opinions will be respected. In their research on school reform, Patricia Wasley, Robert Hampel, and Richard Clark (1997) found that the most successful schools were characterized by open communication among all members of the staff. Civil discourse and openness to honest internal and external feedback were important elements of the communication patterns in such schools.

From the perspective of teachers, one of the factors of greatest importance in terms of the quality of the work culture is the extent to which one feels connected not just to others at one's grade level but to staff throughout the school. This feeling of connectedness helps to provide emotional support through personal and professional challenges that are bound to arise. In the case of many first-year teachers, unless they completed their student teaching at the school in question or worked at the school previously in some other capacity, the new teacher is not only in a new work environment, but a new home, away from college, away from family and friends, paying student loans or a car payment, confronting all of the viruses a first-year teacher encounters—you get the picture.

Another critical factor is the sense of connectedness to the school's goals and the progress being made toward those goals. Teachers and students do really know if a principal genuinely believes that all children can find success. It shows in how they celebrate, in their symbolic actions, in whether they know students by name, and in whether they are making progress.

Secret 3: Maintain a Disciplined Focus

Effective leaders have a clear sense of purpose. They center their actions and the actions of others on the organization's mission and goals. They also pay attention to systemic barriers that, if properly addressed, can amount to mere speed bumps. Most importantly, they shield themselves and the staff

from the distractions of a minor crisis or a passing fad. This commitment to a clear purpose has emerged as an important factor in previous research on high-performing districts. In the late 1980s, Joseph Murphy and Philip Hallinger (1986, 1988) examined the leadership roles of superintendents in twelve effective school districts in California. Among the leadership practices that emerged as significant, three relate to the skill of maintaining a disciplined focus:

- *Setting goals and establishing expectations and standards.* Goals in these districts tended to focus on curriculum and instruction, and there was a strong belief that the district goals and the behavior of its leaders could influence district and school activities.
- *Establishing an instructional and curricular focus.* These districts had both a greater degree of attention to instructional and curricular activities and a greater degree of superintendent involvement in these activities.
- *Ensuring consistency in technical core operations.* Internal consistency in the areas of curriculum and instruction was prevalent in these districts, and leaders saw themselves as key agents for maintaining this consistency.

Secret 4: Manage Efficiently, in Order to Lead Effectively

It is critical for leaders to avoid the situation described by Paul V. Bredeson (1996) as the "managerial activity trap that ensnares all but the most savvy of administrators" (p. 245). It is difficult to focus on a shared vision of academic excellence if the schools are perceived as poorly staffed, disorganized, overcrowded, lacking in basic supplies, or dirty. Effective principals must possess specific organizational skills to enable them to work more efficiently in order to successfully lead their schools and districts. Importantly, they must ensure that the schools' priorities are adequately supported.

Although Harriet Tyson's 1994 study of the working conditions of teachers in the United States was completed 20 years ago, many teachers would report similar problems today. In 1994, Tyson identified some of those conditions as low pay, large classes, a lack of supplies, an absence of administrative support, unsafe buildings, no quiet place to work, and mundane, sometimes demeaning chores. Effective leaders must have an appreciation of the work lives of teachers, and ensure that resources are adequately managed so that they feel supported and capable of being successful. Notes Tye (2000), "Being sure they have what they need in order to do good work—not only materials and equipment but space and time as well—seems a logical starting point" (p. 136).

Secret 5: Choose Optimism

To create a better future for their organizations and their students, effective school leaders are engaged in consciously picturing, choosing, and creating a better future. Such a viewpoint reflects Albert Bandura's (2001) social cognitive theory, in which he posits that one's belief in his or her ability to accomplish a specific task affects both personal and collective efficacy. Such leadership contributes to what Wayne K. Hoy (2003) describes as "mindful and enabling school structures" (p. 99), in which "school leaders know better than most that they must develop a capacity to detect and bounce back from mistakes" (p. 98). A feature common to leaders in high-performing settings is their cultivation of resiliency of spirit.

Choosing optimism and going out of one's way to reinforce the positive has a powerful influence on school culture, for both students and adults. Messaging external to the school tends to be experienced by those within the school as unfairly negative. School leaders can counter this by accentuating progress toward goals while still being honest about the work that still needs to be done. Principals and other leaders find much more success in telling teachers what is working instructionally than focusing on what is not working. Principals find much more success in reinforcing the good things that students are doing, rather than by focusing on their shortcomings or by punishing them into being better citizens. While research indicates that a positive, caring, and responsive environment is likely to more effectively promote learning, especially for disadvantaged students, this is not the type of environment that disadvantaged students tend to experience. Leaders need to strive to create caring environments where students are valued for who they are and what they can become. Leaders' optimism must be founded on high expectations for students and a belief that students must be meaningfully engaged in the life of the school.

The choice of optimism is reflected in one's approach toward goal setting. A challenge is to establish goals that are owned by the entire staff, worth doing in a meaningful way, and attainable yet somewhat beyond the school's current level of performance. Based upon their research on the practices of schools that were most effective in meeting the needs of African American and Hispanic students, Rosemary Papalewis and Rex Fortune (2002) found that principals "with a strong commitment to their school's mission ensure that everyone identified with the school is aware of and fully committed to the school's direction" (p. 13). Such a commitment requires not only that the school's practices be aligned with the school's goals but also an outward-focused belief on the part of leaders and others that the goals can be attained.

A study in 2004 completed by Bobbie J. Greenlee and Darlene Y. Bruner examined the differences in work cultures of schools with high and low student achievement. Asserting that schools with stronger work cultures were settings typified by greater interdependency and customer focus, the authors found that staff members in schools with relatively higher achievement were more involved in planning, program development, and staff development. Moreover, high-achieving schools demonstrated statistically higher scores in ratings of visionary leadership, information systems, human resource development, and customer success and satisfaction. Greenlee and Bruner noted that, in higher-achieving schools, principals communicate the vision and the direction of the school by words and deeds to all whose cooperation may be needed to accomplish school goals. Innovations and contributions of teachers are recognized. The environment supports design and redesign of programs and experimenting with options to meet the needs of the students (p. 75).

Conclusion

Picture a school leader exiting the state capitol building after spending time with legislators and heading to the rows upon rows of cars in a vast parking lot. Reaching the car, he pushes the button on the key fob. The car does not beep in reply. The door does not succumb to his efforts to open it. He clicks again. Nothing. "Great," he thinks. The battery must be dead. He attempts to put the key in the lock, but finds that it won't fit. Somehow, he reaches the conclusion that someone has vandalized his car, jamming something into the door lock so his key will not fit.

On a different day, our leader is rushing to get to church. His wife is upstairs, so he rifles through her purse to find the checkbook so that he can write out a check for the offering. He goes through every nook, cranny, and secret compartment in her purse. No checkbook can be found. He calls upstairs, "Hey, are you sure the checkbook's in your purse?" He dumps the contents on the dining room table. Many interesting artifacts emerge, but no checkbook is found.

At times we look, without really seeing.

The pressure to improve student performance on state-mandated tests causes many educators to focus on entirely the wrong things. Experience teaches us the following:

- In the extreme, some leaders have been known to tolerate or encourage unethical or even unlawful practices related to testing.
- Not as extreme, but equally pernicious, are other examples of misguided efforts to improve performance. Educational leaders sometimes believe that blaming or browbeating teachers will improve subpar performance. Such practices may yield short-term gains, but there is little evidence that a school improvement plan built on a foundation of blame would be a sustainable and effective long-term strategy.
- In other instances, well-intentioned leaders place their hopes in the use of a simplistic classroom observation checklist to point out deficiencies in teaching performance. Entire systems have been built around the premise that the practice of regularly monitoring classrooms using a checklist of exemplary teaching behaviors will be sufficient to lead to a proliferation of exemplary teaching everywhere. There are certainly benefits to using an inventory of building-wide needs to develop a school plan for professional development, but a checklist alone will not adequately serve to improve instruction. This, too, may produce short-term gains, but prioritizing teaching and learning through a checklist approach to managing classroom practice will not produce deep or lasting change.

Had the school leader described earlier been a tad more observant when he went to unlock his car, he might have noticed that not only was he trying to unlock another person's car, but he was not even in the right section of the parking lot. If he had exercised more keen attention to details, he might have noticed that it was not his wife's purse that he had emptied onto the counter but his daughter's. At times we look, without really seeing.

As school leaders, we lead distracted and harried lives. If, to address the challenge of improving academic achievement for all students, we focus on what appear to be direct and simple solutions such as the misguided strategies identified earlier, then we will not lead our schools to develop the capacity for reinvention and renewal. Easy answers rarely solve complex problems. Instead, in our desire to focus on the goal of improved student achievement, we need to focus on the secrets of creating positive work cultures:

1. Prioritizing teaching and learning

2. Building strong connections through being present and responsive

3. Maintaining a disciplined focus

4. Managing efficiently

5. Choosing optimism

Finally, what should be evident from this chapter is that, while we can point out the secrets of creating positive work cultures, organizational improvement is not the outcome of a superintendent or a principal working in isolation to "secretly improve" (Cuban, 1984, p. 147) the institution. The challenges of schooling all of America's children are great, so great that any leader who attempts to individually and independently reform a school or a district, absent the perspective and engagement of others, is likely to do more damage than good. The most effective leaders recognize that their best work is done through and with others, and that such work comes about in a healthy, fulfilling, and rewarding work culture.

Key Chapter Terms

Capacity building: Strategies intended to systematically develop skills and practices that will empower individuals in the organization to more effectively fulfill the overarching purposes of the organization.

Cultural norms: Unwritten rules guiding individual behavior that are typical of a particular setting.

Culture: The informal beliefs, behaviors, and expectations that are characteristic of a particular organization or setting.

Entrepreneurship: The desire and ability to plan, develop, and manage innovative approaches to the organization's work, as well as the risks that come with innovation.

Formal leaders: Individuals with position authority, such as the principal, assistant principal, or dean of students.

Informal leaders: Individuals whose leadership is heeded by virtue of their reputation, experience, or prestige within the group.

Instructional leadership: A construct of leadership based on an individual leader's deep knowledge of effective instructional practice and ability to guide and support teaching behaviors.

Positive work culture: Patterns of beliefs, attitudes, and styles of interaction that reflect contentment, purposefulness, fulfillment, and commitment.

Reductionist: A viewpoint or approach that reduces inherently complex issues to simple terms or slogans.

Standards and accountability reform movement: A wave of reforms initiated in the 1980s and strengthened by the No Child Left Behind Act. Standards-based reforms generally involve specifying learning outcomes representing what students are expected to know and do, assessments that measure student performance against these outcomes, and accountability measures with rewards or sanctions for schools, school systems, or individuals.

Transformational leadership: A construct of leadership that reflects the capability to collaboratively engage staff in building and transforming the organization's capacity to fulfill its mission and to sustain continuous improvement after the leader is gone.

References

Bandura, A. (2001). Social cognitive theory: An agentic perspective. *Annual Reviews of Psychology, 52*, 1–26.

Bredeson, P. V. (1996). Superintendents' roles in curriculum development and instructional leadership: Instructional visionaries, collaborators, supporters, and delegators. *Journal of School Leadership, 6*(3), 243–264.

Burns, J. M. (1978). *Leadership.* New York, NY: Harper & Row.

Bushaw, W. J., & Lopez, S. J. (2012). Public education in the United States: A nation divided. *The Phi Delta Kappa/Gallup Poll of the Public's Attitudes Toward the Public Schools.* Retrieved from : http://pdkintl .org/wp-content/blogs.dir/5/files/2012-Gallup-poll-full-report.pdf

Cheng, Y. C. (1993). Profiles of organizational culture and effective schools, school effectiveness and school improvement. *International Journal of Research, Policy and Practice, 4*(2), 85–110.

Cuban, L. (1984). Transforming the frog into a prince: Effective schools research, policy, and practice at the district level. *Harvard Educational Review, 54*(2), 129–151.

Elmore, R. F. (2003). A plea for strong practice. *Educational Leadership, 61*(3), 6–10.

Feistritzer, C. E. (2011). *Profile of teachers in the U.S. 2011.* Washington, DC: National Center for Education Information. Retrieved from http://www .ncei.com/Profile_Teachers_US_2011.pdf

Fullan, M. (2001). *Leading in a culture of change.* San Francisco, CA: Jossey-Bass.

Fullan, M. (2008). *The six secrets of school change.* San Francisco, CA: Jossey-Bass.

Greenlee, B. J., & Bruner, D. Y. (2004). Why school culture both attracts and resists whole school reform. *Essays in Education, 10.* Retrieved from http://www .usca.edu/essays/vol102004/greenlee.pdf

Hallinger, P. (2003). Leading educational change: Reflections on the practice of instructional and transformational leadership. *Cambridge Journal of Education, 33*(3), 329–351.

Hoy, W. K. (2003). An analysis of enabling and mindful school structures: Some theoretical, research, and practical consideration. *Journal of Educational Administration, 41*, 87–108.

Kardos, S. M., Johnson, S. M., Peske, H. G., Kauffman, D., & Liu, E. (2001). Counting on colleagues: New teachers encounter the professional cultures of their schools. *Educational Administration Quarterly, 37*(2), 250–290.

LaRocque, L., & Coleman, P. (1991). Negotiating the master contract: Transformational leadership and school district quality. In K. Leithwood & D. Musella (Eds.), *Understanding school system administration: Studies of the contemporary chief education officer* (pp. 96–123). New York, NY: Falmer.

Little, J. W. (1990). The persistence of privacy: Autonomy and initiative in teachers' professional relations. *Teachers College Record, 91*(4), 509–537.

Murphy, J., & Hallinger, P. (1986). The superintendent as instructional leader: Findings from effective school districts. *Journal of Educational Administration, 24*(2), 213–236.

Murphy, J., & Hallinger, P. (1988). Characteristics of instructionally effective school districts. *Journal of Educational Research, 81*(3), 175–181.

Papa, R., English, F., Davidson, F., Culver, M., & Brown, R. (2013). *Contours of great leadership: The science, art, and wisdom of outstanding practice.* Lanham, MD: Rowman and Littlefield Education.

Papalewis, R., & Fortune, R. (2002). *Leadership on purpose: Promising practices for African American and Hispanic students.* Thousand Oaks, CA: Corwin.

Peterson, K. (1999). Time use flows from school culture: River of values and traditions can nurture or poison staff development hours. *Journal of Staff Development, 20*(2), 16–19. Retrieved from http://learningforward.org/docs/jsd-spring-1999/peterson202.pdf?sfvrsn=2

Rose, S. (2012). *Third grade reading policies.* Reading/Literacy P-3. Denver, CO: Education Commission of the States. Retrieved http://www.ecs.org/clearinghouse/01/03/47/10347.pdf

Schein, E. H. (1992). *Organizational culture and leadership* (2nd ed.). San Francisco, CA: Jossey-Bass.

Sergiovanni, T. J. (1984). Leadership and excellence in schooling. *Educational Leadership, 41*(5), 4–13.

Tye, B. B. (2000). *Hard truths: Uncovering the deep structure of schooling.* New York, NY: Teachers College Press.

Tyson, H. (1994). *Who will teach the children? Progress and resistance in teacher education.* San Francisco, CA: Jossey-Bass.

Wasley, P., Hampel, R., & Clark, R. (1997). The puzzle of whole-school change. *Phi Delta Kappan, 78*(9), 690–697.

Further Readings

Achinstein, B. (2002). Conflict amid community: The micropolitics of teacher collaboration. *Teachers College Record, 104*(3), 421–455.

This study uses two case studies of urban high schools to examine the nature of teacher collaboration. The author notes that conflict is a natural by-product of close interaction in the workplace, and many in the education setting are unprepared to cope with disagreement and dissent.

Berliner, D., & Biddle, B. (1995). *The manufactured crisis: Myths, fraud, and the attack on America's public schools.* Reading, MA: Addison-Wesley.

Although this book was published twenty years prior to publication of the present work, it still provides key insights into criticism of public schools and includes data to support the conclusion that American schools continue to improve over time.

Blase, J., & Blase, J. (2000). Effective instructional leadership: Teachers' perspectives on how principals promote teaching and learning in schools. *Journal of Educational Administration, 38*(2), 130–141.

The authors conducted a study of over 800 teachers in order to identify the characteristics of principals that helped to improve classroom instruction. The study illustrates the importance of reflective conversations with teachers and prioritizing.

Bogler, R. (2001). The influence of leadership style on teacher job satisfaction. *Educational Administration Quarterly, 37*(5), 662–683.

A significant finding of this research was that teachers' perceptions of job-related prestige, self-esteem, autonomy, and professional development contribute more to job satisfaction than other factors. A conclusion that can be reached from this work is that to increase teachers' satisfaction, leaders must pay attention to the ways in which their role and their conduct affect teachers. Through leadership that is more collaborative and participative, principals can improve the positive feelings of teachers regarding their vocation.

Bolman, L. G., & Deal, T. E. (1997). *Reframing organizations* (2nd ed.). San Francisco, CA: Jossey-Bass.

This text is one of the seminal works in the field of educational leadership. The book describes a four-frame model including the structural frame, the human resource frame, the political frame, and the symbolic frame.

DuFour, R. (2004). Culture shift doesn't happen overnight—or without conflict. *Journal of Staff Development, 25(*4), 63–64.

DuFour asserts that cultures that produce high levels of student learning are those in which the principal's leadership is focused on effectively empowering staff, delegating authority, and developing collaborative decision making. In such settings, leadership can be fluid and situational, depending upon the problem that needs solving and the varied expertise of staff. Principals must work to shape norms of behavior by creating processes for monitoring student learning and intervening to give struggling students additional time and support, by establishing expectations that guide teachers' work while still preserving considerable autonomy in implementation, and by taking a stand when an individual violates the underlying values of the school's culture.

English, F. & Papa, R. (2010). *Restoring human agency to educational administration: Status and strategies.* Lancaster, PA: ProActive.

This text includes arguments for reinventing the profession of educational leadership as a catalyst for social change. It also includes an analysis of current approaches to doctoral research.

Fullan, M., Bertani, A., & Quinn, J. (2004). New lessons for districtwide reform. *Educational Leadership, 61,* 42–46.

This article summarizes findings from research on the change process underway in several school districts in the United States and Canada. These findings point to the importance of creating work cultures that are highly participative, collaborative, and driven by a deep sense of moral purpose. Large-scale capacity building is possible in settings where relationships are characterized by respect, integrity, and competence.

Louis, K. S., & Wahlstrom, K. (2011). Principals as cultural leaders. *Phi Delta Kappan, 92*(5), 52–56.

Some conceptualize a "turnaround" principal as a heroic leader who singularly wills a school to become something that it has not yet become. The authors of this article argue that principals are most effective as shapers of culture when their influence fosters interconnectedness and mutual responsibility for finding solutions to the problems schools face. They summarize three findings from a study of school cultures: (1) Principals must create conversations about classroom practices that are associated with improved student learning; (2) principals must seek out the best ideas from teachers and parents and creating opportunities for others to engage in deciding how to implement these ideas; and (3) principals must earn teachers' trust, as this trust provides the foundation for learning for both students and adults.

Marks, H. M., & Louis, K. S. (1999). Teacher empowerment and the capacity for organizational learning. *Educational Administration Quarterly, 35,* 707–750.

This study of organizational learning and teacher empowerment was conducted in 24 elementary, middle, and high schools, eight at each grade range. One significant finding was that in schools with a greater capacity for organizational learning, teachers are more likely to be engaged in decisions related to their work lives. The findings in this study are consistent with other findings by these authors regarding the role of teacher empowerment as one of a small number of school improvement traits that when focused on teaching and learning, can produce learning gains for students.

Petersen, G. J. (1999). Demonstrated actions of instructional leaders: An examination of five California superintendents. *Education Policy Analysis Archives, 7,* [online] 18. Retrieved from http://epaa.asu.edu/ojs/article/view/553/676

A growing body of research indicates that superintendents' instructional leadership can have a significant impact on student outcomes. This article reports on research into the leadership behaviors of five California superintendents recognized for their instructional leadership. The research was conducted by interviewing the superintendents, principals, and school board members.

Scheurich, J. J., Skrla, L., & Johnson, J. J. (2000). Thinking carefully about equity and accountability. *Phi Delta Kappan, 82*(4), 293–299.

As state-level accountability policies influenced the development of the No Child Left Behind Act, a discussion unfolded regarding the relationship between such policies and efforts to increase educational equity. The authors examine this relationship, which continues to have a significant influence on policy debates at the state and federal levels.

Sosik, J. J., & Megerian, L. E. (1999). Understanding leader emotional intelligence and performance: The role of self-other agreement on transformational leadership perceptions. *Group and Organization Management, 24*(3), 367–390.

It is important for leaders to seek 360-degree feedback to ensure they have an accurate picture of how they are perceived by others. Sosik and Megerian conducted research on the relationship between the self-perceptions of 63 managers, the perceptions of them held by subordinates, the emotional intelligence of leaders, and leader performance. This article examines the manner in which self-awareness varies in relation to these factors.

Togneri, W. (2003). *Beyond islands of excellence: What districts can do to improve instruction and achievement in all schools*. Washington, DC: Learning First Alliance.

This document, produced by an alliance of organizations representing parents, teachers, principals, administrators, local and state boards of education, and colleges of education calls on policymakers and practitioners to address the challenge of improving student achievement by focusing on improvement strategies across entire school systems rather than in isolated settings. Five high-poverty school districts that were making strides in improving achievement were studied through more than 200 individual interviews, 15 school visits, and 60 focus groups. Seven factors that are essential to improvement were identified.

Wagner, T. (2001). Leadership for learning: An action theory of school change. *Phi Delta Kappan, 82*(5), 378–383.

Wagner expands on the ways that effective leaders make changes that are aimed at improving learning for all students—what he refers to as an "action theory" of change. He describes how to create organizational capacity for sustaining change, which of necessity is the first step that any leader should consider when undertaking significant reform efforts. He asserts that leaders must clearly understand and engage staff in discussions on the need for change, create a sense of ownership while adhering to a credo of "No shame, no blame, no excuses" and create time for educators to understand and discuss disaggregated student data.

27

NEW SOUTH REALITIES

Demographics, Cultural Capital, and Diversity

TAWANNAH G. ALLEN
Fayetteville State University

DIONNE V. MCLAUGHLIN
North Carolina Central University

Ms. Sargent, a highly competent first-grade teacher, has been teaching for more than 20 years. Her bright, well-organized classroom, which is visually stimulating, features "word walls," strategically displayed letters and numbers, a centrally placed carpet with a map of the world on it, and a stage. Other elements include carefully grouped book baskets and the use of pocket charts for guided reading groups.

During the class period allotted to literacy, Ms. Sargent works with groups of five students to review a story. Before they begin the discussion of each story, she asks if there are any questions they would like to ask. Students also complete a "picture walk" that includes a close examination of all of the illustrations. They discuss each book's genre (e.g., animal, fantasy) and contemplate the habits of its characters. After pauses to "frame" unfamiliar words, the students reread each story silently to themselves. When they are finished, Ms. Sargent asks them questions about what

they have found interesting about the book and reminds them of her expectation that they ask themselves questions about what they are reading.

In all of these ways, Ms. Sargent provides her students with the **cultural capital** they need to fully engage in the books they read. Rather than assuming prior knowledge about the topic of the story and launching a discussion as if students already have this knowledge, Ms. Sargent involves her students in a process that helps them to obtain the necessary knowledge by engaging in lively, two-way discussions about the text. During the pre-reading discussion, Ms. Sargent provides background information for her students.

Ms. Sargent also helps her students to make connections to the texts by providing them with specific facts and identifying experiences that enable them to make clear and purposeful associations with the books. This insightful teacher had this to say about her philosophy:

NOTE. The teacher, assistant superintendents, and principals quoted in this chapter are African American or Native American educators in North Carolina, working primarily in rural areas. All but one have 5 or more years of experience. All of their names are pseudonyms.

I want children to see learning as a puzzle. Teaching is about making them curious: Then there is less work I have to do. They do the work. If they are doing it because you make them do it, you're fighting them all day. If you get a child to be curious, they will do the learning. If the work is too easy, they become careless. If it is too hard, they can't do it. Teaching is a mission and a privilege.

This example illustrates the impact of **effective** instruction and the role that teachers can play by intentionally passing on knowledge, skills, and dispositions that increase their students' access to cultural capital and ultimately academic achievement.

The demographics of the United States have rapidly been changing due to the large-scale immigration to the United States from Latin America and Asia (Johnson, 2006). The expected future growth of non-White, ethnic minority groups in the U.S. population can be characterized as the browning and graying of America, with Latinos expected to constitute a majority of the U.S. population within a few decades (Johnson, 2006).

Between 2000 and 2010, the U.S. population increased by an estimated 24.8 million, with the concentration of this growth primarily being situated in the South (Johnson & Kasarda, 2011). The South accounted for about 51.4% of this growth, followed by the West, which captured only roughly one third of growth during this same period. The Northeast and Midwest states experienced slow population growth, with only 6.5% and 9.4% of the net population growth, respectively (**Table 27.1**).

Region	Absolute Population Change	Percentage of Total
United States	27,323,632	100%
Northeast	1,722,862	6.5%
Midwest	2,534,225	9.4%
South	14,318,924	52.0%
West	8,747,621	32.0%

Table 27.1 Shares of Net Population Growth, by Region, 2000–2010

SOURCE: U.S. Census Bureau (2011).

Migration to the South accounted for an estimated net influx of 2.3 million migrants from 2008 to 2009, with nearly all major demographic groups represented in this trend (Johnson & Kasarda, 2011). Assuming this rate of growth continues, it has been predicted that the White population will fall below 50% by 2050; the most significant growth of non-Whites is expected among Latinos and Asians, combined with modest growth among African Americans (Johnson & Kasarda, 2011).

From fall 2001 through fall 2011, the number of White students enrolled in prekindergarten through 12th grade in U.S. public schools decreased from 28.7 million to 25.6 million, and their share of public school enrollment decreased from 60% to 52%. In contrast, the number of Latino students enrolled during this period increased from 8.2 million to 11.8 million students, and their share of public school enrollment increased from 17% to 24%. The number of Black students enrolled during this period fluctuated between 7.8 million and 8.4 million, and Black students' share of public school enrollment decreased from 17% in 2001 to 16% in 2011. In 2002, the Latino share of public school enrollment exceeded the Black share and has since remained higher than the Black share in each subsequent year through 2011.

More than three quarters (76%) of native-born Latino students attend school in the "established" Latino states—those states that have traditionally higher concentrated populations of Latinos, identified as California, Texas, Arizona, New Mexico, Colorado, Illinois, New York, Pennsylvania, and New Jersey (Pew, 2010). An additional 13% live in the "new" Latino states—Florida, Georgia, Massachusetts, Nevada, North Carolina, Oregon, Virginia, and Washington—that more recently began to experience an influx of Latinos (Pew, 2010). This current explosion is indicative of the type of growth expected within the next few decades and is not exclusive to North Carolina's public schools.

This chapter explores how six North Carolina public school systems accommodate the demographic shifts reflected in their classrooms. These districts acknowledge the challenges that they have encountered in educating diverse populations, especially Latino students. These counties were selected because they have experienced exponential growth (in excess of 61% over 10 years from 2000 to 2010) in their African American and Latino populations (see **Table 27.2**).

County	2000 Latino Population	2010 Latino Population	Growth (%)
County 1	10%	13%	73%
County 2	15%	21%	62%
County 3	6%	11%	132%
County 4	4%	7%	109%
County 5	5%	8%	82%
County 6	11%	16%	61%

Table 27.2   Growth of Latino Population in Six North Carolina Counties

SOURCE: Pew Research Hispanic Center (2010).

North Carolina as a Microcosm of the Changing Complexion of the United States

From 2001 to 2011, the number of minority students increased throughout the United States from 47.7 million to 49.5 million, with non-White students becoming the majority in public schools in the South and West. Overall, White students made up 51.7% of enrollment in public elementary and secondary schools; Blacks, 15.8%; Latino, 23.7%; Asians and Pacific Islanders, 5.1%; and American Indians and Native Alaskans, 1.1%; and two or more races, 2.6%. The number of Latino students enrolled increased in all four regions, with the largest increase in their share of public school enrollment (8%) occurring in the South. The share of Black student enrollment was 24% in the South and 5% in the West. The number of Asian/Pacific Islander students increased in all regions, with the largest increase occurring in the South.

North Carolina is facing the new reality of an increasing Latino population. From 2000 to 2010, its Latino population grew by an explosive 111% (U.S. Census Bureau, 2012). North Carolina's growth rate can serve as an indicator of potential growth in other southern and northeastern states. As their numbers grow, Latinos will become a more significant presence in K-12 and college classrooms. Clearly, like other public education systems, North Carolina cannot

wait to address the needs of this steadily growing population. Nationally, from 1993 to 2010, the enrollment of Latino students in public elementary schools has increased by more than 150%, compared to 20% for African American students and 10% percent for White students.

A burgeoning number of minority students are not achieving academic success in U.S. public schools. Children need access to high-quality early education to gain the skills that are necessary for starting kindergarten ready to learn. However, cost, access, and other barriers keep African American and Latino children out of high-quality early education classrooms. Such education is crucial in order to close the **achievement gap** for African American and Latino students.

The current achievement gap between African American and Latino students and their White counterparts has been well documented. The effects of these performance differences are catastrophic in fourth grade (see **Figure 27.1**). Poor reading skills can be a cause of poor math performance, due to math end-of-grade assessments being comprised of word problems. The achievement gap appears in both elementary and secondary schools. In 2010, about 72% of North Carolina's Latino high school students graduated 10 points below the graduation rates of White students and 2 points behind African Americans (Dewett, 2013). Thus, it becomes important to examine how to successfully educate African American and Latino students and close the reading and mathematics achievement gap for these fast-growing minority groups. In this chapter, we describe this achievement gap in terms of the disparity in academic performance between groups according to income, gender, and cultural background.

African American and Latino Underachievement Through the Lenses of Cultural and Social Capital

In this chapter, the authors draw upon social and cultural theories to explore the challenges that the six counties in North Carolina are experiencing as they implement institutional changes designed to meet the needs of their African American and Latino students. Minority students in North Carolina enter school

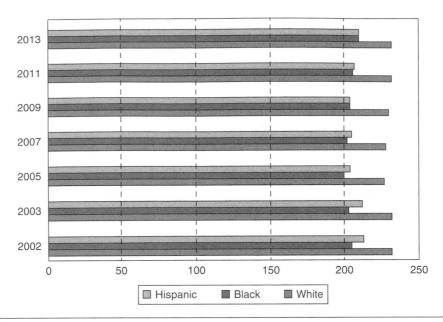

Figure 27.1 North Carolina Fourth-Grade Reading Score Gaps, by Race

SOURCE: Created by the authors using data from the North Carolina Department of Public Instruction.

with a culture that differs from the dominant school culture. Their classmates, teachers, and school administrators often lack understanding or knowledge about African American and Latino culture. The result is a mismatch for educators charged with educating African American and Latino students and increasing their academic success. Fostering an understanding about the social and cultural capital of African American and Latino students is imperative in order to improve their educational outcomes. The current public education system treats the social and cultural capital of minority students as deficient and as less valuable than the dominant culture.

Perry, Steele, and Hilliard (2003) elucidated aspects of Ogbu's (1986) cultural difference theory, which holds that cultural adaptation must precede skill development and intellectual competency. Rather than assuming that skill development and the acquisition of intellectual competency occur simultaneously with cultural adaptation, cultural difference theorists (e.g., Davidson, 1992; Delgado-Gaiten, 1987; Erickson, 1976) insist that cultural adaption is a precursor. Perry and colleagues (2003) also indicated that history and politics have a distinct role in the education of African Americans. She questioned the extent to which culture inhibits the education of minority children, particularly

when teachers confuse cultural differences with deficits. In her discussion of Pierre Bourdieu's (1973) examination of the relationship between culture and inequality and the value added through cultural codes disseminated in schools, Perry wrote,

> Cultural capital is socially inherited cultural competence that facilitates achievement in school. It is unequally distributed, and like economic capital, it has an exchange value. In other words, culture, whether viewed as objective forms (books, works of art), practices (museum visits, concerts), or the institutional currency of academic credentials, is susceptible to treatment in terms of the laws governing macro- and microeconomic relationships. (Perry et al., 2003, p. 67)

Bourdieu (1973) claimed that, because the education system presupposes the possession of cultural capital and few students possess it, there is a great deal of inefficiency in "pedagogic transmission" (i.e., teaching). This inefficiency occurs because students simply do not understand the information their teachers are trying to convey.

Other definitions of cultural capital include Kincheloe's (1999) statement that it "involves ways of dressing, acting, thinking, or representing oneself" (p. 222). English and Steffy (2002) defined cultural capital as "the lived experiences and linguistic, conceptual knowledge, skills and dispositions prized by a specific culture, which are available to be purchased within it by consumers and patrons; and which are also ultimately embedded in schools and the tests in use in schools" (p. 18).

Unlike cultural capital, which is focused on individual experiences, **social capital** consists of aspects of social organization through which productive relationships and networks are developed and nurtured. These relationships provide and facilitate access to opportunities and advantageous outcomes; their maintenance is ongoing. Social capital gives people the ability to achieve things they would not be able to achieve without it. It incorporates three components: the obligation and expectations of reciprocity in social relationships, norms and social control, and information channels (Coleman, 1988). Bourdieu (1973) used the terms *habitus* and *field* to describe inequalities in the people's ability to acquire and develop social capital. Habitus is a system of dispositions, whereas field is a structured system of social relations at the micro and macro levels. Only when the habitus and field are aligned can African American and Latino parents and their children enjoy the advantages associated with social capital. Ideally, parents use their social capital to promote their children's educational achievement, for example, when African American and Latino parents may use social networks to gain information on how to seek educational resources for their children, experience valuable interactions with other parents during school-sponsored activities, or engage in parent-teacher conferences. The next section explores how the lack of social capital networks can impact student **underachievement**.

Descriptions of African American and Latino Underachievement

Many African American and Latino children entering kindergarten already lag behind their classmates in reading and mathematics. Latino students as a group have the lowest level of education and the highest dropout rate of any group of students in the United States. A number of factors negatively impact their achievement. Ferguson (2003) noted inadequate access to early education programs as well as inadequate levels of family income, low levels of parental

education, and high rates of poverty and single-parent households as one of the most resounding factors. Gándara (2004) suggested that residential mobility, lack of peer support for academic achievement, racial and ethnic stereotyping, low teacher expectations, inequality in K-12 schools, and limited English ability are also to blame.

While the above-mentioned issues are certainly factors in underachievement, they do not represent the whole story. The lack of **cultural sensitivity** among teachers and administrators, **subtractive schooling processes**, at-risk school environments, and the lack of qualified teachers also contribute to the underachievement of African American and Latino students.

Cultural Sensitivity and Latinos

Latinos can be White, Black, or indigenous, though many are of mixed-race heritage. Latinos are a heterogeneous group of people that faces many contradictions and tensions. Many Latinos are American citizens who were born in the United States or Puerto Rico. Others do not have legal residency. Latino students often must become bilingual or resolve to be monolingual. Many Latino students are bicultural, straddling two worlds—at home and at school. Suárez-Orozco and Páez (2002) wrote that part of understanding Latino culture is learning that it has roots in more than 12 different countries, with distinct backgrounds based on class, race, and skin color. The cultural background of White, upper-middle-class, third-generation Cuban Americans differ considerably from that of newly arrived Mexican immigrants. Latinos do not constitute a race. Outside of the United States, persons of Hispanic descent are not identified as Latino or Hispanic, but are described in terms of their country of origin, for example, as Puerto Rican, Salvadoran, or Colombian. Noguera (2008) found that many first-generation Latinos have a desire to work hard and see value in making sacrifices to obtain their goals. Second- and third-generation Latinos tend to be socialized, to be less optimistic, and less willing to buy into the hope of the American Dream, as they have to contend with poverty and racial oppression. It is important for educators to understand how first-generation Latino students become acclimated to life in the United States and how they make sense of immigration issues that target undocumented immigrants. Second-generation Latinos face different issues. Some may not identify at all with their parents' country of origin. It is vital not to make assumptions but to get to know the Latino students who are part of each school's unique Latino population. The students' language ability, literacy level, or parental background should not inhibit the teachers' expectations concerning their potential.

Subtractive Schooling Processes

The experience of being stripped of important social and cultural resources and of having these resources devalued by teachers and administrators is a common one for African American and Latino students in U.S. schools. The results of this experience, which include increased vulnerability to adverse academic outcomes, are also familiar. At times, authority figures within the dominant culture attempt to acculturate minorities without fully considering all of the possible consequences of their attitudes and procedures. Devaluation is generally manifested as a failure to acknowledge the cultures and prior experiences that minority students bring to school. Course topics that do not reflect the accomplishments of minority students or even negate them promote feelings of disconnect and the inability to relate to course materials and assignments. When classroom teachers label African American and Latino students as uneducable or as low achievers on the basis of their dress, speech, and friends, this rejection perpetuates the cycle of marginalization. Marginalization serves as a consequence for not ascribing to the dominant culture within the school.

Academic Stratification

School structure may perpetuate the underachievement of African American and Latino students. **Academic stratification** or grouping based upon specific criteria or characteristics is commonly practiced, as is cultural tracking. For example, students whose cultures are not valued may be sorted into lower academic tracks, particularly if their academic abilities and achievement are perceived to be lower as well. In these situations, only minority students who display the behaviors of the dominant culture are allowed to enroll in college preparatory academic tracks; the remaining students are relegated to vocational courses.

Academic stratification is based on the premise that in order for low-performing students to achieve success, they must be separated from other students and taught a simplified curriculum. Stratification exposes students to unequal levels of academic content and discourse, as well as teacher quality. These factors can produce significantly different academic outcomes for students, depending on the academic tracks they are assigned to. High-achieving students continue to move ahead, unhampered by their peers, as students who have been identified as low achievers fall further behind. This approach widens the achievement gap.

At-Risk School Environments

It is common for minority students to be viewed as problematic and for their achievement to be critiqued using a deficit model. Bronfenbrenner (1979) suggested a paradigm shift in which the term *at-risk* would be applied to school environments instead of labeling only those who attend the schools as at-risk. The premise behind this shift is that changing a school's environment or culture is far easier than changing the students in attendance. In addition, expanding the label to include schools themselves acknowledges that teachers, administrators, and school culture also influence whether certain students are thought to be at-risk. Factors that may cause a school's environment to be considered as at-risk include poor building and equipment maintenance, low expectations for student achievement, high expulsion and disciplinary referral rates, alienating classroom environments, and poorly qualified or incompetent teachers.

Lack of Qualified Teachers

Ironically, schools with high minority populations are often staffed with teachers who have the least amount of such experience; these teachers may not even be fully credentialed. Although such teachers are required to undergo additional training to obtain full certification, they may not be comfortable employing evidenced-based strategies to meet their students' needs. This lack of teacher preparedness means that teacher-education programs should be restructured to produce teachers who have a sound understanding of how to work with minority students.

Effectively Educating African American and Latino Students

African American and Latino students will become academically **successful** when negative epistemologies regarding them are changed with counternarratives and when culturally appropriate instruction is provided. As has been stated, from 2000 to 2010, many rural counties in North Carolina have experienced exponential growth (in excess of 61%) in their Latino population (U.S. Census Bureau, 2012). Administrative narratives from North Carolina assistant superintendents and principals presented in this chapter offer templates for districts that not only have had huge surges in their Latino and/or African American population but also are struggling to create positive settings in which African American and Latino students can flourish.

This chapter examines the challenges that counties with growing African American and Latino populations are experiencing as they strive to educate African American and Latino students and the strategies and resources that they have utilized. The academic performance and needs of African American and Latino students are discussed, as are possible explanations of achievement gaps in their counties and schools and the knowledge, skills, dispositions, and linguistic abilities that are needed in order for African American and Latino students to be successful. The challenges that districts with growing African American and/or Latino populations experience can be redefined by examining the following themes:

- Addressing beliefs about who deserves to be helped by using counternarratives
- Educating children whose parent are believed to devalue education
- Finding staff/faculty who look like the children in our buildings
- Distinguishing between the language and ability needs of English language learners (ELLs)
- Instituting systematic approaches to reform

In his poem "The Second Coming," William Butler Yeats (1921/1998) stated, "The best lack all conviction, while the worst are full of passionate intensity." Research-based solutions that address strategies for improving achievement for African American and Latino students are widely available. What is lacking in some cases is the will or the conviction needed to implement lasting comprehensive solutions. Questioning the legitimacy of a student's right to be educated impacts the treatment of African American and Latino students. To what extent are African American and Latino students ostracized, ignored, or rebuffed as they seek to be educated?

One of the educators interviewed, Dr. Bennington, stated, "There is absolutely the belief of some that you should not be allowed to take advantage of our public system if you are undocumented or not born here." Mr. Sanford commented that "We have the traditional conservative culture where some believe minorities are not supposed to be educated or succeed or they are not valued." Both Dr. Bennington and Mr. Sanford described beliefs held by some staff members in their respective counties about what students have a right to be educated.

Dr. Rudolph shared statements made in his presence by faculty members in his district who apparently equate being Latino with being undocumented. "For some reason, they feel it's OK to say this to me. They don't call them Hispanics; they call them Mexicans, and [one person] said, 'They need to go back where they came from.' I fix that if they say it in my presence." By making these statements in the presence of a central office administrator, these teachers revealed their disregard for distinct Latino cultures and openly ignored the fact that many of their Latino students are U.S. citizens.

Ms. Chandler concurred. "Across the county, some expect all students to learn. Others view Latinos as not worth the time because they'll move to other areas very soon. Our [Latino] students enter without having basic skills. [They] can be transient and often [have] no English [proficiency]." Ms. Mangum did not raise the issue of whether Latino students deserved to be helped but did note that mobility and language issues affect the performance of Latino students. "Hispanics move quite often due to the huge farming areas throughout the county. We have four districts within this county, and some Hispanics have attended all districts. Their limited English is the primary issue with their performance." Part of the authors' work is examining through professional development deepseated beliefs that some faculty and staff have about Latino students and whether Latino students deserve to have the assistance needed to be academically successful. While other comments were made about educating African American students, the comments about belonging and who deserved to be educated were primarily directed towards Latino students.

Changing Teachers' Epistemologies

Teachers' belief systems and perceived structural systems (epistemologies) matter. Martin (2007) stated that teachers' epistemologies, including beliefs about natural ability and merit, impact their effectiveness with minority students. Whether they have been consciously or unconsciously adopted, epistemologies also directly affect how administrators treat students. Perry et al. (2003) advised educators at all levels to study theories of achievement/underachievement and to articulate their own belief systems; they noted that what teachers believe about achievement will impact how they teach students of color.

Two theories documented by Perry et al. (2003) are particularly useful in explaining racial minority underachievement: cultural difference theory and social mobility theory. The changes in one's social and economic position over time are defined as social mobility (Riddle, 2013). According to cultural difference theory, the academic failure of racial minorities is predicated on mismatches between home and school cultures (Gándara, 2004).

Using Counternarratives

Effective teachers introduce counternarratives that are in opposition to the dominant society's notions about the intellectual inferiority of African Americans and Latinos. Perry et al. (2003) defined counternarratives as messages passed consistently and intentionally on in a group setting. Antiracist counternarratives are an important part of effectively educating African American and Latino students (Martin, 2007).

Educating Children Whose Parents Are Believed to Devalue Education

Dr. Xavier stated, "Latinos live for the now, but there are small pockets of parents, Black, Native Americans, and Latinos, who value education. Their educational progression is determined by their socioeconomic status (SES). Even our affluent farmers want better for their children." Dr. Xavier described the impact of extreme poverty on her parents' ability

to provide their children with better experiences. She also added that many parents in her rural county have not had positive experiences with schools.

Dr. Xavier did not provide evidence to substantiate her claim that Latinos live for the now or for her assertion that only small pockets of Blacks, Native Americans, and Latinos value education. It is unclear why Dr. Xavier and some of the other assistant superintendents devoted so much attention to criticizing parents and accusing them of not caring about their children's education.

Ms. Mangum stated,

Poverty is an issue for us. A lot of our parents have negative experiences about school and they pass their experiences on. Many of our current teachers were their teachers. Parent support is always a problem, along with resources because of the size and varied needs of our students is always a problem. We are a typical rural farming county. Many of our parents need parenting skills themselves due to their own low skills.

Mr. Sanford commented,

Education is not valued in many of our kids' homes nor is it a priority that is passed down. Now Ds or Fs are acceptable. When I was in school, your grades determined Christmas and birthday gifts. Kids don't have the motivation to do well because they still get rewarded no matter what the grades or behaviors. Parents are interested in the education of their kids in the lower grades, but not as much when they get to middle or high school. I think because they too dropped out of school around that age.

When asked to describe the culture of the county where she worked and the culture's effect on the performance of African American and Latino students, Dr. Xavier said,

Some don't value education so they don't instill that value in their children. Some in the county think it's OK for kids not to learn. The affluent parents want their kids to do well and often have the dollars and resources for them to get what they need to succeed. Parents and kids alike should know that we expect our teachers to use basic literacy and math skills to learn within all content areas. We know the demographics of the county. We expect kids to come and at least try to learn. We expect parents to support us as we try to teach their kids.

Studies have found strong correlations between parental involvement and academic achievement (Lee & Bowen, 2006). Parental involvement takes the form of attendance at parent-teacher conferences, participation in parent-teacher organizations, and engagement in volunteer activities at their children's schools. Within the home, parental involvement includes helping with homework assignments and projects, discussing daily school experiences, and structuring home activities to include school content and an academic focus.

Levels of parental involvement vary based upon amounts of engagement. In turn, engagement may vary according to ethnic background. For example, parents in nondominant groups may be less involved with school-based activities. Negative educational experiences, unfamiliarity with or lack of knowledge about schools and their practices, limited English skills, and lack of understanding of educational jargon (in any language) are the most common reasons for reluctance in school involvement (Lee & Bowen, 2006).

It is surmised that the parents' limited involvement in school or engulfment in poverty has influenced the conclusions that were drawn about devaluing school. Focusing on a litany of parental limitations is counterproductive. As leaders, our focus should be on how we educate African American and Latino children, not on disparaging their families and underscoring their shortcomings. Being uneducated, living in poverty, or not attending parent-teacher meetings should not be equated with devaluing education. We need to focus our attention on what we can change in schools—our approach to working with the children in our classrooms and the educators in our buildings. Why would we really work to educate children if we truly believed that even their own parents did not care

about their education? These types of assumptions need to be challenged.

Finding Faculty That Look Like the Children in Our Buildings

Teacher shortages in the United States, especially for teachers who are capable of teaching ELLs, are increasing. Many current teachers are monolingual and are therefore not prepared to address the needs of students whose primary language is not English. District administrators commonly believe that minority teachers and educators are difficult to find. Fostering positive recruiting relationships with teacher preparations programs located at historically Black institutions (HBCUs) or Hispanic-serving institutions (HSIs) dramatically increases the chances of being able to hire minority teachers in districts with high numbers of Latino and African American students. Custodial staff and teacher assistants should be considered as candidates for grow-your-own initiatives in all districts (see **Sidebar 27.1**).

Dr. Rudolph shared a story about recruiting a Latino male teacher from another county to teach Algebra I. He added that the teacher's students performed exceptionally well on standardized tests because of how tenacious this teacher was about parent communication. "I had growth every year in my school when I was a principal—every measure you want to look at and people asked me why. I went out and found folks that looked like the children in my building." Minority teachers exist, but finding them depends on where we are looking. If we continue to recruit at the same colleges and universities, we will continue to employ the same types of teachers from

---

Sidebar 27.1 A Checklist for Working With Minority Students and Their Families

- Despite the past educational experiences of parents, they still understand the importance of education and want the best education for their children.
- Valuing a diverse staff offers unspoken validation to students of diverse cultures.
- Commit to "growing your own" from your cadre of support staff to help diversify your personnel. Active recruitment efforts include Hispanic-serving institutions and historically Black colleges and institutions.
- Language difference does not constitute language deficit.
- Effective educational reform permeates policies, procedures, and practices to become institutionalized.

the same racial/ethnic backgrounds. We should begin to build relationships with career services offices in HBCUs and HSIs.

Dr. Bennington observed, "We're at a point where we're going to have more Latino students than African American students. They need mentors that look like them and talk like them; they need opportunities beyond athletics." Ms. Mangum added, "The problem is many of our teachers cannot relate to the needs of many of our parents or students. [We need] more diverse teachers and for our current teachers, more professional development on how to work with minority students." Though not specifically referring to hiring minority teachers and administrators, Dr. Xavier underscored the importance of hiring highly skilled teachers in her rural county. "Exposure to literacy experiences. Prerequisites for reading skills. African Americans, Native Americans, and Latinos enter school already about two years behind White kids. Many of our teachers don't know how to deal with, teach kids how to read if they enter school not knowing. Exposure to rich culture is what is missing." Dr. Rudolph asserted that having a diverse staff contributed to increasing the achievement of African American and Latino students in his building when he was a principal. He and other assistant superintendents called attention to the importance of a diverse cadre of mentors, bilingual staff, and the critical importance of building relationships with local HBCUs and HSIs that could lead to diverse hiring practices. Dr. Rudolph added that he believed that "Latinos and African Americans fare better when there is someone in the building that they can identify with." Strategies that lead to creating successful learning environments for African American and Latino students include addressing beliefs about who deserves to be helped by using counternarratives, educating children whose parents are believed to devalue education, and locating and hiring educators from diverse racial backgrounds that are representative of the student body.

Distinguishing Between the Language and Ability Needs of English Language Learners

It is vital to accurately assess the needs of ELLs and not confuse second language acquisition with a disability. Districts need teachers trained in second language acquisition who can discern the difference between language and ability. Dr. Bennington stated,

We don't have enough teachers who are able to communicate with our second language learners. We have not yet mastered the ability to determine if students are struggling because of Exceptional Children (EC) issues or if they are in fact slow learners in their native language.

Ms. Chandler added, "More bilingual teachers. More reading focus, not much differentiation other than ESL is provided. Our district treats them all [Latino students] as low performing. Only difference really acknowledged is language disparity." Ms. Chandler also mentioned the importance of hiring more bilingual staff. In her response, she did not specify hiring bilingual Latino staff but mentioned the value of having people on staff who could communicate in Spanish with Latino students who are monolingual.

One challenge for counties with limited bilingual staff is the ability to accurately assess the language needs of ELLs so that they are not mistakenly diagnosed. Dr. Bennington stated,

The first thing people want to say is that they are second language learners. That is why they are not doing well. Let's do wholesale assessment before we decide. In most districts we have some staff members who really get it.

Infusing a Systematic Approach to Reform

The development of a **systematic approach to reform** is critical to successfully addressing the achievement issues of Latino students. Once successful reform is developed and implemented, school and district administrators need to assess how to best implement the initiatives systemwide and account for variations in implementation. According to Mr. Sanford, "We have not done much differently for Latinos other than the implementation of English as a Second Language (ESL) program. Since both African Americans and Latinos are underachieving, we've continued to do the same for both populations." Dr. Rudolph shared his frustration with looking at data at the beginning of the year and discussing the gaps with the leadership team but not implementing a plan to address the gaps. Dr. Bennington concurred. He is anxious to create a consistent plan that will be followed each year, and he added,

We need to make sure it informs our decisions at every level. "They are going to have to speak to the gaps in their school improvement plans. In our learning walks, we'll be looking at how engaged our students are.

Central office administrators acknowledged that some initiatives had resulted in a modicum of success with specific target groups. What was missing was a comprehensive district plan to address the needs of African American and Latino students that was implemented with fidelity because staff believed that it was right for kids.

Systematic reform should include the infusion of best practices. Effective teachers of African American and Latino students are aware of possible problems minority students have had in school, but they do not allow past performance to dictate their potential. Effective teachers treat their minority students as if they are already high achievers. Ferguson (2008) listed ways that teachers treat students differently based on whether they are perceived to be high achievers or low achievers. Effective teachers avoid these behaviors.

> For low achievers, these include waiting less time for them to answer; giving them the answers or calling on someone else, rather than trying to improve their responses by offering clues or repeating or rephrasing questions; accepting inappropriate behavior or incorrect answers; criticizing them more often for failure; praising them less often for success; failing to give feedback to their public responses; paying less attention; calling on them less often with questions; seating them further from the teacher; demanding less from low achievers (teaching them less, providing unsolicited help); interacting with them more in private than public, and monitoring and structuring their activities more closely; in grading tests and assignments, not giving them the benefit of the doubt in borderline cases. (p. 95)

Effective systematic reform includes the utilization of **culturally responsive instruction**.

Culturally Responsive Instruction

Latino and African American students in U.S. public schools achieve higher levels of academic success in classrooms that reflect their prior knowledge and cultural backgrounds and when teachers connect course content with their present (social) realities and interests (Gay, 1999; Martin, 2007). Scheurich and Skrla (2003), who describe the importance of **culturally responsive teaching**, contend that many White teachers who are otherwise well-meaning

unconsciously harbor negative beliefs about minority students and are therefore unable to recognize the assets that students of color bring to the classroom. According to Gay (1999), teachers should develop effective learning environments for African American and Latino students by managing classroom discourse, providing culturally relevant conceptual examples, delivering appropriate curricula, and creating positive classroom climates.

Teachers control the discourse in their classrooms. The degree to which culturally diverse students participate in classroom discourse depends upon turn-taking rules, student attention levels and attention-getting behaviors, wait time for teacher responses, length of speech exchanges with teachers, student ability to question proposed learning strategies, and other student feedback mechanisms (Conchas, 2001). Teachers should extend wait times, integrate active learning strategies, and incorporate questions that require higher order thinking skills (Conchas, 2001). Students must be supplied with opportunities to "talk through learning tasks together—posing questions, finding solutions, and demonstrating mastery" (Moschkovich, 1999). These approaches and strategies have been found to promote learning by African American students (Moschkovich, 1999).

As they convey the meaning of abstract concepts, pertinent skills, facts, and principles, teachers must use various examples, illustrations, and anecdotes. In the absence of culturally relevant examples, learning opportunities for African American and Latino students are limited. As research on other minority students has shown (Gay, 1999), African American and Latino students are more likely to learn when classroom experiences are connected to their cultural experiences (Gay, 1999). Educating teachers about the history, cultural traditions, and background of Latino students is essential if teachers are to be capable of introducing ethnically diverse, antiracist content.

Although the United States has advanced the ideal for more than a century that a high-quality public education is the birthright of all American children, public schools cannot fulfill this noble purpose unless everyone (parents, policymakers, and the general public) commit to sustaining education as a public trust and a promise to future generations (Nieto, 2005, p. 1).

Appendix A: Interview Questions for Assistant Superintendents

Name: **Gender:**   **School Name:**

Introductory statement:

Thank you for your willingness to participate in our study and do this interview with me today. This study will investigate how six southern counties are supporting the surging Latino student population. Your comments will be treated as strictly confidential; no names will ever be linked directly to your comments, so no one else will know what you said.

Please feel free to say as much or as little as you like in response to my questions. There is no right answer—I just want to know what you think.

During this interview, I will be taking notes using a notepad or, if permissible, I would like to use a laptop computer. If you would prefer I not use a laptop, I can simply use written notes. What is your preference?

1. How many years have you been an assistant superintendent?

2. How many years have you been an assistant superintendent in this district?

3. How many years of experience did you have as a principal or other central office position?

4. Where did you attend college and what degrees did you earn?

5. What do you consider to be your race or ethnicity?

6. How many faculty/staff do you have in the district?

7. How many Latino faculty/staff do you have in the district?

8. What is the current number of Latino students in your district?

9. Briefly tell me about the performance of the Latino students in your district.

10. If there is a gap, why do you think the performance of Latino students lags behind White students in your district?

11. What are some of the needs that Latino students in your district have?

12. What are some of the challenges that your district has encountered as you have tried to meet these needs?

13. In 2000, the Latino population in your district was _____. It has now grown to _____. What additional resources has your district allocated to support Latino students?

14. What additional resources would Latino students in your district benefit from receiving?

15. What are one or two successful strategies that your district has utilized to support the academic performance of Latino students?

16. How would you describe the culture of your county? How, if at all, does the county's culture affect the performance of Latino students?

17. What should Latino students know about the expectations of _____ County teachers in order to be successful?

18. What knowledge and skills are needed for students to be successful in your county?

19. What linguistic ability and dispositions are needed for students to be successful in your county?

20. What institutional changes would improve the district's ability to better accommodate the needs of students?

NOTE: These interview questions were developed by the authors of this chapter for use with administrators at public schools in North Carolina and have not been previously published.

Appendix B: Interview Questions for Principals

Name: **Gender:**   **School Name:**

Introductory statement:

Thank you for your willingness to participate in our study and do this interview with me today. This study will investigate how six southern counties are supporting the surging Latino student population. Your comments will be treated as strictly confidential; no names will ever be linked directly to your comments, so no one else will know what you said.

Please feel free to say as much or as little as you like in response to my questions. There is no right answer—I just want to know what you think.

During this interview, I will be taking notes using a notepad or, if permissible, I would like to use a laptop computer. If you would prefer I not use a laptop, I can simply use written notes. What is your preference?

1. How many years have you been a principal?

2. How many years have you been a principal in this district?

3. How many years of experience did you have as an assistant principal?

4. Where did you attend college and what degrees did you earn?

5. What do you consider to be your race or ethnicity?

6. How many faculty/staff do you have in your building?

7. How many Latino faculty/staff do you have your building?

8. What is the current number of Latino students in your building?

9. Briefly tell me about the performance of the Latino students in your building.

10. If there is a gap, why do you think the performance of Latino students lags behind White students in your school?

11. What are some of the needs that Latino students in your school have?

12. What are some of the challenges that your building has encountered as you have tried to meet these needs?

13. In 2000, the Latino population in your district was _____. It has now grown to _____. What additional resources has your district allocated to support Latino students?

14. What additional resources would Latino students in your school benefit from receiving?

15. What are one or two successful strategies that your district or school has utilized to support the academic performance of Latino students?

16. How would you describe the culture of your school? How, if at all, does the school's culture affect the performance of Latino students?

17. What should Latino students know about the expectations of _____ School teachers in order to be successful?

18. What knowledge and skills are needed for students to be successful in your school?

19. What linguistic ability and dispositions are needed for students to be successful in your school?

20. What institutional changes would improve the district's ability to better accommodate the needs of students?

NOTE: These interview questions were developed by the authors of this chapter for use with administrators at public schools in North Carolina and have not been previously published.

Key Chapter Terms

Definitions of terms utilized throughout this chapter are vital to understanding the purpose of this research. The most important terms to understand are academic stratification, achievement gap, cultural capital, culturally responsive instruction, and cultural sensitivity.

Academic stratification: The process of sorting or tracking students into levels or high school tracks based upon expected academic attainment.

Achievement gap: The persistent disparity of a number of educational measures between the performances of groups of students, especially groups defined by socioeconomic status (SES), race/ethnicity, and gender.

Cultural capital: The values, beliefs, and dispositions obtained from family and peers.

Cultural sensitivity: The awareness that cultural differences and similarities exist and have an effect on values, learning, and behaviors.

Culturally responsive instruction: Instruction that makes meaningful connections to the diverse backgrounds of classroom students while emphasizing rigorous curricula and high expectations for achievement.

Culturally responsive teaching: Developing an understanding of the importance of culturally responsive teaching is imperative for the success of minority students. Helping educators develop sociocultural consciousness (an understanding that one's way of thinking, behaving, and being is influenced by race, ethnicity, social class, and language) coupled with the desire to learn about their students' past experiences, home and community cultures, and experiences both in and outside of school all help to build positive relationships. Using a variety of teaching strategies that help students construct knowledge, build on their personal and cultural strengths, and examine the curriculum from multiple perspectives are instrumental in promoting inclusive classroom environments.

Social capital: The ability to develop and nurture productive relationships and networks that provide access to opportunities and advantageous outcomes.

Subtractive schooling processes: The stripping or devaluing minority youth of important social and cultural resources, resulting in their being viewed as deviant from the dominant culture.

Successful and effective: These terms, which were used interchangeably in this chapter, refer to communication and behaviors that promote academic success. For high school students, academic success is defined as the sum of interactions in subject-matter classrooms that help students succeed in class and learn the material that is presented and discussed.

Systematic approach to reform: Knowledge of how a system interacts with specific component subsystems, boundaries, inputs and outputs, feedback, and relationships is imperative when making changes to a school district's culture. In the U.S. education system, the school is the central institution of public instruction. However, schools include many components that interact, including teaching, administration, and finance. Any worthwhile reform initiatives must take a systematic approach if they are to achieve maximum effectiveness.

Underachievement: Discrepancy between a child's school performance and his or her actual ability. This word should not be used as a label for a child but rather a description of a child's current academic progress.

References

Bourdieu, P. (1973). Cultural reproduction and social reproduction. In R. Brown (Ed.), *Knowledge, education, and cultural change,* (pp. 71–112). London, England: Tavistock.

Bronfenbrenner, U. (1979). Beyond the deficit model in child and family policy. *Teachers College Press*, 81, 95–104.

Coleman, J. S. (1988). Social capital in the creation of human capital. *American Journal of Sociology*, 94, 95–120.

Conchas, G. (2001). Structuring failure and success: Understanding the variability in Latino school engagement. *Harvard Educational Review, 71*(3), 475–504.

Dewett, D. (2013, March 20). *Left off the path: Latinos and high school graduation.* Retrieved from http://wunc.org/post/left-path-latinos-and-high-school-graduation

English, F. W., & Steffy, B. E. (2002). *Deep curriculum alignment.* Lanham, MD: Scarecrow.

Ferguson, R. (2003). Teachers' perceptions and expectations and the Black-White test score gap. *Urban Education, 38*(4), 460–507.

Ferguson, R. (2008). *Toward excellence with equity: An emerging vision for closing the achievement gap.* Cambridge, MA: Harvard Education.

Gándara, P. (2004). *Latino achievement: Identifying models that foster success.* Davis: University of California.

Gay, G. (1999, November). *Including at-risk students in standards-based reform.* Paper presented at the second meeting of the Mid-continent Research for Education and Learning Diversity Roundtable (MCREl), Aurora, CO.

Johnson, J. (2006). People on the move: Implications for US higher education. *The College Board Review,* 209, 43–49.

Johnson, J., & Kasarda, J. (2011, January). *Six disruptive demographic trends: What census 2010 will reveal.* Chapel Hill, NC: Frank Hawkins Kenan Institute of Private Enterprise.

Kincheloe, J. (1999). *How do we tell the workers? The socioeconomic foundations of work and vocational education.* Boulder, CO: Westview.

Lee, J.-S., & Bowen, N. (2006). Parent involvement, cultural capital, and the achievement gap among elementary school children. *American Educational Research Journal, 43*(2), 193–218.

Martin, D. (2007). Beyond missionaries or cannibals: Who should teach mathematics to African American children? *High School Journal, 91*(1), 6–28.

Moschkovich, J. (1999). Understanding the needs of Latino students in reform-oriented mathematics classrooms. In L. Ortiz-Franco, N. Hernandez, & Y. De La Cruz (Eds.), *Changing the faces of mathematics: Perspectives of Latinos* (pp. 5–12). Reston, VA: National Council of Teachers of Mathematics.

Nieto, S. (2005). *Why we teach.* New York, NY: Teachers College Press.

Noguera, P. A. (2008). *The trouble with Black boys and other reflections on race, equity, and the future of public education.* San Francisco, CA: Jossey-Bass.

Perry, T., Steele, C., & Hilliard, A. (2003). *Young, gifted, and Black: Promoting high achievement among African-American students.* Boston, MA: Beacon Press.

Pew Research Hispanic Center. (2010). *Census 2010.* Retrieved from http://www.pewhispanic.org/census-2010/

Riddle, R., (2013). Social mobility and education. In S. Ward (Ed.), *A student's guide to education studies,* (pp. 23–35). New York, NY: Routledge.

Scheurich, J. J., & Skrla, L. (2003). *Leadership for equity and excellence.* Thousand Oaks, CA: Sage.

Suárez-Orozco, M. & Páez, M. M. (2002). *Latinos: Remaking America.* Berkeley, CA: University of California Press.

U.S. Census Bureau. (2011). *Population change for the United States, regions, states, and Puerto Rico: 2000 to 2010.* Retrieved from http://www.census.gov/prod/cen2010/briefs/c2010br-01.pdf

U.S. Census Bureau News. (2012, December). *U.S. census bureau projections show a slower growing, older, more diverse nation a half century from now.* Retrieved from https://www.census.gov/newsroom/releases/archives/population/cb12-243.html

Yeats, W. B. (1998). The second coming. In W. Harmon (Ed.), *The classic hundred poems.* New York, NY: Columbia University Press. (Original work published 1921).

Further Readings

Browne, J. R. (2012). *Walking the equity talk.* Thousand Oaks, CA: Sage.

This book shows how culturally courageous leadership by all school community stakeholders can help achieve equitable learning opportunities and outcomes for all students.

Singleton, G. (2013). *More courageous conversations about race.* Thousand Oaks, CA: Corwin.

This text demonstrates the positive outcomes for students and their schools when educators have the will, the skill, and the knowledge to sustain courageous conversations about race. It explicitly embraces other people of color in the drive for racial equity and illustrates how the courageous conversations protocol can be applied to their circumstances.

Singleton, G., & Linton, C. (2005). *Courageous conversations about race: A field guide for achieving equity in schools.* Thousand Oaks, CA: Corwin.

Many educators are acutely aware of the statistical gaps in achievement between different racial groups. Examining the achievement gap through the prism of race explains the need for candid, courageous conversations about race so that educators may understand why performance inequity persists and learn how they can develop a curriculum that promotes true academic parity.

PART X

POLITICS, ELECTIONS, AND ACCOUNTABILITY

28

School Leadership and Politics

Catherine Marshall

University of North Carolina, Chapel Hill

Darlene C. Ryan

Glenwood Elementary School, Chapel Hill, North Carolina

Jeffrey E. Uhlenberg

Guilford County Schools, Greensboro, North Carolina

Principals' frequent refrains are "every day brings a new political demand," and "ultimately, I am the one who's responsible." This chapter provides an overview of what principals need to know to manage the challenges of such political demands and responsibilities.

Power, Conflict, and Leaders as Political Actors

Many central office administrators believe that principals and superintendents are terminated not for student achievement (although they should be), but for their **politics**—or for political reasons. School leaders must acknowledge the political, the power struggles, and the battles over fundamental differences in **values**. A school is a political system that has both real and symbolic resources—ranging from pencils and salaries to status, access, power, and prestige.

School politics is mostly about manipulating and bargaining over who gets what—and who controls who

gets what. Principals who ignore politics or perform as if school leadership centers on technical competencies will leave themselves, their staff, their parents, their communities, and their students vulnerable.

Whether they see playing politics as a dance, a game, a craft, or a frustration, they do have to reckon with power, conflicts of values and interests, and political actors. Often, the challenges they face are **wicked problems**.

Society's Wicked Problems Land on Principals' Shoulders

Handling problems is a primary role of the principal, and there is an expectation that ultimately the principal is responsible. Challenges increase when these problems are complex and full of obstacles that are "wicked" (Rittel & Webber, 1973, p. 160). Wicked problems often have no clear solution and may involve conflicting values or perceived mistakes that carry consequences (pp. 161–166). They never go away because they come from chronic challenges, such as poverty, violence, the tendency for people to take care of their self-interests and ignore others, and the like (Head & Alford, 2008).

The following are examples of wicked problems that principals have to manage:

- Dealing with high-poverty schools evaluated by student proficiency on state tests
- Acknowledging parent groups with issue-specific agendas
- Cracking down on bullying while also the addressing underlying causes
- Working with ineffective, tenured teachers protected by union representation
- Building an effective staff with common vision while receiving placements, such as teachers or assistant principals, who are being shifted around by the district
- Investing the time to develop new teachers while also ensuring students receive adequate instruction
- Navigating the lines of jurisdiction between principals and school resource officers
- Promoting academic excellence while sponsoring successful athletic programs
- Balancing an open, inviting school with safety precautions
- Retaining an ethical culture in the midst of high-stakes testing

Principals quickly learn that the problems they face are often wicked in nature. They are expected to support their teachers, advocate for their students, market their schools, raise their test scores, encourage parent involvement, keep their buildings safe, promote diversity, address personnel issues, and much, much, more. No day is ever the same for a principal except for one guarantee: Every day, principals will contend with a wicked problem.

Power, Principals' Roles, and the Organizational Realities of Schools

Being politically wise and strategic means actively engaging in the political environment. Three roles a politically wise leader takes to manage issues and problems are the diplomat/negotiator, political strategist, and the executive. The executive principal brings the facts and data to discussions as promoter of neutral decision making (Marshall & Gerstl-Pepin, 2005). However, schools are organizations

whose realities make every decision political. In order for the principal to work effectively as a political strategist, the person must always keep in mind the powerful forces and context of issues.

The hypothetical case below demonstrates how the leader navigates school politics in the three roles.

Political Realities: Roles of the Wise Leader in Navigating Decision Making

Principal Jewel had a quite intense meeting with a parent who wanted his child moved from a classroom because he did not feel the child's needs were being met. She knew that her assistant principal, Ms. Normal, had also met with the parent. The child had not qualified for the advanced class based on assessments, and the parent was attempting to negotiate using his connections, knowing that his child would benefit greatly from advanced programming (or placement).

A joint meeting of the administrators and parent was set up. During the meeting, the parent had difficulty articulating why the student's needs were not being met, and both administrators reported that the parent made "irrational and disrespectful comments."

A second meeting was held with both administrators, the expert district support personnel, and the parent. The parent was very agitated; Ms. Jewel had intense reactions to the parent's behavior, but she remained calm.

The assistant principal, Ms. Normal, reflected, "I'm sure that such behavior would not be tolerated in the parent's place of business. I admired how you stood by your decision and your beliefs and stayed calm."

Ms. Jewel's resolute control of her emotions enabled her to diplomatically navigate this intense political environment. Assistant Principal Normal learned from seeing the behaviors of the politically wise leader in choosing among the roles of diplomat/negotiator, political strategist, and the executive as described by Catherine Marshall and Cynthia Gerstl-Pepin (2005). Ms. Jewel used much skill and tact in responding to this irate parent's demands for special privileges. Strategically, the principal understood the threat posed by the angry parent. When the parent was not satisfied, the principal took an executive role, enabling her to defuse the situation through behind-the-scenes work and to bring the data and research to the discussion to facilitate neutral decision making.

This case required navigating to preserve equity values and instructional procedures, calling upon district personnel for outside reinforcements and anticipating and fending off power plays. Principals' power lies in comprehension of the organizational realities and creating alliances from among constituents who believe the principal has influence and can win (Yukl & Van Fleet, 1992). Crafty politicians can create win-win solutions and project a caring, facilitative approach. In an ideal environment, open lines of communication facilitate team building, maximize effectiveness, and contribute to social justice. Ironically, the open lines of communication and caring can create avenues for power plays by individuals and/or groups.

The reality of schools is that teachers, hourly support staff (e.g., custodians, cafeteria workers, office staff, teaching assistants), students, and parents/guardians each have their own agendas. Constructing a collective sense of what is best for the group requires great wisdom, critical communications, and caring leadership (Sernak, 1998). Typically, there are no simple, "right" responses or decisions to the personal agendas presented by individuals or groups. The principal must care enough to delve into the situations through the lenses of the diplomat (listen, remain calm, and negotiate in a courteous and respectful way), strategist (analyze the players and the underlying interests), and the executive (make a decision that is neutral, timely, clear, and in the best interest of the students).

Organizational Realities

As principals seek to address wicked problems, they see that schools constitute loosely coupled and open systems. So leaders have to ask questions such as "Where are the internal bases of power?" and "what external influences are at play?"

Schools as Loosely Coupled Organizations

Loosely coupled systems such as school systems are connected and interdependent, but also retain their "own identity . . . and some physical or logical separateness" (Weick, 1976, p. 3). For instance, principals operate under the direction of superintendents

but retain a degree of autonomy in their own schools. Likewise, teachers, who are positional subordinates of the principal, often have greater expertise in their subject areas and exercise a great deal of independent judgment in their classrooms. "The 'looseness' of structures in educational organizations produces 'space' that may promote political activity" (Blase, 1991, p. 3). People can be **street-level bureaucrats**, deciding on their own whether or not to comply with directives. An example of the opposite of **loose coupling** would be a tightly coupled organization such as the military, where directives come from leaders and are carried out by subordinates with high accountability and oversight.

There are advantages to loose coupling, such as the flexibility to respond in ways tailored to the context. In a school with a high number of Spanish-speaking parents, the principal might redirect funding for office support or Title I to hire a part-time bilingual receptionist. A high school with a ninth grade dropout problem might rework staffing to create an insulated ninth grade academy.

However, when individual schools select different programs or textbooks, it is very difficult for the district to monitor implementation for effectiveness. When principals give differing instructions deadlines, it is difficult to know which is real. A school with weak academic performance but a media-savvy principal may get more favors from school district administrators. Loose coupling can create challenges; for example, it may make efforts to navigate district-level politics a bit of a game of survival of the fittest, favoring the "squeaky wheel."

Schools as Open Systems

Schools are open systems in that leaders cannot control budgets, and educational demands often come from state legislative action. They cannot control the local economy or population growth, yet these are huge factors in their operations (Pfeffer & Salancik, 1978/2011.)

At the school level, there may be external influences such as parent groups, community organizations, or teachers' associations. For instance, a church group may offer to run a free after-school tutoring program at the school, but school administrators may suspect that the group may engage in evangelism with the students. A partnership with a local university may pressure the school to allow for research in the school that creates additional work for teachers. Principals need to be aware of external groups' vested interests so that they can manage and direct external involvement.

Political Dynamics in Schools

Political dynamics contribute to the complexity or wickedness of the problems principals will encounter. Three concepts help in deciphering the politics of schools.

Arenas for Decision Making

Principals have a good deal of power in establishing the setting and context for decision making since school sites have no clear designation of where and how such decision making should take place. The dance of power and politics in those sites is often quite free-form, without clear choreography. Venues for decision making could be as a public staff meeting, a formal leadership team meeting, a more exclusive meeting of the principal and a few trusted staff, or a PTA meeting with a few influential parents. Even a brief hallway encounter and a seemingly innocuous question such as "Can I leave a bit early for an appointment?" is in many ways a **policy** arena as well, in that all decisions the principal makes are watched and taken as precedent. With each case, Tim Mazzoni (1991) says, the **arena** involves "key actors, relevant resources, incentives for action, influential relationships, and governing rules—and hence winners and losers," and "establishing the arena for a decision is a fundamental political strategy" (p. 116) as it determines the rules under which decisions will be made. Recalling that schools are loosely coupled organizations with multiple power bases, principals stay attuned to other arenas such as discussions in the teacher's lounge and parking lot, or departmental meetings, the superintendent's council, a school board meeting, or a state legislative subcommittee. It is key to recognize when and where decisions are being made and how that influences who has access, who sets the agenda, and other levers of control. In working to ensure that decisions are inclusive and reflect the needs of often unrepresented groups such as students or Spanish-speaking parents, the context and venue matter and can be key considerations in coping with wicked problems.

Micropolitics in Schools

A principal's ability to recognize power situations and contexts within the relationships in the political network and to use that understanding as a basis for action requires identifying formal and informal power groups, value systems, and appropriate behaviors.

Principals may engage in political maneuvering in negotiations with district officials or by making sure to touch base with a central office administrator in a monthly principals' meeting and remind them of any requests that have been made. These interactions can be very important but are often episodic. Within the school building, **micropolitical** maneuvering is constant. Betty Malen (1995) describes these micropolitical interactions as "the overt and covert processes through which individuals and groups in an organization's immediate environment acquire and exercise power to promote and protect their interests" (p. 147).

Principal-Parent Interactions

Principals' formal decision arenas might include such venues as site-based decision making teams that include parent representation, advisory councils, or an individual education plan meeting with a parent discussing a child's special education services. Principals' positional leverage influences the selection of representatives, setting of the agendas, and the teachers' general inclination to side with the principal to keep decisions in the hands of "professionals" (Malen, 1995, pp. 150–151). Parent representation in formal arenas can be superficial to create the impression of parent involvement. Including parents and giving them a substantive voice in formal decision arenas, especially in schools with low-income and minority parents, requires a deliberate effort and may even require training for principals.

Often, the principal's primary objective is to manage and minimize **conflict**. Thus, the primary influence of parents is in informal interactions rather than in the almost scripted formal decision arenas more tightly under the principal's control. The principal's efforts to arbitrate disputes and prevent conflicts expanding beyond the school—to the media, the central office, or school board members—often lead to accommodating individual parents. However, such compromises are often viewed by teachers as undermining their authority, and they may lower morale and erode teacher's commitment. Such "individualized, private agreements" allow "select parents to exert influence . . . in ways that are unfair to less vocal or powerful constituencies" (Malen, 1995, p. 154). Principals must recognize that every decision they make will be watched and viewed as precedent; compromises to accommodate parents are expedient, but may "erode [rather than deal with] fundamental challenges, and thereby reinforce existing patterns of power and privilege" (Malen, 1995, p. 154).

Principal-Teacher Interactions

The primary work of schools, teaching students, is done by the teachers. Principals and teachers negotiate the boundaries of their influence in "territorial (e.g., schoolwide, classroom bounded) and topical domains (e.g., budget, personnel, curriculum, instruction)" (Malen, 1995, p. 154). Principals tend to view some areas, such as budgets, personnel issues, and schoolwide policies, as their jurisdiction, while teachers seek to protect their control over other areas such as their classroom instruction. The typical understanding is that teachers concede a significant say in school-level policy decisions in order to retain greater discretion within their classrooms.

Similar to parents, teachers interact with principals in both formal and informal arenas. Principals can control decision-making processes in formal decision arenas through such strategies as "controlling the agenda content, meeting format, and information flow" (Malen, 1995, p. 155). In formal arenas such as site-based decision making, teachers can become frustrated with token input, while principals can become weary of the time-consuming work and loss of control from participatory processes. However, these formal decision arenas are "symbols of teachers' right to a voice in a decision" (Malen, 1995, p. 155).

Leaders may see professional learning communities (PLCs) as arenas for communicating powerful messages about values and goals. PLCs can break down teacher isolation and make teacher conversations more public. In such a public arena, the leader should be attuned to the conflicts, debates, and competitions emanating from that arena. While teachers are expected to work collaboratively to address learning (Dufour, Eaker, & Dufour, 2005), the PLC approach opens a new policy arena where debate and competition may occur (under the guise of collegial collaboration). Teachers have long been the directors of their teaching. Such a stronghold is difficult to

shift as can be seen in resistance, anxiety, or ritual compliance rather than true group collaboration and accountability for the learning of all students. Administrator accountability for implementation of the PLC structures can also take on the power dynamics between the administration and teachers among teachers (Talbert, 2010).

Informal interactions between principals and teachers also carry micropolitical dynamics. In a study of how teachers view and respond to principals, Blase (1989) focused on the ways teachers engage with principals.

Open principals are characterized as holding high but reasonable expectations, being honest and nonmanipulative; being communicative; being collegial, approachable, supportive, and collaborative in their decision making (Blase, 1989, pp. 384–385). Strategies such as diplomacy, conformity, and putting in extra work were associated with open principals.

Closed principals are described with such attributes as being authoritarian, inaccessible, nonsupportive, as well as having other negative traits such as being egocentric, unfriendly, and intimidating.

In general, teachers were more likely to seek the principal's support and less likely to behave in a self-protective manner with open principals, whereas "strategies practiced with closed principals were typically more covert, indirect, and subtle" (Blase, 1989, p. 398). The truth of the matter is that most often principals are not categorically closed or open, but these perceptions can vary from teacher to teacher and from issue to issue. Often, within the same building, the same principal could be rated closed by some teachers and open by others. Todd Whitaker (2003), in *What Great Principals Do Differently,* offers guidance in how to respond to teacher perceptions. First, ask the question, "What will my best teachers think?" (p. 68). Follow-up questions include the following: If my best teachers don't think something is a good idea? What are the chances that the rest of the faculty will accept it? And what are the chances that it is a good idea?

Learning the Assumptive Worlds Rules

Powerful understandings are embedded in schools' **assumptive worlds**. Assumptive worlds are the "unwritten rules and undefined understandings about roles" (Marshall & Gerstl-Pepin, 2005, p. 12).

They are the sometimes shocking rules that leaders learn by observation, by trial and error, or through advice when they leave teaching to become administrators. Navigating in assumptive worlds will either foster or inhibit the ability of the principal to cope with dilemma-laden situations, express values, perform duties, and build relationships, as illustrated in **Table 28.1**.

Clearly, these assumptive worlds rules stop leaders from taking initiative or proposing ideas that would challenge their peers' traditional ways of thinking and doing things.

Situation	*Rule*
Need to determine rights and responsibilities	**Rule 1: Limit risk taking** Focus energies on safe projects, improving the school without causing major changes or inviting strong opposition.
	Rule 2: Remake policy quietly Overlook, evade, or loosely interpret externally imposed policies that do not work well for their school.
Acceptable and unacceptable values	**Rule 1: Avoid moral dilemmas** Deal with problems quietly rather than taking a stand.
	Rule 2: Do not display divergent values Publically support and articulate the party line such as district policies or initiatives, *regardless of personal beliefs and even if in reality you are quietly "remaking" the policy.*
Patterns of expected behavior	**Rule 1: Commitment is required** Superiors expect commitment and loyalty from their direct reports. *Make sure you follow the chain of command and do not skip over levels of leadership.*
	Rule 2: Don't get labeled as a troublemaker Take care in directly challenging District policies. *Start at the lowest level possible to solve a problem.*
	Rule 3: Keep disputes private Handle disagreements privately, and resolve them at the school level if at all possible.
	Rule 4: Cover all your bases Be sure to take care of responsibilities that reflect on superiors.
Conditions affecting political relationships	**Rule 1: Build administrator team trust** Support and cooperate with superiors. *Especially important in building trust is giving your superiors a heads-up so they are not caught unawares if you expect a problem cannot be kept from reaching central office.*
	Rule 2: Align your turf Work to gain involvement in tasks, such as district project teams, that are important to your superiors. *Take time to ask and learn what your superiors value and prioritize.*

Table 28.1 Assumptive Worlds of School Administrators—The "Rules"

SOURCE: Adapted from Marshall, C. & Hooley, R. (2006). *The assistant principal: Leadership choices and challenges* (2nd ed.). Thousand Oaks, CA: Corwin Press, pp. 55–58.

Principal-Central Office Interactions and Assumptive Worlds Rules

To a large degree, unwritten rules of assumptive worlds are enforced upon subordinates in subtle ways. In the school building, the principal has that power. In dealings with the central office, however, the principal becomes a follower rather than an enforcer of the rules.

When a Principal Calls Central Office

In smaller districts, a principal's route to solving problems and keeping them quiet has more to do with relationships, with a positive rapport translating to the central office staff "having your back" and handling multiple roles such as combining supervision of elementary curriculum with overseeing Title I implementation. In larger districts with resources and departmentalization, finding the right specialist is often key, and a problem can often be resolved without involving a principal's superiors.

When the principal assists central office superiors in following the rules of assumptive worlds, conveying deference to their positions will smooth the way. Also, one principal described the "beating the bus home" strategy, meaning that if the principal can speak with a parent about a child's misbehavior before the bus drops off the child at home, the child has to defend against the principal's or central office's version of an event, rather than vice versa. Similarly, if having a complaint or other issue reach the central office is unavoidable, it is always preferable to be the first to explain the situation. Then the central office staff member can sound knowledgeable rather than being caught off guard. The principal must also follow the chain of command so that no one's turf is violated.

When Directives Come From Above

The principal's role, often, is implementation. In these situations, principals need to be a buffer between multiple initiatives or directives coming from above, protecting their teachers from becoming overwhelmed. Often, directives for a new curriculum, for character education, and for service learning programs come all at once!

Principals manage these directives. They can spread out tasks across different staff or departments or time the release of the information so teachers have time to process each assignment. Principals can create release time by working out class coverage so teachers can attend to district expectations. Determining which initiatives can be done well enough and which need thorough implementation, prioritizing by which have the most direct impact on student achievement, is another way to filter district directives. Principals can filter directives by framing them—for example, framing the Response to Intervention initiative as the kinds of things, such as tutoring and data collection, that staff do. Thus, a principal can articulate and support the priorities of the school superintendent while at the same time protecting teachers—a win-win situation.

School Boards

Boards of education vary from the highly partisan to the relatively united, from taking a hands-on approach to deferring to the superintendent. School board members can be engaged or passive, supportive, or confrontational. Principals must understand what the school board is prioritizing and which school board members feel a vested interest in a particular school. Strategic principals develop positive relationships with school board members, by including them in school events or through personal connections. Caution is needed, though: Such actions could be perceived as violations of assumptive world's rules.

The Actors in the Dramas of School Politics

The dance of leadership is one of the metaphors for describing "the micropolitical nature of the principal's' relationship with different dance partners as they move across a number of fields" (Ehrich & English, 2013, p. 5). Whether the metaphor is that of the stage or the dance floor, the battle, or a chess game, the drama is full of an array of demanding actors—from cliques of teachers to secretaries to board members but also from new challenges presented daily.

As agents of the government, school leaders play the political role of negotiating how the curricula convey messages about values such as patriotism, national character, and other cultural values. Decisions about allowing certain clubs and activities, providing access to parent groups or businesses or agencies may be political hot buttons.

What Are the Sources of a Leader's Power?

Leaders' positional power comes from having been placed in a position with prescribed responsibilities. That power erodes quickly if the leader cannot demonstrate other key types of power. Expert power comes from evidence of training, experience, and from having walked in the shoes of those who would be followers—so principals gain the power of expertise and credibility from having been a teacher or administrator before, from having degrees, from having managed crowds at football, and even from having been a parent. Personal power, often called charisma, comes from interpersonal skills, from demonstrations of ability to command respect of other powerful people and sometimes just from charm and good looks.

Student Power

Students are ever-present stakeholders. What do students want and what power do they have? Students wield their power as individuals by acting out (e.g., wearing baggy pants or tank tops in defiance of dress codes or skipping school); often, these are the acts of kids who want attention or who are exploring their identities.

Given that schooling is mandatory, their power is quite constrained. Students working in coalitions, however, can exercise more power. Their demands may be for more field trips or chocolate milk in the cafeteria, and principals wisely use student governments to manage such demands. However, a gang is also a coalition, with roots in neighborhoods and with dangerous and even criminal activities, so leaders have to decide whether to involve social workers, parents, counselors, or juvenile justice systems and which district policies apply. Also, students' demands can openly and directly defy policy, as when students feel a teacher is unfair or does not like them, and students begin to collaborate to undermine the teacher's authority through classroom disruptions or refusing to participate. Students can also protest policies by more organized means, such as petitions or even staged walkouts or boycotts in more extreme circumstances.

Teachers' Power

Teachers have perhaps the most vested interests since this is their lifetime career commitment, entwined with their personal investment in their professional certification and their professional associations like those for reading teachers and special education teachers. It's also entwined with their community status, their homes, and their mortgages—and of course, their love of kids and their subject matter. Bottom line is their interests are employment, hopefully joyful or at least satisfying, safe, fair, secure, and healthy; respect and flexibility to manage their own work; and a decent paycheck and benefits.

Politics rears up in the maneuvers and power plays of individuals and groups of teachers when there is competition for budget items or for favors. The teacher angling for forgiveness about frequent tardiness, the English department seeking more regarding expenditures for curriculum materials, and the principal wanting that unsafe gymnasium torn down and replaced are all competing for scarce resources and to protect what is valuable to them.

As in all politics, leaders use their power to distribute benefits and favors, also known as the patronage system. The benefits may seem small to outsiders. Leaders can grant something like the permission to bring one's young child to school after hours or to have the earliest lunch period. Leaders' dispensing benefits can get very close to matters that are in teacher contracts, though, such as extra pay for after-school activities. As described above, teachers' respond to open and closed principals with varying political responses.

Unions

With unions, principals' political skills are required to negotiate and interpret, where possible, any disputes over the who-gets-what quandaries that arise. A week's worth of political skills may be spent in conflicts over whether teachers should get extra pay for advising clubs or oversize classes or in finessing the questionable creativity of the newspaper advisor or theater teacher. Union reps wield power and stand ready to advise a teacher with an unanswered complaint and to file grievances when complaints pile up, with the threat of strikes or arbitration. Leaders and union reps maintain their respective power bases so that, when needed, they can mount a good fight. However, in right-to-work states unions are less powerful, and teachers are more easily controlled. While teacher unions' power has swayed elections in the 20th century, that power is now under attack, being presented in the media as a main cause for problems and expenses of schooling. (See **Sidebar 28.1**.)

School Staff

Woe be to the principal who forgets the interests and powers of staff, be it secretaries, cafeteria workers, bus drivers, or cleaning staff. Loyal secretaries are political advisors, both within the school and in relations with the wider community, keeping the leader aware of impending or simmering teacher tensions or potential threats or crises created by outside events and being the diplomats and first responders to phone calls from irate or drunk parents and surprise visits from micromanaging board members. They can help the leader amass personal power when they cue the leader to pay attention to the teacher whose wife is undergoing chemotherapy or the student debate team that gets so little attention. Conversely, secretaries can simply withhold their insights and do great damage to the leader's power.

Similarly, a range of support staff, counselors, social workers, the school nurse, and teacher aides mediate and link in ways that lessen tensions and meet needs. They are key political allies for the

leader who can then portray the school as calm and caring—for example, about tensions at the time of statewide testing, kids who really need clean clothes before going to class, or kids whose parents never explained about menstruation.

Cafeteria workers, custodial workers, and bus drivers know their community, their students, and their teachers so they can contribute to the portrayal of an orderly, neat, healthy, and safe system with clean corridors, caring people, and efficient bus services. They pass judgment on the art teacher whose room is a mess and on the kids whose homes have yards with broken-down trucks. But the astute political leader amasses credits with them so that they attend to monitoring trash, lining up kids, and providing for the needs of struggling kids. Often, these actors' insider, native knowledge of the history and families in the community are crucial assets for a leader new to the area.

Parents

Relationships with the volunteers, parents, students, and staff are one aspect of the micropolitical environment in which relational experiences create the interaction of values and beliefs.

Parents are often the most powerful in their abilities to pressure for their interests and needs. The gripe may be about the way in which a discipline situation was handled, the recent cutbacks in fourth-grade teacher aides, the fact that one school has

Sidebar 28.1 Political Realities: Who Controls Personal Days?

This political reality case illustrates one kind of political tension that can arise even when bureaucratic rules and contracts cover seemingly simple situations:

Even though she kept quiet about it at school, Susan was an active member of the local group fighting against new legislative controls on women's rights to control their reproductive lives. She was well aware that some of their parents and board members' values were on the other side of the proposed legislation so this was risky. She really wanted to be part of the rally at the state capitol building, which was on a school day. When she submitted the proper form requesting a personal day, her principal pulled her aside and asked her the purpose. First, she said, firmly, "Well, as the form says, it is personal." She immediately saw his anger. He was accustomed to listening to teachers confiding their woes about health scares, family demands, and then like the good patriarch/politician, granting their request as a favor, with sympathy. So he felt he had to draw the line because Susan was trying to take away that power. To Susan, though, she was exercising her rights within the contract and her free speech rights as a citizen. She stood her ground but was relieved when the TV cameras never focused on her at the rally.

dual-language programming and others do not, or access to advanced/honors tracked courses. Regardless of the difficulties that might present in these political situations, the research is clear that parent involvement positively influences student learning (Hallinger, Bickman, & Davis, 1996).

Because principals know they should encourage and foster parental involvement, they must be proactive in creating an atmosphere of welcome and avenues for communication. Effective principals have routines for parent input at PTA or School Improvement Team (SIT) meetings. Principals should be prepared for and accepting of parents interfacing personally with the principal, either in impromptu settings such as school events (ballgames, concerts, field days) as well as the scheduled parent conference or phone call.

Most directly supportive of students and parents is parent involvement directly with the classrooms (Cotton & Wikelund, 1989). To caution, family math nights and the like are attuned to White middle-class parents; leaders' approaches must be innovative for outreach to less privileged groups (Lopez, Scribner, & Mahitivanichcha, 2001). Building relationships and lines of communication are political strategies building a foundation to ward off difficulties or misunderstandings.

Powers of the Central Office, Community, and School Board

The superintendent and school board use their appointed and elected positional power to assert the right to make and enforce decisions, including those about hiring and evaluating principals and about how to manage districtwide political forces. They may or may not serve as buffers when a principal has political challenges that get out of hand or gets embroiled in a conflict-laden debate that spills out past the walls of the building. They may or may not have good working relationships through which to create any united front when the need arises.

District leaders are cautious about anything that would offend powerful constituents. Usually the source of power is money, which can be in the form of large contributions to scholarships for local high school graduates or food for the baseball team (or the withdrawal of the same). Leaders may forget the clout of business and property owners—until they want to expand the middle school with athletic fields so close that they would annoy residents of an affluent neighborhood. Even small businesses make demands, as when the convenience store owner demands that school officials make the high school students behave or a major employer who provides a number in town gets upset when his two sons never get above third string on the football team.

Advocacy and Interest Groups

An array of groups may lobby for their particular special interests. Some are fledgling, inspired by a new idea or gripe, as illustrated in **Sidebar 28.2**. The interest may be cultural, as when an increased immigrant population pushes for cultural opportunities or

Sidebar 28.2   Political Realities: Parents as Lobbyists

After the school board discontinued the dual-language program at a local elementary school, citing budget constraints, parents rallied with an email group. Many meetings ensued, with the principal and the central office, with lengthy and well-attended, noisy public forums, and with lobbying school board members through personal visits. Months after submitting a proposed plan for continuous support of the program, the parents won! The school board voted to keep the program and got the principal to develop a subcommittee of the PTA. This group had created powerful and outspoken coalitions among parents and had even presented a well-researched document citing studies on dual-language benefits.

Power relationships with parents range from those who feel entitled to those who have been silenced and often require a delicate balance of counseling as well as facilitating positive future communications. Both proactive and reactive communications might be urgent, with deadlines, and with a particular audience. With the difficult parent, a personal prompt phone call is strategically more effective than an email or letter. Likewise, if the superintendent calls, return the call as quickly as possible.

events reflecting their country of origin, such as soccer, ethnic-themed theater, or readily available vegetarian food. To educators, many of these demands seem extreme, fringe, or nutty. Some educators may be passionate about other concerns, such as protecting children from books with themes that, in their minds, condone or promote evolution, Communism, same-sex relationships, promiscuity, witchcraft, racial mixing, or women's rights. They may object to anything that they see as undermining American traditions by encouraging government intrusion through programs such as vaccinations or school record keeping. Zealots come in many forms; many have the backing of religious movements and national advocacy organizations. Some are local associates of national groups, with national and well-established platforms. For example, the American Civil Liberties Union's state and local associates stand ready to take a stand and may threaten a lawsuit over issues such as prayer in schools. The National Women's Law Project will readily provide resources when locals protest any undermining of the rights of women and girls. Consequently, school leaders may get messages and phone calls from a variety of advocacy and **interest groups** who are making such demands. Catherine Lugg's (2001) work on the power of religious groups provides illustrations.

Often, the demands of such groups will fester until they go directly to the school board or superintendent and/or the local press. Principals may even be drawn into lawsuits when those political demands are not resolved. Principals' political roles include avoiding or managing these kinds of demands at their site level whenever possible. In the dynamics of districts, they seek to keep such challenges at their level rather than ask for the central office expertise and advice from district lawyers or professional associations that could clarify their options. Rather than go through official channels (and risk being seen as vacillating), they often ask a trusted colleague, with a kind of unstated pact to keep their request for advice quiet.

The Larger Context: State, Federal, and Global Actors

State and federal policy changes, laws passed, or mandates that are sent down, often without clear guidelines for implementation, leave leaders to struggle with how to comply without clear directions. This could be in the form of new testing from the state school board, budget cuts from the state legislature, or a new law that more rigidly restricts social promotion. In such cases, as well as with decisions from the local school board, an important role of the principal is to pay attention, listen, and try to anticipate possible outcomes so that the school staff is not caught by surprise. In their open systems, they use loose coupling, and they frame the change in ways that tailor and buffer to maintain equilibrium and calm.

Even global forces affect school leaders. Sometimes national political rhetoric ramps up the pressure on schools to be more globally competitive. Sometimes international exchanges of ideas, spread through ramped up technology, influences thinking about how schools should be run, as when "New Public Management . . . emphasizes privatization, outsourcing, and high-stakes accountability . . . narrowing the curriculum to those content areas measured by standardized achievement test scores (Crow & Weindling, 2010, p. 140). So the politically astute leader is constantly tuning in to networks of information. He or she keeps abreast of the hum of rumors to detect facts and shared beliefs that could provoke conflict or disrupt.

Politics and the Career

Playing the Promotion Game

Political dynamics involve the distribution of power and authority, the nature of the **hierarchy**, coalitions, recruitment patterns, and the organization's unwritten code of conduct, that is, "the norms, values, myths . . . that govern individual behavior" (Foster, 1986, 159–160). Further, school administrators learn what is forbidden and what is allowed. Newcomers are socialized quickly into these understandings; they learn so that they can get what they need. They learn to function within the sanctions of the assumptive worlds (see **Table 28.1**) so they will be seen as loyal, having congruent values, and knowing about avoiding disputes and disruptions.

Power, access, and rewards are distributed unequally and not necessarily according to merit, need, or effort. Some see that they can take risks and can expect rewards; others see that they have characteristics that make them unlikely to move up. For school administrators seeking to move up the ladder, competence and credentials are not enough for the political game of competition among peers vying for a limited number of upwardly mobile positions. Good mentors are wonderful but not enough. Aspirants who play the game well find ways to get the attention of superiors and to amass a list of **sponsors** who will promote their name and give them advance notice of potential vacancies.

Principals and Self-Interest

Principals are people. They have goals, aspirations, and ambition, as well as mortgages, families, and obligations. Principals, like all others, are in part motivated by self-interest. This self-interest is a political arena where those seeking to be promoted follow the assumptive world rules so that they will be viewed as effective and as viable candidates. Whereas teaching is largely a lateral profession, with options of changing subject or grade level but typically no hierarchy, school administrators have a professional ladder to climb.

Career Hierarchies and Evaluations

In the career ladder of school administration, assistant principals are at the bottom, entry level. There can be negative speculation about an administrator who stays an assistant principal for too long. A status and pay hierarchy among principals is based on level and size of school, with large high schools being the most visible positions. A school's academic performance can also carry a prestige factor, with high-performing schools often hailed as the flagship schools in a district, even if more affluent socioeconomics or other external factors are a primary reason for high test scores. In the central office, the position of director is often seen as a lateral move or even slightly below a principalship, but the director position is often the gateway into higher central office positions such as assistant superintendent. Conversely, moving downward such as from a large middle school to a small elementary school could be viewed as a demotion.

Principal evaluations are often based on standards such as those of the Interstate School Leaders Licensure Consortium. Typically, such standards cover a variety of areas from instructional leadership to more managerial tasks, but the theme throughout is the notion of principal as executive. An assistant superintendent or similar level typically does a principal's evaluations, whether or not they have first-hand knowledge of the principal's school, but in general evaluations are perceptions formed by sporadic interactions and metrics such as test scores, out of school suspension rates, staff attendance, or

Sidebar 28.3   Political Realities: Navigating Assumptive Worlds Rules

Principal Savvy knew that his assistant principal had interviewed for the principal position, which had created tensions initially. But in his third year as principal, Mr. Savvy gave time to mentoring the assistant principal, George, to achieve his aspirations of becoming a principal.

Savvy illustrated how he guided George:

"I have made clear to him through words and actions there are certain ways of talking and choices he'd better avoid. I take him aside and tell him which battles to avoid, whether it is in transportation battles, special education placement, teacher evaluations, or cafeteria overcrowding, and even whom to talk to (and to avoid) at district meetings. Once he had a neat idea for working with problem students, but I took him aside and told him, 'Don't make it look like you think you know better than the higher-ups. They're the ones who are supposed to come up with such ideas.' And once when the superintendent invited him and a few others to his golf game, George stupidly said he needed to be at his daughter's dance recital. I admire that, but he's got to know how to show his loyalty. He can't make too many mistakes and ruin his chances."

As discussed by Marshall and Gerstl-Pepin (2005), a mentor, internships, and lots of trial and error train leaders navigating in assumptive worlds; their navigation skills will either foster or inhibit a leader's ability to garner respect and power, to build relationships, and be viewed as fitting in with the political realities of the career.

school climate surveys. While not in and of themselves a determining factor in a principal's opportunities for promotion, evaluations can be used as a tool to substantiate a demotion or removal of a principal. In other words, it is political. (**Sidebar 28.3**).

Challenges for Women and Minorities in Administration

The skewed power relationship can be viewed through the gender and ethnicity of persons filling the principalship and the assistant principalship. Women and minorities still struggle to move from the assistant principalship to the principalship and above, reflecting societal assumptions that leadership is for White males. The Equal Employment Opportunity Commission (EEOC) completed questionnaire surveys in 1974, 1976, and 1978 compiling data for principals and assistant principals. Statistics in 1976 revealed only 7.6% minority men in principalships and 12.6% in assistant principalships. Women comprised 13% of principalships and 18.3% of assistant principalships with 2.6% and 5.4% respectively of those being minorities.

The percentages have risen since then. Still, a study on educational career path for administrators in North Carolina revealed males were four times more likely than women to become principals directly (without serving as assistant principals) and over three times more likely to become assistant principals (Brown et al., 2004). The report also indicates that the number of minority teachers is declining, creating a potential deficit of future leadership candidates. By 2006, the percentage of men in the combined category for principals and assistant principal positions was 46%. Women, at 54%, were now employed at a higher rate. Yet that increasing gender equity declines when one looks at the higher status positions. And the number of Whites in these roles is still very high, at 73%, showing negligible progress toward racial equity.

Further, women and minorities' complaints are often silenced. They sense the politics of evaluations, their need for mentors and sponsors; recognizing dominance of White males in the top leadership, they learn assumptive world's rules to avoid being labeled troublemakers and to comply with dominant values. Consequently, aspiring and politically astute leaders

will avoid associating with public displays demanding gender and race equity in the profession. This politics of denial creates conformity; thus, the chance to benefit from any alternative views from women and minorities is lost.

Exercising Power While Promoting Instruction, Democracy, and Community

Leaders strategically balance between the ideals of community involvement and democracy and the realities of political pressures, all the while directing schools to be places that enhance student learning! A bureaucratic table of organization structures authority and lends legitimacy to the leader's uses of power relationships (English, 2005; Marshall & Scribner, 1991). Leaders manage within a system with boundaries, assumptions, rules, customs, traditions, and habitual ways of thinking, and the first responsibility of these leaders is to maintain stability within the organization. Leaders' work on controlling communication serves to systematically create cohesion among the potentially conflicting power structures. Leaders' political duties include monitoring and promoting calm within these disputed areas, whether they are taking place at the boundary between the soccer and the baseball fields or at the boundary between the parents who believe in keeping some divisions among people in communities and those who believe in inclusive community.

However, each of the identifiable groups in the system wants things from the leader. Their expectations create competition for specific group or personal value systems to prevail. The competition may be carried out in the school grounds, at classroom doors, in the principal's office, district office, and school board meeting arenas. School leaders monitor and adjudicate those competitions. Some competitions are abstractions, such as inclusiveness, democratic participation and rights, community, collaboration, esprit de corps, and a school's history and identity and traditions.

Principals monitor the physical boundary between the athletic fields and any threats from surrounding neighborhoods or the interactions of students with local stores. At the same time, principals monitor the symbols and the heroes connected to the school— and the meanings of communally collaborative inclusiveness, as in making families feel welcome and supporting the student successes in assemblies, field days, honor societies, drama performances, and graduation events.

Leaders use public communication avenues to keep a continuous control over the messages about the school, whether by a weekly memo, celebrating the accomplishments of individuals, or just the morning announcements.

Leaders construct their own communication systems among allies and among the various levels of power relationships. Whom do they call or email? Their personalized network likely includes an assortment of peers, mentors, and friends who are trusted to help handle threatening or embarrassing challenges. However, leaders are strategic about widening the circle of communication to seek the voices and concerns to be heard, both for improved decision making and for acting diplomatically for decisions on such tough issues.

Circles of communication that deliberately include voices often left out of decisions demonstrate a "power to" style—an orientation that sees power as shared. As Brunner and Schumaker (1998) note, a principal exercising "power to" will work cooperatively with various groups and, through multilateral negotiations and compromises, may be able to identify problems, new opportunities, and policies that will be good for all stakeholders. "Power over" is characterized by hierarchy, control over resources, use of coercion, and other direct assertions of authority. Such leaders make sure that issues that threaten their interests do not see the light of day. In general, men are more likely to view power as a means of social control, whereas women in leadership more often use "power to." Solving complex social problems using a collaborative power to approach, would work best for wicked problems in the education context.

Politically Astute Communications

Leaders in open systems try to control all messages coming to and going from the school. Beyond just news reporting in papers, radio, and television, in this world of instant communications (e.g., email, social media) leaders must be on top of messages sent out to the public they serve, creating consistency about smooth procedures and expectations.

Several particularly political approaches that are among the effective principal communication recommendations are

- incorporating stakeholder views in shared decision-making processes,
- engaging in open and democratic dialogue with multiple stakeholders, and
- distributing leadership to facilitate improved communication about the change process. (Stronge, Richard, & Catano, 2008)

At the same time, leaders seek to control the dialogue. All communications build the vision and mission of the school and create the micropolitical interface between the administration (principal/assistant principal), teachers, teaching assistants, custodians, cafeteria workers, office/clerical staff, and students. The leader is effectively establishing arenas for promoting a platform—that is, a set of beliefs (just as political candidates do) when he or she talks and sends out messages in individual conversations and in collective meetings. These happen in teacher meetings, teacher assistant meetings, principal/assistant principal meetings, and custodian meetings. The leader who understands the power of that platform creation will pay attention to planning, choosing words, and setting up **allies and coalitions** who will spread and monitor the expectations and values (Bloom & Krovetz, 2001).

Politically astute communication skills are essential for balancing the tension between ideals of democracy and principals' need to manage power relationships. Principals interface strategically between the democratic systems situated at the district level and the school level, yet principals use power relationships (Marshall & Scribner, 1991) to engage in communications and to manage conflicts. They balance a democratic model with a power-based approach to defuse conflicts and competition and to maintain a semblance of order and calm.

Politics and Leadership for Social Justice

Leaders' work is managing symbols, buffering, interpreting and modifying directives, and allocating resources—more like politicians' work than the work of apolitical managers or bureaucrats. As such, these politicians are constantly sending out signals about the mission and the values. A **social justice** advocacy leader's vision incorporates assertive actions regarding the marginalized populations. That leader is constantly on alert for the silenced voices, the unmet needs, and the tendency to ignore truly difficult problems. That leader not only talks about social justice values, he or she sets up systems and personnel for monitoring the school's efforts with the homeless, poor, people of color, immigrants or ESL students, and those whose gender or sexual orientation puts them at disadvantage. The voices and needs of such individuals and groups are often pushed aside or silenced. Leaders could use texts by Jim Scheurich and Linda Skrla (2003) and Catherine Marshall and Maricela Oliva (2010) with PLCs working on social justice. Principals must anticipate the political ramifications of such social justice advocacy stances. (See **Sidebar 28.4**.)

Rather than giving in to the temptation to bury or gloss over such challenges or to allow their community to make excuses, that leader finds ways to intervene. This means putting time and resources to make sure the school is on alert to notice any instance of students falling through the cracks, be it the overrepresentation of certain students in suspension or special education, too few girls taking advanced math, or the tendency to attend to the squeaky wheel parents but fail to notice the ones who cannot make time for PTA. This will result in political ramifications: When it appears that schools are redistributing the goodies, there will be **backlash**. Principals have to

Sidebar 28.4   Several Strategies for Changing Beliefs and Behaviors

Leaders must practice strategies for anticipating and managing likely backlash, such as:

- taking a low-key approach, building personal relationships, and then slowly winning over opponents;
- disrupting equilibrium by overt challenges to dominant assumptions and practices; and
- co-opting the disruptions created from on high, taking them as openings to change behaviors and assumptions.

What can a leader do to champion supports for those whose needs are seldom heard or provided for? Several strategies can work. In some instances, leaders can convert people who would create roadblocks into allies, slowly and gradually, by continuous low-key personal discussions. This can result in the accumulation of coalitions in support of an agenda or a program or an item in the budget to meet the unmet needs. Corridor conversations with individual teachers and parents, talking with them about that need, asking how they see it in daily realities with their students, can lead to slow-simmering movements, perhaps joined by business allies, local concerned citizens, perhaps a school board member, culminating in getting the issue into the arena for policy discussion.

In contrast, the leader decides that the low-key strategy will have no effect and that kids will continue to fall through the cracks, so it will be necessary to disrupt the equilibrium. While risky, the strategy of deliberately provoking conflict and backlash can ultimately result in changed assumptions. The wise leader plans for that backlash, knows that the school and community will need time to cope, finds ways to manage the newly introduced values and provides for the newly legitimized needs, with the expectation that eventually a new equilibrium will develop. This risk taker may get labeled troublemaker—or could get visibility as an outstanding leader.

A third politically strategic approach is co-optation. Leaders might use the latest dictates from on high, which will create disruptions and conflicts anyway, and interpret them as a basis for pushing for social justice agendas. For example, the leader could use the mandates for accountability to state standards, data-driven decision making, a district-generated alarm about the achievement gap, or a court-ordered monitoring of the district's allocations of resources for classrooms with high concentration of minority students. Or perhaps the state department of education or a consultant firm is creating lots of buzz about culturally proficient instruction or equity auditing. That buzz, or that dictate, creates an opening that leaders can interpret to set up tasks and reorientations of belief systems so that educators, the students, and the community will then move toward social justice agendas. The force and legitimacy of the mandate or directive will open the possibility that the leader capitalizes upon. The system's loose coupling (mentioned earlier) will allow a clever leader to maneuver tasks, resources, and ways of framing issues so that the school will be oriented toward social justice. That leader might even get away with saying, "I know it is disruptive, but you all know we have to do this and here's how we can do it and make it work best for us."

have ways of fending off the flak from parents accustomed to privilege and access and students and teachers who assume that no gay girl can be prom queen or that it is a waste of counselor time to help certain students get a winter coat, or get to college.

Backlash

Counselors, school social workers, and the school improvement team can be social justice allies, and of course all school staff must get the message that there will be no regression to old often-heard assumptions that "some kids aren't meant to make it." But principals envisioning their school within the larger political context—their community, particular stakeholders, their central office and board, their state's legislators and their professional associations, will generate momentum toward this social justice advocacy. Educators who know the realities of schools and students' lives can be allies. However, social justice advocacy is risky, often defying assumptive worlds rules by defying dominant values. (See **Sidebar 28.5**.)

Social justice advocacy leadership requires careful political strategizing and constant monitoring. It may result, too, in getting fired. The social justice advocacy leader is directing the school to create access for all. Bill Foster (1986) reminds us of the larger goal: "Each administrative decision carries with it a restructuring of a human life; this is why administration at its heart is the resolution of moral decisions," and "administrators . . . engage in an effort to develop, challenge, and liberate human souls" (p. 33). To keep this in mind, while constantly making political moves and while focusing on student achievement is a wickedly challenging task.

Wicked Problems Revisited

Working with the students, parents, staff, teachers, and district administration, principals must view these interactions as political and then create politically aware strategies and platforms to lead schools to pursue learning and also pursue social justice. Sometimes, the principal will take on the role of facilitator who choreographs effective conversations, shared decision making, and solution finding. The leader's political strategies will greatly affect, in any specific situation, whether he or she will be viewed by others as effective. Those strategies require skills in consensus building and negotiation, conflict resolution, effective communication, community relations, identifying stakeholders, and even marketing. This chapter provides political scenarios and concepts the leaders should use for dealing with conflicting values or the power plays of resistant, complacent, or enraged constituents. In addition, the chapter provides background for building capacity for politically astute management of the newest mandates and policies.

Sidebar 28.5 A Social Justice Advocacy Leader Is More Than Just a Good Leader

George Theoharis, (2007) in "Social Justice Educational Leaders and Resistance: Toward a Theory of Social Justice Leadership," shows how good leaders work with publics, speak of success for all children, empower staff, and so on. Politically, though, a social justice advocacy leader will attend to power and politics with intention to create inclusiveness and to address equity issues. Some elements of such leadership include the following:

- Demonstrate cultural respect
- End segregated and pull-out programs
- Ensure that diverse students have access to core curriculum
- Know that school cannot be great until the students with the greatest struggles have the same opportunities, both academically and socially, as their more privileged peers
- Seek strength from other activist administrators
- See all data through a lens of equity
- See that community building and differentiation are tools for mutual success
- Be entwined with the community

As Marshall and Scribner (1991) say, principals comprehending the micropolitical environment will have the best chance of shaping powerful forces within and outside of schools and constructing a social environment for student success, equity, and constituent satisfaction.

Key Chapter Terms

Allies and coalitions: People who can be counted on to speak or act to support a particular decision or help to strategize to make decisions and procedures that move toward a common goal. Often, these are temporary, focused on one target; they cannot be relied upon for accomplishing another goal, another day.

Arena: The place where decisions are made. Changing the arena can impact who has control or influence and what the rules are for a decision-making venue.

Assumptive worlds: The unstated rules of the game; unwritten and undefined understandings about roles or practices.

Backlash: Overt or hidden challenge to decisions that take privileges or resources from people and try to spread out those resources more equally.

Conflict: Friction caused by disagreements about who should decide on goals or procedures or who should get the best of scarce resources—often just an unspoken tension between or among people but sometimes outright physical challenge.

Hierarchy: Organizational structure that establishes a rank order of positions based on status or authority.

Interest groups: Formed because of their commonality of needs, values, or goals, these organizations have leaders, procedures, and money so that they can effectively lobby to get their way in districts, states, and national government decisions.

Loose coupling: Organizations whose component parts, such as central office and the individual schools in a district, are connected and interdependent, but each part retains its own identity, as well as some degree of separateness and autonomy.

Micropolitics: The often subtle interactions or political ideologies of social systems at the school level (students, parents, staff, teachers, and administration).

Policy: A set of plans or actions agreed upon by a government or agency that is determined by the dominant values of the system

Politics: The managing and manipulation of power to influence or control the distribution of limited resources and the prioritization of values and policy directions, in a setting where there are conflicting values.

Social justice advocacy: Assertive articulation of goals and interventions to constantly reduce inequities.

Sponsors: People in positions of authority or influence who are able to assist in obtaining favorable results, such as resources or promotions.

Street-level bureaucrats: Employees making decisions on their own initiative or discretion about how they carry out their work.

Values: The principles or standards that are intrinsically important to a person or group of persons.

Wicked problems: Complex, enduring social problems with no clear solution involving multiple interests and conflicting values.

References

Blase, J. (1989). The micropolitics of the school: The everyday political orientation of teachers toward open school principals. *Educational Administration Quarterly, 25*(4), 377–407.

Blase, J. (Ed.). (1991). *The politics of life in schools: Power, conflict, and cooperation.* Newbury Park, CA: Sage.

Bloom, G., & Krovetz, M. (2001). A step into the principalship. *Leadership, 30*(3), 12–13.

Brown, A., Chung, C. H., Gates, M., Gosh-Dastidar, B., Guarino, C., & Santibañez, L. (2004, May). Career paths of school administrators in North Carolina: Insights from an analysis of state data. *Rand Education.* Retrieved from http://www.rand.org/pubs/technical_reports/2005/RAND_TR129.sum.pdf

Brunner, C. C., & Schumaker, P. (1998). Power and gender in the "new view" public schools. *Policy Studies Journal, 26*(1), 30–45. doi:10.1111/j.1541–0072.1998.tb01923.x

Cotton, K., & Wikelund, K. R. (1989). *Parent involvement in education.* Washington, DC: U.S. Department of Education, Office of Educational Research and Improvement.

Crow, G. M., & Weindling, D. (2010). Learning to be political: New English headteachers' roles. *An Interdisciplinary Journal of Educational Policy and Practice, 24*(1), 137–158. doi:10.1177/0895904809354495

DuFour, R., Eaker, R., & DuFour, R. (2005). *On common ground: The power of professional learning communities.* Bloomington, IN: Solution Tree.

Ehrich, L. C., & English, F. W. (2013). Leadership as dance: A consideration of the applicability of the 'mother' of all arts as the basis for establishing connoisseurship. *International Journal of Leadership in Education: Theory and Practice, 16*(4), 1–28. doi: 10.1080/13603124.2012.696282

English, F. W. (Ed.). (2005). *The Sage handbook of educational leadership: Advances in theory, research, and practice.* Thousand Oaks, CA: Sage.

Equal Employment Opportunity Commission. (1974). *Elementary-secondary staff information—biennial.* Washington, DC: Government Printing Office.

Equal Employment Opportunity Commission. (1976). *Elementary-secondary staff information (EEO-5) annual survey* [Unpublished data]. Washington, DC: Government Printing Office.

Equal Employment Opportunity Commission. (1978). *Elementary-secondary staff information (EEO-5) annual survey* [Unpublished data]. Washington, DC: Government Printing Office.

Foster, W. (1986). *Paradigms and promises.* Buffalo, NY: Prometheus.

Hallinger, P., Bickman, L., & Davis, K. (1996). School context, principal leadership, and student reading achievement. *Elementary School Journal, 96*(5), 527–549.

Head, B., & Alford, J. (2008, March 28). Wicked problems: The implications for public management. *International Research Society for Public Management.* Retrieved from http://www.irspm2008.bus.qut.edu.au/papers/documents/pdf2/Head%20-%20Wicked%20Problems%20HeadAlford%20Final%20250308.pdf

Lopez, G. R., Scribner, J. D., & Mahitivanichcha, K. (2001). Redefining parental involvement: Lessons from high-performing migrant-impacted schools. *American Educational Research Journal, 38*(2), 253–288.

Lugg, C. A. (2001). The Christian right: A cultivated collection of interest groups. *Educational Policy, 15*(1), 41–57.

Malen, B. (1995). The micropolitics of education: Mapping the multiple dimensions of power relations in school politics. In J. D. Scribner & D. H. Layton (Eds.), *The study of educational politics: The 1994 commemorative yearbook of the politics of education association* (pp. 147–170). Bristol, PA: Taylor & Francis.

Marshall, C., & Gerstl-Pepin, C. (2005). *Re-framing educational politics for social justice.* Boston, MA: Pearson Education.

Marshall, C., & Hooley, R. (2006). *The assistant principal: Leadership choices and challenges* (2nd ed.). Thousand Oaks, CA: Corwin.

Marshall, C., & Oliva, M. (2010). *Leadership for social justice.* Boston, MA: Pearson Education.

Marshall, C., & Scribner, J. D. (1991). It's all political: Inquiry into the micropolitics of education. *Education and Urban Society, 23*(4), 347–355.

Mazzoni, T. L. (1991). Analyzing state school policymaking: An arena model. *Educational Evaluation and Policy Analysis, 13*(2), 115–138.

Pfeffer, J., & Salancik, G. R. (2011). External control of organizations: A resource dependence perspective. In J. M. Shafritz, J. S. Ott, & Y. S. Yang (Eds.), *Classics of Organizational Theory,* (7th Ed.) Boston, MA: Wadsworth. (Original work published in 1978)

Rittel, H. W., & Webber, M. M. (1973). Dilemmas in a general theory of planning. *Policy Sciences, 4*(2), 155–169.

Scheurich, J. J., & Skrla, L. (2003). *Leadership for equity and excellence.* Thousand Oaks, CA: Corwin.

Sernak, K. (1998). *School leadership: Balancing power with caring.* New York, NY: Teachers College.

Stronge, J. H., Richard, H. B., & Catano, N. (2008). *Qualities of effective principals.* Alexandria, VA: ASCD.

Talbert, J. E. (2010). Professional learning communities at the crossroads: How systems hinder or engender change. In M. Fullan, A. Hargreaves, & A. Lieberman (Eds.), *International handbook of educational change* (Vol. 3, pp. 555–571). Dordrecht, The Netherlands: Springer.

Theoharis, G. (2007). Social justice educational leaders and resistance: Toward a theory of social justice leadership. *Educational Administration Quarterly, 43*(2), 327.

Weick, K. E. (1976). Educational organizations as loosely coupled systems. *Administrative Science Quarterly, 21*(1), 1–19.

Whitaker, T. (2003). *What great principals do differently: Fifteen things that matter most.* Larchmont, NY: Eye on Education.

Yukl, G., & Van Fleet, D. D. (1992). Theory and research on leadership in organizations. In M. D. Dunnette & L. M. Hough (Eds.). *Handbook of industrial and organizational psychology* (Vol. 3, 2nd ed., pp 147–197). Palo Alto, CA: Consulting Psychologists.

Further Readings

Black, J. A., & English, F. W. (1986). *What they don't tell you in schools of education about school administration.* Lancaster, PA: Technomic.

Told in straightforward and cynical but reality-based style, this text gives advice on how to handle the array of bad actors encountered by school leaders. It seems to recommend using take-charge displays of power rather than facilitative leadership and does little with social justice issues, but it is still a useful how-to book.

Corson, D. (Ed.). (1995). *Discourse and power in educational organizations.* Cresskill, NJ: Hampton.

This collection of chapters reveals a range of ways to see how words and dialogue are used as power plays in schooling. Leaders (and followers) will find this very useful for recognizing subtle displays of power.

Dufour, R., Eaker, R., & Dufour, R. (2005). *On common ground: The power of professional learning communities.* Bloomington, IN: Solution Tree.

The authors construct the vision and mission of finding common ground through teacher collaboration in professional groups called professional learning communities to improve student achievement.

Foster, W. (1986). *Paradigms and promises.* Buffalo, NY: Prometheus.

The traditional ways of viewing organizations and leadership are tossed aside so that the author can set up his demonstration that for leadership to be democratic and moral and to move people toward a socially just society, leaders must take a critical stance and must defy the norms of the administrative profession. Scary, but inspiring!

Fullan, M., & Hargreaves, A. (1996). *What's worth fighting for in your school.* New York, NY: Teachers College.

Recognizing when and how to take action on issues in the school are important skills for the principal. The authors address such skills not only for the principal but for teachers as well.

Ginsburg, M. B. (Ed.). (1995). *The politics of educators' work and lives.* New York, NY: Garland.

This collection of chapters emphasizes the ways that so many people involved in schooling are acting politically. So the reader sees how teachers are political in their work lives both in the United States and around the world, how the status of women in leadership is a political matter, and how teachers are politically active.

Hartzell, G. N., Williams, R. C., & Nelson, K. T. (1995). *New voices in the field.* Thousand Oaks, CA: Corwin.

Assistant principals and novice principals will find solace as they read examples and get advice from their peers who describe their initial encounters with the sometimes shocking demands, realities, and dilemmas of leaders' responsibilities.

Kosmoski, G., & Pollock, D. (2003). *Managing difficult, frustration and hostile conversations.* Thousand Oaks, CA: Corwin.

Full of cases with strategies for managing the stress and the resolution, this book is all too real. Still the advice "forewarned is forearmed" is reason enough to use this book, as it reminds readers that they must have strategies for managing the unethical, the ranting, and the drunk, as well as the times when they themselves make mistakes.

Marshall, C., & Gerstl-Pepin, C. (2005). *Re-framing educational politics for social justice.* Boston, MA: Pearson.

This politics textbook provides answers to the question, "What if I hate the way current policies are framed?" One chapter, "Being Politically Wise and Strategic," discusses the dilemmas encountered when actively engaging in the political environment.

Marshall, C., & Hooley, R. (2006). *The assistant principal: Leadership choices and challenges.* Thousand Oaks, CA: Corwin.

Examining the micropolitics of entry-level administration provides essential understandings of policies, power systems, and leadership styles.

Marshall, C., & Oliva, M. (2010). *Leadership for social justice.* Boston, MA: Pearson Education.

Leaders can use this book for basic information regarding equity issues as well as for strategies, training, and motivation to pay attention to social justice. Some chapters are designed to be curricula useful in professional development sessions for educators and communities.

Marshall, C., & Scribner, J. D. (1991). The micropolitics of education. *Education and Urban Society, 23*(4), 347–355.

The edition of the journal responded to questions, issues, and topics related to the micropolitics of schools and research surrounding power contexts and groups.

Pellicer, L. O. (2003). *Caring enough to lead: How reflective thought leads to moral leadership.* Thousand Oaks, CA: Corwin.

The book offers vignettes and stories to assist the principal with visualizing important concepts around leadership and the politics of being a leader.

Scheurich, J. J., & Skrla, L. (2003). *Leadership for equity and excellence.* Thousand Oaks, CA: Corwin.

Believing that schools can be attuned to our pursuit of equity and social justice, these authors show how leaders can use specific tools, such as curriculum alignment, accountability, and data-driven decision making to erase school system inequities. Particularly useful are the equity audit strategies illustrated and the strategies for social justice leaders to sustain themselves as they encounter resistance.

Sernak, K. (1998). *School leadership: Balancing power with caring.* New York, NY: Teachers College.

The book tells the story of a principal's struggle to create a caring school environment while facing the issues of equity, power, and politics.

Stronge, J. H., Richard, H. B., & Catano, N. (2008). *Qualities of effective principals.* Alexandria, VA: ASCD.

The text provides strategies and resources for a principal to use in creating a cohesive and effective school environment. Principals can establish a roadmap for sustaining personal leadership and distributing leadership.

Whitaker, T. (2003). *What great principals do differently: Fifteen things that matter most.* Larchmont, NY: Eye on Education.

This book gives advice on how to successfully lead and interact with staff and parents in the micropolitical environment of a school, presented in an accessible, ready-to-apply format.

Whitaker, T., & Fiore, D. J. (2001). *Dealing with difficult parents and with parents in difficult situations.* Larchmont, NY: Eye on Education.

Includes practical tools and language to build relationships and credibility with parent community.

29

PRODUCING "EVIDENCE"

Overcoming the Limitations of the Market, Competition, and Privatization

CHRISTOPHER LUBIENSKI

University of Illinois

JANELLE SCOTT

University of California, Berkeley

ELIZABETH DEBRAY

University of Georgia

One of the major debates playing out right now in the United States is over the appropriate role of the government vis-à-vis the private sector in public education. This debate around schooling often becomes quite acrimonious, with participants making moral claims for their perspectives on issues like **choice** and **competition** or accusations about the unethical position of their opponents. Yet even as such debates play out, they focus on issues for which we have empirical insights. However, the empirical evidence is itself not only often disputed, but frequently serves as the center of a new political economy of knowledge production for use in public policy making.

This chapter focuses less on the veracity of claims—either moral or empirical—and instead focuses on the ways empirical knowledge is produced, packaged, and propagated to the public at large and to policymakers. It discusses the current paucity of evidence supporting what can be called "incentivist" policies in education, not as an accusation but as the obstacle that a number of interests, individuals, and organizations supporting these policies must overcome through strategic action around research, production, and use. This analysis explores the tasks faced by the groups and alliances advocating for incentivist policies as they seek to assert an empirical basis for their agenda. It considers the different roles that various groups play in this larger endeavor and the implications for knowledge, production, and use.

Of course, these issues about the role of markets and governments are contentious, where debates are not limited to substantive issues but also cover semantic ones because of the symbolic value of words (or labels) like **privatization**. The following section discusses these concerns about language and concepts and explains the distinctions and dynamics of these concepts for the present purposes of better understanding research advocacy on these issues. Then it describes the set of incentivist policies that are the focus of this analysis, identifying their common elements, and in the third section, offering a brief survey of the empirical evidence on charter schools, vouchers, and teacher and student incentives. In the fourth part we sketch out our understanding of the emerging political economy of research production and consumption as is evident around market-oriented proposals, focusing on the agenda and actors advocating for incentivist approaches. In the fifth section we look at patterns of policy advocacy and highlight in particular the role of different groups in producing counterevidence in support of the incentivist agenda. The penultimate section moves toward a more theoretical understanding of how the different actors advocating for these policies work in a coalition and identifies some of the key roles and functions. The concluding discussion considers the calls for markets for education and notes the pitfalls of relying on idea brokers within the marketplace of ideas.

Markets, Competition, and Privatization in Education

Terms such as *markets*, *competition*, and *privatization* are often used rather loosely in current discussions of education reform. In such an ideologically charged environment, that can lead to an imprecision that becomes very problematic. For instance, before becoming the foremost critic of the current wave of education reform, Diane Ravitch (1996) (then a fellow at the Hoover Institution) denied that charter schools represented a form of privatization, noting that

> the schools are funded by public dollars, are authorized by legislation, and are accountable to public authorities. By contrast, privatization occurs when a public facility is transferred to private owners, who are accountable to their stockholders, not to public authorities. (p. 23)

More recently, though, after reevaluating the evidence, Ravitch (2013) has come to the conclusion that charter schools are an integral part of a wider privatization movement. While seemingly contradictory, in fact, both positions are correct. Charter schools do not meet the classic definition of privatization seen in, say 1980s Latin America, where state-owned enterprises were transferred to private owners. Yet it is difficult to deny that the substantial shift in control of publicly financed schools from elected school boards to private school management companies does not represent a significant diminishment of public authority (Lubienski, 2013). Thus some specificity, or at least some shared understanding, is warranted around the terminology used to discuss these issues.

While, as a global phenomenon, the term *privatization* has come to have multiple and sometimes contradictory connotations, in the context of education policy, we can distinguish between *privatization of schools* and *privatization of school governance*. In the first instance, individual schools are transferred from public ownership, control, or governance to private interests. In the second case, systems are reoriented to introduce a significant private component of ownership, control, or governance. This distinction is useful because current reforms do not necessarily reflect traditional modes of privatization in individual cases, but they do in aggregate. For instance, in most cases, charter schools are started not when public schools are turned over to private (and especially for profit) interests. However, seen in the context of the closing of neighborhood public schools in, for example, Chicago, Detroit, or in New Orleans (where 90% of students in the public sector attend charter schools), we are seeing urban systems increasingly run by private, nongovernmental entities (Lubienski, 2013).

Furthermore, privatization is distinct from **marketization**, where conditions are introduced to a system in order to bring market-style incentives to bear on schools. Such conditions can apply to both private and public sector schools. That is, even schools that are not privately run might be compelled to act more like private businesses to compete in a market-style environment. Of course, as some have noted, markets for education are not "pure" markets, if such a thing exists (Merrifield, 2000). Instead, in view of continued public funding, regulation, and compulsory consumption, they are better thought of as "quasi-markets" (Bartlett, 1993) or "second-best markets" (Lubienski, 2006) that rely on essential mechanisms from markets to refashion the system.

Although there are many preconceptions, assumptions, and assertions about what makes a marketized system, there are some essential key components. Functioning markets require flexibility for consumers in the form of choice between different options so that they may then impose discipline on producers by threatening to exit for another option. In education, of course, this is typically conceived of as families having alternatives besides the assigned neighborhood public school. Yet in instances where producers have power and are able to select students, as has been evident in a number of contexts, markets are thought to be misfiring (Lauder et al., 1999; Parry, 1997; Walford, 1997). Thus, producers are expected to compete for the patronage of consumers. In situations where there are monopolies, collusion, cooperation, or coercion between providers, competition is thwarted and producers have little incentive to respond to consumers' demands (Finn, 2008). At the same time, simply introducing multiple providers and giving consumers the opportunity to choose between them does little if producers do not have the **autonomy** to innovate and differentiate the options they offer consumers.

In fact, each one of these factors is essential but insufficient in itself for fashioning a functioning education market. Certainly, market-oriented reformers note that public education resembles a government monopoly of taxpayer funds for education (Greene et al., 2008; Kolderie, 1990), but replacing a state monopoly with a private monopoly would not be expected to change conditions substantially for students. Schools can differentiate between themselves based on, say, the professional visions of their faculty, but such differentiation is largely meaningless if families have to enroll their children in the schools to which they are assigned. If families can choose between different schools but those schools are lazy monopolists that are funded regardless of enrolment trends, for example, they may have no reason to compete to attract and satisfy families, thus removing a critical driver for innovation and improvement. And if schools can compete but are hamstrung by excessive regulation that limits their range of actions, they lack the autonomy to respond to consumer preferences as best fits local circumstances.

The Promise of Incentivism

Focusing on these mechanisms, market-oriented theorists and reformers have been advancing a number of proposals and policies over the last quarter century on the logic that such measures bring market-style dynamics into the monopolistic public sector.

Typically, such measures focus largely on the choice mechanism. Indeed, advocates frequently push for a range of school choice schemes that enable parents to choose options beyond their local public school. While there are debates about the degree to which such policies represent forms of privatization (Carnoy, 2000; Chubb & Moe, 1990; Lubienski, 2013; Ravitch, 1996, 2013), such discussions are incomplete in the current reform context. In fact, choice should be considered along with a number of policies promoted by reformers that fall under the general category of what some have called **incentivism**, which essentially adopts key aspects of market models for organizing and driving improvements within education (Greene et al., 2008; Lubienski, Scott, & DeBray, 2011; Stern, 2008).

In particular, these incentivist policies adopt one or more of the key aspects of a market theory for education: choice, competition, and/or autonomy (C. Lubienski & S. T. Lubienski, 2005; Walberg, 2000). The programs then move forward under the premise that individuals and organizations in marketized environments will sense and respond to incentives in ways that match their own self-interest. Top-down mandates, directives, and regulations are not only unnecessary but undesirable, ineffective, and often counterproductive according to this thinking. Under this assumption of the rational, self-interested agent, theorists argue that incentives can be arranged in ways that can shape the behavior of organizations and individuals to promote many specific outcomes (Moe, 2008). If policymakers want greater efficiencies, incentives can be arranged toward that end. If a district desires a higher level of outcomes, leaders can create competitive incentives that work toward that goal. If a community wants more equitable access, policymakers can shape incentive structures that support that objective.

This thinking is evident in a number of policies and proposals put forth in the current wave of market-oriented education reform. As noted, choice programs certainly reflect this thinking, with school choice schemes—from open-enrollment programs and charter schools to vouchers and tax credits—echoing the idea that choice is helpful not only for choosers but can compel providers to improve, innovate, and offer a wider range of services (Hoxby, 2002). Teacher compensation policy proposals can also display incentivist designs. Teacher tenure is portrayed as an impediment to effective teaching, since it shields teachers from competitive incentives. On the other hand, merit pay for teachers advances from the notion that differential pay will motivate teachers to adopt more effective practices that they would not otherwise embrace (Gonring, Teske, & Jupp, 2007). This thinking even extends to pay schemes for students, where pay for performance programs have been established to incentivize desired behaviors like attendance and good grades (Dillon, 2011; Fryer, 2010; Sandel, 2012).

Many of the discussions of these types of reforms have centered on the question of whether or not these approaches privatize education (Ravitch, 1996, 2013). Although there are different conceptions of the term, it is not clear that infusing incentives into the public system represents a form of privatization as traditionally defined (Lubienski, 2013). On the other hand, it would be foolish to ignore the fact that reforms such as charter schools are transferring substantial segments of the publicly governed system to private management. Rather than getting immersed in the question of what constitutes privatization and how current reform proposals may or may not match those definitions, suffice it to say that both proponents and skeptics of these reforms acknowledge that such reforms create a market system, drawing on incentivist assumptions about how individuals and organizations will behave in competitive environments (Davies, Quirke, & Aurini, 2006; Greene et al., 2008; Walberg & Bast, 2003).

Empirical Evidence on Incentivist Policies

While incentivist approaches to education reform are appealing in their simplicity, adopting choice, competition, and autonomy in creating marketized environments for education, they are also comprehensive in that they can be applied to a number of facets of education. Furthermore, several of them have some longevity, having been around enough to develop a substantial track record: For instance, some charter schools and voucher programs have been in operation for over two decades (Lubienski & Weitzel, 2010). In view of the attractive and even compelling logic of incentivism, as well as its obvious appeal for many policymakers, a brief review of the empirical record on these policies is in order.

Charter Schools

As schools of choice, these autonomous schools are expected to compete for students, offering better educational options for students. Laws allowing charter schools have been adopted in 42 states and the District of Columbia, and expansion of the schools has been encouraged by the federal government. However, most of the large-scale studies on these schools find them to be performing at a level no better than and, in some cases, beneath those of demographically similar public schools (Bettinger, 2005; Bifulco & Ladd, 2006; Booker, Gill, Zimmer, & Sass, 2008; Braun, Jenkins, & Grigg, 2006a; Hanushek, Kain, Rivkin, & Branch, 2007; C. Lubienski & S. T. Lubienski, 2013). A number of smaller scale studies of local programs in particular cities have found some effect, at times substantial (Angrist et al., 2011; Hoxby & Murarka, 2007; Hoxby & Rockoff, 2004). Yet there are reasons to be careful with such studies, as they often have very small, nonrepresentative samples of schools and faced methodological hurdles (Baker & Ferris, 2011; Reardon, 2009).

Vouchers

Vouchers allow families to use public funding to send their children to private schools and have been adopted in various forms in several states. This focus on expanding choice to include independent, nonpublic schools has a contentious history since the first modern program was introduced in Milwaukee over two decades ago, with the Cleveland program going to the U.S. Supreme Court, which ruled in 2002 that it was constitutional. Yet most research on the impacts of these programs finds little to no effect on student learning. With the exception of a small group of scholars (Greene, 2001; Greene, Howell, & Peterson, 1997; Peterson, Howell, & Greene, 1999; Wolf et al., 2010; Wolf, 2013), most independent research is much more sober in its findings (Rouse, 1998; Rouse & Barrow, 2009; Witte, 2000), with some early supporters of these programs now changing their minds in view of this evidence (Dodenhoff, 2007; Stern, 2008).

Merit Pay for Teachers

A number of incentivists have proposed linking teacher compensation to the learning growth of their students. These proposals, supported by federal policy, advance from the logic that innovation and productivity would be increased if teachers' efforts were rewarded on an individual basis, rather than tying compensation to seniority (Brill, 2011; From, 1999; Gonring et al., 2007; Gratz, 2009). Yet some skeptics have raised questions about the technical obstacles of distinguishing teachers' efforts from other input factors or the cooperative nature of teachers' work (Cohen & Murnane, 1985; Sandel, 2012). Two recent experiments in New York City and Nashville failed to find achievement gains from these programs (Green, 2011; Otterman, 2011; Springer et al., 2010).

Pay for Performance

Programs providing incentives to students for certain desired behaviors have been around for some time, with cash payment programs more common in developing countries, where they are designed to serve as a replacement for income a family could have received by sending the child into the workforce (de Janvry, Finan, Sadoulet, & Vakis, 2006). Yet there is very little data on systematic policies to incentivize student behavior—in essence making part of the payoff to education more immediate, rather than a matter of delayed gratification—despite the fact that such programs are spreading (Guernsey, 2009). In a recent randomized trial, rewards to students for outcomes had no effect on those outcomes, although rewards for other "input" behaviors did make a difference on outcomes (Fryer, 2010). While many economists are excited about the potential of such incentives, some psychologists are concerned that incentivizing intrinsic rewards can have perverse consequences (Deci, 1975; Guernsey, 2009; Schwartz, 2007).

While there have been debates about the nuances of these findings for these different policies, with the exception of a small group of research advocates, most observers agree that the outcomes of these reforms are not particularly compelling and certainly do not meet the expectations that reformers had originally set out for them (Dodenhoff, 2007; Ravitch, 2009; Stern, 2008; Weitzel & Lubienski, 2010).

Nonetheless, many individuals, organizations, and interests continue to push for these policies. In the remainder of this analysis, we focus on the activities of such advocates, considering the factors that shape their strategies around research evidence on incentivist reforms. In doing this, much of what we discuss draws on our preliminary findings from a large-scale longitudinal study of advocacy organizations' efforts to shape research evidence for use in policy making (Lubienski et al., 2011).

A New Political Economy of Research Evidence?

Especially in some fields, including education, the desired link between evidence on a problem and solution, on the one hand, and policymakers' responses, on the other, has never been as direct and apparent as might be expected in an ideal world. Instead, education has been chronically plagued by fads, charlatans, and ideological agendas that advance in lieu of, and often in spite of, evidence on their effectiveness (Buchholz, 1931/1971; Cuban, 2001; Palmaffy, 1999). Certainly, policymakers have some cause to claim that research reports on education interventions are frequently not particularly useful—that they may often lack rigor, timeliness, applicability, and may raise more questions than they answer.

Nonetheless, there are two points worth making with regard to the issue of research use. First, as we demonstrate below, well-placed advocates have been notably active in collecting and advancing evidence under the assumption that this can substantively alter policymakers' positions on issues (or that policymakers' more symbolic use of such research may at least require evidence to support policymakers' prior positions). Second, policymakers themselves have, in recent years, been demanding better evidence under the assumption that they need this in order to make better policy. This is evident, for instance, in the focus on data-driven decision making and the rise of the effective philanthropy movement, which ties funding to evidence of effectiveness. It is also demonstrated in federal initiatives such as No Child Left Behind, which famously focused attention on evidence-based research and reoriented federal education research funding toward randomized trials. Thus, despite traditional concerns about the paucity of direct use of research evidence in education policy, both research consumers (policymakers) and research providers (advocacy organizations) demonstrate a desire that research evidence be used in policy making.

The Incentivist Agenda

If policy making is to be based in evidence of effectiveness, in light of weaknesses in the evidence base for incentivist policies noted previously, advocates for incentivism face a substantial challenge in advancing their policy agenda. Since a reading of the research literature does not appear to provide compelling evidence of the effectiveness of more market-oriented models for education, incentivist advocates must produce such evidence, cherry-pick or spin current evidence to support their claims, and/or undermine extant findings that challenge their agenda.

Incentivist Actors

As would be indicated under the Advocacy Coalition Framework (Sabatier & Jenkins-Smith, 1999), the alliances advocating for incentivist reforms are not monolithic but instead overlap in their support on some specific issues and differ on others. Indeed, within the broader range of incentivist policies, we see examples of organizations working together on some specific efforts, while such alliances either fall apart or even turn into opposition on other issues. For instance, some groups, such as the Friedman Foundation and Parent Revolution, find common cause on the general idea of choice and, more specifically, charter schools but disagree on the question of vouchers for private schools. Nevertheless, there are some prominent groups that illustrate the multiple types of organizations active in promoting different incentivist policies (DeBray-Pelot, Lubienski, & Scott, 2007).

Drawing on a number of sources, the lists of major players in the incentivist coalition(s) include national philanthropies that fund research, advocacy, and implementation, such as the Gates, Walton, and Broad foundations, along with more local organizations, such as the Daniels Fund, the Piton Foundation, and the Donnel-Kay Foundation. Other organizations are more closely associated with research production or packaging, including traditional think tanks such as the Brookings Institution, the Heartland Institute, and the Fordham Institute, as well as the Mackinac Center or the Pelican Institute at the state and local levels. Newer organizations within traditional academic institutions, often receiving funding from these philanthropies, also play such a role, including the Cowen Institute at Tulane University, the Program on Education Policy and Governance (PEPG) at Harvard University, and the Department of Education Reform at the University of Arkansas. A number of organizations, also typically funded by the aforementioned philanthropies, use evidence produced by these and other research outfits in the coalition in focusing on advocacy; these would include groups that work to convince the public, convince policymakers, or elect policymakers, such as the Center for Education Reform (CER), StudentsFirst, and Stand for Children.

Policy advocacy (and in some instances political activity) is also evident from a number of education training and management organizations—many also funded by these philanthropies—including Teach for America (and their political training partner, Leadership for Educational Equity), The New Teacher Project, KIPP schools, and New Schools for New Orleans. Still other organizations, including the Center for American Progress, Democrats for Education Reform, and Parent Revolution, work largely in the policy realm to promote incentivist policies. Finally, an underexamined but increasingly important area that deserves attention for advancing incentivist reform is media, both new and old. Incentivists operate media outlets such as *School Reform News* and more scholarly venues such as *Education Next,* as well as online outlets such as redefinED. But we are also seeing evidence of incentivist efforts through funding and promotion of films such as the pro-charter-school documentary *Waiting for Superman* and the fictional film *Won't Back Down.*

This brief sketch of organizations working within an advocacy coalition around various forms of incentivist policies is not meant to be exhaustive but indicates that the distinctions between the different types of functions often overlap and are not always clear—although one common element appears to be a discernible group of funders. Nevertheless, this overview suggests that there are multiple functions that need to be served by member groups within that coalition.

Patterns of Strategic Efforts in Advocacy for Incentivist Policies

As noted, in advancing an evidence-based argument for incentivist reforms in lieu of a compelling research base, coalition partners have a number of tasks to which they need to attend as part of a strategy of beefing up empirical claims while negating research challenges to those claims. In that regard, different elements of the coalition can take the leading or supporting role depending on the particular strategic effort in question. In discussing some of these roles, we do not intend to lump all these different groups together in a coalition's efforts, since as we noted regarding advocacy coalitions in general, various member groups might participate in, or even be opposed to, a coalition's efforts depending on the specific issue. Still, it is instructive to consider how the actions of some of these groups exemplify patterns of advocacy and thus the broader strategies of incentivist coalitions.

Obviously, funding agencies play an essential part in the creation and sustenance of key elements of a coalition (Scott & Jabbar, 2013). They support research entities as well as advocacy and lobbying groups. Moreover, even if they stay out of direct political action, they can fund groups that work to promote referenda or to elect candidates favorable to their agenda. More recently, funding agencies have been promoting incentivist arguments by funding or producing feature length films, with other member organizations in the coalition working to promote the film. For instance, Walden Media, owned by Philip Anschutz, helped produce the pro-charter vehicle *Won't Back Down*, which was then featured or promoted by coalition partner organizations such as the Fordham Institute and Parent Revolution, which organized screenings.

Counterevidence Production

In addition to their roles in funding, political lobbying, and even entertainment (Reckhow, 2013; Rich, 2004), another activity of incentivists is counterevidence production—efforts to undermine the emergence of any research that challenges the market-oriented agenda. Several examples of this tactic suggest a wider strategy. (See **Sidebar 29.1**.)

Sidebar 29.1 When Research Raises Red Flags

Especially in politicized fields like education policy, where there are controversial questions often addressed through highly technical methods, there are sometimes competing studies offering conflicting findings—even when researchers look at the same data. In these cases, readers who aren't necessarily experts in those methods are implicitly asked to trust the researcher or the organization publishing the study.

Short of learning sophisticated statistical methods, how can you tell which ones are real studies and which ones are pushing an agenda? Well, you can't, really. But you can get a sense of the veracity of technical studies by considering some of the following factors. No single one of these factors is in itself wrong or sufficient for detecting the snake oil. But combinations of these can be useful, especially if you look at research coming from a particular source over time.

The study is not peer reviewed: Researchers submit their work to be reviewed anonymously by other experts as a way of ensuring integrity and quality in research. Many advocacy reports bypass this process or publish in fake journals that are really magazines or don't use peer review. In some cases, non-peer-reviewed publications could still have good quality control through the editing process. But notice if the editors are all of the same ideological stripe.

The study was funded by an advocacy organization: Researchers will swear that their results are not influenced by the group funding them. And they may often be right. Certainly, many researchers have to get funding wherever they find it, and many funders are not pushing a particular agenda. But ask yourself, when a controversial funding organization with a particular advocacy agenda gets involved, are they likely to invest in studies that undercut their agenda?

The researcher has a history of advocacy: When someone has a developed track record of promoting a particular position, it is not likely that he or she will suddenly find some sense of objectivity. Especially if that researcher has been called out in the past for questionable methodological decisions or always comes to the same conclusion when others see mixed results, beware.

The data and methods are not clearly explained: You don't need to be an expert in the methodological approach to notice if researchers adequately describe the data and method used to arrive at their conclusions. Is it at least stated so that other people who are experts can try to replicate the study? And beware of press releases and media accounts that do not provide an adequate basis to judge.

There is a "consensus": Studies typically add to existing knowledge, so that results quite often affirm and expand on prior studies. That's not to say that some new findings, especially on less settled questions, can't turn our collective wisdom on its head. But that happens pretty rarely, and readers should be cautious until other researchers start to

(Continued)

Sidebar 29.1 (Continued)

affirm those results. At the same time, beware of advocates who claim there is a consensus on issues that are actually quite controversial.

The citations are one-sided: Good research typically looks at an issue from multiple perspectives, at least in framing the question. A quick look at the citations used in a study can tell you whether they come from diverse sources or whether the new study is simply contributing to an echo chamber of yes men agreeing with each other. Also, are the citations from reputable sources?

Christopher Lubienski

Milwaukee Vouchers

When the state of Wisconsin originally implemented the Milwaukee voucher program, it included an official evaluation of the academic impact of the vouchers on students and commissioned a researcher who was himself not opposed to vouchers to conduct the evaluation (Witte, 2000; Witte, Thorn, & Pritchard, 1995). Yet when this official evaluation found virtually no effect for students, voucher proponents at PEPG and later at the University of Arkansas attacked that evaluation and conducted a secondary analysis of the data using methods and analysis that were quite questionable, finding substantial effects— at a crucial time when the program was being reviewed by the courts (Greene & Peterson, 1996; Greene, Peterson, & Du, 1997, 1998).

Cleveland Vouchers

Similarly, the state of Ohio commissioned an official evaluation of its voucher program in Cleveland, and that evaluation came to the conclusion the program did not have a significant effect on achievement (Metcalf et al., 1998; Metcalf, West, Legan, Paul, & Boone, 2003). Once again, PEPG researchers offered an alternative analysis that was much more optimistic about the benefits of the program (Greene et al., 1997). While this alternative analysis was forcefully criticized for misrepresenting data in order to promote vouchers (Metcalf, 1998), the program was eventually found to be constitutional by the U.S. Supreme Court.

Charter School Performance

After it was unable to obtain raw data from the National Assessment of Educational Progress (NAEP) on charter schools, the American Federation of Teachers released an analysis based on less comprehensive online NAEP data, finding that charter schools were performing poorly compared to other public schools (Nelson, Rosenberg, & Van Meter, 2004). Within days, a number of scholars, most of them associated with incentivist groups, took out a full page advertisement in the *New York Times* criticizing the study for, among other things, not being peer reviewed (Various Scholars & CER, 2004). Soon after that, Caroline Hoxby, a Hoover Institution scholar who had signed on to the ad, released findings that charter schools were outperforming other public schools (Hoxby, 2004a, 2004b). The research was criticized for errors and was never published but still received substantial media attention (Carnoy, Jacobsen, Mishel, & Rothstein, 2005; Roy & Mishel, 2005).

Private School Performance

Later, following up on the NAEP data, two much more comprehensive, federally funded studies found that district-run public schools were, in fact, outperforming private schools and charter schools once demographic differences were considered (Braun, Jenkins, & Grigg, 2006b; S. T. Lubienski & C. Lubienski, 2006). Again, within weeks of the latter study's publication, PEPG produced a reanalysis of the data, arguing that private schools instead outperform public schools (Peterson & Llaudet, 2006). Again, the reanalysis had multiple methodological problems and was not published in a peer-reviewed outlet, even though one of the authors had signed on to the *New York Times* ad that criticized the AFT study for not being peer reviewed (C. Lubienski & S. T. Lubienski, 2006).

Charter School Effects

In 2009, the Center for Research on Education Outcomes (CREDO) at Stanford University released a study of charter schools in 16 states, finding that, in over 80% of the cases, charter schools were performing at a level beneath or essentially equal to that of matched traditional public schools (Raymond & CREDO, 2009). The study garnered substantial attention. Within 2 months, Hoxby released a memo attempting to undermine the CREDO findings and then, a month later, a much more optimistic set of findings on charter schools in New York City, despite methodological concerns (Hoxby, 2009; Hoxby, Murarka, & Kang, 2009; Reardon, 2009).

While debates are an important part of scholarly inquiry and researchers often get into methodological squabbles, the point is not who is correct on these issues but the patterns around the discussions of these research reports. For years, incentivist organizations have been promoting an argument through scholarly publications, op-eds, entertainment media, and advertising claiming that marketized education produces greater opportunities and results. Interestingly, when evidence emerges—including rigorous research and official evaluations of these programs—that does not support the narrative, incentivist organizations have moved swiftly to neutralize any negative impact. In the cases described above, this has tended to be done rather quickly after the release of the offending evidence, by scholars at prestigious institutions but also with funding from incentivist philanthropies. Notably, the counter-report is often questioned by independent scholars and does not typically go through a peer-review process.

Toward a Theory of Advocacy Coalitions in Advancing Education Reforms

Arguments for choice are often based in moral arguments about what is ethically appropriate or socially desirable. For instance, some argue that teacher tenure is unfair because it protects incompetence and ineffectiveness (Stossel, 2006). Others have pointed to the injustice of forcing children to attend the failing school in their neighborhood (Holt, 1999; King, 1997).

While such arguments can be particularly persuasive in putting a human face on an abstract issue, the advocacy around incentivist reforms has more typically focused on whether or not these programs work in the sense of improving student outcomes, such as scores on standardized tests. Yet as noted, the evidence on this issue is heavily contested and far from compelling. Nevertheless, these advocacy coalitions often appear to arrange themselves around proving the effectiveness of specific policies within the incentivist framework.

Some key elements of the patterns of advocacy for incentivist policies to move toward a better understanding of how advocacy coalitions operate. More specifically, we examine the production of evidence and counterevidence to advance the incentivist agenda of marketized education, focusing on some organizations active in this effort. Certainly, it is important to keep in mind that such coalitions are dynamic, fluid, and ephemeral (Sabatier & Jenkins-Smith, 1999). Groups will work together in parallel or in concert on efforts around specific policy issues. But the membership and longevity of such alliances depends on the particular situation and policy specifics in question. Partnerships are not permanent and may disintegrate over changes in strategy or circumstances.

Within these advocacy coalitions, different organizations are serving various functions. Certainly, the efforts of a discernible set of philanthropies are evident throughout the coalition. Groups like the Walton Foundation and the Broad Foundation provide support for specific research projects, as well as sustaining funding for organizations that produce research (Rich, 2004). Moreover, they are involved in supporting the dissemination of research evidence and counterevidence, often by funding advocacy organizations that convey claims both to the public and to policymakers.

While funders are integral in nurturing different elements within the coalition, the organizations that produce the evidence supporting incentivist reforms or counterevidence to undermine any research that challenges the incentivist agenda provide the ammunition necessary to make efficacy claims about market-oriented policies. The examples of counterevidence production discussed earlier highlight three such university-based organizations in particular.

PEPG at Harvard University was founded by Paul Peterson, who has describes himself as a "Jedi attacker" challenging the public education monopoly and supporting school choice and has trained a number of other incentivist-oriented researchers who have taken positions in academia (Mezzacappa, 2006; Peterson, 1990, p. 73). PEPG receives funding from the Bradley, Walton, and Friedman foundations and, as noted previously, produces research papers that invariably find benefits for incentivist policies or challenge research that does not.

The Department of Education Reform at the University of Arkansas was founded in 2005 in part by a gift from the Walton Foundation, with $20 million in funding for endowed professorships (Schmidt, 2011; Smith & Brantley, 2005). The entity hosts the School Choice Demonstration Project and trains emerging researchers. Faculty there have been notably successful in placing opinion pieces in a wide range of newspapers and for a time created the *Education Working Paper Archive,* which was established as "an online, refereed, scholarly archive."

The Hoover Institution at Stanford University is associated with a number of conservative and free market causes and includes the Koret Task Force on K–12 Education, funded in part by the Bradley Foundation. One of its primary endeavors is *Education Next,* a professionally produced "journal of opinion and research" that tends to publish articles and essays supportive of market-based policies or that attempt to undercut findings that do not support these policies. The editor is also the director of PEPG, and the editorial board includes many signatories of the *New York Times* ad attacking the AFT study on charter school performance, including the author of the reports on charter schools but no known skeptics of incentivist policies. Such an infrastructure associated with established academic institutions provides substantial credibility to scholarship emerging in advocacy coalitions that promote incentivist reform and allows such research to be published and promoted without going through independent peer-review processes.

Finally, in light of this notable knowledge production, we are also seeing the rise of **intermediary organizations** (IOs) that serve as brokers in conveying research evidence from these and other knowledge producers to policymakers (Lubienski et al., 2011). This intermediary function of selecting, translating, and selling research evidence is not necessarily performed by single, discrete entities, since some larger, more comprehensive organizations such as the Gates Foundation play multiple roles in moving information from funding, production, and dissemination, and others, like PEPG or the Koret Task Force, are active in promoting their own work. Nevertheless, organizations that operate specifically as intermediaries nicely illustrate this function.

For instance, CER compiles evidence supporting the incentivist agenda in areas such as charter schools with the idea of translating and promoting this research for both a wider audience and for policymakers. In doing this, CER receives support from the Anschutz, Bradley, Broad, Gates, and Walton Foundations, as well as many others. It produces state rankings and grades of charter school laws and selective collections and questionable interpretations of research produced by other organizations (CER, 2003, 2010). Another group that serves a similar function is the American Legislative Exchange Council (ALEC), which brings together state legislators with corporate and philanthropic interests; these interest groups must pay substantial fees to

---

Sidebar 29.2   Habits of Highly Effective IOs

Higher impact intermediary organizations are—for better or worse—those that typically exhibit some of the following attributes:

Well networked across a range of organizations, including funders, researchers, media, and policymakers

Bilingual in that they are conversant in the languages of both research and policy but especially the latter

Adept at employing multiple types of media, both new and traditional, to reach their intended audiences

Focused on an issue or specific set of issues where they are known to have some degree of expertise

Well funded . . . of course

participate in its meetings. Funders include or have included the Bradley, Gates, and Walton foundations, as well as Walmart. In education, as on other issues, ALEC offers model legislation to policymakers that promotes incentivist policies such as school choice, charter schools, and vouchers. Moreover, ALEC regularly publishes a synthesis of research favorable to its agenda (e.g., Ladner & Myslinski, 2013).

As with all these types of organizations within the incentivist advocacy coalition, there are many more examples, too numerous to describe or even list here in a complete or comprehensive manner. However, the examples provided demonstrate the ways that these different functions can be served within an advocacy coalition. (See **Sidebar 29.2**.)

Conclusion: Caveat Emptor

Within the marketplace of ideas in a liberal democratic society, we can consider the roles of buyers and sellers in providing information that has substantive or even symbolic value in policy debates. As in many markets for consumer goods and services, the possibility of informational asymmetries exists, where one party to a transaction has access to important information to which the other party is not privy. When the buyer is in such a position, the seller is at a disadvantage and is more likely to miss out on potential gains.

On the other hand, when the seller is the beneficiary of asymmetrical information, the buyer is at a disadvantage—not knowing about other options, for instance, or the production processes or relative quality of a good or service. This is actually a very common situation, where consumers have no way to evaluate the quality of particular goods before purchasing them. They have to rely on surrogate information such as advertising, reputation, recommendations, past experiences, or just faith. Certainly there are correctives to support markets despite these imperfections. For instance, accreditation, reviews, and licensing are all attempts to balance out informational asymmetries.

But brokers, or salespeople, can also play a key role in this—for better or for worse. Such agents can provide valuable insights and expertise to a buyer who is not familiar with a specific market, matching producers with consumers in ways that are mutually

beneficial. For instance, a person getting into a specialized market such as art collection or stock trading may use a broker to help navigate unknown and potentially treacherous transactions. Similarly, salespeople can help shoppers understand and find what they are looking for, offering insights on brands, product quality, and other people's experiences. At the same time, such brokers have informational advantages over consumers they could also exploit. Thus, salespeople are also known for sticking consumers with overpriced, poor-quality purchases that they did not want or need. Even though there are correctives built into the system, the old admonition—*caveat emptor*—remains: Buyer beware.

If we can envision the emerging political economy in areas such as education research production as a marketplace of ideas, it makes sense to consider the actors playing the roles of producers, consumers, and brokers. Regardless of whether research evidence is produced for substantive or symbolic consumption in the policy-making process, it appears that much production, at least in the policy areas discussed earlier, is moving toward alternative sources such as new entities housed in universities but that do not typically deal with traditional academic quality control processes. At the same time, a new group of intermediary agents has emerged to serve the broker function. While this development is still at an early stage, there appears to be some initial evidence that some of these intermediaries are playing the salesperson role within the coalition advocating for incentivist policies—making a pitch rather than translating for policymakers seeking the best evidence. In fact, much of this sort of research evidence is quite technical and requires interpretation for a larger audience, reflecting the informational asymmetries that put research consumers at a disadvantage. Moreover, inasmuch as IOs operate within larger advocacy coalitions, it could be that they have an additional advantage and incentive to promote the ideas from their partners and allies because, as with business operations, they work within a vertically integrated system.

This marketplace of ideas, especially in education policy, is relatively and increasingly unregulated as production moves away from traditional forms of quality control such as peer review. And mechanisms such as accreditation have not yet been established in this area to correct informational advantages enjoyed by the sellers. As incentivist advocacy for market-based policies promotes claims about the effectiveness of these approaches despite a dearth of compelling evidence supporting them, it places quite a burden on these coalitions to sell their agenda. Buyer beware.

Key Chapter Terms

Autonomy: Operational latitude enjoyed by local organizations over resource allocation, policies, and so on, often created through deregulation.

Choice: Consumer-style selection of schools, typically by parents who are expected to shop for the best fit for their child.

Competition: Conditions generated as schools pursue strategies to attract students who might otherwise attend another school.

Incentivism: A reform idea that education policies can be arranged to encourage individuals and organizations to pursue their self-interest and, in doing so, lead to optimal benefits for all.

Intermediary organizations: Entities that function to select, interpret, and promote—or otherwise broker—research evidence between research producers and consumers.

Marketization: Where conditions are introduced to a system in order to subject schools to market-style incentives, often by creating more competitive institutional environments.

Privatization: Shifting public entities to individual or nonpublic ownership or control. In education, this can mean privatization of schools but more often involves privatization of school governance, since the schools themselves are not put under private ownership, but private interests are given greater control over them.

References

Angrist, J. D., Cohodes, S. R., Dynarski, S. M., Fullerton, J. B., Kane, T. J., Pathak, P. A., & Walters, C. (2011). *Student achievement in Massachusetts' charter schools.* Cambridge, MA: Harvard University.

Baker, B. D., & Ferris, R. (2011). *Adding up the spending: Fiscal disparities and philanthropy among New York City charter schools.* Boulder, CO: National Education Policy Center.

Bartlett, W. (1993). Quasi-markets and educational reforms. In J. LeGrand & W. Bartlett (Eds.), *Quasi-markets and social policy* (pp. 125–153). London, England: Macmillan.

Bettinger, E. P. (2005). The effect of charter schools on charter students and public schools. *Economics of Education Review, 24*(2), 133–147.

Bifulco, R., & Ladd, H. F. (2006). School choice, racial segregation, and test-score gaps: Evidence from North Carolina's charter school program. *Journal of Policy Analysis and Management, 26*(1), 31–56.

Booker, K., Gill, B. P., Zimmer, R., & Sass, T. R. (2008). *Achievement and attainment in Chicago charter schools.* Santa Monica, CA: RAND.

Braun, H., Jenkins, F., & Grigg, W. (2006a). *A closer look at charter schools using hierarchical linear modeling* (No. NCES 2006–460). Washington, DC: National Center for Education Statistics.

Braun, H., Jenkins, F., & Grigg, W. (2006b). *Comparing private schools and public schools using hierarchical linear modeling* (No. 2006–461). Washington, DC: National Center for Education Statistics.

Brill, S. (2011). *Class warfare: Inside the fight to fix America's schools.* New York, NY: Simon & Schuster.

Buchholz, H. E. (1971). *Fads and fallacies in present-day education.* Freeport, NY: Books for Libraries Press. (Original work published 1931)

Carnoy, M. (2000). School choice? Or is it privatization? *Educational Researcher, 29*(7), 15–20.

Carnoy, M., Jacobsen, R., Mishel, L., & Rothstein, R. (2005). *The charter school dust-up.* Washington, DC: Economic Policy Institute.

Center for Education Reform. (2003). *Charter school laws: Scorecard and rankings.* Washington, DC: Center for Education Reform.

Center for Education Reform. (2010). *Annual survey of America's charter schools.* Washington, DC: Center for Education Reform.

Chubb, J. E., & Moe, T. M. (1990). *Politics, markets, and America's schools.* Washington, DC: Brookings Institution.

Cohen, D. K., & Murnane, R. J. (1985). *The merits of merit pay.* Washington, DC: National Institute of Education.

Cuban, L. (2001). *Oversold and underused: Computers in the classroom.* Cambridge, MA: Harvard University Press.

Davies, S., Quirke, L., & Aurini, J. (2006). The new institutionalism goes to the market. In H.-D. Meyer & B. Rowan (Eds.), *The new institutionalism in education* (pp. 103–122). Albany: State University of New York Press.

de Janvry, A., Finan, F., Sadoulet, E., & Vakis, R. (2006). Can conditional cash transfer programs serve as safety nets in keeping children at school and from working when exposed to shocks? *Journal of Development Economics, 79,* 349–373.

DeBray-Pelot, E., Lubienski, C. A., & Scott, J. T. (2007). The institutional landscape of interest group politics and school choice. *Peabody Journal of Education, 82*(2–3), 204–230.

Deci, E. L. (1975). *Intrinsic motivation.* New York, NY: Plenum Press.

Dillon, S. (2011, October 2). Incentives for advanced work let pupils and teachers cash in. *New York Times.* Retrieved from http://www.nytimes.com/2011/10/03/education/03incentive.html

Dodenhoff, D. (2007). *Fixing the Milwaukee public schools* (WPRI Report). Thiensville: Wisconsin Policy Research Institute.

Finn, C. E. J. (2008, February 27). Lessons learned. *Education Week, 27,* 28, 36.

From, A. (1999, Fall). Where we stand: New Democrats' 10 key reforms for revitalizing American education. *Blueprint Magazine.* Retrieved from http://www.dlc.org/ndol_ci8e10.html?kaid=110&subid=900023&contentid=1203

Fryer, R. G. (2010). *Financial incentives and student achievement.* Cambridge, MA: Harvard University Press.

Gonring, P., Teske, P., & Jupp, B. (2007). *Pay-for-performance teacher compensation.* Cambridge, MA: Harvard Education Press.

Gratz, D. B. (2009). *The peril and promise of performance pay.* Lanham, MD: Rowman & Littlefield.

Green, E. (2011). Study: $75M teacher pay initiative did not improve achievement. Retrieved from http://gothamschools.org/2011/03/07/study-75m-teacher-pay-initiative-did-not-improve-achievement/

Greene, J. P. (2001). The hidden research consensus for school choice. In P. E. Peterson & D. E. Campbell (Eds.), *Charters, vouchers, and public education* (pp. 83–101). Washington, DC: Brookings Institution.

Greene, J. P., Carroll, T. W., Coulson, A. J., Enlow, R., Hirsch, E. D., Ladner, M., . . . Stern, S. (2008, January 24). Is school choice enough? *City Journal.* Retrieved from http://www.city-journal.org/2008/forum0124.html

Greene, J. P., Howell, W. G., & Peterson, P. E. (1997). *An evaluation of the Cleveland Scholarship Program* (Occasional papers). Cambridge, MA: Program on Education Policy and Governance, Harvard University.

Greene, J. P., & Peterson, P. E. (1996). *Methodological issues in evaluation research: The Milwaukee school choice plan* (Occasional papers). Cambridge, MA: Program on Education Policy and Governance, Harvard University.

Greene, J. P., Peterson, P. E., & Du, J. (1997). *Effectiveness of school choice: The Milwaukee experiment* (Occasional paper no. 97–1). Cambridge, MA: Program on Education Policy and Governance, Harvard University.

Greene, J. P., Peterson, P. E., & Du, J. (1998). School choice in Milwaukee: A randomized experiment. In P. E. Peterson & B. C. Hassel (Eds.), *Learning from school choice* (pp. 335–356). Washington, DC: Brookings Institution.

Guernsey, L. (2009, March 2). Rewards for students under a microscope. *New York Times,* p. 1D.

Hanushek, E. A., Kain, J. F., Rivkin, S. G., & Branch, G. F. (2007). Charter school quality and parental decision making with school choice. *Journal of Public Economics, 91*(5–6), 823–848.

Holt, M. (1999). *Not yet "free at last": The unfinished business of the civil rights movement: Our battle for school choice.* Oakland, CA: Institute for Contemporary Studies.

Hoxby, C. M. (2002). *School choice and school productivity (or could school choice be a tide that lifts all boats?)* (Working paper no. w8873). Cambridge, MA: National Bureau of Economic Research.

Hoxby, C. M. (2004a). *Achievement in charter schools and regular public schools in the United States.* Cambridge, MA: Harvard University and National Bureau of Economic Research.

Hoxby, C. M. (2004b). *A straightforward comparison of charter schools and regular public schools in the United States.* Cambridge, MA: Harvard University.

Hoxby, C. M. (2009). *A statistical mistake in the CREDO study of charter schools.* Stanford, CA: Stanford University. Retrieved from http://credo.stanford.edu/reports/memo_on_the_credo_study%20II.pdf

Hoxby, C. M., & Murarka, S. (2007). *New York City's charter schools overall report.* Cambridge, MA: New York City Charter Schools Evaluation Project.

Hoxby, C. M., Murarka, S., & Kang, J. (2009). *How New York City's charter schools affect achievement.* Stanford, CA: Stanford University.

Hoxby, C. M., & Rockoff, J. (2004). *The impact of charter schools on student achievement: A study of students who attend schools chartered by the Chicago Charter School Foundation.* Cambridge, MA: Harvard University.

King, A. C. (1997, September 11). Fighting for school choice: It's a civil right. *Wall Street Journal.* Retrieved from http://media.hoover.org/sites/default/files/documents/0817928723_350.pdf

Kolderie, T. (1990). *Beyond choice to new public schools* (Policy Report No. 8). Washington, DC: Progressive Policy Institute.

Ladner, M., & Myslinski, D. (2013). *Report card on American education.* Washington, DC: American Legislative Exchange Council.

Lauder, H., Hughes, D., Watson, S., Waslander, S., Thrupp, M., Strathdee, R., & Simiyu, I. (1999). *Trading in futures: Why markets in education don't work.* Buckingham, England: Open University Press.

Lubienski, C. (2006). School diversification in second-best education markets: International evidence and conflicting theories of change. *Educational Policy, 20*(2), 323–344.

Lubienski, C. (2013). Privatizing form or function? *Oxford Review of Education, 39*(4), 498–513.

Lubienski, C., & Lubienski, S. T. (2005). *Re-examining a primary premise of market theory: An analysis of NAEP data on achievement in public and private schools* (No. 102). New York, NY: National Center for the Study of Privatization in Education.

Lubienski, C., & Lubienski, S. T. (2006). *Report on "on the public-private school achievement debate" from the program on education policy and governance at Harvard University.* Tempe: Educational Policy Research Unit, Education Policy Studies Laboratory, Arizona State University.

Lubienski, C., & Lubienski, S. T. (2013). *The public school advantage: Why public schools outperform private schools.* Chicago, IL: University of Chicago Press.

Lubienski, C., Scott, J., & DeBray, E. (2011, July 22). The rise of intermediary organizations in knowledge production, advocacy, and educational policy. *Teachers College Record* (ID No. 16487). Retrieved from http://www.tcrecord.org

Lubienski, C., & Weitzel, P. (2010). Two decades of charter schools: Shifting expectations, partners, and policies. In C. Lubienski & P. Weitzel (Eds.), *The charter school experiment: Expectations, evidence, and implications* (pp. 1–14). Cambridge, MA: Harvard Education Press.

Lubienski, S. T., & Lubienski, C. (2006). School sector and academic achievement: A multi-level analysis of NAEP mathematics data. *American Educational Research Journal, 43*(4), 651–698.

Merrifield, J. D. (2000). *Commentary: Education reforms typically ignore root causes.* Oakland, CA: Independent Institute.

Metcalf, K. K. (1998, September 23). Commentary—Advocacy in the guise of science: How preliminary research on the Cleveland Voucher Program was "reanalyzed" to fit a preconception. *Education Week, 18,* 34, 39.

Metcalf, K. K., Boone, W., Stage, F., Tait, P., Stacey, N., & Mueller, P. (1998). *Evaluation of the Cleveland Scholarship Program: Second year report.* Bloomington: Indiana Center for Evaluation, Indiana University.

Metcalf, K. K., West, S. D., Legan, N. A., Paul, K. M., & Boone, W. J. (2003). *Evaluation of the Cleveland scholarship and tutoring program: Summary report 1998–2002.* Bloomington: Indiana University.

Mezzacappa, D. (2006). *Market forces: Professor Paul Peterson's influential protégés.* Washington, DC: Education Sector. Retrieved from http://www.educationsector.org/publications/market-forces-professor-paul-petersons-influential-prot%C3%A9g%C3%A9s

Moe, T. M. (2008). Beyond the free market: The structure of school choice. *Brigham Young University Law Review, 2008*(1), 557–592.

Nelson, F. H., Rosenberg, B., & Van Meter, N. (2004). *Charter school achievement on the 2003 National Assessment of Educational Progress.* Washington, DC: American Federation of Teachers.

Otterman, S. (2011, July 17). New York City abandons teacher bonus program. *New York Times.* Retrieved from http://www.nytimes.com/2011/07/18/education/18rand.html

Palmaffy, T. (1999, October 22). Are school consultants worth it? Many get big bucks, say critics, for very little. *Investor's Business Daily.* Retrieved from http://www.investors.com/stories/IF/1999/Oct/22/23.html

Parry, T. R. (1997). How will schools respond to the incentives of privatization? Evidence from Chile and implications for the United States. *American Review of Public Administration, 27*(3), 248–269.

Peterson, P. E. (1990). Monopoly and competition in American education. In W. H. Clune & J. F. Witte (Eds.), *Choice and control in American education: Vol 1. The theory of choice and control in education* (pp. 47–78). London, England: Falmer Press.

Peterson, P. E., Howell, W. G., & Greene, J. P. (1999). *An evaluation of the Cleveland Voucher Program after two years.* Cambridge, MA: Program on Education Policy and Governance, Harvard University.

Peterson, P. E., & Llaudet, E. (2006). *On the public-private school achievement debate* (No. PEPG 06–02). Cambridge, MA: Program on Education Policy and Governance, Harvard University.

Ravitch, D. (1996, January/February). In deep denial. *The New Democrat,* 21–23.

Ravitch, D. (2009). *The death and life of the great American school system: How testing and choice are undermining education.* New York, NY: Basic Books.

Ravitch, D. (2013). *Reign of error: The hoax of the privatization movement and the danger to America's public schools.* New York, NY: Random House.

Raymond, M. E., & Center for Research on Education Outcomes. (2009). *Multiple choice: Charter school performance in 16 states.* Stanford, CA: Stanford University.

Reardon, S. F. (2009). *Review of "How New York City's charter schools affect achievement"* (Think Tank Review). Boulder, CO: National Education Policy Center.

Reckhow, S. (2013). *Follow the money: How foundation dollars change public school politics.* Oxford, England: Oxford University Press.

Rich, A. (2004). *Think tanks, public policy, and the politics of expertise.* Cambridge, England: Cambridge University Press.

Rouse, C. E. (1998). Private school vouchers and student achievement: An evaluation of the Milwaukee Parental Choice Program. *Quarterly Journal of Economics, 113*(2), 553–603.

Rouse, C. E., & Barrow, L. (2009). School vouchers and student achievement: Recent evidence, remaining questions. *Annual Review of Economics, 1,* 17–42.

Roy, J., & Mishel, L. (2005). *Advantage none: Re-examining Hoxby's finding of charter school benefits* (Briefing paper no. 158). Washington, DC: Economic Policy Institute.

Sabatier, P. A., & Jenkins-Smith, H. C. (1999). The advocacy coalition framework: An assessment. In P. A. Sabatier (Ed.), *Theories of the policy process* (pp. 117–166). Boulder, CO: Westview Press.

Sandel, M. J. (2012). *What money can't buy: The moral limits of markets.* New York, NY: Farrar, Straus and Giroux.

Schmidt, G. N. (2011, June 2). Wal-Mart "scholars" at the University of Arkansas prove, once again (again!), that the Walton family's voucher and pro-"choice" ideologies are beautiful good and true . . . *Substance News.* Retrieved from http://www .substancenews.net/articles.php?page=2305

Schwartz, B. (2007, July 2). Money for nothing. *New York Times,* p. 19A.

Scott, J., & Jabbar, H. (2013). Money and measures: The role of foundations in knowledge production. In D. Anagnostopoulos, S. A. Rutledge, & R. Jacobsen (Eds.), *The infrastructure of accountability: Data use and the transformation of American education* (pp. 75–92). Cambridge, MA: Harvard Education Press.

Smith, D., & Brantley, M. (2005, July 28). Conservative think-tanker to head UA school-reform operation. *Arkansas Times.* Retrieved from http://www .arktimes.com/arkansas/conservative-think-tanker-to-head-ua-school-reform-operation/ Content?oid=867264

Springer, M. G., Ballou, D., Hamilton, L., Le, V.-N., Lockwood, J. R., McCaffrey, D. F., . . . Stetcher, B. M. (2010). *Teacher pay for performance: Experimental evidence from the project on incentives in teaching.* Nashville, TN: National Center on Performance Incentives at Vanderbilt University.

Stern, S. (2008, Winter). School choice isn't enough. *City Journal, 18,* 1. Retrieved from http://www.city-journal .org/2008/2018_2001_instructional_reform.html

Stossel, J. (2006, January 13). Stupid in America: How lack of choice cheats our kids out of a good education. *20/20.* Retrieved from http://abcnews.go .com/2020/Stossel/story?id=1500338

Various Scholars, & Center for Education Reform. (2004, August 25). Charter school evaluation reported by The New York Times, fails to meet professional standards. *New York Times.* Retrieved from https:// www.edreform.com/wp-content/uploads/2013/04/ NY-Times-Ad-Ed-Week-Version.pdf

Walberg, H. J. (2000, July 12). Market theory of school choice. *Education Week, 19,* 46, 49.

Walberg, H. J., & Bast, J. L. (2003). *Education and capitalism: How overcoming our fear of markets and economics can improve America's schools.* Stanford, CA: Hoover Institution Press.

Walford, G. (1997). Diversity, choice, and selection in England and Wales. *Educational Administration Quarterly, 33*(2), 158–169.

Weitzel, P., & Lubienski, C. (2010). Grading charter schools: Access, innovation, and competition. In C. Lubienski & P. Weitzel (Eds.), *The charter school experiment: Expectations, evidence, and implications* (pp. 15–31). Cambridge, MA: Harvard Education Press.

Witte, J. F. (2000). *The market approach to education: An analysis of America's first voucher program.* Princeton, NJ: Princeton University Press.

Witte, J. F., Thorn, C., & Pritchard, K. (1995). *Fifth year report: Milwaukee Parental Choice Program.* Madison: Wisconsin Department of Public Instruction.

Wolf, P., Gutmann, B., Puma, M., Kisida, B., Rizzo, L., Eissa, N., & Carr, M. (2010). *Evaluation of the DC Opportunity Scholarship Program: Final report.* Washington, DC: U.S. Department of Education.

Wolf, P. J. (2013, January 28). Minnesota falls behind on school choice. *Star-Tribune.* Retrieved from http:// www.startribune.com/opinion/ commentaries/188596381.html

Further Readings

DeBray, E., Scott, J., Lubienski, C., & Jabbar, H. (2014). Intermediary organizations in charter school policy coalitions: Evidence from New Orleans. *Educational Policy, 28*(2), 175–206.

This article develops a framework for investigating research use, using an "advocacy coalition framework" and the concepts of a "supply side" and "demand side." The authors examine (a) the role of intermediaries in producing information and research syntheses for local, state, and/or federal policymakers; (b) the extent of policymakers' demand for such research and information; and (c) the extent to which local and national coalitions of organizations appear to be influential in research use. The authors map preliminary findings about how intermediary organizations are connected to national groups, as well as how research is shared within coalitions.

Jabbar, H., Goldie, D., Linick, M., & Lubienski, C. (2014). Using bibliometric and social media analyses to explore the "echo chamber" hypothesis. *Educational Policy, 28*(2), 281–305.

Intermediary organizations are promoting research using a variety of traditional and nontraditional media. Given the current policy arena, it is critical to reexamine the research underlying current reforms and to determine whether there is an "echo chamber" effect, where a small and often unrepresentative sample of studies is repeatedly cited to create momentum around a reform. Using bibliometric methods and examining social media activity by intermediary organizations, the preliminary evidence suggests the presence of an echo chamber effect in policy debates.

Lubienski, C., Scott, J., & DeBray, E. (2011, July 22). The rise of intermediary organizations in knowledge production, advocacy, and educational policy. *Teachers College Record* (ID Number: 16487). Retrieved from http://www.tcrecord.org

This commentary examines the rise of intermediary organizations that "broker" research for policymakers and considers the implications for traditional forms of knowledge production.

Lubienski, C., Scott, J., & DeBray, E. (2014). The politics of research use in education policymaking. *Educational Policy, 28*(2), 131–144.

This article considers how changing historical conditions can shape institutional demands on and for research production, promotion, and use and how policymakers and other information consumers sort through competing claims. The authors compare the relative role of research use in education policy to other issues, such as climate science, and highlight the growing role of intermediate actors as they shape research use. They offer an overview of the understanding of research use in education and point to the need to explore new theoretical frameworks and methodologies. The essay ends with an overview of the papers in the issue.

Lubienski, C., Weitzel, P., & Lubienski, S. T. (2009). Is there a "consensus" on school choice and achievement? Advocacy research and the emerging political economy of knowledge production. *Educational Policy, 23*(1), 161–193.

A number of school choice advocates claim that there is a research consensus indicating that vouchers for private schools lead to higher academic achievement. The authors note limitations inherent in different methodological approaches to this question, focusing on the shortcomings of randomization as an exclusive "gold standard" for research on the issue of achievement in school choice plans. The concluding discussion reconsiders the question of a consensus, highlighting the emerging research environment that bypasses traditional review processes and emphasizes instead the promotion of ideas to support policy agendas.

30

THE CHANGING NATURE OF TEACHERS' UNIONS AND COLLECTIVE BARGAINING

TODD A. DEMITCHELL

University of New Hampshire

Wisconsin, in 1959, captured the attention of workers throughout the United States by passing the first state public sector collective bargaining law allowing public employees, including teachers, to bargain collectively with their public employer. This started the heyday of public sector collective bargaining in which all states except for five (Georgia, North Carolina, South Carolina, Texas, and Virginia) either required school boards to bargain with the teachers' exclusive representative or permitted local districts to do so (Sanes & Schmitt, 2014, p. 5). However, just over a half a century later, the nation once again focused on Wisconsin in February and March of 2011, when thousands of workers descended on the state capitol for a different purpose. This time they came not to celebrate their victory of 1959 but to save that victory. Workers, including teachers, arrived, some with children in tow, carrying signs, banging drums, and loudly proclaiming their opposition to pending legislation on collective bargaining and the status of their unions. As a backdrop to the protest, Democratic senators decamped to another state, denying the Republican governor and the Republican majority in the Senate the quorum necessary to pass the Wisconsin Budget Repair Act, also known as Act 10. This act was designed to address the deficit in the state's budget. Governor Scott Walker cast the argument as repairing the budget and addressing the deficit, while for many the subtext and result was an overt assault on public sector unions. Act 10 withstood litigation brought by the Madison teachers' union when the Wisconsin Supreme Court upheld the law in a 5 to 2 decision in *Madison Teachers, Inc. v. Walker* (July 31, 2014).

Collective bargaining is a creature of the law; it is created by law, changed by law, and eliminated by law. Walker's legislation changed the collective bargaining law by limiting public sector bargaining to just wages, not terms and conditions of employment, with a requirement that any raise over the consumer price index must be referred to the voters for a referendum vote. In addition, the bill forced the union to hold an election recertifying it every year; it allowed employees who benefit from the collectively bargained contract not to pay a fee for the union's work performed on their behalf; public employers under the bill were restricted from collecting the dues of the union members; and the legislation eliminated all collective bargaining rights for employees in the University of Wisconsin System. Proponents of the governor's bill characterized the legislation as loosening the stranglehold of unions and protecting the taxpayers' pocketbook from the avarice

---

NOTE: Portions of this entry are adapted from DeMitchell (2011).

of the voracious appetite of union bosses. Public sector unions were under siege.

Union leaders and their rank-and-file members, such as classroom teachers, and other supporters responded by exclaiming that Walker's real goal was to bust public employee unions, leaving the worker without protection from the will and whim of the public employer and turning them out of the middle class. They asserted that they were being unfairly targeted as the reason for the economic recession and argued that their contracts were bilaterally negotiated and not unilaterally forced on the public. To be vilified for accepting the contract with provisions that the school board approved is unfair and a rewriting of the realities of a bilaterally agreed upon contract, union members and supporters asserted.

While unions in general, and teachers' unions in particular, have long been the subject of political attacks, the level of negative characterization of teachers as individuals is without precedent. For example, *The New Republic* titled an online article, "Why Public Employees Are the New Welfare Queens" (Cohn, 2010). Two commentators wrote on the Wisconsin situation stating, "We conclude with our lament about the tone of the general public discourse. Teachers have become leeches, hooligans, and thugs in the public discourse" (DeMitchell & Parker-Magagna, 2012, p. 14). In many instances, teachers felt that they were under siege whether they were union members or not.

Beyond the Wisconsin Budget Repair Act: Money, Power, and Relevance

The Wisconsin Budget Repair Act was about money and about the power and relevance of public sector unions. The act restricted the scope of what is bargainable to just wages, required a yearly vote of the membership on whether to keep the union as the exclusive representative, and eliminated **agency shops**, in which members of the bargaining unit either must be union members or pay a fee to the union for bargaining their wages and benefits. Opponents argued these provisions did little to close the budget deficit but did much to harm unions. Public sector unions had already agreed to greater contributions to benefits and wage concessions demanded by the governor, but the bill moved forward, raising the question of whether he sought concession or capitulation from the unions.

Wisconsin led the way in the retrenchment of the role of public sector unions and the rewriting of collective bargaining laws, and several states followed, with varying outcomes. For example, Ohio passed legislation restricting public sector collective bargaining, but it was overturned by a statewide referendum by a significant margin. Tennessee eliminated bargaining for teachers and banned the use of union dues for lobbying state lawmakers. Several states developed legislation establishing right-to-work (RTW) states in which teachers do not have to pay any union dues for the bargaining that the union does on their behalf, thus, according to the union, allowing free riders—individuals getting something for nothing instead of taking responsibility for what they receive. Proponents argue that RTW protects the employee from the union. New Hampshire's RTW legislation failed, but Michigan's prevailed, and Indiana's RTW was upheld by the Seventh Circuit Court of Appeals. Kansas initiated RTW legislation but dropped it in 2013.

Critics of teachers' unions, while always present, seem to have grasped an available megaphone and added their voice to the legislators seeking a change in the calculus between public employees and public employers. For example, Terry Moe (2011), a professor of political science and senior fellow at the Hoover Institution at Stanford University, stated, "The pivotal question for the future of American education is, will the problem of union power ever get resolved so that the nation's schools can actually be organized in the best interests of children?" (p. 14).

Unions and school districts must adjust to the changing social and economic environment. Public sector collective bargaining laws were typically passed to foster harmonious relations between the public employer and its public employees who provide a governmental service. Will the reduction of union power and its elimination in some instances foster harmonious relations? Or is harmony in the workplace no longer the goal? To understand the changing nature of teachers' unions and collective bargaining, we must first start with what unions do.

What Unions Do

Public education is the most heavily unionized occupation in the United States. In the last 50 years, teachers' unions have impacted the governance of America's public schools. The two teachers' unions have become major policy and political players not only at the local school district level but also at the state and national levels. In those states that have public sector bargaining laws, governance has become bilateral on the issues of wages, benefits, and terms and conditions of employment.

The National Education Association (NEA) is the largest of the two teachers' unions with a membership of just over 2.5 million active members, and the American Federation of Teachers (AFT) has a membership of around 900,000. These numbers do not include teachers who may work under union-bargained contracts but pay an agency fee instead of joining the union, adding to the influence of the unions.

A Brief History

The NEA and AFT grew from different traditions, which initially shaped their approach to unionization and collective bargaining. For its first 100 years, the late 1850s to the late 1950s, NEA was considered and considered itself a professional organization. It was not dominated by classroom teachers; rather, its leadership tended to be superintendents, college presidents, and college professors. It was concerned with elevating the stature of education and educators.

The AFT, by contrast, has always seen itself as a teachers' union. The AFT "was organized by teachers, the membership was composed of teachers, and most important, the leadership came from classroom teachers" (Streshly & DeMitchell, 1994, p. 9). While the NEA focused on professionalism, the AFT argued that teachers first needed higher wages and better benefits; professional stature could wait and wages would follow. Nicholas Murray Butler, president of NEA at the turn of the century, called the Chicago Federation of Teachers, the forerunner of the AFT, "insurrectionists" and "union labor grade teachers" (Murphy, 1990, p. 54). "The NEA thought collective bargaining would destroy professionalism. . . . In contrast, the AFT pointed out that teachers would gain respect because at last their salaries would be commensurate with their preparation" (Murphy, 1990, pp. 209–210).

During the 1960s, particularly after the New York teachers strike led by Al Shanker of the AFT, NEA was forced to shift its focus more strongly toward teachers' interests if it was to remain competitive. This shift seriously challenged the NEA's long-cherished concept of professionalism. "Teachers wanted higher salaries and better benefits, not necessarily a higher standard of respect" (Streshly & DeMitchell, 1994, p. 10). To remain competitive with the AFT, the NEA changed its philosophy and tactics. It began to look and act more like the AFT.

Today, major differences of values and mission between the nation's two largest unions have faded, and both AFT and NEA clearly see themselves as advocates and representatives of classroom teachers and as unions. In fact, although the two unions have remained separate on a national level, in some states the two unions' state-level affiliates have merged. New York, Montana, Minnesota, Florida, and North Dakota have entered into merger agreements. This development bears watching to see if the mergers result in a common, effective voice for the teachers of those states.

Both major teachers' unions have become powerful participants in the nation's educational policy debates, where they make their voices heard regarding the interests of teachers, providing teachers' views about educational practice. The NEA and the AFT, through bargaining, impact the structure of public education. In fact, even in states that prohibit collective bargaining, the negotiated salary schedule that reflects level of graduate education and seniority is pervasive. Similarly, collective bargaining has influenced due process in dismissals, transfers of employees, benefits, class sizes, the allocation of preparation times, and the processing of **grievances**. A number of these practices, while bargained for in states that allow for it, influence the practices in states and school districts that do not. There is more congruence between unionized schools and non-unionized schools than there are differences. Consequently, it can reasonably be asserted that the impact of the AFT's and the NEA's positions are felt across the nation's schools and school districts.

Collective Bargaining and Public Education: The Context

All unions, including teachers' unions, exist primarily to protect and enhance the social and economic welfare of their members. Teachers' unions advance their members' interests chiefly through collective bargaining with school districts. They are primarily organizations that assist teachers to pursue their shared self-interests—legitimate interests that, unions assert, teachers were less likely to successfully pursue on their own. At their core, unions pursue the self-interests of their members through collective action. A union sells its service to a specific group of employees by arguing that the employee will be better off with the union representing his or her self-interests than without it. Unions operate like other service organizations: They provide a service that individuals may not be able to efficiently and effectively get on their own. They provide or sell a service to their membership through their dues; they are spokespersons and advocates for their members. School districts speak for, advocate for, and bargain for the students and the community. This allows the bargaining table to be symmetrical, with each side representing its constituency, with neither party representing the legitimate interests of the other.

Prior to the emergence of collective bargaining in the public schools in the 1960s, following the lead of Wisconsin, teachers were largely powerless on their own to improve their working conditions or their economic status. Salaries, benefits, hours of employment, class sizes, and assignment and transfer procedures were set by school boards and enforced by administrators. In some cases, state law and school board policy allowed representatives of the teachers (usually the union, because employees can join unions as an allied right of association) to meet and confer or, as some union wags have described it, meet and defer or meet and beg. This process did not result in a legally binding document that identified rights and responsibilities for both parties.

Subjects of Bargaining: Mandatory, Permissive, and Prohibited

When the National Labor Relations Act (NLRA) was passed by Congress in 1935, it pertained only to private sector employees and employers. Public employees could join unions, but the unions were precluded from forcing the public employer to the bargaining table. This changed when states started passing public sector collective bargaining laws that allowed public employees to select an exclusive representative who would speak for them at the bargaining table. The unilateral decision making of the employer was replaced by the bilateral decision making of the bargaining table on wages, benefits, and terms and conditions of employment.

In all states that have adopted collective bargaining in the public education sector, state law governs the relationship between teachers' unions and school districts. These laws differ somewhat from state to state, but in general they require school districts to bargain in good faith with the teachers' exclusive representative over teachers' wages and benefits and other terms and conditions of employment. In many states, school districts bargain collectively with other employee groups as well, including bus drivers, clerical workers, custodians, and principals.

Most, if not all, states preclude elected school boards from bargaining over educational policies with the unions. This does not mean that unions cannot influence school boards' policy decisions; rather a union cannot compel a school board to abdicate its legal responsibility to set educational policy or delegate that responsibility to the teachers' union. As the New Jersey Supreme Court explained in *Ridgefield Park Education Association v. Ridgefield Park Board of Education* (1978), "The very foundation of representative democracy would be endangered if decisions of significant matters of government policy were left to the process of negotiations, where citizen participation is precluded" (p. 287).

Of course, it is sometimes difficult to differentiate between what constitutes a nonbargainable policy and what is considered a mandatory topic for negotiation at the collective bargaining table. The Supreme Court of Alaska, in a consolidation of three cases over what is bargainable, used class size as an example of the difficulty of ascertaining whether a topic is a subject of bargaining or prohibited from bargaining. The court wrote:

> The question of class size affects directly the amount of work a teacher must perform. But the determination of optimum class size is quite basic to school policy and management, and potentially has a substantial impact on the school district's personnel expenditures (Kenai Peninsula Borough School District v. Kenai Peninsula Education Association, 1977, p. 423).

The court further stated that an analysis of other school issues "yields equally indefinite answers" (p. 423). The court held that class size was a prohibited subject of bargaining. Typically, however, school districts are required to bargain with their unions over matters pertaining to teachers' economic well-being

Sidebar 30.1   Subjects of Bargaining

Mandatory Subjects

These are subjects that are required by state law to be bargained by both parties. If one of the parties refuses to bargain a mandatory subject of bargaining, it is considered a violation of the collective bargaining law or an **unfair labor practice**. Wages and benefits are clearly mandatory subjects of bargaining. Working conditions are considered a mandatory subject of bargaining, but which working conditions are considered mandatory are defined by the individual states through their public employee boards.

Permissive Subjects

Permissive subjects may be voluntarily bargained, but they are not required subjects of bargaining. These are conditions that are typically controlled by the employer. They cannot be bargained to **impasse**, and the refusal to bargain over a permissive subject of bargaining does not constitute an unfair labor practice.

Prohibited Subjects

Subjects of bargaining that violate public sector collective bargaining law are prohibited subjects. For example, policy that is reserved for the discretion of the school district is a prohibited subject of bargaining, and any such bargained provision is void and unenforceable.

An example of how different states define the subjects of bargaining, either through statute or case law, is how states treat bargaining of teacher evaluation:

- Mandatory subject of bargaining—California
- Permissive subject of bargaining—New Hampshire
- Prohibited subject of bargaining—Indiana

and **bread-and-butter issues**. "The troubling question is what other items are bargainable" (p. 422; see **Sidebar 30.1**).

The Role of Union Member and Professional Teacher

The conundrum for teachers is that while their union advocates and bargains for their self-interests, teachers are professionals who provide a valuable service in the best interests of their students. Teachers tend to see themselves and describe themselves as professionals. Typically, they do not define themselves as union members but they become union members when threats to their work, their livelihood, and their security arise. How do teachers fit these two roles, of professional and union member, together?

For the great majority of teachers, the crush of the workday in the classroom consumes their time and energy. Cooper and Liotta (2001) write that while "teachers in many communities are union members, they still see themselves and their work as primarily professional—helping children to learn. They identify with their students and the needs of their students" (p. 109). For most teachers, the reality of the classroom forces the role of professional front and center. Comments such as, "I am a professional, this is my professional judgment, and I need to be treated as a professional" are heard more often in schools than the comment, "I am a union member." Teachers seek to present themselves to the public as professionals.

Professionalism is built around expert knowledge. The work of the professional teacher is complex and not routine. It involves the exercise of discretion. Teaching involves a standard of practice recognized and adhered to by the practitioners but applied in varying contexts, even within the same school district. Professionals use their judgment and take actions within the accepted standards of the profession that are in the best interests of the client, patient, or student. The focus of the professional is the best interests of the "other" and not the "self." Unions seek to secure the self-interests of members. Professions are predicated on acts designed to further the interest of the patient, client, or student and not the professional. Both the interests of the professional and the interests of the "other" are legitimate, and both are in tension with one another.

Casey Cobb, now a professor at the University of Connecticut, and this author conducted a nationwide study of randomly selected teachers. The overarching research question was, "[Are] teachers' unions and collective bargaining compatible with teacher perceptions of professionalism?" (DeMitchell & Cobb, 2006, p. 19). The study found that teachers have a tangled view of how their professionalism fits within the context of a unionized workforce. They perceive that union activity and professional activity are compatible. They would not, however, turn first to the union to meet their professional needs. They tend to believe that the contract protects their professional activities but also believe that the contract does not foster quality teaching, cannot address the creative aspects of teaching, and that teaching quality cannot be standardized into a

contract; however, they perceive that the contract protects their professional activities.

Teachers tend to believe that they need to be protected. The union and the contract appear to act as buffers between teachers and administrators; however, that buffer also can be a barrier for some teachers. The comments from teachers over the issue of protection reveal a tension between the realities of union protection and a lamentation about that protection. Teachers see the limits of how a contract impacts their teaching, yet they believe that given that limitation, they still prefer the contract and the union. When faced with difficult choices that highlight the inherent conflict between the self-interest represented by the union and the other-directed interest of professionalism, many teachers retreated to a safe harbor of neutral on a 5-point Likert-type scale, unwilling to take a position that forced them to confront the difficult choice.

Teachers are professionals. How their professionalism meshes with union membership and bargained contracts is tangled. **Sidebar 30.2** summarizes the second part of the research that defines the themes that emerged from the two prompts on support and harm.

Sidebar 30.2   Teacher Perceptions of Unions

The following are themes with examples of responses from teachers to prompts:

Unions SUPPORT professionalism in the following ways:	Unions HARM professionalism in the following ways:
Protection "Protect you from inept administrators."	**Blind Protection** "Automatically defending teachers whether they are right or wrong."
Advocacy "In this era of 'scripted teaching,' I am assured my right to teach students in creative and effective ways."	**Work of the Union** "Unions focus on money, making teachers seem self-serving and unprofessional."
Support "Require professional development as part of the contract."	**Divisiveness** "Creates adversarial atmosphere."
	The Union Label "I don't hold banners/pickets . . . not what I do if it's for self-interest."

SOURCE: Based on DeMitchell and Cobb (2007).

The challenge of providing an important public service as a professional emerged with the passage of state collective bargaining laws that defined teachers as members of a collective bargaining unit. The adopted legal definition of a public sector union, in many ways, placed teachers in both the professional classroom and the union labor hall.

The Industrial Labor Model

When the public sector collective bargaining laws were passed, the predominant labor-management mold was the industrial union of the teamsters, autoworkers, and coal miners. The procedures for conflict resolution, the definition of management and labor, and their respective rights were all borrowed, in many cases word for word, from the private labor sector, which embraced the industrial labor model. This initial choice of models to use for the public sector has had major consequences for education, given the uniqueness of public schools and a work force that struggles with the issue of professionalism.

Us and Them

In order to bargain, there must be two parties who have differences to be settled through collective bargaining. The industrial union model tends to heighten the differences, thus requiring formal negotiations. It is essentially an adversarial process that fosters an us-and-them mentality. Collective bargaining assumes a conflict of interest and a community of interest. Teachers' interests are pursued by the union, and the interests of the students and the community are the province of the school board. Both sets of interests are legitimate, and both are separate. Not everything in the work setting that is good for teachers is good for students and vice versa. Without a conflict of interest, there is nothing to bargain; agreement has already been achieved. If there is no community of interest, reaching agreement may be difficult to impossible. How to find and expand the sweet spot of community is the challenge.

When the industrial labor model is applied to education, teachers become labor and administrators become management. The fact that both groups are educators with common goals and values is lost in this model. "The separateness of some work activities performed by teachers and administrators is emphasized, and not the commonality of purpose, roots, interests, or overlapping functions" (DeMitchell & Fossey, 1997, p. 21). Consequently, the emphasis on separateness places a great premium on conflict management within the labor relations and bargaining the contract. This focus on conflict management is further enhanced because collective bargaining is a system for creating agreement when trust is low, and the union members believe that they must be protected by a legally binding instrument that spells out in some detail the rights and responsibilities of their employment. Labor contracts, therefore, must be explicit, unambiguous, and provide for enforcement. These requirements may emphasize the conflicts of interest and diminish the community of interest. This is so fundamental that the absence of conflict actually "arouses anxiety and uncertainty among both union leaders and school managers who fear that they will be seen as having 'gone soft'" (Kerchner & Mitchell, 1988, p. 237).

Policy and Teaching

Workers relinquished control over the outcomes of the product of their work with the advent of industrial unionism. Decisions about what is produced and how it is produced passed into the hands of management. Industrial workers are divorced from the formation of policy; all they can do is implement it. Kerchner, Koppich, and Weeres (1997) note, "Collective bargaining invests in the union the obligation to enhance and protect the rights of its members. It implicitly invests in management the responsibility for the health of the educational enterprise" (p. 137). Under the industrial union model, teachers, like factory line workers, are only supposed to perform a labor function; they are not supposed to influence the outcome of the product. We know that this is not the reality of teaching. Classroom teachers' daily work with students is a translation and reconfiguring of policy to meet the highly individualized contexts of their classroom. Educators do not turn out mass produced widgets; teaching is a highly complex process calling for the use of judgment. Classroom teachers fashion and adapt policy with the myriad decisions they make daily. Teachers are not divorced from policy, as the industrial union labor model would have us believe; they influence, adapt, and implement policy (DeMitchell, 2010, p. 39).

Formalization, Standardization, and Centralization

The work of teachers and the relationship between teachers and the school district is reduced, in large part, to a written contract. Reduction has consequences. The outcomes include a formalization of the relationship between teacher and administrator as mediated by the contract. Formalization leads to a standardization of expectations and work, which leads to centralization so that standardization can be achieved across the various schools of the school district.

Reducing the relationship to a written contract, which in many school districts is literally reduced to a size that could fit in a pocket, helped to formalize the relationships. Comments such as, "I have to check on the contract before we proceed further" catches educators in a web of rules. The contract becomes a mediating force between teacher and principal. Individual responses to specific needs are often replaced with a response that fits within the contract. The contract formalizes relationships because it is an enforceable, written instrument that replaces informal understandings between teachers and administrators.

The results of collective bargaining are the standardization and centralization of teachers' work. This standardization is not the same as professional standards developed through rigorous examination of practice, which comports with the accepted literature, which forms the core knowledge of a profession. Standardization in collective bargaining occurs because the elements of the contract apply equally to all members of the union at all times and in all places. How the contract is interpreted and enforced in one school must be consistent with how it is interpreted and enforced in all of the schools of the district. This need for standardization leads to centralization since the contract must be administered uniformly. Since the contract is between the union and the school board, both parties are charged with its uniform application.

Uniformity is enforced at the central office by both union and school district officials through the formal grievance process and the informal and sometimes guarded relationship that often develops between union officials and district-level administrators. Both parties to the contract seek uniform application of the contract; otherwise, instability might ensue, thus endangering the labor peace achieved by the contract. "Both the union and the district office administrators seek to centralize and standardize

Figure 30.1 Outcomes of Collective Bargaining

behavior through consistent rule interpretation, scrutiny, and enforcement" (DeMitchell, 1993, p. 79). Uniqueness or the context of unique teaching environments is typically not accommodated in collective bargaining agreements. (See **Figure 30.1**.)

Many, if not most teachers, are union members who also consider themselves to be professionals. Unlike some of their private sector counterparts, such as autoworkers, teamsters, and coal miners, teachers apply their expertise in a nonscripted, nonrote fashion to a nonuniform group of students in a dynamic work setting nested in a community that seeks to exert influence over their daily decisions. A school setting is not the work setting of the United Autoworkers. In the industrial model of collective bargaining, can the richness of teaching be reduced to the confines of a contract that standardizes behavior, treats all teaching situations uniformly, and centralizes authority?

Good Faith and Disputes

Good Faith

Collective bargaining requires the union bargaining team and the school district's bargaining team to meet in good faith to exchange **proposals** and counterproposals with the aim of arriving at a mutually agreed upon contract, which is a framework for reciprocal rights and responsibilities. Once a contract has been agreed upon, it becomes legally binding and enforceable through state law through grievances and unfair labor practices.

Good faith bargaining does not require that either side must agree to a change or alteration in their bargaining position. Good faith bargaining does not preclude hard bargaining. It does, however, require each party to come to the table with a mind accessible to persuasion. It requires that each side consider the other's proposals and not reflexively reject proposals without consideration of how it may be acceptable. The intention must be to find a basis for an agreement. Neither party can just simply go

Sidebar 30.3   Duty to Bargain in Good Faith

There is a mutual obligation on the part of management and labor to bargain in good faith. Typically, this places a mutual obligation to meet at reasonable times and to confer in good faith with respect to wages, hours, and other terms and conditions of employment. This obligation does not compel either party to agree to a proposal or require them to make a concession.

The practical rules for bargaining in good faith are as follows:

- Approach bargaining with a mind accessible to persuasion.
- Follow procedures that will enhance the prospects of a negotiated settlement.
- Be willing to discuss freely and fully your respective claims and demands. When such claims and demands are opposed by the other side, be prepared to justify your claims with reason.
- Explore with an open mind proposals for compromise or other possible solutions of differences. Make an effort to find a mutually satisfactory basis for agreement.

through the motions. It is possible to bargain in good faith and still reach an impasse in bargaining.

How do the parties bargain in good faith? Teachers and administrators come to the bargaining table seeking to secure, to expand, and to protect their interests. This is legitimate and it is the essence of bargaining. But how do the parties meet their self-interests while finding the community of interest they both need? (See **Sidebar 30.3**.)

Two very useful and practical approaches came out of the Harvard Negotiation Project, *Getting to Yes* (Fisher & Ury, 1983) and *Getting Together* (Fisher & Brown, 1988). The focus of these two books is not just on getting a contract. The success of bargaining is not predicated upon signing the contract. Success is determined by whether the employee-employer relations are enhanced and improved or, at a minimum, not harmed. Bargaining is not a success if one side or the other is angry at the end of bargaining and has a score to settle in the next round.

In *Getting Together: Building Relationships as We Negotiate*, Roger Fisher and Scott Brown (1988) describe six principles that help negotiating parties bargaining cope with differences and build relationships:

1. It helps to balance reason with emotion. "We need both reason informed by emotion and emotion guided and tempered by reason" (p. 10).

2. Understanding helps. "Unless I have a good idea of what you think the problem is, what you want, why you want it, and what you think is fair, I will be groping in the dark for an outcome that will meet your interests as well as mine" (p. 10).

3. Good communication helps. "Inquire, consult, and listen. We both participate in making decisions" (p. 40).

4. Being reliable helps. "It tends to build trust and confidence" (p. 40). "My communication with you is not worth much if you do not believe me" (p. 11).

5. Persuasion is more helpful than coercion. "The more coercive the means of influence, the less likely it is that the outcome will reflect both of our concerns, and the less legitimate it is likely to be in the eyes of at least one of us" (p. 12).

6. Mutual acceptance helps. "Accept the other as worth dealing with and learning from" (p. 40).

Enforcement of Rights and Responsibilities: Grievances and Unfair Labor Practices

As mentioned earlier, the collective bargaining agreement codifies rights and responsibilities for members of the bargaining unit and the school district's administration. The enforcement of these rights and responsibilities is important if the contract is to be implemented uniformly and fairly. When conflict arises, and it does, between the two parties, grievances and unfair labor practices are two legal mechanisms that are used to resolve the conflict.

Grievances

A grievance is an allegation of a misapplication, misinterpretation, or violation of a specific section of the contract. It is not a disagreement with any decision that a school administrator makes. All conflicts are not grievances. Grievances that access the grievance procedures of the contract must be contained to addressing problems arising from the application and/or interpretation of the contract. To use the grievance procedure for any and all disagreements is to expand the contract without the benefit of bargaining. The grievance process was fashioned through the collective bargaining process to specifically address problems associated with conflict regarding the implementation of the contract.

Essentially, the grievance section of the contract is a conflict resolution strategy. The process is clearly defined with steps and time lines for each step. The grievance procedure provides a process by which the parties can explore and ascertain the extent and application of the rights and responsibilities contained in the contract. Because the grievance procedure is specific to the contract in which it is found, the author strongly advises that the grievance process be reserved for disputes over the implementation of the contract. The grievance process should not be used as a general conflict resolution strategy (DeMitchell, 2010, pp. 50–52).

The grievance process becomes unwieldy when it is used to solve all problems and misunderstandings that arise that are not a specific violation or misapplication of the contract. A broad use of the contract grievance process to resolve noncontract disagreements has the potential to misuse the process, turning it into a cudgel rather than a process. A misuse of the grievance process may expand the contract without the benefit of bargaining. Grievances should be confined to the job they were created to do—apply the contract consistently and fairly within the agreed upon conditions of employment. Grievances often end in **arbitration** as the last step of the process. Arbitration related to the enforcement of a contract is called rights arbitration. When arbitration is used to settle a contract, it is called interest arbitration.

Arbitration of a grievance is either advisory or binding. This is a permissive subject of bargaining. Advisory arbitration results in a written position delivered by the arbitrator, an outside party selected by both parties. As its name implies, advisory arbitration is the opinion of the arbitrator. It does not carry the weight of legal authority, compelling the

implementation of the arbitrator's decision. In other words, an advisory decision is just exactly what is meant by the definition of advisory; the parties can accept it or reject it. An advisory opinion cannot be imposed on the parties. Because advisory arbitration cannot compel either party to accept the opinion, unions typically prefer binding arbitration so that a decision that goes in their favor cannot be dismissed by the school board.

Binding arbitration, on the other hand, is a quasi-judicial opinion; it must be implemented by both parties. It is less of a problem-solving character assisting the parties and more of a judicial character. An arbitrator's task is to interpret the contract and apply it to the dispute/grievance. Most collective bargaining contracts include language that states that the arbitrator shall have no power to alter, add to, or subtract from the specific language of the contract. It is assumed that all sections of a contract are subject to arbitration unless there is explicit language in the contract removing a section from arbitration. This is called positive assurance.

The arbitration hearing is more of a courtroom hearing in which the advocates for both parties extensively prepare, evidence is presented, and witnesses are questioned. Arbitrators use three elements: the language of the contract, the intent of the parties, and **past practice** to reach a decision.

Unfair Labor Practices

Another labor dispute mechanism is an **unfair labor practice.** Similar to grievances, either the union or the school district can file an unfair labor practice with the appropriate public sector labor board. However, an individual unit member of the union can file a grievance against her or his union. When this occurs, it is usually an allegation that the union failed to provide **fair representation** to the member.

While a grievance is an allegation of a violation of the contract, an unfair labor practice is an allegation of a violation of the state public sector collective bargaining law. Unfair labor practices are state specific, with each state defining what constitutes an unfair labor practice. A violation of good faith bargaining by making a unilateral change in wages, benefits, or terms and conditions of employment is a common unfair labor practice. Another is interfering with the union's right to exclusive representation through management either offering inducements or threats to members of the bargaining unit.

The Future of Unions and Collective Bargaining

Teachers' unions and collective bargaining were battered by politics and endured a backlash in the early part of second decade of the 21st century. For example, in Wisconsin the passage of Act 10, the restrictive collective bargaining law, resulted in a significant decline in union membership with public employees opting out of their union. From 2011 to 2012, there was a 13 percentage point decline in public sector union membership (Gilbert, 2013).

While unions and public sector collective bargaining have recently been bruised and battered, they still exist, and school administrators and teachers must understand the policies, politics, and processes of labor relations in education, which includes unions and collective bargaining. For example, following Walker's success in Wisconsin in reducing the power of public sector unions, Governor John Kasich of Ohio found his Wisconsin-style legislation, SB 5, defeated by the voter's in the state by a margin of 61% to 39%. The legislation would have reduced public sector bargaining rights and eliminated the right to strike as well as the right to binding arbitration (Prokopf, 2013, p. 1402). The headstone for public sector unions should not yet be carved.

While collective bargaining appears to be here for the foreseeable future, it faces challenges. Unions face the challenge of securing the self-interest of their members while moving the teaching occupation toward greater professional standing. School districts also face a challenge from the retrenchment of labor relations. Martha Parker-Magagna and this author raised questions about the changing dynamics in Wisconsin: Would the employer seize the moment to keep or improve relations with its teachers? Or would the employer grab the opportunity to impose its will on its employees? Will school boards and administrators seek to improve relations and build the collegiality we know is necessary in schools? The conflict of interest will remain; will the community of interest be expanded through conscious effort? We asked, "Will the new theme song in labor relations be the

old Rolling Stones song 'Under My Thumb'?" (DeMitchell & Parker-Magagna, 2012, p. 7). Because many teachers believe that a union protects them from school administrators' arbitrary decisions, will an overreaching school board and administration bring teachers back into the union fold?

Similarly, will the teachers' unions rise to the challenges they are facing? At a minimum, unions must join with administrators to roll back the impact of the industrial labor template superimposed on public education: "Teachers labor but they are not laborers" (DeMitchell, 2010, p. 132). Strikes, work to rule, and filing frivolous grievances are intended to act as levers to gain acquiescence from management, but they ill serve the profession and public education. Working together, teachers and administrators, the union and the school district, can reduce or break the hold of the ill-fitting industrial labor model and replace it with a more flexible, professional mold for labor relations in education. The agenda for change can, at a minimum, include reducing the exaggerated differences of us and them, substituting flexibility for standardization, a rethinking of the role of seniority, and broadening the concept of what and not just who must be protected.

In the DeMitchell and Cobb (2007) study of professionalism and unionism, teachers identified protection by the union as both supporting professionalism and harming professionalism. The responding teachers asserted that they needed protection from inept administrators and arbitrary action. They also argued that blind protection of the incompetent was troubling. Unions must protect the due process of their members, but they must also protect quality teaching by evincing a willingness to be an ally for securing a quality education that is offered by professionally competent teachers. Employment must not trump the provision of quality educational services.

The task of reframing the industrial model to make it comport with the realities of providing an important professional service of teaching is most challenging. Acknowledging and accepting that conflicts of interest are real and legitimate while vigorously pursuing and building the community of interest and upholding teachers', administrators', school boards', parents', and community members' share is not easy; if it were, it would already have been done. However, difficulty should not obstruct the path to better labor relations designed to provide high-quality educational services to the children of the community. The stakes are high, and the commitment to address these issues must be equally high.

Key Chapter Terms

Agency shop: A requirement that all employees in the unit pay dues or fees to the union to defray the costs of providing representation. This is different from a closed shop, which requires an employee to be a union member in order to be hired. A closed shop is a violation of the National Labor Relations Act, Civil Service Reform Act, and the various state collective bargaining statutes.

Arbitration: At its core, arbitration is a form of dispute resolution. It is an alternative to court action. It is either advisory—either party can reject the opinion, or binding—in which case both parties must accept the decision.

Bread-and-butter issues: This term is generally used to describe those issues that affect the everyday lives of individuals. In collective bargaining it refers to wages, benefits, and terms and conditions of employment.

Fair representation: The union's duty to represent the interests of all unit employees without regard to union membership. Unions cannot discriminate against members in its formulation or implementation of the contract.

Good faith bargaining: The duty to approach negotiations with a sincere resolve to reach a collective bargaining agreement, to be represented by properly authorized representatives who are prepared to discuss and negotiate on any condition of employment, to meet at reasonable times and places as frequently as may be necessary and to avoid unnecessary delays, and in the case of the agency, to furnish upon request data necessary to negotiation.

Grievance: An alleged violation, misapplication, or misinterpretation of a specific section of the collective bargaining agreement.

Impasse: When the parties have reached a deadlock in negotiations they are said to have reached an impasse in negotiations. If bargaining on any subject is still proceeding, impasse cannot be declared. Impasse proceedings typically involve mediation and fact finding.

Past practice: Existing practices sanctioned by use and acceptance that are not specifically included in the collective bargaining agreement. Often, it is used to clarify the language of the contract. The strength of a past practice is the absence of challenge to the practice. Arbitrators use evidence of past practices to interpret ambiguous contract language.

Proposal: A formal statement of one party's proposed language to be inserted into the contract. It is given to the other party at the bargaining table. If a proposal is agreed to by both parties, that language is signed off as approved (tentative agreement).

Unfair labor practice: An alleged violation of the state public employment law. An unfair labor practice is heard before the state public employment board, the agency charged with the implementation of the state public employment law. It is different from a grievance in that a grievance is predicated on the contract, whereas an unfair labor practice is predicated on the state's public sector collective bargaining law.

References

Cohn, J. (2010, August 8). Why public employees are the new welfare queens. *The New Republic.* Retrieved from http://www.tnr.com/blog/jonathan-cohn/76884/why-your-fireman-has-better-pension-you

Cooper, B. S., & Liotta, M. (2001). Urban teachers unions face their future: The dilemmas of organizational maturity. *Education and Urban Society, 34,* 101–118.

DeMitchell, T. A. (1993). Collective bargaining, professionalism, and restructuring. *International Journal of Education Reform, 2,* 77–81.

DeMitchell, T. A. (2010). *Labor relations in education: Policies, politics, and practices.* Lanham, MD: Rowman & Littlefield.

DeMitchell, T. A. (2011). Labor relations and the challenges of leading. In F. W. English (Ed.), *The SAGE handbook of educational leadership* (2nd ed., pp. 381–394). Thousand Oaks, CA: Sage.

DeMitchell, T. A., & Cobb, C. D. (2006). Teachers: Their union and their profession. A tangled relationship. *West's Education Law Reporter, 212,* 1–20.

DeMitchell, T. A., & Cobb, C. D. (2007). Teacher as union member and teacher as professional: The voice of the teacher. *West's Education Law Reporter, 217,* 25–38.

DeMitchell, T. A., & Fossey, R. (1997.) *The limits of law-based school reform: Vain hopes and false promises.* Lanham, MD: Rowman and Littlefield.

DeMitchell, T. A., & Parker-Magagna, M. (2012). "A law too far?" The Wisconsin Budget Repair Act: Point. *West's Education Law Reporter, 275,* 1–15.

Fisher, R, & Brown, S. (1988). *Getting together: Building relationships as we negotiate.* Boston, MA: Houghton Mifflin.

Fisher, R, & Ury, W. (1983). *Getting to yes: Negotiating agreement without giving in.* New York, NY: Penguin Books.

Gilbert, C. (2013, February 9). The politics of Wisconsin's declining union membership. *Milwaukee Wisconsin Journal Sentinel.* Retrieved from http://www.jsonline.com/blogs/news/190545131.html

Kenai Peninsula Borough School District v. Kenai Peninsula Education Association, 572 P.2d 422–423 (Alaska 1977).

Kerchner, C. T., Koppich, J. E., & Weeres, J. G. (1997). *United mind workers: Unions and teaching in the knowledge society.* San Francisco, CA: Jossey-Bass.

Kerchner, C. T., & Mitchell, D. E. (1988). *The changing idea of a teachers' union.* New York, NY: Falmer Press.

Madison Teachers, Inc. v. Walker, 2014 WI 99. Retrieved from http://media.jrn.com/documents/Wisconsin_Supreme_Court_Ruling_Act_10.pdf

Moe, T. (2011). *Special interests: Teacher unions and America's public schools.* Washington, DC: Brookings Institution.

Murphy, M. (1990). *Blackboard unions: The AFT and NEA, 1900–1980.* Ithaca, NY: Cornell University Press.

Prokopf, D. (2013). Public employees at the school of hard Knox: How the Supreme Court is turning public-sector unionism into a history lesson. *William Mitchell Law Review 39,* 1363–1403.

Ridgefield Park Education Association v. Ridgefield Park Board of Education, 393 A.2d278 (N.J. 1978).

Sanes, M., & Schmitt, J. (2014, March). *Regulation of public sector collective bargaining in the states.* Washington, DC: Center for Economic and Policy Research. Retrieved from http://www.cepr.net/documents/state-public-cb-2014–03.pdf

Streshly, W. A., & DeMitchell, T. A. (1994). *Teacher unions and TQE: Building quality labor relations.* Thousand Oaks, CA: Corwin.

Further Readings

Cooper, B. S., & Liotta, M. (2001). Urban teachers unions face their future: The dilemmas of organizational maturity. *Education and Urban Society, 34,* 101–118.

This article explores the issues that teachers' unions encounter in urban settings. It provides a view of the challenges that unions face as they confront the push for educational reform.

DeMitchell, T. A. (2010). *Labor relations in education: Policies, politics, and practices.* Lanham, MD: Rowman & Littlefield Education.

This book covers the major aspects of the impact of teachers' unions and collective bargaining on education. It provides a history of the rise of teacher unions, discusses the challenges presented by a unionized faculty, and presents the nuts and bolts practical applications of negotiating, implementing, and enforcing a contract. It also has a full simulation that can be used to practice bargaining a contract.

DeMitchell, T. A., & Cobb, C. D. (2006). Teachers: Their union and their profession. A tangled relationship. *West's Education Law Reporter, 212,* 1–20.

Their quantitative analysis of teacher responses sought to understand how teachers make sense of their role as a professional and the role of a member of a union. They found that teachers overwhelmingly believe they are better off with the union and its contract than without the union. However, a contract does not easily impact the professional task of teaching.

DeMitchell, T. A., & Parker-Magagna, M. (2012). "A law too far?" The Wisconsin Budget Repair Act: Point. *West's Education Law Reporter, 275,* 1–15.

Mawdsley, R. D., Russo, C. J., & Mawdsley, J. L. (2012). "A law too far?" The Wisconsin Budget Repair Act: Counterpoint. *West's Education Law Reporter, 275,* 16–22.

These two companion pieces discuss Wisconsin Governor Scott Walker's legislation that focused national attention on public sector unions in general

and teacher unions in particular. The point offers a critique of the legislation, which the authors contend was designed to cripple the public sector unions. The counterpoint asserts that the shift in Wisconsin can be viewed as a bellwether shifting the debate from teachers' unions protecting jobs to focusing on the best interests of children.

Hess, F. M., & West, M. R. (2006). *A better bargain: Overhauling teacher collective bargaining for the 21st century.* Cambridge, MA: Cambridge Program on Education Policy & Governance.

The two authors call for a break from the industrial model upon which public sector bargaining was built. They consider it an anachronism in the 21st century. They call for the elimination of work rules that are obstacles to teacher professionalism and effective administration of schools and a retooling of security safeguards.

Keane, W. G. (1996). *Win/win or else: Collective bargaining in an age of public discontent.* Thousand Oaks, CA: Corwin.

Interest-based bargaining is an attempt to reduce the influence of the industrial labor relations model that institutionalizes conflict as a primary condition of bargaining. This useful book applies the concepts of getting to yes to education. Keane writes, "The basic premise of bargaining in a win/win mode is the assumption that both parties see the best interests of their constituents most efficiently served by helping the other party meet the interests of its own constituents simultaneously" (p. 36).

Kenai Peninsula Borough School District v. Kenai Peninsula Education Association, 572 P.2d 422–423 (Alaska 1977).

This is example of an early case in which state courts struggled with what a school district was required to bargain. The Supreme Court of Alaska ruled that salaries, fringe benefits, the number of hours worked, and the amount of leave time were negotiable, but other matters that affected educational policy were not. The court provided a list of bargainable and nonbargainable subjects.

Kerchner, C. T., Koppich, J. E., & Weeres, J. G. (1997). *United mind workers: Unions and teaching in the knowledge society.* San Francisco, CA: Jossey-Bass.

The authors offer a vision of teachers' unions reorganized around the concept of teachers as knowledge workers. They focus on moving the locus of control over teaching closer to teachers. Unions play a different role but occupy a critical position as teachers assume more responsibility for quality education. An interesting read

is juxtaposing Myron Lieberman and this piece, both published in the same year but each using a different lens to view the role of unions in educational reform.

Kerchner, C. T., & Mitchell, D. E. (1988). *The changing idea of a teachers' union.* New York, NY: Falmer Press.

Kerchner and Mitchell, influential commentators in the area of collective bargaining in education, discuss the parameters of how public sector bargaining can change in response to emerging challenges in education.

Liberman, M. (1997). *The teacher unions: How the NEA and the AFT sabotage reform and hold students, parents, teachers, and taxpayers hostage to bureaucracy.* New York, NY: Free Press.

Myron Liberman, a one-time candidate for president of the AFT, started off as proponent of teacher unionization but reversed course in his views on the impact of unionization on public education. This book is a good representation of the arguments that he makes against the power and reach of teachers' unions. Among his suggestions to "weaken the grip" of the national teachers' unions is legislation that offers teachers the option of choosing to join local-only teachers' unions.

Loveless, T. (Ed.). (2000). *Conflicting missions? Teachers unions and educational reform.* Washington, DC: Brookings Institution.

Tom Loveless gathers a number of teachers' union researchers and commentators to provide multiple perspectives on the intersection of teachers' unions and educational reform. The book is the result of a multiple-day conference held at the Harvard Kennedy School of Government. It is a wide-ranging discussion.

McDonnell, L. M., & Pascal, A. (1988, April). *Teacher unions and educational reform.* Santa Monica, CA: RAND.

This is an early study of how unions react to educational reform. Union leaders who get too far out in front of their rank-and-file members run the risk of losing their leadership positions. Teachers, in this study, want their leaders to focus on bread-and-butter issues with concern for union-driven or -supported educational reform taking a trailing position.

Megel, C. J. (1957). A teacher union leader views problems. *Teachers College Record, 59,* 26–31.

This is an early discussion from the viewpoint of a classroom teacher and former four-term president of the AFT. It provides a blueprint of the issues faced by teachers (salary, tenure, retirement, sick leave, discipline, and the right to bargain) in the mid-20th century and serves as an outline for the rise of public sector bargaining, which would soon follow.

Moe, T. (2011). *Special interests: Teacher unions and America's public schools.* Washington, DC: Brookings Institution.

Terry Moe is a vocal critic of teacher unions. He argues that unions are not solely responsible for the nation's education problems but they are at the "heart" of its problems. He places the major blame for ineffective public school organization on the power of unions. For a short video of Terry Moe discussing his ideas on teacher unions based on his book, see "Terry Moe on teacher union power" available on YouTube at http://www.youtube.com/watch?v=Q-zctmMbvaI.

Murphy, M. (1990). *Blackboard unions: The AFT and NEA, 1900–1980.* Ithaca, NY: Cornell University.

This is an excellent history of the rise of teachers' unions. The separate lines between the inception, growth, and convergence of the two major teachers' unions are deftly drawn. An interesting discussion is the importance of the "fiend in petticoats" to the rise of the AFT.

Ridgefield Park Education Association v. Ridgefield Park Board of Education, 393 A.2d 278 (N.J. 1978).

The New Jersey Supreme Court captured the reason why public policy is generally considered a prohibited subject of bargaining. The court wrote, "The very foundation of representative democracy would be endangered if decisions of significant matters of government policy were left to the process of negotiations, where citizen participation is precluded" (p. 287).

Russo, C. J. (2013). Collective bargaining in public education: "It was the best of times, it was the worst of times" for teacher unions. *West's Education Law Reporter, 291*, 545–561.

Professor Russo reviews the political events in Wisconsin and Ohio in 2011 and 2012 that pertain to each state's response to public sector unions and collective bargaining. The article also presents suggestions for reforming teacher bargaining, including reducing the political power of teachers' unions; restrictions on nonunion members paying for agency fees for the work of the union in bargaining a contract; making it harder, in a nod to the failed recall referendum of Governor Walker of Wisconsin, to recall public officials; and allowing more shared decision making on policy issues. The article also reviews the argument for higher salaries for teachers.

Sanes, M., & Schmitt, J. (2014, March). *Regulation of public sector collective bargaining in the states.* Washington, DC: Center for Economic and Policy Research. Retrieved from http://www.cepr.net/documents/state-public-cb-2014–03.pdf

This Center for Economic and Policy Research brief provides a brief introduction to public sector collective bargaining. It includes useful tables for firefighters, police, and teachers on legislation on the right to bargain, wage negotiations, and the right to strike by state. It also provides an appendix of laws.

Appendix

Getting Started in Your Educational Leadership Career

Associations and Journals

Joining professional associations is a key to a career in educational leadership and management. Membership in such groups will bring one into important professional and social relationships that are essential to continuing career professional development and advancement. The associations and journals in this section are national and international. The only associations listed are those you may join as an individual. Some associations, such as the University Council for Educational Administration (UCEA), accept only institutional memberships and are not listed. However, UCEA does publish an outstanding journal that can be accessed online and that is shown in this section.

Many associations, such as the American Association of School Administrators (AASA), Association for Supervision and Curriculum Development (ASCD), National Association of Elementary School Principals (NAESP), National Association of Secondary School Principals (NASSP), and National Council of Professors of Educational Administration (NCPEA), have state affiliates. If you go to the national association's website, you can see if there is an affiliate for your state and it will provide information about joining. In almost all cases, you must join the state and the national as separate memberships. Some state affiliates also have their own conferences apart from the national conference. Attending a state conference is an excellent way to get started in putting together a cadre of professional friends that are important for career networking.

Some of the best journals for school site administrators are published by national associations. These are shown in this section. If you do not wish to join a national association but want to have access to its journals, there are usually procedures to subscribe or purchase articles independently from association membership. Nearly all association journals also have iPad and Kindle applications.

National and International American Administrative Educational Associations

American Association of School Administrators (AASA)
1615 Duke Street, Alexandria, Virginia, 22314
703-528-0700
info@aasa.org
http://www.aasa.org/

The AASA is primarily known as the superintendents' national association. However, school site administrators may also join. The AASA was founded in 1865 just months after the assassination of President Abraham Lincoln. Originally known as the National Association of School Superintendents, it merged in 1870 with the National Teachers Association. which eventually became the National

Education Association (NEA). As part of the NEA it was known as the Department of Superintendence until 1937, when it became the AASA. It left the NEA in 1972.

The AASA is governed by an elected governing board and executive committee. It holds an annual conference, publishes a variety of journals and books, and every 10 years releases a study of the American superintendency that has become an important source on the changing values and demands of the superintendency in the United States. The AASA also has affiliates in 48 of the 50 states as well as relationships with the Canadian Association of School System Administrators and the Association for the Advancement of International Education.

American Education Research Association (AERA)
1430 K St., NW, Suite 1200, Washington, DC 20005
202-238-3200
www.aera.net

Despite the fact that AERA's main membership consists largely of researchers and professors, there are still many school leadership practitioners who belong to it and attend its annual conference. AERA's publications are among the very best in the field. AERA was founded in 1916 and includes international members. It is led by a council consisting of the president, the president-elect, the immediate past president, the vice presidents of divisions, six at-large members, a graduate student representative, a special interest group representative, and the executive director, who serves without a vote. The divisions of AERA that most often are of interest to school practitioners are Division A: Administration, Organization and Leadership; Division B: Curriculum Studies; Division C: Learning and Instruction; and Division L: Education Policy and Politics.

Association for Supervision and Curriculum Development (ASCD)
1703 North Beauregard St.
Alexandria, Virginia 22311
800-933-2723 or 703-578-9600
www.ascd.org

The Association for Supervision and Curriculum Development (ASCD) was founded in 1943 as the result of a merger between the NEA's Society for Curriculum Study and the Department of Supervisors and Directors. It became independent of the NEA in 1972. It is governed by a 21-member board of directors on which the executive director and its president also serve. ASCD is an international organization and also has state affiliates. Its membership is open to teachers, principals, supervisors, central office administrators, and professors. It has an annual conference and a strong professional development and publishing program. It is an excellent "starter" professional organization for the beginning school site administrator.

Flagstaff Seminar: Educational Leaders Without Borders
25 Creek Rock Circle, Sedona, Arizona 86351
928-284-4015
www.educationalleaderswithoutborders.com

This is an international association of scholars and practitioners dedicated to getting all children around the world into school, especially girls. Educational leaders must become emboldened to step out of the school/state nexus so that they become true leaders without borders, ensuring that greater equality is the result for all children and their families. The basic principles of the Flagstaff Seminar (FS) are that all children have a right to go to school, that education should draw out of humans the potentialities of a progressive humanity that is inclusive and respectful of difference, that schools are a leveraging institutional force for greater equality and opportunity, and that educational leaders can and must be more than agents of the state in perpetuating the socioeconomic status quo.

National Association of Elementary School Principals (NAESP)
1615 Duke St., Alexandria, Virginia 22314
703-684-3345
www.naesp.org

The National Association of Elementary School Principals (NAESP) was founded in 1921 by a group of principals interested in establishing a national forum for leadership at the K-8 level. It is the only national administrative association solely focused on issues before elementary and middle school principals. It is governed by a 14-member board of directors and an executive director. It hosts an annual conference, and its publications include a widely read national journal. It also has state affiliates that a school site administrator can join separately.

National Association of Secondary School Principals (NASSP)
1904 Association Drive, Reston, Virginia 20191
703-860-0200
www.principals.org

Created in 1916, NASSP's mission has been to promote excellence in school leadership. Its membership is open to middle school and high school principals and assistant principals. NASSP runs an annual convention and releases books and other publications, among the most famous of which is *Breaking Ranks: The Comprehensive Framework for School Improvement,* released in 2011. The organization has also created a Center for New Principals (CNP) where members can find advice and tips from experienced principals. There is also a free helpline for new principals. The National Honor Society and the National Junior Honor Society were created in 1921 and 1929, respectively, by NASSP. The organization also sponsors the National Association of Student Councils, which seeks to promote civil service among students to their schools and communities.

National Council of Professors of Educational Administration (NCPEA)
John W. Porter Building, Suite 304
Eastern Michigan University
Ypsilanti, Michigan 48197
734-487-0255
www.ncpeaprofessor.org

The National Council of Professors of Educational Administration (NCPEA) is the oldest organization of professors of educational administration in the nation. It was established in 1947. It is open to membership from school site practitioners who may also attend the organization's annual summer conference. Many of the professors in NCPEA are former school practitioners. The organization also has state affiliates and an independent publishing arm of print and e-books. Its blog, "Talking Points," discusses the issues of the day at http://ncpeapublications.blogspot.com.

Professional Journals for the School Site Educational Leader

Professional reading is essential to stay abreast of current developments in education. Without constant attention to professional development, a school site administrator can quickly become dated. Staying current is an investment in one's career. The journals listed are some of the most popular ones and range from topical treatments and reviews to more in-depth and scholarly analyses. Some of the journals are published by educational associations, and access to them comes with membership. They are listed here because they can also be accessed or purchased separately.

Some terms should be explained. An *academic journal* is primarily written by and for professors and researchers. A *nonacademic journal* is aimed at a largely practitioner audience. Some journals are mixed in this respect. A *refereed journal* (sometimes called "peer reviewed") is one in which the content is evaluated by independent, usually anonymous, judges to determine its accuracy and perspective. If a journal is refereed the judges or evaluators are usually "blind"; that is, an author does not know who is going to be reviewing and rating his or her paper. Nearly all top-rated academic journals are "blind refereed." Most practitioner-centered journals are not refereed, and the decision to publish is determined by the journal's editorial staff.

Education Week

This newspaper is dedicated to covering national and international issues in education. It does feature stories on graduation rates and publishes very useful information in chart and graph form, which can be useful in comparing a leader's school or school system with others in the nation. *Education Week* is published 37 times per year by Editorial Projects in Education, which is located at 6935 Arlington Road, Suite 100, Bethesda, MD 20814-5287. Its phone number is 301-280-3100. The newspaper has received foundation support from the Carnegie Corporation of New York, the Ford Foundation, the Bill and Melinda Gates Foundation, the GE Foundation, the Wallace Foundation, and the Walton Family Foundation, among others. Its website is www.edweek.org. Articles cover a very wide range of topics. It is billed as "American Education's Newspaper of Record." *Education Week* is a nonacademic, nonrefereed publication of general interest to all educators and to members of the public who are interested in educational issues.

Educational Administration Quarterly

Educational Administration Quarterly is the flagship publication of the University Council for Educational Administration (UCEA). It is an academic, refereed publication and focuses mainly on research and conceptual issues in educational administration. Articles are much longer and more detailed than those found in more contemporary, practitioner-focused publications. The journal is published five times each year by SAGE. Information is available at eaq.sagepub.com

Educational Leadership

This is the flagship journal for ASCD and it is written for practitioners, teachers, principals, superintendents, and professors. Its circulation is estimated at more than 100,000. About 75% of the articles are unsolicited. It is considered a nonacademic, non-peer-reviewed journal. Articles are practical, current, and reader friendly. You can subscribe independently of joining ASCD. Digital subscriptions are available for use with the iPad, iPhone, Android, and Kindle devices. More information is available at www.ascd.org/publications/educational-leadership.aspx

eJournal of Education Policy

The *eJournal of Education Policy* was established in the fall of 2000. The journal is an open access journal and free to use. It is an excellent resource for the beginning school site administrator. It is an academic, refereed journal and is published twice a year, in the fall and spring. Special editions are also a part of publication. The editor is Dr. Shadow Armfield. The journal may be accessed at http://nau.edu/COE/eJournal; the address is P.O. Box 5774, Flagstaff, AZ 86011. The phone number is 928-523-7651. The journal is affiliated with the Directory of Open Access Journals (DOAJ).

NASSP Bulletin

The *Bulletin* of the National Association of Secondary School Principals is the award-winning official journal of NASSP. It is peer reviewed but not considered an academic journal. It is, however, focused on the issues middle school and high school principals face every day. NASSP makes articles available on OnlineFirst, which allows articles to be viewed before they are published in the journal. The *Bulletin* is published by SAGE; information about the journal is available at the NASSP website at http://www.nassp.org/knowledge-center/publications/nassp-bulletin

NCPEA Educational Leadership Review

Educational Leadership Review (ELR) is published by the National Council of Professors of Educational Administration (NCPEA). It is an academic and refereed journal and is published in the spring and fall of each year. Articles are usually 5,000 words and scholarly in content. While it is considered an outlet for research on leadership, the articles deal with practical leadership issues. For information go to http://www.ncpeapublications.org/subscriptions.html

Phi Delta Kappan

The *Kappan* is perhaps the most widely read and influential nonacademic educational journal in the United States. It is published by Phi Delta Kappa, the honorary educational fraternity. The *Kappan* can be read on the Web at kappanmagazine.org or pdk.sagepub.com. Many libraries offer online access to current and back issues of this journal. Abstracts and the full text of all *Kappan* articles from November 1915 to the most recent 3 months are available. There is also an iPad edition that can be obtained in the App Store. Phi Delta Kappa sponsors the annual Gallup Poll of the Public's Attitudes Toward the Public Schools and publishes the results in the *Kappan*. The content of the journal is reader friendly and nontechnical.

Principal

Principal is a magazine published by the National Association of Elementary School Principals (NAESP). Articles are between 1,500 and 2,000 words. The magazine is nonacademic and non-refereed but highly readable and practical. Articles are available at the NAESP website at www.naesp.org

INDEX

AASA (American Association of School Administrators), 186, 487–488

A-B-A-B approach to monitoring, 80

Abandonment (of an activity or project), 261–262, 264, 270

Abbott, M., 92, 94

A-B-C curriculum alignment, 114–115, 114 (figure)

Ability grouping, 60–61, 140, 247 (sidebar). *See also* Academic stratification; Tracking

Ableism, 73–74, 76, 82

Abnormality and normality, 73. *See also* Normal, concept of

Absenteeism, 72 (sidebar), 352. *See also* Attendance

Abuse, child. *See* Child abuse

Academic achievement. *See* Achievement, student

Academic journal, meaning of, 489

Academic language proficiency, 93, 98

Academic performance:
    bullying and, 289
    charter schools and, 330, 332
    class size and, 250
    for homeschoolers, 362
    under No Child Left Behind, 175–176
    SEL programming for, 378
    See also Achievement, student

Academic readiness, 377, 382. *See also* Readiness

Academic stratification, 422, 430. *See also* Ability grouping; Tracking

Access:
    advocacy for, 380
    and distribution of power and rewards, 445–446
    to instructional materials, 220
    to knowledge, 203, 208
    to online learning, 214–215, 216, 217, 219–220, 368
    to preschool education, 275, 421

Accountability:
    achievement and, 171, 173, 174, 175, 180, 182
    in budgeting, 259, 260, 264, 267
    caring classrooms in tension with, 403
    for charter schools, 330, 331
    credit recovery and, 216
    discourse of, 136, 147
    era of, 141
    government-based pressures on, 174
    high stakes landscape of, 173, 332
    inside-out and outside-in, 404
    in a managerial control model, 6–7
    A Nation at Risk and, 173

No Child Left Behind and, 6, 175, 205, 333
    test scores, politics, and, 164
    work culture and, 403–404, 406, 408

Accountability measures, in school turnaround, 389, 391–398, 398 (table)

Accoutrements of leadership, 25–28, 27 (table), 33. *See also* Management/leadership dyad

Achievement, student:
    accountability and, 171, 173, 174, 175, 180, 182
    attendance and, 352–353
    bullying and, 290
    in charter schools, 281, 282, 332, 335
    class size and, 250
    classroom instruction and, 390
    cultural and social capital for, 420–421
    defined as a key term, 182, 270, 399
    distance learning and, 214
    emotional disturbances and, 376
    evidence of, 169
    grade point average and, 173
    historic analysis of, 171–174
    instructional time and, 173
    leadership and, 390, 404
    learning behaviors for, 375
    legislation of, 181
    meanings of, 169–171
    merit pay and, 459
    under No Child Left Behind, 175, 176–177, 277, 378
    online/blended learning and, 214
    parental involvement and, 424–425, 444
    per-pupil spending and, 250
    in public versus charter schools, 282
    in public versus homeschooling, 368–369
    in public versus private schools, 281
    questions to ask about, 169, 170, 171 (sidebar)
    school quality and, 173, 277
    social-emotional development and, 378
    teacher evaluation and, 220
    turnaround school initiative for, 389–397, 398 (table)
    voucher programs and, 280, 281, 462
    work cultures of schools and, 410
    See also Achievement gap(s)

Achievement gap(s):
    causes of, 276–280
    closing of, crucial to do so, 419
    closing of, suggestions for, 180–182

college graduation and, 179
counseling services for reduction of, 377
culture and, 112–113, 172, 174, 181
curriculum alignment for reduction of, 114, 115
defined as a key term, 129, 192, 282, 430
and family background factors, 276, 277–280
gender and, 182
high school graduation and, 179
historic analysis of, 171–174
income achievement gap, 179, 182
international, 112, 179–180
language and, 112, 121
learning barriers and, 277–280
Matthew Effect in, 171
A Nation at Risk impact on, 172–174
No Child Left Behind and, 175, 277
in North Carolina, 419, 420 (figure), 423, 426
opportunity gap versus, 139–140
poverty and, 172, 175, 179, 180, 181, 277–278, 421
preschool readiness and, 276
race/ethnicity and, 112, 178–179, 189, 192–193, 275–279, 419
racial isolation and, 278
school cheating scandals affected by, 189, 191
social class and, 112, 113, 276–277, 278, 279
socioeconomics of, 112–113, 171–172, 175, 179, 275–278
See also Achievement, student; Assessment competency gap;
  Digital divide; Opportunity gap
Achievers, level of, as perceived by teachers, 427
ACLU (American Civil Liberties Union), 445
Act 10 (Wisconsin Budget Repair Act), 471,
  472, 481
Action research, 143
Actionable knowledge, 154
Active listening, 348
Activity budgeting, 263, 270
Actors in school politics, 441–445
ADA (Americans with Disabilities Act), 219, 292, 295, 314
ADA (average daily attendance), 352
Adequacy and school finance, 241–242, 244, 251, 253
Adequate yearly progress (AYP):
  attendance rates in, 352
  fraudulent misrepresentations for, 188
  NCLB sanctions and, 189
  prescribed indicators of, 175–176
  school cheating scandal and, 186
  turnaround schools and, 391
  validity and reliability of, 174–175
  See also Waivers, from NCLB provisions
Administrators. *See* Central office; Leadership; Principals;
  Superintendents
Adult learners, understanding of, 26, 27 (table)
Adult-led cheating. *See* School cheating scandals
Advanced degrees, and teacher effectiveness, 251
Advanced placement (AP) courses, 61, 84, 140, 181, 214,
  231, 363
Advisory arbitration, 480
Advocacy Coalition Framework, 460
Advocacy committees, 125–126
Advocacy groups, in school politics, 445

AERA (American Education Research Association), 488
Affluent schools, 333
African American students:
  achievement gap and, 189, 275, 276, 279, 419
  in charter schools, 335
  control of their own education by, 337
  and cultural construct of "acting White," 135, 141
  in demographic shifts, 419
  disproportionate discipline referrals for, 84, 142
  disproportionate representation in special education, 84
  education of, for subservience to Whites, 336
  expulsion of, 315
  and health-related learning barriers, 279
  in the history of achievement gaps, 172, 173
  in lower student tracks, 275
  practices that meet the needs of, 410
  and the right to be educated, 423
  in so-called failing schools, 333
  strategies in effective education for, 423–427
  underrepresented in AP and honors courses, 84
  See also African American underachievement; Black students;
    Students of color
African American underachievement:
  and cultural capital for achievement, 419–421
  factors that contribute to, 421–422
  and social capital for achievement, 421
African Americans:
  and *Brown v. Board of Education*, 172
  classification of, 130
  population projections in U.S. for, 418
  See also Blacks
African peoples, deculturalization of, 336
AFT (American Federation of Teachers), 281, 282, 330,
  462, 473
Age medians, by racial/ethnic group, 119–120
Agency shops, 472, 482
Agenda moving, GAMEing for, 43 (sidebar)
Agenda-pushing research, recognizing, 461–462 (sidebar)
Aggression, micro-, 75, 76, 81, 84
Agriculture, U.S. Department of, 252
AIDS, 42
AIM (accessible instructional materials)
  centers, 220
Airasian, Peter W., 156, 157, 159, 160, 163
Al Otaiba, Stephanie, 94
Alabama, 364
Alaska, 105
Alaska Natives, 121, 130, 131, 419
Alcohol:
  abuse of, 279, 315
  random testing for, 311, 313
Alfonso, Vincent, 96
Alger, Horatio, 200
Allen, Louise Anderson, 137
All-English approaches, 123
Allensworth, E., 390
Allies and coalitions, 448, 451. *See also* School politics
Allocation of resources:
  in budgeting, 257, 258–259, 260, 261, 262–268, 270

school finance and, 239, 240–242, 246, 247, 249–252

    teacher allocation, 267, 269, 395, 396–397

    See also School finance

Allocative efficiency, 241, 253

Alpha coefficient, 158, 160

Alphabetic principle, 89

Alternate forms reliability, 159

Ambrose, Susan A., 144

American Association of School Administrators (AASA), 186, 487–488

American Bar Association, 323

American Civil Liberties Union (ACLU), 445

American Council on Education, 130

American Dream, 336, 421

American Education Research Association (AERA), 488

American Enterprise Institute, 110

American Federation of Teachers (AFT), 281, 282, 330, 462, 473

American Indians, 121, 130, 131, 419. *See also* Native Americans

American Recovery and Reinvestment Act, 177

American School Counselor Association (ASCA), 375, 377, 380, 382

Americans with Disabilities Act (ADA), 219, 292, 295, 314

America's Promise Alliance, 350

Amish community, 366–367

Anderson, S. E., 390

Anger management, 324, 374, 375

Anonymity in cyberbullying, 291, 323

Anschutz Foundation, 464

Anti-bullying curricula, 374 (figure), 377, 378–379

Anti-bullying legislation, 291–292, 293, 323. *See also* Bullying and the law

Antiracist content, 427

Antiracist counternarratives, 424

Anti-Semitism, 294

Anyon, J., 276

Anyon, Jean, 333

Anytime/anywhere learning, 199, 206, 207, 208–209, 215. *See also* Ubiquitous learning

AP (advanced placement) courses, 61, 84, 140, 181, 214, 231, 363

Appiah, Kwame Anthony, 15

Apple, Michael, 333, 337

Approach-specific best practices, 146–147

APS (Atlanta Public Schools), 186–187, 188–189, 190, 191

Arbitration, 438, 442, 480, 482

Architecture, for virtual education, 202

Arenas for school politics, 438, 439, 446, 447, 448, 451

Arizona, 26, 418

Arizona K12 Center, 67

Arkansas, 119, 121

Armfield, Shadow, 490

Armstrong, Lance, 185

Arreaga-Mayer, C., 92, 94

Art Instruction Schools, 211

Artful leadership, 13, 26–27, 27 (table), 28 (sidebar), 33

Articles of Confederation, 11

Artiles, A. J., 93

Arts, the, 111, 274, 374, 375

Asante, Molefi Kete, 337

ASCA (American School Counselor Association), 375, 377, 380, 382

ASCD (Association for Supervision and Curriculum Development), 487, 488, 490

Asian American students:

    achievement gap and, 189, 276

    enrollment data for, 121, 419

    and Whites, in higher student tracks, 275

Asian Americans:

    median age in the U.S. for, 120

    population projections in U.S. for, 418

Asians, classification of, 130–131

Assertion, as a social skill, 375

Assessed value, and property taxes, 244

Assessment competency gap, 180

Assessments:

    in budgeting, 262, 263, 264–265, 266

    daily, impact of, 180

    defined as a key term, 165

    formative, 89, 98, 217, 392

    inter-user consistency in, 155

    multiple types needed, 192

    under No Child Left Behind, 176, 177

    for online and blended learning, 216, 217

    questions to ask about, 171 (sidebar)

    self-, by students, 144, 146, 147

    self-, by teachers, 220

    and tests differentiated, 153, 154

Assistant principals, in the career hierarchy, 446, 446 (sidebar), 447. *See also* Principals

Association for Supervision and Curriculum Development (ASCD), 487, 488, 490

Association for the Advancement of International Education, 488

Associations, professional, 487–489

Assumptive worlds, defined as a key term, 451

Assumptive worlds rules, 439–441, 445, 446, 447, 450

    for four situations, 440 (table)

    navigation of, 446 (sidebar)

Asymmetrical information, 465

Asynchronous environment, 201, 202, 206, 209, 213, 215

Asynchronous instruction, defined as a key term, 221

Atlanta Public Schools (APS), 186–187, 188–189, 190, 191

At-risk school environments, 421, 422

At-risk students, 90, 91, 93, 94, 141

Attendance:

    consistent, 343, 344, 354–355

    engagement, self-regulation, and, 352–353

    essential nature of, 343, 354

    exemption from laws on, 364, 366–367

    funding tied to, 344

    incentives for, 345

    rate of, for NCLB, 176

    reasons for concern about, 346

    See also Discipline, student

Attention levels, 427

Audits:
    community audit, 75, 76, 81–82
    equity audit, 180–181
Australia, 26, 27 (table)
Authority:
    defined as a key term, 33
    in the management/leadership dyad, 22 (figure), 25
Autism, 295
Autobiography, reflective, 67
Autonomy:
    of charter schools, 331, 458
    defined as a key term, 466
    for innovation, 457
    in market theory, 457, 458
    for principals, 437
    as a psychological need, 406
    in small learning communities, 376
    for teachers, 24, 402
    in the workplace, 8
Avatars, 229
Average daily attendance (ADA), 352
Awareness, self-. *See* Self-awareness
Awareness, social, 378
AYP. *See* Adequate yearly progress (AYP)

Baby boomer generation, 11, 15, 406
Back stage behavior, 45–46, 45 (figure)
Backlash, 449–450, 449 (sidebar), 451
Backloading, 115, 116
Backpack activities, 65, 76
Bakia, M., 214
Balance test (in an organization), 232, 233
Bandura, Albert, 410
Barbour, C., 393
Bargaining:
    collective (*see* Collective bargaining)
    in school politics, 435
Barnes, Aaron, 88
Baroody, Karen, 354
Barrett, Judi, 59
Barriers to learning. *See* Learning barriers, overcoming
Barriers to positive work cultures, 409
Barry, B., 114
Barth, Roland, 10–11, 12
Barton, Paul, 179
Batdorff, M., 332
Beabout, Brian, 12
Beating the bus home strategy, 441
Beckett, Lois, 186
Behavior, student. *See* Student conduct
Behavioral approach to monitoring, 80
Behaviors and beliefs, strategies for changing, 449 (sidebar)
Belfiore, G., 390
Beliefs:
    dichos (folk sayings) and, 129 (sidebar)
    informed skepticism on, 181
    strategies for changing, 449 (sidebar)
    of teachers, about minority students, 424
    of teachers, and school quality, 401

virtual education and, 201
in the workplace, 402, 406, 408, 410
Bell, Derrick, 335
Bell, Taylor, 227
Bell, Terrel, 35–36, 111, 173
Bell v. Itawamba County School Board (2012),
    227–228
Bender, W. N., 93
Bender, William, 91
Benefits, employee:
    collective bargaining on, 472, 473, 474, 475 (sidebar)
    expenditures for, in public education, 241 (figure)
Benign insensitivity, 75
Benjamin, Harold, 105
Bentham, Jeremy, 44, 49, 333
Berkeley High School Diversity Project, 179
Berla, Nancy, 63
Berlin wall, 202
Berliner, D., 333
Berman, Paul, 8
Best practices:
    for all students at any given time and setting, 139
    careful discernment of, 30–33
    as checklists, 142
    context and, 140, 141, 142, 145
    context and, as key to, 139
    critique of, 136–142
    as defensible practices, 136, 141, 142, 147
    defined as a key term, 33, 147, 355
    for developmentally appropriate practice, 353
    dimensions of, 144–147
    equity issues and, 135, 136, 138 (sidebar), 139–140, 142
    ethics and, 136, 137, 141, 142, 147
    misuse of, 141–142
    poor implementation of, 140–141
    power issues and, 136, 139, 140
    professional judgment and, 399
    progressive and constructivist principles of, 144
    roots of, 136
    social justice and, 136, 140, 142, 147
    strategies for use of, 142–143
    for students with disabilities, 219
    in systematic reform, 427
    theoretical challenges to, 136–138
Bethel School District v. Fraser (1986), 226, 227, 229, 230
Betterment through change, 136
Bible, the, 24, 30, 182, 359, 365
Biddle, B., 333
Big data, 240
Biggers, Neal, 228
Bigotry, 141, 345
Bilingual education, 93, 121, 123, 124. *See also* English as a
    second language (ESL); English language learners (ELLs);
    Second language
Bilingual intermediary organizations, 464 (sidebar)
Bilingual newsletters, 128
Bilingual staff members, 426, 437
Bilingual teachers, 426
Bill & Melinda Gates Foundation, 103, 334, 464, 465

Binding arbitration, 480
Bing Translator, 128
Bioecological approach:
  background for, 71–73, 74
  in community building, 349
  learning strategies in, 79, 80–81, 82
  policies and rules ecologies in, 76–78, 82
  social, cultural, economic ecologies in, 74–76
  teaching strategies in, 78–80
  See also Social ecological perspective
Birth weights, 179, 279
Bisexual profile, 229. *See also* Sexual orientation
Black colleges and universities, historically (HBCUs), 425, 425
    (sidebar), 426
Black educators, 336, 337
Black students:
  achievement gap and, 178–179, 192–193, 275–279
  in charter schools, 336
  childhood poverty and, 121, 277
  childrearing learning barriers for, 278, 279
  cyberbullying of, 323
  discipline referrals for, high rate of, 82
  dropout rates for, 122
  enrollment data for, 121, 418, 419
  and health-related learning barriers, 279
  in voucher programs, 281
  See also African American students; Students of color
Blackboard, software, 208
Blacks:
  classification of, 130
  median age in the U.S. for, 120
  poverty data for, 121, 277
  See also African Americans
Black-White achievement gap, 178–179, 192–193, 276, 277.
    See also Black students; White students
Blame and blaming, 123, 190, 191, 411
Blanchard, Kenneth, 31
Blank, Martin J., 348
Blase, J., 439
Blended learning:
  accessibility to, 214, 216, 220
  for credit recovery, 217
  data on, 212
  defined as a key term, 213, 221–222
  as disruptive innovation, 211, 221
  for personalized instruction, 215–216
  planning for, 218–221
  potential of, 204
  privacy concerns in, 216
  questions to ask about, 218–219
  special education and, 220
  student-teacher ratio in, 217
  See also Online learning
Blind protection, by unions, 476 (sidebar), 481
Blind refereeing, 489
Blind to self behavior, 44–45, 45 (figure), 46
Block, M. E., 162, 163
Blogs, 213, 227, 228
Bloom's Taxonomy, 115, 374, 382

*Board of Education of Independent School District No. 92 of
    Pottawatomie County v. Earls* (2002), 301
Boards of education:
  in school politics, 438, 441, 443, 444, 444 (sidebar), 445
  teachers' unions and, 474, 477, 478, 480, 481
Bobbitt, Franklin, 3, 5–6, 8, 9, 10, 104–105
Bode, Boyd, 105
Bode, Patty, 333
Bolton, Cheryl, 31–33, 33 (figure)
Bond, Guy L., 138
Bonding, sense of, 379
Bonds, financial, 245, 253
Boser, Ulrich, 178
Bourdieu, P., 110, 112
Bourdieu, Pierre, 104, 113, 115, 420, 421
Bowles, Samuel, 333
Boxed curriculum, 364, 370. *See also* Online learning
Boyatzis, Richard, 349
Boyd, Drew, 27, 28
Boys. *See* Males
Bradley Foundation, 464, 465
Brain development:
  different rates of, 82
  impeded by malnutrition, 279
  for self-regulation and focus, 353
  See also Development
Brain research, for best practices, 137
Brainstorming, 144
Braun, Henry, 281, 282
Bread-and butter issues, 475, 482
Bredeson, Carmen, 409
Brick-and-mortal school:
  computer labs in, 216, 217
  credit recovery courses in, 216
  the digital school and, 199, 200–203, 205, 206, 207
    (*see also* Digital schools)
Bridges, Michael W., 144
Brigham Young University, 30–31
Broad Foundation, 334, 463, 464
Brokers, in the marketplace of ideas, 464, 465
Bronfenbrenner, U., 422
Bronfenbrenner, Urie:
  and the bioecological approach, 71, 73, 74, 76, 349, 354
  and ecological systems theory, 61, 62 (figure)
  See also Bioecological approach
Broward County Public Schools, 317, 318 (figure)
Brown, K. M., 391, 392, 393
Brown, Monica R., 55
Brown, R., 31, 407
Brown, Ric, 22
Brown, Scott, 479
Brown v. Board of Education (1954), 172, 200, 278, 335. *See
    also* Racial desegregation
Browning and graying of America, 418. *See also* Demographic
    shifts for U.S. education
Browsers, Internet, 201, 202, 203
Bruner, Darlene Y., 410
Brunner, C. C., 448
Bryk, A. S., 390

Buckley, Jack, 330
Budde, Ray, 330
Buddin, Richard, 282
Budget, defined as a key term, 270
Budgeting, 257–272
    as an art, 258–259
    budget cuts and, 185, 257, 261, 264, 445
    efficiency, effectiveness, and, 260–261, 262
    expectations and, 257, 258, 259, 270
    functions of the budget, 261
    levels or types of, 262–265, 265 (table)
    NCLB, CCSS, and, 258
    performance-based, 264–270
    productivity and, 259, 261, 262, 264, 265, 270
    questions to ask in, 262, 266
    RTT programs and, 178
    state revenue reductions and, 257–258
    steps for, 259
    See also Fund distribution; Revenue generation; School
        finance
Bulletin of the NASSP (journal), 490
Bullycide, 290. *See also* Suicide
Bullying:
    achievement and, 290
    anti-bullying curricula, 374 (figure), 377, 378–379
    anti-bullying legislation, 291, 293, 323
    and community norms and values, 42
    cyber- (*see* Cyberbullying)
    data on, 322, 322 (figure), 323, 324 (figure), 379
    defined as a key term, 325, 355, 382
    defined by the federal government, 290
    discriminatory, 293–295
    as an erosion of feeling safe, 345
    and exploiting diversity as a deficit, 74
    forms of, 321
    gender and, 294–295, 321–322, 322 (figure), 323
    guidelines for prevention and response in, 42
    insidious nature of, 314, 379
    laws and (*see* Bullying and the law)
    off campus, 290
    and responsibility to protect students, 295–296
    schoolyard, 83, 321
    seriousness of, 289, 290, 321
    suicide by victims of, 289–290, 291, 323
Bullying and the law:
    court decisions on due process, 292–293
    court decisions on equal protection, 293–294
    discriminatory bullying/harassment, 293–295
    federal statutes, 292, 294–295
    list of court decisions and statutes, 305
    state policies and statutes, 291–292
    student speech and, 291, 323
    See also Bullying
Bureaucracy:
    in the management/leadership dyad, 22, 23, 24, 25
    as networks (*see* Networks (of people))
    positive and negative connotations of, 39
    shifting from, for virtual education, 201, 207
    Weber's (Max) ideal model for, 6

Bureaucrats, street-level, 240, 254, 437, 451
Burger, Warren, 366
Burns, James MacGregor, 405
Burns, Rebecca C., 60
Bursuck, W. D., 374
Buses, school. *See* School bus transportation
Bush, George H. W., 12
Bush, George W., 12, 135, 141, 174
Butler, Nicholas Murray, 473

C-A-B curriculum alignment, 115
Calendar, school, 76, 215. *See also* School day flexibility
California:
    accoutrements research database and, 26
    collective bargaining law in, 475 (sidebar)
    educational alternatives in, laws on, 363
    as an established Latino state, 418
    Hispanic population in, 119, 120 (table)
    limits on strip searches in, 300
Calkins, A., 390
Callahan, Raymond, 12
Cameras, security, 312, 320 (table), 321
Canadian Association of School System Administrators, 488
Capacity building, 108–109, 347, 404, 405, 411, 450
Capital:
    cultural (*see* Cultural capital)
    intellectual, 202, 203
    social, 421, 430
Capital construction and maintenance, 245
Capital expenses, 245, 253
Career building and advancement:
    network formation and, 40
    network navigation for, 42, 43 (sidebar), 46–47 (sidebar), 47
Career ladder, and school politics, 445–447
Career readiness, 105, 106, 109
Carey, J., 380
Caring:
    in leadership, 437
    in relationships, 56, 391
    schools as places of, 307, 350–351, 403, 410, 443
    teachers as, 56, 353
Caring environment:
    for a positive work culture, 410
    in school turnaround, 389, 391–398, 398 (table)
Carnegie Foundation, 182
Carnegie units, 173, 182
Carter, Suzanne, 62
Caruso, Guy, 141
Case law:
    defined as a key term, 235
    and legal precedents, importance of, 225–226
    list of court decisions for, 236, 305
    See also Bullying and the law; Search and seizure court
        decisions; Social media and case law; Speech/expression
        and case law
Categorical programs, 91, 248–249, 253
Catholic private schools, 281
C-B-A curriculum alignment, 115
CBM (curriculum-based measurement), 89, 90, 91, 93, 98

CCSS. *See* Common Core State Standards (CCSS)
CCSSO (Council of Chief State School Officers), 7, 105, 106, 110
Ceballos, Richard, 233
Cell phones, 83, 206, 291, 301–303, 321. *See also* Smartphones
Center for American Progress, 178
Center for Education Reform, 464
Center for Effective Discipline, 314
Center for Mental Health in Schools, 348
Center for Research on Education Outcomes, 463
Center on Education Policy, 176
Central Intelligence Agency, 40
Central office:
    in the formal grievance process, 478
    school finances and, 239, 242
    in school politics, 435, 438, 441, 444, 445, 446
Central tendency of data, and ecological fallacies, 138–139
Chain of command, 44, 440 (table), 441
Change, technological. *See* Technological change
Change time, in interventions, 80
Charisma, 442
Charter management organizations (CMOs), 329, 331
Charter schools:
    accountability for, 330, 331
    arguments pro and con, 331–334
    characteristics of, 329–330
    critical race theory on, 335–336, 337
    cultural capital and, 334–335
    data on, 329, 336
    defined as a key term, 282, 338
    empirical evidence on, 458
    as a form of privatization, 456
    funding for, 249, 258, 329, 332, 363
    goals of, 330
    history of, 330–331
    for homeschoolers, 363
    incentivism and, 457, 458, 460
    liberty associated with, 242
    main tenets of, 330
    powerful interests served by, 335–336
    questions to ask about, 331, 331 (sidebar), 337
    segregation contributed to by, 282, 334, 335–336
    students as a form of property in, 336
    traditional schools compared to, 281, 282, 330, 332, 335, 458, 462, 463
Chat technology, 213, 321, 380
Cheating scandals. *See* School cheating scandals
Cheng, Yin Cheong, 406
Chicago Public Schools, 225
Chieppo, Charles, 111
Child abuse, 314, 365, 367, 368
Child deficit model, 95, 96, 98. *See also* Deficit model
Child development:
    and the brain, 82, 279, 353
    ecological systems theory on, 61–62
    See also Development
Child find mandate, 95, 98
Child neglect, 365, 367
Child poverty rate, 277. *See also* Poverty

Child-centered education, 362. *See also* Student-centered learning
Childrearing barriers to learning, 278–279. *See also* Parenting
Children of color, 175, 274, 280, 361, 362. *See also* Ethnicity; Race; Students of color
Children's rights, 365, 445. *See also* Privacy; Search and seizure court decisions; Speech/expression and case law
Chinn, Philip C., 335
Choice:
    defined as a key term, 466
    in incentivist policies, 457, 460, 463
    See also School choice
Chomsky, Noam, 333
Christensen, Clayton, 212
Christensen, John, 31
Christians in the homeschooling movement, 361, 362, 364, 365
Church and state, constitutional separation of, 280
Church groups, 76, 437. *See also* Communities
Circuit breaker, personal risk, and decision making, 32
Citizenship:
    charter schools and, 332
    diverse goals of, 16
    homeschooling and, 360, 361, 365, 367, 369
    neoliberalism and, 136
    schooling for, 4, 14, 280
    soft skills in, 84
    See also Democracy
City of Ontario, California v. Quon (2010), 226
Civil rights, 147, 219, 298, 299
Civil Rights Act, 179, 292, 294, 295, 314
Civil rights movement, 361
Civil society, and homeschooling, 368. *See also* Democracy
Clandinin, D. Jean, 67
Clark, Richard, 409
Class, social. *See* Social class
Class size:
    control, power, and, 78
    NEA for reduction in, 281
    student achievement and, 250
    and teachers as remediation sources, 394–395
    tension of values in decisions on, 242
    See also Student-teacher ratio
Classical test theory, 157, 158
Classroom climate, 145–146, 427
Classroom community, 64, 66, 144, 349. *See also* Communities
Classroom environment:
    alienating, 422
    effective teaching and, 55, 56, 57, 58, 67
    toxic, 145
    welcoming, 65–66
    See also Classroom management
Classroom management:
    class size, control, and power in, 78
    for culturally responsive teaching, 427
    democratic classroom community and, 144
    foundational elements of, 56–58
    importance of, 55–56
    rules in, 82
    scenarios on, 57, 58

whole classroom, whole child, and, 68
See also Classroom environment; Discipline, student
Classroom observation, 14, 26, 79, 80, 220–221, 411. *See also* Teachers, evaluation of
Cleveland Public School system, 390
Cleveland voucher program, 280, 281, 458, 462
Clifford, M., 393
Climate of fear, 188–189, 192 (sidebar)
Climate of performance and success. *See* Turnaround initiative in North Carolina
Clinton, Bill, 12
Closed inquiry, 146
Closed principals, 439, 442
Clune, William, 249
CMOs (charter management organizations), 329, 331
Coalitions and allies, 448, 451. *See also* School politics
Cobb, Casey, 476, 476 (sidebar), 481
Codes of ethics, 154–155, 321
Coefficients:
    alpha, 158, 160
    correlation, 159
    of equivalence, 159
    reliability, 157, 158, 159, 160, 161, 164
    of stability, 158, 159
    of stability and equivalence, 159
    validity, 164
Cognitive demand, 79, 82
Cognitive development, 58–59. *See also* Development; Metacognition
Cognitive developmental differences, 71, 82–83
Cognitive riches, and the Matthew Effect, 171
Coherent school improvement models, 9, 15
Coleman, James S., 250
Coleman, Peter, 405
Coleman Report, 250, 253, 276
Coley, Richard, 179
Collaboration:
    in adopting positive school conduct, 351, 352
    in advocacy, 125
    attention needed for, 354
    in best practices, 139, 141, 142, 143, 144, 147
    in budgeting, 260, 266, 270
    in collective responsibility for learning, 124
    community building and, 348–349
    for counseling services, 380
    culture of, fostered by leaders, 346
    cycles of, 124
    in positive work cultures, 402, 404, 405, 406, 408, 409
    school community built on, 344
    for school counseling, 377, 378, 379, 380
    school staff in, 376, 378
    among students, and best practices, 141, 142, 143, 144, 147
    among students, for student power, 442
    among students, in online learning, 213
    between students and teacher, 60
    among teachers (*see* Teacher collaboration)
    between teachers and principals, 376
    in a turnaround school initiative, 392

Collaborative practices, defined as a key term, 355
Collective bargaining:
    bargainable subjects in, 474–475, 475 (sidebar)
    conflict of interest assumed in, 477, 481
    the contract in, 472, 476, 477, 478–480
    as a creature of the law, 471
    future of, 481
    good faith bargaining, 478–479
    impact of, 473
    laws on, 474, 475 (sidebar), 477, 480, 481
    principles for coping in, 479
    restricted in the public sector, 472
    See also Teachers' unions
College and career readiness, 105, 106, 109, 369. *See also* Readiness
College and Career Readiness Standards, 106
College completion rates, 122, 126
College graduation and the achievement gap, 179
Colleges, HBCU (historically Black colleges and universities), 425, 425 (sidebar), 426
Colonial America, 11, 200, 361, 365
Colorado, 418
Columbine High School, 290, 317, 321
Common Core:
    common only to a select group, 113
    cultural factors and, 110, 111, 112–113
    curriculum alignment and, 115
    as a de facto national curriculum, 103
    flash points for, 109–114
    as one cultural lens among many, 115
    See also Common Core State Standards (CCSS); Common curriculum
Common Core of Data, 130, 131
Common Core standards, defined as a key term, 116
Common Core State Standards (CCSS):
    budgeting impact of, 258
    capacity building for, 108–109
    cultural factors and, 104
    debate over the rigor of, 111
    development of, 105–106
    for economies of scale, 218
    effective teaching strategies and, 59 (sidebar)
    high school redesign under, 204
    implementation materials for, 109
    online/blended learning and, 218
    and previous rounds of reform, 10
    primary rationale for, 106
    Race to the Top support for, 178
    supplementary materials for, 106–107
    tests linked to, 104, 258 (*see also* Standardized tests; State tests)
    See also Common curriculum
Common curriculum, 103, 104–105. *See also* Common Core; Common Core State Standards (CCSS)
Common school movement, 280, 361
Commonalities of leaders, 26. *See also* Accoutrements of leadership
Communal leadership, 22 (figure)
Communication:

in family partnerships and involvement, 63–65, 125, 126–128

family preferences for ways of, 127

global network for, 206

in online learning, 216

in positive work cultures, 407, 408–409, 410, 411

school politics and, 437, 439, 444, 447–448

two-way, 73, 80, 84, 126

Communication, electronic. *See* Blogs; Email; Instant messaging; Internet; Social media; Social media and case law; Texting

Communities:

    barriers to learning overcome by, 74, 75–76, 81–82

    barriers to learning set up by, 72 (sidebar)

    classroom community, 64, 66, 144, 349

    conduct, attendance, and discipline supported by, 355

    confidence of, in school budgeting, 259

    in decision making processes, 73

    in ecological system spheres of influence, 61–62

    engagement of, in Epstein's model, 73, 75, 83

    engagement of, to legitimize reform, 354

    expectations of, from NCLB, 258

    family involvement facilitated by, 126

    of Hispanic school populations, 125, 126–127, 128

    in network formation, 41, 42

    norms, values, fit, and, 42

    as a panoptic mechanism, 44

    school services and, 377 (figure)

    school staff links to, 443

    as school support systems, 348

    schools as part of, 81–82

    small, neighborhood schools in, 214

    visits to, by school personnel, 75–76

    volunteers from, 75, 84–85, 126

    See also Neighborhoods; School community

Community audit, 75, 76, 81–82

Community building, for school safety and stability, 347–349

Community centers, online/blended learning in, 214, 216, 218

Community engagement, 73, 75, 83, 354. *See also* Communities

Community of learners, 350

Comparability:

    defined as a key term, 253

    under Title I (ESEA), 246, 246 (sidebar), 253

Compelling state interest, 297, 303

Compensation, financial. *See* Salaries and benefits; Salary schedules; Teacher salaries; Wages

Competence:

    assessment competency gap, 180

    continuum of, 170, 170 (figure)

Competition:

    in budget decision making, 260, 442

    charter schools and, 281, 331, 458

    defined as a key term, 466

    Friedman (Milton) on, 331

    global, free market education as, 203

    incentives and, 457–458

    public school improvement and, 280, 331

    in school politics, 446, 447

Completion rates:

    college completion rate, 122, 126

high school completion rates, 130, 273–274

    See also Dropout rates

Comprehension, reading, 89, 93, 94, 98, 144. *See also* Reading

Compton, D. L., 96, 97

Compulsory attendance laws, defined as a key term, 370

Compulsory public education, 274–275, 365, 366–367

Compulsory school attendance:

    enacted across the U.S., 352

    exemption from, 364, 366–367

    See also Attendance

Computer labs, 213, 214, 215, 216, 217

Computer-based games, 199

Concept mapping, 144, 145

Concurrent validity, 163, 163 (figure), 164

Conditions:

    of performance, for tests and items, 114, 115

    of testing, 154, 155, 157–158, 159, 160, 164

Conduct, defined as a key term, 355. *See also* Student conduct

Confidence intervals, 161

Confidentiality, 76, 380. *See also* Privacy

Conflict, defined as a key term, 451

Conflict minimization, 438

Conflict of interest, in collective bargaining, 477, 481

Conflict resolution, 126, 324, 374, 477, 480

Connected text fluency, 89

Connelly, F. Michael, 67

Connick v. Myers (1983), 232–233

Consensus decision making, 269

Conservative Christian private schools, 281

Conservative Christians, 361, 362, 363

Consistency:

    in applying all rules, 296

    in attendance, 343, 344, 354–355 (*see also* Attendance)

    in classroom management, 57–58

    in communications to parents, 63

    in discipline programs, 77–78, 325

    internal, 159

    inter-user, 155

    of measurement, 157, 158 (*see also* Reliability)

    in test scores across time, 158

Constant or systematic error, 157, 165

Constitution, U.S. *See* U.S. Constitution

Constitutional rights:

    to due process (*see* Due process rights)

    and non-constitutional rights, 232

    searches and (*see* Search and seizure court decisions)

    to speech/expression (*see* Free speech)

    See also Separation of church and state; U.S. Constitution; U.S. Constitution amendments

Construct validity, 162–164, 163 (figure)

Construction and maintenance, revenue for, 245

Constructivist:

    defined as a key term, 68

    and progressive principles of best practices, 144

    Vygotsky (Lev) as, 58

Construct-related validity evidence, 162–163

Consultants, 12, 40

Consumption tax, 244, 253

Content-related validity, 163, 163 (figure), 164

Context:
  accoutrements and, 26
  of best practice studies, 31
  of best practices, 139, 140, 141, 142, 145
  of decision making, 33, 33 (figure)
  importance of, 3, 4, 5, 8, 13, 15, 16
  leadership agenda within, 26
  leadership practice and, 29–30
  in the management/leadership dyad, 22 (figure), 24
  and validity, for tests, 162
Contingency alternatives, in budgeting, 264
Continuous improvement, unrealistic expectations of, 29, 34
Contracts:
  under collective bargaining, 472, 476, 477, 478–480
  master, 405
Control:
  best practices as a mechanism of, 137
  over one's own education, 215, 337
  and power dynamics, 78
  in school politics, 435, 437, 438–439, 443, 447–448
  See also Power
Controlled access to schools, 319 (table), 321
Controlled substances in schools, 315. *See also* Drugs
Contructivist and developmental teaching, 144
Convergent validity, 162–163, 163 (figure)
Conversations, parent-child, 278–279. *See also* Discourse
Coons, John, 249
Cooper, B. S., 475
Cooperation, as a social skill, 375
Co-optation, for changing beliefs and behaviors, 449 (sidebar)
Core values in decision making, 32–33
Corporal punishment, 293, 314–315
Corporate takeover of schools, 332, 334. *See also* Privatization
Correlation coefficient, 159
Correspondence programs, 211, 364, 370. *See also* Distance
  learning
Corrigan-Halpern, P., 393
Corruption, culture of, 26
Cost-benefit analysis:
  in budgeting, 260, 261, 262, 263, 265–266
  defined as a key term, 271
Cost-to-effectiveness ratio, 217
Co-teaching, 220
Council of Chief State School Officers (CCSSO), 7, 105,
  106, 110
Counseling, school. *See* School counseling
Counterevidence, for undermining research, 461–463
Counternarratives, 423, 424, 426
Country of origin, 421, 445
Coursera, 206
Court decisions, lists of, 236, 305, 327, 372. *See also* Bullying
  and the law; Homeschooling; Search and seizure court
  decisions; Social media and case law; Speech/expression
  and case law; Supreme Court of the U.S.
Court services near schools, 76
Cover schools, 364, 370
Covey, Stephen, 30–31
Craigslist, 234
Cranston, Neil, 26, 27 (table)
Crawford, James, 123

Creationism, teaching of, 110
Creative intelligence, 143
Creativity:
  imaginativeness and, 27 (table)
  in the management/leadership dyad, 22 (figure), 23
  See also Imaginativeness; Innovation
Creshan v. Hart County Board of Education (1977), 311
Criminal background checks, 321
Criminal prosecutions, 191, 235
Crisis in education, as a myth, 273–274, 332
Crisis intervention, 380, 382–383
Criterion-referenced approach, 277
Criterion-related validity, 162, 163–164, 163 (figure)
Critical intelligence, 142–143
Critical race theory (CRT), 335–336, 337, 338
Cronbach, Lee, 156
Cronbach's alpha, 158, 160
CRT (critical race theory), 335–336, 337, 338
Cubberley, Ellwood, 240
Cultural adaptation, 420
Cultural arbitrary:
  Common Core as, 113, 115
  and the control of schooling, 334
  defined as a key term, 116, 338
  and the single curriculum, 104
Cultural brokers, school counselors as, 377
Cultural capital:
  achievement gap and, 112–113
  charter schools and, 334–335
  curriculum alignment and, 114, 115
  defined as a key term, 116, 338, 430
  definitions of, 420–421
  for engaging in books, 417–418
  for facilitating achievement, 420–421
Cultural competence, 181
Cultural difference theory, 420, 424
Cultural diversity, 75, 122, 296
Cultural factors, 74–76
  in achievement gaps, 112–113, 172, 174, 181
  for best practices, 139, 140, 141
  bullying, harassment, and, 296
  in choosing homeschooling, 361
  Common Core/CCSS and, 104, 110, 111, 112–113
  community, the network, and, 47 (sidebar)
  in content-related validity, 163
  in curricular outcomes, 105
  in curriculum alignment, 114, 115
  in curriculum content selection, 110, 111
  deculturalization, 336
  in democracy, 258
  differences confused with deficits, 420
  dominant culture, 334, 420, 422
  in ethical codes, 154
  family culture, 125, 127–128
  funds of knowledge in, 83
  in Hispanic population growth, 120, 122, 123, 124–129
  human culture as a construct, 104, 112
  in interactive learning, 58
  leadership practice and, 29–30
  no natural culture, 116

norms, authority, and, 25
oral culture, 128
organizational culture, 402, 405–406
and overcoming learning barriers, 71, 72 (sidebar)
professional culture, 346, 402, 404, 405, 406, 407
reading delay and, 88
response to intervention (RTI) and, 88, 92–93, 96, 97
rules, making adjustments, and, 11
school culture (*see* School culture)
shared culture, 405–406
subcultures, need to know intimately, 15
in virtual education, 201
work culture (*see* Work cultures, positive)
See also Context; Culture
Cultural leadership, 405, 405 (figure)
Cultural norms, 408, 411
Cultural resources, devaluing of, 422
Cultural sensitivity, 421–422, 430
Cultural tracking, 422. *See also* Tracking
Culturally responsive curriculum, 124, 427
Culturally responsive instruction, 427, 430
Culturally responsive teaching, 427, 430
Culture:
    of corruption, 26
    defined as a key term, 412
    of fear, 188–189
    of learning, 202, 330
    nature of, 402
    shared, 405–406
    word cluster diagram of, 402 (figure)
    See also Cultural factors
Culver, M., 31, 407
Curiosity, intellectual. *See* Intellectual curiosity
Curricular rigor, 111–112
Curriculum:
    boxed, 364, 370
    common, Bobbit's approach to, 104–105
    common, in Jefferson's Virginia, 103
    culturally responsive, 124, 427
    defined as a key term, 116
    determined by those in power, 333
    hidden, for future roles of students, 333–334
    multicultural, 329
    A Nation at Risk impact on, 173
    national, from a common set of standards, 103
    No Child Left Behind impact on, 175, 177
    outcomes specified in, 105–106
    and standards, distinction between, 106–107, 107 (table)
    values and cultural factors in content selection for, 110
Curriculum alignment, 114–115, 116
Curriculum flash points, for the Common Core, 110–114
Curriculum-based measurement (CBM), 89, 90, 91, 93, 98
Custodial factors, and divorce, 64 (sidebar), 76
Customer focus, 410
Cut points, 277. *See also* Cut scores; Cutoff scores
Cut scores, 176, 177, 182. *See also* Cut points; Cutoff scores
Cutbacks in budgets. *See* Budgeting
Cutoff scores, 113–114. *See also* Cut points; Cut scores
Cyber schools, 363, 364, 370. *See also* Digital schools; Virtual schools

Cyberbullying:
    as a barrier to learning, 71, 72 (sidebar)
    court decisions on, 294
    data on, 323, 324 (figure)
    defined as a key term, 83, 325
    definitions of, 290, 321, 322–323
    devastating impact of, 291, 323
    electronic media for, 290, 291
    escape from, difficulty of, 292
    and exploiting diversity as a deficit, 74
    gender and, 321, 323
    legislative responses to, 291–292, 323
    off campus, 290
    as passive aggression, 314
    as private speech, 291
    race and, 323
    seriousness of, 289, 290
    on social media, 71, 74, 83, 290, 291, 294, 314, 323
    social violence and, 314
    suicide by victims of, 291, 323
    See also Bullying; Bullying and the law
Cycle of inquiry, 143

Daily class schedules, 215. *See also* School day flexibility
Daniels, Harvey, 135, 137, 144, 146
DAP (developmentally appropriate practice), 351, 353, 355
Darling-Hammond, Linda, 139, 282
Data Accountability Center, 94
Data-driven decision making:
    in RTI programs, 90
    in school turnaround, 389, 392–398, 398 (table)
Davidson, Adam, 12
Davidson, F., 31, 407
Davidson, Frank, 402 (figure)
Davis, Michael J., 229
Davis v. Monroe County Board of Education (1999), 293, 295
Dawson, P., 390
DCPS (District of Columbia Public Schools), 187–188, 190, 191
D/discourse and d/discourse, 42
De facto segregation, 172, 182, 275
De jure segregation, 172, 182
Deaths. *See* Fatalities
Decision making:
    balance of factors in, 32–33
    consensus, 269
    data-driven, 90, 389, 392–398, 398 (table)
    defined as a key term, 83
    English and Bolton study of, 31–33
    in Epstein's model, 73, 75, 76, 77
    participatory, 260, 266, 270, 271 (*see also* Collaboration)
    responsible, 378
    in school politics, 436–437, 438–439, 444, 448, 450
    shared, 72 (sidebar), 375–376, 383
Decisions in case law. *See* Case law
Deculturalization, 336
Deductions, income tax, 243
Dee, T., 390
Deep student-centered learning, 350
Defense, U.S. Department of, 263

Defensible practices, 135, 136, 138, 141, 142, 147. *See also* Best practices
Deficit mindset, avoidance of, 112–113
Deficit model:
    child deficit model, 95, 96, 98
    defined as a key term, 83
    and diversity as deficit, 74, 82
    list of deficits in, 73
    under No Child Left Behind, 175
Deficit thinking, 74, 78, 83, 396
Definitions, theoretical and empirical, 156, 162, 165
Delgado, Richard, 335
Deliberate indifference standard, 293, 294, 295, 303
Deming, W. Edwards, 260
DeMitchell, Todd A., 476, 476 (sidebar), 481
Democracy:
    in the classroom community, 144
    and continuous remaking of social fabric, 105
    education as investment for, 12
    goals of, 16
    impact of homeschooling on, 359, 368, 369
    literacy and numeracy demanded in, 258
    relevance of Dewey (John) for, 14
    social hierarchy in conflict with, 113
    See also Citizenship
Demographic shifts for U.S. education:
    in enrollment, by racial/ethnic groups, 120–121, 418, 419
    in enrollment, by region, 419
    in population, by racial/ethnic groups, 119, 418
    in population, by region, 418, 418 (table)
    See also North Carolina, demographic shifts in
Denial, politics of, 447
Denton, Carolyn, 94
Dependability, 75, 83, 156
Derrida, Jacques, 41
Desegregation, racial. *See* Racial desegregation
DeShaney v. Winnebago County Dept. of Social Services (1998), 292, 295
Design, universal, 220
Deskilling and simplifying, by best practices, 137
Devaluation:
    of education, 424, 425
    of social and cultural resources, 422
Development:
    any person's, 71–73
    of the brain, 82, 279, 353
    cognitive, Piaget's theory of, 58–59
    cognitive developmental differences, 71, 82–83
    ecological systems theory on, 61–62
    of empathy in children, 349
    ethical, 352
    ever-expanding ecologies and, 71–73
    proximal, 60, 145
    of social skills, 375
    social-emotional, 71, 84, 378
    See also Learning barriers, overcoming
Developmental and contructivist teaching, 144
Developmental Reading Assessment (DRA), 89
Developmentally appropriate practice (DAP), 351, 353, 355
DeVon, Holli A., 162, 163

Dewey, Cynthia, 107 (table)
Dewey, John:
    on children, 15
    continued relevance of, 14
    on the control of individual actions, 354
    on creative intelligence, 143
    on habits of mind, 75, 83
    on learning from mistakes, 4
    on the need for education, 354
    on recalcitrant attitudes, 345
    on social interactions, 58, 59
Dexter, Douglas D., 94
DIBELS (Dynamic Indicators of Basic Early Literacy Skills), 89
Dichos (folk sayings), 128, 129 (sidebar)
Differentiated instruction:
    and barriers to learning, 72 (sidebar)
    driven by achievement data, 392 (sidebar), 393
    for educational productivity, 217
    for effective teaching, 60–61
    for gifted students, 375
    in RTI programs, 91
    in traditional versus online settings, 215
Diffusion theory, 200–201, 202
Digital contents of cell phones, searching of, 301
Digital divide, 138 (sidebar). *See also* Technology
Digital schools:
    brick-and-mortal schools and, 199, 200–203, 205, 206, 207
    and decentralization of learning, 200
    and disruptive trends, 203
    and the flatteners, 202–203
    infrastructure of global learning for, 200–201
    locus of learning in, 203–205
    MOOCs in, 202, 205–206
    for personalized learning, 205
    trend line for, 199–200
    for ubiquitous learning, 206–207
    See also Blended learning; Cyber schools; Online learning; Virtual schools
Digital-rich environment, 200
Dimmitt, C., 380
DiPietro, Michele, 144
Diplomat/negotiator, in school politics, 436, 437
Direct instruction, 59 (sidebar), 60, 61, 138 (sidebar), 141, 204, 279
Disabilities, students with. *See* Students with disabilities
Discipline, student:
    and bullying or harassment, 291, 295, 296, 323
    disproportionate rates among African Americans/Blacks, 82, 84, 142
    essential nature of, 343, 354
    methods for support of, 351–352
    monitoring of data on, 72 (sidebar), 77
    as an opportunity to teach, 351
    parent involvement and, 63
    police involved in, 316, 317
    reasons for being concerned about, 346
    rule and policy assessment based on, 77–78
    on school buses, 312–313
    in search and seizure court decisions, 298–299, 300
    self-, 343, 351–352, 353, 354

for speech/expression, case law on, 226–232
structuring the environment and, 56
teaching of, 345
in a turnaround school initiative, 391, 393, 394, 396,
    398 (table)
See also Attendance; Classroom management; Corporal
    punishment; School safety; Student conduct
Disciplined focus, 409. *See also* Purpose, sense of
Discipline-specific best practices, 146
Discourse:
    of accountability, 136, 147
    of best practices, 136, 142
    culturally responsive, 427
    D/discourse and d/discourse, 42
    defined as a key term, 147
    neoliberal, 136–137
    pedagogy as, 21, 34
    See also Counternarratives
Discrepancy formula, 88, 95, 96, 98
Discriminant validity, 162, 163, 163 (figure)
Discriminatory harassment or bullying, 293–295
Discussion boards, 213, 215
Disenfranchised groups, 179, 333, 335. *See also* Marginalized
    groups
Disputes, 438, 440 (table), 442. *See also* Arbitration; Grievances
Disruption of equilibrium, 449 (sidebar)
Disruption test, for speech/expression:
    for a district attorney as litigant, 233
    in drafting anti-bullying legislation, 291
    for students as litigants, 226, 227, 228, 229, 230, 231, 323
    for teachers as litigants, 232, 234
    See also Speech/expression and case law
Disruptive innovation, 200, 202, 211, 221
Distance:
    geographic, 206, 215, 278
    of homes from schools, 72 (sidebar), 75, 262
    physical, 199, 206, 207, 208, 278, 290
    psychological, 199, 207, 208
    social, 290
    transactional, 199, 206–207, 215
    virtual, 208
Distance learning, 211–212, 213, 214. *See also* Blended
    learning; Correspondence programs; Online learning
Distributive leadership, 24, 404
District of Columbia Public Schools (DCPS), 187–188, 190, 191
Diversity:
    and a common curriculum, 104
    cultural, 75, 122, 296
    cultural competence and, 181
    as deficit, 74
    intolerance for, and moral panic, 74
    linguistic, 92–93, 122, 307
    in needs, 88, 137, 270
    respect for, 81
    school safety and, 345
    in the school staff, 426
    single curriculum concept and, 104
    among teachers, 425–426
    underemphasized by ecological fallacies, 138
    See also Language

Division of labor, 6, 105
Divorced parents, 64 (sidebar), 76
Do no harm, first (*primum non nocere*), 141, 154, 180
Domestic pesticides, 279
Dominant and subordinate groups:
    counternarratives to the dominant group, 424
    education, subservience, and, 336
    marginalization and, 422
    norms and values of, 42
    parental involvement level and, 425
    in school culture, 419–420, 422
    social class and, 113
    and what is normal, 41, 49
    See also Hegemony; Privileged groups
Doninger, Avery, 228
Doninger v. Niehoff (2009, 2011), 228, 231
Doyle, Fred, 232
DRA (Developmental Reading Assessment), 89
Drake, Susan M., 60
Dreeben, Robert, 22
Dress codes, 229, 232, 320 (table), 442
Drivers of school buses, 308, 310, 311, 312–313
Dropout, defined as a key term, 130
Dropout rates, 122, 130, 131, 189, 379. *See also*
    Completion rates
Drug testing:
    data on, 319 (table), 321
    random, 301, 310, 311, 313
Drugs:
    abuse of, 227, 315
    in search and seizure court decisions, 296, 297, 299, 300,
        301, 304
Dual language education, 123, 444 (sidebar). *See also* Bilingual
    education
Duchnowski, A. J., 374
Duchnowski, Albert, 376
Due process rights:
    and the effects of bullying, 292–293
    of students, 228, 230
    of teachers, 473, 481
    See also Fourteenth Amendment (U.S. Constitution)
Dues, union, 471, 472, 474
Duke, D. L., 393
Duncan, Arne, 329, 334
Dyad, management/leadership, 22–25
Dykstra, Robert, 138
Dynamic Indicators of Basic Early Literacy Skills (DIBELS), 89
Dynamic management/leadership dyad, 22–25
Dyslexia, 95

Early childhood education, 275, 353, 421. *See also* Preschool
    programs
Early Childhood Longitudinal Survey of Kindergartners
    (ECLS-K), 179
Early exit bilingual education, 123. *See also* Bilingual
    education
Early-dismissal days, 408
Earnings. *See* Household income; Income gaps; Salaries and
    benefits; Salary schedules; Teacher salaries; Wages
Easton, J. Q., 390

ECLS-K (Early Childhood Longitudinal Survey of Kindergartners), 179
Ecological approaches. *See* Bioecological approach; Ecological systems theory; Social ecological perspective
Ecological fallacies, 138–139
Ecological systems theory, 61–62, 62 (figure), 68. *See also* Bioecological approach; Social ecological perspective
Economic confidence, 259, 259 (figure), 271
Economic factors:
    in achievement gap, 112–113, 171–172, 175, 179
    and curriculum content selection, 110
    "haves" and "have-nots" in America, 278
    in Internet access and online learning, 214, 216, 217–218
    as learning barriers, 72 (sidebar), 74
    and the myth of a suffering economy, 274
    scientific management and, 6
    See also Budgeting; School finance
Economic versus social values, 136
Economies of scale, 217–218
Education:
    of children as a financial investment, 12
    as an equalizer, 169, 276
    as an equalizer (revisionist interpretation), 336
    function of, 113
    as an industry, 104
    main purpose of, 191
    not a U.S. constitutional right, 308
    as a political endeavor, 40
Education, U.S. Department of, 221, 273, 281, 282, 329
Education Amendments Act of 1972, 292, 294–295, 314
Education Finance Statistics Center, 243
Education First (consulting firm), 390
Education Trust (organization), 377, 383
Education Week (newspaper), 489–490
Education welfarism, 362
Educational Administration Quarterly (journal), 490
Educational attainment data, 120
Educational crisis, as a myth, 273–274
Educational leadership. *See* Leadership
Educational Leadership (journal), 490
Educational Leadership Review, NCPEA (journal), 490
Educational opportunity. *See* Equal educational opportunity; Inequities
Educational productivity, 217–218
Educative versus miseducative experiences, 14
EEOC (Equal Employment Opportunity Commission), 447
Effective and successful, defined as key terms, 430
Effective leaders, characteristics of, 347, 409–410. *See also* Leadership
Effective teaching, 55–68
    classroom management and, 55–58
    for closing achievement gaps, 182
    components of, yearly changes in, 235
    family partnerships and, 61–66
    in Finland, 180
    for increasing cultural capital, 418
    inequitable distribution of, 181
    less, in higher needs schools, 252
    of minority students as high achievers, 427

no one right way of, 138
    in online courses, 220–221
    reflective teaching and, 66–67
    scenarios on, 55, 57, 58, 63, 64
    strategies for, 58–61, 82
    years of experience and, 251
Effectiveness:
    appropriateness versus, 141–142
    efficiency and, 6, 10, 260–261, 262
Effectiveness ratio (cost to effectiveness), 217
Efficiency:
    allocative, 241, 253
    defined as a key term, 253
    economic confidence and, 259
    effectiveness and, 6, 10, 260–261, 262
    social, 9, 10
    technical, 241, 254
    as a value in school finance, 241, 244, 247 (sidebar)
Egg crate school, 23
Ehren, B., 92
Ehrich, Lisa, 26, 27 (table)
Eisenhower, Dwight, 12
Eisner, Elliot, 4
eJournal of Education Policy, 490
El Paso Independent School District (EPISD), 188, 190, 191
Elasticity (or responsiveness) of taxes, 244, 245 (table), 253
E-learning days, 216
Elective classes, 403
Electricity consumption, as an economic indicator, 274
Electronic communication. *See* Blogs; Email; Instant messaging; Internet; Social media; Social media and case law; Texting
Electronic data and privacy, 375. *See also* Privacy
Elementary and Secondary Education Act (ESEA):
    Gun-Free Schools Act tied to, 315
    in the history of achievement gaps, 172
    impact of, 200
    NCLB as 2001 reauthorization of, 338
    school finance and, 242, 246
    Title I of (*see* Title I (ESEA))
    See also No Child Left Behind (NCLB) Act
Elementary schools:
    gender imbalance among teachers in, 182
    general student service trends in, 374 (figure), 375
    in North Carolina turnaround initiative, 390–398
ELLs. *See* English language learners (ELLs)
Elmore, Richard F., 404, 407, 408
Email:
    case law and, 227, 228
    cyberbullying in, 290, 323, 324 (figure)
    in online learning, 213
    in school counseling, 380
Emotional climate, of the classroom, 145
Emotional commitment, of students to each other, 350
Emotional disturbances. *See* Students with emotional disturbances
Emotional harm, as a form of school violence, 313
Emotional literacy, 349
Emotional safety, 307, 324
Emotional support, 409

Empathy, 290, 349

Empirical definitions, 156

Employee salaries. *See* Salaries and benefits; Salary schedules; Teacher salaries; Wages

Engineering, science integrated with, 146

England, 31–32, 321. *See also* Great Britain; United Kingdom

English, Fenwick W.:
 and Bolton, on decision-making practices, 31–33, 33 (figure)
 on critique, 3, 10
 on cultural capital, 334, 420
 on illusion in school reform, 5
 on management/leadership common elements, 22 (figure)
 and Papa, on accoutrements of leadership, 27 (table)
 and Papa, on commonalities of leaders, 26
 and Papa and others, on highly effective leaders, 407
 on scientific management, 3, 6, 11

English as a second language (ESL):
 bilingual education compared to, 123
 defined as a key term, 130
 ELLs and, 121, 383
 and language versus ability, confusion about, 426
 professional development in, 124
 response to intervention (RTI) and, 94
 See also Bilingual education; English language learners (ELLs); Second language

English immersion programs, 123, 131

English language arts:
 bridging home-forms and school-forms of, 74–75
 under CCSS, 59 (sidebar), 107, 109, 111, 218, 258
 micro-aggression in instruction on, 75
 for students with emotional disturbances, 374
 See also Reading

English language learners (ELLs):
 achievement gap and, 121
 in charter schools, 332, 336
 data on, 121
 defined as a key term, 130, 283, 383
 as high-cost students, 282
 language spoken at home and, 121
 and language versus ability, confusion about, 426
 program options for, 123
 response to intervention (RTI) for, 87, 92–93
 in small learning communities, 376
 See also Bilingual education; English as a second language (ESL); Second language

Enlightenment, the, 136

Enrollment data and projections, 120–121, 122, 266, 418, 419. *See also* Demographic shifts for U.S. education

Entrepreneurship, 401, 402, 412

EPISD (El Paso Independent School District), 188, 190, 191

Epistemologies of teachers, 424

Epstein, Joyce L.:
 and benefits of family involvement, 63
 and the family/community involvement model, 72–73, 75, 76, 77, 83, 84

Epstein, M. H., 374

Equal educational opportunity, 273, 274–275, 280. *See also* Achievement gap(s); Inequities

Equal Employment Opportunity Commission (EEOC), 447

Equal protection clause, 292, 303–304

Equalizing plans, 248

Equity:
 best practices and, 135, 136, 138 (sidebar), 139–140, 142
 in class size decisions, 242
 defined as a key term, 253
 family advocacy for, 125
 horizontal, 241, 253
 leadership in seeking, 27 (table)
 in participatory decision making, 260
 systemic, frameworks for, 180–181
 in the testing process, 155
 as a value in school finance, 241, 244, 246 (sidebar), 247, 247 (sidebar)
 vertical, 241, 247, 254
 See also Inequities

Equity audits, 180–181

Equity II, 241, 253

Equivalence and stability reliability, 159

Equivalency certificate, 122, 130

Equivalent forms reliability, 159

Eric M. v. Calon Valley Union School Dist. (2009), 308

Ernst, D. M., 162, 163

Errors:
 as important forms of learning, 79
 in the testing process, 155–156

Ervin, Ruth A., 88

Erwin, Jonathan C., 56

ESEA. *See* Elementary and Secondary Education Act (ESEA)

ESL. *See* English as a second language (ESL)

Essential life skills, 353

Esteem, as a psychological need, 406

Estimation of reliability, 157–160

Ethical codes, 154–155, 321. *See also* Ethics

Ethical development, 352

Ethical meeting of diverse needs, 137

Ethical responsibility, 156, 158

Ethical values, 129 (sidebar)

Ethically defensible practices, 136, 141, 142, 147. *See also* Best practices

Ethics:
 and arguments for choice, 463
 codes of, 154–155, 321
 defined as a key term, 165
 morals and, 154
 of responsibilities to children, 295–296, 303
 tests and (*see* Ethics of testing)
 See also Unethical practices

Ethics of testing:
 defined as a key term, 165
 principles of, 155
 reliability and, 154, 156, 157, 158, 164
 school cheating scandals and, 187
 validity and, 154, 164

Ethnic isolation, 282. *See also* Racial segregation

Ethnic slurs, correcting of, 126

Ethnicity:
 achievement gap and race/ethnicity, 112, 178–179, 189, 192–193, 275–279, 419

of administrators, 447
bullying based on, 294
and curriculum content selection, 110
data disaggregation by, 125
in the deficit model, 73
honoring differences in, 81
poverty rate by race/ethnicity, 120, 121, 277
verbal violence based on, 314
See also Demographic shifts for U.S. education; Minorities;
    Minority students
Ethnic/racial groups. *See* Racial/ethnic groups
Ethos, professional, 405
ETV (educational television), 211–212
Eurocentric education, 337–338
Evaluation of principals, 446–447
Evaluation of students. *See* Assessments; Test scores; Tests
Evaluation of teachers. *See* Teachers, evaluation of
Evans, Katherine, 230–231
Evans v. Bayer (2010), 230–231
Event dropout rate, 122, 130. *See also* Dropout rates
Evergreen Education Group, 212
Evidence:
    for incentivist policies (*see* Incentivist policies)
    for objectivity, 155
    for reliability, 156, 158
    in search and seizure, 297, 298, 300, 302
    for validity, 161, 162–164
Evidence-based instruction, 88, 96
Evidence-based intervention, 87, 88, 89, 90, 96, 98
Evidence-based pedagogical techniques, 374
Evidence-based practice:
    best practices and, 135, 136, 141–142, 147
    to support CCSS, 107
    See also Best practices
Evidence-based research, 459
Evidence-based student service trends, 375–376, 378
Evolution, teaching of, 110
Excellent practice, 135, 147. *See also* Best practices
Exclusionary rule, 297
Excused absences, 352
Executive role in school politics, 436, 437, 446
Executive-elite schools, 333
Exosystem, 61–62, 62 (figure)
Expectations:
    in budgeting, 257, 258, 259, 270
    in classroom management, 56–57, 58
    communication of, 63, 65
    general best practices and, 145
    high, as set by CCSS, 106
    high, communicated to students and families, 123–124
    high, difficulty in meeting, 204
    high, in a safe, inviting environment, 355
    high, in school turnaround, 389, 391–398, 398 (table)
    outlined by standards, 106, 116
    that all students can learn, 93
Expenditures. *See* Budgeting; School finance
Experiential learning, under best practices, 144
Experimental research design, 136, 137
Expert knowledge, 475

Expert power, 25, 442
Expertism, 12
Expression and speech rights. *See* Speech/expression and
    case law
Expulsion and suspension rates, 189
External analysis of construct validity evidence, 162

Fables, and follower relations, 24, 25
Face validity, 163, 163 (figure)
Facebook, 203, 225, 227–228, 229, 230, 232, 233, 235, 291,
    294, 323
Face-to-face instruction:
    and distance technology on snow days, 216
    included in blended learning, 213
    online compared to, 204–205, 214, 215, 217, 218, 219–221
    and wireless schooling, 199
Facilitative leadership, 404
Factory models of schooling, 23. *See also* Scientific management
Faculty. *See* Teachers
Failing schools:
    charter schools as possible solution to, 330, 333
    and the education debt, 179
    under NCLB, 176, 189, 280
    supposed, 332 (*see also* Myths)
Fair representation by teachers' unions, 480, 482
False positives, in RTI screening, 95, 97
Familial rights, 361. *See also* Children's rights; Parental rights,
    in homeschooling
Families:
    achievement gap and, 276, 277–280
    advocacy for, 124–126
    engagement of, to legitimize reform, 354
    in Epstein's model, 72–73
    funds of knowledge for, 83
    in Hispanic school populations, 123, 124–125, 126–129
    literacy and, 63, 64–65, 128, 278
    minority, checklist for working with, 425 (sidebar)
    in overcoming learning barriers, 72, 76, 80–81
    school counseling and, 380
    and student homework, 63, 73, 125, 126, 279, 425
    student services and, 374, 375, 376, 377 (figure)
    welcome and support for, 448
    See also Family partnerships; Home environment; Parents
Family advocacy committees, 125–126
Family culture, 125, 127–128
Family involvement, 126–128
    development and support of, 126–127
    dichos (sayings) for, 128, 129 (sidebar)
    and familiarity with school operations, 125
    for lowering learning barriers, 72–73
    planning for, 63–66
    See also Families; Family partnerships
Family partnerships:
    building of, 61–63
    planning for, 63–66
    in student-centered learning, 350
    See also Families; Family involvement
Family tree (Stammbaum), in network formation, 40–41
Family/parent meetings, 63, 66, 126

Family/parent newsletters, 63, 64 (figure), 65, 126, 128
FAPE (free appropriate public education), 295
Farkas, George, 171
Fatalities:
    in homeschooling families, 367
    in school bus transportation, 308, 310, 313
    in school violence, 313, 315 (*see also* School shootings)
    See also Murder and homicide
Fear:
    about traditional schools, 364
    climate of, 188–189, 192 (sidebar)
    in school cheating scandals, 187, 188–189, 190, 192, 192
        (sidebar)
Federal and state roles. *See* Government roles in education;
        States, U.S.
Federal funding:
    portion of all education funding from, 243
    Tenth Amendment constraints on, 242
    Title I for, 242, 246 (*see also* Title I (ESEA))
Federal income tax, 242, 243. *See also* Income taxes
Federal Motor Vehicle Safety Standards, 311
Federalist system, 242, 243, 253
Federalization of education policy, 174. *See also* Government
        roles in education
Feedback:
    in budgeting, 260, 262, 264, 266
    in CCSS development, 106
    in culturally responsive teaching, 427
    explicit, to support student conduct, 351
    in navigating a network, 43 (sidebar)
    from peers, for teachers, 79–80
    in positive work cultures, 408, 409
    prioritized and targeted, 145
Female/male ratio in some teaching areas, 182
Females:
    gendered roles for, 83
    inequities for, and rebirth of homeschooling, 361
    underrepresented in advanced science courses, 142
    See also Gender; Girls, rights of; Women
Ferguson, R., 421, 427
Fewless, Joseph, 298
Fewless v. Board of Education of Wayland Union Schools
        (2002), 298, 299
Fey, Patricia, 164
Field and habitus, in acquiring social capital, 421
Field-specific best practices, 146
Fighting, as a common form of violence, 314. *See also* Bullying;
        School violence
Finance, school. *See* School finance
Financial stewardship, 265
Finland, 180, 277
Finn, Chester, 111
First, do no harm (*primum non nocere*), 141, 154, 180
First Amendment (U.S. Constitution), 226, 227, 228, 229, 230,
        231, 233, 234, 235, 289, 303. *See also* Speech/expression
        and case law
First-year teachers. *See* New teachers
Fiscally dependent districts, 247–248, 253
Fiscally independent districts, 247

Fisher, Roger, 479
Fit (political construct):
    defined as a key term, 48
    in network formation, 40–42
    in network navigation, 44, 45, 47, 47 (sidebar)
Fixing approach, the, 73
Flagstaff Seminar: Educational Leaders Without Borders, 488
Flanagan, Dawn, 96
Flat grants, 247, 253
Flatteners, the, 202–203, 204
Fletcher, Jack, 93, 94
Flipped classroom, 213, 222
Flipped instruction, 138 (sidebar)
Florida:
    AFT/NEA merger in, 473
    discipline for off-campus harassment in, 291, 323
    Hispanic population in, 119, 120 (table), 121
    as a "new" Latino state, 418
    voucher program in, 280, 281
    zero tolerance reevaluated in, 317
Florida Virtual School, 212
Flouri, Eirini, 351
Focus, disciplined, 409. *See also* Purpose, sense of
Follower relations, in management/leadership dyad, 22 (figure),
        24–25
Foreign language courses, 214. *See also* Bilingual education
Foreign language law, 366
Formal and informal arenas, 438, 439
Formal and informal leaders, 402, 404, 412. *See also* Leadership
Formalization, and collective bargaining, 478
Formative assessments, 89, 98, 217, 392
Formative-reflective assessment, 144
Fortner, C. K., 391, 392, 393
Fortune, Rex, 410
Forumlas, funding, 218, 246, 247, 249, 257, 344
Foster, Bill, 450
Foster, William, 21
Foucault, Michel, 41, 42, 44, 49, 333
Foundation (funding mechanism), 247, 253
Fourteenth Amendment (U.S. Constitution), 228, 292–294, 366
Fourth Amendment (U.S. Constitution), 226, 290, 296–297, 298,
        301, 302, 303
France, 112, 274, 313
Frankenberg, Erica, 336
Fraser, Mathew, 226
Frederick, Joseph, 227
Free appropriate public education (FAPE), 295
Free market education, 203
Free speech:
    bullying and, 291, 303
    case law on, 226–228, 230–233, 235
    school politics and, 443 (sidebar)
    See also First Amendment (U.S. Constitution); Speech/
        expression and case law
Freeman, Alan, 335
French, John, 25
Frenkel, Edward, 111
Friedman, Milton, 280, 331
Friedman, Thomas, 202

Friedman Foundation, 464
Friend, M., 374
Friendship, 62 (figure), 375
Front stage behavior, 44, 45, 45 (figure), 47 (sidebar)
Frontloading, 115, 116
Fuchs, Douglas, 90, 96, 97
Fuchs, L. S., 96, 97
Fuchs, Lynn, 87
Fuchs, Lynn S., 90, 96
Fulfillment, sense of, 406
Fullan, Michael, 8, 406, 408
Fuller, Howard, 281
Functionalist paradigm, 21
Fund distribution:
    for charter schools and vouchers, 249
    federal role in, 246 (*see also* Title I (ESEA))
    funding formulas for, 218, 246, 247, 249, 257, 344
    mechanisms for, 247–249
    state role in, 247–249
    See also Budgeting; Revenue generation; School finance
Fundamental Christians, 362. *See also* Christians in the
    homeschooling movement
Funding for education. *See* Allocation of resources; Budgeting;
    Fund distribution; Funding formulas; Revenue generation;
    School finance
Funding formulas, 218, 246, 247, 249, 257, 344
Funds of knowledge:
    community audit of, 81
    deficit model and, 83
    defined as a key term, 83
    dichos (sayings) as, 129 (sidebar)
    of distinctive communities, 73
    learning and, 78, 80, 84
    schools removed from, 74
    as a social-cultural influence, 71
Futurity, visioning of, 26, 27 (table)

Gabbard, David, 332
Gable, Robert, 158
Galinsky, Ellen, 353
Gallup Poll, 264
Game theory, 32, 34
Game-based learning, 204, 205
GAMEing (Getting the Attention of Movers Early), 43
    (sidebar), 48
Games, computer-based, 199
Gaming, harassment while, 324 (figure)
Gándara, P., 421
Gangs, 302, 442
Gaps:
    achievement (*see* Achievement gap(s))
    assessment competency, 180
    defined as a key term, 182
    between "haves" and "have-nots," 276, 278
    income, 179, 182, 278
    opportunity, 140, 142, 179, 180
    understanding, 206–207
Garber, Barry L., 231
Garcetti, Gil, 233

Garcetti v. Ceballos (2006), 231, 233
Garcia, Juanita, 180
Garcia, Lorenzo, 187, 188, 190, 191
Garcia, P., 393
Garcia, Shernaz B., 92, 93
Gardner, Howard, 24
Garner, Mary, 164
GASing (Getting the Attention of a Superior), 43 (sidebar), 48
Gass, Jamie, 111
Gates Foundation, 103, 334, 464, 465
Gay, G., 427
Gay, Lorraine R., 156, 157, 159, 160, 163
Gay principals, 41. *See also* Sexual orientation
Gay students, 42, 293, 450. *See also* Sexual orientation
G.C. v. Owensboro Public Schools (2013), 302
GDP (gross domestic product), 274, 275, 283
G.D.S. v. Northport-East Northport Union Free School District
    (2012), 294
GED (General Educational Development) certificate, 122, 130
Gee, James Paul, 42, 49
Gender:
    achievement gap and, 182
    of administrators, 447
    bullying and, 294–295, 321–322, 322 (figure), 323
    and curriculum design for current jobs, 105
    honoring differences in, 81
    imbalanced, in some teaching areas, 182
    power and, 83
    as a protected classification, 293
    verbal violence based on, 314
    See also Females; Males; Sexual harassment
Gender socialization, 74
Gendered roles, 71, 83. *See also* Sexual identity
General best practices, 144
General Educational Development (GED) certificate, 122, 130
General Spearman-Brown prophecy formula, 159–160
General student services:
    data and privacy in, 373–375
    elementary school trends in, 375
    secondary school trends in, 375–377
    special education and, 373–375, 376
    systems perspective of, 377 (figure)
    taking action in, 381–382 (vignette), 381 (sidebar), 382
        (sidebar)
    See also School counseling; Special education
Geographic distance, 206, 215, 278
Georgia:
    Atlanta cheating scandal in, 186–187, 188–189, 190, 191
    as a "new" Latino state, 418
    per-pupil weights and funding in, 247, 248 (table)
Gerard, M. R., 64 (sidebar)
Germany, 112, 274
Gerstl-Pepin, C, 446 (sidebar)
Getting the Attention of a Superior (GASing), 43 (sidebar), 48
Getting the Attention of Movers Early (GAMEing), 43
    (sidebar), 48
G.I. Bill, 172
Gifted students, 171, 374–375
Gintis, Herbert, 333

Girls, rights of, 445. *See also* Females
Giroux, Henry, 21, 334
Glasgow, Neal A., 140
Glass, Gene, 104
Glickman, Carl, 348
Glines, Marissa, 299
Global communication network, 206
Global educational system:
    the flatteners and, 202–203
    infrastructure of, 200–201
    locus of learning in, 203–205
    MOOCs in, 205–206
    See also Digital schools
Global forces, on school politics, 445
Global learning, 200–201, 205–206. *See also* Digital schools
Goal displacement, 4, 10, 16
Goffman, E., 44, 45
Gold standards:
    experimental research design as, 136
    randomization as, 470
    standardized tests as, 174
    teaching effectiveness in Finland as, 180
Goldenberg, Jacob, 27, 28
Goleman, Daniel, 349
Gollnick, Donna M., 335
Good faith bargaining, 474, 478–479, 479 (sidebar), 482
Good practice, 135, 147. *See also* Best practices
The Good Shepherd (film), 40
Goodman, S. D., 88
Google, 7, 128, 203
Gordon, Mary, 349
Government employment. *See* Public employees
Government roles in education:
    in the Common Core, 110–111
    in federalization of education policy, 174
    homeschooling as a reaction to, 361, 362, 365, 368
    A Nation at Risk and, 172–174
    school politics and, 445
    in the states (*see* States, U.S.)
    vis-à-vis the private sector, 455 (*see also* Incentivist policies)
Government roles through federal legislation. *See* Americans with Disabilities Act (ADA); Education Amendments Act of 1972; Elementary and Secondary Education Act (ESEA); Individuals with Disabilities Education Act (IDEA); Individuals with Disabilities Education Improvement Act (IDEIA); No Child Left Behind (NCLB) Act; Race to the Top (RTT); Rehabilitation Act
Grade point average, 164, 173
Graded school, creation of (1848), 23
Graduate Record Exam (GRE), 273
Graduation rates:
    compulsory school attendance and, 352–353
    credit recovery and, 216
    improvement in, 273
    as an NCLB indicator, 176
    race/ethnicity and, 189, 419
Gramsci, Antonio, 332, 334
Grandparents, 279
Grassroots leaders, 24

Gray, L. H., 175
Graying and browning of America, 418. *See also* Demographic shifts for U.S. education
GRE (Graduate Record Exam), 273
Great Britain, 112. *See also* England; United Kingdom
Great teachers, 55, 67–68. *See also* Effective teaching
Greene, J., 390
Greenlee, Bobbie J., 410
Greenwood, C., 92, 94
Grievances:
    defined as a key term, 482
    under a union contract, 473, 478, 479–480
Griffiths, Dan, 43
Grigg, Wendy, 281, 282
Griswold v. Connecticut (1965), 297
Gross domestic product (GDP), 274, 275, 283
Group counseling, 379–380
Group dynamics, 40, 44, 49, 71. *See also* Networks (of people)
Grouping of students. *See* Ability grouping; Academic stratification; Tracking
Groups, dominant. *See* Dominant and subordinate groups
Guenther, W., 390
Guggenheim, Davis, 330
Guidance counselors, 374, 377. *See also* School counseling
Guided inquiry, 146
Gun-Free Schools Act, 315
Guns. *See* Weapons
Guskey, Thomas, 169
Guthrie, James, 173

Habit changing, 80–81
Habits of mind, 75, 79, 83
Habitus and field, in acquiring social capital, 421
Haertel, Edward, 164
Hakuta, Kenji, 92
Hall, Beverly, 186–187, 188–189, 190
Hallinger, Philip, 405, 409
Hamilton, Alexander, 11
Hamilton, Clyde H., 316
Hamilton, Leah, 204
Hammons, Sherman Lee, 235
Hammons v. State (2010), 235
Hampel, Robert, 409
Harassment:
    discriminatory, 294, 295
    electronic, 291
    gaming and, 324 (figure)
    guidelines for prevention of, 296
    messaging for, 324 (figure)
    off-campus, 291, 323
    protected classes in court decisions on, 293
    racial, 294
    retaliation for, 290
    sexual, 293, 295, 315
    of students with disabilities, 295
    See also Bullying; Bullying and the law
Hargreaves, David, 354
Harlacher, Jason, 88
Harris, Douglas, 171, 173, 174

Harris, Eric, 317
Harris, M., 156, 157, 161
Harvard Negotiation Project, 479
Harvill, Leo, 157
Hate website, 228
"Haves" and "have-nots," 276, 278. *See also* Economic factors
Hawaii, 243
Hawley, Nikki, 110
Hayden, S. J., 162, 163
Hazelwood School District v. Kuhlmeier (1988), 226, 227
HBCUs (historically Black colleges and universities), 425, 425 (sidebar), 426
Head Start program, 172, 179, 200
Hegemony, 41, 48, 49, 332, 334, 338
Helplessness, feeling of, 112, 290, 396
Henderson, Anne T., 63
Henry, G. T., 391, 392, 393
Henson, Kenneth T., 351, 352
Herman, R., 390
Herrera v. Santa Fe Public Schools (2013), 300
Herrington, Carolyn, 171, 173, 174
Heuristics (rules of thumb), 30, 31–33, 241
Hibel, Jacob, 171
Hicks, Cathy D., 140
Hicks, Larry R., 229
Hierarchy:
    and the career ladder, 446–447
    defined as a key term, 451
    of leadership forces, 405, 405 (figure)
    political dynamics and, 445
    power-over style and, 448
    in roles, 22 (figure), 23
High schools:
    completion rates for, 130, 273–274
    credit recovery in, 216–217
    daily class schedules in, 215
    dropouts from (*see* Dropout rates)
    graduation from, and the achievement gap, 179
    graduation rates of, 176, 273
    in North Carolina turnaround initiative, 390, 391
    online learning in, 212, 213, 215, 216–217
    redesign of, 204
    response to intervention (RTI) in, 93–94
    See also Secondary schools
High-cost students, definition of, 282
Higher education:
    free MOOC courses in, 215
    graduation, achievement gap, and, 179
    in HBCUs, 425, 425 (sidebar), 426
    K-12 systems partnered with, 6
    See also College and career readiness; College completion rates
High-stakes testing:
    accountability and, 173, 174–177, 178, 180, 332–333, 403, 445
    as a cause of cheating, 189
    defined as a key term, 338
    school readiness and, 275
    school-year timing for, 216
    statistical reliability and, 161
    See also Tests
Hilliard, A., 420, 424
Hispanic ethnic category, 130
Hispanic students:
    in the achievement gap, 173, 278
    and childrearing learning barriers, 278
    cyberbullying of, 323
    in lower tracks, 275
    practices that meet the needs of, 410
    underrepesented in AP and honors courses, 84
    See also Latino students
Hispanic U.S. population growth, 119–133
    advocacy for families in, 124–126
    challenges and solutions in, 120–128
    culture and, 120, 122, 123, 124–129
    demographics of, 120 (table), 121, 418, 419, 423
    dropout rates, completion rates, and, 122
    enrollment projections under, 120–121
    family involvement and, 126–128
    high-quality instruction and, 123–124
    language and, 120–129
    poverty and, 120, 121, 123–126
    See also Demographic shifts for U.S. education; Latino students; Latinos
Hispanic-serving institutions (HSIs), 425, 426
Historically Black colleges and universities (HBCUs), 425, 425 (sidebar), 426
Hodges, Rita A., 348
Holistic counseling programs, 377
Holistic learning, 144
Home educators:
    characteristics of, 362
    defined as a key term, 370
    roles of, 363, 364, 367, 369
    See also Homeschooling
Home environment:
    achievement gap and, 112
    curriculum alignment and, 114, 115
    family partnerships and, 61, 63, 64–65, 66
    for flipped instruction, 138 (sidebar)
    for Hispanic school population, 120, 121, 126, 127–128
    Internet and online-learning access in, 214, 216
    language spoken in, 120, 121, 126, 127–128
    school environment bridged to, 74–75, 76
    support learning in, 73, 84
    See also Families; Family involvement; Family partnerships; Homework; Parents
Home language, 120, 121, 126, 127–128
Home location, distance of schools from, 72 (sidebar), 75, 262
Home School Legal Defense Association (HSLDA), 362, 363
Home visits, 76, 127, 373
Homeschooling, 359–370
    arguments against, 359, 365, 367–369
    arguments for, 359, 365, 366–367
    court decisions on, 366–367
    data on, 360, 360 (table), 361, 367, 370
    defined as a key term, 370
    funding for, 363

history of, 359, 361–362, 365

legal issues in, 362, 363–364, 365–369

as a mainstream movement, 362, 364

options for, 212, 362–365

parental rights and, 359, 361, 365–367, 369

reasons for choosing, 359, 360, 362, 364, 365

religion and, 360, 361, 362, 364, 365, 366–367

as a social movement, 361, 368, 369

traditional schools compared to, 368–369

Homeschooling's Invisible Children, 368

Homework:

families and, 63, 73, 125, 126, 279, 425

flipped classroom and, 213, 222

volunteers to help with, 75, 85

See also Home environment

Homicide and murder, 313, 314, 367

Honors courses, 84. *See also* Advanced placement (AP) courses

Hord, Shirley M., 143

Horizontal equity, 241, 253

Horn, M. B., 212

Household income, 120

Hoxby, Caroline, 462, 463

Hoy, Wayne K., 410

HSIs (Hispanic-serving institutions), 425, 426

HSLDA (Home School Legal Defense Association), 362, 363

Hubbard, Glenn, 12

Huerta, Dolores, 110

Hughes, Charles, 94

Human agency, development of, 26, 27 (table), 28 (sidebar)

Human capitalist ideology, 333

Human leadership, 405, 405 (figure)

Human rights, 147. *See also* Social justice

Humor, and classroom management, 56

Hunger, 279

Hunt, James B., 105

Hunt Institute, 105

Hurricane Katrina, 330

Hybrid learning, 199, 205, 213. *See also* Blended learning

Hyde, Arthur, 135, 137, 144, 146

Iceland, 277

ID badges, 319 (table), 321

IDEA. *See* Individuals with Disabilities Education Act (IDEA)

IDEIA. *See* Individuals with Disabilities Education Improvement Act (IDEIA)

Identity:

in competing for followers, 24

in the essence of leadership, 26

fit, network formation, and, 41, 42

linguistic, 127–128

multiple identities, 41

school, 447

sexual, 73, 74, 81, 83

student, 442

Ideology, 21, 33–34, 62

Iliescu, D., 156, 157, 161

Illinois, 119, 120 (table), 418

Imaginativeness, 26–27, 27 (table), 28 (sidebar). *See also* Creativity; Innovation

Immigration:

cultural opportunities and, 444–445

data on, 104

family culture and, 127

in the industrial era, 361

language and, 74

the undocumented as targets in, 421–422

U.S. demographic shifts and, 418

Immorality, 12, 234. *See also* Moral issues

Impasse, 475 (sidebar), 479, 482

In re O'Brien (2013), 233–234

iNACOL (International Association for K-12 Online Learning), 216, 218, 219 (sidebar)

Incapacities, trained, 4, 16

Incarceration of youth, increases in, 316

Incentivism, 457, 458, 460, 466. *See also* Incentivist policies

Incentivist policies:

advocacy strategy for, 460–463

counterevidence production for, 461–463

empirical evidence on, 458–459

in the marketplace of ideas, 465–466

terminology for discussion of, 456–457

theoretical understanding of, 463–465

See also Charter schools; Merit pay; Open-enrollment programs; Pay for performance; Tax credits; Voucher programs

Income. *See* Household income; Income gaps; Salaries and benefits; Salary schedules; Teacher salaries; Wages

Income gaps, 179, 182, 278

Income taxes:

characteristics of, 243, 245 (table)

consumption tax and, 244

deductions for, 243

defined as a key term, 253

marginal tax rates for, 243 (table)

Incremental budgeting, 263–264

defined as a key term, 271

example of, 264 (table)

NCES characteristics of, 265 (table)

Indecent or lewd speech, 226, 227, 230

Independent study programs, 363

Indiana, 111, 472, 475 (sidebar)

Indifference, deliberate, 293, 294, 295, 303

Indirect mechanisms, and testing, 164

Indirect violence, 314

Individualized education program, 294

Individualized learning, 203–205, 364

Individuals with Disabilities Education Act (IDEA):

in bullying court decisions, 292, 294, 295

general student services and, 373

online learning and, 219, 220

as a shaper of American education, 200

Individuals with Disabilities Education Improvement Act (IDEIA):

defined as a key term, 98

RTI and, 87–88, 92, 94–95, 96

special education student services and, 373

Industrial labor model, 477–478, 481

Inequities:
  in acquiring social capital, 421
  in advanced placement class representation, 84
  in advanced science course representation, 142, 449
  in discipline referrals, 82, 84, 242
  in distribution of power, access, and rewards, 445–446
  in education, as motivation for homeschooling, 361
  for females, 142, 361
  in Internet and online access, 214, 216, 219
  for males, 82, 84, 142
  for minorities and children in poverty, 273, 280
  perpetuated by those in power, 333
  in per-pupil spending, 275
  in preschool education access, 275, 421
  social, root cause of, 337
  in special education placement, 84, 88, 181
  in taxes, 244, 258
  in teacher salaries, 275
  in tracking, 275
  for the underserved (*see* Underserved, the)
  See also Achievement gap(s); Equity
Informal and formal arenas, 438, 439
Informal and formal leaders, 402, 404, 412. *See also* Leadership
Informants, tips from, and search and seizure, 298
Information asymmetries, 465
Information sharing, 7
Informed skepticism, 181
In-forming, 203
Ingham, Harry, 44, 45 (figure), 49
Inkelas, Moira, 355
Inner locus of control, 349, 351. *See also* Self-discipline
Inner-city blight, 179
Innovation:
  best practices and, 137, 138 (sidebar)
  diffusion theory on, 200–201, 202
  disruptive, 200, 202, 211, 221
  in engaging students to learn, 199
  in finding a problem for a solution, 28
  the flatteners and, 202
  learning from, 15
  limited by state purpose and object codes, 250
  as a priority of Race to the Top, 177
  problem solving for, 403
  risk and, 5
  See also Creativity; Imaginativeness
Inquiry labs, 146
Inquiry-based learning, 142, 144
Insensitivity, benign, 75
Inside the box, thinking, 23, 27–28
Inside-out and outside-in accountability, 404
Insourcing, 203
Instant messaging, 228–229, 302, 323, 324 (figure). *See also* Texting
Instruction, quality of. *See* Effective teaching
Instructional leadership, 404–405, 412
Instructional supplies, expenditures for, 241 (figure)
Instructional time, 55, 173, 352, 397. *See also* School calendar; School day flexibility
InTASC (Interstate Teacher Assessment Support Consortium) standards, 59, 66, 67

Integrated curriculum, 60
Integrated professional cultures, 407
Integrative (trans-disciplinary) units, 144
Intellectual capital, 202, 203
Intellectual curiosity, 26, 27 (table), 28 (sidebar)
Intellectual safety, 324
Interactive learning, 58–59, 59 (sidebar), 60, 144
Interest arbitration, 480
Interest convergence, 335–336, 337, 338
Intergenerational mobility, 169
Intermediary organizations (IOs), 464, 464 (sidebar), 466
Internal analysis of construct validity evidence, 162
Internal consistency reliability, 159–160
International achievement gaps, 112, 179–180
International Association for K-12 Online Learning (iNACOL), 216, 218, 219 (sidebar)
International Principal Centers, 11
International Reading Association, 89
International Test Commission, 154
International test score comparisons, 111
Internet:
  access to, for homeschoolers, 368
  access to, inequities in, 214, 216
  awareness of learning strategies for, 79
  brevity of messages on, 24
  browsers for, 201, 202, 203
  in the digital school, 199, 201, 204, 206
  electronic language translators on, 128
  the flatteners and, 202, 203
  global learning environment of, 204
  homeschoolers and, 368
  social media on (*see* Social media; Social media and case law)
  See also Online learning
Internet-based educational system, 200
Internships, 446 (sidebar)
Interobserver reliability, 160
Interpersonal communication skills, 408, 442
Interpretations of test results, 155, 156, 159, 160, 161, 164. *See also* Judgments based on test results
Interpreters, language, 128
Interrater reliability, 160
Interscorer reliability, 160
Interstate School Leaders Licensure Consortium (ISLLC), 7, 8, 9–10, 16
Interstate Teacher Assessment Support Consortium (InTASC) standards, 59, 66, 67
Inter-user consistency, 155
Intervention, response to. *See* Response to intervention (RTI)
Intimate partner violence, 377. *See also* Spousal abuse
Intimidation, in school cheating scandals, 189, 190
Investment, education as, 12
Invisible omniscience, sentiment of, 44, 49
Involvement of families. *See* Family involvement; Family partnerships; Parents
IOs (intermediary organizations), 464, 464 (sidebar), 466
Iowa, 300
IQ measures, 88, 96
ISLLC (Interstate School Leaders Licensure Consortium), 7, 8, 9–10, 16

Ispas, D., 156, 157, 161
Italy, 274, 350
Items (on tests), types and quality of, 160
Itinerant teachers, 214, 215

Jackson, Jesse, 315
Jacobson, Reuben, 348
Jaffe, Barbara, 235
Japan, 112, 274
Jay, John, 11
J.C. v. Beverly Hills Unified School District (2010), 231
Jefferson, Thomas, 103, 200, 369
Jencks, Christopher, 276
Jenkins, Frank, 281, 282
Jenlink, P., 9 (table)
Jennings, Jack, 176
Jewish student, bullying of, 294
Johari Window, 44–46, 45 (figure), 47 (sidebar), 49
Johnson, C. W., 212
Johnson, Lyndon B., 172
Johnson, Spencer, 31
Johnson, Susan Moore, 407
Jones, R., 65
Journals (for teacher reflection), 66, 67
Journals (professional), 489–490
Journey or quest, leadership as, 26, 27 (table)
J.S. ex rel v. Bethlehem Area School District (2002), 226
J.S. v. Blue Mountain School District (2011), 229–230
Judgments based on test results, 79, 153, 155, 156, 161. *See also*
    Interpretations of test results
Justice:
    family advocacy for, 125
    racial justice, 335, 338
    social (*see* Social justice)
J.W. v. DeSoto County School District (2010), 302

K¹² International Academy, 364, 370
Kadmas v. Dickinson Public Schools (1988), 308
Kame'enui, Edward J., 95
Kamenetz, Anya, 205
Kamps, Debra, 92, 94
Kansas, 257–258, 258 (figure)
Kappan (journal), 489
Kardos, Susan, 407
Kasich, John, 481
Katrina (hurricane), 330
Kauffman, David, 407
Kena, G., 122
Kennedy, Anthony, 226
Kennedy, John F., 169
Kentucky, 119, 121, 212
Kerchner, C. T., 477
KewalRamani, A., 122
Khan Academy, 215
Kincheloe, J., 332, 420
Kincheloe, J. L., 143
Kindergarten rule, 241
Kitsch management books, 30, 31, 33, 34
Kleinfeld, Judith, 79

Kliebard, H., 9
Klinger, J. K., 93
Kluck, M. L., 155
Klump v. Nazareth Area School District (2006), 302, 303
Knowing, multiple frames of, 27 (table)
Knowledge:
    access to, 203, 208
    actionable, 154
    banking of, 353
    expert, 475
    from external authorities, 14
    influence based on, 25
    information and, 154
    internalization of, 58
    organization of, 144–145
    power and, 12
    prior knowledge, 66–67, 140, 144, 417, 427
    of results, in budgeting, 260
    rich, in the craft of school people, 12
    right knowledge, 110
    scientific, 136
    self-, 155, 337
    values important to, 205
    whose, 333, 337
Knowledge linking, 203
Known unknowns, 4, 15
Koehler, Matthew J., 201
Kohn, Alfie, 56, 350, 352
Koller, Daphne, 206
Koppich, J. E., 477
Koret Task Force on K-12 Education, 464
Kostas-Polston, E., 162, 163
Kotter, John, 344, 347
Kowalski, Kara, 228
Kowalski v. Berkeley County Schools (2011), 228
Kozol, Jonathan, 275
KR-20 (Kuder-Richardson 20), 160
Krashen, Stephen, 123
Kristapovich, P., 122
Kuder-Richardson 20 (KR-20), 160
Kuhn, Thomas, 202, 206
Kutash, K., 374
Kutash, Krista, 376

Labor unions. *See* Collective bargaining; Teachers' unions;
    Unions
Ladson-Billings, Gloria, 79, 179, 335
Lampedusa, Frank, 234
Lancastrian model of schooling, 23
Land, Anna, 234
Land Ordinance of 1785, 365
Land v. L'Anse Creuse Public School Board of Education
    (2010), 234
Language:
    ability versus, confusion about, 426
    achievement gap and, 112, 121
    and analysis of student failure, 78
    bilingual education, 93, 121, 123, 124
    in the deficit model, 73

Hispanic population growth and, 120–129
honoring differences in, 81
literacy and vocabulary as, 79
and overcoming learning barriers, 72 (sidebar), 74–75
reading delay and, 88
in RTI programs, 88, 89, 91–93, 94, 95
spoken at home, 120, 121, 126, 127–128
submersion in, 123, 131
translators and interpreters for, 74, 128
See also English as a second language (ESL); English
    language learners (ELLs); Language minority children;
    Reading; Second language
Language acquisition, 93, 95, 124, 126, 426
Language minority children, 120, 121, 123–124, 126, 129. *See
    also* Hispanic U.S. population growth; Language
LaRocque, Linda, 405
Lash, D., 390
Late exit bilingual education, 123. *See also* Bilingual education
Latino students:
    achievement gap and, 275, 276, 278, 419
    bicultural backgrounds of many, 421
    in charter schools, 335, 336
    childhood poverty and, 277
    in demographic shifts, 120 (table), 121, 418, 419
    graduation rates of, 419
    and health-related learning barriers, 279
    and the right to be educated, 423
    in so-called failing schools, 333
    strategies in effective education for, 423–427
    See also Hispanic students; Latino underachievement
Latino underachievement:
    and cultural capital for achievement, 419–421
    factors that contribute to, 421–422
    and social capital for achievement, 421
Latinos:
    to be the U.S. majority group, 418
    classification of, 130
    described by country of origin, 421
    as a heterogeneous group, 421
    poverty rate for, 277
    states most prominent for, 120 (table), 121, 418, 419
    See also Hispanic U.S. population growth
Law cases. *See* Bullying and the law; Court decisions, lists of;
    Search and seizure court decisions; Social media and case
    law; Speech/expression and case law; Supreme Court of the
    U.S.
Law enforcement personnel. *See* Police officers; School resource
    officers (SROs)
Lawrence Public Schools, 257–258, 258 (figure)
Layshock, Justin, 230
Layshock v. Hermitage School District (2011), 230
Lazzara, D. J., 162, 163
Leadership:
    accoutrements of, 25–28, 27 (table), 33
    for all situations and all people, 14
    artful, 13, 26–27, 27 (table), 28 (sidebar), 33
    authority and, 22 (figure), 25
    big "L" and little "l" of, 13–15
    caring, 437

in closing the achievement gap, 180–182
commonalities in, 26
creativity and, 22 (figure), 23
cultural, 405, 405 (figure)
distributive, 24, 404
in the doing, 13
effective, characteristics of, 347, 409–410
essence of, 26
every action of daily life included in, 47
facilitative, 404
false dichotomy with management, 22
first lesson of, 26
follower relations in, 22 (figure), 24–25
formal and informal, 402, 404, 412
hierarchy of forces in, 405, 405 (figure)
human, 405, 405 (figure)
instructional, 404–405, 412
legitimacy, power, and, 25
in the management/leadership dyad, 22–25, 22 (figure)
moral factors and, 3, 9, 26, 405, 406
networks and (*see* Networks (of people))
not confined or defined by an organization, 23
participatory, 376
in physical and conceptual spaces, 21
for positive work cultures, 401–411
power/sanctions in, 22 (figure), 25
as a quest or journey, 26, 27 (table)
role legitimacy in, 22 (figure), 24
school politics and, 435–451
shared, 404, 405
six elements of, 406
in solutions to school cheating, 191–192, 192 (sidebar)
symbolic, 405, 405 (figure)
technical, 405, 405 (figure)
transactional, 25, 351
transformational (*see* Transformational leadership)
in turnaround efforts, importance of, 390
as values driven, 27 (table)
Leadership narratives, 24
Leadership standards, 7, 8, 9–10, 16
Leadership/management dyad, 22–25, 22 (figure)
Leadership/management paradox, 3–16, 22 (figure)
Learner-centered approach, 147. *See also* Student-centered
    learning
Learner's ecology, 71. *See also* Bioecological approach
Learning:
    attention important for, 353–354
    being in charge of one's, 353
    blended (*see* Blended learning)
    under constructivist principles, 144
    culture of, 202, 330
    decentralization of, 200
    in the digital school, 199–207
    global, 200–201, 205–206
    hybrid, 199, 205, 213
    individualized, 203–205, 364
    inquiry-based, 142, 144
    interactive, 58–59, 60, 144
    lifelong, 4, 181, 205, 408

motivation to promote, 145
not equal for all children, 113
online (*see* Digital schools; Online learning)
personalized, 200, 201, 203–205, 215 (*see also* Personalized instruction)
problem-based, 146–147
as a puzzle, 418
readiness for, 74, 215, 217 (*see also* Readiness)
safety in, 289–290 (*see also* School safety)
self-awareness of, 72 (barrier), 79, 80
software-based, 204–205
student-centered, 144, 147, 350, 362
virtual, 199, 205 (*see also* Digital schools)
See also Effective teaching
Learning barriers, overcoming, 71–85
bioecological approach to, 71–81
learning strategies for, 79, 80–81, 82
optimistic approach as the key to, 81
and policies and rules ecologies, 76–78, 82
questions on barriers in your school, 72 (sidebar)
and social, cultural, economic ecologies, 74–76
teaching strategies for, 78–80
Learning communities. *See* Professional learning communities (PLCs); Small learning communities (SLCs)
Learning disabilities, students with. *See* Students with learning disabilities
Learning environment:
for African American and Latino students, 426, 427
classroom climate and, 145–146
effective teaching and, 56, 67
equitable, 251
homeschooling and, 364
leadership committed to, 355
online, 204, 206 (*see also* Digital schools; Online learning)
physical barrier to, 207
rules in, 76–77, 78, 82
safe and secure, 289, 297, 303
school climate and, 307
stereotypes in, 145
student-centered, 350
synchronous and asynchronous, 201
trust in, 82
See also Bullying; Classroom management
Learning management system (LMS), 212, 216, 222
Learning online. *See* Digital schools; Online learning
Learning strategies for overcoming barriers, 72 (sidebar), 79, 80–81, 82
Leaving no child behind, 332. *See also* No Child Left Behind (NCLB) Act
Lee, Chungmei, 282
Lee, Jaekyung, 175
Legal issues. *See* Bullying and the law; Constitutional rights; Privacy; Search and seizure court decisions; Social media and case law; Speech/expression and case law; Supreme Court of the U.S.; U.S. Constitution; U.S. Constitution amendments
Legal precedents, importance of, 225–226
Leithwood, K., 390
Length, test, 160

Levels:
of budgeting, 262–265
of reliability, 157, 160–161
Levy, M. K., 393
Lewd or indecent speech, 226, 227, 230
Liberal left, the, 361
Liberty:
defined as a key term, 253
and the due process clause, 292, 304
as a value in school finance, 242, 244, 246 (sidebar), 247 (sidebar)
Libraries:
bilingual books in, 128
cultural representativeness of, 125
number of, 274
online/blended learning in, 213, 214, 216, 218
public, 76, 213, 216, 274
smart library, 199
virtual, 201
Life skills, seven essential, 353
Lifelong learning, 4, 181, 205, 408
Lincoln, Abraham, 24–25, 200
Line-item budgeting, 262, 265 (table)
Line-item documents, school budgets as, 260
Linguistic skills and foundation, 123. *See also* Language
Linguistically sensitive engagement, 127, 128, 129
Linguistic diversity, 92–93, 122, 307. *See also* Language
Linguistic identity, 127–128
LinkedIn, 225
Liotta, M., 475
Lipton, Martin, 337
Listening:
CCSS standards on, 59 (sidebar)
and the collaborative spirit, 348
leadership and, 26, 28 (sidebar)
Literacy:
balanced approach to, 137
demands for improvement in, 258
emotional literacy, 349
family, the home, and, 63, 64–65, 128, 278
and overcoming learning barriers, 79
response to intervention (RTI) and, 89, 91, 92, 94, 95
science literacy, 146, 147
scriptural literacy, 359
Little, Judith Warren, 402
Little things, the, 13–14
Liu, Edward, 407
LMS (learning management system), 212, 216, 222
Lobbying, 444–445, 444 (sidebar), 461, 472
Local funding:
additional, raised by districts, 249
portion of all U.S. education funding from, 243
See also Property taxes
Local option sales tax (LOST), 245, 253
Locke, John, 12, 200, 205
Longstaff, J., 92, 94
Looking without seeing, 411
Loose coupling, 10, 437, 438, 445, 449 (sidebar), 451
Losen, Daniel J., 93

LOST (local option sales tax), 245, 253
Louis, K. S., 390
Louis, Karen, 8
Louisiana, 7–8, 114
Lovett, Marsha C., 144
Low birth weights, 279
Low-income children:
    charter schools and, 330
    childrearing learning barriers for, 278
    computer access for, 214, 216
    cumulative disadvantages for, 280
    health-related learning barriers for, 279
    as high-cost students, 282
    many unprepared to learn, 275
    relatively inexperienced teachers for, 92
    student services to, 376
    Title I and Head Start help for, 172, 200
    See also Poverty
Lubienski, Christopher, 462 (sidebar)
Luft, Joseph, 44, 45 (figure), 49
Lugg, Catherine, 445
Lundin, Stephen C., 31
Luppescu, S., 390
Lutheran private schools, 281

MacGillivray, Laurie, 64
Machine metaphors, 28–29, 34
Mackinnon, Anne, 204
MacLeod, Jay, 112
Macrosystem, 61, 62, 62 (figure)
Maday-Karageorge, T., 393
Madison, James, 11
Madison Teachers, Inc. v. Walker (2014), 471
Madoff, Bernie, 185
Maenad, R., 390
Magnet schools, 330
Mail correspondence courses, 211. *See also* Correspondence
    programs
Maintenance and construction, revenue for, 245
Majority minority, 135, 418. *See also* Demographic shifts for
    U.S. education
Male/female ratio in some teaching areas, 182
Malen, Betty, 438
Males:
    in administrative positions, 447
    African American, overrepresented in discipline referrals,
        82, 84
    African American, overrepresented in special education, 84
    gendered roles for, 83
    See also Gender
Malnutrition, 279–280
Maloney, L., 332
Management:
    authority in, 22 (figure), 25
    in the doing, 13
    false dichotomy with leadership, 22
    follower relations in, 22 (figure), 25
    language of, and leadership, 7
    legitimacy, power, and, 25

in the management/leadership dyad, 22–25, 22 (figure)
    and necessity as a virtue, 13
    power/sanctions in, 22 (figure), 25
    reclaimed to its rightful place, 15
    role relationships in, 22 (figure), 23–24
    See also Principals; Superintendents
Management, classroom. *See* Classroom management
Management/leadership dyad, 22–25, 22 (figure). *See also*
    Accoutrements of leadership
Management/leadership paradox, 3–16, 22 (figure)
Managerial control model, 6–7
Managerial mystique, 3, 4, 12, 16
Managerial perfectionism, 28–29, 34
Mandates:
    on budget cuts, 257
    defined as a key term, 271
    top-down, ineffectiveness of, 457
    without clear guidelines, 445
Mann, Horace, 361
Manning, E., 122
Marginalization:
    abolishing/avoiding, 142, 146
    by the digital divide, 138 (sidebar)
    of discourses on democratic roles of education, 136
    by the dominant culture, 422
    perpetuation of, 338
    of qualitative and mixed methods research, 136, 137
    of students, 146
    systemic, 140
Marginalized groups:
    charter schools for, 329
    economic initiatives for, 172
    education as an equalizer for, 169
    learning climates for, 145
    social justice for, 147, 449
    See also Disenfranchised groups; Oppressed groups
Market-driven model of pedagogy, 334
Marketization:
    defined as a key term, 466
    privatization compared to, 456
    See also Incentivist policies; Privatization
Marketized system, components of, 456–457. *See also*
    Incentivism
Market-oriented education models, 457–458, 460, 463–464. *See
    also* Incentivist policies
Markets, pure, quasi-, and second-best, 456
Marshall, C., 446 (sidebar), 451
Marshall, Catherine, 449
Marshall, Thurgood, 231, 232
Martin, D., 424
Marzano, Ana S., 56
Marzano, Robert, 347
Marzano, Robert J., 56
Massachusetts, 111, 200, 365, 418
Massive open online courses (MOOCs), 202, 205–206, 208, 215
Master contract, 405. *See also* Contracts
Materiel, 259, 271
Mathematics:
    achievement gap in, 419

achievement test for advanced placement in, 162 (sidebar)
"acting White" cultural construct and, 135, 141
advanced, limited in small schools, 214
backpack activities for, 65
best practices in, 135, 141
under CCSS, 59 (sidebar), 107, 111, 218, 258
in charter versus traditional schools, 282
in conservative Christian schools, 281
females underrepresented in advanced courses, 449
gender imbalance among teachers of, 182
international test scores for, 111
NAEP scores for, 177, 278, 281, 282
under No Child Left Behind, 174, 176, 177
under Race to the Top, 178
response to intervention (RTI) for, 89
stable standardized test scores for, 274
for students with emotional disturbances, 374, 376
The Matrix (film), 39, 47–48
Matthew Effect, 171, 174, 182
Matthews, A., 88
May, J., 332
McCarran, John, 188
McGlinchey, M. T., 88
McKee, Annie, 349
McLaughlin, Milbrey Wallin, 8
McNulty, Brian, 347
McShane, Michael, 110
Means, B., 214
Measurement error, 157–158
Measures and measurement:
    in budgeting, 260, 261, 262, 263, 264, 267
    as creating a form of imprisonment, 333
    reliability, validity, and (*see* Reliability; Validity)
    standards for, 6
    See also Test scores; Tests
Mechanistic view of leadership, 28–29
Media, the:
    cheating scandals covered by, 185–186, 187–188, 190
    homeschooling reported by, 362
    incentivist reform advanced by, 460
    influence on children from, 61
    moral panic and, 71, 77
    school violence covered by, 313
    teachers' union power as presented by, 443
    U.S. schools far better than reported by, 273
Media-rich environment, 199. *See also* Digital schools
Medical doctors, 28
Meehl, Paul, 156
Meeting after the meeting, 40. *See also* Networks (of people)
Mehta, Jal, 207
Melaville, Atelia, 348
Men, gendered roles for, 83. *See also* Males
Mendez Barletta, L., 93
Mental health services, 376, 377
Mentoring:
    for career moves, 446, 446 (sidebar), 447
    community involvement in, 75
    from diverse mentors, 426
    for gifted students, 374

in navigating a network, 43 (sidebar)
    for persistence development, 79
    in positive work cultures, 409
    for small, neighborhood schools, 214
    volunteering expanded into, 73
    See also Tutoring; Volunteers
Merit pay, 24, 458–459
Merrow, John, 187, 188, 191
Merton, Robert, 171
Mesosystem, 61, 62, 62 (figure)
Messaging. *See* Instant messaging; Texting
Messick, Samuel, 161, 162
Metacognition:
    best practices and, 144, 146
    defined as a key term, 83–84
    of flipped content, 138 (sidebar)
    gifted students and, 375
    student awareness required by, 79
    See also Cognitive development
Metal detectors, 320 (table), 321
Metaphors, 25, 28–29, 34
MetLife, 185
Meyer, C., 393
Meyer v. Nebraska (1923), 366
Michigan, 300, 472
Michigan Virtual School, 217
Michlin, M., 390
Micro-aggression, 75, 76, 81, 84
Micromanagement, 397, 443
Micropolitics, 438, 439, 441, 443, 448, 451
Microsoft Office, 199
Microsystem, 61, 62, 62 (figure)
Microteaching, 124
Middle schools:
    gender imbalance among teachers in, 182
    in North Carolina turnaround initiative, 390, 391, 393
    response to intervention (RTI) in, 93–94
Middle-class schools, 333
Miles, Karen Hawley, 354
Mills, C. Wright, 11–12
Mills, Geoffrey E., 143
Milwaukee voucher program, 280, 281, 458, 462
Minnesota, 119, 310, 331, 473
Minorities:
    in administration, challenges for, 447
    demographic shifts for, 418
    as teachers, 425–426, 447
Minority students:
    charter schools for, 281, 282, 330, 332
    cultural arbitrary and, 334
    cultural capital of, 334–335, 420
    curriculum alignment effect on, 114
    demographic shifts for, 419
    and families, checklist for working with, 425 (sidebar)
    health-related learning barriers for, 279
    how to work with, 426
    many unprepared to learn, 275
    overrepresented in special education, 88
    in post-World War II era, 172

and the right to be educated, 423
in the RTI context, 88, 93
social capital of, 420
and teacher beliefs on natural ability and merit, 424
teachers with least experience for, 422 (*see also* New
    teachers)
treated as high achievers, 427
See also Language minority children
Mintzberg, Henry, 14
Miscall, B., 390
Miseducative versus educative experiences, 14
Mishra, Punya, 201
Mission statement, everyone involved in, 347. *See also* Vision
Missouri, 114, 300
Mixed methods research design, marginalization of, 136
Mixed motive test, 232
Mixed-ability grouping, 61. *See also* Ability grouping;
    Differentiated instruction
Mizzen, Tim, 438
Mobile devices:
    for anytime/anywhere/ubiquitous learning, 203, 215
    digital schools and, 199, 200, 201, 206
    See also Smartphones
Modernism, 136, 137
Modules, in budgeting, 264, 264 (table), 267
Moe, Terry, 472
Moll, L. C., 73
Momaday, N. Scott, 26–27
Monitoring, progress. *See* Progress monitoring in RTI
Monitoring, self-. *See* Self-awareness
Monopolies, 331, 457, 464
Montana, 473
Montgomery, J., 92
Monthly/weekly newsletters, 63, 64 (figure), 65, 126
MOOCs (massive open online courses), 202, 205–206, 208, 215
Moore, S., 390
Moral, all education as, 14
Moral authority, 25
Moral compass, fidelity to, 48
Moral issues:
    in avoiding dilemmas, 440 (table)
    in best practices, 136
    in child well-being, 295–296, 303
    in choice, 463
    in decision making, 32, 450
    in homeschooling, 360
    in leadership, 3, 9, 26, 405, 406
    and the power elite, 12
    in social media, 225
    and spheres of influence, 62, 62 (figure)
Moral panic, 71, 74, 77, 84, 316
Moral values, 26, 129 (sidebar)
Morale:
    of educators, 192, 438
    of staff, in school turnaround, 389, 391–393, 396–397,
        398 (table)
Morgan, Paul, 171
Mormon Church, 30, 31
Morrill Act, 200

Morrow v. Balaski (2013), 293
Morse v. Frederick (2007), 227, 229, 289
Moses, Lyria Bennett, 226
Moss, Connie, 180
Moyle-Wright, P., 162, 163
Mt. Healthy City School District Board of Education v. Doyle
    (1977), 232
Muhammad, Elijah, 336, 337
Multicultural contributions to school safety, 345
Multicultural curriculum, 329
Multicultural lens, 115. *See also* Cultural factors
Multicultural school advocacy committees, 125
Multicultural training, 124
Multitiered model of RTI, 89, 90, 93–97. *See also* Response to
    intervention (RTI)
Munley, James M., 229
Murder and homicide, 313, 314, 367
Murphy, J., 213
Murphy, Joseph, 3, 8–9, 9 (table), 409
Murphy, R., 214
Music program, incremental budgeting for, 264, 264 (table)
Myers, Sheila, 232–233
Myspace, 225, 227, 228, 229, 230, 231, 234
Myths:
    about corporal punishment, 314–315
    about U.S. public schools, 273–274, 332

NAACP, 317
Nabozny, Jamie, 293
NAEP. *See* National Assessment of Educational Progress
    (NAEP)
NAESP (National Association of Elementary School Principals),
    487, 488–489, 490
Nagin, Ray, 185
Napier v. Centerville City Schools (2004), 312
Narratives. *See* Counternarratives; Leadership narratives
NASDPTS (National Association of State Directors of Pupil
    Transportation Services), 308, 311, 312
NASSP (National Association of Secondary School Principals),
    487, 489, 490
NASSP Bulletin (journal), 490
A Nation at Risk:
    charter schools, opportunity, and, 331
    claims of unmet economic needs by, 274
    defined as a key term, 252, 338
    impact of, 172–174, 189, 240
    international test scores and, 111
    No Child Left Behind and, 175
National Assessment of Educational Progress (NAEP):
    in achievement gap analysis, 179
    charter school online data from, 462
    for charter/traditional school comparisons, 281, 282
    ELL and non-ELL scores on, 121
    improvement of scores on, 273, 274
    Massachusetts student scores on, 111
    in NCLB assessment program, 177
    poor versus non-poor children's scores on, 278
National Association of Elementary School Principals (NAESP),
    487, 488–489, 490

National Association of School Psychologists, 92, 379

National Association of School Resource Officers, 319

National Association of Secondary School Principals (NASSP), 487, 489, 490

National Association of State Directors of Pupil Transportation Services (NASDPTS), 308, 311, 312

National Association of Student Councils, 489

National Center for Education Statistics (NCES):
   on budget levels, 265 (table)
   on bullying, 321–323, 322 (figure), 324 (figure)
   on core academic classes, 173
   on data organization and compilation, 375
   on distance education, 212, 213
   on dropout rates, 122
   on homeschooling, 360, 360 (table)
   on local/state/federal portions of funding, 243
   on school crime and safety, 319–320 (table), 321
   on school enrollment, 120, 121

National Center on Student Progress Monitoring, 90

National Center on Universal Design for Learning, 220

National Commission on Excellence in Education, 111, 172–173, 240. *See also A Nation at Risk*

National Council of Professors of Educational Administration (NCPEA), 487, 489, 490

National Council of Teachers of English, 89

National Dissemination Center for Children with Disabilities, 95

National Education Association (NEA), 218, 281, 311, 473, 487–488

National Governors Association, 105, 110

National Highway Traffic Safety Administration (NHTSA), 308, 310, 311–312

National Home Education Research Institute (NHERI), 362

National Labor Relations Act, 474

National Materials Accessibility Standard, 220

National Parent Teacher Association. *See* PTA

National Policy Board of Educational Administration (NPBEA), 7

National PTA. *See* PTA

National Reading Panel, 89

National Research Council, 146

National Standards for School Counseling Programs, 378, 383

National Traffic and Motor Vehicle Safety Act, 310

National Women's Law Project, 445

Native Alaskan students, 419. *See also* Alaska Natives

Native Americans, 275, 424, 426. *See also* American Indians

Native language:
   academic language and, 93
   family culture and, 127–128
   learning ability in one's, 426
   second language and, 123, 130, 131
   See also English as a second language (ESL); English language learners (ELLs); Second language

Native peoples. *See* Alaska natives; American Indians; Native Americans

Natural law, Locke (John) on, 200

NCES. *See* National Center for Education Statistics (NCES)

NCLB Act. *See* No Child Left Behind (NCLB) Act

NCPEA (National Council of Professors of Educational Administration), 487, 489, 490

NCPEA Educational Leadership Review (journal), 490

NEA (National Education Association), 218, 281, 311, 473, 487–488

Neal ex rel. Neal v. Fulton County Board of Education (2000), 293

Nebraska, 212, 366

Needs assessment, program, 381–382 (vignette)

Negligent school bus driving, 311, 312–313

Negotiator/diplomat, in school politics, 436, 437

Neighborhood schools:
   Internet access in, 213
   requirements to attend, 280
   small, course availability at, 214–215
   in suburban areas, 252

Neighborhoods:
   barriers to learning set up by, 72 (sidebar)
   influence on children by, 61, 62 (figure)
   urban, concentrated poverty in, 179
   visits to, 75–76, 127
   See also Communities

Neoliberal agenda, 334

Neoliberal discourse, 136–137

Neoliberal education policies, 26

Neoliberalism, 136–137

Netscape, 202

Networks (of people), 39–49
   all U.S. education systems built on, 40
   fit (political construct) and, 40–42, 44, 45, 47, 47 (sidebar)
   formation of, 40–42
   leadership and, 40, 42, 43 (sidebar), 44, 45, 47 (sidebar), 48
   navigation of, 42–47
   N/networks and n/networks, 42, 43 (sidebar), 49
   panopticon, Johari Window, and, 42, 44–46, 46–47 (sidebar)
   social, and funds of knowledge, 81
   social, student support from, 75

Neuroscience, 137, 220

Nevada, 418

New Hampshire, 472, 475 (sidebar)

New Jersey, 243, 300, 418

New Jersey v. T.L.O. (1985), 297–298, 299, 300, 301, 302

New Mexico, 418

New Orleans, 330

New teachers:
   at high needs schools, 246 (sidebar), 251–252, 422
   positive work culture for, 407, 408, 409

New York City, 275, 300, 317

New York State, 104, 119, 120 (table), 418, 473

News media. *See* Media, the

Newsletters, parent/family, 63, 64 (figure), 65, 126, 128

Next Generation Science Standards, 146

NHERI (National Home Education Research Institute), 362

NHTSA (National Highway Traffic Safety Administration), 308, 310, 311–312

Nieto, Sonia, 333

Nilekani, Nandan, 202

Nixon, Richard, 187

N/networks and n/networks, 42, 43 (sidebar), 49. *See also* Networks (of people)

No Child Left Behind (NCLB) Act:
    accountability and, 6, 175, 205, 333
    achievement defined and measured under, 176–177, 277
    achievement gap and, 277, 280
    AYP and (*see* Adequate yearly progress (AYP))
    basic skills focus of, 375
    choice provisions of, 280
    defined as a key term, 193, 338
    as ESEA 2001 reauthorization, 338
    evidence-based research emphasized by, 459
    failure of, indicator for, 189
    funding under, 175, 176
    Gun-Free Schools Act and, 315
    impact of, 174–175, 176–177, 258
    impact of, on general student services, 375
    impact of, on school counselors, 377
    managerial perfectionism and, 28–29
    mandates of, 175
    opportunities that existed prior to, 13
    prescribed indicators or adequacy under, 175–176
    RTI and, 87, 88, 89, 92
    school cheating scandals and, 186, 189
    scientific management and, 6
    standardized tests under, 176, 186, 189, 280
    waivers from requirements of, 28–29, 110, 177, 189
    in a wave of reforms, 412
    See also Leaving no child behind
Noble, Paul, 22
Noddings, Nel, 56
Noguera, P. A., 421
Noguera, Pedro, 179
Nolly, Glenn, 180
Nomological network, 156, 162, 165
Nonacademic journal, meaning of, 489
Non-constitutional and constitutional rights, 232. *See also* U.S.
        Constitution
Non-English language learners, 121
Non-English language speakers, ESL for. *See* English as a
        second language (ESL)
Non-English speaking countries, 162 (sidebar)
Non-English speaking homes, 283
Non-native English language speakers, 121
Non-rational theories, 239
Normal, concept of:
    as a barrier to learning, 73
    in the deficit model, 73, 83
    defined by the dominant group, 41
    differences as, 75
    in gendered roles, 83
    See also Deficit model
Norman, Marie K., 144
Norm-referenced tests, 88, 97, 98, 277
Norms and values of a dominant group, 42. *See also* Values
Norms in the workplace, 402, 404, 405, 406, 407, 408
North Carolina:
    achievement gap in, 419, 420 (figure), 423, 426
    gender in principalships in, 447
    graduation rates in, 419
    Latino population growth in, 119, 121, 419, 419 (table), 423

    as a "new" Latino state, 418
    student-teacher ratio, for funding in, 247
    turnaround initiative in, 390–399
North Carolina, African American and Latino students in:
    cultural capital for achievement by, 419–421
    effective education for, 423–427
    interview questions for study of, 428–429
    social capital for achievement by, 421
North Carolina, demographic shifts in:
    data on, 119, 121, 419, 419 (table), 423
    strategies to meet the challenges of, 423–427
North Carolina State Board of Education, 29
North Dakota, 473
Northwest Ordinance of 1787, 365
No-smoking policies, 297
Novice-oriented professional cultures, 407. *See also*
        New teachers
NPBEA (National Policy Board of Educational Administration), 7
Numeracy, 258. *See also* Mathematics

Oakes, Jeannie, 275, 337
Obama, Barack, 45, 177, 188, 329
Obama administration, 12, 110, 334
Object and purpose codes, for funds, 250
Objectivity, 155–156, 165, 461 (sidebar). *See also* Subjectivity
O'Brien, Jennifer, 233–234
Obscene language or gestures, 226, 227, 232. *See also* Profanity;
        Vulgar language
Observation, classroom, 14, 26, 79, 80, 220–221, 411. *See also*
        Teachers, evaluation of
Observed score, 157, 158
OECD (Organization for Economic Co-operation and
        Development), 275
Off-campus activity and speech, 227, 229, 230, 231, 290, 291,
        313, 323
Off-formula funding, 249
Offshoring, 203
Ogbu, J. U., 420
Ohio, 312, 472, 481
Oklahoma, 111, 363, 364
Old Deluder Satan Act, 200, 365
Oliva, Maricela, 449
Omnibus Transportation Testing Act, 311
One best method or one right way, 30, 33, 138. *See also* Best
        practices
Oneself, understanding of, 26
One-size fits all model, 27 (table), 82, 261
One-to-one laptop/tablet programs, 216
Online courses:
    in-house development of, 215
    MOOCs as, 202, 205–206, 208, 215
    See also Online learning
Online learning:
    access to, 214–215, 216, 217, 219–220, 368
    assessments for, 216
    boxed curriculums in, 364, 370
    for credit recovery, 216–217
    data about, 211, 212
    data collection systems linked to, 216, 217

defined as a key term, 212, 222
as disruptive innovation, 211, 221
face-to-face compared to, 204–205, 214, 215, 217, 218, 219–221
as fifth generation distance learning, 212
for homeschoolers, 364
learning strategies for, 79
opportunities and concerns for, 213–217
for personalized instruction, 215–216
planning for, 215–216, 218–221
privacy concerns in, 216
productivity of, 217–218
questions to ask about, 218–219
Socratic method in, 204
special education and, 219–220
standards for, 218, 219 (sidebar)
student-teacher ratio in, 217
synchronous or asynchronous, 213
See also Blended learning; Digital schools; Internet; Social media
Open inquiry, 146
Open principals, 439, 442
Open systems, 437–438, 445
Open-ended leadership, 27 (table). *See also* Intellectual curiosity
Open-enrollment programs, 457
Open-mindedness, 26, 345. *See also* Intellectual curiosity
Operational definitions, 156, 165
Operational efficiencies, 261
Operational expenses, 245
Opportunity, equal. *See* Equal educational opportunity; Inequities
Opportunity gap, 140, 142, 179, 180
Oppressed groups, 336. *See also* Disenfranchised groups; Marginalized groups
Optimism, in positive work cultures, 410
Oral culture, 128
Orderly environment, in school turnaround, 389, 391–398, 398 (table)
Oregon, 366, 418
Orfield, Gary, 93, 282, 332
Organization for Economic Co-operation and Development (OECD), 275
Organization of knowledge, 144–145
Organizational boundaries, 23, 24
Organizational culture, 261, 402, 405–406. *See also* School culture; Work cultures, positive
Orman, Sheryl, 65
Ortiz, Alba A., 92, 93
Osburn, Joe, 141
Other-directed interests and self-interests, 476
Outside the box, thinking, 26, 27
Outside-in and inside-out accountability, 404
Outsourcing, 202, 261, 445
Overrepresentation:
of African Americans and Hispanics in lower student tracks, 275
of African Americans and Latinos in failing schools, 333
of African Americans/Blacks in discipline referrals, 82, 84, 142

of minorities, in special education, 84, 88
See also Underrepesentation

Pacheco, M., 125, 126
Pacific Islanders, 121, 130–131, 419
Pacing guides for teachers, 215
Packages, program unit, 267, 268 (figure), 269, 270
Páez, M. M., 421
Panic, moral. *See* Moral panic
Panoptic mechanisms, 44, 49. *See also* Panopticon
Panopticon, 42, 44, 47 (sidebar), 49, 333
Papa, Rosemary, 22, 26, 27 (table), 31, 407
Papa accoutrements of leadership, 27 (table)
Papalewis, Rosemary, 410
Paradigm shifts:
in communication, 206
technological implementation as, 202
for the term "at-risk," 422
Paradox, leadership/management, 3–16, 22 (figure)
Parens patriae doctrine, 365, 367, 370. *See also* Compulsory public education
Parental rights, in homeschooling, 359, 361, 365–367, 369
Parent-child conversations, 278–279
Parent-directed education, 359. *See also* Homeschooling
Parent/family newsletters, 63, 64 (figure), 65, 126, 128
Parenting:
barriers to learning and, 278–279
defined as a key term, 84
Epstein (Joyce) on, 63, 73, 84
family involvement and, 63, 73
See also Parents
Parents:
anti-bullying involvement by, 379
child safety as a concern of, 307, 313 (*see also* School safety)
conferences with, 64 (sidebar), 66, 75, 128, 408, 421, 425
disparaging comments about, 424–425
divorced, 64 (sidebar)
education level of, 278, 279
in Hispanic school population, 125–128, 129 (sidebar)
homeschooling and, 359–370
for improving student self-awareness, 80–81
involvement in homework by, 63, 125, 279, 425
involvement of, as predictor student success, 126, 424, 444
involvement of, giving the impression of, 438
kinds of schools wanted by, 405
as lobbyists, 444 (sidebar)
occupation of, 278
principal-parent interactions, 438–439
response to intervention (RTI) and, 92, 95, 96, 97
in the school community, 352
school counselors and, 375
in school politics, 436–439, 441, 443–444, 444 (sidebar), 447
social capital of, and achievement, 421
in spheres of influence, 61, 62, 62 (figure)
student attendance supported by, 352
student services and, 375, 376
teacher partnerships with, 61–66
teacher selection and, 252
in a turnaround school initiative, 392, 393, 394, 395, 396

as volunteers, 65, 75
work environment of, 62, 62 (figure)
See also Families; Family involvement; Home environment
Parents Involved in Community Schools v. Seattle School District No. 1 (2007), 252
Parent-teacher associations. *See* PTA
Parent-teacher conferences, 64 (sidebar), 66, 75, 128, 408, 421, 425
Parent-teacher partnerships:
    defined as a key term, 68
    the family and, 61–66
    in a turnaround school initiative, 392, 394
    See also Families; Parents
Parker-Magagna, Martha, 481
Parochial schools, 258. *See also* Private schools; Religious private schools
Participatory decision making, 260, 266, 270, 271. *See also* Collaboration
Participatory leadership, 376
Participatory management, 260
Partnerships:
    for deep, student-centered learning, 350
    defined as a key term, 355
    family, 61–66, 350
    inter-firm, core features of, 354
    parent-teacher, 61–66, 68, 392–394
    systems building and, 354
    See also Family involvement
Part-time students, 360 (table), 363, 368
Passeron, Jean-Claude, 104, 113, 115
Past practice, 14, 480, 482
Pat-down searches, 300–301
Patronage system, 442
Pattison, Stephen, 28
Paul, Harry, 31
Pay for performance, 458, 459
Payne, A. M., 296
PBIS (Positive Behavioral Interventions and Supports), 394, 396
PBL (problem-based learning), 146–147
Pearson correlation, 164
Peavey, Fran, 181
PECOTA (Player Empirical Comparison and Optimization Test Algorithm), 4
Peddiwell, J. Abner, 105
Pedhazur, Elazar J., 162–163
Pedhazur-Schmelkin, Liora, 163
Peer review, 461 (sidebar), 462, 463, 464, 465, 489, 490
Pennsylvania, 170, 418
PEPG (Program on Education Policy and Governance), 460, 462, 463–464
Perfectionism, managerial, 28–29, 34
Performance conditions for tests, 114, 115
Performance pay. *See* Pay for performance
Performance-based budgeting, 264–270
    advantages of, 265–266, 270
    defined as a key term, 271
    framework for, 266
    NCES characteristics of, 265 (table)
    priorities and funding levels for, 269–270

program unit packages in, 267, 268 (figure), 269, 270
    when to use, 265
Performing arts, 374, 375
Permissiveness, warnings about, 173
Per-pupil allocations, 249
Per-pupil facilities, 275
Per-pupil funding, 239, 247, 248 (table), 249, 257, 363
Per-pupil spending, 250, 275, 282
Per-pupil state aid, 258 (figure)
Per-pupil tax revenue, 248
Per-pupil weights, 247, 248 (table)
Perry, T., 420, 424
Persistence rate, 130. *See also* Dropout rates
Personal days, politics of, 443 (sidebar)
Personal power, 442, 443
Personalized instruction, 215–216, 217. *See also* Personalized learning
Personalized learning:
    in the digital school, 203–204, 205
    distinctive nature of, 200
    emerging software for, 201
    online and blended courses for, 215
    See also Personalized instruction
Personnel salaries. *See* Salaries and benefits; Salary schedules; Teacher salaries; Wages
Persons per vehicle, as an economic indicator, 274
Peske, Heather G., 407
Pesticides, 279
Peters, Thomas, 31
Peterson, Kent D., 402, 402 (figure)
Peterson, Paul, 280–281, 463
Pew Hispanic Center, 11, 119, 121
Phelps, Sarah, 230–231
Phi Delta Kappan (journal), 490
Philanthropies, 460, 463
Philanthropists, 334, 336
Philbrick, John, 23
Phillips, Meredith, 276
Phone calls to parents, 64, 126, 444. *See also* Cell phones; Smartphones
Phonemic awareness, 89
Phonics, 89. *See also* Reading
Phonological awareness, 89
Photobucket, 230
Physical distance, 199, 206, 207, 208, 278, 290
Physical harm, in school violence, 313. *See also* Bullying
Physical safety, 307
Piaget, Jean, 58–59
Pickering, Marvin, 231
Pickering v. Board of Education of Township High School District 205 (1968), 231–232, 233
Pierce v. Society of the Sisters (1925), 366
PISA (Programme for International Student Assessment), 111
Platform, in school politics, 448
Player Empirical Comparison and Optimization Test Algorithm (PECOTA), 4
PLCs. *See* Professional learning communities (PLCs)
Point of view, in reading standards, 108

Police officers:
    involved in school disciplinary matters, 316, 317
    noted in court decisions, 226, 229, 230, 297, 301–302
    See also School resource officers (SROs)
Policies:
    ecologies, barriers, and, 72 (sidebar), 76–78, 82
    learning-friendly, 82
    school politics and, 438, 439, 440 (table), 442, 445
Policy, defined as a key term, 451
Political elite, 334
Political speech, 226. *See also* Speech/expression and case law
Political strategists, in school politics, 436, 437
Politics:
    accountability, test scores, and, 164
    of assigning teachers and students to schools, 252
    blind eye turned to challenges of, 48
    Common Core and, 104, 110–111, 113–114, 115
    in the control of schooling, 334
    defined as a key term, 451
    of denial, 447
    and education as a political endeavor, 40
    fit and (*see* Fit (political construct))
    homeschooling and, 361–362, 363
    of human capitalist ideology, 333
    inequality perpetuated by, 333
    micropolitics, 438, 439, 441, 443, 448, 451
    in network formation, 40–41
    in network navigation, 42, 45, 46, 47, 47 (sidebar)
    of schools (*see* School politics)
    in student weights for funding, 247
    in tax policy, 243, 244
    work culture of schools and, 403
Popper, Karl, 205
Population shifts. *See* Demographic shifts for U.S. education
Positional power, 444
Positive Behavioral Intervention programs, 291
Positive Behavioral Interventions and Supports (PBIS), 394, 396
Positive work cultures. *See* Work cultures, positive
Posttraumatic stress disorder (PTSD), 315
Poverty:
    achievement gaps and, 172, 175, 179, 180, 181, 277–278, 421
    concentrated, 278
    data on, 120, 121, 277
    in the deficit model, 73
    gifted students in, 374
    in the growing Hispanic population, 120, 121, 123–126
    long-term, 277
    No Child Left Behind and, 175
    rates of, 120, 121, 277–287
    as a source of wicked problems, 436
    unequal opportunity and, 273, 280
    War on, 172
    See also Low-income children
Powell, Colin, 23
Power:
    authority as a source of, 33
    best practices and, 136, 139, 140
    control, class size, and, 78
    curriculum determined by those with, 333

defined as a key term, 34
disciplinary, 44
of a dominant group, 41
expert power, 25, 442
in gendered roles, 83
in interest convergence, 335
knowledge and, 12
in the management/leadership dyad, 22 (figure), 25
margins of tolerance and, 44
personal power, 442, 443
positional power, 444
and relevance, of public sector unions, 472
in school politics, 435, 436–439, 441, 442–448
shared power, 448
sources and types of, 442–445
sovereign power, 44
to terminate, 44, 47
Power elite, the, 12
Power over and power to (styles or orientations), 448
Practice and theory, bridge between, 48
Praxis, 143
Precedents, legal, importance of, 225–226. *See also* Case law
Predictive validity, 163, 163 (figure), 164
Prefrontal cortex, 353. *See also* Brain development
Pregnancy, and health-related barriers to learning, 279
Premature births, 279
Preschool programs, 92, 275, 276, 350, 421. *See also* Early childhood education
Primum non nocere (first, do no harm), 141, 154, 180
Principal (magazine), 490
Principal Centers, International, 10
Principals:
    budget-cut stress on, 185
    collaboration with teachers, 376
    electronic media and, 225–232, 235
    evaluation of, 446–447
    evaluation of teachers by, 220
    as factory supervisors, 23
    gender of, 447
    NAESP and, 487, 488–489, 490
    NASSP and, 487, 489, 490
    open and closed, 439, 442
    positive work cultures and, 401, 403, 404, 405, 407–410, 411
    school cheating that involves, 186, 187, 188, 190, 191
    school finance dynamics for, 242, 243, 247 (sidebar)
    in school politics, 435–451
    as the school-community link, 347
    for supporting student conduct, 351
    in a turnaround school initiative, 391–399, 398 (table)
    See also Superintendents
Prior, J., 64 (sidebar)
Prior, Jennifer, 62 (figure)
Prior knowledge, 66–67, 140, 144, 417, 427
Priority rankings, in budgeting, 269–270, 269 (table)
Prison:
    home imprisonment, 368
    panopticon for, 44
    for a school cheating scandal, 191

school-to-prison pipeline, 316, 319
for sexually explicit text messages, 235
Privacy:
balanced with school safety, 297
for dispute handling, 440 (table)
online learning and, 216
right to, and Fourth Amendment, 297
and search and seizure decisions, 296–303
for student services data, 375
teaching and, 402
of texting, 226
See also Fourth Amendment (U.S. Constitution)
Private school affidavit, 363
Private schools:
accountability of, 259
homeschooling and, 363, 364
public funding for, 258, 280
public schools compared to, 281, 462
See also Voucher programs
Private selves, in the Johari Window, 45–46
Private speech, cyberbullying as, 291. *See also* Cyberbullying;
Free speech
Privatization:
charter schools and, 332, 334, 456
critical race theory on, 335–337
defined as a key term, 466
incentives and, 458
international issues and, 445
as a label, 455
marketization compared to, 456
the marketplace and, 280–282
operational efficiency from, 261
as similar to slavery, 336
See also Charter schools; Incentivist policies; Marketization;
School choice
Privileged groups, 112, 113, 275, 361, 450 (sidebar). *See also*
Dominant and subordinate groups
Probable cause, in search and seizure, 296, 297, 301, 304
Problem-based learning (PBL), 146–147
Productivity:
attributes for, 262
budgeting and, 259, 261, 262, 264, 265, 270
defined as a key term, 271
of online and blended learning, 217–218
Profanity, 229, 231. *See also* Obscene language or gestures
Professional associations, 487–489
Professional culture, 346, 402, 404, 405, 406, 407. *See also*
Professionalism
Professional development:
on advocacy, 125–126
best practices for selection of, 142
for building trust, 348
CCSS and, 109, 258
in response to intervention (RTI), 91
role-based, 407
strong, assumptions for, 124
time available for, 408
in a turnaround school initiative, 394
Professional ethos, 405

Professional journals, 489–490
Professional learning communities (PLCs):
best practices and, 139, 143
principles of, 143
in school politics, 439
social justice as a target of, 449
in a turnaround school initiative, 392, 394, 396
Professionalism:
AFT, NEA, and, 473
and its fit with union membership, 475–477, 481
teacher perceptions of, 476, 476 (sidebar)
Profiling, of deficits, 73
Program budgeting, 263, 265 (table)
Program needs assessment, 381–382 (vignette)
Program on Education Policy and Governance (PEPG), 460,
462, 463–464
Program unit packages, 267, 268 (figure), 269
Programme for International Student Assessment (PISA), 111
Progress monitoring in RTI, 89, 90, 91, 92, 93, 94–95, 96, 97
Progressive and constructivist principles of best practices, 144
Progressive taxes, 244, 245, 245 (table), 253
PROMISE initiative, for redirecting children, 317
Promising practice, 87, 135, 139, 147. *See also* Best practices
Property, in the due process clause, 292, 304
Property owners, and school politics, 444
Property taxes:
characteristics of, 242, 244, 245 (table), 246 (sidebar)
countries not dependent on, 179
defined as a key term, 253
in mechanisms for funding, 248, 249
See also Local funding
Proposals, in bargaining, 478, 479 (sidebar), 482
ProPublica, 186
Protected classes, under equal protection claims, 293
Protection by teachers' unions, 476, 476 (sidebar), 477, 481
Protection of children:
children's rights and, 365
from harassment and bullying, 295–296
homeschooling and, 367–369
Proto, B., 390, 391, 393
Proverbs, 31, 33, 128, 129 (sidebar)
Proximal development, 60, 145
Prudence, in the use of public funds, 259, 259 (figure)
Psychological bullying, 321. *See also* Bullying
Psychological distance, 199, 207, 208
Psychological harm, 313, 314
Psychological safety, 307, 324
Psychologists, school, 80, 92, 95–96, 324, 374
Psychometric properties, 155, 156. *See also* Tests
PTA, 125, 438, 444, 444 (sidebar), 449
PTSD (posttraumatic stress disorder), 315
Public choice theories, 239
Public education, early American history of, 11, 200, 361
Public education, failings of:
homeschooling as a reaction to, 362, 364
myths about, 273–274, 332
See also Failing schools
Public education, traditional. *See* Traditional public schools
Public employees:

collective bargaining for, 471, 474
as litigants in case law, 231–235
See also Public sector unions; Teachers; Teachers' unions
Public good, public education as, 206. *See also* Homeschooling
Public libraries, 76, 213, 216, 274. *See also* Libraries
Public school buses. *See* School bus transportation
Public sector employees. *See* Public employees
Public sector unions:
collective bargaining restricted for, 471, 472
collective bargaining subjects for, 475 (sidebar)
declining membership in, 481
exclusive representation by, 474
power and relevance of, 472
teacher professionalism and, 477
See also Public employees; Teachers' unions
Public self, the, 44. *See also* Front stage behavior
Pullout programs, 91, 98
Punishment as a barrier to ethical development, 352
Pupil-teacher ratio. *See* Student-teacher ratio
Purchased inputs, 240, 250, 253
Purchased services, expenditures for, 241 (figure)
Pure markets, 456
Purpose, sense of, 26, 403, 408, 409
Purpose and object codes, for funds, 250
P.W. et al v. Fairport Central School District (2013), 294

Q Sort methodology, 269, 271
Quadrants of the Johari Window, 44–46, 45 (figure), 47 (sidebar)
Qualified immunity, 293, 304
Qualitative research design, marginalization of, 136, 137
Quality control, 260, 465
Quality improvement, 261, 270, 271
Quantitative experimental design, as privileged, 136, 137
Quasi-markets, 456
Quest or journey, leadership as, 26, 27 (table)
Quincy, Massachusetts, 23
Quon, Jeff, 226

Race:
achievement gap and, 112, 178–179, 189, 192–193, 275–279, 419
assigning students to schools by, 252
bullying/harassment based on, 294
CRT at the intersection of education and, 335
and curriculum content and design, 105, 110
cyberbullying data by, 323
data disaggregation by, 125
in the deficit model, 73
honoring differences in, 81
poverty rate by, 120, 121, 277
as a protected classification, 293
reading delay and, 88
social class, tracking, and, 275
verbal violence based on, 314
See also Critical race theory (CRT); Demographic shifts for U.S. education
Race to the Top (RTT):
accountability and, 333
Common Core adoption aided by, 110

key priority areas in, 177
reforms and shortcomings of, 178
as a slogan, 337
Racial desegregation, 172, 200, 278, 330, 335. *See also Brown v. Board of Education* (1954); Racial segregation
Racial isolation, 277, 279, 282, 336. *See also* Racial segregation
Racial justice, 335, 338
Racial minorities. *See* Minorities; Minority students
Racial resegregation, 275
Racial segregation:
achievement gap and, 278
charter school contribution to, 282, 334, 335–336
community norms, values, and, 42
de facto, 182
de facto, still in existence, 172, 275
de jure, 172, 182
as racism, 84
resegregation, 275
See also Brown v. Board of Education (1954); Racial desegregation
Racial slurs, correcting of, 126
Racial/ethnic groups:
defined as a key term, 130–131
See also African American students; African Americans; Alaska Natives; American Indians; Asian American students; Asian Americans; Black students; Blacks; Hispanic U.S. population growth; Latino students; Latinos; Pacific Islanders; White students; Whites
Racially motivated hostility, micro-aggression as, 75
Racism:
ableism and, 73
antiracist strategies, 424, 427
as a barrier to learning, 71
CRT analysis of, 335, 338
defined as a key term, 84
institutionalized and seen as normal, 335
in rules, 82
Racist blogs, 227
Radio, for distance learning, 211
RAND Corporation, 282, 335
Random drug testing, 301, 310, 311
Random error, 157, 158, 159, 165
Random searches, 301, 310, 311, 313. *See also* Search and seizure court decisions
Rathbun, A., 122
Rational choice theory (RCT), 32, 33, 34
Ratner v. Loudoun County Public Schools (2001), 315–316
Raven, Bertram, 25
Ravitch, Diane, 281, 335, 456
RCT (rational choice theory), 32, 33, 34
Readiness:
academic, 377, 382
for college and career, 105, 106, 109, 369
to learn, 74, 215, 217
preschool, 276
for school, 92, 275, 276, 278, 286
Reading:
achievement gap in, 121, 419
in CCSS, 59 (sidebar), 108, 109, 111

in charter versus traditional schools, 282
to children, and family background, 278
content-related validity and, 163
differentiated instruction in, 60–61
early intervention for, 94
essential components of instruction in, 89
gender imbalance among teachers of, 182
integrated instruction for, 59–60
NAEP scores for, 121, 177, 278, 281, 282
under No Child Left Behind, 174, 176, 177
parent/child activity in, 65 (sidebar), 278
under Race to the Top, 178
requirements for, and limits on recess, 403
response to intervention (RTI) for, 87–98
specialists in, 374
stable standardized test scores for, 274
strategic, 144
Reading comprehension, 89, 93, 94, 98, 144. *See also* Reading
Reading delay, 88
Reading First initiative, 89
Reading-writing classroom workshop, 144
Ready, Douglas, 170
Reagan, Ronald, 173
Reardon, Sean, 179
Reasonable suspicion standard, 297–298, 299, 300, 302–303
Recertification elections, for unions, 471
Recess, 58, 403
Recruiting of teachers, 425–426
Redding, S., 390
Redding, Savana, 299
Reductionism, 27 (table)
Reductionist approaches, 29, 412
Reed-Danahay, Deborah, 113
Reeves, Todd, 175
Refereed journal, meaning of, 489
Reflective practitioners, 143
Reflective teaching, 66–67, 68
Reform initiatives, historical analysis of, 171–174
Reggio Emilia (Italy), 350
Regressive taxes, 244, 245, 245 (table), 253
Rehabilitation Act, 219, 292, 295, 314
Relational trust, 389, 391–398, 398 (table), 399
Reliability:
    alternate forms, 159
    as a characteristic of test scores, 160
    defined as a key term, 165
    equivalence and stability, 159
    equivalent forms, 159
    estimation of, 157–160
    ethics and, 154, 156, 157, 158, 164
    evidence for, 156, 158
    factors affecting, 160, 164
    internal consistency reliability, 159–160
    levels of, acceptable, 157, 160–161
    measurement error and, 155–158
    not a guarantee of validity, 162 (sidebar)
    scorer-rater, 160
    split-half, 159–160
    test-retest, 158–159

Reliability coefficient, 157, 158, 159, 160, 161, 164
Religion:
    advocacy and, 445
    attendance exemptions based on, 364
    and curriculum content selection, 110
    freedom of, 359
    homeschooling and, 359, 360, 361, 362, 364, 365, 366–367
    honoring differences in, 81
    as a protected classification, 293
    verbal violence based on, 314
Religious private schools, 281. *See also* Parochial schools; Private schools
Rentner, Diane Stark, 176
Reproduction, social. *See* Social reproduction theory
Reproductive rights, 443 (sidebar)
Republican democracy, 258. *See also* Democracy
Republican National Committee, 110
Research, real versus agenda-pushing, 461 (sidebar)
Research designs, privileged and marginalized, 136, 137
Research-based instruction, 87, 88–89, 96, 98
Research-based interventions, 93, 95
Research-based policy, 175
Research-based practice, 25, 30, 135, 147. *See also* Best practices
Research-based reading instruction, 89, 98
Research-based strategies, 330, 373, 423
Resegregation, 275. *See also* Racial segregation
Resource allocation. *See* Allocation of resources
Respect:
    between adults and students, 344
    built in the school community, 350
    in classroom cohesiveness, 56
    family culture of, 127
    implemented by school leaders, 345
    in the testing process, 155
Response to intervention (RTI), 87–100
    components of, 88–90
    defined as a key term, 98
    for English language learners, 87, 92–93
    future of, 94–97
    general education and, 87–88, 90, 91, 92, 94, 95, 96, 98
    IDEA and, 87–88, 92, 94–95, 96, 98
    impact on classroom performance, 94
    No Child Left Behind and, 88, 89, 92
    parent involvement in, 92, 95, 96, 97
    principles of, 88, 93
    response time for, 80
    roles in, 90–92, 95–96
    school politics and, 441
    smart RTI, 96–97
    systemic reform under, 87–88, 97–98
    See also Reading; Special education
Response to Intervention Action Network, 88
Responsiveness (elasticity) of taxes, 244, 245 (table), 253
Restructuring and abandonment, 261–262, 264
Retrofitting, 103, 220
Revenue enhancement, 261, 264, 266
Revenue generation:
    for capital construction, 245

goal of, 243
local/state/federal portions of funding, 243
taxes for, 242, 243–245
taxes for, and four values of finance, 244
taxes for, and taxing authority, 247–248
Tenth Amendment and, 242
See also Budgeting; Fund distribution; School finance
Revenues, defined as a key term, 271
Revisionist interpretation:
   in critical race theory, 335–336, 336–337
   defined as a key term, 338
Reynolds, Cecil R., 95
Rhee, Michelle, 187–188, 190, 191
Rice, Thomas, 355
Rich getting richer, 171. *See also* Achievement gap(s)
Ridgefield Park Education Association v. Ridgefield Park Board of Education (1978), 474
Right knowledge, 110
Rights arbitration, 480
Right-to-work laws, 443, 472
Rigor, curricular, 111–112
Riley v. California (2014), 301–302, 303
Rinaldi, Claudia, 93
Roberts, Greg, 90, 91
Roberts, John, 227, 289
Robinson, Ken, 4
Rogers, E. M., 201, 202
Role legitimacy, 22 (figure), 24
Roles:
   assumptive worlds rules on, 439–441
   gendered, 71, 83
   identity and, 41
   in the management/leadership dyad, 22 (figure), 23–24
   in RTI programs, 90–92, 95–96
   See also Government roles in education
Romney, Mitt, 45
Roosevelt, Franklin, 24
Rose v. Nashua Board of Education (1982), 308
Ross, E. Wayne, 332
Ross, T., 122
Rothman, Robert, 105
Rothstein, Richard, 112, 276
Rowe, Deborah W., 64
Rowley, Glenn, 158, 159
R.S. v. Minnewaska Area School District No. 2149 (2012), 229
RTI. *See* Response to intervention (RTI)
RTT. *See* Race to the Top (RTT)
Rubin, Beth, 275
Rubino, Christine, 235
Rubino v. City of New York (2013)., 235
Rudebusch, J., 92
Rueda, Robert, 92
Rules:
   assumptive (*see* Assumptive worlds rules)
   balanced with individual rights, 77
   cultures and, making adjustments for, 11
   ecologies approach to, 76–78, 82
   as educative, not as control, 78
   learning-friendly, 82

for success in n/networks, 43 (sidebar)
Rules of thumb. *See* Heuristics (rules of thumb)
Rural households, limited Internet access for, 214, 216
Rutherford Institute, 316

The Saber-Tooth Curriculum (by Harold Benjamin), 105
Safe school, 303, 307–308, 316, 317, 324–325. *See also* School safety
Safford Unified School District v. Redding (2009), 299, 300
Salaries and benefits:
   expenditures for, 240, 241 (figure), 249–250, 261
   See also Salary schedules; Teacher salaries; Wages
Salary compensation asymmetry, 267, 271
Salary schedules, 23–24, 251, 254, 267, 473. *See also* Salaries and benefits; Teacher salaries; Wages
Sales taxes:
   characteristics of, 242, 244, 245 (table)
   as a consumption tax, 244
   defined as a key term, 254
   local option added to, 245, 253
Salmonowicz, M. J., 393
Salter, S. E., 380
Sameness, structural, 7
Samples and sampling, 158, 160, 163
Samson, Jennifer, 93
San Diego Unified School District v. Commission of Professional Competence (2011), 234
Sanchez, Claudia, 120 (table)
Sanctions, in the management/leadership dyad, 22 (figure), 25
Sandy Hook Elementary School, 317, 346
SAT (Scholastic Aptitude Test), 164, 172, 273, 274
Savery, John R., 147
Sayeski, Kristin L., 55
Scales, and construct validity, 162
Scapegoating, in school cheating scandals, 190
Scarlet letter effect, 174. *See also* Accountability
Schaughency, A., 88
Schedule, school. *See* Instructional time; School day flexibility
Schein, Edgar H., 402, 402 (figure)
Scheurich, J. J., 427, 449
Scheurich, James Joseph, 180
Schneider, Mark, 330
Scholastic Aptitude Test (SAT), 164, 172, 273, 274
Schon, Donald, 66
School advocacy committees, 125–126
School boards. *See* Boards of education
School budgets. *See* Budgeting
School Bus Safety Amendments of 1974, 310
School bus transportation, 308–313
   bus drivers for, 308, 310, 311, 312–313
   discipline and, 312–313
   litigation on, 310–311
   seat belts for, 311–312, 313
   stop arm violations against, 308–309 (table), 310
School calendar, 76, 215. *See also* Instructional time; School day flexibility
School cheating scandals, 185–195
   causes and effects of, 187–191
   prevention of, 191–192, 192 (sidebar)

the worst, 186–187, 188–189, 190
School choice:
  balancing needs under, 246 (sidebar)
  defined as a key term, 283
  homeschooling and, 361, 362
  liberty associated with, 242
  in market-style dynamics, 457
  NCLB provisions for, 280
  origin of the concept, 330
  public school problems and, 282
  See also Charter schools; Open-enrollment programs; Tax
    credits; Voucher programs
School Choice Demonstration Project, 464
School climate:
  bullying and, 296, 379
  defined as a key term, 325
  negative, 315
  positive, 379
  for promoting safe schools, 307–308, 324, 325
  See also School culture; School safety
School community:
  building of, teacher support for, 349 (sidebar)
  built by daily community meetings, 350
  built on collaborative practices, 344
  for a common goal, 354
  parents emphasized in, 352, 355
  for school safety and stability, 345, 346, 347–349
  values of, shared vision based on, 351
  See also Communities
School counseling:
  advocacy and leadership in, 378, 380
  anti-bullying curricula in, 378, 379
  expanded role of, 377
  group counseling in, 379–380
  technology and, 380–381
  wraparound counseling in, 380
  See also General student services
School culture:
  can-do spirit for, 401
  dominant culture in, 419–420, 422
  family/home culture and, 125, 424
  of high-quality instruction, 123, 124
  and school safety and stability, 325, 344, 345, 346, 347
  student conduct and, 351
  in a turnaround school initiative, 391, 393, 395, 398
  unique in each school, 401, 402
  work culture and, 401, 403, 404, 405, 406, 407, 410
  See also Organizational culture; School climate; Work
    cultures, positive
School day flexibility, 215, 332, 392, 408. *See also* Instructional
    time; School calendar
School desegregation. *See Brown v. Board of Education* (1954);
    Racial desegregation
School finance:
  checklist for, 252
  distribution of funds in, 245–249
  the four values in, 241–242, 244, 246–247 (sidebar)
  revenue generation in, 242–245
  salaries/benefits in, 240, 241 (figure), 249–250
  and shift to resource allocation, 239, 240–241, 251–252
  student achievement and, 250, 251
  taxes and, 242, 243–245, 245 (table), 247–248
  the teacher factor in, 239, 242, 246, 247, 249, 250–252
  See also Budgeting
School Improvement Team (SIT), 444
School persistence rate, 130. *See also* Dropout rates
School politics, 435–454
  actors in, 441–445
  assumptive worlds rules in, 439–441, 440 (table), 445, 446,
    447, 450
  balance of ideals with, 447–448
  in career events, 445–447
  case study in, 436–437
  dynamics of, 438–441
  micropolitics in, 438, 439, 441, 443, 448, 451
  organizational factors and, 436–438
  roles of the leader in, 436–437
  for social justice, 437, 448–450, 449 (sidebar), 450 (sidebar)
  wicked problems in, 435–436, 438, 448, 451
  women, minorities, and, 447
  See also Politics
School psychologists, 80, 92, 95–96, 324, 374
School readiness. *See* Readiness
School resource officers (SROs), 290, 296, 316, 317, 319, 436.
    See also Police officers
School safety:
  balanced with students' rights, 289, 297, 303
  bullying as a danger to, 345
  communities of supportive adults for, 354–355
  counseling involvement in, 378
  dimensions of, 307, 324
  effective school leaders for, 343–344, 346–347
  in electronic data, 375
  indicators of, 324–325
  partnerships for, 349–350
  positive student engagement for, 353
  prevention as critical to, 346
  school community building for, 347–349
  in school transportation, 308–313
  and security, variety of measures for, 319–320 (table), 321
  stability and (*see* School stability)
  strategy implications for administrators, 324–325
  violence and, 313–316
  zero tolerance policies for, 315–317
  See also Attendance; Bullying; Bullying and the law;
    Discipline, student; School resource officers (SROs);
    School violence; Search and seizure court decisions;
    Student conduct
School shootings:
  bullying and, 290, 321
  case law reference to, 229
  corporal punishment and, 315
  international, 313
  moral panic and, 74, 84
  oversensitivity to, 317
  zero tolerance as a response to, 316
School stability:
  all participants involved in, 346

bullying as a danger to, 345
communities of supportive adults for, 354–355
community building for, 348–349
with effective school leaders, 346–347
positive student engagement for, 353
as a sense of permanence, 346
transformational leadership for, 343–344, 346
See also School safety
School staff:
bilingual, 426, 437
in collaboration for counseling services, 378
in collaboration for student services, 376
diversity in, 426
family involvement and, 126, 127, 128, 129 (sidebar)
in positive work cultures, 403, 404, 405, 406, 408, 409, 410
professional development for, 124
in school politics, 443
See also Principals; Teachers
School stakeholders:
defined as a key term, 355
See also Boards of education; Communities; Families;
Government roles in education; Parents; Principals;
School staff; States, U.S.; Students; Superintendents;
Teachers
School turnaround:
defined as a key term, 399
research on, 389–390
research on, in North Carolina, 390–399
School uniforms, 320 (table). *See also* Dress codes
School violence:
bullying as (*see* Bullying)
crisis intervention in, 380
data on, 313
forms of, 313–315
learning opportunity disrupted by, 343
long-term effect of, 314, 315
shootings (*see* School shootings)
See also Zero tolerance
School vouchers. *See* Voucher programs
Schools:
as evolving systems, 88
function and purpose of, 4, 9, 113, 401, 405
identity of, 447
as loosely coupled organizations, 437, 438
as open systems, 437–438
as political systems, 435
primary work of, 439
in spheres of influence, 62, 62 (figure)
as workplaces, 401 (*see also* Work cultures, positive)
School-to-prison pipeline, 316
Schoolwide practice, defined as a key term, 355–356
Schoolyard bullying, 83, 321. *See also* Bullying; Cyberbullying
Schumaker, P., 448
Schwandt, Thomas A., 142
Science:
advanced, limited in small schools, 214
gender imbalance among teachers of, 182
literacy in, 146, 147
NAEP scores for, 274

natural, best practice instruction in, 146
underrepresented females in advanced courses, 142, 449
Scientific knowledge, 136
Scientific management:
best practices and, 30, 136
Bobbitt (Franklin) and, 3, 5–6
defined as a key term, 16
language of, 3, 6, 7, 8
legacy of, 11
recently proposed reforms compared to, 10
See also Best practices; Factory models of schooling
Scientific method, 6, 25, 105, 155–156. *See also* Reliability;
Validity
Scientifically based practice, 135, 141–142, 147. *See also* Best
practices
Scorer-rater reliability, 160
Scores, test. *See* Test scores
Scotland, 313
Screening, universal. *See* Universal screening
Scribner, J. D., 451
Scriptural literacy, 359
Search and seizure court decisions:
and avoiding Fourth Amendment violations, 298
for cell phones, 301–303
decisions listed, 305
probable cause in, 296, 297, 301, 304
reasonable suspicion in, 297–298, 299, 300, 302–303
special needs doctrine and, 301
strip searches, 298, 299–300
unreasonable searches, 296, 300–301, 303
Search warrants, 233, 296, 297, 301–302, 304
Seat belts, for school buses, 311–312, 313
Seating areas, in the classroom, 66
Sebring, P. B., 390
Second language:
acquisition of, confused with a disability, 426
English as a second language (ESL), 94, 121, 124, 130,
383, 426
native language and, 93, 123, 130, 131, 426
and reading skill needs, 61
response to intervention (RTI) and, 93, 94, 95
See also English as a second language (ESL); English
language learners (ELLs); Language
Secondary schools:
general student service trends in, 374 (figure), 375–379
response to intervention (RTI) in, 93–94
See also High schools
Second-best markets, 456
Section 504 (Rehabilitation Act), 219, 292, 295, 314
Secular humanism, 359, 370
Security, school. *See* School safety
Security cameras, 312, 320 (table), 321
Security of electronic data, 375. *See also* Privacy
Sedwick, Rebecca, 323
Segregation, racial. *See* Racial segregation
SEL (social emotional learning), 374 (figure), 377, 378, 383
Selective tradition, 333, 337
Self-actualization, 406
Self-assessment, 144, 146, 147, 220

Self-awareness:
  and overcoming learning barriers, 72 (sidebar), 75, 79, 80–81, 82
  SEL programs for, 378
  See also Metacognition
Self-control, 353, 356, 375, 383
Self-critical attitude, 205, 208
Self-directed learners, 146
Self-discipline, 343, 351–352, 353, 354. *See also* Self-regulation
Self-education, 200
Self-esteem, 369
Self-image, 405
Self-interest, 436, 446
Self-interests:
  of bargaining parties, 479
  of union members, 473–474, 475, 476, 481
Self-knowledge, 155, 337
Self-management, 378
Self-monitoring, 44, 49, 80–81
Self-motivation, 214, 217
Self-regulation, 44, 349, 351, 353, 354, 356, 370. *See also* Self-discipline
Seniority, 23–24, 459, 473, 481
Sentiment of invisible omniscience, 44, 49
Separate but equal status, 172, 182
Separation of church and state, 280
Sergiovanni, T. J., 405, 405 (figure)
Sergiovanni, Thomas, 3, 4, 16
Servicemen's Readjustment Act, 172
Sesame Street (television program), 211
The 7 Habits of Highly Effective People (by Stephen Covey), 30–31
Sexist rules, 82
Sexual content, case law on:
  for blogs, 227
  for social media, 229, 230, 234
  for a speech, 226
  for texting, 226, 235
Sexual harassment, 293, 295, 315
Sexual identity, 73, 74, 81, 83
Sexual orientation, 293, 314, 345, 449. *See also* Bisexual profile; Gay principals; Gay students
Sexual violence, 314
Shanker, Albert, 330, 473
Shared assumptions, 406
Shared beliefs, 406. *See also* Beliefs
Shared culture, 405–406
Shared decision making, 72 (sidebar), 375–376, 383. *See also* Collaboration
Shared information, 7
Shared leadership, 404, 405
Shared power, 448
Shared responsibility, 402
Shared values, 406. *See also* Values
Shared vision, 139, 351, 404, 405, 408–409
Shaywitz, Sally E., 95
Shipman, Neil, 11
"Shocks the conscience," 292–293, 304
Shootings, school. *See* School shootings
Shor, Ira, 110

Shujaa, Mwalimu, 336
Shunning, 42, 314
Siblings, influence on children by, 62 (figure)
Siegel-Hawley, Genevieve, 336
Silver, Nate, 4, 5, 13, 14
Simon, Philip P., 230
Simplifying and deskilling, by best practices, 137
Single best way, 138. *See also* One best method or one right way
Single salary schedule, 251, 254. *See also* Salary schedules
SIT (School Improvement Team), 444
S.J.W. v. Lee's Summit R-7 School District (2012), 227
Skepticism, informed, 181
Skrla, L., 427
Skrla, Linda, 180, 449
Slade v. New Hanover County Board of Education (1971), 311
Slavery, 336, 337
SLCs. *See* Small learning communities (SLCs)
Small learning communities (SLCs), 215, 330, 373, 374 (figure), 376, 383
Small schools, online learning in, 214–215, 217
Smart library, 199
Smart RTI, 96–97
Smartphones, 199, 301. *See also* Cell phones
Smiley, Tavis, 190
Smith, Mary Lee, 164
Smith v. Guildford Board of Education (2007), 293
Smith v. Half Hollow Hills Central School District (2002), 293
Smoking, 279, 297. *See also* Tobacco use
Snow days, 216
Social awareness, 378
Social capital, 420, 421, 430
Social change, 201, 405
Social class:
  achievement gap and, 112, 113, 276–277, 278, 279
  and curriculum content selection, 110
  dominant, 113
  inequities, perpetuated by schools, 333–334
  race, tracking, and, 275
  school segregation by, 278
  See also Dominant and subordinate groups; Socioeconomic factors
Social climate, of the classroom, 145
Social cognitive theory, 410
Social competence curriculum, 378, 379–380
Social construction, 26, 41, 48, 334
Social destiny, 5
Social distance, 290
Social ecological perspective, 379. *See also* Bioecological approach
Social efficiency, 9, 10
Social emotional learning (SEL), 374 (figure), 377, 378, 383
Social inequities, root cause of, 337
Social justice:
  advocacy for, 449, 450, 450 (sidebar), 451
  best practices and, 136, 140, 142, 147
  charter schools and, 329, 333
  counseling for, 377
  defined as a key term, 147
  leadership accoutrements and, 26, 27 (table)

school politics for, 437, 448–450, 449 (sidebar), 450 (sidebar)
  beyond schools, 16
  your capacity for, 28 (sidebar)
Social media:
  cyberbullying on, 71, 74, 83, 290, 291, 294, 314, 323
  defined as a key term, 235
  enormous impact of, 225
  homeschooler access to, 368
  knowledge gathering from, 203
  See also Facebook; Myspace; Social media and case law;
      Twitter; YouTube
Social media and case law:
  background for, 225–226
  list of court decisions on, 236
  public employees as litigants in related cases, 231–233
  students as litigants in, 227–228, 229–231
  students as litigants in, precedents to, 226–227
  teachers as litigants in, 233–235
  See also Blogs; Email; Instant messaging; Social media;
      Texting
Social mobility theory, 424
Social networking websites. *See* Social media; Social media and
    case law
Social reproduction theory, 333
Social resources, devaluing of, 422
Social responsibility, 154
Social values, 136
Social violence, 314
Social workers, 80, 346, 374, 376, 380, 442, 443, 450
Social-emotional development, 71, 84, 378. *See also*
    Development
Socialization:
  gender socialization, 74
  homeschooling and, 361, 368
  into school politics, 445
Social/moral panic, 71, 84. *See also* Moral panic
Society of the Sisters, 366
Sociocultural theory, 58, 61, 68
Socioeconomic factors:
  achievement gap and, 112–113, 171–172, 175, 179, 275–278
  in curriculum alignment, 115
  inequality perpetuated by, 333
  influence of, 13
  prestige, test scores, and, 446
  schools, students, and families affected by, 74
  See also Cultural factors; Poverty; Social class
Socratic method, 204
Software blackboard, 208
Software pedagogy, 203
Software system of education, 200–201. *See also* Digital schools
Software-based learning, 204–205
Solution-focused counseling, 379
Souter, David, 299, 300
South Carolina, 110, 111, 119, 121, 300
South Dakota, 243
The South (U.S.), demographic shifts in, 418, 419. *See also*
    North Carolina
Sovereign power, 44
Spanierman, Jeffrey, 234

Spanierman v. Hughes (2008), 234
Spanish *dichos*, 128, 129 (sidebar)
Spanish language:
  in family involvement programs, 126, 128, 129 (sidebar)
  spoken at home, 120
  spoken by parents, 437, 438
  spoken by school staff, 426
Speaking/listening, CCSS standards on, 59 (sidebar)
Spearman-Brown prophecy formula, 159
Special education:
  ableism and, 73
  African American males disproportionately in, 84
  in charter schools, 332, 336
  constant referral and placement rates in, 94
  general student services and, 373–375, 376
  high-cost students in, 282
  inequitable patterns of placement in, 84, 88, 181
  online learning and, 219–220
  reduction in referrals to, 90, 91, 93, 94
  RTI and, 87, 88, 90–97
  See also Students with disabilities; Students with learning
      disabilities
Special needs doctrine, 301, 302, 304
Special relationship doctrine, 292, 293
Specialists, in RTI programs, 87, 90, 91–92, 94, 95–96
Speech and language pathologists, 91–92
Speech/expression and case law:
  for blogs, 227, 228
  bullying and, 291, 323
  for email, 228
  for instant messaging, 228–229
  limits on freedom of expression, 227
  for personal websites, 226–227
  for social media, 227–228, 229–231, 233–235
  students as litigants in, 226–231, 291
  teachers as litigants in, 231–232, 233–234, 235
  for texting, 226, 235
  See also Free speech
Spencer, Herbert, 110
Spending. *See* Budgeting; School finance
Spheres of influence, in ecological systems, 61–62, 62 (figure)
Split-half reliability, 159
Sponsors, for career moves, 446, 447, 451
Sports, 215, 301, 374
Spousal abuse, 314
Spring, Joel, 333
Springer, Matthew, 173
Squatrito, Dominic J., 234
SROs (school resource officers), 290, 296, 316, 317, 319, 436
Stability coefficient, 158
Stability of measurement, 158. *See also* Equivalence and
    stability reliability
Staff, school. *See* School staff
Stakeholders, school. *See* School stakeholders
Stammbaum (family tree), in network formation, 40–41
Standard error of measurement, 161, 165
Standardization:
  in collective bargaining, 478
  standards and, 6, 14

Taylor (Frederick) and, 16
   of test/assessment procedures, 155
Standardized performance measures, 242
Standardized tests:
   adult-led cheating on, 186, 187, 188, 189, 192 (sidebar)
   capacity building compared to, 404
   for certifying achievement, 174
   cheap and easy implementation for, 403–404
   for homeschooled students, 362
   improvement of scores on, 274
   under No Child Left Behind, 176, 186, 189, 280
   norm-referenced tests as, 98
   school politics and, 445
   teacher evaluation linked to, 178
   teacher salary and tenure linked to, 25
   See also Assessments; State tests; Test scores; Tests
Standards:
   of accessibility, 220 (*see also* Access)
   CCSS (*see* Common Core State Standards (CCSS))
   College and Career Readiness Standards, 106
   for counseling programs, 377, 378
   and criteria for achievement, 170
   and curriculum, distinction between, 106–107, 107 (table)
   developing standards versus, 8–10, 9 (table), 14
   and the difference between rules and customs, 11
   financial pressures from, 258
   high versus impossible, 29
   InTASC standards, 59, 66, 67
   ISLLC standards, 7, 8, 9–10, 16
   Murphy (Joseph) on, 3
   Next Generation Science Standards, 146
   No Child Left Behind and, 175, 177
   for online programs, 218, 219 (sidebar)
   and quest for a center, 8, 9 (table)
   for school buses and drivers, 310, 311
   standardization and, 6, 14
   state, assessments of, 88
Standards-based reform, 240, 252, 254, 377, 412. *See also A Nation at Risk*; Standards
Starratt, Robert, 12, 14
State income taxes, 242, 243. *See also* Income taxes
State tests:
   for the Common Core, 104, 258
   costs of, 258
   cut points/cut scores/cutoffs for, 113–114, 176, 177, 182, 277
   and focusing on the wrong things, 411
   for No Child Left Behind, 186
   online courses and, 216
   RTI and, 88
   school politics and, 445
   See also Standardized tests
State-created danger, doctrine of, 292–293, 295
States, U.S.:
   attendance policy regulated by, 352
   bullying policy and statutes in, 291, 323
   charter schools legislation in, 331, 458
   collective bargaining laws of, 471, 472, 473
   Common Core and, 104–111, 113–114, 115
   compulsory education laws in, 364, 365

   course credits in, 216
   devolving authority to, 242
   fund distribution by, 246, 247–249
   funding formulas used by, 218, 246, 247, 249, 257, 344
   homeschooling and, 362, 363–364, 366–367, 368
   legal and coercive power of, 22
   A Nation at Risk impact on, 174
   online learning programs of, 212, 213, 216, 217
   police forces or SROs in, 317
   public schools established by, 200
   purpose and object codes for funding in, 250
   under Race to the Top, 177–178
   revenue generation by, 243–245
   revenue reductions in, 257–258
   right-to-work laws of, 443, 472
   taxes in, 243–245, 247–248
   Tenth Amendment on powers reserved to, 242
   tests (*see* State tests)
   tuition tax credits offered by some, 280
   unfair labor practices defined by, 480
   See also Government roles in education
Status dropout rate, 122, 130, 131
Steele, C., 420, 424
Stefancic, Jean, 335
Steffy, B. E., 420
Stefkovich, Jacqueline A., 77
Stereotypes:
   best practices and, 141
   deficit model and, 73, 74
   of homeschooling parents, 360
   in the learning environment, 145
   misperceptions and, 76
   racial and ethnic, 421
Stewart, J., 393
Stop arm (school bus) violation survey, 308–309 (table), 310
Stovall, David, 335
Strategic reading, 144
Strategist, in school politics, 436, 437
Stratification, academic, 422, 429. *See also* Ability grouping; Tracking
Street-level bureaucrats, 240, 254, 437, 451. *See also* Bureaucracy
Strike, Kimberly, 347
Strike, right to, 481
Strikes, teacher, 442, 473
Strip searches, 298, 299, 300. *See also* Search and seizure court decisions
Structural sameness, 7
Structured English immersion, 123, 131
Student achievement. *See* Achievement, student; Achievement gap(s)
Student advocates, 378
Student conduct:
   appropriate versus acceptable, 350
   connections, intersections, and, 354
   essential nature of, 343, 354
   and mutual respect in adults and children, 344
   reasons for being concerned about, 346
   support for, 350–351

See also Attendance; Discipline, student
Student identity, 442
Student learning. *See* Learning; Learning barriers, overcoming; Learning environment
Student power, 442
Student self-assessment, 144, 146, 147
Student self-awareness, 72 (barrier), 75, 79, 80, 82, 83–84
Student services. *See* General student services; School counseling
Student-centered learning, 144, 147, 350, 362
Students:
    assignment of, to classrooms, 247
    assignment of, to teachers, 251, 252
    collaboration among, 141, 142, 143, 144, 147, 213, 442
    control over their learning, 215, 337
    effective teaching of (*see* Effective teaching)
    a form of property in charter schools, 336
    funding weights for, 247, 254
    impact of adult-led cheating on, 191
    as litigants in case law, 226–231
    online learning for (*see* Blended learning; Online learning)
    and pay for performance, 458, 459
    personal websites of, 226–227
Students of color:
    failures (alleged) of equal opportunities for, 280
    failures of public education for, 362
    harsh disciplinary action for, 315
    increased incarceration of, 316
    inequities for, and rebirth of homeschooling, 361, 362
    racial segregation and, 336
    SAT taken by, 273
    and teacher belief systems, 424
    unrecognized assets of, 427
    well behind the White and wealthy, 175
    See also Ethnicity; Race
Students with disabilities:
    bullying and harassment of, 295
    in the deficit model, 73
    No Child Left Behind and, 175
    online learning for, 219–220
    See also Special education; Students with learning disabilities
Students with emotional disturbances, 374, 376
Students with learning disabilities:
    bullying of, 295
    in charter schools, 332
    effective teaching of, 61
    identification of, 87, 88, 95, 96, 98
    online learning for, 219–220
    RTI and, 87–89, 91, 93–97
    See also Special education; Students with disabilities
Student-teacher ratio, 217, 242, 247. *See also* Class size
Studer, J. R., 380
Studies, real versus agenda-pushing, 461 (sidebar)
Suárez-Orozco, M., 421
Subjectivity, 155, 160. *See also* Objectivity
Submersion, as a language option, 123, 131
Subordinate groups. *See* Dominant and subordinate groups
Subscales, and construct validity, 162
Subsidiarity, 242, 254

Substitute teachers, 344
Subtraction strategy, in imagination, 27
Subtractive schooling processes, 421, 422, 430
Successful and effective, defined as key terms, 430
Sufficiency and school finance, 241–242, 244
Sugarman, Stephen, 249
Suicide:
    by bullying/cyberbullying victims, 289–290, 291, 323
    PTSD and, 315
    school-associated, decline in, 313
    thoughts of, 302
Sumi, W. C., 374
Summers, Larry, 12
Superintendents:
    in bureaucratic networks, 40–45, 43 (sidebar), 46–47 (sidebar)
    characteristics of successful, 31
    and education for African Americans and Latinos, 423, 424, 426, 428
    leadership/management paradox and, 5, 7, 11, 15
    positive work culture and, 405, 409, 411
    in school cheating scandals, 186, 188, 191
    in school politics, 435, 437, 441, 444
    in social media court decisions, 229, 230, 231, 232, 234
    See also Principals
Supplement, not supplant, 246, 254
Supplies, instructional, expenditures for, 241 (figure)
Supply chaining, 203
Support for learning at home:
    defined as a key term, 84
    to overcome learning barriers, 73, 74–75, 76, 81
    See also Families; Home environment; Homeschooling; Parenting; Parents
Support staff. *See* School staff
Supreme Court of the U.S.:
    Bethel School District v. Fraser (1986), 226, 227, 229, 230
    Brown v. Board of Education (1954), 172, 200, 278, 335
    City of Ontario, California v. Quon (2010), 226
    Connick v. Myers (1983), 232–233
    Davis v. Monroe County Board of Education (1999), 293, 295
    DeShaney v. Winnebago County Dept. of Social Services (1998), 292, 295
    Garcetti v. Ceballos (2006), 231, 233
    Griswold v. Connecticut (1965), 297
    Hazelwood School District v. Kuhlmeier (1988), 226, 227
    Kadmas v. Dickinson Public Schools (1988), 308
    Meyer v. Nebraska (1923), 366
    Morse v. Frederick (2007), 227, 229, 289
    Mt. Healthy City School District Board of Education v. Doyle (1977), 232
    New Jersey v. T.L.O. (1985), 297–298, 299, 300, 301, 302
    Parents Involved in Community Schools v. Seattle School District No. 1 (2007), 252
    Pickering v. Board of Education of Township High School District 205 (1968), 231–232
    Pierce v. Society of the Sisters (1925), 366
    Riley v. California (2014), 301–302, 303
    Safford Unified School District v. Redding (2009), 299, 300
    Tinker v. Des Moines Independent School District (1969), 226, 227, 228, 229, 230, 231, 291, 323

Wisconsin v. Yoder (1972), 366
Survival Spanish course, 128
Suspension and expulsion rates, 189
Symbolic leadership, 405, 405 (figure)
Synchronous environment, 201, 202, 209, 213
Synchronous instruction, defined as a key term, 222
Systematic approach to reform, 426–427, 430
Systematic or constant error, 157, 165
Systematic variance, 158
Systems:
    ecological systems theory, 61, 62, 62 (figure), 68
    loosely coupled, 437 (*see also* Loose coupling)
    open, 437–438, 445
    in student services, 377 (figure)
Systems building, 344, 348, 349, 354
Systems within systems, 349, 354

Talented students, 374. *See also* Gifted students
Targeted feedback, 145
Task unification strategy, 27–28
Tate, William, 335
Tax base equalization, 248
Tax credits, 280, 283, 457
Tax reform, 244. *See also* Taxes
Taxes:
    characteristics of, 245 (table)
    defined as a key term, 254
    elasticity of, 244, 245 (table), 253
    income taxes, 242, 243, 245 (table), 253
    inequities in, 244, 258
    progressive, 244, 245, 245 (table), 253
    property (*see* Property taxes)
    rate limits for, 259
    regressive, 244, 245, 245 (table), 253
    for revenue generation, 242, 243–245
    sales (*see* Sales taxes)
    taxing authority for, 247–248, 257
    use taxes, 245
Taylor, Frederick, 6, 16, 30, 33, 136
Taylorism, 30, 136. *See also* Scientific management
Teach and test, 182. *See also* Test scores; Tests
Teacher collaboration:
    best practices and, 139, 143
    for counseling services, 378
    between general and special educators, 220
    between general and specialist educators, 90, 91, 95, 97
    for general student services, 376
    online, 212
    PLCs and, 392, 439
    school community building and, 348
    with students, 60
Teacher compensation. *See* Salaries and benefits; Salary
    schedules; Teacher salaries
Teacher education programs. *See* Teacher preparation programs
Teacher effectiveness. *See* Effective teaching
Teacher evaluation. *See* Teachers, evaluation of
Teacher experience, years of, 251, 267, 271, 407
Teacher experience index, 267, 271
Teacher preparation programs, 61, 125, 203, 214, 422, 425

Teacher salaries:
    disparities in, 275
    investment in, to attract excellence, 251
    merit pay in, 24, 458–459
    role relationships and, 23–24
    student test scores tied to, 25
    See also Salaries and benefits; Wages
Teacher strikes, 442, 473
Teacher tenure:
    as an impediment to effectiveness, 457–458
    student test scores tied to, 25
    transfer options and, 252
    unfairness of, 463
    in wicked problems, 436
    See also Teachers, evaluation of
Teacher-focused instruction, 78–79
Teachers:
    as advocates, 125–126
    allocation of, 267, 269, 395, 396–397
    assignment of, to schools, 251–252, 395, 396
    attendance (consistent) of, 344
    autonomy for, 24, 402
    beliefs and attitudes of, and school quality, 401
    bilingual, 426
    caring, 56, 353
    as a changing workforce, 406–407
    characteristics of, 403
    collaboration among (*see* Teacher collaboration)
    customization and, 204
    as cyberbullying targets, 291
    in the digital school, 199–205, 206–207
    dismissal or termination of, 231, 234, 235
    diversity among, 425–426
    enrollment projection challenges for, 123–128, 129 (sidebar)
    as entrepreneurs, 402
    epistemologies of, 424
    as facilitators of systems, 349
    as factors in school finance, 239, 242, 246, 247, 249, 250–252
    as the greatest factor in student achievement, 251
    itinerant, 214, 215
    lack of time felt by, 408
    lifelong learning for, 408
    as litigants in case law, 231–232, 233–235
    minorities as, 425–426, 447
    new, 246 (sidebar), 251–252, 407, 408, 409
    observation of (*see* Classroom observation)
    in online and blended learning, 212–221
    policy not divorced from, 477
    in positive work cultures, 401–403, 405–411
    pressure on, 189, 190
    primary work of schools done by, 439
    in professional learning communities, 139, 143, 392, 439
    as public employees, 231–232, 234, 235
    recruiting of, 425–426
    school cheating involving, 186, 187, 190, 191
    school cheating solutions and, 191, 192, 192 (sidebar)
    school counselors and, 375
    in school politics, 437–439, 441–443, 447, 448
    shortages of, 425

social media and, 225, 230–231, 233–235
students assigned to, 251, 252
substitute, 344
in a turnaround school initiative, 391–397, 398 (table)
working conditions for, 409–410 (*see also* Work cultures, positive)
years of experience for, 251, 267, 271, 407
Teachers, evaluation of:
  collective bargaining on, 475 (sidebar)
  in online programs, 219, 220–221
  Race to the Top and, 178
  role relationships and, 24
  student achievement and, 220
  test scores linked to, 104, 178, 334
  See also Classroom observation; Merit pay; Teacher salaries
Teachers' unions, 471–482
  bargainable subjects for, 474–475, 475 (sidebar)
  collective bargaining and, 471, 473–475, 477–480
  the contract and, 472, 476, 478–480
  future of, 481
  good faith bargaining and, 478–479
  grievance process and, 473, 478, 479–480
  history of, 473
  in the industrial labor model, 477–478, 481
  in the management/leadership dyad, 24, 25
  professionalism, and its fit with, 475–477, 481
  professionalism, NEA, AFT, and, 473
  protection by, 476, 476 (sidebar), 477, 481
  role of, 473–474
  in school politics, 442–443
  teacher assignment to schools, and, 252
  unfair labor practices and, 480–481
  on vouchers and charter schools, 281, 282
  See also Public sector unions
Teaching, effectiveness of. *See* Effective teaching
Teaching, simplified and deskilled by best practices, 137
Teaching, virtual, 199, 200, 204, 208. *See also* Digital schools
Teaching to the test, 189. *See also* Test scores; Tests
Team approach, in a turnaround school initiative, 392, 394, 396.
    See also Collaboration
Technical efficiency, 241, 254
Technical leadership, 405, 405 (figure)
Technique-specific best practices, 146–147
Technological change:
  and decentralization of learning, 200
  and the flatteners, 202–203
  for infrastructure of global learning, 200–201
  in the locus of learning, 203–205
  MOOCs in, 202, 205–206
  trend line for, 199–200
  for ubiquitous learning, 206–207
Technological Pedagogical Content Knowledge (TPACK) model, 201
Technology:
  access to, 214, 216, 380 (*see also* Access)
  for administering tests, 258
  best practices and, 137, 138 (sidebar)
  in the capital budget, 245
  as a catalyst, 205

for flipped instruction, 138 (sidebar)
to increase educational productivity, 217
as integral to education, 207
law lagging behind, 226
privacy and, 226, 375
school counselor use of, 380
See also Internet; Online learning; Social media;
    Technological change
Telephone calls to parents, 64, 126, 444. *See also* Cell phones;
    Smartphones
Television, educational (ETV), 211–212
Tennessee, 212, 472
Tenth Amendment (U.S. Constitution), 242, 254
Tenure, teacher. *See* Teacher tenure
Test bias, 155, 165
Test preparation factories, some schools as, 189
Test scores:
  accountability, politics, and, 164
  achievement gap, language, and, 121
  achievement gap, socioeconomics, culture, and, 112–113
  adult-led cheating on, 185–191
  cut points, 277
  cut scores, 176, 177, 182
  cutoff scores, 113–114
  increasing, best practices for, 141–142
  and intended effects of testing, 164
  international, for U.S. comparisons, 111
  interpretation of, 155, 156, 159, 160, 161, 164
  judgments based on, 79, 153, 155, 156, 161
  leadership effectiveness linked to, 26
  measurement error and, 157–158
  observed and true, 157–158
  teacher evaluation linked to, 104, 178, 334
  teacher salary and tenure linked to, 25
  See also Reliability; Tests; Validity
Testing environment, 160
Test-retest reliability, 158–159
Tests:
  appropriateness of, 154, 156, 161–162, 163, 164
  and assessments differentiated, 153, 154
  CCSS linked to, 104, 258 (*see also* Standardized tests;
      State tests)
  cheating and (*see* School cheating scandals)
  commercial selling of, 104
  conditions of testing, 154, 155, 157–158, 159, 160, 164
  costs of testing, 258
  in curriculum alignment, 114–115, 114 (figure)
  daily, impact of, 180
  defined as a key term, 165
  and effects of testing, 164
  error in the testing process, 155–156
  ethics and, 154–155, 156, 157, 158, 164, 165
  GRE, 273
  high-stakes (*see* High-stakes testing)
  instructional investigation of, 79
  length of, 160
  limitations of, 79, 165
  under No Child Left Behind, 175, 176, 177
  norm-referenced, 98

preparation practices for, 115, 189
questions to ask about, 154
reliability and (*see* Reliability)
SAT, 164, 172, 273, 274
standardized (*see* Standardized tests)
state (*see* State tests)
strengths of, 165
teach and test, propensity to, 182
validity and (*see* Validity)
See also National Assessment of Educational Progress
    (NAEP); Test scores
Texas:
    Common Core and, 105
    designation of curriculum content in, 110
    El Paso cheating scandal in, 188, 190, 191
    as an established Latino state, 418
    Hispanic population in, 119, 120 (table), 121
    homeschooling in, 363
    test cutoff scores in, 113
Text messages, in confiscated cell phones, 302–303
Texting:
    case law and, 226, 235
    cyberbullying via, 290, 314, 323, 324 (figure)
Theoharis, George, 450 (sidebar)
Theoretical definitions, 156, 162, 165
Thinking inside the box, 23, 27–28
Thinking outside the box, 26, 27
Thomas B. Fordham Institute, 111
Thompson, C. L., 391, 392, 393
Threats, idle, in classroom management, 57–58
Tiered model, of RTI, 89, 90, 93–97. *See also* Response to
    intervention (RTI)
Time:
    instructional, 55, 173, 352, 397
    respect for teachers', 408
    See also School calendar; School day flexibility
Time and motion studies, 30. *See also* Scientific management
Time-bound learning, 201
Tinker test, on disruptive speech, 226. *See also* Disruption test,
    for speech/expression
Tinker v. Des Moines Independent School District (1969), 226,
    227, 228, 229, 230, 231, 291, 323
Title I (ESEA):
    comparability under, 246, 246 (sidebar), 253
    defined as a key term, 254
    funds withheld from, 315
    in the history of achievement gaps, 172
    per pupil allocation under, 239
    school politics and, 437, 441
    supplement, not supplant under, 246, 254
    Tenth Amendment and, 242
    for vertical equity, 241
    See also Elementary and Secondary Education Act (ESEA)
Title II (Americans with Disabilities Act), 314
Title VI (Civil Rights Act), 292, 294, 295, 314
Title IX (Education Amendments Act of 1972), 292, 293,
    294–295, 314
T.K. v. New York City Department of Education (2011), 295
T.L.O. (*New Jersey v. T.L.O.*, 1985), 297–298, 299, 300, 301, 302

Tobacco use, 319 (table). *See also* Smoking
Toolbox metaphor, 29, 81
Tooms Cyprès, Autumn, 45 (figure)
Torgesen, Joseph K., 94
Tourists, sales taxes on, 244
Townsend, C., 393
Townsend, L. W., 391, 392, 393
Toyama, Y., 214
TPACK (Technological Pedagogical Content Knowledge)
    model, 201
Tracking, 60, 125, 275, 283. *See also* Ability grouping;
    Academic stratification
Traditional public schools:
    charter schools compared to, 281, 282, 330, 332, 335, 458,
        462, 463
    defined as a key term, 338
    homeschooling as a response to, 362, 364
    homeschooling compared to, 368–369
    private schools compared to, 281, 462
    See also Public education, early American history of; Public
        education, failings of
Trained incapacities, 4, 16
Transactional distance, 199, 206–207, 215
Transactional leadership, 25, 351
Transactional management, 22 (figure)
Transactional theory, 206–207, 208
Trans-disciplinary (integrative) units, 144
Transformational leadership:
    bringing out the best in others, 346
    characteristics of, 343–344
    defined as a key term, 412
    instructional leadership and, 404, 405
    management and, 22 (figure), 25
    school-community link and, 347
Transformative intellectuals, 142
Transforming School Counseling Initiative (TSCI), 377, 378,
    383
Translational validity, 162, 163, 163 (figure)
Translators, language, 74, 128
Transparency:
    in actions against bullying, 296
    in budgeting, 260, 262, 266, 270
    in school finance, 240
    in the testing process, 155, 164
Transportation, school. *See* School bus transportation
Transportation, U.S. Department of, 310
Traub, Ross, 158, 159
Traumatic events, 315, 377
Trigger-reaction monitoring, 80
Truancy laws, 352
True score, 157–158, 161, 165
Trumbull, E., 125, 126
Trust:
    building of, 440 (table)
    built by daily school community meetings, 350
    built by professional development, 348
    in the classroom, 56
    encouragement, high standards, and, 85
    family culture of, 127

family involvement and, 63
industrial labor model and, 477
in the learning environment, 82
in networks, 45, 46 (sidebar)
organizational, and decision making, 32
relational, 389, 391–398, 398 (table), 399
required for learning, 78
T.S. v. State of Florida (2012), 300
TSCI (Transforming School Counseling Initiative), 377, 378, 383
Tucker, P. D., 393
Tuition, expenditures for, 241 (figure)
Tuition tax credits, 280, 283, 457
Turnaround, defined as a key term, 399
Turnaround initiative in North Carolina:
    background for, 389–390, 391
    case studies for, 393–397
    contributions to low performance in, 393
    data on, 390, 393, 395
    factors in performance and success in, 398 (table)
    principals' strategies for, 393–397
    the three themes of, 391–397
    your leadership actions, 397 (sidebar)
    your school's challenges and conditions, 392 (sidebar)
Turnaround school, defined as a key term, 399. *See also* Turnaround initiative in North Carolina
Tutoring:
    for homeschooling, 363
    with native language speakers, 128
    for overcoming learning barriers, 75, 79, 81, 82, 85
    in RTI programs, 90
    in student services, 374
    See also Mentoring; Volunteers
T.V. v. Smith-Green Community School Corporation (2011), 230
Twitter, 24, 45, 203, 225, 291, 323
Two-way bilingual education, 123. *See also* Bilingual education
Two-way communication, 73, 80, 84, 126. *See also* Communication
Tyack, David, 12
Tye, Barbara Benham, 401, 408, 410
Tyler, Ralph, 8
Tyler Rationale, 8
Tyson, Harriet, 409

Ubiquitous learning:
    as anytime/anywhere learning, 199, 206
    defined as a key term, 208–209
    in the digital school, 201
    global communication for, 206
    mobile devices for, 203
    See also Anytime/anywhere learning
UCEA (University Council for Educational Administration), 8, 487, 490
Udacity, 206
UDL (universal design for learning), 220
Umbrella schools, 364, 370
Unconstitutionality, 299, 301. *See also* Constitutional rights; U.S. Constitution; U.S. Constitution amendments

Underachievement, defined as a key term, 430. *See also* Achievement gap(s); African American underachievement; Latino underachievement
Underrepesentation:
    of African Americans and Hispanics in AP and honors courses, 84
    of females in advanced math courses, 449
    of females in advanced science courses, 142, 449
    of low-income or rural homes with broadband service, 214
    See also Overrepresentation
Underserved, the:
    charter schools and, 330, 332, 334, 335, 336
    critical race theory and, 335, 336
    lifted to positions of power, 337
    negative school experiences for, 189
    prepared for work under the powerful, 336
Understanding gap, between teachers and learners, 206–207
Unethical practices, 141, 154, 157, 411. *See also* Ethics; Ethics of testing
Unfair labor practices, 475 (sidebar), 480, 482
Unions:
    dues for, 471, 472, 474
    fair representation by, 480, 482
    future of, 481
    industrial labor model of, 477–478, 481
    public employee (*see* Public sector unions)
    role of, 474
    teachers' (*see* Teachers' unions)
United Kingdom, 32, 274. *See also* England; Great Britain
Universal design for learning (UDL), 220
Universal screening:
    defined as a key term, 98
    in RTI, 89, 90, 93, 94, 95, 96, 97
Universities, HBCU (historically Black colleges and universities), 425, 425 (sidebar), 426
Universities and colleges. *See* College and career readiness; College completion rates; Higher education
University Council for Educational Administration (UCEA), 8, 487, 490
Unknown, Johari quadrant of, 45 (figure), 46
Unknowns, known, 4, 15
Unreasonable searches, 296, 300–301, 303. *See also* Search and seizure court decisions
Uploading, 202
Urine samples, 301
U.S. Constitution:
    education a fundamental right not recognized by, 308
    public education left to the states by, 11
U.S. Constitution amendments:
    First Amendment, 226, 227, 228, 229, 230, 231, 233, 234, 235, 289, 303
    Fourth Amendment, 226, 290, 296–297, 298, 301, 302, 303
    Tenth Amendment, 242, 254
    Fourteenth Amendment, 228, 292–294, 366
U.S. Department of Agriculture, 252
U.S. Department of Defense, 263
U.S. Department of Education, 221, 273, 281, 282, 329
U.S. Department of Transportation, 310
U.S. Supreme Court. *See* Supreme Court of the U.S.

Us-and-them mentality, in the industrial labor model, 477, 481
Use taxes, 245
Uyeda, Kimberly, 355

Validation Committee, in CCSS development, 106
Validity:
　concurrent, 163, 164
　construct, 162–164
　construct, model of, 163 (figure)
　content-related, 163, 164
　convergent, 162–163
　criterion-related, 162, 163–164
　defined as a key term, 165
　discriminant, 162, 163
　as an ethical issue, 154
　evidence for, 161, 162–164
　face validity, 163
　factors affecting, 164
　not guaranteed by reliability, 162 (sidebar)
　predictive validity, 163, 164
　systematic error and, 157
　translational, 162, 163
Validity coefficient, 164
Valued, feeling of being, 56, 58
Values:
　arts in the curriculum and, 111
　best practices and, 136, 143
　of a community, 41
　core, in decision making, 32–33
　curricular outcomes entrenched in, 105
　and curriculum content selection, 110
　defined as a key term, 451
　divergent, 440 (table)
　ethical, 129 (sidebar)
　examination of one's own, 126, 127
　fit, community, and, 42
　knowledge evolution, and, 205
　leadership driven by, 27 (table)
　modernist, 136
　moral, 26, 129 (sidebar)
　objectivity and, 155
　in school finance, 241–242, 244, 246–247 (sidebar)
　social, 136
　in spheres of influence, 62, 62 (figure)
　in the workplace, 402, 405, 406, 407, 408
Variance, in test score analysis, 157, 158
Vaughn, Sharon, 87, 90, 91, 93, 94, 96
Verbal bullying, 321. *See also* Bullying
Verbal violence, 314
Veronia School Dist. 47J v. Acton (1995), 301
Vertical equity, 241, 247, 254
Veteran-oriented professional cultures, 407
Victimization, 290, 296, 377, 379. *See also* Bullying
Video lessons online, 215
Video logs (vlogs), 213
Videoconferencing, 211–212, 214, 380
Vietnam War, 226, 361
Violence:
　data on, 313, 377
　school (*see* School violence)
Virginia, 103, 212, 220, 317, 418
Virginia Tech massacre, 229
Virtual classroom, 201. *See also* Digital schools
Virtual distance, 208
Virtual education system, 200–201, 202, 205, 206, 208. *See also* Digital schools
Virtual learning, 199, 204, 205, 207, 208. *See also* Digital schools
Virtual schools, 201, 203, 213, 363, 364
　defined as a key term, 370
　in Florida, 212
　in Michigan, 217
　in Virginia, 212, 220
　See also Cyber schools; Digital schools
Virtual teaching, 199, 200, 204, 208. *See also* Digital schools
Vision:
　anchored to imagination and creativity, 27 (table), 28 (sidebar)
　shared, 139, 351, 404, 405, 408–409
Visionary leadership, 410
Visual arts, 374, 375
Vocabulary development, 59 (sidebar), 79, 93, 279. *See also* Reading
Vocational destiny, 5
Voltaire, 12
Voluntary racial segregation, 84. *See also* Racial segregation
Volunteering, defined as a key term, 84–85. *See also* Volunteers
Volunteers:
　barriers to learning overcome by, 75, 81–82
　community members as, 75, 84–85, 126
　family involvement and, 73, 126
　in homeschooling, 364
　parents as, 65, 75
　preparation for, 72 (sidebar)
　for supporting student conduct, 350, 351
　volunteer leaders, 24
　See also Mentoring; Parent-teacher partnerships; Tutoring
Voucher programs:
　academic achievement under, 280, 281, 462
　in Cleveland, 280, 281, 458, 462
　empirical evidence on, 458, 462
　funding mechanisms for, 249, 258
　incentivism and, 457, 460
　liberty associated with, 242
　in Milwaukee, 280, 281, 458, 462
　for school competition, 331
Vouchers, defined as a key term, 283
Vulgar language, 227, 228, 229, 230, 295. *See also* Obscene language or gestures
Vygotsky, Lev, 58, 60, 61

Wages:
　collective bargaining on, 471, 472, 473, 474, 475 (sidebar)
　See also Salaries and benefits; Salary schedules; Teacher salaries
Wagner, Mary, 374
Wahlstrom, K. L., 390
Wait times, in speech exchanges, 427